all the friction.
none of the static.

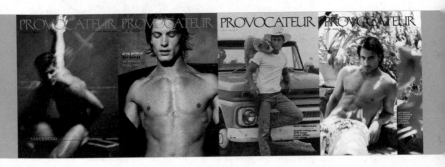

PROVOCATEUR ™

subscribe @ 1-800-959-9843

The collectable bi-monthly magazine dedicated to the Art & Culture of Man is available at bookstores and newsstands everywhere. Cover price $11.95. Subscribe now and save.
1 year (6 issues), $49. 2 years (12 issues), $86. http://alluvial.com

Giving You the Tools to Find Your Way OUT

With information about area bars, bookstores, lodgings and more in over 65 different gay-friendly destinations in the U.S., Canada and Germany, a Columbia FunMap® is the perfect pocket-sized, gay travel companion.

Choose Any Four FunMaps® for $8.00 or a FunMap® TravelPak of all available maps for only $18.00.

(*Check maps from list below. Then copy this page and send it to Columbia FunMap, 118 East 28 Street, New York, NY 10016, or call us at 212-447-7877.*)

❑ Atlanta
❑ Baltimore
❑ Berlin, Germany
❑ Boston
❑ Chicago
❑ Fort Lauderdale
❑ Frankfurt, Germany
❑ Hawaii
❑ Karlsruhe, Germany

❑ Key West
❑ Long Island
❑ Los Angeles
❑ Miami/Miami Beach
❑ Manhattan
❑ Mannheim, Germany
❑ Milwaukee/Wisconsin
❑ Montréal
❑ Munich, Germany

❑ New Jersey
❑ New Orleans
❑ Northeast Resorts
❑ Palm Springs
❑ Philadelphia
❑ Provincetown
❑ Providence
❑ Québec
❑ Rehoboth Beach

❑ San Diego
❑ San Francisco
❑ Seattle
❑ Stuttgart, Germany
❑ Toronto
❑ Washington, DC

❑ Please rush me the maps indicated above. ❑ Please send me a FunMap TravelPak.

Enclosed please find a check for $_____.

Name _____

Address _____ City _____ State _____ Zip _____

Columbia FunMap® Corp.
mapping the gay & lesbian world
118 East 28 Street, New York City 10016 212-447-7877 Fax 212-447-7876

ODYSSEUS

The International Gay Travel Planner™

'97/98 Edition

The World's
Most Comprehensive
Guide of accommodations & travel
USA / INTERNATIONAL
For Gay men & Lesbians

Eli Angelo
Joseph H. Bain
Editors

Robert Richards...Cover Illustration
Jose Arroyo...Male Photography
Joseph H. Bain...Maps
Eli Angelo, Tim Nugent......................................Marketing & Sales

ODYSSEUS ENTERPRISES LTD.
Port Washington, New York

ODYSSEUS ENTERPRISES LTD.
P.O. Box 1548
Port Washington, New York 11050

Library of Congress Catalog
Card Number: 84-62555

ISBN: 1-881536-03-3

ISSN: 0883-3664

The listing, photo, or illustration of any individual, business, group
or organization in **Odysseus '97/98** does not indicate or
imply their sexual orientation is homosexual, nor
that they encourage or discourage gay patronage.

CONTENTS

V. Contents
IV. Foreword -
English, French,
Spanish, Russian,
Japanese
XI. Key to abbreviations
/ disclaimer
XIII. ODYSSEUS Travel
Supplement

U. S. A.

1. U.S.A.
2. ALASKA
4. ARIZONA
8. ARKANSAS
9. CALIFORNIA
41. COLORADO
44. CONNECTICUT
46. DELAWARE
48. DISTRICT OF
COLUMBIA
53. FLORIDA
71. GEORGIA
73. GUAM
75. HAWAII
88. ILLINOIS
93. INDIANA
96. LOUISIANA
101. MAINE
102. MARYLAND
104. MASSACHUSETTS
113. MICHIGAN
115. MINNESOTA
117. MISSOURI
118. NEVADA
121. NEW HAMPSHIRE
122. NEW JERSEY
126. NEW MEXICO
131. NEW YORK
149. NORTH CAROLINA
151. OKLAHOMA
153. OREGON
155. PENNSYLVANIA
159. PUERTO RICO
163. RHODE ISLAND
165. SOUTH CAROLINA
167. TENNESSEE
169. TEXAS
175. UTAH
176. VERMONT
177. VIRGIN ISLANDS (US)
180. VIRGINIA
182. WASHINGTON
183. WISCONSIN

CANADA

185. CANADA
186. ALBERTA
188. BRITISH COLUMBIA
190. NOVA SCOTIA
191. ONTARIO
197. QUEBEC
211. SASKATCHEWAN

INTERNATIONAL

213. ALBANIA
214. ANTIGUA
215. ARGENTINA
223. ARUBA
224. AUSTRALIA
237. AUSTRIA
240. BAHAMAS
241. BARBADOS
242. BELARUS
243. BELGIUM
250. BELIZE
252. BERMUDA
253. BOLIVIA
254. BRAZIL
259. BRITISH VIRGIN ISL.
261. BULGARIA
263. CAYMAN ISLANDS
264. CHILE
266. CHINA
268. COLOMBIA
271. COOK ISLANDS
272. COSTA RICA
276. CROATIA
277. CUBA
278. CURAÇAO
279. CYPRUS
281. CZECH REPUBLIC
287. DENMARK
290. DOMINICAN REPUBLIC
291. EGYPT
293. ESTONIA
294. FIJI
295. FINLAND
297. FRANCE
312. FRENCH POLYNESIA
314. GERMANY
329. GHANA
330. GREECE
358. GRENADA
359. GUATEMALA
360. HONDURAS
361. HONG KONG
364. HUNGARY
366. ICELAND
367. INDIA
369. INDONESIA
377. IRELAND (EIRE)
380. ISRAEL
387. ITALY
405. JAMAICA
406. JAPAN
419. JORDAN
420. KOREA (SOUTH)
421. LATVIA
422. LITHUANIA
423. LUXEMBOURG
424. MACAU
425. MALAYSIA
426. MALTA
427. MARTINIQUE
428. MEXICO
442. MONACO
443. MOROCCO
446. NEPAL
447. NETHERLANDS
461. NEW CALEDONIA
462. NEW ZEALAND
465. NORWAY
467. PANAMA
468. PARAGUAY
469. PERU
470. PHILIPPINES
472. POLAND
474. PORTUGAL
478. ROMANIA
479. RUSSIA
486. SAINT MARTIN
487. SAUDI ARABIA
488. SEYCHELLES
489. SINGAPORE
491. SINT. MAARTEN
492. SLOVAKIA
493. SLOVENIA
494. SOUTH AFRICA
501. SPAIN
529. SRI-LANKA
530. ST. BARTHELEMY
531. ST. KITTS/NEVIS
532. SURINAM
533. SWEDEN
537. SWITZERLAND
544. SYRIA
545. TAIWAN
547. TANZANIA
548. THAILAND
555. TRINIDAD & TOBAGO
556. TUNISIA
557. TURKEY
562. UKRAINE
564. UNITED ARAB EMIRATES
566. UNITED KINGDOM
575. NORTHERN IRELAND
576. SCOTLAND
579. URUGUAY
580. VANUATU
581. VENEZUELA
584. YEMEN
585. ZIMBABWE

APPENDIXES

586. Airlines
586. Bookstores
591. Lodging
592. Mail Order
593. Maps
593. Publications
598. Railroads
599. Rent-A-Car
599. Reservation Services
599. Tour Operators
599. Travel Agents
604. Travel Insurance
604. Advertisers Index
605. 97/98 Calendar

CONTENTS

ongratulations, by purchasing our 13th edition of **ODYSSEUS** - The "All-In-One" International Gay Travel Planner ™ guide, you have demonstrated that you are or wish to become an experienced traveler. Thus, you take your gay travel seriously and you appreciate the quality of the travel information that has been associated with **ODYSSEUS** since it was first published in 1984.

The cover of **ODYSSEUS** '97/98 represents and salutes with pride the **1998 GAY GAMES** in Amsterdam. This special sports and cultural event will take place in Amsterdam, the "Gay Capital of the World", from August 1 - 8, '98. More than 10,000 participants and over 100,000 spectators from around the world are expected to be in attendance. This will be the last large 'Gay & Lesbian Event of the Century'. With such a great demand for rooms in Amsterdam, anyone who plans to be a part of the celebrations, should make their travel arrangements as soon as possible.

If "Getting there is Half the Fun", **ODYSSEUS** is where you should turn before you travel. Find out about all those difficult and essential travel tips, to help you get as much out of your international travels as possible. **ODYSSEUS** has created a travel planner guide that is clearly written and easy to use. Complete with a wealth of information on how to visit the latest travel destinations, meet new friends, have a great time in the bars / clubs, restaurants and fitness establishments. You will find the best beaches, relax in comfortable surroundings and enjoy delectable cuisine, all in an exclusively gay or gay-friendly atmosphere.

In **ODYSSEUS**, we are listing for you more than a short indiscriminate listing for establishments. Our marketing staff has traveled the world to check-out first hand the world's most popular gay and lesbian resorts in destinations such as: Mykonos, Ibiza, Sitges, Gran Canaria, to name just a few - other locations can be found throughout our publication. With this very personal visit, we bring to you many properties and the latest information about what's 'the-best-out-there'. Thus making your travel plans and decisions much easier.

The 13th edition is fully revised and up-dated, plus **ODYSSEUS** Travel is making available to you our 14 years of experience in the gay travel industry. Including our exclusive connections with resorts, hotels, bed & breakfasts. Ranging from elegant 'Five-Star' world-class resorts to the more affordable. Regardless of your tourist classification, we always make sure that gay and lesbian travelers are most welcome and that adequate facilities are offered. For over 14 years, hundreds of thousands of gay and lesbian travelers around the globe have booked their travels and enjoyed their dream vacations, thanks to **ODYSSEUS**. Whether you are planning your 'Honeymoon' in Hawaii, a 'Singles Escapade' in Paris or Amsterdam, 'Sun & Fun' on the Greek Islands or the world's most 'Outrageous' gay nightlife in Ibiza; **ODYSSEUS** is your best source for what the "Gay Travel World" has to offer.

Our close contacts with hotels, resorts and travel suppliers worldwide; allows us to offer to you our reader, a wealth of knowledge through the **ODYSSEUS WORLDWIDE RESERVATIONS SYSTEM** (OWRS). We also offer rooms and flights for the 1998 GAY GAMES in Amsterdam. Your travel agent or you yourself can easily book any accommodation mentioned in the **ODYSSEUS** guide by contacting us directly.

TOLL-FREE USA/Canada: (800) 257-5344
WORLDWIDE: (516) 944-5330
E•MAIL: odyusa/owrs@odyusa.com or
INTERNET: http://www.odyusa.com/index.html

We normally confirm reservations in 24 hrs, but since we prepay the accommodations in-advance, we request a minimum of 14 days notice for most reservations. For special events and holidays a minimum notice of 4 - 6 months is suggested. Contact us today for full details.

Please keep writing to us with your suggestions for improvements or information that we should include or not in **ODYSSEUS** '98/99. If we include and use the information that you have provided to us in writing, we will send you a complimentary copy of **ODYSSEUS** '98/99. Please send your correspondance to: Odysseus Enterprises Ltd., Dept. Ody98/99, PO Box 1548, Port Washington, NY 11050 (USA) or Email: odyusa/info@odyusa.com . Once again we thank you for selecting ODYSSEUS '97/98, as your passport for a "Travels Without Frontiers"© . Enjoy discovering the new age of gay travel, that will take you on a fantastic journey to destinations around the globe. As we get closer to the year 2000, we at **ODYSSEUS** may even someday take our readers to gay and gay-friendly establishments to destinations on the Moon, Mars and beyond...

Enjoy Your Magical Gay Vacations ! ™

élicitations, en achetant notre 13ième édition du guide **ODYSSEUS** - *L'Agenda "Tout-Dans-Un" International de Voyage Gay* ™, *vous avez démontré que vous êtes ou souhaitez devenir un voyageur expérimenté. Donc, vous prenez au sérieux vos voyages gay et vous appréciez la qualité de l'information touristique associée avec* **ODYSSEUS** *depuis la première édition de 1984.*

*La page couverture d'***ODYSSEUS** *'97/98 représente et rends fièrement hommage aux* **"1998 GAY GAMES'** *d'Amsterdam. Ces sports spéciaux et événements culturels auront lieu à Amsterdam, la "Capitale Gay du Monde", du 1 - 8 août, '98. Plus de 10,000 participants et 100,000 spectateurs d'autour du monde sont attendus pour l'occasion. Ce sera le dernier grand 'Événement Gay & Lesbienne du Siècle'. Avec une telle demande pour l'hébergement à Amsterdam, quiconque forme le projet de faire partie des célébrations, devra faire les arrangements nécessaires aussitôt que possible.*

La préparation de votre voyage fait déjà partie du plaisir des vacances; et **ODYSSEUS** *est le conseiller rêvé pour les planifier. Vous y découvrirez une foule de renseignements essentiels et difficiles à obtenir autrement sur "tout-ce-que-vous-auriez-dû-savoir" pour vous aider à profiter au maximum de votre voyage.* **ODYSSEUS** *a créé un agenda-guide de voyage rédigé clairement et facile à utiliser. C'est un guide complet avec une richesse d'informations sur l'art de visiter les destinations de voyage en vogue, comment rencontrer des nouveaux amis et avoir du bon temps dans les bars / clubs, restaurants et établissements de sport et de santé. Vous trouverez les meilleures plages, vous vous délasserez dans des environnements confortables tout en savourant une cuisine délectable. Tout cela dans une atmosphère exclusivement gay ou gay-amicale.*

Chez **ODYSSEUS** *nous inscrivons plus qu'une courte liste non-vérifiée d'établissements. Notre personnel voyage partout dans le monde pour connaître de première main les endroits de villégiatures gay et lesbiennes les plus populaires dans des destinations telles que: Mykonos, Ibiza, Sitges, Gran Canaria, pour n'en nommer que quelques-unes. D'autres emplacements se retrouvent tout au long de notre publication. Avec ce critère de qualité nous vous suggérons ainsi beaucoup d'endroits merveilleux et l'information la plus récente sur ce qu'il y a de mieux à découvrir. Cela facilite l'organisation de votre voyage et rend vos décisions plus facile à prendre.*

La 13ième édition est rêvisée complètement et '**ODYSSEUS Travel**' *vous fait bénéficier de nos 14 années d'expérience dans l'industrie du voyage gay. Y compris nos contacts exclusifs avec endroits de villégiatures, hôtels et gîtes et déjeuners. De l'élégant 'Cinq Etoiles' de première classe au plus accessible; peu importe votre classification touristique, nous nous assurons que les voyageurs gay et lesbiennes sont toujours bienvenus et que des accomodations adéquates sont offertes. Pour plus de 14 années, des centaines de milliers de voyageurs gay et lesbiennes de partout ont réservé leurs voyages et ont aimé leurs vacances de rêve, merci à* **ODYSSEUS**. *Si vous organisez votre 'Lune de Miel' à Hawaii, une 'Escapade de Célibataires' à Paris ou Amsterdam, un festival 'Soleil & Plaisir' aux Iles grecques ou une 'Vibrante' vie nocturne gay à Ibiza,* **ODYSSEUS** *est votre meilleure source sur ce que le "Monde du Voyage Gay" peut vous offrir.*

Nos contacts privilégiés avec hôtels, sites de villégiatures et fournisseurs de voyage, nous permettent d'offrir à nos lecteurs, une richesse de connaissances grâce à '**ODYSSEUS WORLDWIDE RESERVATIONS SYSTEM**' *(OWRS). Nous offrons aussi des chambres et des vols pour les '1998 GAY GAMES' à Amsterdam. Votre agent de voyages ou vous-même pouvez réserver facilement pour toutes les destinations mentionnées dans le guide* **ODYSSEUS** *en nous contactant directement.*

SANS-FRAIS USA/Canada: *(800) 257-5344,*
MONDIAL: *(516) 944-5330,*
E•MAIL: *odyusa/owrs@odyusa.com*
INTERNET: *http://www.odyusa.com/index.html*

Nous confirmons normalement les réservations dans les 24 hrs, mais étant donné que nous payons d'avance ces réservations nous demandons un délai minimum de 14 jours avant votre date d'arrivée pour la plupart des réservations. Pour les événements spéciaux et périodes des fêtes un avis minimum de 4 - 6 mois est suggéré. Contactez-nous aujourd'hui pour plus de détails.

Continuez à nous écrire vos suggestions pour l'amélioration du guide ou toutes informations que nous devrions inclure ou non dans **ODYSSEUS** *'98/99. Si nous incluons et utilisons l'information que vous nous avez fournie par écrit, nous vous enverrons un exemplaire gratuit d'***ODYSSEUS** *'98/99. S.V.P. adressez votre correspondance à: Odysseus Entreprises Ltd., Dept. Ody98/99, PO Box 1548, Port Washington, NY 11050 (USA) ou Email: odyusa/info@odyusa.com . Une fois encore, merci d'avoir choisi* **ODYSSEUS** *'97/98, comme votre passeport pour "Voyages Sans Frontières"©. Découvrez le nouvel âge du voyage gay, cela vous conduira sur un itinéraire de destinations et voyage autour du monde. Comme nous approchons de l'année 2000,* **ODYSSEUS** *amènera peut-être un jour ses lecteurs dans des établissements gay et gay-amicaux sur la Lune, Mars et au-delà...*

Aimez Vos Vacances Magiques Gay ! ™

elicitaciones, por adquirir nuestra 13va edición de **ODYSSEUS** - El Plan "Todo-En-Uno" Internacional de Viajes Gay ™ guía, has demostrado que eses o deseas ser un experto viajero. Por lo tanto, toma seriamente tu guía de viajes gay y apreciaras la calidad de la información de los viajes que están asociados con **ODYSSEUS** desde su primera publicación en 1984.

La portada de **ODYSSEUS** '97/98 presenta y saluda con orgullo los **'1998 GAY GAMES'** en Amsterdam. Estos eventos especiales tanto deportivos como culturales se desarrollarán en Amsterdam, la "Capital Gay del Mundo", desde el 1 al 8 de agosto 1998. Se espera la asistencia de más de 10,000 participantes y por encima de 100,000 espectadores al rededor del mundo. Este será el último y más grande 'Evento de Gay & Lesbianas del Siglo'. Con una demanda tan grande de habitaciones en Amsterdam, alguien que planee ser parte de las celebraciones debería hacer sus arreglos de viaje lo más antes posible.

Si "La Quieres Pasar Muy Divertido", **ODYSSEUS** es donde debes acudir antes de viajar. Encontrarás todo aquello difícil y esencial para un viaje. **ODYSSEUS** ha creado una guía viajera claramente diseñada y fácil de usar. Llena de una información muy rica, como visitar cualquier destino, encontrar nuevos amigos, pasar un buen tiempo en bares / clubes, restaurantes o tiendas. Encontrarás las mejores playas, descansar en ambientes confortables y deleitar del arte culinario, todo en una atmósfera exclusivamente gay o con amigos de los gay.en **ODYSSEUS** hemos incluido más que un listado de establecimientos. Nuestro personal de mercadeo ha viajado alrededor del mundo para observar primeramente los resorts para gay y lesbianas más populares del mundo, destinos como: Mykonos, Ibiza, Sitges, Gran Canaria, para nombrar algunos - otros destinos pueden ser encontrados a través de nuestra publicación. Con estas visitas personales, les brindamos muchas oportunidades y la más reciente información acerca de "que es lo mejor ahí". Así hacemos su plan de viajes y decisiones más fácil.

La 13va edición fue revisada totalmente, además que **'ODYSSEUS Travel'** te ofrece sus 14 años de experiencia en la industria turística gay. Incluyendo nuestras conexiones exclusivas con resorts, hoteles, hospedaje con desayuno. Abarcando desde resort muy elegantes de 'Cinco Estrellas' hasta los más económicos. Indiferentemente de su clasificación turística, siempre nos aseguramos que los viajeros gay y lesbianas que sean bienvenidos y que les ofrezcan medios adecuados. Por más de 14 años, cientos de millares de turistas gay y lesbianas alrededor del globo han reservado sus viajes y disfrutaron las vacaciones de sus sueños, gracias a **ODYSSEUS**. Si planeas tu 'Luna de Miel' en Hawaii, un 'Escape Solitario' en París o Amsterdam, 'Sol y Diversión' en las Islas Griegas o el mundo lo más 'Extravagante' de las noches gay en Ibiza, **ODYSSEUS** te ofrece la mejor fuente de información para "Viajar en el Mundo Gay".

Nuestro estrecho contacto con hoteles, resorts y proveedores alrededor del mundo nos permite ofrecer a nuestros lectores gran cantidad de opciones a través del **'ODYSSEUS WORLDWIDE RESERVATIONS SYSTEM'** (OWRS). También ofrecemos habitaciones y vuelos para los **'1998 GAY GAMES'** en Amsterdam. Tu agencia de viajes o por ti mismo puedes fácilmente tramitar cualquier reservación mencionada en la guía **ODYSSEUS** contactándonos directamente.

TOLL-FREE USA/Canadá: (800) 257-5344,
MUNDIAL: (516) 944-5330,
E•MAIL: odyusa/owrs@odyusa.com
INTERNET: http://www.odyusa.com/index.html

Normalmente confirmamos reservaciónes en 24 horas, pero cuando se se debe pagar la reservación por adelantado, requerimos avisar con un mínimo de 14 días para la mayoría de las reservaciones. Para eventos especiales y fiestas sugerimos notificar de 4 a 6 messes. Contáctenos hoy para major detalles.

Por favor envíenos por escrito sus sugerencias para mejorar o alguna información que ustedes puedan incluir o eliminar en **ODYSSEUS** '98/99. Si nosotros incluimos y usamos la información que nos has proporcionado, te enviaremos una copia de **ODYSSEUS** '98/99 como agradecimiento. Por favor envía tu correspondancia a: **Odysseus Enterprises Ltd.**, Dept. Ody98/99, PO Box 1548, Port Washington, NY 11050 (USA) o Email: odyusa/info@odyusa.com . Una vez más queremos agradecerte por seleccionar **ODYSSEUS** '97/98, como su pasaporte par un "Viajes Sin Fronteras"©. Disfruta descubriendo la nueva era de los viajes gay, te llevaremos a un viaje fantástico a diferentes destinos alrededor del globo. En tanto que estamos más cerca del año 2000, **ODYSSEUS** podría algún día llevar a nuestros lectores a establecimientos gay con destinos en la Luna, Marte y más allá...

¡ **Disfruta Tus Vacaciones Mágicas Gay** ! ™

ODYSSEUS 97/98

Поздравляем! Покупкой 13 издания нашего Всемирного гей-справочника для путешественников Вы доказали, что уже имеете некоторый опыт в путешествиях или, по крайней мере, собираетесь его приобрести! В силу этого Вы серьезно относитесь к предстоящим Вам поездкам и цените качество туристической информации, понятие, неразрывно ассоциирующееся с ODYSSEUS с момента его первого выхода в свет в 1984 г.

Обложка нынешнего издания с гордостью посвящается Геевским Олимпийским Играм 98 (1 – 8 августа) в Амстердаме, «голубой» столице мира. Ожидается свыше 10.000 участников и 100.000 зрителей со всего мира. Это будет последнее крупное гей-событие ХХ века. Из-за большого спроса на гостиницы в Амстердаме всякий, кто хотел бы приехать на Игры, должен позаботиться о планировании своей поездки заранее.

Перед тем, как отправиться в путь, загляните в ODYSSEUS. Здесь есть вся необходимая Вам информация для того, чтобы использовать Вашу поездку на все 100! Наш справочник хорошо написан, им просто пользоваться. Море полезной информации: как попасть в самые популярные среди геев места отдыха, встретить новых друзей, в каких клубах, ресторанах и спортзалах лучше всего проводить время. Расслабьтесь на лучших пляжах, насладитесь комфортом и изысканной кухней лучших ресторанов – исключительно геевских или, по крайней мере, «дружелюбных» по отношению к нам.

ODYSSEUS предлагает больше, чем просто краткий перечень заведений. Наши сотрудники много поездили по миру, чтобы из первых рук получить информацию о наиболее популярных курортах для геев и лесбиянок. Вот только некоторые из них – Миконос, Ибица, Ситчес, Гран Канария. Все остальные курорты Вы найдете в нашем справочнике. Только для Вас мы предлагаем эксклюзивную и самую свежую информацию обо всем самом лучшем в геевском мире, помогая тем самым решить – куда же, в конце концов податься?!

13 издание ODYSSEUS является утонченным и дополненным. В Вашем распоряжении весь наш 14-летний опыт в гей-туризме, включая уникальные связи с курортами, пансионами и гостиницами, от элегантных пятизвездных всемирно-известных курортов до более доступных по ценам. Мы можем Вас заверить, что какой бы «звездности» ни была гостиница, рекомендуемая нами, она будет соответствовать данной категории и Вам всегда там будут рады. В течение 14 лет сотни тысяч геев и лесбиянок со всего мира заказывали свои поездки через нас и, благодаря нам, смогли действительно насладиться своим отпуском. Планируете ли Вы провести медовый месяц на Гаваях, в одиночку пройтись по Парижу или Амстердаму, повеселиться под солнцем Греции или же насладиться известной всему миру ночной гей-жизнью на острове Ибица, ODYSSEUS всегда предложит Вам наилучшую информацию о том, что есть в нашем мире для геев.

Наши тесные связи с гостиницами и туроператорами по всему миру позволяют нам, читатель, предложить все богатство нашего опыта через ВСЕМИРНУЮ СЕТЬ БРОНИРОВАНИЯ ODYSSEUS. Мы также предлагаем размещение и авиабилеты на Геевские Олимпийские Игры 1998 в Амстердаме. Вы или Ваш турагент легко можете заказать любой тип размещения из упомянутых в ODYSSEUS, связавшись напрямую с нами. Бесплатный телефон (США/Канада) – (800) 257-5344. Телефон для остальных стран: (516) 944-5330.

E-mail: odyusa@odyusa.com
Internet: http://www.odysa.com/index.html

Как правило, мы подтверждаем бронирование в течение 24 часов, но, поскольку мы должны оплачивать размещение заранее, мы просим присылать Ваши заявки минимум за 14 дней. Если речь идет о каких-либо событиях или периоде отпусков, мы рекомендуем бронировать поездку минимум за 4 – 6 месяцев.

Мы просим Вас писать нам о тех изменениях и информации, которые нам по Вашему мнению следовало бы включить в Справочник или исключить из него. Вы можете посылать информацию обычной или электронной почтой, а также оставлять сообщения на нашей странице в Интернете. Если мы включим Вашу информацию в наш справочник, Вы получите бесплатный экземпляр ODYSSEUS 98/99. Пожалуйста, направляйте всю корреспонденцию по следующему адресу:

Odysseus Enterprises Ltd., Dept. ODY98/99, PO Box 1548,
Port Washington NY 11050–1548 (USA).
E-mail: odyusa@odyusa.com

Еще раз благодарим Вас за то, что Вы выбрали ODYSSEUS 97/98 как Ваш пропуск в «Туризм без Границ». Откройте для себя новую эру в гей-туризме, фантастику путешествий по всему миру. Чем ближе мы приближаемся к 2000 году, тем вероятнее, что в ODYSSEUS как-нибудь предложим нашим читателям посетить гей-заведения на Луне, Марсе и так далее...

Насладитесь Вашим волшебным гей-путешествием!

１９９７／９８年度オデッセウス序説：
　この度は、１９９７／９８年度の第１３版「オデッセウス国際ゲイ総合ガイドブック」をご購入頂き、誠に有り難うございました。当社は、１９８４年の初版以来大多数の読者の支持を獲得してきました。

　今回発行分の表紙は、１９９８年８月初旬にオランダのアムステルダムで開催の「ゲイ・ゲーム」を記念して制作されています。皆様ご存知の通りアムステルダムは、「ゲイの世界の首都」と呼ばれ、世界中からの競技参加者は 10,000 名を越え、また競技期間中は 100,000 名の観客動員が見込まれています。２０世紀最後を飾るゲイ・レズビアンのイベントを見逃さないために、是非お早めに旅程及び宿泊のプランを立てられるよう、お勧め致します。

　オデッセウスでは、他にも、旅行者のよきガイド役として、人気の高いビーチ・バー・クラブ・レストランの最新情報をご紹介しております。最新かつ最高の情報を提供するという当社の編集方針に基づいて制作された、このガイドブックを充分にご活用下さい。

　なお、本誌読者への特典として、１９９８年８月開催のゲイ・ゲーム観戦旅行者用に、フライト及びホテルの予約を受け付けます。以下の電話番号で、直接お申し込み下さい。また、電子メールでも承ります。最後に、本誌をご購入頂き、厚く御礼申し上げます。

　TEL（５１６）９４４－５３３０
　E-mail : odyusa/owrs@odyusa.com

◆ Following please find some of the most commonly used abbreviations in this guide:

A/C = Air Conditioning
C/H = Central Heating
IGTA = International Gay Travel Assoc.
AGLTA = Australian Gay Travel Assoc.
TAC = Travel Agent Commission
W/ = With

Breakfast:
AB = American Breakfast
CB = Continental Breakfast
ChB = Chinese Breakfast
CnB = Canadian Breakfast
DB = Dutch Breakfast
EB = English Breakfast
FB = French Breakfast
GB = German Breakfast
HB = Hawaiian Breakfast
IB = Irish Breakfast

IsB = Israeli Breakfast
JB = Japanese Breakfast
RB = Russian Breakfast
TB = Tropical Breakfast
b = buffet
H/B = Half Board (2 meals included, breakfast + lunch or breakfast + dinner)

Clientele:
GM = Gay men
GW = Gay women
GMW = Gay men and women
AW = All welcome

Credit Cards:

CC# = Credit Card number
AMEX = American Express
MC = Master Card
DC = Diners Club
DISC = Discover
EC = Euro Card

DON'T FORGET!

The hotel prices in this edition are given as a price range only and are not exact. All prices mentioned in **Odysseus '97/98** are subject to change without notice.

All prices must be reconfirmed at the time of reservation.

DISCLAIMER

ODYSSEUS ENTERPRISES LTD., CANNOT BE HELD RESPONSIBLE FOR THE QUALITY OF SERVICES OR PRODUCTS MENTIONED IN THIS GUIDE.

ALTHOUGH EVERY EFFORT IS MADE TO ENSURE THE ACCURACY OF THE TRAVEL INFORMATION AND HOTEL RATES APPEARING IN THIS GUIDE, IT SHOULD BE KEPT IN MIND THAT INFORMATION DOES CHANGE DURING AND AFTER PUBLICATION.

ALL MAPS IN THIS GUIDE ARE NOT TO SCALE AND THE LOCATION OF A BUSINESS ON THE MAP IS ONLY APPROXIMATE.

WE WELCOME COMMENTS PERTAINING TO ANY INACCURACIES OF INFORMATION AND / OR QUALITY OF PRODUCTS AND SERVICES EXPERIENCED BY OUR READERS IN ORDER TO EVALUATE THEIR LISTING IN FUTURE EDITIONS.

JOSE ARROYO

INTENSITY
PHOTOGRAPHY

FINE ART FIGURE PHOTOGRAPHY
213 . 467. 0475
2021 N CHEREMOYA AVENUE . LOS ANGELES CA 90068
INTERNET MAIL: jarroyo@aol.com

ODYSSEUS

TRAVEL SUPPLEMENT

GREECE • SPAIN • TURKEY • HAWAII
EUROPEAN CITY BREAKS
SPECIAL EVENTS & TOUR PACKAGES   **13th year**

Discover **Santorini,** a postcard perfect island in the Cyclades only 45 min. flight from Mykonos. The Caldera-type volcano, volcanic lava and stones give Santorini its characteristic wild beauty, and wild riot of colors. Santorini is an important stop for cruise ships in the Aegean Sea. The island is more conservative than Mykonos, and it is mostly oriented towards straight honeymoon type tourism. However, Odysseus clients can enjoy the beauty of the island while staying at the charming **Kavalari Hotel** situated in Fira on the Caldera Cliff with terraces looking on to the volcanic islets, or at **Dana Villas, Grotto Villas** or **Sun Rocks Apts** in Firostefani within a short walk from **Fira Town** along the scenic promenade.

HOTEL KAVALARI

Hotel Kavalari commands a central location in Fira Town. Originally a Captain's House, the converted hotel is built on the rock and completely in tune with its dramatic surroundings. Enjoy the hotel's traditional style guest rooms in local architecture and gusto. Each room features a double or twin bed, full bath, phone, radio and fridge. Deluxe rooms are spacious accommodating from 2-4 people, with extra living space area, small kitchenette, and panoramic views. Its superb furnishings and all the modern amenities will satisfy even the most denmanding guest. Breakfast is served on the terrace overlooking the magnificent Aegean Sea with view of the famous volcano. Airport transfers available on request. Odysseus clients have always enjoyed a warm welcome at the Hotel Kavalari.

DANA VILLAS

A group of studios and apartments perched on the rim of the cliff in Fira, yet away from the noisy center, facing the sea and the Volcano island. The villas have been reconstructed in traditional architectural style and can accommodate 2-6 persons. They are all fully equipped with modern bathrooms and kitchenette. Enjoy panoramic views and breathtaking sunset from your own terrace. **Grotto Villas** are adjacent to Dana Villas sharing a pool. They offer different size villas in typical island style ranging from studios to 2 bedroom apts.

SUN ROCKS

Traditionally designed elegant villa-apts fully furnished. Spacious terrace overlooking the Aegean Sea. Pool and sundecks.

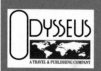

MYKONOS

Mykonos is the world's most famous gay holiday resort destination in the Cyclades, situated 1 hour flight from Athens. Mykonos Town is an architectural gem, with marshmallow white houses, narrow paved alleyways and a postcard pretty waterfront lined with authentic island tavernas, shops and galleries. Mykonos offers romantic beauty found nowhere else on earth with fantastic sunsets, and white Cycladean windmills. The island boasts some of the finest beaches in Greece and is justly famous for its legendary gay nude beaches and nightlife. **ODYSSEUS** has the best connections on the island of Mykonos since 1986, assuring our clients the best properties and the finest service. Many of our clients enjoy their Mykonos vacation so much that they keep coming back.

▼ The season in Mykonos is generally from mid April to the end of October. July and August are the busiest months; hotel rooms must be booked months in advance.

▼ Gay travelers prefer to stay in Mykonos Town close to shops, tavernas and the legendary gay nightlife. The Gay / Nude beaches are outside town and can be reached by bus from town, or by boat from the port.

▼ All the properties that we represent offer central in town, or beach location, with warm gay friendly atmosphere. Andromeda Residence and Mykonos Blu are the most upscale; Anastasios Sevasti, Apolonia Bay and Hotel Elysium are traditional hotels; the hotel Elena is suggested for the economic minded single gay travelers.

ANDROMEDA RESIDENCE

Andromeda Residence consists of 30 fully air-conditioned luxurious studios, maisonettes and villas, arrange in six two-story buildings in an excellent location, 5 minutes walk from the center of Mykonos Town. Amenities include: large sparkling swimming pool with extensive sundeck, poolside bar, a superb restaurant, 12 hrs room service, full reception, direct dial phones, and travel assistance. The highest quality of materials have been used to provide the best possible traditional atmosphere and decoration.

ANDROMEDA
Residence
Mykonos

Due to the great demand for holiday booking at the "Andromeda Residence" we recommend to reserve your units at least 10 weeks in advance. Availability and details of the units are available from Odysseus.

"Andromeda Residence" offers a superb quality and service immeasurably superior to anything one is likely to find on the island.

ODYSSEUS clients are invited to enjoy a welcome drink at the bar on arrival.

HOTEL ELYSIUM

Attractive Myconean style hotel in traditional color. The hotel is situated in a convenient downtown location up on the hill near the School of Art with a panoramic view over the old city of Mykonos and the Aegean Sea. All rooms have private bath or shower, ceiling fans, hairdryer, phone, stereo music, refrigerator, safe box, and color satellite TV. Some rooms have a private balcony and seaview as well. The hotel has a pool, jacuzzi, poolside bar, and a fully equipped Fitness Center with sauna. There is an attractive breakfast room/lounge. A warm welcome is extended to ODYSSEUS clients for a perfect holiday in Mykonos.

ANASTASSIOS SEVASTI

Anastassios Sevasti is a Myconian style hotel in a quiet, elevated area near the School of Art, overlooking the blue Aegean Sea and the town. It is a short 10 min. walk from the center of town. All guest rooms have balconies, private bath, telephone, Hi-Fi stereo music, refrigerator, safe deposit and air-conditioning. The hotel has a beautiful swimming pool with sundecks and poolside bar. There is also a Gym room for those who wish to keep in shape. ODYSSEUS customers enjoy a friendly welcome atmosphere, buffet breakfast, and a complimentary pick up service from the airport.

HOTEL ELENA

Small, intimate hotel with traditional colors. The hotel is available on a bed and breakfast basis and is located in the center of town close to the Amphitheater and the Andromeda, some 7 min. walk from the port. All rooms have private bath or shower, and some a private balcony and seaview as well. There is an attractive breakfast room/lounge, although breakfast and drinks can also be taken on the terrace. ODYSSEUS clients have stayed at this hotel since 1986 and have spoken highly of the warm Greek hospitality extended to them by the owners.

MYKONOS BLU

The most luxurious Mykonos 5-star resort hotel in a tranquil beachside setting with panoramic views of the Gulf of Psarou, only 5 km / 3 mi from Mykonos Town. Island style bungalows and bungalow suites in gardens with private bath, balcony, hairdryer, phone, satellite TV, refrigerator, safe deposit box, A/C. Indoor and outdoor dining, pool, pool taverna and pool snack bar, cocktail bar and room service. Mykonos Blu offers a gracious welcome to **ODYSSEUS** customers to make your holiday a lasting memory.

ATHENS

Athens, the capital of Greece is a bustling Mediterranean city with white-washed houses, large avenues, busy street cafes, interesting flea-markets for the bargain hunters, and the home town of the ancient Acropolis with its Classical temples. Visit the Agora, the Theatre of Dionysus and the Temple of Zeus. Athens with its ancient port Piraeus are your getaway to the magnificent Greek Islands. Most of the islands are within a short 1 hour flight from the capital. In Athens we offer two hotels: The Athenian Inn, a comfortable and friendly hotel near the famous Kolonaki Square, the trendy Tsakaloff Street and some of Athens best gay bars. The elegant 5-star Andromeda Athens is an excellent choice for the most discerning travelers. It is conveniently located in Athens business district near the USA embassy.

AIRFARE
Ask about special airfares
to Athens and the Greek Islands from
major USA cities

SIGHT-SEEING TOURS

Athens
(1/2 day)
Sounion
(1/2 day)
Delphi
(full day)
Other tours
available
on request

ANDROMEDA ATHENS

Elegant, intimate and luxurious five-star hotel in the best Old World tradition. The most exclusive "Boutique style" hotel in town. Conveniently located in the business heart of Athens, off Vassilisis Sofias Ave., near the USA Embassy. The **Andromeda Athens** offers 30 designer rooms, suites, studios and penthouses with color satellite TV, mini-bar, direct-dial phones, air-conditioning and central heating. Carpets from Persia, pastel studio works from Italy, and art pieces from famous designers welcome the guests in Andromeda Athens. Gourmet Italian restaurant "Michelangelo" offers a cosmopolitan atmosphere and is open for lunch and dinner. Warm welcome is extended to all **ODYSSEUS** customers.

Amenities:
Superb Italian
restaurant and bar,
color satellite TV,
mini bars,
24 hrs room service,
laundry, valet service,
safety deposit boxes,
hairdryer, phones
in all bathrooms.
private guide, limo service
upon request

ATHENIAN INN

Athenian Inn is a charming renovated tourist class hotel in the heart of Athens, right in the fashionable Kolonaki area near all major city attractions, clubs, restaurants and shopping. The hotel features large fully air-conditioned rooms and suites with twin or double beds, private shower, balconies with view of the Lycabettus Hill, and attractive breakfast room / lounge. Excellent accommodating staff and warm welcome is always extended to ODYSSEUS customers who stay at this hotel.

athenian inn
your home in Athens

ST. GEORGE LYCABETTUS HOTEL

Deluxe landmark hotel in Kolonaki, the most exclusive quarter of Athens. Byzantine, Victorian and Greek art displays throughout the hotel. 167 rooms with priv. bath. phone, CTV, A/C. Some rooms with balcony and views of the Acropolis. Amenities: restaurant, cafe, bar, rooftop pool. Walk to gay bars and clubs, elegant shopping and restaurants.

CRETE

Crete is the southernmost and the largest of all the Greek Islands. It offers infinite variety of attractions from its magnificent beaches to the snow covered highest peaks. In Crete ODYSSEUS offers accommodations in Heraklion at the Hotel Atlantis for those who wish to visit the nearby Minoan ruins of Knossos. For a perfect beach holiday enjoy your stay at Casa Delfino or the Hotel Halepa in the Hania on the West Coast with its picture perfect Venetian Harbor, lovely secluded beaches, tavernas, bars and lively nightlife.

HOTEL ATLANTIS

Elegant four-star hotel in a central location near the Archeological Museum with views of the sea and harbor. 160 rooms with priate bath, phone, double bed, heating/air-conditioning, mini-bar, some with terrace. Restaurant, bar, roof terrace with snack bar, solarium and health studio.

CASA DELFINO

Modern complex of luxurious living quarters incorporated into an attractive historical environment. Casa Delfino is located in the Old Town near the Venetian Harbor. Fully furnished air-conditioned apartments-suites with refrigerator, stove. Easy access to beaches.

HALEPA HOTEL

New Classical style historic hotel in the beautiful, quiet and historic suburb of Hania. It is close to the sea within walking distance of the beach. 40 comfortable rooms and suites with private bath, phone, breakfast lounge and sun terrace.

RHODES

The island of **Rhodes** belongs to the god **Helios** (Sun) according to the ancient Greek Mythology. The island is a vacation paradise for sunseekers. The city of Rhodes will amaze you with its bustling medieval town, shopping, nightclubs, discos and gambling casino. 15 min. south of Rhodes is the famous Faliraki nude beach. Further south is beautiful Lindos with its famous acropolis, lovely beaches, and vibrant nightlife. ODYSSEUS offers a variety of accommodations in Rhodes Town and Lindos.

LINDOS MARE

First class luxury resort hotel near Lindos village, built in the hillside with a panoramic view of Vlicha Bay, 100 m. / yards from the sea. All rooms with terrace, balcony and Sea View, full bath, refrigerator, phone, radio, air-conditioning. Amenities: lounge, restaurant, bar, pool, snack bar, mini market.

AEGEAN COCKTAIL CRUISE

Discover the yachting world of the Greek Islands by joining a small mixed group of passengers. Sail among dozens of exciting and unique islands full of natural beauty, fantastic beaches, and age old history. Yachts are approximately 100-140 ft. in length accommodating less than 30 passengers in air-conditioned staterooms with private bath en suite. The yachts have excellent crew, food, service and great deal of fun. Enjoy a 7-Day Friday-Friday **Cyclade Islands Cruise** with your lover or friends, into a magic journey with clean air, blue sky, and crystal-clear waters. Departure/Return: Port of Piraeus (Athens). Islands visited: Piraeus - Kea, Paros, Santorini, Ios, Heraklia, Naxos, Delos, Mykonos, Tinos - Piraeus. Departures are March - October. Rates include: American breakfast, lunch or dinner, welcome cocktail, captain's dinner, tour leader on board, transfers to and from the yacht. Not included: port taxes, drinks on board, optional excursions, gratuities for the crew. We can arrange flights from any USA city and extensions on the Greek Islands.

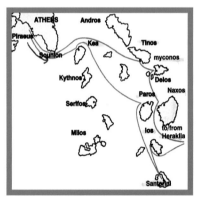

or similar yachts

or similar yachts

The yacht is a motor sailer type that combines tradition and luxury. She accommodates up to 30 passengers in 10 luxury cabins with Upper and Lower single beds, double beds, or two lower beds. All cabins offer en suite facilities, air condition, telephone and stereo. The elegantly appointed saloon is ideal for entertaining and relaxing. Separate accommodation for the crew of 7. Cruising speed: about 12 knots.

SPECIAL CONDITIONS FOR ALL CRUISES: Although cruise itinerary is almost always followed as indicated, on occasions circumstances such as exceptionally bad weather, the captain may make required changes at his discretion. The Company reserves the right to cancel any cruise, in which case the full fare will be refunded. Please call for prices and departure dates.

or similar yachts

ISTANBUL TURKEY

Istanbul is a delight for the senses evoking fantasies out of the Arabian Nights. It is a magic combination of the ancient and the new. Here the exotic Orient meets the progressive West at the meeting point of Europe and Asia. Istanbul has great monuments and museums: Aya Sofia, the Byzantine Great Church now serving as a museum; The Blue Mosque, famous for its magnificent blue Iznik tiles; as well as Topkapi, and the Grand Bazaar. The gay scene is low key with few bars and clubs around Taksim Square. **Odysseus** offers in Istanbul a fine selection of hotels chosen for their quality and central location to major tourist attractions and the gay nightlife. We can also arrange transfers, city tours and cruises by friendly English speaking guides.

AIRFARE
Ask about special airfare to Istanbul from major USA cities

çemberlitas bath

CITY TOURS

Full Day Classic Istanbul
visit to Byzantion Hippodrome, Blue Mosque, Saint Sophia, lunch at Topkapi Palace, visit Topkapi Museum, Underground Cistern and Grand Bazaar

Full Day Classic Istanbul with Hammam (Turkish Bath)
Same as above plus visit to a typical Turkish Bath

Full Day Istanbul-Bosphorous
boat trip on the Bosphorous and a lunch at a fish restaurant, visit the Asian part of Istanbul and the Camlica Hill. Sightseeing the modern part of Istanbul, Taksim and Beyoglu.

Topkapi Museum

gulette

ISTANBUL NIGHTLIFE
8pm-midnight
Enjoy dinner at Hacibaba or Sarnic restaurants, night tour of two "all welcome" type bars, or gay bars, clubs of the Taksim Square area + one drink per person in bars with English speaking guide.
Pick up and return to your hotel.

In addition to tourist services in Istanbul, **ODYSSEUS** is pleased to offer to our customers various other travel arrangements for individuals and small groups to any destination of interest anywhere in Turkey. Whether you are interested in photography, cultural expeditions, historical sites, national parks, yachting, or biblical tours, our ground service operator in Turkey will do the best to make your holiday in Turkey a wonderful and hassle free experience. We can work out for you any tour program or goulette cruise to fit your budget and schedule.

HOTEL ARCADIA

The Hotel Arcadia is an elegant four-star hotel in an authentic 19th century building. It offers traditional Turkish hospitality. Located right on Sultanahmet Square, the hotel commands beautiful views of St. Sophia and the Blue Mosque, and it is only 500 m / 1/2 mi. from the famous Grand Bazaar and Topkapi Museum. 48 rooms and 7 suites are elegantly decorated with CTV, phone, minibar, C/H, A/C, safe deposit, hairdryer. Restaurant, Lobby Cafe Bar. Young and dynamic staff, 24 hrs room service. Many ODYSSEUS clients have already stayed at the Hotel Arcadia and enjoyed its fine amenities and service.

Enjoy the panoramic view of the Sea of Marmara from the Panorama Restaurant, or a delightful feast of Turkish cuisine at the Arcadia Restaurant.

AMSTERDAM

Amsterdam is a graceful city with beautiful canals, historic buildings, world class art museums, and colorful flower markets. A city where **The Queen** is always a symbol of admiration. This is Europe's most popular city break destination for gay and lesbian travelers. From the Houses with boys to the Leather Clubs, Amsterdam got it all. The liberal spirit of the city combined with a civilized tolerance will make your stay in Amsterdam both fun and uncomplicated. **August 1-8, 1998** the Gay Games will be in Amsterdam. This will be the largest international sports, culture and friendship event of the century. ODYSSEUS offers selected gay hotels in Amsterdam for the Gay Games period including flights from Major USA cities.

HOTEL EDEN

Delightful and friendly three-star hotel in the heart of Amsterdam on the famous Amstel Canal. 300 rooms with private bath, CTV, phone, and hairdryer. All the important sights and attractions are within walking distance. The legendary gay nightlife is only a short walk away.

HOTEL KRASNAPOLSKY

Elegant first-class four-star hotel in the center of Amsterdam on the famous Dam Square near the Royal Palace. 429 comfortable rooms and suites with CTV (CNN), phone, A/C, minibar, trouser press, 24 hrs. room service. Restaurants (4), Sushi bar, lounge & hair salon.

TULIP INN

Modern three-star hotel in five Art Deco style buildings in the heart of Amsterdam close to the Flower Market, Royal Palace and Central Train Station. All 208 rooms have private bath, hair dryer, phone, CTV and A/C. Brasserie, bar and parking. The hotel enjoys a central location close to public transportation, gay clubs, and tourist attractions.

CENTRE APTS
Amsterdam

High quality individually decorated self-catering studios and one-bedroom apartments near the Central Train Station and the leather bars scene off the Damrak. Each with double bedroom, lounge, kitchen, microwave and dishwasher. The larger apartments have a separate single bedroom for a third guest.

AMSTERDAM CONNECTION

Fully furnished self-catering studios and one-bedroom apts in the center of the city and only minutes away from gay bars and clubs. Most units with full bath, living room, CTV, tape cassette player, tea and coffee making facilities. Use of full large kitchen and dining room.

HOTEL ORFEO

Popular all male gay hotel in the center of Amsterdam's restaurants and entertainment area, few steps from the Kerkstraat gay scene. 20 rooms with shared or private bath. The rooms with private bath are larger wirh, phone, CTV, and refrigerator. Amenities include: breakfast lounge, bar and sauna. Own key. Free maps and information about the Amsterdam Gay Scene. Fully furnished apartments are available nearby. The hotel's central location and the friendly service of the management and staff make the Hotel Orfeo an excellent and affordable choice for your accommodations needs in Amsterdam.

Christmas & New Year
Min. 7 nights stay
Easter
Min. 5 nights stay
Reception Open:
8:00am-24:00 (midnight)

ITALY

Italy is one of the world's most fascinating destinations. This age old land is blessed with beautiful landscapes, rich history, and magnificent ancient monuments of one of the greatest centers of Western Civilizations. There is always something special for you in Italy whether your interest is in the Opera, art, religion, or Italian cuisine. **ODYSSEUS** offers individually selected charming hotels in Italy's most popular destinations: **Hotel Veneto** in Rome, **Hotel Basilea** in Venice and **Hotel Duomo** **and Hotel Delle Tele** in Florence. These hotels offer high standards, friendly service, and excellent location for sight seeing or nightlife.

HOTEL BASILEA

Venice

Comfortable three-star hotel overlooking a typical venetian canal in the historical heart of Venice. CTV, phone, A/C, hair dryer, minibar. Near Railway Station house, Garage and Air Terminal. 15 min. from St. Mark's square.

Florence

HOTEL DUOMO

Situated right in Cathedral Square with magnificent views of the Duomo, it offers the comfort of a modern hotel with warm and friendly atmosphere. CTV, phone, minibar, priv. bath, A/C. Beautiful breakfast lounge.

HOTEL DELLE TELE

Elegant comfortable three-star hotel in the heart of the city decorated with paintings on canvas. The hotel is located a short stroll from the Cathedral and the Train Station. All rooms with CTV, phone, minibar, priv. bath, A/C. Beautiful breakfast lounge.

HOTEL VENETO

Completely refurbished three-star hotel between the famous Via Veneto and the Air Terminal. Walk to Villa Borghese, Spanish Steps, Vatican and all tourist attractions. Comfortable rooms with CTV, phone, A/C, and mini-bar. Breakfast lounge, American bar.

Rome

PARIS   FRANCE

Paris is the historical, political and cultural capital of France. It is a delightful city with historical monuments, large Avenues, sidewalk cafes, gourmet restaurants, and fashion shops and boutiques. Paris will captivate you with its exuberant *joie de vivre*, eternal charm and youthful vitality. Visit the oldest parts of Paris - Ile de la Cité and the Ile St.-Louis right in the middle of the Seine. The Left Bank is famous for the Latin Quarter extending from the Luxembourg Gardens and the Panthéon to the Seine including the fashionable St. Germain de Près and Blvd. St. Michel. On the Right Bank you will find "the Marais", the bohemian center of Paris and the "Gay Village" of the French Capital. The "marais" offers many popular gay bars, clubs, coffee shops and restaurants.

▼ Gay travelers prefer to stay in the Marais, the renovated art and culture center of Paris where the gay nightlife is at its best and most of the gay clubs, bars and restaurants are within a short walking distance.

▼ We are pleased to offer three quality hotels in Paris: The **Axial Beaubourg**, the **Hotel Saintonge**. Both hotels are well situated in the Marais. The **Hotel Rive Gauche** is located in the Latin Quarter off St. Germain de Prés.

AXIAL BEAUBOURG

The **Axial-Beaubourg** is a charming three star hotel in the Marais, the 'gay village' of Paris. The hotel offers sparkling clean freshly decorated rooms in an historic building, with remote control CTV, phone, and private bath with hairdryer. Double rooms have large double beds. Breakfast is served in the breakfast cellar. The hotel offers good quality amenities and services. Easy public transportation near the hotel will connect you anywhere in Paris. Walking distance to the **Pompidou Art Center**, the famous **Latin Quarter**, the **Opera** and the **Louvre Museum**.

HOTEL SAINTONGE

Situated in a peaceful street in the **Marais**, the Hotel Saintonge offers the comfort of its 23 rooms all with direct dial phones, automatic alarm clock, mini-bar, safe deposit box, and CTV. Enjoy your breakfast at the hotel's breakfast lounge and leisurely explore all the charms of the historic quarter. Gay clubs and bars are all within walking distance. Warm welcome is extended to **ODYSSEUS** customers from the management and staff of the Hotel Saintonge.

HOTEL RIVE GAUCHE

Economy two-star hotel off the fashionable St. Germain de Prés in the antique dealers district of the trendy Latin Quarter. Walk to prestigious Cafés, Jazz clubs and restaurants. 21 rooms with priv. bath, CTV, phone.

Sophisticated and cosmopolitan, **Ibiza** is a beautiful and gentle island popular with the international jet setters, fashion designers and trendy gay tourists. Enjoy the medieval **'Old Town'** Dalt Vila with its unique fairytale-like atmosphere, packed with 24 hrs. bars, clubs and restaurants. By day sunbath *'au naturel'* on the famous nude beach 'Es Cabellet' near Las Salinas where the action is 'hot'. Nearby **Playa Figueretes**, 1 mi. / 1.5 km from Ibiza Town, is a modern beach resort with wide sandy beach, large hotels, restaurants, and shops. The travel season in Ibiza is May-October. Most gay travelers prefer to stay in Ibiza Town where the gay nightlife is easily accessible. In the heart of the **'Old Town'** Odysseus offers the charming Navila Aparthotel, and in Figueretes the popular all male **Hotel Marigna**.

NAVILA APARTHOTEL

Renovated apartments in a 300 years old mansion in the heart of Old Town. Individually decorated spacious one-bedroom apartments with living room, kitchen/dining area and full bath. Spectacular views, modern comfort, CTV, air-condition, rooftop swimming pool with sundecks, own key. Walk to gay clubs, bars and restaurants. The best in Ibiza Town.

Apartahotel
NAVILA

HOTEL MARIGNA

With 44 rooms the **Hotel Marigna** is the largest GAY-HOTEL in Europe. It is ideally located in Figueretas, about 15 min. walk from the Old Town of Ibiza and the gay scene. All rooms are tastefully furnished with private bath or shower, phone and bahama fans. The largest double rooms are very comfortable with balcony, fridge and CTV. The Hotel Marigna offers 3 bars, huge breakfast room, cozy TV lounge, and a roof top sundeck with panoramic view of the Sea and the Old Town. A pool with poolside bar is located nearby and can be used free of charge by the hotel guests. Enjoy afternoon tea and evening dinner at the Marigna-terrace. ODYSSEUS clients are offered a warm and friendly welcome.

SITGES

A seaside holiday resort some 40 km / 25 mi. southwest of Barcelona along the coast. Sitges is a mecca for young Europeans, a great weekend escape for Barcelonans, and a major gay summer destination. Sitges offers great beaches, including a famous gay nude beach, dynamic gay nightlife, and an outrageous Carnival with many gay followers in February which climax in Tuesday's mostly gay late-night parade. The high season lasts from July to September when the resort is in full swing. Accommodations can be a problem during the high season, therefore it is recommended that you plan your travel to Sitges well in advance to secure your room at your favorite gay hotel. **ODYSSEUS** offers to our clients the best accommodations choice in Sitges: The Hotel Romantic, La Renaixença, Montserrat Hotel and the Oasis Apts. All in the heart of town walk to the beach, clubs and the train station.

HOTEL ROMANTIC & LA RENAIXENÇA

The Hotel Romantic occupies 3 adjacent 19th century villas, conserved and restored in the style of the period. Collection of paintings, ceramics and sculptures make the Hotel Romantic an exquisite living work of art. Some rooms have a terrace overlooking the gardens.

The hotel is ideally located on a quiet street near public transportation, shops and entertainment. Gay Beach and nightclubs are all within walking distance. La Renaixença is an all male gay hotel near the Hotel Romantic with rooftop sundeck.

ODYSSEUS clients have stayed at these hotels since 1986 and have spoken highly of their friendly atmosphere and traditional Catalunyan hospitality. Welcome drink is offered to **ODYSSEUS** customers at the charming "Romantic Corner" bar.

GRAN CANARIA

Gran Canaria is one of the Canary Islands situated off the southern coast of Morocco. Playa del Ingles / Maspalomas is a year round tropical paradise in the south of Gran Canaria with more than 350 sunny days per year. **High Season: November - January.** The resort with its wide sans dunes, secluded nude beaches, palm trees, vibrant nightlife, and duty free shopping is popular with European gays. The gay nude beach is at the far end of the official nude beach where beautiful bodies bath and tan side by side on **Maspalomas Beach**. To explore this beautiful island and enjoy its constantly changing landscapes, rent a car or a roofless jeep, fill it with low-tax gas, and cruise around on your own. In Maspalomas we offer two all-male gay resorts: **Los Robles Bungalows** and **Villas Blancas**; in Sonnenland - **Vista Bonita**. For those who wish to be on their own in town close to the Yumbo Center and the nude beach we can offer studios and apartments that accommodate from 1-4 people.

AIRFARE: Complete packages including flights are available to Gran Canaria from Amsterdam, London or New York

LOS ROBLES

Well established all male gay resort complex of 21 coonected bungalows set in a landscaped tropical garden in the quiet Campo Internacional area. Each bungalow has one bedroom, living room, kitchen, full bath, patio, and in house CTV (movies). Amenities: large pool, poolside bar, clothing optional sunbathing area. Walk to the gay dunes of Maspalomas, beaches and nightlife.

VISTA BONITA

All male gay complex of 20 brightly colored, terraced villas and penthouses, built on two floors. The ground floor consists of a living room, kitchenette and a patio. The upper floor has twin-bedded room with balcony overlooking the pool, and a full bath. The villas accommodate 1-3 people, and two in the penthouse. A sliding glass from the living room leads into the gardens, swimming pool, and the clothing optional sunbathing area. Excellent bus and taxi service close to the complex which is located in Sonnenland.

VILLAS BLANCAS

Exclusively for gay men, Villas Blancas is popular with international clientele. The complex consists of 24 bungalows with a living room, full bath, kitchen and patio. Amenities: swimming pool, poolside bar, sundecks, and clothing optional sunbathing area. Located in Maspalomas it is near beaches, dunes and gay nightlife in Playa del Ingles.

AIRFARE
Complete package including round trip charter flights are available from London or New York
Call ODYSSEUS for prices and schedule

MADRID / BARCELONA

Madrid is the administrative and cultural capital of Spain. It is the major airport of entrance for most foreign visitors. Explore the city's rich historical heritage, impressive monuments, plazas, parks and museums. For a perfect holiday or business at the Iberian capital ODYSSEUS offers the charming **Hotel Atlantico** on the famous Gran Via avenue in the heart of Madrid's main shopping centre near Madrid's main gay nightlife center, or the **Hotel Madrid** near the Plaza del Sol.

HOTEL ATLANTICO

Charming three-star hotel with amenities far superior to it category. 60 spacious rooms beautifully decorated in individual style, all with modern bathrooms, air-conditioning, minibar, security box, and CTV. 24 hrs laundry delivery and car-park only 50 m. away. Short walk to gay bars and clubs.

Barcelona is the cosmopolitan art and cultural capital of Catalunya. It is extremely beautiful with Gothic and Art Nouveau buildings, large parks, wide avenues, and the historic Ramblas. In Barcelona enjoy your stay at the Palatial style **Hotel Granvia** on the famous Gran Via avenue near the Plaza Cataluña.

HOTEL GRANVIA

Atmospheric and colorful Victorian style three-star hotel in historic palace. Central location near the Ramblas, Plaza Cataluña and Commercial Center of Barcelona. Walk to gay bars and clubs. 54 rooms with private bath, phone, minibar, air-conditioning. Restaurant, terrace café, antique filled salon.

BELIZE

Belize is a small Central American country sharing borders with Mexico and Guatemala. The population is a mixture of Creole, Indians and Mayas. Explore the country's fresh water lagoons, Caribbean cays with beautiful sandy beaches, forested mountains, nature reserves, and Mayan antiquity everywhere you go. The climate is warm year round with temperatures reaching 35°c (95°F). Mountain Pine Ridge of Western Belize is a large Forest Reserve with orchids, butterflies, beautiful river scenery and high waterfalls. The Mayan city of Caracol - a National Monument Reservation can be visited in the area. ODYSSEUS is pleased to offer the unique **Blancaneaux Lodge** a peaceful oasis deep in the enchanted Mountain Pine Ridge.

BLANCANEAUX LODGE

Share the beauty of Francis Ford Coppola's mountain retreat for honeymooners or special friends. 14 thatched-roof cabanas and luxury villas overlook waterfalls and pools. The interior design is uniquely different incorporating colonial and antiques. Visit magnificent Caracol, jungle river trips, horseback riding and mountain biking. Amenities: natural pools, hiking trails and gourmet restaurant feature authentic Italian cuisine and seafood.

Bali the most famous of all the 13,677 islands that makes up the country of Indonesia is also popularly known as "Morning of the World" . It is an exotic 90 mi. / 145 km island with olive green rice terraces, palm trees, tropical flowers and beautiful sandy beaches. The island offers a mixture of Hindu and Moslem cultures, 20,000 temples, 60 religious and spiritual holidays a year, and over 2,000 different dance troupes. Kuta, the main beach town attracts many gay holiday makers and resembles a mini-Thailand. Bali will fascinate you with its unique atmosphere that is gay friendly and completely offbeat. In Bali ODYSSEUS is proud to offer to our clients the world-class **Hotel Santika Beach** with its superb amenities and friendly service.

HOTEL SANTIKA BEACH

Located on the beach at Tuban **Hotel Santika Beach** offers Balinese hospitality, world class service and comfort. All rooms, bungalows and suites have private bath, CTV, phone and are situated within luxurious gardens. Suites with private pools are available. Amenities: swimming pools, and three restaurants. To clients staying at Hotel Santika Beach we can offer the services of a local Gay travel supplier for airport transfers, local tours, and gay nightlife orientation.

THAILAND

Thailand is one of the most fascinating countries in the world. Located in South East Asia it shares borders with Malaysia, Mynamar, Laos and Cambodia. Thailand is mostly a Buddhist country with excellent hotels and resorts, great beaches, interesting cuisine, exotic temples, vibrant nightlife and excellent shopping. Most gay travelers arrive in Bangkok, the country's capital and after a few days continue to the gay beaches of the picture perfect resorts of **Phuket** on the Andaman Sea, or **Pattaya** (154 km / 97 mi.) south of Bangkok. If you have more time visit **Chiang Mai** in the north for another Thai experience and explore its gentle, easygoing people, culture and cuisine. **ODYSSEUS** offer a selection of great accommodations for gay travelers throughout Thailand.

Bangkok

HOTEL MALAYSIA

Friendly and affordable six-story hotel with 120 tastefully furnished air-conditioned rooms in a central area of Bangkok near foreign embassies and gay nighttime entertaining spots. Amenities: pool, lounge, and coffee shop.

Pattaya

LE CAFÉ ROYALE

Elegant gay hotel & restaurant in the heart of Pattaya's gay nightlife near the beach. Beautiful rooms and suites with priv. bath, CTV, phone and mini-bar. 24 hrs. room service

AMBIANCE INN

Luxurious gay hotel in the heart of Pattaya's gay nightlife near the beach. 34 luxurious rooms with priv. bath, CTV, phone and mini-bar. 24 hrs. room service, coffee shop & nightclub.

Phuket

ROYAL PARADISE

A landmark luxury hotel on the famous shopping and gay nightlife of Patong Beach. 250 deluxe rooms, queensize beds, full bath, minibar, phone, CTV, most with private balcony and seaview. Amenities: restaurants, bar, coffee shop, disco, pool, sauna, health club.

UNITED STATES OF AMERICA

AREA: 3,623,420 sq. mi. (9,384,658 sq. km)
POPULATION: 255,000,000
CAPITAL: Washington D.C.
CURRENCY: US dollar ($)
OFFICIAL LANGUAGE: English
MAJOR RELIGIONS: Protestantism, Roman Catholicism, Judaism
Telephone: 1
Nat'l Holiday: Independence Day, July 4
Official Time: 5-8 hrs behind G.M.T.
Electricity: 117 volts, 60 cycles

Measurements: English system
Visas: visitor's visa required from almost any foreign visitor to the USA
Major Airlines: Delta, United, TWA, US Air

LAW REGARDING HOMOSEXUALITY:
Homosexual acts between women are not mentioned in the law. The legal status of male homosexuality varies from one state to another. Generally, it is legal in the northern states and illegal in the south. For information about the existence or non existence of Sodomy Law by state, refer to the introduction for each individual state. The main topic of gay legal rights concerns Gay Marriages. The Hawaii Supreme court ruled in 1993 that the denial of marriage licenses to same-gender couples is discriminatory, thus opening the door to legalization of same-sex marriage in Hawaii. However, a federal anti-gay marriage bill is in firm opposition to a nationwide same-sex marriage. In the meantime Gay Commitment ceremonies are popular in the USA as a substitute to legal marriages.

© Odysseus Enterprises Ltd. 1997

ALASKA

ANCHORAGE

◆ **Population:** 570,000
◆ **Capital:** Juneau
◆ **Time Zone:** Alaska Standard Time Zone (1 hr. behind PST); The far reaches of the Aleutian Islands and Saint Lawrence Island are in the Hawaii-Aleutian Time Zone
◆ **No Sodomy Law**
◆ **Legal drinking age:** 21

ANCHORAGE   ℂ   **907**

✈ Anchorage Int'l Airport (ANC)
5 mi. / 8 km SW

LOCATION: South central Alaska at the head of the 220 mi. / 354 km Cook Inlet.

POPULATION: 230,000

CLIMATE: Winters are long and cold with plenty of snowfall. January has 8 hours of functional daylight and average temperature of 20°F (-7°c). Spring begins in April; Summers are pleasant with a July average of 65°F (18°c). In June there are 24 hours of functional daylight.

Gay & Lesbian Visitor Information
Gay & Lesbian Helpline: 258-4777

DESCRIPTION: Alaska's largest city combines spectacular setting, Russian and Native American heritage, and big city amenities. It's airport is an international hub served by many

domestic and international flights. Anchorage is a starting point to explore the state's rich wildlife and magnificent wonders of nature. The gay scene is small with only two clubs catering to gay clientele in Anchorage.

BARS ♈ RESTAURANTS ♯

● Bars/Clubs (GMW): **The Raven** (276-9672); **The Wave**, dance bar, drag shows, 3103 Spenard Rd. (561-9283).

● Restaurants (AW): **Akaihana**, Japanese restaurant & Sushi bar, 930 W. 5th Ave. (276-2215); **Downtown Deli & Café**, omelettes, Reindeer Stew, fresh Alaskan Seafood, 525 W. 4th Ave. (276-7116); **Gwennie's**, Old Alaska style, Reindeer Omelettes, smoked salmon, Alaskan King crab, 4333 Spenard Rd. (243-2090); **Illusions**, bakery, 807 'G' St. (276-8458); **La Mex**, Mexican & American food, 900 W. 6th Ave. (274-7678); **O'Brady's**, burgers and beers, Chugach Square, 6901 E. Tudor Rd. (338-1080) and Diamond Square, 800 E. Diamond (344-8033).

λ SERVICES λ

● Erotica (G/S): **Adults Only Bookstore**, 3956 Spenard Rd. (243-0697); **La Sex Shoppe**, 305 W. Diamond Blvd. (522-1987); **Swinger Bookstore**, 710 W. Northern Lights Blvd., (561-5039).

● Gift Store (AW): **Apone's T-Shirt Cache**, T-Shirts, Sears Mall (272-1007); **Artique**, art gallery, 314 G St. (277-1663); **Once in a Blue Moose**, gifts, toys, books, Alaskan products, 547 W. 4th Ave. (276-0021).

● Personal Phone Line (GM): ✪ **Anchorage Confidential Connection**, meet local guys! Record, listen, respond to ads free (563-MEET) free access code 8060.

● Pharmacy (AW): **Professional Infusion Pharmacy**, 725 Northway Dr. (279-8055).

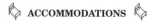 ACCOMMODATIONS

ANCHORAGE HOTEL
330 E. St., Anchorage AK 99501. Tel: (907) 272-4553. Fax: (907) 277-4483. TYPE: *Hotel*. CLIENTELE: All Welcome. LOCATION: Heart of old downtown. 31 rooms w/priv. bath, CTV, phone, refrigerator, parking. Rates: $79-$179. DESCRIPTION: Small historic hotel.

○ AURORA WINDS

7501 Upper O'Malley, Anchorage AK 99516.
Tel: (907) 346-2533. Fax: (907) 346-3192.
Email: awbnb@alaska.net. TYPE: *Bed & Breakfast.* HOST: James & Bill. CLIENTELE:
Mostly gay men & women. LOCATION: On the
hillside overlooking Anchorage on 2 acres of
secluded property.

* Suites: 5 (1BR) w/priv. bath, sitting area
* Rooms: 2 family rooms
* Rooms for non smokers
* CTV, VCR, phone, refrigerator, hairdryer
* Kitchenette: available
* Bed Types: twin, queen size, king size
* Hot Tub, full gym, sauna, free parking
* Clothing optional policy
* Billiard room, Theatre room, fireplaces (4)
* Recreation: cross country & downhill skiing,
  horseback riding, golf, tennis
* Gay Bars: in Anchorage (15 min.)
* Health Club: 10 min.
* Airport: 17 min., taxi, car rental
* Reservations: deposit or CC guarantee
* Cancellation Policy: deposits are fully
  refundable with 7 day notice; deposit is
  forfeited if cancelled less than 5 days
  before arrival
* Open: Year round
* Rates: $95-$175 (May-Sept. 30)
  $55-$125 (Oct - Apr. 30) w/CB
* Tax: 8%
* *TAC:* 10%

DESCRIPTION: Elegant Bed & Breakfast
resort in contemporary style with Alaskan
ambiance. Guest rooms and suites are lavishly decorated and individually furnished with
all modern amenities. Enjoy the outdoor 8-per-
son jacuzzi or relax with a glass of wine by the
fireplace. Expanded continental breakfast is
available in room or full breakfast in the dining
room. *IGTA*

DAYS INN

321 E. 5th Ave., Anchorage AK 99501. Tel:
(907) 276-7226. Fax: (907) 278-6041. TYPE:
Motor Inn. CLIENTELE: All Welcome. LOCA-
TION: Downtown. 118 rooms w/priv. bath, CTV
(CNN), phone, cafe, bar. Airport: 7 mi. / 11 km
(free shuttle). Open: Year round. Rates: $49-
$129. *TAC:* 10%. DESCRIPTION: Motor Inn.

THE LODGE at EAGLE RIVER

P.O. Box 90154, Anchorage AK 99509. Tel:
(907) 278-7575. Fax: (907) 278-1010. TYPE:
Guest House. HOST: Pinkie Bailey. CLIEN-
TELE: All Welcome. LOCATION: 10 mi. / 16 km
from the city limits of Anchorage in a forest on
Mount Magnificent near Chugach State Park.

ARIZONA

◆ **Population:** 2,720,00
◆ **Capital:** Phoenix
◆ **Time Zone:** Mountain
◆ **Sodomy Law**
◆ **Legal drinking age:** 21

PHOENIX   ✆ 602

✈ Sky Harbor Int'l Airport (PHX)
4 mi. / 6 km SE

LOCATION: In the "Valley of the Sun" in southern Arizona, 116 mi. (186 km) northwest of Tucson, and 290 mi. (464 km) southeast of Las Vegas, Nevada.

POPULATION: 765,000

CLIMATE: Dry desert climate. The average mean temperature is 70°F (21°c) in the Spring, 54°F (12°c) in the Winter, and 95°F (35°c) in the summer.

VISITOR INFORMATION
Phoenix & Valley of the Sun CVB
Tel: (602) 254-6500

Gay Visitor Information
G&L Community Center
3136 N. 3rd Ave.
Tel: (602) 234-2752

DESCRIPTION: Phoenix, the capital of Ari-

zona is the nation's eighth largest city and an important gateway to the Pacific Rim. Phoenix combines the spirit of the American West with the sophistication and energy of the East. The city center is modern, but the suburbs retain a distinguished western look. Visit: **Desert Botanical Garden**, 1201 N. Galvin Parkway, a showcase of desert plants with an annual Cactus Show in February; **Heard Museum**, 22 E. Monte Vista Rd., anthropology and primitive art with Eskimo and American Indian art. Explore the **Red Rocks Country** between Phoenix and Sedona following I-17 north, or U.S. 60 northwest.

BARS ♈ RESTAURANTS 🍴

● Bars/Clubs (GM): **Ain't Nobody's Biz**, 3031 E. Indian School #7 (224-9977); **Apollo's**, karaoke, theme parties, 5749 N. 7th St. (277-9373), a motorcycle type cruise bar; **BS West**, 7125 5th Ave., Scottsdale (945-9028); **Cash Inn Country**, country-western club,2120 E. McDowell (244-9943); **Charlie's**, country-western dance bar & restaurant, 727 West Camelback (265-0224); **Country Club**, country-western bar & grill, 4428 N. 7th Ave. (264-4553); **Desert Rose**, dance club, cocktails, 4301 N. Seventh Ave. (265-3233); **Detour**, cruise bar, 4102 East Thomas Rd., (224-9471); **Eagle**, sports club, 4351 N. 7th St. (285-0833); **Foster's**, dance club, entertainment, 4343 N. 7th Ave. (263-8313); **Harley's 155**, leather/levi dance bar, 155 West Camelback Rd. (274-8505); **JC's Fun One**, bar, lounge, Karaoke, 5542 No. 43rd Ave. (939-0528); **Metro**, dance club, 4102 E. Thomas (224-9457); **Options**, 5111 No. 7th st. (263-5776); **Pookie's Cafe**, music video bar & grill, 1540 N. 7th St. (277-2121); **Pumphouse**, 4132 E. McDowell (275-3509); **307 Lounge**, female impressionists, entertainment, 222 E. Roosevelt (252-0001); **Trax**, leather, 1724 E. McDowel Rd. (254-0231); **Wink's**, cocktail bar/cabaret, 5707 N. 7th St. (265-9002); **The Works**, 7223 E. 2nd St., Scottsdale (946-4141).

● Bars/Clubs (GW): **The Cat Walk**, nightclub for women, 3-level dance floor, every wednesday, 4102 E. Thomas Rd. (224-9457); **Incognito**, dance club, 2424 E. Thomas (955-9805); **Nasty Habits**, live entertainment, female strippers, drag shows, 3108 E. McDowell (267-8707).

● Restaurants (AW): **Avanti**, elegant Italian, 2728 E. Thomas St. (956-0900); **Café Unique**, espresso, deserts, live entertainment, art gallery, 4700 N. Central, Suite 105 (279-9691); **Common Ground**, health food, courtyard dining, 7125 E. 5th Ave., Scottsdale (970-4746); **Ed Debevic's Diner**, Chicago style, Town & Country Shopping Center in Phoenix, 2102 E.

Highland Ave. (956-2760); **Los Olivos**, Mexican, 7328 E. 2nd St., Scottsdale (946-2256); **May West**, open 24 hrs., 1825 E. University Drive, Tempe (966-2761); **Petit Café**, French, 7340 Shoeman Lane, Scottsdale (947-5288); **Ruth's Chris Steak House**, American favorites at moderate prices, 2201 E. Camelback Rd. (957-9600); **Shorty'z**, breakfast & lunch cafe, 801 N. 1st St. (253-1985); **Vincent Guerithault on Camelback**, contemporary southwestern, 3930 E. Camelback (224-0225).

λ SERVICES λ

● Adult Erotica (GM): **The Adult Shoppe**, videos, books, magazines, open 24 hrs, 7 days a week, 111 S. 24th St. (306-1130); **Book Cellars**, novelties, videos, twin theatres, sexy lingerie, 2103 W. Camelback (249-9788) also other locations; **Castle Boutique**, safer sex superstore, 300 E. Camelback Rd. (266-3348) also other locations; **Mass Hysteria**, adult toys, 140 W. Camelback Rd. (264-3321).

● Health Club (GM): **Flex Complex**, entertainment complex with health club, 1517 S. Black Canyon (271-9011).

● Personal Phone Line (GM): ✪ **Phoenix Confidential Connection**, meet local guys! Record, listen, respond to ads free (252-3333) free access code 8060; ✪ **Personal Chat Line** call to meet new people nationwide (900) 526-5050 ext:1057.

● Theater (GMW): **Berlitz Gallery Theatre**, gay & lesbian plays, 113 Park Central Mall (263-0587).

ACCOMMODATIONS

ARIZONA SUNBURST INN
6245 N. 12th Pl., Phoenix, AZ 85014. Tel: (602) 274-1474. TYPE: *Bed & Breakfast.* HOSTS: Bill and Wayne. CLIENTELE: Gay men only. LOCATION: Central Phoenix, between 12th St., & Bethany Home. 7 rooms (2 priv./ 5 shared shower), phone, CTV, gym, jacuzzi, clothing optional policy. Rates: $60-$80. Tax: 10.625%. *TAC:* 10%. DESCRIPTION: All male clothing optional resort.

✪ **B&B INN ARIZONA**
13802 N. Scottsdale Rd., Scottsdale, AZ 85254. Tel: (602) 368-9250. Toll Free (800) 266-7829. Email: president@bnbreservations.com. TYPE: *Accommodations Service.* CLIENTELE: All Welcome. LOCATION: Arizona and throughout the country. DESCRIPTION: Free reservation

service for thousands of bed & breakfasts, inns and ranches throughout the country. This free service can be accesses on the WEB at http://bnbreservations.com.

DESERT FERREN
P.O. Box 5550, Carefree, AZ 85377. Tel: (602) 488-1110. TYPE: *Bed & Breakfast.* HOST: Darrell. CLIENTELE: Gay/Straight. LOCATION: 25 mi / 40 km north of Phoenix. 6 rooms, pool, sundeck, clothing optional. Rates: $69-$139. Tax: 11%. **TAC:** 10%. DESCRIPTION: Simply furnished oversized rooms in a Spanish hacienda type villa.

HERITAGE INN
401 N. 1st St., Phoenix, AZ 85004. Tel: (602) 258-3411. Fax: (602) 258-3171. TYPE: *Motor Inn.* CLIENTELE: Mostly Straight. LOCATION: Downtown near Convention Center and financial district. 161 rooms. DESCRIPTION: Superior tourist class hotel in a convenient central location.

RODEWAY INN
3400 Grand Ave., Phoenix, AZ 85017. Tel: (602) 264-9164. Fax: (602) 264-7633. TYPE: *Motor Inn.* CLIENTELE: Mostly Straight. LOCATION: Across the street from Grand Central Station, 1 mile from downtown. 132 rooms. DESCRIPTION: Standard tourist class motor inn in a convenient location.

SEDONA   ℭ   520

✈ Sedona Regional Airport
Sky Harbor Int'l Airport (PHX)
Pulliam Field Airport (FLG)

LOCATION: In the Coconino National Forest, 100 mi. / 160 km north of Phoenix, 30 mi. / 48 km south of Flagstaff, 2-2.5 hrs (120 mi. / 192 km) from the Grand Canyon's South Rim, and 267 mi. / 430 km southeast of Las Vegas (NV).

POPULATION: 11,000

CLIMATE: Dry, temperate and sunny desert climate. The average high temperature is 74°F (23°c), while the mean low is 50°F (10°c).

Gay & Lesbian Visitor Information
Gay & Lesbian Alliance: (520) 526-6098

DESCRIPTION: Originally a pioneer settlement, Sedona is a vibrant community known for its achievements in the fields of the visual, performing and literary arts. The area's beauty

combined with a healthy climate makes it an excellent year round destination resort.

BARS ♈ RESTAURANTS 🍴

● Restaurants (AW): **Armond's Expresso Bar**, coffees & ice creams, Tlaquepaque Market Place (282-6019); **Cups Coffee House**, deli-style meals, informal, 1670 W. Hwy 89A (282-2531); **El Rincon** Restaurante Mexicano, Navajo & Arizona inspired Mexican cuisine (inexpensive), Hwy 179 at the Bridge, in Tlaquepaque Arts & crafts Village (282-4648).

λ SERVICES λ

● Health Clubs (AW): **Sedona Health Spa**, health club, Gym, heated pool, jacuzzi at Los Abrigados Resort, 160 Portal Lane (282-5108).

🔑 ACCOMMODATIONS 🔑

LOS ABRIGADOS
160 Portal Lane, Sedona, AZ 86336. Tel: (602) 282-1777. TYPE: *All-suite Resort.* CLIENTELE: Mostly Straight. LOCATION: 10 min. from the heart of Sedona, and attractions. 175 suites, restaurant, lounge, health spa.

TUCSON   ℭ   520

✈ Tucson Int'l AP (TUS) 12 mi. / 19 km SE

LOCATION: Southern Arizona at the foot of the Catalina mountains, 120 mi. (192 km) southeast of Phoenix.

POPULATION: 330,000

CLIMATE: Desert climate with a long hot, dry and sunny season from April to October. High temperatures of 90°F (32°c) and over are common. Winter mean temperature in January is a comfortable 50°F (10°c). Tucson offers 350 days on sunshine year round.

DESCRIPTION: Desert Oasis, the oldest continually inhabited settlement in the USA, Tucson is snugly nestled in a valley surrounded by mountains. It offers a unique blend of a comfortable western living, colorful desert setting, and big city attractions.

BARS ♈ RESTAURANTS 🍴

● Bars/clubs (GM): **Ain't Nobody's Biz**, 2900

E. Broadway (318-4838); **Club Congress**, 311 E. Congress (622-8848); **Graduate**, 23 W. University (622-9233); **Hours**, 3455 E. Grant Rd. (327-3390); **IBT's**, 616 No. 4th Ave. (882-3053); **It's 'bout Time**, country-western dance bar, drag show, 4th Ave (882-3053); **The Plug**, 2520 No. 6th Ave. (623-6969); **Shanti**, 300 E. 6th St. (622-7107); **Stonewall/Eagle**, leather cruise bar, 2921 No. First Ave. (624-8805); **Venture Inn**, 1239 No. 6th Ave. (882-8224); **Wingspan**, 422 No. 4th Ave. (624-1779).

● Restaurants (AW): **Capriccio**, Italian cuisine, professional atmosphere, 4825 N. First Ave. (887-2333); **Solarium**, seafood, moderate, 6444 E. Tanque Verde Blvd. (886-8186); **Jerome's**, Creole and Cajun menu, 6958 E. Tanque Verde Rd. (721-0311).

λ SERVICES λ

● Personal Phone Line (GM): ✪ **Tucson Confidential Connection**, meet local guys! Record, listen, respond to ads free (791-7000) free access code 8060.

 ACCOMMODATIONS

A ROYAL SUN
1015 N. Stone Ave., Tucson, AZ 95705. Tel: (520) 622-8871. Fax: (520) 623-2267.TYPE: *Highway Motor Inn.* CLIENTELE: All Welcome. LOCATION: N. Stone Ave. & Speedway Blvd. Short distance to the many of Tucson's gay clubs and bars. Walk to the University of Arizona. 59 rooms w/priv. bath, CTV, phone, VCR, refrigerator, 20 suites w/jacuzzi tub, restaurant, outdoor pool, hot tub, sauna, gym. Rates: $99-$180. Tax: 9.5%. *TAC:* 10%. DESCRIPTION: Excellent accommodations, very private, convenient location. *Best Western*

EL CONQUISTADOR
10000 No. Oracle Rd., Tucson AZ 85737. Tel: (602) 544-5000. TYPE: *Deluxe Resort.* CLIENTELE: Mostly Straight. LOCATION: Catalina Mountain foothills. 434 rooms w/priv. bath, 100 suites, 24 hrs room service, restaurant, health club, Rates: $95-$240. *TAC:* 10%. DESCRIPTION: Mega resort with Spanish and Native American architecture.

PUEBLO INN
350 S. Freeway, Tucson, AZ 85745. Tel: (602) 622-6611. TYPE: *Motel.* CLIENTELE: Gay/Straight. LOCATION: Near the Tucson Convention Center. 171 rooms w/priv. bath, 5 suites, pool, cafe, lounge, free parking. Open: Year round. Rates: $39-$125. *TAC:* 10%. DESCRIPTION: Basic motor inn.

TORTUGA ROJA
2800 E. River Rd., Tucson, AZ 85718. Tel: (602) 577-6822. TYPE: *Bed & Breakfast.* HOST: Carl. CLIENTELE: Gay men & women. LOCATION: 7mi./ 11km to downtown Tucson. 1 cottage, 2 rooms. DESCRIPTION: Cozy retreat on 4 acres.

ARKANSAS

♦ **Population:** 2,300,000
♦ **Capital:** Little Rock
♦ **Time Zone:** Central
♦ **Sodomy Law**
♦ **Legal drinking age:** 21

EUREKA SPRINGS   ✆ 501

DESCRIPTION: Small Victorian Spa town clinging to the side of the Ozarks Mountains.

BAR ☿ RESTAURANT ❙❙

● Bar/Restaurants (AW): **Celebrity Club**, live entertainment, 75 Prospect (Crescent Hotel) (253-9766); **Center Street**, 10 Center Street (253-8071); **Plaza**, Continental menu, art collection, 55 S. Main St. (253-8866); **Victorian Sampler**, American cuisine in a restored Victorian Mansion, 33 Prospect St. (253-8374).

⬡ ACCOMMODATIONS ⬡

GREENWOOD HOLLOW RIDGE
Route 4, Box 155, Eureka Springs, AR 72632. Tel: (501) 253-5283. TYPE: *Bed & Breakfast.* HOST: S.J. Young. CLIENTELE: Gay men & women only. 4 rooms, sundeck, jacuzzi, clothing optional. PWA discount. Rates: $45-$65; DESCRIPTION: Country home on 5 acres.

LITTLE ROCK   ✆ 501

✈ Regional Airport (LIT) 4 mi. / 6 km SE

LOCATION: In the heart of Arkansas on the Arkansas River.

POPULATION: 67,000

CLIMATE: Modified continental climate. Winters are temperate with a January average of 40°F (4°c). Summers are long and humid with a July average of 80°F (27°c).

Gay/Lesbian Visitor Information
Gay/Lesbian Switchboard: 375-5504

DESCRIPTION: Little Rock is surrounded by rolling hills, picturesque lakes, rivers and forested wilderness. Located in the heart of the mid-south, it reflects a unique blending of the old south and the new southwest.

❖ **SPECIAL EVENTS: All Arabian Horse Show**, 2nd weekend in April, Barton Coliseum; **Riverfest**, Performing arts festival, memorial day weekend.

BARS ☿ RESTAURANTS ❙❙

● Bars/Clubs (GM): **Back Street**, cruise bar, 1021 Jessie Rd. (664-2744).

● Bar/Club (GMW): **Christopher's Lounge**, piano bar, 601 Center St. (376-8301); **Discovery III**, 1021 Jessie Rd. (664-4784).

● Bar/Club (GW): **Silver Dollar**, pub, 2710 Asher Ave. (663-9886).

⬡ ACCOMMODATIONS ⬡

HOLIDAY INN - CITY CENTER
617 S. Broadway, Little Rock, AR 72201. Tel: (501) 376-2071. Fax: (501) 376-7733. TYPE: *Hotel.* CLIENTELE: Mostly Straight. LOCATION: Downtown, 5 blocks from Convention Center. 280 rooms w/priv. bath, phone CTV, A/C, restaurant. Rates: on request.

LITTLE ROCK INN
601 S. Center, Little Rock, AR 72203. Tel: (501) 376-8301. Fax: (501) 372-1150. TYPE: *Hotel.* CLIENTELE: Gay Welcome. LOCATION: Centrally located in downtown. All rooms w/priv. bath. bar popular with gay clientele.

CALIFORNIA

Russian River
Sacramento
SAN FRANCISCO
SAN JOSÉ
SANTA BARBARA
W. HOLLYWOOD
LOS ANGELES
LONG BEACH
PALM SPRINGS
LAGUNA BEACH
SAN DIEGO

- **Population:** 23,700,000
- **Capital:** Sacramento
- **Time Zone:** Pacific
- **No Sodomy Law**
- **Legal drinking age:** 21

LAGUNA BEACH ✆ 714

✈ John Wayne Airport, Orange County (SNA)

LOCATION: On the steep hills overlooking the Gulf of Santa Catalina and the Pacific Ocean. South of Los Angeles, 8 mi. / 13 km south of Newport Beach.

POPULATION: 17,900

CLIMATE: Mild Winters with daily temperatures between 60°F-75°F (16°c-24°c). The nights are 20°F (6°c) cooler. Summer temperatures are comfortable, reaching 83°F (28°c) during the day and dropping to 63°F (17°c) at nights.

VISITOR INFORMATION
Chamber of Commerce: (800) 877-1115

Gay/Lesbian Visitor Information
Laguna Outreach: (714) 497-4237

DESCRIPTION: Beach resort and bohemian art colony halfway between Los Angeles and San Diego. Overlooking the Pacific Ocean and the Gulf of Santa Catalina, Laguna Beach epitomizes California chic. Local artists display their crafts in the Irvine Bowel.

❖ **SPECIAL EVENTS: Festival of Arts** July-August, California's oldest and most famous outdoor art show. Many valuable paintings and sculptures of local artists are shown and sold during the duration of the festival; **LATA Championships**, GLTA tennis tournament, Sept. 1-4 (310-435-4490).

❖ Gay Beach: For the surf and sand try the gay **West Street Beach** at the south end of the Laguna, opposite West St. near the **Little Shrimp**.

BARS 🍸 RESTAURANTS 🍴

● Bars/Clubs (GMW): **Boom Boom Room** and **Tap Room** at the **Coast Inn** (494-7558); **Little Shrimp**, bar/restaurant, 1305 S. Coast Hwy, (494-1111); **Main Street**, 1460 S. Coast Hwy (494-0056); **Newport Station**, 1945 Placentia, Costa Mesa (631-0031).

● Restaurants (AW): **Cafe Zoolu**, California cuisine, 860 Glenneyre (894-6825); **Cottage**, 308 N. Coast Hwy; **Cafe Zinc**, 350 Ocean Ave. (494-6302); **Coast Inn Café**, cafe style food, 1401 S. Coat Hwy (494-7588); **Dexter's**, 2892 So. Coast Hwy (897-8912); **Dizz's As Is**, 2794 S. Coast Hwy (494-5250); **Golden Peacock**, Chinese, 410 Broadway (494-0446); **Laguna Feast**, Mexican, 801 Glenneyre St. (494-0642); **Mark's**, California cuisine, 858 S. Cost Hwy (494-6711); **Royal Thai Cuisine**, 1750 S. Coast Hwy (494-8424); **Taco Loco**, Mexican taco bar, 640 S. Coast Hwy (497-1635); **Tivoli Terrace**, hillside setting with view of the Festival of Art in the summer, 650 Laguna Canyon Rd. (494-9650).

λ SERVICES λ

● Jewelry Store (GMW): ○ **Jewelry by Poncé**, specializing in Commitment and Pride rings (traditional, rainbow, triangles); body jewelry, watches, unique gifts. Visit our store or call 800-969-RING for brochures. Wholesale inquiries welcome. URL: www.jewelrybyponce.com. Email: jewelry@jewelrybyponce

● Leather Shop (GMW):**Leather Connection**, 540 So. Coast Hwy, Suite 106 (494-3394).

● Personal Phone Line (GM): ○ **Laguna Beach Confidential Connection**, meet local guys! Record, listen, respond to ads free (539-7000) free access code 8060.

 ACCOMMODATIONS

COAST INN

1401 So. Coast Highway, Laguna Beach, California 92651. Tel: (714) 494-7588. TYPE: *Motel*. CLIENTELE: Gay men & women. LOCATION: Above the beach in Laguna's gay district. 23 rooms, restaurant, bar. Rates: $49 - $139. Taxes: 10%. California Deco style.

○ BEST WESTERN LAGUNA BRISAS SPA HOTEL

1600 S. Coast Hwy, Laguna Beach, CA 92651. Tel: (714) 497-7272. Toll Free (800) 624-4442. Fax: (714) 497-8306. TYPE: *Resort Complex*. MANAGER: Leslie Peterson GM. CLIENTELE: All Welcome. LOCATION: Central location on Pacific Coast Hwy, between Los Angeles and San Diego. Take I-5 or 405 Freeway, exit Hwy 133 south to PCH, turn left, head (1) mile south. Cross street is Bluebird Canyon.

* Rooms: 64 w/priv. whirlpool spa
* Rooms for smokers and non smokers
* CTV, phone. refrigerator, C/H, A/C, hair dryer, safe box (at hotel back office)
* Suite (1), Cottage (1): 1 BR w/living room, full bath, king size spa, patio
* Bed Types: double, king size, queen size
* Services: maid service, laundry, wheelchair access, elevator
* Pool, sundeck, jacuzzi
* Free Parking, pets w/prearrangement
* Beach: 2 min. (mixed)
* Gay Bars: 2 min.
* Health Club: 3-5 min. (mixed)
* Airport: 20 min. taxi, super shuttle
* Train Station: 15 min., taxi
* Languages: English, German, Spanish
* Reservations: credit card guarantee or prepayment (room & tax in full)
* Cancellation Policy: 48 hrs. advance notice
* Credit Cards: MC/VISA/AMEX/DISC/DC
* Open: Year round
* Rates: $139-$279 / (off) $99-$229 w/CB
* Tax: 10%
* Check in 3:00pm / check out 12 noon
* *TAC:* 10%
* Email: LagunaBrisasSpaHotel@worldnet.att.net
* WEB: http://www.travelweb.com./thisco/bw/05537/05537_b.html

DESCRIPTION: Picturesque seaside resort hotel. Guest rooms feature classic California decor with casual furniture, artwork and private spa. Some units with partial ocean views. Amenities include: open air sundeck with panoramic view of the Pacific Ocean, outdoor heated pool and spa. Complimentary continental breakfast and morning newspaper. *Best Western, Dag, Sabre, Apollo*.

HOTEL ST. MAARTEN

696 So. Coast Hwy, Laguna Beach, CA 92651. Tel: (714) 494-1001. TYPE: *Hotel*. CLIENTELE: Gay/straight. LOCATION: Heart of Laguna Beach. 55 rooms w/priv. bath. DESCRIPTION: Hotel with bed & breakfast ambiance. Restaurant and Piano bar popular with the gay community.

LONG BEACH   ℰ   310

✈ Long Beach Municipal AP
10 mi. / 16 km N of Long Beach
24 mi. / 38 km SE of Los Angeles

LOCATION: Orange County, 24 mi. / 38 km South of Los Angeles.

POPULATION: 380,000

**Gay/Lesbian Visitor Information
The Center Long Beach**
2017 E. Fourth St.
Tel: (310) 434-4455

DESCRIPTION: Long Beach was once one of America's premier seaside resorts. Today, it is a modern port city with a gleaming skyline. Take a day cruise to **Santa Catalina Island**.

BARS Y RESTAURANTS

● Bars/Clubs (GM): **Brit**, English pub, 1744 E. Broadway (432-9742); **Broadway**, video dance club, 1100 E. Broadway (432-3646); **Falcon**, 1435 East Broadway; **Club Broadway**, neighborhood bar and grill, 3348 E. Broadway (438-7700); **Club 740**, dance club, drag shows, Mexican restaurant, 740 E. Broadway (438-7705); **5211 Club / Inspiration**, cruise bar,video games, open 24 hrs. on weekends 5211 N. Atlantic (423-9860; **Executive Suite**, dance club, male strippers, 3428 E. Pacific Coast Hwy (597-3884); **Floyd's**, country-western bar, 2913 E. Anaheim St., (433-9251); **Mineshaft**, leather/levi cruise bar, 1720 E. Broadway (436-2433); **Pistons**, leather bar, **Ripples**, cruise bar, 5101 E. Ocean Blvd. (433-0357); **Silver Fox**, karaoke video bar, mature clientele, 411 Redondo Ave. (439-6343); **Wolfe's**, levi/leather, outdoor patio, 2020 Artesia Blvd. (422-1928); **Utopia**, dance club, restaurant, popular on weekends, 145 W. Broadway (432-7202).

● Bars/Clubs (GMW): **Executive Suite**, 3248 E. Pacific Coast Hwy (597-3884); **Ripples**, 5101 E. Ocean Blvd. (433-0357); **Whistle Stop**, neighborhood bar, 5873 N. Atlantic Ave. (422-7927).

● Bar/Club (GW): **Club Broadway**, 3348 E. Broadway (438-7700); **Executive Suite**, 3428 E Pacific Coast, dance club, (597-3884); **Que Sera Sera**, dance club, DJ music, 1923 E. 7th St. (599-6170).

● Restaurants (AW): **Details**, 740 E. Broadway (437-7705); **Double Rainbow**, pastries, gourmet ice creams, 5375 E. 2nd St. (433-2212); **Los Trez Amigos**, 2030 Fourth St. (434-9117); **Papa Bear's Cafe**, 1538 E. Broadway (435-7364).

λ SERVICES λ

● Clothing: **De Santis**, 3840 Atlantic Ave. (428-

3927); **Trende Uomo**, 115 Pine Ave. (590-9423).

● Health Club (GM): **Club 1350**,sauna, porno videos, JO parties, 510 W. Anaheim, Wilmington (830-4784).

● Novelties: **Hot Stuff**, 2121 E. Broadway (433-0692); **Taylor Flag & Banner**, gay pride flags (425-0869).

● Personal Phone Line (GM): ✪ **Long Beach Confidential Connection**, meet local guys! Record, listen, respond to ads free (421-9231) free access code 8060.

● Videos (GMW): **Broadway Video**, 2130 E. Broadway (438-8919).

ACCOMMODATIONS

ROYAL HOTEL
431 E. Broadway, Long Beach CA 90802. Tel: (310) 495-0633. TYPE: *Hotel*. CLIENTELE: Gay Welcome. LOCATION: Centrally located near Elm Avenue. DESCRIPTION: Budget hotel, free HBO, Parking. Rates: $45 and up.

LOS ANGELES   ⓒ

DOWNTOWN / HOLLYWOOD /	213
WEST HOLLYWOOD (see separate section)	
COASTAL COMMUNITIES	310
SAN FERNANDO VALLEY /	818
BURBANK / NORTH HOLLYWOOD	

✈   Los Angeles Int'l Airport (LAX)
    15 mi. / 24 km SW

LOCATION: Los Angeles sprawls over 460 sq. mi. (1177 sq.km) of Southern California in a basin formed and confined by the Pacific Ocean on the southwest, the San Gabriel Mountains on the northeast and desert on the east.

POPULATION: City 3,040,000
                    Metro 7,478,000

CLIMATE: Mild winters with daily temperatures from 60°F (16°c) to 75°F (24°c) and nights some 20°F (6°c) cooler. Summers are warm and dry with temperatures of 80°'sF (28°c) during the day dropping to around 63°F (17°c) at night. The hottest season is August - September. Average annual rainfall is 14" (350mm); rainiest season is November - March.

VISITOR INFORMATION
Greater Los Angeles VCB
Tel: (213) 624-7300

Gay/Lesbian Visitor Information
Gay & Lesbian Community Center
1625 N. Schrader Blvd.
Los Angeles CA 90028
Tel: (213) 993-7400

DESCRIPTION: Los Angeles is the second largest city in the USA. It is a sprawling conglomerate of intermingling communities, each maintaining its own identity and character. **Hollywood**, lies entirely within the city limits, but you can travel less than 3 miles (5km) from the City Hall and find yourself in an independent town, or travel as far as 25 mi (40km) and still remain within the city limits. Los Angeles is a city of freeways, where the use of a car is most essential.

Los Angeles thrives on tourism. It offers many attractions: **Chinatown**, **T.V. Studio** and **Movie Tours**, **Exposition Park**, **Farmer's Market**, **Griffith Park**, **Disneyland**, **Universal Studios** - the world's largest motion picture and television production center; **Knott's Berry Farm**, and **J. Paul Getty Museum**.

For gay visitors Los Angeles is one of the most appealing destinations in the U.S.A. Its charm revolves around the mystique of Hollywood, and the lure of the sun and beaches. The **"City of Angels"** has some of the smartest shops, restaurants, and night clubs that the West Coast has to offer. The drawback is that a car is essential to move around in Los Angeles, the clubs and bars are not at any walking distance, and public transportation is mostly unreliable.

Of interest to gay visitors: **West Hollywood** (see information under the West Hollywood section), **Hollywood**, and **Silver Lake**. **West Hollywood** is home for a large and active gay community. Its shops and galleries are always a pleasure to explore. **Hollywood** offers some of the city's most popular gay bars, restaurants, discos, and shops along the never ending Santa Monica Blvd., Melrose and Highland Avenues, provide enough action for the most demanding gay travelers. **Silver Lake** is a multiethnic community with gay owned businesses along Hyperion Avenue, Sunset Boulevard, Santa Monica, and Manyanita. **Manhattan Beach**, 15 min. from LAX airport by taxi or car, is a charming neighborhood of shops, restaurants, and coffeehouses near the municipal pier.

❖ Beaches: Los Angeles is famous for its beautiful beaches and sexy surfers. **Marina del Rey** has a lovely coastal strip. It is a popular beach destination for tourists, as well as a "gateway" for the entire Los Angeles metropolitan area; the popular **Venice Beach** is only a short stroll away.

❖ SPECIAL EVENT: **Gay Rodeo** every year on the last weekend of March; ◯ **Gay & Lesbian Tennis Tournament (LATA)** every Labor Day weekend. For info: (310) 576-4855.

BARS ♈ RESTAURANTS ¶¶

Los Angeles has many gay bars and clubs in different parts of the city. Each is geared to a select clientele; their ambience reflects various West Coast attitudes. This list contains a few popular bars to get you started.

● Bars/clubs(GM): ☞ **Hollywood** (213/310) - **Circus Disco**, dance club popular with latinos, gay Tue. & Fri. only, 6655 Santa Monica Blvd. (462-1291); **Jox**, 10721 Burbank Blvd. (760-9031); **Mugi**, dance bar, popular with Asians, 5121 Hollywood Blvd. (462-2039); **Pedro's Grill**, popular salsa dance club, gay every Wed., 1739 No. Vermont (660-9472); **Probe**, late night dance club with special parties and

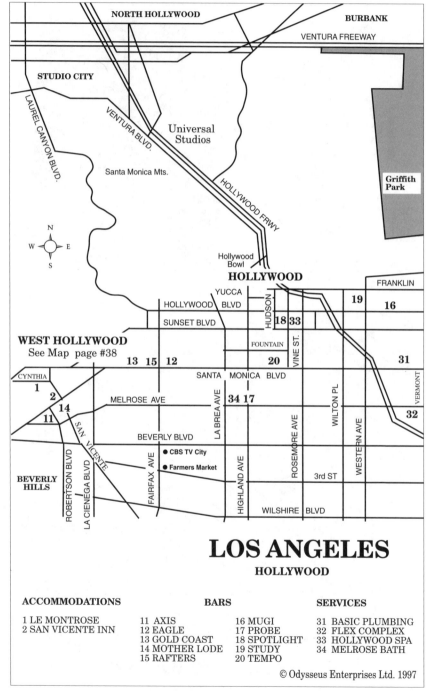

LOS ANGELES
HOLLYWOOD

ACCOMMODATIONS	BARS	SERVICES
1 LE MONTROSE	11 AXIS	31 BASIC PLUMBING
2 SAN VICENTE INN	12 EAGLE	32 FLEX COMPLEX
	13 GOLD COAST	33 HOLLYWOOD SPA
	14 MOTHER LODE	34 MELROSE BATH
	15 RAFTERS	
	16 MUGI	
	17 PROBE	
	18 SPOTLIGHT	
	19 STUDY	
	20 TEMPO	

© Odysseus Enterprises Ltd. 1997

events, 836 N. Highland Ave. (461-8301); **Salsa Con Clase**, live salsa music, 1038 S. Hill St. Downtown at the Mayan (368-6594); **Spotlight**, bar and cocktail lounge, 1601 N. Cahuenga Blvd. (467-2425); **Study**, 1723 N. Western (464-9551); **Tempo**, latin dance club,5520 Santa Monica Blvd. (466-1094).

☞ **Los Angeles Metro** (213) - **Annex Club**, 8355 LaBrea, Inglewood (310-671-7323); **Catch One**, dance club, 4067 W. Pico (734-8849); **The Connection**, 4363 Sepulveda Blvd. (310-391-6817); **Downtowner**, men's happy hour club, One Wilshire Bldg., ground fl., 624 S. Grand Ave. (622-3300); **Plaza**, latino dance club, 739 LaBrea (939-0703); **Plush Pony**, latin dance club,drag shows, 5261 Alhambra St., El Sereno (224-9488).

☞ **Silverlake** (213) - **Le Bar**, latino dance club, drag shows, 2375 Glendale Blvd. (660-7595); **Bunkhouse**, popular beer busts, 4519 Santa Monica Blvd. (667-9766); **Cuffs**, leather/levi cruise bar, 1941 Hyperion Ave. (660-2649); **Detour**, levi cruise bar, 1087 Mazanita (664-1189); **Gauntlet II**, macho cruise bar, 4219 Santa Monica Blvd. (669-9472); **Houstons**, live entertainment, piano bar, restaurant, cabaret, 2538 Hyperion Ave. (661-4233); **Hyperion**, disco and strippers, 2810 Hyperion Ave (660-1503); **Silverlake Lounge**, strictly latino dance club, 2906 Sunset Blvd. (663-9636).

● Bars/Clubs (GM):☞ **Studio City** (818) - **Apache**, 11608 Ventura Blvd., open 7 days/week 3pm-2am, (506-0404); **Oasis**, piano bar, 11916 Ventura Blvd. (980-4811); **Oil Can Harry's**, C&W dance club, 11502 Ventura Blvd. (760-9749); **Queen Mary**, dance club, drag shows, 12449 Ventura Blvd. (506-5619).

● Bars/Clubs (GM): ☞ **North Hollywood / Van Nuys** (818) - **Bullet**, levi/leather cruise bar, 10522 Burbank Blvd. (760-9563); **Driveshaft**, neighborhood bar, 13641 Victory Blvd., Van Nuys (782-7199); **Escapades**, dance club, entertainment, 10437 Burbank Blvd. (508-7008); **In Touch East**, dance club, 10437 Burbank Bl. (508-7008); **Lodge**, dance club, 4923 Lankershim (769-7722); **Mag Lounge**, piano bar, 5248 Van Nuys Blvd., Van Nuys (981-6693);**Oxwood Inn**, dance club, 13713 Oxnard St., Van Nuys (997-9666); **Rawhide**, C&W dance club, beer busts, 10937 Burbank (760-9798).

● Bars/Clubs (GW): ☞ **North Hollywood** (818) - **Club 22**, dance bar with lounge, 4882 Lankershim Blvd. (760-9792); **Rumors**, 10622 Magnolia Blvd. (506-9651).

● Restaurants (GMW): ☞ **Hollywood** (213) -
Il Piccolino, Italian cuisine, 641 N. Highland
Ave. (936-2996); **Fellini's on Melrose**,
Continental Italian, 6810 Melrose Ave. (936-
3100); **Gate of India**, Tandoori Indian cuisine,
7300 Sunset Blvd. (874-6673); **Kafe Kafka**,
French /Italian dishes, brilliantly bizarre setting, 6069 Sunset Blvd. (464-3938); **Off Vine**,
restaurant in historic Hollywood home, 6263
Leland Way (962-1900); **Zumaya's**, Mexican
cuisine, 5722 Melrose Ave. (464-0624).

☞ **Silverlake** (213) - **Buzz Coffeehouse**,
3932 Sunset Blvd. (913-1021); **Casita del
Campo**, 1920 Hyperion Ave. (662-4255); **El
Conquistador**, Mexican cuisine, 3701 Sunset
Blvd. (666-5136); **Da Giannino**, Italian cui-
sine, 2630 Hyperion Ave. (664-7979); **Glorias
Café**, California cuisine, 3603 Sunset Blvd.
(664-5732).

λ SERVICES λ

● Adult Shop (G/S):**Drake's**, xxx videos, body
jewlery, erotic cards, open 24 hrs., 7566 Melrose
Ave. (651-5600).

● Health Clubs (GM): **Compound**, 5636
Vineland Ave., North Hollywood (818-760-
6969) 24 hrs..; **Flex Complex**, 4424 Melrose
Ave., Hollywood (663-5858) full gym & pool;
Hollywood Spa, 1650 N. Ivar Ave, Hollywood
(213-463-5169) 24 hrs..; **Melrose Baths**, 7269
Melrose Ave., Hollywood (213-937-2122) IGHC,
24 hrs..; **Midtowne Spa**, 615 Koler St., LA
(213-680-1838), private club, 24 hrs..; **Roman
Holiday**, 14435 Victory Blvd., Van Nuys (818-
780-1320) 24 hrs..; **Steamworks**, 2107 43th
St., LA (213-845-8992) 24 hrs..

● Jewelry Store (GMW): ✪ **Jewelry by
Poncé**, specializing in Commitment and Pride
rings (traditional, rainbow, triangles); body
jewelry, watches, unique gifts. Visit our store or
call 800-969-RING for brochures. Wholesale
inquiries welcome. URL: www.jewelryby-
ponce.com. Email: jewelry@jewelrybyponce

● Personal Phone Line (GM): ✪ **Los Angeles
Confidential Connection**, meet local guys!
Record, listen, respond to ads free (213) 734-
7822. free access code 8060.

● Sex Club (GM): ✪ **Basic Plumbing**, LA's
hottest and most sexual private men's club,
sundeck, clothing optional. Opens 12 noon Sat
& Sun.; 8:00pm Mon-Fri, 1924 Hyperion Ave.
(953-6731).

☖ ACCOMMODATIONS ☖

MAGIC HOTEL
7025 Franklin Ave., Hollywood, CA 90028. Tel:
(213) 851-0800. TYPE: *Hotel.* CLIENTELE: All
Welcome. LOCATION: Near the Chinese
Theatre. 40 suites. Rates: $65-$95. *TAC:* 10%.
DESCRIPTION: All suite apartment hotel.
Large suites with kitchens, and economy rooms.

ORCHID SUITES
1753 N. Orchid Ave., Hollywood, CA 90028. Tel:
(310) 874-9678. TYPE: *Hotel.* CLIENTELE: All
Welcome. LOCATION: Downtown Hollywood,
directly behind Mann's Chinese Theatre. 39
suites w/priv. bath, CTV, phone, kitchen with
dining area. Rates: from $65.

SEA VIEW INN
3400 Highland Ave., Manhattan Beach, CA
90266. Tel: (310) 545-1504. Fax: (310) 545-
4052. TYPE: *Mote.* CLIENTELE: All Welcome.
LOCATION: Centrally located in Southern
California. 20 rooms w/priv. bath. Rates: on
request. DESCRIPTION: Ocean view rooms
around a courtyard and pool.

OAKLAND/BERKELEY ✆ 510

✈ Oakland Int'l Airport (OAK)
San Francisco Int'l AP (SFO)

LOCATION: 10 mi. / 16 km, east across the
bay from San Francisco.

POPULATION: Oakland 350,000
Berkeley 120,000

CLIMATE: Average temperatures are on the
cool side year round; they rarely rise above
70°F (21°c) or fall below the mid 40°F's (7°c). As
a general rule, September and October are the
warmest months and January is the coldest.

**Gay/Lesbian Visitor Information
Pacific Center:** (510) 841-6224
2712 Telegraph Ave.
Berkeley CA 94705

DESCRIPTION: Across the Bay Bridge from
San Francisco, Berkeley is a cosmopolitan city;
the home of the famous **University of
California**, one of the oldest and largest in the
country; Oakland is a busy port and industrial
center. The **Oakland Museum** features rich
material on California art and history.

BARS ♈ RESTAURANTS 🍴

● Bars/Clubs (GMW): **Bella Napoli**, dance bar, 2330 Telegraph Ave. (893-5552); **Bench & Bar**, bar & restaurant, Sun. brunch, 120 11th St. near Oak (444-2266); **Cable's Reef**, dance bar, cruising, 2272 Telegraph Ave. (451-3777); **Town & Country**, bar, 2022 Telegraph Ave. (444-4978); **White Horse**, dance bar, 6551 Telegraph Ave. Oakland (652-3820).

● Restaurants (AW): **Gulf Coast Grill**, grilled Chicken and seafood,historic building in old Oakland, 736 Washington St. (836-3663); **Osumo**, Japanese restaurant & Sushi bar, 532 Grand Ave. (834-7866).

λ SERVICES λ

● Erotica (G/S): **Adult Books & Videos**, 2298 Monument Blvd., Pleasant Hill (676-2982); **Good Vibrations**, 2504 San Pablo Ave, Berkeley (841-8987); **Passion Flower**, 4 Yosemite Ave., (Oakland (601-7750).

● Health Club (GM): **Steamworks**, sauna, porno videos, relax cabins, 2107 4th St., Berkeley (845-8992)

● Personal Phone Line (GM): ✪ **Oakland Confidential Connection**, meet local guys! Record, listen, respond to ads free (814-6699) free access code 8060.

🗝 ACCOMMODATIONS 🗝

CLARION SUITES
1800 Madison St., Oakland, CA 94612. Tel: (510) 832-2300. Fax: (510) 832-7150. TYPE: *All Suites Hotel.* CLIENTELE: All Welcome. LOCATION: Downtown hotel near business district and BART station.

* Suites: 50 w/priv. bath
* CTV, phone, minibar
* Maid & room service, wheelchair access
* Restaurant, valet parking
* Gay Bars: 20 min. by car
* Airport: 13 mi / 20 km, taxi
* Open: Year round
* Rates: $89-$160
* *TAC:* 10%

DESCRIPTION: Art-deco style boutique. All suites hotel in a central location. Good connection to San Francisco by metro system or public transportation.

PALM SPRINGS   © 760

✈ Palm Springs Municipal Airport (PSP)

LOCATION: 115 mi. / 184 km east of Los Angeles off I-10 in the California desert.

POPULATION: 32,000

CLIMATE: Hot and dry desert climate. Winter temperatures are pleasant and average 75°F (24°c); Summer temperatures are high and may reach 110°F (43°c).

**Gay/Lesbian Visitor Information
DGTG (Desert Gay Tourism Guild)**
Tel: (888) 200-4469

DESCRIPTION: Palm Springs is a year round vacation town. Exotic palm trees, high mountains, clear blue skies and fascinating desert create a serene, away-from-it all feeling. A favorite winter residence of the leisure class and the movie set, it has developed its own resident and politically influential gay community.

The resort is composed of three communities: **Cathedral City, Palm Springs**, and **Rancho Mirage**. Palm Springs is fashionable with neat streets, and lovely shops and boutiques. Rancho Mirage and Cathedral City are younger with a casual, laid-back atmosphere.

Take the world-famous aerial tramway up to the 8500 ft. (2590 m.) snow-covered peaks in the **San Jacinto Mountains** for a spectacular view of the region. Los Angeles, San Diego and Las Vegas are all within driving distance.

❖ SPECIAL EVENT: **Palm Springs International Film Festival**, January 9-26, 1997 (778-8979); **Palm Springs Open**, GLTA tennis tournament, Nov. 24-26 (778-8352).

BARS ♈ RESTAURANTS 🍴

● Bars/clubs (GM): **C.C. Construction**, cruise bar/restaurant with patio, 68-449 Perez Rd., C.C. (324-4241); **Choices**, entertainment complex, special events, 68-352 Perez Rd. C.C. (321-1145); **Delilah's**, DJ and country dancing, 68-657 Hwy 111 C.C. (324-3268); **Iron Horse Saloon**, country-western dance club, 36-650 Sun Air Plaza, C.C. (770-7007); **Richards**, Piano bar, 68-599 Hwy 111 C.C. (321-2841); **Streetbar**, party bar, 224 E. Arenas Blvd. P.S.

(320-1266); **Sweetwater Saloon**, bar/restaurant, live entertainment, 2420 N. Palm Canyon Dr. P.S. (320-8878); **Tool Shed**, 600 E. Sunny Dunes P.S. (320-3299); **Village Pub**, full bar, restaurant, entertainment, 266 S. Palm Canyon, P.S. (323-3265); **Wolfs Den**, man's cruise bar, big patio, leather shop, bears and big men welcome, 67-625 Hwy 111 C.C. (321-9688).

● Bar/Club (GMW): **Shame on the Moon**, 68-cocktails and dining, 805 Hwy 111 C.C. (324-5515).

● Bar/Club (GW): **Delilah's Nightclub**, 68-657 Hwy 111, C.C. (324-3268).

● Restaurants (GMW): **Ashai**, Japanese cuisine, Sushi bar, 330 N. Palm Canyon Dr. (323-0920); **Billy Reed's**, American food and bakery, 1890's decor, 1800 N. Palm Canyon Dr. P.S. (325-1946); **Dates Cafe**, light meals and sandwiches, 67-670 Carey Rd. C.C. (328-7211); **Don & Sweet Sue's**, vegetarian selections, homemade cuisine, 68-955 Ramon Rd. C.C. (770-2760); **Donetello**, Italian cuisine, 196 S. Indian Canyon, P.S. (778-5200); **Europa**, romantic dining, at the Villa Royale Inn, 1620 Indian Trail, P.S. (327-2314); **Golden Triangle**, New York style restaurant, Thai, French and Italian food,

68-805 Hwy 111 C.C. (324-9113); **Mortimer's**, California & French cuisine, 2095 N. Indian Canyon Drive, P.S. (320-4333); **Raphael's**, Pasta house, 266 S. Palm Canyon, P.S. (320-8344); **Red Tomato**, Italian, 68784 Grove St. at Hwy 111, C.C., (328-7518); **Shame on the Moon**, cocktails and dining, 68-805 Hwy 111, C.C. (324-5515); **Silas' on Palm Canyon**, continental cuisine, intimate dining, 664 N. Palm Canyon Dr. (325-4776); **Village Pride**, traditional coffeehouse, 214 E. Arenas Rd., P.S. (323-9120); **Village Pub**, happy hour, casual dining, 266 S. Palm Canyon, P.S. (323-3265); **Wilde Goose**, Continental cuisine, 67-938 Hwy 11, C.C. (328-5775).

λ SERVICES λ

● Adult Bookshops (G/S): **Hidden Joy**, 68-424 Commercial Rd., C.C. (328-1694); **Perez Books**, 68-366 Perez Rd C.C. (321-5597); **World Wide Books**, 68-300 Ramon Rd., (321-1313).

● Art Gallery (AW):**Desert Art Source**, art & sculpture, 41-801 Corporate Way, Ste #7, P.D. (346-7893).

● Clothing (G/S): **Gaymart**, gym wear, adult videos, 305 E. Arenas, P.S. (320-0606); **R&R**

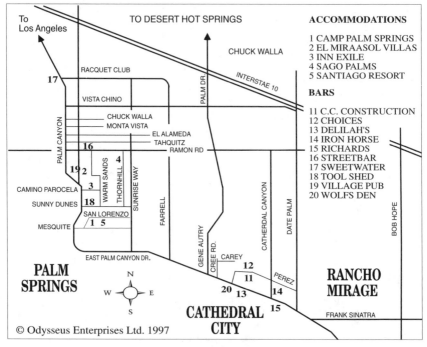

To Los Angeles

TO DESERT HOT SPRINGS

CHUCK WALLA

RACQUET CLUB

17

VISTA CHINO

CHUCK WALLA
MONTA VISTA
EL ALAMEDA
TAHQUITZ
RAMON RD

16

PALM DR.

INTERSTAE 10

19 2
CAMINO PAROCELA
SUNNY DUNES
MESQUITE

4
WARM SANDS
THORNHILL
SUNRISE WAY
3
18
SAN LORENZO
1 5

PALM CANYON

FARRELL

EAST PALM CANYON DR.

PALM
SPRINGS

N
W ✦ E
S

© Odysseus Enterprises Ltd. 1997

GENE AUTRY
CREE RD.
CAREY
12
20 11
13   14

CATHEDRAL 15
CITY

CATHERDAL CANYON
DATE PALM

PEREZ

RANCHO
MIRAGE

FRANK SINATRA

BOB HOPE

ACCOMMODATIONS

1 CAMP PALM SPRINGS
2 EL MIRAASOL VILLAS
3 INN EXILE
4 SAGO PALMS
5 SANTIAGO RESORT

BARS

11 C.C. CONSTRUCTION
12 CHOICES
13 DELILAH'S
14 IRON HORSE
15 RICHARDS
16 STREETBAR
17 SWEETWATER
18 TOOL SHED
19 VILLAGE PUB
20 WOLFS DEN

Menswear, 333 N. Palm Canyon Dr. P.S. (320-3007).

● Gifts (GMW): **Moonlighting**, gay pride gift store, 67-580 E. Palm Canyon Dr., C.C. (323-8830);

● Gym (G/S): **Body Balance**, sensitive body-work, massage (323-7347); **Gold's Gym**, 4070 Airport Center Drive.

● Erotica (G/S): **Hidden Joy**, books, magazines, videos, open 24 hrs., 68-424 Commercial Rd., C.C. (328-1694); **Perez Video & Books**, 68-366 Perez Rd., C.C. (321-5597).

● Health Clubs (GM): **Palm Springs Athletic Club**, 543 S. Palm Canyon Dr., P.S. (323-7722).

● Health Clubs (AW): **A Buff & Beyond**, salon & spa, massage, facials, full body waxing, 68-733 Perez Rd. #6, C.C. (770-5900).

● Maps (GMW): ✪ **Columbia Fun Maps**, free Gay & Lesbian guide maps to Palm Springs, Los Angeles, San Diego and 63 destinations across the USA, Canada and the US Virgin Islands, 118 E. 28th St., suite #308, New York NY 10016. (212) 447-7877. Fax: (212) 447-7876.

● Personal Phone Line (GM): ✪ **Palm Springs Confidential Connection**, meet local guys! Record, listen, respond to ads free (322-9200) free access code 8060.

● Sex Club (GM): **The Gravel Pit**, private men's playground, open Fri. & Sat. 9pm - dawn, 68774 Summit (off Perez), C.C. (324-9771).

⌂ ACCOMMODATIONS ⌂

✪ CAMP PALM SPRINGS
722 San Lorenzo Rd., Palm Springs, CA 92264. Tel: (619) 322-CAMP. Reservations Toll Free 1 (800) 793-0063. Fax: (619) 322-5699. TYPE: *Reort Complex*. HOST: Dwight Hanna GM. CLIENTELE: Gay men only. LOCATION: Warm Sands gay district, 3 blocks south of downtown Palm Springs. Mountain views.

* Rooms: 17 w/priv. bath (13 dbl / 4 quad)
* Suites: 4 (3-bedroom) w/living room,
  full bath, kitchen, patio
* Smoking allowed in rooms
* CTV, VCR, phone, C/H, A/C,
  cooking facilities, outdoor cooling
* Maid service

* Wheelchair access
* Pool, sundeck, gym, jacuzzi
* Clothing optional policy
* Parking: free (some off street)
* Pets: prearrangement required
* Gay bars: 3 minutes
* Health Club: 6 minutes
* Airport: Palm Springs 5 min. free pick up
* Reservations: 50% deposit
* Cancellation: 72 hours, 2 weeks on holiday
* Credit Cards: MC/VISA/AMEX
* Open: Year round
* Rates: $69-$299; (off) $69-$199 w/CB
* Tax: 10% (room tax)
* Check in 2 pm / check out 11 am
* *TAC:* 10% (Poolside studios only)

DESCRIPTION: Private four season resort for men set on 1/2+ acre of landscaped gardens. Spacious studios, and luxurious 3 bedroom suites. Erotic ambiance. *IGTA*

✪ EL MIRASOL VILLAS
525 Warm Sands Drive, Palm Springs CA 92264. Tel: (619) 327-5913 or (800) 327-2985. Fax: (619) 325-8931. TYPE: *Resort Complex*. HOST: John B. Turner, owner. CLIENTELE: Gay men, lesbians and bisexuals. LOCATION: On Warm Sands Drive at Ramon Road.

* Rooms: 6, Suites: 3; 2 (1BR), 1 (2BR)
  full bath, kitchen, patio/terrace, safe box
* Smoking allowed in rooms, Wheelchair access
* CTV, VCR, phone, refrigerator, C/H, A/C
  cooking facilities, maid & laundry service
* Clothing optional around 1 of 2 pools
* Swimming pools (2), sun deck, jacuzzi
* Gay bars: 4 blocks
* Health Club: 1/2 mi. / 800 m (mixed)
* Airport: 1 mi. / 1.6 km free pick up
* Languages: English, French, Spanish
* Reservations: CC# guarantee
* Cancellation: 7 day notice
* Credit Cards: MC/VISA/AMEX/DISC/DC
* Open: Year round
* Rates: $95-$280 w/CB + lunch
  call for summer and fall specials
* Tax: 10%. *TAC:* 10%
* Email: mirasol@mail.gte.net
* Web: http://homel.gte.net/mirasol

DESCRIPTION: A private resort for those seeking the finest service, setting, and ambiance. Spacious rooms and individually decorated suites with all modern amenities. Breakfast and lunch are served poolside. Gym passes, refreshments complementary all day. Uniformed staff. Palm Spring's most relaxing gay resort. Established in 1975.

pools • jacuzzi • steamroom

Gymnasium

complimentary breakfast luncheon

545 Warm Sands Drive
Palm Springs • CA 92264
reservations: 800 962 0186
fax: 619 320 5745

a man's resort   clothing is always optional

* Studios: 26 sgl/dbl w/priv. bath
* Smoking allowed in rooms
* CTV, VCR's, phone
* C/H, A/C, refrigerator
* Suites: 5, 1BR w/living room, full bath,
  CTV, VCR, phone, refrigerator, C/H, A/C
* Bed type: king size; wheelchair access
* Restaurant: **Skivvies** vegatarian
* Pools, gym, jacuzzi, steam room
* Houseman service, free off street parking
* Clothing optional policy, no pets
* Gay bars: a few blocks
* Health club: 1 mi. / 2 km (mixed)
* Airport: 1.5 mi. / 2.5 km, taxi
* Reservations: CC# guarantee
* Cancellaion: min. 3 days notice
* Credit cards: MC/VISA/AMEX/DIS/DC
* Open: Year round
* Rates: $83-$114 w/CB; Tax: 10.1%
* Check in time - vary / check out 12 noon
* *TAC:* 10%
* Email: innexile@earthlink.com
* Web: www.innexile.com

DESCRIPTION: Modern southwest resort. Tastefully decorated rooms, and one-bedroom suites with living room and full bath in soothing Desert colors with king size beds. Dramatic views of the mountains. Complimentary breakfast, afternoon luncheon and Happy Hour. Enticing atmosphere where clothing is always optional. *IGTA*

ENCLAVE
641 San Lorenzo Rd., Palm Springs, CA 92264. Tel: (619) 325-5269. TYPE: *Hotel.* CLIENTELE: Gay men only. LOCATION: East of Palm Canyon Drive, near downtown Palm Springs. 12 rooms w/priv. bath, garden, pool, jacuzzi. Rates: $89-$129; (off) $46-$65. DESCRIPTION: Private compound with keyed entry. Tastefully decorated rooms and suites, most with fully appointed kitchens and private patios.

HARLOW CLUB HOTEL
175 E. El Alameda, Palm Springs, CA 92262. Tel: (619) 323-3977. TYPE: *Resort Complex.* CLIENTELE: Gay Men Only. LOCATION: Central. 15 rooms w/priv. bath, CTV, phone, A/C. *TAC:* 10%. DESCRIPTION: Spanish hacienda and bungalows built in the early '30s and set in rambling, tropical gardens.

✪ INN EXILE
545 Warm Sands Drive, Palm Springs, CA 92264. Tel: (619) 327-6413. or (800) 962-0186. Fax: (619) 320-5745. TYPE: *Resort Complex.* HOST: John Kendrick. CLIENTELE: Gay men only. LOCATION: Centrally located in the famous Warm Sands area.

✪ SAGO PALMS
595 Thornhill Rd., Palm Springs, CA 92264. Tel: (760) 323-0224 or (800) 626-SAGO. Fax: (760) 323-0224. TYPE: *Guest House.* OWNER: Bill. CLIENTELE: Gay men only. LOCATION: Warm Sands area corner Thornhill & Ramon.

* Rooms: 7 (smoking allowed)
* CTV, VCR, refrigerator, A/C,
  cooking facilities, fireplace
* Suite (1), Apartments (5), 1BR (3)
  Living room, full bath, kitchen, patio
* Bed Type: king size
* Maid and laundry service
* Pool, sundeck, gym, jacuzzi
* Clothing optional policy
* Parking: free (off street), No pets
* Gay Bars: walking distance
* Health Club: nearby
* Airport: 2 mi. / 3 km, taxi
* Reservations: 1 night deposit
* Open: Year round
* Rates: $74-$149 w/AB
* Taxes: 10.1%
* Check In 2:00 pm / Check Out 12 noon
* *TAC:* 15%

DESCRIPTION: Deluxe private resort hotel. Suites with full kitchen & fireplace. Misting system around pool. Breakfast served poolside. Mountain views. Complimentary wine or champagne upon arrival.

○ **SANTIAGO RESORT**

650 San Lorenzo Rd., Palm Springs, CA 92264-8108. Tel: (619) 322-1300, Toll Free (800) 710-7729. Fax: (619) 416-0347. TYPE: *Resort Complex*. HOST: Scott Neil, owner. CLIENTELE: Gay men only. LOCATION: Central, immediately south of downtown Palm Springs.

* Suites: 10 w/priv. bath + sitting alcove
* Suites: 3 w/full kitchen & full bath
* Studios: 10 w/priv. bath
* Smoking allowed in rooms
* CTV, VCR, phone
* Refrigerator, C/H, A/C
* Houseman service, wheelchair access
* Pool, sundeck, jacuzzi, outdoor pavillion with fire place, free parking
* Clothing optional policy
* Gay Bars: 5 min. (by car)
* Health Club: 10 min. (by car), Gold's Gym
* Airport: 10 min. taxi
* Languages: English, French
* Reservations: 1 night deposit
* Cancellation: minimum 3 day notice
* Credit Cards: MC/VISA/AMEX/DISC
* Open: Year round
* Rates: $89-$119 w/CbB
* Tax: 10% city tax
* Check in 1:00 pm / check out 11:00 am
* Email: santiagops@earthlink.net
* URL: http://www.prinet.com/santiago
* *TAC:* 10%

DESCRIPTION: Palm Spring's most spectacular private resort. Choose from poolside, courtyard or terrace suites or studios, all professionally designed and distinctively appointed. Standard luxuries include a 50' diving pool, outdoor cooling mist, king beds w/feather duvets, shower massages, refrigerators and microwaves. Expanded Continental breakfast, luncheon, film library and Gold's Gym passes are all complimentary. Definitely for the discriminating traveler. *IGTA*

WARM SANDS VILLAS
555 Warm Sands Drive, Palm Springs, CA 92264. Tel: (619) 323-3005 or (800) 357-5695. Fax: (619) 323-4006. TYPE: *Resort Complex*. HOSTS: Georg & Sidi. CLIENTELE: Gay men only. LOCATION: Central Warm Sands area. 26 rooms, 4 cottages, CTV VCR, phone, refrigerator DESCRIPTION: A private men's resort in 50's style charm.

RUSSIAN RIVER   ✆ 707

✈ San Francisco Int'l Airport (SFO)
Oakland Int'l Airport (OAK)

LOCATION: 70 miles (112km) north of San Francisco along the Russian River and California Hwy 116.

POPULATION: 6,000 (in rural Sonoma)

CLIMATE: Warm summers with average temperature of 75°F (24°c); Winter temperatures are in the upper 50°sF (14°c).

DESCRIPTION: The Russian River is a popular destination for recreational vacations and a getaway for the San Francisco area gay men and women. It offers serenity and peaceful in a rural river setting. The nearby wine country is one of the loveliest in California.

ϒ BARS ϒ

● Bar/Club (GM): **Jungle**, 16135 River Rd. (869-1400); **Rainbow Cattle Co.**, Main St. Gerneville (869-0206).

● Bars/Clubs (GMW): **Burdon's**, 15405 River Rd.(869-2615); **Coffee Bazaar**, 1405 Amstrong Woods Rd. (869-9706); **Molly Brown's Saloon**, 14120 Old Cazadero Rd. (869-0511).

● Restaurants (AW): **Little Bavaria**, German cuisine, 15025 River Rd., Guerneville (869-0121); **Sweet's River Grill**, 16251 Main St., Guerneville (869-3383).

λ SERVICES λ

● Personal phone Line (GM): ✪ **Russian River Confidential Connection**, meet local guys! Record, listen, respond to ads free (522-5001) free access code 8060.

🗝 ACCOMMODATIONS 🗝

APPLEWOOD
13555 Hwy 116, Guerneville, CA 95446. Tel: (707) 869-9093. TYPE: *Bed & Breakfast*. HOST: Jim Caron. CLIENTELE: All Welcome. LOCATION: 1/2 mi / 800 m south of Guerneville. 16 rooms w/priv. bath, CTV, VCR, phone, A/C, C/H, pool,sundeck.Rates: $125-$250. Tax: 9%. *TAC:* 10%. DESCRIPTION: Deluxe accommodations in a Mediterranean style villa with garden court.

FERN FALLS
5701 Austin Creek Rd., P.O. Box 228, Cazadero, CA 95421. Tel: (707) 632-6108. Fax: (707) 632-6216. TYPE: *Guest House*. HOSTS: Darrel & Peter. CLIENTELE: Mostly Gay. LOCATION: Russian River Resort area. DESCRIPTION: Private turn-of-the century remodelled cabins amidst redwoods on a year round creek with a natural waterfall and private swimming hole.

FIFES RESORT
16467 River Road, P.O. Box 45, Guerneville CA 95446. Tel: (707) 869-0656. TYPE: *Resort*. CLIENTELE: Gay men & women. LOCATION: Russian River Resort area. Rustic cabins, pool, river beach, TV lounge, restaurant.

INN at OCCIDENTAL
3657 Church St., Occidental, CA 95465. Tel: (707) 874-1047. TYPE: Guest House. CLIENTELE: All Welcome. LOCATION: Heart of Sonoma County, 8 mi. / 13 km to Russian River. DESCRIPTION: Elegant 1870's wine country Inn. 8 guest rooms w/priv. bath, antique decor. Rates: $95-$195.

RUSSIAN RIVER RESORT
16390 Fourth at Mill St., Guerneville, CA 95446. Tel: (707) 869-0691. TYPE: *Resort*. CLIENTELE: Gay men only. LOCATION: 5 min. walk from the Russian River. 24 rooms w/priv. bath, CTV, restaurant, bar, spa and pool, sundeck.DESCRIPTION: Full service resort in contemporary design.

SACRAMENTO   ✆ 916

✈ Metropolitan AP (SMF) 12 mi. / 20 km NW

LOCATION: Northern California, about 80 mi. / 128 km northeast of San Francisco.

POPULATION: 370,000

Gay/Lesbian Visitor Information
Lambda Community Center: 442-0185

DESCRIPTION: Capital of the State of California since 1854, Sacramento is known as the "Camelia Capital of the World". Historically, Sacramento played an important role during the gold rush era.

BARS ϒ RESTAURANTS 🍴

● Bars/Clubs (GM): **Faces**, bar & nightclub, 2000 K St. (448-7798); **Mercantile Saloon**,

1928 L St. (447-0792); **Town House**, 1517 21st St., (441-5122).

● Bars/Clubs (GMW): **Joseph's Town & Country**,2062 Auburn Blvd. (649-9248); **Silver Spur**, 2721 Broadway (457-2070).

● Bar/Club (GW): **Buffalo Club**, 1831 S. St. (442-1087).

● Restaurants (GMW): **Cafe Lambda**, at the Lambda Community Center, 1931 'L' St. (442-0185). Others (AW): **Ernesto**, Mexican, 1901 16th St. (441-5850); **Firehouse**, Continental cuisine in Old Sacramento, 1112 2nd St. (442-4772); **Lemon Grass**, Thai/Vietnamese cuisine, 601 Monroe St. (486-4891); **Marakech**, Moroccan menu, 1833 Fulton Ave. (486-1944); **Rick's**, diner, 2322 'K' St., (444-0969).

λ SERVICES λ

● Erotica (G/S): **Adult Discount Center**, 1800 Del Paso Blvd. (920-8659); **L'Amour Shoppe**, 2531 Broadway (736-3467).

● Health Club (G/S): **Valentis**, pool, gym, weights, 921 11th St. (442-2874).

● Personal Line (GM): ✪ **Sacramento Confidential Connection**, meet local guys! Record, listen, respond to ads free (489-2300) free access code 8060.

 **ACCOMMODATIONS**

HARTLEY HOUSE INN
700 22nd St., Sacramento, CA 95816-4012. Tel: (916) 447-7829. TYPE: *Bed & Breakfast*. HOST: Randy Hartley. CLIENTELE: All Welcome. LOCATION: 22nd & G Streets. 5 rooms w/priv. shower. Rates: $79-$145 w/AB. *TAC:* 10%.

PONDEROSA INN
1100 H St., Sacramento, CA 95814. Tel: (916) 441-1314. TYPE: *Motor Inn*. CLIENTELE: All Welcome. LOCATION: 1 block from City Hall, 2 blocks from the Capitol, near gay scene.

* Rooms: 98 w/priv. bath
* CTV (movies), phone, hair dryer
* Rooms for non-smokers, wheelchair access
* Restaurant, lounge, pool, sauna, parking
* Gay Bars: walking distance
* Airport: 10 mi. / 16 km
* Rates: $80-$95. *TAC:* 10%

DESCRIPTION: Downtown motor inn in a convenient location.

SAN DIEGO   ✆ 619

✈ Lindbergh Field Int'l Airport (SAN)

LOCATION: On the shores of the Pacific Ocean near Tijuana (Mexico). About 100 mi. / 160 km southeast of Los Angeles.

POPULATION: Metro area 1,862,000

CLIMATE: Excellent climate year round. Average daily temperature is 70°F (21°c). Winters are mild with temperatures in the mid 60°F's (18°c). Summers are beautiful, with temperatures reaching 76°F (24°c) and dropping at night to 64°F (18°c). August and September are the warmest months.

VISITOR INFORMATION
San Diego CVB
Tel: (619) 232-3101. Fax: (619) 696-9371

Gay Visitor Information
Lesbian & Gay Community Center
3916 Normal St., Hillcrest
Tel: (619) 692-4297

DESCRIPTION: San Diego is California's second largest city (the 6th largest in the nation). A magic combination of a modern metropolis and a year round resort town. The region is famous for its healthy climate, fascinating desert setting, lively harbor, and miles of sandy beaches. It is also the U.S.A.'s largest Naval Air station on the West Coast.

Visit: **Old Town San Diego**, a six block area with many of the original buildings dating from the first half of the 19th century. The Old Town is famous for its excellent restaurants offering Mexican specialties and an interesting shopping area; the **Bazaar Del Mundo**, designed in 1930 in a California style offers folk art, antiques, and jewelry; **Sea World**, watch penguins and other aquatic creatures doing acrobatics; **Maritime Museum**; **San Diego Museum**; and the world famous **San Diego Zoo** in the beautiful **Balboa Park**, with its 3,200 animals living mostly outdoors, check the **Heart of the Zoo II**, the largest Zoo exhibit ever built.

The **Gaslamp Quarter**, a renovated quarter with shops, offices, restaurants and cafes, is centered around Fifth and Market. **Tijuana** (Mexico) is only 17 mi. / 28 km away by freeway or trolley. San Diego has many gay bars, restaurants and discos, most are along University Avenue in Hillcrest and Park Blvd.

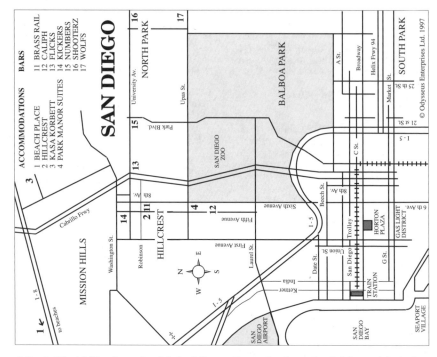

❖ Beach: **Black's Beach**, gay beach in La Jolla north of San Diego. Take Genesee exit off I-5, go west cross Torrey Pines and proceed right at the glider port sign.

❖ SPECIAL EVENT: **San Diego Open XI**, July 4-7, GLTA tennis tournament (692-4274).

BARS 𝗬 RESTAURANTS 🍴

● Bars/Clubs (GM): **Bourbon St.**, leather, piano bar, 4612 Park Blvd. (291-0173); **Brass Rail**, video dance bar, latin ambience, 3796 5th Ave. (298-2233); **Caliph**, piano bar and lounge, mature crowd, 3100 Fifth Ave. (298-9495); **Cheers**, leather/levi, pool table, 1839 Adams Ave. University Heights (298-3269); **Eagle**, leather cruise bar, 3040 N. Park Way (295-8072); **Flicks**, video disco, students and military, 1017 University Ave. (297-2056); **The Hole**, cruise bar, 2820 Lytton St. (226-9019); **Kickers**, country-western dance club, 308 University Ave. Hillcrest (491-0400); **Matador**, neighborhood bar, beach crowd, 4633 Mission Blvd. (483-6943); **Number One Fifth Ave**, Piano bar, live entertainment, professional crowd, 3845 5th Ave. (299-1911); **Numbers**, video bar, 3811 Park Blvd., Hillcrest (294-4789);

Pecs, after hours 'macho' dance club, leather and uniform nights, 2046 University Ave. (296-0889); **Rich's**, dance club, 1051 University Ave. (295-0750); **Shooter'z**, sports bar popular Fri. night, 3815 30th St., (574-0744); **West Coast Construction Co.**, popular disco, 2028 Hancock St. (295-3724); **Wolf's**, cruise bar, 3404 30th St. (291-3730); **Wolfs**, leather cruise bar, backroom party, 3404 30th St., at Upas (291-3730).

● Bars/clubs (GW): **David's Place**, coffeehouse for positive people and their friends, 3766 5th Ave. (294-8908); **North Park Country Club**, 4046 5th Ave. (563-9051).

● Restaurants (GMW): **A Taste of Aloha**, Hawaiian, 420 Robinson Ave. Suite D/E, Hillcrest. (692-9145); **Bayou Bar & Grill**, Cajun, 329 Market St., downtown (696-8747); **Beyond**, Szechuan, 618 5th Ave. (238-2328); **Bravo**, Mediterranean cuisine, 895 4th Ave. (234-8888); **California Cuisine**, 1027 University Ave. (543-0790); **Crest Café**, 425 Robinson, Hillcrest (295-2510); **Hamburger Mary's**, sandwiches, salads, 308 University Ave., Hillcrest (491-0400); **Liaison**, bistro food, sunday brunch, 2202 4th Ave. (234-5540); **Redwing**, Mexican bar & grill, 4012 30th St., (North Park) (281-8700); **La Salsa**, Mexican, 1010

University Ave., Hillcrest (296-4847); **Sally's**, cocktails, lunch & dinner daily, 1288 University Ave. (291-1288); **Star of India**, buffet lunch, vegetarian, 423 F St. (544-9891).

λ SERVICES λ

● Adult bookstores (G/S): **"F" Street**, adult books, cinema, 24 hrs., 1202 University Ave., Hillcrest (298-0854); **Gemini**, 5265 University Dr., (287-1402).

● Cinema (AW): **Guild Theatre**, new & foreign films, 3827 Fifth Ave., Hillcrest (295-2000); **Hillcrest Cinema**, 3965 Fifth Ave. Hillcrest (299-2100); **Park Theatre**, new & foreign films, 3812 Park Blvd., Hillcrest (294-9264).

● Fitness Center (G/S): **Bodybuilders Gym**, 3647 India St. (299-2639); **The Hillcrest Gym**, 142 University Ave., (299-PUMP).

● Health Club (GM): **Club Mustang**, 2200 University Ave. No. Park (297-1661); **Club San Diego**, largest sauna complex in San Diego, VIP suites, lockers, private rooms, 3955 4th Ave. (295-0850); **Dave's Club**, 4969 Santa Monica Ave. (224-9011); **Vulcan Steam & Sauna**, 805 West Cedar St. (238-1980).

● Massage (GM): **Kurt**, private certified massage (293-3657).

● Personal phone Line (GM): ✪ **San Diego Voicemale**, meet local guys! Browse, match, chat. Try it free (692-1299) free access code 8060.

◈ ACCOMMODATIONS ◈

✪ THE BEACH PLACE

2158 Sunset Cliffs Blvd., San Diego, CA 92107. Tel: (619) 225-0746. TYPE: *Guest House /Rental Apts.* HOST: Dan & Joff. CLIENTELE: Gay men & women. LOCATION: 4 blocks from the beach.

* Rooms: 4, Apartments: 4
* Smoking allowed
* Maid service, cooking facilities
* CTV (adult gay videos)
* Sundeck, jacuzzi, clothing optional
* Free parking, pets w/prearrangement
* Beach: 4 blocks (mixed)
* Gay Bars: 5 min. drive
* Health Club: 6 blocks (gay)
* Airport: 10 min. (free pick up)
* Train Station: Amtrak, 10 min.
* Reservations: 1 night deposit
* Cancellation: 48 hrs

Rooms   Suites   Spa
Continental Breakfast

KASA KORBETT
bed & breakfast

Where a guest is at home!

1526 Van Buren Avenue
San Diego, CA 92103
(800)757-KASA

* Open: Year round
* Rates: $50-$75
* **TAC:** 10%

DESCRIPTION: Fully equipped small one-bedroom apartment complex with private decks for natural sunbathing and garden near sandy beach. Convenient location and easy access to the Black's beach (gay beach).

✪ HILLCREST INN

3754 Fifth Ave., San Diego CA 92103. Tel: (619) 293-7078 or (800) 258-2280. Fax: (619) 293-3861. TYPE: *Hotel.* HOST: Roger Williams Mgr. CLIENTELE: Mostly Gay. LOCATION: On 5th Ave., 1 1/2 blocks south of University in the heart of the gay Hillcrest area.

* Rooms: 45 dbl w/priv. bath or shower
* Bed types: twin, double, queen size
* Rooms for non-smokers
* CTV, phone, safety box, garden, balcony, sundeck, jacuzzi, cooking facilities
* Business fax/phone facilities
* Wheelchair access, no pets
* Maid service, parking (paid, off street)
* Beach: 10 min. (mixed)
* Gay Bars: many nearby (2 min. walk)

* Health Club: 2 blocks (gay) Hillcrest Gym
* Airport: 15 min., taxi
* Train Station: Amtrak 10 min., taxi
* Reservations: 1 night deposit
* Cancellation: 72 hrs
* Credit Cards: MC/VISA/AMEX/DISC/EC/JCB
* Open: Year round
* Rates: $49-$55 (breakfast not included)
* Check in 2 pm / check out 12 noon
* **TAC:** 10%

DESCRIPTION: 3-story facility built around a central courtyard with separate sunning patio and jacuzzi. Security gates. Large int'l following. 10 gay bars within walking distance. *IGTA*

✪ KASA KORBETT

1526 Van Buren Ave., San Diego, CA 92103. Tel: (800) 757-5272. Fax: (619) 298-9150. TYPE: *Bed & Breakfast in Private Home.* HOST: Bob Korbett. CLIENTELE: Gay men & women. LOCATION: Quiet residential neighborhood connected by a pedestrian bridge to the popular Hillcrest/Uptown area.

* Rooms: 2 w/shared bath
* Rooms for non smokers
* CTV, VCR, phone, refrigerator, cooking facilities, hair dryer
* Suite: 1, full bath, fireplace
* Bed Type: queen size
* Dining room, patio deck, jacuzzi
* Maid & room service, wheelchair access
* Parking: off street, No pets
* Beach: 12 mi. / 19 km (gay)
* Gay Bars: walking distance
* Health Club: 1/2 mi. / 800 m
* Airport: Lindbergh Field 3 mi. / 5 km
* Airport Transportation: free pick up, taxi
* Train Station: Santa Fe (Amtrak) San Diego Stat'n, 2 mi. / 3 km (free pick up)
* Reservations: one night deposit (first week for an extended stay)
* Season: Year round
* Rates: $59 - $89 w/CB (tax included)
* Check In 12:00 noon / check out (as needed)

DESCRIPTION: A 70 year old, comfortable craftsman-design house. The Southwest bedroom features a queen-sized bed, the New England Cottage room has a full size brass bed. The two guest rooms share one bath. The exotic Key West Suite features a queen-sized bed, fireplace and its own private bath.

✪ PARK MANOR SUITES

525 Spruce St., San Diego, CA 92103. Tel: (619) 291-0999. Toll Free (800) 874-2649. Fax: (619) 291-8844. TYPE: *Hotel.* CLIENTELE: Equal

Gay / Straight. LOCATION: 6th Ave. and Spruce
St., across from Balboa Park in Hillcrest.

* Suites: 80 w/priv. bath
  sgl/dbl 80 / triple 45 / quad 11
* Smoking allowed in rooms
* CTV, phone, refrigerator, safe box, cooking
  facilities, hair dryer
* Studios: 58, 1BR and 2BR (11 each) w/full
  bath, kitchen, patio/terrace
* Bed Types: twin, king size, queen size
* Services: maid, laundry
* Wheelchair access elevator
* Restaurant & Bar: Inn at the Park, conti-
  nental cuisine, lounge, live entertainment
* Parking: free (off street)
* Pets: w/prearrangement
* Beach: 10 min. (gay/nude)
* Gay Bars: 5 min.
* Health Club: 5 min (Hillcrest Gym)
* Airport: San Diego Int'l 10 min.
* Languages: English, French, Spanish, Italian
* Reservations: Credit Card # guarantee
* Cancellation Policy: 24 hrs prior to arrival
* Credit Cards: AMEX/MC/VISA/DISC
* Season: Year Round
* Rates: $99 - $169 w/CB
* Check In 3:00 pm / Check Out 12:00 noon
* Taxes: 10.5%
* *TAC:* 10%

DESCRIPTION: Restored hotel built in 1926. 7
story, Italian Renaissance style. All rooms offer
"Old World Charm", full kitchens, dining areas,
private baths and sleeping quarters. *IGTA,
GSDBA*

SAN DIEGO PRINCESS RESORT
1404 W. Vacation Rd., San Diego, CA 92109.
Tel: (619) 274-4630. TYPE: *Resort Hotel.*
CLIENTELE: All Welcome. LOCATION: On 44
acre island in the heart of San Diego's Mission
Bay Aquatic Park.

* Rooms: 462 w/priv. bath
* Rooms/suites for smokers and non smokers
* Suites: 93
* CTV, phone, A/C, patio/lanai, kitchenette
* Restaurants, bars, pools, health club
  free parking, wheelchair access
* Airport: 7 mi. / 11 km
* Gay Bars: car required
* Beach: on the beach
* Open: Year round
* Rates: $130 - $2,200
* *TAC:* 10%

DESCRIPTION: Elegant resort complex featuring single level cottage style buildings near
sandy beaches. Tennis, golf and boat rentals
available.

SAN FRANCISCO   ✆ 415

✈ San Francisco Int'l Airport (SFO)
  Oakland Int'l Airport (OAK)

LOCATION: The city lies on 40 hills ranging
from sea level to 929 ft. (280 m) at the tip of the
narrow peninsula bordered on the west by the
Pacific Ocean and on the east by the San Francisco Bay.

POPULATION: City 680,000; Metro 3,255,000

CLIMATE: Cool year round; temperatures
rarely rise above 70˚F (21˚c) or fall below the
mid 40˚F's (7˚c). September and October are
the warmest months.

VISITOR INFORMATION
SF CVB
Tel: (415) 974-6900.
Fax: (415) 227-2602

Gay/Lesbian Visitor Information
Pacific Center / Berkeley
Tel: (510) 841-6224

DESCRIPTION: San Francisco is one of the
most beautiful cities in the world. It's architecture is a mixture of Victorian, Edwardian, Oriental and Mediterranean. Explore the charm of
San Francisco's **"Painted Ladies"** - Victorian
Houses in the tradition of the late 19th century.
America's legendary fun loving city, is also an
important industrial and financial center. The
financial district is known as the "Wall Street
of the West", and the port is one of the busiest
in the U.S.A.

San Francisco is the Gay Capital of the U.S.A.
Gay people live and take equal share in the political and financial life of their city. Rainbow colored flags are proudly displayed on homes and
businesses. San Francisco maintains some distinct gay neighborhoods: **Castro** - the gay center
of the city, consists of two blocks, Castro Street
south of Market, and two blocks of 18th Street
both sides of Castro and the surrounding residential neighborhoods. In this area you may find,
shops, restaurants, and art deco movie theatres.

Other 'gay' neighborhoods of interest are: the
commercial section of **Polk Street**, with its
shops, bars, restaurants; the **South of Market**
area between Market Street and Janes Hick
Skyway around Folsom, Howard, and Harrison
Sts. near 8th and 9th Sts. with leather, Levi-
leather bars; Height Street just east of the Golden

State Park; and the trendy Pacific Heights area of tree-lined streets, beautiful Victorian homes and mansions. Visit: **Alcatraz Island**; **Chinatown** - the most densely populated Asian community in the country; **Japantown**, explore the best of Japan only few blocks from downtown; **Fishermen's Wharf** a tourist recreation center with boutiques, shops, seafood restaurants and a great view of the bay; **The Golden Gate Bridge** and **Park** offers a magnificent views of the city and harbor as does **Lombard Street** and **Telegraph Hill**.

❖ **SPECIAL EVENT: Gay Pride Celebration**, last Sunday in June; '96 USGO, GLTA tennis tournament, May 1996 (Memorial Day Weekend) (668-8132).

BARS ♈ RESTAURANTS 🍴

● Bars/Clubs (GM): ☞ **Castro - Badlands**, cruise bar, 4121 18th St. (626-9320); **Bear**, 440 Castro St. (861-9427); **Castro Country Club**, alternative to the bar scene, no alcoholic drinks, relaxed and friendly atmosphere, 4058 18th St. at Hartford (552-6102); **Castro St. Station**, party bar, 456 Castro St., (626-7220); **Daddy's**, levi/leather cruise bar, 440 Castro St. (621-8732); **Detour**, leather/levi, 2348 Market (861-6053); **Eagle**, heavy duty leather cruise bar, 1398 12th St. (626-0880); **Edge**, popular Leather/Levi cruise bar, 4149 18th St., (863-4027); **Esta Noche**, Latin hombres galore, popular on weekends 3079 16th St. (861-5757); **Men's Room**, 3988 18th St., at Noe (861-1310); **Metro**, video bar/Chinese restaurant, 3600 16th St., (431-1655); **Midnight Sun**, the oldest gay video bar in the country, 4067 18th St. (703-9750); **Motorwerks**, leather bar, 4 Valencia St. (864-7208); **Night Shift**, video cruise bar, 469 Castro; **Pendulum**, primarily African-American clientele, cruisy on weekends, 4146 18th St.(863-4441).

● Bars/Clubs (GM): ☞ **Folsom - Club Universe**, the most popular gay dance club in the city, 177 Townsend St. (985-5241); **Colossus**, dance club, special events, 1015 Folsom St., (431-2697); **Jackhammer**, cruisiest bar in town, 290 Sanchez St. (252-0290); **Pleasure dome**, the largest disco in SF, late Sunday tea dance, 177 Townsend (985-5256).

● Bars/Clubs (GM): ☞ **Pacific Heights - Alta Plaza**, jazz music, handsome guys, 2301 Fillmore (922-1444)

● Bars/Clubs (GM): ☞ **Polk - Cinch Saloon**, 1723 Polk St. (776-4162); **Giraffe Lounge**,

friendly video bar, 1131 Polk St. (474-1702); **Kimo's**, 1351 Polk St. (885-4535); **Lion Pub**, Sacramento at Divisadero (567-6565); **Motherlode**, transgender and transvestite bar, 1002 Post St. (928-6006); **N'Touch**, cruisy Asian bar, open 3pm, Tuesday night karaoke, 1548 Polk St. (441-8413); **Polk Gulch**, 1100 Polk St. (771-2022); **QT Bar**, live music, cute male strippers, 1312 Polk St. (885-1114); **Swallow**, gay piano bar with sing-a-longs, mature clientele, 1750 Polk St. (775-4152).

● Bars/Clubs (GM): ☞ **Soma (Downtown)** - **The Box**, dance club, 715 Harrison St. at 3rd St. (972-8087); **Hole in the Wall**, cool biker bar, 289 8th St. near Folsom (431-4695; **Jackhammer**, the cruisiest bar in town, Tue,. is red hanky night, 290 Sanchez St. (252-0290); **Lone Star**, bears and bikers, 1354 Harrison (863-9999); **Pleasuredome**, the largest disco in San Francisco, special events, late Sunday tea dance, 177 Townsend St. (985-5256); **SF Eagle**, leather bar, patio, best Sunday from 2pm-9pm, 398 12th St., (626-0880); **Stud**, popular bar, fun crowd, 399 9th at Harrison (863-6623); **Time**, dance club, 715 Harrison St. (675-5661); **Watering Hole**, leather/levi's cruise bar, restaurant, 1145 Folsom St. (864-0300).

● Bars/clubs (GW): **Catwalk**, bi-monthly dance club, go-go dancers, downtown location (337-4962); **Club Confidential**, cocktail bar, girls in drag queens, Embassy Lounge, 600 Polk St., (885-0842); **Club Q**, dance club, first Friday of every month, 77 Townsend at 3rd St. (985-5241); **Comme Nous**, speakeasy for dykes, 139 8th at Minna (553-8719); **Diva**, dance club, go-go dancers, 314 11th St. at Folsom (487-6305); **G-Spot**, dance club, go-go female dancers, 278 11th St. at Folsom (337-4962); **Hollywood Billiards**, semi-cruisy pool hall, 61 Golden Gate St. at Market (252-9643); **Litter Box**, dance club with attitude-free atmosphere, 1190 Folsom at 8th St. (431-3332); **Mad Magda's**, cafe style atmosphere, 579 Hayes St. (864-7654); **Red Dora's**, dyke-owned establishment, cafe atmosphere, 485 14th St. near Guerrero (626-2805); **Wilde Side**, oldest Lesbian bar in San Francisco, 424 Cortland (647-3099).

● Restaurants (GMW): **Akimbo**, 116 Maiden Lane, 3rd Fl. (433-2288); **Artemis**, women's restaurant, 1199 Valencia St. (821-0232); **Bagdad Cafe**, popular diner, some vegetarian selections, 2295 Market St. (621-4434); **Bombay**, Indian cuisine, 2217 Market St. (861-6655); **Cafe Flore**, Paris style sidewalk cafe, Noe at Market St. (621-8579); **Carta**, international cuisine, 1772 Market & Octavia (863-

Visit San Francisco before you leave your house.

WWW.FYISF.COM

Your web guide to San Francisco clubs, restaurants, shopping, entertainment listings, and more.

And when you're here...

The tourist magazine that's user-friendly with updated entertainment listings every week!

FYI-0999
(415) 394-0999

To find out what's hot in San Francisco, call this number.

Brought to you by the *San Francisco Bay Guardian*, the best weekly newspaper in California

www.sfbg.com

Free every Wednesday in racks and stores all over town.

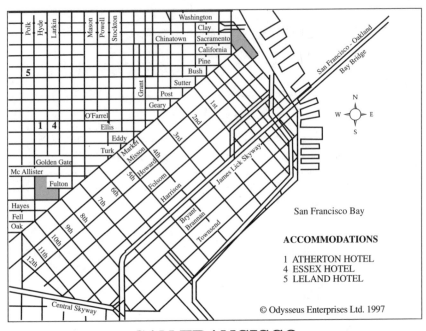

ACCOMMODATIONS

1 ATHERTON HOTEL
4 ESSEX HOTEL
5 LELAND HOTEL

© Odysseus Enterprises Ltd. 1997

SAN FRANCISCO

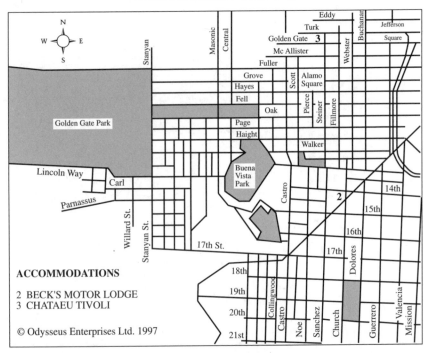

ACCOMMODATIONS

2 BECK'S MOTOR LODGE
3 CHATAEU TIVOLI

© Odysseus Enterprises Ltd. 1997

The Hotel

A charming European style hotel located in the heart of San Francisco

Conveniently located near
all major attractions.
Beautifully appointed rooms
all with private baths,
color TV,
and direct dial phones.
Abbey Room Bar
The Atherton Grill Restaurant
Complimentary morning
coffee.
Complimentary weekday
morning Limo service.

Proudly Serving The
Gay Community
For 15 Years

685 Ellis Street, San Francisco, Ca. 94109
Tel. 415-474-5720 / Fax. 415-474-8256
Toll-Free 800-474-5720

3516); **Castro Country Club**, cafe and non-alcoholic bar, 4058 18th St., (552-6102); **Castro Hibachi**, Japanese, 4063 18th St. (863-0484); **Castro Gardens**, 558 Castro St., (621-2566); **Josie's**, cabaret, restaurant, 3583 16th St. (861-7933); **Marcello's Pizza**, 420 Castro St. (863-3900); **Metro**, Hunan Chinese at the **Metro Bar** in Castro (431-1655); **Miss Pearl's Jam House**, Caribbean-Hispanic, 601 Eddy St. (775-5267); **Monda**, 2032 Polk St. (923-9984); **Orphan Andy's**, diner open 24 hrs., 3991 17th St. (864-9795); **The Rooster**, Int'l cuisine, 1101 Valencia St. at 22nd (824-1222); **Ryan's**, California cuisine, 4230 18th St. (621-6131); **Valentine's**, weekend brunch, vegetarian specialties, 1793 Church St. (285-2257).

λ SERVICES λ

● Gay Store (GM): ✪ **The Bear Store**, retail outlet featuring Bearaphenalia, videos and sexual lifestyle products, 367 Ninth St., (552-1506) or 800-234-3877.

● Health Clubs (GM): **City Athletic Club**, full service health club, open: M-F 6:00am-10:00pm, Sat-Sun 9:00am-8:00pm, 2500 Market St., (552-6680); **Eros**, Sex playrooms, sauna, video lounge, massage, 2051 Market St. (864-3767); **Market Street Gym**, popular gym in the heart of Castro, 2301 Market St. (626-4488); **Muscle Gym**, free wights, universal training, 346 Hayes St. (863-4701) and 2275 Market St. (863-4700); **Pacific Heights Health Club**, free wights, training, 2356 Pine St. (563-6694).

● Health Club (GW): **Osento, gym**, sauna, massage, 955 Valencia St. (282-6333); **Women's Training Center**, health club, gym, 2164 Market St. at Sanchez (864-6835).

● Leather (GM): **A Taste of Leather**, Leather & Erotica Emporium, 317-A 10th St. (252-9166); **Johnson Leather**, 1833 Polk (775-7393); **Leather Masters**, custom leather, B&D equipment, toys, novelties, 969 Park Ave. (293-7660).

● Personal Phone Line (GM): ✪ **San Francisco Voicemale**, meet local guys! Browse, match, chat. Try it free (247-5555) free access code 8060.

● Publications (AW):✪ **SF Bay Guardian**, the best weekly newspaper in California. Free every Wednesday in stores all over town. Internet: www.fyisf.com. (394-0999)

 ACCOMMODATIONS

✪ ATHERTON HOTEL

685 Ellis St., San Francisco, CA 94109. Tel: (415) 474-5720 or (800) 474-5720. Fax: (415) 474-8256. TYPE: *Hotel*. CLIENTELE: All Welcome. LOCATION: Downtown Polk area, 1/2 mi / 800 to Castro, 4 blocks to Civic Center.

* Rooms: 75 w/priv. bath
  sgl/dbl (up to 75) / triple 6 / quad 4
* Bed Types: twin, double, king size, queen
* Rooms for non smokers
* Phone, C/H, safe box
* Services: maid, laundry, elevator
* Restaurant: **Atherton Grill** (American)
* Bar: **Abbey Room**, English style pub
* Parking: paid (off street)
* Beach: 1.5 mi. / 2.4 km (mixed)
* Gay Bars: 2 blocks
* Health Club: 4 blocks
* Airport: SF Int'l (SFO) 16 mi. / 25 km
* Train Station: Amtrack 1 mi. / 1.6 km
* Languages: English, French, Spanish, Portugese, Tagalog, German
* Reservation: 1 night deposit
* Cancellation: 24 hrs. in advance or deposit forfeit
* Credit Cards: MC/VISA/AMEX/DC/DISC/JCB
* Open: Year round
* Rates: $69-$119; (off) 59-$99. Tax: 14%
* Check in time 3pm / check out 12 noon
* **TAC:** 10%

DESCRIPTION: Built in 1927, renovated to maintain the "Old San Francisco" feel. Abbey Room pub open nightly. Atherton Grill on mezzanine offers breakfast, lunch, dinner and Sunday brunch. *IGTA*

✪ BECK's MOTOR LODGE

2222 Market St., San Francisco, CA 94114. Tel: (415) 621-8212, or (800) 227-4360. Fax: (415) 241-0435. TYPE: *Motel*. MANAGER: Irene Fontaine. CLIENTELE: Gay/Straight. LOCATION: Castro area near M° Church St.

* Rooms: 57 w/priv. bath
  dbl 35/ triple or quad 22
* Rooms for smokers (36) and nonsmokers (21)
* CTV (movies), phone, A/C (10), C/H, safe box, refrigerator, balcony
* Maid service, sundeck, wheelchair access
* Free parking (on premises)
* Beach: 3 mi. / 5 km
* Gay Bars: 2 blocks
* Health Club: across the street (mixed)
* Airport: 12 mi. / 19 km, taxi, shuttle
* Languages: English, Spanish, French,Tagalog
* Reservations: 1 night deposit
* Cancellation: 48 hrs.
* Credit Cards: MC/VISA/AMEX/DISC/DC

$\mathcal{B}eck's$ motor lodge

In San Francisco   Stay in the City. And near Friends.

Located at the foot of Twin Peaks on outer Market Street in the Castro Area.
➤ Large comfortable rooms at economical rates ➤ Free Parking ➤ Sundeck
➤ Fireplace Units ➤ Free cable movies in your room ➤ Launderette ➤ Nearby
restaurants and shops ➤ Direct public transportation and sightseeing tours
leave right from your door ➤ Minutes from UC Medical Center ➤ Free
in-room coffee ➤ Refrigerator in all rooms ➤ Major credit cards accepted

2222 Market Street, San Francisco CA 94114 (415) 621-8212
RESERVATIONS: 1-800-227-4360

* Open: Year round
* Rates: $86-$110; (off) $72-$100
* Tax: 12%. **TAC:** 10%
* Check In 2:00 pm / Check out 12 noon

DESCRIPTION: Three-story motel with large comfortable rooms, spacious bathrooms and Queen or king size beds. Complimentary in room coffee daily. Two units with fireplace. Excellent Castro location.

✪ THE CHATEAU TIVOLI

1057 Steiner, San Francisco CA 94115. Tel: (415) 776-5462, Toll Free (800) 228-1647. Fax: (415) 776-0505. TYPE: *Bed & Breakfast*. MANAGER: Chris Clarke, GM. CLIENTELE: Equally Gay/Straight. LOCATION: Centrally located, 7 blocks south of Pacific Heights, 4 blocks southwest of Japan Center, 3 blocks north of Alamo Square.

* Rooms: 8; 4 w/priv. 4 w/shared bath
  sgl 6 / dbl 2 (phone in all rooms)
* Suites: 2 (1BR + 2BR), dining room
* Bed Types: double, king size, queen size
* Maid service, Parking: on street
* Gay Bars: walking distance
* Beach: 2 mi. / 3 km (mixed)
* Gay Bars: 10 blocks

The Chateau Tivoli

Experience San Francisco's romantic Golden Age of Opulance in the world's most beautiful 'Painted Lady'

**1057 Steiner Street
San Francisco CA 94115
Tel: (415) 776-5462

(800) 228-1647**

* Health Club: 10 blocks (mixed)
* Airport: SFO 12 mi. / 20 km, taxi, shuttle
* Metro: 1 block
* Reservations: credit card guarantee
* Cancellation Policy: $10 fee for 7 days or more, 1 night fee for less than 7 day notice
* Credit Cards: VISA/MC/AMEX
* Open: Year round
* Rates: $100 - $200 w/CB
  Mon-Fri Continental + breakfast;
  Weekend Champagne brunch
* Taxes: 14% state tax
* Check in 2:00 pm / Check out 12:00 pm

DESCRIPTION: Fully restored Landmark Victorian mansion. All guest rooms are lavishly decorated in American or French Renaissance furniture, antiques and objets d'art. Enjoy expanded continental breakfast during the week and champagne brunch on weekends

✪ ESSEX HOTEL

684 Ellis St., San Francisco, CA 94109. Tel: (415) 474-4664 or (800) 453-7739. Fax: (415) 441-1800. TYPE: *Hotel*. HOST: Jean Chaban, Mgr. CLIENTELE: All Welcome. LOCATION: Downtown, corner of Ellis and Larkin Sts near Union Sq., Cable Car, theaters, Opera Plaza, Polk St. and gay nightlife.

* Rooms: 100, 50 w/priv., 50 w/shared bath. Smoking allowed in rooms
* TV, phone, safe box, C/H
* Bed Types: twin, queen size
* Maid service, elevator. Parking (paid)
* Beach: 4 mi. / 6 km (mixed)
* Gay Bars: 2 blocks (Polk Street)
* Health Club: 3 blocks (mixed)
* Airport: 17 mi. (27 km), AP shuttle, taxi
* Languages: English, French, German
* Cancellation: 24 hrs.. notice
* Credit Cards: MC/VISA/AMEX/EC
* Open: Year round
* Rates: $59-$79. Tax: 12% *TAC:* 10%
* Check In 12 noon / Check Out 12 noon

DESCRIPTION: Newly renovated with high quality furnishings. Charming and affordable European-style rooms in the heart of downtown. Palatial lobby with marble floor and French antiques. 24 hrs.. front-desk and multilingual staff.

✪ LELAND HOTEL

1315 Polk St., San Francisco, CA 94109. Tel: (415) 441-5141 or (800) 258-4458. Fax: (415) 775-8322. TYPE: *Hotel*. HOST: Brian Murrian GM. CLIENTELE: Mostly Gay. LOCATION: Corner of Polk and Bush Sts. 1 block to Cable

Cars, near Japantown, Chinatown, Opera, Theatres, and public transportation.

* Rooms: 93; 72 w/priv., 36 w/shared bath
* Apartments: 15 w/cooking facilities
* CTV, phone, maid service, parking
* Beach: 20 minutes
* Gay Bars: 10 ft. / 3 m
* Airport: 30 min., taxi, limo, bus
* Reservations: 1 night deposit
* Credit Cards: MC/VISA/AMEX
* Rates: $30 - $58. *TAC:* 10%

DESCRIPTION: Large budget hotel complex in the center of Polk St. District. Unpretentious, friendly w/clean, moderately priced rooms. *IGTA*

RENOIR HOTEL
45 McAllister St., San Francisco, CA 94102. Tel: (415) 626-5200 or Toll Free (800) 576-3388. Fax: (415) 626-5581. TYPE: *Hotel.* CLIENTELE: All Welcome. LOCATION: Downtown San Francisco, McAllister at Market, 10 min. from Castro St. on Market Street Trolley.

* Rooms: 128 w/priv. bath. Suites:3 (1BR)
* Rooms for smokers and non smokers
* CTV, phone, safe box, AM/FM clock radios
* Maid, room and laundry service
* Wheelchair access, elevator
* Restaurant: **Renoir Cafe**
* Bar: **McDonald Pub** (gay bar)
* Parking: paid, off street. No pets
* Beach: 7 mi. / 11 km (mixed/nude)
* Gay Bars: in house, other nearby
* Health Club: 1 block (YMCA central)
* Airport: SFO 17 mi. / 27 km
* Languages: English, Tagalog, German, French, Spanish, Cantonese, Mandarin
* Reservation: required
* Cancellation: 24 hrs. prior to arrival
* Credit Cards: MC/VISA/AMEX/DISC/DC/EC/JCB
* Open: Year round
* Check in time 3pm / check out 11am
* Rates: $84-$109; (off) $49-$89, Suites $99-$150. Tax: 12%. *TAC:* 10%

DESCRIPTION: European style newly renovated Historical Landmark located between Gay areas and tourist attractions. Comfortable and tastefully furnished rooms and suites with queen, king, or double beds.

SAN FRANCISCO VIEWS
379 Collingwood St., San Francisco, CA 94114. Tel: (415) 282-1367. TYPE: *Guest House.* CLIENTELE: Mostly Gay. LOCATION: Top of Collingwood near the intersection of 21st Street (2nd house from the corner). 2 rooms, 2 suites. Rates: on request. DESCRIPTION: Spanish-style former private residence. Indoor lounge with fireplace, kitchen and dining room.

SAN JOSÉ   © 408

✈ San José Int'l AP (SJC) 2 mi. / 3 km NW

LOCATION: South end of San Francisco Bay, 50 mi / 80 km from San Francisco.

POPULATION: 785,000

Gay/Lesbian Visitor Information
Billy DeFrank Center: 293-2429

DESCRIPTION: San José is known as the "Capital of the Silicon Valley". It is an important electronics, computers and aerospace center. Visit **The Egyptian Museum** (947-3636); and the famous **San Jose Museum of Art**, 110 S. Market St. (294-2787).

BARS ♈ RESTAURANTS 🍴

● Bars/clubs (GM): **641 Club**, 641 Stockton Ave. (998-1144); **Bucks**, 301 Stockton Ave. (296-1176); **FX**, 400 S. 1st St. (298-9796);**Mac's Club**, 349 S. 1st St., (998-9535); **Renegades**, 393 Stockton (275-9902);**The Saint**, cruise bar, 170 W. St. John St. (947-1667); **Selections**, 1984 Oakland Rd. (428-0329).

● Restaurants (AW): **Bo Town**, Chinese/ Vietnamese, 409 S. 2nd St. (295-2125); **Emile's**, French, 545 S. 2nd St. (289-1960); **Hamburger Mary's**, restaurant/bar, 170 W. St. John St. (947-1667); **Tacos Al Pastor**, 400 S. Bascom Ave. (275-1619).

λ SERVICES λ

● Erotica (G/S): **l'Amour Shoppe**, 447 S. 1st St. (298-2173); **Leather Masters**, 969 Park Ave. (293-7660).

● Health Club (GM): **Watergarden**, gym, sauna, 24 hrs., 1010 The Alameda (275-1215)

● Personal phone Line (GM): ✪ **San José Confidential Connection**, meet local guys! Record, listen, respond to ads free (532-3000) free access code 8060.

🖋 ACCOMMODATIONS 🖋

HOTEL DE ANZA
233 W. Santa Clara St., San José. Tel: (408) 286-1000. TYPE: *Hotel*. CLIENTELE: All Welcome. LOCATION: Downtown San José. 100

rooms w/priv. bath, 6 suites w/jacuzzi, minibar, CTV, VCR, A/C, C/H, room service, Italian restaurant, exercise room. Rates: $130 - $160. Tax: 10% *TAC:* 10%. DESCRIPTION: Art Deco style hotel.

WEST HOLLYWOOD   © 310

✈ Los Angeles Int'l Airport (LAX) 15 mi. / 24 km SW, or Burbank

LOCATION: Centrally located in the Greater Los Angeles area, tucked between Beverly Hills on the west and Hollywood on the east. Convenient to Santa Monica, downtown Los Angeles and the San Fernando Valley.

POPULATION: 36,000

CLIMATE: See Los Angeles

VISITOR INFORMATION
W. Hollywood CC: (310) 858-8000

Gay/Lesbian Visitor Information
Gay & Lesbian Community Services Ctr.
Tel: (213) 464-7400

DESCRIPTION: West Hollywood is a small urban village surrounded by the nation's second largest metropolitan area. The 'Creative City' has a large gay/lesbian population and it is the 'hottest' destination for international gay and lesbian travelers. Many bars, clubs, shops and restaurants are clustered along the famous Santa Blvd. West Hollywood offers the convenience of a small town with the sophistication of a large metropolis. Unlike Los Angeles you do not need a car to enjoy West Hollywood and the endless nightlife scene.

❖ **SPECIAL EVENT: Gay Pride Parade**, Last Sunday in June.

BARS ♈ RESTAURANTS 🍴

● Bars/Clubs (GM): **Axis**, popular dance club, multiple bars, erotic dancers, 653 N. La Peer Dr. (659-0471); **Backlot**, cabaret, shows, videos, 657 N. Robertson (at Studio 1) (659-0472); **Bar One**, exclusive bar, celebrity clientele, 9229 Sunset Blvd.; **Eagle**, Levi cruise bar, pool table, 7864 Santa Monica Blvd. (654-3252); **Gold Coast**, Neighborhood cruise bar, 8228 Santa Monica Blvd. (656-4879); **Hunter's**, cruise pool bar, 7511 Santa Monica Blvd. (213-850-9428); **Love Lounge**,live music, go-go dancers, 657 N.

Robertson Blvd. (659-0472); **Micky's**, dance club, 8857 Santa Monica Blvd. (657-1176); **Mother Lode**, friendly cruise bar, cocktail hours, 8944 Santa Monica Blvd. (659-9700); **Numbers**, bar/restaurant, some boys for hire, 8029 Sunset (656-6300); **Rafters**, country/western, 7995 Santa Monica Blvd.; **Rage**, high energy dance club, videos, Wed. The Troopers (camp drag), 8911 Santa Monica Blvd. (652-7055); **Revolver**, video bar, hot crowd, opens daily 4pm, Fri./Sat. Beautiful men night, videos, 8851 Santa Monica Blvd., (550-8851); **Spike**, leather/levi bar, 7746 Santa Monica Blvd. (654-3336); **Trunks**, sports video bar, pool table, 8809 Santa Monica Blvd. (652-1015).

● Bars/Clubs (GMW): **7702 SM Club**, live DJ, pool table, 24 hrs., 7702 Santa Monica Blvd. (654-3336); **Axis**, video dance club, 652 N. LaPeer Dr. (659-0471); **Love Lounge**, Disco, showbar, 657 N. Robertson (652-5926); **Revolver**, video cabaret, 8851 Santa Monica Blvd.

● Bar/Clubs (GW): **Club 7969**, 7969 Santa Monica Blvd. (654-0280); **The Palms**, dance bar, 8572 Santa Monica Blvd. (652-6188)

● Restaurants (GMW): **Baja Buds**, Mexican cuisine, 8575 Santa Monica Blvd. (659-1911); **Benevenuto**, Italian cuisine, 8512 Santa Monica Blvd. (659-8635); **Bossa Nova**, Brazilian cuisine, 685 N. Robertson Blvd. (657-5070); **Checca**, French/Italian, 7323 Santa Monica Blvd. (850-7471); **Club Cafe**, healthy low fat cuisine, 8560 Santa Monica Blvd. (659-6630); **Figs**, American cuisine, 7929 Santa Monica Blvd. (654-0780); **French Quarter**, American & Continental cuisine, 7985 Santa Monica Blvd. (654-0898); **Melrose Place**, California cuisine, 650 N. La Cienega Blvd. (657-222); **Montage Bistro**, California & Int'l cuisine, 8730 Santa Monica Blvd., Ste. F (289-8187); **L'Orangerie**, haute French cuisine, 903 N. La Cienega Blvd. (652-9770); **Stella's Café**, Vegetarian specialties, 8711 Santa Monica Blvd. (657-5820); **Tandoori Nights**, Tandoori dishes, 8165 Santa Monica Blvd. (848-8626); **Yukon Mining Co.**,American cuisine, Gold Rush-themed dining room, 24 hrs., 7328 Santa Monica Blvd. (851-8833).

λ SERVICES λ

● Adult Bookshop (G/S): **Drake's**, xxx videos, body jewelry, erotic cards, 8932 Santa Monica Blvd. (289-8932); **The Pleasure Chest**, 7733 Santa Monica Blvd. (650-1022);

● Gift Shop (GMW): **۞ Dorothy Surrender**, West Hollywood's #1 Gift Shop! All kind of gifts

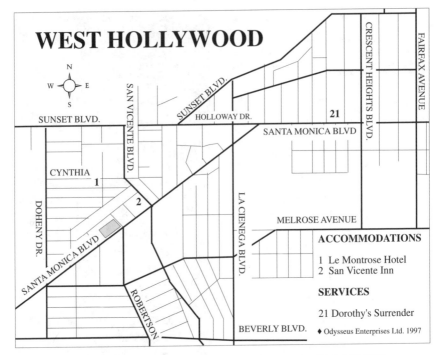

WEST HOLLYWOOD

N
W — E
S

SUNSET BLVD.

SAN VICENTE BLVD.

SUNSET BLVD.

HOLLOWAY DR.

SANTA MONICA BLVD

CRESCENT HEIGHTS BLVD.

FAIRFAX AVENUE

21

CYNTHIA
1

2

DOHENY DR.

SANTA MONICA BLVD.

ROBERTSON

LA CIENEGA BLVD.

MELROSE AVENUE

BEVERLY BLVD.

ACCOMMODATIONS

1 Le Montrose Hotel
2 San Vicente Inn

SERVICES

21 Dorothy's Surrender

♦ Odysseus Enterprises Ltd. 1997

---

for all kind of people, books, magazines, cards, T-Shirt, Gay Pride gifts, jewelry, CD's etc., 7985 Santa Monica Blvd. #111, Tel: (213-650-4111), Fax: (213-656-2667).

● Clothing Store (GMW): **Don't Panic**, quality T-shirts and sweat shirts, 802 N. San Vicente (1-800-45-PANIC).

● Health Club/Gym (GM): **The Athletic Club**, 8560 Santa Monica Blvd. (659-6630); **Sports Connection**, 8612 Santa Monica Blvd.; **World Gym**, 8560 Santa Monica Blvd. (659-6630)

● Jewelry Store (GMW): ○ **Jewelry by Poncé**, specializing in Commitment and Pride rings (traditional, rainbow, triangles); body jewelry, watches, unique gifts. Visit our store or call 800-969-RING for brochures. Wholesale inquiries welcome. URL: www.jewelryby-ponce.com. Email: jewelry@jewelrybyponce

● Personal Phone Line (GM): ○ **West Hollywood Confidential Connection**, meet local guys! Record, listen, respond to ads free (854-6666) free access code 8060.

● Pharmacy: **Capitol Drugs**, 8578 Santa Monica Blvd. (289-1125); **Vee's Pharmacy**,

8609 Santa Monica Blvd. (657-5180).

● Publication: ○ **Provocateur**, elegant homo-erotic art magazine, stunning male nude photographs, 8599 Santa Monica Blvd., West Hollywood, CA 90069. Tel: (800) 959-9843 or (310) 659-6654. URL: http://alluvial.com.

ACCOMMODATIONS

○ LE MONTROSE HOTEL

900 Hammond St., West Hollywood, CA 90069. Tel: (310) 855-1115 or Reservations (800) 776-0666. Fax: (310) 657-9192. TYPE: *First Class All Suite Hotel*. CLIENTELE: All Welcome. LOCATION: Heart of West Hollywood on a quiet lane. Above Santa Monica Blvd., one block east of fashionable Beverly Hills.

* Suites: 125 w/priv. facilities
* CTV, VCR, phone, wet bar, fireplace private balcony, cooking facilities
* Business phone/fax facilities
* Room service, twice daily maid service
* Complimentary fruit & beverage upon arrival
* Wheelchair access
* Meeting room & business center
* Restaurant: Continental cuisine

* Roof garden w/heated pool & jacuzzi
* State of the art Health Club, free tennis
* Gay bars: walking distance
* Beaches: 10 mi. / 16 km west (mixed)
* Airport: 12 mi. / 19 km north of LAX
* Credit Cards: all major credit cards
* Open: Year round
* Rates: $160-$475. Corporate rates on request
* Check in 3 pm / check out 12 noon
* Tax: 13%
* *TAC:* 10%

DESCRIPTION: Delightful Art Nouveau style hotel featuring spacious suites, excellent amenities and friendly service. 41 Junior Suites with Queen size beds and a living room; 68 Executive Suites with King size bed, living/dining area w/kitchenette; and 14 one-bedroom suites with King size bed, living/dining area w/kitchenette. Packages available. Ask for the "Bed & Breakfast" and "Weekend" packages. Enjoy the roof garden pool, excellent restaurant and convenient central location.

PARK SUNSET HOTEL

8462 Sunset Blvd., West Hollywood, CA 90069. Tel: (213) 654-6470. Fax: (213) 654-6470. TYPE: *Hotel.* CLIENTELE: All Welcome. LOCATION: In the heart of the Sunset Strip.

* Rooms: 84 w/priv. bath, Suites: 18
* CTV (VCR), phone, hair dryer,safe some w/fully equipped kitchens
* Room & maid service, laundry facilities
* Restaurant, heated pool, sundeck
* Gay Bars: many nearby
* Airport: 35 min.
* Rates: $75-$140
* *TAC:* 10%

DESCRIPTION: Contemporary moderate first class hotel near the Comedy Store. Public and tour buses stop at the hotel's door.

RAMADA WEST HOLLYWOOD

8585 Santa Monica Blvd., West Hollywood, CA 90069. Tel: (310) 652-6400. Fax: (213) 652-2135. TYPE: *Hotel.* CLIENTELE: Gay/Straight. LOCATION: Near Beverly Hills, Century City & Hollywood, convenient to the area gay scene

* Rooms: 177 w/priv. bath; Suites: 22
* CTV, (VCR's available), phone, A/C
* Restaurants & Shops
* Pool, Sundeck, health club
* Room & maid service, free parking
* Gay Bars: walking distance
* Airport: 15 mi. (24 km)
* Credit Cards: MC/VISA/AMEX/DC/CB
* Open: Year round
* Rates: on request.

* *TAC:* 10%

DESCRIPTION: High-tech design business oriented hotel with spacious modern rooms. Elegant loft suites are available with wet bars.

✪ SAN VICENTE INN

845 San Vicente Blvd., West Hollywood, CA 90069. Tel: (310) 854-6915. TYPE: Inn *Resort.* HOSTS: Terry & Rocky. CLIENTELE: Gay men only. LOCATION: 1/4 street block north of Santa Monica Blvd.

* Rooms: 20 rooms, (16 w/priv. bath, 4 shared)
* Suites: 10 suites, Cottages: 4
* CTV, VCR, phone, refrigerator
* Room service
* Pool, sun deck, clothing optional policy
* Gym, jacuzzi
* Free parking
* Gay bars: many nearby
* Airport: 35 min.
* Pets: Prearrangement required
* Open: year round
* Reservations: One night credit card deposit
* Cancelation policy: 7 days
* Check in 11 am, check out 1 pm
* Rates: $59-$149,
  Continental breakfast included
* Tax: 13%.
* *TAC:* 10%.

DESCRIPTION: Gay owned and operated bed & breakfast in West Hollywood. Intimate atmosphere.

SUNSET PLAZA HOTEL

8400 Sunset Blvd., West Hollywood, CA 90069. Tel: (213) 654-0750. Fax: (213) 650-6146. TYPE: *Hotel.* CLIENTELE: All Welcome. LOCATION: On the famous Sunset Strip near West Hollywood Gay scene.

* Rooms: 86 w/priv. bath
* 2-room suites available
* CTV (VCR), phone, electronic safe, refrigerator, some w/kitchen
* Room & Valet service
* Heated pool, sundeck
* Free parking
* Gay bars: many nearby
* Airport: 35 min.
* Rates: $65-$165.
* *TAC:* 10%

DESCRIPTION: Attractive hotel on the famous Sunset Strip. Public transportation and tour buses at the door.

COLORADO

Galena (920-6905); **Silver Nugget**, bar & restaurant, Hyman Ave., Mall (925-6905); **The Trippler**, bar & restaurant, 535 E. Dean (925-4977).

♦ ACCOMMODATIONS ♦

ASPEN B&B
311 West Main St., Aspen, CO 81611. Tel: (303) 925-7650. Fax: (303) 925-5744. TYPE: *Bed & Breakfast.* CLIENTELE: All Welcome. LOCATION: Conveniently located on free shuttle bus line, 5 blocks from downtown. 38 rooms w/priv. bath. DESCRIPTION: Contemporary lodge with an impressive atrium lobby. Some rooms have balcony or jacuzzi.

HOTEL ASPEN
110 W. Main St., Aspen, CO 81611. Tel: (303) 925-3441. Fax: (303) 920-1379. TYPE: *Hotel.* CLIENTELE: All Welcome. LOCATION: In downtown Aspen, 3 blocks to Aspen Mall. 45 rooms w/priv. bath. DESCRIPTION: Superior first class downtown hotel. All rooms with custom-designed furniture, some with balcony, terrace, or jacuzzi. Lobby lounge with scenic views.

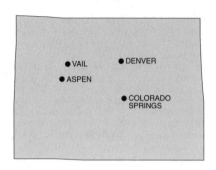

♦ **Population:** 2,900,000
♦ **Capital:** Denver
♦ **Time Zone:** Mountain
♦ **No Sodomy Law**
♦ **Legal drinking age:** 21

ASPEN   ✆ 303

✈ Sardy Field AP (DEN) 4 mi./ 6km North

LOCATION: Heart of Western Colorado's White National forest near Snowmass Village, 200 mi. / 320 km southwest of Denver.

POPULATION: 4,000

CLIMATE: Mountainous, high altitude weather can be chilly at any time; cold with snow in the winter.

**Gay/Lesbian Visitor Information
Aspen G&L Community**
Tel: (303) 925-9249

DESCRIPTION: Old Victorian town with history going back to the Silver boom of the 1880's. Today, it is a major ski resort and a playground of celebrities. Nearby Snowmass is a group of condos and hotels built around a ski mountain.

BARS ▼ RESTAURANTS ¶¶

● Bars/clubs (G/S): **Double Diamond**, 450 S.

COLORADO SPRINGS   ✆ 303

✈ Municipal Airport (COS) 7 mi. / 11 km SE

LOCATION: Northern Colorado on a mile-high plateau east of the Rocky Mountains.

POPULATION: 285,000

CLIMATE: Pleasant climate with mild temperatures for a city in this latitude and elevation. Dry sunny summers and long winters. January high temperatures are in the 40's F (4°c); Summer high temperatures in August can reach 82°F (28°c).

DESCRIPTION: Colorado Springs, at the foot of Pikes Peak, was founded as a summer playground and health resort. It is a conservative community with a small gay presence.

BARS ▼ RESTAURANTS ¶¶

● Bars/clubs (GMW): **Hide & Seek Complex**, 4 bars and restaurant, 512 W. Colorado (634-9303); **Hour Glass Lounge**, mostly lesbians, 2748 Airport Rd. (471-2104); **Penthouse**, 1715 N. Academy Blvd. (597-3314); **True Colors**, 1865 N. Academy Blvd. (637-0773).

⚑ ACCOMMODATIONS ⚑

EMBASSY SUITES
7290 Commerce Center Dr., Colorado Springs, CO 80970. Tel: (719) 599-9100. TYPE: *All Suite Hotel.* CLIENTELE: All Welcome. LOCATION: Monument Creek Commerce Center. 207 suites w/priv. bath, A/C, living room, wet bat, microwave, refrigerator, restaurant, pool, sauna, steam room. Rates: $99-$140. *TAC:* 10%. DESCRIPTION: Superior first class all suite hotel.

DENVER   ✆ 303

✈ Stapleton Int'l Airport (DEN)

LOCATION: At an elevation of more than 6,000 ft. / 1,820 km on the eastern slope of the Rocky Mountains.

POPULATION: City 493,000;
                       Metro 1,800,000

CLIMATE: Mild climate. Summers are cool with July average of 73°F (23°c). Winters are cold with January average of 30°F (-2°c). Springs are stormy, wet and cloudy. Average annual rainfall 16" (406 mm) and snowfall 60" (1.5 m).

Gay/Lesbian Visitor Information
G&L Community Center: 837-1598

DESCRIPTION: Denver the "Queen City of the Plain" lies on the slopes of the Rocky Mountains. Settled in 1858, the city developed from a tiny gold-hungry mining town to a cosmopolitan city. Besides being a Western center of business and commerce, Denver offers excellent cultural events which include the **Denver Symphony** and the **Denver Repertory Theatre**. The local museum - **Denver Art Museum** is well known for its fine art exhibits. Visit: The **Civic Center** at Colfax and Broadway Avenues, a green oasis in the heart of the city; the **Colorado Governor's Mansion**, 8th Ave. and Pennsylvania. **Denver Botanic Gardens**, 1005 York Street, lovely landscaped area with herbs, roses and Japanese style gardens. If you visit Denver in January don't miss the annual **National Western Stock Show**, the world's largest livestock exhibition. Events include professional and amateur rodeo, horse shows and the best cattle contest. The events take place at the **Denver Coliseum**, I-70 and Washington Streets. For shopping and quality dining in downtown Denver visit **Larimer Square** and the **16th Street Mall**.

BARS ▼ RESTAURANTS ▮▮

● Bars/clubs (GM): **BJ's Carousel**, bar/restaurant, 1380 S. Broadway (777-9880); **Brick's**, 1600 E. 17th Ave. (377-5400); **Charlie's**, dance club, restaurant, country/western, 900 E. Colfax (839-8890); **Garbo's**, restaurant, piano bar, Sunday brunch, 116 E. 9th Ave. (837-8217); **Compound**, 145 Broadway (722-7977); **Metro Express**, 314 E. 13th Ave. (894-0668); **Mike's**, 60 S. Broadway (777-0193); **Paradise Garage**, 2975 Fox St. (292-5671); **The Raven**, leather/levi cruise bar, 2217 Welton; **R&R**, cocktail lounge western/levi style, 4958 E. Colfax (320-9337).

● Bars/Clubs (GMW): **The Bobcat**, 1700 Logan (830-0535); **The Den**, bar & restaurant, 5110 W. Colfax Ave. (534-9526); **Detour**, dance bar & restaurant, 551 E. Colfax Ave. (861-1497); **Highland Bar**, dance bar, show, restaurant, 2532 15th St. (455-9978).

● Restaurants: **Basil's Cafe**, health food, 30 S. Broadway (698-1413); **Lautrec's**, restaurant/cabaret, 266 S. Downing (777-1991); **Matchmaker**, Chinese, 1480 Humboldt (839-9388); **Surf City**, bar & grill, 1175 E. Colfax Ave. (830-0715); other suggested restaurants: **Fins Restaurant and Oyster Bar**, 1401 Larimer (571-1150); **The Little Russian Cafe**, Russian Cuisine and European deserts, at Larimer Sq. courtyard, 1430 Larimer (595-8600); **Imperial**, Chinese, 1 Broadway (698-2800).

λ SERVICES λ

● Erotica (GM): **Crypt Cinema**, all-male movies, videos, open 24 hrs., 139 Broadway (778-6584); **Heaven Sent Me**, 1855 Gaylord (331-8000); **Pleasure Entertainment Center**, 127 S. Broadway (722-5852).

● Health Clubs (GM): **Midtown Spa**, 2935 Zuni St. (458-9909); **Denver Swim Club**, open 24 hours, 6923 E. Colfax (321-9399); **Broadway Bodywork**, fitness club for men and women, 160 S. Broadway (722-4342).

● Personal Phone Line (GM): ✪ **Denver Voicemale**, meet local guys! Browse, match, chat. Try it free! (831-8330) free access code 8060.

⚑ ACCOMMODATIONS ⚑

○ VICTORIA OAKS INN

1575 Race St., Denver, CO 80206. Tel: (303) 355-1818 or Toll Free (800) 662-OAKS. Fax: (303) 662-6257. TYPE: *Bed & Breakfast.* HOST: Clyde Stephens. CLIENTELE: Mostly Gay. LOCATION: On a residential street, 1 mi. (1.5 km) from downtown, close to shopping, parks, museums and all tourist attractions.

* Rooms: 9; 1 w/priv., 8 w/shared bath
  Suite: 1, cooking facilities in all units
* CTV Lounge, phone, C/H
* Garden, sundeck, maid service, parking
* Gay Bars: 5 min. walk
* Airport: 10 min. drive, taxi
* Train Station: 5 minutes
* Reservations: 1 night deposit, CC guarantee, 1 week cancel policy
* Credit Cards: AMEX/MC/VISA/DISC/DC
* Open: Year round
* Rates: $45-$85 w/breakfast.
* *TAC:* 10%

DESCRIPTION: Beautifully restored Victorian Mansion with urban convenience, providing upscaled accommodations and personalized service. The best accommodations choice in Denver for the gay travelers. *IGTA*

Toll Free (800) 662-OAKS

**1575 Race Street
Denver, Colorado 80206
303/355-1818**

VAIL   ✆ 303

✈ Eagle County Airport

LOCATION: One hundred miles / 160 km west of Denver on Interstate 70.

POPULATION: 2,300

CLIMATE: Continental mountainous climate. Spring average temperatures are 49°F (9°c), 79°F (24°c) in the summer, 50°F (10°c) in the Fall, and 40°F (4°c) in the winter.

VISITOR INFORMATION
Vail Resort Association
Tel: (800) 824-5737

DESCRIPTION: A year round mountain resort in the scenic White River National Forest. The resort is one of the finest skiing resorts in North America with beautiful European-style pedestrian village, sophisticated shopping, restaurants and other diversions. Skiing is available in winter on Vail and Beaver Creek Mountain. The rest of the year area recreation include: golf, tennis, hot-air balloon rides, river rafting, scenic gondola rides, hunting and fishing.

BARS ♀ RESTAURANTS ⑪

There is no organized gay/lesbian nightlife scene in Vail. However the following establishments may be considered for social drinking or dining: **Bart & Yeti's**, American cuisine in a rustic log cabin atmosphere, Lionshead (476-2754); **Cafe Arlberg**, skier's buffet lunch, in the Lodge at Vail (476-5011); **Cyrano's**, Pacific Grill dinner, tropical beers, cocktails and the hottest dance club in Vail downstairs, 298 Hanson Ranch Rd. (476-5551).

BAR ♀ RESTAURANT ⑪

● Bar/Restaurant (G/S): **Sweet Basil**, 193 E. Gore St., Drive (476-0125).

⬟ ACCOMMODATIONS ⬟

HOLIDAY INN AT VAIL
13 Vail Rd., Vail, CO 81657. Tel: (303) 476-5631. Fax: (303) 476-6879. TYPE: *Hotel.* CLIENTELE: Mostly Straight. LOCATION: 200 yards/m from ski lifts, walking distance of Vail Village. 120 rooms. DESCRIPTION: Attractive first class lodge in a central location to the ski lifts and Vail Village.

CONNECTICUT

- ◆ **Population:** 3,100,000
- ◆ **Capital:** Hartford
- ◆ **Time Zone:** Eastern
- ◆ **No Sodomy Law**
- ◆ **Legal drinking age:** 21

HARTFORD   ℱ 860

✈ Bradley Int'l Airport (BDL)

LOCATION: In the heart of New England's Connecticut Valley.

POPULATION: 140,000

CLIMATE: Continental climate. Summers are mild with a July average temperature of 74°F (23°c); winters are cold and snowy with an average January temperature of 28°F (-2°c).

Gay/Lesbian Visitor Information
G&L Community Center: (860) 724-5542

DESCRIPTION: The Greater Hartford area is an important manufacturing center and the "Insurance capital of the World" with more than 52 insurance companies.

BARS ⅄ RESTAURANTS 🍴

● Bar/Club (GM): **Sanctuary**, cruise bar, 2880 Main St. (724-1277).

● Bars/Clubs (GMW): **Chez Est**, dance bar, 458 Wethersfield Ave. (522-3243); **Choices**, dance club, 8 No. Turnpike Rd., Wallingford (949-9380); **Nick's**, dance bar, professional crowd, 1943 Broad St. (522-1573).

● Restaurant (AW): **Reader's Feast**, bookstore with coffee shop, 529 Farmington Ave (232-3710).

λ SERVICES λ

● Personal Phone Line (GM): ✪ **Hartford Confidential Connection**, meet local guys! Record, listen, respond to ads free (293-3969) free access code 8060.

📭 ACCOMMODATIONS 📭

HOLIDAY INN - DOWNTOWN
50 Morgan St., Hartford, CT 06120. Tel: (860) 549-2400. Fax: (860) 549-7844. TYPE: *Hotel*. CLIENTELE: Mostly Straight. LOCATION: Near Hartford Civic Center. 359 Rooms, 4 Suites, CTV, phone, A/C, pool & fitness room, 14 mi. / 23 km to airport, Gay bars: nearby. Rates: $75 - $95. *TAC*: 10%. A multiple story hotel.

RAMADA INN CAPITOL HILL
440 Asylum St., Hartford CT 06108. Tel: (860) 246-6591. Fax: (860) 728-1382. TYPE: *Motel*. CLIENTELE: Mostly Straight. LOCATION: 1 block from the Civic Center. 96 Rooms, 4 Suites, CTV, phone, A/C, parking, 14 mi. / 23 km to airport, Gay bars: nearby, Season: Year round, Rates: $75 - $95. *TAC*: 10%. Attractive motor hotel in a convenient central location.

NEW HAVEN   ℱ 203

✈ Tweed-New Haven Airport (HVN)

LOCATION: A university and port town on the Long Island Sound, only 75 mi. / 120 km north of New York City.

POPULATION: 130,000

CLIMATE: Continental. Summers are mild with a July average of 74°F (23°c); winters are snowy cold with a January average of 28°F (-2°c).

DESCRIPTION: Typical New England port town with a rich historical heritage (founded in 1638); the home town of **Yale University** (founded in 1701).

BARS 🍸 RESTAURANTS 🍴

● Bars/Clubs (GM): **The Bar**, 254 Crown St. (495-8924).

● Bars/Clubs (GMW): **168 York St. Café**, bar/restaurant, 168 York St. (789-1915); **The Chapel Pub**, 1150 Chapel St. (789-8612); **DV8**,148 York St. (865-6206).

● Restaurants (GMW): **168 York St. Café**,168 York St. (789-1915). Other (AW): **Robert Henry's**, elegant, imaginative American cuisine, near the Yale Campus, 1032 Chapel St. (789-1010); **Delmonaco's**, Italian restaurant, 232 Wooster St. (865-1109).

 ACCOMMODATIONS

COLONY INN
1157 Chapel St., New Haven CT 06511-4892. Tel: (203) 776-1234. Fax: (203) 772-3929. TYPE: *Hotel*. CLIENTELE: Mostly Straight. LOCATION: Adjacent to Yale University. 86 Rooms, CTV, phone, A/C, restaurant, parking, 10 min. to airport, Gay bars: nearby, Season: Year round, Rates: $79 (sgl) - $400 (suite w/parlor) *TAC:* 10%. Modern five-story hotel.

HOLIDAY INN - YALE U.
30 Whalley Ave., New Haven CT 06511. Tel: (203) 777-6221. Fax: (203) 772-1089. TYPE: *Motor Inn*. CLIENTELE: Mostly Straight. LOCATION: Adjacent to Yale University, near downtown., 156 Rooms, 6 Suites, CTV, phone, A/C, restaurant, pool, parking, 5 mi. / 8 km to airport, Gay bars: nearby, Season: Year Round, Rates: $69 - $99. *TAC:* 10%. Standard Motor

Inn adjacent to Yale University.

MYSTIC ✆ 203

✈ Groton/New London Airport

LOCATION: Southeastern Connecticut.

DESCRIPTION: Old whaling port founded in 1654. Mystic is a popular tourist destination due to a fascinating reconstruction of the town's 19th century seaport. For those interested in Casino gambling, the **Foxwood Casino**, the largest on the East Coast with its slot machines and table games is located nearby in Ledyard on Indian Reservation. Open 24 hrs. State Road #2, Ledyard. For gay nightlife, travel to nearby New London.

BARS 🍸 RESTAURANTS 🍴

● Bar/Club (GMW): **Frank's Place**, 9 Tilley St. New London (443-8883).

● Restaurant (AW): **Flood Tide**, seafood, c/o Inn at Mystic (536-8140).

 ACCOMMODATIONS

THE INN at MYSTIC
US1 & State #27, Mystic, CT 06355. Tel: (203) 536-9604. TYPE: *Hotel*. CLIENTELE: All Welcome. LOCATION: Set on 13 acres overlooking Mystic Harbor. 68 rooms, 4 suites. DESCRIPTION: Renovated Colonial Mansion with turn-of-the-century furnishings and ambience.

DELAWARE

REHOBOTH BEACH

♦ **Population:** 600,000
♦ **Capital:** Dover
♦ **Time Zone:** Eastern
♦ **No Sodomy Law**
♦ **Legal drinking age:** 21

DELAWARE SHORE ℂ 302
REHOBOTH BEACH

✈ Salisbury, Maryland, Airport (SBY)
Washington National Airport (DCA)

LOCATION: Delaware's Eastern Shore on the Atlantic Ocean. 2 hours from Washington D.C., Philadelphia and Baltimore.

POPULATION: Rehoboth Beach 1,730

CLIMATE: Hot, humid in the summer with sea breezes. Cold stormy winters.

DESCRIPTION: Miles of sandy beaches make Delaware's eastern shore a major summer resort center.

❖ Gay Beaches: **North Shores**, north on First toward Cape Henlopen State Park; **Poodle Point**, Prospect on the beach.

BARS ♉ RESTAURANTS 🍴

● Bars/Clubs (GMW): ✪ **Renegde**, dance club, restaurant, entertainment complex, 4274

Highway 1 (227-4713); **Back Porch Cafe**, 59 Rehoboth Ave. (227-3674); **Blue Moon**, bar & restaurant, 35 Baltimore Ave. (227-6515).

● Restaurant (GMW): ✪ **Good & Plenty**, American restaurant at the Renegade Motel, 4274 Hwy 1 (227-1222). Others (AW): **Back Porch Café**, 59 Rehoboth Ave. (227-3674); **Blue Moon**, 35 Baltimore Ave. (227-6515); **The Deli**, New York style, 32 Wilmington (226-2088); **Surfside Diner**, 137 Rehoboth (226-0700).

λ SERVICES λ

● Clothing: **Boxers & Drawers**, 36 Baltimore (227-4887); **Sãeno**, 1st & Wilmington (227-2882); **Splash**, 2 Penny Lane Mall (227-1927).

● Personal Phone Line (GM): ✪ **Delaware Confidential Connection**, meet local guys! Record, listen, respond to ads free (478-4330) free access code 8060.

 ACCOMMODATIONS 🏠

RAMS HEAD INN
RD2, Box 509, Rehoboth Beach, DE 19971-9702. TEL: (302) 226-9171. TYPE: *Bed & Breakfast*. HOST: Carl & Jim. CLIENTELE: Gay Men Only. 7 rooms, pool & sundeck (clothing optional). Season: Year round.

REHOBOTH GH
40 Maryland Avenue, Rehoboth Beach, DE 19971. Tel: (302) 227-4117. TYPE: *Guest House*. HOST: Bill Courville. CLIENTELE: Mostly Gay. LOCATION: Rehoboth Beach. 12 rooms w/shared bath. DESCRIPTION: Victorian guesthouse.

✪ RENEGADE RESORT
4274 Hwy 1, Rehoboth Beach, DE 19971. Tel: (302) 227-1222. Fax: (302) 227-4281. TYPE: *Resort Complex*. HOST: Wayne, Mgr. CLIENTELE: Gay men & women. LOCATION: Rte 1, just outside downtown Rehoboth.

* Rooms: 28 w/priv. bath
* Suites & Apartments: available
* Rooms for smokers and non smokers
* CTV, phone, A/C
* Bed Types: twin, king size
* Services: maid, room, laundry
* Restaurant: **Good & Plenty** (American)
* Dance bar: **The Renegade**
* Pool, sundeck, free parking
* Beach: 1 mi. / 1.6 km (gay)
* Gay Bars: on premises, other nearby
* Health Club: 1 mi. / 1.6 km (mixed)

* Airport: Philadelphia or Washington DC
  2 hrs. (car rental)
* Train Station: Wilmington 2 hrs.
* Cancellation: 48 hrs.
* Credit Cards: MC/VISA
* Open: Year round
* Rates: $85-$120 / (off) $35-$55 w/CB
  high season May-Oct. / Low Season Oct.-Apr.
* Tax: 8%
* Check in 3 pm / check out 12 noon

DESCRIPTION: The Renegade offers modern guest accommodations, intimate restaurant, high tech dance club, 6 bars to serve you, swimming pool and karaoke lounge.

✪ THE SHORE INN

703 Rehoboth Ave., Rehoboth Beach, DE 19971. Tel: (302) 227-8487, Toll Free (800) 597-8899. TYPE: *Bed & Breakfast*. HOSTS: Ben & Michael, owners. CLIENTELE: Gay men & women only. LOCATION: 5 1/2 blocks from center of town. 3/10 mi. / 480 m. from exit Hwy 1A.

* Rooms: 14 w/priv. bath
  (5) dbl / (8) 2 x dbl / 1 (king)
* Smoking allowed in rooms
* CTV, phone, refrigerator, A/C, maid service
* Pool, sundeck, jacuzzi
* Clothing optional policy
* Parking: free off street, no pets
* Beach: 1/4 mi. / 400 m
* Gay Bars: 5 1/2 blocks
* Health Club: 1 block (mixed)
* Airports: 100 mi. / 160 km
* Reservations: 1 night deposit
* Cancellation Policy: 7 day notice
* Credit Cards: MC/VISA/AMEX/DISC
* Open: Year round
* Rates: $95 - $135 / (off) $50-$75 w/CB

* Taxes: 8%
* Check in 2:00 pm / Check out 11:00 am

DESCRIPTION: 2 story B&B Inn with tastefully decorated single rooms downstairs and double rooms and a large suite on second floor. A super continental breakfast is served in the Krystal Room. Friday and Saturday Happy Hours.

DISTRICT OF COLUMBIA

WASHINGTON

◆ **Population:** 640,000
◆ **Capital:** Washington
◆ **Time Zone:** Eastern
◆ **Sodomy Law**
◆ **Legal drinking age:** 21

WASHINGTON, DC   ✆ 202

✈ National Airport (DCA)
Dulles Int'l Airport (IAD)

LOCATION: On the east Coast of the Continental U.S.A., notched out of the State of Maryland on the Potomac River.

POPULATION: Metro - 3,036,000
City - 640,000.

CLIMATE: Summer - hot and humid. Spring and fall - warm days, cool nights. Winter - cold with snowstorm and occasional icy rains.

VISITOR INFORMATION
Washington CVB
1575 I (Eye) St. NW, Suite 250
Washington, D.C. 20005

Gay/Lesbian Visitor Information
Hotline: (202) 833-3234

DESCRIPTION: The Capital of the Nation, Washington is one of the leading tourist attractions in the U.S.A. It is clean, spacious, workaholic, with the nation's highest level of education.

The famous architectural style of the city's Federal buildings and monuments in the **Capitol Hill Area** including the **Supreme Court Building, Library of Congress, Botanic Gardens** and the **Union Station**. But the reason most visitors come is the **White House** and other famous sites nearby. The **Washington Monument**, the **Lincoln Memorial** and other major sites are located at **The Mall**, a two mile stretch of green between these landmarks. After a decade of planning the **U.S. Holocaust Memorial Museum** is now open to the public, 100 Raoul Wellemberg Place SW (488-0400).

For gay visitors, Washington D.C. offers a rich and diversified nightlife scene, with trendy bars, restaurants and dance clubs. Many establishments are located in the **Dupont Circle** area, which is comparable to New York's **Chelsea**, near the intersection of 22nd and P Streets NW.

❖ **SPECIAL EVENT: Capital Classic IV,** GLTA tennis tournament, Sept. 16-18 (703-281-1483).

BARS ♈ RESTAURANTS 🍴

● Bars/Clubs (GM): **Annex**, video cruise bar, next door to Badlands (upstairs); **Badlands**, video/dance bar, 1415 22nd St., NW (296-0505); **The Circle**, tavern, dance bar, nightclub, 1629 Connecticut Ave. NW (462-5575); **Cobalt**, bar & lounge, corner 17th and 'R' Sts NW (232-6969); **Delta Elite**, dance bar, 3734 10th St., NE (529-0626); **Edge-Wet**, dance club, erotic dancers, 56 'L' St., SE (488-1202); **The Fireplace**, 22nd & 'P' St. NW (293-1293); **Fraternity House**, dance bar, videos, 2122 'P' St. NW (223-4917); **Green Lantern**, 1335 Green Court NW; **J.R's**, bar & grill, popular with college students, 1519 17th St., NW (328-0090); **La Cage**, show bar, go-go dancers, 18 'O' St., SE (554-3615); **Mr. P's**, dance cruise bar, 2147 P St., NW (293-1064); **Ozone**, party club, Fri. go-go boys, 1214 18th St., NW (293-0303); **Phase One**, dance bar, 525 8th St., SE (544-6831); **Remington's**, country-western bar, 639 Pennsylvania Ave SE (543-3113); **Wet**, erotic dancers, 52 'L' St. SE (488-1200); **Ziegfeld's**, male strippers, 1345 Half Street SE (554-5141).

● Bars/Clubs (GMW): **Escándalo (Lone Star West)**, show bar, drag, 2122 'P' St., NW (822-8909); **Grand Poohbah**, video bar, 20011 14th St. NW (588-5709); **Larry's Lounge**, 1836 18th St., NW; **Tracks**, high energy cruise video dance bar, 1111 First St., SE (488-3320); **Ziegfields**, male strippers, 1345 Half St., SE (554-5141).

a perfect fit

Metro Arts & Entertainment Weekly

HUMOR | NEWS | POLITICS | REVIEWS | GOSSIP | INTERVIEWS | AND MORE

Washington's only queer entertainment weekly

1649 Hobart Street NW, Washington, DC 20010; (202) 588-5220, fax (202) 588-5219

ODYSSEUS '97/98

● Bars/clubs (GW): **Hung Jury**, dance bar, 1819 'H' St. NW (279-3212); **Phase One**, 525 8th St. SE (544-6831).

● Restaurants (GMW): **Annie's**, 24 hrs. steakhouse, 1609 17th St. NW (232-0395); **Café Blanca**, 1523 17th St., NW (986-3476); **Cafe Luna**, pizza, pasta etc. , 1633 P St., NW (387-4005); **Cusano's**, casual dining, 1613 17th St, NW (319-8757); **Food For Thought**, vegetarian, great deserts, 1738 Connecticut Ave. NW (797-1095); **Greenwood**, modern American cooking, 1990 'R' St., NW (833-6572); **Herb's**, special Sunday brunch, 17th & Rhode Island Ave. NW (333-HERB); **Howard's Grill**, 613 Pennsylvania Ave SE (543-2850); **La Fonda**, Mexican, 1639 R St., N.W. (232-6965); **Las Cruces**, New Mexico cuisine, 1524 'U' St., (328-3153); **2 Quail**, American, 320 Mass. Ave. NE (543-8030); **Mali**, Thai, 1805 18th St. NW (986-5124); **Pop Stop**, coffee house, 1513 17th St. NW (328-0880); **Shepherds**, restaurant/bar, 1527 17th St., NW (328-8193); **Skewers**, Middle Eastern restaurant & bar, 1633 P St. NW (387-7400); **Straits of Malaya**, Malaysian, 1836 18th St., NW (483-1483); **Sala Thai**, 2016 P St. NW (872-1144); **Wild Oats**, Sunday brunch, 539 8th St., SE (547-9453); **Windows**, Italian cuisine, corner 17th and 'R' (328-3222).

● Restaurants (AW): **La Fourchette**, French seafood, 2429 18th St., NW (332-3077); **The Islander**, Caribbean, 1762 Columbia Rd. NW (234-4955); **Roof Terrace**, American cooking, French provincial decor, located in the *Kennedy Center for the Performing Arts Bldg.* 2700 F St., NW (833-8870) view of the Potomac River; **The Fairfax Bar**, English tea 3-5pm, delicate sandwiches and pastries, in authentic English decor, at the Ritz-Carlton Hotel (293-2100); **Madurai**, vegetarian, cheap food, 3318 M St. NW (333-0997); **Mr. L's & Sun**, Chinese and NY style Jewish Deli, 5018 Connecticut Ave. NW (244-4343).

λ SERVICES λ

● Cinema (GM): **The Follies**, erotic movies, strippers, 24 'O' St. SE (484-0323).

● Erotica (G/S): **Pleasure Chest**, toys, lingerie, videos, 1063 Wisconsin Ave. NW Georgetown (333-8570) and 1710 Connecticut Ave. NW Dupont Circle (483-3297).

● Gifts (GMW): **The Second Floor**, variety store, 2147 'P' St., NW (822-3984).

● Health Club (GM): **Club Washington**, 24 hour health club with sauna, gym, snack bar, 20 'O' St., SE (488-7317); **Crew Club**, free weights, gym, tanning, nudist friendly, open 24 hrs., 1321 14th St., NW (319-1333); **Glorious Health Club**, 24 'O' St., SE (863-2770).

● Leather Shop (G/S): **Leather Rack**, 1723 Connecticut Ave. NW (797-7401).

● Massage (GM): **Fantastic Massage**, HIV discount, (488-5883); **Frank's Massage**, certified therapist, Swedish, sports (797-8535).

● Personal Phone Line (GM): ✪ **District of Columbia Confidential Connection**, meet local guys! Record, listen, respond to ads free (408-7878) free access code 8060.

● Publication (GMW): ✪ **Metro Arts & Entertainment Weekly (MW)**, Washington's only gay & lesbian entertainment guide, look for us at family-friendly establishments throughout the Metropolitan Area. 1649 Hobart St., NW, Washington, D.C. 20010. Tel: (202) 588-5220. Fax: (202) 588-5219.

🔖 ACCOMMODATIONS 🔖

CAPITOL HILL
101 5th St. N.E., Washington, D.C. 20002. Tel: (202) 547-1050 TYPE: *Guest House*. HOST:

Antonio Cintra. CLIENTELE: All Welcome. LOCATION: 6 blocks to Union Station. 10 rooms w/shared bath. Rates: $39-$110. Tax: 13%. *TAC:* 10%.

THE CARLYLE SUITES
1731 New Hampshire Ave., NW, Washington, DC 20009. Tel: (202) 234-3200. Fax: (202) 387-0085. TYPE: *Hotel.* CLIENTELE: All Welcome. LOCATION: 3 blocks from Dupont Circle. 170 suites. DESCRIPTION: All suites hotel in a central location.

EMBASSY INN
1627 16th St., NW, Washington DC 20009. Tel: (202) 234-7800. Fax: (202) 234-3309. TYPE: *Hotel.* CLIENTELE: All Welcome. LOCATION: Near Dupont Circle. 38 rooms w/priv. bath, CTV, phone, A/C. DESCRIPTION: Federalist style European Inn.

THE GOVERNOR'S HOUSE
Rhode Island Ave., at 17th St., NW, Washington, DC 20036. Tel: (202) 296-2100. Fax: (202) 331-0227. TYPE: *Hotel.* CLIENTELE: All Welcome. LOCATION: On the 'Gay' 17th St. corridor. 5 blocks from the White House. 152 rooms. DESCRIPTION: First class Holiday Inn hotel in the heart of the gay scene.

ST. JAMES
950 24th St., NW, Washington DC 20037. Tel: (202) 457-0500. Fax: (202) 659-4492. TYPE: *All-suite Hotel.* CLIENTELE: All Welcome. LOCATION: Off Washington Circle near Georgetown. 196 suites, cooking facilities, A/C, parking, Rates: $129-$199. *TAC:* 10%. DESCRIPTION: Elegant one-bedroom suites featuring fully furnished living and dining room, king or queen size bed and marble bath.

✪ THE KALORAMA GUEST HOUSE
At Kalorama Park
1854 Mintwood Place NW, Washington, DC 20009. Tel: (202) 667-6369. Fax: (202) 319-1262. TYPE: *Bed & Breakfast.* INNKEEPERS: John, Tami & Charlotta. CLIENTELE: All Welcome. LOCATION: Mintwood Place off of 19th St. Close to downtown Washington DC and Dupont Circle. Short taxi ride to National monuments, museums and nightlife.

* Rooms: 31; 12 w/priv. bath, 19 w/shared sgl 1 / 20 dbl / 6 triple / 4 quad
* Rooms for non smokers
* Phone, refrigerator, C/H, A/C
* Suites: 2 (2BR) w/full bath
* Bed Types: single, twin, double, queen
* Maid service, paid (off street) parking, no pets
* Gay Bars: 6 blocks

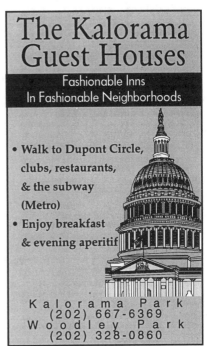

The Kalorama Guest Houses

Fashionable Inns
In Fashionable Neighborhoods

• **Walk to Dupont Circle, clubs, restaurants, & the subway (Metro)**

• **Enjoy breakfast & evening aperitif**

Kalorama   Park
(202) 667-6369
Woodley   Park
(202) 328-0860

You are *always* welcome at the

WILLIAM LEWIS HOUSE
Washington's Finest Bed & Breakfast
Warm, Cozy, Convenient
Close to 17th St. and Dupont Circle
Minutes from the Mall
Close to Metro
Great Restaurants Nearby

(202) 462-7574
(800) 465-7574
Visa and Master Card Accepted
Smoking Permitted in the Garden

* Health Club: 4 blocks (mixed)
* Airport: 10 mi. / 16 km, taxi, bus, subway
* Train Station: Amtrack 2 mi. / 3 km
* Metro: 5 blocks
* Languages: English, Spanish
* Reservations: credit card # to hold room
* Cancellation: 14 days notice no charge
* Credit Cards: MC/VISA/AMEX/DISC
* Open: Year round
* Rates: $60 - $105 / (off) $50-$95 w/CB
* Taxes: 13% sales tax + $1.50 hotel tax
* Check in by 8:30 pm M-F / 7:30 pm S-S
  Check out 11 am
* **TAC:** 10%

DESCRIPTION: Victorian townhouse on a quiet, residential street. The vibrant Adams Morgan and Dupont Circle neighborhoods are just moments away. Enjoy antique furnishings, continental breakfast and evening aperitif. *IGTA*

✪ THE KALORAMA GUEST HOUSE
At Woodley Park
2700 Cathedral Ave. NW, Washington DC 20008. Tel: (202) 328-0860. Fax: (202) 328-8730. TYPE: *Bed & Breakfast.* INNKEEPERS: Mike & Mary Ann. CLIENTELE: All Welcome. LOCATION: Close to downtown Washington DC, corner of Cathedral Ave, & 27th St. Short taxi ride to National monuments, museums and nightlife.

* Rooms: 19; 12 w/priv. bath, 7 w/shared
  sgl 1 / dbl 16 / triple 1 / quad 1
* Totally non-smoking, C/H, A/C
* Suite: 1BR w/full bath
* Bed Types: single, twin, double, queen size
* Maid service, Parking: paid, off street
* No Pets
* Gay Bars: 8 blocks
* Health Club: 8 blocks (mixed)
* Airport: 10 mi. / 16 km, taxi, bus, metro
* Train Station: Amtrack 2 mi. / 3 km
* Subway: 3 blocks
* Reservation: credit card # to hold room

* Cancellation Policy: 14 day notice no charge
* Credit Cards: MC/VISA/AMEX/DISC/DC
* Open: Year round
* Rates: $60-$105 / (off) $50-$95 w/CB
* Taxes: 13% sales tax + $1.50 hotel tax
* Check in by 8:30 pm M-F / 7:30 pm S-S
  Check out 11 am
* **TAC:** 10%

DESCRIPTION: Victorian townhouse on a quiet, residential street. The vibrant Adams Morgan and Dupont Circle neighborhoods are just moments away. Enjoy antique furnishings, continental breakfast and evening aperitif. *IGTA*

✪ THE WILLIAM LEWIS HOUSE
1309 'R' St., NW, Washington DC 20009. Tel: (202) 462-7574 or Toll Free (800) 465-7574. Fax: (202) 462-1608. TYPE: *Bed & Breakfast.* HOSTS: David Holder / Theron White. CLIENTELE: Mostly gay men. LOCATION: Between 13th & 14th on 'R'. 3 blocks from 'U' St. M°, near Dupont and McPhearson Sq.

* Rooms: 4 w/shared bath (2/bath)
* Phone, C/H, A/C, maid service
* Sun deck, free parking (permits provided)
* Gay Bars: 4 blocks
* Health Club: 4 blocks (mixed)
* Airport: Washington Nat'l 5 mi. / 8 km
* AP Transportation: taxi, bus, subway
* Metro: Union Station 1 mi. / 1.6 km
* Reservations: deposit require
* Credit Cards: MC/VISA
* Open: Year round
* Rates: $65 - $75 + tax, CB incl.
* **TAC:** 10%
* Check in 3:00pm / check out 12:00 noon

DESCRIPTION: A classically inspired and beautifully restored house built after the turn of the century. The bedrooms and bathrooms include many fixtures and decorations original to the house and lots of antiques. Warm hospitality and friendly atmosphere.

FLORIDA

◆ **Population:** 9,750,000
◆ **Capital:** Tallahassee
◆ **Time Zone:** Eastern
◆ **Sodomy Law**
◆ **Legal drinking age:** 21

COCOA BEACH   ℂ 407

✈ Orlando Int'l Airport, 60 min. east
Regional Airport (MLB), 20 min. south

LOCATION: On a narrow sandy beach along the Atlantic Ocean, south of Cape Canaveral.

BARS ♈ RESTAURANTS ¶¶

● Bar (GMW): **Blondies**, 5450 N. Atlantic Ave. (783-5339); **Mango Tree**, restaurant, 118 N. Atlantic Ave. (799-0513).

ACCOMMODATIONS

TRIANGLE PALMS
131 Sunny Lane, Cocoa Beach, FL 32931. Tel: (407) 799-2221. TYPE: *Guest House.* HOSTS: John, Tony or Jeff. CLIENTELE: Gay men & women only. LOCATION: South of the Cape Canaveral. 14 rooms. Rates: on request.

DAYTONA BEACH   ℂ 904

✈ Regional Airport (DAB), 3 mi. / 5 km south west of Daytona Beach

LOCATION: Northern Florida's East Coast.

POPULATION: 259,000

CLIMATE: Humid subtropical. Winters are pleasant with a January average of 54°F (12°c). Summers are hot with Tropical rain showers, with a July average of 81°F (27°c).

DESCRIPTION: Year-round beach vacation, resort and surfers paradise with 18 mi. / 40 km of golden sandy beaches. The public beach is world famous and attracts over 7 million visitors each year.

❖ **SPECIAL EVENTS:** Auto and stock-car races: the **Daytona 24 Hours** and **Daytona 500** in February at the **Daytona International Speedway**, 1801 Speedway Blvd. (254-6767).

BARS ♈ RESTAURANTS ¶¶

● Bars/Clubs (GMW): **Barracks/Officers Club**, leather/levi cruise bar, 952 Orange Ave. (254-3464); **Beach Side**, 415 Main St. (252-5465).

● Bars/Clubs (GMW): **7-69 Restaurant & Lounge**, 769 Alabama (253-4361); **Barndoor**, 615 Main St. (252-3776).

● Restaurants (AW):**Aunt's Catfish's**, seafood restaurant, 4009 Halifax Dr. (767-4768); **Hungarian Village**, Hungarian & American cuisine, 424 S. Ridgewood (253-5712).

ACCOMMODATIONS

DAYTONA INN SEABREEZE
730 N. Atlantic Ave., Daytona Beach, FL 32118. Tel: (904) 255-5491. TYPE: *Hotel.* CLIENTELE: All Welcome. LOCATION: Beachfront. 98 rooms, 16 suites, 35 efficiencies w/priv. bath, phone, CTV, A/C, coffee shop, outdoor pool, free parking. Rates: from $85. *TAC:* 10%. DESCRIPTION: Tourist class beach hotel.

NAUTILUS INN
1515 S. Atlantic Ave., Daytone Beach, FL 32118. Tel: (904) 254-8600. TYPE: *Hotel.* CLIENTELE: All Welcome. LOCATION: Beachfront, 5 mi / 8 km from the airport. 90 rooms w/priv. bath, phone, CTV, in room safe,

microwave, refrigerator, balcony, wheelchair access, outdoor pool, free parking. Rates: from $89. *TAC:* 10%. DESCRIPTION: Moderate first class resort hotel.

FT. LAUDERDALE   ℂ 954

✈ Ft. Lauderdale - Hollywood Int'l Airport (FLL) 2 mi. / 3 km south

LOCATION: Southeast Florida on the Atlantic Ocean.

POPULATION: City 153,000;
            Metro 1,014,000

CLIMATE: Warm and pleasant year round. Average winter temperature is 69°F (20°c). Average summer temperature 82°F (28°c).

Gay/Lesbian Visitor Information
G&L Community Center: 463-9515

DESCRIPTION: Fort Lauderdale offers the famous Gold Coast beaches, abundant sunshine, and busy nightlife. This "Venice-like" resort city is well situated for a pleasant holiday in South Florida. Ft. Lauderdale's new image is of shiny skyscrapers, designer shops, and an improved beach front promenade. It is only a 3 1/2 hour drive from **Disney World** and **Epcot Center**, 40 miles / 64km from the **Everglades National Park**, and within driving distance of **Miami, South Beach, Key West, the Palm Beaches**, and **The Kennedy Space Center**.

❖ **SPECIAL EVENT: Clay Court Invitational / Charity Classic**, GLTA tennis tournament, Feb. 16-19 (776-4365).

BARS 🍴 RESTAURANTS 🍴

● Bars/Clubs (GM): **Adventures**, C&W cruise bar, 303 SW 6th St. (782-9577); **Bus Stop**, video bar, game room, hot male dancers, 2203 S. Federal Hwy. (761-1782); **Bills**, neighborhood bar, 1243 NE 11th Ave. (525-9403); **Boots**, all male cruise bar, 901 S.W. 27th Ave. (792-9177); **Cathode Ray**, popular video/cruise bar, 1105 E. Las Olas Blvd. (462-8611); **The Copa**, Florida's #1 entertainment complex, disco, 624 S.E. 28th St., Ft. Lauderdale, (463-1507); **Eagle**, leather bar, 1951 Powerline Rd (462-6380); **Electra**, high tech dance club, 1600 SE 15th Ave. (764-8447); **End Up**, cocktail lounge,

3521 W. Broward Blvd. (584-9301); **Hideaway**, 2022 N.E. 18th St. (566-8622); **Johnny's**, male strippers/hustler bar, 1116 W. Broward Blvd. (522-5931); **Jungle**, video bar & cabaret, male dancers, 545 S. Federal Hwy (832-9550); **Matrix**, video bar at Saint (see below), **Ramrod**, levi/leather uniform bar, 1508 NE 4th Ave. (763-8219); **Saint**, cruise bar, crowded on Saturdays, dance club, 1000 W. State Rd., (525-7883).

● Bar/club (GMW): **825**, entertainment club, 825 E. Sunrise Blvd. (524-3333).

● Bar/club (GW): **Other Side**, 2283 Wilton Dr., Wilton Manors (565-5538).

● Restaurants (GMW): **Chardees**, restaurant, bar, entertainment, open 7 days, 2209 Wilton Drive (563-1800); **Corral**, restaurant & lounge, 1727 N. Andrews Ave. (767-0027); **The Deck**, 401 N. Atlantic Blvd. (467-7315); **Food Lovers**, American café, 1576 E. Oakland Park Blvd., (566-9606); **Garden**, bar & grill, 4240 Galt Ocean Dr. (564-1999); **Hi-Life Cafe**, 3000 N. Federal Hwy (563-1395); **La Rezza**, seafood restaurant, 1506 E. Commercial Blvd. (491-1983); **Tropics**, restaurant, piano bar, cabaret, 2000 Wilton Dr. Wilton Manors (537-6000).

λ SERVICES λ

● Erotica (GMW): **Catalog X**, adult oriented sex toys, magazines, videos, 850 NE 13th St. (524-5050).

● Health Clubs (GM): **The Club**, steamroom, sauna, full gym, sundecks, TV lounge, open 24 hrs., 400 W. Broward Blvd. (525-3344); **Clubhouse II**, 2650 E. Oakland Park Blvd. open 24hrs., (566-6750); **Oceanside Gym**, mixed clientele, 3001 SE 5th St.; **Triangle Club**, free lockers, 405 E. Oakland Park Blvd. (763-4911).

● Publication (GMW) ✪ **Hot Spots**, Florida's largest gay entertainment publication, 5100 NE 12th Ave., Ft. Lauderdale, FL 33334. (305) 928-1862. Toll Free (800) 522-8775. Fax: (305) 772-0142. Internet: http://www.hotspotsmagazine.com.

● Shopping (GMW): **Effxx**, manswear, 1117 N. Federal Hwy (537-2056); **Pride Factory**, gifts, cards, magazines, 710 W. Broward Blvd. (463-6600); **Trader Tom's**, swimwear, clothing, pride items, 914 N. Federal Hwy (524-4759).

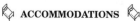 ACCOMMODATIONS

On Beautiful Fort Lauderdale Beach

King Henry Arms Motel

A small, clean, quiet and congenial gay
motel just steps from the ocean.
A tropical setting with patio, heated pool,
privacy fence and barbecue. Amenities
include direct-dial telephone, cable
television, private bath, in-room safe and
refrigerator. Some units have kitchens.
Meet new friends over continental
breakfast on the patio.

Your Hosts: Don and Roy

543 Breakers Avenue
Fort Lauderdale, FL 33304

(954) 561-0039
USA and Canada:
1-800-205-KING

Please write or call for a free
brochure and rate information.

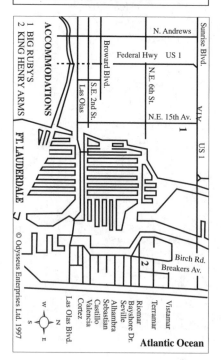

BIG RUBY'S Tropical Guesthouse
908 NE 15th Ave., Ft. Lauderdale, FL 33304.
Tel: (954) 523-7829. Fax: (954) 731-1593. TYPE:
Bed & Breakfast. HOSTS: Derek or Allen.
CLIENTELE: Gay men only. LOCATION: Popular 'Gay area' between Las Olas and Sunrise Blvd., close to beach, bars and clubs.

* Rooms: 10 w/priv. bath. Suites: 3
* CTV, VCR, phone, refrigerator, safe box, C/H, A/C, cooking facilities
* Room & maid service, laundry service
* Wheelchair access, free parking
* Bar: **Ruby's Lounge**
* Pool, sundeck, clothing optional policy
* Beach: 5 min. (gay beach)
* Gay Bars: 5-10 minutes
* Health Club: 5 minutes (Club Body Center)
* Airport: 15 min, limo service
* Rates: $55-$115; (off) $25-$65
* Tax: 10%. **TAC:** 10%

DESCRIPTION: Tropical guesthouse with a large pool and lush garden. Clean, comfortable tastefully appointed rooms. Very reasonable prices especially during the off season. Friendly and relaxed atmosphere.

✪ KING HENRY ARMS

543 Breakers Ave., Ft. Lauderdale, FL 33304.
Tel: (954) 561-0039. Toll Free 1 (800) 205-
KING. TYPE: *Motel.* HOST: Don Keller & Roy
Leger. CLIENTELE: Mostly Gay. LOCATION:
On Ft. Lauderdale beach near the ocean.

* Rooms: 6 w/priv. bath
  3 dbl/ 1 triple / 2 quad
* CTV, phone, refrigerator, A/C
* Suites: 6 (one bedroom)
* Living room, Full bath, kitchen, CTV, phone, refrigerator, C/H, A/C
* Smoking allowed in rooms and suites
* Pool, sun deck, maid service, free parking
* Beach: 300 ft. / 100 m (mixed)
* Gay Bars: 2 mi. / 3 km
* Health Club: 1 mile / 2 km (mixed)
* Airport: 6 mi. (10 km) taxi, shuttle
* Train Station: 3 mi. / 5 km taxi, bus
* Reservations: 25% deposit
* Cancellation: 25% or 48 hrs.
* Credit Cards: MC/VISA/AMEX/DISC
* Open: Year round
* Rates: $77 - $99 / (off) $45-$60 w/CB
* Tax: 9%. **TAC:** 10%
* Check in 1 pm / Check out 11 am

DESCRIPTION: Two-story motel with home-like atmosphere. Hotel rooms, efficiencies & one-bedroom suites. Fully equipped kitchens in efficiencies and one-bedroom suites. *IGTA.*

KEY WEST   © 305

✈ Key West Int'l Airport (EYW)

LOCATION: An island at the southwestern tip of the Florida Keys (a chain of small islands). It is the southernmost point in the Continental U.S.A.

POPULATION: 30,000 (permanent)
                          60,000 (in season)

CLIMATE: Tropical and steady during the year, warm and humid. Average winter temperature is 70°F (21°c) with only 6 rainy days in February. The average summer temperature is 84°F (29°c). The average annual rainfall is 38" (950 mm).

Gay/Lesbian Visitor Information

○ **Key West Business Guild**
Box 1208, Key West, FL 33041
Tel: 1 (800) 535-7797
Fax: (305) 294-3273
Internet WEB site:
http://key-west.com/gaykw/kwbg

DESCRIPTION: Key West, also known as the 'Conch Republic' after a local large sea snail, is one of the most popular vacation destinations for American and International gay travelers. Tourists from Europe, the Far East and South America come to discover the charms of Key West filling **Mallory Square** at Sunset and packing the **Conch Train** on tours. The city is compact in size. Everything is within walking distance. **Duval St.** is the **Old Town**'s main drag with upscale restaurants, cafes, and shops selling tropical clothing, art, perfumes and foods from around the world. It is also your best orientation indicator; everything in Key West is judged by its proximity to Duval Street.

Key West has its share of tourist sites and museums: visit **Hemingway House**, where the reputable nobel writer lived and produced many of his masterpieces, 907 Whitehead St. If you are in a military mood check the **Lighthouse Military Museum**, 938 Whitehead St..; **Ripley's Believe It or Not!** museum at the former Strand Theatre on Duval St.; **Key West Lighthouse**, restored tower and museum, 938 Whitehead St. (294-0012); **Key West Aquarium**, one of the oldest aquariums in the USA, 1 Whitehead St. (296-2051); **Audubon House and Tropical Gardens**, graceful house surrounded by gardens and native plants, 205 Whitehead St. (294-2116).

You're among friends.

fabulous
the gay destination
KEYWEST

For *the* 52 page color guide & map call the Key West Business Guild at 1-800-535-7797. Visit our web site at: http://key-west.com/gaykw/kwbg

Key West is an openly gay town. Gay men and Lesbians, both residents and visitors, are the mainstay of the island's economy. Visitors enjoy a sense of freedom that results from the island's geographical location - far from the mainland and deep into the ocean. Key West dances to a different beat from the mainland; the Key West community is tolerant, and everybody lives according to the motto "Live and let live".

There is a large selection of gay owned and oriented facilities that include resorts, guest houses, restaurants, discos, bars, etc. Most guest houses have their own pools as an alternative to the public beaches. Key West is ideal for a memorable vacation in a relaxed, carefree, gay friendly, tropical corner of paradise.

❖ **TRAVEL SEASON INFORMATION**: The high season in Key West is in the winter roughly from mid December until the end of April; Summer is the low season when the rates are at their lowest, the summer season is from the end of May until the beginning of November. Anything in between is the medium season with rates in the middle.

❖ **SPECIAL EVENTS: Old Island Days**, mid January - March, celebrates the city's historical heritage; **Gay Art Festival**, June; **Women In Paradise** July; **Womenfest '96**, Sept. 4-10, 96 (305-296-4238); **Fantasy Fest** October.

BARS ♈ RESTAURANTS 🍴

● Bars (GM): **Cafe Exile**, cocktail bar, 700 Duval St., (296-0991); **801 Bar**, live entertainment, Sunday bingo, piano bar, 801 Duval St., (294-4737); **One Saloon**, 3 bars, dance club, male dancers nightly, 524 Duval St. (294-3064), **Numbers**, bar, nude male dancers, 1020 Truman Ave. (296-0333).

● Club (GMW): **The Club**, nightly entertainment and dancing at La Te Da, 1125 Duval St. (296-6706); **The Epoch**, popular dance club, garden bar, nightly entertainment, formerly The Copa, 623 Duval St. (296-8522); **Voo Doo**, dance bar, outdoor patio, 700 Duval St. (292-4606).

● Bar (GW): **416 Café**, 416 Applerouth Lane (296-9483); **Club International**, 900 Simonton St. (296-9230).

● Restaurants (AW): **Applelrouth Grill**, 416 Applerouth Lane (296-9483); **The Buttery**, local favorite, Continental Cuisine, 1208 Simonton St.; **Cafe des Artistes**, French style seafood, 1007 Simonton St., (294-7100); **Cafe Europa**, German pastries, desserts, 1075 Duval St. (294-5443); **Dim Sum**, 613 1/2 Duval Street, moderately priced exotic menu from the far east (294-6230); **Five Star**, small, informal Cuban restaurant, 1100 Packer St. (296-0650); **Lighthouse Cafe**, seafood, Florida specialties, 917 Duval St. (296-7837); **Louie's Backyard**, Key West's best known restaurant, eclectic menu and seafood, expensive, 700 Waddell St. (294-1061); **Mango's**, vegetarian meals, cocktail bar, nightly specials, 700 Duval St. (292-4606); **La-te-da**, restaurant, sunday tea dance, 1125 Duval St. (296-6706); **La Trattoria**, 524 Duval St., casual, French/Italian cuisine (294-7863); **The Quay**, 12 Duval St., fresh local Keys seafood specialties and a selection of International Coffee and great desserts (294-4446); **Pier House**, regional specialties, 1 Duval St. (294-9541); **Savannah**, good home cooking, outdoor tropical gardens, 915 Duval St. (296-6700); **Sippin'**, coffee house, pastries, 424 Eaton St. (293-0555); **Square One**, American cuisine, piano bar, 1075 Duval St. (296-4300); **Trattoria Venezia**, Italian & French cuisine, 524 Duval St. (296-1075); **Viva's**, Int'l cuisine, 903 Duval St. (296-3138).

λ SERVICES λ

● Business Guild (GMW): ✪ **Key West Business Guild**, non-profit organization representing over 400 gay/lesbian owned and gay friendly businesses committed to catering to the gay & lesbian travelers, P.O. Box 1208, Key West, FL 33031. Tel: (305) 294-4603 or Toll Free (800) 535-7797. Fax: (305) 294-3273.

● Cruises (GM): **Asylum**, reef sail (294-4524); **Clione**, gay sail charter (296-1433); **Miss Sunshine**, gay party boat (296-4608).

● Erotica (G/S): **Alligator News & Books**, 716 Duval St. (294-4004); **Key West Videos**, 528 Duval St. (292-4113).

● Gifts (G/S): **Bodyscapes Gallery**, male nude photography, 507 Southard at Duval; **Greetings from Key West**, 1075 Duval St. (294-1733); **Key West Aloe**, 524 Front St. (294-5592).

● Gym (G/S): **Duval Square Health & Fitness**, mostly straight.

● Leather (GM): **Leather Master**, custom hand made leather erotica, gay novelties, 418A Appleroute Lane (292-5051).

● Medical (GMW): **Immune Care**, special medical services for HIV positive travelers, 520 Southard St. (296-4990).

● Real Estate (AW): **Key West Realty**, 1109 Duval St. (294-3064).

● Shopping (AW): **Annex**, menswear and accessories, 705 Duval St. (296-9800); **Fast Buck Freddie's**, 500 Duval St. (294-2007); **Greffitti**, clothing and accessories for men, 701 Duval St. (294-8040); **Zero**, progressive clothing for men, 624 Duval St. (294-3899).

ACCOMMODATIONS

▼ **HOTEL TAX:** Hotel prices in Key West are normally quoted net without taxes. The tax rate is 11% which must be added to the hotel room price.

✪ ALEXANDER'S

1118 Fleming St., Key West, FL. 33040. Tel: (305) 294-9919. Toll Free (800) 654-9919. Fax: (305) 295-0357. E-mail: alexghouse@aol.com TYPE: *Guest House.* HOST: Bill & Mike. CLIENTELE: Gay men & women. LOCATION: Historical Key West, few blocks from shops, restaurants, bars, and discos.

* Rooms: 15, 13 w/priv. shower, 2 w/shared dbl 12 / quad 3
* Smoking allowed in rooms, maid service
* CTV, VCR, phone, refrigerator, safe box, A/C, hair dryer
* Suite (1), Apartment (1): 1BR, living room, full bath, kitchen, patio/terrace
* Bed Types: king size, queen size
* Pool, sundeck, clothing optional policy
* Parking, No Pets
* Beach: 1 mi. / 1.6 km (mixed)
* Gay Bars: 6 blocks
* Health Club: 8 blocks (mixed)
* Airport: Key West Int'l 2.5 mi. / 4 km taxi
* Train Station: Miami (FL) 150 mi. / 240 km
* Reservations: 1 night deposit; holidays and special events 2 nights deposit
* Cancellation Policy: 14 day normal / 30 day holiday period + special events
* Credit Cards: MC/VISA/AMEX/DISC
* Open: Year round
* Rates: $120 - $250 / (off) $80 - $180 w/CB (expanded). Taxes: 11.5%
* Check in 2:00pm / Check out 12:00 noon
* *TAC:* 10%

DESCRIPTION: Restored early 1900's Conch house in tropical setting. Each of the rooms and suites is uniquely decorated in a tasteful Key West casual elegance. Select rooms have private verandahs or decks. Complimentary continental breakfast is served poolside each morning. *IGTA*

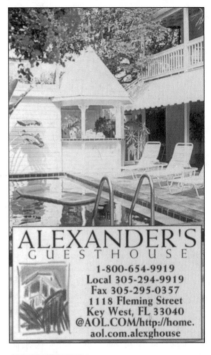

ALEXANDER'S
G U E S T H O U S E
1-800-654-9919
Local **305-294-9919**
Fax **305-295-0357**
1118 Fleming Street
Key West, FL 33040
@AOL.COM/http://home.
aol.com.alexghouse

ANDREWS INN
Zero Walton Lane, Key West, FL 33040. Tel: (305) 294-7730. TYPE: *Inn & Cottages.* CLIENTELE: All Welcome. LOCATION: Old Town. DESCRIPTION: Rooms and cottages with phone, CTV, and priv. bath.

COCONUT GROVE
817 Fleming St., Key West, FL. 33040. Tel: (305) 296-5107. TYPE: *Bed & Breakfast.* HOST: Meir & Michael. CLIENTELE: Gay men only. LOCATION: Heart of Old Town, DESCRIPTION: White gingerbread mansion.

COLOURS
410 Fleming St., Key West, FL. 33040. Tel: (305) 294-6977. Fax: (305) 534-0362. TYPE: *Guest House.* CLIENTELE: Mostly Gay. LOCATION: Heart of Old Key West. 12 rooms. DESCRIPTION: Victorian Mansion.

CORAL TREE INN
822 Fleming St., Key West, FL 33040. Tel: (305) 296-2131. TYPE: *Guest House.* HOST: Graeme Smith. CLIENTELE: Gay men only. LOCATION: Center of town. DESCRIPTION: Historic Inn. 11 rooms.

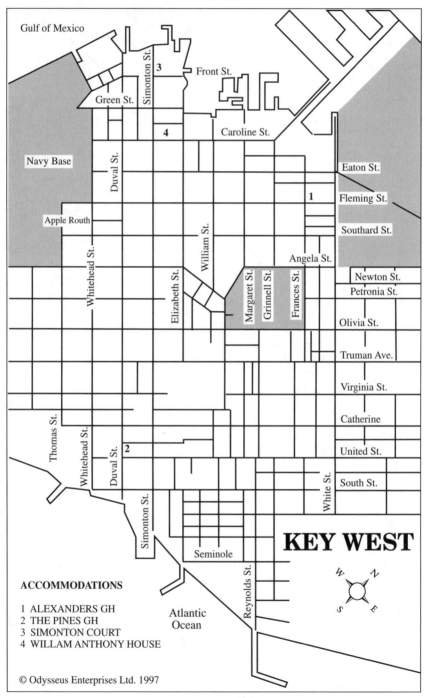

Gulf of Mexico

Simonton St.

3

Front St.

Green St.

4

Caroline St.

Navy Base

Duval St.

Eaton St.

Fleming St.

1

Apple Routh

Southard St.

Whitehead St.

William St.

Angela St.

Elizabeth St.

Margaret St.

Grinnell St.

Frances St.

Newton St.

Petronia St.

Olivia St.

Truman Ave.

Virginia St.

Thomas St.

Whitehead St.

Duval St.

2

Catherine

United St.

White St.

South St.

Simonton St.

KEY WEST

Seminole

Reynolds St.

W — N — E — S

ACCOMMODATIONS

1 ALEXANDERS GH
2 THE PINES GH
3 SIMONTON COURT
4 WILLAM ANTHONY HOUSE

Atlantic
Ocean

© Odysseus Enterprises Ltd. 1997

CURRY HOUSE
806 Fleming St., Key West, FL 33040. Tel: (305) 294-6777. TYPE: *Guest House.* HOSTS: Carl or Stephen. CLIENTELE: Gay men only. LOCATION: Old Town near Duval St. DESCRIPTION: Old Victorian home. 9 rooms.

CYPRESS HOUSE
601 Caroline St., Key West, FL. 33040. Tel: (305) 294-6969. TYPE: *Guest House.* HOST: Arthur. CLIENTELE: Gay men only. LOCATION: Old Town near Duval St. DESCRIPTION: Victorian mansion. 16 rooms.

HERON HOUSE
512 Simonton St., Key West, FL. 33040. Tel: (305) 294-9227. TYPE: *Bed & Breakfast.* HOST: Fred Geibelt. CLIENTELE: All Welcome. LOCATION: Heart of Old Town. DESCRIPTION: "Conch" style houses 19 rooms.

ISLAND HOUSE
1129 Fleming St., Key West, FL. 33040. Tel: (305) 294-6284. TYPE: *Guest House.* HOST: Dean Babula. CLIENTELE: Gay men only. LOCATION: In downtown. End of Fleming St. 34 rooms. Rates: on request.

KEY LODGE MOTEL
1004-A Duval St., Key West, FL 33040. Tel: (305) 296-9915. Fax: (305) 296-9750. TYPE: *Motel.* CLIENTELE: All Welcome. LOCATION: Old Town. DESCRIPTION: Individually decorated motel rooms and heated pool.

THE KNOWLES HOUSE
1004 Eaton St., Key West, FL 33040. Tel: (305) 294-0980. Fax: (305) 294-3273. TYPE: *Guest House.* HOSTS: Steve Smith & Paul Morray. CLIENTELE: Mostly Gay men & women. DESCRIPTION: 1880's Conch home in Old Town. Pool, A/C, CTV, CBb.

LIME HOUSE
219 Elizabeth St., Key West, FL. 33040. Tel: (305) 296-2978. TYPE: *Guest House.* HOST: Jim. CLIENTELE: Gay men only. LOCATION: Old Town. 11 rooms. Rates: on request.

NEWTON STREET STATION
1414 Newton St., Key West, FL 33040. Tel: (305) 294-4288. TYPE: *Guest House.* HOST: John Adams. CLIENTELE: Gay Men Only. LOCATION: Old Town near Pearl St. DESCRIPTION: 7 rooms. Rates: $55-$115.

OASIS GUESTHOUSE
823 Fleming St., Key West, FL. 33040. Tel: (305) 296-2131. TYPE: *Guest House.* HOST: Robb Adams. CLIENTELE: Gay men only.

LOCATION: Old Town. DESCRIPTION: Restored 1895 mansion.

THE PILOT HOUSE
414 Simonton St., Key West, FL. 33040. Tel: (305) 294-8719 or (800) 648-3780. Fax: (305) 294-9298. TYPE: *Guest House.* HOST: Ed Cox. CLIENTELE: Gay men only. LOCATION: center of Old Town. DESCRIPTION: Otto Mansion with standard queen bedrooms, two queen bedroom, master suite, penthouse and copula bedroom; Poolside Cabana with queen and king bedrooms; Duval Suites with garden views and Duval balconies. 12 unique units some with kitchen minibar, and jacuzzi. Pool, sundeck, garden. Rates: $135-$300 season; $80-$175 summer.

✪ THE PINES
521 United St., Key West, FL. 33040. Tel: (305) 296-7467 or Toll Free (800) 282-PINE (7463). Fax: (305) 296-3928. TYPE: *Guest House.* HOSTS: Jim & Tom. CLIENTELE: Gay men & women only. LOCATION: Old Town, 1/4 block from Duval St. Short walk to shops, restaurants and gay nightlife.

*   Rooms: 15 w/priv. bath
    10 sgl or dbl / 5 dbl or quad

* Smoking allowed in rooms
* CTV, phone, refrigerator, A/C, maid service
* Pool, sundeck, jacuzzi
* Clothing optional policy
* Parking: free, off street
* Beach: 10 min. walk (mixed)
* Gay Bars: 5 blocks
* Health Club: 3 blocks (mixed)
* Airport: 10 min., taxi
* Reservations: 2 nights or 50%
* Cancellation: $20; 10 day non refundable
* Credit Cards: MC/VISA/AMEX/DC/DISC
* Open: Year round
* Rates: $95-$175; (off) $60-$100 w/CB
* Tax: 11.5%
* Check in 2pm / check out 11am
* *TAC:* 10%

DESCRIPTION: Exclusively gay Tropical style guest house with clean comfortable rooms on twin levels. Enjoy one of the largest pools on the island, multi-level sundecks, and a spacious hot tub. Friendly and congenial atmosphere. *IGTA, KWIA, KWBG*

SEA ISLE
915 Windsor Lane, Key West, FL. 33040. Tel: (305) 294-5188. TYPE: *Resort Complex.* HOSTS: Randy & Jim. CLIENTELE: Gay men only. LOCATION: Old Town 3 blocks from Duval.

* Rooms: 17 sgl & 5 dbl w/priv. bath: 2 Suites
* CTV, phone, A/C, refrigerator
* Maid service, wheelchair access
* Pool, sundeck, gym, jacuzzi, clothing optional
* Free parking
* Health Club & Gay Bars: nearby
* Rates: $110-$175 season; $75-125 (off).
* *TAC:* 10%

DESCRIPTION: Popular resort complex with week-end cocktail parties. *IGTA, KWBG.*

○ SIMONTON COURT
320 Simonton St., Key West FL 33040. Tel: (305) 294-6386 or (800) 944-2687 (USA). Fax: (305) 293-8446. TYPE: *Historic Inn & Cottages.* HOST: Bill & Mike. CLIENTELE: Mostly Gay men & women. LOCATION: Central. 1 block off Duval St., 3 blocks from Mallory Square.

* Rooms: 10 dbl w/priv. bath
* Suites: 4, Cottages: 6
* One-bedroom (4); Two-bedroom (5)
* Smoking allowed in rooms
* Soundproof rooms, balcony, garden
* CTV/VCR, phone, cooking facilities (some), A/C, C/H, fans, safety box, refrigerator
* Maid and laundry service
* Parking: paid available

* 3 heated pools, sundeck, jacuzzi
* Beach: 1/2 mi. / 800 m (mixed)
* Gay Bars: 3 blocks
* Health Club: 4 blocks
* Airport: 3 mi. / 5 km, taxi, shuttle
* Reservations: 1 night deposit
* Cancellation: 14 days for refund
* Credit Cards: MC/VISA/AMEX/DISC/EC/JCB
* Open: Year round
* Rates: $150-$350; (off) $100-$200 w/CB
* Tax: 11%
* Check In: 2:00pm / Check Out: 11:00am
* *TAC:* 10%

DESCRIPTION: Upscaled and sophisticated Historic Inn and Cottages built in the 1880's and lovingly restored. Three distinct types of accommodations are offered: the Mansion, the Cottages and the Inn. *IGTA*

○ WILLIAM ANTHONY HOUSE
613 Caroline St., Key West, FL 33040. Tel: (305) 294-2887, Toll Free (800) 613-2276. Fax: (305) 294-9209. TYPE: *Guest House.* HOSTS: Tony Minore & William Beck. CLIENTELE: Equal Gay/Straight. LOCATION: Central Old Town, 1 1/2 blocks from Duval St., between Simonton & Elizabeth Sts. Walking distance to all attractions.

* Suites: 4, Rooms: 2, all w/priv. bath + Cottage
* Rooms for non smokers
* CTV, phone, refrigerator, C/H, A/C bahama fans, microwave oven, coffee maker
* Maid service, wheelchair access
* Spa pool, sundeck, free parking, no pets
* Beach: nearby (mixed)
* Gay Bars: 3 blocks, minutes away
* Health Club: 4-5 blocks
* Airport: Key West Int'l 10 min. drive
* Reservations: 1-2 nights deposit
* Cancellation: 14 days
* Credit Cards: MC/VISA/AMEXDISC
* Open: Year round
* Rates: $125-$245; (off) $79-$150 w/CB + Social Hour
* Taxes: 11.5%
* Check in 2:00pm / Check out 11:00am
* *TAC:* 10%

DESCRIPTION: Beautifully restored historic Inn in a tropical garden setting. Winner of two awards for preservation and new construction. The Ramon Navarro guest suites are spacious with kitchenette, sitting & dining area; one suite has a separate bedroom. All rooms and suites have queen beds. *KWBG, KW Innkeepers Assoc., KWCC.*

Queer Across America and Southern Florida, too.

Let Columbia FunMaps® lead the way. Our FunMaps® are available through most gay & lesbian frequented locations or order Travel Paks directly from Columbia FunMaps®.

Columbia FunMap®

118 East 28 Street, New York, NY 10016

212-447-7877

WILLIAM ANTHONY HOUSE

Award winning, beautifully renovated Historic Inn with 4 luxury suites and 2 guest rooms, all with private baths, Queen beds, A/C, kitchenettes, spa, gardens, pond, porches & decks. Excellent quiet location, handicap accessible. Complimentary breakfast & social hour.

"The Sweetest Stay"
(305) 294-2887 • (800) 613-2276
613 CAROLINE ST., KEY WEST, FL 33040

SIMONTON COURT
The Island Resort
Historic Inn & Cottages

Secluded Rendezvous

Quiet. Romantic. A block from Duval Street in Key West.

For more information call:
1-800-944-2687

MIAMI/MIAMI BEACH   ✆ 305

✈ Miami Int'l Airport (MIA)
7 mi. / 11 km from downtown

LOCATION: On the Southeast Atlantic and Florida's Gold Cost.

POPULATION: Miami 352,000;
Miami Beach 90,300

CLIMATE: Subtropical marine with average temperature of 82°F (28°c). In the summer and fall there are frequent, but brief showers. The annual rainfall is 60" (150 cm).

Gay/Lesbian Visitor Information
South Beach Business Guild
Tel: (305) 534-4763

DESCRIPTION: Miami is a vibrant tropical showcase. Its nightlife varies from the exotic and glittering to the subtle and intimate. During the day recreation and sports facilities abound, especially beach and water sports. Miami has developed industrial, commercial and service related industries, many with important ties to Latin and South American countries.

Miami Beach or 'South Beach' is known for its newly renovated art-deco hotels and resorts, sidewalk cafes, and wide sandy beaches. **Coconut Grove** is the area's tropical version of New York City's famous Greenwich Village. Latin influence dominates the cultural and business life and beat of this city. The Spanish language is the main language spoken in many residential neighborhoods and business areas.

Visit the **Miami Seaquarium, Miami Wax Museum, Monkey Jungle, Metro Zoo Parrot Jungle, Planet Ocean**, and **Viscaya** plus the Beach. **South Beach** is a popular destination for the international gay travelers is **South Miami Beach**, also known as **SoBe**. A two-square mile historic district with classic '30s architecture, trendy shops and boutiques and gorgeous beaches at the southern tip of Miami Beach.

❖ **Gay Beaches:** the popular gay beaches are located at the 12th and 21st streets.

❖ **SPECIAL EVENT: Miami Art Deco Open**, GLTA tennis tournament, Jan. 13-16 (674-9338).

BARS ⵂ RESTAURANTS 🍴

➤ **Miami**
● Bars/Clubs (GM): **Boardwalk**, piano bar, male strip club, 17008 Collins Ave., No. Miami Beach (949-4119); **Cactus Lounge**, 2041 Biscayne Blvd. (576-8089); **O'Zone**, dance club, 6620 Red Rd., SW 57th Ave.,(667-2888); **Southpaw Saloon**, den of the bears and their friends, 7005 Biscayne Blvd. (758-9362); **Sugar's**, leather/levi video nightclub in North Miami Beach, 17060 W. Dixie Hwy (751-7775).

● Bars/Clubs (GMW): **Eclipse**, dance/show bar, 1969 71st St., Miami Beach (861-0965); **On the Waterfront**, bar/restaurant and entertainment nightspot, 3615 N.W. South River Dr. (635-5500).

● Bars/Clubs (GW): **Cheers**, bar, dance club, 1224 S. Dixie Hwy, Hollywood (667-4753).

● Restaurants (AW): **The Bistro**, French, 2611 Ponce de Leon Blvd. Coral Gables (442-9671); **Joe's Stone Crab**, seafood, 227 Biscayne St., Miami Beach (673-0365); **Malaga**, Cuban, 740 S,W. 8th St., Miami (858-4224); **Latin American Cafeteria**, Cuban fast food 24 hrs., 2940 Coral Way, Coral Gables (448-6809).

➤ **South Beach**
● Bars/Clubs (GM): **Hombre**, men's indoor/ outdoor cruise bar, 925 Washington Ave. (538-7883); **Kremlin**, 727 Lincoln Rd. (673-3150); **Loading Zone**, leather, cruise bar, 1426A Alton Rd. (531-5623); **Salvation**, trendy dance video bar, 1771 West Avenue (673-6508); **Twist**, dance club, 1057 Washington Ave. (538-9478); **Westend**, cruise bar, DJ music nightly, 942 Lincoln Rd. (538-9378).

● Bar/Clubs (GMW): **Club Deuce**, 222 14th St. (673-9537); **Paragon**, popular dance club, 245 22nd St. (531-5265); **Tavern on the Beach**, 18th St., & the Ocean; **Lazy Lizard Lounge**, bar/restaurant, 646 Lincoln Rd.; **Torpedo**, 634 Collins Ave. (538-2500).

● Restaurants (GMW): **Big Pig**, coffee club, light deserts, 214 Española (534-3700); **Casbah**, New American, Spa cuisine at the Shore Club Ocean Resort, see hotels listing (538-7811); **Gertrude's**, coffee shop in art gallery setting, 826 Lincoln Rd. (538-6929); **Key East**, 647 Lincoln Road Mall (672-3606).

λ   SERVICES   λ

➤ **Miami**
● Health Club (GM): **Club Body Center**, gym, message, hair salon, restaurant, open

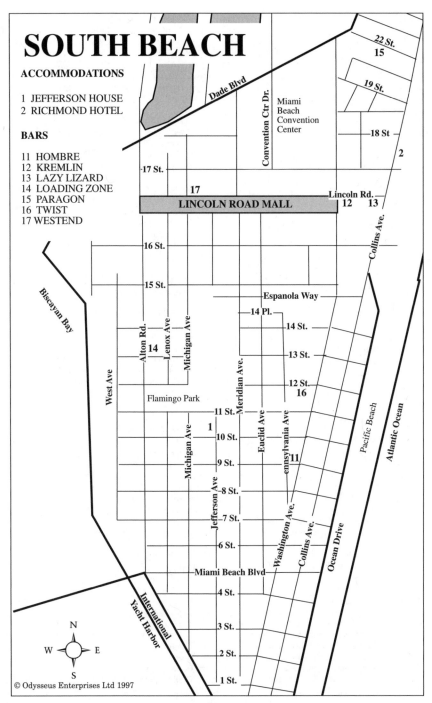

SOUTH BEACH

ACCOMMODATIONS

1 JEFFERSON HOUSE
2 RICHMOND HOTEL

BARS

11 HOMBRE
12 KREMLIN
13 LAZY LIZARD
14 LOADING ZONE
15 PARAGON
16 TWIST
17 WESTEND

Dade Blvd

Convention Ctr Dr.

Miami Beach Convention Center

22 St.
15

19 St.

18 St

2

17 St.

17

LINCOLN ROAD MALL

Lincoln Rd.
12 13

Collins Ave.

16 St.

15 St.

Biscayan Bay

Espanola Way

14 Pl.

14 St.

West Ave

Alton Rd.

Lenox Ave

Michigan Ave.

14

13 St.

Meridian Ave.

12 St.
16

Flamingo Park

11 St.

Euclid Ave

Pennsylvania Ave

Pacific Beach

Atlantic Ocean

Michigan Ave

1

10 St.

9 St.

11

Jefferson Ave

8 St.

7 St.

Washington Ave.

Collins Ave.

Ocean Drive

6 St.

Miami Beach Blvd

4 St.

International Yacht Harbor

3 St.

2 St.

N
W — E
S

1 St.

© Odysseus Enterprises Ltd 1997

24hrs., 2991 Coral Way (448-2214).

● Health Center (G/S):**Health Testing Center**, confidential AIDS testing, 10621 N. Kendall Dr. (947-0707).

● Personal Phone Line (GM): ✪ **Miami Confidential Connection**, meet local guys! Record, listen, respond to ads free (999-9200) free access code 8060.

➤ **South Beach**

● Clothing (GMW): **Cabana Joe**, men's clothing, 1200 Ocean Dr. (532-4510); **Don't Panic**, 1249 Washington Ave., (531-7223); **Ete**, 1419 Washington Ave. (672-4742); **Tommy at the Beach**, 458 Ocean Drive (538-5717).

● Erotica (GMW): **GW**, 718 Lincoln Road Mall (534-4763).

● Gym (G/S): **Bodytech**, 12th & Washington.

 ACCOMMODATIONS

➤ **South Beach**

COLOURS THE MANTELL GUEST INN
255 West 24th St., Miami Beach, FL 33140. Tel: (305) 532-9341 or (800) ARRIVAL. Fax: (305) 534-0362. TYPE: *Hotel*. CLIENTELE: Mostly Gay. LOCATION: 24th St. enter off Pine Tree / Dade Blvds.

* Suites: 25+ w/priv. bath
* Smoking allowed, non-smokers rooms
* CTV, phone, refrigerator, safety deposit, A/C, some w/balcony, garden
* Pool, ocean beach, sundeck, gym
* Maid service, parking
* Beach: 1 block (mixed)
* Gay Bars: 1-12 blocks
* Airport: 8 mi. / 13 km
* Languages: English, French, Spanish
* Reservation: 2 nights minimum
* Cancellation: 14 days for refund less $25 cancellation fee
* Credit Cards: MC/VISA/AMEX/DISC
* Open: Year round
* Rates: $79-$159; (off) $49-$119 w/CbB
* *TAC:* 10%

DESCRIPTION: Historic Art Deco hotel completely renovated providing stunning resort for travelers wanting the comfort of home with uniquely appointed rooms, kitchenettes, some terraces with views. Experience the difference...*"Not just a place, but a state of mind."*
SBBG, IGTA,CC,KWBG

GOLDEN SANDS HOTEL
6901 Collins Ave., Miami Beach, FL 33141. Tel: (305) 866-8734. USA/Canada - (800) 932-0333. Fax: (305) 866-0187. TYPE: *Beach Resort Complex*. HOST: Friendly Staff. CLIENTELE: All Welcome. LOCATION: 69th St. & Collins Ave directly on the beach, walk to restaurants, shopping and nightlife.

* Rooms: 102 w/priv. bath sgl 10/dbl 80/ triple 6/ quad 6
* Smoking allowed in rooms
* CTV, phone, A/C, safety deposit, refrigerator
* Fax/phone facilities, maid & room service
* Bar: cocktail lounge, pool bar, live music
* Restaurant: **Joe's** German/American cuisine
* Pool, ocean beach, sun deck
* Clothing optional policy, Parking (paid)
* Beach: on the beach (mixed)
* Gay Bars: 2-4 mi. / 3-6 km
* Health Club: one block (fitness center)
* Airport: Miami 12 mi. / 19 km
* Bus Stop: at the door
* Languages: German, English, French, Hebrew, Spanish, Portuguese
* Credit Cards: MC/VISA/AMEX/DISC
* Open: Year round
* Rates: $47-$97; (off) $47-$67 w/AbB
* *TAC:* 10-15% (negotiable)

DESCRIPTION: Art-deco beach resort complex with fine amenities and service in the heart of trendy Miami Beach. Convenient and safe bi-level parking attached to the hotel.

✪ JEFFERSON HOUSE
1018 Jefferson Ave., Miami Beach, FL 33139. Tel: (305) 534-5247. Fax: (305) 534-5247 ext #8. TYPE: *Bed & Breakfast*. HOSTS: Jeffrey & Jonathan. CLIENTELE: Mostly gay men & women. LOCATION: Heart of Miami Beach, between 10th and 11th St., on Jefferson Avenue south of Flamingo Park.

* Rooms: 7 w/bath (5 dbl/1 triple/ 1 quad)
* Smoking allowed in rooms
* CTV, phone, A/C, C/H
* Suite: 1 (1BR)
* Bed Types: double, queen size
* Maid service, pool, sundeck, garden area
* Beach: 6 blocks (gay/mixed)
* Gay Bars: 4 blocks
* Health Club: 6 blocks (gay, mixed)
* Airport: Miami Int'l. 20 min, taxi, bus
* Languages: English, Spanish
* Reservations: 1 night deposit
* Cancellation: 14 days notice
* Credit Cards: MC/VISA/AMEX
* Open: Year round

* Rates: $95-$150; (off) $75-$120 w/AB
* Tax: 11.5%
* Check In 3:00 pm / Check Out 12:00 noon
* **TAC:** 10%

DESCRIPTION: Bed & breakfast in the heart of Deco South Beach. Walk to Gay Beach, Bars, and Restaurants. Full breakfast served on the sun deck overlooking the tropical garden and pool. Free local phone and maid service, with laundry facilities available. *IGTA*

❍ RICHMOND HOTEL

1757 Collins Ave., Miami Beach, FL 33139. Tel: (305) 538-2331, Toll Free (800) 327-3163. Fax: (305) 531-9021. TYPE: *Hotel.* CLIENTELE: All Welcome. LOCATION: Ocean front on Collins Ave. between the Raleigh & Delano hotels. 2 short blocks from the Convention Center.

* Rooms: 99 w/priv. bath
* Rooms for smokers and non smokers
* CTV, phone, safe box, A/C, hair dryer
* Suites: 6 (1BR), Bed Type: queen size
* Services: maid, room, laundry dry cleaning, wheelchair access, elevator
* Restaurant: **Verandah** (southern American)
* Pool, ocean beach, sun deck, gym, jacuzzi
* Parking (paid valet), no pets
* Beach: on the beach, 5 blocks to gay beach
* Gay Bars: 5 blocks
* Health Club: 3 blocks (mixed)
* Airport: Miami Int'l, 7 mi. / 11 km
* Train Station: Amtrak (Hialeah) 12 mi. / 19 km
* Languages: Spanish, French, Italian, English
* Reservations: 1st night deposit + tax
* Cancellation Policy: 48 hrs.
* Credit Cards: MC/VISA/AMEX/DC
* Open: Year round
* Rates: $145-$285 / (off) $125-$230 w/CB
* Taxes: 11.56%
* **TAC:** 10%

DESCRIPTION: Completely restored ocean front art deco masterpiece in the heart of South Beach. Small gem with excellent amenities, service, privacy, and great food at reasonable prices. Best location for a gay and lesbian holiday.

SHORE CLUB OCEAN RESORT

1901 Collins Ave., Miami Beach, FL 33139. Tel: (305) 538-7811. Fax: (305) 531-1158. TYPE: *Resort Complex.* CLIENTELE: Mostly Gay. LOCATION: Oceanfront corner of 19th St. & Collins Ave. 226 rooms, CTV, phone, minibar, safe box, C/H, A/C, clothing optional sun-bathing area. DESCRIPTION: 23-story 1940's style full service beachfront resort complex.

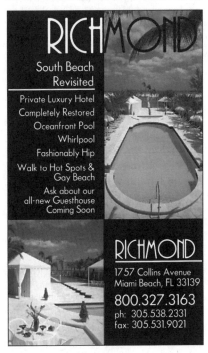

ORLANDO   ✆ 407
KISSIMMEE

✈ Orlando International Airport (MCO)

LOCATION: In central Florida, half way between Tampa on the West Coast and Daytona Beach on the East Coast on I-4.

POPULATION: 112,300.

CLIMATE: Tropical and humid with frequent afternoon showers and thunderstorms. Average winter low temperature is 52°F (11°c), average summer high temperature is 90°F (32°c).

VISITOR INFORMATION
Orlando/Orange County CVB
Tel: (407) 363-5800
Fax: (407) 363-5899

Gay/Lesbian Visitor Information
(407) 843-4297 (24 hrs)

DESCRIPTION: Orlando is an internationally acclaimed winter resort and a 'gateway' to **Disney World, Epcot Center**, and the **MGM Studios**, about 15 mi. / 24 km southwest on Lake Buena Vista. Visit: **Sea World** on I-4, between Orlando and the Walt Disney World, **Circus World**, southwest on US-27 at I-4, **Hall of Fame Wax Museum**, 14 min. southwest of Orlando on SR 528; **Florida Festival** across from the Sea World features entertainment,shopping, and restaurants.

BARS ⟂ RESTAURANTS ¶¶

● Bars/clubs (GM): **The Club**, spectacular showcase of dance-hall technology that provides a stimulating party environment for every conceivable species of nightlife, 578 N. Orange Ave., downtown Orlando (426-0005); **City Lights**, cruise bar, disco, 3400 S. Orange Blossom Trail (422-6826); **Connections**, 1517 N. Orange Blossom Trail (841-4030); **Eagle**, levi/leather cruise bar, 3400 S. Orange Blossom Trail (843-6334); **Stable**, Levi/leather bar at the **Parliament House**, 410 N. Orange Blossom Trail (425-7571).

● Bars/clubs (GMW): **Cactus Club**, 1300 Mills Ave. (894-3041); **Full Moon Saloon**,500 N. Orange Blossom Trail (648-8725); **Power House Disco**, 410 N. Orange Blossom Trail (425-7571).

● Disco (GW): **Faces**, dance bar, 4910 Edgewater Dr. (291-7571).

● Restaurant (GMW): **Dug Out**, American cuisine at the **Parliament House**, 410 N. Orange Blossom Trail (425-7571).

λ SERVICES λ

● Health Club (GM): **New Image Fitness Center**, 3400 S Orange Blossom Trail (420-9890).

● Personal Phone Line (GM): ✪ **Orlando Confidential Connection**, meet local guys! Record, listen, respond to ads free (354-3005) free access code 8060.

ACCOMMODATIONS

DOUBLETREE GUEST SUITE RESORT
Walt Disney World Village, 2305 Hotel Plaza Blvd., Orlando 32830. Tel: (407) 934-1000. TYPE: *All Suite Resort Hotel.* CLIENTELE: All Welcome. LOCATION: Inside Walt Disney World Village.

* Suites: 229 w/priv. bath, separate bedroom and living room. Suites for non smokers
* CTV (3), phone, wet bar, refrigerator, microwave oven, hair dryer
* Wheelchair access, room service, parking
* Restaurants, bar, deli, pool, jacuzzi, gym
* Complimentary transportation to Disney theme parks
* Airport: Orlando 20 min.
* Open: Year round
* Rates: $110 - $235. Tax: 10%, *TAC:* 10%

DESCRIPTION: The only all-suite hotel inside Walt Disney World. Newly renovated spacious 1BR suites with fine amenities.

GARDEN COTTAGE
1309 E. Washington St., Orlando, FL 32801-2153. Tel: (407) 894-5395. Fax: (407) 894-3809. TYPE: *Cottage.* OWNERS: Lisa & Sherry. CLIENTELE: Gay men and women only. LOCATION: Downtown Orlando, 4 blocks east of Lake Eola. 1BR cottage in historic gay neighborhood. Rates: $70-$80. *TAC:* 10%. *See our ad in the Market Place.* Email: talmadge@aol.com

PALM BEACH   ✆ 407

✈ Palm Beach Int'l Airport

LOCATION: About 50 mi / 80 km north of Ft. Lauderdale. On the northern end of an island with Lake Worth to the west and the Atlantic Ocean to the east.

DESCRIPTION: Palm shaded elegant residential and resort communities. West Palm beach offers exclusive shopping areas and famous restaurants and nightlife.

BARS ⅄ RESTAURANTS 🍴

● Bars/clubs (GM): **Chatters**, 2677 Forest Hill Blvd., W. Palm Beach; **Chez 421**, 421 North Lake Blvd., No. Palm Beach; **Choices**, 21073 Powerline Rd., Boca Raton; **5101**, 5101 S. Dixie Hwy, W. Palm Beach; **Hurricane**, 425 25th St. W. Palm Beach; **H.G. Rooster's**, 823 Belvedere Rd., W. Palm Beach; **Heartbreaker**, 2677 Forest Hill Blvd., W. Palm Beach; **Inn Exile**, 6 So. J St., Lake Worth; **Kozlow's**, 6205 Georgia Ave., W. Palm Beach; **Paradise**, bar/restaurant, 1745 NW 2nd Ave. Boca Raton; **Tilt**, 1920 S. Federal Hwy, Delray Beach.

● Restaurants (GMW): **Down Dixie**, 3815 S. Dixie Hwy, W. Palm Beach; **Paradise**, bar/restaurant, 1745 NW 2nd Ave. Boca Raton. Others (AW): **Café l'Europe**, elegant French, expensive,jacket (dinner), 150 Worth Ave., 2nd fl., of Esplanade (655-4020); **Charley's Crab**, fresh seafood, 456 S. Ocean Blvd. (659-1500); **The Dining Room**, Continental cuisine, at the Brazilian Court Hotel, 301 Australian Ave. (659-7840); **The Restaurant**, Southeast regional menu, at the Ocean Grand Hotel, 2800 S, Ocean Blvd. (582-2800).

🔑 ACCOMMODATIONS 🔑

HIBISCUS HOUSE
501 30th St., W. Palm Beach, FL 33407. Tel: (407) 863-5633. TYPE: *Guest House*. CLIENTELE: Gay men. LOCATION: Downtown near the gay scene. 3 rooms, 1 suite, 1 poolside studio, clothing optional weekends. DESCRIPTION: Historic mansion listed on the National Register.

ST. PETERSBURG   ℂ   813

✈ St. Petersburg International Airport (PIE); Tampa Int'l Airport (TPA)

LOCATION: Florida's west coast, on the southern half of the Pinellas Peninsula.

DESCRIPTION: One of Florida's largest cities and an important West Coast tourist center.

BARS ⅄ RESTAURANTS 🍴

● Bars/clubs (GM): **DT's**, 2612 Central Ave.

(327-8204); **Golden Travel**, 10604 Gandy Blvd., (577-7774).

● Bars/Clubs (GMW): **The Connection**, 3100 3rd Ave. N. (321-2112); **Hank's Hideaway**, dance club, 8302 W. 4th; **The Saint**, dance club, 10568 Gandy Blvd. (579-1570).

🔑 ACCOMMODATIONS 🔑

GARDEN GUESTHOUSES
920 4th St., So., St. Petersburg, FL 33701. Tel: (813) 821-3665. TYPE: *Guest House*. HOST: Jay or Gene. CLIENTELE: Mostly Gay. LOCATION: Downtown. DESCRIPTION: Key West style complex. 10 rooms, 2 suites, 2 cottages, 6 apts.

CAPE HOUSE INN
2800 Pass-A-Grille Way, St. Petersburg Beach, FL 33706. Tel: (813) 367-6971. TYPE: *Bed & breakfast*. HOSTS: Ron or Rich. CLIENTELE: Mostly gay. LOCATION: Tip of St. Pete Beach. 3 rooms. Rates: on request.

TAMPA   ℂ   813

✈ Tampa Int'l Airport (TPA); St. Petersburg International Airport (PIE)

LOCATION: On Florida's central West Coast across the Old Tampa Bay.

DESCRIPTION: Tampa is a business oriented community 30 min. from beautiful beaches of the Gulf of Mexico. Major attractions: **Busch Gardens, Florida Aquarium**, and **Tampa Coliseum**. **Disney World** and **Winter Haven** are only one hour away.

**Gay & Lesbian Visitor Information
The Community Center**
P.O. Box 173582
Tampa, FL 33672-1582
Tel: (813) 824-7940

BARS ⅄ RESTAURANTS 🍴

● Bars/clubs (GM): **Angel's**, 4502 S. Dale Mabry (831-9980); **Annex**, cruise leather bar, 2408 W. Kennedy Blvd. (254-4188); **Club 2606**, cruise leather bar, 2606 N. Armenia Ave. (875-6993); **City Side**, 3810 Neptune St. (254-6466); **Howard Avenue Station**, dance bar, 3003 N. Howard Ave. (254-7194).

● Bars/Clubs (GMW): **Baxter's**, dance club, 4010 S. Dale Mabry Hwy (831-6537); **Bridge**

Club, dance bar, 5519 1/2 W. Hillsboro Ave.;
The Cove, 3703 Henderson Blvd. (875-3290);
Track's, video dance bar, 1430 E. 7th Ave.
(247-2711).

λ SERVICES λ

● Health Club (GM): **Club Tampa Baths**, 215
N. 11th St. (223-5181).

● Personal Phone Line (GM): ✪ **Tampa Voicemale**, meet local guys! Browse, match, chat.
Try it free. (626-6699) free access code 8060.

● Video Store (GMW): **MC Film Festival
Video Store**, quality gay & lesbian videos (not
xxx), 117 So. Hyde Park Avenue (258-8083).

ACCOMMODATIONS

DAYS INN (Conference Center)
515 E. Cass St., Tampa FL 33602. Tel: (813)
229-6431. TYPE: *Motor Inn*. CLIENTELE: All
Welcome. LOCATION: Heart of downtown. 180
rooms, 18 suites. DESCRIPTION: Moderate
first class motor inn. Convenient location to
access local gay bars and nightlife.

DAYS INN (Busch Gardens Main Gate)
2901 E. Busch Blvd., Tampa FL 33612. Tel:
(813) 933-6471. TYPE: *Motor Inn*. CLIENTELE:
All Welcome. LOCATION: Within walking distance of Busch Gardens & Adventure Island.
179 rooms. DESCRIPTION: Two-story motor
inn near Tampa's major tourist attractions.

GEORGIA

ATLANTA

- **Population:** 5,500,000
- **Capital:** Atlanta
- **Time Zone:** Eastern
- **Sodomy Law**
- **Legal drinking age:** 21

TENNIS CHAMPIONSHIPS

THE PEACH 1997

ATLANTA, GA

The Premier Stop on the GLTA Circuit

Call: (404) 766-5824

ATLANTA   ✆   404

✈ William B. Hartsfield Int'l AP (ATL)

LOCATION: Northwest Georgia at the intersection of I-20, I-75 and I-85 and the rail and air hub of the south.

POPULATION: City 425,000;
Metro 1,820,000

CLIMATE: Mild and temperate with temperatures varying between 25°F (-4°c) in the winter and 60°F (16°c) in the spring and fall. Summer temperatures vary between the low 70's°F (23°c) and high 80°'sF (29°c) with 70% humidity.

Gay/Lesbian Visitor Information
Atlanta Gay Center
63 12th St., Atlanta GA 30309
Tel: (404) 876-5372
Helpline (404) 892-0661 (6pm-11pm)

DESCRIPTION: Atlanta, the capital of the state of Georgia, is the commercial, industrial and financial giant of the southeast U.S. It is also an important cultural center. The city's nightlife is concentrated on the north side. The midtown business district along the lively

Peachtree Street near Piedmont Park has several gay establishments.

Visit: **State Capitol**, Capitol Square; **Martin Luther King Jr National Historic Site**, a two-block area in memory of the black civil rights leader (524-1956); **Fox Theatre**, one of the most lavish movie theatres in the world, 660 Peachtree St. NE (892-5685); **Atlanta State's Farmers Market**, 10 mi. S on I-75 in Forest Park, the largest farmers' market in the Southeast; **Six Flags Over Georgia**, family entertainment center with rides, shows and attractions, 7561 Six Flags Pkwy. (948-9290).

❖ **SPECIAL EVENT:** ❂ **Atlanta Peach Tennis Tournament**, annual GLTA tennis tournament, Labor Day Weekend (766-5824).

BARS Ⓨ RESTAURANTS ⑪

● Bars/Clubs (GM): **Armory**, dance/show, outdoor garden bar, 636 Juniper NE (881-9280); **Backstreet**, disco, young crowd, open 24 hrs., 845 Peachtree St. NE (873-1986); **Blake's**, yuppie, professional clientele, 227 10th St. (892-5786); **Bulldog**, leather bar/restaurant, hot sexy male dancers, 893 Peachtree St. NE (872-3025); **Chaps**, country/western bar, 917

Peachtree St. (815-0606); **Guys & Dolls**, video bar, male nude dancers, 2788 East Ponce de Leon Ave., Decatur (377-2956); **Eagle**, leather bar, 306 Ponce de Leon Ave. NE (873-2453); **The Heretic**, leather/levi dance club, 2069 Cheshire Bridge (325-3061); **March**, dance club, male strippers, 550C Amsterdam Ave. (872-6411); **Masquarade**, dance club, 695 North Ave., NE (577-8178); **Metro**, hot male dancers, 48 6th St., (874-9869); **Spectrum**, dance club, 1492B Piedmont (875-8980).

● Bars/clubs (GMW): **Model T**, C&W dance club, 872-2209); **Pearl Garden**, 111 Luckie St. (659-4055); **Phoenix**, country/western, 567 Ponce de Leon (892-7871); **Revolution**, dance club, 293 Pratt Rd. (816-5455); **Scandals**, 1510-G Piedmont Rd. NE (875-5957); **Velvet**, dance club, 89 Park Place (681-9936); **Visions**, 2043 Cheshire Bridge Rd. NE (248-9712).

● Restaurants (AW): **Bridgetown Grill**, creative Caribbean, 689 Peachtree St. (873-5361); **Café Diem**, popular café, great hangout for the bohemian set, 640 N. Highland Ave. (607-7008); **Gourmet Grill & Bar**, steaks, seafood, Peachtree Battle Shopping Center (266-8477); **Mambo**, authentic Cuban, 1402 N. Highland Ave. (876-2626); **Marquito's**, Mexican, 8610 Roswell Rd. (642-1296); **Marra's Seafood Grill**, excellent seafood, 1782 Cheshire Bridge Rd. (872-0114); **Pad Thai**, 1021 Virginia Ave. (892-2070); **Rainbow Café**, vegetarian, 2118 N. Decatur (633-3538); **South of France**, country French, 2345 Cheshire Bridge Rd. (325-6963); **The 3rd Act**, dining and entertainment showplace, 595 Piedmont Ave. at North Ave. (897-3404); **Tortillas**, Mexican, 774 Ponce de Leon Ave. (892-3493); **Vickery's**, Creole-Italian, great atmosphere, 1106 Crescent Ave. (881-1106).

λ SERVICES λ

● Erotica (GMW): **CondomArt**, 632 N. Highland (875-5665); **Mohawk Leather**, at Eagle Saloon, 306 Ponce de Leon Ave. (873-2453).

● Health Club/Gym (G/S): **Better Bodies**, 931Monroe Drive, Midtown Promenade (881-6875); **Flex**, sauna, pool, juice bar, 76 4th St. (815-0456); **Genesis Fitness**, 3861 Peachtree Road NE (237-9133); **Peachtree Center Athletic Club**, 227 Cortland St. (523-3833); **World Class Gym**, 1859 Cheshire Bridge Rd. (892-0287).

● Personal Phone Line (GM): ✪ **Atlanta Confidential Connection**, meet local guys! Record, listen, respond to ads free (870-8830) free access code 8060.

● Variety Store (GMW): **Brushstrokes**, 1510-J Piedmont Ave. NE, Ansley Square (876-6567).

ACCOMMODATIONS

BILTMORE PEACHTREE
330 Peachtree St., Atlanta, GA 30308. Tel: (404) 577-1980 or (800) 241-4288. Fax: (404) 688-3706. TYPE: *Hotel.* CLIENTELE: All Welcome. LOCATION: Downtown Peachtree St., 94 rooms w/priv. bath. CTV, phone, refrigerator, safe box, C/H, A/C, microwave kitchen, maid service, elevator, parking. Credit Cards: MC/VISA/AMEX/DISC/DC. Rates: $69-$125 w/CB. Tax: 13%. DESCRIPTION: Comfortable hotel in a central downtown location.

BILTMORE SUITES HOTEL
30 5th St., Atlanta, GA 30308. Tel: (404) 874-0824 or (800) 822-0824. Fax: (404) 804-8710. TYPE: *All Suite Hotel.* CLIENTELE: All Welcome. LOCATION: North Avenue train station, 3 blocks from the Fox Theatre. 72 suites w/priv. bath. CTV, phone, refrigerator, C/H, A/C, cooking facilities, jacuzzi, maid, laundry service, elevator, paid parking. Gay Bars: 2 blocks. Credit Cards accepted. Rates: $69-$225 w/CB Tax: 13%. *TAC:* 10% DESCRIPTION: First class All Suite Hotel.

DAYS INN PEACHTREE
683 Peachtree St. NE. Atlanta, GA 30308. Tel: (404) 874-9200. FAX: (404) 873-4245. TYPE: *Hotel.* CLIENTELE: All Welcome. LOCATION: Midtown, opposite Fox Theatre. Rooms: 142 w/priv. bath. Suites: 2. CTV, phone, balcony, wheelchair access, sauna, parking. Gay Bars: nearby. Credit Cards accepted. Rates: $59 - $170. *TAC:* 10% DESCRIPTION: Tourist class downtown hotel near the local gay scene.

INN AT THE PEACHTREES
330 W. Peachtree, Atlanta, GA 30308. TEL: (404) 577-6970. FAX: (404) 659-3244. TYPE: *Motor Hotel.* CLIENTELE: All Welcome. LOCATION: Midtown near the Convention center. 101 rooms w/priv. bath. CTV, phone, A/C, restaurant, parking. Gay Bars: many nearby. Rates: $79-$120. *TAC:* 10%. DESCRIPTION: Motor hotel with strium courtyard.

QUALITY INN HABERSHAM
330 Peachtree St., NE, Atlanta, GA 30308. Tel: (404) 577-1980. TYPE: *Hotel.* CLIENTELE: Mostly Straight. LOCATION: 2 blocks from Peachtree Center. 91 rooms w/priv. bath. CTV, phone, wet bar, A/C, health Spa, parking. Gay bars nearby. Credit Cards accepted. Rates: $115 -$145. *TAC:* 10%. DESCRIPTION: Quiet first class hotel near Peachtree Center.

GUAM

Agana

- ◆ **Population:** 106,000
- ◆ **Capital:** Agana
- ◆ **Languages:** English, Chamorro and Taglog English is spoken by almost everyone
- ◆ **Time Zone:** West Central Pacific
- ◆ **Age of Sexual Consent:** 16
- ◆ **Legal drinking age:** 18

GUAM   © 671

✈ Guam Int'l AP (GUM)
3 mi. / 5 km NE of Agana

LOCATION: About 1,400 mi. / 2,240 km east of the Philippines in the west Central Pacific

CLIMATE: Tropical oceanic climate with temperatures averaging 80°F (27°c). Northeasterly winds produce a cooling effect. Rainfall is abundant with an annual figure of 80"-100" (2,000-2,500mm). The rainiest season lasts from May to November. Highly destructive Typhoons may strike during the wet season.

VISITOR INFORMATION
Guam Visitor Bureau
P.O. Box 3520
Agana GU 96910 (USA)

Gay/Lesbian Visitor Information
GLG (G&L Community of Guam)
P.O. Box 26920
Agana GU 96921 (USA)

DESCRIPTION: Guam is an important U.S. military base . The island is 30 mi. / 50 km long and 4-8 mi. / 6-13km wide. With its beautiful secluded beaches, jungles and sunny weather, Guam has an excellent vacation value. Guamanians make half of the island population; the rest are Hawaiians, Philippinos, and a large number of North Americans, most of whom are U.S. military personnel. Guam is a thriving and enjoyable tourist destination. The island has fully recovered from the devastating typhoons of 1992 and the earthquake of 1993. In Guam you can explore primitive villages and a unique western lifestyle steeped in ancient Micronesian culture. Until recently, gay life on Guam was rather subdued. Today, there is a growing American-style gay scene but discretion is necessary. The island's gay men and lesbians generally prefer to hide their sexual orientation because the island is small and they do not wish to reveal their sexuality to their relatives and friends.

❖ Gay Beaches: the area adjacent to Guam's most popular beach bars (on the northern end of Tumon's bay strip) **Tahiti-Rama** and **Wet Willie's; Reef Hotel Beach,** quiet beach area between the Reef and Okura hotels with shade trees and rocky coves; **Fai Fai Beach** lush, secluded beach in north west Guam (north of Tanguisson beach park. Sometimes frequented by gays and nudists.

❖ Public Cruising (AYOR): **Ipao Beach Park,** near Hilton Hotel, Tumon. This is Guam's only active "Cruising" spot, at night only (21:00-3:00). Frequented by "quick sex" fans, it is dark and occasionally dangerous; **Bank of Hawaii** (Parking Lot), Marine Dr. Tamuning, late night hangout for transvestites and hustlers.

BARS ⵖ RESTAURANTS ⵙ

The gay scene in Guam is mostly active and at its best during the week-end (Fri/Sat/Sun).

● Bars/Clubs (GMW): **Club Margie,** meeting place for military and local gays, frequented by transvestites and their admirers, Marine Drive, Anigua; **Club Sophia,** rustic karaoke lounge bar, (heterosexual) sex videos, mixed clientele, "pick-up" bar but not everybody is gay, Dededo Center Complex, Rte 1, Dededo; **Jakob's,** Japanese style Karaoke lounge, the only gay bar in the Tumon Bay tourist area, 340 San Vitores Rd., Tumon across from the Hilton Hotel (646-9510); **TJ's,** noisy but well appointed hotel bar and restaurant, mixed clientele, live music nightly, Hyatt Hotel,

Tumon; **The Underground** (Club Paradise), dance club, popular on weekends, crowd mostly gay, young, male, local and "trendy", Marine Dr. Tamuning, near Blockbuster Video (635-INFO ext. 888).

● Restaurants (AW): **Dai Ichi Hotel Coffee Shop**, 24 hrs. popular with tourists and locals; **Denny's** and **King's**, 24 hrs. American style diners in Tamuning. Both are popular with the nightclub crowd on weekend nights after the clubs close down; **Linda's Café**, unremarkable food, smoky and run-down but can be cruisy after the clubs close, Marine Dr., East Agana.

λ SERVICES λ

● Erotica (G/S): **Playboy Gift Shop**, novelties, erotic videos, magazines, viewing booths are notorious meeting places. North end of San Vitores Rd. Tumon (649-8963).

ACCOMMODATIONS

GUAM DAI-ICHI HOTEL
801 Pale San Vitores Rd., Tumon. Tel: (671) 646-5881. Fax: (671) 646-6729. TYPE: *First Class Hotel Complex.* CLIENTELE: Mostly Straight. LOCATION: On Tumon Beach. 367 rooms w/priv. bath, A/C, phone, CTV, restaurants, night club, coffee shop, disco. Rates: $120-$260. *TAC:* 10%.

GUAM HILTON
Ipao Beach, Tamuning. Tel: (671) 646-1835. Fax: (671) 646-6038. TYPE: *Superior First Class Hotel.* CLIENTELE: All Welcome. LOCATION: On the famous Ipao Beach, 10 min. from downtown. 694 rooms w/priv. bath, 32 suites, A/C, CTV, phone, 24 hrs. room service, restaurant, lounge, disco, pool, tennis, private beach. Rates: $185-$750. *TAC:* 10%

REEF HOTEL
1317 San Vitores Rd., Tumon Bay. Tel: (671) 646-6881. Fax: (671) 646-5200. TYPE: *Superior First Class Hotel.* CLIENTELE: All Welcome. LOCATION: Overlooking Tumon Bay, 1 mi / 2km from the airport. 458 rooms w/priv. bath, CTV (CNN), minibar, priv. balcony, restaurants, coffee shop, pool with poolside bar, tennis. Lively and popular with cruisy beach. Rates: $190 - $260. *TAC:* 10%

HAWAII

- ◆ **Population:** 1,000,000
- ◆ **Capital:** Honolulu
- ◆ **Time Zone:** Pacific - 2 hours
- ◆ **No Sodomy Law**
- ◆ **Legal drinking age:** 21

HAWAII ISLAND

✈ Keahole AP (KOA) or Gnrl Lyman Field AP (ITO), 2 mi. southeast of Hilo.

CAPTAIN COOK   ✆ 808

LOCATION: 18 mi. / 29 km south of Kailua-Kona town, and 68 mi. / 110 km from Volcano National Park.

CLIMATE: Subtropical with a mean winter temperature of 68°F (20°c) and a summer mean of 77°F (28°c). Trade winds keep the nights cool even in mid-August.

DESCRIPTION: The country south of Kailua-Kona is a lush tropical paradise of Coffee and Macadamia nut groves, papaya, banana and mango trees. The beautiful shore is dotted with historic sites. Sunsets tend to be strikingly beautiful and romantic.

 ACCOMMODATIONS

✪ R.B.R. FARMS

P.O. Box 930, Captain Cook, HI 96704. Tel/Fax: (808) 328-9212. Toll Free 1 (800) 328-9212.

TYPE: *Bed & Breakfast.* HOSTS: Bob & Jane. CLIENTELE: Gay Men & Women. LOCATION: Old Macadamia Nut and Coffee Plantation, southwestern coast of Hawaii so. of Kona.

- * Rooms: 5, 1 w/priv., 4 w/shared bath.
- * Rooms for non-smokers
- * Cottage: 1, Apt: 1 w/cooking facilities
- * CTV, phone (reception), safety deposit
- * Bahama fans, balcony, garden
- * Recreation: swimming, horseback riding, snorkeling, sailing, diving
- * Pool, sundeck, hot-tub, jacuzzi
- * Clothing optional policy
- * Special diets, room & maid service, parking
- * Beach: 2 mi. / 3 km (nude beach)
- * Gay Bars: 10 mi. / 16 km
- * Health Club: 10 mi. / 16 km (straight)
- * Airport: 26 mi. (42 km), car rental
- * Reservations: 50% deposit required
- * Cancellation: 14 days prior to arrival
- * Credit Cards: MC/VISA
- * Open: Year round
- * Rates: $60 - $150 w/AB
- * **TAC:** 15%

DESCRIPTION: A renovated old plantation home, very private and secluded. A popular place to relax and get away from it all, just minutes from black sands beach and snorkeling. *IGTA*

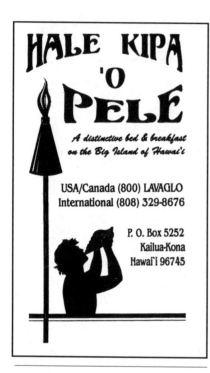

HALE KIPA 'O PELE

*A distinctive bed & breakfast
on the Big Island of Hawai'i*

USA/Canada (800) LAVAGLO
International (808) 329-8676

P. O. Box 5252
Kailua-Kona
Hawai'i 96745

KAILUA-KONA   ✆ 808

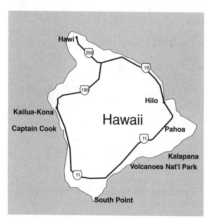

LOCATION: On the central western coast of Hawaii - The Big Island near the Keahole airport and the beach.

DESCRIPTION: Kailua-Kona is a tiny resort center of the delightful Kona Coast "the vaca-

tion paradise of Hawaiian royalty". Enjoy sunshine year round, beautiful beaches, great surfing, shopping and fine restaurant. For a spectacular adventure take a dive aboard the submarine *Atlantis* which takes passengers 80 to 100 ft. below the waters of Kona Bay.

 **ACCOMMODATIONS**

❍ HALE KIPA 'O PELE

P.O. Box 5252, Kailua-Kona HI 96745. Tel: (808) 329-8676 or Toll Free (800) LAVAGLO. TYPE: *Bed & Breakfast.* CLIENTELE: Mostly gay men & women. LOCATION: Palani Road in Kailua-Kona city.

* Rooms: 2 (dbl) w/priv. bath (non-smoking) Smoking permitted on Lanai's (patios)
* Suite: 1, Cottage: 1 (1BR) living room, full bath, kitchen, patio/terrace
* Cottage includes: CTV, VCR, refrigerator, cooking facilities
* Maid service, free parking, sun deck, jacuzzi
* Beach: 7 mi. / 11 km (gay/nude)
* Gay Bars: 5 mi. / 8 km
* Airport: Keahole, 9 mi. / 14 km, car rental
* Reservations: 50% deposit
* Cancellation: 2 weeks notice, or if room rebooked for full refund
* Credit Cards: MC/VISA/AMEX
* Open: Year round
* Rates: $65-$115. Tax: 10% w/B. *TAC:* 15%
* Check in 2pm / check out 12 noon

DESCRIPTION: Tropical plantation style bed & breakfast. The house surrounds an open-air atrium with lava rock waterfall, and koi pond. Each room-suite has its own private entrance. Full panoramic view from the covered wooded lanai. *IGTA*

❍ ROYAL KONA RESORT

75-5852 Alii Drive, Kailua-Kona HI 96740. Tel: (808) 329-3111 or Toll Free (800) 774-5662. Fax: (808) 329-7230. TYPE: *Hotel.* HOST: Cameron Hewines. CLIENTELE: All Welcome. LOCATION: South End of Kailua-Kona within walking distance to the village.

* Rooms: 452 w/priv. bath
  76 sgl / 376 dbl / triple / quad
* Rooms for smokers and non smokers
* CTV, phone, refrigerator, safe box, A/C
* Restaurants, bar, shops, pool
* Maid & room service, laundry service, wheelchair access, elevator, paid parking,
* Beach: 2 mi. / 3 km (mixed/nude)
* Gay Bars: 1 mi. / 2 km
* Health Club: 1 mi. / 2 km (The Club)

* Airport: Keahole Int'l 9 mi. / 14 km
* Languages: English, French, Filipino, Japanese
* Cancellation: 48 hrs.
* Credit Cards: MC/VISA/AMEX/DISC/DC/ EC/JCB
* Open: Year round
* Rates: $155-$390. Tax: 10.17%. *TAC:* 10%
* Check in 3pm / check out 12 noon

DESCRIPTION: Moderate deluxe full service creatively designed multistory resort overlooking Kailua Bay. Close to historical sites, fine restaurants and shopping. Comfortable rooms with Hawaiian decor. Oceanfront dining, entertainment and Dreams of Polynesia Luau show.

PAHOA   ℂ 808

LOCATION: 30 min. by car south from Hilo on route 130.

DESCRIPTION: The Big Island's South eastern Coast is famous for its natural beauty, magic volcanoes, black-sand beaches and seasonal dolphin and whale watching. The Village of Pahoa is known for its boutiques of local art.

BARS ⅄ RESTAURANTS 🍴

● Bar/Club (GM): **The Godmothers**, at the Village of Pahoa.

✪ KALANI ECO-RESORT

RR2 Box 4500, Pahoa Beach Rd., HI 96778. Tel: (808) 965-7828. Toll Free (800) 800-6886. Fax: (808) 965-9613. TYPE: *Resort Complex*. HOST: Richard Koob, Dir. CLIENTELE: Mostly gay men & women. LOCATION: 45 min. from Hilo Airport, take Hwy 11 to 130; by-pass Pahoa; at Kalapana take Hwy 137 to sign.

* Rooms: 35; 20 w/priv., 15 w/shared bath 20 dbl / 10 triple / 5 quad
* VCR, cooking facilities
* Rooms for non-smokers (smoking outdoors)
* Cottages: 7, 2BR w/living room, refrigerator
* Services: maid, laundry, wheelchair access
* Restaurant, disco, shop (gifts, nature crafts)
* Pool, sundeck, gym, sauna, jacuzzi
* Clothing optional policy
* Free parking, no pets
* Beach: 1 mi. / 1.6 km (mixed/nude)
* Gay Bars: 10 mi. / 16 km (Pahoa)
* Health Club: 10 mi. / 1.6 km (Pahoa)
* Airport: Hilo, 30 mi./ 48 km (taxi, car rental)
* Languages: English, German, French, Spanish, Japanese
* Reservations: 1 night deposit
* Cancellation: up to two weeks prior to arrival, full refund less $20 service fee
* Credit Cards: MC/VISA/AMEX/DC
* Rates: $45-$95; camping $15-$40 w/CB
* Open: Year round
* *TAC:* 10%
* Email: kh@ILHawaii.net
* WEB: http://randm.com/kh.html

DESCRIPTION: Kalani Eco-Resort is a tropical get-away offering fun adventures, comfortable accommodations, healthful cuisine and annual gay events. Vacation paradise on the sunny southeast coast of Hawaii Island, the state's largest conservation area. *IGTA, Hawaii Visitors Bureau, Hawaii Eco-Tourism Assoc.*

✪ The VOLCANO RANCH

13-3775 Kalapana Hwy., Pahoa, HI 96778. Tel: (808) 965-8800. TYPE: *Guest House / Resort Complex*. HOST: Loran Lee, owner. CLIENTELE: Gay men and women only. LOCATION: 30 min. by car south of Hilo near Kalapana black sand beach and the Kilauea Crater.

* Rooms: 4 w/priv. bath
* Bunkhouse: for budget guests
* Rooms for non smokers

Hawaii: 79, top right.

* CTV, VCR, refrigerator, C/H,
  cooking facilities, hairdryer, lanai
* Bed Types: single, twin, queen size
* Maid service, off street parking, no pets
* Pool, sundeck, sauna, jacuzzi, steam rooms
* Clothing optional policy
* Recreation: holistic therapy/massage
* Beach: 10 min (gay/nude)
* Gay Bars: 3 mi. / 5 km
* Health Club: 3 mi. / 5 km to gym in Pahoa
* Airport: Hilo, 30 min., car rental, pick up (fee)
* Languages: English, Spanish, French, German
* Reservations: $100 deposit
* Cancellation: 50% with 30 days notice
* Open: Year round
* Rates: $20 - $120 / (off) $20-$90 w/CB
* *TAC:* 10%

DESCRIPTION: Hawaii's newest gay playground. Only place with natural steam baths/caves, including an active 24 hrs "public" steam cave. 25 acres of privacy (nudity OK) with rain forests, trails, panoramic ocean views, nearby nude beach & thermal pools. See the glow of the volcano at night, swim in thermal pools heated by the volcano. Luxurious yet affordable gay inn and bunkhouse in Hawaii.

VOLCANO   © 808

LOCATION: Southeastern Hawaii the Big Island near the Hawaii Volcanoes National Park, 40 minutes from Hilo.

DESCRIPTION: National park with rain forest, active volcanos, and lava flows. This is the enchanting home of "Madame Pele". Nearby volcano village has a growing colony of artists and carftspeople, most of them from the Big Island. The Volcano Art Center offers self-guiding tapes " Tale of Old Hawaii" for those who wish to explore the volcano at their own pace.

 ACCOMMODATIONS

CHALET KILAUEA
P.O. Box 998, Volcano, HI 96785. Tel: (808) 967-7786. TYPE: *Inn.* CLIENTELE: All Welcome. LOCATION: In cool upcountry Volcano Village. Rooms: 4 w/priv. bath. Rates: $135-$295. DESCRIPTION: Offering elegant atmosphere. Enjoy fireside tea service, marble bath with en suite jacuzzi. Friendly, attentive service.

LODGE AT VOLCANO
P.O. Box 998, Volcano, HI 96785. Tel: (808) 967-8214 or (800) 736-7140. TYPE: *Bed & Breakfast.*

Mahina Kai

(Moon over Water)

**Corporate Retreat
Bed & Breakfast Beach Villa
on the Garden Island of
Kauai**

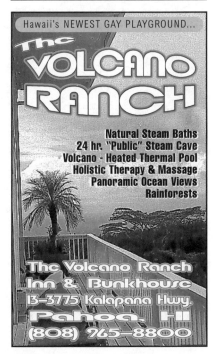

Mahina Kai

Box 699, Anahola HI 96703
Tel: (808) 822-9451 Fax: (808) 822-9451
Toll Free: (800) 337-1134

CLIENTELE: All Welcome. LOCATION: Off Hwy 11 at the end of Ama Uma U St., 7 mi. / 11 km from the Volcanoes National Park. 7 rooms, 2 suites w/priv. bath, CTV, VCR, refrigerator, cooking facilities. Rates: $85-$125. Tax: 10.17%. *TAC:* 10%. DESCRIPTION: Ranch style lodge on 30 acres.

VOLCANO B&B

P.O. Box 998, Volcano, HI 96785. Tel: (808) 967-7779 or (800) 736-7140. Fax: (808) 967-8660. TYPE: *Bed & Breakfast.* CLIENTELE: All Welcome. LOCATION: Off Hwy 11 on Keonelehua Road. 5 rooms, 1 suite (2BR), CTV, phone, refrigerator, free parking. Rates: $45-$64. Tax: 10.17%. *TAC:* 10%. DESCRIPTION: Country home on landscaped grounds.

KAUAI ISLAND

✈ Lihue Municipal Airport (LIH)

Hawaii's northernmost island known as the Garden Island. The island has a staunch individuality and a cautious attitude towards tourism development.

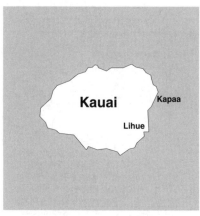

VISITOR INFORMATION
Hawaii's Visitors Bureau
Tel: 1-800-AH-KAUAI

ANAHOLA   © 808

LOCATION: Northeast Kauai on a beautiful Coconut Coast.

BAR Ⴘ RESTAURANT ¶¶

● Bar/Restaurant (G/S): **Buzz's Steak & Lobster**, serves lunch and dinner daily to a mixed clientele, daily happy hour and entertainment, 484 Kuhio Hwy., Kapaa Kauai (822-7491).

🖏 ACCOMMODATIONS 🖏

✪ MAHINA KAI

4933 Aliomanu Rd., Box 699, Anahola, Kauai, HI 96703. Tel: (808) 822-9451 or (800) 337-1134. Fax: (808) 822-9451. TYPE: *Bed & Breakfast / Rental Apts.* HOSTESS: Trudy Comba. CLIENTELE: Mostly gay men & women. LOCATION: In terraced hillside garden overlooking beautiful Anahola Bay.

* Rooms: 3 (1 sgl / 2 dbl)
* phone, refrigerator, safe box, cooking facilities, fax/computer, smoking outside
* Apartments: 2BR, living room, full bath, kitchen, patio/terrace, CTV, VCR, refrigerator, safe box, cooking facilities
* Bed types: twin, double, queen size
* Lagoon Pool, jacuzzi, hot tub
* Clothing optional policy, Free parking
* Beach: 100 ft. / 30 m (mixed)
* Gay bars: 6 mi. / 10 km
* Health Club: 6 mi. / 10 km (mixed)
* Airport: Lihue, 30 min. ($15 charge for PU)
* Languages: English, French
* Reservations: 1 night deposit
* Payment: travel checks, checks, cash
* Season: Year round
* Rates: $95-$150. Tax: 10.7% w/CB.
* *TAC:* 10%
* Check in: any time / check out: 12 noon

DESCRIPTION: Asian-Pacific country villa with 2 bedrooms, one of the most unique homes in Kauai. Also private 2 room self catering apartment. Perfect for workshops, retreats, weddings and special occasions.

KAPAA   © 808

LOCATION: Mid-way on the eastern coast of the island of Kauai off Hwy 56, about 20 min. north of the main airport in Lihue.

DESCRIPTION: A pretty village with lush tropical landscape, art galleries, shops, restaurants and lovely secluded beaches nearby. Enjoy a tour boat trip on the **Wailua River**. The **Wailua Falls** near the Fern Grotto area are spectacular and not to be missed. Visit: **Kauai Village Museum & Gift Shop** for authentic made-in-Hawaii arts and crafts and native products.

❖ Gay Beaches: **Donkey Beach**, the only "official" gay beach on Kauai, located just beyond the 11-mile marker north of Kealia on Kuhio Highway. Park along the side of the road or drive through the sugarcane fields towards the beach; **Ke'e Beach**, North shore most popular beach best for sunset watching, end of Kuhio Highway; **Lumaha'i Beach**, splendid white sand beach, west of Hanalei just before the Lumaaha'i River.

BAR ⅄ RESTAURANT 🍴

● Bar/Club (G/S): **Side Out**, 4-1330 Kuhio Hwy.

● Restaurants (AW): **Bull Shed**, steak & seafood, 796. Kuhio Ave. (822-3791); **The King and I**, Thai restaurant, 4-901 Kuhio Hwy (822-1642); **Kintaro**, authentic Japanese, 4-370 Kuhio Ave. (822-3341); **Margaritas**, wonderful margaitas and outdoor patio, Kuhio Hwy (822-1808); **A Pacific Cafe**, fresh seafood, Asian cuisine, Kauai Village Shopping Center (822-0013); **Wailua Marina**, one of the most popular restaurants on Kauai, Wailua River State Park (822-4311).

λ SERVICES λ

● Organization (GMW): **Lambda Aloha**, social organization which plans events during the year, write for their free newsletter, P.O. Box 921, Kapaa HI 96746.

● Publication (GMW): **The Freedom Network**, political journal for Kauai's sexual minorities, P.O. Box 921, Kapaa, HI 96746. (822-7171).

ACCOMMODATIONS

ALOHA KAUAI B&B
156 Lihau St., Kapaa, HI 96746. Tel: (808) 822-6966. Toll Free (800) 262-4652. TYPE: *Bed & Breakfast*. HOST: Charles Walker. CLIENTELE: Gay men & women. LOCATION: In the hills above the town of Kapaa and the Wailua River.

* Rooms:4 (dbl); 2 w/priv., 2 w/shared bath
* Rooms for non smokers
* CTV, VCR, maid and room service
* Pool, free parking, no pets
* Beach: 9 mi / 13 km (gay nude beach)
* Gay Bars: 5 mi. / 8 km
* Health Club: 4 mi. / 6 km (straight)
* Open: Year round
* Rates: $60-$85 w/AB, Tax: 10%. *TAC:* 10%

DESCRIPTION: Expansive 4-bedroom open home with spectacular views of Wailua River canyon. Quiet, casual and peaceful.

○ KAUAI COCONUT BEACH

Coconut Plantation, P.O. Box 830, Kapaa, HI 96746. Tel: (808) 822-3455 or Toll Free (800) 222-5642. Fax: (808) 822-1830. TYPE: *Resort Complex*. HOSTESS: Sandy Phipps. CLIENTELE: All Welcome. LOCATION: Oceanfront on Waipouli Beach in Kapaa.

* Rooms: 312 w/priv. bath.
* Suites: 2
* Rooms for smokers and non smokers
* CTV, phone, refrigerator, safe box, A/C
* Maid & room service, laundry service, wheelchair access, elevator
* Restaurants, bar, shops
* Pool, sundeck, jacuzzi, free parking
* Beach: on the beach (mixed)
* Gay Bars: 3 mi. / 5 km
* Health Club: 1/2 mi. Hammerhead Gym
* Airport: Lihue 8 mi. / 13 km
* Languages: English, Japanese, French, Italian, Filipino
* Reservations: 1 night
* Cancellations: 72 hrs. prior to arrival
* Credit Cards: MC/VISA/AMEX/DISC/JCB
* Open: Year round
* Rates: $125-$210. Tax: 10.17%
* Check in 3pm / check out 12 noon
* *TAC:* 10%

DESCRIPTION: Oceanfront resort with the regal essence of Hawaiian plantation. Newly decorated rooms and suites and a wide variety of full-service amenities.

KILAUEA   ℭ 808

DESCRIPTION: A small resort town in Northern Kauai. **Kauapea Beach** a fine coral sand beach backed by jungle cliff. **Kalihiwai Bay**, where the river meets the shore, is one of Hawaii's best beaches.

ACCOMMODATIONS

PALI KAI
P.O. Box 450, Kilauea, HI 96754. Tel: (808) 828-6691. TYPE: *Bed & Breakfast*. HOST: Jane or Barbara. CLIENTELE: Mostly Gay Women. LOCATION: On a hilltop overlooking the ocean. 3 rooms.

MAUI ISLAND
✈ Kahului Airport (OGG)

HAIKU   ✆ 808

 ACCOMMODATIONS

✪ KAILUA MAUI GARDENS

SR 1, Box 9, Haiku, Maui HI 96708. Tel: (808) 572-9726. Toll Free (800) 258-8588. Fax: (808) 572-5934. TYPE: *Cottages/House Rentals.* HOST: John Montfort, owner. LOCATION: Two acres of tropical gardens on Maui's North Shore near Maui's major attractions.

* Rooms: 7, 5 w/priv., 2 w/shared bath
* Cottages: 3 (1BR) w/living room, jacuzzi, kitchen, patio/terrace
* CTV, VCR, phone, refrigerator, cooking facilities, hair dryer
* Bed types: queen and king-size beds
* Laundry facilities, wheelchair access
* Pool, sundeck, jacuzzi, parking
* Beach: 1 hr. (mixed/nude)
* Gay Bars: 1/2 hr.. (mixed bars)
* Health Club: 1/2 hr. (Valley Isle Fitness)
* Airport: 30 min. (taxi, car rental)
* Reservations: 25% deposit
* Cancellation Policy: 30 day / 50%
* Open: Year round
* Rates: $60-$200 Tax: 10%.
* *TAC:* 10%

DESCRIPTION: Deluxe house and cottage rentals on a private estate. Units vary from studio with full bath to a 3BR, 2 baths house with full kitchen and ocean view lanai.

HANA   ✆ 808

LOCATION: On the southeastern coast of Maui., 10 mi. (16km) to the Haleakala Crater.

 ACCOMMODATIONS

HANA PLANTATION HOUSES
P.O. Box 489, Hana, Maui, HI 96713. Tel: (808) 248-7867. TYPE: *Rental Apartments.* HOST: Blair. CLIENTELE: Gay/Straight. LOCATION: in Hana. 9 apts. Rates: on request.

KIHEI   ✆ 808

LOCATION: In the heart of the Kihei-Wailea coastal beach area of southern Maui. 15 min. by car to Kahului airport.

DESCRIPTION: A sunny stretch of a marvelous beach area on the unspoilt island of Maui. Kihei has the best and some of the least crowded beaches in the state. Many conveniences grace the area with excellent dining and shopping.

❖ Gay Beach: the popular gay nude beach at **Makena** is nearby at the south end of Kihei.

λ SERVICES λ

● Wedding Ceremonies (AW): ✪ **Royal Hawaiian Weddings**, offer many plans for different types of ceremonies starting at $189, Box 424, Puunene, HI 96784. Tel: (800) 659-1866, Fax: (808) 875-0623.

● Surfing School (AW): ✪ **Maui Surfing School**, learn to surf in one lesson technique, Box 424, Puunene, HI 96784. Tel: (800) 851-0543, Fax: (808) 875-0623.

 ACCOMMODATIONS

✪ ANDREA & JANET's

MAUI VACATION CONDOS
Box 424, Puunene, HI 96784. Tel: (808) 879-6702 or Toll Free (800) 289-1522. Fax: (808) 879-6430. TYPE: *Oceanfront Condominiums.* HOSTESS: Andi Thomas & Janet Renner. CLIENTELE: All Welcome. LOCATION: Kihei, Maui.

* Condos: 1BR & 2BR
* Living room, full bath, kitchen, patio, terrace, washer/dryer
* Pool, sundeck, sauna, jacuzzi, free parking
* Beach: on the beach, 6 mi. / 10 km from gay nude beach

* Gay Bars: 6 mi. / 10 km
* Health Club: 1 mi. / 1.6 km
* Airport: Kahului 8 mi. / 13 km, taxi, car rent
* Reservations: 2 nts deposit
* Cancellation: 2 weeks
* Credit Cards: MC/VISA/DISC
* Open: Year round
* Rates: $85-$125 Tax: 9.2%
* Check in 12 noon
* *TAC:* 10%

DESCRIPTION: Oceanfront deluxe condos with all amenities. Recreation: tennis, golf, windsurfing, fine dining, shopping. Just bring your swimsuit. *IGTA*

O ANFORA's DREAMS

Kihei, HI. Correspondence: PO Box 7403, Los Angeles, CA 90004. Tel: (213) 737-0731 or (800) 788-5046. Fax: (818) 224-4312. TYPE: *Condominium Rentals.* HOST: Dale Jones. CLIENTELE: All Welcome. LOCATION: Middle of Kihei on Ma'alea Bay on the west side of Maui.

* Condos w/living room, full bath, kitchen, patio/terrace, CTV, phone, refrigerator, A/C
* Smoking allowed, maid service
* Bed Types: single, twin, double, queen
* Pool, sundeck, sauna, jacuzzi
* Pets: with prearrangement
* Beach: 200 ft. / 60 m. (mixed)
* Gay Bars: 15-20 min.
* Health Club: 5 min. (mixed)
* Airport: Kahului 15-20 min.
* Deposit: 50%
* Cancellation: $100 over 30 days prior, less than 30 days forfeit
* Credit Cards: MC/VISA
* Open: Year round
* Rates: $65-$450   Tax: 10.17%
* Check in 2:00 pm / check out 11:00 am
* *TAC:* 10%

DESCRIPTION: Single condos to elegant beach front homes all with pool and jacuzzi. Completely furnished.

LAHAINA   © 808

✈ Kapalua Airport (West Maui)

LOCATION: Western Maui Coast.

DESCRIPTION: Lahaina is a plantation town and an historic Landmark with a distinctive 19th century and early 20th century architectural charm. The area around Lahaina offers

beautiful beaches, shopping and nightlife.

λ SERVICES λ

● Travel (GMW): O **Gay Hawaii Excursions**, activities and tours for all the Hawaiian islands designed exclusively for gays and/or lesbians: dinner cruises, helicopter tours, horseback riding, snorkeling at Molokini crater, sunset sails, bike down Halekale crater, 256 Front St., Lahaina, HI 96761. (808) 667-7466. (800) 311-4460. Fax: (808) 667-5401. Albert Molina, *IGTA*

 ACCOMMODATIONS

O KAHANA BEACH RESORT

4221 Lower Honoapiilani, Lahaina HI 96761. Tel: (808) 669-8611 or Toll Free (800) 222-5042. Fax: (808) 669-1656. TYPE: *Condominiums / Hotel.* HOST: Lalo Fernandez. CLIENTELE: All Welcome. LOCATION: 6 mi / 10 km north of Lahaina, oceanfront on Kahana Beach.

* Studios: 81 w/priv. bath
* Suites: 11 (1BR)
* Smoking allowed in rooms
* CTV, phone, refrigerator, safe box, A/C, cooking facilities
* Wheelchair access
* Maid service, elevator
* Restaurant & Bar: **Eriks** seafood
* Pool, free parking
* Beach: on the beach (mixed)
* Gay Bars: 6 mi. / 10 km
* Health Club: 6 mi. / 10 km
* Airport: Kapalua, 3 mi. / 5 km, rental car main airport Kahalui 35 mi. / 56 km
* Reservations: 1 night deposit
* Cancellation: 72 hrs. prior to arrival
* Credit Cards: MC/VISA
* Open: Year round
* Rates: $120-$210. Tax: 10.17%
* Check in 3pm / check out 12 noon
* *TAC:* 10%

DESCRIPTION: Standard economy 12 story highrise on the beach with mostly studios and 1BR units, all with ocean views.

O MAUI KAI Condominiums

106 Kaanapali Shores Pl., Lahaina, HI 96761. Tel: (808) 667-3500 or (800) 367-5635. Fax: (818) 667-3660. TYPE: *Condominiums.* CLIENTELE: All Welcome. LOCATION: North Kaanapali Beach, next door to Embassy Suites.

* Condos: 56
* Rooms for non smokers

* CTV, phone, refrigerator, A/C
* Maid service, laundry service
* Bed types: twin, double, queen size
* Pool, spa, sun deck, jacuzzi, parking
* Airport: Kahului, 1 hr., taxi
* Reservations: 2 nights deposit
* Cancellation Policy: 14 days prior /
  Xmas 30 days prior
* Credit Cards: MC/VISA
* Open: Year round
* Rates: $135-$265 / (off) $120-$245
* Tax: 10.17%.
* **TAC:** 10%
* Check in 3:00 pm / Check out 12:00 noon

DESCRIPTION: Oceanfront condominium complex on Kaanapali Beach facing Molokai and Lanai. Air-conditioned studios, 1BR, 1BR corner and 2BR units with all modern amenities including fully equipped kitchens. Guests can enjoy BBQ facilities, paperback library, outdoor shower and sundeck.

✪ PLANTATION INN

174 Lahainaluna Rd., Lahaina, HI 96761. Tel: (808) 667-9225. Toll Free (800) 433-6815. Fax: (808) 667-9293. TYPE: *Bed & Breakfast.* HOST: Charles Robinson, Mgr. LOCATION: 30 min. from Kahului airport, west/northwest on Hwy 380, left on 30 "Lahaina".

* Rooms: 15 dbl w/priv. bath
* Suites: 4 w/living room, full bath, jacuzzi (2),
  kitchen (3), patio/terrace (3)
* Smoking allowed in rooms
* CTV, VCR, phone, refrigerator, safe box,
  A/C, cooking facilities (limited), hairdryer
* Bed type: queen size, maid service
* Restaurant: **Gerard's** - contemporary French
* Pool, sundeck, jacuzzi, free parking, no pets
* Beach: 2 mi. / 3 km
* Gay Bars: 17 mi. / 28 km
* Health Club: 2 blocks
* Airport: 27 mi. / 43 km, taxi, bus, van service
* Reservations: 3 night deposit
* Cancellation: 30 day notice,
  $25 fee on all refunds
* Credit Cards: MC/VISA/AMEX/DC/DISC/JCB
* Open: Year round
* Rates: $119-$219 / (off) $104 - $195
  w/full or CB. Taxes: 10.17%
* Check in 3:00 pm / check out 12:00 noon
* **TAC:** 10%

DESCRIPTION: A unique country Inn blending gracious turn-of-the century architecture with designer accommodation. Each room is individually furnished with its own unique decor, including antique stained glass, hardwood floors, brass and/or canopy beds.

✪ ROYAL LAHAINA RESORT

2780 Kekaa Drive, Lahaina HI 96761. Tel: (808) 661-3611 or Toll Free (800) 447-6925. Fax: (808) 661-3538. TYPE: *Resort Complex.* HOST: Epi Rabanal. CLIENTELE: All Welcome. LOCATION: On Kaanapali Beach, 4 mi. / 6 km from historic Lahaina.

* Rooms: 592 w/priv. bath
* Suites 26 / Cottages 135
* Rooms for smokers and non-smokers
* CTV, phone, refrigerator, safe box, A/C
  cooking facilities (on request)
* Maid & room service, laundry service .
* Wheelchair access, elevator
* Restaurants, bar, shops
* Pool, jacuzzi, paid parking
* Beach: on the beach (mixed)
* Gay Bars: 4 mi. / 6 km
* Health Club: 4 mi. / 6 km (World Gym)
* Airport: Kapalua 8 mi. / 13 km rental car
* Languages: English, Spanish, German,
  Japanese, Filipino
* Reservations: 1 night
* Cancellation: 72 hours prior to arrival
* Credit Cards: MC/VISA/AMEX/EC
* Open: Year round
* Rates: $195-$315. Tax: 10.17%
* Check in 3pm / check out 12 noon. **TAC:** 10%

DESCRIPTION: Resort complex on 27 tropical acres of Kaanapali Beach featuring elegantly appointed rooms, private cottages, and suites. Good quality accommodations and service.

OAHU ISLAND
✈ Honolulu Int'l Airport (HNL)

HONOLULU   ✆ 808

LOCATION: On the island of Ohau 2,400 miles (3,840 km) from the U.S. mainland in the middle of the Pacific Ocean.

POPULATION: City 325,000;
Ohau 710,000

CLIMATE: Mild marine tropical, with a slight seasonal change. Winter is hot with a January mean temperature of 72˚F (22˚c). Summer is

slightly hotter with a July average of 80˚F (27˚c). Annual rainfall is 23" (575 mm), with few thunderstorms. Its location just south of the tropic of cancer assures mildness and warmth year round.

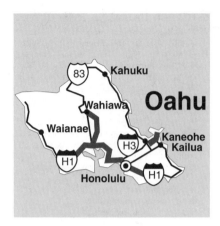

VISITOR INFORMATION
Hawaii Visitors Bureau: (808) 923-1811

Gay/Lesbian Visitor Information
Tel: (808) 926-1000 24 hrs.

DESCRIPTION: Honolulu is the island's largest city, the state's capital, commercial center and a tourist's paradise. The city stretches along the narrow coastal plain between **Pearl Harbor** and **Koko Head**. The harbor is the heart of the old town; it dwells in the downtown banking and trade area at the Financial Plaza.

The Oriental District on Nuuanu and River Sheets, creates an exotic atmosphere with chinese markets, herb shops, and craftsmen plying their trades. **Waikiki**, a fashionable resort area, is the core of the state's tourist industry with deluxe hotels and sandy beaches. Here is also the "**Kuhio District**" or the gay village of Waikiki. Visit the **Polynesian Cultural Center**, only one hour's drive from Waikiki for an authentic show case of the South Pacific. For info call: 1-800-367-7060.

❖ Beaches: favorite with tourists is the **Waikiki Beach**. The gay beach is at the **Queen Surf Beach** going towards Diamond Head on Kalakaua Ave. A straight beach frequented by gays is the **Royal Hawaiian Hotel beach**.

BARS ▾ RESTAURANTS ▮▮

● Bars/Clubs (GM): **Banana's**, 2139 Kuhio Ave., #125 (922-6262); **Dirty Mary's**, dance bar, restaurant, 2109 Kuhio Ave. (922-6722); **Fusions**, dance club, cocktails, 2260 Kuhio Ave., Third Floor (924-2422); **Garbo's**, 2260 Kuhio St., 2nd fl., (922-1405); **Hula's**, dance/cocktail

bar, 2103 Kuhio Ave. (923-0669); **Metropolis**, country & western, 611 Cook St., (593-2719); **Question Mark II**, 1401 Kalakua Ave; **Trixx**, bar, music and pool next to Hula's, 2109 Kuhio Ave.; **Windows**, candlelit tables, Eaton Square, Hobron & Eaton (946-4442); **Xtensions**, Lewers between Kuhio & Kalakaua.

● Restaurants (GMW): **Buzz's Steak & Lobster**, 225 Saratoga Rd., (923-6762); **Club 58**, 2139 Kuhio Ave. (922-6588); **The Godmother**, Italian cuisine, 339 Saratoga Rd., Waikiki (922-6960); **Hamburger Mary's Grill**, 2109 Kuhio Ave., Waikiki (922-6722); **Piece of Eight**, 250 Lewers St. (923-6646); **Rudy's Waikiki Pasta Co.**, 2280 Kuhio Ave., (923-5949). **Keo's Thai Cuisine**, exotic Thai cuisine, 625 Kapahulu Ave. (737-8240); **Singha Thai Cuisine**, 1910 Ala Moana Blvd., (941-2898). Other restaurants (AW): **Fisherman's Wharf**, fresh seafood, 1009 Ala Moana Blvd. (538-3808); **Wo Fat**, authentic Chinese cuisine, 115 N. Hotel St. (537-6260). Also try the buffet and Polynesian show at the **Polynesian Cultural Center**, one hour drive from Honolulu for transportation call Waikiki Hotels (293-3333 for reservation).

λ SERVICES λ

● Boutique: **80% Straight**, 2131 Kuhio Ave., (923-9996); **Pet Boy**, 2117 Kuhio Ave., (924-3376).

● Health Club (GM): **Koko Pacific**, 2139 Kuhio Ave, Waikiki (923-1852). (G/S) **Pacific Beach Hotel**, mixed health club, 2490 Kalakaua Ave., 2nd Fl.

● Limousine (GMW): **Honolulu's Pride Taxi & Tour**, personalized Airport transfers. Advance booking 1-(800)-330-5598 (24 hrs).

● Personal phone Line (GM): ✪ **Hawaii Confidential Connection**, meet local guys! Record, listen, respond to ads free (596-7222) free access code 8060.

● Videos (GMW): **Diamond Head**, 870 Kapahulu Ave. (735-6066); **Movieland**, 1695B Kapiolani Blvd. (941-1023)

🖐 ACCOMMODATIONS 🖐

✪ COCONUT PLAZA HOTEL

450 Lewers St., Honolulu, HI 96815. Tel: (808) 923-8828. Toll Free (800) 882-9696. Fax: (808) 923-3473. TYPE: *Hotel.* MANAGER: Eric Nissen General Manager. CLIENTELE: All Welcome. LOCATION: Central, corner of Lewers St., and Ala Wai Blvd.

* Rooms: 80 w/priv. bath
  20 sgl/ 20 dbl / 20 triple / 20 quad
* Suites: 10 executive suites
* Rooms for smokers and non smokers
* CTV, phone, refrigerator, safe box,
  A/C, cooking facilities, hairdryer
* Maid service, Laundry service,
  wheelchair access, elevator
* Pool, sundeck, gym, parking (paid), no pets
* Beach: 4 blocks (mixed) 24 Hour Fitness
* Gay Bars: 1 block
* Health Club: 3 blocks (mixed)
* Airport: Honolulu Int'l, 11 mi. / 18 km
* Languages: English, Japanese
* Reservations: 1 night deposit
* Cancellation: 72 hrs.
* Credit Cards: MC/VISA/AMEX/DISC/JCB
* Open: Year round
* Rates: $85-$150 w/CB
* Taxes: 10.17%   *TAC:* 10%
* Check in 3:00 pm / Check Out 12:00 noon

DESCRIPTION: Charming gay friendly boutique hotel in the heart of Waikiki. The
Coconut Plaza hotel offers a pleasant alternative to larger resorts and the hurried pace of
Waikiki through its gracious warmth in accommodations and service. Guest rooms feature
kitchenettes and private lanais.

HOTEL HONOLULU
376 Paoakalani St., Honolulu, HI 96815. Tel: (808)
926-2766. TYPE: *Hotel.* CLIENTELE: Mostly
Gay. LOCATION: Two blocks from Waikiki
Beach, in the Kuhio gay district. 15 studios, 9
suites all with private bath, phone, A/C, rooftop
garden and sundeck, parking. Cooking facilities available. Rates: on request. DESCRIP-
TION: Gay hotel recreating the essence of
Hawaii during the late 30's.

OCEAN RESORT HOTEL WAIKIKI
175 Paoakalani Ave., Honolulu, HI 96815-3743.
Tel: (808) 922-3861. Toll Free (800) 367-2317.
Fax: (808) 924-1982. TYPE: *Hotel.* CLIEN-
TELE: All Welcome. LOCATION: 1 block from
the famous Waikiki Beach and the Honolulu
Zoo on the corners of Kuhio and Paoakalani
Avenues. Diamond Head end of Waikiki.

* Rooms: 451 w/priv. bath. Suites: 7
  261 sgl/dbl / 190 quad
* Rooms for smokers and non smokers
* CTV, phone, refrigerator, safe box, A/C
* Cooking Facilities: kitchenettes (Pali Tower)
* Maid & Room service
* Laundry service, elevator
* Mala Restaurant: American/Japanese
* Punawai Lounge: cocktail lounge/karaoke
* Shops, pool, sun deck

* Parking: paid, off street
* Beach: 1 block (mixed)
* Gay Bars: 4 blocks
* Health Club: 1 block (mixed)
* Airport: Honolulu Int'l, 12 mi. / 19 km
* Airport Transportation: taxi, bus, shuttle
* Languages: English, Japanese, German,
  Filipino, and Chinese
* Reservations: 1 night deposit
* Cancellation Policy: 3 days (72 hrs) prior to
  arrival. If notice is not received one night
  deposit will be forfeited
* Credit Cards: MC/VISA/AMEX/DISC/DC/JCB
* Open: Year round
* Rates: $86-$150; (off) $76-$140
* Breakfast not included, available in restaurant
* Taxes: 10.17% hotel room & state tax
* Check in 3:00pm / Check out 12:00 noon
* *TAC:* 10%

DESCRIPTION: Moderately priced hotel with
clean, comfortable and friendly atmosphere.
The hotel is accessible by public city bus, within a short walking distance from Kapiolani
Park, Waikiki Aquarium, Kodak Hula Show
and Diamond Head Crater, yet away from the
hustle and bustle. Hotel is comprised of two
towers; the Diamond Tower with 261 rooms,
and the Pali Tower with 190 kitchenette rooms.

ILLINOIS

CHICAGO ●

- ◆ **Population:** 11,500,000
- ◆ **Capital:** Springfield
- ◆ **Time Zone:** Central
- ◆ **No Sodomy Law**
- ◆ **Legal drinking age:** 21

CHICAGO   © 312

✈ Chicago O'Hare Int'l Airport (ORD)
Midway Airport (MDW)

LOCATION: On the southwest, southern tip of Lake Michigan in the midwest of the U.S.A.

POPULATION: City 3,000,000;
                     Metro 7,100,000

CLIMATE: Continental and variable. Summers are hot and humid, winters are freezing with temperatures reaching 0°F (-18°c) with abundant amount of snow.

VISITOR INFORMATION
Chicago CVB: (312) 567-8500

Gay/Lesbian Visitor Information
(312) 975-1212

DESCRIPTION: Chicago is the spirited, hard working cultural and financial center of the Midwest. For some people, Chicago is the "Windy City", others like to call it the "Queen City" of the Lakes. Architects admire the distinguished "Chicago Style", scholars love it for being a major educational and University Center. Gay people appreciate Chicago's thriving gay culture and nightlife in the Old Town and the New Town areas.

The business center of Chicago - the Loop, occupies six-square-blocks of tall historic buildings encircled by an elevated train system. Here are the headquarters of some of the largest and most respected Fortune 500 companies in the U.S.A. Chicago's elegant retail stores running north of the Chicago River to Oak Street Beach. Museums are located at Roosevelt Road: **Field Museum of Natural History**, **Shedd Aquarium**, and the **Adler Planetarium**. **Chinatown** is a few miles south of the Loop, beginning on South Wentworth Ave. at Cermak. **Lincoln Park** delightfully landscaped with green lawns and shady corners is perfect for recreation or sports. It is popular with the gay community who frequently organize picnics and other events in the Park. **Lake Michigan**, east of the Park, is a great place to escape the heat of the summer.

❖ Gay beach - **Belmont Rocks**, is near Lincoln Park, 2 blocks from Belmont and Broadway.

❖ **SPECIAL EVENTS**: ✪ **Chicago Indoor International Tennis Classic**, August 4-6 (929-6463); ✪ **Int'l Mr. Leather Contest**, 5 nights of hot Leather Action, each year in May, 5015 N. Clark St., (878-6360).

BARS ☿ RESTAURANTS 🍴

● Bars/Clubs (GM): **Anvil**, 1137 W. Granville; **Buck's Saloon**, 3439 N. Halsted (525-1125); **Cell Block**, leather bar, 3702 No. Halsted (665-8064); **Charlie's**, country/western dance bar, 3726 N. Broadway (871-8887); **Chicago Eagle**, leather/cruise bar, Tuesdays Leather Nights, 5015 N. Clark St. (728-0050); **Cocktail**, video-bar, great music and ambiance, 3359 N. Halsted; **Dandy's**, intimate piano bar, live entertainment, 3729 N. Halsted (525-1200); **Lucky Horseshoe Lounge**, male dancers, strippers, 3169 N. Halsted (404-3169); **Manhandler**, late night club, 1948 N. Halsted Ave. (871-3339); **Manhole**, leather cruise bar, 3458 N. Halsted (975-9244); **Man's Country**, adult entertainment complex, hot male strippers, 5015 N. Clark (878-2069); **Numbers**, 6406 N. Clark (743-5772); **Qwest**, dance club, 2554 W. Diversey; **Roscoe's**, bar/tavern/cafe, Sunday Tea Dance, 3354-56 N. Halsted (281-3355); **Sidetrack**, popular video bar, 3349 N. Halsted (477-9189); **Spin**, dance club, young clientele, 800 W. Belmont (327-7711); **Temptations**, male strippers, comedy shows, 10235 W. Grand Ave. (455-0008); **Touché**, levi/leather cruise bar, 6412 N. Clark

(465-7400); **Vortex**, largest dance club in Chicago, 3631 N. Halsted (975-0660).

● Bars/clubs (GMW): **Baton Show lounge**, female impersonators, 436 N. Clark St. (644-5269); **Berlin**, high-energy video dance club, 954 W. Belmont (348-4975); **Buddies'**, restaurant and video bar, 3301 N. Clark (477-4066); **Cell Block**, leather cruise bar, 3702 N. Halsted (665-8064); **Dandy's**, piano bar, 3729 N. Halsted (525-1200); **Chicago Eagle**, home to the International Mr. Leather, 5015 N. Clark (728-0050); **Different Strokes**, video bar, 4923 No. Clark (989-1958); **Gentry**, cabaret nightly, bar & cafe, close to downtown hotels, 712 N. Rush Street (664-1033); **Glee Club**, 1543 No. Kingsbury (243-2075); **Inn Exile**, video nightclub, 5758 W. 65th St. (582-3510).

● Bars/clubs (GW): **Lost & Found**, 3058 W. Irving Park Rd. at Albany (463-9617); **Paris Dance**, dance bar/restaurant, 1122 W. Montrose (769-0602); **Temptations**, 10235 W. Grand, Franklin Park (847-455-0008); **The Other Side**, 3655 N. Western (404-8156).

● Restaurants (GMW): **Arnold's**, Irving Park at Broadway (929-3338); **The Bagel**, restaurant & deli, 3107 N. Broadway (477-0300); **Bucktown Café**, 1750 W. North Ave. (342-8700); **Buddies'**, 3301 N. Clark (477-4066); **Caeser's**, Mexican, low fat and vegetarian dishes, 3166 N. Clark (248-2835); **Cas and Lou's**, authentic Italian, tri-level dining, 3457 W. Irving Park (588-8445); **Fireplace Inn**, Old Chicago steakhouse, 5739 N. Ravenswood (878-5942); **Julie Mai's - Le Bistro**, French / Vietnamese, 5025 N. Clark (784-6000); **Lolita Café**, Mexican cuisine, 4404 No. Clark St. (561-3356); **Mike's**, full service cafe, 3805 N. Broadway (404-2205); **Rhumba**, Brazilian cuisine, 3631 N. Halsted; **Siam Corner**, Thai cuisine, 3374 N. Clark (528-2572); **Villa Toscana**, 3447 N. Halsted St. (404-2643); **Waterfront**, seafood, 16 West Maple (943-7494); ✪ **Way to Work**, coffee shop at the City Suites Hotel (see hotel information).

λ SERVICES λ

● Erotica (GMW): **Banana Video**, 4923 N. Clark (561-8322); **Bijou Theatre**, all male cinema, 24 hrs.,1349 N. Wells (943-5397); **Cupid's Treasures**, love boutique, 3519 N. Halsted (348-3884); **Nationwide Video**, two locations - 843 1/2 W. Belmont (525-1222) and 736 W. Irving Park (871-7800); **Pleasure Chest** 3143 N. Broadway (525-7151); **Specialty Video**, 5225 N. Clark (878-3434) and 3221 N. Broadway (248-3434).

● Gifts (GMW): **Gay Mart**, Chicago's largest

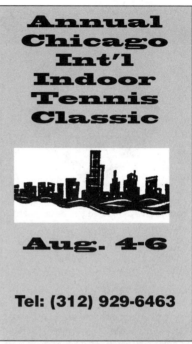

Downtown Chicago Without the
Downtown Price

Cass HOTEL

Surrounded by Chicago's finest
restaurants, shops and entertainment.

Clean
Comfortable $ **49** 00 plus tax
Rooms From
Only:

Reservations and information:
312-787-4030
Toll free reservations:
800-CASS-850 (227-7850)

640 North Wabash Avenue, Chicago, IL 60611
Fax: 312-787-8544

* Bed Types: single, double
* Cafe and lounge
* Maid service, elevator, no pets
* Beach: 10 blocks (mixed)
* Gay Bars: 2 blocks
* Airport: O'Hare / Midway 25-30 min.
* Subway: 2 blocks
* Train Station: Amtrak 10 min. by cab or bus
* Credit Cards: MC/VISA/AMEX
* Open: Year round
* Rates: from $49 + Tax. *TAC:* 10%
* Check in 1:00pm / check out 12:00 noon

DESCRIPTION: The vintage Cass Hotel offers
reasonably priced clean, comfortable rooms, in
Chicago's historic River North neighborhood.

gay & lesbian gift store, 3457 N. Halsted (929-
4272); **Paper Trail**, 5307 N. Clark (275-2191).

● Health Clubs (GM): **Bodyshop**, full service
health club, open: M-F 6:00am-10:00pm, Sat.
6:00am-8:00pm, Sun. 6:00am-6:00pm, 3246 N.
Halsted St., (248-7717); **Man's Country**, club,
patio, 24 hrs., 5017 N. Clark St., (878-2069);
Man's World, 4740 N. Western (728-0400);
Unicorn Club, all male bathhouse, open 24
hrs, clean, safe, 3246 N. Halsted St. (929-6080).

● Leather Shop (G/S): **Male Hide Leathers**,
leather accessories, 2816 N. Lincoln Ave. (929-0069).

 **ACCOMMODATIONS**

❍ CASS HOTEL

640 N. Wabash Ave., Chicago IL 60611. Tel: (312)
787-4030, Toll Free (800) CASS-850 (227-9850).
Fax: (312) 787-8544. TYPE: *Hotel.* CLIENTELE:
All Welcome. LOCATION: Historic River North
neighborhood, two short blocks from Chicago's
"Magnificent Mile" with easy access to shopping,
entertainment and nightlife.

* Rooms: 175 w/priv. bath
* Smoking allowed in rooms
* CTV (HBO), phone, safe box, C/H, A/C

❍ CITY SUITES HOTEL

933 W. Belmont Ave., Chicago IL 60657. Tel:
(312) 404-3400. Toll Free (800) CITY-108. Fax:
(312) 404-3405. TYPE: *Hotel.* CLIENTELE: All
Welcome. LOCATION: North Side, close to fine
dining, shopping, entertainment and the elevated train for easy downtown access. Short
walk to gay clubs and bars.

* Rooms: 15 sgl w/priv. bath, CTV, phone, A/C
* Suites: 30 dbl (1BR, living room)
* CTV, phone, refrigerator, safe box, C/H, A/C
* Rooms/suites for smokers and non-smokers
* Maid & room service, elevator
* Disco: **Berlin** (nearby)
* Parking: paid, Pets: w/prearrangement
* Beach: 6 blocks (mixed)
* Gay Bars: many nearby (walking distance)
* Health Club: gym nearby
* Airport: O'Hare Int'l 10 mi. / 16 km
* Metro: Belmont-Howard Dan Ryan Line
  130 ft / walking distance
* Reservations: CC# or 1 night deposit
* Cancellation: 24 hrs. in advance
* Credit Cards: MC/VISA/AMEX/DC/DISC
* Open: Year round
* Rates: $85 - $99 w/CB. Tax: 14.9%. *TAC:* 10%
* Check in time 2pm / check out 12 noon

DESCRIPTION: European style hotel with the
casual elegance and ambiance of Chicago during the roaring 20's. Graciously appointed
rooms and suites decorated in period furniture
and artwork. Complimentary newspaper delivered to your room daily.

❍ PARK BROMPTON INN

528 W. Brompton, Chicago, IL 60657. Tel: (312)
404-3499. Toll Free (800) PARK-108. Fax: (312)
404-3495. TYPE: *Hotel.* CLIENTELE: All Welcome. LOCATION: Near Lincoln Park & Lake
front. Minutes from downtown via scenic Lake

Here, the notion of atmosphere extends far beyond the walls of our hotels.

Set in picturesque surroundings on Lincoln Park and the Near North Side, three distinguished hotels stand ready to welcome you as the Neighborhood Inns of Chicago.

Each hotel is situated in the heart of the gay community, amid a charming neighborhood filled with eclectic shopping, theatre, dining and nightlife, with downtown attractions still just minutes away.

And our reasonable everyday rates carry no restrictions, so you can afford to take in our atmosphere, again and again.

Rooms and Suites

$**79** $**99**

from   to

Rates valid through March 31, 1998 (based on single occupancy)

NEIGHBORHOOD INNS *of* CHICAGO

555 West Surf
800-SURF-108
312-528-8400

528 W. Brompton
800-PARK-108
312-404-3499

933 W. Belmont
800-CITY-108
312-404-3400

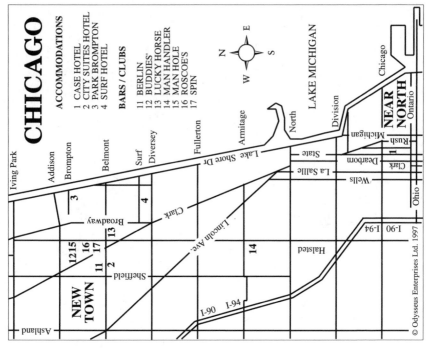

Shore Drive, steps from gay bars and clubs.

* Rooms: 30 w/priv. bath w/CTV, phone, A/C
* Suites: 22 (1BR) living room, full bath, kitchen, CTV, phone, A/C, safe box
* Smoking allowed in rooms/suites
* Maid service, elevator, paid parking
* Pets: w/prearrangement
* Beach: across the street (mixed)
* Gay Bars: many nearby (walking distance)
* Health Club: 2 blocks (mixed)
* Airport: O'Hare Int'l 10 mi. / 16 km
* Metro: Addison "L" stop, 4 blocks
* Reservations: CC# guarantee or deposit
* Cancellation: 24 hrs. in advance
* Credit Cards: MC/VISA/AMEX/DC/DISC
* Open: Year round
* Rates: $79-$99 w/CB, Tax: 14.9%. *TAC:* 10%
* Check in time 2pm / check out 12 noon

DESCRIPTION: Quaint English style Inn. Guest rooms and suites decorated with Dickensian touch like poster beds and tapestry furnishings. Larger suites feature butler pantries with microwave, refrigerator and wet bar. Complimentary newspaper delivered to your room daily.

✪ THE SURF HOTEL

555 West Surf St., Chicago IL 60657. Tel: (312) 528-8400. Toll Free (800) SURF-108. Fax: (312) 528-8483. TYPE: *Hotel*. CLIENTELE: All Welcome. LOCATION: Chicago's lakefront, only 10 min. from downtown, steps from gay bars and clubs.

* 55 rooms w/priv. bath, 20 sgl / 31 dbl
* Suites: 4 (1BR), living room, full bath
* Smoking allowed in rooms/suites
* CTV, phone, A/C
* Maid & room service, elevator, paid parking
* Pets: w/prearrangement
* Beach: 3 blocks (mixed)
* Gay Bars: many nearby (walking distance)
* Health Club: nearby
* Airport: O'Hare Int'l, 10 mi. / 16 km
* Metro: Diversey, Howard Dan Ryan Line 5 blocks
* Reservations: CC# guarantee or deposit
* Cancellation: 24 hrs. in advance
* Credit Cards: MC/VISA/AMEX/DC/DISC
* Open: Year round
* Rates: $79-$99 w/CB. Tax: 14.9%. *TAC:* 10%
* Check in time 2pm / check out 11am

DESCRIPTION: Small and intimate 19th century Parisian style boutique hotel, decorated with French impressionist oil paintings and period wall coverings. Newspaper delivered to your room daily. Full room service available. *IGTA*.

INDIANA

SOUTH BEND

INDIANAPOLIS

◆ **Population:** 5,500,000
◆ **Capital:** Indianapolis
◆ **Time Zone:** Eastern/Central
◆ **No Sodomy Law**
◆ **Legal drinking age:** 21

INDIANAPOLIS   ℭ 317

✈ Indianapolis Int'l Airport (IND)

LOCATION: In central Indiana.

POPULATION: 775,000

CLIMATE: Continental and variable climate. Summers are warm and humid with July average of 75°F (24°c); winters are moderately cold with a January average of 28°F (-2°c). Pleasant springs and falls.

VISITOR INFORMATION
The Indianapolis City Center
Tel: (317) 237-5200

Gay/Lesbian Information Service
(317) 253-4297

DESCRIPTION: Indianapolis is the state capital and the largest city in Indiana. This Mid-Western town is a major grain and cattle market. In spite of its agricultural image, Indianapolis is also associated with sports. It is the hometown of the famous annual 500 mi.

(805 km) automobile race at the Indianapolis Motor Speedway, and has some of the best amateur sports facilities. Purdue University, the home of the Indiana University Medical Center is a world pioneer in medical research.

Visit: **State Capitol**; City Market - renovated market place with ethnic foods, 222 E. Market St.; **Union Station**; **Hoosier Dome**, 200 S. Capitol; **Indiana State Museum**, 202 N. Alabama St. (232-1637); **Indianapolis Museum of Art**, 1200 W. 38th St., (923-1331); **Indianapolis Zoo**, in downtown 1200 W. Washington (638-8072).

BARS Y RESTAURANTS ¶¶

● Bars/Clubs (GM): **Boing**, every Sunday night at the Vogue, 6259 College Ave.; **Five O One Tavern**, country style, 501 N. College Ave. (632-2100); **Metro**, restaurant & nightclub, 707 Massachusetts Ave. (639-6022); **Our Place**, cruise bar, 231 E. 16th (638-8138); **Unicorn**, male dancers, 122 W. 13th St., (262-9195).

● Bars/Clubs (GMW): **Brother's Bar & Grill**, 822 N. Illinois (636-1020); **The Ten**, 1218 N. Pennsylvania St. (638-5802); **Tomorrow's**, bar/restaurant, 2301 N. Meridian (925-1710).

● Bar/Club (GW): **151 Club**, dance club, exotic female dancers, 151 W. 14th St. (767-1707).

● Restaurants (GMW): **Brother's Bar & Grille**, 822 N. Illinois (636-1020); **Jimmy's**, 924 No. Pennsylvania (638-9039); **Varsity**, 1517 N. Pennsylvania (635-9998). Other (AW): **Key West Shrimp House**, seafood, nautical decor, 2861 Madison Ave. (787-5353); **Maxi**, Northern Italian, 36 S. Pennsylvania (631-6294).

λ SERVICES λ

● Erotica (GMW): **Gay Emporium**, videos, magazines, 115 N. New Jersey St.

● Health Clubs (GM): **Club Indianapolis**, sauna, gym, videos, 620 N. Capitol (635-5796); **The Works**, sauna, gym, videos, 4120 N. Keystone Ave. (547-9210).

● Personal Phone Line (GM): **❍ Indianapolis Confidential Connection**, meet local guys! Record, listen, respond to ads free (791-1234) free access code 8060.

● Publication (GMW): **❍ Outlines**, out & about Indiana for gay men and lesbians, 133 W.

Market St. #105, Indianapolis, IN 46204. (317) 574-0615. Fax: (317) 574-0228.

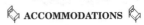

ACCOMMODATIONS

EMBASSY SUITES DOWNTOWN
110 West Washington St., Indianapolis, IN 46202. Tel: (317) 236-1800. TYPE: *Suite hotel*. CLIENTELE: Mostly Straight. LOCATION: Near the Hoosier Dome, 2 blocks from Market Square.

* Suites: 360 all with private bath
* CTV, phone, minibar, microwave
* Wheelchair access
* Restaurant, lounge
* Pool, whirlpool, sauna, steam room
* Retail shopping mall, free parking
* Gay Bars: 15 minutes
* Airport: 7 miles (11km), free transfer
* Credit Cards: MC/VISA/AMEX
* Season: Year round
* Rates: $110-$160 w/full breakfast
* *TAC:* 10%

DESCRIPTION: All suite hotel with semiformal furnishings and 18 story atrium lobby with waterfall and trees.

HILTON AT THE CIRCLE
31 W. Ohio, P.O. Box 1966, Indianapolis, IN 46204. Tel; (317) 635-2000. TYPE: *Hotel*. CLIENTELE: Mostly Straight. LOCATION: At Monument Circle 2 blocks to all the sports arenas. 371 rooms w/priv. bath, 45 suites, CTV, phone, A/C, restaurant, health club, pool. Gay bars: 15 min. Airport: 8 mi. / 13 km. Rates: on request. DESCRIPTION: Superior first class hotel with distinctive rooms and fine amenities.

RAMADA INN DOWNTOWN
501 Washington St., Indianapolis, IN 46204. Tel: (317) 635-4443. TYPE: *Motor hotel*. CLIENTELE: Mostly Straight. LOCATION: At the State Capital and Convention Center. 232 w/priv. bath, CTV, phone, restaurant, pool, parking. Gay bars: 15 min. Airport: 7 mi. / 11 km. Rates: on request. DESCRIPTION: Conveniently located motor hotel, recently renovated.

SOUTH BEND   ✆ 219

✈ Michiana Regional Airport (SBN)
4 mi. / 6 km NW

LOCATION: North central Indiana, east of Chicago and Lake Michigan.

POPULATION: South Bend - 285,000
                  Mishawaka - 42,000

CLIMATE: see Chicago

DESCRIPTION: South Bend is the home of the **University of Notre Dame**. Its industrial image is balanced with parks and nature trails. The **East Race Waterway** in downtown is one of the few man made whitewater raceways in the world. Kamm's Island Inn, a gay guest house in Mishawaka, is only a short distance away.

BARS Y RESTAURANTS 🍴

● Bars/Clubs (GMW): **Seahorse II**, dance bar, cabaret, 1902 Western Ave. (237-9139); **Starz**, dance/show bar, 1505 Kendall (288-7827); **Truman's**, nightclub, piano bar, 100 N. Center at the **Kamm's Island Inn** (see description below) (259-2282).

● Restaurants (AW): **The Carriage House**, elegant dining in a converted 1850's church, Continental, 24460 Adams Rd., (272-9220); **Tippecanoe Place**, fine dining in a restored Mansion, some antiques, steaks & seafood, 620 W Washington St. (234-9077).

λ SERVICES λ

● Erotica (GM): **Pleasureland Museum**, 918 S. Michigan St. (288-9797); **Pleasureland**, 114 Mishawaka Ave. (259-6776).

 ACCOMMODATIONS 🔑

KAMM's ISLAND INN
100 N. Center, Box 35, Mishawaka, IN 46544. Tel: (219) 256-1501 or (800) 955-5266. TYPE: *Motel*. HOST: Ginger Gravenor. CLIENTELE: Gay men & women. LOCATION: In Mishawaka's historical Kamm's Brewery near South Bend.

* Rooms: 28 w/priv. bath
* Phone, CTV, A/C, C/H
* Cooking Facilities, Maid Service
* Wheelchair Accessibility
* Bar & Disco: **Truman's**
* Free Parking, Pets w/prearrangement
* Gay Bars: nearby
* Airport: 8 mi. / 13 km
* Credit Cards: MC/VISA/AMEX/DISC
* Season: Year round
* Rates: $37.50-$95

DESCRIPTION: Motel & Chicago style entertainment complex.

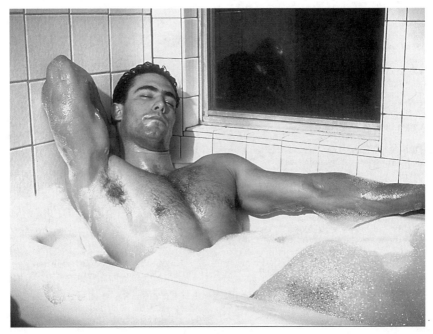

LOUISIANA

◆ **Population:** 4,300,000
◆ **Capital:** Baton Rouge
◆ **Time Zone:** Central
◆ **Sodomy Law**
◆ **Legal drinking age:** 18

BATON ROUGE ✆ 504

✈ Metropolitan Airport (BTR) 8 mi. NE

LOCATION: About 100 miles / 160 km northwest of New Orleans.

POPULATION: 500,000 (metropolitan)

CLIMATE: See New Orleans

DESCRIPTION: The historic Capital City and gateway to Louisiana's famous **Cajun Country** (west of the city) and **Plantation Country** (north of the city). The name Baton Rouge in French refers to the red stick which marked the boundary between two Indian tribes. Explore the city's famous 'southern hospitality' and sample a true 'flavor' of Louisiana. Visit the **State Capitol Building** and 'Catfish Town', a huge covered market with dozens of shops and restaurants located on Government Street.

❖ **SPECIAL EVENT: Spanish Town Mardi Gras Parade**, fun parade with gay & lesbian groups participating, end of February.

BARS ⅄ RESTAURANTS 🍴

● Bars/clubs (GM): **Blue Parrot**, 450 Oklahoma St. (267-4211); **Buddies**, 450 Oklahoma St. (346-1191); **George's**, party club, 860 St. Louis (387-9798); **Hideaway**, 7367 Exchange Pl. (923-3632); **Mirror Lounge**, 111 3rd St. (387-9797); **Time Zone**,7th & Main (344-9714); **Traditions**, 2183 Highland Rd. (344-9291).

● Bar/club (GMW): **Argon**, 2160 Highland Rd. (336-4900).

● Restaurants (AW): **The Chinese Restaurant**, elegant Chinese, 1710 Nicholson Dr. (387-9443); **Don's**, Seafood & Steakhouse, 6823 Airline Hwy. (357-0601); **Mulate's**, famous Cajun restaurant with live Cajun music, 8322 Bluebonnet Rd. (767-4794); **Ralph & Kacoo's**, largest seafood restaurant in the south, Bluebonnet at I-10 (766-2113).

🔖 **ACCOMMODATIONS** 🔖

GENERAL LAFAYETTE MOTEL
427 Lafayette St., Baton Rouge, LA 70802. Tel: (504) 387-0421. TYPE: *Motel*. CLIENTELE: Mostly Straight. LOCATION: Downtown just off the Mississippi River, near Capitol. 137 rooms. DESCRIPTION: Superior tourist class motel in a convenient location.

NEW ORLEANS ✆ 504

✈ Moisant Int'l Airport (MSY)

LOCATION: Near the Gulf of Mexico, on a 5 mile (8km) strip between the Mississippi River and Lake Pontchartrain.

POPULATION: 581,000.

CLIMATE: Subtropical, tempered and moistened by the Gulf winds. Summers are hot and humid with average highs in the 90°sF (32°c). Winters are rainy with lows in the 40°sF (7°c). Spring and fall are pleasant with temperatures in the mid 60°sF (18°c). Humidity averages 76% for the year.

Gay/Lesbian Visitor Information
L&G Community Center: 522-1103

DESCRIPTION: New Orleans is a city of Jazz and Mardi Gras. The famous 18th century **Vieux Carré** (French Quarter) is a popular tourist destination with honky-tonk bars, boutiques, restaurants and cabarets. Visit: **Riverwalk**, shopping mall complex; **Jackson Brewery**, renovated beer brewery with restaurants and speciality shops; **The Esplanade** - fashionable shopping center in the Louisiana World Exposition style near the airport.

The city of Blanche DuBois has a spicy gay nightlife right on **Bourbon St.** in the heart of the **"French Quarter"** to match its famous Cajun cuisine. New Orleans is the birthplace of the Jazz. Check out **Preservation Hall** at 726 Peter St., for authentic New Orleans Jazz.

❖ **SPECIAL EVENTS: Bayou Women's Tennis Tournament**, GLTA tennis tournament, October 20-22 (482-4807); **Mardi Gras Celebrations**, officially opens two weeks before Fat Tuesday, Mardi Gras starts the day before lent begins, mid to end of February; **Jazz & Heritage Festival**, rhythm and blues Festival, last weekend of april.

BARS ♈ RESTAURANTS 🍴

● Bars/clubs (GM): **Bears & Boots**, male strippers, 2601 Royal & Franklin (945-7006); **Bourbon Pub**, cruise bar, 801 Bourbon St. (529-2107); **Cafe Lafitte in Exile**, video bar open 24 hrs. 901 Bourbon St. (561-6724); **Corner Pocket**, male strippers, 24 hrs, 940 St. Louis (568-9829); **Double Play**, 439 Dauphine (523-4517); **Full Moon**, 424 Destrehan Harvey (341-4396); **Golden Lantern**, 1239 rue Royale (529-2860); **Good Friends**, popular happy hour, 740 Dauphine (566-7199); **Oz**, male strippers, 800 Bourbon St. (593-9491); **Parade**, New Orleans largest gay dance club, erotic performances,803 St. Ann corner of Bourbon St., (529-2107); **Phoenix**, cruise bar, 941 Elysian Fields Ave., (945-9264); **Rawhide**, leather levi cruise bar, 740 Burgundy St. (525-8106); **Sterling Club**, 700 Burgundy (522-1962); **Wolfendale's**, mostly African-American clientele, male strippers and drag shows, 834 N. Rampart (524-5749); **Ziggies**, 718 No. Rampart St. (566-7559).

● Bars/clubs (GMW): **Angles**,2301 N, Causeway, Metairie (948-6288); **Big Daddy's**, 2513 Royal (948-6288); **Country Club**, 634 Louisa St. (open Summer only) 2 bars, hot tub (944-6452); **Footloose**, dance club, entertainment, 700 N. Rampart (524-7654); **Mint**, bar, entertainment, 504 Esplanade (525-2000); **MRB**, male erotic dancers, 515 Philip St. (586-064); **Phoenix**, levi/leather bar, Men's Room bar upstairs, 941 Elysian Fields (945-9264).

● Bars/club (GW): **Charlene's**, oldest lesbian club in town, 940 Elysian Field (945-9328).

● Restaurants (AW): **Arnaud's**, french / Creole menu, wine bar, Sun Jazz brunch, 813 rue Bienville, French Quarter (581-4422); **Bayona**, Mediterranean cuisine, 430 rue Dauphine (525-4455); **Bayou Ridge Cafe**, casual dining, 437 Esplanade Ave. (949-9912); **Cafe Lafayette**, Cajun cuisine, 717 Orleans St. (571-4655); **Cafe Marigny**, gourmet coffees and pastries, 1913 rue Royale (945-4472); **Cafe Sbisa**, Sunday Jazz brunch, 1011 rue Decatur (522-5565); **Quarter Scene**, open 24 hrs, 900 Dumaine at Dauphine (522-6533); **Sebastian's Little Garden**, 538 St. Philip St. (524-2041); **Versaille**, French, Creole cuisine, wine cellar, 2100 St. Charles Ave. (524-2535).

λ SERVICES λ

● Cinema (GM): **Cine Royale Theatre**, all male X-Rated films, 921 Canal St. (524-9111).

● Health Clubs (GM): **The Club** , sauna, gym, videos, 24 hrs., 515 Toulouse (581-2402); **Midtowne Spa**, 24 hrs, 700 Baronne St., (566-1442).

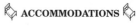 ACCOMMODATIONS

CHATEAU HOTEL
1001 Chartres St., New Orleans, LA 70116. Tel: (504) 524-9636. Fax: (504) 525-2989. TYPE: *Hotel*. CLIENTELE: All Welcome. LOCATION: French Quarter.

* Rooms: 45 w/priv. bath
* Suites: 6 individually decorated
* CTV (CNN), phone, A/C, hairdryer
* Wheelchair access, limited room service
* Poolside cafe, bar, outdoor pool, parking
* Gay bars: walking distance
* Airport: 30 min.
* Open: Year round
* Rates: $79-$150
* Tax: 11%
* *TAC:* 10%

DESCRIPTION: Stylish motor hotel in an historic building. Good service & amenities.

FRENCH MARKET INN
501 Decatur St., New Orleans, LA 70130. Tel: (504) 561-5621. Fax: (504) 566-0160. TYPE: *Boutique Inn*. CLIENTELE: All Welcome. LOCATION: French Quarter, 3 blocks from Bourbon Street.

* Rooms: 68 w/priv. bath
* CTV (movies), phone, A/C

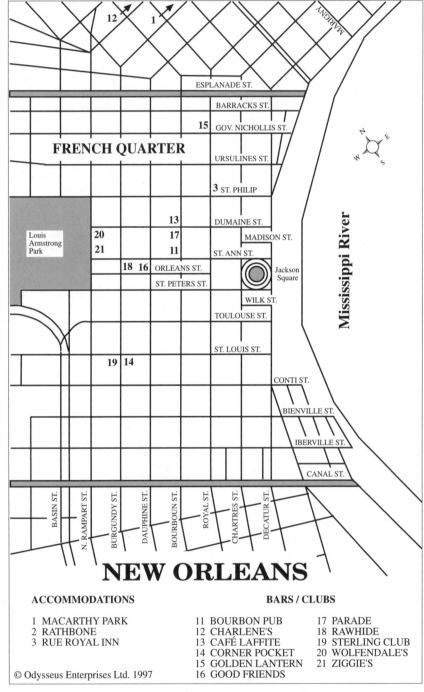

ESPLANADE ST.

BARRACKS ST.

15 GOV. NICHOLLIS ST.

FRENCH QUARTER

URSULINES ST.

3 ST. PHILIP

13 DUMAINE ST.

20   17   MADISON ST.

21   11   ST. ANN ST.

Louis Armstrong Park

18 16 ORLEANS ST.

ST. PETERS ST.

Jackson Square

WILK ST.

TOULOUSE ST.

ST. LOUIS ST.

19 14

CONTI ST.

BIENVILLE ST.

IBERVILLE ST.

CANAL ST.

Mississippi River

BASIN ST.
N. RAMPART ST.
BURGUNDY ST.
DAUPHINE ST.
BOURBOUN ST.
ROYAL ST.
CHARTRES ST.
DECATUR ST.

NEW ORLEANS

ACCOMMODATIONS

1 MACARTHY PARK
2 RATHBONE
3 RUE ROYAL INN

© Odysseus Enterprises Ltd. 1997

BARS / CLUBS

11 BOURBON PUB
12 CHARLENE'S
13 CAFÉ LAFFITE
14 CORNER POCKET
15 GOLDEN LANTERN
16 GOOD FRIENDS

17 PARADE
18 RAWHIDE
19 STERLING CLUB
20 WOLFENDALE'S
21 ZIGGIE'S

* Maid service, parking, priv. courtyard
* Gay bars: walking distance
* Airport: 15 mi. / 24 km
* Open: Year round
* Rates: $78-$150
* *TAC:* 10%

DESCRIPTION: Charming boutique Inn. All rooms and suites in 18th century decor.

LANDMARK
FRENCH QUARTER HOTEL
920 North Rampart St., New Orleans, LA 70116. Tel: (504) 524-3333 or (800) 535-7862. Fax: (504) 522-8044. TYPE: *Hotel.* LOCATION: French Quarter corner of St. Philip St. walk to restaurants, shops and attractions.

* Rooms: 100 w/priv. bath
  sgl 21 / double 79
* Rooms for smokers and non smokers
* CTV, phone, refrigerator, safe box, A/C
* Maid, room, laundry service, wheelchair access, elevator, paid parking, pool
* Restaurant: **Jazz Garden** (breakfast only)
* Bar: **Jazz Alley** - creole deli style sandwiches
* Beach: 1 hour
* Gay Bars: 3 blocks
* Health Club: 3 blocks (mixed)
* Airport: 30 - 45 minutes
* Languages: English, French, Spanish & Russian
* Reservation: CC# guarantee
* Cancellation: 48 hrs
* Credit Cards: MC/VISA/AMEX/DC/DISC
* Open: Year round
* Rates: $89-$135; (off) $69-$135
* Tax: 11% + $1 occupancy tax
* Check in time 3pm / check out 12 noon
* *TAC:* up to 10%

DESCRIPTION: Quaint European style hotel with an ambiance you'll never forget. Recently renovated spacious rooms and lobby. Beautiful courtyard with luscious pool that lights up at night.

✪ MACARTY PARK
3820 Burgundy St., New Orleans, LA 70117-5708. Tel: (504) 943-4994. Toll Free (800) 521-2790. Fax: (504) 943-4999. TYPE: *Guest House.* HOST: John, owner. CLIENTELE: Mostly gay men & women. LOCATION: 5 min. to French Quarter.

* Rooms: 8 w/priv. bath (1 w/jacuzzi)
  6 dbl / 1 triple/ 1 quad
* Smoking allowed in rooms
* CTV, phone, refrigerator (some rooms)
  C/H, A/C, cooking facilities (some rooms)

Rue Royal Inn

Economical units to large balcony suites with jacuzzi.
$60 - $125

800-776-3901
Fax 504-558-0566

* Suite (1), Cottage (2) 1BR (3) w/living room, full bath, kitchen, patio/terrace
* Bed Types: twin, double, king size, queen size, 4 poster
* Maid service, free parking (off street)
* Pets: w/prearrangement only
* Pool, sundeck, gym, clothing optional policy
* Beach: 1 hr. (mixed)
* Gay Bars: 2 minutes
* Health Club: 5 minutes (mixed)
* Airport: 20 min. / 15 mi.
* Train Station: Amtrak, 10 min.
* Languages: English, French
* Reservations: 1 night deposit
* Cancellation: 7 days for full refund
* Credit Cards: MC/VISA/AMEX
* Rates: $59 - $115; (off) $45-$115 w/Expanded CB
* Tax: 11% + $1
* Check in time 2pm / check out 12 noon
* *TAC:* 10%

DESCRIPTION: Classic Victorian guesthouse in a National Historic District of New Orleans. Beautiful bright guest rooms and fully equipped cottages furnished primarily in antique, reproduction and traditional style accented by beautiful collection of art. Relax, swim, party, and play in the in ground heated pool 24 hrs a day.

✪ RATHBONE INN
1227 Esplanade Ave., New Orleans, LA 70116. Tel: (504) 947-2100 or (800) 947-2101. Fax: (504) 947-7454. TYPE: *Guest House.* HOST: Bob & Dick. LOCATION: On Esplanade Avenue, 1-1/2 blocks outside the French Quarter.

* Rooms: 9 w/priv. bath; Suites: 2 sgl 5; dbl 5; triple 4.
* Smoking allowed, cooking facilities
* A/C, C/H, balcony, CTV (in room), phone,
* Garden, free parking;
* Pets: w/prearrangement
* Gay Bars: 8 blocks
* Health Club: 12 blocks
* Airport: 20 mi. / 32 km
* reservations: 1 night deposit
* Cancellation: 48 hrs. notice
* Credit Cards: MC/VISA/AMEX/DC/EC
* Open: Year round
* Rates: $75-$125
* *TAC:* 10%

DESCRIPTION: Restored 1850's Greek Revival style mansion. All rooms have kitchenettes, some have interesting architectural details and high ceilings.

✪ RUE ROYAL INN
1006 Royal St., New Orleans, LA 70116. Tel: (504) 524-3900 or (800) 776-3901. Fax: (504) 558-0566. TYPE: *Guest House.* HOST: Bob Feldman & Dick Mole. CLIENTELE: Equal Gay/Straight. LOCATION: Heart of the French Quarter. Corner of Royal and St. Philip Sts.

* Rooms: 17 w/priv. bath. Suite: 1 sgl 6; dbl 6; triple 11. Smoking allowed
* CTV, phone, A/C, C/H, Cooking Facilities
* Business phone/fax facilities
* Maid service
* Parking (paid), security
* Pets: w/prearrangement
* Gay Bars: 2 blocks
* Health Club: 6 blocks
* Airport: 20 mi. / 32 km, taxi, limo
* Train Station: 2 mi. / 3 km
* Reservations: 1 night deposit
* Cancellation: 48 hrs. notice
* Credit Cards: MC/VISA/AMEX/DISC/DC
* Open: Year round
* Rates: $60 - $125
* *TAC:* 10%

DESCRIPTION: Historic Creole townhouse. Accommodations range from economical courtyard units to large balcony suites with jacuzzi tub. All units have small refrigerators.

MAINE

PORTLAND

OGUNQUIT

- ◆ **Population:** 2,126,000
- ◆ **Capital:** Augusta
- ◆ **Time Zone:** Eastern
- ◆ **No Sodomy Law**
- ◆ **Legal drinking age:** 20

OGUNQUIT   ✆ 207

✈ Portland Int'l Jet Port (PWM) in Portland (ME) (40 mi. / 64 km); or Logan Int'l Airport (BOS) in Boston (MA) (65 mi. / 104 km)

LOCATION: 69 mi. / 110 km north of Boston (MA), and 30 mi. / 48 km south of Portland.

POPULATION: 1,500

CLIMATE: Continental. January temperature is 30°F (-1°c), and in July 75°F (24°c).

DESCRIPTION: Ogunquit is a popular summer resort, especially among artists. It has 3 long miles / 5 km of sandy beaches, and a mile of rocky shore to the south. The town has craft shops, galleries, and restaurants.

BARS ▼ RESTAURANTS ▮▮

● Bars/clubs (GMW): **The Club**, 52 Main Street, bar, restaurant and disco catering to gay men (646-6655); **Front Porch**, piano bar, Ogunquit Square (646-3976); **Maxwell's Pub**, 27 Main St. (6460-2345).

● Restaurants (AW): **The Lobster Shack**, Perkins Cove (646-2941), or the **Ogunquit Lobster Pond**, Rte. 1 North, (646-2271). **Black Swan**, Rte. 1 North (646-4811).

ACCOMMODATIONS

CLIPPER SHIP
P.O. Box 236, Ogunquit, ME 03907. Tel: (207) 646-9735. TYPE: *Bed & Breakfast.* CLIENTELE: Gay/Straight. LOCATION: 1 block from center of town. 30 rooms.

LEISURE INN
6 School St., Box 2113, Ogunquit, ME 03907-2113. Tel: (207) 646-2737. TYPE: *Guest House.* LOCATION: In town. 10 rooms.

OGUNQUIT HOUSE
7 Kings Hwy., Box 1883, Ogunquit, ME 03907. Tel: (207) 646-2967. TYPE: *Bed & Breakfast.* CLIENTELE: Gay/Straight. LOCATION: At the edge of town. 10 rooms.

PORTLAND   ✆ 207

✈ Portland Int'l Jet Port (PWM)

LOCATION: Along the Willamette River on Casco Bay at Southeast ME.

DESCRIPTION: The "City of Roses", Portland is known for its beauty, quality of life, and conservation of historical sites and monuments.

BARS ▼ RESTAURANTS ▮▮

● Bars/clubs (GMW): **Blackstones**, 6 Pine St., (772-9244); **Chart Room Saloon**, mostly men, 117 Spring St. (774-9262); **Limelight**, dance club, 3 Spring St. (773-3315); **Woodfords Cafe**, cafe & bar, 129 Spring St. (772-1374).

● Restaurant (AW): **Atwater**, 360° panoramic view of the town, 30th fl. of US Bancorp Tower, 111 SW 5th Ave. expensive (220-3600).

ACCOMMODATIONS

HOLIDAY INN - Downtown
88 Spring St., Portland, ME 04101. Tel: (207) 775-2311. TYPE: *Hotel.* CLIENTELE: All Welcome. LOCATION: Downtown near gay bars. 246 rooms w/priv. bath, CTV, phone, fitness center, pool, sauna. Rates: $90-$130. *TAC:* 10%. DESCRIPTION: First class hotel.

MARYLAND

BALTIMORE

ANNAPOLIS

DC

◆ **Population:** 4,250,000
◆ **Capital:** Annapolis
◆ **Time Zone:** Eastern
◆ **Sodomy Law**
◆ **Legal drinking age:** 21

ANNAPOLIS   ℰ   301

✈ Baltimore-Washington Int'l Airport(BWI)

LOCATION: About 25 mi. / 40 km south of Baltimore on the Chesapeake Bay.

POPULATION: 32,000

CLIMATE: see Baltimore

`DESCRIPTION**: The Capital of Maryland, the 'Jewel on the Chesapeake' and the home of the **Naval Academy**, Annapolis is a fascinating town with more than 300 years of history.

BARS ▼ RESTAURANTS 🍴

● For gay bars and restaurants travel to Baltimore or Washington D.C. about 30-45 min. away.

● Restaurants (AW): **Busch's Chesapeake Inn**, seafood, 321 Revell Hwy. (757-1717); **Cafe Normandie**, French style cafe, seafood, Maryland Crab dishes, 195 Main St. (263-3382); **Carol's Creek Cafe**, specialize in local seafood, 410 Severn Ave., Eastport (263-8102).

✥ ACCOMMODATIONS ✥

ANNAPOLIS MARRIOTT WATERFRONT
80 Compromise St., Annapolis MD 21401. Tel: (301) 268-7555. Fax: (301) 269-5864. TYPE: *Hotel*. CLIENTELE: Mostly Straight. LOCATION: Downtown waterfront on the Annapolis Harbor, one block from the historic district.

* Rooms: 150 w/priv. bath. Suite: 1
* CTV, phone, A/C
* Restaurant, cafe, entertainment
* Airport: 20 mi. / 32 km, taxi, shuttle
* Gay Bars: 30 mi. / 48 km
* Credit Cards: MC/VISA/AMEX/JCB
* Open: Year round
* Rates: $115 - $270
* **TAC:** 10%

DESCRIPTION: Annapolis' only waterfront hotel offering high standard accommodations and fine service. Walk to the Naval Academy, antique Shops, galleries and restaurants.

BALTIMORE   ℰ   301

✈ Baltimore-Washington Int'l AP (BWI)

LOCATION: 45 miles / 72 km northeast of Washington D.C. on Chesapeake Bay.

POPULATION: City 786,800
                         Metro 2,175,000

CLIMATE: Mild weather influenced by the Chesapeake Bay and the Ocean. Late summer and early fall is marked by hurricanes and severe thunderstorms. January average is 33˚F (1˚c), and July average is 77˚F (25˚c). Annual rainfall is 40" (1016 mm), and annual snowfall is 22" (55 cm).

Gay/Lesbian Visitor Information
G&L Community Center: 837-5445

DESCRIPTION: Baltimore is Maryland's largest city and the home town of Francis Scott Key the author of "The Star-Spangled Banner". It is a modern financial, industrial and fishing center, yet unlike neighboring Washington, D.C., it has a provincial, down to earth charm.

Discover the **Inner Harbor** with its art buildings, shops, restaurants and cafes. For a panoramic view of the city and the port visit the **World Trade Center** observation deck.

Visit: **Star-Spangled Banner Flag House** and the **1812 War Museum**, 844 E. Pratt St.; The house has been restored in authentic Federal period style and displays a replica of the original flag; **Washington Monument**, Charles & Monument Sts.; **Edgar Allan Poe House**; the **National Aquarium**, pier 3 at Pratt St., unique display of tropical rain forest, Atlantic coral reef, and exotic fishes.

BARS ♈ RESTAURANTS 🍴

● Bars/clubs (GM): **Allegro's**, video dance club, 1101 Cathedral St., (837-3906); **Atlantis**, male strippers, 615 The Fallsway (727-9909); **Baltimore Eagle**, Leather/levi cruise bar, 2022 No. Charles St. (823-2453); **Central Station**, video bar/restaurant, 1001 No. Charles St., (752-7133); **Drinkery**, 205 W. W. Read St. (669-9820); **Hippo**, video bar, 1 West Eager St. (547-0069); **Lynn's**,774 Washington Blvd. (727-8924); **Park Sportsman Bar**, 412 Park Ave. (727-8935); **P.T. Max**, cruisy levi/leather bar and restaurant, 1735 Maryland Ave. (539-6965); **Senator**, 614 N. Howard St., quiet bar for older gay men (727-9620); **Stagecoach**, piano bar, 1003 N. Charles St. (547-0107); **Unicorn**, gay pub, 2218 Boston St. (342-8344); **Zippers**, 519 Gorsuch Ave. (366-9006).

● Bars/clubs (GMW): **Mardi Gras**, 228 Park Ave, (727-8878); **P.T. Max / The Gallery**, dance club, videos, drag shows, Maryland Ave. (539-6965).

● Restaurants (GMW): **Acropolis**, Greek cuisine, 4714-4718 Eastern Ave. (675-3384); **The Buttery**, 1 E. Centre St. (837-2494); **Cafe Diana**, coffee house, 3215 N. Charles St. (889-1319); **Central Station**, 1001 N. Charles St. (752-7133); **City Cafe**, 1001 Cathedral St. (539-4252); **The Gallery**, studio restaurant, from fried chicken to backfin crab cakes, Sunday brunch, 1735 Maryland Ave. (539-6965); **Louie's**, 518 N. Charles St. (962-1225); **Mount Vernon Stable & Saloon**, 909 N. Charles St. (685-7427). Others (AW): **CoChin**, Vietnamese,

800 No. Charles St. (332-0332); **Cultured Pearl Cafe**, Mexican cuisine, 1114 Hollins St. (837-1947); **L'École**, 19-21 Gay St., part of the International Culinary Arts Institute, run by its students, specializes in Maryland seafood, (752-1446); **Thai Restaurant**, seafood specialty, 1032 Light St., at Inner Harbor (539-5611).

λ SERVICES λ

● Community Center (GMW): **Gay & Lesbian Community Center**, for events and activities call the G&L Switchboard, 241 W. Chase St., (837-5445).

● Personal Phone Line (GM): ✪ **Baltimore Confidential Connection**, meet local guys! Record, listen, respond to ads free (653-6900) free access code 8060.

● Publication (GMW): ✪ **Baltimore Gay Paper**, #1 Gay & Lesbian paper in Maryland, P.O. Box 22575, Baltimore, MD 21203. (410) 837-7748. Fax: (410) 837-8512.

 ACCOMMODATIONS

MOUNT VERNON HOTEL
24 W. Franklin St., Baltimore MD 21201. Tel: (410) 727-2000. Fax: (410) 576-9300. TYPE: *Hotel.* CLIENTELE: All Welcome. LOCATION: Historic Mt. Vernon, 8 blocks from the Inner Harbor (trolley service). 189 rooms, CTV, phone, A/C. DESCRIPTION: Tourist class 9-story hotel operated by the Baltimore Int'l Culinary College. Nice rooms, great service and a central location. Easy walk to the Inner Harbor and all the gay clubs.

TREMONT HOTEL
8 E. Pleasant St., Baltimore MD 21202. Tel: (410) 576-1200. Fax: (410) 685-4215. TYPE: *All Suite Hotel.* CLIENTELE: All Welcome. LOCATION: 6 blocks from Inner Harbor, near the gay scene. 60 suites, DESCRIPTION: Fully equipped suites with kitchenettes and special amenities.

MASSACHUSETTS

● BOSTON
P'TOWN ●

◆ **Population:** 5,750,000
◆ **Capital:** Boston
◆ **Time Zone:** Eastern
◆ **No Sodomy Law**
◆ **Legal drinking age:** 21

BOSTON   © 617

✈ Logan Int'l Airport (BOS)

LOCATION: On the Atlantic Ocean and the Boston Harbor, at the mouth of the Charles and Majestic Rivers.

POPULATION: City 563,000;
                   Metro 2,763,000

CLIMATE: The seasons in Boston are distinct. Summers are warm with a July average of 75°F (24°c). Winters can be cold and snowy with a January average of 29°F (-2°c). Spring and fall are mild to crispy cool. Rain is plentiful with annual rainfall of 43" (1075 mm), and snowfall of 42" (1.05 m) annually.

Gay/Lesbian Visitor Information
G&L Community Center: 247-2927

DESCRIPTION: Boston is the Capital of Massachusetts, and the largest city in New England. It is one of the nation's most vibrant cities and a popular tourist destination. The city presents a fascinating mosaic of a proud past and present where the old mingles with the new.

Boston today is a thriving intellectual and cultural center with many prestigious institutions e.g.: **Harvard University, Massachusetts Inst. of Technology** (M.I.T.), as well as the **Radcliff College** and many others.

Boston is easy to explore by walking. Follow the historic **Freedom Trail** in Boston and the **Heritage Trail** in Cambridge. The **Black Heritage Trail** celebrates the history of Boston's black community between 1800 and 1900. Visit the **Museum of Fine Arts**, the **Symphony Hall**, Museum of **Science**, the **New England Aquarium**, and the Universities. For shopping, dining, and night life rolled in one area, try the **Back Bay** area from Arlington Street to Boston University. Visit the historical sites of **Bunker Hill, Fanenhil Hall, Old North Church,** The **U.S.S. Constitution** and **J.F.K. Library**.

❖ The Boston gay and lesbian community is one of the better organized in the nation. The liberal and tolerant attitude for which the State of Massachusetts' people and politicians are known for, has greatly helped the community to ascertain itself culturally and politically.

BARS ☡ RESTAURANTS 🍴

● Bars/clubs (GM): **Avalon**, dance club, 21 Boylston Place (351-2583); **Boston Eagle**, levi/leather cruise bar, 520 Tremont St. (542-4494); **Campus**, dance club, Thur. for gay men only, 21 Brookline St., Cambridge (864-0400); **Chaps**, dance/cruise bar, 27-31 Huntington Ave. (266-7778); **Chicago Saloon**, video bar, 10 Westland Ave. (536-6396); **Jacques**, drag shows, 79 Broadway (338-9066); **Jox**, sports bar,69 Church St. (423-6969); **Luxor**, video cruise bar, 69 Church St. (423-6969); **Napoleon Club**, 52 Piedmont St. (338-9595); **Paradise**, 180 Mass Ave. (864-4130); **Quest**, dance video bar, 1270 Boylston St. (424-7747); **Ramrod**, levi/leather cruise bar, 1254 Boylston St. (266-2986); **Sporters**, 228 Cambridge St. (742-4084); **Underground**, dance club, 79 Warrenton (542-1981).

● Bars/clubs (GMW): **Club Cabaret**, female impersonators, 209 Columbus Ave. (536-0966); **Playland**, 21 Essex St. (338-7254); **Quest**, 1270 Boylston (424-7747);

● Bar/club (GW): **Esmé**, Sundays for women, 3 Boylston Place (482-7799); **Girl Bar**, Friday night for women at Bobby's, 69 Canal St., (248-9520).

● Restaurants (AW): **Club Cafe**, restaurant and lounge, 209 Columbus Ave. (536-0966);

Downtown Cafe, 12 LaGrange St. (338-7037); Geoffrey's, cafe/bar, 578 Tremont St. (266-1122);La Trattoria, Italian cuisine, 288 Cambridge Street (227-0211); Mario's, 69 Church St. (542-3776); Other (AW) Anthony's Pier 4, seafood restaurant, 140 Northern Ave. (423-6363); St. Botolph, 99 St. Botolph St. (266-3030).

λ SERVICES λ

● Erotica (GMW): Art Cinema, 204 Tremont St. (482-4661); Movie Place, video rentals, 526 Tremont St., (482-9008).

● Health club (GM): Metropolitan Health Club, 209 Columbus Ave. (536-3006); Mike's Gym II, 1A Waltham St. (338-6677); Safari Club, full gym, lockers, private rooms, 90 Wareham St., 2nd fl. (292-0011).

● Maps (GMW): ✪ Columbia Fun Maps, free Gay & Lesbian guide maps to Boston, Los Angeles, San Diego and 63 destinations across the USA, Canada and the US Virgin Islands, 118 E. 28th St., suite #308, New York NY 10016. (212) 447-7877. Fax: (212) 447-7876.

● Personal Phone Line (GM): ✪ Boston Confidential Connection, meet local guys! Record, listen, respond to ads free (494-5454) free access code 8060.

● Reservation Service (GMW): ✪ Just Right Reservations, hotels, inns, and guest houses in Boston, Provincetown, and New York City. Office hours: Mon-Fri 9am-4pm EST. James Koumpouras, managing partner, 18 Piedmont St., 2nd Fl. (423-3550).

ACCOMMODATIONS

✪ OASIS GUEST HOUSE

22 Edgerly Road, Boston, MA 02115. Tel: (617) 267-2262. Fax: (617) 267-1920. TYPE: *Bed & Breakfast*. HOST: Joe Haley. CLIENTELE: Mostly Gay. LOCATION: Back Bay area. Convention Ctr stop on Green Line. Near corner Boylston/Mass. Avenues.

* Rooms: 16; 5 w/shared, 11 w/priv. bath
  2 sgl / 13 dbl/ 1 triple, rooms for non smokers
* CTV, phone, A/C,C/H, balcony, sundeck
* Business fax/phone facilities
* Parking, maid service
* Gay Bars: walking distance
* Health Club: walking (gay)
* Airport: 5 mi. (8 km),taxi, limo, bus
* Reservations: 1 night deposit

* Cancellation: 14 days
* Credit Cards: MC/VISA/AMEX
* Open: Year round
* Rates: $50-$78; (off) $45-$62 w/CB
* *TAC:* 10%

DESCRIPTION: Two renovated Back Bay Townhouses in the heart of Boston. The lobby, living room and outdoor sundecks are handsomely appointed. Walk to museums, shopping, nightlife and restaurants. Fine accommodations for less than major hotels *IGTA, BBBB.*

THE COLONADE
120 Huntington Ave., Boston, MA 02116. Tel: (617) 424-7000. TYPE: *Hotel.* CLIENTELE: All Welcome. LOCATION: Historic Back Bay area.

* Rooms: 288 w/priv. bath. Suites: 11
* CTV, phone, A/C, minibar
* 24 hrs room service
* Restaurant, bar, outdoor cafe
* Rooftop pool, gym,
* Parking garage
* Gay Bars: walking distance
* Airport: 6 mi. / 8 km
* Open: Year round
* Rates: $195-$225
* *TAC:* 10%

DESCRIPTION: Elegant first class hotel.

THE COPLEY HOUSE
239 W. Newton St., Boston, MA 02116. Tel: (617) 236-8300. TYPE: *Hotel.* CLIENTELE: All Welcome. LOCATION: Behind Prudential Center, 2 blocks from Copley Square. 53 studios w/priv. bath, CTV, phone, full kitchen, dining area, 1BR apartments, wheelchair access. Open: Year round. Rates: $85-$100. *TAC:* 10%. DESCRIPTION: Residential-style studios and apartments near clubs, bars and restaurants.

PROVINCETOWN   ✆ 508

✈ Municipal Airport (PVC)

LOCATION: Provincetown is located at the tip of Cape Code, 128 mi. / 204 km southeast of Boston by land, 40 mi. / 64 km by sea.

POPULATION: 3,400 (20,000 in the summer)

CLIMATE: Slightly milder than that of Boston. January average is 33˚F (0˚c), and July 77˚F (25˚c). Rainfall is 40" (1000 mm), snowfall is less than 20" (0.5 m).

Gay/Lesbian Visitor Information
Provincetown Business Guild
Tel: (508) 487-2313 or (800) 637-8696

DESCRIPTION: Provincetown is a beach resort at the tip of Cape Code. Historically it was the first landing place of the pilgrims in 1620. The monument that symbolizes this event stands erect on the town hill. Once a whaling port, the town today is home to a substantial fishing fleet and a thriving art colony. Tourism is the town's main industry with a large share of gay & lesbian travel. Summer is the high season when tourists arrive *en masse* to enjoy the beaches and the town's nightlife.

Miles of white sandy beaches line the harbor and the ocean sides of the peninsula. Along the "Back Shore", from peaked Hill Bars to Race Point, surf coasters find striped bass from May to mid October. A visitor center for Cape Code National Seashore is located at Province Lands, off Race Point Road. Dune buggy tours operate daily from 8:30 am to dusk, charter boats are available too, check locally for details.

Spend summer days leisurely walking up and down **Commercial Street**, checking the shops, cruising the crowds, or join the high energy T-dances at the **Boatslip**. At night there is plenty of excitement in the bars, cabarets or discos. For intimate dining, there are excellent restaurants to choose from.

❖ **TRAVEL SEASON INFORMATION:** Provincetown is basically a summer resort. The season picks up from Memorial Day Weekend (last Monday in May) through Labor Day Weekend (1st Monday in September). Memorial Day Weekend, 4th of July Weekend and Labor Day Weekends are the busiest.

❖ **SPECIAL EVENTS:** August 18-25 is *Carnival* time with shows, parties and lots of fun; October 11 is **Gay & Lesbian Rights Day**; October 18-20 **Women's Weekend** (dates change each year to coincide with the weekend); November 10 celebrating and re-enacting the **landing of the Pilgrims** and lighting up the **Monument** on Thanksgiving Eve. For further information call the **Provincetown Business Guild** (487-2313) or **Just Right Reservations** (617-423-3550).

❖ **HOW TO GET THERE:** By boat (3 hours trip) - from Boston Harbor, leaving Boston at 9:30 am arriving in Provincetown at 12:30 pm. From Provincetown the boat leaves daily at 3:30 pm arriving in Boston Harbor at 6:30 pm. By Air - take **Cape Air** flights from Boston to

142 Bradford Street
Provincetown, MA 02657

800 • 965 • 1801
508 • 487 • 9810

Continental Breakfast

Sun Decks • Ample Parking

One Block from Beach

Spectacular views of
Provincetown Harbor

One Block from Town Center

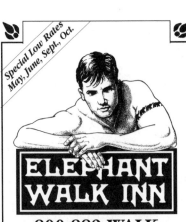

*Special Low Rates
May, June, Sept., Oct.*

ELEPHANT WALK INN

800-889-WALK

Distinctive, Affordable Accommodations
Private Baths • TVs • Fridges
Parking • Sundeck • Breakfast
Optional A/C • Brochure

**156 Bradford Street
Provincetown, MA 02657**
(508) 487-2543   (800) 889-9255

*Accommodations
in the heart of
Provincetown*

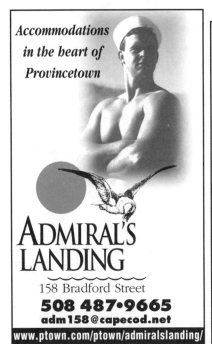

ADMIRAL'S LANDING

158 Bradford Street
508 487•9665
adm158@capecod.net
www.ptown.com/ptown/admiralslanding/

INN & ANNEX
6 DYER • 8 DYER

BENCHMARK INN, debuting
April 1997 promises top-notch comfort
and style. Luxuries include fireplaces,
whirlpool baths, wet bars and stunning
harbor views. **BENCHMARK INN —**
The Best Is For You.

BENCHMARK ANNEX
A cozy, quiet gem with thoughtful
amenities and moderate tariffs –
perfect for your Provincetown getaway
6-8 Dyer Street • 508 487-7440

TOLL FREE 1 888 487-7440
www.CapeCodAccess.com/benchmark/

PROVINCETOWN CENTRAL

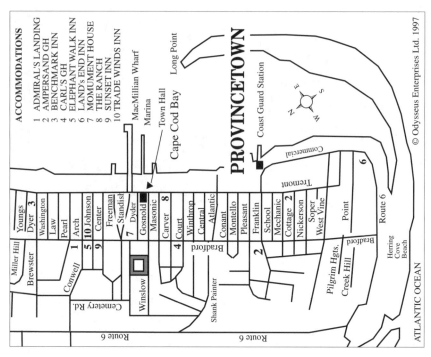

Provincetown and back. The flight takes about 30 minutes.

BARS ♈ RESTAURANTS 🍴

During the summer, Provincetown's gay nightlife is at its best. The bars and clubs close at 1:00 am.

● Bars/Clubs (GM): **The Boatslip**, bar/lounge/ restaurant and P'town's legendary T-Dance daily at the beach front pool, 161 Commercial St. (487-1669); **Atlantic House**, bar/disco, 4-6 Masonic Place (487-3821); **Backstreet**, bar/disco, at the Gifford House, 9-11 Carver St., (487-0688); **Crown & Anchor**, cabaret, disco and leather club, 247 Commercial St.

● Bar/Club (GMW): **Love Shack**, 67 Shack Painter Rd. (487-4444); **Post Office Cabaret**, bar/lounge, top-name entertainment, 303 Commercial St. (487-3892); **Tavern at the Red Inn**, 15 Commercial St. (487-0050).

● Bar/Club (GW): **Pied Piper**, disco, T-dances, 193 Commercial St., (487-1527).

● Restaurants (GMW): **The Boatslip**, Ameri-

can cuisine, seafood specialties, view of the harbor, 161 Commercial St. (487-1669); **Cafe Blase**, sidewalk cafe, 328 Commercial St. (487-9465); **Fat Jack's**, fine dinning, casual ambience, 335 Commercial St. (487-4822); **Front Street**, Continental, 230 Commercial St. (487-9715); **Landmark Inn**, seafood, intimate dining, 404 Commercial St. (487-9319); **The Martin House**, intimate dining in a restored 18th century house, 157 Commercial St. (487-2276); **The Moors**, American/Portuguese, Bradford St. (487-0840); **Napi's**, seafood, vegetarian, 7 Freeman St. (487-1145); **Post Office Cafe**, casual, economic, 303 Commercial St. (487-3892).

λ SERVICES λ

● Clothing (GMW): **Don't Panic**, large selection of original T-shirts and sweat shirts, 192 Commercial St. #4 (487-1280).

● Gifts (GMW): **Pride's**, books, clothing, 182 Commercial St. (487-1127); **Recovering Hearts**, books and gifts, 4 Standish St. (487-4875); **Zeus Limited**, collectables and decorative accessories, 169 Commercial St. (487-3096).

● Health Club (AW): **Mussel Beach Health**

Club, clean health club for men & women, free-weight, cardiovascular equipment, 56 Shank Painter Rd., (next to A&P) (487-0001); **Provincetown Gym**, 333R Commercial St. (487-2776).

● Museum (AW): **Pilgrim Monument** and **Provincetown Museum**, history of the *Mayflower* and the Pilgrim Fathers, Town hall (487-1310).

● Reservation Service (GMW):✪ **Just Right Reservations**, hotels, inns, and guest houses in Boston, Provincetown, and New York City. Office hours: Mon-Fri 9am-4pm EST. James Koumpouras, managing partner, 18 Piedmont St., 2nd Fl. (617-423-3550).

 ACCOMMODATIONS

✪ ADMIRAL's LANDING

158 Bradford St., Provincetown, MA 02657. Tel: (508) 487-9665. Fax: (508) 487-4437. TYPE: *Bed & Breakfast*. HOST: Chuck Anzalone, innkeeper. CLIENTELE: Gay men & women. LOCATION: Centrally located in the East End on Bradford & Pearl Sts, 3 blocks from the Town Center.

* Rooms: 8, 6 w/priv., 2 w/shared bath
* Studios: 2 w/refrigerator, cooking facilities
* Smoking allowed in rooms
* Bed types: twin, king, queen
* Maid service, sun deck, free parking
* Pets w/prearrangement (studios only)
* Beach: 1 block (harbor beach)
  1 mi / 1.6 km (gay beach)
* Gay Bars: 5 min. walk
* Health Club: 3/4 mi. / 1 km
* Airport: 1 1/2 mi. / 3 km, free pick up
* Languages: English
* Reservations: 50% deposit
* Cancellation: within 14 days refund -10% if room is re-rented
* Credit Cards: MC/VISA
* Open: Year round
* Rates: $74-$109; (off) $34-$89 w/CB
* Check in 2:00 pm / Check out 11am
* Tax: 8%
* *TAC:* 10%
* Email: adm158@capecod.net
* WEB: http://www.ptown.com/ptown/ admiralslanding

DESCRIPTION: A Greek revival home from the 1840's, centrally located one block from the harbor. A variety of distinctively decorated rooms and pet-friendly studio efficiencies available year round. Continental breakfast served in common rooms or patio, afternoon snacks, off-street parking. *PBG, CC*

✪ AMPERSAND GH

6 Cottage St., PO Box 832, Provincetown, MA 02657. Tel: (508) 487-0959. TYPE: *Guest House*. HOST: Ken Johnson, owner. CLIENTELE: Mostly gay men & lesbians. LOCATION: West End of Provincetown. A 10 min. walk from the center of town.

* Rooms: 9 w/priv.; 2 w/shared bath
  11 doubles / 1 studio w/cooking facilities
* Smoking allowed in rooms
* Refrigerator, C/H, maid service
* Sundeck, free parking
* Beach: 1/2 mi. / 800 m. (gay)
* Gay Bars: 5 min. walk
* Health Club: 5 min. walk
* Airport: 1.5 mi. / 2 km, taxi
* Reservations: 50% deposit
* Cancellation Policy: refunded less10% for cancellation within 3 weeks of arrival date. Less than 3 weeks non refundable
* Open: Year round
* Credit Cards: MC/VISA/AMEX
* Rates: $71-$121 / (off) $51-$71 w/CB. Tax: 8%
* Check in 1:00 pm / Check out 11:00 am

DESCRIPTION: Gracious mid-nineteenth century Greek revival home in the West End of Provincetown. Second story sundeck with water views. Rooms, studio, apartment and 2 & 3 room suites available all furnished in a careful blend of contemporary and restored antiques.

✪ BENCHMARK INN & ANNEX

6-8 Dyer St., Provincetown, MA 02657. Tel: (508) 487-7440. Toll Free (888) 487-7440. Fax: (508) 487-7442. TYPE: *Bed & Breakfast*. HOSTS: Park & Neil. CLIENTELE: Mostly gay men & women. LOCATION: Central to Commercial Street.

* Rooms: 14; 5 w/priv., 5 w/shared bath
  4 w/jacuzzi. rooms for non smokers
* CTV, VCR, phone, refrigerator, safe box, C/H, A/C, hair dryer
* Suite: 1 BR, full bath, jacuzzi, kitchen, patio
* Bed Types: double, queen size
* Maid service, pool, sundeck, free parking
* Beach: 1.5 mi. / 2 km (mixed,nude)
* Gay Bars: 8 min. walk
* Health Club: 10 min. walk (gay/mixed)
* Airport: 5 mi. / 8 km (free pick up)
* Bus/Ferry: 5 min. walk
* Languages: English
* Reservations: 50% deposit
* Cancellation Policy: 10% penalty with 10 or more days advance notice
* Credit Cards: MC/VISA/AMEX/DISC
* Open: Year round
* Rates: $75-$245 / (off) $55-$165 w/CB*

* Expanded continental with room delivery
* Check in 2:00 pm / Check out 11:00 am
* Tax: 8%. *TAC:* 10%

DESCRIPTION: Deluxe Bed & Breakfast in a central location. Fireplaces, jacuzzis, superb harbor views, private balconied entrances, fresh flowers. *IGTA, PBG, CC.*

BOATSLIP BEACH CLUB
161 Commercial St., Box 393, Provincetown, MA 02657. Tel: (508) 487-1669. TYPE: *Resort Complex.* HOST: Peter & Jim. CLIENTELE: Mostly Gay. LOCATION: On the beach, near the center of town. 45 rooms, restaurant, disco, private beach, parking. DESCRIPTION: All male resort w/waterfront or poolside rooms.

THE CAPTAIN'S HOUSE
350A Commercial St., Provincetown, MA 02657. office: (508) 487-9353; guests only: (508) 487-9794. TYPE: *Guest House.* HOST: Jeff Hitchcock. CLIENTELE: Gay men (women welcome). LOCATION: Center of town. 11 rooms. DESCRIPTION: A century old guest house.

✪ CARL'S GUEST HOUSE
68 Bradford St., Provincetown, MA 02657. Tel: (508) 487-1650. Toll Free (800) 348-CARL. TYPE: *Guest House.* HOST: Carl. CLIENTELE: Gay men only. LOCATION: Central Provincetown, corner of Bradford & Court Sts. 2 blocks to the Boatslip.

* Rooms: 14; 3 w/priv., 11 w/shared bath
  sgl 3 / dbl 11. rooms for non smokers
* CTV, VCR, refrigerator, C/H, A/C
* Bed Types: single, double, queen size
* Pool, sun deck, clothing optional policy
* Free parking (off street); no pets
* Beach: 2 blocks (gay)
* Gay Bars: 2 blocks
* Health Club: 2 blocks
* Airport: 2 mi. / 3 km, taxi
* Credit Cards: VISA/MC
* Open: Year round
* Rates: $60 - $120 / (off) $30-$75. Taxes: 8%
* Check in 9am-9pm / Check out 11am

DESCRIPTION: Comfortable, clean, and affordable guest house. Gently landscaped, flowered yards. Catering to easy going, gentle guys. "Where strangers become friends".

✪ ELEPHANT WALK INN
156 Bradford St., Provincetown, MA 02657. Tel: (508) 487-2543. Toll Free (800) 889-9255. TYPE: *Bed & Breakfast.* HOST: Len Paoletti, owner. CLIENTELE: Mostly gay men & women. LOCATION: Central, near the inter-

section of Conwell & Bradford Sts. One block from Commercial St.

* Rooms: 8 w/priv. bath
  sgl 2 / dbl 4/ triple 1 / quad 1
* Smoking allowed in rooms
* CTV, VCR, phone, refrigerator, C/H, A/C
* Bed types: king, queen, 4 poster
* Maid service, sun deck, free parking, no pets
* Beach: 1 block. 1 mi. / 1.5 km (gay beach)
* Gay Bars: 5 min. walking
* Health Club: 12 blocks (mixed)
* Airport: 1 1/2 mi. / 3 km, free pick up
* Languages: English
* Reservations: 50% deposit
* Cancellation Policy: deposits refundable only if room rerented for time of original reservation
* Credit Cards: MC/VISA/DC/DISC
* Open: mid April - mid December
* Rates: $89 - $95 w/CB. Tax: 8%
* Check in 12 noon / check out 11:00 am
* *TAC:* 10% (off season only excluding holidays)

DESCRIPTION: A mission/craftsman house built in 1917 in a convenient location. Guest rooms are spacious, well appointed and furnished in eclectic mixture of antiques. Enjoy continental breakfast in the front lounge or up on the open air sundeck. *PBG, CC*

THE FAIRBANKS INN
90 Bradford St., Provincetown, MA 02657. Tel: (508) 487-0386 or (800) FAIRBANK. TYPE: *Guest House.* HOST: Adam. CLIENTELE: All Welcome. LOCATION: Center of town. DESCRIPTION: 200 year old ship captain's house. 16 rooms.

LAMPLIGHTER INN
26 Bradford St., Provincetown, MA 02657. Tel: (508) 487-2529. Fax: (508) 487-0079. TYPE: *Guest House.* HOSTS: Steve & Brent. CLIENTELE: Mostly Gay. LOCATION: On Rte 6-A, in the West End, one block from Beach, between Pleasant & Franklin Sts. 10 rooms.

✪ LAND's END INN
22 Commercial St., Provincetown, MA 02657. Tel: (508) 487-0706. Toll Free (800) 276-7088. TYPE: *Bed & Breakfast.* HOST: Anthony Arakelian, Mgr. CLIENTELE: All Welcome. LOCATION: Quiet West End area perched atop Gull Hill overlooking Cape Code Bay..

* Rooms: 16 w/priv. bath, 1 w/jacuzzi
* Suites: 2
* No Smoking allowed inside building
* Phone, refrigerator (in common living room)
* Bed types: single, double, queen size
* Sundeck, free parking, no pets

* Beach: walking distance (mixed)
* Gay Bars: 1/2 mi. / 800 m.
* Airport: 10 min. taxi
* Reservations: 50% no later than 7 days after reservation was made
* Cancellation Policy: 15% charge for cancellation received 14 days prior to arrival
* Credit Cards: MC/VISA
* Open: Year round
* Rates: $120-$190 (rooms); $285 (suite) (off season) $87-$165 (rooms); $185 (suite)
* Check in after 12:30 / check out 11:00 am

DESCRIPTION: Built in the turn of the century Land's End Inn is tastefully furnished with beautiful antiques, stained glass and collection of oriental wood carvings. Enjoy a quiet retreat in a comfortable and friendly ambiance. *Mass. Lodging. Assoc.*

✪ MONUMENT HOUSE

129 Bradford St., Provincetown, MA 02657. Tel: (508) 487-9664. Toll Free (888) 487-9664. Fax: (508) 487-3446. TYPE: *Bed & Breakfast.* OWNER: Park Davis. CLIENTELE: Mostly gay men & women. LOCATION: Centrally located to Commercial St.

* Rooms: 6; 2 w/priv., 4 w/shared bath dbl 5 / triple 1
* Rooms for non smokers
* CTV, phone, refrigerator, C/H, hairdryer
* Bed Types: large doubles, queen size
* Maid service, free parking, sun deck
* Beach: 1 mi. / 1.6 km (mixed/nude)
* Gay Bars: 1 block
* Health Club: 6 blocks (mixed)
* Airport: 4 mi. / 6 km (free pick up)
* Bus (1 block); ferry from Boston (1 block)
* Languages: English
* Deposit: 50%
* Cancellation Policy: 10% with 10 day notice
* Credit Cards: MC/VISA/AMEX/DISC
* Open: Year round
* Rates: $69-$99 / (off) $39-$69 w/CB
* Check in 1:00 pm / Check out 11:00 am
* Tax: 8%. *TAC:* 10%

DESCRIPTION: Charming 1840's home. Queen beds, fresh flowers. Complimentary beverages, roof deck, library, garden patio. Very central to commercial Street. *IGTA, PBG*

✪ THE RANCH

198 Commercial St., Provincetown MA 02657. Tel: (508) 487-1542. Toll Free (800) 942-1542. Fax: (508) 487-7442. TYPE: *Guest House.* OWNER: Park Davis. CLIENTELE: Gay men only. LOCATION: Central location corner of Commercial & Carver Sts. Walk to gay bars,

clubs and restaurants.

* Rooms: 20 w/shared bath
  sgl 5 / dbl 14 / triple 1
* Smoking allowed in rooms
* Lounge w/CTV, VCR, phone, refrigerator
* Bar & Fireplace, sundeck, maid service
* Bed Types: single, twin, double, queen size
* Parking: paid
* Beach: 1 mi. / 1.6 km (gay/mixed/nude)
* Gay Bars: walk to all
* Health Club: 2 min. walk
* Airport: 4 mi. / 6.4 km, taxi
* Bus/Ferry: from Boston 5 min. walk
* Reservations: 50% deposit
* Cancellation: 10% with 10 day notice
* Credit Cards: MC/VISA/AMEX
* Open: Year round
* Rates: $49-$79 / (off) $29-$59
  w/morning coffee
* Check in 2:00 pm / check out 11:00 am
* Tax: 8% (room tax)
* **TAC:** 10%

DESCRIPTION: A Provincetown landmark and the choice for men in need of economic lodging. Make and renew friendships at the street side patio, sun deck and handsome lounge. Spotless bathrooms and comfortable bedrooms offer street, town and bay view. *PBG*

✪ SUNSET INN

142 Bradford St., Provincetown, MA 02657. Tel: (508) 487-9810. Toll Free (800) 965-1801. TYPE: *Guest House.* HOST: Joel Tendler, Mgr. CLIENTELE: Mostly gay men & women. LOCATION: Centrally located near Commercial Street in a quiet location.

* Rooms: 20; 8 w/priv., 12 w/shared bath
  dbl 13 / triple 4 / quad 3
* Smoking allowed in rooms
* Bed Types: twin, double, queen size
* Maid service, free parking
* Sun deck
* Beach: 1 block (Mixed)
* Gay Bars: 3 blocks
* Health Club: 8 blocks (mixed)
* Airport: 4 mi. / 6 km (free pick up)

* Languages: English
* Reservations: 2 nights deposit
* Cancellation Policy: 15 days before arrival
  for a full refund
* Credit Cards: MC/VISA/DISC
* Open: 4/15-10/31
* Rates: $58-$95 / (off) $38-$68 w/CB
* Check in 1:30 pm / Check out 11:00 am
* Tax: 8%. **TAC:** 10%

DESCRIPTION: Charming 1850 Captain's home offering comfortable and quiet rooms just one block to town center. Meet hotel guests in the Common Room, or rest on the sundeck with beautiful harbor views. *PBG, CC*

✪ TRADE WINDS INN

12 Johnson St., Provincetown, MA 02657. Tel: (508) 487-0138. Fax: (508) 487-9484. TYPE: *Guest House.* HOST: Jeff Cazzoll Mgr. CLIENTELE: Mostly gay men & women. LOCATION: Central between Commercial and Bradford Sts toward the East End of town.

* Rooms: 16; 12 w/priv., 4 w/shared bath
  1 room w/jacuzzi; sgl 1 / dbl 12 / triple 3
* Rooms for smokers and non smokers
* CTV, VCR, refrigerator, safe box (in office)
  C/H, hairdryer
* Hot tub, patio areas
* Bed Types: twin, double, queen size
* Maid service, off street parking, no pets
* Beach: 1.5 mi / 2 km
* Gay Bars: 6 blocks
* Health Club: 10 blocks (mixed)
* Airport: 2 mi. / 3 km, taxi
* Deposit: 50% deposit
* Cancellation Policy: 15% fee
* Credit Cards: MC/VISA/AMEX
* Open: Year round
* Rates: $70 -$180 / (off) $55-$130 w/CB
* Check in 2:00pm / Check out 11:00 am
* Tax: 8%

DESCRIPTION: One of Provincetown's most gracious Inns. All rooms with contemporary furnishings, tile baths, wood stove and fireplace. Unwind and meet other guests in a relaxed atmosphere.

MICHIGAN

DOUGLAS
SAUGATUCK

DETROIT

ANN ARBOR

- ◆ **Population:** 9,300,000
- ◆ **Capital:** Lansing
- ◆ **Time Zone:** Eastern/Central
- ◆ **No Sodomy Law**
- ◆ **Legal drinking age:** 21

ANN ARBOR   ✆ 313

✈ City Airport (DET)
  Metropolitan Airport (DTW)

LOCATION: Southeastern lower peninsula of Michigan, about 30 mi. / 48 km west of Detroit.

POPULATION: 109,000

DESCRIPTION: Ann Harbor is a pretty college town and a center for the research and high-tech industry. It is the home of the University of Michigan.

❖ **SPECIAL EVENTS: Ann Arbor Summer Festival**, Performing arts Festival at the University of Michigan, June - early July (995-7281); **Street Art Fair**, 4 days of arts and crafts exhibition and street fair, mid July.

BARS ⅄ RESTAURANTS 🍴

● Bar/club (GMW): **The Nectarine**, 516 E. Liberty (994-5436).

● Restaurants (AW): **Bella Ciao**, Italian menu, outdoor dining, 118 W. Liberty St. (995-2107); **Gandy Dancer**, fresh seafood. 401 Depot St. (769-0592).

 ACCOMMODATIONS

See Detroit. To stay in town check the following hotels.

BELL TOWER HOTEL
300 So. Thayer, Ann Arbor MI 48104. Tel: (313) 769-3010. TYPE: *Hotel.* CLIENTELE: All Welcome. LOCATION: On the University of Michigan Campus. 66 rooms and suites w/priv. bath, CTV, phone, twice daily maid service, French restaurant. Rates: $92-$210. *TAC:* 10% DESCRIPTION: Quality first class hotel. Rooms and suites individually furnished in rich English decor.

CAMPUS INN
615 E. Huron St., Ann Arbor MI 48104. Tel: (313) 769-2200. TYPE: *Hotel.* CLIENTELE: All Welcome. LOCATION: Near the University of Michigan, walking distance to Power Center for the Performing Arts. 201 rooms w/priv. bath, CTV, phone, A/C, outdoor pool, sauna, restaurant, free parking. Rates: $89-$240. *TAC:* 10%. DESCRIPTION: Moderate first class hotel.

DETROIT   ✆ 810

✈ City Airport (DET)
  Metropolitan Airport (DTW)

LOCATION: In Southeast Michigan, stretching out along the Detroit River between Lakes Erie and St. Clair, opposite the Canadian city of Windsor, Ontario.

POPULATION: City 1,100,000
          Metro 4,500,000

CLIMATE: The seasons are distinct. Summers are hot and humid with an average July temperature of 69°F (21°c); fall and spring are on the cool side with an average temperature of 42°F (6°c); winters are cold with plenty of ice and snow and an average January temperature of 30°F (-1°c).

Gay/Lesbian Visitor Information
Affirmation: (810) 398-4297

DESCRIPTION: Detroit or "Motor Town" is the famous automobile capital of the USA and the hometown of car makers like Ford, Chrysler and General Motors. It is America's most important industrial city after Chicago;

an important inland port; and the birthplace of the famous Detroit Sound.

Visit the **Renaissance Center**, an impressive architectural complex designed by the celebrated architect John Portman; **Millender Center** is a modern complex that includes offices, hotel, stores and restaurants; the **Eastern Market**, is a picturesque European-style open air market, Russell St. at Fisher Fwy.

BARS Y RESTAURANTS ¶

Most of the gay scene is concentrated north of downtown, along Woodward North between McNichols in the south and W. 7-Mile Rd. in the north.

● Bars/clubs (GM): **Back Pocket**, cruise bar, restaurant, 8832 Greenfield Rd. (272-8374); **Backstreet**, dance bar, 15606 Jor Rd. (272-8959); **Deck**, dance bar, drag shows, 14901 E. Jefferson (822-1991); **Detroit Eagle**, leather bar, 1501 Holden (873-6969); **Gigi's**, dance bar, 16920 W. Warren (584-6525); **Tiffany's**, 17436 Woodward Ave. (883-7162).

● Bars/clubs (GMW): **Cruisin' Again**, 1641 Middlebelt Rd.,Inkster (729-8980); **Numbers**, 17518 Woodward Ave. NE (868-9145); **Other Side**, 16801 Plymouth Rd. (836-2324); **Times Square Station**, 1431 Times Square (963-0874); **Zippers**, 6221 East Davison (892-8120).

● Bars/clubs (GW): **Railroad Crossing**, dance bar, 6640 E. 8-Mile Rd. (891-1020); **Splash**, dance bar, 14526 W. Warren (582-0639).

● Restaurant (AW): **Backstage**, restaurant/dinner theatre, 17630 Woodward Ave. (869-3988); **Salute**, restaurant & bar, 17546 Woodward NE (867-1390). Other restaurants include: **Sheik**, Lebanese cuisine, 316 E. Lafayette St. (964-8441): **La Cuisine**, authentic French cuisine, 417 Pelissier St., Windsor (Canada) (519-253-6432).

λ SERVICES λ

● Erotica (G/S): **Complex Video**, 1333 W. 8 Mile Rd. (341-5322); **Irving Art Theatre**, 21220 Fenkell (531-2368): **24 Hr Video Rental**, 17520 Woodward N. (869-9524).

● Health Club (GM): **TNT Health Club**, sauna, gym, videos, 13333 W. 8-Mile Rd. (341-5322).

● Personal Phone Line (GM): ✪ **Detroit**

Confidential Connection, meet local guys! Record, listen, respond to ads free (962-7070) free access code 8060.

 **ACCOMMODATIONS**

QUALITY INN
1 W. 9 Mile Rd., Hazel Park, Detroit 48030. Tel: (810) 399-5800. Fax: (810) 399-2602. TYPE: *Motor Inn*. CLIENTELE: Mostly Straight. LOCATION: 10 mi. / 16 km from downtown. 212 rooms w/priv. bath, informal restaurant, pool, free parking. Rates: $49-$69. *TAC:* 10%. DESCRIPTION: Moderate first class motor inn in a convenient location.

DOUGLAS ℅ 616
SAUGATUCK

✈ Kent County Airport (GRR)

LOCATION: Eastern shore of Lake Michigan and the Kalamazoo River, 30 miles / 48 km southwest of Grand Rapids, and 160 miles / 258 km northeast of Chicago, Illinois.

CLIMATE: Summers are hot and humid with lake breezes, winters are harsh with abundance of snow. Average temperatures are similar to those in Detroit.

DESCRIPTION: The twin towns - Douglas and Saugatuck are lake summer resorts for the Mid West.

 **ACCOMMODATIONS**

DOUGLAS DUNES
333 Blue Star Hwy, Douglas, MI 49406. Tel: (616) 857-1401. TYPE: *Motel*. HOST: Lawrence. CLIENTELE: All Welcome. LOCATION: In Douglas. 69 rooms, restaurant, bar, disco. Rates: on request.

THE KIRBY HOUSE
294 W. Center, Douglas MI 49406. Tel: (616 521-2904. TYPE: *Rental Apts*. HOSTESSES: Loren or Marsha. CLIENTELE: Equal Gay/Straight. LOCATION: Corner of Blue Star Hwy & Center St. 7 rooms, 2 apts. DESCRIPTION: Queen Anne Victorian residence.

SAUGATUCK LODGES
Box 279, Saugatuck MI 49453. Tel: (616) 857-4269. TYPE: *Hotel*. CLIENTELE: Gay men & women.

MINNESOTA

MINNEAPOLIS ST. PAUL

- ◆ **Population:** 4,100,000
- ◆ **Capital:** St. Paul
- ◆ **Time Zone:** Central
- ◆ **Sodomy Law**
- ◆ **Legal drinking age:** 21

MINNEAPOLIS ✆ 612
ST. PAUL

✈ Minneapolis/St-Paul Airport (MSP)

LOCATION: The "Twin Cities" are at the confluence of the Mississippi and Minnesota Rivers.

POPULATION: Minneapolis 371,000
St. Paul 270,000.

CLIMATE: Continental with wide variations of temperature, ample summer rainfall, and snowfall in the winter.

Gay/Lesbian Visitor Information
Helpline: 822-8661

DESCRIPTION: Minneapolis is across the Mississippi river from St. Paul, the capital of Minnesota. St. Paul is a city of diversified industry and lovely residential neighborhoods. Minneapolis is the commercial center of the Upper Midwest, clean with modern highrise corporate buildings, a University town with a clean-cut Yuppie image. It is an important agricultural center for America's cattle and grain.

Visit the **Nicollet Mall** - a world-famous shopping promenade; **IDS Tower**, the tallest bldg. (57 stories) between Chicago and the West Coast; **Minneapolis Institute of Art**, 2400 3rd Ave. S. with art collection covering American and European art; and the **University of Minnesota** on the banks of the Mississippi, the largest single campus in the USA; **Bell Museum of Natural History**, 17th Ave. & University Ave. SE (373-2423); **Minneapolis Grain Exchange**, 400 S. 4th St. S. (338-6212). Both cities offer lakes, parks and skiing nearby.

❖ **SPECIAL EVENT: North Country Tennis Classic III**, May 3-5 (724-5515).

❖ **Gay Beach: 32nd Street Beach** at Lake Calhoun (32nd St., and W. Calhoun Blvd.); **Bare Ass Beach**, along the Mississippi River (on E. River Parkway, across from the Shriner's Hospital).

BARS ᵧ RESTAURANTS 🍴

The gay scene in Minneapolis is located in or around Hennepin Ave., northeast of the Nicollet Mall.

● Bars/clubs (GM): **Brass Rail**, mature clientele, 422 Hennepin Ave. (333-3016); **19 Bar**, pub, 19 W. 15th St., (871-5553); **Saloon**, dance sports bar, 830 Hennepin Ave. (332-0835); **Town House**, country/western entertainment complex, 1415 University Ave., St. Paul (646-7087).

● Bars/clubs (GMW): **Gay 90's**, entertainment complex, restaurant, bars and strip and drag shows, 408 Hennepin Ave. (333-7755); **Innuendos**, espresso bar, 510 N. Robert St. St. Paul; **Rumors**, dance bar, 490 N. Roberts St., St. Paul (224-0703); **Metro**, cocktail lounge, dance floor, Sunday brunch, 733 Pierce Butler Route, St. Paul (489-0002).

● Restaurants (GMW): **Bar X Press**, expresso bar, 1008 Marquette Ave. (371-9882); **La Covina**, Mexican,1570 Selby Ave. (St. Paul (645-5288); **Ruby's Cafe**, 1614 Harmon Pl. (338-2089). Other (AW): **Black Forest Inn**, German cuisine, 1 E. 26th St. (872-0812); **Blue Moon Cafe**, 3822 E. Lake St, St. Paul; **Café Brenda**, gourmet vegetarian restaurant; 300 1st Ave. N. (342-9238); **Café Zev**, popular after bar crowd, 1362 La Salle; **Cafe Wyrd**, popular with the young and attractive crowd, 1600 W. Lake St.; **Jax Café**, Continental, 1928 University Ave. NE (789-7297); **Nye's Polonaise Room**, Polish, 112 Hennepin Ave. (379-

2021); **Times Bar & Cafe**, popular Sunday jazz brunch, 11th St. & Nicollet.

λ SERVICES λ

● Erotica (GM): **Broadway**, books, videos, sex toys, large gay section, 24 hrs., 901 Hennepin Ave. (338-7303); **Fantasy House**, 81 S. 10th St. (333-6313); **Sex World**, 241 2nd Ave. N. (672-0556).

● Health Club (GM):**Body Quest**, sauna, gym, videos, 245 N. Aldrich Ave. N. (377-7222).

● Personal Phone Line (GM): ✪ **Minneapolis Confidential Connection**, meet local guys! Record, listen, respond to ads free (338-4700) free access code 8060.

 ACCOMMODATIONS

✪ HOTEL LUXEFORD SUITES

1101 LaSalle Ave., Minneapolis, MN 55403. Tel: (612) 332-6800 or (800) 662-3232. Fax: (612) 332-8246. TYPE: *Hotel.* CLIENTELE: All Welcome. LOCATION: In downtown Minneapolis, 11th and LaSalle, one block from Nicollet Mall and Orchestra Hall.

* Suites: 230 1BR w/priv. bath
  sgl 110 / dbl 120
* Suites for smokers and non-smokers
* CTV (2), phone, refrigerator, wet bar, microwave, some with whirlpool
* Room & maid service, laundry service, wheelchair access, elevator
* Restaurant: **Café Luxeford**, American
* Bar: **Crowley's** Jazz Club
* Exercise room, sauna, jacuzzi
* Parking (paid), valet service
* Gay Bars: 3 blocks
* Health Club: 1 block (mixed) YWCA
* Airport: MSP 12 mi. / 19 km, AP Express
* Reservations: required
* Cancellation: 4 pm day of arrival
* Credit Cards: MC/VISA/AMEX/DISC/DC/JCB
* Open: Year round
* Rates: from $99. Tax: 12%
* Check in time 4pm / check out 11am
* *TAC:* 10%

DESCRIPTION: Superior first class hotel featuring elegantly furnished 230 spacious suites. The location is perfect just one block off Nicollet Mall for fashionable shopping and entertainment. Highly recommended for your business or pleasure stay.

MISSOURI

● St. Louis

◆ **Population:** 5,117,000
◆ **Capital:** Jefferson City
◆ **Time Zone:** Central
◆ **Sodomy Law**
◆ **Legal drinking age:** 21

ST. LOUIS   © 314

✈ Lambert/St. Louis Airport (STL)

   10 mi / 16 km northwest

LOCATION: At the confluence of the Missouri and the Mississippi rivers, slightly east of the geographic center of the United States.

POPULATION: City: 397,000
                    Metro 2,500,000

CLIMATE: Modified Continental with wide variations of temperature. Hot and humid summers with ample summer rainfall. July average temperature is in the 80°sF (25°c). Winters are relatively mild with an average January temperatures of 30°s (-2°c).

Gay/Lesbian Visitor Information
Hotline: 367-0084

DESCRIPTION: St. Louis is one of the oldest settlements in the Mississippi Valley. Emerged from a steamboat era it is today a cosmopolitan and diverse destination. Visit the observation deck in the top of the famous **Gateway Arch**; the **Anheuser-Busch Brewery** - the world's largest in a complex of art deco buildings recently designated a National Historic Landmark; the **Missouri Botanical Garden** and the **National Museum of Transport**.

BARS RESTAURANTS

● Bars/clubs (GM): **Eagle / Outpost**, levi/ leather cruise bar, 17 S. Vandeventer (535-4100); **Fallout**, dance bar, 1324 Washington (421-0003); **Merlies**, drag show, 2917 S. Jefferson (664-1066).

● Bars/clubs (GMW): **Bacchus**, 6 Sarah St. (531-1109); **Clementines**, bar and restaurant, 2001 Menard (664-7869); **Club 747**, 1624 Delmar (621-9030); **Complex**, video dance club, 3511 Chouteau (772-2645); **Drake**, 3502 Papin (865-1400); **Fallout**, video dance club, 1324 Washington (421-0003); **Front Page**, cruise bar, 2330 Menard Ave. (664-2939); **Loading Zone**, 16 S. Euclid (361-4119); **Magnolias**, video dance club, 5 Vandeventer (652-6500);

● Bar/club (GW): **Attitudes**, video dance club, 4100 Manchester (534-3858); **Ernie's Class Act**, dance club, restaurant, 3756 S. Broadway (664-7869); **Gabriel's**, 6901 S. Broadway (832-0656).

● Restaurants (GMW): **Angles**, at the Complex, 3511 Chouteau (772-2645); **Niner Diner** at Magnolias, 5 Vandeventer (652-6500); **Oh, My Darlin' Cafe**, at Clementines, 2001 Menard (664-7869).

🖋 ACCOMMODATIONS 🖋

DRURY INN (Union Station)
201 S. 20th St., St. Louis, MO 63103. Tel: (314) 231-3900. TYPE: *Hotel*. CLIENTELE: All Welcome. LOCATION: Downtown. 180 rooms w/priv. bath, 17 mini-suites, microwave, refrigerator, loveseat, rooms for nonsmokers, restaurant, indoor pool, free parking. Rates: $83-$113. Tax: 13.85%. *TAC*: 10%. DESCRIPTION: Superior tourist class hotel in a convenient location.

NEVADA

- RENO

LAS VEGAS

LAUGHLIN

- ◆ **Population:** 800,000
- ◆ **Capital:** Carson City
- ◆ **Time Zone:** Pacific
- ◆ **Sodomy Law**
- ◆ **Legal drinking age:** 21

LAS VEGAS   ✆ 702

✈ McCarren Int'l Airport (LAS)

LOCATION: Southern Nevada near the Arizona border.

POPULATION: 465,000

CLIMATE: Dry desert climate. Summers are hot with average July temperatures of 90°F (32°c). Winters are moderate with average January temperatures of 50°F (10°c).

Gay/Lesbian Visitor Information
The Center: 733-9800

DESCRIPTION: Las Vegas is the entertainment/gambling capital of the world. In its early days it was a small oasis on the route to California. Founded by Mormon settlers, it experienced its first economic expansion during the legendary Silver Rush Period. Today, Las Vegas is one of the fastest growing cities in the USA attracting millions of visitors to its plush casinos, from high rollers to everyday people. Everyone can find something to its taste in Las Vegas: gambling activities, world-class entertainment, great selection of low-priced all-you-can-eat buffets at the casinos, elegant dining places, circus acts, or even 24hrs. Wedding Chapels for those who can not wait a second longer to Say I do. (Someone should come up with the idea to establish the world's first 24hrs. Gay/Lesbian Wedding Chapel in Las Vegas). Yes, Las Vegas can be tacky as hell, but it will certainly keep you busy and entertained. Nearby attractions include: **The Hoover Dam**, 726 ft. (220 m), one of the highest built dams in the world; **Lake Mead**, great water sports recreation area.

❖ Gay/Nude Beach: take Lake Mead Blvd. So. from Nellis Ave., when you reach North Shore Rd., (Dead End) go left, drive to the 8.0 mi. marker, make right hand turn. From that point take all left turns on the gravel road. As you reach the Lake Park, walk to your left to the third cove - relax and enjoy.

BARS ♈ RESTAURANTS ❡❡

● Bars/clubs (GM): **Angles**, video cruise bar, 4633 Paradise Rd., (791-0100); **Backstreet**, country/western bar, open 24 hrs., 5012 S. Arville Rd. (876-1844); **Badlands**, country & western cruise/dance bar, 953 E. Sahara Ave., #22B (792-9262); **The Buffalo**, levi/leather bar, 4640 Paradise Rd. (733-8355); **The Eagle**, levi & leather bar, slots, pool table, 24 hrs., 3430 E. Tropicana (458-8662); **Good Times**, piano bar, disco, lounge, popular with collegiate crowd, 1775 E. Tropicana (736-9494); **Snick's Place**, beer bust, slots, open 24 hrs., 1402 S. 4th St. (385-9298).

● Bars/clubs (GMW): **Backdoor**, 1415 E. Charleston Blvd. (385-2018); **Gipsy**, alternative dance club, 4605 Paradise (731-1919).

● Bar/clubs (GW): **Curve**, 4633 Paradise Road (791-1947); **Faces**, 701 E. Stewart (386-7971).

● Restaurants (AW): there are no gay restaurants in Las Vegas. Most of the casinos feature several restaurants ranging from the popular, low priced all-you-can-eat buffet to quality medium range and elegant dining. Some suggestions include - **Andre's**, French cuisine, 401 S. 6th St. (385-5016); **Gigi's**, French cuisine, expensive, Bally's Casino, 3645 Las Vegas Blvd., So. (739-4111); **Garcia's**, Mexican cuisine, 1030 E. Flamingo Rd. (731-0628); **Golden Wok**, Chinese cuisine, 504 S. Decatur Blvd. (878-1596).

λ SERVICES λ

● Erotica (G/S): **Desert Adult Books**, video

arcade, novelties, 24 hrs., 4350 Las Vegas Blvd. N. (643-7982); **Flick Adult Theatre**, 24 hrs., 719 E. Fremont (386-0250); **Pure Pleasure**, adult books, videos, 24 hrs. 3177 S. Highland Dr.; **Talk of the Town**, videos, arcade, 24 hrs, 1238 Las Vegas Blvd., So (385-1800).

● Personal Phone Line (GM): ✪ **Las Vegas Confidential Connection**, meet local guys! Record, listen, respond to ads free (693-6800) free access code 8060.

 **ACCOMMODATIONS**

EXCALIBUR HOTEL & CASINO
3850 Las Vegas Blvd. So., Las Vegas, NV 89109-4300. Tel: (702) 597-7700. TYPE: *Hotel/Casino*. CLIENTELE: Mostly Straight. LOCATION: on the South end of the Las Vegas Strip. 4032 rooms w/priv. bath. Rates: $45-$89. *TAC:* 10%. DESCRIPTION: Extravagant castle-like mega casino complex.

✪ **LAS VEGAS B&B**
Las Vegas, NV 89104. Tel: (702) 384-1129. TYPE: *Bed & Breakfast*. HOST: Ole. CLIENTELE: Gay men only (women welcome). LOCATION: Two blocks off the strip.

* Rooms: 3, 1 w/priv., 2 w/shared bath
  2 dbl / 1 triple, rooms for non smokers
* CTV, VCR, phone, C/H, A/C
* Maid, room & laundry services
* Pool, sundeck, sauna, jacuzzi, hot tub
* Clothing optional policy
* Parking: free (off street)
* Pets: w/prearrangement only
* Beach: 28 mi. / 45 km (gay/nude)
* Gay Bars & Health Club: 5 min.
* Airport: Mc Carran Int'l 15 min.
* Train St'n: AmTrack, 10 min.
* Languages: English, German, French, Danish, Norwegian, Swedish
* Reservation: 50% deposit
* Cancellation: full refund w/8 days notice
* Open: Year round
* Rates: $49 - $98 w/AB Tax: 8%
* *TAC:* 10%

DESCRIPTION: Private B&B featuring European decor and fine amenities, set in a lush garden with tropical birds, greenhouse and hot tub. The Innkeeper is a professional European chef (Liberace's former chef). Dinners and snacks available upon request.

LUXOR HOTEL & CASINO
3900 Las Vegas Blvd. So., Las Vegas NV 89119. Tel: (702) 262-4000. TYPE: *Hotel & Casino*. CLIENTELE: All Welcome. LOCATION: On

the Strip. 2533 rooms, 251 suites, restaurants, casino, pool, health club. Rates: $59-$89 *TAC:* 10%. DESCRIPTION: Egyptian themed Pyramid casino with replicas of Egyptian artifacts.

THE MIRAGE
3400 Las Vegas Blvd. So., Las Vegas NV 89109. Tel: (702) 791-7111. Fax: (702) 791-7446. TYPE: *Hotel & Casino*. CLIENTELE: Mostly Straight. LOCATION: In center of Strip, 1-1/2 mi. from the convention center. 3,049 rooms w/priv. bath. Rates: $79 - $600. *TAC:* 10% DESCRIPTION: The strip's most exclusive casino. Exotic decor; dolphin shows; white tigers; erupting volcano, and water falls.

LAUGHLIN   ℂ **702**

✈ Laughlin Airport (NV)
Bullhead City Airport (AZ)

LOCATION: 100 mi. / 160 km south of Las Vegas, across the Colorado River from Bullhead City (AZ).

POPULATION: 4,500

CLIMATE: See Las Vegas

DESCRIPTION: A fast growing little gambling town on the Colorado River. The town offers a mile long drive dotted with casino hotels. Not particularly gay, but fun to explore when you are in the area.

BARS ⅄ RESTAURANTS ¶¶

● Bar (G/S): **Lariat Saloon**, 1161 Hancock Rd., Bullhead City (AZ) (602-758-9741).

● Restaurants (AW): try the restaurants and buffets at the casino hotels.

 **ACCOMMODATIONS**

COLORADO BELLE
2100 S. Casino Dr., Laughlin NV 89028. Tel: (702) 298-4000. Fax: (702) 298-8165. TYPE: *Casino Hotel*. CLIENTELE: All Welcome. LOCATION: On the Colorado River. 1238 rooms, 38 suites. restaurants, bars, entertainment, pools, spa, free parking. Rates: $55-$89. *TAC:* 10%. DESCRIPTION: Replica of a Mississippi Paddlewheeler.

RAMADA EXPRESS
2121 S. Casino Dr., Laughlin NV 89029. Tel:

(702) 298-4200. Fax: (702) 298-4619. TYPE: *Casino Hotel.* CLIENTELE: All Welcome. LOCATION: On the Colorado River. 406 rooms, restaurants, entertainment, pool. Rates: $25-$54. *TAC:* 10%. DESCRIPTION: Railroad theme casino hotel with 2 working trains for guest use on property.

RENO   *©* 702

✈ Cannon Int'l Airport (RNO)

LOCATION: Western Nevada near Lake Tahoe and the California border.

POPULATION: 120,000

CLIMATE: Abundant sunshine throughout the year. Temperatures are mild and fluctuate some 45°F (7°c) between the high and low during the day. Winter mean temperature is 32°F (0°c) in January. Summer mean temperature is 69°F (21°c) in July. Average annual rainfall is only 7" (175 mm); snow fall is 27" (0.68m).

VISITOR INFORMATION
Reno-Sparks CVA: 827-7600

DESCRIPTION: Reno is known both as the "Biggest Little City in the World and the "Divorce Capital of the World", due to a six month divorce law on the books since 1861. Casino gambling began in 1931 when the state of Nevada legalized gambling, however, the casinos have industry has grown rapidly only after World War II. Today large casinos with 24 hour gambling and entertainment are Reno's main attraction. Visitors can enjoy world class hotels, big name entertainment, and the outdoor activities of nearby Lake Tahoe.

BARS ♟ RESTAURANTS ♟♟

● Bars/clubs (GM): **Bar West**, bar, dancing, pool, open 4 pm, 210 W. Commercial Row (786-0878); **Five Star Saloon**, bar, slots, pool table, deli, dancing, 24hrs., 132 West St. (329-2878); **Shouts**, bar, slots, 24 hrs., 145 Hillcrest St. (829-7667); **1099 Club**, video bar, slots, 24 hrs., 1099 S. Virginia (329-1099); **Visions**, night-

club, slots, swimming pool, 24hrs., 340 Kietzke Lane (786-5455).

● Bars/clubs (GMW): **Alley Club**, 24 hrs, mostly men, 100 N. Sierra (333-2808); **Bad Dollys**, pool table, dancing, 535 East 4th St. (348-1983),

● Restaurant (AW): **Glory Hole**, steaks and seafood, 4201 W. 4th St. (786-1323); **Ichiban**, Japanese cuisine/Sushi bar, 635 N. Sierra (323-5550); **Rumpus Room**, Italian cuisine, bar, slots, 24hrs., 424 E. 4th St. (323-7756).

λ SERVICES λ

● Health Club (GM): **Steves**, private club, 24hrs., 1030 W. 2nd St. (323-8770).

🏠 ACCOMMODATIONS 🏠

HARRAH'S RENO
219 N. Center St., Reno, NV 89520. Tel: (702) 786-3232, or (800) 648-3773. Fax: (702) 788-3703. TYPE: *Deluxe Hotel & Casino.* LOCATION: In the heart of downtown Reno casino district. 565 rooms. 69 suites, restaurants, entertainment, lounges, pool, health club, sauna, jacuzzi, gay bars nearby, Rates: $89-125. Suites $135-475. Tax 9%. *TAC:* 10%. DESCRIPTION: *"The Better People Place"* know for its high quality, service, fine restaurants, and entertainment.

PEPPERMILL HOTEL & CASINO
2707 S. Virginia St. Reno, NV 89502. Tel: (702) 826-2121 or (800) 648-6992. Fax: (702) 825-5737. TYPE: *Hotel & Casino.* LOCATION: 1 mi. from the downtown.

* Rooms: 631 w/ priv. bath. Suites: 36
* Wheeelchair Accessibility
* Restaurants, cabaret lounge
* Pool, sauna, exercise room
* Airport: 1 mi., free shuttle
* Gay Bars: nearby
* Open: Year round
* Credit Cards: AMEX/DC/DIS/MC/VISA
* Rates: $65-115; Suites $200-400. Tax 9%
* *TAC:* 10%

DESCRIPTION: Quality highrise casino hotel.

NEW HAMPSHIRE

- ◆ **Population:** 921,000
- ◆ **Capital:** Concord
- ◆ **Time Zone:** Eastern
- ◆ **No Sodomy Law**
- ◆ **Legal drinking age:** 20

CENTRE HARBOR ✆ 603

✈ Laconia Airport

 ACCOMMODATIONS

RED HILL INN
RFD #1, Box 99M, Centre Harbor, NH 03226.
Tel: (603) 279-7001. TYPE: *Country Inn.*
HOST: Rick & Don. CLIENTELE: Gay
Welcome. LOCATION: On Route 25, 2 hrs.
north of Boston. DESCRIPTION: Restored
mansion overlooking mountains. 21 rooms.
Rates: $85-$150. Tax: 8%. *TAC:* 15%

MANCHESTER ✆ 603

✈ Municipal Airport (MHT) 5 mi. / 8km SE

LOCATION: Southeastern New Hampshire.

DESCRIPTION: Year round resort town near
the **Green Mountain National Forest**.

BARS ♊ RESTAURANTS 🍴

● Bars/Clubs (GMW): **Club Merrimac**, 201
Merrimac (623-9362); **Front Runner**, 490
Chestnut St., (623-6477); **Sporters**, bar &
restaurant, 361 Pine St. (668-9014).

ACCOMMODATIONS

HOLIDAY INN
700 Elm St., Manchester NH 03101. Tel: (603)
625-1000. TYPE: *Hotel.* CLIENTELE: All
Welcome. LOCATION: Downtown off I-293.
250 rooms w/priv. bath, 10 suites, CTV, phone,
A/C, restaurant, coffee shop. Rates: $78-$120.

QUEEN CITY MOTOR INN
140 Queen City Ave., Manchester NH 03103. Tel:
(603) 622-6444. TYPE: *Motel.* CLIENTELE: All
Welcome. LOCATION: 2 minutes from downtown.
45 rooms w/priv. bath. Rates: $50-$65. *TAC:* 10%.

PORTSMOUTH ✆ 603

✈ Municipal Airport (MHT) Manchester

LOCATION: Southeastern New Hampshire on
the Atlantic Ocean.

♊ BARS ♊

● Bars/Clubs (GMW): **Blue Strawberry**, 29
Ceres St. (431-6420); **Desert Hearts**, Rte. 1,
Bypass North (431-5400); **Members**, 53 Green
St. (436-9451).

ACCOMMODATIONS

HOLIDAY INN
300 Woodbury Ave., Portsmouth NH 03801.
Tel: (603) 431-8000. TYPE: *Motel.* CLIEN-
TELE: All Welcome. LOCATION: near Pease
AFB. 130 rooms, room service, restaurant,
gym, pool, parking. Rates: $75-$120. *TAC:*
10%. DESCRIPTION: Smart motor inn.

SISE INN
40 Court St., Portsmouth, NH 03801. TYPE:
Inn. CLIENTELE: All Welcome. LOCATION:
Center of historic area. 34 rooms, 9 suites
w/priv. bath, CTV/VCR, phone, A/C, C/H.
Rates: $69-$89. DESCRIPTION: Elegant
Queen Anne Inn dating from 1881. All rooms
and suites tastefully decorated with period furniture and wall coverings.

NEW JERSEY

ATLANTIC CITY

- ◆ **Population:** 7,370,000
- ◆ **Capital:** Trenton
- ◆ **Time Zone:** Eastern
- ◆ **No Sodomy Law**
- ◆ **Legal drinking age:** 21

ATLANTIC CITY   ✆ 609

✈ Bader Municipal Airport (AIY);
  Pomona Airport (ACY) 12 mi. NW

LOCATION: In southern New Jersey on the Atlantic Ocean. 145 mi. / 230 km south of New York City and 70 mi. / 112 km southeast of Philadelphia.

POPULATION: 40,200

CLIMATE: Summer highs in the mid 80"sF (29°c), winter lows in the mid 20"sF (-4°c). Ocean breezes moderate the city's climate.

VISITOR INFORMATION
Atlantic City CVB
Tel: (609) 348-7100

DESCRIPTION: A world-class holiday and casino gambling resort on the U.S. East Coast. Flashy nightlife, all-star entertainment, and fine restaurants are the city's major attractions. Most of the Casinos are located near, or on the Boardwalk and are within walking distance of each other. The **Taj-Mahal** Hotel/Casino is one of the largest casinos and enter-

tainment centers in the world.

❖ Visit: **The Boardwalk**, a lovely promenade along the Atlantic Ocean; **Absecon Lighthouse**, built in 1857, contains an interesting marine museum in its base; Amusement Piers; **Lucy the Margate Elephant**, an 1881 wooden elephant; the famous Casinos, and the boat-shaped shopping center with boutiques, cafes and restaurants.

♣ Gambling is the main reason why millions of visitors come to Atlantic City each year. However, you can also enjoy the beaches and the ocean for swimming and water sports in the summer.

❖ **HOW TO GET HERE:** The most economic way to reach Atlantic City is via the **Greyhound** bus service from New York City or Philadelphia. **Amtrak** has train service from New York City, Washington, Baltimore & Philadelphia.

BARS ♈ RESTAURANTS 🍴

● Bars/clubs (GM): ✪ **Rendezvous Revisited Lounge**, cruise bar, drag shows Sundays, strippers Tuesdays and Saturdays, 137-139 So. New York Ave. (347-8539); ✪ **Studio Six**, high energy video/dance club, top entertainment recording artists and celebrities, open 10:00 pm till dawn, (balcony bar) big screen TV, secure parking, 14 So. Mt. Vernon Ave. (348-3310); ✪ **Surfside Deck Bar**, open May - October, noon, frozen drinks, sundeck, lounge chairs, pool, next to Studio Six, T dance every Sunday 4:00 pm, 18 S. Mt Vernon Ave.; **Reflections**, cocktails, S. Carolina Ave. at the Boardwalk (345-1115).

● Bar/Club (GMW): ✪ **Brass Rail Tavern**, bar/restaurant open 24 hrs, ladies night Fridays, movie night Mondays, 14 So. Mt. Vernon Ave., bar/restaurant, open 24 hours (348-0192).

● Restaurants (AW): You'll have no problem finding a good restaurant or buffet to your liking in Atlantic City. Each casino offers a mind boggling variety from all-you-can-eat buffet to plush international dining. Some general recommendations include: **Cafe 96**, Continental and specialty cuisine, lunch & dinner, gay friendly, below Surfside Resort Complex, parking available, 18 S. Mt. Vernon Ave. (343-1444); **Dock's Oyster House**, Tuesdays - Sundays, seafood, gay friendly; 2405 Atlantic Ave. (345-0092); **Le Palais**, expensive French restaurant

Surfside

Atlantic City, New Jersey

Resort Hotel

50 Rooms and the Hottest Club in South Jersey!
STUDIO SIX Video Dance Club • Brass Rail Tavern
Surfside Sun Deck • Swimming Pool
American Grille Bar B Que • Cafe 96 Resaurant

Rooms Available with:
Private Tile Bathrooms with
Hair Dryers
Remote Color TV, Refrigerator

Open Year Round
"A Place for All Seasons"

The Surfside Resort Hotel, Sun Deck Bar & Pool
is centrally located.
One Block to the Beach & Boardwalk, Walk to all Gay Bars,
Right next to STUDIO SIX & Brass Rail Tavern
Healthclub
Walk to the Casinos

| Call For |
| Free Brochure |

Atlantic City is the #1 tourist destination!
Gambling • Cabaret • Headline Entertainment •
World Class Restaurants • White Sand Beaches
Party All Night, Atlantic City Never Closes!

Video Dance Club
STUDIO SIX
Where Entertainers Are Entertained

For Reservations & Information
609-347-0808   fax 609-344-5244
10-18 S. Mt. Vernon Ave • Atlantic City, NJ 08401

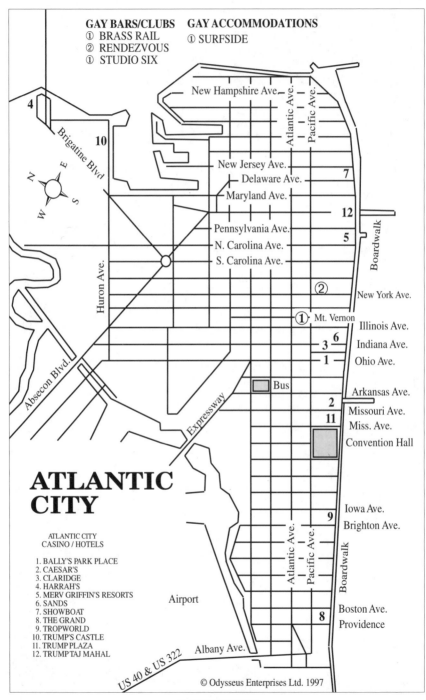

GAY BARS/CLUBS
① BRASS RAIL
② RENDEZVOUS
① STUDIO SIX

GAY ACCOMMODATIONS
① SURFSIDE

New Hampshire Ave.

Atlantic Ave.
Pacific Ave.

Brigatine Blvd

10

4

N E S W

New Jersey Ave.
Delaware Ave.
Maryland Ave.

7

12

Pennsylvania Ave.
N. Carolina Ave.
S. Carolina Ave.

Boardwalk

Huron Ave.

5

② New York Ave.

① Mt. Vernon Illinois Ave.

3 6 Indiana Ave.

1 Ohio Ave.

Absecon Blvd.

Bus Arkansas Ave.

2 Missouri Ave.

11 Miss. Ave.

Convention Hall

Expressway

ATLANTIC CITY

ATLANTIC CITY
CASINO / HOTELS

1. BALLY'S PARK PLACE
2. CAESAR'S
3. CLARIDGE
4. HARRAH'S
5. MERV GRIFFIN'S RESORTS
6. SANDS
7. SHOWBOAT
8. THE GRAND
9. TROPWORLD
10. TRUMP'S CASTLE
11. TRUMP PLAZA
12. TRUMP TAJ MAHAL

9 Iowa Ave.
Brighton Ave.

Atlantic Ave.
Pacific Ave.
Boardwalk

Airport

8 Boston Ave.
Providence

US 40 & US 322 Albany Ave.

© Odysseus Enterprises Ltd. 1997

ODYSSEUS '97/98

at Resorts Hotel & Casino; **Momma Motts**, Italian cuisine & seafood, next door to Rendezvous Revisited, 151 S. New York Ave. (345-8218); **Peking Duck House**, Chinese, gay friendly, 2801 Atlantic Ave (344-9090).

λ SERVICES λ

● Personal Phone Line (GM): ✪ **Atlantic City Confidential Connection**, meet local guys! Record, listen, respond to ads free (663-7900) free access code 8060.

 **ACCOMMODATIONS**

HARRAH'S HOTEL & CASINO
1725 Brigantine Blvd., Atlantic City NJ 08401. Tel: (609) 441-5000. Fax: (609) 344-2974. TYPE: *Casino Hotel.* CLIENTELE: All Welcome. LOCATION: Bayfront. 760 rooms w/priv. bath, 244 atrium suites, 24 hrs. room service, restaurants, bars, theatre, casino. Rates: $120-$180. *TAC:* 10%. DESCRIPTION: Deluxe contemporary style casino resort.

✪ SURFSIDE RESORT COMPLEX
18 So. Mt. Vernon Ave., Atlantic City, NJ 08401. Tel: (609) 347-0808. Fax: (609) 344-5244. TYPE: *Hotel.* HOST: Friendly staff. CLIENTELE: Gay men only. LOCATION: Central location, 1/2 block to jitney stop or bus, near Post Office, shopping, casinos and the beach.

* Rooms: 50 w/priv. bath
* Smoking allowed in rooms
* CTV, phone, A/C, C/H
* **Cafe 96**: breakfast, lunch & dinner; **John's American Grill** open summers on deck
* Bars: **Surfside Six Bar** (full liquor bar) & **Brass Rail** - next door 24 hrs.
* Disco: **Studio Six** (10:00 pm till dawn)
* Pool, outdoor sundeck w/full service bar
* Recreation: world famous boardwalk

* 12 casinos within walking distance
* Free parking (off street)
* Beach: 1 1/2 blocks
* Gay Bars: next door
* Health Club: walking distance
* Train Station: walking distance
* Airport: 15 minutes by taxi
* Credit Cards: MC/VISA/AMEX
* Open: Year round
* Rates: $65-$145; (off) $55-$125
* *TAC:* 12%

DESCRIPTION: Upscaled accommodations for gay men in the heart of Atlantic City. All rooms have refrigerators, remote Color TV, and sparkling clean private tiled bath with hair dryers. Deluxe rooms are available with wet bar, microwave oven and coffee maker. Outside rooms offer large picture windows overlooking the large sundeck and pool. Group rates on request.

TRUMP's TAJ MAHAL
1000 Boardwalk, Atlantic City, NJ 08401. Tel: (609) 449-1000. Fax: (609) 449-5501. TYPE: *Hotel/Casino.* CLIENTELE: Mostly Straight. LOCATION: Overlooking the beach and the boardwalk.

* Rooms: 1250 w/priv. bath
* Rooms for non-smokers
* CTV, phone, mini-bar, A/C
* Wheelchair accessibility
* 24 hrs. room service, maid service
* 16 restaurants & lounges
* Casino, Health Club, pool
* Beach: on the beach
* Gay Bars: walking distance
* Airport: 10 mi. / 16 km
* Open: Year round
* Credit Cards: MC/VISA/AMEX/JCB
* Open: Year round
* Rates: $115-$625
* *TAC:* 10%

DESCRIPTION: Eye-catching Tower Hotel & Casino complex.

NEW MEXICO

TAOS ●
SANTA FE●
● MADRID
ALBUQUERQUE ●

◆ **Population:** 1,300,000
◆ **Capital:** Santa Fe
◆ **Time Zone:** Mountain
◆ **No Sodomy Law**
◆ **Legal drinking age:** 21

ALBUQUERQUE   ℭ 505

✈ Albuquerque Int'l Airport (ABQ)

LOCATION: In the Rio Grande Valley, 55 mi. / 88 km southwest of Santa Fe, surrounded by mountains.

POPULATION: 340,000

CLIMATE: Arid continental. Sunny and dry with mild winters and hot summers. Average January temperatures in the mid 30°sF (2°c); and July temperatures in the 90"°sF (35°c).

Gay/Lesbian Visitor Information
Helpline : (505) 266-8041

DESCRIPTION: Surrounded by mountains Albuquerque is a growing town, and the home of the University of New Mexico. The dry sunny climate and mild winters have contributed to the reputation of Albuquerque as a year round health resort. Visit the **Old Town** with its lovely Spanish flavor; the **Maxwell Museum of Anthropology** with emphasis on Indian culture of the Southwest; **Fine Arts**

Center and the **Indian Pueblo Cultural Center**, 2401 12th St. NW, owned and operated by 19 indian pueblos of New Mexico. Nearby attractions include the **Turquoise Trail** a superb mountain scenery route between Albuquerque and Santa Fe; **Madrid**, a nearby community of artists, writers and film makers *(see additional information under Madrid in this section)*; and **Cerrillos** a quaint village known for its antiques and collectible shops.

❖ **SPECIAL EVENT: ZIA Rodeo**, gay rodeo, Sept. 3-5.

BARS ⟑ RESTAURANTS ⑪

● Bars/clubs (GM): **AMC**, leather bar, 7209 Central Ave. NE (255-4022); **Club on Central**, 10030 Central SE (291-1550); **Foxes**, dance bar, 8521 Central Ave. NE (255-3060); **The Ranch**, country / western man's bar, 8900 Central St. SE (275-1616).

● Bars/clubs (GW): **Corky's**, private dance club, 2428 San Mateo Place NE (881-9985); **Cricket's**, show bar, 5509-11 Central NW (836-2088).

● Restaurants (AW): **Chef du Jour**, American cuisine, 119 San Pasquale SW (247-8998); **Chianti's**, Italian, 5210 San Mateo NE (881-1967); **Monroe's**, Mexican, 1520 Lomas NW (242-1111) or 6051 Osuna NE (881-4224).

λ SERVICES λ

● Clothing (AW): **Hillson's**, western wear, 8800 Central SE (268-5070); **Western Warehouse**, 6210 San Mateo NE (883-7161).

● Erotica (G/S): **Harris Newsstand**, gay videos, magazines, 1301 San Mateo NE (260-0356); **Mr. Peepers**, 24 hrs., 4300 Edith Blvd. NE (343-8063).

● Leather (G/S): **Falcon Leather**, leather boots, 146 Washington Ave. SE (260-0900); **The Leather Shoppe**, erotic leather, 4217 Central NE (266-6690).

● Personal Phone Line (GM): ⊙ **Albequerque Confidential Connection**, meet local guys! Record, listen, respond to ads free (837-1300) free access code 8060.

🖾 ACCOMMODATIONS 🖾

BARCELONA COURT HOTEL
900 Louisiana Ave. NE, Albequerque   NM 87110. Tel: (505) 255-5566. TYPE: *Hotel*.

CLIENTELE: All Welcome. LOCATION: Financial District. 164 suites w/priv. bath, CTV, phone, wet bar, kitchens, tropical atrium, indoor and outdoor pools, fitness room. Rates: $75-$95. DESCRIPTION: All Suite hotel, 4 blocks from regional shopping mall.

DAVE's
P.O. Box 27214, Albuquerque, NM 87125-7214. Tel: (505) 247-8312. TYPE: *Bed & Breakfast.* HOST: Dave. CLIENTELE: Mostly Gay. LOCATION: 1.5 mi. / 2.4 km north of Old Town. 2 rooms.

ROYAL HOTEL
4119 Central Ave., Albuquerque, NM 87108. Tel: (505) 265-3585. Fax: (505) 260-1950. TYPE: *Hotel.* CLIENTELE: Mostly Straight. LOCATION: 8 blocks from State Fairgrounds and 4 mi. / 6 km to City Center. 70 rooms w/priv. bath, 10 suites, 3 studios w/full kitchen, CTV, phone, A/C, mini-bar, wheelchair access, restaurant & cocktail lounge, pool, jacuzzi & saunas, airport: 3 mi. / 5 km. Rates: $56-$95. *TAC:* 10%. DESCRIPTION: Superior tourist class motel in a convenient location.

MADRID ✆ 505

✈ Albuquerque Int'l Airport (ABQ)

LOCATION: In a valley near the Ortiz Mountains, 28 mi. / 45 km south of Santa Fe.

POPULATION: 425

CLIMATE: Sunny and dry desert climate with dust storms. The hottest month is July with temperatures reaching 90°F (32°c), however low humidity and cool nights make the heat bearable.

Gay/Lesbian Visitor Information
Diva Divine : (505) 438-4360

Internet: www.virtualmadrid.com
or kumo.swcp.com/showem/madrid/index.html

DESCRIPTION: Madrid is a tiny town on the historic and scenic Tuquoise Trail between Santa Fe and Albuquerque. The oldest coal mining town in New Mexico became a ghost town in the 50's. The town was later revived in the mid 70's by a group of colorful pioneers. The local residents have artistic and cultural inclination with about 30% gay, lesbian, bisexual or transgendered. Explore the town's numerous shops, cafes and art galleries. Visit

Madrid's **Coal Mine Museum** for a fascinating journey into the past; enjoy entertainment, benefit drag shows and holiday traditions at the **Mineshaft Tavern**. Madrid will fascinate you with its unique unspoiled charm and genuine joyous love of diversity, audacity and color.

BARS ♈ RESTAURANTS 🍴

● Bar/club (GMW): **Mineshaft Tavern**, old west style club, music and entertainment, Open daily - 11am-2am, 2846 State Hwy 14 (473-0743).

● Restaurants (GMW): **Blondie's**, home cooking diner, some vegetarian, southwestern hospitality, open: 8am - 6pm, 2849, Ste Hwy 14 (438-2772); **Java Junction**, coffee and gift shop, accommodations upstairs, Open: 8am - 7pm; 2855 State Hwy 14 (438-2772); **Mineshaft Tavern**, C&W tavern & restaurant, Open 11am-2am, 2846 State Hwy 14 (473-0743).

λ SERVICES λ

● Clothing (AW): ✪ **Woofy Bubbles Woowear**, unisex artwear for the body. From funky, cool hats, to vests, tunics, jackets and coats. All handmade by artist, open daily 10am - 5pm or call for appointment, 2872 State Hwy 14 (471-1083). Correspondence: PO Box 258, Cerrillas, NM 87010.

● Erotica (AW): ✪ **Diva Divine**, exotic, esoteric gift boutique celebrating the sensual with body products, gifts, erotic and spiritual jewelry, books, B&D toys, leather & PVC clothing and accessories, adult sex toys. A luscious emporium of smells, sounds and colors. Open daily - 10am - 5pm, 2850 State Hwy 14 (438-4360). Email: diva@nets.com

● Furniture (AW): ✪ **Impatient Artifacts**, Spanish and Colonial style pine furniture, wrought iron candle holders, and gift items, open daily 10am - 5pm except Tues, 36 Main St. (474-6878). Correspondence: #34 Back Road, Madrid NM 87101.

● Galleries (AW): ✪ **Apache Kid & Standing Bear**,antique native American articrafts,decorative items and ethnic art, open daily - 10am - 5pm, 2874 State Hwy 14 (474-3945); ✪ **Jack of All Arts**, 'feel good' art gallery with a whimsical mix of fun and fine art, monthly shows and themes, Open daily - 11am - 5pm, 2870 Hwy 14, Tel/Fax (505) 474-4044; **Madrid Folk**, local

art gallery, Open Thu-Mon 10am - 5pm, 2839 State Hwy 14 (471-2754); **Madrid Treasures**, unique hard to find antiques & collectibles, Open daily 10am - 5pm, 2821 State Hwy 14 (471-0553); ✪ **Primitiva**, handcrafted furniture, imports, gifts and accessories, Open daily 10am - 5:30pm, 2860 State Hwy 14 (471-7904).

🔑 ACCOMMODATIONS 🔑

JAVA JUNCTION
2855 Hwy 14, Madrid NM 87010. Tel: (505) 438-2772. TYPE: *Bed & Breakfast.* CLIENTELE: Gay/Straight. LOCATION: West side of Main St. DESCRIPTION: Victorian style bed & breakfast in the heart of historic Madrid. 2 suites. Large outside smoking terrace. Rates: $55-$65 w/CB

MADRID LODGING
14 Opera House Rd., Madrid NM 87010. Tel: (505) 471-3450. TYPE: *Bed & Breakfast.* CLIENTELE: All Welcome. LOCATION: In the Old Opera House in the center of Madrid. 2 room suite in a private home. Decks with view of Santa Fe. Outdoor jacuzzi. Rates: $55-$65 w/CB served in your room.

SANTA FE　　🕿　505

✈ Santa Fe Municipal Airport

LOCATION: Northern New Mexico in the Rio Grande Valley with the Jemez Mountains to the west and the Sangre de Cristo range of the Rockies to the east. Santa Fe is 59 miles / 94 km northeast of Albuquerque.

POPULATION: 50,000

CLIMATE: Sunny and dry desert climate with dust storms. The hottest month is July with temperatures reaching 90˚F (32˚c), however low humidity and cool nights make the heat bearable.

VISITOR INFORMATION
Chamber of Commerce
Tel: (505) 983-7317

DESCRIPTION: Santa Fe is the capital of New Mexico and the oldest capital of the nation. The population here is a mix of Spanish, Indian and Anglo, and the same goes for the dominating culture. The locals call their city "The City Different" and they are proud of its unique history, and perfect weather.

❖ **SPECIAL EVENTS: Santa Fe Rodeo,** for cowboys and cowboy lovers, mid July. Cultural events include the **Santa Fe Art Festival,** with a **Bach Festival** in February, Film Festival in April, and **Festival of the Arts** in October.

BARS 𝖸 RESTAURANTS 🍴

● Bars/clubs (GMW): **Edge,** 135 W. Palace, 3rd Fl. (966-1700).

● Restaurants (AW): **The Compound,** elegant award winning French Restaurant requiring formal dress, excellent but expensive; **Coyote Café,** contemporary ethnic cuisine, 132 W. Water St. (983-1615); **Hall of Fame,** western grill, vegetarian specialties, 319 So. Guadalupe (982-2565); **The Pink Abode,** 406 Old Santa Fe Trail (983-7712) authentic Spanish/Mexican cuisine.

🔑 ACCOMMODATIONS 🔑

ELDORADO A CLARION HOTEL
309 W. San Francisco St., Santa Fe, NM 87501. Tel: (505) 988-4455. TYPE: *Hotel.* CLIENTELE: Mostly Straight. LOCATION: Near the historic Plaza in downtown. 218 rooms w/priv. bath. 18 Suites. CTV, phone, A/C, wheelchair access, restaurants, pool, sauna, massage. Credit Cards: MC/VISA/AMEX/CB/DC. Rates: $115 - $250 (suite). *TAC:* 10%. DESCRIPTION: The most elegant hotel in town. Colorful decor, Indian motifs. Luxurious, well designed rooms, views of the city.

✪ INN of the TURQUOISE BEAR

342 E. Buena Vista St., Santa Fe, NM 87501-4423. Tel: (505) 983-0798. Toll Free (800) 396-4104. Fax: (505) 988-4225. E-mail: bluebear @roadrunner.com. TYPE: *Bed & Breakfast.* HOSTS: Ralph Bolton & Robert Frost. CLIENTELE: Mostly gay men & women. LOCATION: Quiet area, walk to Plaza (6 blocks), gay nightlife (3 blocks), galleries, museums, Indian Market; short drive to ski area, S.F. opera.

* Rooms: 10; 8 w/priv. bath, 2 w/shared bath dbl 8 / triple 2
* CTV, VCR, phone, refrigerator, C/H, kiva fireplace, hair dryer
* Bed Types: double, large (oversized) double, king size, queen size
* Maid service, wheelchair access (1 room)
* Recreation: hiking, skiing nearby
* Clothing optional policy, jacuzzi (soon)
* Parking: free (off street)
* Pets: w/prearrangements
* Gay Bars: 8 blocks
* Health Club: 2 mi. / 3 km (mixed)

* Airport: Albuquerque 55 mi. / 88 km
* Airport Transportation: shuttle
* Languages: Spanish, French, Norwegian
* Reservations: 50% deposit
* Cancellation: 14 days prior to arrival
* Credit Cards: MC/VISA/AMEX/DISC
* Season: Year round
* Rates: $90 - $210 / (off) $80 - $175 w/CB (expanded)
* Taxes: 10.25%
* Check In 3:00pm / Check out 12:00 noon
* *TAC:* 10%

DESCRIPTION: Authentic Adobe on a secluded acre at the historic estate of the poet, Witter Bynner, who "set the standard of being gay in Santa Fe". Experience southwest gay history in the home where Bynner hosted D.H. Lawrence and many other celebrities. *IGTA*

TAOS   © 505

✈ Albuquerque Int'l Airport (ABQ)

LOCATION: Northern New Mexico, on a high plateau flanked by mountains.

DESCRIPTION: Art colony in one of New Mexico's most scenic areas. The heritage of this historic town is an exotic mixture of Indian, Spanish and Anglo American.

BARS RESTAURANTS

● Restaurant (AW): **Apple Tree**, seafood and New Mexican dishes, 123 Bent St. (758-1900); **Casa de Valdez**, Southwestern Menu, 1401 Paseo del Pueblo Sur (758-8777); **El Patio de Taos**, outdoor dining, atrium fountain, fine art, bar open till midnight, 121 Teresino Lane, near Plaza (758-2121); **Villa Fontana**, Northern Italian cuisine, outdoor dining, 5 mi / 8 km N on NM522 (758-5800); **Wild & Natural Cafe**, 812-B Paseo del Pueblo Norte (751-0480).

ACCOMMODATIONS

CASA BENAVIDES INN
137 Kit Carson Rd., Taos NM 87571. Tel: (505) 758-1772. TYPE: *Bed & Breakfast Inn*. CLIENTELE: All Welcome. LOCATION: Near Taos Plaza. 28 rooms w/priv. bath, no smoking. Rates: $80-$195. DESCRIPTION: Beautifully restored Inn comprising former art gallery. Original works of art throughout.

HISTORIC TAOS INN
125 Paseo del Pueblo Norte, Taos NM 87571. Tel: (505) 758-5776. TYPE: *Historic Inn.* CLIENTELE: All Welcome. LOCATION: Downtown near Taos Plaza. 39 rooms w/priv. bath, CTV, phone, A/C, kiva fireplace, restaurant, bar, library, pool, jacuzzi, free parking. Rates: $75-$160. DESCRIPTION: Restored inn from 1800. Each room uniquely decorated in Southwestern style.

THE RUBY SLIPPER
P.O. Box 2069, Taos, NM 87571. Tel: (505) 758-0613. TYPE: *Bed & Breakfast.* HOST: Beth Goldman. CLIENTELE: Mostly Gay. LOCATION: 6 blocks west of Taos Plaza. 7 rooms.

TAOS STONE HOUSE
P.O. Box DD, Valdez NM 87580. Tel: (505) 776-2146. TYPE: *Guest House.* HOST: Noel Stone. CLIENTELE: Gay men & women. LOCATION: 10 min. from Taos Ski Valley. Rates: on request.

NEW YORK

ALBANY
●
CATSKILL MTS
●
NEW YORK ● LONG ISLAND
●
FIRE ISLAND

◆ **Population:** 17,560,000
◆ **Capital:** Albany
◆ **Time Zone:** Eastern
◆ **No Sodomy Law**
◆ **Legal drinking age:** 21

ALBANY   ✆ **518**

✈ County Airport (ALB) 8 mi. / 13 km NW

LOCATION: Upstate NY on the Hudson River, 155 mi. / 248 km north of Manhattan (NYC).

POPULATION: 102,000.

DESCRIPTION: Capital of New York State

and the seat of the State government. Visit the **State Capitol**, **State University** and the **Performing Arts Center** at the **Empire State Plaza**.

BARS ▼ RESTAURANTS ¶¶

● Bars/clubs (GM): **Oh Bar**, 304 Lark St. (463-9004); **Water Works Pub**, 76 Central Ave. (465-9079).

● Bars/clubs (GMW): **Club Oz**, 326 Central Ave. (434-4288); **Longhorns**, 90 Central Ave.; **Power Company**, 238 Washington Ave. (465-2556).

● Restaurant (AW): **Jack's Oyster House**, Continental cuisine, 42 State St. (465-8854).

λ SERVICES λ

● Video Shop (G/S): **Video Central**, videos and magazines, 37 Central Ave. (463-4153).

 ACCOMMODATIONS

HOWARD JOHNSON LODGE
Rte 9W Southern Blvd., Albany NY 12209. Tel: (518) 462-6555. Fax: (518) 462-2547. TYPE: *Motor Inn.* CLIENTELE: All Welcome. LOCATION: Exit 23 off New York Thruway, 12 mi / 19 km from airport. 177 rooms w/priv. bath, phone, CTV (movies), 5 suites, restaurant, coffee shop, pool, sauna, tennis, free parking. Rates: $68-$150. Tax: 11.2%. *TAC:* 10%.

FIRE ISLAND   ✆ **516**

✈ John F. Kennedy Int'l Airport (JFK)
   La Guardia Airport (LGA)
   MacArthur Airport (ISP) (L.I.)

LOCATION: Across the Great South Bay off southern Long Island's Atlantic shore, on a long and narrow strip of land.

POPULATION: 15,000

CLIMATE: Same as New York City with extra sea breeze.

VISITOR INFORMATION
Cherry Grove Chamber of Commerce
Cherry Grove, NY 11782
Tel: (516) 597-6040

DESCRIPTION: Fire Island is a national seashore, a barrier beach, 32 mi / 51 km long encompassing undeveloped land, beautiful beaches, and about 17 resort communities, 2 of which are gay (Cherry Grove & The Pines). Both gay communities are mixed (gay men & women). **Cherry Grove** is a small bohemian town, with some 200 wooden houses. In the summer it is known as "Pleasure Island" when it is invaded by pleasure-seeking gay tourists from all over America and Canada. The summer ends with the famous Miss Fire Island Contest. The 'Meat Rack' is a 24 hrs. cruising area between the Grove and the Pines. **The Pines**, the youngest community looks like a European resort with its harbor's floral borders, modern houses, apartment complexes and swimming pools. Real Estate values in The Pines compare favorably with Beverly Hills.

❖ **HOW TO GET THERE**: from New York City, catch the L.I. Railroad from Penn Station to Sayville. In Sayville catch the ferry for a twenty min. ride to Cherry Grove or the Pines on Fire Island. For ferry information call (516) 589-0810.

BARS ♟ RESTAURANTS 🍴

➤ The Pines (516)

● Bars/clubs (GMW): **Island Club**, piano bar, dancing, Fire Island Blvd., & Picketty Ruff Walk; **Botel**, the Pines (597-6131); **The Pavillion**, T-dance, Picketty Ruff at Fire Island Blvd. (597-6131).

● Restaurants (GMW): **Cultured Elephant**, Yacht Club (Botel) (597-6010); **Island Club Bistro**, Lower Mall next to the Loft, (597-6001); **Yacht Club**, Harbor Walk (597-6010).

➤ Cherry Grove (516)

● Bars/clubs (GMW): **Chery's**, outdoor piano bar, Bayview Walk (597-6820); **Ice Palace**

(597-6600); **El Mostro**, dance club, Ocean Walk, Cherry Grove (597-7455).

● Restaurants (GMW): **Mallory Square**, Cherry Grove Ferry Terminal (589-8628); **Michael's**, open 24 hrs., Dock Walk (597-6555); **Top of the Bay** Dock Walk at Bay Walk, 7-11pm daily, (597-6699).

λ SERVICES λ

➤ Fire Island Pines (516)

● Ferry Service (AW): daily departures in the summer from Sayville (LI) to Cherry Grove from 7a - 8:30p. Departure from Grove: from 7:25a-9p (almost every hour). Daily departures from Sayville to the Pines from 7a-8:30p. For more info call (516) 589-0810.

● Real Estate (GMW): ✪ **Bob Howard Real Estate**, Fire Island Pines rental and sales, 97 Fire Island Blvd., P.O. Box 5297, Fire Island Pines, NY 11782-0999. (516) 597-9400. Fax: (516) 597-9575. Bob Howard; ✪ **Fire Island Land Co.**, weekly, monthly, seasonal rentals of apartments and houses by the sea. A licensed real estate broker for your fun in the sun, P.O. Box 4161, Cherry Grove, NY 11782-0995. (597-6040) Paul or David; ✪ **Island Properties**, Real Estate and Management Corp., rentals, sales. Mailing address: May-Oct. P.O. Box 5272, 37 Fire Island Blvd., Fire Island Pines, NY 11782-5272. Nov.-Apr. P.O. Box 790, Wainscott, NY 11975-0790. Tel: (516) 597-6900. Carole or Cheri.

 ACCOMMODATIONS

✪ BELVEDERE HOTEL
P.O. Box 4026, Cherry Grove, NY 11782. Tel: (516) 597-6448. TYPE: *Hotel/Rental Apartments*. HOST: John Eberhardt. CLIENTELE: Gay men only. LOCATION: On Bayview Walk, near the corner of Maryland Walk, overlooking the bay in the eastern section of Cherry Grove.

* Rooms: 40, 30 w/priv., 10 w/shared bath
  35 db / 5 quad
* Smoking allowed in rooms
* CTV, VCR, refrigerator
* Wheelchair accessible
* Clothing optional policy
* Pool, sundeck, gym, hot tub, jacuzzi
* Beach: 300 yards / 300 m
* Gay Bars: 10 min. walk
* Health Club: on premises
* Airport: 5 mi. (8 km), taxi + ferry
* Train Station: Sayville (L.I.R.R.)

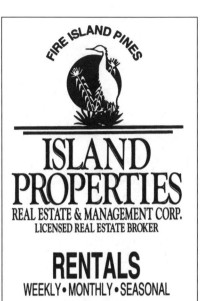

* Reservations: 50% deposit required
* Cancellation: 7 days before arrival
* Credit Cards: MC/VISA/AMEX
* Open: May 1 - October 1
* Rates: $80-$200 + tax
  w/Cb on weekend (sun+holidays)
* Check in 1 pm / Check out 11 am

DESCRIPTION: Charming Italian Venetian style hotel amidst a beautifully landscaped European garden with statutes and fountains. Guest rooms are furnished with antiques and period decor. Complimentary fresh coffee every morning. The Belvedere has been a Fire Island Community Landmark since 1950.

✪ CAROUSEL GH

P.O. Box 4001, Cherry Grove, NY 11782-0998.
Tel: (516) 597-6612. HOSTESS: Tricia Mgr.
TYPE: *Guest House*. CLIENTELE: Mostly Gay.
LOCATION: In Cherry Grove on Holly Walk.

* Rooms: 11 w/shared bath
  2 sgl / 9 dbl
* Smoking allowed in rooms
* Rooms for non smokers
* Beach: 300 ft. / 100 m (mixed)
* Gay Bars: 2 min. walk
* Airport: LI McArthur in Islip, 30 min.
* Train Station: Sayville
* Reservations: 50% deposit
* Cancellation: with 14 days, 80% of deposit
  is refunded, no exceptions
* Credit Cards: MC/VISA/AMEX
* Open: May - Fall
* Rates: $61 - $175 w/CB
* Check in 2:00pm / Check out 11:30am

DESCRIPTION: Charming guest house set in a flowering garden, just 300 ft. / 100 m from the white sands of the ocean.

CHERRY GROVE BEACH HOTEL
Fire Island, Cherry Grove, NY 11782, P.O.Box 537, Sayville, NY 11782. Tel: (516) 597-6600. TYPE: *Hotel*. CLIENTELE: Mostly Gay. LOCATION: In the heart of Cherry Grove.

* Rooms: 58 w/priv. bath
* Rooms for smokers and non smokers
* CTV, VCR, phone, refrigerator, safe box,
  C/H, A/C, cooking facilities
* Maid service, wheelchair access
* Bar & Disco: **Ice Palace**
* Pool, sundeck, gym, sauna
* Clothing optional policy
* Beach: 200 ft. / 70 m (gay/nude beach)
* Gay Bars: 200 ft. / 70 m
* Airport: MacArthur-Islip 9 mi. / 14 km
* Train Station: Sayville LIRR 5 mi. / 8 km

* Reservations: 50% deposit
* Cancellation: 14 days in advance
* Credit Cards: MC/VISA/AMEX/DISC
* Open: May 1 - October 1
* Rates: $69.69 - $399.69 / (off) $39.69-$199.69
* Tax: 9 1/4% *TAC:* 20%
* Check in Time 3pm / Check out 12 noon

DESCRIPTION: Fire Island's largest hotel. Choose between economy and deluxe rooms with kitchenette. Ask about additional nights at $19.96.

HUDSON RIVER VAL. ✆ 914
CATSKILL MTS ✆ 518

✈ Albany County Airport (ALB)

DESCRIPTION: The Hudson River Valley area and The Catskill Mountains, roughly 2 1/2 hrs. drive north of New York City include some of the country's wildest and most pristine natural parks south of Maine.

BARS Ⴤ RESTAURANTS ¶¶

● Bars/Clubs (GMW): **Barz**, 327 Rte 9W, Upper Nyack (914-353-4444); **Club Fix**, Rte 9, Wappingers Falls, Dutchess Shopping Plaza (914-297-1585).

● Restaurants (GMW): **Catskill Rose**, Rt. 212, Mt. Tremper, just west of Woodstock (914-688-7100); **Coven Cafe**, 162 Main Street, Nyack (914-358-9829); **Sandy's**, 325 North Main St. Port Chester (914-939-0758).

ACCOMMODATIONS ❧

POINT LOOKOUT
Rt. 23, E. Windham, NY. Tel: (518) 734-3381. TYPE: *Restaurant & Inn*. CLIENTELE: All Welcome.

RIVER RUN
Main Street, Fleishmans, NY 12430. TEL: (914) 254-4884. TYPE: *Bed & Breakfast*. HOST: Larry Miller. CLIENTELE: All Welcome. LOCATION: Edge of the Catskill Forest. DESCRIPTION: Queen Ann Victorian guest house. 7 rooms. Rates: $50-$90. Tax: 6%. *TAC:* 10%.

UJJALA's
2 Forest Glenn, New Paltz NY 12561. TEL: (914) 255-6360. TYPE: *Bed & Breakfast*. CLIENTELE: All Welcome. DESCRIPTION: Victorian Country Inn.

LONG ISLAND ✆ **516**

✈ MacArthur Airport Islip (ISP)

LOCATION: Long Island stretches 120 mi. / 193 km east by northeast from the edge of Manhattan to the dunes of Montauk.

POPULATION: 7,000,000 (including Brooklyn & Queens which are part of New York City).

Gay/Lesbian Visitor Information
Nassau Hot Line (NOW): 485-8902

CLIMATE: see New York City

DESCRIPTION: A long and narrow island stretching from Great Neck on the border with Queens (NYC) to Montauk in the East. It is composed of two counties: Nassau and Suffolk, Nassau being closer to New York City.

Long Island offers lovely state parks, quaint historic villages, and lovely harbours with fine seafood restaurants, shops and galleries. Northeastern Long Island has developed a reputable wine country with first class vineyards that offer Old World touch to their region. Long Island has a large and established gay community with many bars, discos and clubs in various locations. Large communities exist in Huntington, Port Washington, and a few other towns.

❖ Gay Beaches: Miles of clean sandy beaches have always been the island's best treasures. For gay visitors we recommend: **Jones Beach**

State Park, "Field 6A", located east of Field 6, thousands of gay sun - worshippers congregate each summer, off south end of Wantagh or Meadowbrook Parkways; **Robert Moses State Park**, Fire Island; **East Hampton Beach**, 5 mi. / 8 km of sandy beach stretching from Georgica Pond on west to 2 Mile Hollow Road on east; **Fowler Beach**, on Flying Pt. Rd., South Hampton; and of course the famous gay beaches at the **Pines** and **Cherry Grove** (see information under Fire Island).

BARS ⅄ RESTAURANTS ¶¶

➤ **Nassau (516)**

● Bars/clubs (GMW): **Beret's**, LI's newest and most popular club, great DJ, dance floor, bar and lounge, always crowded Thursdays and Saturdays, 272 Post Ave. Westbury (997-4400); **Chameleon**, 4020 Long Beach Rd., Island Park (889-4083); **Libations**, 3547 Merick Rd., Seaford (679-8820); **Pal Joey's**, neighborhood bar, slightly older crowd, 2457 Jerusalem Ave., N. Bellmore (785-9301). **Silver Lining**, the dinosaur of Long Island clubs at 20+ years, excellent DJ, always popular on Wednesdays and Fridays, but open Wed-Sun, 175 CherryLane, Floral Park (488-5193).

● Club (GW): **Bedrock**, women's disco, 121 Woodfield Ave., West Hempstead (486-9516).

➤ **Suffolk (516)**

● Bars/clubs (GM): **Bunkhouse**, 192 Montauk Hwy, Sayville (567-2865); **Club Swamp & The Annex**, club & disco, Montauk Hwy, Wainscott, Route 27A (537-3332); **LI Eagle**, very popular with the leather crowd, 94 No. Clinton Ave., Bay Shore (968-2750).

● Bars/clubs (GMW): **Blanche**, cocktail lounge, 47-2 Boundary Ave., So. Farmingdale (594-6906); **Club 608**, bar, open 7 days at 8pm, 608 Sunrise Hwy, West Babylon (661-9580); **Fanny's**, 7 Price Rd., Rocky Point (744-4290); **St. Marks Place**, dance club for men and women, crowded on Saturdays, 6550 Jericho Turnpike, Commack (499-2244); **Thunders / The Loft**, Long Island's Friday night hotspot for men and women, excellent DJ, dance floor, piano bar, patio, 1017 E. Jericho Tpke, Huntington Station (423-5241).

● Club (GW): **Forever Green**, women's disco, 841 N. Broome Ave., Lindenhurst (226-9357).

● Restaurants: **Annex** (GM), at Swamp's bar, Montauk Hwy, Wainscott (537-3332); **Bayman's Catch** (AW), seafood, 220 N. Main St., Sayville (589-9744); **Silver Spoon** (GMW), 56 Sunrise Hwy, Merrick (377-4437).

⅄ SERVICE ⅄

● Adult Shop (G/S): **Heaven Sent Me**, books, magazines, videos and toys, Open: 24 hrs. / 7 days, 108 Cain Dr., Brentwood (434-4777).

● Cinema (G/S): **Cinema Arts Centre**, Community cinema featuring quality award winning films, many on gay & lesbian subjects, 423 Park Ave., Huntington (423-8610).

● Personal Phone Line (GM): ✪ **Long Island Confidential Connection**, meet local guys! Record, listen, respond to ads free (496-4444) free access code 8060.

● Publications (GMW): ✪ **Long Island Pride Press**, informative communications resource for the Long Island (NY) gay & lesbian community. Publishers of **LIPP** and the **Long Island Pride Guide** distributed free every Pride Month (June), P.O. Box 2303, N. Babylon, NY 11703. Tel: (516) 225-7900. Fax: (516) 225-7918.

● Travel (GMW): ✪ **Odysseus Publishing & Travel**, publishers of Odysseus the Int'l Gay & Lesbian Travel Planner. Also reservation service for int'l gay resorts. Box 1548, Port-Washington, NY 11050. (516) 944-5330 or (800) 257-5344. Fax: (516) 944-7540 or (800) 982-6571.

◈ ACCOMMODATIONS ◈

CENTENNIAL HOUSE
13 Woods Lane, E. Hampton NY. Tel: (516) 324-9414. TYPE: *Guest House*. HOST: Harry & David. CLIENTELE: All Welcome. LOCATION: Central near the beach. Rates: on request. DESCRIPTION: A small Victorian style B&B.

THE INN AT MEDFORD
at exit #64 L.I.Exwy, 2695 RT 112, Medford, L.I., NY 11763. Tel: (516) 654-3000 or (800) 626-7779. Fax: (516) 654-1281. TYPE: *Hotel*. HOST: Richard Yaeger GM. CLIENTELE: All Welcome. LOCATION: Centrally located between NYC and the Hamptons on Exit 64 on the L.I.E. 76 rooms, 8 suites w/priv. bath, CTV, phone, C/H, A/C, bar, pool, gym. DESCRIPTION: Friendly Inn with "A touch of Old Santa Fe".

NEW YORK CITY © 212/718

MANHATTAN   212
BROOKLYN/QUEENS/STATEN ISLAND   718

✈ John F. Kennedy Int'l Airport (JFK)

15 mi. / 24 km Southeast,
50-60 min. to downtown
La Guardia Airport (LGA)
8 mi. / 13 km northeast
30-45 min. to downtown
Newark Int'l Airport (EWR) (NJ)
16 mi. / 26 km southwest
45-60 min. to downtown

LOCATION: Northeastern coast of the U.S.A on the Atlantic Ocean.

POPULATION: Metro - 7,071,000
                     Manhattan 1,430,000

CLIMATE: Average low 27°F (-3°c) in the winter with occasional snowfall; hot and humid summer with an average high of 85 c); Cool fall/spring seasons with average temperature in the 50°sF (12°c).

VISITOR INFORMATION
New York CVB
Tel: (212) 397-8222

Gay/Lesbian Visitor Information
Gay & Lesbian Switchboard
Tel: (212) 777-1800 (noon-midnight)

L & G Community Center
208 West 13th St., New York NY 10011
Tel: (212) 620-7310

DESCRIPTION: New York City - the 'Big Apple', is the most exciting and diverse city on Earth. It is a bustling metropolis that proudly enjoys its position as the world capital of culture, entertainment, dining, shopping and sightseeing. NYC offers wonderful museums, art galleries, music and dance performances. Some of the better known museums are - **Gugghenheim Museum**, int'l art center, 1071 Fifth Ave. (423-3500); **Metropolitan Museum of Art**, Fifth Ave., & 82nd St. (535-7710); **New York Film Academy**, 375 Greenwich (941-4007); **Statue of Liberty Museum**, Liberty Island NY (363-3200).

The City is composed of five boroughs - **The Bronx, Brooklyn, Manhattan, Queens**, and **Staten Island**. New York is the city where gay

liberation began with the events at Stonewall. As a visitor to you will appreciate the variety of attractions and the numerous establishments that cater to gay men and lesbian clientele. In spite of the size of the city it is one of the few USA cities where visitors do not need to rely on a car. The public transportation is relatively affordable and easily accessible from and to almost any point of interest in the city.

The following New York City areas are of major interest to gay and lesbian visitors:

❖ **Chelsea**, New York City's premier gay district, an eclectic residential neighborhood in the West 20's between 7th and 10th Avenues half way between Greenwich Village and Mid-Town's Theatre District. Chelsea has a substantial gay population and has been transformed into New York City's largest gay & lesbian residential and entertainment center. Chelsea offers fine gay and lesbian owned hotels, guest houses, bars, clubs, restaurants & theatres.

❖ **Columbus Ave**, on the west side of Central Park between 65th and 79th Streets (one block over from Central Park West), is a desirable neighborhood among the more affluent in the gay community. It offers a profusion of trendy boutiques, shops, restaurants, bars and many other diverse businesses, many of which are gay owned.

❖ **Greenwich Village**, a bohemian residential quarter in lower manhattan which extends from 14th St. south to Houston St. and from Washington Square west to the Hudson River. The "village" is home to artists, writers and a large gay community.

● **Theatres**: New York is famous for its theatre productions. Broadway - known as the "**Theatre District**" is located near **Times Square** and features world-class theatre and musical productions. Tickets for Broadway and Off Broadway productions are available through Telecharge (212) 239-6200.

❖ Gay Beaches: **Jones Beach** on Long Island; **Fire Island**, the gay 'Mecca' for those who want to escape the humdrum of city life in the summer, is located just off the south shore of Long Island along the Atlantic, about 60 to 90 minutes drive east of New York City.

❖ **SPECIAL EVENTS: New York's Gay & Lesbian annual Pride March**, last Sunday in June. The march originated in 1970 to commemorate the Stonewall Riots of June 27-29,

1969. The New York march is the largest annually held Gay & Lesbian civil rights event in the world; ✪ **Liberty Open 1997**, Int'l G&L tennis tournament, July 4-7 (4th of July weekend) (802-4768); **Greenwich Village Halloween Parade**, largest public celebration of Halloween in the USA, fun, gay, colorful Mardi Gras style parade, Oct. 31.

BARS Y RESTAURANTS ¶¶

Most New York City gay bars are located in Greenwich Village, Chelsea, or the Upper West Side near Columbus Circle. However, some bars and discos exist in other parts of Manhattan and the boroughs.

● Bars/Clubs (GM):
☞ **Chelsea** (212) - ✪ **Splash**, friendly bar with live entertainment nightly and the Big Apple's most attractive men, busy every night by 10:00pm, 50 West 17th St. (691-0073); **Break**, popular on Tuesday's, video cruise bar, pool rooms and backyard patio/terrace, 232 8th Ave. (22nd) (627-0072); **Barracuda**, 50's style cruise bar, drag shows, 275 W. 22nd (645-8613); **Champs**, crowded cruise bar, gym-boy scene, gets busy by 11:00pm, 17 W. 19th St. (633-1717); **Eagle**, for the NYC leather scene, 142 11th Ave. (691-8451); **King**, three-level men's dance club, very cruisy darkroom, sexy theme nights, Underwear Party on Sundays, 579 Ave. of the Americas (366-5464); **Rawhide**, cruise leather bar, 212 8th Ave. at 21st (242-9332); **Rome**, Multilevel megabar with ancient Roman theme, popular on weekends, go-go men, 290 8th Ave. at 24th (242-6969) **Roxy**, former roller rink with two bars, mixture of muscle men and drag queens, roller skating Tuesdays, dancing Saturdays, 515 W. 18th St. (645-5156); **Spike**, levi/leather bar, 11th Ave. at 20th (243-9688); **Tunnel**, monster club with after hours party, go-go men, VIP lounge, bathroom bar, 220 12th Ave. (695-4682).

☞ **Greenwich Village** (212) - **Boots & Saddle**, cruise bar, 76 Christopher St. (929-9684); **Dugout**, western levy cruise bar, 185 Christopher (242-9113); **Hangar**, cruise neighborhood bar, go-go boys, 115 Christopher St. (627-2044); **J's Hangout**, sex club, dark rooms, J.O. caves, after hours dancing and cruising, 675 hudson at 14th St.; **Julius**, 159 W. 10th St. (929-9672); **Lure**, leather bar, 409 West 13th St., (741-3919); **Monster**, 80 Grove St., (924-3558); **Pieces**, video, piano bar, 8 Christopher St. (929-9291); **Stonewall**, 53 Christopher St. (463-0950); **Two Potato**, mostly African-American clientele, strippers, drag shows, 145 Christopher St. (255-0286);

Open every day from 4 p.m. to 4 a.m.
HAPPY HOUR
Monday to Saturday
4 p.m. to 8 p.m
2 for 1

SPLASH BAR
50 W. 17th. Street, off 6th. Ave. N.Y.C.

ODYSSEUS '97/98

BRUNCH
216 Seventh Avenue (22-23)
GARDEN
New York City   212-242-7900
LIVE DJ
Community
BAR & GRILL

TY's, friendly neighborhood gay saloon, 114 Christopher St. (741-9641); **Uncle Charlie's**, cruise bar, gym type crowd, go-go dancers, 56 Greenwich Ave. (255-8787).

☞ **East Side** (212) - ✪ **The Web**, New York City's only Upper East Side video/laser disc music dance club with multi-national clientele, 40 E. 58th St. (308-1546); **Bridge Bar**, slick and cruisy hangout, 309 E. 60th St. (223-9104); **Tool Box**, video/cruise bar, 1742 2nd Ave. (427-3106); **Townhouse**, bar/restaurant, professional clientele, 236 E. 58th St. (754-4649).

☞ **East Village** (212) - Palladium, Junior Vasquez's NYC home on Saturdays, excessively popular, 126 East 14th St., (473-7171); **Boiler Room**, 86 E. 4th St. (254-7536); **Boy Bar**, cruise bar, entertainment, 15 St. Marks Pl. (674-7959); **Cake**, casual homo hangout, 99 Ave. B (674-7957); **Crowbar**, popular alternative bar, attractive local crowd, 339 E. 10th St. (420-0670); **Dick's Bar**, video bar, 192 2nd Ave. (475-2071); **Tunnel Bar**, dance/cruise bar, popular with East Village artists, 116 First Ave. (777-9232); **Wonder Bar**, 505 E. 6th St. (777-9105).

☞ **Tribeca** (212) - **Altar**, leather bar, 161 W. Broadway (571-7272).

☞ **West Side** (212) - **The Works**, most popular Westside video bar, great international music, wide-screen televisions, pool table and video games, Sunday Beer Blast, call for nightly specials, 428 Columbus Ave. (at 81st) (799-7365); **Coqtales**, 730 8th Ave., at 45th St., (560-9961); **Candle Bar**, leather/western, 309 Amsterdam Ave. (874-9155); **Falcon Club**, 42 W. 33rd St. (279-0179); **Savoy**, Times Square bar behind the Port Authority, body contests on Weekends, 335 W. 41st St at 9th Ave. (560-9635).

● Bars/Clubs (GMW):

☞ **Greenwich Village** (212) - **Dick's Bar**, 192 2nd Ave., (388-0689); **Eighty Eight**, show bar, cabaret, 228 W. 10th St. (924-0088); **Fat Cat**, mainly womyn's piano bar, 281 W. 12th St. (243-9041); **Mike's Club**, neighborhood bar and cafe, 400 W. 14th St. at 9th Ave. (691-6606); **Nuts & Bolts**, cocktail lounge, piano bar, male dancers, 101 7th Ave., So. (620-4000); **Two Potato**, 145 Christopher St. (242-9340); **Wonder Bar**, East Village mixed bar, 505 E. 6th St. (777-9105).

☞ **East Side** (212) - **G.H. Club**, bar for mature clientele, 353 E. 53rd St. and 1st Ave. (223-9752); **Pegasus Bar**, cafe, restaurant, cabaret, 119 E. 60th St. (888-4702).

☞ **Midtown** (212) - **Buster's**, neighborhood bar, 129 Lexington Ave. at 29th St. (684-8832); **Don't Tell Mama**, cabaret / showbar, 343 W. 46th St. (757-0788).

☞ **Brooklyn** (718) - **1 Hot Spot**, friendly bar, sizzling dance club, weekend shows. The hottest spot under the Brooklyn bridge, 1 Front St., Brooklyn Heights (852-0139); **Spectrum**, multi-level video dance bar and entertainment complex, 802 64th St. (238-8213).

☞ **Queens** (718) - ☞ **Astoria**: **Krash**, male strippers, drag shows, 34-48 Steinway St at 35th Ave. (937-2400). ☞ **Forest Hills/Kew Gardens**: a fashionable neighborhood in Queens where many professional and affluent gay people live. **BS**, 113-24 Queens Blvd. (Forest Hills) video-bar, D.J. music (263-0300); **Boulevard**, night club, open 7 days 9pm-4am, 2 blocks east of Old Hatfields, 137-65 Queens Blvd., Briarwood (739-2200). ☞ **Jackson Heights**: mixed neighborhood, large hispanic and gay population. **Bachelors Tavern**, 81-12 Roosevelt Ave. (458-3131); **Friend's Tavern**, American-Latino bar, 78-11 Roosevelt Ave. (397-7256); **Llamarada**, latin club with Latin and American music, friendly atmosphere, 82-20 Baxter Ave., Jackson Heights (779-7200); **Montana Saloon**, western bar, 40-08 74th St.,

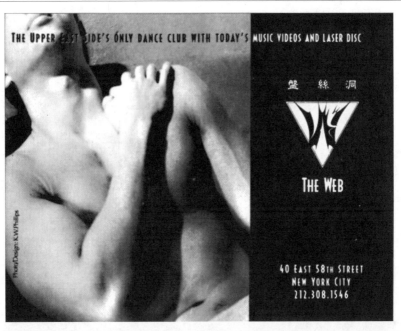

at Broadway (429-9356). ☞ **Woodside: Lucho's Club**, Latino night club, drag shows, dancing, 38-19 69th St. (899-9048).

● Bars/clubs (GW):

☞ **Greenwich Village** (212) - **Clit Club**, dance club, 432 W. 14th St. (529-3300); **Crazy Nanny**, mostly lesbians, video bar, pool tables, 21 7th Ave. So. (366-6312); **Cubbyhole**, small women's bar, 281 W. 12th St. (243-9041); **Henrietta Hudson**, video bar, 438 Hudson St. (243-9079); **Light Wisdom & Sound**, Saturday Night club, 229 West 28th St (645-6479); **Meow Mix Bar**, popular dyke bar with a great jukebox, open Tue-Sun, 269 E. Houston St. (254-1434); **Rubyfruit**, bar & grill, 531 Hudson St. (929-3343); **Wonder Bar**, hangout for lipstick lesbos and their admirers, 505 E. 6th St. (777-9105).

☞ **Upper East Side** (212) - **Julies**, professional women, 204 East 58th St., (688-1294).

● Restaurants (GMW):

➤ **Chelsea** (212) - ✪ **Community Bar & Grill**, upscale inviting restaurant, eclectic menu, Nouvelle American Cuisine, divers selection of daily specials, 216 Seventh Ave. (between 22-23rd sts) (242-7900); **Cafe "Q"**, 192 8th Ave. (627-2166); **Claire**, Seafood, Key West style, 156 7th Ave. (255-1055); **Man Ray**, contemporary American, 169 **Moran's**, steakhouse, 146 10th Ave. (627-3030); **Tiziano Trattoria**, Italian fare, fish and seafood, 165 8th Ave. (989-2330).

➤ **Greenwich Village** (212) - **Chez Ma Tante**, French bistro, 189 W. 10th St. (620-0223); **Elephant & Castle**, American food, 68 Greenwich Ave. (243-1400); **The Paris Commune**, 411 Bleecker St. (929-0509); **Rosolio Restaurante**, Tuscan cuisine, 11 Barrow St. (645-9224); **Soup's Café**, 210 W. 10th St. (727-7499); **Woody's**, bar & restaurant, 140 7th Ave., So. (242-1200).

➤ **Mid-Town** (212) - **West Side Chef**, authentic Chinese cuisine in a gay friendly atmosphere, 315 W. 57th St. (541-8999); **Chez Suzette**, French, 363 W. 46th St., (974-9002); **Uncle Nick**, Greek cuisine, 747 9th Ave. (245-7992); **Pegasus**, cafe & espresso bar, 119 E. 60th St. (888-4702); **Townhouse**, bar, restaurant, 206 E. 58th St. (826-6241). Other (AW): **Bistro at Trump Tower**, Italian menu, chic 5th Ave. ambience, cascading water falls, 725 Fifth Ave. (832-1555); **Russian Tea Room**, Russian cuisine, next to Carnegie Hall, popular with performing artists, 150 W. 57th St., (265-0947); **Victor's Café 52**, Cuban, fresh Seafood, 236 West 52nd St., (586-7714).

➤ **Upper West Side** (212) - **Josie's**, 300 Amsterdam Ave. (769-1212); **Niko's Mediterranean**, Greek cuisine, 2161 Broadway at 76th St. (873-7000); **Royal Canadian Pancake House**, 2286 Broadway (873-6052); **Sidewalkers**, 12 W. 72nd St. (799-6070).

➤ **Flushing** (Queens) (718) - For inexpensive, yet delightful authentic Chinese cuisine skip China Town and check the restaurants in Flushing (Queens) last stop on the number 7 train from Times Square. My favorites are: **Bamboo Garden**, vegetarian Taiwanese, wonderful cuisine with delicious meat substitutes for cholesterol restricted diets, moderate, 41-28 Main St. (463-9240); **Happy Dumpling**, try their steamed corn buns, 135-29 40th Rd. (445-2163); **Szechuan Capital**, 135-28 Roosevelt (762-0950).

λ   SERVICES   λ

● Clothing (G/S): **Village Army Navy**, 328 Bleecker St. (242-6665); **Chelsea Army Navy**, 110 8th Ave. (645-7420); 1598 Second Ave. (737-4661).

● Erotica (GM): ✪ **Christopher St. Book Shop**, serving the needs of the gay community

for over 25 years in the "Gay Village", 500 Hudson at Christopher St., (463-0657); ✪ **Les Hommes Book Shop**, 217 W. 80th St., (Btwn. B'way & Amsterdam), "THE" All-Male Uptown Bookstore, open 24 hrs.; ✪ **Unicorn**, All male erotica, exclusively for gay men, 277-C West 22nd St. (924-2921); **Ann St. Entertainment Center**, mixed, Quality erotica in the heart of New York's Financial Center, 21 Ann St. (Broadway & Nassau) (267-9760); **Eros**, male cinema, 8th Ave. between 45 & 46 (221-2450); **Gaiety Theatre**, go-go boys and porn films, 201 W. 46th St. (221-8868); **7th Avenue Playhouse**, 12:00 noon - 6am 7 days a week, two private lounges, 28 7th Ave., So. (229-0418).

● Gifts/Cards: **Candle Shop**, 118 Christopher St. (989-0148); **Come Again**, erotic emporium, 353 E. 53rd St. (308-9394); **Crystal Gardens**, 21 Greenwich Ave. (727-0692); **Greetings**, 45 Christopher St. (242-0424); **Rainbows & Triangles**, 192 8th Ave. (627-2166).

● Health Care (AW): **Village Apothecary**, all prescriptions filled, in the heart of Greenwich Village, 346 Bleecker St., (807-7566); **Health on Christopher**, vitamins, herbs, health food, 9 Christopher St. (691-7955); **MacKay Drugs**, 55 5th Ave. (627-2300).

● Health Clubs (GM): **American Fitness Center**, mixed clientele, 128 8th Ave. (627-0065); **Body by Serge**, 692 Greenwich St. (675-1179); **East Side Sauna**, open 24 hrs., 227 E. 56th St. (753-2222) (mid-town); **Spa 227**, sauna, 227 East 56th St., 3rd floor (754-0227); **Wall Street Sauna**, 1 Maiden Lane (233-8900) (downtown); **Chelsea Gym**, mostly gay, 267 West 17th St. (255-1150).

● Leather Store (G/S): **Leather Man**, 111 Christopher St. (243-5339); **The Noose**, 261 West 19th St. (807-1789).

● Maps (GMW): ✪ **Columbia Fun Maps**, free Gay & Lesbian guide maps to Manhattan, Los Angeles, San Diego and 63 destinations across the USA, Canada and the US Virgin Islands, 118 E. 28th St., suite #308, New York NY 10016. (212) 447-7877. Fax: (212) 447-7876.

● Publications (GMW): ✪ **Gayellow Pages**, community resource guide with listings of bars, clubs, lodging, organizations, helplines, and legal / professional resources for gay men and lesbians, local and nationwide editions, PO Box 533, Village Station, NY 10014-0533. (674-0120). Fax: (212) 420-1126.

● Records (AW): **Disc-O-Rama**, 186 W. 4th St. (206-8417); **Tower Records**, 692 Broadway (505-1500); Triton, 247 Bleecker St. (243-3610).

● Sightseeing (AW): **Circle Line**, 3 hrs. sightseeing cruise around Manhattan, West 42nd St., at the Hudson River (563-3200); **Liberty Helicopters**, flight tours over Manhattan, daily from 9:00 am - 9:00 pm (800-542-9933); **New York Apple Tours**, visit NYC's major tourist sites, hotel pick-ups between 8:30 am-10:00 am. (800-876-9868).

● Tanning Salons (AW): **The Beach**, 112 Christopher St. (924-8551); **Beach Bum Tanning**, 224 W. 4th St. (366-4853); **The Coast**, 53 Greenwich Ave. (675-9009).

● Reservation Service (GMW): ✪ **Just Right Reservations**, hotels, inns, and guest houses in Boston, Provincetown, and New York City. Office hours: Mon-Fri 9am-4pm EST. James Koumpouras, managing partner, 18 Piedmont St., 2nd Fl. (617-423-3550).

● Travel Services (GMW): ✪ **Odysseus Travel**, Holiday reservations in Greece (all islands) - accommodations, cruises, sightseeing tours, yacht charters (Specialize in Athens, Mykonos, Santorini); Spain - Canary Islands, Ibiza, Sit-

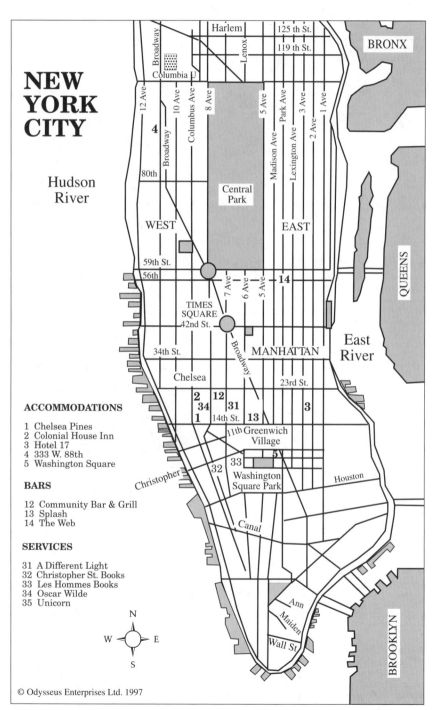

NEW YORK CITY

Hudson River

ACCOMMODATIONS

1 Chelsea Pines
2 Colonial House Inn
3 Hotel 17
4 333 W. 88th
5 Washington Square

BARS

12 Community Bar & Grill
13 Splash
14 The Web

SERVICES

31 A Different Light
32 Christopher St. Books
33 Les Hommes Books
34 Oscar Wilde
35 Unicorn

N
W — E
S

© Odysseus Enterprises Ltd. 1997

ODYSSEUS '97/98

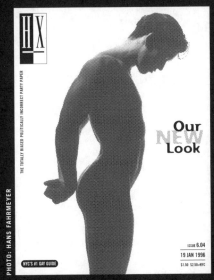

ges; Italy - Rome, Florence, Venice, Taormina
(Sicily); France - Paris, Cannes, Nice; Holland -
Amsterdam; Mexico - Puerto Vallarta, Acapulco, Cancun; Israel, Turkey, Argentina, Brazil,
Costa Rica. **AMSTERDAM GAY GAMES
1998 PACKAGES (AUG.1-8, '98) from JFK.
Call now for reservations!** Individualized and
attentive service. P.O. Box 1548, Port Washington, NY 11050. Tel: (516) 944-5330 or (800) 257-
5344. Fax: (516) 944-7540 or (800) 982-6571.
Email: odyusa@odyusa.com. Internet: http://w-
ww.odyusa.com. **Serving the Gay & Lesbian
community since 1984.** *IGTA, ASTA*

 ACCOMMODATIONS

❂ CHELSEA PINES INN

317 W. 14th St., New York NY 10014. Tel:
(212) 929-1023. Fax: (212) 620-5646. TYPE:
Bed & Breakfast. OWNER: Jay B. Lesiger.
CLIENTELE: Gay men and women. LOCA-
TION: On the border of Greenwich Village and
Chelsea. Between 8th and 9th Avenues. Conve-
nient to all transportation.

* Rooms: 24 dbl; 4 w/priv. bath, 11 w/shared,
  8 w/semi priv. bath
* Smoking allowed in rooms
* CTV (movies), phone, A/C, C/H, refrigerator
* Safe in office
* Bed Types: double, queen size
* Business fax/phone facilities
* Daily maid service, no pets
* Parking: paid off street; garden
* Beach: 1 hour (gay)
* Gay Bars: 1/2 block
* Health Club: 2 blocks
* Airports: JFK, LGA, NWK 30 min. to 1 hour
* Airport Transportation: taxi, bus
* Languages: English
* Reservations: Credit Card guarantee
  or 1 night deposit
* Cancellation: 7 days prior to arrival
* Credit Cards: MC/VISA/AMEX/DIS/DC/CB
* Open: Year round
* Rates: $75 - $99 (plus tax) w/ expanded CB
* Taxes: 13.25% + $2 per night
* Check In 2:00 pm / Check out 12:00 noon
* **TAC:** 10%
* Email: cpiny@aol.com

DESCRIPTION: A comfortable, charming Bed
and Breakfast in the heart of 'Gay New York'.
Guest rooms are pleasantly appointed. All
rooms and common areas are decorated with
absolutely fabulous vintage movie posters.
Walk to gay bars, shops, restaurants. " The
best-known accommodations in the city... it's a
great deal!" *Fodors Gay USA guide*

✪ COLONIAL HOUSE INN

318 W. 22nd St., New York, NY 10011. Tel: (212) 243-9669, Toll Free (800) 689-3779. Fax: (212) 633-1612. TYPE: *Guest House.* HOSTS: Vinny and Dave. Owner: Mel Cheren. CLIENTELE: Gay men & women. LOCATION: Conveniently located in the heart of gay Chelsea, only a few minutes away from Midtown and within walking distance of Greenwich Village.

* Rooms: 20; w/private or shared bath
* Smoking allowed in rooms
* CTV, phone, A/C, C/H, safety deposit
* Business phone/fax facilities, maid service
* Rooftop sundeck (clothing optional), gym
* Parking: on street, or 1/2 block to self pay garage
* Pets: w/prearrangement
* Beach: 1 hr, car needed
* Gay Bars: 1/2 block
* Health Club: several within a few blocks
* Airport: 30 min. (LGA/JFK) taxi, bus
* Languages: German, French, Spanish, Italian
* Reservations: 1 night deposit
* No Credit Cards accepted
* Cancellation: 48 hrs
* Open: Year round
* Rates: $65 - $99 w/CB
* *TAC:* 10%

DESCRIPTION: A charming European style bed & breakfast. Featuring fully renovated clean and comfortable rooms, some with refrigerators and fireplaces. The Colonial House Inn has established a flawless reputation for its high standards and excellent service. The Inn of choice by International travelers, and awarded the Editor's Choice award by Out and About magazine as New York City's best bed & breakfast for 3 years running. *IGTA*

✪ HOTEL 17

225 E. 17th St., New York NY 10003. Tel: (212) 475-2845. Fax: (212) 677-8178. TYPE: *Hotel.* HOST: Friendly Staff. CLIENTELE: Gay/ Straight. LOCATION: On 17th St., between 2nd & 3rd Ave., Safe East Side area, near Union Square Subway.

* Rooms: 125; 6 w/priv.; 119 w/shared bath
* Smoking allowed in rooms
* CTV, phone (public) / buzzer (in room) refrigerator (some); A/C (some)
* Maid service, elevator
* Sundeck (limited nude sunbathing)
* Close to Stuyvesant Park
* Parking: off street
* Gay Bars: 5 min. walk
* Health Club: 5 min. (Better Bodies)
* Airport: LGA 30 min.
  JFK 60 minutes, taxi

* Open: Year round
* Rates: $65-$90/day; $125 - $575/ week

DESCRIPTION: Artsy budget hotel. Half of the hotel is filled with resident actors and models, the other half consists of international tourists. Good location for the NYC gay scene.

INCENTRA VILLAGE HOUSE
32 Eighth Ave., New York, NY 10014. Tel: (212) 206-0007. TYPE: *Guest House*. CLIENTELE: Gay men & women. LOCATION: In Greenwich Village near Christopher St. 12 studios, CTV, phone. DESCRIPTION: Renovated 1841 Townhouse. Rooms are decorated in period style. Most have double beds and fireplaces.

○ 333 W. 88TH ASSOC.
333 West 88th St., New York NY 10024. Tel: (212) 724-9818. Toll Free (800) 724-9888. Fax: (212) 769-2686. TYPE: *Rental Rooms & Apartments*. HOST: Albert. CLIENTELE: Mostly gay men & women. LOCATION: Upper West Side near Columbus Circle, Metropolitan Museum and Lincoln Center. 1 room w/priv. bath, 2 suites. CTV, phone, refrigerator, C/H, A/C. Rates: $70 - $118. Tax: 8.25% (for less than one week stay). Weekly / Monthly rates available on request. DESCRIPTION: Beautifully furnished hosted and unhosted rooms and apartments. Good subway and bus transportation nearby.

TRAVEL INN HOTEL
515 West 42nd St., New York NY 10036. Tel: (212) 695-7171.TYPE: *Hotel*. MANAGER: Glenn Isaacs. CLIENTELE: All Welcome. LOCATION: Midtown near the Port Authority Bus Terminal, and Broadway Theaters. 159 rooms w/bath. Rates: $99-$180 (no breakfast). DESCRIPTION: AAA property. Oversized modern rooms, outdoor pool with roof top sun deck.

WASHINGTON SQUARE HOTEL
103 Waverly Place, New York, NY 10011-9194. Tel: (212) 777-9515. TYPE: *Hotel*. CLIENTELE: All Welcome. LOCATION: Heart of Greenwich Village on Washington Sq. park.

* Rooms: 60 w/shared or priv. bath
* CTV, phone, A/C, restaurant
* Bed Types: twin, queen, king size
* Check in: 3 pm / Check out: 12 noon
* Gay Bars: walking distance
* Airports: 30-40 min. by taxi
* Open: Year round
* Credit Cards: MC/VISA/AMEX
* Rates: $110-$190 w/CB
* *TAC:* 10%

DESCRIPTION: Centrally located hotel to the nightlife of the Greenwich Village. All rooms with private bath. Deluxe rooms have been renovated.

NORTH CAROLINA

● RALEIGH

● CHARLOTTE

◆ **Population:** 6,200,000
◆ **Capital:** Raleigh
◆ **Time Zone:** Eastern
◆ **Sodomy Law**
◆ **Legal drinking age:** 21

CHARLOTTE   ✆ 704

✈ Douglas Int'l Airport (CLT)
5 mi. / 8 km west of Charlotte

LOCATION: Southern Piedmont, an area of rolling hills between the mountains to the west and the Coastal Plains to the east.

POPULATION: 350,000

CLIMATE: Temperate, modified considerably by the ocean. Summer is warm and humid with a July average of 80°F (28°c). Winters are mild with a January average of 48°F (9°c).

Visitor Information
Charlotte CVB: (704) 334-2282

Gay/Lesbian Visitor Information
(704) 535-6277 (6:30-10:30pm)

DESCRIPTION: The largest metropolis in the Carolinas. It is an historic town, home of the University of North Carolina and a major center for the textile industry.

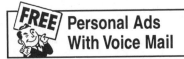

Y BARS Y

● Bars/clubs (GMW): **Brass Rail**, 3707 Wilkinson Blvd. (399-8413); **Charger's**, 3217 The Plaza (339-0500); **Scorpio**, hot erotic dancers, showclub, 2301 Freedom Drive (373-9124).

● Bars/clubs (GW): **Ye Olde Wishing Café**, 1501 Elizabeth Ave. (339-0350).

λ SERVICE λ

● Bookstore (GMW): ✪ **White Rabbit Books & Things**, 314 Rensselaer Ave. #1. (377-4067).

 ACCOMMODATIONS

CITY CENTER INN
601 N. Tyron St., Charlotte 28202. TEL: (704) 333-4733. TYPE: *Motor Inn.* CLIENTELE: All Welcome. LOCATION: 5 blocks from downtown. 120 rooms, CTV, A/C, Pool, free parking. Rates: $40-$80. *TAC:* 10%

DURHAM   ℂ 919

Y BARS Y

● Bars/clubs (GMW): **Boxers**, piano bar, entertainment, 5504 Chapel Hill Blvd. at Straw Valley (489-7678); **Power Company**, dance club, show nights, 315 W. Main St. (683-1151).

λ SERVICE λ

● Adult Videos (G/S): **Atlantis Video News**, 522 E. Main St. (982-7469); **Venus**, 1720 New Raleigh Rd. (598-3264).

GREENSBORO   ℂ 910

Y BARS Y

● Bars/clubs (GMW): **Babylon**, dance club, 221 South Elm St. (275-1006); **The Palms**, 413 N. Eugene St. (272-6307); **Warehouse 29**, country/western, ladies night each Thursday at the **Loading Dock** patio bar, 1011 Arnold St. (333-9333).

RALEIGH   ℂ 919

✈ Raleigh/Dutham Airport (RDU)
12 mi. / 19 km northwest of Raleigh

LOCATION: In the transition zone between the Coastal Plain and the Piedmont Plateau of North Carolina.

POPULATION: 180,000

CLIMATE: see Charlotte

Visitor Information
Greater Raleigh CVB: (919) 834-5900

Gay/Lesbian Visitor Information
G&L Helpline: (919) 821-0055

DESCRIPTION: The Capital of North Carolina, the seat of the government, and an educational center. Raleigh relatively small, with a relaxed residential flavor and nearly two centuries of history.

Y BARS Y

● Bars/clubs (GMW): **1622**, private club, exotic dancers, entertainment, 1622 Glenwood Ave., (832-9082); **CC Now**, bar, pool, parties,313 W. Hargett St. (755-9599); **Legends**, lively nightclub with high energy entertainment, 330 West Hargett St. (831-8888).

λ SERVICE λ

● Bookstore (GMW): ✪ **White Rabbit Books & Things**, 309, W. Martin St. (856-1429).

● Publication (GMW): ✪ **The Front Page**, The Carolina's premiere Gay & Lesbian newspaper, up-to-date information on the local gay & lesbian scene. P.O. Box 27928, Raleigh, NC 27611. Tel: (919) 829-0181. Fax: (919) 829-0830.

ACCOMMODATIONS

BROWNESTONE HOTEL
1707 Hillsborough St., Raleigh, NC 27605. TEL: (919) 828-0811. TYPE: *Hotel.* CLIENTELE: All Welcome. LOCATION: Adjacent to NC State University, 5 min. to State Capitol. 194 rooms w/priv. bath, phone, CTV, outdoor pool, apartments available. Rates: $62-$95. *TAC:* 10%.

OKLAHOMA

● TULSA

●OKLAHOMA CITY

◆ **Population:** 3,050,000
◆ **Capital:** Oklahoma City
◆ **Time Zone:** Central
◆ **Sodomy Law**
◆ **Legal drinking age:** 21

OKLAHOMA CITY   ✆ 405

✈ Will Rogers World Airport (OKC)

LOCATION: In the geographic center of Oklahoma State.

POPULATION: 403,000

CLIMATE: Continental climate influenced by the Gulf of Mexico. Summers are long, hot with tornadoes and a July average of 82˚F (28˚c). Winters are mild with a January average of 36˚F (2˚c). Annual snowfall is only 9" (22cm).

VISITOR INFORMATION
Oklahoma City CVB
Tel: (405) 278-8963

Gay Visitor Information
(405) 447-4297 (7pm-midnight)

DESCRIPTION: Oklahoma City is the State capital. Once a barren mid-western prairie, the city is a modern, prospering city siting on one of the nation's largest oil fields. Cattle and grain continues to keep the old western tradition alive. Visit the **National Cowboy Hall of Fame** & **Western Heritage Center**, 1700 NE 63rd St. (478-2250); **Oklahoma Heritage Center**, restored mansion converted into a museum, 201 NW 14th St., (235-4458); **Frontier City**, western theme park, 11601 NE Expy (478-2412); and the famous **Oklahoma National Stock Yard**, auction of livestock (235-8675). The gay scene in Oklahoma City is conveniently located on a strip along 39th Street. between Barnes and N. Penn. Here you can find most of the city's gay establishments.

BARS ☕ RESTAURANTS 🍴

● Bar/club (GM): **Tramps**, 2201 NW 39th St. (528-9080).

● Bars/clubs (GMW): **Angles**, video dance club, 2117 NW 39th St. (524-3431); **Bunk House**, bar & restaurant, 2800 NW 39th St. (943-0843); **Hi Lo Club**, beer busts, entertainment, 1221 NW 50th (843-1722); **KA's**, beer bust daily, 2024 NW 11th St. (525-3734); **Park**, video bar, 2117 NW 39th St. (528-4690); **Wreck Room**, after hours dance club, 2127 NW 39th St. (525-7610).

● Bars/clubs (GW): **Coyote Club**, ladies club, Wed-Sun. 5pm-2am, 2120 NW 39th St., (521-9533).

● Restaurant (GMW): **Bunk House**, bar & restaurant, 2800 NW 39th St. (943-0843); **Gusher's**, serving American food with entertainment on Saturday nights at the Habana Inn; **The Kitchen**, next to Coyote Club on NW 39th St.

🏠 ACCOMMODATIONS 🏠

HABANA INN
2200 NW 39th Expy., Oklahoma City, OK 73112. Tel: (405) 528-2221. TYPE: *Motel*. CLIENTELE: Mostly Gay. LOCATION: Near downtown. 172 rooms, restaurant, bar, pool. Rates: on request.

DAYS INN NORTHWEST
2801 NW 39th St., Oklahoma City OK 73112. Tel: (405) 946-0741. Fax: (405) 942-0181. TYPE: *Motor Inn*. CLIENTELE: All Welcome. LOCATION: 10 minutes from downtown.

* Rooms: 192 w/priv. bath
* CTV, phone, refrigerator
* Restaurant, club, pool, free parking
* Gay Bars: nearby
* Airport: 13 mi. / 21 km
* Rates: $45-$60

DESCRIPTION: Superior tourist class motor inn.

TULSA $\mathcal{C}$ 918

✈ Tulsa Int'l Airport (TUL)
9 mi. / 15 km northeast of Tulsa

LOCATION: Lies along the Arkansas River at an elevation of 700 ft / 210 m in Northeastern Oklahoma.

POPULATION: 370,000

CLIMATE: Continental characterized by rapid temperature changes. Winters are mild with a January average of 38°F (4°c). Summers are hot with temperatures of 100°F (38°c) frequently experienced in July-Sept. Tornadoes are common during the summer.

VISITOR INFORMATION
Tulsa CVB
Tel: (918) 585-1201

Gay & Lesbian Visitor Information
(918) 743-GAYS (8-10pm)

DESCRIPTION: Historic city on the Arkansas River. The second largest in Oklahoma. Its energy oriented economy evolves around oil, tourism and education. Considering that this is the home town of Oral Roberts University, Tulsa has a refreshingly vivid gay nightlife.

BARS 𝚼 RESTAURANTS 🍴

● Bars/clubs (GMW): **Bad Boyz Club**, male dancers daily, 1229 S. Memorial (835-5083); **Concessions**, 3340 S. Peoria St. (744-0896); **Lola's**, 2630 E. 15th St. (749-1563); **Metropole**, 1902 E. 11th St. (587-8811); **Silver Star Saloon**, 1565 S. Sheridan (834-4234); **Tool Box**, 1338 E. 3rd St. (584-1308).

● Restaurants (AW): **Atlantic Sea Grill**, fresh seafood, 8321-A E. 61st St. (252-7966); **Jamil's**, Lebanese menu, 2833 E. 51st St. (742-9097); **Ursula's Bavarian Inn**, German cuisine, outside beer garden, 4932 E. 91st Ave. (496-8282).

 ACCOMMODATIONS

DOUBLETREE HOTEL
616 W. 17th St., Tulsa OK 74127. TEL: (918) 587-8000. TYPE: *Hotel*. CLIENTELE: All Welcome. LOCATION: Downtown business area next to the Convention Center. 418 rooms w/priv. bath, restaurant, cafe, indoor swimming pool, health club, free parking. Rates: $102-$122. *TAC:* 10%. DESCRIPTION: First class sleek conventions oriented hotel.

COMFORT SUITES
8338 61st St., Tulsa, OK 74133. TEL: (918) 254-0088. TYPE: *All Suite Hotel*. CLIENTELE: All Welcome. LOCATION: In-town near shopping mall, 11 mi / 18 km from airport. 50 suites w/priv. facilities, refrigerator, CTV, phone, restaurant, bar, outside swimming pool, fitness room. Rates: $60-$105. *TAC:* 10%

OREGON

- **Population:** 2,700,000
- **Capital:** Salem
- **Time Zone:** Mountain/Pacific
- **No Sodomy Law**
- **Legal drinking age:** 21

EUGENE   © 541

✈ Mahlon Sweet Airport (EUG) 8 mi. NW

LOCATION: Central western Oregon, on the west bank of the Willamete River.

POPULATION: 112,000

DESCRIPTION: Home of the University of Oregon, Eugene offers state parks, national forests, and trails for biking, hiking or jogging.

BARS ♟ RESTAURANTS 🍴

● Bars/clubs (GMW): **Club Arena**, 959 Pearl St., (683-2360).

● Restaurants (AW): **Sweetwaters**, Pacific Northwest regional cuisine, 1000 Valley River Way (341-3462); **Govinda's Vegetarian Buffet**, international vegetarian menu, 270 W. 8th St. (686-3531).

λ SERVICES λ

● Erotica (G/S): **Exclusively Adult**, 1166 S. 'A' St. (726-6969).

🏳 ACCOMMODATIONS 🏳

CAMPUS INN
390 E. Broadway, Eugene, OR 97401. Tel: (541) 343-3376. TYPE: *Motor Inn.* CLIENTELE: All Welcome. LOCATION: Adjacent to the University of Oregon Campus.

- * Rooms: 60 w/priv. bath
- * CTV, phone, A/C, rooms for non smokers
- * Pool, restaurants nearby, parking
- * Airport: 15 mi. / 24 km taxi
- * Train Station: Amtrak 1/2 mi / 800m
- * Rates: $45-$65. *TAC:* 10%

DESCRIPTION: Budget motor inn.

EUGENE HILTON
66 E. Sixth Ave., Eugene, OR 97401. Tel: (541) 342-2000. TYPE: *Hotel.* CLIENTELE: All WElcome. LOCATION: Downtown near the Center for the Performing Arts.

- * Rooms: 270 w/priv. bath, Suites: 12
- * CTV (CNN), phone, A/C, C/H
- * Restaurants, coffee shop, health club indoor pool, wheelchair access
- * Airport: 9 mi. / 14 km free shuttle
- * Rates: $110 - $145. *TAC:* 10%

DESCRIPTION: First class hotel, part of a new downtown complex.

PORTLAND   © 503

✈ Portland Int'l Airport (PDX) 9 mi. NE

LOCATION: In Northwestern Oregon, along the Willamette River, some 110 mi. / 160 km from the Pacific Ocean.

POPULATION: 1,250,000

CLIMATE: Rainy in the winter, marked by relatively mild temperatures and cloudy skies with a January average temperatures of 38°F (3°c); Long pleasant summers with ample precipitation with an average July temperatures of 67°F (15°c). Fall and Spring are transitional

VISITOR INFORMATION
Portland Visitors Assoc.
26 SW Salmon, 97204-3299
Tel: (503) 275-9750

Gay/Lesbian Visitor Information
L&G Pride: 232-8233

DESCRIPTION: A beautiful city, known as the "City of Roses". Portland often ranks highly on the "quality of Life" surveys. Public parks abound, development is strictly monitored, and the waterfront is kept for all to enjoy. The city is divided into east and west by the Willamette River. The east side is unappealing, while the west side and downtown are more elegant. The city is connected by 11 bridges.

❖ Portland is a city made for walking. Visit on the west side the **Portland Center for the Performing Arts**; the **Old Town**, a restored shopping and browsing area in downtown; **Washington Park** and the **Washington Park Zoo**. On the east side visit the **Crystal Springs Rhododendron Gardens** and the **Mt. Tabor Park**.

BARS ⅋ RESTAURANTS ¶¶

● Bars/clubs (GM): **Boxx's**, video bar, 1035 SW Stark (226-4171); **CC Slaughter's**, 1014 SW Stark St. (248-9135); **City Nightclub**, 13 NW 13th Ave. (224-2489); **Crow**, 4801 SE Hawthorne (232-2037); **Dirty Duck**, tavern, 439 NW 3rd (224-8446); **Embers**, show bar/restaurant, 110 NW Broadway (222-3082); **Scandals**, 1038 SW Stark (227-5887); **Silverado**, 1217 SW Stark (224-4493); **Starky's**, neighborhood lounge/restaurant, 2913 SE Stark (230-7980); **Three Sisters**, 1125 SW Stark St. (228-0486).

● Bars/clubs (GMW): **Choice's**, 2845 SE Stark (236-4321);**Hobo's**, dining and entertainment nightly, 120 NW 3rd St. (224-3285).

● Restaurants (GMW): **Hobo's**, dining and entertainment nightly, 120 NW 3rd St. (224-3285); **Old Wives' Tales**, vegetarian, lesbian clientele, 1300 E. Burnside St. (238-0470); **Silverado**, at the Silverado bar, 1217 SW Stark (224-4493); Others (AW) **Atwater's**, expensive, Northwest menu, 360-degree view from the top of the US Bancorp Tower, 111 SW 5th Ave. (220-3600); **Bush Garden**, Japanese cuisine, 900 SW Morrison, downtown (226-7181); **Café des Amis**, moderate, French cuisine, 1987 NW Kearny (295-6487); **Chart House**, prime rib, seafood, panoramic view of Portland, 5700 SW Terwilliger Blvd. (246-6963); **Jake's Famous Crawfish**, moderate, seafood catering since 1892, 401 SW 12th (226-1419); **Pazzo**, grilled seafood, pizzas, at the Vintage Plaza Hotel, 422 SW Broadway (228-1515); **Zen**, Japanese, 90 SW Salmon (222-3056).

λ SERVICES λ

● Erotica (G/S): **Fantasy for Adults Only**, 24 hrs. adult store, videos, 3137 NE Sandy Blvd. (239-6969).

● Health Clubs (GM): **Club Portland**, sauna, 24 hrs., 303 SW 12 (227-9992); **Olympic Steambath Downtown**, 509 SW 4th Ave. (227-5718).

● Personal Phone Line (GM): ☼ **Portland Confidential Connection**, meet local guys! Record, listen, respond to ads free (221-0009) free access code 8060.

🔑 ACCOMMODATIONS 🔑

BENJAMIN STARK HOTEL
SW 1022 Stark, Portland, OR 97205. Tel: (503) 274-1223. TYPE: *Hotel*. CLIENTELE: Gay/Straight. LOCATION: Downtown, in the heart of the gay scene. Sgl/dbl rooms w/shared bath. Rates: on request.

CYPRESS INN (Downtown)
809 SW King Ave., Portland, OR 97205. Tel: (503) 226-6288 or reservations: (800) 255-4205. TYPE: *Motor Inn*. CLIENTELE: Mostly Straight. LOCATION: Downtown near Japanese Gardens and Washington Park Zoo.

* Rooms: 82 w/priv. bath
* Refrigerator, telephone, CTV, parking
* Gay Bars: nearby
* Airport: 10 mi. / 16 km
* Transportation: free van transfer
* Rates: $48-$79 w/CB. *TAC:* 10%

DESCRIPTION: Tourist class motor inn in a convenient downtown location.

IMPERIAL HOTEL
400 SW Broadway at Stark, Portland, OR 97205. Tel: (503) 228-7221 or (800) 452-2323. Fax: (503) 223-4551. TYPE: *Hotel*. CLIENTELE: Mostly Straight. LOCATION: Downtown near shopping, business and the gay scene.

* Rooms: 168 w/priv. bath, non-smoker rooms
* CTV, phone, A/C, parking
* Wheelchair access, restaurant, lounge
* Free Covered Parking
* Gay Bars: walking
* Airport: 10 mi. / 16 km
* Transportation: shuttle/charge
* Credit Cards: MC/VISA/AMEX
* Rates on Request. *TAC:* 10%

DESCRIPTION: First class hotel in a convenient location. Some rooms with king-size beds.

PENNSYLVANIA

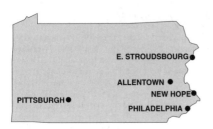

- ◆ **Population:** 11,870,000
- ◆ **Capital:** Harrisburg
- ◆ **Time Zone:** Eastern
- ◆ **No Sodomy Law**
- ◆ **Legal drinking age:** 21

ALLENTOWN   ℂ   610

✈ Allentown Airport (ABE)
4 mi. / 6 km northeast of Allentown

LOCATION: In the Lehigh Valley of Eastern Pennsylvania, the heart of Pennsylvania Dutch country.

POPULATION: 110,000

DESCRIPTION: A thriving city with roots in early American history. Some of the area's historic homes are open to the public on weekends. Great weekend escape for those interested in shopping, antiquing or art.

BAR ¥ RESTAURANT ⑪

● Bar/club (GMW): **Stonewall**, disco, restaurant, piano lounge, game area, 28-30 N. 10th St. (432-0215).

🏳 ACCOMMODATIONS 🏳

RADISSON HOTEL AMERICUS CTR
6th & Hamilton Sts., Allentown, PA 18101. TEL: (610) 434-6101. TYPE: *Hotel.* CLIENTELE: All Welcome. LOCATION: Heart of the Financial District. 50 rooms and 35 suites

w/priv. bath, hair dryer, jacuzzi, phone, CTV, A/C, restaurant, lounge, piano bar. Gay bar: walking distance. Rates: $78-$108. *TAC:* 10%. DESCRIPTION: First class Landmark hotel.

E. STROUDSBOURG   ℂ   717

🏳 ACCOMMODATIONS 🏳

RAINBOW MOUNTAIN
RD #8, Box 8174, E. Stroudsbourg, PA 18301. Tel: (717) 223-8484. Fax: (717) 421-3453. TYPE: *Rustic resort.* CLIENTELE: Gay men & women. LOCATION: Pocono Mountains, 46 lodges, 16 cottages, restaurant, bar, disco, pool. Mountain resort on 85 acres.

NEW HOPE   ℂ   215

✈ Allentown, Pennsylvania AP (ABE);
Philadelphia International AP (PHL)

LOCATION: In Bucks county of eastern Pennsylvania on the Delaware River. 40 mi. / 64 km north of Philadelphia, and 65 mi. / 104 km southwest of New York City.

POPULATION: 1,500

CLIMATE: Winter temperatures range from an average low of 23°F (-5°c) to a high of 38°F (3°c) in December. Summer temperatures vary from an average low of 65°F (18°c) to a high of 86°F (30°c) in July.

DESCRIPTION: Historic and artistic old town on the banks of the Delaware River. New Hope attracts many visitors to its unique antique shops, flea markets, art galleries, museums, quaint restaurants and small guest houses.

BARS ¥ RESTAURANTS ⑪

● Bars/clubs (GM): **Cartwheel**, bar/restaurant, 347 Old York Rd. (862-0880); **Prelude**, dance bar/restaurant, 408-A Old York Rd. (862-3600); Bars for gay men & lesbians: **Raven**, bar/restaurant at the hotel (862-2081).

🏳 ACCOMMODATIONS 🏳

BACKSTREET INN
144 Old York Rd., New Hope, PA 18938. TEL:

(215) 862-9571. TYPE: *Bed & Breakfast Inn.*
CLIENTELE: All Welcome. LOCATION: 8 minutes walk from centre of town. 7 rooms w/priv.
bath, A/C, no TV or phones in room, secluded
pool. Rates: $60-$120. *TAC:* 10%

HACIENDA INN
36 W. Mechanic St., New Hope, PA 18938. TEL:
(215) 862-2078. TYPE: *Motel.*CLIENTELE: All
Welcome. LOCATION: Center of village. 30
rooms, A/C, CTV, phone, restaurant, bar, pool,
patio. Rates: $45-$85. DESCRIPTION: Small
Spanish style motel.

LEXINGTON HOUSE
New Hope, 6171 Upper York Rd., PA 18938.
Tel: (215) 794-0811. TYPE: *Bed & Breakfast.*
HOST: Alex. CLIENTELE: Gay men & women.
LOCATION: In the fork of two country roads
near New Hope. 6 rooms. DESCRIPTION: His-
toric house circa 1749.

PHILADELPHIA   ✆ 215

✈ North Philadelphia Airport (PNE)
Philadelphia Int'l Airport (PHL)

LOCATION: Eastern Pennsylvania border on
the banks of the Delaware and the Schuylkill
Rivers, about 83 miles / 130 km southwest of
New York City.

POPULATION: Metro 4,720,000

CLIMATE: The Appalachian Mountains and
the Atlantic Ocean have a moderating effect on
the city's climate. Summers are hot and humid
with average July temperature of 78°F (26°c).
Winters are cold with average January temperature of 32°F (0°c). Snowfall is 20" (0.5m).

VISITOR INFORMATION
Philadelphia CVB
1515 Market St., Ste 2020
(215) 636-3323 or 800-CALL-PHL

Gay/Lesbian Visitor Information
Gay Switchboard: (215) 546-7100
Lesbian Hotline: (215) 225-5110

DESCRIPTION: Philadelphia, the "City of
Brotherly Love", is the birthplace of the United
States. In 1787 representatives of the colonies
gathered in Independence Hall to produce the
constitution and elect Philadelphia as the new
capital of the independent colonies. In 1800 the
seat of government moved to Washington DC,
and Philadelphia started to loose some of its

industry and economy to New York City.

Today, Philadelphia embraces both the glory of
the past with a well planned modern urban
development. Of interest to visitors: **Independence Hall**, between 5th and 6th Streets on
**Independence Square; Liberty Bell Pavil-
lion**, where the cracked Bell and the symbol of
Freedom and Liberty is displayed under a glass
structure; **Franklin Institute Science
Museum** and **Planetarium**, 20th St., and
Benjamin Franklin Pkwy - a national memorial to Benjamin Franklin and an interesting science and computer center; **Second Bank of
U.S. Portrait Gallery**, 420 Chestnut St., the
most important gallery in the U.S.A. devoted to
the nation's founding fathers; and the **New-
market**, between Pine and Lombard Streets,
on both sides of 2nd St., a busy shopping center
with boutiques, ice cream parlors, restaurants,
and cafes.

❖ The Gay Scene in Philadelphia is concentrated in a Downtown Philadelphia area
bounded from north to south by Chestnut and
Pine Streets, and from the east to west by 17th
and 9th Streets. Many of the popular gay bars,
clubs and restaurants are in the fashionable
Rittenhouse Square area around Rittenhouse
Square and City Hall. Generally speaking the
downtown area is formed as a simple grid
where most of the north-south streets are numbered and east-west streets are named. (Broad
St., is the equivalent of 14th St.).

BARS ♈ RESTAURANTS ♉

● Bars/clubs (GM): **247 Bar**, piano bar, male
dancers, 247 S. 17th St. (545-9779); **Backstage**, dance club, 614 4th St. (627-9887); **Bike
Stop**, leather/levi dance bar, 206 S. Quince St.
(627-1662); **Key West**, club, entertainment,
207 S. Juniper St. (545-1578); **Post**, levi/
leather bar, 1705 Chancellor St. (985-9720);
Raffles, disco/restaurant, 243 S Camac St.,
(545-6969); **Rodz**, bar/restaurant, 1418 Rod-
man St., (735-2900); **12th Air Command**,
dance club, 254 S. 12th St. (545-8088); **Two-
Four Club**, after hours dance bar, 204 S.
Camac St. (735-5772); **Uncle's**, 1220 LOcust
St. (546-6660); **Venture Inn**, mature clientele,
bar/restaurant, 255 S Camac St. (545-8731);
Westbury, bar/restaurant, 261 S. 13th St.,
(546-5170); **Woody's**, bar/restaurant, 202 S.
13th St. (545-1893).

● Bars/clubs (GMW): **24 Club**, after-hours
club, 204 S. Camac St. (732-5562);**Venture
Inn**, bar/restaurant and English Pub, 255 So.
Comac St. (545-8731).

● Bar (GW): **Hepburn's,** nightclub/restaurant, 254 S. 12th St. (545-8484).

● Restaurants (G/S): **Astral Plane,** 1708 Lombard St. (546-6230); **Backstage,** Continental, 614 S 4th (627-987); **Diner on the Square,** 19th at Spruce (735-5787); **Esmeralda's,** 2nd at Bainbridge St. (925-9117); **The Inn Philadelphia,** historic restaurant, classic & modern cuisines, 251-253 S. Camac St. (732-2339); **Shing Kee,** Chinese, 52 N. 9th St. (829-8983); **Venture Inn,** 255 S. Camac St. (545-8731); **Vezzo,** Italian cuisine, 530 South St. (925-3006); **Waldorf Cafe,** American cuisine, 20th & Lombard St. (985-1836).

λ SERVICES λ

● Erotica (GM): **Adonis Cinema,** videos, private booths, theatre, 2026 Sansom St. (557-9319); **Excitement Video,** 249 Market St. (925-8900); **Sansom Cinema,** all male entertainment,120 S. 13th St. (545-9254).

● Erotica (GMW): **Adam & Eve,** videos, magazines, cards, open 24 hrs., 133 So. 13th St. (925-5041); **The Leather Rose,** 201 So. 13th St., (985-2344); **The Pleasure Chest,** 2039 Walnut St. (561-7480).

● Health Care: **Medical Tower Pharmacy,** 255 So. 17th St. (545-3525).

● Health Clubs (GM): **Chancellor Athletic Club,** 1220 Chancellor St. (545-4098); **CBC Club Philadelphia,** 120 S. 13th St. (735-9568); **Panorama Club (AW),** 1500 Locust St.

● Personal Phone Line (GM): **۞ Philadelphia Confidential Connection,** meet local guys! Record, listen, respond to ads free (875-9900) free access code 8060.

✑ ACCOMMODATIONS ✑

CUNARD-HOTEL ATOP BELLEVUE
1415 Chancellor Ct., Philadelphia, PA 19102. Tel: (215) 893-1776. TYPE: *Deluxe Hotel.* CLIENTELE: Mostly Straight. LOCATION: Corner of Broad and Walnut. 173 rooms, rates on request.

HOLIDAY-INN MIDTOWN
1305-11 Walnut St., Philadelphia, PA 19107. Tel: (215) 735-9300. TYPE: *Moderate First Class Hotel.* CLIENTELE: Mostly Straight. LOCATION: In busy area, 6 blocks from Liberty Bell, near gay scene. 161 rooms. Rates: on request.

WARWICK HOTEL
1701 Locust St., Philadelphia, PA 19103. Tel: (215) 735-6000 or (800) 523-4210. Fax: (215) 790-7766. TYPE: *Deluxe Hotel.* CLIENTELE: All Welcome. LOCATION: Corner of 17th and Locust Streets. 153 rooms w/priv. bath, CTV, phone, A/C, C/H. Rates: from $145/day. DESCRIPTION: Landmark hotel, the "Grand Boutique Hotel" of Philadelphia.

PITTSBURGH ℂ 412

✈ Greater Pittsburgh Int'l Airport (PIT)

LOCATION: Southwest Pennsylvania on the banks of three rivers: the Alleghany the Mononghela and the Ohio Rivers.

POPULATION: 423,000

CLIMATE: Humid, continental type. Winters are cold and snowy with average mean temperature for January of 28°F (-2°c). Summer are mild with average mean temperature for July of 72°F (22°c). Annual rainfall is 36" (914mm), and annual snowfall is 45" (1.14m).

Gay/Lesbian Visitor Information
Community Center: (412) 422-0114

DESCRIPTION: Pittsburgh is known as the "Smoky City" or the "Iron City", remnant images from the industrial revolution and the post WW II era. Today, thanks to a tough anti-smoking campaign and fine architectural reconstruction, the once dismal "Golden Triangle" has become a viable area with lovely parks. The city is known for the famous **Pittsburgh Symphony Orchestra.** You can see the orchestra and other cultural events at the **Heinz Hall,** 600 Penn Ave., a restored movie theater with excellent acoustics and decor.

BARS Υ RESTAURANTS ♨

● Bars/clubs (GM): **Jazi's,** 1241 Western Ave. (323-2721); **Holiday Bar,** 4620 Forbes Ave. (682-8598); **Pegasus,** dance bar, drag shows, cocktail hour, 818 Liberty Ave. (281-2131).

● Bars/clubs (GMW): **Brewery Tavern** at the **Brewer's Hotel,** 3315 Liberty (681-7991); **Donnie's Place,** 1226 Herron Ave. (682-9869); **New York, New York,** piano bar and restaurant, 5801 Ellsworth (661-5600);

● Restaurants: **New York, New York,** mixed,

5801 Ellsworth (661-5600); **Sidekicks**, 931 Libert Ave. (642-4435). Other restaurants: **Le Pommier**, French cuisine, country French decor, 2104 E. Carson St., (431-1901); **Samurai**, Japanese Steak House, 2100 Greentree Rd., (276-2100); **Station Square Cheese Cellar**, fondues, imported cheeses, European decor, #25 Freight House Shops, Station Sq. (471-3355).

λ SERVICES λ

● Erotica: **Blvd. Videos**, 346 Blvd. of the Allies (261-9119); **Golden Triangle News**, 816 Liberty Ave. (765-3790).

● Health club (GM): **Arena Health Club**,

2025 Forbes Ave. (471-8548).

● Personal Phone Line (GM): ✪ **Pittsburgh Confidential Connection**, meet local guys! Record, listen, respond to ads free (553-2300) free access code 8060.

 ACCOMMODATIONS

RAMADA HOTEL
1 Bigelow Sq., Pittsburgh PA 15219. Tel: (412) 281-5800. TYPE: *Hotel.* CLIENTELE: Mostly Straight. LOCATION: Downtown. 300 suites, CTV, phone, A/C, pool, sauna, gym, restaurant. DESCRIPTION: All suites hotel in a convenient location. Suites are available in 1 and 2 bedroom units and junior suites.

PUERTO RICO

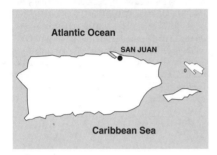

Atlantic Ocean

SAN JUAN

Caribbean Sea

◆ **Population:** 3,680,000
◆ **Capital:** San Juan
◆ **Time Zone:** Atlantic
◆ **Sodomy Law**
◆ **Legal drinking age:** 21

Puerto Rico is a Commonwealth of the U.S.A. The population is bilingual speaking both Spanish and English. The U.S. dollar is the local currency. The legal system is also the same as in the United States. Puerto Rico offers a balmy climate, a strong Latin culture, exotic beaches, rain forests, unique activities, and the best gay nightlife in the Caribbean.

SAN JUAN   ✆ **787**

✈ Isla Grande Airport (SIG)
San Juan Luis M. Marin Int'l (SJU)
5 mi. / 8 km east

LOCATION: Northwest of the island, which lies between the Atlantic Ocean and the Caribbean Sea.

POPULATION: 1,000,000

CLIMATE: Tropical with plenty of sunshine, trade winds, and an average daily temperature of 77°F (25°c).

VISITOR INFORMATION
Puerto Rico Tourism Co: (800) 223-6530

DESCRIPTION: The oldest city under the American Flag established in 1521. Spanish forces built massive city walls around the city in the 17th century to protect San Juan from attacks. Today, sun, sea and balmy weather make San Juan an ideal holiday destination.

The beaches are perfect and so are the 'hot' latin hunks on the beaches.

Old San Juan has been artistically restored and is both interesting and fun to visit. The **Old Quarter** is a masterpiece blend of Old Spanish houses and courtyards along neatly cobble stoned streets where you can find many fine restaurants, and art galleries. The **Condado** section is one of the busiest in the city.

Ashford Avenue is the main thoroughfare and it is lined with boutiques, restaurants, and nightclubs. Many of the hotels and clubs are located in the Condado area. The gay beach is only a short walk away. Visit: the **Old City** to appreciate the historic sites and monuments. Some of the most famous are: **Plaza Colon** with the statue of Christopher Columbus. **Casa Blanca** which is also a Museum of Cultural Center; the **San Juan Church** the second oldest Roman Catholic church in America. Also of interest is the **La Fortaleza** the official residence of the Governor of Puerto Rico, and the **El Morro** fortress with a magnificent view of the New San Juan and the Atlantic Ocean.

❖ Gay Beaches: **Condado Beach**, infront of the Atlantic Beach Hotel, accessed through calle Vendig & Ashford; **Ocean Park Beach** infront of the Ocean Park GH, accessed through Atlantic Place & McLeary Ave.

♣ Entertainment (AW): Gambling casinos offer slot machines and table game action. All the casinos operate between noon and 4am. Some of the Casinos are: **Caribe Hilton Int'l**, San Jerónimo Grounds (721-0303); **Clarion Hotel**, 600 Fernandez Juncos Ave., Miramar (721-4100); **Condado Plaza**, 999 Ashford Ave. (721-1000); **Dutch Inn**, Condado 55, San Juan (721-0810); **El San Juan Hotel**, Isla Verde Ave., Carolina (791-7777); **Sands Hotel**, Isla Verde (791-6100). The new casino resort **El Conquistador** is located in Las Croabas, 31 mi. / 50 km east of San Juan.

❖ Side Trips: a trip to **Bacardi Rum Factory**, is only a brief ferry ride across the bay from Old San Juan to the Catano Plant. To arrange a trip you call (788-1500); **El Yunque** is the only rain forest in the United States, and it is only 30 minutes drive from downtown. The 28,000 acre forest features stunning mountain vistas, lush flora and waterfalls. To arrange your trip call (887-2875).

BARS ♈ RESTAURANTS 🍴

● Bars/clubs (GM): **Abbey**, calle Cruz #251,

Old San Juan (725-7581); **The Barefoot**, Condado beach front bar & restaurant, happy hour with nightly drawings, #2 Calle Vendig (724-7230); **Kenny's**, special events, performance artists, pool, disco, restaurant, Carretera de Rio Oiedras a Caguas km 23.2; **Krash**, 'hottest' cruise dance bar on the island, young, good-looking Latin crowd, 1257 Ponce de Leon, Santurce (722-1131); **TJ's**, Happy Hour, Male Revues, 1203 Ponce de Leon; **Vibrations**, 'hot' levi/leather cruise bar, good music and 'steamy' latin videos, 51 Barranquitas, across from the American Airlines office; **Video Bar**, cruise bar, 1130 Ashford, Condado.

● Bars/clubs (GMW): ✿ **Deck Bar**, popular after noon Happy Hour on the beach, calle Vendig 1 at Atlantic Beach Hotel (721-6900); **Industria**, disco, 1512 Fernandez Juncos, Santurce (726-5809); **Junior's**, latin music/videos, calle Condado #202, Parada 17-1/2, Santurce; **Norman's**, Carretera 318 Barrio Maresua, San Geman; **La Zafra**, popular pub/bar, calle San José #54, Old San Juan.

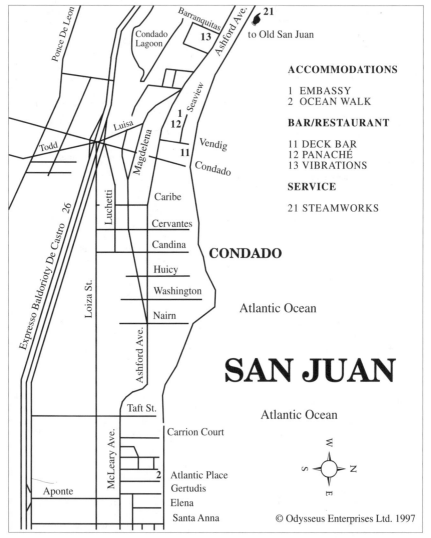

ACCOMMODATIONS

1 EMBASSY
2 OCEAN WALK

BAR/RESTAURANT

11 DECK BAR
12 PANACHÉ
13 VIBRATIONS

SERVICE

21 STEAMWORKS

CONDADO

Atlantic Ocean

SAN JUAN

Atlantic Ocean

© Odysseus Enterprises Ltd. 1997

● Bar/club (GW): **Taboo**, calle Loiza 1753, Santurce.

● Restaurants (G/S): **Barefoot**, Beach front, American, #2 Vendig St. (724-7230); ○ **Ocean Walk**, American style on the beach, 1 Atlantic Place (728-0855); ○ **Panaché**, innovative gourmet Southern French cuisine, fresh grilled or broiled seafood daily, across from the Embassy Guest House (see listing), 1127 Calle Seaview (725-2400); ○ **Sandy Beach**, American style breakfast & lunch, #1 Vendig St., at the Atlantic Beach Hotel (721-6900). Others

(AW): **Aladdin**, Middle Eastern, 1018 Ave. Ashford (721-7366); **Caruso**, Italian, Ave. Ashford #1104 (723-6876); **Chart House**, steak-seafood, expensive, Ashford #1214 (728-0110); **Miramar**, Chinese, good and inexpensive, Vendig #6 (724-0074); **El Patio de Sam**, 102 San Sebastian St., Old San Juan (723-8802); **Restaurant #Uno**, Argentinian, Avda Condado 56 (721-5572).

λ SERVICES λ

● Gym (G/S): **Muscle Factory**, 1302 Ashford Ave. (721-0717).

● Health Club (GM): **Steamworks**, bathhouse. Open: Mon-Thu 4:00pm-7:00am, weekends open 24 hrs, 205 Calle Luna, 2nd fl., Old San Juan, (725-4993).

ACCOMMODATIONS

ATLANTIC BEACH HOTEL
Calle Vendig #1, San Juan, P. R. 00907, (787) 721-6900. Fax: (787) 721-6917 TYPE: *Hotel.* CLIENTELE: Mostly Gay. LOCATION: Heart of the Condado on the 'Gay Beach'. 10 min. to Old San Juan.

* 37 rooms: 27 w/priv., 10 w/shared bath
* Smoking allowed, wheelchair access
* CTV, phone, safety box, A/C
* Restaurant, bar, sundeck, jacuzzi
* Business phone/fax facilities
* Maid service, free parking
* Beach: on 'Gay Beach'
* Gay Bars: walking distance
* Health Club: walking distance
* Airport: 20 min., bus, taxi, AP Van
* Languages: English, Spanish
* Reservations: 1 night deposit
* Cancellation: 10 days or 1 day charge
* Credit Cards: MC/VISA/AMEX/DISC/DC
* Open: Year round

* Rates: $75 - $110 / (off) $60-$90
  breakfast not included. **TAC:** 10%

DESCRIPTION: Contemporary beachfront hotel. Rooms are tastefully furnished, carpeted with newly remodeled bathrooms. Coin laundry and ironing facilities. PRTC endorsed. *IGTA*

○ EMBASSY

Calle Seaview #1126, San Juan, P.R. 00907. Tel: (787) 725-8284 or 725-2400. Fax: (787) 725-2400. TYPE: *Guest House.* HOST: Thierry & Jacques. CLIENTELE: Mostly Gay. LOCATION: Center of the famous Condado Beach, 5 min. from Old San Juan.

* Rooms: 13 w/priv. bath. Suite: 1
* Smoking allowed in rooms
* Cooking facilities, safety deposit
* CTV, phone (public), A/C
* Sundeck, garden, balcony
* Fax facilities
* Maid Service, free parking
* Restaurant: **Panaché -** French
* Beach: 50 ft. (15 m) across the street
* Gay Bars: all nearby
* Health Club: 3 blocks
* Airport: 15 min. / taxi, limo, bus
* Reservations: 2 night deposit
* Cancellation: 72 hrs. prior to arrival
* Languages: English, French, Spanish
* Credit Cards: MC/VISA/AMEX
* Open: Year round
* Rates: $65 - $105, (off) $45 - $85.
* **TAC:** 10%

DESCRIPTION: Gracious guesthouse in tropical setting. Individually decorated rooms with fine amenities. Only steps away from the ocean and activities. *IGTA*

○ OCEAN WALK

Atlantic Place No. 1, San Juan, PR 00911. Tel: (787) 726-0445, 728-0855 or (800) 468-0615. Fax: (787) 728-6434. TYPE: *Guest House.* HOSTS: Karl & Jim. CLIENTELE: Mostly Gay. LOCATION: On the beach in Ocean Park.

* Rooms: 40; 34 w/priv. bath, 6 w/shared
  4 sgl / 34 dbl / 2 triple, Apartments: 3
* CTV, phone, A/C, safety deposit
* Business phone/fax facilities
* Bar & grill, pool & 3 sundecks
* Maid service; parking: off street
* Pets: w/prearrangement
* Gay Bars: 5 minutes
* Health Club: 5 min. (mixed)
* Languages: English, Spanish, German, French
* Airport: 3 mi. / 5 km, taxi, limo, bus
* Reservations: 2 night's deposit
* Cancellation: 15 days full refund
* Credit Cards: MC/VISA/AMEX/DISC/EC
* Open: Year round
* Rates: $50-$120; (off) $35-$80 w/CB.
* **TAC:** 10%

DESCRIPTION: Charming ambience of Spanish decor in a lush, tranquil, romantic tropical setting. Yet walking distance to all the action. Safe and secure economy singles to garden studio apartments. A perfect environment for females and their friends and gay men who just want to lay back in a casual atmosphere on San Juan's best beach. *IGTA*

RHODE ISLAND

- ◆ **Population:** 950,000
- ◆ **Capital:** Providence
- ◆ **Time Zone:** Eastern
- ◆ **Sodomy Law**
- ◆ **Legal drinking age:** 21

NEWPORT   ✆ 401

✈ Providence Airport (PVD)

LOCATION: On an island in the Rhode Island Bay, along the northeastern coast of the U.S.

POPULATION: 29,600.

CLIMATE: Moderate, due to the vicinity of the Atlantic Ocean. Winter average is 48°F (9°c), summer average is 76°F (24°c). Fall and Spring temperatures are in the mid 60°'s (17°c).

VISITOR INFORMATION
Newport County Chamber of Commerce
Tel: (800) 326-6030

DESCRIPTION: The Yachting capital of the USA combining history and Nature's beauty. Newport was founded by men who fled religious intolerance on land that was bought from the Indians. After the Civil War, Newport gained popularity as a summer resort for wealthy New England families. Today you can still see the magnificent mansions that served as summer residences for the rich and famous of New England.Newport is also a home base for the U.S. Navy.

Visit: **The Newport Historical Society Museum**; The **Touro Synagogue National Historic Site** — one of the oldest synagogues in the U.S. (built circa 1763); The Mansions and Palaces of wealthy families, open to the public, are worth visiting; and the **Automobile Museum** for a fine collection of antique and classic automobiles. Recreation: swimming, boating, yachting, fishing.

BARS ▼ RESTAURANTS ¶¶

● Bar/clubs (GM): **David's**, 28 Prospect Hill St. (847-9698); **Raffles**, bar/disco, 3 Farewell St. (847-9663).

● Restaurants (AW): **The Ark**, American/English, 348 Thames St. (849-3808); **The Black Pearl**, dockside atmosphere, gourmet French (846-5264); **Clarke Cook House**, Continental, elegant colonial decor, Bannister's Wharf (849-2900).

 ACCOMMODATIONS

HYDRANGEA HOUSE
16 Bellevue Ave., Newport, RI 02840-3206. Tel: (401) 846-4435. TYPE: *Bed & Breakfast.* CLIENTELE: Equal Gay / Straight. LOCATION: Bellevue Ave. in the heart of the historic pedestrians district. 6 rooms.

MELVILLE HOUSE INN
39 Clarke St., Newport RI 02840. Tel: (401) 847-0640. TYPE: *Bed & Breakfast.* CLIENTELE: Gay/Straight. LOCATION: Heart of Newport Historic District one block from the harbor front. 7 rooms.

PROVIDENCE   ✆ 401

✈ T.F. Green Airport (PVD)

LOCATION: Eastern Rhode Island, centering around the junction of the Woonasquatucket and Moshassuck rivers.

POPULATION: 156,000

CLIMATE: see Newport.

Gay/Lesbian Visitor Information
Helpline: (401) 751-3322

DESCRIPTION: The capital of the smallest state in the US. became an important maritime port in the 18th century. Historic Providence is concentrated around the central Kennedy Plaza. Providence is the hometown of **Brown University**, the seventh oldest college in the USA; the **Museum of R.I. History**, 110 Benevolent St., presents exhibits relating to the state's history (331-8575).

BARS Y RESTAURANTS ¶¶

● Bars/clubs (GM): **In Town**, 95 Eddy St. (751-0020); **Tramps**, 70 Snow St. (421-8688); **Yukon Trading Co.**, dance bar, male dancers, 124 Snow (274-6620).

● Bars/clubs (GWM): **Galaxy**, disco, 123 Empire St. (831-9206); **Generation X**, 235 Promenade St. (521-7110).

● Restaurants (AW): **Rue de L'Espoir**, bar/restaurant, many lesbians, 99 Hope St., (751-8890); **Hemenway's Seafood Grill**, fresh seafood from around the world, 1 Old Stone Square (351-8570).

λ SERVICES λ

● Erotica (G/S): **Upstairs Bookshop**, 206 Washington St. (272-3139).

● Personal Phone Line (GM): ✪ **Providence Confidential Connection**, meet local guys! Record, listen, respond to ads free (553-2300 free access code 8060.

ACCOMMODATIONS

HOLIDAY INN DOWNTOWN
21 Atwells Ave., Providence, RI 02903. Tel: (401) 831-3900. TYPE: *Hotel*. CLIENTELE: Mostly Straight. LOCATION: At Broadway and Atwells Avenues, adjacent to Civic Center.

* Rooms: 274 w/priv. bath. Suites: 11
* CTV, phone, A/C, wheelchair access
* Restaurant, lounge, pool, jacuzzi
* Room & maid service, parking
* Gay Bars: walking distance
* Airport: 8 mi. (13 km)
* Credit Cards: MC/VISA/AMEX/CB/DC
* Open: Year round
* Rates: $97 - $185
* *TAC:* 10%

DESCRIPTION: Thirteen-story hotel in a convenient location.

SO. CAROLINA

MYRTLE BEACH ●

CHARLESTON ●

HILTON HEAD ●

◆ **Population:** 3,200,000
◆ **Capital:** Columbia
◆ **Time Zone:** Eastern
◆ **Sodomy Law**
◆ **Legal drinking age:** 21

CHARLESTON   *✆* 803

✈ Charleston Int'l Airport (CHS)

LOCATION: On a peninsula midway along the South Carolina coast line.

POPULATION: 277,000

CLIMATE: Moderate tempered by the Ocean. Summer is warm and humid with July mean temperature of 80°F (27°c). Winters are mild with average temperature in January of 49°F (9°c).

VISITOR INFORMATION
The Charleston Trident CC
Tel: (800) 853-8000

DESCRIPTION: Charleston is an aristocratic Southern city with pre-civil war houses, mansions, churches and cobbled stone streets. The old section is known as the "**Old Walled City**". It offers historical sites, galleries, mansions, and lovely southern gardens. Some of the mansions are open to the public. **The Washington House**, 87 Church St., displays a collection of period furnishings; **The Charleston Museum**, 360 Meeting Place, claims to be the oldest museum in the USA; **Fort Sumter**, in the Charleston Harbor, is a Civil War symbol.

● Gay Beach: **Folly Beach**.

BARS ♈ RESTAURANTS ♟

● Bars/clubs (GMW): **Arcade**, dance bar, 5 Liberty St., (723-4347); **Dudley's**, 346 King St., (723-2784); **Treehouse**, 348A King St. (723-9945).

● Restaurants (G/S): **Carolina's**, seafood, 10 Exchange St. (724-3800); **Colony House**, in historic district, seafood & steaks, 35 Prioleau St. (723-3424); **82 Queen**, seafood and regional Low Country dishes, 82 Queen St. (723-7591).

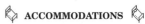 ACCOMMODATIONS

✪ CHARLESTON BEACH
P.O. Box 41, 118 West Arctic Ave., Folly Beach, SC 29439. Tel: (803) 588-9443. TYPE: *Guest House*. HOSTS: Butch or Betty, Mgrs. CLIENTELE: Gay Men & Women only. LOCATION: Twenty minutes from historic Charleston, directly on the ocean.

* Rooms: 9 dbl; 2 w/priv., 7 w/shared bath
* Refrigerator, C/H, A/C
* Smoking allowed in rooms
* Suite: 1 (1BR) w/kitchenette, CTV, VCR,

* Refrigerator, C/H, A/C
* Pool, sun deck, jacuzzi, clothing optional
* Parking: free off street, No pets
* Beach: 100 yards / meters (straight) gay beach 3 mi. / 5 km
* Gay Bars: 20 min. drive
* Health Clubs: 8 mi. / 13 km (straight)
* Airport: 23 mi / 37 km, taxi, car rental
* Train Station: 20 mi. / 32 km
* Reservations: 1 night deposit
* Cancellation Policy: 2 weeks notice no charge; 1 week notice 1 night charge; 24 hrs. notice charge for entire visit
* Credit Cards: MC/VISA/DISC
* Open: Year round
* Rates: $69-$99 / (off) $45-$75 w/AB
* Check in 3:00 pm / Check out 11:00 am
* Taxes: 10%. *TAC:* 10%

DESCRIPTION: Large beach house on the Atlantic Ocean with sun porch and sun deck facing the ocean on 2nd floor. Extensive decking with flowers in the back yard with 8 men hot tub and a swimming pool surrounded by privacy fence. Complimentary cocktail every evening between 5:30 pm and 6:30 pm.

CHARLESTON COLUMNS
#8 Vanderhorst St., Charleston, SC 29401. Tel: (803) 722-7341. TYPE: *Guest House.* HOSTS: Frank & Jim. CLIENTELE: Gay men & women. LOCATION: 1/2 block off King St. in the city's Historic District. 4 rooms.

"1854" B&B
34 Montagu St., Charleston, SC 29401. Tel: (803) 723-4789. TYPE: *Bed & Breakfast.* HOST: Terry C. Cox. CLIENTELE: Gay/Straight. LOCATION: Central historic district. 2 self-catering suites. Priv. entrance. Rates; $95-$115. *TAC:* 10%.

HILTON HEAD   *©* 803

✈ Municipal Airport (HHH)
Savannah Int'l AP, GA (SAV) 35 mi. / 56 km

LOCATION: Southeast South Carolina, just north of the Georgia border on the Atlantic.

POPULATION: 25,000

DESCRIPTION: Hilton Head is a year round resort island with 12 miles of beaches, and a delightful climate year round.

☿ BAR ☿

● Bars/clubs (GMW): **Moon Jammers**, 1

Heritage Plaza, Pope Ave. (842-9195).

 ACCOMMODATIONS

SEA CREST OCEANSIDE INN
1 N. Forest Beach, Hilton Head, NC 29938. Tel: (803) 785-2121. TYPE: *Motel.* CLIENTELE: All Welcome. LOCATION: Oceanfront, walk to gay bars. 90 rooms w/priv. bath, CTV, phone, restaurant, pools, parking. Rates: $49-$160. *TAC:* 10%. DESCRIPTION: Moderate first class motel resort.

MYRTLE BEACH   *©* 803

✈ Myrtle Beach Jetport (MYR)
2 mi. / 3 km south

LOCATION: On the Atlantic Ocean just south of the North Carolina border.

POPULATION: 25,000

DESCRIPTION: Myrtle Beach is one of the most popular seaside resorts of the Atlantic Coast with white sandy beaches, boardwalk, seafood restaurants and millions of summer holiday makers.

❖ Gay Beach: **beach at 82nd Ave.**

❖ SPECIAL EVENT: **Sun Fun Festival**, first week of June.

BARS ☿ RESTAURANTS ॥

● Bars/clubs (GMW): **3rd South Lounge**, 1102 3rd Ave. S. (444-2766); **Illusions**, 1012 S. Kings Hwy (448-0421); **Time Out**, 520 8th Ave. N. (448-1180).

● Restaurants (AW): **Bistro**, Continental & Seafood, 73rd Ave. N. at Ocean Blvd. (449-5125); **Italian Peasant**, 6003 N. US 17 Business (449-3031); **Sea Captain's House**, seafood, 3000 N. Ocean Blvd. (448-8082).

 ACCOMMODATIONS

DAYS INN MYRTLE BEACH
Oceanfront at 77th Ave., N. Myrtle Beach, FL 29577. Tel: (803) 449-7431. TYPE: *Motel.* CLIENTELE: All Welcome. LOCATION: Quiet location at Myrtle Beach north end near gay beach. 99 rooms w/priv. bath, CTV, phone, A/C, pool with poolside bar, parking. Rates: $59-$99. *TAC:* 10%. DESCRIPTION: Superior tourist class motel in a convenient beach location.

TENNESSEE

◆ **Population:** 4,591,000
◆ **Capital:** Nashville
◆ **Time Zone:** Eastern/Central
◆ **Sodomy Law**
◆ **Legal drinking age:** 21

KNOXVILLE   ℰ   423

✈ McGee Tyson Airport (TYS)

LOCATION: East Tennessee Valley.

POPULATION: 184,000

CLIMATE: Mild mountain climate. Stormy and humid summers with an average July temperatures of 80°F (27°c); winters are mild with an average January temperatures of 40°F (4°c).

VISITOR INFORMATION
Knoxville CVB: 523-7263

Gay/Lesbian Visitor Information
Helpline/MCC: 521-6546

DESCRIPTION: The first capital of Tennessee and a frontier outpost on the edge of the Cherokee Indian nation. Today, it is a modern town and a gateway to the wilderness of the Smoky Mountains.

❖ **SPECIAL EVENTS:** the **Dogwood Arts Festival**, a two week celebration in April in the town's **Market Square Mall**.

BARS ⟑ RESTAURANTS ⑂

● Bars/clubs (GMW): **Carousel II**, dance bar, cabaret, 1501 White Ave. SW (522-6966); **Old Plantations**, 837 N. 5th Ave. (637-7132); **Trumps**, disco, mostly lesbians, 4541 Kingston Pike (385-9898).

● Restaurants (AW): **Regas**, Continental, 318 N. Gay St., (637-9805); **L & N Seafood Grill**, 401 Henley St., (971-4850); **Morrison's Cafeteria**, self-service buffet, moderate, West Town Mall, 10 mi. W on US 11, West Hills Exit (693-0383).

ACCOMMODATIONS

HYATT REGENCY KNOXVILLE
500 Hill Ave., Knoxville, TN 37901. Tel: (615) 637-1234. TYPE: *Hotel*. CLIENTELE: Mostly Straight. LOCATION: Opposite the Knoxville Civic Auditorium. 386 rooms, CTV, phone, A/C, balcony. DESCRIPTION: Pyramid-shaped, eight story atrium lobby, hotel situated on the sweep of the Tennessee River. Convenient location to explore the gay scene.

MEMPHIS   ℰ   901

✈ Memphis Int'l Airport (MEM)

LOCATION: Southwest Tennessee on the Mississippi River on the border with Arkansas.

POPULATION: 646,000

CLIMATE: Mild climate. The average temperature is 80°F (27°c) in the summer, and 43°F (6°c) during the winter season.

VISITOR INFORMATION
CVB: 576-8181

Gay/Lesbian Visitor Information
Switchboard: 728-4297

DESCRIPTION: Old South town with a name that means "Place of Good Abide". It is the world's largest cotton market with flashy expressways and a modern Civic Center. Visit: **Old Beale St.** where W.C. the "father of the blues" composed his famous songs; **Graceland Mansion**, 3764 Elvis Presley Blvd., is the former abode of the famous "king of Rock 'N' Roll" with memorabilia collections.

BARS ⟑ RESTAURANTS ⑂

● Bars/clubs (GM): **Apartment**, cruise bar, 343 Madison Ave. (525-9491); **Cross Roads**,

168   TENNESSEE

dance club, 102 N. Cleveland (725-8156); **Edge**, 532 S. Cooper (272-3036); **Five-O-One Bar**, C&W dance club, 111 No. Claybrook (726-4767); **J-Wag's**, cruise bar, disco, restaurant, 1268 Madison Ave. (725-1909); **Pipeline**, show/dance bar, 1382 Poplar Ave. (726-5263).

● Bar/club (GW): **WKRB in Memphis**, disco, cabaret, male/female impersonators, 1528 Madison (278-9321).

● Restaurants (AW): **J-Wag's**, bar/restaurant, open 24 hrs., gay men only, 1268 Madison (725-1909). Other restaurants: **Bombay Bicycle Club**, patio dining, 2120 Madison (726-6055); **Justines**, French menu, fresh seafood, expensive, jacket & tie, 919 Coward Pl., (527-3815).

 ACCOMMODATIONS

MEMPHIS TRAVELODGE
265 Union Ave., Memphis, TN 38103. Tel: (901) 527-4305. TYPE: *Motel*. CLIENTELE: Mostly Straight. LOCATION: Downtown near the Greyhound bus terminal. 73 rooms, CTV, phone, A/C, Coffee shop, pool, parking. DESCRIPTION: Budget motel.

THE PEABODY HOTEL
149 Union Ave., Memphis, TN 38103. Tel: (901) 529-4000. Reservations: (800) 732-2639. TYPE: *Deluxe Hotel*. CLIENTELE: Mostly Straight. LOCATION: Downtown. 454 w/priv. bath. Suites: 24, CTV, phone, A/C, restaurants, Deli, lounge, piano bar, Health Club, pool, jacuzzi. DESCRIPTION: Deluxe landmark hotel with upscaled amenities for business and pleasure.

NASHVILLE   ℭ 615

✈ Metropolitan Airport (BNA)

LOCATION: On the Cumberland River in the middle of Tennessee.

POPULATION: 456,000

CLIMATE: Mild climate year round. Summer average temperatures are 78°F (26°c), and winter's average temperatures are 40°F (4°c).

VISITOR INFORMATION
Nashville CVB: 259-3900

DESCRIPTION: Colorful state capital of Ten-

nessee and a must destination for country music lovers. Known as *"Music City USA"* it has interesting Greek Revival architecture, a major religious center.

Visit: **Opryland**, recreational park, 10 mi. E on I-40 (889-6700); **Grand Ole Opry**, live radio show, 2802 Opryland Dr., (889-9490); **Music Village USA**, 4 Country Music Museums, 20 mi. N. via I-65 (822-1800); **Country Music Hall of Fame Museum**, 4 Music Sq. E. (256-1639).

BARS ♈ RESTAURANTS 🍴

● Bars/clubs (GM): **Chute**, leather/cruise bar, 2535 Franklin Rd., (297-4571); **Converstaions**, cruise bar, 923-C Main St. (228-4447); **Crazy Cowboy**, country style, 2311 Franklin Rd., (269-5318); **Victor/Victoria's**, disco, 111 8th Ave. (244-7256);

● Bar (GW): **Ralph's**, 515 2nd Ave. (256-9682).

● Restaurants (AW): **Chute**, 2535 Franklin Rd. (297-4571); **Victor/Victoria's**, 111 8th Ave. (244-7256). Others: **Maude's Courtyard**, seafood, Jazz Sunday Brunch, 1911 Broadway (320-0543); **New Orleans Manor**, seafood buffet, 1400 Murfeesboro Rd., (367-2777); **Morrison's Cafeteria**, self-service buffet, 1000 Two Mile Pkwy. in Rivergate Mall (859-1359); **Townhouse Tea Room**, outdoor dining, in historic mansion decorated with antiques, affordable, 165 8th Ave. N. (254-1277).

 ACCOMMODATIONS

RAMADA INN - DOWNTOWN
840 James Robertson Pkwy, Nashville, TN 37203. Tel: (615) 244-6130. TYPE: *Motor Inn*. CLIENTELE: Mostly Straight. LOCATION: Near the State Capitol. 180 w/priv. bath. 4 suites, CTV, phone, A/C, restaurant, lounge, pool. DESCRIPTION: Motor Inn in a convenient location. Economic prices.

STOUFFER NASHVILLE
611 Commerce St., Nashville, TN 37203. Tel: (615) 255-8400. TYPE: *Hotel*. CLIENTELE: Mostly Straight. LOCATION: At the City's Convention Center Complex. 673 w/priv. bath. 34 suites, CTV, phone, A/C, restaurant, lounge, pool, whirlpool, sauna. DESCRIPTION: Striking high-rise hotel offering upscaled amenities and service. Rooms with king or queen size beds. Suitable for business and upscaled travelers.

TEXAS

FT. WORTH ● ● DALLAS

SAN ANTONIO ● ● AUSTIN
HOUSTON ●
● GALVESTON ●

CORPUS CHRISTI
●

- ◆ **Population:** 14,230,000
- ◆ **Capital:** Austin
- ◆ **Time Zone:** Central/Mountain
- ◆ **Sodomy Law**
- ◆ **Legal drinking age:** 21

AUSTIN   *©* **512**

✈ Robert Mueller Municipal AP (AUS)

LOCATION: 180 mi. / 290 km south of Dallas, and 150 mi. / 240 km northwest of Houston at the foot of the Highland Lakes chain with Lake Austin and Town Lake flowing through the heart of the city.

POPULATION: 345,500

CLIMATE: Summer average temperature is 84°F (29°c), 52°F (11°c) in the winter, and around the upper 60°'sF (20°c) during the fall and spring.

Gay/Lesbian Visitor Information
Austin Stonewall Chamber of Commerce
Tel: 707-3794

DESCRIPTION: Austin, the capital of Texas, was founded in 1839 and named after the leader of the first American colony in Texas. Unlike most other cities in Texas, Austin is compact and easy to get around walking. Visit: **The State Capitol**; **Governor's Mansion**; museums, and the beautiful Town Lake for

fishing, hiking, camping, or boating. In the summer, cool off at the **Barton Spring Pool** - a miniature fresh water artificial lake at the **Zilker Park**.

BARS ▼ RESTAURANTS 🍴

Most of the local gay scene is concentrated in the area northeast of the Colorado River between 4th and 9th Sts. and confined on the west by Guadalupe, and on the east by Hwy. 35.

● Bars/clubs (GM): **Blue Flamingo**, 617 Red River (469-0014); **'Bout Time**, 9601 N. I-35 (832--5339); **Chain Drive**, leather bar, 504 Willow St. (480-9017); **Charlie's**, disco / party bar, 13th & Lavaca Ave. (474-6481); **DJ's**, 611 Red River (476-3611); **5th Street Station**, dance club, karaoke nights, 2pm - 2am daily, 505 E. 5th (478-6065); **Kansas**, 213 West 4th (480-8686); **Oilcan Harry's**, 211 W. 4th (320-8823); **Proteus**, 611 E. 6th (472-8922).

● Bar/club (GW): **Nexus**, largest women's bar in Texas, 401 E 2nd St., (495-9553).

● Restaurants (NG): **Newport's Seafood**, seafood, overlooking Town Lake, 98 San Jacinto Blvd. (472-3474); **Oasis Cantina del Lago**, Mexican, huge dining complex, 6550 Comanche Trail on Lake Travis (266-2441).

λ SERVICES λ

● Adult Cinema (GM): **Cinema West**, all male theatres; open 7 days 11-02, 2130 So. Congress (442-5719).

● Health Club (GM): **Midtown Spa**, open 24 hrs., 5815 Airport Blvd., (302-9696).

🏠 ACCOMMODATIONS 🏠

AUSTIN CREST HOTEL
111 E. 1st St., P.O. Box 2187, Austin, TX 78701. Tel: (512) 478-9611. TYPE: *Hotel*. CLIENTELE: Mostly Straight. LOCATION: Near the State Capitol.

- * Rooms: 287 w/priv. bath; Suites: 24
- * CTV, phone, A/C
- * Wheelchair accessible
- * Restaurant, lounge
- * Pool, terrace
- * Maid & room service
- * Gay Bars: walking distance
- * Airport: 4 mi. (7 km)
- * Credit Cards: MC/VISA/AMEX/CB/DC
- * Open: Year round

* Rates: $68 - $135
* *TAC:* 10%

DESCRIPTION: 12-story hotel with well appointed rooms in a convenient location.

GUEST QUARTERS HOTEL-AUSTIN 303 West 15th St., Austin, TX 78701. Tel: (512) 478-7000. Fax: (512) 478-5103. TYPE: *All Suite Hotel*. CLIENTELE: Mostly Straight. LOCATION: 2 blocks from State Capitol and 6 blocks from the University of Texas.

* Suites: 191 (1-2 bedroom)
* Restaurant w/patio
* Recreation area w/pool and whirlpool
* Gay Bars: nearby
* Airport: 5 mi. (8 km), free transfer
* Credit Cards: MC/VISA/AMEX/DC/CB
* Rates: $99 - $115
* *TAC:* 10%

DESCRIPTION: All suite hotel for the business traveler. Complimentary Continental breakfast.

DALLAS   © 214

✈ Love Field Airport (DAL)
Dallas / Ft. Worth Airport (DFW)

LOCATION: North-central Texas, about 250 mi. / 400 km from the Gulf of Mexico.

POPULATION: 905,000

CLIMATE: Humid Subtropical with hot summers. Average July temperature 85°F (29°c). Winters are mild with average January temperature of 45°F (7°c). Very little snowfall.

Gay/Lesbian Visitor Information G&L Community Center: 528-9254

Gayline: 368-6283
Lesbian Line: 528-2426

DESCRIPTION: Commercial and industrial urban center with ultra modern highrise buildings, wide avenues, theatres, museums, luxury hotels, and shopping centers. The town has gained international reputation as an oil rich city partially due to the success of the "Dallas" episodes on TV.

Visit: **Dallas Museum of Natural History** - interesting exhibits of pre-historic Texas, Cullum Blvd. & Grand Ave. (670-8457); **Dallas**

Aquarium, 1st & M.L. King Jr Blvd. **(670-8457); The Science Place (428-8352); Dallas Museum of Art**, 1717 N. Harwood (922-0220); **Dallas Market Center Complex** - the World's largest wholesale merchandise market, 2100 Stemmons Frwy. (655-6100); **University of Dallas** - liberal arts, art galleries, Northgate Rd. & Tom Braniff Dr. in Irving (721-5000); **Dallas Theatre Center** (526-8857).

❖ **SPECIAL EVENTS: Oak Lawn Tennis Championship**. GLTA tennis tournament, October 7-9 (214-520-9611); **Virginia Slims**, the famous women's tennis tournament late Feb-early March in Moody Coliseum on campus of Southern Methodist University (692-2000); the **Scarborough Faire Renaissance Festival**, recreates a 16th-century English village for 7 weekends (late Apr- early June) (937-6130).

BARS ♉ RESTAURANTS 🍴

The gay scene in Dallas is located in the Oak Lawn area on Cedar Springs.

● Bars/clubs (GM): **Anchor Inn**, 4024 Cedar Springs (526-4098); **Big Daddies**, cruise bar, 3913 Cedar Springs (528-4098); **Crews Inn**, dance bar, 3215 N. Fitzhugh Ave. (526-9510); **Hidden Door**, friendly sports and motorcycle bar, 5025 Bowser (526-0620); **Ice Factory**, dance club, 4117 Maple Ave. (521-2024); **Moby Dick**, cocktail bar, open noon daily, 4011 Cedar Springs Rd. (520-6029); **Numbers**, 4024 Cedar Springs (521-7861); **Round Up Saloon**, C&W dance bar, 3914 Cedar Springs (522-9611); **TMC**, leather/levi, 3014 Throckmorton (380-3808); **Village Station**, entertainment complex, male strippers, drag shows, 3911 Cedar Springs (526-7171); **Zippers**, male dancers, 3333 North Fitzhugh (526-9519).

● Restaurants (GMW): **JR's**, 3923 Cedar Springs (528-1004), or **Ciao's** adjacent to JR's. Other (AW): **Casa Dominguez**, Mexican cuisine, 2127 Cedar Springs (742-4945); **Josef's** Seafood, char-broiled fish, seafood, 2719 McKinney Ave. (826-5560); **L'Ambiance**, French cuisine, jacket for dinner, 2408 Cedar Springs (748-1291); **Newport's Seafood**, mesquite-grilled seafood, in the Brewery, West End Historic district, 703 McKinney (954-0509); **Highlands Park Cafeteria**, buffet, sugar-free deserts, inexpensive, 4611 Cole St. (526-3801).

λ SERVICES λ

● Health Clubs (GM): **The Club**, private men's club & sauna, 2616 Swiss (821-1990); **Midtowne Spa**, 2509 Pacific (821-8989).

● Publication (GMW): **This Week In Texas Magazine (TWIT)**, Texas' Leading Gay & Lesbian Publication since 1975, published weekly. News, entertainment and classifieds, the best source for what's on in Texas, 3300 Reagan St., Dallas, TX 75219. (214) 521-0622. Fax: (214) 520-8948.

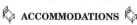

ACCOMMODATIONS

HOWARD JOHNSON LODGE NORTH-CENTRAL
10333 N. Central Pkwy, Dallas, TX 75213. Tel: (214) 363-0221. TYPE: *Motor Inn.* CLIENTELE: Mostly Straight. LOCATION: 10 min. from downtown.

* Rooms: 161 w/priv. bath
* CTV,phone, A/C,
* Restaurant, lounge
* Pool, tennis club
* Gay Bars: car needed
* Airport: 10 minutes
* Credit Cards: MC/VISA/AMEX/CB/DC
* Season: Year round
* Rates: $55 - $85.
* *TAC:* 10%

DESCRIPTION: Motel style accommodations in a convenient location.

INN ON FAIRMOUNT
3701 Fairmount, Dallas, TX 75219. Tel: (214) 522-2800. Fax: (214) 522-2898. TYPE: *Inn.* CLIENTELE: Mostly Gay. LOCATION: 1/2 block south of Oaklawn Ave., at Welborn. 6 rooms w/priv. bath. DESCRIPTION: Elegant Inn furnished with antiques and providing modern comfort at the heart of 'Gay Dallas'.

OMNI MELROSE HOTEL
3015 Oak Lane at Cedar Springs, Dallas, TX 75219. Tel: (214) 521-5151. TYPE: *Hotel.* CLIENTELE: Mostly Straight. LOCATION: 5 minutes from central business district and local gay scene.

* Rooms: 185 w/priv. bath; Suites: 35
* CTV, phone, A/C
* Wheelchair accessibility
* Restaurant, Piano bar, parking
* Gay Bars: nearby
* Airport: 7 min., free limo service
* Credit Cards: MC/VISA/AMEX/CB/DC
* Rates: $135 - $750.
* *TAC:* 10%

DESCRIPTION: Elegant Old-World hotel in a convenient location. Suitable for business or upscaled travelers.

FORT WORTH   ✆ 817

✈ Dallas/Ft. Worth Int'l Airport (DFW)
   17 mi. / 27 km northeast
   Dallas Love Field AP (DAL)
   42 mi. / 67 km east

LOCATION: 30 mi / 45 km west of Dallas.

POPULATION: 500,000

DESCRIPTION: Simpler and smaller than Dallas, Ft. Worth is an important center for the cattle, oil, grain, computer and aircraft industries. Visit: **Sundance Square**, historic dining and entertainment district between Houston & Main Sts; **Ft. Worth Stockyards National Historic District**, renovated district with Western-style shops, nightclubs and restaurants, Exchange & Main Sts.

BARS ☗ RESTAURANTS 🍴

● Bars/Clubs (GM): **Copa Cabana**, 1002 S. Main (336-8911); **Corral Club**, 621 Hemphill (335-0196); **DJ's**, 1308 St. Louis (927-7321); **Magnolia Station**, 600 W. Magnolia (332-0415); **651 Club**, 651 S. Jennings (332-0745); **Square Room**, 2308 W. 7th St. (336-1410).

● Restaurants (AW): **El Rancho Grande**, Mexican, 1400 N. Main St. (624-9206); **Tours 7th St. Cafe**, regional specialties, 3500 W. 7th St. (870-1672).

ACCOMMODATIONS

WORTHINGTON HOTEL
200 Main St., Ft. Worth, TX 76102. Tel: (817) 870-1000. TYPE: *Hotel.* CLIENTELE: All Welcome. LOCATION: Downtown at historic Sundance Square. 507 rooms w/priv. bath, CTV, phone, A/C, 24 hrs. room service, restaurants, bar, indoor pool. Rates: $145-$170. *TAC:* 10%

GALVESTON   ✆ 409

✈ Scholes Field (GLS), 3 mi (5 km) SW
   Ellington Field, Houston (EFD)
   40 mi. / 64 km northwest

LOCATION: 40 mi. southeast of Houston on the Gulf of Mexico.

POPULATION: 60,000

DESCRIPTION: Galveston is an historic resort town with miles of sandy beaches, fishing piers, seafood restaurants and international seaport.

BARS ♈ RESTAURANTS 🍴

● Bars/Clubs (GM): **Kon-Tiki**, 315 23rd at Tremont (763-6264); **Longfellow's**, 2405 Post Office (763-8800).

● Restaurants (AW): **Clary's**, seafood, 8509 Teichman Rd. (740-0771); **Wentletrap**, Continental, 2301 Strand at Tremont (765-5545).

◈ ACCOMMODATIONS ◈

VICTORIAN CONDO HOTEL
6300 Seawall Blvd., Galveston TX 77551. Tel: (409) 740-3555. TYPE: *Condominium Resort Hotel.* CLIENTELE: All Welcome. LOCATION: 50 ft. / m from the beach near 61st Street. 220 one and two bedroom units for 4 - 6 people, BBQ area, outdoor pools, whirlpools, lighted tennis courts, laundry and maid service, free parking. Rates: $69-$210. *TAC:* 10%

HOUSTON   ✆ 713/281

✈ Hobby Airport (HOU)
Intercontinental Airport (IAH)

LOCATION: Southeast Texas, 50 mi. / 80 km inland from the Gulf of Mexico.

POPULATION: Metro - 3,000,000

CLIMATE: Marine climate with temperatures modified by ocean breezes. Winters are mild with a January average of 52°F (11°c). Summers are hot and humid with a July average of 83°F (28°c). Annual rainfall is 48" (120 mm) without snow.

VISITOR INFORMATION
Great Houston CVB
Tel: (800) 231-7799 (US)

Gay/Lesbian Visitor Information
Switchboard: (713) 529-3211

DESCRIPTION: Houston grew from a provincial timber, cotton and cattle town to a major port and the 'Energy Capital' of the world. It is also an important intellectual and cultural center with over 25 colleges and universities, medical center, the famous Space Center, and center of the arts. Visit: **NASA Space Center** - a fascinating center with displays of objects and technology related to the conquest of the outer space; **Astrodome Astroworld**; and the **Museum of Fine Arts**. For shopping try the **Post Oak Galleria Shopping Mall** on Houston's west side. Houston's gay scene is located in the Montrose area, near Montrose Blvd. and Westheimer Rd.

❖ **SPECIAL EVENTS: GLTA Houtex Tennis Tournament** (GMW), 2nd weekend in November, Houston Tennis Club, 929 Allston St. (789-1818); If you are into the cowboy scene check the **Houston Livestock Show Parade & Rodeo** (AW) at the **Astrodome** (late Feb. - early March).

BARS ♈ RESTAURANTS 🍴

● Bars/Clubs (GM): **Brazos River Bottom**, country/western bar and restaurant, 2400 Brazos (528-9192); **Gentry**, male strippers, variety shows, bad boys dance every night, 2303 Richmond (520-1861); **Heaven**, high energy disco, 810 Pacific at Grant (521-9123); **J.R's**, popular dance bar mostly yuppie clientele, 808 Pacific (521-2519); **Montrose Mining Co.**, cruise bar, 805 Pacific (429-7488); **Pacific Street**, leather bar, men in Cages, 710 Pacific (523-0213); **Rascals**, 1318 Westheimer (942-2582)' **Rich's**, high energy disco, 2401 San Jacinto (759-9606).

● Restaurants (AW): **Cafe Artiste**, creative Cajun, 1601 W. Main at Mandell (528-3704); **Bistro 224**, Continental cuisine, 224 Westheimer (529-3224); **Brothers Cafe**, coffee bar, 4005 Montrose (526-1319); **Cafe Anthony**, Italian cuisine, 4315 Montrose at Richmond (529-8000); **Java Java Cafe**, fresh pastas, 911 W. 11th St. (880-5282); **Shiva**, Indian, 2514 Times Blvd., in Rice Village (523-4753).

λ SERVICES λ

● Adult Shop (G/S):**Video X Hits**, adult superstore, 24 hrs., 610 Loop So. (640-1339).

● Cinema (GM): **French Quarter**, all-male cinema, 3201 Louisiana (527-0782).

● Clothing (G/S): **Appearances**, jeans/sportswear, 1340 Westheimer (521-9450); **Basic Brothers**, 1232 Westheimer (522-1626); **Pueblo to People**, 4809 Montrose (526-6591).

● Health club (GM): **Body Balance**, 2425

Sunset (520-9916); **Club Houston**, weights, steam bath, video rooms, open 24 hrs., 2205 Fannin (659-4998); **Fitness Exchange**, free weights, aerobics, training, dry saunas, 3939 Kirby St., at 59 South (524-9932); **Midtowne Spa**, video rooms, pool, 24 hrs., 3100 Fannin St (522-2379).

● Massage (GM): **Altruistic Touches** (523-9153); **Essential Touch**, 3100 Richmond (942-0923).

● Pharmacy (AW): **Stat Script Pharmacy**, 4101 Greenbrier, Ste 235 (521-1700).

 **ACCOMMODATIONS**

HYATT REGENCY HOUSTON
1200 Louisiana St., Houston, TX 77002. Tel: (713) 654-1234. TYPE: *Hotel*. CLIENTELE: Mostly Straight. LOCATION: Near Civic Center.

* Rooms: 1000 w/priv. bath; Suites: 52
* CTV, phone, A/C
* Restaurants, Rooftop pool & sundeck
* Gay Bars: car needed
* Airport: 45 minutes
* Credit Cards: MC/VISA/AMEX/CB/DC
* Rates: $110 - $149.
* **TAC:** 10%

DESCRIPTION: 30 story hotel, convention center suitable for business or upscaled travelers.

MONTROSE INN
408 Avondale, Houston TX 77006. Tel: (713) 520-0206. TYPE: *Bed & Breakfast*. HOST: Henry McClurg. CLIENTELE: Gay men only. LOCATION: Near Westheimer & Whitney. 5 rooms, 1 w/priv. bath, CTV, VCR, phone, refrigerator, C/H, A/C. Rates: $39-$69. Tax: 15%. *TAC:* 10%. Basic guesthouse near gay scene.

RODEWAY INN
5820 Kathy Freeway, Houston, TX 77007. Tel: (713) 526-1071. TYPE: *Motel*. CLIENTELE: Mostly Straight. LOCATION: 1 block from Memorial Park.

* Rooms: 110 w/priv. bath; Suites: 2
* Coffee Shop: 24 hrs., Swimming Pool
* Gay Bars: car needed
* Airport: 40 minutes
* Credit Cards: MC/VISA/AMEX/DIS
* Open: Year round.
* Rates: $39-$65.
* **TAC:** 10%

DESCRIPTION: Tourist class motel in a convenient location.

SAN ANTONIO   ✆ 210

✈ San Antonio Int'l Airport (SAT)

LOCATION: Between the Edwards Plateau and the Gulf Coastal Plains of South-central Texas.

POPULATION: 1,100,000

CLIMATE: Warm sunny summers with average high in July of 82°F (27°c); and mild winters with average high in January of 62°F (17°c). The city receives about 25" (635 mm) of rain; the wetter periods are May-June and Sept.-October.

Gay/Lesbian Visitor Information
Gay Switchboard: 734-2833
Lesbian Info: 828-5472

DESCRIPTION: San Antonio is now ranked among the nation's ten largest cities. Having played a key role in Texas' independence from Mexico 155 years ago, the city is one of the most historically significant in the USA. Visit the **Alamo**, the most famous structure in the city and the symbol of independence for all of Texas; the **Paseo del Rio** (River Walk), San Antonio's downtown main attraction with quaint cobblestone walkways, variety of European-style sidewalk cafés, specialty boutiques, nightclubs and gift shops. **The River Walk** is the site of the city's many scheduled events and Festivals; **Fiesta Texas** theme park.

BARS ᵀ RESTAURANTS ¶¶

● Bars/clubs (GM): **Cowboys**, country/western style, 622 Roosevelt Ave. (532-9194); **Eagle Mountain**, country/western, 1902 McCullough (733-1516); **The Saint**, dance club, female impersonators, 1430 N. Main (225-7330); **Silver Dollar**, country/western style, 1418 No. Main (227-2623); **Sparks**, video bar, male dancers, 8011 Webbles (Walzem) (653-9941); **2015**, neighborhood bar, male dancers, 2015 San Pedro (733-3365); **Wild Club**, go-go boys, drag show, 820 San Pedro (226-2620); **Woody's**, video bar, 826 San Pedro (227-2789).

● Bars/clubs (GMW): **Bonham Exchange**, San Antonio's largest dance club, 411 Bonham (271-3811); **Country Club**, country dance bar, 115 General Krueger Blvd. (344-9720); **Miriam's**, dance club, 115 General Krueger (308-7354).

● Bar/club (GW): **Nexus** , dance bar, 8021 Pinebrook (341-2818); **Riddums**, lesbian nightclub, 10221 Desert Sands (366-4206).

● Restaurants (AW): **Alamo Station** 1150 S. Alamo (271-7791); **Beauregard Café**, 320 Beauregard (223-1388). For fine Mexican ambiance and fare visit **El Mercado**, a large indoor shopping area patterned after a Mexican market place. **El Mercado** is part of the city's Market Square with its Mexican restaurants and farmer's market.

λ SERVICES λ

● Videos (G/S): **Encore Video**, 8546 Broadway #160 (821-5345).

 ACCOMMODATIONS

ADELYNNE'S SUMMIT HAUS & SUMMIT HAUS II
427 W. Summit, San Antonio, TX 78212. Tel: (210) 736-6272, Toll Free (800) 972-7266. Fax: (210) 737-8244. TYPE: *Bed & Breakfast*. HOSTESS: Adelynne H. Whitaker. CLIENTELE: All Welcome. LOCATION: 5-8 minutes north of Riverwalk/Downtown.

* Rooms: 5; 3 w/priv., 2 w/shared bath
* CTV, phone, refrigerator, C/H, A/C
* Suite 1, Cottage 1 (2BR) living room, full bath, kitchen, patio/terrace, sundeck
* Maid service, laundry service, free parking
* Gay Bars: 1-2 mi. / 3 km
* Health Club: 2 mi. / 3 km (mixed)
* Airport: San Antonio Int'l 5 mi. / 8 km
* Metro: 50 m / yards
* Languages: English, German
* Reservations: 1 night deposit
* Cancellation: 7 days, $10 admin. charge
* Credit Cards: MC/VISA/AMEX
* Open: Year round
* Rates: $67.50 - $150 w/AB, Tax: 15%
* *TAC:* 10%

DESCRIPTION: 1920's residence elegantly furnished in period Bidermeire furniture, linens and porcelains. Cottage decorated in period 18th-19th century French & English. Persian oriental rugs, King, Queen and Full beds. Shared yards, decks, fireplaces. *AAA / SABBA*

CROCKETT HOTEL
320 Bonham St., San Antonio, TX 78205. Tel: (512) 225-6500. Fax: (512) 223-6613. TYPE: *Moderate Deluxe Hotel*. CLIENTELE: Mostly Straight. LOCATION: Central location opposite the Alamo.

* Rooms: 202 w/priv. bath. Suites: 9
* CTV, phone, wheelchair accessibility
* Restaurants (2), bar, atrium
* Pool, Roof sundeck w/hot tub
* Gay Bars: walking distance
* Airport: 9 mi. / 15 km
* Credit Cards: MC/VISA/AMEX/DC
* Open: Year round
* Rates: $75 - $120. *TAC:* 10%

DESCRIPTION: Traditional landmark hotel listed on the National Historic Register with true old-Texas flavor. Caters to small groups and tourists.

THE PAINTED LADY
620 Broadway, San Antonio, TX 78215. Tel: (210) 220-1092. TYPE: *Guest House*. HOST: Cindy. CLIENTELE: Mostly Gay. LOCATION: Downtown San Antonio, 4 blocks from the Alamo and Riverwalk. 9 individually appointed suites.

LA QUINTA MOTOR INN
7202 S. Pan am Expwy. San Antonio TX 78221. Tel: (210) 271-0001. Fax: (210) 228-0663. TYPE: *Motel*. CLIENTELE: Mostly Straight. LOCATION: Adjacent to Market Sq. near Riverwalk and Alamo.

* Rooms: 122 w/priv. bath
* CTV, phone, A/C
* Pool & poolside restaurant/bar
* Gay Bars: car needed
* Airport: 9 mi. / 15 km
* Credit Cards: MC/VISA/AMEX/DC
* Open: Year round
* Rates: $68 - $90. *TAC:* 10%

DESCRIPTION: Tourist class moderately priced motel in a convenient location.

UTAH

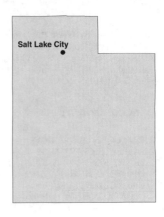

Salt Lake City
●

- ◆ **Population:** 1,800,000
- ◆ **Capital:** Salt Lake City
- ◆ **Time Zone:** Mountain
- ◆ **Sodomy Law**
- ◆ **Legal drinking age:** 21

SALT LAKE CITY   *℃*   801

✈ Salt Lake City Int'l Airport (SLC)
3 mi. / 5 km west

LOCATION: Spectacular setting on Great Salt Lake with the Wasatch Mountains to the east and the Ogirrh mountains to the west.

POPULATION: 160,000

CLIMATE: Rigorous desert climate with four well defined seasons. Summers are hot and dry with cooler nights, Winters are cold but not severe. Fall is short and Spring is longer and stormier.

Gay & Lesbian Visitor Information
UTAH Stonewall Center
770 South 300 West, SLC 84101
Tel: 539-8800

DESCRIPTION: Once a desert wilderness, Salt Lake City was founded by Mormon settlers who escaped religious persecution. The city is laid out in a grid fashion, with Temple Square at the center.

BARS Y RESTAURANTS 🍴

● Bars/Clubs (GM): **Vortex**, members club, #32 Exchange Place, downtown (521-9292); **Deerhunter**, primarily a men's bar, 636 South 300 West (363-1602); **Kings**, dance club, 108 South 300 West (521-5464); **The Sun**, dance club, light show, 702 West 200 South (531-0833).

● Bars/Clubs (GMW): **Brass Rail**, 103 27th St., Ogden (399-1374); **Bricks**, dance club, 579 West 200 South (328-0255); **Radio City**, 147 South State St., (532-9327); **The Trapp**, country/western, 102 South 600 West (531-8727).

● Bars/Clubs (GW): **Paper Moon**, private Womyn's club, 3424 South State St., (466-8517)

● Restaurants (NG): **La Fleur de Lys**, French cuisine, 39 Post Office Place, 340 S. 39 West (359-5753); **Old Salt City Jail**, steak, seafood, in an early brewery old country jail style, 460 S. 1000 E. St. (355-2422).

λ SERVICES λ

● Health Club (GMW): **14th Street Gym**, steam room, hot tub, weights, 1414 West 200 South (363-2029).

● Massage (GM): **Creative Touch Salon**, 2147 East 3300 South (466-9666).

● Videos (GMW): **Video One**, large selection of gay/lesbian films, 484 South 900 West (539-0300).

🏨 ACCOMMODATIONS 🏨

AARDVARKS B&B
249 W. 400 South (Office), SLC UT 89104. Tel: (801) 533-0927. Fax: (801) 533-0926. TYPE: *Bed & Breakfast.* CLIENTELE: Gay men & women. LOCATION: Right in downtown. 6 rooms, CTV, VCR, phone, restaurant. Rates: $40-$80. *TAC:* 5%. DESCRIPTION: 3 story Victorian private home.

COURTYARD BY MARRIOTT
130 West 400 South, SLC UT 84101. Tel: (801) 531-6000. TYPE: *Hotel.* CLIENTELE: All Welcome. LOCATION: Downtown location. 96 rooms and suites w/priv. bath, CTV, phone, work area, restaurant, indoor pool, jacuzzi, exercise room. Rates: $79 - $120. Tax: 10.72%, *TAC:* 10%. DESCRIPTION: Residential style hotel, no bell boy or reception office.

VERMONT

● **STOWE**

◆ **Population:** 511,450
◆ **Capital:** Montpelier
◆ **Time Zone:** Eastern
◆ **No Sodomy Law**
◆ **Legal drinking age:** 18

STOWE   ✆   802

✈ Burlington Int'l Airport (BTV)

LOCATION: Northern Vermont Lamoille County on State Route 100, near the intersection of the Little River and the West Branch River, 36 mi. / 58km east of Burlington.

POPULATION: 583

CLIMATE: Cool summers and long, cold snowy winters.

VISITOR INFORMATION
Stowe Area Association: 253-7321

DESCRIPTION: Charming New England village in the Green Mountains. **Mt. Mansfield**, Vermont's highest peak and a popular ski recreation area is only a few miles away giving Stowe its reputation as the "Ski Capital of the East."

BARS ☿ RESTAURANTS ⍩

● Bar (GMW): Stowe has no gay bars. **Pearl's**, dance bar, 135 Pearl St. (863-2343) is in nearby Burlington.

● Restaurants (NG): **Swisspot Restaurant**, Swiss specialties, on SR 100 (253-4622): **Topnotch At Stowe** on Rte. 108 (253-8585); **Whiskers**, steak/seafood, 1-1/2 miles (2 km) northwest on SR 100 (253-8996).

⌂ ACCOMMODATIONS ⌂

BUCCANEER COUNTRY LODGE
3214 Mountain Rd., Stowe VT 05672. Tel: (802) 253-4772 or Toll Free (800) 543-1293. Fax: (802) 253-4782. TYPE: *Motel style B&B.* HOST: Bill Dangelo. CLIENTELE: Equal Gay/Straight. LOCATION: Heart of Stowe on Rt 108 (Mountain Rd.) corner of Edson Hill Rd.

* Rooms: 12 w/priv. bath
* CTV, phone, refrigerator, C/H, A/C, cooking facilities
* Suites: 4 (1BR) living room, full bath, kitchen, patio/terrace
* Maid service, free parking, outdoor heated pool (summer), outdoor jacuzzi (year round)
* Beach: 15-20 min. (mixed)
* Gay Bars: 30-40 min.
* Health Club: 2 mi. / 3 km (Stowe Gym)
* Airport: Burlington Int'l 35 min
* Languages: English, Spanish, French
* Reservations: 50% or 1 night deposit
* Cancellation: 15 day notice (non-holiday) 30 day notice (holiday)
* Credit Cards: MC/VISA
* Open: Year round
* Rates: $69-$225 w/B; (off) $45-$79
* Tax: 7% VT tax, 13% service
* Check in time 3pm / check out 11am
* *TAC:* 10%

DESCRIPTION: Award winning 3-diamond facility. Deluxe accommodations include guest rooms and suites. Minutes to skiing and all outdoor recreational activities.

TRAPP FAMILY LODGE
Luce Hill Rd., Stow VT 05672. Tel: (802) 253-8511 or reservations: (800) 826-7000. Fax: (802) 253-8511. TYPE: *Alpine Lodge.* CLIENTELE: Mostly Straight. LOCATION: In Stowe. 93 rooms w/priv. bath, most with balcony, pool, sports center. Rates: $85-$140. *TAC:* 10%. DESCRIPTION:Famous Austrian style Alpine lodge owned by the legendary Von Trapp family from the "Sound of Music".

U.S. VIRGIN ISLANDS

ATLANTIC OCEAN

ST. THOMAS

ST. JOHN

CHARLOTTE AMALIE

CHRISTIANSTED

FREDERIKSTED

ST. CROIX

CARIBBEAN SEA

◆ **U.S. Territory**
◆ **Population:** 95,400
◆ **Capital:** Charlotte Amalie
◆ **Time Zone:** Atlantic

SAINT CROIX   ✆ **809**

✈ Alexander Hamilton Airport (STX)
Seaplane Base, Christiansted (SSB)

LOCATION: Northeastern part of the Caribbean, east of Puerto Rico. St. Croix is the easternmost point of the U.S.A. and it is also the largest island lying entirely in the Caribbean Sea.

POPULATION: 31,780
Frederiksted 1,600; Christiansted 3,000

CLIMATE: Comfortable year round. Winter is warm with an average mean temperature of 77°F (25°c). Summer is hot with steady trade winds and an average temperature of 82°F (28°c).

DESCRIPTION: Scattered across the glittering waters of the Caribbean, 1,100 mi. / 1,760 km southeast of Miami lie the US Virgin Islands. The (US) Virgin Islands are territories rather than states, but their residents are American citizens. **St. Croix** is one of the three islands that combines to form the U.S. Virgin Islands into a Caribbean paradise. The other two islands are **St. Thomas** and **St. John**.

St. Croix is the largest island and an ideal place to escape the crowds of St. Thomas and the isolation of St. John. The low-lying island of rolling hills was once the main sugar-producing source of the New World. Many of the old Danish plantation homes and sugar mills have been restored to function as hotels and restaurants. **Christiansted**, the main town of the island, is a compact town with old Danish buildings designated a National Historic site. **Frederiksted** on the west end the atmosphere is sleepy and somewhat less popular with straight tourists. St. Croix claims 47 diving sites, and an underwater garden - **Buck Island Reef**.

❖ Gay Beach: check out the beach adjacent to the On The Beach Hotel.

BARS ♉ RESTAURANTS 🍴

● Bar (AW):✪ **Club Comanche**, popular cocktail bar and restaurant, 1 Strand St. Christiansted (773-0210); **Last Hurrah**, 67 King St. Frederiksted.

● Restaurants (AW): **Blue Moon**, Jazz Club, bistro & restaurant, seafood, on the waterfront in historic Frederiksted (772-2222); ✪ **Club Comanche**, excellent native & continental cui-

⟨X⟩Club Comanche

Enjoy the charm of Old Danish Main House; Open air dining Native and Continental cuisine; relax on the pool terrace overlooking the harbour

Club Comanche

1 Strand St., Christiansted, St. Croix USVI 00820
Tel/Fax: (809) 773-0210
Toll Free: (800) 524-2066

sine, 1 Strand St. Christiansted (773-0210);
Golden China, Chinese, 28 King Cross St.,
(773-8181); **Junies**, seafood West Indian style,
132 Peter's Rest (773-2801); **Top Hat**, elegant,
Danish smorgasbord on Sundays, located on
Company St. in Christiansted (773-4322).

 ACCOMMODATIONS

✪ CLUB COMANCHE

1 Strand St., Christiansted, St. Croix, USVI
00820. Tel/Fax: (809) 773-0210. Toll Free (800)
524-2066. TYPE: *Hotel*. HOSTS: Mary & RJ
Boehm. CLIENTELE: All Welcome. LOCA-
TION: In the heart of town overlooking the
harbor, 2 min. from superb beach.

* Rooms: 40 w/priv. bath
  sgl 20/ dbl 16/ triple 4
* Rooms for smokers and non smokers
* CTV, VCR, A/C, refrigerator
* Suites: 4 (2BR)
* Bed Types: single, twin, double, large
  (oversized) doubles, king size, 4 poster
* Bar, restaurant, shop, large seawter pool
* Recreation: massage, horseback riding,
  watersports, diving packages and scuba
  certification classes.
* Pets: prearrangement required
* Beach: 2 min. (mixed)
* Airport: 10 min.
* Reservations: 1 day deposit
* Cancellation Policy: 4 days
* Credit Cards: MC/VISA/AMEX
* Open: Year round
* Rates: $60 - $150 / (off) $45-$100
* Taxes: 8%
* Check in 2 pm / check out 12 noon
* *TAC:* 10%
* Email: comanche@island.vi
* URL: http://www.usvi.net/hotel/comanche

DESCRIPTION: Beautiful 235 year old Inn.
Tastefully furnished large quaint rooms with
high ceilings. Individually decorated suites
overlooking the harbor with full kitchen facilities and upstairs bedroom.

ON THE BEACH RESORT

P.O. Box 1908, Frederiksted, St. Croix USVI
00841. Tel: (809) 772-1205. Toll Free 1 (800)
524-2018. Fax: (809) 772-1757. TYPE: *Resort
Complex*. HOST: Bill Owens. CLIENTELE:
Gay men & women. LOCATION: On white
sandy beach 1/2 mi. (800 m) from town. Rates:
season $85-$180, off $50-$110. *TAC:* 10%.
DESCRIPTION: 20 unit beachfront hotel,
kitchen, balcony, private bath, A/C, pool, bar
and restaurant. *IGTA, AAA*

PRINCE STREET INN

402 Prince St., Frederiksted, St. Croix, USVI
00840. Tel: (809) 772-9550. TYPE: *Guest
House*. HOST: Paul or Charlotte Pyles. CLIEN-
TELE: All Welcome. LOCATION: Historic
Frederiksted, intersection of Hill & Prince
Streets in Frederiksted. 5 suites. DESCRIP-
TION: Historic Danish Villa with fully
equipped suites in a garden setting. Beaches
and restaurants nearby. Children allowed.

KING CHRISTIAN HOTEL

59 Kings Wharf, Charistiansted, St Croix,
USVI 00822. Tel: (809) 773-2285. TYPE: *Hotel*.
CLIENTELE: Equal Gay/Straight. LOCA-
TION: On the waterfront in historic Christiansted. 39 rooms w/priv. bath, bar, restaurant, pool, sundeck. Rates: $80-$135. Danish
style hotel.

ST. JOHN   ℂ 809

✈ Cyril E. King Airport (STT) 90 min.
   Cruz Bay ferry to St. Thomas, 20 min.

LOCATION: About 5 mi. / 8 km east of St.

Thomas just across the Pillsbury Sound.

DESCRIPTION: The smallest and least populated of the three main US Virgins. St. John is
bordered by a rocky coastline, with secluded
crescent-shaped bays, white sandy beaches and
interesting wildlife and birdlife. St. John is a
popular stop over for boating in the US Virgins
with beautiful sheltered coves for anchorages,
swimming and extended holidays.

❖ Beach: **Solomon Beach**, nude beach, walking distance from Cruz Bay.

 ACCOMMODATIONS

GALLOWS POINT SUITE RESORT

Cruz Bay. Tel: (809) 776-6434. TYPE: *All-Suite
Resort*. CLIENTELE: All Welcome. LOCA-
TION: Oceanfront in lush tropical grounds. 60
suites w/priv. bath, 4 villas, w/living room, dining room, fully equipped kitchen, loft suites,
maid and room service, restaurant, 2 bars, outdoor pool, free parking. Near restaurants, duty
free shopping, walk to nude beach. Rates:
$160-$425. DESCRIPTION: Elegant beachfront resort with attractively decorated suites
and villas. Excellent location and very private.

ST. THOMAS   © 809

✈ Cyril E. King Airport (STT)
Seaplane Base, Charlotte Amalie (SPB)

LOCATION: In the heart of St. Thomas southern coast.

POPULATION: 12,000

CLIMATE: see St. Croix

DESCRIPTION: The capital of the US Virgin Islands is a scenic harbor and a duty-free paradise. Visit **Fort Christian**, the oldest standing structure on St. Thomas (built 1671), now serving as a museum; **Government House**, on Government Hill; **St. Thomas Synagogue**, two blocks from Main Street, second oldest synagogue in this part of the world (completed 1833), in a remarkable Spanish-moorish style architecture; **Market Square**, the infamous slave market of the 17th century at the west end of Main Street, now a market for flowers, herbs and produce; **Frenchtown**, gallic style settlement on the harbor's western shore.

❖ Beaches: **Little Magen's Beach**, clothing optional beach (AYOR); **Morningstar Beach**, popular with local gays and gay tourist.

BARS ⟁ RESTAURANTS ⟨⟩

● Bars/clubs (G/S): **R&R Nightclub**, dance club, late night bar menu, inside Lemon Grass Café, downtown Charlotte Amalie (777-1877).

● Restaurant (AW): **Café Normandie**, rue de St. Bathelemy, Frenchtown (774-1622); **Diamond Barrel**, Seafood, 18 Norre Gade, Charlotte Amalie (774-5071); **Entre Nous**, elegant French for romantic dinner, Bluebeard's Castle, near town (776-4050); **Provence**, Dinner, happy hour, piano bar, Frenchtown (777-5600); **Virgilio's**, Italian, 18 Main St., Charlotte Amalie (776-4920); **Zorba's**, Greek dishes, Isle of Mykonos decor, 1854 Hus, Government Hill (776-0444).

⟨ ACCOMMODATIONS ⟨⟩

HOTEL 1829
PO Box 1567, Charlotte Amalie, USVI 00801. Tel: (809) 776-1829. Fax: (809) 776-4313. TYPE: *Hotel*. CLIENTELE: All Welcome. LOCATION: Town center, above shopping area in Government Hill overlooking the harbor. 15 rooms w/priv. bath, 3 suites, phone, CTV, A/C. Rates: $50-$250. *TAC*: 10%. DESCRIPTION: A private mansion now designated a national historic site. Beautifully restored rooms and suites with view of the harbor.

VIRGINIA

RICHMOND ●
NORFOLK●
VIRGINIA BEACH●

♦ **Population:** 5,346,800
♦ **Capital:** Richmond
♦ **Time Zone:** Eastern
♦ **Sodomy Law**
♦ **Legal drinking age:** 18

NORFOLK *©* **757**
VIRGINIA BEACH

✈ Norfolk Int'l Airport (ORF)

LOCATION: The Chesapeake Bay immediately to the north, and the Atlantic Ocean to the East.

POPULATION: 800,000

CLIMATE: Four-season climate suited for year-round outdoor activities. Outside of the track of hurricanes and tropical storms. Winters are mild with a January average temperature of 40°F (4°c); Summers are warm, humid and long with an average July temperatures of 78°F (26°c).

DESCRIPTION: Norfolk is a seaport town with a bustling business trade center and active gay nightlife. Visit the **Norfolk Botanical Gardens** on Azalea Garden Rd.; and the **Norfolk Naval Base**, one of the largest concentration of Naval Force in the world. Nearby is **Virginia Beach** a beautiful beach resort town with over 28 miles (45 km) of golden sandy shoreline. The resort offers fine restaurants, specialty shops and the famous

Boardwalk, a 2-mile oceanfront promenade with festival atmosphere. Recreational activities vary from deep sea fishing to sailing, windsurfing and more. For the culturally inclined there are festivals, special events, theatre and arts. History lovers will discover an area rich in historical heritage dating back to 1607. Nearby **Williamsburg** is a delightful place to explore a restored 18th century Colonial heritage with people in 18th-century attire. Visit the **Virginia Marine Science Museum** and the **Virginia Beach Center for the Arts.**

❖ **SPECIAL EVENTS:** July-September **Nightly Boardwalk Entertainment;** July 11-26 **Canadian-American Festival;** September 4-7 **Gran Prix Virginia Beach** includes mini-Grand Prix Auto race, offshore Grand Prix Boat Race, fireworks and entertainment.

BARS ⅄ RESTAURANTS ⑪

➤ **Norfolk**
● Bars/Clubs (GM): **Garage**, cruise bar/restaurant, 731 Granby St. (623-0303); **Late Show**, private club, 11th St., (bet. Monticello & Granby) (623-3854).

● Bars/Clubs (GW): **Charlotte's Web**, 6425 Tidewater Dr. (853-5021); **Hershee**, restaurant, dance bar, 6117 Sewells Point Rd. (853-9842); **Ms. P**, 6401 Tidewater Drive (853-9717).

● Restaurant (AW): **Charlie's**, 1800 Granby St. (625-0824).

➤ **Virginia Beach**
● Bars/Clubs (mostly GM): **Ambush**, restaurant/cruise video bar, 2838 Virginia Beach Blvd. (498-4301); **Danny's**, dance club, 2901 Baltic Ave. (428-4016).

● Restaurants: all the gay bars offer some kind of food service. Others (AW): **Captain George's**, seafood buffet, 1956 Laskin Rd, 31st St. (428-3494); **Corner Market**, Pub & restaurant, Sunday brunch buffet, West Great Neck Rd. (481-5511); **Hot Tuna Bar & Grill**, 2817 Shore Drive (481-2888); **Morrison's Cafeteria**, cheap but good cafeteria, 1532 Laskin Rd.; **The Lynnhaven Fish House Restaurant**, Shore Drive & Starfish Rd. (481-0003); **39th St. Seafood Grill**, 39th St. & Oceanfront (428-1711).

λ SERVICES λ

➤ **Norfolk**
● Gym (M/F): **Mid-Town Muscle**, 102 West

Olney Rd. (640-1496).

● Gifts/Novelties: **Max Images**, 537 W. 21st St. (622-3701); **Personal Touch**, 733 Granby St. (622-4438).

● Leather Boutique: **Gears**, 425 Monticello at the Anvil (622-4438).

 ACCOMMODATIONS

CORAL SAND MOTEL
2307 Pacific Ave., Virginia Beach, VA 23451. Tel: (757) 425-0872. TYPE: *Motel.* HOST: Gene Nixon. CLIENTELE: Mostly gay men & women. LOCATION: One block off Hwy 44 at the heart of the beach.19 rooms. **DESCRIPTION:** Virginia Beach's only gay and lesbian resort motel.

HOWARD JOHNSON WATERSIDE
700 Monticello Ave., Norfolk, VA 23510. Tel: (757) 627-5555. Fax: (804) 533-9651. TYPE: *Hotel.* CLIENTELE: All Welcome. LOCATION: Downtown across from the Scope Convention center.

* Rooms: 345 w/priv. bath
* CTV, phone, A/C
* Maid & room service, wheelchair access
* Restaurant, pool, shops, parking
* Gay bars: some within walking distance
* Airport: 8 mi. / 13 km, taxi
* Open: Year round
* Credit Cards: MC/VISA/AMEX
* Rates: $60 - $90
* *TAC:* 10%

DESCRIPTION: Moderate first class hotel in the heart of the gay scene.

RICHMOND   ℭ 804

✈ Richmond Int'l Airport (RIC)
7.5 mi. / 12 km southeast of Richmond

LOCATION: Heart of Eastern Virginia.

DESCRIPTION: Virginia's Capital, Richmond is an historic city. Founded in 1607 as a trading post, it soon flourished thanks to its tobacco industry. The older neighborhoods are today a living museum of Virginia's great Colonial past. The historic warehouses of **Shockoe Slip**, at E. Cary and 13th St., now feature trendy art galleries, boutiques and fine restaurants.

BARS Y RESTAURANTS ¶¶

● Bars/Clubs (GM): **Club Colours**, 534 N. Harrison St. (353-3776); **Fielden's**, private club, 2033 W. Broad St. (359-1963).

● Bar/Club (GW): **Babes**, 3166 W. Cary St. (355-9330).

● Restaurant (GMW): **Casablanca**, innovative American cuisine, 6 E. Grace St. (648-2040).

 ACCOMMODATIONS

BERKELEY HOTEL
1200 E. Cary St. Richmond, VA 23210. TEL: (804) 780-1300. Fax: (804) 343-1885. TYPE: *Hotel.* CLIENTELE: All Welcome. LOCATION: Historic Shockoe Slip area of downtown.

* Rooms: 56 w/priv. bath. Suite: 1
* CTV, phone, room service
* Restaurant, lounge, pool, health club
* Gay Bars: some nearby
* Airport: 5 mi. / 8 km
* Rates: $114-$138
* *TAC:* 10%

DESCRIPTION: European style hotel in the heart of historic Richmond.

COMFORT INN (Midtown)
3200 W. Broad St., Richmond, VA 23230. Tel: (804) 359-4061. Fax: (804) 359-3189. TYPE: *Motel.* CLIENTELE: All Welcome. LOCATION: Near I-64 & I-95, 2 mi. / 3 km from downtown.

* Rooms: 159 w/priv. bath.
* Suites: 8
* Rooms for non smokers
* CTV, phone, room service, A/C (some)
* Restaurant, lounge, pool, gym
* Free parking, wheelchair access
* Gay Bars: some nearby
* Airport: 5 mi. / 8 km
* Rates: $60-$90 w/CB
* *TAC:* 10%

DESCRIPTION: Six story motel in a convenient location.

LINDEN ROW INN
100 E. Franklin St., Richmond, VA 23219. Tel: (804) 783-7000. TYPE: *Hotel.* CLIENTELE: All Welcome. LOCATION: Downtown. 70 rooms w/bath. Greek revival Victorian Inn.

WASHINGTON

● SEATTLE

- ◆ **Population:** 4,130,000
- ◆ **Capital:** Olympia
- ◆ **Time Zone:** Pacific
- ◆ **No Sodomy Law**
- ◆ **Legal drinking age:** 21

SEATTLE   *Ⓒ* 206

✈ Sea-Tac Int'l Airport (SEA)

LOCATION: On Puget Sound on the north-west Pacific Coast of Washington.

POPULATION: City 493,800; Metro 1,606,800

CLIMATE: Mid-latitude coastal climate. Summers are pleasant, and winters are mild.

Gay & Lesbian
Visitor Information
GSBA: 443-4722

DESCRIPTION: The largest metropolis of the U.S. Pacific Northwest. Modern Seattle is built upon several hills ranging from sea level to 450 ft. (136 m), between Lake Washington and Puget Sound.

❖ **SPECIAL EVENT: Evergreen Tennis Championships**, July (4th of July Week End) (323-2336).

BARS ☿ RESTAURANTS 🍴

The gay scene in concentrates in the First Hill and Capitol Hill area.

● Bars/clubs (GM): **Brass Connection**, bar/restaurant, 722 E. Pike (322-7777); **The Cuff**, leather/uniform bar, 1533 13th Ave. (323-1525); **Eagle**, cruise leather bar, 314 E. Pike St. (624-2612); **Madison Pub**, 1315 E. Madison St. (325-6537); **Neighbours**, night club, restaurant, 1509 Broadway (324-5358); **Spag's**, 1118 E. Pike St. (322-3232).

● Bars/clubs (GMW): **Double Header**, dance bar, mature crowd, 407 2nd Ave. South (464-9918); **Hamburger Mary's**, bar/restaurant, 401 Broadway Ave. (325-65650; **Re-Bar**, dance bar/cabaret, 1114 Howell St. (233-9873); **Trumpers**, 1500 E. Madison (328-3800).

● Bars/clubs (GW): **Off Ramp Cafe**, entertainment complex, 109 Eastlake East (628-0232); **Wildrose Tavern**, 1021 E. Pike (324-9210).

● Restaurants (AW): **Aoki**, Japanese grill & Sushi bar, 621 Broadway E. (324-3633); **Encore**, restaurant & lounge, 1518 11th Ave. (324-6617); **George's**, Greek/American, 1901 4th Ave. (622-5631); **Hamburger Mary's**, 401 Broadway Ave. (325-65650; **Neighbours**, 1509 Broadway (324-5358); **Kokeb**, Ethiopian, 926 12th Ave. (322-0485); **Poor Italian Café**, Virginia St. at Second Ave. (441-4313).

λ SERVICES λ

● Erotica (GM): **The Crypt**, leather, sex toys, videos, 1310 E. Union St. (325-3882).

● Health Clubs (GM): **Basic Plumbing**, 1104 Pike St. (682-8441); **Club Seattle**, 24 hrs., 1520 Summit Ave., open 24 hrs (329-2334); **Club Z**, 1117 Pike St. (622-9958); **South End Steam Bath**, 115-1/2 1st Ave. S., at Pioneer Square (223-9091).

● Personal Phone Line (GM): ✪ **Seattle Voice-male**, meet local guys! Browse, match, chat. try it free. (515-4000) free access code 8060.

🖾 ACCOMMODATIONS 🖾

INN AT VIRGINIA MASON
1006 Spring St., Seattle WA 98104. Tel: (206) 583-5453 or reservations: (800) 283-6453. Fax: (206) 223-7545. TYPE: *Hotel.* CLIENTELE: Mostly Straight. LOCATION: Downtown Pike Place market near waterfront. 79 rooms, 3 suites, CTV, phone, A/C, wheelchair access,bar, restaurant, courtyard cafe. DESCRIPTION: Elegant first class hotel with traditionally styled room. Garage parking and fitness center nearby.

WISCONSIN

GREEN BAY

MADISON

MILWAUKEE

♦ **Population:** 4,706,000
♦ **Capital:** Madison
♦ **Time Zone:** Central
♦ **No Sodomy Law**
♦ **Legal drinking age:** 19

GREEN BAY   ℂ 414

✈ Austin Strauble Airport (GRB) 8 mi. SW

LOCATION: Eastern Wisconsin on Green Bay.

POPULATION: 180,000

DESCRIPTION: Historic trading center. Home of the University of Wisconsin-Green Bay, and the "Green Bay Packers" professional football team.

BARS 🍸 RESTAURANTS 🍴

● Bars/clubs (GMW): **Brandy's**, 1126 Main St. (800-311-3197); **Cheecks**, 232 S. Broadway (430-9854); **Napalese Lounge**, 515 S. Broadway (432-9646); **Jayes**, 1106 Main (435-5476); **Sass**, 840 S. Broadway (437-7277).

● Restaurants (AW): **Eve's Supper Club**, steak, seafood, 2020 Riverside Dr. (435-1571); **Zimmani's**, pastas and salad, 2809 S. Oneida St. (499-3327).

🔸 ACCOMMODATIONS 🔸

DAYS INN
406 N. Washington St. at Hwy 141, Green Bay, WI 54304. Tel: (414) 435-4484. Fax: (414) 435-4484. TYPE: *Hotel.* CLIENTELE: All Welcome. LOCATION: Downtown.

* Rooms: 98 w/priv. bath. Suites: 4
* CTV, phone, wheelchair access
* Restaurant, lounge, pool
* Gay Bars: some nearby
* Airport: 5 mi. / 8 km
* Open: Year round
* Rates: $60-$75   *TAC:* 10%

DESCRIPTION: Tourist class hotel adjacent to the Port Plaza Mall.

EMBASSY SUITES
333 Main St., Green Bay, WI 54301. Tel: (414) 432-4555. Fax: (414) 432-0700. TYPE: *All Suite Hotel.* CLIENTELE: All Welcome. LOCATION: Connected to the Port Plaza Mall.

* 223 suites w/priv. bath
* CTV, phone, wheelchair access
* Restaurant, lounge, pool
* Gay Bars: some nearby
* Airport: 5 mi. / 8 km
* Open: Year round
* Rates: $97-$145   *TAC:* 10%

DESCRIPTION: Eight-story first class all suite hotel in a central location.

MADISON   ℂ 608

✈ Dane County Airport (MSN) 5 mi. NE

LOCATION: West of Milwaukee in southern WI, between Lake Mendota and Lake Monona.

POPULATION: 180,000

Gay/Lesbian Visitor Information
G&L Hotline: (608) 255-4297

DESCRIPTION: University town with a rich historical and architectural heritage.

BARS 🍸 RESTAURANTS 🍴

● Bars/clubs (GMW): **Manouvres**, 150 S. Blair (258-9918); **Shamrock**, 117 W. Main St. (255-5029); **Geraldines**, 3052 E. Washington (241-9335); **Greenbush**, 914 Regent (257-2874); **R**

Place, 121 W. Main (257-5455).

⟨⟩ ACCOMMODATIONS ⟨⟩

RAMADA INN
3841 E. Washington Ave., Madison, WI 53704.
Tel: (608) 244-2481. TYPE: *Motor Inn*. CLIEN-
TELE: All Welcome. LOCATION: On Hwy 151,
3 mi / 5 km from airport. 194 rooms w/priv.
bath, phone, CTV, A/C, indoor pool & jacuzzi.
Rates: $65-$95. *TAC:* 10%

MILWAUKEE   ℂ   414

✈ General Mitchell Airport (MKE)

LOCATION: West shore of Lake Michigan, 50
miles / 80 km north of Chicago.

POPULATION: 636,000

CLIMATE: Changeable weather with influence of the nearby lake. January average is
19°F (-7°c). Summers are clear with average in
July of 70°F (21°c). Annual rainfall is 29" (736
mm), and annual snowfall is 45" (1.14m).

Gay/Lesbian Visitor Information
Gay Hotline: (414) 444-7331

DESCRIPTION: Milwaukee, derived from the
Indian word 'Millioki' meaning "gathering
place by the water", is the beer capital of the
nation, an industrial center, and a major port.
The city began as a French trading post
between Chicago and Green Bay. It was later
settled by English, followed by influx of immi-
grants from Germany, Austria, East Europe
and Scandinavia. By the mid 19th century the
community incorporated as a city.

Visit the **Milwaukee Art Museum**, 750 N.
Lincoln Memorial Dr. - exhibits of old American
and contemporary art; **Port of Milwaukee**
and boat tours; **Captain Frederick Pabst
Mansion**, 2000 W. Wisconsin Ave., an impressive restored mansion of the late head of a
brewing company; **Milwaukee County Zoo**,
10001 W. Bluemound Rd., and **Mitchel Park**
featuring exotic floral exhibits in futuristic
looking horticultural domes, 524 S. Layton Blvd.

❖ **SPECIAL EVENTS: Oktoberfest**, the country's biggest beer festival, September / October.

BARS ⅄ RESTAURANTS ❢❢

The bar scene is relatively spread out with
some concentration south of the Amtrak station area along 1st and 2nd streets.

● Bars/clubs (GM): **Ballgame**, cruise video
bar, 196 S. 2nd St. (273-7474); **Boot Camp
Saloon**, cruise leather/levy bar, 209 E. National (643-6900); **C'est la Vie** cruise bar, younger
clientele, 231 S 2nd St. (291-9600); **La Cage**,
video dance bar, drag shows, 801 S. 2nd St.
(383-8330); **M&M Club**, piano bar, Restaurant
(lunch/dinner daily), 124 N. Water St. (347-
1962); **This is It**, professional clientele, 418 E.
Wells St. (278-9192).

● Bars/clubs (GMW): **Club 219**, dance bar,
male strippers, 219 S. 2nd St. (271-3732);
Grubb's Pub, at La Cage, 801 S. 2nd St. (383-
8330); **Loose Ends**, 4322 W Fond du Lac (442-
8469); **M&M Club**, piano bar/restaurant, 124
N. Water (347-1962).

● Bars/clubs (GW): **Fannie's**, popular lesbian
bar, disco & restaurant, DJ and entertainment
on weekends, 200 E. Washington Ave. (643-
9633); **Nitengales**, disco restaurant, men welcome, 2022 W. National (645-1830); **Station II**,
1534 W. Grant (383-5755).

● Restaurants (GM): **Glass Menagerie** at the
M&M bar, 124 N Water St. (347-1962). Other
(AW): **Turner's**, a century old tavern, seafood
specialties, 1034 N. 4th St. (273-5590); **Toy's
Chinatown**, Cantonese cuisine, 830 N. 3rd St.
(271-5166).

⅄ SERVICES ⅄

● Erotica (GM): **J&R News**, open 24 hrs., 831
N 27th St. (344-9686).

● Personal Phone Line (GM): ✪ **Milwaukee
Confidential Connection**, meet local guys!
Record, listen, respond to ads free (224-6462)
free access code 8060.

⟨⟩ ACCOMMODATIONS ⟨⟩

**HOWARD JOHNSON
PLAZA HOTEL**
611 W. Wisconsin Ave., Milwaukee WI 53203.
Tel: (414) 273-2950. Fax: (414) 273-7662.
TYPE: *Hotel*. CLIENTELE: Mostly Straight.
LOCATION: Downtown, near MECCA convention center, Performing Arts Center, University
of Wisconsin. 248 w/priv. bath, 18 Suites. CTV,
phone, A/C. DESCRIPTION: Ten-story hotel in
a convenient location.

CANADA

AREA: 3,851,787 sq. mi. (9,976,139 sq.km)
POPULATION: 27,300,000
CAPITAL: Ottawa, Ontario
CURRENCY: Canadian $ (CAN$)
OFFICIAL LANGUAGE: English, French
MAJOR RELIGIONS: Protestantism, Roman Catholicism

Telephone: 1
Nat'l Holiday: Canada Day, July 1
Official Time: 5-8 hrs behind G.M.T.

Electricity: 110 volts
Exchange Rate: 1US$ = CAN$1.34
National Airline: Air Canada

LAW REGARDING HOMOSEXUALITY: The legal minimum age for consensual homosexual activity is 18 years. Canada's constitution protects gays and lesbians from discrimination and the following jurisdictions have non-discrimination laws on the basis of sexual orientation: Canada (Federal), BC, Yukon, Sask., Manitoba, Ontario, Québec, & Nova Scotia.

● *Federal Tax Saving Tips for Foreign Visitors to Canada:* A 7% GST Federal tax on all goods and services is in effect. Hotels, guest houses and bed & breakfasts levy a service tax on their guests. Non-resident visitors can claim full rebate of the GST paid on accommodations and goods (except alcohol, tobacco or gasoline) purchased in Canada and taken home. Claims can be made at duty-free shops, where visitors receive rebates in Canadian funds. Visitors can mail original receipts along with a claim form to Revenue Canada. Forms are available at participating duty-free shops and many hotels, retail shops, and tourist attractions.

ALBERTA

● EDMONTON

● CALGARY

◆ **Population**: 2,545,500
◆ **Capital**: Edmonton
◆ **Time Zone**: Mountain
◆ **Legal drinking age**: 18

CALGARY   *©*   403

✈ Calgary Int'l Airport (YYC)

LOCATION: In the foothill of the Canadian Rockies in southern Alberta.

POPULATION: 754,000

CLIMATE: Cold snowy winter with an average temperature of 5°F (-15°c) in January. Summers are mild with an average temperature of 66°F (18°-20°c) in July.

Gay/Lesbian Visitor Information
G&L Community Service: 234-8973

DESCRIPTION: Calgary is the highest of Canada's big cities, 3,439 ft. / 1,042 m high with the snow capped Rockies to the west. It is the only metropolis in the world founded by a police force. The local population refer to their city as "cowtown". The city's growth is related to the oil boom of the 80's. It is safe and friendly for locales and visitors. Many mountain ski resorts and golf resorts are only a short distance away.

BARS ▼ RESTAURANTS 🍴

● Bars/clubs (GM): **Boyztown**, 213 10 Ave. SW (265-2028); **Metro/Rekroom**, disco, 213 10th Ave. SW (265-2028); **Trax**, country/western cruise bar, 1130 10th Ave. SW (245-8477).

● Bars/clubs (GMW): **Auburn Saloon**, 712-I St., SE (266-6628); **Backlot**, 209 10 Ave. SW (265-5211); **Detour**, dance club, 318 17th Ave. SW (228-7999); **Money-Pennies** (GW), 111 15 Ave SW (263-7411); **Rooks Bar & Beanerie**, lounge bar and dance club, mostly women, 112-16th Ave. NW (277-1922).

● Restaurants (GMW):**Arena Cafe**, 310-17 Ave. SW (228-5730); **Auburn Saloon**, 712-1 St., SE (266-6628); **Chickenhawks**, 550-11 Ave. SW (263-7177); **Diva Cafe**, 1154 Kensington Cr NW (270-3739); **Folks Like Us**, bistro, 110-10 St. NW (270-2241); **Grabbajabba**, 1610-10 St. SW (244-7750); **Money-Pennies**, mostly women, 111 15 Ave SW (263-7411); **Victoria's**, restaurant, 306-17 Ave SW (244-9991).

λ SERVICES λ

● Health Club (GM): **Goliaths**, 308 17th Ave. SW (rear) (229-0911).

● Leather (GMW): **B&B Leatherworks**, custom fetish clothing, 6802 Ogden Rd. SE (245-0411).

● Publication (GMW): ✪ **qc Magazine**, Alberta's premier gay & lesbian lifestyle magazine. Check out the event calender while you are in town. PO Box 64292, 5512 4 St. NW Calgary AB T2K 6J1. Tel: (403) 630-2061. Fax: (403) 275-6443. Email:qcmag@nucleus.com

● Video Stores (G/S): **After Dark**, 1314 I St. SW (279-3730).

🏰 ACCOMMODATIONS 🏰

BLACK ORCHID MANOR
1401 2nd St., NW, Calgary AB T2M 2W2. Tel: (403) 276-2471. TYPE: *Bed & Breakfast*. CLIENTELE: Gay men & women. Rates: from CAN$40-$65.

FOXWOOD
1725 12th St. SW, Calgary AB T2T 3N1. Tel: (403) 244-6693. TYPE: *Bed & Breakfast*. CLIENTELE: Gay men & women. Rates: from CAN$50-$65.

THE PALLISER
133 9th Ave. SW, Calgary AB T2P 2M3. Tel: (403) 262-1234. TYPE: *Hotel*. CLIENTELE: Mostly Straight. LOCATION: Directly connected to Calgary Tower in downtown. 403 rooms w/priv. bath, CTV, phone, A/C, parking, restaurant, lounge, Health Club. Rates: $150 - $190.

DESCRIPTION: Renovated first class hotel with elegant lobby near the Centre of Performing Arts.

RADISSON PLAZA
110 9th Ave. SE, Calgary AB T2G 5A6. Tel: (403) 266-7331. Fax: (403) 262-8442. TYPE: *Hotel*. CLIENTELE: All Welcome. LOCATION: Downtown near Calgary Convention Center, opposite Train Station. 366 rooms and suites w/priv., bath, CTV, phone, minibar, restaurant, country bar. Rates: $139-$300.

EDMONTON   ✆ 403

✈ Edmonton Int'l AP (YEG) 21 mi. / 34 km South

LOCATION: In the heart of Alberta, some 350 mi. / 560 km north of the US border, on both sides of the North Saskatchewan River.

POPULATION: 600,000

CLIMATE: Sunny, windy and cool. Midsummer temperatures are in the mid 70°sF (23°c).

Gay/Lesbian Visitor Information
G&L Information: 488-2711

DESCRIPTION: Edmonton is the provincial capital. It is also the technological and scientific center of the Canadian oil industry.

BARS ☕ RESTAURANTS 🍴

● Bar/club (GM): **Boots 'n Saddle**, cruise bar, 10242 106th St. (423-5014); **Buddy's Pub**, 10112 124 St. upstairs (488-6636); **Rebar**, 10551 Whyte Ave. (433-3808)

● Bar/club (GMW): **Roost**, 10345 104th St. (426-3150); **Shakespear's**, frequent women only events, upstairs 10306 112th St. (429-7234).

● Restaurants (GMW): **Boystown Cafe Gallery**, 10116 - 124 St., (488-6636); **Java Dabba Doo**, 10304 100 St. (413-9417);**Cook & Gardener Cafe**, 10345 106 St. (421-7044). Other (AW): **Ah-Menn**, mixed Continental, 10115-104 St. (496-9061); **Bistro Praha**, Czech cuisine, 10168 - 100A St. (424-4218); **Cafe Select**, French/Continental, 10018 - 106 St. (423-0419); The **Crêperie**, 10220-103rd St. (420-6656); **Café Budapest**, Hungarian cuisine, 10145-104th St. (426-4363); **La Ronde**, revolving restaurant atop the ivory tower of the Château Lacombe, 101st St. (428-6611); **Rigoletto's**, Italian/Continental, 10044-101A Ave. (429-0701).

🔑 ACCOMMODATIONS 🔑

AMBASSADOR MOTOR INN
10041 106th St., Edmonton, AB T5J 1G3. Tel: (403) 423-1925. Fax: (403) 424-5302. TYPE: *Motor Inn*. CLIENTELE: All Welcome. LOCATION: Downtown. 76 rooms w/priv. bath, CTV, phone, A/C, C/H, restaurant, tavern, parking. Rates: (CAN) $45-$49. DESCRIPTION: Budget motel near the train station and gay bars.

DELTA EDMONTON
10222 102nd St., Edmonton AB T5J 4C5. Tel: (403) 429-3900. Fax: (403) 428-1566. TYPE: *All Suite Hotel*. CLIENTELE: All Welcome. LOCATION: Downtown at the Eaton Center Shopping Mall. 169 suites, CTV, phone, A/C, jet tub, mini bar, restaurant, gym, sauna. Open: Year round. Rates: (CAN) $180. DESCRIPTION: Quality one and two bedroom all suite hotel.

FANTASYLAND HOTEL
17700 87th Ave., Edmonton AB T5T 4V4. Tel: (403) 344-3294. TYPE: *Unique First Class Theme Hotel*. CLIENTELE: All Welcome. LOCATION: West Edmonton Mall. 355 rooms w/priv. bath, CTV, phone, A/C, jacuzzi, mini-bar, cafe, lounge, restaurants, amusement park, ice rink, wheel. Rates: (CAN) $118-$220. *TAC:* 10%.

BRITISH COLUMBIA

VANCOUVER ISLAND

● VANCOUVER

VICTORIA

◆ **Population**: 3,282,000
◆ **Capital**: Victoria
◆ **Time Zone**: Pacific
◆ **Legal drinking age**: 19

VANCOUVER   ℂ 604

✈ Vancouver Int'l Airport (YVR)

LOCATION: Canada's south-west Pacific Coast and the Strait of Georgia, 110 miles / 176 km north of Seattle, WA.

POPULATION: 1,602,000

CLIMATE: Mild with pleasant summers and autumns. The average mean temperature for July is 63°F (17°c). Winters are wet with ground fogs and cloudiness, but snowfalls are rare.

Gay/Lesbian Visitor Information
Vancouver G&L Center: 684-6869

DESCRIPTION: Vancouver is recognized as one of the world's most beautiful cities. **Stanley Park** is the city's major landmark, a landscaped 1000-acres park with beaches and manicured lawns.

❖ Gay Beach: **Wreck Beach**, isolated stretch of unspoiled nude beach below Point Grey Cliffs, off North West Marine Drive. Also popular with straights.

BARS ♈ RESTAURANTS 🍴

● Bars/clubs (GM): **Celebrities**, dance bar, male strippers, 1022 Davie St. (689-3180); **Chucks**, leather/levy, at the Heritage House Hotel (685-7777); **Denman Station**, cruise bar, 860 Denman St., (669-3448); **Numbers**, video/dance bar, 1042 Davie St., (685-4077); **Odyssey**, dance bar, 1251 Howe St. (685-5256); **Shaggy Horse**, cruise bar, male strippers, 818 Richards St. (688-2923).

● Bars/clubs (GMW): **Dufferin Hotel**, drag shows, male strippers, 900 Seymour St. (683-4251); **Ms. T's**, mixed dance bar, 339 W. Pender St. (682-8096).

● Restaurants (GMW): **Hamburger Mary's**, open 24 hrs., 1202 Davie St. (687-1293); **Cafe Luxy**, Persian cuisine, 1235 Davie St., (681-9976); **Oasis**, restaurant & piano bar, 1240 Thurlow St., upstairs (685-1724); **Rocks Cafe**, 1098 Davie St. (685-1724); Other restaurants **Saigon**, Vietnamese/Vegetarian, 1500 Robson (682-8020); **Old Spaghetti Factory**, Italian cuisine, 53 Water St., Gastown (684-1288); **A Taste of Jamaica**, exotic West Indian fare, 841 Davie St.

λ SERVICES λ

● Health Clubs (GM): **F212° Steam,**, sauna club, 971 Richards St. (877-4765); **Club Vancouver**, steam room, dry sauna, private rooms, open 24 hours daily, 339 W. Pender (681-5719); **Hastings Steam & Sauna**, 766 E. Hastings (251-5455); **Richards St. Service Club,**1169 Richards St. (684-6010).

🔑 ACCOMMODATIONS 🔑

ROSELLEN SUITES
2030 Barclay St., Vancouver, B.C. V6G 1L5. Tel: (604) 689-4807. TYPE: *All Suite Hotel*. CLIENTELE: All Welcome. LOCATION: Heart of Vancouver, one block from Stanley Park, near shopping, gay clubs and downtown.

* Suites: 30 (1-2BR)
* CTV, phones (2), 24 hrs. voice mail, Stereo/cassette players, kitchen, microwave oven, smoke detector, dishwasher (in all 2BR suites)
* Full housekeeping, laundry/dry cleaning parking, guest passes to fitness club
* Gay Bars: walking distance
* Airport: 1/2 hr. by car, taxi, shuttle
* Open: Year round
* Rates: CAN $140-$230

* Weekly & Monthly rates available
* Minimum Stay: 3 nights
* Tax: 7% GST / 10% PRT.
* *TAC:* 10%

DESCRIPTION: Contemporary residential style all-suite hotel located beside Stanley Park. Spacious one and two bedroom apartments with all modern comfort and amenities. One bedroom suite is 600 sq.ft. (55 sq.m.); two-bedroom apartment is 800 sq.ft. (73 sq.m.); two-bedroom executive is 1,000 sq.ft. (91 sq.m.) with 2 baths, fireplace; two-bedroom director is 1,150 sq.ft. (105 sq.m.) with 2 bath and fireplace.

SYLVIA HOTEL
1154 Gilford St., Vancouver B.C. V6G 2P6. Tel: (604) 681-9321. TYPE: *Hotel.* CLIENTELE: All Welcome. LOCATION: On beautiful English Bay, two blocks from Stanley Park.

* Rooms: 115 w/priv. bath
* Suites: 17 (1-2BR w/kitchen)
* CTV, phone, C/H
* Room service, wheelchair access, parking
* Restaurant, bistro, cocktail lounge
* Gay Bars: walking distance
* Airport: 10 mi. / 16 km, bus, taxi
* Open: Year round
* Rates:CAN$65 - CAN$170
* Tax: 7% GST / 10% PRT.
* *TAC:* 10%

DESCRIPTION: Tourist class 8 story hotel in a scenic location on English Bay. Excellent location and affordable prices.

VICTORIA   © 604

✈ Victoria Int'l Airport (YYJ)

LOCATION: On the southeast tip of Vancouver Island, off Canada's Pacific Coast.

POPULATION: 287,900

CLIMATE: Moderate. In winter, temperatures rarely decline below 40°F (4°c).

Gay & Lesbian Information
Island G&L Line: 598-4900

DESCRIPTION: Major port and tourist resort on Vancouver Island. Victoria has the most British atmosphere of any city this side of the Atlantic. It is famous for its beautifully landscaped gardens, public parks, and turn-of-the-century architecture.

BARS ▼ RESTAURANTS

● Bars/clubs (GMW): **Rumours**, mixed cabaret/showbar, 1325 Government St. (385-0566).

● Restaurants (AW): **Millos**, Greek cuisine, waiters in Greek costumes (love those hunks in mini-skirts!!!), 716 Burdett St. (382-4422); **Chez Pierre**, authentic French cuisine, in the heart of old town, 512 Yates St. (388-7711); **Pablo's**, Spanish cuisine, near the Inner Harbour, 225 Quebec St. (388-4255); **Olde England Inn**, English mixed grill, 429 Lampson St. (388-4353); **Da Tandoor**, Indian restaurant with dining patio, 1010 Fort St. (384-6333); **Wong's**, Chinese cuisine, 548 Fisgard St. (381-1223).

λ SERVICES λ

● Health Clubs (GM): **Garden Baths**, 660 Johnson St. (383-6623).

ACCOMMODATIONS

EMBASSY MOTOR INN
520 Menzies St., Victoria BC V8V 2H4. Tel: (604) 382-8161. Fax: (604) 382-4224. TYPE: *Motor Inn.* CLIENTELE: All Welcome. LOCATION: Downtown, 1 block from the ferry. 103 rooms w/priv. bath, 15 suites, CTV, phone, pool, sauna, free parking. Rates: (CAN) $59-$120. DESCRIPTION: First class motel in a convenient location near ferries, Parliament buildings and museum.

EMPRESS HOTEL
721 Government St., Victoria, BC V8W 1W5. Tel: (604) 384-8111. Fax: (604) 381-5959. TYPE: *Hotel.* CLIENTELE: Mostly Straight. LOCATION: Downtown overlooking Inner Harbour and in center of business and shopping district.

* Rooms: 481 rooms w/priv. bath
* CTV, phone, A/C, hair dryer
* Room & maid service
* Wheelchair access, parking
* Restaurants, (Salon de Thé),
* Glass enclosed indoor pool
* Health Club, sauna, gym & whirlpool,
* Airport: 17 mi. / 27 km,
* Gay Bars: some nearby,
* Credit Cards: MC/VISA/ AMEX/ CB/DC,
* Open: Year round,
* Rates: (CAN) $110-$245. *TAC:* 10%.

DESCRIPTION: A gracious landmark, turn of the century, hotel surrounded by beautiful gardens. All rooms and suites are beautifully appointed. Rooms for non-smokers available.

NOVA SCOTIA

Halifax

- ◆ **Population**: 874,100
- ◆ **Capital**: Halifax
- ◆ **Time Zone**: Atlantic
- ◆ **Legal drinking age**: 19

HALIFAX   ✆   902

✈ Halifax Int'l Airport (YHZ)
26 mi. / 42 km northeast of Halifax

LOCATION: Atlantic Canada on Bedford Basin, the world's second largest natural harbor. Halifax is connected to Dartmouth via the MacDonald & MacKay bridges.

POPULATION: 115,000

CLIMATE: Cold snowy winter with an average temperature of 20°F (-7°c) in January. Summers are mild with an average temperature of 68°F (25°c) in July.

DESCRIPTION: The Capital of Nova Scotia is a compact and cosmopolitan city with a delightful combination of history and modern urbanism. Founded in 1749 Halifax is a rapidly growing commercial center. The Halifax-Dartmouth metropolitan area is the business, educational and cultural centre of Maritime Canada. Halifax has a busy harbor front with pubs, shops,

museums, parks, and universities. Year round activities include: Jazz and street performers, outdoor festivals, cultural and sporting events.

❖ **SPECIAL EVENTS: Gay Pride Week**, last Sunday in June; **International Buskerfest** August; **Halifax Halloween Mardi Gras** street festival with dances and parades, late October.

BARS ⼂ RESTAURANTS 🍴

● Restaurants (AW): **Five Fishermen**, seafood, 1740 Argyle St. (422-4421); **Halliburton House Inn**, elegant restaurant specializing in exotic game and fresh Atlantic seafood, 5184 Morris St. (420-0658).

λ SERVICES λ

● Erotica (G/S): **Atlantic News**, 5560 Morris St. (429-5468).

● Health Club (GM): **Apollo Sauna Club**, 1547 Barrington (423-6549).

 ACCOMMODATIONS

WAVERLY INN
1266 Barrington St. Halifax B3J 1Y5. Tel: (902) 423-9346. Fax: (902) 425-0167. TYPE: *Hotel.* CLIENTELE: All Welcome. LOCATION: On Barrington Street in downtown Halifax within walking distance of the harbor.

- * Rooms: 32 w/priv. bath
- * CTV, phone, A/C, C/H, jacuzzi tubs
- * 24 hrs telephone and message service
- * Self-service breakfast room, free parking
- * Gay Bars: walking distance
- * Airport: 26 mi. / 42 km (taxi)
- * Open: Year round
- * Rates: (CAN) $65-$75 w/CB
- * Tax: 18.77%
- * *TAC:* 10%

DESCRIPTION: Historic City Inn with the beauty and charm of yesteryear. This Inn was Oscar Wilde's favorite lodge in Halifax.

HALLIBURTON HOUSE INN
5184 Morris St., Halifax NS B3J 1B3. Tel: (902) 420-0658. TYPE: *Hotel.* CLIENTELE: All Welcome. LOCATION: Historic downtown.

ONTARIO

- ◆ **Population**: 10,085,000
- ◆ **Capital**: Toronto
- ◆ **Time Zone**: Eastern
- ◆ **Legal drinking age**: 18

LONDON   ✆ 519

✈ London Airport (YXU) 7 mi. / 11 km NE

LOCATION: In southwest Ontario on the Thames River. 190 km / 118 mi. from Toronto.

POPULATION: 381,500

CLIMATE: Cold winters modified by the Great Lakes with average temperatures in January of 25°F (-4°c). Summers are warm and sunny with an average temperatures in July of 75°F (24°c)

VISITOR INFORMATION
London VCB: (800) 265-2602

Gay Visitor Information
Gayline: (519) 433-3551

DESCRIPTION: A University town on the Thames River and the largest city in southwestern Ontario. The city recaptures the flavor of the British capital with names like **Hyde Park**, **Trafalgar Square**, and the famous London red double-decker buses. Visit the **Museum of Indian Archaeology** and **Lawson Indian Village** which is devoted to 11,000 years of Indian culture and history in Ontario, 1600 Attawandaron Rd., off Wonderland Road No,(473-1360); the **Royal Canadian Regiment Museum**, in historic Wolseley Hall at

Oxford & Elizabeth Sts. features exhibits about regimentals history and battles from the Northwest rebellion to Korea (660-5102).

BARS ♈ RESTAURANTS 🍴

● Bars/clubs (GMW): **Halo Club**, club & community center, 649 Colborne St., (433-3762); **Lacey's Tavern**, neighborhood bar, 355 Talbot St. (645-3197); **52nd Street Bar** at Clarence St., women, men welcome.

● Restaurants (AW): **Michaels on Thames**, local favorite overlooking the river, French/Continental cuisine, 1 York St. (672-0111); **Anthony's**, seafood specialists, 434 Richmond St. (679-0960); **The Horse & Hound**, intimate and elegant dining, in Hyde Park (472-6801); **Le Taste Vin**, best wines from the world's finest wineries, 171 Queens Ave. (432-WINE).

λ SERVICES λ

● Health Club (GM): **The Junction**, unique complex for men only situated half way between Toronto and Detroit. Fully licensed bar w/fireplace, restaurant, sauna, whirlpool, gym, open 24 hrs., 722 York St. (438-2625).

ACCOMMODATIONS

DELTA LONDON
325 Dundas St., London ON N6B 1T9. Tel: (519) 679-6111. Fax: (519) 679-3957. TYPE: *Hotel*. CLIENTELE: Mostly Straight. LOCATION: Central downtown location, 4 blocks from train station.

- * Rooms: 250 w/priv. bath. Suites: 8
- * CTV, phone, A/C
- * Restaurants, piano bar, Atrium lobby
- * Japanese garden with Sushi bar
- * Pool, sauna, gym,
- * Room & maid service, parking
- * Gay Bars: some nearby
- * Airport: 6 mi. / 10 km
- * Reservations: CC# guarantee
- * Credit Cards: MC/VISA/AMEX/DC
- * Open: Year round
- * Rates: (CAN) $95 - $165. *TAC:* 10%

DESCRIPTION: Attractive hotel occupying an old armory in a central location for the discriminating travelers.

NATIONAL TRAVELLERS
636 York St., London ON N5W 2S7. Tel: (519) 433-8161. Fax: (519) 433-5448. TYPE: *Motel*. CLIENTELE: All Welcome. LOCATION: Down-

town near Club London Sauna. 7 blocks from train station.

* Rooms: 89 w/priv. bath
* CTV, phone, A/C, restaurant, lounge
* Gay Bars: nearby
* Airport: 6 mi. / 10 km, taxi
* Season: Year round
* Rates: (CAN) $39-$45. ***TAC:*** 10%

DESCRIPTION: Tourist class motel.

NIAGARA FALLS ✆ 416

✈ Greater Buffalo Int'l AP (BUF) USA
Lester B. Pearson Int'l Airport (YYZ)
Toronto / CANADA

LOCATION: On the USA/Canada boarder near Buffalo (NY). One hour southeast from Toronto and 20 minutes northwest of Buffalo.

DESCRIPTION: The Niagara Falls are widely known as the 7th natural wonder of the world. Millions of people visit the Falls annually. Although the US side is very commercial, the Canadian side has graceful parks and gardens. Niagara Falls is a four-season resort popular with straight couples and honeymooners.

BARS RESTAURANTS

● Bar (GM): **Gusto's**, gay bar in St. Catherines, only 10 min. drive away, 203 Carlton St. (685-0524).

● Restaurants (AW): **Table Rock Restaurant**, scenic view and good food, near the Canadian Horseshoe Falls (354-3631); **Victoria Park Restaurant**, terrace setting, fine food and a renovated downstairs cafeteria (356-2217); **Hungarian Village Restaurant**, Hungarian specialties, 5329 Ferry St. (356-2429); **Happy Wanderer**, German Specialties, 6405 Stanley Ave. (354-9825).

ACCOMMODATIONS

COMFORT SUITES IMPERIAL
5851 Victoria Ave., Niagara Falls, ON L2G 3L6. Tel: (416) 356-2648. Fax: (416) 356-4068. TYPE: *Hotel.* CLIENTELE: Mostly Straight. LOCATION: 2 blocks from the falls. 104 rooms w/priv. bath, CTV, phone, A/C, pool, gym, dining room, bistro, lounge. DESCRIPTION: Commercial hotel within walking distance of the falls. Some rooms have VCR and jacuzzi.

MICHAEL'S INN
5599 River Rd., Niagara Falls, ON L2E 3H3. Tel: (416) 354-2727. TYPE: *Motor Inn.* CLIENTELE: Mostly Straight. LOCATION: Overlooking the Niagara Falls on Niagara River Gorge, adjacent to Rainbow Bridge. 130 rooms w/priv. bath, pools, sauna.

OTTAWA ✆ 613
HULL (QC) ✆ 819

✈ Ottawa Int'l Airport (YOW)

LOCATION: Eastern Ontario on the Québec border, and the west side of the Ottawa River.

POPULATION: Ottawa - 920,000
Hull - 60,700

CLIMATE: Same as northern USA. Summer temperatures are in the 80°'sF (26°c), and winter lowest temperatures can reach -2°F (-16°c).

Gay/Lesbian Visitor Information
Pink Triangle Services: 563-4818

DESCRIPTION: Ottawa, the capital of Canada, sits high on top of a bluff overlooking the confluence of the Ottawa, Gatineau, and the Rideau Rivers. The **Gothic Parliament** building dominates the skyline. Ottawa was selected the site for the Canadian capital in 1858 by Queen Victoria as a compromise for the rivalry between Montréal and Toronto. The downtown is divided into an eastern and western section by the Rideau Canal. Ottawa offers excellent antique shopping. Explore the **Stittsville Market**, about 10 min. west of Ottawa for antiques and collectibles.

Visit: **Parliament Hill**, the **Supreme Court**, the **National Gallery**, and the **National Museum of Man** in the western area, and **Ottawa University**, **Byward Market**, the **Canadian War Museum**, and the **Canadian Mint** in the eastern part of the city. Across the river in Québec lies the twin city of **Hull** with its great French restaurants and vibrant nightlife.

❖ **SPECIAL EVENTS: Lesbian, Gay & Bisexual Pride Week**, June 20-27.

BARS RESTAURANTS

● Bars/clubs (GM): **Cell Block**, leather crowd, 340 Somerset W., upstairs, (594-0233); **Centretown Pub**, 340 Somerset St. W (594-0233); **Club**

363, popular dance club, male strippers 363 Bank St. (237-0708); **Le Club**, mini-dance club, 77 rue Wellington, Hull (819/777-1411); **Pub Bar**, 175 Promenade du Portage, Hull (771-8810).

● Bars/clubs (GMW): **After Stonewall**, 105 4th Ave (567-2221); **Briefs**, 151 George (241-9668); **Icon**, dance club, open Thurs-Sat 8pm-3am, 366 Lisgar St.; **Market Station**, bar & bistro, 15 George (562-3540); **Le Pub**, 175 Promenade du Portage, Hull (771-8810); **Silhouette**, piano bar,340 Somerset W. (594-0233); **Wilde**, 631 Somerset St. (567-4858).

● Bars/clubs (GW): **Coral Reef Club**, dance bar, Fri.-Sat. only, 30 Nicolas St. (234-5118); **The Club House**, Fri.-Sat. womyn only, 77 Wellington St., Hull (777-1411); **The Inner Circle**, Sat. nights, 433 Slater St. (567-5213); **Lavendar Laundrette**, Saturday night club for womyn, 318 Lisgar St., 2nd Fl (233-0152)..

● Restaurants (GMW): **DeLuxe Café**, chicken and sandwiches, 279-283 Dalhousie St. (233-4181); **Centretown Pub**, 340 Somerset St. W. (594-3560); **Eddy's Diner**, 326 Elgin St. (232-4800); **News Café**, basic pasta dishes, Elgin Street (657-6397). Other (AW): **Marrakech**, Moroccan, 356 McClaren Street (234-5865); **La Roma**, moderately priced Italian restaurant, 673 Somerset Street West (234-8244).

λ SERVICES λ

● **Armand Pagé**, 241 Buyère St. (564-1074); **Women's Place**, upstairs of Armand Pagé (789-2155).

● Erotica (G/S): **Clasixxx Videos**, 1940 Bank St. (523-9962); **Variétés Erotiques**, 61 Eddy, Hull (771-8994).

● Health Club (GM): **Club Ottawa**, gym, dry sauna, private rooms, beer, wine and liquor served, open 24 hrs. every day, 1069 Wellington St. (722-8978) *Visa*; **Steamworks**, sauna, video rooms, 24 hrs, 487 Lewis St. (230-8431).

ACCOMMODATIONS

CAPITAL HILL HOTEL & SUITES
88 Albert St., Ottawa ON K1P 5E9. Tel: (613) 235-1413. TYPE: *Hotel*. CLIENTELE: All Welcome. LOCATION: Adjacent to the National Art Gallery, walk to bars and clubs. 150 rooms and suites. Rates on request.

RIDEAU VIEW INN
177 Frank St., Ottawa, ON K2P 0X4. Tel: (613) 236-9309. TYPE: *Bed & Breakfast*. CLIENTELE: Gay/Straight. LOCATION: Heart of Ottawa, near the Rideau canal, Parliament Hill, shopping, restaurants and bars, 7 rooms.

TORONTO   ℱ 416 / 905

✈ Lester B. Pearson Int'l Airport (YYZ)

LOCATION: Western shore of Lake Ontario, 248 mi. / 397 km southwest of Ottawa, and 100 mi. / 160 km northwest of Buffalo N.Y.

POPULATION: 3,893,000

CLIMATE: Changeable but tempered by the vicinity to the lake. Summers are mild with average temperature for July of 70°F (21°c). Winters are snowy and cold with average temperature of 24°F (-4°c).

VISITOR INFORMATION
Metro. Toronto CVA: (800) 363-1990

Gay/Lesbian Visitor Information
Phoneline: (416) 964-6600

DESCRIPTION: The seat of the government for the province of Ontario, Toronto is an Indian word meaning 'meeting place'. It is the political, industrial and commercial center of Canada with a considerable concentration of manufacturing, finance, and population along the shore of Lake Ontario in southern Ontario. Toronto's population used to be predominantly of British origin, but now it is a kaleidoscope of nationalities.

The city is clean and safe with very little street crime. Yonge Street is the city's lively main street with fashionable stores, restaurants, and boutiques. All streets numbering east and west start here. Toronto's Theatre District is the second largest in North America, outside New York.

● Toronto has a dynamic gay/lesbian community. The '**Gay Village**' is at the heart of the city bordered by Bay St. to the west, Parliament to the east, Gerrard to the south and Bloor to the north.

● Visit: the 1,815-foot (550 m) **CN Tower**, the world's tallest free-standing structure; the **Sky Dome** sports complex on Front St.; **Black Creek Pioneer Village**, a re-created traditional rural Ontario village; the **Art Gallery of Ontario** featuring old masters and contempo-

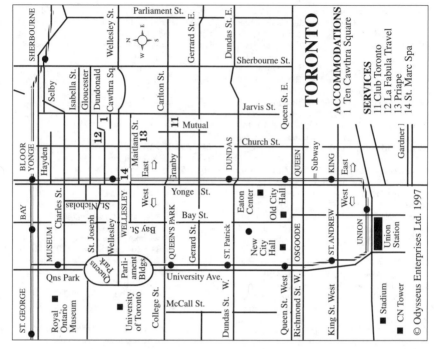

rary Canadian art; Picturesque **Queen's Park** in downtown; and the famous **Metro Toronto Zoo** with over 4,000 animals in climate-controlled pavilions. For shopping check **Yonge St.** and **Yorkville.** Toronto is home for the world's largest underground city with hundreds of shops, restaurants, and business centers which is naturally very busy and popular during the cold winters.

❖ **SPECIAL EVENT: Canadian G&L Tennis Open,**GLTA tennis tournament, May 17-20 (921-7993).

BARS ♈ RESTAURANTS 🍴

Toronto has an attractive gay scene. The '**Gay Village**' is located in an area known as **Molly Wood's Bush** corner of Church and Wellesley.

● Bars/clubs (GM): **Bar 501**, 501 Church St. (944-3272); **Barn**, neighborhood bar, 83 Granby (977-4684); **Black Eagle**, leather cruise bar, 459 Church St. upstairs (413-1219); **Boots**, dance bar, 592 Sherbourne St. (921-0665); **Bul dog**, bar & restaurant, 457 Church St. (923-3469); **Crews**, video bar, patio, 508 Church St. (972-1662); **Remingtons**, entertainment com-

plex, male strippers, non-stop daily, 379 Yonge St., at Gerrard (977-2160); **Sailor**, 465 Church St: **Sneakers**, cruise bar, 502 Yonge St.; **Toolbox**, leather cruise bar, 508 Eastern Ave. (466-8616); **Trax V**, piano bar, cabaret, 529 Yonge St. (962-8729); **Woody's**, nightclub, open daily 11:30am, 467 Church St. (972-0887).

● Bar/Club (GMW): **Colby's**, entertainment complex, 5-9 St. Joseph (961-0777).

● Bar/club (GW): **The Rose Café**, dance bar, restaurant, 547 Parliament St., (928-1495).

● Restaurants (GMW): **The Rose Café**, light meals, 547 Parliament St.. (928-1495); **The Fabulous Bakery Café**, Italian bakery open 24 hrs., 635 Bay St. at Edward (593-1423); **The Fare Exchange**, Italian, 4 Irwin Ave. (923-5924); **The 457**, Sunday brunch buffet, 457 Church St. (923-3469); **The Diner**, 9 Isabella St. (960-1200); **Jennie's**, chic restaurant, open patio, 360 Queen E. (861-1461); **Living Well**, restaurant & bar, 692 Yonge St. (922-6770); **Masrani's**, vegetarian, 200 Carlton (969-9986); **Il Pappagallo**, Spanish tapas, grill & pasta, 538 Church St. (960-6161); **Second Cup**, sandwiches, pastries, exotic coffees, 548 Church St.; **Teriyaki King**, Japanese Café

& Restaurant, 538 Parliament St. (925-6957); **Windows**, Italian, 562 Church St. (962-6255).

λ SERVICES λ

● Boutique/Clothing (GMW): **Out on the Street**, 551 Church St. (967-2759).

● Distributor/Wholesaler (GMW): **J.A.L. Enterprises Ltd.**, guides and erotica, Box 14, Toronto, ON M4Y 2E3. Tel: (416) 979-0499.

● Escort (GM): ✪ **Dreamdates**, perfect for any occasion, social or intimate (567-5028).

● Health Clubs (GM): ✪ **Club Toronto**, Toronto's oldest, friendliest, and most popular sauna. In ground whirlpool, wet and dry sauna, adult video lounge, large screen TV lounge, Sunday poolside B.B.Q, 231 Mutual St. (977-4629); **Barracks**, 56 Widmer St. (593-0499); **The Spa**, 66 Maitland (925-1571); **St. Marc Spa**, health club, gym, 543 Yonge St., top floor, open 24 hrs (927-0210).

● Travel: ✪ **La Fabula Travel & Tours**, 551 Church St. (920-3229) or (800) 661-5605.

● Videos/Mail Order (GM): ✪ **Priape**, Toronto's #1 Gay Superstore, 465 Church St., Toronto ON M4Y 2C5 (586-9914).

🏳️ ACCOMMODATIONS 🏳️

✪ TEN CAWTHRA SQUARE

10 Cawthra Square, Toronto, ON M4Y 1K8. Tel: (416) 966-3074. Toll Free (800) 259-5474. Fax: (416) 966-4494. TYPE: *Bed & Breakfast*. HOSTS: Frank or Ric. CLIENTELE: Mostly gay men & women. LOCATION: Gay Village location.

* Rooms: 3 (doubles) w/shared bath
* Rooms for non smokers
* CTV, VCR, refrigerator, safe box, C/H, A/C cooking facilities, hair dryer
* Jacuzzi, clothing optional policy
* Parking: off street (paid)
* Pets: w/prearrangement
* Beach: 1 km / 0.6 mi. (gay/straight)
* Gay Bars: 5 min. walk
* Health Club: 8 min. walk
* Airports: 2-25 km / 1-15 mi., taxi, bus or express/subway
* Train station: 2 km / 1 mi.
* Subway: 2 blocks away
* Languages: English, American sign language
* Reservations: 1 day or 1/3 of stay deposit

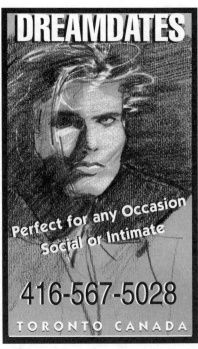

* Cancellation Policy: 1 day non refundable for confirmation
* Credit Cards: MC/VISA/AMEX
* Open: Year round
* Rates: CAN$79-$125 w/CB
* Tax: 7% (Goods & Service Tax - GST)
* Check in 2:00 pm / Check out 11:00 am
* *TAC:* 10%
* Email: host@cawthra.com

DESCRIPTION: Elegantly restored Edwardien residence with traditional furnishings. Tucked away beside a quiet park barely one block from the core of Toronto's vibrant gay village and two blocks from the best subway system in North America. Minutes to everything.

HOTEL SELBY
592 Sherbourne St. Toronto, ON M4X 1L4. Tel: (416) 921-3142. TYPE: *Hotel*. CLIENTELE: Mostly Gay. LOCATION: Central. 67 rooms, bar, disco, restaurant. Rates: on request.

HOTEL VICTORIA
56 Yonge St., Toronto, ON M5E 1G5. Tel: (416) 363-1666. TYPE: *Hotel*. CLIENTELE: All welcome. LOCATION: Heart of downtown Toronto. 48 rooms w/priv. bath. Rates: (CAN) $85-$105 w/CB. *TAC:* 10%. DESCRIPTION: European style with good amenities and service.

WINCHESTER GH
35 Winchester St., Toronto, ON M4X 1A6. Tel: (416) 929-7949. TYPE: *Guest House*. CLIENTELE: Gay men & women. LOCATION: Central, minutes to gay bars & clubs. 3 rooms, 1 suite, hot tub.

WINDSOR   ✆ 519

✈ Windsor Airport (YQG) 6.5 mi. / 10 km SE

LOCATION: Southern Ontario, at the tip of the peninsula on the USA border south of Detroit (MI). It is linked to Detroit via the Ambassador Bridge.

POPULATION: 192,083

DESCRIPTION: Cosmopolitan city with French influence. The city offers large city amenities and nightlife. The gay scene is small, but nearby Detroit offers many venues for gay men and lesbians.

BARS ☿ RESTAURANTS 🍴

● Club (GM): **Happy Tap**, male strippers, 1056 Wyandotte St. E (256-8998); **Silhouttes**, 1880 Wyandotte E. (252-0887).

● Restaurants (AW): **Cook Shop**, Italian, 683 Ouellette Ave. (254-3377); **Lucky Kitchen**, Chinese, 754 754 Ouellette Ave. (253-7255).

λ SERVICES λ

● Health Club (GM): **Vesuvio Steam Bath**, 563 Brant St. 24 hrs. (977-8578).

 ## ACCOMMODATIONS

ROSE CITY INN
430 Ouellette Ave., Windsor ON N9A 1B2. Tel: (519) 253-7281. TYPE: *Hotel*. CLIENTELE: All Welcome. LOCATION: Downtown, adjacent to the Windsor-Detroit Tunnel.

* Rooms: 147 w/priv. bath
* CTV, A/C, phone
* Room service, cocktail lounge
* Indoor pool, laundry service, free parking
* Rates: (CAN) $55-$95

DESCRIPTION: Multi-story downtown hotel.

QUEBEC

- ◆ **Population**: 6,896,000
- ◆ **Capital**: Québec
- ◆ **Time Zone**: Eastern
- ◆ **Legal Drinking Age**: 18

MONTRÉAL   ℂ 514

✈ Dorval Int'l Airport (YUL)
Mirabel Int'l Airport (YMX)

LOCATION: On the Island of Montréal and other small islands at the confluence of the St. Lawrence and Ottawa rivers, 170 mi. / 271km southwest of Québec City, and 126 mi. / 202 km east of Ottawa and 381 mi. / 613 km north of New York City.

POPULATION: 3,127,000

CLIMATE: Cold winter with abundance of snowfall; the average temperature for January is 16°F (-8°c). Summers are cool and pleasant with average temperature for July of 70°F (22°c).

Gay/Lesbian Information
Gayline (English)   : (514) 931-8668
Gai Écoute (French): (514) 521-1508

Community Centre
C.C.G.L.M.: 528-8424
2035 Amherst, main floor

DESCRIPTION: Montréal is Canada's most popular destination and the world's second largest French speaking city. Known as "Paris of North America" it proudly preserves its French roots and heritage. More than 5.6 mil-

lion visitors from the USA selected Montréal as their favorite destination.

Montréal spreads out at the foot of **Mont Royal** on an island in the middle of the **St. Lawrence River**. In the cold winter Mont Royal comes alive with skiers and skaters who challenge the freezing temperatures, while downtown life continues undisturbed in the sheltered underground. All the underground businesses are linked together by the Métro system.

The City has several centers. The downtown business center is located along René Lévesque, the Place Ville-Marie, and Dorchester Square. The large department stores are along Ste. Catherine St. West. The district around Boulevard St.-Laurent and rue St. Denis is a popular commercial strip with many cafes, restaurants, bars, and straight discos.

Visit: **Old Montréal**, a restored section of the city with buildings dating back to the 17th, 18th and 19th centuries. Old Montréal offers a lively scene with sidewalk cafes, street musicians, artists, and local cabarets; **Nôtre Dame**, Montréal's famous neogothic basilica built in 1829 which has one of the largest bells in North America; **The Botanical Gardens** - rank third largest in the world, with magnificent collection of rare exotic species and bonsai; For a bird-eye perspective of the city visit Montréal's **Olympic Stadium** with the world's tallest inclined tower offering a breathtaking view as far away as 50 mi. / 80 km around; The Olympic Park was the site of the 21st. Olympic Games which includes a funicular (cable-car); **La Ronde** is an exhibition and amusement site which takes place every summer on the original grounds of the 1967 World's Fair; **Ile Ste-Hélène**, the place where Montréalers go to escape city life year round; **The Alcan Aquarium** has an exciting collection of marine life. And of course don't miss a ride in the Montréal subway (Métro) system, which is extraordinarily clean, modern and efficient.

❖ Entertainment: **Casino de Montréal**, enjoy an evening of games of chance, slots and table games, proper attire needed, at the the city's first European-style casino, **Palais de Civilisation**, Old French Pavilion from Expo '67 (Terre des Hommes); for a good laugh visit the first international **Museum of Humour** in a former brewery, 2111 Blvd. St. Laurent (845-4000); **Museum of Archeology & History**, Place Royale (Old Quarter).

❖ **SPECIAL EVENTS: Just For Laugh Festival**, the world's largest comedy event, July

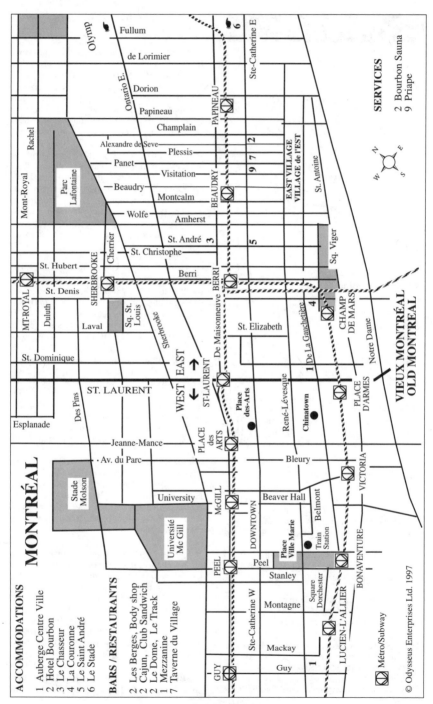

MONTRÉAL

ACCOMMODATIONS
1 Auberge Centre Ville
2 Hotel Bourbon
3 Le Chasseur
4 La Couronne
5 Le Saint André
6 Le Stade

BARS / RESTAURANTS
2 Les Berges, Body shop
2 Cajun, Club Sandwich
2 Le Dome, Le Track
1 Mezzanine
7 Taverne du Village

SERVICES
2 Bourbon Sauna
9 Priape

Métro/Subway

© Odysseus Enterprises Ltd. 1997

ODYSSEUS '97/98

22-Aug. 1 (845-3155); **Festival International de Jazz**, July 1-22 at the "Jazz Village" around the Place des Arts at the Complexe Desjardins (514) 871-1881; **Fireworks Festival**, May -June).

BARS 𝖸 RESTAURANTS 🍴

Most of the gay scene in Montréal is located on the east side of the busy Ste-Catherine E., in the **Gay East Village** / *Village de l'Est.* between Blvd. St. Laurent and de Lorimier.

● Bars/clubs (GM): ✪ **La Track**, cruise bar, disco, rock music, large terrace, casino video poker machine, 1584 Ste-Catherine E. (521-1419); ✪ **Taverne du Village**, cruise video bar, outdoor terrace and pool table, casino video and poker machine, 1366 Ste-Catherine E. (524-1960); **Adonis**, male strippers, 1681 rue Ste-Catherine Est. (521-1355); **Agora**, cruise bar, billard, karaoke (sat.), 1160 Mackay (934-1428); **Barzan**, 4910 St-Laurent (847-8850); **Bar Fly**, sports bar, restaurant, 124 Prince Arthur E. (843-3271); **Black Eagle**, leather cruise bar, pool, video, 1315 Ste-Catherine E. (529-0040); **Bolo**, country/western, 1822 ave. Mont-Royal Est (521-0820); **California**, 1412 rue Ste-Élizabeth (843-8533); **Campus**, male strippers, 1111 rue Ste-Catherine Est (725-5211); **City-bar**, bar, café, 3820 St.-Laurent (499-8519); **Club Date**, piano bar, karaoke (Mon/Tue), 1218 Ste-Catherine est (521-1242); **Fun Spot**, dance bar, drag shows, 1151 Ontario E. (522-0416); **Max**, dance/cruise bar, 1166 Ste-Catherine E. (598-5244); **Météor**, bar, restaurant, 1661 Ste-Catherine Est (523-1481); ✪ **Mezzanine**, lounge bar overlooking the spa area at the Auberge du Centre Ville, 1070 rue Mackay (938-9393); **Mystique**, 1424 rue Stanley (844-5711); **Paco Paco**, 451 rue Rachel Est (499-0210); **Relaxe**, 1309 Ste-Catherine Est; **Rocky**, bar, tavern, 1673, Ste-Catherine Est; **Stud**, male strippers, (598-8243);1812 rue Ste-Catherine Est; **Taboo**, male strippers, pool tables, 1950 boul. de Maisonneuve Est (597-0010); **Taverne Gambrinus**, cruise bar, young clientele, 1151 Ontario E. (522-0416).

● Bars/clubs (GMW): ✪ **Cajun**, New Orleans style piano bar at the **Hotel Bourbon**, casino video poker machine, 1578 Ste-Catherine E. (523-4679); **L'Entre-Peau**, bar/cabaret, 1115 rue Ste-Catherine Est (525-7566);**Les Folichons**, dance club, cabaret, 1669 Ste-Catherine E. (597-0814); **Lezard**, 4177 St. Denis (289-9819); **Metropolis**, dance club, 59 rue Ste-Catherine Est (288-2020); **Mississippi**, entertainment complex, cabaret, drag shows, 1592 Ste-Catherine E. (523-4679).

● Bars/clubs (GW): ✪ **Le Dome**, womyn's bar, casino video poker machine, inside terrace and 2nd floor, from 9 pm to closing, 1364 Ste-Catherine E. (524-1960); **Cabaret Sapho**, dance club, live shows, 2017 rue Frontenac (523-0292); **O'side**, 4075 B. St-Denis (849-7126); **P'town**, 1364 rue Ste-Catherine E. (524-1584); **Sisters**, dance club, 1456, Ste-Catherine Est.

● Restaurants (GMW): ✪ **Body Shop**, bar, cafe, fast food, casino video poker machine, 1550 St-Catherine Est (523-4679); ✪ **Club Sandwich**, 50's style American diner, excellent food, 24 hrs. at the **Hotel Bourbon**, 1578 Ste-Catherine East (523-4679); ✪ **Les Berges**, Continental, at the Auberge Centre-Ville, 1070 rue Mackay (938-9393); ✪ **Cajun**, bar/restaurant, 2nd Fl. 1574, Ste-Catherine Est (523-4679); **Ambiance**, Salon de Thé, popular with lesbians, 1874 Notre-Dame W. (939-2609); **Aux Lilas**, Libanese cuisine, 1285 boul. de Maisonneuve E (527-4109); **Binnerie du Village**, 2008 Amherst (525-1121); **Bistro l'Un & L'Autre**, French/Continental, 1641 Amherst (597-0878); **Callipyge**, nouvelle cuisine québécoise, 1493 Amherst (522-6144); **Canarelli**, Italian, 2181 Ste-Catherine E. (521-1817); **Citibar**, Vietnamese cuisine, 1603 rue Ontario Est (525-4251); **Chablis**, Restaurant, bar, gourmet Spanish and French cuisine 1641 St. Hubert (523-0053); **Le Clandestin**, restaurant, bar, *Fondue Bourguignonne*, 1799 rue Amherst (528-7918); **La Colombe**, French cuisine, 554 rue Duluth Est (849-8844); **La Fondue à François**, fondu au fromage, bouguignonne, 1256 rue Ontario (527-7639); **Grappa**, Italian cuisine, wine cellar, 1560 Ste-Catherine E. (523-4679); **L'Exception**, chili, salads, sandwiches, 1200 St. Hubert (282-1282); **Jardin de Mékong**, Vietnamese, 1330 Ste-Catherine E. (523-6635); **Kilo Café**, 1495 St. Catherine Est (596-3933); **Kim Foo**, Chinese buffet, 2971 Sherbrooke E. (597-1515); **La Marivaude**, French cuisine, 1652 Ontario E. (522-9897); **Modigliani**, French/Italian cuisine, 1874 rue Plessis (522-0422); **Mongolie Grill**, oriental cuisine, 1180 Wolfe (526-0605); **Mozza**, 1208 Ste-Catherine Est (524-0295) also 1256 Ontario Est (527-7639); **Napoleon**, 1694 Ste-Catherine Est (523-2105); **Nêga Fulô**, Brazilian cuisine, 1257 Amherst (522-1554); **Pied de Poule**, roasted chicken, 3945 St-Denis (288-1000); **Pierre du Calvet**, classic French, 405 rue Bonsecours (282-1725); **Le Planète**, solar cooking, 1451 Ste-Catherine E. (528-6953); **Planète Hollywood**, health food, 1349 La Fontaine (523-3991); **Au Poulet Doré**, 340 Sainte Catherine E. (288-2441); **Rave**, cafe, 1351 Ste-Catherine Est (528-0630); **Stromboli**, Italian cuisine, 1019 Mont-Royal E. (528-5020).

λ **SERVICES** λ

● Advertising: ✪ **New World Marketing Group (N.W.M.G)**, publicity for magazines, travel guides and publications, Box 42-D, Stn "M", Montréal, QC H1V 3L6. (899-0054).

● Association (GMW): ✪ **Guilde d'Affaire Montréal Business Guild**, GAMBG, POB 42-G, Stn "M", Montréal QC H1V 3L6.

● Adult Shop: ✪ **Priape**, Montréal's #1 gay store and mail order, now also #1 in Toronto (see information in Toronto section). Odysseus products on sale, 1311 Ste-Catherine E. (521-8451); **Wega Videos**, 930 Ste-Catherine Est (987-5993).

● Clothing / Mail Order (G/S/M): **Fireboy**, erotic accessories for men only. For your **Free Catalog** write to: Fireboy, CP/Box 116 Succ. P.A.T., Montréal, QC H1B 5K1; **Choc Monsieur**, men's underwear, jeans, 1881 Ave. Mont-Royal Est (521-7558); **Joe Blo**, 1412 de la Visitation (597-2330).

● Escorts (GM): ✪ **Agence Flèche**, escort, dancer or a companion for the night and day, 24 hrs./7 days (521-7708).

● Health Clubs (GM): ✪ **Aux berges**, large sauna and hotel complex (see information under accommodations), 1070 rue Mackay (938-9393); ✪ **Bourbon Sauna**, c/o Hôtel Bourbon, steam room, TV room, x rated movies, 1578 Ste-Catherine E. (523-4679); **Le 456**, popular health club complex, pool, sauna and full gym, snack bar, also private cabins with shared bath, 456 de la Gauchetière West (871-8341); **Sauna 5018**, xxx videos, sauna, jacuzzi, heated terrace, 5018 St-Laurent (277-3555); ✪ **Sauna-Centre-Ville**, directly in the heart of the village, popular sauna on 2 floors, lockers, single/double rooms, common shower, dry sauna, steam bath, whirlpool, snack-bar & video, 1465 St-Catherine East (524-3486); **Bain Colonial**, dry and steam sauna, gym, massage, 3963 Colonial Ave.. (285-0132); **Sauna du Plateau**, 961 Rachel Est (528-1679); **Oasis Spa**, the sauna for the young men in Montréal, 1390 Ste-Catherine E. (521-0785); **Sauna St. Hubert**, 6527, St. Hubert (277-0176): **Sauna St. Marc**, large sauna on 2 floors, lockers, whirlpool, dry sauna, video, snack bar, 1168 Ste-Catherine E., Montréal (525-8404); **Stone Gym**, 1440 Ste-Catherine St., West (corner of McKay).

● Massage (GM): ✪ **Tropicales**, California body rub, 24 hrs./ 7 days (521-7708).

● Party Organizers (GMW): ○ **Fondation B.B.C.M**, organizers of the best and biggest annual gay benefit parties in Canada: **Le Bal de Boys** (New Year); **Red** (February); **Wild & Wet** (May); **Twist** (Gay Pride August); **Black & Blue** (October), 800, René-Lévesque O, Suite 450 (875-7026) Fax: (514) 875-9323.

● Publication: **RG**, Les Éditions HMX Inc., C.P. 5245, Succ. C, Montréal, QC H2X 3M4 (523-9463), Fax: (523-2214).

● Reservations (GMW): ○ **Cachet Accommodations Network (C.A.N)**, booking service for Canada, Box 42-A, Stn "M", Montréal, QC H1V 3L6. (254-1250).

● Shopping (AW): **Key West**, brand name watches and sun glasses,150 Ste-Catherine W. (844-9411)

● Videos/Mail Order (GM): ○ **Priape** Montréal's #1 gay Superstore - sexy clothing, leather, videos, books, gifts etc., gay owned and operated since 1974, 1311 Ste-Catherine E., Montréal, QC H2L 2H4 (521-8451) or call Toll Free (800) 461-6969. Fax: (521-1309). **Le Club International**, 529 Ontario Est (282-1899); **Wega Video**, best selection in gay movies from the largest gay video store in Montréal, 930 Ste-Catherine E. (987-5993).

 ACCOMMODATIONS

ANGELICA
1074 St. Dominique, Montréal, QC H2X 2W2. Tel: (514) 875-5270. Fax: (514) 281-9288. TYPE: *Bed & Breakfast*. HOSTESS: Linda. CLIENTELE: Gay men & women. LOCATION: Central between the "Gay Village", the Old City and downtown. M° St. Laurent or Champs de Mars.

* Rooms: 6; 1 w/priv., 5 w/shared bath
* Apartment: 1BR w/living room, full bath, kitchen, patio. Rooms for non-smokers
* CTV, VCR, phone, refrigerator, safe box, C/H, cooking facilities
* Maid & room service, laundry, paid parking
* Gay Bars: 5 min. walk
* Health Club: 5 min (gym 456)
* Airport: Dorval, 20 min. drive
* Train Station: 5 min. Central Station
* Languages: English, French, Portuguese, (some) Italian
* Reservations: 1 night deposit or CC#
* Cancellation: 48 hrs.
* Credit Cards: MC/VISA
* Open: Year round
* Rates: (CAN) $55-$95 w/full CanB.
* *TAC:* 11%

DESCRIPTION: Two recently renovated greystone homes built circa 1830. Each room is decorated in a different theme: Angel, Jungle, Aztek. Good atmosphere and friendly hosts.

✪ AUBERGE CENTRE VILLE

1070 Mackay, Montréal, QC H3G 2H1. Tel: (514) 938-9393 or Toll Free (800) 668-6253 (CAN/USA). Fax: (514) 938-1616. TYPE: *Hotel*. HOST: Serge. CLIENTELE: Gay men only. LOCATION: Heart of downtown, corner of René-Levesque Blvd. near Peel St. M° Lucien L'Allier.

* Rooms: 42; 21 w/priv., 21 w/shared bath 42 dbl / Smoking allowed in room
* CTV, phone, A/C, C/H
* Sauna, sundeck, balcony, garden
* Clothing optional policy
* Maid, room, laundry service, free parking
* Restaurant: **Les Berges** Continental
* Bar: **Le Mezzanine** lounge bar
* Shop: man toys
* Beach: 3 mi. / 5 km (mixed river beach)
* Gay Bars: 500 ft. - 1/2 mi. (Gay Village)
* Health Club: 1 block (Stone Gym)
* Airport: Dorval / Mirabel 25 min.
* Train Station: Central Station 6 blocks
* Languages: French, English, Spanish

* Reservations: 1 night deposit,
* Cancellation: till 6:00 pm date of arrival
* Credit Cards: MC/VISA/AMEX/DC/ CB/DISC/ER
* Open: Year round
* Rates: (CAN) $65-$110 w/CB (tax included)
* *TAC:* 10%

DESCRIPTION: Montreal's premier all male hotel and sauna, popular with international clientele. The hotel has been completely renovated in 1995. All rooms are soundproof with one or more double beds. Amenities include community showers, roof sundeck, large sauna and sunny garden terrace.

AU BON VIVANT

1648 rue Amherst, Montréal, QC H24 3L5. Tel: (514) 525-7744. Fax: (514) 525-2874. TYPE: *Bed & Breakfast*. HOST: Marcel. CLIENTELE: Gay men only. LOCATION: Gay village, 2 1/2 blocks from M° Berri UQAM, 1 1/2 blocks from St. Catherine near all tourist attractions.

* Rooms: 3 w/shared bath
* No smoking
* Maid and laundry service
* Gay Bars: 1 1/2 blocks
* Airport: Dorval 20 min.
* Languages: French, English, Spanish

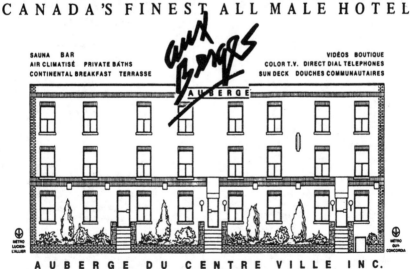

CANADA'S FINEST ALL MALE HOTEL

SAUNA   BAR
AIR CLIMATISÉ   PRIVATE BÁTHS
CONTINENTAL BREAKFAST   TERRASSE

VIDÉOS   BOUTIQUE
COLOR T.V.   DIRECT DIAL TELEPHONES
SUN DECK   DOUCHES COMMUNAUTAIRES

AUBERGE DU CENTRE VILLE INC.
1070 MACKAY, MONTREAL H3G 2H1
(514).938.9393   1.800.668.6253

MONTREAL'S
• BED AND BREAKFAST •

In the heart of the Gay Village near all the activities and fun.

"RECOMMENDED BY FRIENDS FOR FRIENDS"

1-800-451-2238

New Administration
1567 rue Saint-André,
Montréal, (QC) H2L 3T5

---

* Reservation: deposit required
* Cancellation: 72 hrs. full refund
* Credit Cards: MC/VISA/AMEX
* Rates: (CAN) $60-$90;
  (off) $40-$75 w/CB
* Tax: 7% GST 6.5% PST
* Check in time 3pm / check out 12 noon
* *TAC:* 10%

DESCRIPTION: Small intimate bed & breakfast. The use of color, persian carpets, antiques and comfortable beds create a warm, calming and inviting atmosphere. Breakfast served in the country kitchen or summer patio.

✪ HÔTEL BOURBON

1574 Ste-Catherine E., Montréal, QC H2L 2J2. Tel: (514) 523-4679. Toll Free (800) 268-4679. Fax: (514) 523-1599. TYPE: *Hotel.* HOST: Friendly Staff. CLIENTELE: Gay men & women. LOCATION: East downtown, corner of Champlain & Ste. Catherine E. in the 'Gay Village'. Mº Papineau.

* Rooms: 36; w/priv. bath. Suites: 5
  sgl/dbl/triple/quad rooms
* Smoking allowed in rooms
* CTV, phone, refrigerator
* Safe deposit, A/C,C/H
* Business phone/fax facilities
* Balcony, garden, health club & sauna
* Clothing optional, jacuzzi
* Restaurant: **Club Sandwich** 24 hrs. diner
* Room & maid service, laundry service
* Shop: leather, T-shirts,videos
* Gay Bars: on premises - **La Track**, leather cruise dance bar, **Cajun** lounge; other nearby
* Health Club: on premises, other nearby
* Airport: 5 mi. / 8 km, (Dorval) bus, taxi
* Train Station: Central - 10 minutes
* Languages: French, English
* Reservations: credit card #
* Cancellation Policy: 24 hrs prior to arrival
* Credit Cards: MC/VISA/AMEX/DISC/EN ROUTE
* Open: Year round

* Rates: (CAN) $65 - $210
* Tax: 6.5% + 7% (GST)
* Check in / Check out time: 12 noon
* *TAC:* 10%

DESCRIPTION: Hotel and entertainment complex in the heart of the "gay village". New Orleans decor and style. Standard rooms with twin or double beds, and 5 luxurious suites with air-conditioning, sound system and jacuzzi. Each suite can accommodate from 2-8 guests. Montréal's busiest disco-cruise bar on premises. "A must for the international traveler".

✪ LE CHASSEUR

1567 St.-André, Montréal, QC H2L 3T5. Tel: (514) 521-2238 or Toll Free (800) 451-2238. TYPE: *Bed & Breakfast.* HOST: Danny & Richard. CLIENTELE: Mostly Gay. LOCATION: Downtown Montreal, walking distance to the 'Gay Village', Old City, shopping and more. Mº Berri UQAM.

* Rooms: 8; 1 w/priv., 7 w/shared bath
  sgl 2; dbl 4; triple 2, smoking allowed
* CTV, phone (reception), safety box, balcony
* Maid & room service, free parking
* Gay Bars: 2 min. walk
* Health Club: 15 min. walk
* Airport: 20 min., bus, taxi
* Train Station: Gare Centrale / 10 min.
* Reservations: 1 night deposit
* Cancellation: 48 hrs.
* Languages: French, English
* Credit Cards: MC/VISA
* Open: Year round
* Rates: season (CAN) $49 -$79;
  (off) $39-$59 w/CB
* *TAC:* 10%

DESCRIPTION: Charming European guest house. Easy going friendly atmosphere. "Recommended by friends for friends". Clean and tastefully furnished rooms. Central, secure, discreet and intimate.

LA CONCIERGERIE
1019 Saint Hubert, Montréal, QC H2L 3Y3. Tel: (514) 289-9297. Fax: (514) 289-0845. TYPE: *Bed & Breakfast*. HOST: Michael & Luc. CLIENTELE: Mostly gay men. LOCATION: Between Old Montreal and the East Village. 17 rooms. Rates: on request. DESCRIPTION: Victorian home with European ambiance.

✪ HOTEL LA COURONNE

1029 St-Denis, Montréal, QC H2X 3H9. Tel: (514) 845-0901. Fax: (514) 849-8167. TYPE: *Hotel*. HOST: Jean-Claude Mgr. CLIENTELE: All Welcome. LOCATION: Near Champs de Mars or Berri Mᵒ-UQAM and bus terminal.

* Rooms: 33; 17 w/priv., 16 w/shared bath
  sgl 2 / dbl 25 / quad 6
* Smoking allowed in rooms
* CTV, phone, C/H
* Parking: paid, Pets: w/prearrangement
* Gay Bars: 10 min.
* Airport: Durval 40 min., taxi, bus
* Train Station: 3 metro stops
* Languages: English, French
* Reservations: deposit required
* Cancellation Policy: 24 hrs. notice
* Credit Cards: MC/VISA/AMEX
* Open: Year round
* Rates: CAN$35 - CAN$70
* Taxes: 13.5% (7% GST + 6.5% hotel tax)
* **TAC:** 10%

DESCRIPTION: Small friendly hotel for budget travelers with good price/quality ratio in Old montreal at the entrance to the 'Gay Village'.

LES DAUPHINS
1281 rue Beaudry, Montréal, QC H2L 3E3. Tel: (514) 525-1459. TYPE: *Bed & Breakfast*. HOSTS: Gilles & Daniel. CLIENTELE: Mostly gay men & women. LOCATION: Corner of rue Ste. Catherine near Mᵒ Beaudry. 5 rooms w/shared bath. DESCRIPTION: Montréal turn of the century house.

✪ HOTEL LE SAINT ANDRÉ

1285, rue St-André, Montréal, QC H2L 3T1. Tel: (514) 849-7070, Reservations Toll Free 1 (800) 265-7071. Fax: (514) 849-8167. e-mail: WWW.GAIBEC.com/standre. TYPE: *Hotel*. CLIENTELE: Gay/Straight. LOCATION: "Gay Village" near Old Montréal, close to bus terminal. Mᵒ Berri-UQAM.

* Rooms: 61 dbl w/priv. bath
  2 sgl / 50 dbl / 2 triple / 7 quad
* Smoking allowed in rooms
* Soundproof, mini bar
* CTV, phone, A/C, C/H

HÔTEL DE LA COURONNE

1029, rue St-Denis

Montréal (Québec)

H2X 3H9

Rooms Starting at

$45 CAN

Tél.: 845-0901

Fax: 849-8167

Le Saint·André

Le petit

hôtel

à la touche

européenne

The European

Touch Hotel

1285 rue St-André
Montréal (Québec)
Canada H2L 3T1

Tel: (514) 849-7070
Fax: (514) 849-8167
Toll Free: (800) 265-7071
E-Mail: www.gaibec.com/standre

* Business phone/fax facilities
* Maid service, elevator
* Pets accepted w/prearrangement
* Gay Bars: across the street
* Airport: 15 km / 10 mi. bus, taxi
* Languages: French, English
* Reservation: required
* Cancellation: 24 hrs.
* Credit Cards: MC/VISA/AMEX/DC/DISC/EC
* Open: Year round
* Rates: 5/1-10/31 (CAN)$64.50-$89.50;
   (off) 11/1-4/30 $54.50-$79.50
   w/AB Tax: 14%
* Check in 3 pm / Check out 12 noon
* *TAC:* 10%

DESCRIPTION: Charming completely renovated 3-star hotel in the heart of the "Gay Village". Pleasant lobby, comfortable rooms, and personalized service. Continental breakfast served in your room. Excellent location and service. For business or pleasure the St. André is always an excellent choice.

○ LE STADE B&B

Box 42, Stn. "M", Montréal, QC H1V 3L6. Tel: (514) 254-1250. 24 hrs fax available (please call first). TYPE: *Private Home.* HOST: Enrique & Tim. CLIENTELE: Gay Men & Women only.

LOCATION: New Latin/French quarter close to the Olympic Village/Stadium.

* Rooms: 3 w/shared bath
* CTV (lounge), phone (reception)
* Parking, no pets
* Laundry facilities
* Gay Bars: 10 min. transit
* Airport: 25 min. drive
* Languages: English, French, Spanish
* Reservations: 1 night deposit
* Open: Year round
* Rates: on request w/breakfast

DESCRIPTION: Top floor, private apartment. Quiet residential area, near transit and recreational facilities.

QUÉBEC   © 418

✈ Québec Airport (YQB)

LOCATION: On the North Shore of the St. Lawrence River, 150 mi. / 240 km northeast of Montréal.

POPULATION: 646,000
CLIMATE: Cold snowy winter with a January average of 17°F (-9°c). Summers are cool and pleasant, with a July average of 69°F (21°c).

Gay/Lesbian Information
(418) 522-3301

DESCRIPTION: Québec is the capital of the province and the only walled city in North America. It was the first French settlement in the western hemisphere and the wall was designed to block access from enemies to the city. The city's European flavor is enhanced by old fortifications, museums and theatres, gourmet restaurants, and public parcs. The Gay scene concentrates around the Rue St-Jean in the heart of the local 'gay village'.

❖ SPECIAL EVENT: Winter Carnival is the world's biggest winter celebration, taking place on the first Thursday of February each year since 1955; Summer Festival July 8-18 (692-4540).

BARS ♀ RESTAURANTS ♯

● Bars/clubs (GM): Ballon Rouge, 811 St. Jean (529-6709); Bar de la Couronne, open 7 days, male strippers, 310 de la Couronne (525-6593); Drague, pub, taverne & video bar, shows on Sunday only, 815 St. Augustin (649-7212); Bar

Mâle, neighborhood bar, western atmosphere w/pool table and video games, 770 Côte Ste-Genevieve (523-8279); Studio 157, bar, bistro, 157 Chemin Ste-Foy (529-9958); Taverne Pub, 321 rue de la Couronne (525-5107).

● Bar/club (GMW): Amour Sorcier, café-bar with patio, 789 Côte Ste-Geneviève (523-3395); L'Antre, 698, D'Aguillon (648-9497);Bar L'Eveil, 710 rue Bouvier (628-0610); Fausse Alarme, 161, rue St-Jean (529-0227); Studio 157, piano bar, bars, and restaurant, mixed clientele, 157 Chemin Ste Foy (529-9958).

● Restaurants (GMW): Le Balico, 935 rue Bourlamaque (648-1880); Café Bobon, 481 rue St-Jean (648-6338); Diana, snack bar, open late till 4:00 am, 849 rue St.-Jean (524-5794); Le Hobbit, cafe, restaurant, 700 rue Saint-Jean (647-2677); Chez Victor, 145 rue Saint-Jean (529-7702); Café Zorba, 854 rue Saint-Jean (525-5509).

λ SERVICES λ

● Health Clubs (GM): Centre de Santé, 40, rue Lamontagne (647-3744); Hippocampe, 31 rue McMahon (694-0368); Sauna Bloc 225, sauna, video club, 225 rue St-Jean (523-2562); Sauna St-Jean, large sauna complex, videos, close circuit TV in some rooms, young clientele, open 24 hrs., 920 rue St-Jean, (694-9724).

● Videos (GM): Importation Delta, clothing, videos and guide books, 875, rue St-Jean (647-6808).

 ACCOMMODATIONS

○ AU 727 GUEST HOUSE
727 d'Aiguillon, Québec, QC G1R 1M8. Tel: (418) 648-6766, or (800) 652-6766. Fax: (418) 648-1474. TYPE: Guest House. HOST: Denis Côte. CLIENTELE: Gay men & women only. LOCATION: In Vieux Québec / Old Quebec.

* Rooms: 9; 3 w/priv., 6 w/shared bath
* CTV, phone (public), A/C, C/H
* Maid & room service
* Pets: w/prearrangement
* Gay Bars: corner of street
* Airport: 15 min., taxi
* Train Station: 10 min. walk
* Languages: French, English
* Reservations: 1 night deposit, CC#
* Credit Cards: MC/VISA
* Open: Year round
* Rates: (CAN) $40 - CAN$90 w/F/QB
* TAC: 10%

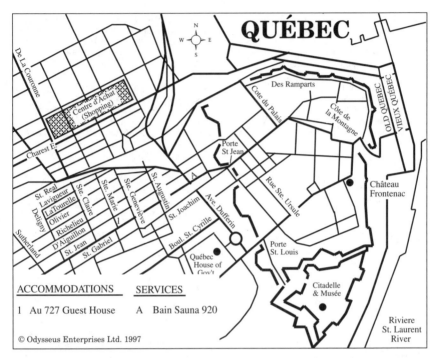

ACCOMMODATIONS

1   Au 727 Guest House

SERVICES

A   Bain Sauna 920

© Odysseus Enterprises Ltd. 1997

DESCRIPTION: A renovated old French style guest house. Friendly and clean. Centrally located for total enjoyment of the local gay scene. Some rooms w/balcony. Massage available.

LE COUREUR DES BOIS
15 Ste-Ursule, Québec, QC G1R 4C7. Tel: (418) 692-1117. TYPE: *Guest House.* HOST: Marc & Jean-Paul. CLIENTELE: Gay Men & Women only. LOCATION: Within the ancient walls of the Old City. 7 rooms. Rates: on request. DESCRIPTION: Simple but tastefully decorated rooms.

QUÉBEC SKI RESORTS

Some recommended ski resorts near Montréal or Québec city include:

MONT BLANC
P.O. Box 122, Saint-Faustin, QC J0T 2G0. One hour northwest of Montréal. 35 trails, 8 lifts. Condominiums and antique decorated rooms.

MONT ORFORD
P.O. Box 248, Magog-Orford QC J1X 2W8. One of the highest vertical drops in Eastern Cana-

da, one hour from Montréal, near the Vermont border. 39 trails, 8 lifts. Slope-side and ski-to-your-door condos.

MONT ST-SAUVEUR
Largest ski resort in the southern Laurantians, only 40 minutes from downtown Montréal. Best night skiing in North America, with 23 lighted runs. Spotlights turn the mountain into a dazzling fairyland (how about this for a description). 14 lifts, 139 trails, 4 mountains, hundreds of boutiques, restaurants, bars, art galleries, antique shops.

ACCOMMODATIONS

MANOIR SAINT-SAUVEUR
USA reservation/information Tel: (516) 944-5330 or (800) 257-5344. Fax: (516) 944-7540. TYPE: *Resort Complex.* CLIENTELE: All Welcome. LOCATION: 40 min. north of Montréal, in the village of St-Sauveur. 225 luxurious rooms w/priv. bath, condos (one or two-bedroom apts) some w/fire-place, restaurants, bar, indoor swimming pool, gym, sauna, health spa. Cross-country and Tube slides packages available. DESCRIPTION: Beautiful resort complex offering unique ski packages. Call for rates.

SASKATCHEWAN

- **Population**: 980,900
- **Capital**: Regina
- **Time Zone**: Central
- **Legal drinking age**: 18

RAVENSCRAG ✆ 306

✈ Regina Airport (YQR) (Saskatchewan)
Medicine Hat Airport (Alberta)

LOCATION: In the southwestern corner of Saskatchewan near the border of Alberta and Montana (USA).

 ACCOMMODATIONS

SPRING VALLEY
Box 10, Ravenscrag, SK S0N 2C0. Tel: (306) 295-4124. TYPE: *Bed & Breakfast and Campground*. HOST: Jim Saville. CLIENTELE: Few Gay. LOCATION: In the soutwestern corner of Saskatchewan, 300 mi. / 480 km from major city. 4 rooms, tipis. Season: April-January. DESCRIPTION: Country B&B.

REGINA ✆ 306

✈ Regina Airport (YQR) (Saskatchewan)

LOCATION: Heart of southern Saskatchewan.

POPULATION: 191,600

CLIMATE: Summers are pleasant with warm dry sunny days and cool evenings. July temperatures average 75°F (24°c). Winters are cold and snowy with a January average of 4°F (-16°c).

Gay/Lesbian Visitor Information
Pink Triangle: 525-6046

DESCRIPTION: Regina is the provincial capital. Although it still has a prairie feeling it is sophisticated and cosmopolitan. The town has some interesting attractions, and good hotels and restaurants, most of them along Victoria Avenue.

Visit: **Wascana Place**, provides public information services and gift shop with local arts and crafts; **Museum of Natural History**, display of regional wildlife history (787-2815); **The Science Center**, fun-filled hand on exhibits in the renovated City of Regina Powerhouse on the north shore of the Wascana Lake (352-5811). If your heart is in the sports visit the **Saskatchewan Sports Hall of Fame**, 2205 Victoria Ave. (780-9232).

❖ **SPECIAL EVENT: Buffalo Days**, first week in August. Old West style celebration, recalls the days of the old west.

BARS ☥ RESTAURANTS

● Bar (GMW): **Scarth St. Station**, dance bar, 1422 Scarth St. (522-7343). (near the bus Depot).

● Restaurants (AW): **Mieka's**, fresh innovative cuisine, 1810 Smith St. (522-6700); **Golf's Steak House**, plush atmosphere, steakhouse fare, 1945 Victoria Ave. (525-5808); **Ozzies**, Cajun cuisine, 2332 11th Ave. (525-555).

ACCOMMODATIONS

PLAINS MOTOR HOTEL
1965 Albert St., Regina SK S4P 2T5. Tel: (306) 757-8661. TYPE: *Motel*. CLIENTELE: Mostly Straight. LOCATION: Downtown location.

* Rooms: 58 w/priv. bath
* CTV, phone, parking
* Restaurant, coffee shop
* Gay Bar: nearby
* Airport: 1 mi. / 1.6 km
* Open: Year round
* Rates: (CAN) $30-$35.
* *TAC:* 10%

DESCRIPTION: Economic motel in a convenient downtown location.

SASKATOON ✆ 306

✈ Saskatoon Airport (YXE) 5 mi. NW

LOCATION: 240 mi. / 385 km northwest of Regina in southern Saskatchewan.

POPULATION: 184,000

Gay/Lesbian Visitor Information
Gay & Lesbian Line: 665-1224

DESCRIPTION: Fast growing frontier town transforming itself into a progressive city on the banks of the Lower Saskatchewan River.

BARS ♟ RESTAURANTS 🍴

● Bar (GMW): **Diva's**, 220 3rd Ave. S. Ste 110 (665-0100).

 ACCOMMODATIONS

BRIGHTON HOUSE
1308 5th Ave. N, Saskatoon, SK. Tel: (306) 664-3278. TYPE: *Bed & Breakfast.* CLIENTELE: Gay men & women. LOCATION: Downtown. DESCRIPTION: Rooms decorated with many antiques.

KING GEORGE HOTEL
157 2nd Ave. St. N, Saskatoon, SK S7K 2A9. Tel: (306) 244-6133. Fax: (306) 652-4672. TYPE: *Hotel.* CLIENTELE: Mostly Straight. LOCATION: Near downtown and Microwave Tower.

* Rooms: 104 w/priv. bath
* CTV, phone, A/C, C/H
* Dining Room, lounge, free parking
* Gay Bar: walking
* Airport: 3 mi. / 5 km
* Rates: (CAN) $39-$47
* *TAC:* 10%

DESCRIPTION: Landmark hotel with pleasant rooms, some with VCR and minibar. Great central location.

ALBANIA

AREA: 11,100 sq. mi. (28,748 sq. km.)
POPULATION: 3,300,000
CAPITAL: Tirana
CURRENCY: Lek (ALL)
OFFICIAL LANGUAGE: Albanian
MAJOR RELIGION: Islam, Roman Catholicism, Albanian Orthodox
Telephone: 355
Official Time: GMT + 1
Nat'l Holiday: Jan. 11, Republic Day
Electricity: 220v / 50c
Exchange Rate: ALL 102 = $1
National Airline: No National Airline

LAW REGARDING HOMOSEXUALITY: Albania has recently decriminalized homosexuality as requested by the member nations of the Council of Europe which Albania wants to join. Consensual gay relationships are allowed and anti-gay violence is prohibited. Male rape or sex with minors remain punishable by law up to 5 years in prison. Many gays though they do not have to fear jail anymore have left Albania since the end of Communism. The few that remain are mostly poor. Some sell sexual services to foreign truckers outside of Tirana. The attitude of the society is mostly hostile towards homosexuals.

TIRANA   © 42

✈   Rinas Airport,
25 km / 15 mi. north-west of Tirana

LOCATION: Central Albania near the Adriatic Coast.

POPULATION: 300,000

CLIMATE: Warm Mediterranean climate. Summers are hot, clear and dry. July is the hottest month, May and October are pleasant. Winters are cool, cloudy and moist.

Gay Visitor Information
Shoqata Gay Albania
(Gay Albania Society)
P.O. Box 104, Tirana

DESCRIPTION: Tirana (Tiranë) is a pleasant city half way between Rome & Istanbul. Founded by Turkish Pasha in 1614. The city is compact with short walking to any point of interest in town. Explore the city's Italian parks, Turkish Mosques, and the age old countryside. For gay men the only public cruising takes place in the park across from the **Hotel Dajti** (AYOR).

BARS ▼ RESTAURANTS ¶¶

● Bars (G/S): **London**, bar and restaurant, Bulevard Dëshmorët e Kombit 51 (near Hotel Tirana).

● Restaurant (AW): **Donika**, near the old 'Ali Kelmendi' Palace of Culture on Bulevardi Stalin (may have changed its name) a short walk from Hotel Tirana.

ACCOMMODATIONS

HOTEL DAJTI
Shetitorja Dëshmorëty Kombit. Tel: (42) 27662. Fax: (42) 32012. TYPE: *Hotel*. CLIENTELE: All Welcome. LOCATION: Central near a cruisy park. Rates: on request.DESCRIPTION: built by the Italians in 1930 the hotel is favorite with foreign businessmen and tourists.

HOTEL EUROPAPARK
Shetitorja Dëshmorëty Kombit. Tel: (42) 42459. Fax: (42) 42458. TYPE: *Hotel*. CLIENTELE: All Welcome. LOCATION: Central on main boulevard. DESCRIPTION: Austrian run hotel, best and most expensive hotel in Tirana. pool. Rates: $130-$170.

HOTEL TIRANA
Skanderberg Square. TYPE: *Hotel*. CLIENTELE: All Welcome. LOCATION: Central. DESCRIPTION: Highrise hotel in a central location. All rooms with private bath.

ANTIGUA

AREA: 171 sq. mi. (443 sq. km)
POPULATION: 76,000
CAPITAL: St. John's
CURRENCY: East Caribbean Dollar (XCD)
OFFICIAL LANGUAGE: English
MAJOR RELIGION: Protestantism
Telephone: 809
Official Time: GMT -4
Nat'l Holiday:
Electricity: 110/220v 60c
Exchange Rate: XCD 2.70 = $1

LAW REGARDING HOMOSEXUALITY: Since its independence in 1981 the island state has a British style parliamentary government. Homosexuality is prosecuted based on the British Law. There are no gay organizations or support groups on the island.

ST. JOHN'S

✈   Bird Int'l AP (ANU), 6 mi. / 10 km NE

LOCATION: Central western coast.

CLIMATE: Typical Caribbean climate with an average year-round temperatures between 75°F - 85°F (23°c-28°c).

DESCRIPTION: Antigua boasts a different beach for each day of the year. Most of the beaches are protected by coral reef. It is a vacation haven with excellent beach resorts and one of the best Caribbean island for mass tourism.

❖ Beaches: **Half Moon Bay** best beach on the island; **Hawksbill Hotel (4th Beach)** the only official nude beach on the island.

🍴 RESTAURANTS 🍴

● Restaurant (AW): **Abracadabra**, Italian cuisine, English Harbor (462-1732); **Albertros**, upscaled Italian, Willoughby Bay (460-3007); **Chez Pascal**, French bistro, St. John's (462-3232); **Coconut Grove**, West Indian, Dickenson Bay (462-1538); **La Perruche**, Cajun, English Harbor (460-3040).

ACCOMMODATIONS

BARRYMORE BEACH CLUB
Runaway Bay, St. John's. Tel: 462-4101. TYPE: *Apartments Complex*. CLIENTELE: All Welcome. LOCATION: Beachfront on Runaway Bay, 2 mi / 3 km from casino and town.

* Apartments: 36 (1&2BR apts)
* Ceiling fan, kitchenette, patio, full bath
* Villas: 3 (3BR) with pool
* Restaurant, bar, free parking, water sports
* Rates: (US) $90-$280

DESCRIPTION: Charming resort complex with tastefully decorated private apartments and villas.

HALF MOON BAY CLUB
Half Moon Bay, St, John's. Tel: 460-4300. TYPE: *All Inclusive Beach Resort*. CLIENTELE: All Welcome. LOCATION: On tropical acres next to the Mill Reef Club.

* Rooms: 100 w/priv. bath
* Phone, ceiling fan, balcony
* Suites: 2 w/sitting room
* Restaurants, lounges, pool, golf, tennis
* Open: Year round
* Rates: (US) $240 - $360

DESCRIPTION: Elegant resort on the islands premier beach location. All inclusive packages include 3 meals daily, all beverages, use of watersports, golf and tennis facilities, evening entertainment, special daily activities, all taxes and gratuities.

TRADE WINDS HOTEL
Dickenson Bay. Tel: 462-1223. TYPE: *All Suite Hotel*. CLIENTELE: All WElcome. LOCATION: Above Dickenson Bay with splendid view of the ocean, 2 mi / 3 km from St. John's.

* Suites: 47 w/priv. bath
* CTV, minibar, balcony, phone
* Maid and room service, parking
* Restaurant, piano bar, pool, sundeck
* Rates: (US) $160 - $220

DESCRIPTION: First class hotel with fine amenities and service.

ARGENTINA

AREA: 1,073,263 sq. mi. (2,779, 741 sq. km)
POPULATION: 33,200,000
CAPITAL: Buenos Aires
CURRENCY: Peso
OFFICIAL LANGUAGE: Spanish (Castellano)
MAJOR RELIGIONS: Roman Catholics
(85%), Protestants (4%), Jewish (2%)
Telephone: 54
Nat'l Holiday: Independence Day, July 9
Official Time: 3 hrs. behind G.M.T.
Electricity: 220 volts, 50 cycles, A.C.
Exchange Rate: 1US$ = Peso 1
National Airline: Aerolíneas Argentinas

LAW REGARDING HOMOSEXUALITY: Homosexuality is not mentioned in the country's Code of Law. The situation is steadily improving since the establishment of democracy in 1983. **CHA** (Comunidad Homosexual Argentina) is very active in changing laws and public acceptance of the gay community. This is good news for local gays, and gay travelers to Argentina. Yet, it is important to realize that while a liberal attitude prevails in large cities, other communities are still very conservative. There are no restrictions on the entry of people with AIDS / HIV into Argentina, however anybody who applies for visa must provide a document stating that he/she does not have any infectious disease.

● National Organizations (GMW): **CHA** (Comunidad Homosexual Argentina), Cochabamba 2454, Piso 1°E (1252) Buenos Eires. Tel: (01) 941-8397; **SIGLA** (Sociedad de Integración Gay Lésbica Argentina), Paraná 122, Piso 2 (1017) Buenos Aires. Tel: (01) 382-4540. Fax: (01) 362-8261.

BUENOS AIRES   ℂ 01

✈ Ezeiza Int'l Airport (EZE)

LOCATION: Eastern Argentina, in the region known as The Pampa, on the River Plate (Río de la Plata), across the river from the Uruguay border.

POPULATION: City: 3,000,000
Metro: 11,000,000

CLIMATE: Buenos Aires lies south of the Equator and the seasons are reversed. Winter runs from June to September with temperatures in the 40°F's (6°c). Summers last from December to March with temperatures in the 80°F's (26°c) with high humidity.

Gay/Lesbian Visitor Information
C.H.A.
(Argentine Homosexual Community)
P.O. Box 1033, Cap. Fed.
Tel: (01) 953-8030. Fax: (01) 383-2212
SIGLA
(Sociedad de Integracion Gay-Lesbica Argentina)
Paraná 122, Piso 2 (1017) Buenos Aires
Tel: (01) 382-4540. Fax: (01) 362-8261.

DESCRIPTION: Buenos Aires the capital of the Republic of Argentina, is known to many of us as the city of Evita Perón. It is a vast Metropolitan agglomeration along the River Plate. Most of the city has now been rebuilt and only a few of the old buildings are left. There is a distinctive European, or French influence on the city's planning and architecture. Plaza De Mayo, is in the heart of the city with the historic Cabildo - the Town Hall. For a panoramic view of the town, try the cocktail lounge at the top floor of the Sheraton Hotel, San Martín 1225 (311-6310). Of interest to visitors: **Pink House** (Casa Rosada), facing the eastern side of **Plaza de Mayo**; **The Cathedral** (La Catedral), site of the first church built in Buenos Aires circa 1620; and the **Colón Theatre**, one of the world's major opera houses.

● Most of the gay nightlife is concentrated on and around **Avenida Santa Fé** and **Av. Callao**. From 7pm - 7am every day the Avenida Santa Fé attracts many gays and lesbians to the many bars, clubs and discos along the avenue. Activity in the bars and clubs starts very late, just before midnight. The 'Hottest' cruising area is right by the **Wilton Palace Hotel**. Gay cruising is also possible at the **Plaza de San Telmo** (on Sundays).

BARS 🍸 RESTAURANTS 🍴

Buenos Aires is probably only second to Rio de Janeiro (Brazil) when it comes to gay nightlife and entertainment. The gay scene is concentrated

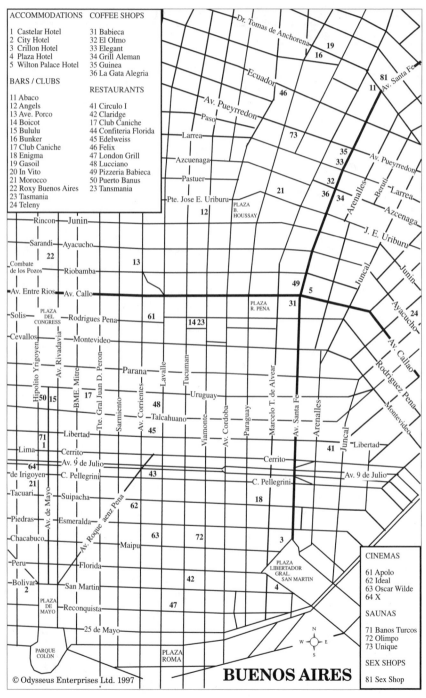

ACCOMMODATIONS   COFFEE SHOPS

1 Castelar Hotel   31 Babieca
2 City Hotel   32 El Olmo
3 Crillon Hotel   33 Elegant
4 Plaza Hotel   34 Grill Aleman
5 Wilton Palace Hotel   35 Guinea
                         36 La Gata Alegria

BARS / CLUBS   RESTAURANTS

11 Abaco   41 Circulo I
12 Angels   42 Claridge
13 Ave. Porco   17 Club Caniche
14 Boicot   44 Confiteria Florida
15 Bululu   45 Edelweiss
16 Bunker   46 Felix
17 Club Caniche   47 London Grill
18 Enigma   48 Lucciano
19 Gasoil   49 Pizzeria Babieca
20 In Vito   50 Puerto Banus
21 Morocco   23 Tansmania
22 Roxy Buenos Aires
23 Tasmania
24 Teleny

CINEMAS

61 Apolo
62 Ideal
63 Oscar Wilde
64 X

SAUNAS

71 Banos Turcos
72 Olimpo
73 Unique

SEX SHOPS

81 Sex Shop

© Odysseus Enterprises Ltd. 1997

BUENOS AIRES

on and around the Avenida Santa Fe which is located northwest of the Plaza de Mayo, at the northern end of the Avenida 9 de Julio which is the main drag in Central Buenos Aires.

● Bars/clubs (GM): **Abaco**, pub, late night show, T. de Anchorena 1347 (824-8550); **After Dark**, pub, Guise 1677, between Soler & Paraguay St., (823-6956); **Angel's**, disco, Viamonte 2168; **Bululu**, Av. Rivadavia 1350 (381-1656); **Bunker**, dance club, Anchorena 1170; **Contramano**, dance club, Rodriguez Peña; **Gasoil**, dance club, male strippers, Anchorena St. 1179 (961-3449); **In Vitro**, Azcuenaga 1007 (824-0932); **Nada**, Laprida 1532 (821-4117); **Tasmania**, bar/restaurant, Pasaje Luis Dellepiane 685, at Viamonte 1600 (374-3177); **Teleny**, piano bar, entertainment, Juncal 2479 (826-4639).

● Bars/clubs (GMW): **Ave Porco**, disco, art gallery, late shows, Av. Corrientes 1980 (953-7129); **Bach Bar**, Juan A. Cabrera 4390, Palermo viejo; **Babilonia**, Guardia Vieja 3360 (862-0683); **Club Caniche**, pub & restaurant, Uruguay 142 (373-2666); **Confusion**, dance club, Avda Scalabrini Ortiz 1721; **Enigma**, dance club, Suipacha 927 near 9 de Julio Ave.; **Morocco**, Hipolito Irigoyen 851, Fri. gay nite (342-6046); **Parakultural**, Chacabuco 1072; **Roxy Buenos aires**, Av. Rivadavia 1910.

● Bars/clubs (GW): **Boicot**, dance club, Pasaje Dellepiane 657 at Viamonte 1600; **Incognito**, pub, Scalabrini Ortiz 1721, open: 10pm; **Las Lunas y Las Autras**, cultural lesbian feminist center, art and languages workshop, movies, library, Maza 1490 , Buenos Aires 1240; **Vivir**, Jufré 162 (777-1314).

● Coffee Shops (AW): **Babieca**, Av. Santa Fe 1790; **Elegant**, Av. Santa Fe 2402; **La Gata Alegría**, Av. Santa Fe 2270; **Grill Alemán**, Av. Santa Fe 2297; **Guinea**, Santa Fe 2478; **El Olmo**, Santa Fe 2304; **Oviedo**, Pueyrredon 1080.

● Restaurants (GMW) **Tasmania**, Pje Luis Dellepiane 685, next door to Boicot (374-3177); **Club Caniche**, pub & restaurant, Thu. gay nite, Uruguay 142 (373-2666); **Puerto Banus**, Ave. de Mayo 1354, pub & restaurant, basement down the corridor to the right (381-7150). Other (AW): **Basilio**, Rawson 26 (950-3038); **Circulo I**, Libertad 1240 (814-0661); **Confiteria Florida Garden**, C. Pellegrini 491; **Claridge**, one of the best restaurants in town, Tucumán 535 (393-7212); **Clark's I**, popular hangout for the Buenos Aires beautiful people, exotic setting and fine food, Junín 1777 (801-9502); **Felix**, fine fish, Italian squid dishes and Codfish, Ecuador 794, Avellaneda (208-2539);

Edelweiss, German specialties, favorite meeting place for artists, Libertad 431 (353-351); **London Grill,** English chop house moderately priced, Reconquista 455 (311-2223); **Lucciano,** Lavalleja 1310 (831-0300); **Pizzeria Babieca,** Av. Santa Fé 1898; **Tasmania,** Pje. Dellepiane 685 (374-3177).

λ SERVICES λ

● Cinemas (GM): **Apolo,** Rodriguez Peña 415; **Biógrafo,** Corrientes 4600; **Blue,** Rivadavia y Nazca; **Ideal,** Suipacha 378; **Once,** Ecuador 54; **Oscar Wilde,** Lavalle 750; **X,** Hipólito Yrigoyen 980.

● Escort/Massage (GM): **Alberto,** massage, home or hotel, (361-7287); **Spartacus,** discreet male escorts, home or hotel, 24 hrs. (825-1804); **Top Boys,** Santa Fe y Callao (813-2010).

● Escort/Massage (GW): **Marcela,** massage (953-9147).

● Sauna (G/S): **Baños Turcos,** c/o Castelar Hotel, Avda de Mayo 1152, near Obelisk; **Olimpo,** Viamonte 750; **Unique,** Pueyrredon 1180 (962-3216).

● Sex Shop (G/S): **Sex Shop,** Av. Santa Fe 2740, 1st. Fl, Loc. 29 (824-3402).

 **ACCOMMODATIONS**

CASTELAR HOTEL
Avda de Mayo 1152, Buenos Aires. Tel: (1) 383-5000. USA/Canada reservations - (800) 257-5344 or (516) 944-5330. Fax: (800) 982-6571 or (516) 944-7540. TYPE: *Hotel.* CLIENTELE: All Welcome. LOCATION: Central near the Obelisk, 3 blocks from financial center. 200 rooms w/priv. or shared bath. Sauna (Baños Turcos) popular with gays. Rates: $60 - $120. *TAC:* 10% (from Odysseus).

CITY HOTEL
Bolivar 160, Buenos Aires 1066. Tel: 34-6481, Telex: 21484. TYPE: *Tourist Class Hotel.* CLIENTELE: Mostly Straight. LOCATION: near Plaza de Mayo. 400 rooms. Rates: $55-$90. *TAC:* 10%. DESCRIPTION: Traditional 12-story tourist hotel in a convenient location. Some rooms are rather simple and on the small side.

CRILLON HOTEL
Avenida Santa Fe 796, Buenos Aires 1059. Tel: 312-8181/92, Fax: 312-9955. TYPE: *Hotel.* CLIENTELE: Mostly Straight. LOCATION: in central shopping area facing Plaza San Martin.

Convenient to the local gay scene.

* Rooms: 96 w/priv. bath. Suites: 12
* CTV, phone, A/C
* Cafeteria, restaurant, nightclub
* Room & maid service
* Gay Bars: walking distance
* Airport: 30 km / 19 mi., taxi
* Credit Cards: VISA/MC/AMEX/DC
* Open: Year round
* Rates: $95 - $170   *TAC:* 10%

DESCRIPTION: Unpretentious older hotel in a central shopping area, near the local gay scene.

PLAZA HOTEL
Calle Florida Buenos Aires 1005. Tel: (1) 311-5011. Fax: (1) 313-2912. TYPE: *Hotel.* CLIENTELE: Mostly Straight. LOCATION: In central location overlooking San Martin Park.

* Rooms: 322 w/priv. bath. Suites: 22
* CTV, phone, A/C, minibar
* Restaurant, pool, gym, sauna
* Room & maid service
* Airport: 10 minutes
* Gay Bars: nearby
* Credit Cards: MC/VISA/AMEX/DC
* Open: Year round
* Rates: (US) $135 - $430.   *TAC:* 10%

DESCRIPTION: Moderate deluxe distinguished hotel in a central location. Modern/traditional decor, comfortable rooms.

✪ WILTON PALACE HOTEL
Callao 1162-1023 Buenos Aires. Tel: (1) 812-9988. USA/Canada reservations: Tel (800) 257-5344 or (516) 944-5330. Fax: (516) 944-7540. TYPE: *Hotel.* CLIENTELE: All Welcome. LOCATION: On Buenos Aires most distinguished street, close to Santa Fe Ave., fashionable shopping and the entertainment district.

* Rooms: 120 w/priv. bath
* CTV, phone, radio, safe box
* Services: maid, room, laundry & dry cleaning, parking garage
* Bar & Coffee shop
* Gay Bars: walking distance
* Airport: 25 min. taxi
* Reservations: through Odysseus
* Open: Year round
* Rates: $130 - $220 w/CB
* *TAC:* 10%

DESCRIPTION: Elegant 4-star hotel with excellent amenities and service. Tastefully decorated guest rooms and public areas. Walk to the Buenos Aires gay scene.

CORDOBA ✆ 051

✈ Pajas Blancas Airport (COR)

LOCATION: Agricultural heart of Northern Argentina, 1 hour flight time, or 192 mi. / 307 km drive northwest of Buenos Aires on Route 9.

POPULATION: 1,200,000

CLIMATE: Pleasant continental climate, with average July temperature of 48°F (8°c), and average January temperature of 75°F (24°c).

VISITOR INFORMATION
Dirección Provincial de Turismo
San Jerónimo 62, 1st. Floor

DESCRIPTION: Córdoba founded in 1573, is the capital of the Córdoba Province, and the third largest city in Argentina. It is a popular tourist destination, second only to that of the coastal area (Mar del Plata). Tourists can enjoy many outdoor activities including horseback riding, swimming, hiking, fishing, in the area health resorts. Gay cruising areas: Pedestrian mall of street 9 de Julio, San Martín, Rivadavia, Rosarjo and Plaza San Martín.

BARS ⏐ RESTAURANTS ¶¶

● Bars/clubs (GM): **Hangar 18**, disco, Blvd. Las Heras 116/118; **La Piaf**, Obispo Ceballos 45, B° San Martín; **Planeta Baja**, San Martin 666 (214-704).

● Restaurants (AW): **Crillón Hotel**; **Florida Grill** (across from the Crillón Hotel); **Jerónimo**, simple, moderately priced and a pleasant restaurant, located next to the Crillón Hotel. The restaurant at the **Hotel Familiar** on S. Jerónimo, near the railway station, is good and rather inexpensive.

λ SERVICES λ

● Health Club (GM): **Sendero**, Tucumán 568.

✑ ACCOMMODATIONS ✑

HOTEL CRILLON
Rividavia 85, Cordoba. Tel: (51) 46093/8, Telex: 51792. TYPE: *Hotel*. CLIENTELE: Mostly Straight. LOCATION: Downtown section, near the local gay scene.

* Rooms: 120 w/priv. bath. Suites: 6
* CTV, phone, A/C
* Restaurant, coffee shop, bar
* Room & maid service
* Gay Bars: mixed bar on premises
* Airport: 15 km / 9 mi., taxi
* Credit Cards: VISA/AMEX/DC
* Open: Year round
* Rates: (US) $70 - $90
* **TAC:** 10%

DESCRIPTION: Pleasant Provincial hotel with attractive public places. All rooms decorated in traditional decor. The Hotel's Bar can be interesting to gay travelers.

GRAN HOTEL DORA
Entre Rios 70, Cordoba 5000. Tel: (51) 212031. Fax: (51) 51744. TYPE: *Tourist Class Hotel*. CLIENTELE: Mostly Straight. LOCATION: Downtown section, 100 m. from San Martin Plaza, the Cathedral and near the local gay scene.

* Rooms: 120 w/private bath
* CTV, phone, A/C
* Restaurant, bar (24 hours, mixed)
* Room & maid service, parking
* Gay Bars: on premises
* Airport: 15 km / 9 mi., taxi
* Reservations: suggested
* Credit Cards: VISA/AMEX/DC
* Open: Year round
* Rates: (US) $65 - $95
* **TAC:** 10%

DESCRIPTION: Provincial hotel with all rooms and public areas decorated in contemporary local artwork. The Hotel is convenient to the gay cruising of Plaza San Martin.

LA PLATA ✆ 01

LOCATION: 40 mi. / 60 km from downtown Buenos Aires.

BARS ⏐ RESTAURANTS ¶¶

● Bar/club (GM): **Bandido**, show bar, Calle 10 and Calle 59.

MAR DEL PLATA ✆ 023

✈ Mar del Plata Airport

LOCATION: On the Atlantic Ocean in Northeastern Argentina, some 400 km / 250 mi. southeast of Buenos Aires.

POPULATION: 540,000. During the summer (late December - early March) the population swells to 2,000,000 due to large influx of visitors and tourists.

CLIMATE: Similar to Buenos Aires with plenty of sea breeze in the summer.

DESCRIPTION: Fashionable seaside resort with 5 mi. / 8 km of beautiful beaches, and one of the largest Casinos in the world. The city burst with life, colors and activities during the summer season. Mar del Plata offers lovely beaches, parks, shopping galleries, inexpensive arts and crafts made by local craftsmen, and of course there is the **Casino** on **Bristol Beach** for the high rollers. The large influx of tourists supports the local gay scene which gets better during the winter from December to March and in July. Generally speaking the local police does not harass gay tourists and establishments.Cruising areas: **Playa Chica**, **Peatonal San Martín**, **Plaza Colón**.

❖ Beaches (popular with gays): Beach of **Plaza Hotel** (in front of the casino); Beach 'Playa Chica' above the rocks, or '**Médanos**'.

BARS 🍸 RESTAURANTS 🍴

● Bars/clubs (GM): **Cream Bar**, Diag. Alberdi 2621 at Cordoba (open daily): **Dicroica**, pub, Bolívar 2152l (open year round); **Extasis**, dance club, Corrientes 2044 (920-338); **Petróleo**, disco, Arenales 2272.

● Restaurants (AW): **Taverna Vaska**, seafood, 12 de Octubre 3301; **Don Pepito**, opposite casino; **Comedor Naturista**, vegetarian, Av. Salta 1571.

λ SERVICES λ

● Erotica (G/S/M): **Cine A**, San Martin & Corrientes (Florida Shopping Mall); **Cine Sex**, video club, sex shop, gay room, Belgrano 2331.

🏮 ACCOMMODATIONS 🏮

GRAN HOTEL PROVINCIAL
Blvd. Martimo 2500, Mar del Plata 7600. Tel: 2-4081/9, Telex: 39844 HPMD. TYPE: *First Class Hotel*. CLIENTELE: Mostly Straight. LOCATION: Adjacent to the Casino building.

* Rooms: 500 w/priv. bath. Suites: 16

* Restaurant & Night Club
* Color TV, Telephone, A/C
* Wheelchair Accessible
* Sauna & Gym
* Room Service & Maid Service
* Distance to Gay Bars: some nearby
* Distance to the Airport: 20 minutes
* Airport Transportation: taxi
* Credit Cards: VISA/AMEX/DC
* Open: Year round
* Rates: (US) $120 - $300
* *TAC:* 10%

DESCRIPTION: A four-star large hotel adjacent to the Casino. Very convenient to nightlife and the beaches. Especially the beach in front of the casino which is popular with gays.

MENDOZA   ✆ 061

✈ El Plumerillo AP (MDZ) 5 mi. NE

LOCATION: Western Argentina close to the Chilean border, at the foot of the Andes.

POPULATION: 700,000

DESCRIPTION: Modern city of low dwellings, thickly planted with trees and gardens. The best shopping is on Avenida Las Heras for souvenirs and handicraft. Mendoza is the the center of the wine making, fruit growing and winter sports. The population is conservative and a "gay lifestyle" is not very well tolerated here. The main cruise area is on the **Ave. San Martín**, between Las Heras & Espejo.

BARS 🍸 RESTAURANTS 🍴

● Club (GM): **Queen**, disco, Ejército de Los Andes 656, (Dorrego) Guaymallen (316-990).

● Restaurants (AW): **Bárbaro**, English spoken, San Martin 914; **Il Tucco**, Emilio Civit 556 (near park gates); **Café de la Gente**, café/bookshop, pleasant atmosphere, Rivadavia 135; **Vecchia Roma**, Italian, España 1617 (231-491).

λ SERVICES λ

● Health Club (mixed): **Sauna of Hotel Aconcagua**, calle San Lorenzo 545 (243833).

🏮 ACCOMMODATIONS 🏮

ACONACAGUA HOTEL
San Lorenzo 545, Mendoza. Tel: (61) 243833.
Fax: (61) 311085. Telex: 55321. TYPE: *Hotel.*
CLIENTELE: Mostly Straight. LOCATION: 7
blocks from downtown.

* Rooms: 160 w/priv. bath
* CTV, phone, A/C
* Restaurant, bar, sauna, pool
* Gay Bars: some nearby
* Airport: 6 mi. / 10 km
* Open: Year round
* Credit Cards: MC/VS/CB
* Rates: on request
* *TAC:* 10%

DESCRIPTION: 4 star comfortable hotel.
Sauna can be interesting. Good restaurant.

PLAZA HOTEL
Chile 1124, Mendoza. Tel: (61) 233000. Telex:
52243 PLAHO. TYPE: *Hotel.* CLIENTELE:
Mostly Straight. LOCATION: City center, facing Independence Plaza.

* Rooms: 86 w/priv. bath
* Telephone, A/C
* Restaurant, bar.
* Rates: (US) $70 - $90.
* *TAC:* 10%.

DESCRIPTION: Centrally located moderate
first class hotel.

ROSARIO   ℂ 041

LOCATION: In the province of Santa Fe, 320 km
/ 200 mi. north of Buenos Aires.

POPULATION: 1,100,000

CLIMATE: Warm from October to early
March; uncomfortably hot from December to
February.

DESCRIPTION: Main city in the province of
Santa Fe, and the third largest in the Republic.
It is a major industrial and export center. The
streets and boulevards are wider than in
Buenos Aires with beautiful parks and open
space. There is some gay nightlife of interest to
international travelers. Cruising areas: **Calle
Peatonal**, **Parque Independencia**, boardwalk along the Paraná River.

BARS ♀ RESTAURANTS ¶

● Bars/clubs (GM): **Contrato Bar**, Alvear 40

bis; **Inizio**, disco, Mitre 1880 (258-878); **Plas-
sa**, Sarmiento 1919; **Scanner**, Alvear 160;
Station G, Avda Rivadavia 2481.

⬧ ACCOMMODATIONS ⬧

HOTEL PRESIDENTE
919 Ave. Corriente. Rosario. Tel: (41) 41245.

RIVERA HOTEL
San Lorenzo 1460, Rosario. Tel: (41) 44460.

SALTA   ℂ 087

LOCATION: Northern Argentina in the
Lerma Valley, 1,600 km / 1,000 mi. from
Buenos Aires by rail or paved road.

POPULATION: 400,000

DESCRIPTION: Salta is a charming colonial
town in a mountainous setting. It is a major
tourist destination with a famous arts and
crafts center. The gay scene is very discreet due
to the conservative and religious nature of the
population. Cruising area: **Plaza 9 de Julio**,
Peatonal Alberdi, **Parque San Martín** overlooking the streets Mendoza or Santa Fe.

BARS ♀ RESTAURANTS ¶

● Bars/clubs (GM): **O'Clock**, disco, La Rioja y
Santa Fe; **Tequila Station**, pub, San Luis 650.

● Restaurants (AW): **La Quincha**, near bus
station with excellent buffet cafeteria; **9 de
Julio**, Urquiza 1020.

λ SERVICES λ

● Cinemas (G/S): **Florida**, Florida 500; **Rex**,
San Martín 1100.

⬧ ACCOMMODATIONS ⬧

SALTA HOTEL
Calle Buenos Aires 1, Salta 4400. Tel: (87) 21-
1011. Fax: (87) 31-0740. TYPE: *Hotel.* CLIEN-
TELE: Mostly Straight. LOCATION: On main
city square, 10 km / 6 mi from airport. 61 rooms
w/bath, CTV, A/C, 24 hrs room service, restaurant w/terrace, coffee shops, pool, bars. Rates:
from US$85/day. DESCRIPTION: Famous
landmark colonial style hotel.

SANTA FE   ✆

BARS ♟ RESTAURANTS 🍴

● Bar/club (GM): **Tudor Taberna**, Javier de la Rosa 320, Barrio Guadalupe.

TUCUMÁN   ✆ **081**

✈ Benjamin Matienzo, 9 km / 4 mi.

LOCATION: Northern Argentina, 19 hrs bus drive from Buenos Aires

POPULATION: 500,000

DESCRIPTION: Capital of the Tucumán province it is also the busiest and largest city in the North. The city was founded by

Spaniards coming from Peru in the 16th century. The gay scene is growing in spite of the generally conservative and sometimes intolerant attitude of the population. Cruising areas: **Calle 25 de Mayo** (Street numbers 300 - 1,000); **Parque 9 de Julio** (at Ave. de los Próceres at night, many TVs); **Plaza Independencia**.

BARS ♟ RESTAURANTS 🍴

● Bar/club (GM): **Enigma Para Vos**, Monteagudo

● Coffee Shops (AW): **Café del Paseo**, 25 de Mayo & Santiago; **Café 25**, 25 de Mayo & Mendoza.

 ACCOMMODATIONS

GRAND HOTEL del TUCUMAN
Av. Soldati 380, Tucuman. Tel: (81) 24-5000. Fax: (81) 22-2596. TYPE: *Hotel*. LOCATION: Opposite Centenario Park. 100 rooms, A/C, restaurant, disco, swimming pool. Rates: on request.

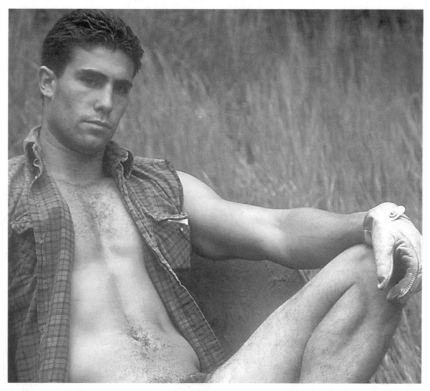

ARUBA

AREA: 70 sq. mi. (180 sq. km)
POPULATION: 66,800
CAPITAL: Oranjestad
CURRENCY: Aruba Guilder (Afl)
OFFICIAL LANGUAGE: Dutch, Papiamento
MAJOR RELIGION: Roman Catholic
Telephone: 297
Official Time: GMT - 5
Nat'l Holiday: Queen's Birthday, April 30
Electricity: 110 volts, 60 cycles
Exchange Rate: 1US$ = Afl 1.79
National Airline: Aruba Air

LAW REGARDING HOMOSEXUALITY:
The legal status of homosexuality is presumed to be similar to that in the Dutch Antilles. Legal between consenting adults, 16 years and older. However, the general attitude of the population is conservative, and discretion is suggested.

ORANJESTAD   © 297

✈ Queen Beatrix Airport (AUA) 10 min. east

LOCATION: Northwestern Aruba, the smallest and westernmost of the Dutch Antilles islands, 15 mi. / 24 km off the Venezuelan coast.

POPULATION: 66,000 (island pop.)

CLIMATE: Year round sunny dry climate with temperatures between 75˚F (24˚c) and 85˚F (29˚c).

VISITOR INFORMATION
Aruba Tourist Bureau
1270 Ave. of the Americas #2212
New York, NY 10020
Tel: (212) 246-3030 / (800) TO ARUBA

DESCRIPTION: The island's capital and one of the busiest towns in the Caribbean. Explore the picturesque Dutch architecture, and duty free shopping. For best buys try the **Aruba Trading Co.** on Main St., Nassaustraat.

The island is famous for its great beaches, notably **Palm Beach** a five-mile stretch of white sand beach where most of the tourist hotels are located. Nightlife centers around the lavish casinos, five are on **Palm Beach**. **The Alhambra Casino & Bazaar**, is an unusual entertainment complex with shops, restaurants, and night spots near the Divi-Divi and the Manchebo Hotels.

❖ Gay Beach: **Eagle Beach**, between La Quinta Resort and Dutch Village Hotel, best between 16 hrs. and sunset; **Malmok**, afternoon by the beach.

BARS ⅄ RESTAURANTS ‖

● Bars (G/S): **Club Visage**, L.G. Smith Blvd. 152; **Manchebo Beach Hotel Bar**, mixed bar, popular during "happy hour"; **Scaramouche**, night club, L.G. Smith Blvd.; **Splash**, night club, L.G. Smith Blvd.

● Restaurants (AW): **Arubian Cuisine**, Holland Aruba Mall (38695); **La Dolce Vita**, Italian restaurant, Nassaustraat (25675); **Bali Restaurant**, exotic restaurant on the pier, off lloyd Smith Blvd. (22131); **The Mill**, seafood, steaks, authentic Dutch Windmill (26300).

 ACCOMMODATIONS

AMERICANA ARUBA
Oranjestad, Aruba. Tel: (297-8) 24500. Fax: (297-8) 23191. TYPE: *Resort Hotel & Casino*. CLIENTELE: Mostly Straight. LOCATION: Beachfront on Palm Beach. 419 rooms w/priv. bath, CTV, oceanview, pool, restaurants, bars, nightclub, casino. Rates: (US) $275-$325. *TAC*: 10%. Superior first class hotel & casino resort.

MANCHEBO BEACH HOTEL
L.G. Smith 55, P.O. Box 564, Oranjestad. Tel: 23444. Fax: 32446. TYPE: *Oceanfront Hotel*. CLIENTELE: Mostly Straight. LOCATION: Manchebo Beach. 71 rooms, bar (interesting during Happy Hour), pool. Rates: (US) $85-$190. *TAC:* 10%. DESCRIPTION: Best Western resort.

AUSTRALIA

AREA: 2,966,136 sq. mi. (7,682,300 sq. km)
POPULATION: 18,173,600
CAPITAL: Canberra
CURRENCY: Australian Dollar (A$)
OFFICIAL LANGUAGE: English
MAJOR RELIGIONS: Protestantism, Roman Catholicism
Telephone: 61
Nat'l Holiday: Australia Day, January 26
Official Time: G.M.T. + 8 to 10 hrs.
Electricity: 220-240 volts
Exchange Rate: 1US$ = A$1.26
Main Airlines: Qantas, Ansett

LAW REGARDING HOMOSEXUALITY:
Laws vary according to the states. Please note the following ages of consent for gay sex: 16 years: in Victoria, South Australia, The Australian Capital Territory (and therefore the Australian Antarctic Territory), and Queensland (anal intercourse has an age of consent of 18 in Queensland). 18 years in South Wales and the Northern Territory. 21 Years in Western Australia. Illegal in Tasmania, although this is currently under review by the Upper House of the Tasmanian Parliament, a bill to decriminalize homosexual 'acts' having been passed by the Lower House.

A.C.T.
AUSTRALIAN CAPITAL TERRITORY

◆ **Population**: 331,800
◆ **Capital**: Canberra
◆ **Time Zone**: Eastern
◆ **No Sodomy Law**
◆ **Legal Drinking Age**: 18+

CANBERRA   ✆ **02**

✈   Canberra Airport (CBR) 3.5 mi. / 6 km E.

LOCATION: Situated between Sydney and Melbourne on the Australian Capital Territory (ACT) on the artificial Lake Burley Griffin.

POPULATION: 175,000

CLIMATE: Dry, cool with July and August the coldest months. Mid to high 20"sc in the summer (mid to high 70"sF), and daily lows close to freezing in the winter between May and October. Rainfall is around 50 mm a month (about 2").

Gay/Lesbian Visitor Information
Gayline: 6247-2726
Lesbian Line: 6247-8882

DESCRIPTION: Canberra, like Washington DC, is a planned city diplomatically situated between Sydney and Melbourne. Canberra, unlike major Australian cities, is orderly and neat with important monuments and government buildings. The city is neatly divided into two parts by an artificially constructed lake - **Lake Burley Griffin**. Canberra is not particularly a gay destination, but it is an important city to visit, enjoy, and absorb the unique culture of the Australian nation.

BARS ♟ RESTAURANTS 🍴

● Bars/clubs (GM): **Falcon X Video Lounge**, cruise bar, 83 Woollongong St. Fishwyk; **Firehouse Nightclub** (G/S), Garema Pl., Canberra City (6257-3631);

● Bars/clubs (GMW): **Heaven**, dance club, Grema Place Civic Center (6257-6180); **Meridian Club**, bar/disco (GMW), 34 Mort St., Braddon (6248-9966); **Tilly's**, bar & restaurant, 13 Wattle St., Lyneham (6249-1543).

● Restaurants (AW): **Burley Griffin Room**, French, panoramic views atop the Lakeside International Hotel (6247-6244); **Burps BYO**, Modern Australian, inexpensive, gay friendly, 9 Lonsdale St., Braddon (6247-8300); **Cafe Pronto**, Italian, inexpensive, gay friendly, 14 Lonsdale St. Braddon (6247-0730); **Peaches**, at Balmey Crescent in Campbell (6249-7333), an award winning restaurant, one of the best in town; **Tilly's**, cafe & bar popular with lesbians, Wattle St. 1 (6249-1543).

🏠 ACCOMMODATIONS 🏠

CANBERRA FOREST
74 Northbourne Ave., P.O. Box 832, Canberra ACT 2601. Tel: (02) 6295-3433. Fax: (02) 95-2119. TYPE: *Motel*. CLIENTELE: Mostly

Straight. LOCATION: Overlooking parklands, New Parliament House. 77 rooms. DESCRIPTION: Motor Inn. Rooms in modern decor near the National Gallery.

LAKESIDE HOTEL
London Circuit, Canberra ACT 2601. Tel: (02) 6247-6244. Fax: (02) 6257-3071. TYPE: *Deluxe Hotel*. CLIENTELE: Mostly Straight. LOCATION: On Lake Burley Griffin near city center. 205 rooms, CTV, phone, A/C, minibar, restaurants, pub, bar, discominibar. DESCRIPTION: Stylish 15 story hotel in a convenient location.

SUBURBAN
89 Wattle St., O'Connor ACT 2601. Tel: (02) 6257-4032. TYPE: *Guest House*. HOST: Tony Sheran. CLIENTELE: Gay men & women only. LOCATION: Central opposite Tilley's Café. Rates: A$40-$75.

N.S.W.
NEW SOUTH WALES

- **Population**: 6,155,000
- **Capital**: Sydney
- **Time Zone**: Eastern

- ◆ **No Sodomy Law**
- ◆ **Legal Drinking Age**: 18+

BERRY **02**

✈ Kingsford-Smith Int'l Airport (SYD)

LOCATION: 125 km / 100 mi. south from Sydney.

 **ACCOMMODATIONS**

TARA
R.M.B. 219 Wattanolla Rd., Berry, NSW. Tel: (02) 4464-1472. Fax: (02) 4464-2265. TYPE: *Guest House*. HOST: Rod Stringer. CLIENTELE: All Welcome. LOCATION: Kangaroo Valley, 2 hrs. south of Sydney. 4 rooms, pool, gym, jacuzzi. Rates: A$70-A$120.

SYDNEY **02**

✈ Kingsford-Smith Int'l Airport (SYD)
6.2 mi. / 10 km S.

LOCATION: Southeastern Australia along the shores of the Pacific Ocean and the Tasman Sea.

POPULATION: 3,400,000

CLIMATE: Temperate and cool year round with average temperature for July in the winter of 54°F (12°c), and average temperature for January in the summer of 70°F (21°c).

Gay/Lesbian Visitor Information
Gay & Lesbian Line: 9360-2211
Gay What's On: 9699-6320

DESCRIPTION: Sydney is a sparkling city with a magnificent harbor and a major international airport for traveling to and from Australia. The unique architectural structure of the Opera House, with its white sharply curving roof, shaped like sails can be compared as a striking monument to the Eiffel Tower or the Statue of Liberty. It is a symbol of the city's rich cultural life. **Sydney Tower** is the tallest structure in Australia rising to an impressing 1,073 ft. (325 m) and offers a magnificent view of the city.

❖ **SPECIAL EVENT: Sydney Gay & Lesbian Mardi Gras** is Sydney's main gay event. It is also the largest gay and lesbian gathering in the world. The annual two week long February celebration includes costumed parades, parties, festivals and lots of fun.

BARS ☥ RESTAURANTS 🍴

Sydney is famous for the great nightlife and wild dance parties. Most of the gay nightlife is concentrated on or around Oxford Street - 'The Golden Mile'.

● Bars/clubs (GM): **Albury Hotel**, restaurant, bar, live entertainment, the largest and most popular in Sydney, 6 Oxford St. (9361-6555); **Beauchamp Hotel**, elegant older style pub, leather/denim mixed crowd in the Base Bar, 267 Oxford St. Darlinghurst (9331-2575); **DCM**, dance club, 33 Oxford St. (9267-7036); **Exchange Hotel**, pub with music and shows, young crowd, 34 Oxford St., Darlinghurst (9331-1936); **Flinders Hotel**, large bar, live entertainment, 63 Flinders St., Darlinghurst (9360-4929); **Midnight Shift**, men only disco, 85 Oxford Street, Darlinghurst (9360-4319); **Oxford Hotel Bar**, pub with a raunchy disco atmosphere, 134 Oxford St. in Taylor Sq. (9331-3467); **Phoenix**, stylish late night bar, Norman St., Darlinghurst, behind the Exchange Hotel (9331-1936); **Stronghold**, over 30's leather bar, 277 Goulburn St., Darlinghurst (9332-2676).

● Bars/clubs (GMW): **Beresford Hotel**, 354 Bourke St., Surry Hills (9331-1045); **Club 77**, 77 William St. East Sydney; **Gilligan's**, cocktail bar, upstairs at the Oxford Hotel; **Newtown Hotel**, 174 King St., Newtown (951-1329).

● Bar/club (GW): **Bank Hotel**, 324 King St. Newtown (9557-1280); **Lava Bar**, Wed. to Sat., Burdekin Hotel, 2 Oxford St., Darlinghurst (9331-3066); **Leichardt Hotel**, cnr Short St. and Balmain Rd., Leichardt (9569-1217); **Oblivion**, at Black Market Regent St., Chippendale; **Sirens**, 12-14 Enmore Rd, Newtown (9519-5877).

● Restaurants: **The Albury Hotel** upstairs, 6 Oxford St. (9331-7430); **L'Au Bergade**, French, 353 Cleveland St., Surry Hills (9319-5929); **Badde Manors**, Glebe Point Rd. (9660-3797); **Bon Cafard**, French cuisine, cnr Liverpool St. & Darlinghurst Rd. (9357-5318); **Cafe Elan**, exotic Vegetarian, 379 Crown St. Surry Hills (9332-3858); **Green Park Diner**, 219 Oxford St. (9357-5391); **JJ's Home Cooking**, mostly lesbian clientele, 357 King St., Newton (9519-7930); **Prasit's Northside on Crown**, Sydney's most famous Thai chef, 413 Crown St., Surry Hills (9319-0748); **70 Please in My Kitchen**, popular with lesbians, 275 Australia St., Newtown (9565-1102); **RamBaa**, 175 Oxford St., Darlinghurst (9360-1963); **Razors Edge**, modern Australian Vegetarian, 129 Enmore Rd., Enmore (9557-5867); **Stronghold**, leather bar and restaurant, 277 Goulburn St., Darlinghurst, Sunday roasts are popular (9332-2627); **Thai Pothong**, 294 King St. Newtown (550-6277).

λ SERVICES λ

● Erotica (GM): **House of Fetish**, specializes in S&M gear, 373 Bourke St., Taylor Square, Darlinghurst; **Numbers**, 95 Oxford St. (upstairs) (9331-6099); **The Toolshed**, (3 locations) Taylor Square; 1st fl.corner of Riley St.,& Oxford St., Darlinghurst (9332-2792); 196 King St., Newtown (9565-1599) (Party tickets for Mardi Gras and Sleaze are issued through the Toolshed by Mardi Gras Pty Ltd.).

● Clothing (GMW): **Ahead in Wigs**, 125 Oxford St., Darlinghurst (9360-1230); **Aussie Boys**, 102 Oxford St., Darlinghurst (9360-7011); **Mephisto Leather**, made to measure leather, 1st fl., 112 Oxford St., Darlinghurst (9332-3218); **S(A)X Leather**, 110A Oxford St., Darlinghurst (9331-6105); **Twisted Sister**, 132a Oxford St., Darlinghurst (9331-5454).

● Gyms (GM): **Fitness Exchange**, at the Sydney Gay & Lesbian Pride center, 26 Hutchinson St., Surry Hills (9331-1333); **Fitness Net-**

work, 256 Riley St., Surry Hills (9211-2799);
City Gym, 107 Crown St., East Sydney (9357-6247); **Newtown Gym**, 294 King St., Newtown (9519-6969).

● Health Clubs (GM): **Bodyline**, 58a Flinders St., Darlinghurst (9360-1006); **King Steam**, 38-42 Oxford St., Darlinghurst (9360-3431); **KKK Sauna**, 83 Anzac Parade (9662-1359).

● Sex Clubs (GM): **The Den**, 1st. fl., 97 Oxford St., Darlinghurst (9332-3402); **Signal**, 2nd fl., corner of Riley St., and Oxford St., Darlinghurst (9331-8830).

● Travel (GMW): ✪ **Jornada**, Australia's largest and most innovative outbound tour operator. Specialists in tailoring individual and group packages to Australia, South Pacific and Asia. Commission payable to agents, level 1, 6 Manning Rd., Double Bay NSW 2028. Tel: (02) 9862-0909, Toll Free (800) 672-120. Fax: (02) 9362-0788. Email: gdholmes@jornada.com.au

  ACCOMMODATIONS

✪ BRICKFIELD HILL

403 Riley St., Surry Hills, Sydney, NSW 2010. Tel/Fax: (02) 9211-4886. TYPE: *Bed & Breakfast Inn*. HOST: Ivano Buoro. CLIENTELE: Mostly gay men & women. LOCATION: East of central railway station, south of intersection of Riley and Foveaux Sts.

* Rooms: 4 (double or single)
  1 w/priv. bath, 3 w/shared bath
* Rooms for non smokers
* CTV, hairdryer, maid service
* Bed Types: double, queen size
* Beach: 15 min. drive to various beaches
* Gay Bars: 3 blocks / 10 min. walk
* Health Club: 2 blocks (Fitness Network)
* Airport: 15 min. taxi, city shuttle bus
* Languages: English, Italian, Japanese, German, French
* Reservations: 1 night deposit
* Cancellation: one week
* Credit Cards: MC/VISA
* Open: Year round
* Rates: US$90-$120 w/CB (extended)

DESCRIPTION: Gay owned and operated. Close to transport, gay districts, restaurants, and sights. A quality breakfast and friendly unobtrusive service. Completely non smoking. Maximum eight guests. *IGTA*

SIMPSONS of POTTS POINT

8 Challis Ave., Potts Point, NSW 2011. Tel: (02) 9356-2199. TYPE: *Hotel*. CLIENTELE: All Wel-

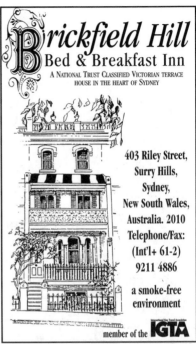

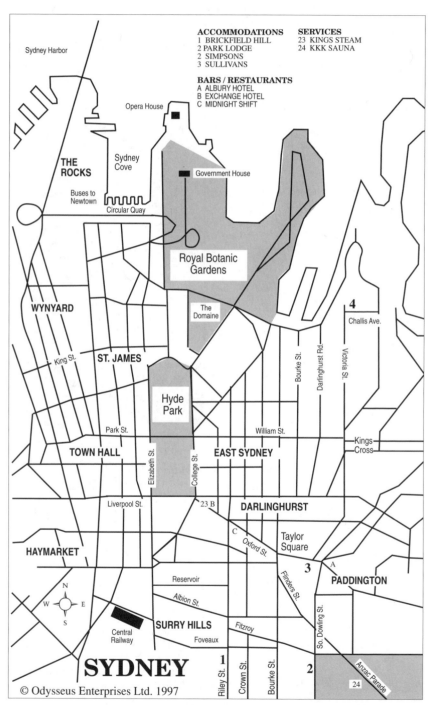

Sydney Harbor

ACCOMMODATIONS
1 BRICKFIELD HILL
2 PARK LODGE
2 SIMPSONS
3 SULLIVANS

SERVICES
23 KINGS STEAM
24 KKK SAUNA

BARS / RESTAURANTS
A ALBURY HOTEL
B EXCHANGE HOTEL
C MIDNIGHT SHIFT

Opera House

THE ROCKS

Sydney Cove

Government House

Buses to Newtown

Circular Quay

Royal Botanic Gardens

WYNYARD

The Domaine

4

Challis Ave.

King St.

ST. JAMES

Bourke St.

Darlinghurst Rd.

Victoria St.

Hyde Park

Park St.

William St.

Kings Cross

TOWN HALL

Elizabeth St.

College St.

EAST SYDNEY

Liverpool St.

23 B

DARLINGHURST

HAYMARKET

C

Oxford St.

Taylor Square

3

A

PADDINGTON

Reservoir

Flinders St.

Albion St.

N
W   E
S

Central Railway

SURRY HILLS

Fitzroy

Foveaux

So. Dowling St.

SYDNEY

1

Riley St.

Crown St.

Bourke St.

2

Anzac Parade

24

© Odysseus Enterprises Ltd. 1997

come. LOCATION: Cosmopolitan Kings Cross area off Victoria Street, 5 min. taxi ride from the heart of Sydney. 14 rooms and suites w/ priv. bath, phone, A/C. Rates: (US) $140-$250. DESCRIPTION: Elegant small hotel with superb decorative detail. Accommodations are in standard or queen size rooms. Cloud Suite has a private spa.

✪ PARK LODGE HOTEL

747 South Dowling St., Moore Park, Sydney NSW 2016. Tel: (02) 9318-2393. Fax: (02) 9318-2513. TYPE: *Hotel.* HOST: Rowen Legge Mgr. CLIENTELE: Gay/Straight. LOCATION: Corner of South Dowling & Thurlow Sts near Cleveland St.

* Rooms: 2 w/shared, 17 w/priv. bath dbl 11 / triple 4/ quad 4
* Smoking allowed in rooms
* CTV, phone, refrigerator, safe box, C/H, A/C, hair dryer
* Bed Types: single, twin, double, king, queen
* Service: maid, room, laundry
* Wheelchair access, courtyard, no pets
* Beach: 15 min. drive (gay/straight)
* Health Club: 1 km (gay/straight)
* Airport: 10 min., taxi
* Train Station: Central Station 5 min. taxi
* Reservations: 1 night deposit
* Cancellation Policy: forfeit deposit if cancelled within 7 days
* Credit Cards: MC/VISA/AMEX/DC
* Open: Year round
* Rates: A$60-A$180
* Check in 2:00 pm / Check out 10 am
* *TAC:* 10%
* Email: pklodge@geko.net.au

DESCRIPTION: Charming 3-star hotel restored to its original elegance. Close to all gay attractions. Well appointed rooms with all amenities. Friendly service. *IGTA, AGLTA*

SIMPSONS of POTTS POINT

8 Challis Ave., Potts Point, NSW 2011. Tel: (02) 9356-2199. TYPE: *Hotel.* CLIENTELE: All Welcome. LOCATION: Cosmopolitan Kings Cross area off Victoria Street, 5 min. taxi ride from the heart of Sydney. 14 rooms and suites w/priv. bath, phone, A/C. Rates: (US) $140-$250. DESCRIPTION: Elegant small hotel with superb decorative detail. Accommodations are in standard or queen size rooms. Cloud Suite has a private spa.

SULLIVANS

21 Oxford St., Paddington NSW 2021. Tel: (02) 9361-0211. TYPE: *Hotel.* CLIENTELE: All Welcome. LOCATION: Heart of Paddington. 66 rooms w/priv. shower, CTV, phone, A/C, tea/coffee making, small refrigerator, pool, parking, room service, maid service, laundry, gay bars

nearby, beach: 6 km / 4 mi (mixed), airport: 11 km / 7 mi. Open: Year round. Rates: $110-$130. *TAC:* 10%. DESCRIPTION: 3-star hotel in a central location. Comfortable rooms, and a delightful garden courtyard. Free guest bicycles.

N.T. (NORTHERN TERRITORY)

---

* **Population:** 176,700
* **Capital:** Darwin
* **Time Zone:** Central
* **No Sodomy Law**
* **Age of Consent for gay sex:** 18
* **Legal Drinking Age:** 18+

DARWIN   © 08

✈ Darwin AP (DRW) 11 mi. / 18 km NE.

LOCATION: Northern Australia along the shores of the Timor Sea.

POPULATION: 79,000

CLIMATE: Hot and dry (winter) or hot and wet (summer). Winter temperatures drop to high 20°sc (high 70°sF), summer temperature is in the 40°sc (104°F). Generally the summers are hot and sticky.

Gay/Lesbian Visitor Information
Darwin Gay Society: 8981-6812

DESCRIPTION: Darwin is a multi-racial town with a heavy drinking, frontier reputation; but, it is also one of the most cosmopolitan and easy-going places in Australia.

♣ Entertainment: Darwin has an elegant world-class casino **Diamond Beach Hotel & Casino**, Gilruth Ave., Mindil Beach 3 km (2 mi.) from Darwin city center. It features elegant accommodations, superb dining and entertainment.

❖ Beaches: **Casuarina Free Beach**-the North end is for nude sunbathing.

BARS Ⴤ RESTAURANTS ¶¶

● Bars/clubs: **Men's Club** (GM), 2 Harriet Pl., (8981-8496); **1990's Nightclub**, 3 Edmunds St. (8981-9761).

● Restaurants (G/S): **Mississippi Queen**,

Creole/Cajun food, 4 Gardiner (8981-3358); **Genghis Khan**, at the Capricornia Motel, 44 East Point Rd. (8981-3883).

 ACCOMMODATIONS

CAPRICORNIA MOTEL
44 East Point Rd., Darwin NT 0801. Tel: (08) 8981-4055. TYPE: *Motel*. CLIENTELE: Gay/Straight. Restaurant, pool. Rates: from (A) $65. Gay managed motel.

TOP END FRONTIER MOTEL
4 Daly Street, Darwin NT 0800. Tel: (08) 8981 6511. Fax: (08) 8941-1253. TYPE: *Motel*. CLIENTELE: Mostly Straight. LOCATION: Corner of Daly/Esplanade in downtown. 47 rooms, CTV, phone, A/C. DESCRIPTION: First class hotel with many bars. A place to mingle with locals.

QLD (QUEENSLAND)

◆ **Population:** 3,316,500
◆ **Capital:** Brisbane
◆ **Time Zone:** Eastern
◆ **No Sodomy Law**
◆ **Legal Drinking Age:** 18+

BRISBANE   © 07

✈ Brisbane Int'l Airport (BNE)
7 mi. / 11 km NE.

LOCATION: The southern East Coast of Queensland on the South Pacific Ocean. The famous Sunshine and Gold coasts are a convenient distance from the city.

POPULATION: 1,489,100.

CLIMATE: Subtropical, mild and warm year round. The coast is warm to hot year round. Winter's are dry and mild with an average temperature of 69°F (20°c); Summers are warm and humid with tropical storms and an average temperature for January of 82°F (28°c).

Gay/Lesbian Visitor Information
Acceptance: 3268-4335

DESCRIPTION: Brisbane's history began when in 1824 the peaceful Brisbane area was selected as the site for a convict settlement for the 'worst class of offenders'. During the days of penal settlement, no free man was allowed within 80 km / 50 mi. of Brisbane. Today, Brisbane is a wonderland for leisure, sun and surf; a getaway to exciting beach resorts such as the Gold Coast, Surfers Paradise, and the Sunshine Coast.

❖ Beaches: Brisbane is mainly a short stopover on the way to the famous beach resorts. To enjoy the beautiful Gold Coast beaches you need to travel 39 miles / 65 km south of Brisbane for fine sandy beaches, seafood restaurants and many attractions.

❖ SPECIAL EVENTS: **Sleazeball**, gay festival in April; **Gay Pride**, one week of celebration around **Stonewall Day** in June; **International Lesbian Day** a one week celebration in October; **Gay & Lesbian Film Festival**, dates vary.

BARS ♼ RESTAURANTS ♨

● Bars/clubs (GM): **Beat**, nightclub 677 Ann St., Fortitude Valley (3252-2543); **Boy World**, 210 Brunswick St. (3252-5690); **Signal**, male to male contact club, open 7 days, 185 Brunswick St., Fortitude Valley (3854-1981); **Terminus**, disco/restaurant, 249 Brunswick St., Fortitude Valley (3252-4920).

● Bars/clubs (GMW): **Hotel Wickham**, 308 Wickham St., Fortitude Valley (3852-1301); **Options**, 18 little Edward St., Spring Hill (3831-4214); **Sportsman Hotel**, 130 Leichhardt St., Spring Hill (3831-2892).

● Bar/club (GW): **Girl World**, Alfred St., Fortitude Valley; **Ruby's**, Waterloo Hotel, Ann St., Fortitude Valley; **The Patch**, Courtyard of the Spring Hill Hotel, cnr Lt. Edward St.

● Restaurant (GMW): **Cafe Babylon**, 142 Boundary St. West End (3846-4505); **Cafe Eiffel**, 346 Brunswick St., (Fortitude Valley (3252-2449); **Carmichael's**, at the Wickham Hotel, 308 Wickham St., Fortitude Valley (3852-1301); **Latin Lovers**, restaurant & bar, 938 Brunswick St., New Farm (3358-1464); **Loaves & Fishes**, seafood, 200 Logan Rd., Buranda (3391-5288); **Paparazzi**, Italian, 697 Ann St. Fortitude Valley (3252-5579).

λ SERVICES λ

● Health Club (GM): **Bodyline**, sauna, gym, massage, movies, rooms, 43 Ipswich Rd., Woolloongabba (3391-4285).

ACCOMMODATIONS

THE ABBEY
160 Roma Rd., Brisbane, QLD 4000. Tel: (07) 3236-1444. Fax: (07) 3236-1134. TYPE: *All Suite Hotel*. CLIENTELE: All Welcome. LOCATION: Downtown opposite Train Station, 6 minutes walk from City Center. 87 suites, restaurant, bar, cafe, pool, spa, sauna, gym. DESCRIPTION: Self-contained suites with excellent service and recreational amenities.

THE ASTOR
35 Astor Terrace, Spring Hill, Brisbane, QLD 4000. Tel: (07) 3839-9022. Fax: (07) 3229-5553. TYPE: *Apartment Hotel*. CLIENTELE: All Welcome. LOCATION: Near Central Train Station. Walking to Gay Nightlife. 35 (1-2 bedroom) apartments, living/dining area, priv. bath, balcony, pool, sauna, table tennis.

GAZEBO HOTEL
345 Wickham Terrace, Brisbane QLD 4000. Tel: (07) 3831-6177. TYPE: *Hotel*. CLIENTELE: Mostly Straight. LOCATION: Downtown near Albert Park, close to the gay nightlife scene. 179 rooms, CTV,phone, A/C, minibar. DESCRIPTION: Mediterranean style.

CAIRNS   © 07

✈ Cairns AP (CNS) 3 mi. / 5 km NW

LOCATION: 5 hrs. drive north of Townsville on the North Queensland Coast; 2 1/2 hour flight from Sydney, 2 hrs from Brisbane on Queensland Coast.

POPULATION: 120,000

CLIMATE: Hot tropical year round. Temperatures average a minimum of 80°F (26°c) and a maximum of 98°F (34°c) from October to May and a minimum of 60°F (15°c) and a maximum of 86°F (28°c) between May & October.

DESCRIPTION: Cairns is the major city of Far North Queensland and a Cosmopolitan center whose architecture is a comfortable blend of old and new. The **Great Barrier Reef** is a major attraction often called the eighth wonder of the world. It supports 400 kinds of coral and 1,500 species of exotic fish in an array of colors. The **Daintree Rainforest and National Park** is located north of Cairns. The **Skyrail** is the world's first rainforest cableway, a 7.5 km / 5 mi. journey to Kuranda enabling visitors to experience the World Heritage Listed Rainforest from an unforgettable perspective.

♣ The **Reef Casino** and Cairns Convention Center provide world class entertainment.

❖ Gay Beach: **Buchans Beach**, gay, mixed, clothing optional, 20 min. north of Cairns.

❖ **HOW TO GET THERE**: Qantas and Ansett flies to Cairns from all cities in Australia; Cairns has an International Airport with flights worldwide. Air-conditioned Buses connect Cairns to Townsville (5 hrs.) and Brisbane (28 hrs.). Efficient rail system runs up the entire east coast of Australia with good standard of service available.

BARS ￥ RESTAURANTS ¶¶

● Bar/Lounge (GMW): **Plantations** indoor and poolside at the "18-24 James" resort (4055-3140); **Rusty's**, at the Commercial Hotel, Sheridan & Spence Sts.

● Restaurants (AW): **Plantations** Int'l cuisine special diets on request at "18-24 James Resort" (4055-3140); **T.K's** coffee shop, 44 Spence St.; **Simply Italian**, 65 Anderson St.; or choose from a wide selection of International restaurants.

ACCOMMODATIONS

"18-24 JAMES"
P.O. Box 7544, Cairns QLD 4870. Tel: (07) 4055-3140. Fax: (07) 4055-3140. TYPE: *Hotel*. CLIENTELE: Gay men & women. LOCATION: 20 min. walk from city center.

* Rooms: 26 w/priv. bath
* Rooms for non smokers
* CTV, VCR, phone, refrigerator, A/C, ceiling fans
* Pool, sundeck, gym, sauna, jacuzzi
* Bar, restaurant, free parking
* Clothing optional policy
* Beach: 25 km / 16 mi (gay/mixed/nude)
* Gay Bars: 2 km / 1.5 mi.
* Health Club: 1 km / 1/2 mi., mixed
* Airport: Cairns Airport 4 km / 3 mi., taxi, or free airport transfers
* Languages: English, Dutch, German, French
* Reservation: 1 night deposit
* Cancellation policy: 7 days full deposit refund; 48 hrs less 10%
* Credit Cards: MC/VISA/AMEX/DC/DISC BANK CARD
* Season: Year round
* Rates: from A$55 w/TbB
* Check In 14:00 / Check out 11:00

DESCRIPTION: Plantation-style complex on 2 floors, surrounding central pool / jacuzzi. Outdoor bar and restaurant area landscaped with Tropical Rain Forest and Palm trees. Rental cars and tour bookings. *AGLTA*

BE BEE'S
P.O. Box 120, Edgehill, Cairns, QLD 4870, Tel: (07) 4032-1677. TYPE: *Resort*. CLIENTELE: Gay Men Only. LOCATION: Mayers St. between Collins Ave. and Greenslopes St. 20 rooms, CTV, pool, clothing optional policy. DESCRIPTION: Units vary from budget rooms to 1 & 2 bedroom apts some with outdoor living areas looking onto the pool.

TURTLE COVE
P.O. Box 158, Smithfield, Cairns QLD 4878. Tel: (07) 4059-1800. TYPE: *Resort*. CLIENTELE: Gay men & women only. LOCATION: On private beach 30 min. north of Cairns.

* Rooms: 26 rooms, 12 suites
* CTV, phone, ceiling fans, refrigerator, tea/coffee making facilities
* Restaurant, pool, sauna
* Clothing optional policy
* Bed Types: single, double, queen
* Beach: 25 km / 16 mi (gay/mixed/nude)
* Gay Bars: 2 km / 1.5 mi.
* Health Club: 1 km / 1/2 mi., mixed
* Airport: Cairns Airport 4 km / 3 mi.
* Open: Year round
* High Season: 6/15-11/30 + 2/15-3/14
* Rates: $95-$180 w/CB
* Check in 2:30 pm / Check out 11 am

DESCRIPTION: Gay resort complex. Private nude gay beach. Accommodations vary from small standard garden units to large ocena view and beachfront units. Rooms are serviced daily. Rates include tropical and continental breakfast.

NOOSA ℂ 07

✈ Brisbane Int'l Airport (BNE)
1-1/2 hrs. south

LOCATION: At the northern end of the Sunshine Coast. Noosa is a combinations of separate centers. Noosa Heads is on the headland, Noosaville a short distance away up the Noosa River.

DESCRIPTION: Popular beach resort, lots of atmosphere, fine views and great beaches. The headland at Noosa is a National Park, and a popular though unofficial nude-bathing beach with many gay followers.

🏳️ ACCOMMODATIONS 🏳️

NOOSA COVE
82 Upper Hastings St., Noosa, QLD 4567. Tel: (07) 5449-2668. TYPE: *Rental Apts*. CLIENTELE: Gay men & women. HOST: Alan Williams. LOCATION: Walk to Noosa Beach. 4 rooms, 3 apts. Fully furnished holiday apts.

OCEAN BREEZE RESORT
Hastings St., Noosa QLD 4567. Tel: (07) 5447-4977. USA/Canada reservation/information Tel: (516) 944-5330 or (800) 257-5344. Fax: (516) 944-7540. TYPE: *Apartment Hotel Complex*. CLIENTELE: All Welcome. LOCATION: Hear of Noose opposite beach. 64 apartments. DESCRIPTION: Attractive resort complex. 1,2, & 3 bedroom apartments are available.

STARDUST
P.O. Box 656, Noosa Heads, QLD 4567. Tel: (07) 5447-4647. TYPE: *Motel*. CLIENTELE: Gay Welcome. LOCATION: 2 km / 1 mi. to gay nude beach. 6 apts, secluded salt pool, sun deck, gym, clothing optional. Rates: $70-$100.

SURFERS PARADISE ℂ 074

✈ Coolangatta Airport (OOL)

DESCRIPTION: The Gold Coast is a continuous strip of hotels, motels and resorts along the Gold Coast highway. **Surfers Paradise** is the centre of the Gold Coast, a jungle of highrise hotels and a skycraper conglomeration that cater to mass market tourism.

♈ BARS ♈

● Bars/Clubs (G/S): **Beat**, 3030 Gold Coast Hwy; **Jupiter's Casino**, bars and lounges of a popular Casino Hotel on Broadbeach Island; **The Tunnel**, popular with gays, Orcham Avenue.

λ SERVICE λ

● Health Club (GM): **Bodyline Gold Coast**, 42 Bundall Rd., Bundall (5492-5944).

🏳️ ACCOMMODATIONS 🏳️

CENTRAL SURFERS
P.O. Box 7260, Gold Coast Mail Center 4217. Tel: (5492-2223). TYPE: *Guest House*. CLIENTELE: Gay men. LOCATION: 2 min. from downtown. 8 rooms, 6 villas. Rates: on request.

S.A. (SOUTH AUSTRALIA)

- ◆ **Population:** 1,475,900
- ◆ **Capital:** Adelaide
- ◆ **Time Zone:** Central
- ◆ **No Sodomy Law**
- ◆ **Legal Drinking Age:** 18+

ADELAIDE   ✆ 08

✈ Adelaide Airport (ADL) 5 mi. / 8 km W.

LOCATION: Southern Australia along the shores of the Indian Ocean and the Gulf St. Vincent. 450 miles / 720 km northwest of Melbourne, Victoria.

POPULATION: 1,081,000

CLIMATE: Winters are temperate with July average of 50°F - 68°F (10°c-20°c). Summers are mild and pleasant with January average of 72°F (21°c).

Gay/Lesbian Visitor Information
Gayline: 8362-3223
Lesbian Line: 8051-9995

DESCRIPTION: The Capital city of South Australia, is known as the "Festival City". It was carefully planned with European style boulevards, green parks, and recreational spaces.

♣ Entertainment: **Adelaide Casino**, North Terrace Blvd., Adelaide (212-2811), one of the most stylish in the Southern Hemisphere offers two gaming levels, bars and elegant restaurants.

❖ Beaches: There are many sandy beaches around Adelaide with excellent swimming and boating facilities. Check **Broadway Beach** in the heart of town and **Estcourt Beach** near West Beach.

❖ Gay Beach: **Maslins**, first legalized gay beach in Australia. Follow the main south road out of Adelaide, past Morphet Vale, over the Onkaparinga River to the Maslin's Beach turn-off, then follow the signs.

❖ **SPECIAL EVENTS**: **Stonewall Celebrations** in June; **Sleazeball**, gay festival in August; **Adelaide Spring Open**, GLTA tennis tournament, September 22-24 (8351-7481); **Festival of**

Life, gay & lesbian festival, late November.

BARS ℐ RESTAURANTS 🍴

● Bars/Clubs (GMW): **Beans Bar**, 258 Hindley St. (8231-9639); Bartoons, Fenn Place, off Hindley St. (8231-9614); **Cloud Nine**, dance club, 123 Gouger St. (8410-2242); **Edinburgh Castle Hotel**, leather/levi bar, Gray St. (8410-1211); **Mars Bar**, dance club, 120 Gouger St. (8231-9639); SRMC, leather cruise bar, 233 Curie St.

● Restaurants (AW): **Mistress Augustine's**, 161 O'Connell (8267-4779); **Astor Hotel**, 437 Pulteney St. (8223-2442); **Witches Brew Cafe**, popular with women, 143 Sturt St. (8212-2459).

λ SERVICES λ

● Health Club (GM): **Pulteney 431**, Sauna with heated pool, snacks, and videos, 431 Pulteney St. (8223 7506).

🔑 ACCOMMODATIONS 🔑

ACCOMMODATIONS CENTRAL
70 Glen Osmond Rd., Parkside, SA 5063. Tel: (08) 8274-1222. Fax: (08) 8272-7371. TYPE: *Rental Apartments*. HOST: Brian Bebbington. CLIENTELE: Gay Welcome. LOCATION: 5 downtown locations and 8 suburban. 40 self-catering apartments. (1-3 bedrooms) Rates: (A) $60-$154.

GREENWAYS APTS.
45 King William Rd., No. Adelaide, SA 5006. Tel: (08) 8267-5903. Fax: (08) 8267-1790. TYPE: *Rental Apts*. HOST: Brenton Smith. CLIENTELE: All Welcome. LOCATION: 1 km / 0.6 mi. north of central city. 24 1,2 or 3 bedroom apts.

GROSVENOR HOTEL
125 North Terrace, Adelaide, SA 5000. Tel: (08) 8231-2961. Fax: (08) 8231 0765. TYPE: First Class Hotel. CLIENTELE: Mostly Straight. LOCATION: Adjacent to Casino, 5 minutes walk from city center. 290 rooms, 8 suites, CTV, phone, A/C, restaurant, bar, gym, sauna, parking.DESCRIPTION: Hotel with classic marble facade near the Casino, Convention Centre complex, and the local gay scene.

HILTON INT'L ADELAIDE
233 Victoria Square, Adelaide, SA 5000. Tel: (08) 8217-0711. TYPE: *Deluxe Hotel*. CLIENTELE: Mostly Straight. LOCATION: Adjacent to SA State Government Offices, near the local gay scene. 380 rooms w/priv. bath. Rates: on request. DESCRIPTION: Elegant contemporary hotel with fine amenities and service.

TASMANIA

- ◆ **Population:** 480,000
- ◆ **Capital:** Hobart
- ◆ **Time Zone:** Eastern
- ◆ **Sodomy Law**
- ◆ **Legal Drinking Age:** 18+

HOBART   ℭ 03

✈ Hobart AP (HBA) 12.5 mi. / 20 km E.

LOCATION: In the south of Australia's southernmost island-state.

POPULATION: 220,000

CLIMATE: The seasons are reversed. Winters are cold and snowy with temperatures often near freezing; Summers are mild with high temperatures rarely over 25°c (77°F).

Gay/Lesbian Visitor Information
Gay Information Line: 6234-8179

DESCRIPTION: Hobart is Australia's second oldest capital city; a colorful town which has managed to combine colonial heritage and modern progress. Gay life in Tasmania is rather subdued, but an energetic gay political activism has developed in Hobart.

BARS ♈ RESTAURANTS ♒

● Bars/clubs (GMW): **La Cage**, bar & disco, mixed clientele, Gladstone St. (6223-8387); **Good Woman Inn** (GW), bar & limited budget accommodations, 186 Argyle St. (344-796).

● Restaurants: **Knopwood's Retreat**, restaurant & bar, Salamanca Palace; **Rockefella's**, 1st floor, 39 Salamanca Place (6223-6530).

ACCOMMODATIONS

THE LODGE ON ELIZABETH
249 Elizabeth St., Hobart. Tel: (03) 6231-3830. Fax: (03) 6234-2566. TYPE: *Guest House.* HOST: Nicholas. CLIENTELE: Gay/Straight. LOCATION: Central City. 10 rooms,CTV, phone, garden, jacuzzi. DESCRIPTION: Colonial style guest house. Oldest home in Hobart City (c 1829).

VIC (VICTORIA)

- ◆ **Population:** 4,521,800
- ◆ **Capital:** Melbourne
- ◆ **Time Zone:** Eastern
- ◆ **No Sodomy Law**
- ◆ **Legal Drinking Age:** 18+

MELBOURNE   ℭ 03

✈ Essendon Airport (MEB); Tullamarine Int'l Airport (MEL) 15 mi. / 24 km NW.

LOCATION: South Victoria by the Indian Ocean overlooking Port Phillip Bay.

POPULATION: 3,100,000

CLIMATE: Mild European style. Temperatures of 25°c-30°c (77°F-86°F) December to April. Earm weather generally lasts through the autumn (March, April, May).

Gay/Lesbian Visitor Information
Gay & Lesbian Switchboard: 9650-7711
Lesbian Line: 9416-0850

DESCRIPTION: Melbourne is a major financial and cultural center and Australia's second largest city. The city offers cosmopolitan shopping centers, sporting events and exciting nightlife. Many parks and gardens add a touch of old world charm to this contemporary and modern city. A popular public transportation here is the tram which provides an inexpensive way to travel around and see Melbourne.

● Beaches: **Middle Park** at **South Melbourne Beach** is a popular gay beach near the **Port Melbourne Lifesaving Club**; **St. Kilda Beach** near the Luna Park.

❖ SPECIAL EVENTS: **Midsumma Festival**, 17 Jan. - 2 Feb., including Carnival; **Melbourne Int'l Lesbian & Gay Film Fetival**, January 31 - February 15, National Theatre, St. Kilda.

BARS ♈ RESTAURANTS ♒

Melbourne's gay scene is located in the St Kilda/Prahran area and the inner northern suburbs of Fitzroy and Collingwood.

● Bars/clubs (GM): **Bassline**, high energy disco, Lower Esplanade, St. Kilda; **Club 80**, cruise leather/levy club, 10 Peel St., Collingwood (9417-2182); **Commerce Club**, 328 Flinders St. (9621-1310); **Diva**, 153 Commercial Rd., Prahran (9826-5500); **Gatehouse**, leather club, 10 Peel St. (9417-2182); **Girl Bar**, 12 McKillop St. (9610-0445); **The Laird**, drinking pub, Mon.-Sat., 149 Gipps St., Abbotsford (9417-2832); **Peel**, dance bar, beer garden, 113 Wellington St. Collingwood (9419-4762); **3 Faces**, dance bar, 143 Commercial Rd., So. Yarra (9826-0933); **Xchange**, bar, disco and restaurant, 119 Commercial Road, South Yarra 3141 (9267-5144).

● Bars/clubs (GW): **Feminique**, Golden Gate Hotel, cnr Coventry & Clarendon Sts, So. Melbourne (9578-0771); **Freedom**, Sarah Sands Motel, 29 Sydney Rd., Brunswick (9387-3872); **Royal Sundays**, Royal Derby Hotel, Bunswick St. & Alexander Pde, Fitzroy (9417-2321).

● Restaurants: **Angel Café**, lesbian owned, men welcome, 362 Brunswick St., Fitzroy, (9417-2271); **Buddy's** at the The Xchange Hotel, restaurant & grill for gay men only, à la carte dinners, 119 Commercial Rd., South Yarra (9267-5144); **Galleon Café**, 9 Carlisle, St. Kilda; **Onions**, vegetarian, nouvelle cuisine, 50 Commercial Rd., (9516-247); **Sukho Thai**, Thai cuisine, 234 Johnston St., (9419-4040); **Taj Mahal**, Indian cuisine, 69 Chapel St., Prahran (951-8155); **Trish's Coffee Lounge**, 126 Peel St., No. Melbourne.

λ SERVICES λ

● Erotica (GMW): **The Beat**, sex shop, guides, leather goods and toys, 157 Commercial Rd., Prahran (9827-8748).

● Gym (AW): **City Baths**, gym, aerobics, swimming pool, cnr Victoria & Swanson Sts (9663-5888); **Muscle World**, serious weight training, 1 Mcllwrick St., Windsor (9529-6161).

● Health clubs (GM): **The Steamworks**, pool, steamroom, sauna, spa, adult-bookshop, lockers, private rooms, refreshments and bar, massage & solarium, 279 Latrobe St. (9602-4493); **Bay City Sauna**, spa, massage, flotation tank, 2/16 Cumberland Drive, Seaford (9776-9279); **Porter St.**, private club, sauna, spa, flotation tank, medical services and therapeutic massage, 55 Porter St. (9529-5166).

● Health club (GW): **The Steamworks**, Special nights for lesbians, please call ahead for exact dates. Swimming pool, steam room, sauna, spa, adult-bookshop, lockers, private rooms, refreshments and bar, massage & solarium, 279 Latrobe St. (9602-4493).

● Leather Shop (GMW): **Leather World**, 157A Commercial Rd., So. Yarra (9827-9974).

 **ACCOMMODATIONS**

CALIFORNIA MOTOR INN
138 Barkers Rd., Hawthorn VIC 3122. Tel: (03) 9818-0281. Fax: (03) 9819-6845. TYPE: *Motel.* LOCATION: Suburban area, 3 mi. / 5 km from Melbourn, convenient to Colleges. CLIENTELE: All Welcome. 80 rooms w/priv. bath, restaurant, bar, pool, off-street parking, 24 hrs reception, close to gay bars, gay owned and operated. Apartments with kitchenettes available. Rates: A$89-$99. *TAC:* 10%

EXCHANGE HOTEL
119 Commercial St., South Yara VIC 3141. Tel: (03) 9867-5144. Fax: (03) 9820-9603. TYPE: *Guest House.* CLIENTELE: Gay Men Only. LOCATION: Heart of the south-of-the-river gay area. 5 dbl rooms w/shared bath, bars, restaurant. Rates: A$45-A$60. DESCRIPTION: Pub style building with two bars downstairs and guest rooms above.

LAIRD HOTEL
149 Gipps St., Collingwood, Melbourne VIC 3067. Tel: (03) 9417-2832. Fax: (03) 9416-0474. TYPE: *Hotel.* HOST: Peter Bond. CLIENTELE: Gay men Only. LOCATION: Melbourne's gay district, adjacent to Collingwood Rail Station. 9 rooms w/shared bath, leather bar. Rates: A$55

LYGON LODGE
220 Lygon St., Carlton, VIC 3053. Tel: (03) 9663-6633. TYPE: *Hotel.* CLIENTELE: All Welcome. LOCATION: Near Melbourne University, 15 min. walk to the center of Melbourne. 69 rooms, CTV, phone, mini-bar. Rates: A$120-$160 w/light breakfast. DESCRIPTION: Renovated hotel offering older style standard rooms or higher standard deluxe rooms all with private facilities.

✪ PALM COURT B & B
22 Grattan Place, Richmond 3121 Victoria. Tel: 0419-777-850 Tel/Fax: +61-3-9427-7365. Postal Address: PO Box 184, East Melbourne 3002 Victoria. *TYPE:* B&B. OWNER: Trevor Davis. CLIENTELE: Gay men & women. LOCATION: Overlooking Melbourne Parkland & Cricket Ground. 4 Rooms 2 doubles, 2 triples, shared bath, CTV, phone, refrigerator, room and laundry service, free parking. 1.5 mi. to gay bars & health club. 3 mi. to beach. Rates: A$ 40-60. DESCRIPTION: Two story restored Victorian home. *(see our ad in Lodging / Marketplace)*

W.A.
WESTERN AUSTRALIA

♦ **Population**: 1,470,000
♦ **Capital**: Perth
♦ **Time Zone**: Western
♦ **No Sodomy Law**
♦ **Legal Drinking Age**: 18+

PERTH   ✆ 08

✈ Perth Int'l AP- (PER) 7 mi. / 11 km NE.

LOCATION: On the banks of the broad Swan River in Western Australia.

POPULATION: 1,262,600

CLIMATE: Wet mild winters, and hot sunny summers. The average January temperature is 80°F (26°c), and average July temperature 55°F (13°c). Average annual rainfall 3600 mm (14").

Gay/Lesbian Visitor Information
Gayline: 9328 9044

DESCRIPTION: Perth is a clean, modern, attractive looking city sitting on the banks of the Swan River with the port of Fremantle 19 km / 12 mi. southwest. The center is compact with the main shopping center on William Street. **North Perth** known as **Northbridge** starts north of the railway line. It is famous for its restaurants, popular hotels and affordable accommodations. It is also the city's gay center.

♣ Entertainment: International Casino on the Swan River just outside the city. **Burnswood Island Resort Hotel & Casino**, Great Eastern Hwy, Perth 6100. Tel: 9362-7777.

● Beaches: Perth claims to have the best beaches and surf of any Australian city, but the most popular with gays are: **Floreat Beach** and **South City** - a nude beach where one can cruise or meet other gays during the early afternoons; **Swanbourne** is the local beach for swimming and sunning in the nude, but it is not necessarily gay. Most of the beaches can be reached via public transportation.

❖ **SPECIAL EVENTS**: **Pride Month**, annual gay and lesbian festival in October; Gay & Lesbian Film Week at the Lumiere Cinema following the Sydney Gay & Lesbian Mardi Gras.

BARS ♈ RESTAURANTS 🍽

The gay scene of Perth is located in Northbridge north of the railway line, or on the other side of the bridge over the railroad tracks from downtown Perth.

● Bars/clubs (GM): **Berlin Club**, young crowd, 89 Miligan St. (9328-9866); **Connections**, popular club, drag show, 81 James St. Northbridge (9328-1870).

● Bars/clubs (GMW): **Click Club**, c/o Orchard Hotel, Wellington and Milligan Sts (9322-2923); **Connections**, dance club, 81 James St., Northbridge (9328-1870); **Northbridge Hotel**, Sat. Sun. pub hours, 198 Brisbane St., Northbridge (9328-5254); **DC's**, fashionable crowd, 160A James St., Northbridge (9227-7950); **The Freezer**, 230 William St., Northbridge (9227-7238).

● Restaurants (GMW): **Plum**, fine food, intimate ambience, 47 Lake St., Northbridge (9328-4264); **Timbuktu**, 620 Beaufort St., Mt. Lawley (9227-9087). Other (AW): **Bohemia**, Yugoslavian, 309 William (9328-7163); **Blue Fin**, seafood, 75 Aberdeen (9328-5370); **Emperor Court**, Chinese, 66 Lake (9328-8860); **Kings Park Garden**, international restaurant overlooking Perth (9321-7655).

🔑 ACCOMMODATIONS 🔑

JEWELL HOTEL
180 Goderich St. (near Hill), Perth WA 6000. Tel: (08) 9325-8488. TYPE: *Hotel*. CLIENTELE: Mostly Straight. LOCATION: Near the Haymarket Center and the Town Hall, convenient to the Northbridge area. rooms: w/shared bath, Gay Bars: nearby, Rates: A$55 sgl - $75. DESCRIPTION: Low budget accommodations in a YMCA run and operated hotel.

SWANBOURNE
5 Myera St., Swanbourne, Perth, WA 6010. Tel: (08) 9383-1981. TYPE: *Guest House*. HOST: Mike or Ralph. CLIENTELE: Gay men & women. LOCATION: 8 km / 5 mi. to Perth. 4 rooms. 10 min. to Beach. Rates: A$55-A$75. DESCRIPTION: Private residence set in tranquil gardens. *TAC*: 10%.

TREE FERN RETREAT
24 Ashton Rise, Woodvale-Perth, WA. Tel: (08) 9309-2982. TYPE: *Bed & Breakfast*. HOST: Lloyd Haven. CLIENTELE: Gay men only. 3 rooms, pool, clothing optional. Rates: on request.

AUSTRIA

AREA: 32,375 sq. mi. (83,851 sq. km)
POPULATION: 7,507,000
CAPITAL: Vienna
CURRENCY: Schilling (Sch.)
OFFICIAL LANGUAGE: German
MAJOR RELIGIONS: Roman Catholicism
Telephone: 43
Nat'l Holiday: 2nd Republic Day, April 27
Official Time: G.M.T. + 1
Electricity: 220 volts
Exchange Rate: 1US$ = Sch. 10.60
National Airline: Austrian Airlines

LAW REGARDING HOMOSEXUALITY:
The minimum legal age for consensual homosexual activity is 18. Homosexuality is discriminated against in Austria and gay liberation has a long way to go in its efforts to make the gay community's voice heard.

INNSBRUCK   ✆   0512

✈ Kranebitten Airport (INN)

LOCATION: In the famous Tyrol region of Western Austria.

POPULATION: 156,000.

CLIMATE: Continental climate. Winters are cold and snowy with an average January temperatures of 28°F (-2°c); summers are pleasant with a July average temperatures of 64°F (18°c).

VISITOR INFORMATION
Städtisches Verkehrsbüro
Tel: (0512) 760-500

Gay/Lesbian Visitor Information
HOSI Tyrol - Tel: (0512) 562-403

DESCRIPTION: Innsbruck, the Tyrol capital, is a beautiful historic city at the junction of two important routes across the central Alps. The city architecture is a mixture of Gothic, Renaissance, Baroque and modern. The city attracts skiers to some of the best known ski slopes in the world. Non skiers appreciate the town's medieval atmosphere and historical attractions.

❖ Gay Beach: **Nudist Beach Hawaii**, exit Kranebitten on A 13. Gay area is located west of the main beach.

BARS ♟ RESTAURANTS ♟

● Bars/clubs (GMW): **Hotel Café Central**, piano bar, mixed clientele, Gilmstraße 5 (5920); **Piccolo Bar**, Seilergasse 2 (582-163); **Savoy - Stüberl**, Höttinger au 26 (287-832);

● Restaurants (AW): **Belle Epoque**, award winning Tirolean restaurant in the Alpotel on the edge of the Old City, Innrain 13 (577-931); **Goethstube**, old wine tavern, Herzog Friedrickstr 6 (586-334); **Ottoburg**, local cuisine, Herzog Friedrichstr. 6 (574-652).

🔯 ACCOMMODATIONS 🔯

HOTEL CAFE CENTRAL
Gilmstraße 5, Innsbruck 6020. Tel: (512) 5920. Fax: (512) 580-310. TYPE: *Hotel*. CLIENTELE: Mostly Straight. LOCATION: In a quiet central area. 87 rooms w/priv. bath, phone, CTV, Viennese Cafe, sauna, solarium, heated indoor pool, DESCRIPTION: Traditional turn of the century hotel.

SALZBURG   ✆   0662

✈ Salzburg Airport (SZG)

LOCATION: On the banks of the Sazach River, near the German border.

POPULATION: 250,000

CLIMATE: See Innsbruck

Gay/Lesbian Visitor Information
HOSI (Salzburg): (0662) 327343

DESCRIPTION: Charming Baroque City on the banks of the Salzach River, and the capital of the province. The Old Town lies on the left bank with its colorful 17th and 18th century buildings, many famous for the grandeur of their architecture. The Bavarian border, is only a short distance away.

BARS Y RESTAURANTS 🍴

● Bars/clubs (GM): **Kupferpfandl**, Paracelsussstraße 14 (875-760); **Weinhaus zum Tiroler**, Steingaße 51 (883-285).

● Bar/club (GMW): **Radlegger's 2-Stein**, Giselakai 9 (880-201).

 ACCOMMODATIONS

PANORAMA HOTEL STEIN
Giselakai 3-5, Salzburg A-5024. Tel: (662) 874-346. TYPE: *Hotel.* CLIENTELE: All Welcome. LOCATION: Town center. 80 rooms w/priv. bath, phone, C/H, restaurant. Season: December - October. Rates: US$80 - US$210. *TAC:* 10% (from Odysseus). DESCRIPTION: Historic hotel in a convenient central location. Extensive view on fortress and old city from the roofgarden-café.

VIENNA   © 01

✈ Schwechat Airport (VIE)

LOCATION: Southeastern Austria with the Danube flowing through the city.

POPULATION: 1,700,000.

CLIMATE: Continental without abrupt changes. The rainy season lasts from mid-October to mid-December. Winters are grim, cold and snowy with average mean temperature in January of 32°F (0°c). Summers are cool, and pleasant with a July average of 66°F (19°c).

Gay/Lesbian Visitor Information

HOSI (Homosexuelle Initiative Wien): 216-6604
Novargasse 40, A-1020 Wien

Rosa Lila Tip: 586-8150
Linke Wienzeile 102

DESCRIPTION: Vienna is an historic city with the glamour of a bygone empire. Impressive baroque and rococo style architecture is still conserved in many old buildings. The city is famous for the musical heritage of its prodigious composers.

Modern Vienna is divided into 23 districts. The inner town is the most important. It is surrounded by the **Ringstrasse**. Visit: **The Opera House**, where the Kärntnerstrasse, the main shopping district, meets the Opera ring; **St. Stephen's Cathedral**, built in 1147 A.D.; **The Hofburg Palace** open to the public with wonderful Habsburg collection; and the **Schönbrunn Castle**, a Viennese version of Versailles on the western outskirts.

For music lovers **The Volksoper** (People's Opera) at the corner of Währinger Strasse and Währinger Gürtel specialize in classical Viennese operetta, For good Jazz, try **Jazzland**, at 29 Franz Josefs Kai.

❖ Side trip is recommended to the **Wienerwald** (Vienna Woods), a lovely forest which inspired some of Johann Strauss most famous waltzes, and **Baden-bei-Wien**, historic Spa and Casino resort which can be reached by taxi from Vienna.

● Entertainment: Vienna offers a sophisticated, elegant gambling casino at the renovated **Palais Esterhazy** near the State Opera, **Casino Cercle Wien**, Estherhazy Palace, Karntnerstraße 41.

BARS Y RESTAURANTS 🍴

● Bars/clubs(GM): **Alexander's Tower**, leather cruise bar, Schönbrunner Straße 25 (581-5890); **Alfi's Goldener Spiegel**, bar and restaurant, Austrian cuisine, Linke Wienzeile 46 entry in Stiegengasse (586-6608); **Alte Lampe**, Vienna's oldest gay bar, Heumülgaße 13 (587-3454); **Blue Boy's**, coffee bar, Pressgaße 30 (586-0888); **Eagle**, leather, uniform and rubber bar, Blümelgaße 1 (587-2661); **Fantasia**, dance club, Schikanedergaße 12 (587-4520); **Heaven**, gay night every 1st Thursday of the month at U4 disco, 12 Schönbrunnerstr. 222 (858-3185); **Mango Bar**, Laimgrubengaße 11 (587-4448); **Nanu**, dance bar, young clientele, Schleifmühlgaße 11 (587-2987); **Nightshift**, leather cruise bar, dark room, Corneliusgaße 8 (586-2337); **Stiefelknecht**, cruise leather bar, Wimmergasse 20 entry in Stolbergg (545-2301).

● Bars/clubs (GMW): **Der Kleiner Traum**, Stauraczgaße 1 (545-5885); **Gay Pride Disco**, at HOSI zentrum, Novargaße 40, Wien 1020 (266-604); **Le Swing**, dance club, Hannovergaße 5 (332-1670); **Why Not**, club disco on two floors, Tiefer Graben 22 (533-1158); **Wiener Freiheit**, dance club, Schönbrunner Straße 25 (586-5938).

● Bar/Club (GW): **Whoopee**, Neustiftgaße 81.

● Restaurants (GMW): **Café Berg**, gay cafe, open all day, Bergaße 8 (319-5720); **Cafe/ Restaurant Willendorf**, vegetarian menu, garden terrace, Linke Wienzeile 102; **Cafe Savoy**, traditional cuisine, Linke Wienzeile 36 (586-7348) Other (AW): **Esposito**, Italian Pizzeria at the Hotel Urania, Obere Weißgerberstr. 7 (713-1711); **Prinz Eugen Rôtisserie**, set in baronial château, International and Nouvelle Cuisine, Hilton Hotel, 2 Landstrasser Haupstrasse (752-652); **Sailer**, old Vienna style, 14 Gersthoferstrasse (472-121). Coffeeshop popular with gay clientele: **Café Savoy**, Linke Wienzeile 36 (567-348).

λ SERVICES λ

● Community Center (GMW): **HOSI-Zentrum**, Nov-argaße 40, Wien 2 (266-604).

● Health Clubs (GM): **Amigos**, cafe/sauna, Müllnergaße 5 (319-0514); **Apollo City Sauna**, two floors sauna complex, Wimbergergaße 34 (938-9855); **Kaiserbründl**, sauna, steam room, darkroom, massage, Weiburggaße 18-20 (513) 3293; **Römersauna**, sauna complex with coffeeshop, relax cabins, videos, Passauer Platz 6, (533-5318).

ACCOMMODATIONS

PENSION WILD
Langegaße 10, Wien 1080. Tel: (1) 435174. USA/Canada reservations - Tel: (516) 944-5330 or (800) 257-5344. Fax: (516) 944-7540. TYPE: *Pension / Rental Apts.* HOST: Peter Wild. CLIENTELE: Equal Gay/Straight. LOCATION: Quietly located in the city center next to the Ringstraße and gay places. M° U2/U3 and tram around the block.

* Rooms: 14; 8 w/priv., 6 w/shared bath
* Apartments: 2
* Sauna, solarium, massage
* Gay Bars: 10-15 min. walking
* Health Club: 5 min. (straight)
* Airport: Vienna Int'l, 12.5 mi / 20 km
* Rates: $110 - $120 w/Cb
* Check in 12 noon / Check out 11:00
* **TAC:** 10% (from Odysseus)

DESCRIPTION: Nice pension with comfortable rooms with cold/hot water. Public shower room. Not luxury but clean and friendly.

URANIA HOTEL
Obere Weißgerberstr. 7, 1030 Vienna. Tel: (1) 713-1711. Fax: (1) 713-5694. USA/Canada reservation/information Odysseus Tel: (516) 944-5330 or (800) 257-5344. Fax: (516) 944-7540 or (800) 982-6571. TYPE: *Hotel.* CLIENTELE: Gay Welcome. LOCATION: Centrally located, tram lines N,0,1,2.

* Rooms: 39 Rooms w/priv. bath
  (7 sgl/ 24 dbl/ 3 triple/ 5 quad)
* Radio, CTV, phone, C/H,
* Room & maid service, parking
* Restaurant: Pizzeria **Esposito**
* Bar: for hotel guests only
* Gay Bars: 10 min.
* Credit Cards: AMEX/EC
* Open: year round
* Rates: (US) $120 - $140 w/CB
* **TAC:** 10% (from Odysseus)

DESCRIPTION: Economically priced tourist hotel known for its many years of service to the international gay travelers in Vienna.

AREA: 5,382 sq. mi. (13,939 sq. km)
POPULATION: 210,000
CAPITAL: Nassau
CURRENCY: Bahamian $ (B$)
OFFICIAL LANGUAGE: English
MAJOR RELIGIONS: Roman Catholicism, Protestantism
Telephone: 809
Nat'l Holiday: Independence Day, July 10
Official Time: G.M.T. - 5
Electricity: 120 volts, 60 cycles
Exchange Rate: US$1 = B$1
National Airline: Bahamasair

LAW REGARDING HOMOSEXUALITY: Homosexuality is illegal in the Bahamas. Under a new Bahamian law sexual intercourse in a public place is punishable by up to twenty years in prison.

NASSAU   *©*   NO AREA CODE

✈ Nassau Int'l Airport (NAS)
  12 mi. / 19 km southwest of Nassau

LOCATION: On the northeastern coast of the New Providence Island with a bridge connection to Paradise Island.

POPULATION: 135,000 (island)

CLIMATE: Constant mild temperatures with an average of 70°F (22°c) year round.

DESCRIPTION: Nassau is the Capital of New Providence and a chief port of entry, less than 60 mi / 96 km east of florida. Visitors come to enjoy the island's famous casinos, nightlife and duty free shopping. For those interested in

Scuba, the reefs and drop-offs close to the shore offer fantastic sites for underwater exploration.

BARS ▼ RESTAURANTS ¶¶

● Bars/clubs (GMW): **City Limits**, one of the most popular gay discos in the Caribbean, also frequented by lesbians, Independence Hwy (393-4076) closed Mon & Tues. Hrs: 10pm-7am.

● Bars/clubs (G/S): **Club Fantasy Disco**, gays don't dance together but socialize, Crystal Palace Casino. Open 7 days, 9-12pm (321-6200); **Club Waterloo**, East Bay St., gays do not dance together. Open 7 days 10pm-10am.; **Drop Off**, frequented by Cruise Ship crews and other happy sailors, Bay St., opposite John Bull. Open Thur.-Sun.; **Orchard Garden**, Village Rd. (393-1297); **Pineapple Lounge**, early crowds, gays can dance together. Open 7 days 7am-6am (326-6942); **West Coast Bar & Grill**, late hour crowds, Open: 7 days 7am-6am (322-8666).

● Restaurants (G/S): **Cabana Bar & Grill**, West Bay St. Open: 7 days 9:30a-midnight. Interesting for gays late in the evening; **Roselawn Café**, Bank Lane & Bay St.; **Orchard Garden**, Village Rd. (393-1297); **West Coast Bar & Grill**, late hour crowds, Open: 7 days 7am-6am (322-8666).

❖ Gay Beach: **Bay Street Beach** (late at night, very risky); **Paradise Island** (in the bushes area).

 ACCOMMODATIONS

THE ORCHARD GARDEN
Village Rd., P.O. Box N-1514,Nassau. Tel: (809) 393-1297. TYPE: *Apartment-Hotel*. CLIENTELE: All Welcome. LOCATION: 2 blocks from Montague Beach and 1 mi. / 1.6 km from Paradise Island Bridge. Public bus to Paradise Island and downtown nearby.

* Studios & Cottages: 34
    12 cottages w/kitchens
* CTV, A/C, balcony, wheelchair access
* Restaurant, bar, outdoor pool
* Free parking, Supermarket nearby
* Gay Bars: some nearby
* Beach: 2 blocks (mixed)
* Airport: 8 mi. / 13 km
* Season: Year round
* Rates: (US) $60-$120
* *TAC:* 10%

DESCRIPTION: Recently renovated tourist class cottages and studios complex in an enclosed 2-acre garden.

BARBADOS

AREA: 166 sq. mi. (430 sq. km)
POPULATION: 250,000
CAPITAL: Bridgetown
CURRENCY: Barbadian Dollar (B$)
OFFICIAL LANGUAGE: English
MAJOR RELIGIONS: Roman Catholicism,
Protestantism
Telephone: 809
Nat'l Holiday: Independence Day, Nov. 30
Official Time: G.M.T. - 4
Electricity: 110 volts, 50 cycles
Exchange Rate: US$1 = B$2
National Airline: BWIA

LAW REGARDING HOMOSEXUALITY:
Homosexuality is illegal in Barbados but the
actual reinforcement of the law is very rare. It
is advisable, however, to take precautions and
be discreet.

BRIDGETOWN   *©* **809**

✈ Grantley Adams Int'l Airport (BGI)

LOCATION: Barbados is the most eastern of
the West Indies islands.

POPULATION: Bridgetown 7,550

CLIMATE: Tropical with slight variation in
temperatures year round. Average annual temperature is in the 80"sF (27˚c).

DESCRIPTION: Independent since 1966,
Barbados was a British colony for over 300
years. It is a beautiful coral island with miles
of great sandy beaches and warm climate year
round. Bridgetown, the capital has a
Trafalgar Square, and the afternoon tea
break is very much a local tradition. Explore

the excellent duty free shops with preference
for British made goods. For Rum lovers,
Mount Gay Rum is produced locally and visitors are welcome to tour the distillery.

BARS RESTAURANTS

● Bars/Clubs (G/S): **John's Night Cap**,
Baxter's Rd., Bridgetown (426-2207); **Mary's
Bar**, Suttle St., Bridgetown; **The Warehouse**,
Cavan's Lane (Bridgetown) (436-2897)

● Restaurant (G/S): **Waterfront Café**, The
Careenage (Bridgetown) (427-0093.

❖ Gay Beaches: **Cattlewash Beach**, on the
east coast between holiday complex and
Barclays Park, discreet nude sunbathing possible; **Long Bay Beach**, near the airport.
Discreet nude sunbathing; **Rockley Beach**
(Accra Beach), cruisy on weekends and
evenings.

ACCOMMODATIONS

ACCRA BEACH HOTEL
Rockley, PO Box 73W, Christ Church. Tel: 435-
8920. Fax: 435-6794. TYPE: *Hotel*. CLIEN-
TELE: All Welcome. LOCATION: Oceanfront
on Accra Beach, 3 mi. / 5 km from Bridgetown.
52 rooms and apartments, CTV, phone, balcony, A/C, restaurant, bar, pool, private beach.
Rates: $90-$120. DESCRIPTION: Tourist class
beach hotel on the cruisy Rockley Beach.

GLITTER BAY
Porter's, St. James. Tel: (809) 422-5555. TYPE:
Deluxe resort. CLIENTELE: All Welcome.
LOCATION: West Coast. 81 rooms and suites
w/living room, kitchenette, panoramic view,
restaurant, bar, 24 hrs. room service. Rates:
$195-$395.

OCEAN VIEW HOTEL
Hastings, Christ Church. Tel: (809) 435-8924.
TYPE: *Hotel*. CLIENTELE: All Welcome.
LOCATION: Sandy beach, 10 mi. / 16 km from
Bridgetown. 30 rooms and suites, phone, CTV,
A/C (some), restaurant, lounge bar. Rates: $65-
$130. DESCRIPTION: Atmospheric hotel in
Colonial building from 1898 furnished with
antiques.

ROMAN BEACH APTS
Miami Beach, Oistins Town, Christ Church.
Tel: 428-7635. TYPE: *Rental Apartments*.
HOST: Fran Roman. CLIENTELE: Gay/
Straight. LOCATION: 3 min. walk to Oistins
Town, 20 min. to Bridgetown. 10 self catering
apts. DESCRIPTION: Budget apartments.

BELARUS

AREA: 80,154 sq. mi. (207,600 sq. km)
POPULATION: 10,200,000
CAPITAL: Minsk
CURRENCY: Belarus Ruble (BRB)
OFFICIAL LANGUAGE: Belorussian, Russian, Polish, Ukrainian, Yiddish
MAJOR RELIGIONS: Eastern Orthodoxy
Telephone: 7
Official Time: GMT +2
Electricity: 127/220 volts, 50c AC
Exchange Rate: 1US$ = BRB 3,270
National Airline:

LAW REGARDING HOMOSEXUALITY: The former Soviet article #121 of the penal code that outlawed homosexuality no longer exists. However inspite of the lifting of the law, gay life remains surpressed due to the prevailing hostile attitude from the general public.

MINSK   ✆   0712

✈ Minsk Airport

LOCATION: Heart of Belarus.

POPULATION: 1,600,000

CLIMATE: Cold winters with frequent snowfalls, temperatures are around 25°F (-4°c); Summers can be warm but rarely too hot with temperatures in the 80's (27°c). The best seasons to visit Belarus are spring and fall.

VISITOR INFORMATION

DESCRIPTION: Minsk the capital is the country's largest industrial, scientific and cultural center. Much of the city was destroyed during WWII, but the old quarter including a 17th century cathedral is undergoing an intensive restoration program. For gays visiting Minsk it is possible to make contacts at the **Park** near the Belarus National-Drama-Theatre; and at **Prospekt Fratsiska Skariny** between the Independence Square and Circus (AYOR). Other possible cruise areas: Main Railway Station and the Main Post Office.

BARS ▼ RESTAURANTS ‖

● Bars/clubs (G/S): **Valerija**, dance club near Post Office; **Prospekt**, cafe and gay dance club, Prospekt Skariny (M° Oktyabrskaya).

● Restaurant (G/S): **Restaurant at Planeta Hotel**, National & European cuisine, 31 Masherova Prospekt.

λ SERVICES λ

● Health Club (G/S): **Bathhouse**, mixed sauna, Moskovaskaja, M° Institute of Culture.

 ACCOMMODATIONS

PLANETA HOTEL
31 Masherova Prospekt, Minsk 220122. Tel: (172) 238587. Fax: (271) 267780. TYPE: *Hotel*. CLIENTELE: Mostly Straight. LOCATION: City Center. 4 km / 2.5 mi. from airport, 5 km / 3 mi. from Train Station. 317 rooms w/priv. bath. cafe, bars, restaurant, health club. Rates: (US) $75 - $130.

BELGIUM

AREA: 11,781 sq. mi. (30,513 sq.km)
POPULATION: 9,860,000
CAPITAL: Brussels
CURRENCY: Belgian Franc (BF)
OFFICIAL LANGUAGE: French, Flemish
MAJOR RELIGIONS: Roman Catholicism
Telephone: 32
Nat'l Holiday: Independence Day, July 21
Official Time: G.M.T. +1
Electricity: 220 volts
Exchange Rate: 1US$ = BF 31
National Airline: Sabena

LAW REGARDING HOMOSEXUALITY:
Homosexuality is legal between consenting
adults 18 years old and over. The majority of
the Belgians oppose to the homosexual lifestyle
for religious reasons, but are relatively tolerant
towards gays and lesbians as individuals.
Brussels has a flourishing gay scene.

ANTWERPEN   ✆ 031

✈ Deurne Airport (ANR)

LOCATION: Large commercial port on the
River Scheldt near the Dutch border.

POPULATION: 920,000

CLIMATE: see Brussels/Amsterdam

Gay/Lesbian Visitor Information
Gay Center (G.O.C.): 233-1071
Dambruggestraat 204

DESCRIPTION: Antwerpen is one of the
largest ports of the world and an important
diamond-cutting center. Visitors can enjoy the
city's glorious past, which is alive in the beau-

tiful Gothic and Renaissance buildings and
cathedrals. Once the headquarter of Flemish
culture, many famous painters resided and created their famous art in Antwerpen. Rubens,
Jordaens, Van Eyck, are some of the better
known artists whose art is displayed in the
city's museums.

Visit: **Cathedral of Our Lady**, a towering
cathedral built in the Barbant Gothic style circa
14th century; **Grote Markt** (Main Square), a
peaceful square in the Italian Renaissance
style; **The Steen**, the oldest building in
Antwerpen (12th century); **Butcher's Guild
House** - a Gothic Palace, which was the headquarters of the Butcher's guild; **Royal Museum of Fine Arts** and the **Rubens' House**.
Three of Antwerpen's main tourist attractions
are: **Antwerpen Port**, the **Diamond Industry**, and the **Zoological Gardens**.

BARS ♈ RESTAURANTS 🍴

The gay scene is located on or near Van
Schoonhovenstraat (yes, grow up and learn
how to pronounce it, you'll need it in Gay
Antwerpen), which is the main road leading
north from the main Central Station in
Antwerpen Center.

● Bars/clubs (GM): **Apollo**, dance club, p/o Las
Mañanas, Ankerrui 34-36 (231-7220); **Bac-
chus**, van Schoonho-venstr. 20 (233-9666);
Boots, leather bar, Van Aerdtsraat 22 (233-
2136); **The Boots**, leather club, tatoo's and
piercing welcome, Van Aerdtstraat 22 (233-
2136); **Borsalino**, popular dance club, Van
Schoonhovenstr. 48 (233-8685); **Cafe Strange**,
Dambruggestraat 161 (226-0072); **Captain
Caveman**, leather bar, Geulincxsstraat 28
(233-4487); **Cpt Caveman**, leather bar,
Geulincxstraat 28; **Den Bazaar**, bar/disco,
Van Schoonhovenstraat 22 (232-9197); **Hanky
Code**, intimate leather bar with summer ter-
race, Van den Wervestraat 69 (226-8172); **Twilight**, Van Schoonhovenstraat 54 (232-6704).

● Bars/clubs (GMW): **Café d'Anvers**,
disco/bar, Verversrui 15 (226-3870); **Envers
d'Envers**, dance bar, most extraordinary disco
decor in Belgium, Waalse Kaai 25 (238-5004);
Fifty-Fifty, Van Schoonhovenstr. 40 (225-
1173); **GOC Gay Center**, bar, restaurant, 204
Dambruggestraat (233-2502); **Playboy**, Van
Schoonhovenstraat 42 (231-6006).

● Restaurants (AW): **Bali**, Indonesian cuisine,
Autolei 217 (militair road) (321-1111); **Preud
Homme**, Suikerrui 28 (233-4200); **Quick**, De
Cninckplein 29 (225 2296); **De Worstepan**,

grill & seafood, Kaasrui 9 (231-7016).

λ SERVICES λ

● Health Clubs (GM): **City Sauna**, Olijftakstraat 35 (234-1925); **Park**, Sanderusstraat 55 (238-3137); **Kouros**, large sauna complex, pool, bar/restaurant, TV room, solarium, Botermelkbaan 50 (658-0937); **SPA 55**, friendly atmosphere, elegant lounge, 5 levels of fun, 55 Sanderusstraat (238-3137) located behind the Justice Palace.

● Sex Shops (GM): **Adonis**, gay video club, Dambruggestraat 174 (226-9151); **Gay Ron**, gay videos, movies, Van Wesenbekerstr. 54 (234-0443).

ACCOMMODATIONS

TOURIST HOTEL
Pelikanstraat 20-22, Antwerpen B-2018. Tel: (3) 232-5870. TYPE: *Hotel.* CLIENTELE: All Welcome. LOCATION: Opposite Central Train Station, 200 yards from Ave. de Keyser. 135 rooms w/priv. bath, CTV, minibar, phone, C/H, restaurant, beer cellar. Rates: (US) $90-$125.

BRUGGE   ✆   050

✈ Brussels Nat'l Airport (BRU)

LOCATION: 50 mi. / 80 km west of Brussels.

POPULATION: 120,000

CLIMATE: Continental. Temperatures vary from 54°F to 72°F in the summer (12°c - 22°c), and 32°F to 43°F in the winter (0°c - 6°c).

Gay Visitor Information
Homocentrum: (50) 334742
BP 131 (8000 Brugge 1)

DESCRIPTION: The historic capital of West Flanders, Brugge is a fascinating museum of the Middle Ages with quaint medieval houses, cobbled streets, misty canals and lively markets. Once an opulent commercial center, Brugge brought many artists and craftsmen from all over Europe to build and decorate its palaces and churches. To explore the city, a walking tour by foot is recommended.

BARS ♈ RESTAURANTS 🍴

● Bars/clubs (GM): **Ravel**, dance club, show

every other Saturday, no entrance fee, Karel De Stoutelaan 172 (315274).

● Bars/clubs (GMW): **Café Mon Paris**, pub, Langestraat 138 (337-287); **Hollywood**, tavern, 'T Zand 33 (337-252); **Locomotief**, pub, Spoorwegstraat 312 (8200 Sint-Michels) (380-123); **Ma Rica Rokk**, Rock house disco popular with students, 'T Zand 6-7-8 (332-424); **Passe - Partout**, tavern during the day and bar in the evening, Sint-Jansstraat 3 (334-742).

● Restaurant (GMW): **Basil Quiches**, Eekhoustraat 6 (345-245).

λ SERVICES λ

● Sauna (GM): **Maurice**, in residential area near Brugge, Turkish bath, sauna, snack bar, Veldstraat 69 (8200 Sint-Michels) (385-757).

ACCOMMODATIONS

HOTEL ACACIA
Korte Zilverstraat 3a, B-8000 Brugge. Tel: (50) 344-411. TYPE: *Hotel.* CLIENTELE: All Welcome. LOCATION: Historic district in the center of town, 50 m / yards from the Market Place.

* Rooms: 30 w/priv. bath
* Junior Suites: 6
* CTV, phone, hairdryer, safe, minibar
* Heated pool, sauna, gym, free parking
* Gay Bars: walking distance
* Train Station: walking distance, taxi
* Open: Year round
* Rates: (US) $160 - $240 w/CB
* *TAC:* 10%

DESCRIPTION: Historic first class hotel in the center of the oldest part of town. Luxury furnished rooms and suites all with private facilities. Excellent amenities and service. Good price/quality level.

BRUSSELS   ✆   02

✈ Brussels Nat'l Airport (BRU)
    8 mi. / 13 km northeast

LOCATION: In the heart of Belgium.

POPULATION: 1,050,000

CLIMATE: Continental. Temperatures vary from 54°F to 72°F in the summer (12°c - 22°c),

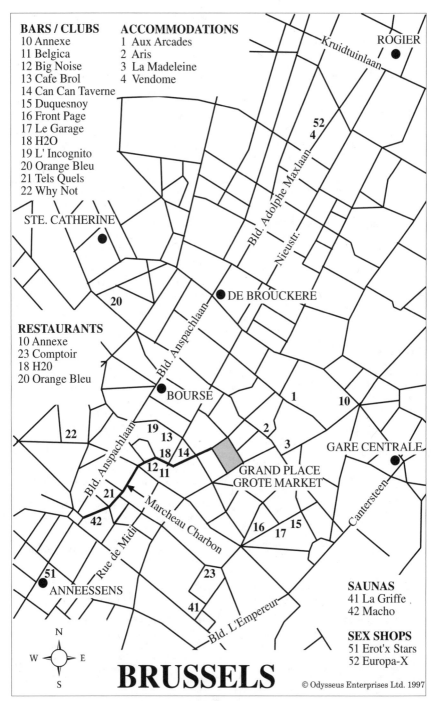

BARS / CLUBS
10 Annexe
11 Belgica
12 Big Noise
13 Cafe Brol
14 Can Can Taverne
15 Duquesnoy
16 Front Page
17 Le Garage
18 H2O
19 L' Incognito
20 Orange Bleu
21 Tels Quels
22 Why Not

ACCOMMODATIONS
1 Aux Arcades
2 Aris
3 La Madeleine
4 Vendome

ROGIER

STE. CATHERINE

DE BROUCKERE

RESTAURANTS
10 Annexe
23 Comptoir
18 H2O
20 Orange Bleu

BOURSE

GARE CENTRALE

GRAND PLACE
GROTE MARKET

ANNEESSENS

SAUNAS
41 La Griffe
42 Macho

SEX SHOPS
51 Erot'x Stars
52 Europa-X

Kruidtuinlaan

Bld. Adolphe Maxlaan

Nieustr.

Bld. Anspachlaan

Bld. Anspachlaan

Marcheau Charbon

Rue de Midi

Cantersteen

Bld. L'Empereur

N
W   E
S

BRUSSELS

© Odysseus Enterprises Ltd. 1997

and 32°F to 43°F in the winter (0°c - 6°c).

Gay/Lesbian Visitor Information
Info Homo: (02) 733-1024

DESCRIPTION: Brussels is the historic, cultural and economic capital of Belgium. Located in the heart of Europe, it has become the major administrative capital of the post-war born European Economic Community. Brussels has a lot more to offer than 'Belgian' fries & beer: beautiful 17th century architecture, the **Grand-Place**, the most beautiful square in the world, The **King's House** (Maison du Roi) built in the 16th century and now contains the **Municipal Museum** with its collections of historical documents.

BARS ♈ RESTAURANTS ▮▮

The gay area of Brussels is located in the Old City (Vieille Ville) near and around the **Grand Place** and **Hôtel de Ville** (Town Hall).

● Bars/clubs (GM): **Annexe**, bar, brasserie, rue des Bouchers, 71-73 (512-3856); **Balmoral**, Place Georges Brugmannplein 21 (347-0882); **Bar à Tapas**, Borgval 11 (502-6602); **Belgica**, Rue du Marché au Charbon 32; **Bump**, dance club, gay parties, rue Blaesstraat 208 (511-9789); **Café Brol**, rue des Pierres/Steenstraat 22 (513-0084); **Cercle 52**, video bar/disco, 52 rue des Chartreux (514-3078); **Can Can Tavern**, the oldest of all gay bars in Bruxelles, rue des Pierres 55 (512-7404); **Démence**, dance club, Rue Blaes 208 (511-9798); **Factory**, dance club, Impasse de la Fidélité 4; **Duquesnoy**, leather cruise bar, 12 Duquesnoy Str. (502-3883); **Dolce**, Petit rue au Beurre 8 (502-7866); **Front Page**, 45 rue Duquesnay (512-7410); **Le Garage**, sunday gay T-dance with drag shows, Rue Duquesnoy 18 (512-6622); **Gémeau**, bar/disco, Rue de Laeken 12 (219-2336); **L'Incognito**, bar, happy hour 19-20 hrs. daily, 36 rue des Pierres (513-3788); **Le Sept**, leather bar/disco, Plattesteen 7 (513-1414); **Why Not**, dance club, leather clientele, theme parties once a month, free entry, 7 rue des Riches-Claires (512-7587).

● Bars/clubs (GMW): **Big Noise**, bar and occasional karaoke nights, 44 rue de Marché au Charbon (512-2525); **La Cita**, 57 rue Marché aux Charbon (513-5959); **Comptoir**, bar/restaurant, Place Vieille Halle aux blés 24-25 (514-0500); **H2O**, 27 rue Marché au Charbon (512-3843); **Orange Bleu**, 29 rue Antoine Dansaert (513-9829); **Tels Quels**, cafe/bar, the meeting place in Bruxelles for gay men and lesbians, 81 rue du Marché au Charbon (512-3234).

● Bars/clubs (GW): **Le Feminin**, disco/bar, Rue Borgval 9 (511-1709); **Sapho**, 1 rue Saint Gery (512-4552).

● Restaurants (GMW): **Annexe**, rue des Bouchers, 71-73 (512-3856); **La Bimbloterie**, fine traditional cuisine, mixed clientele, in one of Brussels oldest areas, rue de Rollebeekstraat 11 (512-7077); **Butte**, 159 Chausée de Waterloo (537-5539); **Chez Maman**, traditional quiches, rue des Grands Carmes (502-8696); **Comptoir**, Place Vieille Halle aux blés 24-25 (514-0500); **Garde-Manger**, local cuisine, rue Washington 151-153 (346-6829); **H2O**, rue du Marché 27 (512-3843); **Maximin**, French, 189 rue de l'Intendant (425-6544); **l'Or Noir**, 45, rue des Pierres (512-6381); **Prime Out**, local cuisine, rue Blaes 109 (511-1312); **Rambûché**, rue de Midi 157 (512-6381); **Orange Bleu**, Italian restaurant, cocktails, rue Antoine Dansaerstraat 29 (513-9829); Others (AW): **Comme Chez Soi**, *mussels, foie gras, and French pastries*, 23 PL. Rouppe (512-2921) expensive; **Aux Armes de Bruxelles**, authentic old world restaurant off the Grand-Place, mostly fish specialties, 13 rue des Bouchers (511-5598) inexpensive.

λ SERVICES λ

● Erotica (GM): **Erot'x Stars**, Boulevard Maurice Lemonnieerlaan 40 (513-9344); **Europa-x**, Blvd. Adolph Maxlaan 60 (219-7140).

● Health Clubs (GM): **Atlantis**, Turkish bath, Finnish sauna, relaxation rooms, bar & restaurant, Wolvertemsesteenweg 74 (270-1186); **La Griffe**, rue de Dinant (512-6251); **Macho 2**, sauna, bar, gym, videos, rue du Marché au Charbon 108 (513-5667); **l'Oasis**, sauna with limited accommodations, fitness room, bars, snack, 10 rue Van Orley Straat (218-0800); **Padoum Center**, sauna, steambath, gay karaoke bar, sexshop, Boulevard Jamarlaan 9 (522-1050).

● Leather (GMW): **Boutique Minuit**, leather clothing and sexy underwear, Galerie de Centre 60 (223-0914).

 ACCOMMODATIONS

HOTEL AUX ARCADES
Rue de Bouchers, Brussels. USA/Canada reservations (800) 257-5344 or (516) 944-7540. Fax: (516) 944-7540. TYPE: *Hotel*. CLIENTELE: All Welcome. LOCATION: Heart of the Old City with many restaurants, bars and clubs around the hotel. Walk to gay bars and clubs.

* Rooms: 40 w/priv. bath
* CTV, phone, C/H, minibar
* Restaurant: local cuisine, elevator
* Airport: 30 min. taxi / train
* Train Station: 5 min. walk
* Gay Bars: walking distance
* Open: Year round
* Rates: (US) $110 - $160 w/CB
* *TAC:* 10% (from Odysseus)

DESCRIPTION: Pleasant 3-star hotel in the center of the Old City. Rooms are large and comfortably appointed. Location can be noisy as it is surrounded by many restaurants, cafes and bars. However, the Old City becomes quiet after midnight. (back rooms are generally quieter). Expanded continental breakfast served in your room.

HOTEL ARIS
78-80 rue Marché aux Herbes, 1000 Bruxelles. Tel: (2) 514-4300. TYPE: *Hotel.* CLIENTELE: All Welcome. LOCATION: Old town location near the Grand-Place.

* Rooms: 55 w/priv. bath
* CTV, phone, A/C, C/H, safe deposit, hairdryer
* Gay Bars: walking distance
* Airport: 14 km / 8 mi.; taxi
* Train Station: 5 min. walk
* Open: Year round
* Rates: (US) $160-$220 w/CbB
* *TAC:* 10% (from Odysseus)

DESCRIPTION: Charming renovated first class hotel in a central Old Town location. Excellent quality and location.

HOTEL CHAMBORD
Rue de Namur 82, Bruxelles B-1000. Tel: (02) 513-4119. TYPE: *Hotel.* CLIENTELE: All Welcome. LOCATION: Fashion and commercial district near Avenue Louise, 10 min. walk from the Grand Place.

* Rooms: 69 w/priv. bath. Suite: 1
* CTV, phone, minibar
* Piano bar, elevator, parking
* Gay Bars: walking distance
* Airport: 14 km / 8 mi.; taxi
* Train Station: 5 min. walk
* Open: Year round
* Rates: (US) $120-$160 w/CbB
* *TAC:* 10% (from Odysseus)

DESCRIPTION: Superior 3-star hotel in a central location. Classic building, pleasantly appointed public areas and guest rooms. Restaurants and clubs within walking distance.

HÔTEL MADELEINE **

Tourist Hotel in the heart of 'Gay Brussels' ★★

USA/CANADA Reservations
1-800-257-5344

H M

HÔTEL VENDOME ***

Quality Hotel in 'Gay Brussels' ★★★

USA/CANADA Reservations
1-800-257-5344

H V

✪ HOTEL LA MADELEINE

Rue de la Montagne 22, B-1000 Bruxelles. Tel: (2) 513-2973. USA/Canada reservations - Tel: (516) 944-5330 or (800) 257-5344. Fax: (516) 944-7540. TYPE: *Hotel.* CLIENTELE: All Welcome. LOCATION: Old City, a few feet from the Grand-Place near the Museum of Fine Arts, Central Train Station and the gay scene.

* Rooms: 52 most w/priv. bath
* CTV, phone, C/H, elevator
* Gay Bars: walking distance
* Airport: 14 km / 8 mi.; taxi
* Train Station: 5 min. walk
* Open: Year round
* Rates: (US) $90 - $140
* *TAC:* 10% (from Odysseus)

DESCRIPTION: Modest 2-star hotel with a listed facade of period architecture in a good central location at the edge of the Old Town. Rooms are simple but comfortable. Hotel completely renovated in 1995.

✪ HÔTEL VENDÔME

Bd. Adolph Max 58, 1000 Brussels. USA/Canada reservations (800) 257-5344 or (516) 944-5330. Fax: (800) 982-6571 or (516) 944-7540. TYPE: *Hotel.* CLIENTELE: Gay welcome. LOCATION: Near Place de Brouckère and Place de la Monnaie of Central Brussels. Close to trains, trams and Buses.

* Rooms: 116 w/priv. bath
* CTV, phone, C/H, minibar, elevator
* Lounges, private garage, veranda
* Gay Bars: many within walking distance
* Airport: 14 km / 8 mi.; taxi
* Open: Year round
* Rates: (US) $110 - $160 w/EbB
* *TAC:* 10% (from Odysseus)

DESCRIPTION: Paris Haussman style 3-star hotel fully renovated in 1994. The hotel offers all the comfort and amenities of a good hotel. Excellent location to enjoy the vibrant gay scene of central brussels. Excellent expanded continental breakfast buffet served in a cozy breakfast room. Most gay bars and clubs only a short walk away.

LIÉGE   ✆ 041

✈ Liege/Bierset Airport (LGG)

LOCATION: Eastern Belgium near the borders with the Netherlands and Germany.

POPULATION: 440,000

CLIMATE: see Brussels

Gay Visitor Information
Paralléle: 342-0056
Rue Surlet 39 (4020)

DESCRIPTION: The third largest city, capital of the province of Liège, and an important University town. According to legend Liège was founded in the 7th century by St. Lambert, Bishop of Maastricht. The city lies at the confluence of the Ourthe and the Meuse (Maas).

BARS ▼ RESTAURANTS ¶¶

● Bars/clubs (GM): **L'Ami Gay**, 33 rue de la Casquette (221-626); **Spartacus**, leather club, 12 rue Saint Jean en Isle (231-259).

● Bars/clubs (GMW): **La Brique**, dance club, 4 rue Laruelle (231-550); **Dr. No**, dance bar, Rue de la Casquette 38 (221-3037); **Le Jaguar**, 37 rue dela Casquette (237-948); **Mama Roma**, 16 rue des Célestines (234-769); **La Scène**, dance club, Rue de la Casquette 1 (221-0548).

● Bars/clubs (GW): **La Jungle**, dance bar, Rue Léon-Mignon 20 (222-0775).

● Restaurants (AW): **La Bonne Franquette**, 152 rue Féronstrée (23 08 81); **Le Brasilia**, restaurant/tavern, Rue Pont d'Avroy 44 (222-1919); **Chez Dimitri**, Greek cuisine, Rue Saint-Jean-en-Isle 6 (223-7456); **Le Comptoir Gourmand**, 13 rue du Mont Blanc (220-516); **L'Italien**, Rue en Bergerue 16 (223-1569).

λ SERVICES λ

● Health Club (GM): **Le 7 Sauna**, 7 rue Celestins (213-921).

● Leather Shop (G/S): **Indoor Dreams**, Rue Souverain-Pont 11 (223-6796).

● Sex Shop (GM): **Rainbow**, videos, movies, Rue de la Cathédrale 9 (221-2611); **Sexy World**, leather, sexy underwear, Rue Souverain-Pont 35 (221-3457).

 ACCOMMODATIONS

DE LA COURONNE HOTEL
Place de Guillemins 11, Liege 4000. Tel: (41) 522-168. Fax: (41) 525-552. TYPE: *Hotel.* CLIENTELE: Mostly Straight. LOCATION: Central location facing the Train Station.

* 78 w/priv. bath. Suite: 1
* CTV, maid & room service
* Gay Bar: nearby
* Airport: 6 km / 4 mi.
* Open: Year round
* Rates: (BF) 2,100 - 2,540.
* *TAC:* 8%

DESCRIPTION: Refined traditional tourist class hotel in a central location.

OSTEND   *(C)* **059**

✈ Brussels Nat'l Airport (BRU)
82 mi. / 130 km southeast of Ostend

LOCATION: North Sea Coast in the province of West Flanders.

POPULATION: 72,000

CLIMATE: see Brussels

Gay/Lesbian Visitor Information
Recht door Zee: 802-674

DESCRIPTION: Seaside resort, the largest in Belgium, and a principal port for passenger and car ferry services to England. Visit the **Old Town** that runs from the commercial docks in the south, north-west to the dike. Attractions include: the **Kuursaal Casino**, Folklore Museum, Marine Museum, Whellington horse racetrack, golf course and sports activities. Ostend is a well known Spa treatment center with its own Thermal Institute.

BARS ▼ RESTAURANTS 🍴

● Bars/clubs (GM): **Calypso**, Groentenmarkt 15 (801-569); **Dali**, bar/hotel, Kadzandstraat 2 (804-360); **Men 4 Men**, dance club, Sint-Franciscusstraat 22 (703-067); **Raphsodie**, St. Franciscusstraat 24 (808-473).

● Bars/clubs (GMW): **JB's**, dance club, Oosttraat 55 (511-892); **Croisette**, Albert 1 Promenade 50a (670-9165); **Valentino**, dance club, Schipperstraat 50 (502-926).

● Restaurants (AW): **Cafe de Flore**, Kursaal (Oostheling); **Le Condor**, Christianstraat 104; **Le Cormoran**, Langestraat 63 (701-160); **Croisette**, seafront restaurant & bar, Italian and light cuisine, Albert 1 Promenade 50a (670-9165); **Pierrot**, Van Iseghemiaan 40F (705-137); **VanEyck**, excellent 5 course menu including wine at affordable price, Hertstraat 10 (703-581).

λ SERVICES λ

● Erotice (GM): **Ero "Adonis"**, videoclub, Dwarstraat 1b (514-301); **Paradise**, Madridstraat 15 (513-672).

● Health Clubs (GM): **Kouros II**, sauna, video room, relax cabines, Peter Benoitstraat 77 (513-455); **Thermos**, Kaaistraat 34 (515-923).

🔑 ACCOMMODATIONS 🔑

ANDROMEDA HOTEL
Kursaal Westhelling 5, Ostend B-8400. Tel: (59) 806-611. Fax: (59) 806-629. TYPE: *Hotel*. CLIENTELE: Mostly Straight. LOCATION: On the Promenade next to the Casino, facing the ocean. 95 rooms w/priv. bath, 10 suites, CTV, phone, balcony, C/H, Wheelchair Accessibility, free parking, restaurant, bar, pool, sauna, 50 m/yards to beach, gay bars nearby, 3 mi. / 5 km to airport, open year round, Rates: BF 4,800 - 8,400. *TAC:* 8%. DESCRIPTION: Most rooms have balconies with seaview. Health Spa programs.

DALI
Kadznadstraat 2, Ostend B-8400. Tel: (59) 804360. TYPE: *Hotel & Tavern*. CLIENTELE: Gay men. LOCATION: Central location. Description: Budget rooms, light meals, ice-cream on terrace.

BELIZE

AREA: 8,867 sq. mi. (22,966 sq. km)
POPULATION: 150,000
CAPITAL: Belmopan
CURRENCY: Belize Dollar (B$)
OFFICIAL LANGUAGE: English, Spanish
MAJOR RELIGIONS: Roman Catholicism, protestantism
Telephone: 501
Nat'l Holiday: National Day, September 10
Official Time: 4 hrs. behind G.M.T.
Electricity: 110/220 volts, 60 cycles
Exchange Rate: 1US$ = B$ 2.00
National Airline: Maya Airways

LAW REGARDING HOMOSEXUALITY: There is no particular law regarding homosexuality. However, it is unadvisable to get involved with minors of less than 18 years old because of the high sensitivity of the local authorities.

BELIZE CITY   *C* 02

✈ Stanley Int'l Airport (BZE)

LOCATION: In the heart of the Eastern Coast of Belize, on the Caribbean Sea.

POPULATION: 50,000

CLIMATE: Hot and humid Caribbean climate, ranging from 67°F to 88°F (19°c - 31°c) year round. Raining season is from May to October; warm dry season lasts from November till April.

VISITOR INFORMATION
Belize Tourist Board,
12 Regent Street, Belize City, Belize

DESCRIPTION: Belize City is one of the old-

est settlements for the English pirates in the 17th and 18th century in the Caribbean. Today, it is the main port and commercial center in Belize. An interesting display of Mayan art can be seen at the **City Museum**. The **Anglican Cathedral** claims to be the oldest of its kind in Central America. There are very few cases of AIDS in Belize, however, you should always protect yourself and your partners. Try to spend as little time as possible in Belize City, although this is a good starting point for exploring the rest of the country. Side trips are recommended to **San Ignacio**, and the Mayan ruins of **Xunantunich**. Also visit **Stann Creek** for its large orange tree plantation and view of the country side.

BARS ⅄ RESTAURANTS 🍴

Gay life in Belize is limited and subdued, therefore any contacts with locals must be dealt with caution. There are no exclusively gay oriented establishments, but most places welcome discreet gays.

● Bar/Club (G/S): **Upstairs Café**, many GI's (AYOR), Queen Street, Belmopan.

● Restaurants (AW): It is highly recommended not to eat in any local restaurant. It is safer to eat local and International cuisine at the **Fort George Hotel** or the **El Centro** hotel and Restaurant.

🏠 ACCOMMODATIONS 🏠

FORT GEORGE HOTEL
2 Marine Parade, P.O. Box 321, Belize City. Tel: (2) 77400. Fax: (2) 73820. TYPE: *Hotel*. CLIENTELE: Mostly Straight. LOCATION: Near the beach, & downtown.

* Rooms: 76 w/priv. bath, Suites: 14
* Phone, CTV, minibar, most w/patio
* 24 hrs room service, maid service, laundry
* Restaurant, bar, roof deck, marina
* Pool w/poolside bar
* Airport: 11 mi. / 18 km
* Open: Year round
* Rates: (US) $99 - $155
* *TAC:* 10%

DESCRIPTION: Colonial style superior first class hotel. Sightseeing arranged to Mayan ruins.

CENTRAL FARM   *C* 92

🦋 ACCOMMODATIONS 🦋

✪ BLANCANEAUX LODGE

Central Farm. USA/Canada Reservations - Tel: (800) 257-5344 or (516) 944-7540. Fax: (516) 944-7540. TYPE: *Mountain Lodge*. OWNER: Fancis Ford Copola. CLIENTELE: All Welcome. LOCATION: In the mountain Pine Ridge Forest Reserve of Western Belize.

* Rooms: 2 lodge rooms w/shared bath
* Cottages: 7, Villas: 5 (9x1BR /5x2BR) living room, full bath,patio/terrace
* Bed Types: twin, double, queen size
* Services: maid, room, laundry
* Restaurant: Italian/Belizean
* Special Diets: vegetarian
* Bar: Jaguar Bar
* Recreation: Jungle river trips, horseback riding, mountain, biking, waterfalls
* Free parking, Pets w/prearrangement

* Beach: river beach nearby, ocean beach 100 mi / 160 km
* Airport: Blancaneaux airstrip on property 2 hrs drive to Belize Int'l AP (80 mi / 128 km)
* Airport Transfers: by arrangement in a 4-wheel drive
* Languages: English, Spanish, Creole, Mayan, Garifuna
* Reservations: through Odysseus
* Open: Nov. 1 - Sept. 30 (closed October)
* Rates: $90-$380 w/CB. Tax: 17%
* Check In 2:00 pm / check out 12:00 noon
* *TAC:* 10% (from Odysseus)

DESCRIPTION: Francis Ford Copola's mountain retreat consists of thatched-roof cabanas and luxury villas overlooking waterfalls and pools. The interior design of each cabana and villa is uniquely different, incorporating colonial and antique furniture and articrafts from Central America. Archaeology, natural history and ecology tours can be arranged.

BLANCANEAUX LODGE
World Class Retreat

Reservations:
(800) 257-5344
Tel: (516) 944-5330
Fax: (516) 944-7540
Email:
odyusa@odyusa.com

BERMUDA

AREA: 21 sq. mi. (54 sq. km)
POPULATION: 70,000
CAPITAL: Hamilton
CURRENCY: Bermuda Dollar (B$)
OFFICIAL LANGUAGE: English
MAJOR RELIGIONS: Protestantism
Telephone: 809
Nat'l Holiday: Independence Day, Sept. 7
Official Time: G.M.T. -5 (or 4)
Electricity: 110 volts / 60 cycles AC
Exchange Rate: 1B$ = US$1
National Airline: British Airways

LAW REGARDING HOMOSEXUALITY: As of June 1994 homosexuality is not a crime and not subject to punishment. The Sodomy law has been repealed. The age of consent is 18 years.

❖ There is not really much that happens in Bermuda for gay men and lesbians. The only way to meet people is private dinner parties or hanging out at **Chaplin Bay Beach** (AYOR) on the south shore.

HAMILTON

✈ Kindley Field Airport (BDA)
   10 mi. / 16 km NE

LOCATION: At the eastern end of Bermuda's Great Sound.

POPULATION: 2,000

CLIMATE: Subtropical with no significant rainy months. There are two distinguished seasons: May-Nov. (summer) with average temperatures of 80°F (26°c); and mid-Nov-March (winter) with average temperatures of 65°F (18°c).

DESCRIPTION: Hamilton, the colony's capital, is a charming pink and white town on the inner shore of the "fishhook".

❖ Beaches: **Elbow Beach** and **Chaplin's Bay**.

♈ BAR ♈

● Bar/Club (G/S): **Casey's**, Queen Street; **Cock & Feather**, Front St.; **Gazebo Bar**, c/o Princess Hotel (see description below).

λ SERVICE λ

● Shop (G/S): **Roomers**, bath accessories and housewares, line of gay/lesbian jewelry and pride/rainbow wear, Queen St.

 ACCOMMODATIONS

HORIZONS
Warwick. Reservation/Information: (516) 944-5330. Fax: (516) 944-7540. TYPE: *Guest House*. CLIENTELE: Mostly Straight. LOCATION: South Shore, 3.5 mi. / 6 km from Hamilton. 10 apartments, bar, lounge, pool. DESCRIPTION: Informal guest house featuring Self-catering apartments and rooms. Beaches, restaurants and entertainment nearby.

ELBOW BEACH HOTEL
South Shore Rd., Paget. Tel: 236-3535. Fax: 236-8043. TYPE: *Resort Hotel*. CLIENTELE: Mostly Straight. LOCATION: On landscaped ground overlooking the popular and cruisy Elbow Beach. 301 rooms w/priv. bath, 17 duplex cottages,CTV, phone, A/C, restaurants, pubs, cafes, pool, Tennis courts, Health Club, sauna, massage, whirlpool, private beach, water skiing, scuba, free parking, on private beach. Rates: $255-$550. *TAC:* 10%. DESCRIPTION: Superior first class resort hotel with duplex cottages scattered along a hillside amongst shade trees and tropical gardens. Rooms and cottages are attractive with modern appointments. Private marble bathrooms some with jacuzzi, bathrobes and hair dryers. Rooms with fax/computer hook-up available.

THE PRINCESS HOTEL
Hamilton. Tel: 295-3000. TYPE: *Hotel*. CLIENTELE: Mostly Straight. LOCATION: Overlooking Hamilton Harbor, 15 min. walk from City's, business center. 450 rooms w/priv. bath, suites & Penthouse suites, CTV, phone, A/C, balcony/patio, restaurants, pub, cocktail lounges. DESCRIPTION: Superior First Class Hotel.

BOLIVIA

AREA: 424,163 sq. mi. (1,098,582 sq. km)
POPULATION: 5,600,000
CAPITAL: La Paz
CURRENCY: Boliviano (B)
OFFICIAL LANGUAGE: Spanish, Quechua
MAJOR RELIGIONS: Roman Catholicism
Telephone: 591
Nat'l Holiday: 5-7 August, Independence
Official Time: G.M.T. - 4
Electricity: 110 volts, 50 cycles AC
Exchange Rate: 1US$ = B4.89
National Airline: Aéreo Boliviano

LAW REGARDING HOMOSEXUALITY:
Homosexuality is not mentioned in the Code of
Law. The age of consent is 17.

LA PAZ ℭ 2

✈ El Alto Int'l Airport (LPB)
8 mi. / 13 km southeast

LOCATION: Western Bolivia, in the Little
Bolivia region, 3,636 m / 12,000 ft. above sea
level in a natural basin.

POPULATION: 1,150,000

CLIMATE: Mountainous. The mean average
temperature is 50°F (10°c) with wide daily variation. Nights are cold and it rains every day
from December to February. The rest of the
year the weather is clear and sunny.

DESCRIPTION: Visitors to the highest capital in the world often feel some discomfort
known as altitude sickness. Most of the Indian
population live on the higher terraces with the
business center and government offices below.

Enjoy the city's unique Indian/Spanish heritage, the magnificent snow covered mountains, Lake Titicaca and mysterious Indian
ruins. La Paz is probably one of the safest cities
in South America, but be aware of pickpockets
and purse snatchers. The Gay scene is almost
non existent. Cruisy areas include: **Plaza San
Francisco, Plaza Mendoza, El Prado &
Plaza P. Velasco.**

🍸 BAR 🍸

● Bar (G/S): **Brasil**, Avda Heroes del Acre 1762
(322-197).

ACCOMMODATIONS

GLORIA HOTEL
Calle Potosi 909, La Paz. Tel: (2) 370010. Fax:
(2) 391-489. TYPE: *Hotel*. CLIENTELE: Mostly Straight. LOCATION: Downtown facing San
Francisco Plaza. 90 rooms, CTV, phone, minibar, refrigerator, restaurant, bar, lounge, Sky
room, gym, free parking. Rate: $60-$80.
DESCRIPTION: Busy superior tourist class
hotel. Many rooms with views.

SANTA CRUZ ℭ 3

✈ Viru Viru Int'l Airport (VVI) 10 mi. / 16 km

LOCATION: Eastern Bolivia, 552 km / 345 mi.
from La Paz by air.

POPULATION: 850,000

CLIMATE: Hot and windy from May to August.
The rainy season is December-February.

DESCRIPTION: The second largest city in
Bolivia and the capital of the Dept. of Santa
Cruz. The region is rich in natural resources.

🍸 BARS 🍸

● Bars/clubs (GWS): **Las Brujas**, Avda Caña-
to; **Line**, Avda 26 de Febrero.

 ACCOMMODATIONS

GRAN HOTEL CORTEZ
Avda Cristobal de Mendoza, Santa Cruz. Tel:
(3) 331-234. Fax: (3) 351-186. TYPE: *Hotel*.
CLIENTELE: Mostly Straight. LOCATION: 6
blocks from downtown. 86 rooms. 11 suites.

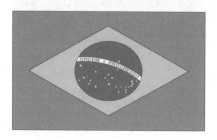

AREA: 3,284,426 sq. mi. (8,506,663 sq. km)
POPULATION: 119,098,000
CAPITAL: Brasilia
CURRENCY: Real (R)
OFFICIAL LANGUAGE: Portuguese
MAJOR RELIGIONS: Roman Catholicism
Telephone: 55
Nat'l Holiday: Independence Day, Sept. 7
Official Time: 3 hrs. behind G.M.T.
Electricity: 220 volts
Exchange Rate: 1US$ = R 1.03
National Airline: Varig

LAW REGARDING HOMOSEXUALITY:
Homosexuality is legal in Brazil. The legal
minimum age for consensual homosexual activity is 18 years. Brazil is a macho oriented society where gays are often discriminated against.

Note: Brazil displays an ambiguous attitude
towards homosexuality. On the one hand it is a
nation with an exuberant gay culture, attracting gay tourists to Rio's legendary Carnavals,
nightlife and sexy beaches. On the other hand
the violence against homosexuals is on the
increase. Brazil's Gay Rights movement is
weak and disorganized, because there are no
laws prohibiting homosexuality in Brazil.
Brazil decriminalized most homosexual acts in
1823. Although more people practice homosexuality in this country, they tend to keep their
sexual orientation secret to avoid exposing
themselves and their families to ridicule.

BRASILIA   🕾 061

✈ Brasilia Int'l Airport (BSB)

LOCATION: 960 km / 600 mi. northwest of Rio
de Janeiro in the uplands of Goiás.

POPULATION: 450,000

CLIMATE: Mild with low humidity. Summer
brings heavy rains, but the air is cool at night.

DESCRIPTION: Brasilia is a man-made capital, constructed in Brazil's interior to draw the
abundant coastal population. Its architecture
was designed by the internationally famous
architect Oscar Niemeyer. An outstanding
example of the modern design is the **Praça
dos Três Poderes** (Square of the Three Powers) where three magnificent buildings house
the three branches of government: the
Supreme Court, the Presidential Palace, and
the Congress. Brasília was designed in the
shape of an airplane, it enjoys fresh, unpollut-
ed air, and plenty of green areas.

❖ Gay beach: try the mineral water pools at the
Parque Nacional.

BARS ⅄ RESTAURANTS 🍴

● Bars/clubs (GM): **Arabeske**, C.L.S. 109,
bloco B, loja 2; **Boite Aquarius**, Edificio
Acropol, loja 12 (225 9928); **Karekas**, C-08 lote
18, loja 2, Taguatinga. If you like English style
pubs (not gay oriented, but who knows what
one can find there) check **Gates Pub**, 403 Sul,
and the **London Tavern**, 409 Sul.

● Restaurants (AW): **Gaff**, French & Brazilian
cuisine, at the Gilberto Salomão Shopping Center; **Restaurante Panoramico**, in the TV
tower building, good food and fine view of the
city; **Aeroporto**, terrace of the International
Airport; for seafood try **Panela de Barro**,
Galeria Nova Ouvidor, Setor Commercial Sul.

λ SERVICES λ

● Health Clubs (G/S): **Apollo**, LN 3, Lote 2,
Taguatinga; **Sauna Hotel Nacional**, c/o Hotel
Nacional, SHS, Lote 1.

ACCOMMODATIONS

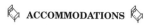

HOTEL NACIONAL
Setor Hoteliero Sul, Lote 1, Brasilia 70322 D.F.
Tel: (061) 226 8180. Telex: 61 1062. TYPE: *Hotel.*
CLIENTELE: Mostly Straight. LOCATION: In
the heart of the capital. 30 rooms, 40 suites,
CTV, phone, restaurants, American bar, night-
club, Finnish sauna & Health Club, pool. Rates:
(US) $86-$110. *TAC:* 10%. DESCRIPTION:
Continental-style superior first class hotel, with
shopping arcade and parking. Check the sauna
and the American bar, but use common sense.

RECIFE   ✆ 081

✈ Guararapes Airport (REC) 8 mi. SW.

LOCATION: Northeast on the Atlantic Ocean, 244 km / 152 mi. north of Maceió.

POPULATION: 1,300,000

CLIMATE: Pleasant tropical climate with dry summers and rainy winters.

DESCRIPTION: A major city on the Atlantic Ocean. Recife offers good beaches, historic sites, artist's and intellectuals' quarter on the Pátio de São Padro, and a fine residential and hotel quarter in the southern suburb of Boa Viagem. The town's Carnaval is famous in Brazil. For gay travelers the place to explore is the colorful colonial **Olinda** a suburb of Recife. This is a charming enclave of historic houses where artists, musicians and writers live and create. Very similar in character to the famous New York's Greenwich Village.

BARS ♈ RESTAURANTS

● Bars/clubs (GM): **Bar Savoy**, Ave. Guararapas 147 (224-2291); **Kibe**, Avda HerculanoBondeira (Pina); **Mustang**, Av. Conde da Boa Vista. In Olinda: **Frutapão**, dance bar, Rua da Sol 349; **Itapoã**, Avda MarkusFreire 897.

● Restaurants (AW): **Le Buffet**, R. do Hospicio; **Maxime**, seafood, Av. Boa Viagem 21; **Mourisco**, best restaurant in Olinda, seafood specialty, 7 Praça Cons. João Alfredo, Olinda (429-1390); **Oficina da Massas**, Italian, Av. Boa Viagem 2232.

λ SERVICES λ

● Health Clubs (G/S): **Club Spartacus**, Rua João Ivo da Silva 95, Madalena (228-6828); **Termas Atenas**, Avda Cons. Aguiar 4790, Boa Viagem; **Termas Olinda**, Avda José Luiz Augusto Moreira 1215,Casa Caida, Olinda (429-4363).

🏠 ACCOMMODATIONS 🏠

INT'L OTHON PALACE HOTEL
Av. Boa Viagem 3722. Recife 51020. Tel: (81) 326-7225. Fax: (81) 325-1967. TYPE: *Hotel.* CLIENTELE: Mostly Straight. LOCATION: On Boa Viagem Beach. 257 rooms w/priv. bath, bars, restaurant, swimming pool. Rates: on request.

RIO DE JANEIRO   ✆ 021

✈ Galeão Int'l Airport (GIG)

LOCATION: East Coast of Brazil along the Atlantic Ocean, slightly above the Tropic of Capricorn, nestled between mountains and a deep blue sea.

POPULATION: City 5,093,237
             Metro 9,018,637

CLIMATE: Warm and comfortable year round. Summer average temperatures in January vary between a low of 73°F (23°c) and high of 84°F (29°c). Winter's average low in July is 63°F (17°c) and the average high is 75°F (24°c).

VISITOR INFORMATION
ATOBA: 331-1527

DESCRIPTION: Rio De Janeiro is a fun loving city; one of the most beautiful in the world. The recent economic problems and inflation rate has put a tremendous strain on the population and increase the gap between the rich and poor. On the streets and public transportation system security for foreign visitors is poor, so be extra careful. The most popular tourist attraction and the city's most recognized symbol is the famous **Statue of Christ**. Inaugurated in 1931 it is standing 120 ft. (40 m) tall on the top of a mountain.

❖ **SPECIAL EVENT: Carnaval Week**, is an extravagant event attracting many visitors to Brazil. During Carnaval the Brazilians are swept in a fast moving, colorful, musical and emotional trans to the exciting rhythm of the samba, which lasts for four days and five nights starting at midnight of the Friday before Ash Wednesday and ends on the Wednesday night. There are number of **gay balls** (warm ups) which attract international followers. The **Grande Gala G** is usually held at the **Help** disco on Copacabana's Avda Atlantica; another **Baille dos Enxutos** is hosted by **Hotel Itália** on Praça Tiradentes (Centro).

❖ Beaches: the city has 16 great sandy beaches with **Copacabana** and **Ipanema** being the most popular with gay travelers. The beach at **Ipanema**, across from the Farme de Almoedo Street by the Garota de Ipanema Bar (at Rua Teixeira de Melo) is very popular with local and visiting gays. The beach area infront of the **Copacabana Palace Hotel** is frequented by gays.

☛ **Note:** Street crimes and muggings are common place. For your personal safety, take cabs at night and be aware and streetwise.

BARS ⅄ RESTAURANTS 🍴

One of the centers of gay life in Rio is the **Galeria Alaska** off Avenida Atlantica in Copacabana. Other gay attractions include the **Cinelandia** and the **Tivoli Amusement Park**. Tivoli Amusement Park features a "gay night" every Saturday, and it can be quite outrageous during Carnaval. Following are some of Rio's popular bars, discos, and cabarets.

● Bars/clubs (GM): **Alibi**, dance club, Barra de Tijuca; **Boemio**, restaurant, bar and nightclub, rua Santa Luzia 760, Centro-Cinelandia (240-7259); **Boy Disco**, Rua Raul Pompeia 94, Copacabana (521-0367); **Club Rio**, bar/restaurant with live entertainment, Travessa Cristiano Lacorte 54, Copacabana (521-6740); **La Cueva**, disco, rua Miguel Lemos 51, Copacabana (237-6757); **Incontru's**, disco, Praça Serzedelo Corrêia 15A, Copacabana (257-6498); **Maxim's**, sidewalk cafe and bar, Avda Atlantica,Copacabana; **Teatro Alaska**, drag show, inside the Galeria Alaska; **Teatro Brigitte Blair**, drag show from 10pm, opposite

The Club Rio on Travessa Cristiano Lacorte.

● Bars/Clubs (GW): **Club Rio** although it is mainly for gay men; **Bohemio** after hours mixed bar for gays and lesbians, rua Santa Luzia 760, Centro (240 7259).

● Restaurants (GMW): **Bohemio**, vegetarian restaurant, Rua Santa Luzia 760 (240-7259); **Rio Jarez**, seafood, Ave. Atlantica 3806 (267-5644). Others (AW): **Chalé**, Rio's best Bahian restaurant, rua da Matriz, 54 (286-0897); **Oxalá**, quick and cheap meals, rua Francisco Serrador (downtown) (242-0256); **Le Relais**, Rio's top French restaurant, Av. General Venancio Flores, 365 (294-2897); **Grottamare**, seafood restaurant, expensive, rua Gomes Carneiro, 132, Ipanema (287-1596); **Del Mare**, seafood, rua Paul Redfern, 37, Ipanema (239-1842); **Maxims**, popular cafe next to the Copacabana Palace, Avda Atlantica; **La Tour**, great view of town and Sugar Loaf, Continental cuisine, moderately priced, rua Santa Luzia, 651 (240-5795).

⅄ SERVICES ⅄

● Cinema (GM): **Astor**, Avda Ministro Edgar Romeiro 236; **Copacabana**, Avda Nossa Sra de Copacabana 801 (Copacabana); **Iris**, rua da Carioca 49; **Palacio**, Rua do Passeio 40, Passeio (240-6541); **Scala**, Praia de Botafogo 320 Botafogo (266-2545).

● Health Clubs (GM): **Nova Termas Leblon**, sauna, rua Barão da Torre 522, Ipanema (287-8899); **Roger's Thermas**, rua Ministro Alfredo Valadão 32, Copacabana; **Termas Ipanema**, rua Barão Jaguaripe 59, Ipanema; .

🔑 ACCOMMODATIONS 🔑

COPACABANA PALACE HOTEL
Av. Atlântica 1702, Rio De Janeiro 22021. Tel: (021) 237-3271. TYPE: *Hotel*. CLIENTELE: Mainly Straight. LOCATION: On the famous Copacabana Beach with all the gay action.

* 223 Rooms w/priv. bath. 102 Suites
* CTV, phone, A/C, minibar
* Bar, restaurants, nightclub
* Pool, sauna, Theatre, room & maid service
* Beach: facing the beach.
* Airport: 4 mi. / 6 km, taxi.
* Credit Cards: MC/AMEX/DC.
* Rates: (US) $240-$380 w/BrB
* *TAC:* 10%

DESCRIPTION: Five star luxury hotel with excellent service in a great beach location, very convenient for upscaled/business travelers.

LUXOR COPACABANA
Av. Atlântica 2554, Rio De Janeiro 22041. Tel: (021) 235-2245. TYPE: *Hotel*. CLIENTELE: Mostly Straight. LOCATION: Excellent location near gay beach.

* Rooms: 123 w/priv. bath. Suites: 4
* CTV, phone, A/C, minibar, in-room safe
* 24 hrs. room service, maid service
* Beach: on the beach.
* Airport: 4 mi. / 6 km, taxi
* Credit Cards: MC/VISA/AMEX/DC
* Open: Year round.
* Rates: (US) $120-$240 w/Bb
* *TAC:* 10%

DESCRIPTION: Pleasent first class hotel with a great Copacabana Beach location.

SALVADOR   ✆ 071

✈ Dois de Julho Airport (SSA)

LOCATION: On the Atlantic Coast, in the province of Bahia 1,700 km / 1062 mi. northeast of Rio.

POPULATION: 1,500,000

CLIMATE: Balmy weather year round with highs in the 80s˚F (29˚c) and lows in the 70s˚F (20˚c). Summers (December - February) can be hot with temperatures in the 90s˚F (30s˚c). Rainy season is from June through September.

Gay/Lesbian Visitor Information
Grupo Gay de Bahia: 243-4902

DESCRIPTION: Salvador is the capital of the state of Bahia. It is the second most popular gay destination in Brazil after Rio de Janeiro. Bahia offers miles of coconut tree lined beaches. The African influence is strongly present in the culture, food, and clothing style of the habitants. The city is full of churches, chapels, and other historic buildings dating back to the 16th century. Visit: **Terreiro de Jesus** - fountain-centered plaza where locals sell arts and crafts; **Church of São Francisco**; and the **Lacerda** elevator which connects the upper and lower cities. Salvador has a large poor population; it can be a rough experience, so be careful with your valuables and documents.

❖ Gay Beaches: **Porto de Barra** & **Farol de Barra**.

❖ **SPECIAL EVENT**: **Carnaval in Salvador**, street event of mass participation in February.

☛ **Note:** Street crimes and muggings are common place. For your personal safety, always take cabs at night and be aware and streetwise.

BARS ⅄ RESTAURANTS 🍴

● Bar/club (GM): **Banana Republica**, disco, Rua Broulio Xavier, Vitoria; **Bastidor**, Beco dos Artistas, Camp Grande; **Bizzaro**, dance club, Largo 2 de Julio, Center; **Holmes**, dance bar, rua Newton Prado 24, Gamboa de Cima (245-2493); **Red Zone**, dance club, Stela Mares.

● Restaurants (AW): **Cantina Lua**, Praça 15 de Novembro, cheap, good atmosphere, live Samba shows; **Ibiza**, rua Alfredo Brito 11; **Palace Hotel**, traditional Portuguese, rua Chile; **O Tempo**, Largo do Pelourinho, cheap restaurant in a charming antique decor; **Restaurante do SENAC**, sponsored by the Center for Professional Training in Tourism and Hospitality, self-service cafeteria in an attractive colonial dining room, authentic Bahian cuisine, Largo do Pelourinho 13/19 (242-5503).

◈ ACCOMMODATIONS ◈

DO FAROL HOTEL
Av. Presidente Vargas 68, Salvador, Bahia 40000. Tel: (71) 247-7611. TYPE: *Hotel*. CLIENTELE: Mostly Straight. LOCATION: Downtown at Farol do Barra Beach (popular with gays). 77 rooms w/priv. bath, CTV, phone, A/C, restaurant, bar, pool, sundeck. Rates: (US) $45 - $80. *TAC:* 10%. DESCRIPTION: Moderate first class hotel. Rooms with twin beds, balconies and refrigerator/bar. Good beach location.

SÃO PAULO   ✆ 11

✈ Congonhas Airport (CGH);
  Guarulhos Int'l Airport (GRU);
  Viracopos Int'l Airport (VCP)

LOCATION: 429 km / 268 mi. southwest of Rio.

POPULATION: 7,000,000

CLIMATE: Moderate. Average summer temperature is 75˚F (23˚c); average winter temperature is 65˚F (17˚c). Rainy season Oct.-March.

DESCRIPTION: The seventh largest, and one

of the fastest growing cities of the world, São Paulo epitomizes the economic and financial pulse of Brazil. The city has a mixture of ethnic groups. The diversification of races, economic development, and traditions makes São Paulo a fascinating metropolis to visit. The main shopping, hotel, and restaurant centre is on **Av. São Luis**, the **Praça da Republìca**, and **Rua Barão de Itapetininga**, the commercial quarter is at the **Triângulo** district. Visit: the Park in **Praça de República**; **Edifício Italía** on the corner of Av. Ipiranga and Av. São Luís is the city's tallest building. It has a rooftop restaurant with a panoramic balcony.

BARS Y RESTAURANTS ¶¶

São Paulo has the liveliest nightlife scene in all of South America and it offers a variety of bars and clubs to gay visitors.

● Bars/clubs (GM): **Anjo Azul**, dance club, Rua Brigadeira Galvão 723 (677-924); **Bug House**, dance club, Rua Santo Antonio 1000, Bela Vista (257-3131); **Bunker**, Rua Brigadeiro Galvão 723, Barra Funda (675-321); **Caneca de Prata**, Avda Vieira de Carvalho 55, Santa Ifigenia (223-6420); **Gent's**, dance club, shows, avda Tbirapuera 1911 (571-1516); **Nostro Mundo**, dance club, Rua da Consoloção 2554, M° Consoloção (257-4481); **Panther Boys**, dance club, Rua Marquês de Itú 182, Vila Buarque (221-4540); **Rave**, nightclub, rua Bela Cintra 1900 (883-2133); **Shock House**, dance club, Rua Rui Barbosa 201, Bela Vista, M° São Joaquim (285-0016); **Sound Factory**, Rua Pe. Bendito de Camargo 351 (293-2481); **Ritz**, Alameda Franca 1082/88, Cerqueira Cesar, Jardim Paulista (820-8599).

● Bars/clubs (GMW): **Casa de Vila**, Rua Girassol 310, Vila Madalena (210-5216); **Malicia**, dance bar, restaurant, Rua de Consolação 2554 (280-1401); **Prohibidu's**, dance club, Rua Amarel Gurgel 253, Vila Buarque, M° Republica (572-3715).

● Bars/clubs (GW): **Bug House**, dance bar, restaurant, Rua Santo Antonio 1000, Bela Vista (257-3131); **Segredu's**, dance bar, Rua Santo Antonio 922 (259-2492); **Setima Arte**, music bar, restaurant, Rua Epitácio Pessoa 32.

● Restaurants (GMW): **Spazio Pirandello**, Italian, Rua Augusta 311 (255-7586). Other: **Café do Bexiga**, Rua Treze de Maio 76, the 'artists quarter'; **Cantina do Piolin**, Italian, Rua Augusta 89 (245 9356). Others (AW): **La Colombe d'Or**, expensive French, Rua Almeda Santos 1165 (287 2431); **Suntory**, Japanese cuisine, Av. Campinas 600 (283 2455).

λ SERVICES λ

● Cinemas (G/S): **Arouche I & II**, Largo do arouche 426 (221-7678); **Art Palacio**, Avda São Paulo 419, Centro (223-2553); **Dom José**, Rua Dom José de Barros (223-5247).

● Health Clubs (GM): **Balneário Alterosas**, Avda de Alterosas 40A (958-1712); **Champion Club**, Largo do Arouche 336 (222-4973); **Ipanema**, rua Santo Antonio 675 (36-5837); **Le Rouge 80**, rua Germaine Burchard 286 (262-1155); **Thermas Lagoa**, sauna, gym, body building, videos, pool, sex shop, Rua Borges Lagoa 287, V. Mariana, M° Santa Cruz (573-9689).

 **ACCOMMODATIONS**

CAESAR PARK
Rua Augusta 1508, São Paulo. Tel: (11) 285 6622. TYPE: *Deluxe Hotel*. CLIENTELE: Mostly Straight. LOCATION: Downtown and Jardins district. 205 rooms w/priv. bath, 17 suites, CTV, phone, A/C, restaurants, cafe, bar, roof top pool, Health Club. Rates: (US) $150 - $500. *TAC:* 10%. DESCRIPTION: International hotel with fine amenities recommended for travelers on business account.

BRITISH VIRGIN ISLANDS

AREA: 59 sq. mi. (152 sq. km)
POPULATION: 12,000
CAPITAL: Road Town (Tortola)
CURRENCY: US dollar (US$)
OFFICIAL LANGUAGE: English
MAJOR RELIGIONS: Roman Catholicism
Telephone: 1
Nat'l Holiday: Commonwealth Day, March 13
Official Time: G.M.T - 5 (6 in winter)
Electricity: 110 volts, 208 volt supply to Tortola
Exchange Rate: 1US$

LAW REGARDING HOMOSEXUALITY: Homosexual acts between women is not mentioned in the British Code of Law. Minimum legal age for consensual homosexual activity for men is 21. The British Virgin Islands is a close knit society, friendly but also conservative.

TORTOLA   ✆ **809**

✈ Beef Island Airport (EIS)
  10 mi. / 16 km east of Road Town

LOCATION: Western British Virgin Islands, 60 mi. / 96 km east of Puerto Rico near the US Virgin Islands.

POPULATION: 10,000

CLIMATE: Constant warm and pleasant temperature cooled by trade winds year round. Temperatures range from 75°F-87°F (22°c-30°c).

VISITOR INFORMATION
BVI Tourist Board
P.O. Box 134, Road Town, Tortola
Tel: (809) 494-3134. Fax: (809) 494-3866

DESCRIPTION: Tortola is the major inhabit-

ed island in the BVI. Discovered by Christopher Columbus in 1493, the English later established control over the islands in the 16th century. Today, it is a major tourist destination for holiday makers in search of sun, sea and unspoiled nature.

❖ **Beaches:** beaches are secluded and rarely crowded. **Cane Garden Bay** is the best on the island; **Long Bay Beach** is on Beef Island near the airport offering a mile long stretch of sandy beach.

❖ **Diving:** The BVI offer some of the most spectacular underwater vistas; **Wreck of the RMS Rhone**, a marine park part of the BVI National Park Trust; **Blonde Rock**, pinnacle between Dead Chest & Salt Island; **Painted Walls**, a shallow dive off the southern point of Dead Chest; **The Chikuzen**, one of the best known dives in the BVI lying at a depth of 75 ft.

❖ **SPECIAL EVENTS: BVI Spring Regatta**, colorful annual yachting event that brings together sailors from all over the world, April 7-9; **BVI Summer Festival**, annual half-month long cultural festival held in Road Town. Nightly entertainment by local musicians, Calypso show, local food festival, July 28 - August 9; **Fall Caribbean Art Festival**, Sept. 26 - Oct. 1.

 ACCOMMODATIONS

ELIZABETH BEACH RESORT
Tortola, BVI. Reservations/information call (800) 257-5344. Tel: (516) 944-5330. Fax: (516) 944-7540. TYPE: *Villa Colony*. CLIENTELE: All Welcome. LOCATION: Hillside near Coconut palm-studded white sandy beach. 3 Villas, 2 or 3 BR, kitchen, living room, large verandah with seaview, daily maid service, private cook available. Rates: on request.

LONG BAY BEACH HOTEL
Road Town, BVI. Reservations/information call (800) 257-5344. Tel: (516) 944-5330. Fax: (516) 944-7540. TYPE: *Cottage Colony*. CLIENTELE: All Welcome. LOCATION: on 50-acre estate near mile-long beach on the north shore. 90 studios, cabanas and 2-5 BR villas, full kitchen, restaurants, bars, pool, tennis, free parking. Rates: on request.

VIRGIN GORDA   ✆ **809**

✈ Virgin Gorda Int'l Airport (VIJ)

Friendly, informal and charming inn, restaurant, bar and intriguing boutique. Now featuring a pool, health club, Jacuzzi, and poolside cafe. We pride ourselves on our excellent food, fine wines and our simple elegant atmosphere. Winner of 1996 Green Hotelier of the Year Environmental Awareness Award.

VIRGIN GORDA

Tel: (809) 495-5544 or (800) 653-9273
Fax: (809) 495-5986
Email: oldeyard@caribsurf.com
Internet: http://www.travelxn.com/oldyard

LOCATION: Northeastern British Virgin Islands.

POPULATION: 2,500

CLIMATE: Constant warm and pleasant temperature cooled by trade winds year round. Temperatures range from 75°F-87°F (22°c-30°c).

DESCRIPTION: A small 8 sq.mi island, the second largest in the cluster of the British Virgin Islands. Virgin Gorda or the "fat virgin" as it was named by Columbus boasts powder white sand beaches, colorful reefs, historic ruins, mountain trails and deep sheltered anchorage.

HOW TO GET THERE: the island is easily reached by flights from San Juan, St. Thomas or Beef Island Airport of Tortola. Regular ferry service links Virgin Gorda to St. Thomas, and Road Town, Tortola.

❖ **Beaches:** the best beaches are the Baths, Virgin Gorda's most famed attractions of granite boulders, grottos and sheltered sea pools for swimming and snorkeling

BARS ☥ RESTAURANTS 🍴

● Bar/Club (AW): ✪ **Olde Yard Inn**, bar, live

entertainment twice weekly in season, Virgin Gorda (495-5544); **Bath & Turtle Pub**, popular pub with twice-daily happy hour, Virgin Gorda Yacht Harbour, Spanish Town (495-5239); **The Mine Shaft**, bar, live entertainment, every Friday is Ladies Night, Virgin Gorda (5-5260).

● Restaurants (AW): ✪ **Olde Yard Inn**, award winning restaurant, classical music,Virgin Gorda (495-5544); **Capriccio de Mare**, Italian style sidewalk cafe Road Town (4-5369); **Peg Leg**, Nanny Cay (4-0028); **The Jolly Roger Inn**, Caribbean cuisine on the water, West End Ferry (495-4559); **The Pusser's Pub**, 2 floors of air-conditioned food and shopping, on Waterfront Drive; **Pusser's Landing**, waterside restaurant near the West End ferries, seafood and steaks (5-4554); **Quito's Gazebo**, bar / restaurant, cool island sound with Hawaiian flavor (5-4837)

🔑 ACCOMMODATIONS 🔑

✪ OLDE YARD INN

P.O. Box 26, The Valley, Virgin Gorda, BVI. Tel: (809) 495-5544. Toll Free (800) 653-9273. Fax: (809) 495-5986. TYPE: *Hotel.* HOSTESS: Jill Kaufman. CLIENTELE: All Welcome. LOCATION: In the Valley, Virgin Gorda, 1 mi. / 1.6 km to Ferry Dock.

* Rooms: 14 w/priv. bath, Suite: 1 (2BR)
  3 dbl / 9 triple /2 quad
* Safe box, A/C (some), hairdryer,
  mini refrigerators (some rooms)
* Maid & room service (breakfast only)
* Restaurant, bar, entertainment, shops
* Pool, sundeck, gym, jacuzzi, free parking
* Beach: 1 mi. / 1.6 km (mixed)
* Health Club: on premises
* Airport: 1 mi. / 1.6 km
* Reservations: 3 night deposit
* Cancellation: 30 days prior to arrival
* Credit Cards: MC/VISA/AMEX
* Open: Year round
* Rates: $145 - $245; (off) $90-$150
  7 night "Not Just for Honeymooners"
  packages available
* Tax: 7% BVI gvmt tax.
* *TAC:* 10%
* E-mail: oldeyard@caribsurf.com.
* Internet: www.travelxn.com/oldeyard

DESCRIPTION: 14 charming rooms with private patios set on a hillside amidst tropical gardens facing the sea. Amenities include: freshwater pool,jacuzzi, Health Club, gazebo library and acclaimed restaurant. This eco-friendly resort is the winner of the 1996 Caribbean Hotel Association Green Hotelier of the Year Environmental Awareness Award.

BULGARIA

AREA: 42,823 sq. mi. (110,912 sq. km)
POPULATION: 9,000,000
CAPITAL: Sofia
CURRENCY: Lev (BGL)
OFFICIAL LANGUAGE: Bulgarian
MAJOR RELIGIONS: Eastern Orthodoxy
Telephone: 359
Nat'l Holiday: March 3, Liberation Day
Official Time: G.M.T. + 2 or 3
Electricity: 220 volts, 50c AC
Exchange Rate: 1US$ = BGL 69
National Airline: Balkan Airlines

LAW REGARDING HOMOSEXUALITY: The law prohibits "scandalous homosexuality" and public manifestation of homosexuality. Violation of these laws can be punishable by up to 5 years in prison. Homosexuality is considered a taboo in the society at large.

SOFIA   ✆ 02

✈ Sofia Airport (SOF) 6 mi. / 10 km east

LOCATION: Western Bulgaria on the high Sofia Plain surrounded by mountains.

POPULATION: 1,000,000

CLIMATE: Warm but not unpleasant even in the summer. January-March is skiing season.

Gay/Lesbian Visitor Information
BULGA
P.O. Box 32, Sofia 1330
Tel: (02) 585271 / Fax: (02) 443804

DESCRIPTION: Sofia is a 5,000 years old city which only a century ago was the oriental capital of the Turkish province of Rumelia. After more than half a century of Communism, the city is slowly adapting to western democracy.

Visit the bazaars, parks, **Alexander Nevski** gold-domed **Cathedral**, the **National Museum of History** and enjoy dinner with folk music and dance. For gay visitors, the cruisy areas in town include: Garden in front of Train Station and the garden behind the Main Library near the University ("Doctors Garden").

BARS ♈ RESTAURANTS

● Bars/clubs (G/S): **Joe**, disco, Studentski Grad, Zimnia Dvorez; **Kamelia**, disco, Slanchev Briag; **Magura Café** (opposite Culture Palace); **Ritam**, Bulgaria St., & Emil Markov; **Vitoshko Lale Café**, Fritof Nansen 7.

● Restaurants (NG): **Lovno Ribarski**, Blvd. Vitosha (near Vasil Kolarov St.)

ACCOMMODATIONS

EVROPA HOTEL
131 Maria Luiza Blvd., Sofia BG-1202. Tel: (2) 31-261. Fax: (2) 320-011. TYPE: *Hotel.* CLIENTELE: Mostly Straight. LOCATION: Centrally near the Train Station.

* Rooms: 608 w/priv. bath. 7 suites
* CTV, phone, wheelchair access.
* Restaurant, bars, Grill room, parking
* Gay Bars: in town
* Airport: 6 mi. / 10 km
* Season: Year round
* Rates: $90-$140 *TAC:* 10%

DESCRIPTION: Modern 16-story hotel in a convenient central location. Walking distance to a cruisy gay garden.

VARNA   ✆ 052

✈ Varna Int'l Airport (VAR)
5.5 mi. / 9 km northwest

LOCATION: Northeastern Bulgaria in the famous Black Sea "Golden Sands" resort area.

POPULATION: 260,000

CLIMATE: Warm but not unpleasant even in the summer when the air is cooled by refreshing sea breezes.

DESCRIPTION: Bulgaria's third largest city

and major port in the tourist resort area of "Golden Sands". The town is elegant and is known worldwide for its seawater spa therapies and beautiful sandy beaches. Visit the 4,000 B.C. necropolis, and the 200 A.D. Roman baths. Drive along the Riviera to the famous resorts of Golden Sands. Casino gambling and Health Spas make the coast a veritable playland for the international jet-set.

❖ Nude Beaches (G/S): **Adam Beach** - men only nudist beach; **Albena Resort**, nudist section behind the Hotel Gergana); **Golden Sands Beach** men's nudist area.

BARS ♉ RESTAURANTS 🍴

● Cafe (AW): **Café Lauta**, infront of the Festivalen Complex (Summer only).

λ SERVICES λ

● Saunas (G/S): **City Baths** near the Moussala Hotel in Main Square; **Hamam**, Avram Gachev St. 3 (behind "Valentina) (223-027); **Mineral Bath No. 1**, Stefan Kjardja St., 1, behind the Cherno More Hotel, 2nd fl.; **Turkish Bath**, Tsar Simeon St. 3 (223-027).

ACCOMMODATIONS

CHERNO MORE HOTEL
G Dimitrov 33, Varna BG-9000. Tel: (52) 232115. Fax: (52) 236311. TYPE: *Hotel*. CLIENTELE: Mostly Straight. LOCATION: City Center. 214 rooms w/priv. bath, Panoramic bi-level restaurant, Nightclub. Rates: $65-$95. *TAC:* 10%.

DROUZHBA RESORT
Varna. Tel: (52) 861491. Fax: (52) 861920. TYPE: *Resort Hotel*. CLIENTELE: Mostly Straight. LOCATION: In large park near Golden Sands & Varna.

* Rooms & Suites: 328 w/priv. bath
* Rooms for non-smokers
* Wheelchair accessibility
* CTV, phone, A/C
* Pools, Spa Therapy Center, Tennis Courts, Gym, Casino
* Beach: 4 mi. / 6 km to Golden Sands
* Airport: 6 mi. / 10 km
* Season: Year round
* Rates: $110- $160.   *TAC:* 10%

DESCRIPTION: Resort complex with extensive resort facilities. A quiet place favored by scientists, intellectuals, writers and older people.

CAYMAN ISLANDS

AREA: 100 sq. mi. (259 sq. km)
POPULATION: 20,000
CAPITAL: George Town
CURRENCY: Cayman Island $ (CI$)
OFFICIAL LANGUAGE: English
MAJOR RELIGIONS: Roman Catholicism
Telephone: 809
Nat'l Holiday: Constitution Day, 1st Mon. in July
Official Time: G.M.T. - 5
Electricity: 110 volts, 60 cycles, A.C.
Exchange Rate: 1US$ = 0.83 CI$
National Airline: Cayman Airways

LAW REGARDING HOMOSEXUALITY: We do not have information about the status of the law regarding homosexuality in this country. There are no reports about particular cases of harassment or legal prosecutions of gay or lesbian tourists.

GEORGE TOWN

✈ Owen Roberts Int'l AP (GCM)
   1 mi. / 1.6 km east of George Town

LOCATION: On the western coast of the Grand Cayman Island.

POPULATION: 8,000

CLIMATE: Caribbean tropical climate year round with constant warm temperatures in the 80°sF (25°c). High travel season is mid-December to mid-April. Hurricane season is from June 1-November 30.

DESCRIPTION: The Cayman islands consist of three islands: **Grand Cayman** where the capital **George Town** is located, **Cayman Brac** and **Little Cayman**. The islands are accessible by air from Miami, flying time is about 70 minutes. **Grand Cayman** the largest island, offers excellent scuba diving, and offshore banking in George Town. The gay scene concentrates in West Bay Rd. The beach of interest to gay travelers is **Seven Mile Beach**, between the Ramada and the Holiday Inn.

BARS ⟓ RESTAURANTS ⟘

● Bars/clubs (G/S): **DJ's**, Coconut Place, West Bay Rd., (947-4234); **Lone Star Bar & Grill**, West Bay Rd.; **Monkey Business**, disco, The Falls, West Bay Rd. (947-4024); **Santiago's**, West Bay Rd. (949-8580); **Run Point Club**, dance club, Rum Point (947-9059); **Silvers-Island Rock**, Ramada Treasure Island, West Bay Rd. (949-7777). **Faces** and **Lord Nelson** on West Bay Road are popular with gays and lesbians.

🗝 ACCOMMODATIONS 🗝

CARIBBEAN CLUB
Seven Mile Beach, Grand Cayman Island. Tel: (809) 947-4099. Fax: (809) 947-4443. TYPE: *First Class Resort*. CLIENTELE: All Welcome. LOCATION: On the beach, 3 mi. / 5 km from George Town. 18 fully equipped 1-2 bedroom villas, satellite TV, A/C, restaurant. Rates: US$160-$430.

CORAL CAYMANIAN APT HOTEL
Seven Mile Beach, Grand Cayman Island. Tel: (809) 947-5170. Fax: (809) 947-5164. TYPE: *Tourist Class Apartment/Hotel Complex*. CLIENTELE: All Welcome. LOCATION: On the beach, 2 mi. / 3 km from downtown. 30 apts. w/priv. bath, A/C, kitchen, restaurant, wheelchair accessible. Open: Year round. Rates: US$90 - US$200. *TAC*: 10%.

RADISSON BEACH RESORT
Seven Mile Beach, West Bay Rd. Tel: (809) 949-0088. Fax: (809) 949-0288. TYPE: *Deluxe Beach Resort*. CLIENTELE: All Welcome. LOCATION: On the beach. 315 w/priv. bath, A/C, STV, telephone, restaurants, bars, swimming pool, Scuba nearby. Rates: US$160-US$860.

CHILE

AREA: 292,257 sq. mi. (756,946 sq. km)
POPULATION: 11,300,000
CAPITAL: Santiago
CURRENCY: Chilean peso (Cp)
OFFICIAL LANGUAGE: Spanish
MAJOR RELIGIONS: Roman Catholicism
Telephone: 56
Nat'l Holiday: Independence Day, Sept. 19
Official Time: G.M.T. - 4
Electricity: 220 volts, 50 cycles, A.C.
Exchange Rate: 1US$ = Cp 419
National Airline: LanChile

LAW REGARDING HOMOSEXUALITY: Chile's penal code outlaws sexual relationships between men and prescribes a prison term of 3-20 years for sodomy between consenting adults (homosexuals or heterosexuals). No one is known to be in prison for sodomy, but the gay community is fighting to repeal the law. According to the president of Chile, Patricio Aylwin, there is no discrimination against lesbians and gays, rather, it's just that "Chileans do not like homosexuals".

SANTIAGO   © 02

✈ Arturo Merino Benitez AP (SCL)
    12 mi. / 19 km northwest of Santiago

LOCATION: In the heartland of Chile within easy reach of the Andean Ski Resorts, the Pacific Beaches, or the international resort of Viña del Mar.

POPULATION: 4,000,000

CLIMATE: Mediterranean climate. Temperatures can reach 33°c (91°F) in January (summer), but fall to -2°c (30°F) in July (winter).

Days are usually hot and nights are cool.

Gay/Lesbian Visitor Information
MOVILH: 562-632

DESCRIPTION: Founded in 1541 by Pedro de Valdivia, it is the fifth largest city in South America, commanding a beautiful site on a wide plain some 600 m / 1,980 ft. above the sea. The Avenida O'Higgins (known as Alameda) runs through the heart of the city. Visit the **Plaza de Armas**, The **Cathedral**, **Pre-Columbian Art Museum** and the **Casa Colorada**.

Note: The society in Chile is known for its strong Catholic and family ties. Gay life in Santiago is 'civilized' in some way, underground and private. As Chile becomes part of the western democratic society, gay life is becoming more open. Santiago is relatively a closely knit city where people know each other. Do not dress feminine, avoid true colors, tight jeans and colorful shirts with flowery patterns. Dress elegant or casual.

In Chile men do not kiss each other (like they do in Argentina or North Africa), and do not hug in public. Gay magazines are in short supply, so bring some with you. No gay or XXX rated movies are available. Condoms can be purchased locally (standard size only and who knows what the quality is). You can not buy KY but vaseline is readily available. Advertisement for Saunas in Chilean papers can be misleading, because they normally mean 'brothels for heterosexuals only'.Chileans are ultra conservative. So play it 'straight', but keep your eyes open.

BARS ㊉ RESTAURANTS ㊉

● Bars/clubs (GM): **Fausto**, Mecca of Chilean gays, safe, cruisy, handsome men, bar, cafe, disco, after 11pm, Avenue Santa Maria 0832; **Fox**, dance bar, Paseo Las Palmas Lugar 19; **Metropolis**, dance club, San Diego 935 (696-9136); **Paradise Disco**, Euclides 1204, Gran Avenida, paradero 2; **Trianon**, Santo Domingo 1998 (698-3019).

● Bars/Clubs (GMW): **Quasar**, nightclub, disco, drag shows, Coquimbo 1458 (711267); **Yo, Claudio**, Santa Lucia 234.

● Restaurants (GMW): **Libro Café**, Purisima, Bellavista Quarter); **Prosit**, fast food, Plaza Baquedano, near Crowne Plaza Hotel. Others: **Coco Loco**, Seafood, 554 Rancagua (491-214); **Giratorio**, revolving rooftop restaurant, impressive night view of Santiago, 2250 Av. 11

de Septiembre (232-1827); **Hamburger Place**, French, Santo Domingo 2096 (698-3019).

λ SERVICES λ

● Health Clubs (mixed): **Banos Catedral**, steam bath, dark rooms, Avda Catedral 2749; **Sauna Miraflores**, 353 Miraflores St.; **Gimnasio**, Calle Condell 372.

ACCOMMODATIONS

GALERIAS HOTEL
San Antonio 65, Santiago. Tel: (2) 384-011. Fax: (2) 330-821. TYPE: *Hotel*. CLIENTELE: Mostly Straight. LOCATION: Adjacent to Municipal Theatre.

* Rooms: 157 w/priv. bath. Suites: 8
* TV, phone, minibar, A/C, wheelchair access
* Restaurant, cafeteria, bar
* Pool, gym,sauna, solarium, massage
* Airport: 8 mi. / 13 km
* Credit Cards: MC/VISA/AMEX/DC
* Rates: (US) $100-$150. *TAC:* 10%

DESCRIPTION: Striking first class hotel in a convenient central location. All rooms are pleasantly appointed and soundproof.

VIÑA del MAR & VALAPARISO   ℭ   32

✈ Arturo Merino Benitez AP (SCL)

LOCATION: On the Pacific Ocean northwest of Santiago.

POPULATION: About 300,000 each

DESCRIPTION: Capital of the V Región, Valapariso is a principal port, a major naval base and the second largest city in Chile. Viña del Mar is just 9 km / 6 mi. north of Valpariso via bus route along the narrow belt between the shore and precipitous cliffs. It is a famous international seaside resort. Major attractions include the Casino and the Annual Song Festival which includes famous latino and European singers.

❖ Gay Beaches: **Caleta Abarca** (next to Hotel Miramar); **Los Marino** (towards Reñaca area); **Las Salinas**, popular with sailors).

BARS ♟ RESTAURANTS 🍴

● Bars/clubs (GM): **Divine**, popular disco, Chacabuco 2687 (255-879) in Vaparaiso. **Scratch**, dance bar, mixed clientele, Old Viña Railway Station, Viña del Mar.

ACCOMMODATIONS

HOTEL ALCAZAR
Alvarez 646, Viña del Mar. Tel: (32) 685112. Fax: (32) 884-245. TYPE: *hotel*. CLIENTELE: Mostly Straight. LOCATION: Central.

* Rooms: 74 w/priv. bath
* CTV, phone, A/C
* Restaurant, Bar
* Rates: Cp 21,200-35,200. *TAC:* 10%

DESCRIPTION: Convenient central hotel. Motel units have private entrances.

MIRAMAR HOTEL
Calete Abarca s/n. Viña del Mar. Tel: (32) 664-077. Fax: (32) 665-220. TYPE: *Hotel*. CLIENTELE: Mostly Straight. LOCATION: On rocky coast at Caleta Abarca Beach overlooking Valparaiso Bay.

* Rooms: 122 w/priv. bath. Suites: 12
* CTV, phone, minibar
* Restaurant, disco, gym, sauna
* Terrace with bay view
* Elegant Casino nearby
* On the Beach
* Rates: (US) $115-2100. *TAC:* 10%

DESCRIPTION: Quality hotel in a convenient location.

CHINA
PEOPLE'S REPUBLIC OF

AREA: 3,692,244 sq. mi. (9,562,904 sq. km)
POPULATION: 980,000,000.
CAPITAL: Beijing
CURRENCY: Yuan
OFFICIAL LANGUAGE: Chinese
MAJOR RELIGIONS: Confucionism, Buddhism, Taoism, Islam
Telephone: 86
Nat'l Holiday:
Official Time: G.M.T. + 8 or 9
Electricity: 220v, 50 cycles, A.C.
Exchange Rate: 1US$ = Yuan 8.32
National Airline: China Airlines

LAW REGARDING HOMOSEXUALITY: Homosexuality is not mentioned in the Code of Law, yet it is considered an offense against the 'principle of harmony' and not well tolerated by the communist authorities. Chinese police have adopted an "ignore and don't ask" approach to gays. Nearly all Chinese gays are closeted and little is known of Chinese lesbians. Persons with HIV/AIDS are not allowed to enter China. They risk expulsion if they try to enter.

BEIJING   © 01

✈ Capital Int'l Airport (PEK)
  14 mi. / 22 km northeast

LOCATION: Center of the Hopeh province in northeastern China.

POPULATION: 8,000,000

CLIMATE: Beijing lies at approximately same latitude as Philadelphia or Madrid. Winters are cold and dry with temperatures often drooping below freezing. The average January temperature is 24°F (-5°c). Summers are oppressively hot and humid with a July average of 80°c (26°c). The best time to visit Beijing is during September and early October. During this short period Beijing remains dry and warm during the day and cool in the evenings.

DESCRIPTION: The capital of the People's Republic of China, Beijing is the political, economic and cultural center of this giant nation. The city is famous for its artificial lakes, parks, temples and cuisine. The famous **Forbidden City** the historic residence of the former Emperors is located within the Tartar City. The **Imperial City** is now the seat of the Communist Government. Visit **Tiananmen Square**, and the **Beijing Zoo**. The gay scene is very subdued and contacts between foreign and local gays and lesbians are almost non existent. Some contacts are possible in luxury tourist hotels.

❖ Public cruising (AYOR) takes place at the following places: **Tiantan Park** (evenings); **Wangfuing Street** and Bathall (evenings); **Worker's Cultural Palace** (evenings).

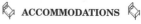 ♈ BAR ♈

● Dance Club (G/S): **Talk of the Town**, 1 Jian Guomenwai Ave., China World Hotel basement, (505-2266).

 ACCOMMODATIONS

CHINA WORLD HOTEL
1 Jianguomenwai Ave., Beijing 100004. Tel: (1) 505-2266. Fax: (1) 505-0828. TYPE: *Deluxe Hotel*. CLIENTELE: Mostly Straight. LOCATION: Heart of diplomatic, financial and commercial district, 15 min. from Forbidden City and Tianamen Square. 743 rooms w/priv. bath, 56 suites, 24 hrs. rooms service, CTV, telephone, A/C, restaurants, bars, disco, Health Club w/gym, sauna, massage, indoor swimming pool. Season: year round. Rates: US$180-$300. *TAC:* 10%.

OLYMPIC HOTEL
52 Baishiqiao Rd., Beijing 100081. Tel: (1) 831-6688. Fax: (1) 831-5985. TYPE: *First Class Hotel*. CLIENTELE: Mostly Straight. LOCATION: Western part of the city near Exhibition Hall & Zoo, convenient to Tianamen Square. 338 rooms w/priv. bath, 56 suites, executive floor, 24 hrs room service, CTV, phone, refrigerator, restaurant, cafe, tennis, gym. Rates: US$60-$120. *TAC:* 10%. DESCRIPTION: 11 story hotel with a magnificent atrium lobby.

NANJING   ℭ   025

✈ Nanjing Airport

LOCATION: Along the northern banks of the Yangtse River at the foothills of the Zijin Mountains. 1157 km / 724 mi. south of Beijing.

POPULATION: 3,000,000

DESCRIPTION: Nanjing ranks among the most pleasant of China's great cities. It is the capital of the Jiangsu Province.

 **ACCOMMODATIONS**

JINLING HOTEL
Xin Jie Kou Sq, Nanjing 210005. Tel: (25) 445-4888. TYPE: *Hotel.* CLIENTELE: Mostly tourists. LOCATION: Downtown, 15 min. from the Yangtse River Wharf. 818 rooms w/priv. bath, phone, CTV, A/C, minibar, 30 suites, restaurants, coffee shop, dance club, pool, sauna, gym, massage, jacuzzi. Rates: $150-$210. DESCRIPTION: Modern tower hotel.

SHANGHAI   ℭ   021

✈ Hongqiao Airport (SHA) 10 mi. / 16 km SE.

LOCATION: Eastern China, on the Huangpu River where it flows into the Yangze estuary .

POPULATION: 12,000,000

CLIMATE: Temperate during Spring and Autumn. Winters are chilly and gray with a January average of 38°F (3°c), while summers are hot and rainy with a July average of 82°F (32°c).

DESCRIPTION: The largest city on the Asian Continent, Shanghai is the country's foremost educational, cultural and commercial center. Unlike Beijing, it offers a cosmopolitan Laissez-Faire attitude with its modern and Western appearance. This is the only major Chinese city with a visible gay presence.

The harbor quarter, known as the "Bund" is the city's major cruising place for local and visiting gays. Other places frequented by gays include: **Waitan** downstream from the Peace Hotel; **Jin An Park** near the Jin Jiang Hotel; and the intersection near the **Quingan Temple.**

 ACCOMMODATIONS

JIN JIANG HOTEL
59 Mao Ming Rd., Shanghai 200002. Tel: (21) 258-2582. Fax: (21) 215-5588. TYPE: *First Class Hotel.* CLIENTELE: Mostly Straight. LOCATION: Set on landscaped gardens in a residential area. 682 rooms w/priv. bath, 97 suites, CTV, phone, A/C, restaurants, bar, nightclub, sauna. Rates: US$60-$450.

PEACE HOTEL
20 E. Nanjing Rd., Shanghai 200002. Tel: (21) 321-1244. Fax: (21) 329-0300. TYPE: *First Class Hotel.* CLIENTELE: Mostly Straight. LOCATION: On the Huangpu River near the Bund. 408 rooms w/priv. bath, 54 suites, CTV, telephone, A/C, Lobby and cafe bar can be cruisy. Rates: US$50 - $200. DESCRIPTION: Old-world hotel, rooms for non-smokers.

XI'AN   ℭ   029

✈ Xi'an Int'l Airport

LOCATION: In the Shaanxi Province inland on the Wei River.

POPULATION: 2.8 million

CLIMATE: Harsh Continental climate with great seasonal variation. The average winter temperature is 34°F (1°c), and the average summer temperature is 82°F (28°c).

DESCRIPTION: Once the largest city in the world, Xi'an served as the capital of 11 dynasties. Today it is the capital of the Shaanxi Provincw. Xi'an is one of the most popular travel destination in China due to the discovery of the Qin tob excavation with the famous terra cotta soldiers. There is not much for gay travelers to do in the city besides tourism, shopping, and exploring the city's antique shops.

 ACCOMMODATIONS

GRAND CASTLE HOTEL
12 Xiduan, Nanloo, Xi'an 710068. Tel: (29) 723-1800. TYPE: *Hotel.* CLIENTELE: Mostly Tourists. LOCATION: Facing the South Gate of the Ming Dynasty. 354 rooms w/priv. bath, 22 suites, CTV, phone, hair dryer, A/C, minibar, gym, sauna, restaurants, bars. Rates: $120-$180. DESCRIPTION: Attractive atrium hotel in a Goose Pagoda shape.

COLOMBIA

AREA: 439,513 sq. mi. (1,138,339 sq. km)
POPULATION: 27,600,000
CAPITAL: Bogotá
CURRENCY: Colombian peso (Cp)
OFFICIAL LANGUAGE: Spanish
MAJOR RELIGIONS: Roman Catholicism
Telephone: 57
Nat'l Holiday: Independence Day, Dec. 17
Official Time: G.M.T. - 5
Electricity: 120v DC
Exchange Rate: 1US$ = Cp 1,003
National Airline: Avianca

LAW REGARDING HOMOSEXUALITY: Homosexuality is not mentioned in the Code of Law and the age of consent for homosexuals and heterosexuals is 18. The attitude of the population is rather hostile and the Police are known to harass the gay population. In Colombia, so-called "disposables" are being routinely murdered by death squads and neo-nazi groups. There is ample evidence of police involvement in the killings. Some of the targets are transvestites, prostitutes, and gay men. The government's human right ombudsman in the city of Barranquilla declared that gay men are "abnormal" .

❑ Colombia is a beautiful country with almost every climate known to man present somewhere within its borders. It enjoys all the flavor and spice of Latin America mixed with the hectic pace of modern society. Though open and progressive compared with some other Latin cultures, it is advisable for gay visitors to observe certain local customs and mannerisms. The society is critical of homosexuality, but tolerates gays and lesbians as long as they remain discreet. Any display of public affection between members of the same sex (even women) is considered an offense to the local population. Foreign visitors need to be watchful for their own safety and security. Watch your pockets, don't wear expensive jewelry, don't wander off alone to unknown places, as it can turn very nasty very quickly.

BOGOTA   © 1

✈ El Dorado Airport (BOG)
7.5 mi. / 12 km east of Bogota

LOCATION: On a high plateau, 8,640 ft./2,618 m above sea level, in the heart of Colombia.

POPULATION: 6,500,000

CLIMATE: Days are pleasant with year round average temperature of 50°F-60°F (10°c-15°c). The rainy season is from May to November.

Gay & Lesbian Visitor Information
Proyecto Lambda: 287-7914

DESCRIPTION: Known as the land of El Dorado, Santa Fé de Bogotá, the capital of the Republic is modern with high rise buildings, large tourist hotels, and wide avenues. Standing tall against the peaks of the Andes in the background, the city is a shocking mixture of opulence and poverty. The gay scene is located in the northwestern part of town near the Avda Jorge Eliécer Gaitán and calle 23.

BARS Y RESTAURANTS ¶¶

● Bars/Clubs (GM): **Boys Club**, Avda Caracas no. 37-68; **Cinema**, Euro-disco, American music, great light show and screen videos, one of the most vibrant clubs in Bogotá, open 10:00-3:00, Carrera 14 #75-46 Thu-Sat; **Class One Club**, dance club, drag shows, Thu-Sun. open 10:00-4:00, Avda Caracas #74-46 (210-0785); **K-OZ**, late night cruise club, Thu-Sat. open: 2:00-5:00 best after 3:00a, Calle 85 #11-18 (257-5443); **Noa Noa Club**, Calle 74 #15-20 (217-4526); **Punto 59**, piano bar with romantic music, Carrera 13 #59-24 Acuario Shopping Center; **Safari's Club**, dance club, strip shows, Avda Caracas #73-26 Thu-Sat. open: 10:00-3:00 (217-8262); **Studio Uno**, video bar, shows, Calle 100 #17A-55 Fri-Sun (256-1710); **Te Odio** (I Hate You), small and elegant bar in the heart of the "Zona Rosa", Calle 80 #13A-28 (618-3337).

● Bars/Clubs (GMW): **Boys Junior**, dance club, Carrera 13A, No. 35-36 (287-0407); **Dali's**, bar with jukebox music, Fri-Sat dancing until 3:00, Carrera 22 #67-30 (235-6516).

● Bars/Clubs (GW): **Agora**, exclusive bar for

lesbians, Carrera 14 #78-78.

● Restaurants (G/S): **Café Oma**, carrera 15, calle 89/90; **Oma Bavaria**, carrera 10, no. 27-91, local 117 (243-8241); **Pierrot**, bar, restaurant, calle 27, no. 5-76, local 2 (334-4292). Others: **El Vegetariano**, calle 22, no. 8-89; **Shamua**, cocktails and American style, calle 85, no. 11-69.

λ SERVICES λ

● Cinemas (G/S): **Coliseo**, Carrera 7 No. 27-46; **Teatro Esmeralda**, Carrera 7, No. 22-20.

● Health Clubs (GM): **Baltimore**, Hotel Maria Isabel, calle 33, carrera 15-17, mixed clientele (245-2650); **Monroe's Club**, Carrera 16A 79-24, El Lago (218-0731);**Hotel Orquidea Real Sauna**, carrera 7, no. 32-16, mixed clientele (285-6020); **Ulises**, carrera 15, no. 32-26 (232-5809).

ACCOMMODATIONS

HOTEL ORQUIDEA REAL
carrera 7 no. 32-16, Bogotá. Tel: (1) 285-6020. Reservations available from Odysseus. Tel: (516) 944-5330. Fax: (516) 944-7540.TYPE: *Hotel*. CLIENTELE: All Welcome. LOCATION: Centrally located near the local gay scene. 166 rooms w/priv. bath, restaurant, pool, gym, sauna. Rates: on request. *TAC:* 10% (from Odysseus). Good hotel in a central location.

CALI   *C* **23**

✈ Alfonso Bonilla Arigon Int'l AP (CLO)
12 mi. / 19 km north of Cali

POPULATION: 2,000,000

CLIMATE: Though hot all year (temperatures hover around 90°F (32°c); it is very cool and pleasant at night.

DESCRIPTION: Cali, the capital of the Valle Dept., is the third largest city in Colombia. It is a bustling city nestled in a beautiful agriculture rich valley. Known as the capital of Salsa Music, Cali enjoys one of the liveliest ambiance in all of Latin America. Every Christmas, the city stages the famous "feria" which is similar in spirit to Rio's Carnaval, though on a smaller scale. The people are friendly and open and there is a considerable gay nightlife to be found.

BARS Y RESTAURANTS 🍴

Most bars listed are for gay men. Although much more relaxed than straight bars it is not recommended that they be used as pick-up joints as most gay men go out in couples or groups. It is essential to have a dancing partner as latin music requires dancing in couples. Cali is famed for its openness and friendliness, and it is not unusual to end up socializing with other men at the bars, though this will not necessarily lead to any sexual adventure. Nightclubs are for dancing the night away, though inside city limits there is a 3 am closing time by law. Do not be openly affectionate with a member of the same sex and be very careful accepting drinks. Unfortunately it is not unknown for people to slip scopolamine into drinks and rub the victim while he is defenseless. All places have a cover charge but this is discounted from your final bill.

● Bars/Clubs (GM): **Amigos**, bar and nightclub, shows every weekends, Calle 15 #16-13 (881-3701); **Articulo 13**, dance club, outside Cali city limit, opens 12-6am, Calle 70 #4N-10; **Chapien**, dance club, young gay crowd, Avda Colombia #6-28 (889-2317); **Charles**, nightclub for gay men and transvestites, nightly shows, strip tease, dancing, Carrera 3 #10-55 (884-2497); **Contragolpe**, dancing and weekend shows, close to main nightlife area of town, excellent location for safety, Calle 17N #6N-30 (661-5851); **El Dollar**, friendly bar and nightclub, Calle 16 #4-09 (889-2547); **Escape**, large and vibrant nightclub, mixed clientele, open Wed-Sat 6:00-3:00, Calle 23B #3N-42 (667-1397); **Exilio**, Cali's best newest gay nightclub, located in industrial area (441-4266); **Golden**, bar, mature clientele, no dancing, friendly crowd, Calle 9 #3-36; **Madonna**, dancing and weekend shows, younger crowd, Avda Colombia #8-74; **Palladium (Romanos)**, one of the best nightclubs in Cali, friendly staff, popular with the large gay Cuban colony in town, Carrera 3 #9-47 1st Fl. (880-4065); **Ulises**, dance club, Avda Colombia 8-47 (816-469).

● Bars/Clubs (GMW): **Relax**, one of Cali's busiest and best nightclubs, discrete location, excellent atmosphere, dancing until 3am weekends only (Thu-Sat).

● Bars/Clubs (GW): **Celeste**, bar, dancing and female shows, Calle 18N #5AN-38 (668-7675); **La Zona Rosa**, bar, dancing and weekend shows, gay men welcome, excellent location, Calle 20N #3N-42 (661-3597).

● Restaurants (AW): **Don Carlos**, seafood, elegant, Carrera 1 #7-53; **La Terraza**, elegant, music and dance, good atmosphere, Calle 16 #6N-14; **Los Gauchos del Sur**, Argentine style grilled meat, Calle 5 about Carrera Carrera 60.

λ SERVICES λ

● Cinema (G/S): **Cine Zaccour**, straight porn, some gay cruise inside, Carrera 2 #11-20 basement. (AYOR).

● Health Clubs (GM): **Cali Club**, Calle 8 #28-21 (558-6505); **Romanos**, Carrera 3 #9-47, 2nd fl. (880-4065); **Spartacus Club**, Carrera 23A #8A15 (557-0764).

● Sex-Shop (G/S): **Universo Sexual**, sex toys, edificio Plaza Versalles,Avda 6N #17-92 2nd fl.

 ACCOMMODATIONS

ARISTI HOTEL
Carrera 9A #10-04. Tel: (23) 822521. TYPE: *Hotel.* CLIENTELE: All Welcome. LOCATION: Within walking distance of residential and shopping area. 168 rooms w/priv. bath, phone, some w/A/C, 24 hrs. room service, restaurants, bar, rooftop garden with swimming pool. Rates: (US) $50-$100. *TAC:* 10%

DANN CALI HOTEL
Avda Colombia #1-40. Tel: (23) 823230. TYPE: *Aparthotel.* CLIENTELE: All Welcome. LOCATION: Walking distance of city center, 90 apartments, rooms w/bath, phone, some balcony, CTV, restaurant, coffee shop, cinema on premises, limited room service, laundry, free parking. Rates: (US) $140 - $190. *TAC:* 10%

PEREIRA   ℂ   63

LOCATION: Heart of Colombia's coffee and cattle growing region.

POPULATION: 480,000

CLIMATE: Year round temperatures in the low 80°sF (28°c).

DESCRIPTION: Capital of the Risaralda Dept. Overshadowd by the green mountains it lies at an altitude of 1,476 m / 4,871 ft. above the Cauca Valley. The city offers artificial lake, parks, quaint cathedrals and a zoo. There are some good clubs and bars for gay men and lesbians. Most require the usual cover charge at the door, all are located near the city center.

BARS ⅄ RESTAURANTS ‖

● Bars/Clubs (GM): **Manhattan**, nightclub, dancing until dawn, Carrera 9 #20-15 (343839); **390 Minutos**, one of the best clubs in town, Calle 18 #10-69 (347-911).

● Bars/Clubs (GW): **Kundry Club**, best known gay club for women, right next to Manhattan, dancing and music every night, weekend female shows, Carrera 9 #20-15 (335-153).

 ACCOMMODATIONS

SORATAMA HOTEL
Carrera 7A #19-20. Tel: (63) 358-650.TYPE: *Hotel.* CLIENTELE: All Welcome. LOCATION: In town center at Plaza Bolivar. 77 rooms w/priv. bath, restaurant, bar. Rates: (US) $50 - $80. *TAC:* 10%.

COOK ISLANDS

AREA: 92 sq. mi. (237 sq. km)
POPULATION: 18,550
CAPITAL: Rarotonga
CURRENCY: NZ($)
OFFICIAL LANGUAGE: Maori, English
MAJOR RELIGIONS: Protestantism
Telephone: 64
Nat'l Holiday: Independence Day, Aug. 4
Official Time: G.M.T. - 10
Electricity: 230v, 50 cycles, A.C.
Exchange Rate: 1US$ = NZ$1.53
National Airline: Polynesian Airlines

LAW REGARDING HOMOSEXUALITY:
The Cook Islands are independent in a "free
association" with New Zealand. They have
sodomy laws on their books based on old New
Zealand legislation. But the laws are never
enforced, and the population is very friendly.
Nude or topless sunbathing may cause offense.

❖ The Cook Islands consist of 15 islands, scattered over some 2 million sq. km / 776,000 sq.
mi. of the Pacific Ocean.

RARATONOGA   ✆ 0682

✈ Rarotonga Airport (RAR)

LOCATION: South Pacific Ocean, about 2,000
mi. / 3,200 km northeast of New Zealand.

POPULATION: 10,200

CLIMATE: Warm and sunny year round. June
to August are the cooler months, Nov.-March is
the hottest season with heavy rain. Temperatures vary between 25°c-29°c (77°F-84°F).

VISITOR INFORMATION
Cook Islands Tourist Authority

6033 West Century Blvd., Suite 690
Los Angeles CA 90045
Tel: (310) 216-2872
or (800) 624-6250

DESCRIPTION: Raratonga is the main
island and the capital of the Cook Islands.
Enjoy watersports, scuba, reef walks and
island tours. For gay visitors the areas where
cruising is possible: **Raratonga Hotel** & the
beach promenade in town.

❖ **HOW TO GET THERE:** International air
services to the Cook Islands are operated by Air
New Zealand, Polynesian Airlines & Air Hawaii.

❖ **SPECIAL EVENTS:** The biggest celebration
is **Constitution Celebrations**, 2 weeks filled
with fun, color and excitement starting August 4.

BARS RESTAURANTS

There is no established gay scene in Rarotonga,
but check the bars, clubs and restaurants at
the **Tamure Resort, Rarotonga Hotel** and
the **Banana Court** bar, Avarua (City Center).

ACCOMMODATIONS

THE RAROTONGAN
P.O. Box 103, Rarotonga, Cook Islands. Tel: 25-
800. USA/Canada reservations: Tel (516) 944-
5330 or (800) 257-5344. Fax: (516) 944-7540
TYPE: *Resort Hotel.* CLIENTELE: All Welcome. LOCATION: On white sand beach 20
min. to town center.

* Rooms: 151 w/priv. bath
* Smoking allows in rooms
* Phone, refrigerator, A/C (some), hair dryer
* Suites: 4, 1BR w/living room, full bath
  patio/terrace
* Bed Types: single, double, large (ovesized)
  doubles, queen size
* Services: maid, laundry, wheelchair access
* Restaurant (local/European); Nu Bar - pool
  side bar (informal)
* Pool, beach/lagoon, free parking, no pets
* Beach: on the beach (mixed)
* Health Club: 15 km / 10 mi. (mixed)
* Airport: 12 km / 7.5 mi., taxi, bus
* Rates: $140-$380 w/TB
* Check in 2:00 pm / check out 12:00 noon
* *TAC:* 10% (from Odysseus)

DESCRIPTION: Superbly laid out resort complex over 6 acres of beach frontage. The beautiful white sandy beach and picturesque tropical
gardens provide a perfect setting for the south
pacific experience.

COSTA RICA

AREA: 19,575 sq. mi. (50,700 sq. km)
POPULATION: 2,250,000.
CAPITAL: San José
CURRENCY: Colón
OFFICIAL LANGUAGE: Spanish
MAJOR RELIGIONS: Roman Catholicism
Telephone: 506
Nat'l Holiday: Independence Day, Sept. 15
Official Time: 6 hrs. behind G.M.T.
Electricity: 110/220v, 60 cycles, A.C.
Exchange Rate: 1US$ = Colón 192
National Airline: Lacsa

LAW REGARDING HOMOSEXUALITY:
Homosexuality is legal in Costa Rica at the age
of 18. One must proceed with caution when
dealing with minors under 18 as it is possible
to get arrested for "contributing to the delin-
quency of a minor" and to be expelled from the
country. Homosexuality is not illegal at the age
of 15 if "previous corruption" exist and this is
also the "effective age" of consent.

❖ *Note:* if you travel to Costa Rica during the
end of the year holiday season it is important
to know that all banks and businesses are
closed between December 22 - January 2. Tours
and excursions can be arranged at certain
hotels during this period.

QUEPOS   ℂ NO AREA CODE

✈ Juan Santamaria Int'l Airport (SJO)

LOCATION: Puntarenas Province on the
Pacific ocean, 155 km/97 mi. south of San José.

POPULATION: 2,200

CLIMATE: Spring-like year round. Temperatures vary slightly. Average temperature is
around 70°F (22°c). Rainy season lasts from
May to November with sporadic rainfall.

DESCRIPTION: Puerto Quepos was built by
United Brands as a banana exporting port.
Today it is a beach resort. Nearby lie the beau-
tiful beaches of Manual Antonio National Park.

❖ Beach: Nude beach, mostly gay, Northwest of
Mariposa Road, over rocks.

BARS ⵑ RESTAURANTS ᴙ

Check the bar and restaurant at the **La Mariposa Hotel**.

🗝 ACCOMMODATIONS 🗝

LA MARIPOSA
P.O. Box 4, Quepos. Tel: 77-03-55 / 77-04-56.
Fax: 77-00-50. TYPE: *Hotel*. CLIENTELE:
Mostly Straight. LOCATION: Beach location in
the Manual Antonio National Park. 10 Rooms:
w/bath, Restaurant & Bar, Maid Service, Off
Street Parking, Rates: (US) $100 - $150. *TAC:*
10%. DESCRIPTION: Hillside Spanish-style
villas situated. Friendly staff.

VILLAS EL PARQUE
Apdo 111, Quepos. Tel: (506) 777-0096. Fax: (506)
777-0538. TYPE: *Apartments with Hotel Service*.
HOSTESS: Susanne. CLIENTELE: Gay/Straight.
LOCATION: Hillside above Manuel Antonio
beach near Quepos. 13 rooms, 16 suites, 2 villas,
restaurant, bar, pool, jacuzzi. DESCRIPTION:
Mediterranean style villas with spectacular view
of Manuel Anthonio Bay & islands. Large balconies, luxurious apartment style suites.

VILLA LA ROCA
Manual Antonio Beach. Tel: (506) 777-1349.
USA/Canada reservations (800) 257-5344 or
(516) 944-5330. Fax: (516) 9544-7540. TYPE:
Guest House. HOST: Don Mgr. CLIENTELE:
Gay men & women. LOCATION: On a hill next
to popular Vista Point.

* Rooms: 5 (double) rooms w/priv. bath
* Smoking allowed in rooms
* Refrigerator, cooking facilities, ceiling fan
* Free parking, no pets
* Beach: 15 min. (gay)
* Airport: Quepos 10 mi / 16 km, bus
* Languages: Spanish, English
* Open: Year round
* Rates: from US$60 w/CB
* Tax: 18.5%
* Check in 2:00 pm / Check out 12 noon
* *TAC:* 10% (from Odysseus)

DESCRIPTION: Comfortable rooms in a large villa type guesthouse with private bathroom with hot water, coffee maker and toaster. Each room has a terrace with magnificent ocean view.

SAN JOSÉ   *C* NO AREA CODE

✈ Juan Santamaria Int'l Airport (SJO)

LOCATION: In the center of Costa Rica spreading over a fertile valley at an elevation of 3000 ft. (1000 m).

POPULATION: 450,000

CLIMATE: Spring-like year round. Temperatures vary slightly from one season to another. Average temperature is 70°F (22°c). No need for air-condition during the summer season. Rainy season lasts from May to November with only sporadic rainfall.

DESCRIPTION: Dynamic, clean, modern city with charming old public buildings, and manicured parks. It is the cultural as well as the commercial center for the whole country. San José is an ideal starting point for visitors to Costa Rica and can be used as a convenient headquarter to explore the rest of the country. The East side of San José is of greater interest to the gay & lesbian visitors than the West side. The **"Plaza de la Cultura"** is the main daytime/early evening gay meeting area.

BARS ▼ RESTAURANTS ¶¶

● Bars/clubs (GMW): **Antros Bar**, small gay bar, Calle 7 & 9 Avda 14; **la Avispa**, popular disco, good fun music, 3 floors, 3 bars, video rooms (non porno movies), once a week dedicated to women only, closed Monday, Calle 1, Ave. 8 & 10 (23-5343); **Cantabrico**, early bar closes midnight, popular with tourists and older gays, Ave. 6, Calle Central and 2nd Ave. (21-5927); **Los Cucharones**, small disco, pleasant atmosphere, lower class clients, some rent, between Calle Central & 1 (33-5797); **Dejavu**, largest disco in San José, popular and crowded on weekends, 2 bars, A/C, good music, young crowd, Calle 2 Aves. 12 & 14; **Jaco Taverna**, go-go boys, good floor shows, closes Sundays, Av. 7, calle 1 & 3; **Monte Carlo**, calle 2 & Avenida 2 (across from Parque Central); **New Yesterday**, large bar/dance club, Ave. 1 between calle 5 and 7 (233-1988); **Risas Bar**, two floors with mixed bars, gays mostly on 2nd floor, disco on weekends, Calle 1, Aves. Central

& 1; **La Taverna**, lovely bar, quiet ambiance, some lesbians, Calle 9 #33, calle Central; **Viva Costa Rica**, restaurant, bar & hotel, mixed clientele, not gay but frequented by gays, Calle 34, Avs. Paseo Colon & 2; **El Unicornio**, Calle 5, Ave. 8 #362 (21-5552).

● Bars/clubs (GW): **La Avispa**, women only once a week, Calle 1, Avs 8&10 (23-5343); **La Taverna**, mostly men, some lesbians, Avda 9 #33E.

● Restaurants (AW): **Hacienda Steak House**, calle 7 and Avenida 2, inexpensive but good; **The Bastille**, French cuisine, expensive but best in the country, on Paseo Colón; **Ile de France**, French cuisine, Intimate, expensive. Calle 5, south of Hotel Balmoral (22-4241).

λ SERVICES λ

● Health Clubs (GM): **De Cameron**, calle 5 & 7, Av. 10; **Leblon**, young crowd, bar, clean but dingy, next door to **Pelaqueria Rodrigo**, calle 9, Av. 1 & 3.

🖻 ACCOMMODATIONS 🖻

APARTMENTS SCOTLAND
Ave. 1 & Calle 27, San Jose. Mailing address: c/o Interlik #102, PO Box 526770, Miami, FL 33152. Tel: (506) 223-0833. Fax: (506) 228-2211. TYPE: Rental Apartments. Hostesses: Marlena or Giana. CLIENTELE: Equal Gay/Straight. LOCATION: Quiet residential area, 10 blocks from center of town.

* Apartments: 25 (one-bedroom)
* Living room, full bath, kitchen, patio
* CTV, VCR, phone, refrigerator, safe box
* Beach 1 1/2 hrs. (mixed)
* Gay Bars: 8 blocks
* Airport: San Jose 30 min. taxi.
* Language: English, Spanish
* Reservations: one week deposit
* Season: Year round
* Rates: weekly US$250-$350: monthly US$600-$800, tax included, no meals.

DESCRIPTION: Simply furnished one bedroom apartment complex. New part has a veranda and gardens. Guests enjoy complete privacy, over night friends are permitted.

COLOURS
Reservations: Tel (305) 532-9341 Correspondence: 255 W. 24th St., Miami Beach, FL 33140. TYPE: *Guest House*. CLIENTELE: Mostly Gay. LOCATION: Blvd. Rohrmoser, few blocks from the Plaza Mayor Mall, 10 min. to

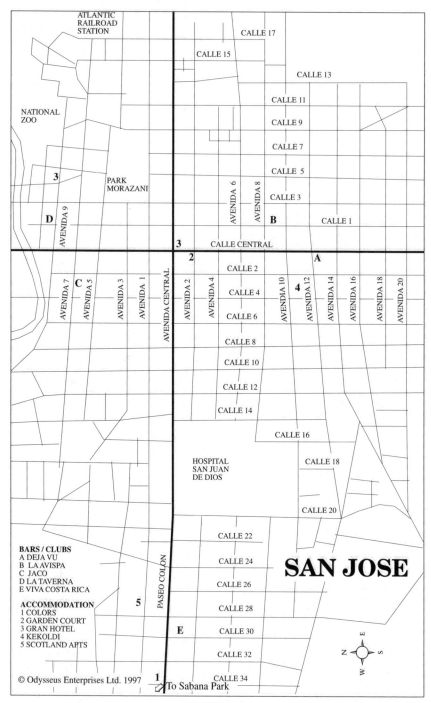

ATLANTIC RAILROAD STATION

CALLE 17
CALLE 15
CALLE 13
CALLE 11
CALLE 9
CALLE 7
CALLE 5
CALLE 3
CALLE 1

NATIONAL ZOO

PARK MORAZANI

AVENIDA 6
AVENIDA 8

3

D AVENIDA 9

B CALLE 1

3 CALLE CENTRAL

2 **A**

CALLE 2
CALLE 4
CALLE 6
CALLE 8
CALLE 10
CALLE 12
CALLE 14
CALLE 16
CALLE 18
CALLE 20
CALLE 22
CALLE 24
CALLE 26
CALLE 28
CALLE 30
CALLE 32
CALLE 34

AVENIDA 7
C AVENIDA 5
AVENIDA 3
AVENIDA 1
AVENIDA CENTRAL
AVENIDA 2
AVENIDA 4
AVENIDA 10
AVENIDA 12 **4**
AVENIDA 14
AVENIDA 16
AVENIDA 18
AVENIDA 20

HOSPITAL SAN JUAN DE DIOS

PASEO COLON

SAN JOSE

5

E

1

To Sabana Park

BARS / CLUBS
A DEJA VU
B LA AVISPA
C JACO
D LA TAVERNA
E VIVA COSTA RICA

ACCOMMODATION
1 COLORS
2 GARDEN COURT
3 GRAN HOTEL
4 KEKOLDI
5 SCOTLAND APTS

© Odysseus Enterprises Ltd. 1997

N E S W

Central San José. 10 rooms w/shared bath. Rates: on request.

GARDEN COURT HOTEL
San José, Costa Rica. Tel: (506) 255-4766. USA/Canada: Tel: (800) 257-5344 or (516) 944-5330. Fax: (516) 944-7540.TYPE: *Hotel*. CLIENTELE: Gay Welcome. LOCATION: Downtown corner of Central St. & 2nd Ave.

* Rooms: 70 w/priv. bath
* CTV, phone, A/C
* Pool, restaurant, bar, parking
* Gay Bars: 10-15 min. walking
* Health Club: 10 min. walking
* Airport: 10 mi / 16 km
* Languages: English, Spanish
* Reservations: 1 night deposit
* Credit Cards: MC/VISA/AMEX
* Rates: from US$60-$90 w/CB
* Check in 2:00 pm / Check out 11 am
* *TAC:* 10% (from Odysseus)

DESCRIPTION: Pleasant holiday complex in a central location with tastefully furnished large air-conditioned rooms, landscaped pool and self-service restaurant. Excellent location and service.

GRAN HOTEL COSTA RICA
San José. Reservations / Information: (516) 944-5330 or (800) 257-5344. Fax: (516) 944-7540. TYPE: *Hotel*. CLIENTELE: All Welcome. LOCATION: Heart of San José between Avenida Central & Calle Central. 110 rooms w/priv. bath, phone, CTV, A/C, room service, 2 restaurants, live shows, casino. Rates: $85-$135. DESCRIPTION: First class quality hotel in a central location. Walk to gay bars and clubs.

❍ JOLUVA
Calle 3B, Avs 9 y 11 #936, San José. Tel: (506) 23 9901. USA - Tel: (609) 298-7965. Fax: (609) 294-2418. TYPE: *Guest House*. HOST: Peter. CLIENTELE: All Welcome. LOCATION: "Barrio Amón" downtown section of San José, near cultural and historic areas of interest.

* Rooms: 8; 6 w/priv., 2 w/shared bath
* sgl 4 / dbl 4
* Smoking allowed in rooms
* CTV, VCR, laundry service
* Gay Bars: 10-15 min. walking
* Health Club: 10 min. walking
* Airport: 10 mi / 16 km
* Languages: English, Spanish
* Reservations: 1 night deposit
* Credit Cards: MC/VISA/AMEX
* Rates: from US$30 w/CB
* Check in 2:00 pm / Check out 11 am

DESCRIPTION: Colonial house with spacious rooms, high ceilings, in newly developing tourist area in downtown. Small group tours up to 6 persons are offered.

HOTEL KEKOLDI
San José, Costa Rica. Tel: (506) 223-3244. USA/Canada tel: (800) 257-5344 or (516) 944-5330. Fax: (516) 944-7540. TYPE: *Hotel*. CLIENTELE: Gay Welcome. LOCATION: Historic Barrio Amón, about 200 m/yards north of Parque Morazán.

* Rooms: 14 w/priv. bath
* Phone, king size beds
* Snack and bar service
* Room and laundry service
* Gay Bars: 10-15 min. walking
* Health Club: 10 min. walking
* Airport: 10 mi / 16 km
* Languages: English, Spanish
* Reservations: 1 night deposit
* Credit Cards: MC/VISA/AMEX
* Rates: from US$40 w/CB
* Check in 2:00 pm / Check out 11 am

DESCRIPTION: Renovated guest house with colorful atmosphere and beautiful paintings by English artist. All rooms with hot water. Young and friendly staff.

CROATIA

AREA: 21, 829 sq. mi. (56,538 sq. km)
POPULATION: 4,800,000
CAPITAL: Zagreb
CURRENCY: Croatian Kuna (Ck)
OFFICIAL LANGUAGE: Croatian
MAJOR RELIGION: Roman Catholicism
Telephone: 38
Nat'l Holiday:
Official Time: G.M.T.
Electricity: 220 volts
Exchange Rate: 1US$ = Ck 5.25
National Airline: Croatia Airlines

LAW REGARDING HOMOSEXUALITY: There is no law against homosexuality. The current age of consent is 14 for heterosexuals, and 18 for homosexuals. Not much information is available about the legal status of homosexuality in Croatia, since the break away from the former republic of Yugoslavia.

ZAGREB ✆ 41

✈ Pleso Airport (ZAG) 11 mi. / 18 km SE

LOCATION: In the heart of Croatia on the river Sava.

POPULATION: 900,000

CLIMATE: Continental. Hot summers and very cold winters. Heavy snowfall with temperatures below freezing.

Gay/Lesbian Visitor Information

Gayline: 245-421

DESCRIPTION: Zagreb is the capital of Croatia. It is attractively laid out with many parks, museums, art galleries and opera house. The city is the site of many music festivals including the Musical Biennale for contemporary music.

The gay scene is rather limited. Some of the bars and discos in the city's large tourist hotels attract gay crowds. Public places where you can cautiously try your luck with gay cruising: **Zrinjevac Park** (at night); **Trg Republike**; and the **Botanical Gardens** (Botanicki vit).

BARS ☕ RESTAURANTS 🍴

● Bars/clubs (GMW): **Bacchus**, small café and bar, Trg. Kralija Tomislava; **Tockica**, Mesnicka ulica; **Tropicana**, popular disco at the Hotel Intercontinental.

● Restaurants (AW): **Café Dubrovnik**, Trg. Republike Sq. Hotel Dubrovnik, 1st Fl.; **Café Tomislav**, Zrinjevac Park; **Splendid**, restaurant, Zrinjevac Park.

λ SERVICES λ

● Health Clubs / Saunas (G/S): **Diana Baths**, Ulica St. 8; **Dom Sportova**, Trg. Doma Sportova.

ACCOMMODATIONS

DUBROVNIK HOTEL
Gajeva Str. 1, Zagreb 41000. Tel: (41) 424-222. Fax: (41) 424-451. TYPE: *Hotel*. CLIENTELE: Mostly Straight. LOCATION: Trg Republike Sq. in downtown area. 269 rooms w/priv. bath, phone, C/H, some TV. Rates: (US) $60-$90. DESCRIPTION: Tourist class hotel with cafe popular with gays.

INTERCONTINENTAL HOTEL
Krsjavoga 1, Zagreb 41000. Tel: (41) 453-411. Fax: (41) 444-431. TYPE: *Hotel*. CLIENTELE: Mostly Straight. LOCATION: Downtown adjacent to commercial center. 457 rooms w/priv. bath, 20 suites, CTV (CNN), phone, A/C, C/H, indoor pool, health club, sauna, massage, solarium, gym, casino, tennis, parking. Rates: (US) $150-$200. *TAC:* 10%. DESCRIPTION: Superior first class hotel and casino. The disco is popular with gay clientele.

CUBA

AREA: 44,206 sq. mi. (114,494 sq. km)
POPULATION: 10,800,000
CAPITAL: Havana
CURRENCY: Cuban peso (Cp)
OFFICIAL LANGUAGE: Spanish
MAJOR RELIGION: Catholicism, Santeria
Telephone: 53
Nat'l Holiday: Jan. 1, Liberation Day
Official Time: G.M.T. - 4
Electricity: 110/120 volts, 60 cycles
Exchange Rate: 1US$ = Cp 1.00
National Airline: Cubana Aviacion

LAW REGARDING HOMOSEXUALITY:
There is no law against homosexuality. Sodomy
laws were eliminated after the revolution, but
made it illegal to "publicly demonstrate homosexual condition". The government passed a
law against harassment based on clothing,
appearance or behavior.

Note: US Citizens should bear in mind that the
US government's Trading with The Enemy Act
prohibits US citizens from engaging in financial
transactions with U.S. dollars in Cuba; it is illegal to spend US$ in Cuba in connection with busi-
ness or recreational trips. Americans are allowed
under the law to spend dollars in Cuba if they are
travelling as journalists or are engaged in educational research. A special license to visit Cuba can
be obtained from the US Treasury Dept. The
penalties for traveling to Cuba under any other
circumstances range from 12 years in prison to
fines of up to $250,000. Prepaid all inclusive
(down to tips and laundry) tours or cruises run by
an operator based in another country allow Americans to avoid spending US dollars in Cuba.

HAVANA

✈ Jose Marti Airport (HAV)

14 mi. / 22 km South

LOCATION: In Northern Cuba, about 125 mi.
/ 200 km south of Key West (FL).

POPULATION: 1,800,000

DESCRIPTION: The Jewel of the Caribbean,
Havana was a bustling metropolis in the 50's
with gambling casinos, nightclubs, and girls and
boys for hire. Today, Havana is a faded image of
itself, destroyed by years of communism and isolation. Visit the **Malecón**, along the ocean and
harbor channel shore between the Vedado section's tourist hotels and the old colonial heart of
the city; **The Prado Boulevard**, a small version of the Champs Elysées, the **Capitol Building**, modeled after Washington's.

Havana has no organized gay nightlife. The
gay scene centers around the **Coppelia Park**
which is devoted to the pleasures of ice-cream
and same sex cruising; across town near the
Capitol Building, older and mostly married
men cruise the **Park Centrale** generally after
dusk or past midnight. The cruise circuit runs
along the south arcade across the street from
the Capitolio, up to Simon Bolivar Ave.

❖ Gay Beach: End of 16th St. near the Karl
Marx Theatre in the **Miramar district**. Here
gay men and lesbians come to sun and socialize
in the warmer months.

BARS ☿ RESTAURANTS 🍴

● Bars/Clubs (GMW): **D'Giovanni**, Old Town;
Kirachi Club, dance club, Verdado.

● Restaurant (AW): **El Pacifico**, calle San
Nicolas, Zanja (central).

📖 ACCOMMODATIONS 📖

HABANA LIBRE HOTEL
L entre 23 y 25 Vedado, Havana. Tel: 30-5011.
TYPE: *Hotel*. CLIENTELE: Mostly Straight.
LOCATION: Near the Waterfront, opposite
Copelia Park.

* Rooms: 572 rooms w/CTV, phone, A/C
* Restaurant, cafeteria, nightclub
* Rooftop bar w/panoramic view
* Pool, sauna, parking
* Season: Year round
* Rates: (US) $68-$120

DESCRIPTION: Famous 25-story hotel Most
rooms with twin beds. Good location for Ice-
cream and some other goodies in the Park.

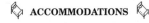

CURAÇAO
NETHERLANDS ANTILLES

AREA: 183 sq. mi. (474 sq. km)
POPULATION: 168,000
CAPITAL: Willemstad
CURRENCY: Antilles florin (NAf)
OFFICIAL LANGUAGE: Dutch, English
MAJOR RELIGION: Roman Catholicism, Protestantism
Telephone: 599
Nat'l Holiday: Autonomy Day Dec. 15
Official Time: G.M.T. -4
Electricity: 110-130 volts; 50 cycles
Exchange Rate: 1US$ = NAf 1.79
National Airline: ALM

LAW REGARDING HOMOSEXUALITY: Homosexual acts are legal between adult men. The age of consent is 16. Generally speaking the attitude of the local population to homosexuality is conservative and less tolerant than it is in the Netherlands.

WILLEMSTAD ✆ 9

✈ Dr. Albert Plesman Airport (CUR)
7 mi. / 11 km north

LOCATION: Southwestern part of the island on the Piscadera Bay.

POPULATION: 100,000

CLIMATE: Yearly sunny-dry with Average annual temperature between 77°F-85°F (24°c-29°c). Average humidity 77%. Average rainfall 21" / 533mm. The Trade winds blow all the time.

VISITOR INFORMATION
Tourist Office: (599-9-61600)
USA: (800) 332-8266

DESCRIPTION: Capital of Curaçao and the Netherlands Antilles, Willemstad is the 7th largest harbor in the world and important trading and cruise ships port. The town is a charming 17th-century replica of Amsterdam in the Tropics. Enjoy free port shopping, low-key friendly casino gambling, pristine beaches and scuba diving nearby. Visit: **Fort Amsterdam**, with its ancient canons and the world's largest "floating bridge"; **Mikve-Israel**, the oldest synagogue in the Western Hemisphere.

❖ Beaches: the island is not famous for its beaches, although there are over 38 beaches to choose from, most of the large hotels have the better beaches. For great visual stimulation go to the **Seaquarium Beach** where all the Dutch Marines go to on their break; **Knip Bay**, about 18 mi. / 29 km outside the city is the Island's most popular beach and is worth the trip.

❖ **SPECIAL EVENTS**: pre-Lenten **Carnival** with costumed parades and Street dancing.

BARS ￥ RESTAURANTS 🍴

● Bars (G/S): **l'Aristocrat**, dance club, Lindbergweg (614-353); Bar at the **Avila Beach Hotel**, popular at Happy Hour during Sunset; **Façade**, dance club, Lindbergweg 32-34; **Rumours**, at the **Lions Dive Hotel**, Bapor Kibra. Gay crowds on Sunday nights.

● Restaurants (AW): **Bistro le Clochard** French Provincial, Brionplein, Otrabanda (62-5666); **Chateau Suisse**, Continental & Dutch, 5 Penstraat (5-5418); **Queen's View**, French cuisine, 15 min. outside town on a hill, Sorsaka 620 (675105).

🔑 ACCOMMODATIONS 🔑

ANVILA BEACH HOTEL
Penstratt 130-134, Willemstad. Tel: (599-9) 614377. Fax: (599-9) 688114. TYPE: *Hotel*. CLIENTELE: Mostly Straight. LOCATION: Oceanfront near town. 90 rooms, 10 suites, CTV, phone, A/C, terrace, restaurant, bar, cafe, tennis, private beach, walking distance to gay bars, Rates: (US) $75-$220. *TAC:* 10%.

LIONS DIVE HOTEL & MARINA
Bapor Kibra z/n, Willemstad. Tel: (599-9) 618100. Fax: (599-9) 618200. TYPE: *Hotel & Marina*. CLIENTELE: All Welcome. LOCATION: Next to Willamsted Public Aquarium. 72 rooms, CTV (CNN), phone, A/C, bahama fans, balcony w/Ocean view, **Rumours** Restaurant/Bar, pool, dive school, gay friendly bar on premises, beach. Rates: US$95-$125. *TAC:* 10%.

CYPRUS

AREA: 3,572 sq. mi. (9,251 sq. km)
POPULATION: 710,600
CAPITAL: Nicosia (Lefcosia)
CURRENCY: Cypriot Pound (C£)
OFFICIAL LANGUAGE: Greek
MAJOR RELIGIONS: Greek Orthodox
Telephone: 42
Nat'l Holiday: Independence Day, Oct. 1
Official Time: G.M.T. +2
Electricity: 240v, 50Hz
Exchange Rate: 1US$ = 0.45 C£
National Airline: Cyprus Airways (CYP)

LAW REGARDING HOMOSEXUALITY:
Homosexual acts between women is not mentioned in the Code of Law. Homosexual acts between men are illegal under section 171 of the Penal Code, with a maximum penalty of 5 years in prison*. There have been prosecution of gay men under this section. The society is conservative and there are no gay and lesbian support groups. *The government of Cyprus has submitted a bill to Parliament to legalize gay anal sex. The European Court of Human Rights ordered Cyprus to decriminalize gay sex in 1992. Cyprus' anti sodomy law violates the European Convention on Human Rights, to which Cyprus is a signatory.

❖ **Note**: The island of Cyprus is currently divided between Greeks in the south and Turks in the north. 58% of the island is Greek, 30% in the north is under Turkish sovereignty. 5% is a no-man land between the two parts.

LIMASSOL   ℭ 05

✈ Paphos Airport (PFO) 37 mi. / 60 km west of Limassol and Larnaca Int'l Airport (LCA) 40 mi. / 65 km northeast of Limassol.

LOCATION: On the South Coast.

CLIMATE: Mild Mediterranean climate. Summers are hot with a maximum of 32°c (90°F) in July; winters are mild with a minimum of 10°c (50°F) in January.

DESCRIPTION: Limassol is the island's largest seaside resort, spreading over 10 mi. / 16 km along the coast. It offers carefree holiday atmosphere, sea front promenade, shopping centers and lively nightlife. Some gay cruising takes place along the central **Anexartisias Avenue**.

❖ Beaches: **Dasoudi Beach**; **Pissouri Beach**, nude beach (5 km / 3 mi.) west of Evdimou; **White Rocks**, between 'Governor's Beach' and 'Agios Georgios Alamanos' Monastery.

BARS ⊤ RESTAURANTS ⏐⏐

● Bars/Clubs (GM): **Alaloum**, bar, 216 Saint Andrews St. (369-726); **Irodion**, mixed clientele, 238 St. Andrews St. (363427); **Jacaré**, tourist area of the city, behind Park Beach Hotel, popular gay meeting point, Popiland 67, Georgiou Yermassoyias (320-635).

λ SERVICES λ

● Health Club (GM): **Spartacus**, 17 Voltaire St., Yermassoyias (Semiramis Complex).

🏳 ACCOMMODATIONS 🏳

L'ONDA BEACH HOTEL
Potamos Yermassoyias. Tel: (5) 321-821. TYPE: *Apartments Resort Complex*. CLIENTELE: All Welcome. LOCATION: On the beach. 22 suites, 44 studios, A/C, CTV, phone, minibar, restaurant, beach bar, heated pool, health club, gym, sauna. Rates: on request.

NICOSIA   ℭ 02

✈ Larnaca Int'l Airport (LCA)
30 mi. / 50 km south

LOCATION: Nicosia (Lefkosia) is located in northern Cyprus. The capital is shared on the border with Turkish Northern Cyprus.

POPULATION: 166,500

DESCRIPTION: The Capital of Cyprus since the 10th century. It is the seat of the government, diplomatic headquarters and cultural center of Cyprus. The Old Town is of great historic interest.

BARS Y RESTAURANTS ¶¶

● Bars/Clubs (GMW): **Bastione**, 6 Athina Ave., (433101); **Garden Café**, opposite Museum.

λ SERVICES λ

● Health Club (GM): **Korkut Hamam**, Belig Pasa Sokak 16 (Arasta).

 ACCOMMODATIONS

CLEOPATRA HOTEl
8 Florina St., Nicosia. Tel: (2) 445-254. TYPE: *Hotel*. CLIENTELE: All Welcome. LOCATION: Downtown. 90 rooms w/priv. bath, CTV, C/H, A/C, restaurants, bar, TV room, parking. Rates: $65-$95. *TAC:* 10%.

KENNEDY HOTEL
70 Regaena St., Nicosia. Tel: (2) 377-777. TYPE: *Hotel*. CLIENTELE: All Welcome. LOCATION: At the Venetian Walls, walking distance of city center. 150 rooms w/priv. bath, CTV, phone, A/C, C/H, restaurants, bars, roof garden, indoor/outdoor pool and terrace. Rates: $90-$140. *TAC:* 10%

PAPHOS   ℂ 06

✈ Paphos Airport (PFO)

5 mi. / 8 km southeast of Paphos

LOCATION: West coast between the Western Troodos Mountains and the Mediterranean Sea.

POPULATION: 28,000

DESCRIPTION: Paphos, known as the 'Playground of Aphrodite' is an historic town entwined with Greek Mythology and the legendary birth of Aphrodite. Paphos offers an attractive harbor, picturesque open-air restaurants and historical sites. Visit the famous **'Aphrodite Rocks'** the birthplace of the goddess with a nearby shrine of the goddess; impressive monasteries, and recently unearthed 3rd century AD mosaics in the harbor area.

Y BAR Y

● Bar/Club (GM): **La Boite 67**, Apostolos Pavlos 116 (harbor location).

 ACCOMMODATIONS

ALEXANDER THE GREAT
Poseidon Ave., Paphos. Tel: (6) 244-000. TYPE: *Resort Hotel*. CLIENTELE: All Welcome. LOCATION: Beachfront in the harbor. 172 rooms w/priv. bath, CTV, phone, A/C, C/H, restaurant, bar, pool, health club, sauna, gym, jacuzzi. Rates: $130-$180. *TAC:* 10%.

CZECH REPUBLIC

AREA: 30,449 sq. mi. (78,864 sq. km)
POPULATION: 10,444,000
CAPITAL: Prague
CURRENCY: Koruna (CSK)
OFFICIAL LANGUAGE: Czech, Slovak
MAJOR RELIGION: Roman Catholicism (30%), Protestantism (8%)
Telephone: 42
Nat'l Holiday: October 28, Independence
Official Time: G.M.T. + 1 or 2
Electricity: 220 volts
Exchange Rate: 1US$ = CSK 26.20
National Airline: CSA

LAW REGARDING HOMOSEXUALITY: Homosexuality is legal. The legal minimum age of consent is 15. There are no laws concerning tourists with HIV/AIDS. Homosexuality is considered a taboo by the majority of the population. Prague is a liberal city where many gay Czechs choose to live.

BRNO   ℭ 05

✈ Brno Airport

LOCATION: In Moravia, where the Carpathians and Bohemian highlands meet, about 3 hrs. southeast of Prague.

POPULATION: 400,000

Gay/Lesbian Visitor Information
Lambda-men: 572937
Lambda-women (Sapfo club): 523712

DESCRIPTION: Historical and cultural center of Moravia. The city enjoyed its Golden Age in the 14th century when the City walls and the Spilberk Castle were built. Today Brno is an important trade center with a charming Old City center.

❖ Public Cruising (AYOR): Park in front of the **Opera House; Ceska Ulice.**

BARS ♈ RESTAURANTS 🍴

● Bars/Clubs (GM): **Gibon Club**, video club, Pekarska 38; **H 46**, cosy bar, daily 17-2:00 hrs., near railway station, Hybesova 46 (324-945); **Philadelphia**, Milady Horakove 1a; **Sklipek u Richarda**, oldest and most popular gay bar & restaurant in town, Sat. 20-06 hrs., closed Jul-Aug., Luzova 29 (572-937).

● Bar/Club (GW): **Autotourist** (Sapfó Klub), lesbian meeting place, irregular terms, call Inge (523-712), Pekarska 24.

λ SERVICES λ

● Erotica (G/S): **Solarcentrum**, sex shop, Pekarska 54 (4321-1555)

● Health Club (G/S): **Lázne Kopecná ulice**, gay sauna.

● Health Service (G/S): **Mestska hygienicka stanice**. Mon. 16-18 hrs., Sypka 25 (4521-2174).

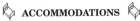 ACCOMMODATIONS

AUSTROTEL GRAND HOTEL
Benesova 18/20, Brno 65783. Tel: (05) 26421. TYPE: *Hotel*. CLIENTELE: Mostly Straight. LOCATION: Downtown near railway station. 102 rooms w/priv. bath, CTV, phone, minibar, 24 hrs. room service, restaurants, bars, disco, casino. Rates: $70-$140.

HOSTKA   ℭ 0411

LOCATION: 50 km / 31 mi. north of Prague on road No. 261 in the Central Bohemian Highlands near Litomerice and the German border.

 ACCOMMODATIONS

AT THE VISCOUNT
Pod nádrazím St. 201, 411 72 Hostka. okr. Litomerice. Tel: (411) 500-808. HOSTS: Emil & Yarda. TYPE: *Bed & Breakfast*. CLIENTELE: Gay/ Straight. LOCATION: Rustic Czech countryside, north of Prague near the German border. 6 rooms w/shared bath, wash basin in each room, restaurant, coffee bar, sauna with minibar and massage (on request), nightclub with Saturday disco and drag show, pool, summer

terraces, free parking. Rates: on request.

KARLOVY VARY   © 017

DESCRIPTION: Karlovy Vary (Karlsbad) is the largest and most famous Spa resort in the Czech Republic. There are 12 major hot springs, each has its own unique therapeutic value. The Spa resort is located in Bohemia of northwestern Czech Republic near the German border.

BARS Y RESTAURANTS ¶¶

● Bar/Club (GM): **Krusne Zakouti**, Na Petrine 4, Tue-Sun 15-24 hrs. (27591).

ACCOMMODATIONS

HOTEL DVORAK
Nova Louka 11, Karlovy Vary 36021. Tel: (17) 24145. TYPE: *Hotel.* CLIENTELE: Mostly Straight. LOCATION: Downtown in the center of the Spa area. 76 rooms w/priv. bath, A/C, CTV, phone, indoor pool, cafe, restaurant, sauna, Health Club, massages. Rates: $90-$160.

OSTRAVA   © 069

LOCATION: In Moravia near the border with Poland.

❖ Gay Beach: **Lazne Hulvaky**, take tram #4,8,9 from the city.

❖ Public Cruising (AYOR): in front of the **Hotel Imperial**.

Gay/Lesbian Visitor Information
Lambda:516-30

BARS Y RESTAURANTS ¶¶

● Bars/Clubs (GM): **U Dzbanu**, dance club/wine bar, Jiraskovo nam daily 10-24, Fri-Sat 20-4, Kuri rynek.

λ SERVICES λ

● Health Club (GM): **Lazne Capkova Sokolovna**, Trida Osvoboditelu.

● Health Service (G/S): **Linka duvery zdravi**, 24 hrs., tel: 234-359.

ACCOMMODATIONS

HOTEL IMPERIAL
Tyrsova 6, Ostrava 70 138. Tel: (69) 236-621. TYPE: *Hotel.* CLIENTELE: All Welcome. LOCATION: Town Center. 126 rooms w/priv. bath, CTV, phone, minibar, restaurant, cafe, bar. Rates: $110-$180. DESCRIPTION: First Class turn-of-the-century hotel. Gay cruising right in front of the hotel.

PLZEN   © 019

DESCRIPTION: Plzen is the famous Beer brewing capital where the smooth Pilsner beer is produced. This medium size town, population 180,000, is located some 60 mi. / 96 km southwest of Prague in Bohemia.

❖ Public Cruising (AYOR): Main Railway Station.

Gay/Lesbian Visitor Information
Help Line: Tue. 14-16 (224-325)

BARS Y RESTAURANTS ¶¶

● Bars/Clubs (GM): **4HP**, Jiraskovo namesti 5 (7242811); **Patrick Klub**, Politickych veznu 31 (225-049); **Studna**, dance club, Machova 14-16; **U Jupitera**, gay bar., disco on Saturdays, daily 10:00-22:00, Palackeho namesti 23.

ACCOMMODATIONS

CONTINENTAL HOTEL
Zbrojnicka 5, Plzen 30 534. Tel: (19) 364-779. TYPE: *Hotel.* CLIENTELE: Mostly Straight. LOCATION: City Center. 53 rooms, some w/priv. bath, phone, CTV, restaurant, coffee shop. Rates: $80-$140.

PRIVATE ROOMS: call Peter (372-27).

PRAGUE   © 02

✈ Ruzyne Airport (PRG)

LOCATION: Heart of Bohemia, in western Czech Republic.

POPULATION: 1,200,000

CLIMATE: Continental climate. Winters are cold and snowy with an average January temperatures of 28°F (-2°c). Summers can be hot with an average July temperature of 70°F (21°c).

Gay/lesbian Visitor Information
AMIGO
Tel/Fax: (02) 684-6548

DESCRIPTION: Prague is an historic, romantic city built on seven hills with graceful bridges, and fairy-tale architecture. Since the peaceful revolution of November 1989, Prague is again the capital of a free nation, but it will take many more generations to get rid of oppressing years of communist rule. Visit **Wenceslas Square** and the **Old Town**; catch a view of Prague from the old **Charles Bridge**, and explore the 1000 years old **Prague Castle**.

Prague is the center of gay life in the Czech Republic. Attitudes toward gays although less severe than in the neighboring Catholic dominated Poland, can not be perceived as liberal in the western sense. People sometimes use the term "freaks" to describe homosexuals. For this reason it is necessary to be discreet.

● Side trips are recommended to the Bahamian Spas of **Karlovy Vary** and **Marianske Lazne** and the many medieval castles in the country.

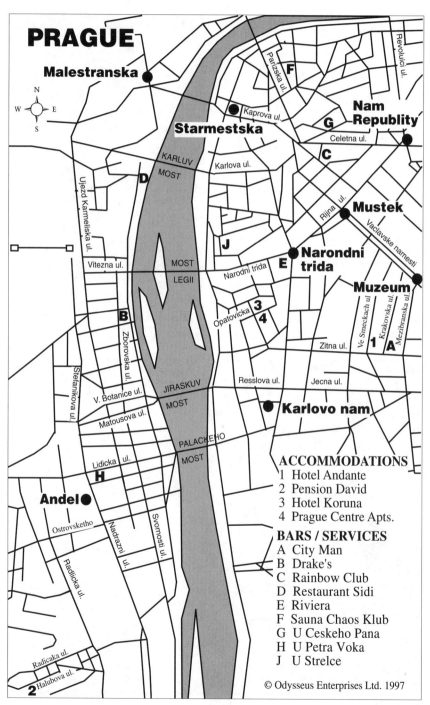

PRAGUE

Malestranska

N
W — E
S

Starmestska

Kaprova ul.

Parizska ul.

F

Nam Republity

G

Celetna ul.

C

KARLUV MOST

Karlova ul.

Ujezd Karmeliska ul.

D

Vitezna ul.

MOST LEGII

Narodni trida

J

E

Narondni trida

Rijna ul.

Mustek

Vaclavske namesti

B

Zborovska ul.

Stefanikova ul.

Opatovicka

3

4

Muzeum

Ve Smeckach ul

Krakovska ul.

Mezibranska ul.

Zitna ul.

1

A

V. Botanice ul.

JIRASKUV MOST

Resslova ul.

Jecna ul.

Matousova ul.

PALACKEHO MOST

Karlovo nam

Lidicka ul.

H

Andel

Ostrovsketho

Nadrazni ul.

Svornosti ul.

Radicka ul.

Radicaka ul.

Halubova ul.

2

Revolucni ul.

ACCOMMODATIONS
1 Hotel Andante
2 Pension David
3 Hotel Koruna
4 Prague Centre Apts.

BARS / SERVICES
A City Man
B Drake's
C Rainbow Club
D Restaurant Sidi
E Riviera
F Sauna Chaos Klub
G U Ceskeho Pana
H U Petra Voka
J U Strelce

© Odysseus Enterprises Ltd. 1997

❖ Public Cruising (AYOR): **Letná Park**; **Main Railway Station**, **Masaryk's Railway Station**, **Vaclavske namesti** and all the central area of the city.

❖ Gay Beach: **Plavecky stadion Podoli (Podoli Sports Stadium)**, the most famous gay haunts in the Czech Republic, a short distance from Prague's city center. 'Soviet' style sports center with several big swimming pools, not only gay, but very interesting, Podolska 74 (4391-513).

BARS 🍴 RESTAURANTS 🍴

● Bars/Clubs (GM): **Bambi Bar**, cocktail bar / escort service, Bonvojova 43 (275-500); **Billiard Club Hugo**, Husitska 5 (534-909); **Crazy**, cocktail bar/escort service, Kloboukova 11 (7935-885/6); **Inkognito**, small cosy bar, Prokpova 18, Prague 3 (270-153); **Mercury**, dance club, drag & strip shows, Kolinska 11 (6731-0603); **Piano Bar**, Milesovska 10; **Sam**, leather club, Cajkovského 34, Prague 3 - Zizkov, open: 18-24; **Stella**, gay pub, Luzicka 10; **Tom's Bar**, small entertainment complex in western style, bars, disco, dark/video room, Pernerova 4, Prague 8, Karlin (232-1170); **U dubu**, beer Pub, popular with older gays, Zahrebska 14 (691-0889); **U Petra Voka**, Na Belidle 40, Prague 5; **U strelce**, popular cabaret with drag shows, Strelecky ostrov, 21-6 hrs.

● Bars/Clubs (GMW): ♻ **The Rainbow Club**, cafe and bar, in the cellar at the Red Peacock, Kamzíková 6, bet. Celetná & Zelezná, near Prague's Old Town Square (2423-3168); **G&L Club**, disco, bar, restaurant, Lublanska 48, Prague 2, open: 17:00-4:00 daily; **Mercury**, small disco, outside city center, Kolinska 11, Prague 3 (673-10603); **Riviera**, most popular gay club in Prague, right in the center of Prague near the National Theatre, pub, wine bar,disco,young people and some hustlers, Narodni 20, Prague 1, open: 20-05 (2491-2249).

● Restaurants (GMW): **Barberina**, expensive gay owned restaurant & bar in the centre of historical town, Melantrichova 10, Prague 1 (261-084); ♻ **Restaurant David**, Czech & International, Summer garden terrace, also hotel, Holubova 5, Prague 5 (549-820). Other (AW) **U Maliru**, picturesque wine tavern, popular with the artist, Maltézské námesti 11, Malá Strana (531-883); **Opera Grill**, small stylish antique decorated restaurant, Czech cuisine, K. Svétlé 35, Staré Mésto (265-508).

λ SERVICES λ

● Cinema (GM): **Drake's**, gay erotic cinema,

video cabins, sex toys, young hustlers. Live strip show every day at 9 pm. Popular calling place for gay men visiting Prague, Petrinska 5, Smichov, Prague 5, non stop (534-909).

● Erotica (GM): **City Man**, Krakovska 2; **Video Erotic Center**, Borivojova 105, Prague 3 (275610); **Rial**, Main Railway Station, Wilsonova ulics; **Video Center**, Americka 14, Prague 2 (253-656); **Video Erotic Studio**, sex shop and video cabins, Jana Zajice 4, Prague 7 (37 7716).

● Health Clubs (GM): **Aqua Club 2000** (Lazne Zizkov), solarium, baths, sauna, sex shop, Husitska 7, Prague 3 (627-8971); **Chaos Club**, Dusni 13 B, Prague 1 (2423-8510); **David Sauna**, Sokolovska 77, Prahas 8 - Karlin, open: 16-04 (232-8789); **Inkognito**, smaller sauna, far from center but very good ambiance, Strelnicna 1969, Prague 8 (858-6616); **Smichov**, nam. 14 rijna 10, Prague 5 (547-164).

● Publication (GMW): ✪ **Amigo**, P.O. Box 60, 180 00 Praha 8, gay & lesbian information service and entertainment monthly magazine, Tel/Fax: (02) 684-6548. Email: amigoint@mbox.vol.cz; ✪ **Czech Mate**, complete guide to all gay & lesbian businesses in the Czech Republic and Slovakia in English, Amigo, P.O. Box 60, 180 00 Praha 8, Tel/Fax: (02) 684-6548. Email: amigoint@mbox.vol.cz; **SOHO Revue**, cultural, social magazine, ORBIS, Vinohradskà 46, CZ-120 41 Praha 2. Tel/Fax: 42-2-25-7891.

ACCOMMODATIONS

HOTEL ANDANTE
Prague 1, Czech Republic. USA/Canada reservations Tel: (516) 944-5330 or (800) 257-5344. Fax: (516) 944-7540 or (800) 982-6571. TYPE: *Hotel.* CLIENTELE: Gay/Straight. LOCATION: Central Prague near Gay scene.

* Rooms: 32 w/bath or shower
* Apartments: (2) 2-bedroom
* CTV, phone, refrigerator, A/C, balcony
* Business phone/fax facilities
* Room & maid service
* Office with secretary service available
* Snack bar: from 11:00am
* Gay Bars: walking distance
* Open: Year round
* Rates: (US) $115-$140 w/CB apartments from $160
* *TAC:* 10% (from Odysseus)

DESCRIPTION: Renovated hotel in the center of Prague. Fully air-conditioned. French restaurant on premises.

✪ HOTEL KORUNA
Prague 1, Czech Republic. USA/Canada reservations Tel: (516) 944-5330 or (800) 257-5344. Fax: (516) 944-7540 or (800) 982-6571. TYPE: *Hotel.* CLIENTELE: All Welcome. LOCATION: Central Prague near Gay scene.

* Rooms: 25 w/shower
* CTV, phone, radio
* Breakfast lounge
* Laundry, maid service
* Parking garage
* Gay Bars: walking distance
* Airport: 25 mins., taxi
* Open: Year round
* Rates: (US) $110 - $160 w/CB
* *TAC:* 10% (from Odysseus)

DESCRIPTION: Renovated hotel in the center of Prague 1. All rooms are clean and comfortable. Walk to restaurant, metro and gay clubs.

✪ PENSION DAVID
Holubova 5, 150 00 Prague 5. Tel: (2) 900-11293 or 900-11294. Fax: (2) 549-820. TYPE: *Hotel.* HOST: Václav Kaftan. CLIENTELE: Mostly Gay. LOCATION: 15 min. from Prague Center with excellent metro and tram connection. M° Radlicka. Tram No. 14 Laurova Stop.

* Rooms: 6 w/shared shower/WC
* Smoking permitted
* Phone, CTV, cooking facilities, C/H
* Safe deposit, balcony, garden, maid service
* Restaurant & Bar: Czech & International
* Shop: maps, china, glass, cards etc.
* Pool, sundeck, free parking
* Beach: 200 m / yards (mixed)
* Gay Bars: 15 min.
* Airport: Prague 8 km / 5 mi., taxi, bus
* Train St'n: Praha - Smichov, 10 min. walk
* Languages: Czech, German, Eng., Russian
* Credit Cards: VISA/AMEX/JCB
* Open: Year round
* Rates: US$57-US$85 w/Bb. *TAC:* 5%

DESCRIPTION: Comfortable 3-star accommodations with sauna, club and restaurant. Garden terrace in summer, swimming pool in season, escort service.

PRAGUE CENTRAL APTS
USA/Canada reservations Tel: (516) 944-5330 or (800) 257-5344. Fax: (516) 944-7540 or (800) 982-6571. TYPE: *Self-catering Apartments.* Quality apartments in Central Prague near the gay scene. Each apartment has kitchen and full bath. Rates: $60-$120/day. Transfers can be arranged from airport or train station. *TAC:* 10%.

DENMARK

AREA: 16,629 sq. mi. (43,069 sq. km)
POPULATION: 5,124,000
CAPITAL: Copenhagen
CURRENCY: Krone (DK)
OFFICIAL LANGUAGE: Danish
MAJOR RELIGION: Protestantism
Telephone: 45
Nat'l Holiday: Liberation Day, May 5
Official Time: G.M.T. +1
Electricity: 220 volts
Exchange Rate: 1US$ = DK 5.47
National Airline: SAS

LAW REGARDING HOMOSEXUALITY:
Homosexuality is legal in Denmark. The legal
minimum age for consensual heterosexual or
homosexual activity is 15. Generally the attitude
of the law enforcing authorities is very liberal
and the Danes have no problems accepting gay
lifestyle. In May 1989 the Danish Parliament
passed the Registered Partnership Act, assuring
gay and lesbian couples similar legal rights as
heterosexual married couples. The same law
allows same sex marriage making Denmark the
first country in the world where homosexual
marriage is legal. The National Danish Organization for Gays & Lesbians (LBL) works closely
with the government authorities to protect and
advance the rights of gay men and lesbians.

ARHUS   ⓒ   86

✈   Tirstrup Airport (AAR)
     23 mi. / 37 km northwest

LOCATION: Centre of Jutland east coast, connected to the European mainland

POPULATION: 580,000

Gay/Lesbian Visitor Information
PAN Information: 8613-1948

DESCRIPTION: Denmark's second largest
city, a lively University town and important
trade center since Viking times. The town is
compact and offers well preserved historic
quarter, entertainment scene and nearby
beaches (during the summer).

BARS ▼ RESTAURANTS

● Bars/Clubs: **A-Men's Club** (GM), Skowejen 7
(8619-1089); **Musikcafeen**, alternative scene
jazz and reggae club, Meljgæde 53; **Pan Café**
(GMW), dance club & café, Jægergåsgade 42, just
south of the railway station, open: 10pm-3am,
Thu. are for women only (8613-4380); **Café Sappho** (GW), Mejlgæde 19.

● Restaurants (AW): **Hollywood Café**, light
meals, Banegårsgæde 47; **China Town**, Chinese
cuisine, Fredensgæde 46 (opp. bus station).

ACCOMMODATIONS

ANSGAR MISSION HOTEL
Banegaardsplads 14, Aarhus DK-8100. Tel:
(86) 124122. TYPE: *Hotel*. CLIENTELE: All
Welcome. LOCATION: Central location adjacent to the train station, SAS terminal, walk to
gay clubs.

* Rooms: 168 w/priv. bath. Suites: 6
* CTV, phone, C/H
* Room and maid service, laundry
* Restaurant, private garden, parking
* Airport: 20 min. (taxi, bus)
* Train Station: walking distance
* Gay Bars: walking distance
* Beach: 4 km / 3 mi.
* Open: Year round
* Rates: $96-$140

DESCRIPTION: Popular older hotel in a central location. Rooms in old and new wings.

COPENHAGEN   ⓒ   31/33

✈ Copenhagen Airport Kastrup (CPH)

LOCATION: Eastern coast of the island of
Sjaelland (Zealand) on the Baltic Sea.

POPULATION: 616,570

CLIMATE: Mild for a Scandinavian country.
Summer temperatures between 61°F and 77°F
(16°c - 25°c). Winter temperatures seldom fall
below 30°F (-1°c).

Gay/Lesbian Visitor Information
PAN Information: 3311-1961

DESCRIPTION: Copenhagen is a dynamic port city and a center for arts, architecture, antiquities and museums. Most of the major city attractions are within a short distance of each other. Public transportation is excellent and the city is safe and relatively crime free. Major tourist attractions: **Tivoli Gardens**, a famous amusement park and a national treasure in operation since 1843 with its world famous landmark - the **Arabian Nights Palace** outlined with colorful sparkling light bulbs. The **Royal Museum of Fine Arts**, sølvgade, with extraordinary collection of Danish arts. **Rosenborg Castle**, a red brick Renaissance style castle from the 17th century; **Christianborg Palace**, Christianborg Slotsplads, house of the Danish Parliament, its Supreme Court and the Royal Reception Rooms. **Ny Carlsberg Glyptothek**, Dantes Plads, one of the most important art museums in Scandinavia; **National Museum**, 12 Frederiksholms Kanal, one of the oldest and largest of its kind in the world. And of course no visit to this city is completed without visiting the world famous beer breweries **Carlsberg** or **Tuborg** for a fascinating demonstration of how barely becomes beer, and a good one as you all know.

Triton

Charming Hotel near Central Station, Tivoli Gardens and Town Hall

USA/Canada Reservations:
1-800-257-5344
TEL: (516) 944-5330 / FAX: (516) 944-7540

BARS ⅄ RESTAURANTS ¶¶

Almost all the gay bars are located in the city center, within walking distance of the **Strøget**, the main pedestrian street in Copenhagen.

● Bars/clubs (GM): **Amigo Bar**, Schonbergsgade 4 (3121-4915); **Can Can**, Mikkel Bryggers Gade 11 (3311-5010); **Central Hørnet** (Central Corner), talk bar, friendly atmosphere, Kattesundt 18; **Cosy Bar**, Studiestræde 24 (3312-7427); **Geomarlix**, dance club, Rådhausstræde 4 (3311-7735); **Masken**, Studiestræde 33; **Men's Bar**, leather cruise bar, Teglgaardstraede 3 (3312-7303); **Metro Place de Clichy**, dance club, Hyskenstraede 10.

● Bars/clubs (GMW): **After Dark**, disco/bar, drag shows, male strippers, Studiestræde 31 (3332-31910).

● Bars/Clubs (GW): **Kvindehuset/Women House**, Gothergade 37, 2nd fl. (3314-2804) for detailed information; **Masken Bar**, Studiestrdræde 33; **Sappho's Salon**, Knabrostræde 3.

● Restaurants (GMW): **Babooshka**, Turesensgade 6(3315-0536); **Cafe Intime**, Allégade 25 (3834-1958); **Flyvefisken**, seafood, vegetarian, Lars Bjørn stræde 18 (3314-9515); **Krasnapol**sky, cafe, restaurant, Vestergade 10 (3332-8800); **La Rose de Tunis**, Vesterbrogade 120; **Teglkroen**, Teglgårdsstr. 17; **Spiseloppen**, Christiania (3157-9558). Other restaurants (AW): **Anva Cafeteria**, 2E Vesterbrogade, a popular Smørrebørd restaurant in a shopping mall, moderately priced, and good food; **Det Grønne Køkken**, 10 Larsbjørns-stræde (127-068), Mediterranean style, near the Tivoli and the Rådhus-plasden; **Fiskekælderen**, popular seafood restaurant, 18 Ved Stranden (122-011).

⅄ SERVICES ⅄

● Cinema (GM): **Club 16**, erotic movies, and sex club daily 09-05, Fri-Sun non-stop, Abel Cathrinesgade 16 (3131-1648); **Club 18**, Istegæde 18.

● Health Clubs (GM): **Amigo**, Studiestræde 31 (3315-3332); **Body Bio**, Kingosgæde 7; **Copenhagen Gay Center**, Istesgæde 36 (3122-2300).

● Leather (GM): **Cruz**, leather works, Studiestræde 29 (3314-9017); **SM-Shop**, Studiestræde 12 (3332-3303).

● Sex Shop (G/S): **Club Kingo**, Kingosgæde 5; **Club 16**, Abel Cathrinsegæde 16; **Copenhagen Gay Center**, also gay sauna and adult movies,

Istedgade 36 (22.23.00); **Men's Shop**, videos, leather, S/M video show, Viktoriagade 24 (3323-1493).

 **ACCOMMODATIONS**

ASCOT HOTEL
Studiestræde 61, DK-1554-V. Tel: 3312-6000. USA/Canada reservations Tel: (516) 944-5330 or (800) 257-5344. Fax: (516) 944-7540 or (800) 982-6571. TYPE: *Hotel*. CLIENTELE: All Welcome. LOCATION: Near city center, walking distance of the famous Tivoli Gardens and City Hall right in the heart of Gay Copenhagen. 140 rooms w/priv. bath, 7 suites, 20 Apts (1-2 bedroom w/kitchenette), CTV (CNN), radio, phone, room/maid service, DESCRIPTION: First class elegant hotel in a restored and modernized turn of the century bathhouse. Rooms are bright and colorful decorated. Rates: $240 - $320. *TAC:* 10% (from Odysseus).

○ HOTEL TRITON
Helgolandsgade 7-11, Copenhagen DK 1653 V. USA/Canada Tel: (800) 257-5344 or (516) 944-5330. Fax: (800) 982-6571 or (516) 944-7540. TYPE: *Hotel*. CLIENTELE: All Welcome. LOCATION: Heart of Copenghagen near Central Station, SAS Air Terminal, Tivoli Gardens

& Town Hall.

* Rooms: 123 w/priv. bath
  37 sgl / 80 dbl / 6 JR suites
* Rooms for non-smokers
* CTV, phone, refrigerator, hair dryer
* Security safe boxes (in lobby)
* Breakfast room, piano bar
* Smoke detectors, automatic fire doors
* Maid service, elevators (2), parking
* Gay Bars: walking distance
* Airport: 10 km / 6 mi. (taxi)
* Open: Year round
* Rates: (US) $115 - $180 w/DbB
  JR Suites $180-$240
* *TAC:* 10% (from Odysseus)

DESCRIPTION: Charming turn-of-the-century 3-star hotel in a central location. All rooms are brightly decorated in Scandinavian design and have non-allergic duvets and synthetic pillows. Good quality accommodations and fine service.

HOTEL WINDSOR
Frederiksborggade 30, 1360 Copenhagen K. Tel: (33) 110-830. TYPE: *Hotel*. HOST: John Larsen. CLIENTELE: Gay/Straight. LOCATION: Central near Israels Plads. 25 rooms all with shared bath. Rates: on request. DESCRIPTION: Simple hotel, moderately priced. Own keys.

AREA: 18,704 sq. mi. (84,443 sq. km)
POPULATION: 5,648,000
CAPITAL: Santo Domingo
CURRENCY: Dominican Peso
OFFICIAL LANGUAGE: Spanish
MAJOR RELIGION: Roman Catholicism
Telephone: 809
Nat'l Holiday: Independence Day Feb. 27
Official Time: GMT - 5
Electricity: 110 volts
Exchange Rate: 1US$ =
National Airline: Dominicana

LAW REGARDING HOMOSEXUALITY: There is no special mention in the law regarding homosexual relations for adults over 18 years. But article 330 of the Penal Code provides for up to two years in prison for violation of decorum and good behavior in public. The police is hostile to gay owned businesses.

SANTO DOMINGO

✈ Las Americas Int'l Airport (SDQ)
18 mi. / 29 km north

LOCATION: On the southern Caribbean coastline of the island, near the lovely Boca Chica beach.

POPULATION: 1,313,000

CLIMATE: Tropical climate with warm days and ocean breezes. Heat is seldom excessive. There is only a slight change between the average summer temperature of 90°F (32°c); and winter's average temperature of 80°F (27°c). Both summers and winters are comfortable.

DESCRIPTION: The capital of Santo Domin-

go was Founded in 1496 by Christopher Columbus' brother, as a stepping stone for further explorations in the New World. Santo Domingo is rich with historical sites related to the early exploration and settlement by Spanish Seafarers. Visit **Old Santo Domingo** on the west bank of the Ozama River which was restored to recreate an authentic 16th century look. A modern glimpse of the city can be taken at the **Plaza de la Cultura** an impressive residential and cultural center. Main public cruise area (AYOR) include: **Plaza Independence** and **Parque Colón**.

❖ Beaches: **Boca Chica Beach**, about 20 min. ride east of the city; **Embassy Beach**, about 30 min. by car from the city.

BARS Ⴤ RESTAURANTS ᵞᵞ

● Bars (GMW): **Broadway**, Avda Duarte 347 (681-8703); **Café Capri**, Avda Tiradentes 20, Naco; **El Bochinche**, bar and disco, c/ El Seybo #20, altos; **Free**, dance club, Avda Ortega y Gasey 13 off Avda J.F. Kennedy (565-8100); **Poussee Bar**, c/ 19 de Marzo #107 (682-7905); **O'Hara's**, dance club, c/ Danae 3, Gascue (682-8408); **Phönix**, c/ Polvorin 10, Zona Colonial

● Restaurants (AW): **El Alcázar**, International cuisine, elegant, designed by Oscar de la Renta in a Moorish motif, at the Santo Domingo Hotel, Av. Abraham Lincoln (221-1511); **Grand Café**, light café fare, DJ nightly, 26 Lope de Vega (541-6655); **Pitiri**, c/ Nicholas de Bar 6, La Esperilla (541-5478);**Reina de España**, Spanish cuisine, seafood specialties, 103 c/. Cervantes (685-2588).

ᨆ ACCOMMODATIONS

CONTINENTAL HOTEL
Maximo Gomez #16, Santo Domingo. Tel: 689-1151. TYPE: *Hotel*. CLIENTELE: All Welcome.
LOCATION: Residential area opposite Palace of Fine Arts, near restaurants & casinos.

* Rooms: 100 w/priv. bath. Suites: 6
* CTV, phone, A/C, some w/ocean view, balcony
* Disco, cocktail lounge, restaurant, pool
* Beach: 1 block
* Gay Bars: walking distance
* Airport: 25 min. taxi
* Open: Year round
* Rates: $69-$120

DESCRIPTION: Modern tourist class hotel in a central location. Free parking.

EGYPT

AREA: 386,659 sq. mi. (1,001,447 sq. km)
POPULATION: 43,000,000
CAPITAL: Cairo
CURRENCY: Egyptian pound (E£)
OFFICIAL LANGUAGE: Arabic
MAJOR RELIGIONS: Islam, Coptic
Telephone: 20
Nat'l Holiday: Revolution Day, June 23
Official Time: G.M.T. +2/3
Electricity: 220 volts, 50 cycles, A.C.
Exchange Rate: 1US$ = E£ 3.39
National Airline: Egyptair

LAW REGARDING HOMOSEXUALITY:
Homosexual acts are not illegal but are not recognized either. As it is the case in most traditional Islamic countries the role of marriage
and family is socially very important. However,
it is not uncommon for men to engage in homosexual conducts.

ALEXANDRIA   ⓒ   03

✈ Nouha Airport (ALY) 5 mi. / 8 km E.

LOCATION: In northern Egypt on the
Mediterranean Sea.

POPULATION: 2,500,000

CLIMATE: Mediterranean climate. Long dry
hot summer with temperatures in the 90˚sF
(35˚c), and short rainy winter. The heat of the
summer can be tempered by cool sea breezes.

DESCRIPTION: Egypt's main port and second largest city is also the most cosmopolitan
and Mediterranean of all Egyptian cities.
Beautiful beaches and comfortable climate
make Alexandria a natural destination for
mass summer exodus from Cairo. Visit the
Museum of the former **Royal Palace**, and

admire the ancient historic ruins. Swimming
and water skiing facilities are readily available. If you are interested in gambling check
the casino at the **Pullman Cecil Hotel/ Casino**, 16 Saad Zaghloul Square (580-7055).

BARS ♈ RESTAURANTS 🍴

There are no gay bars and restaurants, but
most bars at the international hotels maybe
interesting at late hours. You can try the
Admiral Disco at the Admiral Hotel (Ramleh
Station); or the **Amoun Disco** at the Amoun
Hotel (El Mansheya). Restaurants: limit yourself to the good restaurants at the International Hotels, avoid drinking tab water or uncooked
fruit and vegetables.

🗝 ACCOMMODATIONS 🗝

PULLMAN CECIL HOTEL
16 Saad Zaghloul Sq., Ramleh Station. Tel: (03)
807-055. Fax: (03) 807-250. TYPE: *Hotel / Casino*. CLIENTELE: Mostly Straight. LOCA-
TION: City Center overlooking Harbor and the
Park.87 rooms w/priv. bath, CTV (movies),
phone, A/C, restaurant, 24 hrs. coffee shop,
American bar, nightclub, Health Club, casino.
Rates: (US) $65-$120. DESCRIPTION: Superi-
or tourist class hotel & casino in a convenient
central location.

CAIRO   ⓒ   02

✈ Cairo Int'l Airport (CAI)
   14 mi. / 22 km northeast of Cairo

LOCATION: Northern Egypt on the River
Nile, at the apex of the Delta.

POPULATION: 12,500,000

CLIMATE: Hot and dry desert climate year
round, with a slightly cooler and rainy weather
during the short winter months (Dec-Feb). The
average temperature in January is 14˚c (57˚F)
and 27˚c (81˚F) in July.

DESCRIPTION: The largest city in Africa,
Cairo is a mixture of modern and traditional
architecture. It is a third world city par excel-
lence with many buildings and public infrastructure in a state of decay. Central Cairo
around the Tahrir square is overwhelming
with chaotic traffic, large crowds, and the colors and smells of the orient.

Visit the ancient **Pyramids** and **Old Cairo** on the east bank of the Nile. The **Egyptian Museum** is a must with its collection of ancient treasures. For tourists there is the *Sound and Light* show at the Pyramids, and authentic belly dancing and floor show at the famous **Sahara City** near the Pyramids. Gay travelers should bear in mind that contacts are possible but they are not confined to 'gay' establishments as we know them in the west.

BARS ⊤ RESTAURANTS ¶¶

There are no gay bars and restaurants, but most bars at the international hotels maybe interesting at late hours. You can try the bars at the **Cairo Marriott Hotel** or the **Swan Bar** and Lobby Bar at the **Heliopolis Sheraton**, also check the **Riche Café**, Talaat Harb St. (opposite Air-France office), or the **Taverne** at the El Tahrir Square at the Nile Hilton Hotel. Restaurants: limit yourself to the good restaurants at the International Hotels, avoid drinking tap water or uncooked fruit and vegetables.

⬙ ACCOMMODATIONS ⬙

HELNAN SHEPHEARD HOTEL
Corniche El Nil St., Garden City. Tel: (02) 355-3800. TYPE: *Hotel.* CLIENTELE: All Welcome. LOCATION: Residential area off Tahrir Street. 290 rooms w/priv. bath, 30 suites, CTV, phone, A/C, many with balcony, dining room, grill room, nightclub. Rates: from $160/day. DESCRIPTION: Famous hotel in a central location.

NILE HILTON
Tahrir Square, Cairo. Tel: (02) 767-444. Fax: (02) 760-874. TYPE: *Hotel.* CLIENTELE: Mostly Straight. LOCATION: On the East Bank of the Nile next to the Egyptian Museum. Rooms/Suites 433 w/priv. bath, CTV (movies), phone, A/C, wheelchair access, restaurants, bars, disco, casino, pool, Health Club, Tennis. Rates: (US) $140-$180. *TAC:* 10%. DESCRIPTION: Well established hotel in a central location. The hotel bars and sauna can be of interest to gay travelers.

RAMSES HILTON
1115 Corniche El Nil, Cairo. Tel: (02) 744-400. Fax: (02) 757-152. TYPE: *Hotel.* CLIENTELE: Mostly Straight. LOCATION: East bank of the Nile, in the heart of Cairo. Walk to Museum and shopping. Rooms/Suites 842 w/priv. bath, CTV (movies), phone, A/C, wheelchair accessibility, 24 hrs. room service, restaurants, bars, Casino, pool, poolside bar, Health Club. Rates: (US) $140-$180. DESCRIPTION: Striking tower hotel in a convenient location. Easy to take new friends to your room.

TABA

✈ Eilat Airport (Israel) (ETH)
1 mi. / 1.5 km north of Taba

LOCATION: South Sinai Peninsula just north of Eilat and the Israeli/Egyptian border.

DESCRIPTION: One of the Sinai's loveliest spot by the Red Sea close to Eilat. It has great beaches, scuba diving, colorful Bedouin population and laid back atmosphere. For entertainment check out the casino at the Taba Hilton. Crossing the borders to Eilat (Israel) and Jordan (Aqaba) is easy. Short visit visas can be issued at the border crossing.

⬙ ACCOMMODATIONS ⬙

● For additional information about area accommodations and entertainment see Eilat (Israel).

TABA HILTON
Taba Beach, South Sinai. Tel: (2) 763544. TYPE: *Resort Hotel.* LOCATION: Taba Beach north of Eilat. CLIENTELE: All Welcome. 326 rooms w/priv. bath, phone, CTV, minibar, A/C, balcony w/seaview, restaurants, bars, casino, pool, massage, room service. Rates: (US) $110-$160. *TAC:* 10%. DESCRIPTION: Dramatic high rise resort hotel. Popular with Israelis and foreign tourists.

ESTONIA

AREA: 17,413 sq. mi. (45,100 sq. km)
POPULATION: 1,600,000
CAPITAL: Tallinn
CURRENCY: Estonian Kroon (Ek)
OFFICIAL LANGUAGE: Estonian
MAJOR RELIGIONS: Roman Catholicism
Telephone: 37
Nat'l Holiday: Ind. Day, Feb. 24
Official Time: G.M.T. +2
Electricity: 220 volts, 50 cycles, A.C.
Exchange Rate: 1US$ = Ek 11.29
National Airline: Estonian Air

LAW REGARDING HOMOSEXUALITY: The new Estonian Criminal Code does not mention homosexual activity between consenting males. The age of consent has been lowered to 14 for women and 16 for men with no difference between heterosexual or homosexual activity.

TALLINN   ✆   (02)

✈ Ulemiste Airport (TLL) 2.5 mi. / 4 km

LOCATION: Western Estonia on the Baltic sea.

POPULATION: 450,000

CLIMATE: Cold and cloudy winters with freezing temperatures around 30°F (-2°c). Summers are unpredictable with temperatures ranging from 50°F-90°sF (10°-32°c).

DESCRIPTION: The capital of Estonia is ethnically and culturally close to the Finns. Explore the Old Town and visit Palace built by Peter the great for his wife. For possible gay crusing try **Manezhi St.** from the **Hotel Viru** to the right along Narva Maantee St.

Gay/Lesbian Visitor Information
EGL/Voimalus, Box 142, EE-0090 Tallinn 90
Tel: 437710 or 437693

Lesbian Visitor Information
Eesti Lesbiliit, Box 3245, EE-0090, Tallinn 90
Tel: 439-769

BARS 🍷 RESTAURANTS 🍴

● Bars/club (GMW): **Kastani**, disco, 7 Toompuiestee for disco location call EGL Hotline (472-129); **Tooro**, pub/bar, Suur-Karja 18.

● Restaurants (AW): **Café Kloostri Ait**, fashionable cellar café, new hangout in Old Town, 14 Vene (446-887); **Maharaja**, Indian, Raekoja plats 13; **Vana Toomas**, large cellar restaurant, Estonian dishes, Raekoja plats 8; **Viru**, all you can eat buffet, and a la carte menu, Viru väljak 4 (652093); **Toomkooli**, heart Estonian specialties, 13 Toomkooli (446-613).

λ SERVICES λ

● Erotica (GM): **Sexyland**, Gonsiori 3 (open 11-17); **Sexbox**, Kaupmehe 2 entry through Peterburigatan 71 (open 11-19).

● Health Clubs (G/S): **Sauna**, Raua 23; **Sauna**, Lennukigatan.

● Leather Club (GM): **Tallinn's Tom's Club**, Box 5705, EE-003 Tallinn 3.

ACCOMMODATIONS

HOTEL PALACE
Vabaduse Sq. 3, Tallinn. Tel: (2) 444-761. TYPE: *Hotel.* CLIENTELE: Mostly Straight. LOCATION: Historic Old Town. 91 rooms, CTV/VCR, phone, minibar, restaurant, pizzeria, nightclub, sauna, casino, tennis court, parking, 5 km / 3 mi. to airport, 1 km / 800 yards to train station, open year round. Rates: (US) $95-$305. *TAC:* 10%. DESCRIPTION: The best hotel in Tallinn, renovated to 4-star int'l standards by Scandinavian companies.

VIRU HOTEL
4 Viru Sq., Tallinn EE 2400. Tel: (2) 650-300. TYPE: *Hotel.* CLIENTELE: Mostly Straight. LOCATION: 1.5 km from city center, 6 km / 4 mi. to Airport. 458 rooms, 13 suites, CTV, phone, C/H, A/C, restaurant, bar, sauna, open year round. Rates: (US)$ 60-$130. *TAC:* 10%. DESCRIPTION: Moderate first class 22 story hotel with comfortable pine-paneled rooms.

AREA: 7.055 sq. mi. (18,272 sq. km)
POPULATION: 727,000
CAPITAL: Suva
CURRENCY: Fijian Dollar (F$)
OFFICIAL LANGUAGE: Fijian, Hindi,
English
MAJOR RELIGION: Protestantism,
Hinduism
Telephone: 679
Official Time: GMT + 12
Nat'l Holiday: Fiji Day October 10
Electricity: 240 v 50c AC
Exchange Rate: F$1.42 = US$
National Airlines: Air Pacific, Fiji Air

LAW REGARDING HOMOSEXUALITY:
Homosexuality is illegal according to para-
graph 168-170 of the Fiji Penal Code. The maximum penalty for gay sex is up to 14 years in
prison. In reality however, the obsolete law is
on the book only and is not enforced. Fiji is a
popular tourist destination especially for travelers from and to Australia and New Zealand.
Fijians are friendly and have a deep respect for
everyone regardless of sexual orientation.

SUVA   © 42

✈ Nausori AP (SUV) 14.5 mi. / 23 km north
    Nadi Int'l AP (NAN)

LOCATION: Eastern coast of Viti Levu Island

POPULATION: 85,000

CLIMATE: Warm, humid and tropical climate. Average high temperatures vary between
83˚F and 88˚F (28˚c-31˚c) during the summer
months (Dec-March). During the winter temperatures are in a comfortable 70˚F (21˚c).
Most of the rainfall is during the summer. Fiji

is in the heart of the South Pacific cyclone belt
with hurricane season between Nov. and April.

DESCRIPTION: Fiji's capital is one of the
most cosmopolitan cities of the South Pacific. It
represents a mix of cultures and traditions part
Hindu and part Old Colonial British. The population is a melting pot of Indians, Fijians,
Asian and Europeans. Fiji offers excellent duty
free shopping, scuba diving, fine beaches, and
great nightlife.

HOW TO GET THERE: Most international
flights arrive and depart from Nadi Int'l
Airport, about 7 mi. / 11 km north of Nadi Town
on the western coast of Viti Levu.

❖ SPECIAL EVENTS: **Hibiscus Festival** -
traditional dance shows, first week of August
in Suva; **Bula Festival** - dance show festival
in Nadi in the middle of July.

BARS ▼ RESTAURANTS ▮▮

● Bars/Clubs (G/S): **The Dragon**, Victoria
Parade; **Lucky Eddie's**, dance club, 217
Victoria Parade; **O'Reilly's**, 5 McArthur St.
(312-884); **Sugar Shack**, 54 Camavon St. (305-
707); **Traps**, 305 Victoria Parade (312-922).

● Restaurant (AW): **Swiss Tavern**, 16
Kimberley St. (303-233); **Hare Krishna**, popu-
lar Indian/vegetarian, 16 Pratt St. (314-154);
Ming Palace, Chinese, Victoria Parade, Old
Town Hall (315-111).

ACCOMMODATIONS

MAN FRIDAY RESORT
Queens Rd., Naboutini, Korolevu. USA/Canada
reservations: (800) 257-5344 or (516) 944-5330.
Fax: (516) 944-7540. AUSTRALIA - Jornada
800-672-120 or (02) 362-0900. TYPE: *Resort
Complex.* CLIENTELE: Gay men. LOCATION:
Tropical beachfront in Fiji's coral coast near
the village of Namaqumaqua.

* Bungalows: 28 (self contained)
* Restaurant, bar, pool
* Free parking, water sports
* Airport: 90 km / 56 mi. (Nadi Int'l AP)
    about 2 hrs. by bus
* Open: Year round
* Rates: from $190 *TAC:* 10%

DESCRIPTION: The only openly gay resort
complex in the South Pacific on 13 acres of lush
tropical grounds. Enjoy a deep in the salt water
pool naturally heated to 80˚F (27˚c) or exotic
cocktails and fruit at the restaurant and bar.

FINLAND

AREA: 130,128 sq. mi. (337,032 sq. km)
POPULATION: 4,800,000
CAPITAL: Helsinki
CURRENCY: Markka (FM)
OFFICIAL LANGUAGE: Finnish, Swedish
MAJOR RELIGIONS: Protestantism
Telephone: 358
Nat'l Holiday: Independence Day, Dec. 6
Official Time: G.M.T. + 2
Electricity: 220 volts
Exchange Rate: 1US$ = FM 4.54
National Airline: Finnair

LAW REGARDING HOMOSEXUALITY: Homosexuality is legal between consenting adults 18 years old and over. But the law forbids public encouragement of homosexuality. The general attitude of the Finnish in the large cities can be described as tolerant. In smaller communities outside the major cities it is best to be discreet. Finland has banned discrimination based on sexual orientation nationwide. The new law makes unfair treatment of gays criminal offense.

HELSINKI   ✆ 90

✈ Helsinki-Vantaa Int'l Airport (HEL)

LOCATION: On a little peninsula in southern Finland on the Gulf of Finland.

POPULATION: 500,000

CLIMATE: Cold and cloudy winters with temperatures around 30°F (-2°c). Summers are unpredictable and can vary from 50°F (10°c) to the 90°'sF (32°c).

Gay/Lesbian Visitor Information
SETA Tel: (90) 135-8302
Fax: (90) 135-8306

DESCRIPTION: Helsinki, known as the "White City of the North" for the light-colored granite material used for its buildings, is an historic city surrounded by water on three sides. Helsinki is closer culturally to the Baltic States than it is to Scandinavia. Helsinki's harbor is the largest in Finland and handles most of the nation's international commerce. The city is uncrowded with public parks and historic 16th century monuments such as the famous **Senate Square**.

❖ Beaches: Although there are no gay beaches in Helsinki the following places are frequented by gays: **Swimming Stadium**, and the **Seurasaari nudist beach**, and to some extent also the island **Pihljasaari**. For day cruising try **Seurasaari Island** (Park Foiison) a recreational park with beaches.

BARS ♉ RESTAURANTS

● Bars/Clubs (GM): **Botta**, dance club, Museokatu 10 (44 69 40); **Blue Boy**, Eerinkatu 14; **New Faces**, Lord Hotel, Lönnrotsg. 29.

● Bars/Clubs (GW): **Ladies' Night** at Taiteilijoiden klubi, disco for women every other Sat., Ainonkatu 3, open 21-02, (135-8302); **Naisten Huone** (Women's Room), cafe and feminist library, mon-sat, 11 Bullevardi; **New Faces**, dance club (men welcome), Sat. only, Lönnrotinkatu 29.

● Bars/Clubs (GMW): **Club Triangle**, disco with gay-karaoke upstairs, Mon. gay nights at Botta, Museokatu 10, open 22-04; **H2O**, pub with gay summer terrace, Eerinkatu 14, Mon-Sun open 16-02; **Don't Tell Mama**, disco, Annankatu 32, Tue-Sun open 22-03, Mon. closed (694-4043); **Nalle Pub**, Kaarlenkatu 3-5 (701-5543); **Olotila**, Pursimiehenkatu 18 (701-5543); **Stonewall**, dance bar, Eerikinatu 3 9694-4043).

● Restaurants (GMW): **Botta's**, 10 Museokatu; **Senaatin Kellari**, Finnish cuisine, Aleksanterinkatu 22, Senate Square (656-722); **Stockman Dept. Store**, mixed bar/restaurant in the leading Helsinki Dept. Store, open Mon-Sat till 01, sun. closed, Mannerheimintie.

λ SERVICES λ

● Bookstore (GMW): **Baffin Books**, the only gay/lesbian bookstore in Finland, mon-fri 11-20, Sat 11-18, Eerikinkatu 33 (694-7078).

● Health Clubs (GMW): **Töölön uimahalli**,

Topeliuksenkatu 41A (417-761); **Yrjönkadun uimahalli**, mixed sauna and swimming pool, Yrjönkatu 21 (609-81).

● Sex Shops (G/S): **Harness Sin-City**, Kalevankatu28 (700-29204); **Mister Mose'sBoy Shop**, Iso Robertinkatu 38; **Sex 10**, Eerikkinkatu 10 (602-368).

 ACCOMMODATIONS

HOTEL ARTHUR

Vuorikatu 17B, Helsinki 00100. Tel: (0) 173-441. Fax: (0) 626-880. USA/Canada reservations: Odysseus Tel: (516) 944-5330 or (800) 257-5344. Fax: (516) 944-7540, or (800) 982-6571. TYPE: *Hotel*. CLIENTELE: All Welcome. LOCATION: Commercial center of the city. 145 rooms most w/priv. bath/shower, CTV, phone, room service, restaurant, sauna. Rates: (US) $90-$190. **TAC:** 10% (from Odysseus). DESCRIPTION: Modern tourist class hotel in a central location. Quiet and attractively priced for budget travelers.

TAMPERE   ℂ   931

✈ Tampere-Pirkkala Airport (TMP)
9.5 mi. / 15 km SW of Tampere

LOCATION: On the banks of the Tammer River rapids in the Finnish Lakelands.

POPULATION: 400,000

Gay/Lesbian Visitor Information
SETA: 214-8721

DESCRIPTION: The country's second largest city, Tampere boasts more than 180 lakes inside the city limits. Mostly an industrial city, it offers fine theatre and cultural activities. Here you can see the best of Finland's 20 century art collection at the famous **Sara Hildén Museum**, Särkänniemi (231-333).

Ⴠ BARS Ⴠ

● Bars/clubs (GMW): **Amarillo**, dance bar, Hatanpään voltatie 1; **Grandy**, dance club, Satakunnankatu 13; **Mixei**, Otavalan-katu 3, open daily till 02.

ACCOMMODATIONS

TAMPERE HOTEL

Hameenkatu 1, Tampere 33100. Tel: (31) 244-6111. Fax: (31) 221-910. TYPE: *Hotel*. CLIENTELE: Mostly Straight. LOCATION: Downtown near train station. 250 rooms w/bath or shower, few with mini-bars, 2 w/priv. sauna. indoor pool, gym, saunas. Rates: FM 350-600. **TAC:** 10%.

TURKU   ℂ   921

✈ Turku Airport (TKU)

LOCATION: In the Finnish Lakeland, 95 mi. / 152 km west of Helsinki. Easily reached by bus, train or flights.

POPULATION: 225,000

Gay/Lesbian Visitor Information
SETA: 231-0335

DESCRIPTION: The oldest city in Finland and the country's capital until Czar Alexander I moved the seat of government to Helsinki in 1812. Visit the famous **Turku Castle** and Cathedral and fine museums.

❖ Gay Beach: **Ruissalo Saaronniemi**, nude beach on the island of Ruissalo. Walk beyond the camping area.

Ⴠ BARS Ⴠ

● Bars/clubs (GMW): **Jacks & Mikes**, Kauppiaskatu 4; **Time Out**, dance bar, Puutarhakatu 8; **Why Not**, Linnankatu 19.

 ACCOMMODATIONS

RUISSALO SPA HOTEL

Ruissalo Island, Turku SF-201000. Tel: (21) 605-511. Fax: (21) 605-590. TYPE: *Hotel*. CLIENTELE: Mostly Straight. LOCATION: On the island of Ruissalo, nude beach nearby. 130 rooms w/priv. bath, restaurant, bar, fitness room, tennis. Rates: (FM) 580 - 680. DESCRIPTION: Modern hotel in a park-like setting. Convenient to explore the gay action in the nearby nude beach.

FRANCE

AREA: 210,038 sq. mi. (543,998 sq. km)
POPULATION: 53,788,000
CAPITAL: Paris
CURRENCY: French Franc (FF)
OFFICIAL LANGUAGE: French
MAJOR RELIGIONS: Roman Catholicism
Telephone: 33
Nat'l Holiday: Bastille Day, July 14
Official Time: G.M.T. + 1
Electricity: 220 volts
Exchange Rate: 1US$ = FF 4.85
National Airline: Air France

LAW REGARDING HOMOSEXUALITY: Homosexuality is accepted in France. The legal minimum age of consent is 15, but it is not advisable to get sexually involved with under 18 because of possible legal complications. Gay men and lesbians are protected against discrimination on the job. The law also protects HIV+ and PWA against discrimination by employers.

BIARRITZ   ℭ 5

✈ Parme Airport (BIQ)

LOCATION: In the Atlantic Southwest coast of France, near the Spanish border.

POPULATION: 27,500

CLIMATE: Warm sunny summers and cool rainy winters. Winter average temperatures in the 50°sF (10°c) and summer average temperatures in the 80°sF (27°c).

DESCRIPTION: Biarritz is a picturesque fishing village and a fashionable seaside resort in the southwest of France, with lovely beaches and the famous Rock of the Virgin. Nearby is

its sister town **Bayonne** which is practically a continuation of Biarritz with a slightly different flavor. Bayonne is clean, sunny and very Basque. **Capebreton** is a seaside resort some 25 km / 15 mi. north of Biarritz on the Atlantic shore. **St. Martin de Seignaux** is a small village 15 km / 9 mi. north east of Bayonne on R.N. 117.

● Gay beach: **Plage de Miramar**, at the foot of the lighthouse.

BARS Ⓨ RESTAURANTS 🍴

● Bars/clubs (GM): Biarritz - **Bakara**, Place Sainte-Eugénie (5924-0534); **City's Bar**, 31 Av. Verdun (5924-2785); **Le Caveau**, bar/disco, 4, rue Gambetta (5924-1617). Bayonne - **Le James Dean**, 11, rue Vieille-Boucherie, Place Montaut (5959-1964).

● Restaurants (AW): Biarritz - **La Lieutenance**, terrace garden setting, 31, Av. de Verdun (5924-2785). Bayonne - **Restaurant de la Tour**, traditional cuisine, 5 rue de Faures (5959-0567). Capbreon - **Le Cap B**, regional, 1 Av. Georges Pompidou (5872-0800). St. Martin de Seignaux - **La Calèche**, regional cuisine and grill, R.N. 117, Route de Pau, 40390 St. Martin de Seignaux (5956-7362).

ACCOMMODATIONS

LE ST. JAMES
15 rue Gambetta, 64200 Biarritz. Tel: 5924-0636. TYPE: *Hotel*. HOST: Mme. B. Barros. CLIENTELE: Gay/Straight. LOCATION: Centrally located near beaches. 14 rooms. DESCRIPTION: Budget gay friendly hotel.

BORDEAUX   ℭ 5

✈ Merignac Airport (BOD)

LOCATION: Southwest of France, on the banks of the Garonne River just before it joins the Atlantic Ocean.

POPULATION: 220,830

DESCRIPTION: Bordeaux is the former capital of the Dukes of Aquitaine. It is a major port and a commercial center for the famous Bordeaux wines. It is rich with historic monuments: **Quinconces Esplanade**, near and around the Stock Exchange, is a group of 18th century buildings. The most beautiful church in Bordeaux is the **St. André Cathedral** with its embellished bell tower. The local **Fine Arts Museum**, displays a rich collection of 18th and 19th century French paintings.

BARS ⅄ RESTAURANTS 🍴

● Bars/clubs (GM): **Le 18**, dance club, 18 rue Louis de Foix (5652-8298); **Moyen Age**, 8 rue des Ramparts (5644-1287); **TH**, 15 rue Montbazon (5681-3816); **Yellow Moon**, dance club, 6 rue Combes (5651-0079).

● Restaurants : **Le Jardin**, 15 rue Montbazon (5681-3816); **Les Bains Bouffes**, plat du jour, 5 rue Guienne (5652-2662).

⅄ SERVICES ⅄

● Health Clubs (GM): **Sauna Club 137**, sauna, hammam, videos, 137 Quai des Chartrons (5643-1849); **Sauna Ferrière**, hammam, sauna, TV lounge, 18 rue Ferrère (5644-5301).

● Sex Shops: **La Boîte à Films**, 26 rue Rolland (5644-8221); **Love Video**, 221 Cours de la Marne (5691-6855).

🏳 ACCOMMODATIONS 🏳

BURDIGALA HOTEL
115 rue Georges-Bonnac, 33000 Bordeaux. Tel: 5690-1616. TYPE: *Hotel*. CLIENTELE: Mostly Straight. LOCATION: In the heart of the city near the gay scene and other places of interest. 71 rooms.

CANNES   © 4

✈ Côte d'Azure Airport, Nice (NCE)

LOCATION: In the Southeast of France, along the Mediterranean shore

POPULATION: 70,226.

CLIMATE: Mediterranean climate. Hot summers with temperatures in the mid 80"sF (30°c). Cool, windy and wet winters with temperatures in the mid 50°sF (10°c).

DESCRIPTION: Cannes is an elegant French Riviera seaside resort with a magnificent set-

ting overlooking the bay and the flower filled gardens along the Boulevard de la Croisette. The **Old Town** sits on the hill of Suquet overlooking the harbor. Cannes has many beautiful historic churches such as the **Church of Notre Dame d'Espérance**. The **Castre Museum** has a fine collection of Mediterranean archaeology and ancient civilization.

❖ **SPECIAL EVENTS**: Cannes is famous for its international festivals, and the annual carnival. **The International Film Festival** at the Palais des Festivals takes place each year in June, when this chic resort is at its most frenzied. The **MIDEM**, International Music and Record Industry Festival is in January.

❖ Beaches: If you are looking for sun and 'hot' fun, there is a beach you would probably like to explore. This cruisy nude beach is **La Plage de La Batterie**. Take the exit going to Nice on RN 7. Leave the town and watch on your left for the Shell Gas Station near a small parking. Cross the road and take a subway passage. This is a rocky nude beach, but very cruisy; **Ile Sainte-Marguerite**, clothing optional is allowed on the east side facing the Ile Saint-Honorat.

❖ Entertainment: Cannes has three classy casinos - **Casino Croisette** at the Palais de Festivals; **Casino du Palm Beach** (Summer Casino) and the **Carlton Casino** (on the first floor of the Carlton Inter-Continental, 58 Blvd. de la Croisette). All the casinos offer international games, Dinner & Cabaret.

BARS ⅄ RESTAURANTS 🍴

● Bars/clubs (GM): **Bar Basque**, 14, rue Macé (9339-3561); **Extérieur Nuit**, bar, cafe & restaurant, 16 rue du Suquet (9399-2736); **Le Zanzi-Bar**, open 22:00 - 06:00, 85 rue Felix Faure (9339-3075); **Disco 7**, disco, live entertainment nightly, 7 rue Rouguière (9339-1036); **Trois Cloches**, the hottest club/disco in Cannes, 6 rue du Commandant Vidal (9368-3292).

● Restaurants (AW): **Bistrot de la Galerie**, 4 rue Saint-Antoine (9339-9938); **Dauphin**, 1 rue Bivonac Napoléon (9339-2273); **Marais**, 9 rue du Suquet (9338-3919); **Mirabelle**, 24 rue Saint Antoine (9338-7275). Others (AW): **La Croisette**, Italian and local cuisine, 15 rue du Commandant André (9339-8606); **Le Canibal**, Pizzas and flame broiled Seafood/Steaks, 10 rue des Frères Pradignac (9339-2665); **Extérieur Nuit**, bar, cafe & restaurant, 16 rue du Suquet (9399-2736);

🏳 ACCOMMODATIONS 🏳

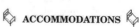

✪ HOTEL DE PARIS

34 Blvd. d'Alsace, 06400 Cannes. Tel: 9338-3069. USA/Canada reservation Tel: (516) 944-5330 or (800) 257-5344. Fax: (516) 944-7540 or (800) 982-6571. TYPE: *Hotel.* CLIENTELE: All Welcome. LOCATION: Center of Cannes near the famous Croisette beach.

* Rooms: 45 w/priv. bath. Suites: 3
* CTV, phone, A/C, soundproof
* Bar, jacuzzi, Hammam, pool
* Gay Bars: walking distance
* Beach: 300 m / yards
* Airport: 30 km / 19 mi., taxi
* Train Station: 500 m / yards
* Open: Year round
* Rates: (US)$120-$290
* *TAC:* 10% (from Odysseus)

DESCRIPTION: Beautiful 3-star hotel in a charming garden setting. Tastefully appointed spacious rooms with all contemporary comfort. Highly recommended for a relaxing holiday.

CHAMONIX   ✆ 4

✈ Cointrin AP Geneva (GVA)
   50 mi. / 80 km northwest of Chamonix

LOCATION: Heart of the French Alps at the foot of the Mont-Blanc, easily accessible from Paris (596 km / 372 mi.), Annecy (95 km / 60 mi.) and Geneva, Switzerland (83 km / 52 mi.).

POPULATION: 9,500

CLIMATE: Continental and mountainous. Cold snowy winters, and mild pleasant summers.

DESCRIPTION: Famous ski-resort at the foot of the majestic Mont-Blanc, the highest mountain in Europe. The snowscapes amid the spires and glaciers of the whole range is spectacular. The lively nightlife, fine French cuisine and the busy gambling casino makes this trendy resort a delight even for non-skiers.

❖ Gay cruising, there is some action in a small forest, known for clothing optional sunbathing **Hameau le Bois** 3.5 km / 2 mi. from Chamonix on Lake Arve, behind the Himalayen bridge.

BAR ♈ RESTAURANT 🍴

● Bar (GMW): at the bar of the **International Hotel**, see description below.

Hôtel de Paris

Cannes
Côte d'Azur
USA/CANADA Reservations
call Odysseus
(800) 257-5344

● Restaurant: **Pizzeria le Napoli**, 233 rue Michel-Croz (5053-2040).

◊ ACCOMMODATIONS ◊

INTERNATIONAL HOTEL
255 Ave Michel-Croz, 74400 Chamonix. Tel: 5053-0060. USA/Canada reservations Tel: (516) 944-5330 or (800) 257-5344. Fax: (516) 944-7540 or (800) 982-6571. TYPE: *Hotel.* CLIENTELE: All Welcome. LOCATION: Center of Chamonix, near all shops, transportation to ski lifts.

* Rooms: 30 w/priv. bath
* CTV, phone, C/H, safety box
* Sauna, jacuzzi, solarium, Health Spa
* Parking, elevator, pets accepted
* Bar, & restaurant: facing the hotel
* Airport: 50 mi. / 80 km (Geneva)
* Season: Closed May 15-June 1
  & Nov. 15 - Dec. 5
* Rates: (US) $110-$240 w/CbB
* *TAC:* 10% (from Odysseus)

DESCRIPTION: Charming 3-star hotel in the center of Chamonix. Tastefully furnished guest rooms and renovated public areas. Car rental, ski passes and sightseeing can be arranged.

LILLE   © 3

✈ Lesquin Int'l Airport (LIL)
5 mi. / 8 km south

LOCATION: Northern France near the Belgian border.

POPULATION: 180,000

Gay & Lesbian Visitor Information
C.R.S.H: 2040-1149

DESCRIPTION: The capital of the North, Lille is an industrial town with traditional heavy plants and a university center. The region is a mix of french & Flemish cultures. Lille offers a nicely established gay nightlife scene.

BARS Υ RESTAURANTS ¶¶

● Bars/clubs (GM): **Loft**, 80 bis rue Bathélémy Delespaul (2042-0586); **Ramponneau**, gay pub, 22 Square du Ramponneau (2074-4990); **Roccambole**, cocktail bar, 11 Place Jacques Louchard (2013-8164).

● Bars/clubs (GMW): **Alles du Désir**, cocktail bar, 57 rue Basse (2055-1133); **Bon Coin**, pub, 36-38 place de la Gare (2021-0001); **Grim Bar**, 165bis rue Solferinbo (2015-8779); **Zenith**, dance club, 74 avenue de Flandre (2089-9229)

● Restaurants (GMW):**Albert II**, 38 rue de Puebla (2057-9151); **Anatole**, 6 rue Anatole France (2055-8751); **Claire de Lune**, 50 rue de Gand (2051-4655).

λ SERVICES λ

● Sex-Shops (G/S): **Cinésex Shop**, 41 rue des Ponts-de-Comines (2006-2583); **Sex Shop Golden Boy**, 4 rue de la Quenette (2006-3026).

📷 ACCOMMODATIONS 📷

MERCURE CENTRE
2 blvd. Carnot, Lille 59800. Tel: (3) 2051-0511. TYPE: *Hotel.* CLIENTELE: All Welcome. LOCATION: Central near the Stock Exchange and the Opera, 300 m / yards from train station. 102 rooms w/priv. bath, CTV, phone, elevator, wheelchair access, grill room & bar. Rates: FF 420 - FF 680.

LYON   © 4

✈ Satolas Airport (LYS)

LOCATION: In southeastern France, at the confluence of two rivers the Saône and the Rhône.

POPULATION: 454,260

CLIMATE: Continental climate. Cold, snowy winters, and rather mild and pleasant summers.

Gay/Lesbian Visitor Information
ARIS: 7827-1010

DESCRIPTION: Once the ancient capital of the Gaul, Lyon is a modern city, the third largest in France. It is a major industrial and silk center. For first time visitors the city projects a cold and grey image. Lyon is a great gastronomic center. You will love the restaurants with their rich variety of local dishes. Enjoy *Fondue Savoyarde*, a blend of local cheeses and *eau de vie* on a cold winter day.

For the gay visitor, Lyon has a good selection of gay bars, discos and restaurants, enough to make your stay enjoyable. Most of the bars are located either near the **Place des Terreaux** (1st) or **Place Bellecour** (2nd).

BARS Υ RESTAURANTS ¶¶

● Bars/clubs (GM): **Bar du Centre**, video bar, 3 rue Simon-Maupin (2nd) (7837-4018); **Boys to Men**, dance club, 38 rue de l'Arbre Sec; **Broad'way**, 9 rue Terraille (1st) (7839-5054); **Quatre**, 4 rue Bellecordière (7837-8966); **Stairway Club**, 2 rue Fernand Rey (7200-2000); **Troubles**, leather cruise bar, 86 Grande Rue de la roix Rousse, M° Croix Rousse (7829-2009); **Verre à Soi**, bar & restaurant, 25 rue des Capucines (7828-9244).

● Club (GMW): **Taverne II**, 12 rue René-Leynaud (7828-2428); **Village Club**, dance club, 6 rue Violi (7207-7262).

● Restaurants (GMW): **Bâteau à Vapeur**, home style, cocktails, 23 rue Royale (1st) (7828-6508); **Brasserie Burdeau,** cuisine Lyonnaise, 5 rue Burdeau (1st) (7828-6603); **Boudinière de Lyon**, specialités Lyonnaise, also bar, 14 rue René-Leynaud (1st) (7828-7151); **La Tirelire**, Lyon style, 14 rue de la Monnaie (2nd) (7837-3742); **Le Verre à Soi**, 25 rue des Capucines (7828-9244).

λ SERVICES λ

● Health Clubs (GM): **Bellecour**, 4 rue Simon Maupin (2nd) (7838-1927); **Mandala**, large elegant Health Club with sauna, swimming pool, gym, bar and TV lounge, 9 rue Boissac (7842-7428) (2nd); **Oasis Club**, 10 quai Jean-Moulin (1st) (7839-0382).

● Sex-Shop: **Oncle Charlie**, gay videos, 2 cinemas, 7 rue Puits Gaillot (1st) (7829-2887).

ACCOMMODATIONS

BEST WESTERN CARLTON
4 rue de Jussieu, 69002 Lyon. Tel: 7842-5651. Fax: 7842-1071. TYPE: *Hotel*. CLIENTELE: Mostly Straight. LOCATION: Near Place Bellecour, Celestins and Terreaux, and the local gay scene. 90 rooms w/priv. bath, balcony, bar, phone, CTV. Rates: (FF) 520-690. DESCRIPTION: 3-star hotel in a convenient location.

MARSEILLE ℭ 4

 Marignane Int'l Airport (MRS)

LOCATION: In the south of France along the Mediterranean coast.

POPULATION: 901,400

CLIMATE: Mediterranean climate. Hot summers. Cool, windy and wet winters.

Gay/Lesbian Visitor Information
S.O.S. Amitié: 9176-1010

DESCRIPTION: Marseille is the second largest city in France. This famous port town was founded over 25 centuries ago by Greek settlers of Massilia. Marseille is the hometown of the national anthem "La Marseillese" which was composed during the French Revolution. Visit the **Old Harbor**, and stroll along the principal street La Canebière to explore busy Mediterranean style sidewalk cafes, restaurants, and shops. From the harbor you can take a boat to the **Château d'If**, made famous by Alexander Dumas popular Novel " The Count of Monte-Cristo".

❖ Gay Beach: sunbath au naturel at Le Mont Rose, an all nude gay cruise beach. Take bus #19 till the last stop, then follow the boardwalk along the sea.

BARS Y RESTAURANTS ¶¶

● Bars/clubs (GM): **Eden**, the oldest gay bar in Marseille, 7 rue Curiol (9147-3006); **Mare aux Diables**, dance club, in Traverse-Bon-Encontre, Allauche near Marseille; **MP Video**, 10 rue Beauvan (9133-6479); **New Cancan**, dance club, 3-5 rue Sénac (9148-5976).

● Restaurants (AW): **La Dent Creuse**, mixed clientele, 14 rue Sénac (9142-0567); **Chez Alex**, Italian cuisine, 43 rue Curiol (9147-8012); **La Bessonière**, traditional, Nouvelle Cuisine, 40 rue Sénac (9194-0843).

λ SERVICES λ

● Health Clubs (GM): **Palmarium**, hammam, sauna, videos, 20 rue Sénac (9147-4393); **MP Sauna**, 82 La Canbière (9148-7251); **Sauna Club**, turkish hammam, sauna, videos, 117 La Canebière (9164-1908).

● Sex-Shops (G/S): **Sexashop**, two locations, 73, La Canbière (9190-7244) and 6 rue Corneille (9133-7191).

ACCOMMODATIONS

HOTEL DU PETIT LOUVRE
19 Canebière, Marseilles 13001. Tel: 9190-1378. USA/Canada reservations Tel: (516) 944-5330. Fax: (516) 944-7540. TYPE: *Hotel*. CLIENTELE: Gay/Straight. LOCATION: Near Old Port and Beaches. 31 rooms w/priv. bath, CTV, phone, A/C, restaurant, bar. DESCRIPTION: Convenient, pleasant 3-star hotel. Half board available.

MONTPELLIER ℭ 4

 Frejorgues Airport (MPL)

LOCATION: In the south of France, some 168 km / 105 mi. west of Marseille.

POPULATION: 210,000

CLIMATE: Balmy Mediterranean climate. Hot summers with temperatures in the high 80°sF (28c); and mild winters with temperatures in the 60°sF (15°c).

DESCRIPTION: Well known University town in the south of France and a major linguistic center where many foreign students learn or

Hôtel Ulysse

**NN

30 rooms
TV, mini-bar, phone
private garage
convenient central location

Reservations: Mr. Leuenberger
338, Av. St. Maur, 34000 Montpellier
Tel: 33-4-6702-0230
Fax: 33-4-6702-1650

brush up their French. **La Grande Motte** is a new resort town some 20 km / 13 mi. southeast of Montpellier. It is famous for its futuristic style pyramid shaped holiday complexes, and fine sand beaches where partial nudism is accepted.

Visit: **Montpellier University**, founded in the 13th century; **Place de la Comédie**, colossal oval square with a fountain surrounded by cafés; **Grand-Rue Jean Moulin**, pedestrian only street; **Musée de Vieux Montpellier**, exhibits pertaining to the city's history; **Musée Fabre**, international collection of 17th and 19th century paintings, on bd. Sarrail by the Esplanade.

BARS Ⴐ RESTAURANTS ¶¶

● Bars/clubs (GM): **Bilitis**, dance club, Rte de Fréjourges (6722-2270); **Cafe de la Mer**, 5 place du Marché aux Fleurs (6760-7965); **Cupidon**, dance club, Rte Nationale 113 (6778-2733); **THT**, video bar, 29 ave. de Castelneau (6779-9617).

● Bar/club (GMW): **Rome Club**, Espace Commerciale du Fréjorgues Est (6722-2270).

● Restaurants (GMW): **La Bodega**, restaurant and bar, 27, rue du fg Saint-James (6741-0698);

Le Colombier, local cuisine, 11, bd de l'Observatoire (6766-0599); **Le Flore**, traditional menu, 2, rue Bonnier-d'Alco (6760-5506); **Les Goélands,** 8 rue de la Petite-Loge (6760-6034). in La Grande Motte - **Chez Fabrice**, brasserie de la Mer, seafood, Quai d'Honneur (6756-7593).

λ SERVICES λ

● Health Clubs (GM): **Hammam Club,** hammam, sauna, gym, videos, 2 rue de la Merci (6758-2206); **Sauna de la Gare**, Finnish sauna, hammam, videos, 8 rue Levat (6758-6142).

🔑 ACCOMMODATIONS 🔑

ALTEA POLYGONE
218 rue du Bastion Ventadour, Montpellier 34000. Tel: 6764-6566. TYPE: *Hotel*. CLIENTELE: Mostly Straight. LOCATION: In the heart of the Polygone quarter next to the Palais des Congress and the Place de la Comedie. 116 rooms w/priv. bath, CTV, phone, minibar. Rates: on request.

HOTEL AZUR
Esplanade de la Capitanerie, Presqu'il du Port, La Grande Motte 34280. Tel: 6756-5600. Fax: 6729-8126. USA/Canada reservations: (516) 944-5330. Fax: (516) 944-7540. TYPE: *Hotel*. HOST: Bernard. CLIENTELE: Gay/Straight. LOCATION: Top of a peninsula near the beach and town center. 20 rooms. DESCRIPTION: Modern 3-star resort hotel on a presqu'il.

HOTEL LE GUILHEM
18, rue Jean-Jacques Rousseau, 34000 Montpellier. Tel: 6752-9090. Fax: 6760-6767. TYPE: *Hotel*. HOST: Eric Charpentier or Catherine. CLIENTELE: Gay/Straight. LOCATION: In the historic center of Montpellier. 33 rooms w/priv. bath. Rates: on request. DESCRIPTION: 16th century building; quite rooms, large terrace with views of the cathedral or the faculty of Medicine.

✪ HOTEL ULYSSE
338 Av. de St. Maur, 34000 Montpellier. Tel: (4) 6702-0230. Fax: (4) 6702-1650. TYPE: *Hotel*. HOST: Bernard, Dir. CLIENTELE: Mostly gay men & women. LOCATION: Near City Center, Railway Station, and A9 motorway exit.

* Rooms: 30 w/priv. bath
  dbl 22 / triple 6 / quad 2
* Rooms for non smokers
* CTV, phone, refrigerator, safe box, hair dryer
* Bed Types: single, twin, double, oversized dbl
* Room service, Free parking

* Beach: 8 km / 5 mi. (gay/nude)
* Gay Bars: 0.8 km / 1/2 mi.
* Health Club: 2 km / 1.5 mi. (gay)
* Airport: Montpellier 3 km / 2 mi.
* Train Station: 50 m / yards
* Languages: French, English, German, Italian, Spanish
* Reservations: FF 200 deposit
* Cancellation Policy: 12 noon
* Credit Cards: MC/VISA/AMEX
* Season: Year round
* Rates: FF 275-325 / (off) FF 250-295 (breakfast not included)
* Taxes: FF 5.50 per person per day
* Check in 19:00 / check out 12 noon
* *TAC:* 10%

DESCRIPTION: 30 comfortable rooms with private facilities and modern amenities in an outstanding convenient location. Underground lockup garages. Hotel Ulysse offers warm welcome and pleasant stay adapted to your lifestyle.

NICE   Ⓛ 4

✈ Côte d'Azur Airport (NCE)
4 mi. / 7 km W.

LOCATION: Southern France, Côte d'Azure-French Riviera, on the beautiful Baie des Anges.

POPULATION: 400,000

CLIMATE: Mediterranean, pleasant year round. Summers can be hot with high humidity with temperatures in the high 80°'sF (30°c).

DESCRIPTION: Seaside resort along the mediterranean with a touch of old Italian architecture and style. The city is famous for its carnivals and festivals. The **Old Town** is where most of the popular restaurants and clubs are and is worth visiting; you can see many valuable paintings at the **Ste.-Reparate Cathedral**; **The Lascaris Palace** presents the remains of an old citadel; The **Flower Market** is very colorful; The **Vieux Port** is small but picturesque, and it offers some interesting seafood restaurants and a popular gay sauna with an easy to find location. Many boats sail from the port of Nice to the Island of Beauty - Corsica.

The fashionable area of Nice is located near the **Promenade des Anglais**. Here you can find the best beaches, restaurants, sidewalk cafés, pedestrian street, banks, and an American Express office. If you like to play in a European

L'ASCENSEUR

PUB • BILLARD • VIDEO
18 BIS, RUE EMMANUEL - PHILIBERT
06300 NICE (PORT)

TÉL 93 26 35 30

casino check the **Casino Ruhl** at the Meridien Hotel. (entry to the slot machines is free of charge and there is also a small bar).

A side trip to **Monaco** is a must. Take the bus from the Central Bus Station (Gare Routière - promenade du Pavillon) it will take you on a 30 min. scenic ride along the coast to the classy principality where you can spend hours at the gambling tables or slot machines. The last bus back from Monte Carlo leaves at about 7:30 PM. You may catch a taxi later sharing ride with few other people.

❖ **SPECIAL EVENT:** The world famous **Carnaval de Nice** takes place in mid-February each year. February 8-23 (97).

❖ Nude Beaches: to reach the cruisy gay nude beach - **Jeteé du Port**, follow a path along the sea going towards Cap de Nice. When you reach a restaurant called **Coco Beach**, go beyond and discover, when the weather is sunny, a wild nude beach with year round heavy cruising.

BARS ☿ RESTAURANTS 🍴

The gay scene in Nice is located near the port

and the Old City.

● Bars/clubs (GM): ✪ **L'Ascenseur**, American style video bar, pub, billiard, video, 18 bis rue Emmanuel Philibert, open 9:00 pm - 2:30 am, (closed Monday), free map of Gay Nice available at the bar (9326-3530) e-mail: ascenceu@pratique.fr.; **Bar Tabac Alberti**, day rendez-vous bar, mixed clientele, 4 rue Alberti (9385-4390); **Blue Boy**, most popular disco in Nice, 9 rue Spinetta (9344-6824); **Factory**, dance club, 26 Quai Lunel (9356-1226); **Morgan**, large place, good music, 3 rue Claudia (9386-8608); **QG**, 2 rue de la Tour (9362-4762); **Le Rusca**, outside terrace open from 9am near the port, 2 rue Rusca (9386-8608);

● Bars/clubs (GW): **Le Baby Doll**, 227, bd. de la Medelaine (9344-8658); **Le Tunnel**, rue de la Tour (9380-8026).

● Bars/clubs (GMW): **Tip Top**, nice bar w/terrace infront of a cruising place (lighthouse) open: 8am - 3am (9326-2288).

● Restaurants (GMW): **La Baron Ivre**, German cuisine, medium priced,6, rue Maraldi (9389-5213); **Le Petit Gourmand**, inexpensive, 3, rue de Suisse (9316-8095); **La Cave**, good cuisine, inexpensive, rue Francis Gallo (9362-4846); **L'Ambigu**, 4, rue du pontin (9385-8841);**Poco Loco**, mexican cuisine, 2 rue Dalpozzo (9388-8583). Others (AW): **Choux-Choux**, regional specialties, 6, rue Maraldi (9389-5213); **Pub 93**, home cooking, 10, bd Lech-Walesa in the port area (9326-9664). Other (AW) - try the restaurants in the Old Town: **Atmosphère**, seafood/local cuisine, 36 cours Saleya (9380-5250); **Au Chapon Fin**, Seafood and local cuisine, 1 rue du Moulin (9380-5692); **Chez les Pêcheurs**, Seafood, authentic bouillabaisse, 18 quai des Docks (Vieux Port) (9389-5661).

λ SERVICES λ

● Health Clubs (GM): **Azur Sauna**, 4 quai papacino (sur le port), good mix of gay/bi-sexual men (9356-2500); **Le Grand Bleu**, sauna, jacuzzi, hammam, video bar relax, UVA, 7, ave. D´sambrois (9380-8180); **Le 7**, most popular sauna in Nice, hammam, videos, 7, rue Foncet (9362-2502); **Sauna du Chateau**, massage, sauna, hammam, 17 rue des Ponchettes (9385-7391).

● Sex-Shop (G/S): **Sex Shop**, large selection of gay videos, some cruising downstairs, 7, rue Massena; **Sex Shop**, 23, rue Belgique.

✎ ACCOMMODATIONS ✎

✪ HOTEL GOUNOD
3 rue Gounod. USA/Canada reservations - Tel: (516) 944-5330 or (800) 257-5344. Fax: (516) 944-7540 or (800) 982-6571. TYPE: *Hotel*. CLIENTELE: All Welcome. LOCATION: Quiet location in the centre of Nice in the "Musician area", steps from the seaside.

* Rooms: 52 w/priv. bath. Suites: 5
* CTV (satellite), phone, A/C
* Use of facilities at the next door Hotel Splendid: restaurant, bar, pool, sauna
* Parking, room & maid service
* Gay Bars: walking distance
* Health Club: walking distance
* Airport: 7 km / 4 mi.
* Train Station: 1 km / 0.6 mi.
* Open: Year round.
* Rates: $120 - $200 w/CB
* *TAC:* 10% (from Odysseus)

DESCRIPTION: Tastefully decorated traditional hotel. All rooms and suites with private bath, balcony some w/hair dryers. Free use of the facilities at the next door 4-star Hotel Splendid.

HOTEL GOUNOD

HOTEL GOUNOD
3, RUE GOUNOD
NICE FRANCE

For a perfect vacation in the French Riviera

USA/CANADA
available from Odysseus
1-800-257-5344
Tel: (516) 944-5330 • Fax: (516) 944-7540

✪ MEYERBEER BEACH

15 rue Meyerbeer, Nice 06000. Tel: 9388-9565. USA/Canada Tel: (800) 257-5344 or (516) 944-5330. Fax: (800) 982-6571 or (516) 944-7540. TYPE: *Hotel*. CLIENTELE: Gay men & women. LOCATION: Near the Promenade des Anglais, casino, markets and shopping.

* Rooms: 16 w/shower/bath
* CTV, phone, kitchenette
* Maid service, Parking nearby
* Beach: 50 m / yards (mixed)
* Gay Bars: walking distance
* Airport: 15 min.
* Rates: ($) 75-$120 w/CB
* *TAC:* 10% (from Odysseus)

DESCRIPTION: Tourist class gay hotel in a central location. Clean and comfortable rooms. Friendly hotel staff will help you with the local gay scene.

PARIS   ⓒ 1

✈ Orly Airport, Orly (ORY)
Charles de Gaulle AP, Roissy (CDG)

LOCATION: Heart of northern France in the historic Ile De France along the banks of the River Sein.

POPULATION: City 2,400,000;
Greater Paris (Ile-de-France) 9,900,000

CLIMATE: Continental. Winter is cold with snowfall in January and February. Average January temperature is 37°F (3°c). Spring is mild and pleasant. Summer is warm and dry with average temperature in July of 64°F (16°c), but temperatures can sometimes reach the mid to high 80°sF (24°c-28°c).

Gay/Lesbian Visitor Information
Centre Gai et Lesbian: 4357-2147
3 rue Keller, Paris 75011

DESCRIPTION: Paris is the universal "City of Lights" and the "City of Love". Its beauty and spirit are inspiring and it is a pleasure to visit Paris again and again. This is the historical, political and cultural center of France with historic, elegant buildings, monuments and large avenues. It is world famous for fashion, design, perfumes, and excellent cuisine.

Paris is divided into two distinctive sections: The **Right Bank** (La Rive Droite) on the 'right bank' of the River Sein, it is commercial, cosmopolitan, and somehow busier than the quiet and subtle **Left Bank** (La Rive Gauche).

There are many special places in Paris. Some of the attractions include The **Eiffel Tower**, The **Arc De Triumph**, The Champs Elysées, The famous **Louvre Museum**, The futuristic shaped **Pompidou Center**, The **Latin Quarter** with its great international restaurants and lively university activities, the prestigious **Sorbonne University**; the charming **Luxembourg Garden**; the artists quarter of **Montmartre** with the splendid **Basilique de Sacre-Coeur** on the top; the decadent **Moulin Rouge** and the naughty sexshops of **Pigalle** and the **Rue Saint Denis**. Many delightful sights and people to discover on your next visit to this ageless city.

● Gay life in Paris is *trés chic*. There are unlimited opportunities for pleasure and entertainment for gay men and lesbians. The gay scene extends all over the metropolitan area, but its heart is in the restored historic district **Le Marais** and **Les Halles** (3rd & 4th districts) with the famous 'gay street' **rue Sainte-Croix-de-la-Bretonnerie**, and the colorful rue des Rosiers; and my favorite rue des Mauvais Garçons (translation: 'Bad Boys Street'). Check out the cute boys while enjoying Cafe crème at the **Beaubourg Café** facing the Pompidou Center on rue Brisemiche (4th).

Another area for entertainment, especially for the beautiful people in the fashion/modeling industry is the **St. Germain de Prés** / **Montparnasse**, (6th) with sidewalk cafes, and restaurants. Don't miss the legendary **Café Flore**, 172 Blvd. Saint Germain (6th) and **Les Deux Magots**, 6 Place St. Germain-de-Prés, both are popular summer cafes full of Parisian grace and intrigue. Sip your demi-tasse or mint-àe l'eau and watch the sexy Parisians go by!

❖ **SPECIAL EVENTS: Europride**, full week of celebrations with special events on Friday and **Gay Pride March** on Saturday, call Odysseus for special arrangements for Paris Europride celebrations at (516) 944-5330 or (800) 257-5344. Email: odyusa@odyusa.com, June 23-30 1997; **Fashion Show** (*Salon de Mode)* first week-end in October. Extremely difficult to book hotel rooms, therefore if you plan to be in Paris during these dates make your hotel reservation a few months ahead of time.

BARS ♉ RESTAURANTS 🍴

● Bars/clubs (GM): **Amnesia Café**, 42 rue

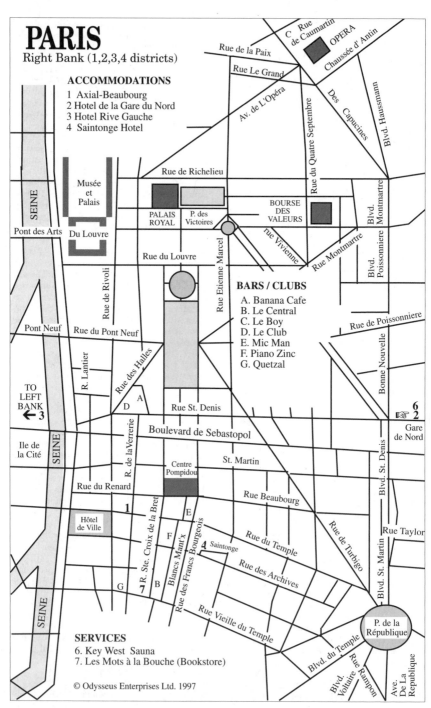

PARIS
Right Bank (1,2,3,4 districts)

ACCOMMODATIONS
1 Axial-Beaubourg
2 Hotel de la Gare du Nord
3 Hotel Rive Gauche
4 Saintonge Hotel

OPERA

Rue de Caumartin

Rue de la Paix

Chaussée d' Antin

Rue Le Grand

Av. de L'Opéra

Des   Capucines

Blvd. Haussmann

Rue du Quatre Septembre

Rue de Richelieu

Musée
et
Palais

PALAIS
ROYAL

P. des
Victoires

BOURSE
DES
VALEURS

Blvd. Montmartre

Blvd. Poissonniere

Du Louvre

SEINE

Pont des Arts

Rue de Rivoli

Rue du Louvre

Rue Etienne Marcel

rue Vivienne

Rue Montmartre

BARS / CLUBS
A. Banana Cafe
B. Le Central
C. Le Boy
D. Le Club
E. Mic Man
F. Piano Zinc
G. Quetzal

Rue de Poissonniere

Pont Neuf

Rue du Pont Neuf

R. Lantier

Rue des Halles

Bonne Nouvelle

TO
LEFT
BANK
← 3

D   A

Rue St. Denis

6
2

Ile de
la Cité

SEINE

R. de la Verrerie

Boulevard de Sebastopol

St. Martin

Blvd. St. Denis

Gare
de Nord

Centre
Pompidou

Rue du Renard

Rue Beaubourg

1

Hôtel
de Ville

E

R. Ste. Croix de la Bret

F

Blancs Mant'x

Rue des Francs Bourgeois

4 Saintonge

Rue du Temple

Rue de Turbigo

Rue Taylor

Blvd. St. Martin

Rue des Archives

G

7

B

SEINE

Rue Vieille du Temple

P. de la
République

SERVICES
6. Key West Sauna
7. Les Mots à la Bouche (Bookstore)

© Odysseus Enterprises Ltd. 1997

Blvd. du Temple

Blvd. Voltaire

Rue Rampon

Ave. De La Republique

Vieille du Temple (4th) (4272-1694); **L'Arène**, bar, lounges, videos, 80 quai de l'hôtel de Ville (4th) (4027-8304); **Banana Café**, bar on two levels, young and trendy, daily go-go boys, piano bar downstairs, 13, rue de la Ferronerie (1st) (4233-3531) M⁰ Châtlet; **Le Bar**, cruise bar, 5 rue de la Ferronerie (1st) (4041-0010) M⁰ Châtlet; **Bar Bi**, 23 rue Ste-Croix de la Bretonnerie (4278-2620); **Le Central**, 33 rue Vieille du Temple (4278-1142) M⁰ Châtlet / Hotel de Ville; **Club 18**, 18 rue de Beaujolais (1st) M° Palais Royal (4297-5213); **Docks**, video leather club, 150 rue St-Maur (11th) M°Gouncourt (4357-3382); **Duplex**, 25, rue Michel le Comte (3rd); **Feeling**, 43 rue Ste-Croix de la Bretonnerie (4th) (4804-7003); **Keller**, leather bar, 14, rue Keller (11th) (4700-0539); **Le London**, disco, 33 rue Lombards (M° Châtlet); **Mec Zone**, leather bar/videos, 27 rue Turgot (9th); **Mic Man**, video bar, 24, rue Geoffrey-l'Angevin (4274-3980) (4th) M⁰ Rambuteau; **One Way**, leather bar, 28 rue Charlot (3rd) (4887-4610); **Piano Zinc**, piano bar/cabaret, 49 rue des Blancs Manteaux, M⁰ Rambuteau (4274 3442); **Quetzal**, cruise bar, small restaurant for lunch, 10, rue de la Verrerie (4th) (4887-9907) M⁰ Châtlet / Hotel de Ville; **Subway**, happy hour daily, 35, rue Ste-Croix-de-la-Bretonnerie (4th) (4277-4110); **Thermilk**, theme based

evenings, friendly atmosphere, 7 rue de la Verrerie (7th) (4478-0818); **Transfert**, leather bar, e3 rue de la Sourdière (1st) (4260-4842); **Trap**, cruise bar, videos, 10 rue Jacob (6th); **Tropic Café**, cocktail bar, heated terrace, 66 rue des Lombards (1st) (4026-3245).

● Dance Clubs (GM): **Club 18**, popular disco, young clientele, show every Tuesday, 18, rue du Beaujolais (1st) (4297-5213); **Le Club**, known for its famous theme parties and colorful ambience, 14, rue St. Denis (1st) (4508-9625); **L'Insolite**, disco where slow and tango is still in fashion, 33 rue des Petits-Champs (1st) (4020-9859); **Palace**, gay T-Dance every Sunday afternoon 17:00, all other days open 23:00, 8, rue du Faubourg-Montmartre (9th) (4246-1087); **Privilège**, gay dance parties on weekends, 3 Cité Bergère (9th) (4770-7502); **Scaramouche**, one of the oldest gay discos in Paris, great late night shows, 44 rue Vivienne (2nd) (4233-2489).

● Bars/clubs (GW): **La Champmeslé**, 4 rue Chabanais (2nd) (4296-8520) M⁰ Pyramides; **Katmandou**, rue de Vieux Colombier 21, international crowd, one of the most elegant womyn's bar in the world (4548-1296); **Le Memory**, dance bar, 12, rue de Ponthieu (8th).

Axial Beaubourg

H Ô T E L ***

modern comfort
central 'gay village' location

Reservations
(800) 257-5344
Tel: (516) 944-5330 • Fax: (516) 944-7540

For more information about the lesbian scene contact **Canal Miel** (4379-6607).

● Restaurants: Paris has many excellent restaurants and it is impossible to cover them all. All restaurants in Paris and for this matter anywhere in France have a rigid schedule for lunch or dinner. In general lunch is served between 12:00 noon and 2:30 pm, and dinner is served between 6:30 pm and 10:30 pm. Do not try to show at a restaurant a minute early or late because they will ignore you.

● Restaurants (GMW): **L'Amazonial**, Sunday brunch, 3, rue Ste-Opportune (1st) (4233-5313); **Auberge de la Reine Blanche**, traditional cuisine, 30 rue Saint-Louis en l'Ile (4th) (4633-0787); **Au Diable des Lombards**, American, 64, rue des Lombards (1st) (4233-8184); **Le Café Chantant**, karaoke cafe, 12, rue du Plâtre (4th) (4887-5104); **Chez Max** (le Trou des Halles), regional, 47, rue Saint-Honoré (1st) (4508-8013); **La Cochonnaille**, good traditional cuisine, 21 rue de la Harpe (5th) (4051-7736); **Fond de Cour**, fine cuisine elegant setting, 3 rue Sainte-Croix-de-la Bretonnerie (4th) (4804-9112); **La Macrobiothèque**, macrobiotic, 17, rue de Savoie (6th) (4325-0496); **Le Marais Ste Catherine**, traditional cuisine, excellent food

and service, 5 rue Caron $th) (4272-3994); **Palmier en Zinc**, classic French, 16, rue des Lombards (4th) (4278-5353); **Petit Prince**, 12 rue Lanneau (5th) (4354-7726); **Vagabond**, 14, rue Thérèse (1st) (4296-2723); **Xica Da Silva**, authentic Brazilien, cocktails, 47, rue des Batignolles (17th) (4293-2298). Others (AW) **Altitude 95**, award winning French restaurant, first floor of the Eiffel Tower, Champs de Mars (4455-0021). For a special lunch or dinner arrangements USA/Canada call (800) 257-5344 or (516) 944-7540; **Jule Verne**, elegant expensive restaurant on the Eiffel Tower, 2nd floor (4555-6144). For a memorable lunch or dinner arrangements USA/ Canada call (800) 257-5344 or (516) 944-7540.

λ SERVICES λ

● Health Club (GM): **Euro Men's Club**, sauna, pool, videos, 10 rue Saint-Marc (2nd) (4233-9263); **IDM**, body building, sauna, suntan, 4 rue du Faubourg Montmartre (9th) daily from 12 noon to 1 am; **Key-West**, large elegant Sauna club with swimming pool, Finnish sauna, private cabins, Video lounge, Solarium and bar, open: 7 days a week 12pm - 1am, 141 rue Lafayette (10th) (4526-3174) M° Gard du Nord; **Mandala**, sauna club, body building, 2 rue Drouot (9th) (4246-6014); **Tilt**, newly renovated sauna on 3 floors, video cabins, massage, relax rooms, 41 rue Sainte Anne (1st) (4296-0743); **Victor Hugo**, sauna, snack bar, videos, 109 avenue Victor-Hugo (16th) (4704-4124).
● Erotic Films: **Banque Club**, videos and movies, 3 floors of action, 23, rue Penthièvre (8th) open daily 4pm - 2am (4256-4926); **Rangers**, erotic movies on large screen, darkroom, cabins, bar, 47, bd Saint-Denis (10th) M° Strasbourg-St-Denis (4239-8330).

● Sex-Shops: **I.E.M.**, three locations, 4, rue Bailleul (1st) (4296-0574), 33, rue de Liège (8th) (4522-6901) and 208 rue Saint Maur (10th) (4241-2141); **VideoVision**, 62 rue de Rome (8th) (4293-6604).

 **ACCOMMODATIONS**

✪ AXIAL-BEAUBOURG

Paris 75004. Information and reservations: Odysseus (516) 944-5330 or (800) 257-5344. Fax: (516) 944-7540 or (800) 982-6571. TYPE: *Hotel*. CLIENTELE: Gay/Straight. LOCATION: In the heart of the Gay Village - the Marais, near the Pompidou Center. M° Hôtel de Ville or Châtlet.

* Rooms: 40, w/priv. bath
* CTV, phone, hair dryer, A/C, C/H

* Room & maid service
* Elegant breakfast cellar
* Gay Bars: walking distance
* Parking: 100 m / yards 24 hrs.
* Airport: 45 min., taxi, RER, bus shuttle
* Season: Year round
* Rates: $150 - $210 w/CB
* *TAC:* 10% (from Odysseus)

DESCRIPTION: Gracious three-star hotel in a renovated Parisian building. All rooms are decorated with brown and peach designer fabrics; double rooms have large queen-size beds. Triple rooms have large double bed plus a fold up single bed. Friendly service in the heart of Paris' Art and Culture center. The gay village of the Marais is at the hotel's doorstep. Excellent public transportation (metro and RER) will take you anywhere in Paris. Walking distance to the Louvre Museum, the Opera, and the Latin Quarter. Recommended for gay/lesbian couples or discreet singles. Odysseus clients have stayed in this hotel since 1989.

○ SAINTONGE HOTEL

Le Marais, Paris 75003. USA/Canada reservations - Tel: (516) 944-5330 or (800) 257-5344. Fax: (516) 944-7540 or (800) 982-6571. TYPE: *Hotel.* CLIENTELE: Gay/Straight. LOCATION: In a quiet residential street in the heart of the Marais, the 'Gay Village' of Paris, near the Picasso Museum, Hotel de Ville, Opéra and many shops and restaurants. M° Filles de Calvaire, Republique.

* Rooms: 23 w/priv. bath. 17 w/dbl bed,
  5 twins and 1 suite for 4 people.
* CTV, phone, minibar, safety box, C/H
* Breakfast cellar, parking nearby
* Gay Bars: walking distance
* Airport: 45 min., taxi
* Languages: French, Spanish, English
* Reservation: through Odysseus
* Season: Year round
* Rates: $110 - $200 w/CB
* *TAC:* 10% (from Odysseus)

DESCRIPTION: Restored 3-star hotel. Guest rooms are calm, comfortable and modern with clean private bath, hairdryer. Beautiful and spacious 2 room suite for 4 people on the top floor with sky lights. Delightful breakfast service at the breakfast cellar every day from 7:30a-10:30a. Friendly management and staff. Many popular gay bars and restaurants only a short walk away.

HOTEL de la GARE DU NORD
33 Rue Saint Quentin, Paris 75010. Tel: (1) 4878-0292. USA/Canada Reservations: Tel:

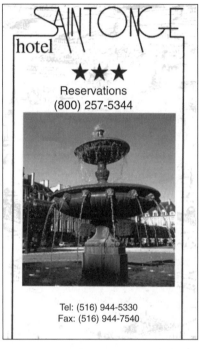

hotel SAINTONGE

★★★
Reservations
(800) 257-5344

Tel: (516) 944-5330
Fax: (516) 944-7540

(516) 944-5660 or (800) 257-5344. Fax: (516) 944-7540 or (800) 982-6571. TYPE: *Hotel.* CLIENTELE: All Welcome. LOCATION: Facing the Gare du Nord, around the corner from the famous Key West Sauna.

* Rooms: 47 w/priv. bath
* CTV, radio, phone, hair dryer
* Elevator, restaurants nearby
* Room & maid service
* Gay Bars: by metro
* Health Club: Key West Sauna nearby
* Airport: 30 minutes
* Train Station/Metro: Gare du Nord
* Open: Year round
* Rates: from (FF) 580
* *TAC:* 10% (from Odysseus)

DESCRIPTION: Renovated 3-star hotel with elevator, bar and restaurant. Conveniently located in the Gare du Nord area for those who wish to enjoy the nearby legendary Key West Sauna (around the corner). Breakfast can be served in your bedroom or in the dining room.

SOLOMIAC   ℂ   5

🔖 ACCOMMODATIONS 🔖

AUBERGE D'ENROSE
32120 Solomiac. Tel: 6265-0142. USA/Canada reservations Tel: (800) 257-5344 or (516) 944-5330. Fax: (800) 982-6571 or (516) 944-7540. TYPE: *Guest House.* HOSTS: Richard & Peter. CLIENTELE: Gay men only. LOCATION: near Toulouse. 5 rooms, 3 apts. Open: year round. High Season April 1 - Sept. 30. Rates: (US) $120 - $140. *TAC:* 10% (from Odysseus). DESCRIPTION: Restored 18th century Farm House.

STRASBOURG   ✆ 3

✈ Entzheim Airport (SXB)

LOCATION: Eastern province of Alsace on the West German border.

POPULATION: 250,000

CLIMATE: Cold and snowy winters with low temperatures -20°F (-22°c); dry and hot summers, pleasant and cool springs and fall.

DESCRIPTION: The ancient capital of Alsace, Strasbourg is an historic city with a mixture of German & French cultures. Modern Strasbourg is the headquarters of the Council of Europe, the home of the European Parliament, and the new capital of Europe.

BARS ♆ RESTAURANTS 🍴

● Bars (GM): **Le Nid d'Espion**, 3 rue de Soeurs (8837-0283); **Warning Bar**, 3 rue Klein (8825-0441).

● Restaurants (GMW): **Antinoos**, inexpensive near the gay sauna, 2, place du Fbg-de-Pierre (8875-1415); **Au Coin du Feu**, 10 rue de la Râpe (8835-4485). Other (AW): **Au Crocodile**, award winning Alsatian cuisine, expensive, 10 rue de l'Outre (8832-1303); **L'Ami Fritz**, good place for Alsatian food in the Petite France area, moderate, 8 rue des Dentelles (8832-8053); **l'Arsenal**, light Alsatian cuisine, moderate, 11 rue de L'Abrevoir (8853-0369); **Strissel**, Alsatian food and wines, traditional decor, inexpensive, 5 Pl. de la Grande Boucherie (8832-1473).

λ SERVICES λ

● Health Clubs (GM): **Oasis Club Sauna**, a sauna/bar/gym complex, 22 rue de Bouxwiller (8823-0319); **Sauna Equateur**, health club and sauna, mostly gay Wednesday - Friday, 5 rue de Roshein (8822-2522).

● Lesbian social group : **La Lune Noire** (Café de femmes), 14 rue des Couples.

🔖 ACCOMMODATIONS 🔖

DE FRANCE HOTEL
20 rue du Jeu-des-Enfants, Strasbourg 67000. Tel: 8832-3712. TYPE: *Hotel.* CLIENTELE: Mostly Straight. LOCATION: Central. 66 rooms, CTV, phone, minibar. Rates: on request. 3-star tourist hotel.

TOULOUSE   ✆ 5

✈ Blagnac Airport (TLS)

LOCATION: Southern Province of Languedoc, close to the Spanish border. 705 km / 440 mi. south of Paris, and 387km /241mi. north of Barcelona (Spain).

POPULATION: 375,000

CLIMATE: Mild Mediterranean with hot sunny summers; cool pleasant winters.

DESCRIPTION: Toulouse is the 4th largest city in France. It is the ancient capital of Languedoc, and a charming southern French town. Explore the town's old quarters, Baroque and Renaissance buildings, cathedrals and palaces, and pretty pink color houses made of terra-cotta brick and red roof tiles. It is a famous University Center, the hometown of the French aerospace industry, and a world famous art center. The gay scene is in the city center between **Place du Pont Neuf** and the **Hôtel de Ville**.

BARS ♆ RESTAURANTS 🍴

● Bars/clubs (GM): **Broadway Club**, disco, 11 rue du Puits Clos (6121-1011); **NYC**, leather disco, 83 Allée Charles-de-Fitte (6159-4645).

● Bar/Club (GMW): **Le New Shanghai**, video bar, Tea-dance, 12 rue de la Pomme (6123-3780).
● Restaurants (GMW): **l'Os à Moelle**, traditional cuisine, rustic decor, 14, rue Roquelaine (6163-1930); **La Comédie**, traditional cuisine, 1 rue Velane (6153-5171); **La Table d'Aline**, steaks and seafood, 7 quai Saint-Pierre (6123-

2407); **le Petit Saint-Germain**, traditional cuisine, 6 rue l'Etoile (6163-1343).

 SERVICES λ

● Health Clubs (GM): **Le Calypso**, 16, rue Bayard (6163-8652); **Le Physic Club**, 14 rue d'Aubuisson (6162-8129); **Le Président**, 38 rue d'Alsace-Lorraine (6121-5218).

● Sex Shop (G/S): **Spartacus**, videos, magazines, leather, toys, 29 rue Héliot (6162-2702).

🗝 **ACCOMMODATIONS** 🗝

GRAND HOTEL DE L'OPERA
1 Place du Capitole, Toulouse 31000. Tel: 6121-8266. Fax: 6123-4104. TYPE: *Hotel*. CLIENTELE: Mostly Straight. LOCATION: Downtown, facing the Opera. 50 rooms w/priv. bath, CTV, phone, A/C. Rates: on request. DESCRIPTION: Moderately priced hotel.

TOURS   ✆ 4

✈ Saint Symphorien AP (TUF)
   4 mi. / 6 km north of Tours

LOCATION: In the famous Loire Valley. 55 min. by fast train from Paris.

POPULATION: 140,000

CLIMATE: Continental. Cool and pleasant summers, cold and snowy winters.

Gay/Lesbian Visitor Information
Maison de Homosexualité: 4720-5530

DESCRIPTION: Major city between the Loire and the Cher. The Loire river was the chosen residence of former French Kings.

BARS 🍸 **RESTAURANTS** 🍴

● Bars/clubs (GM): **Aux Voltigeurs**, 53bis rue du Docteur Fournier (4732-9537); **Fouquet Bar**, 26 rue Jean-Fouquet (4764-1979); **Le Petit Café**, 148 rue Giraudeau (4739-6254).

● Disco (GMW): **Club 71**, Sun. T-dance, 71 rue Georges Courteline (4737-0154).

● Restaurants (AW): **La Grosse Tour**, 14 rue de la Grosse Tour (4738-6949); **Le Passage**, 66 rue Colbert (4761-3234).

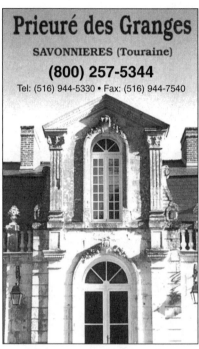

Prieuré des Granges

SAVONNIERES (Touraine)

(800) 257-5344

Tel: (516) 944-5330 • Fax: (516) 944-7540

🗝 **ACCOMMODATIONS** 🗝

✪ PRIEURE DES GRANGES

37510 Savonnières. USA/Canada Reservation/ Information Tel: (516) 944-5330 or (800) 257-5344. Fax: (516) 944-7540 or (800) 982-6571. TYPE: *Guest House/Castle*. HOST: Philippe. CLIENTELE: Equal Gay/Straight. LOCATION: In the heart of the Loire Valley, 10 min. south of Tours on the road of Villandry (D7).

* Rooms: 6 w/priv. bath (4 dbl / 2 triple)
* Suite: 1 (two-bedroom) w/full bath
* Phone, pool, balcony, garden
* Free parking, pets w/prearrangement
* Gay Bars: Tours, 10 min. by car, train
* Airport: Paris 2 hrs. by car or train
* Season: Open April - Nov. 30
  (Closed Dec. - March)
* Rates: (US) $120-$220
* *TAC:* 10% (from Odysseus)

DESCRIPTION: XVII century-old Chateau amidst artistically landscaped park and gardens. All rooms are spacious, decorated with period furniture and antiques. Ideal for a relaxed vacation in France's most celebrated historic region. Warm welcome to Odysseus guests. Recommended by repeated guests.

FRENCH POLYNESIA

AREA: 402 sq. mi. (1,041 sq. km)
POPULATION: 96,000
CAPITAL: Papeete
CURRENCY: French Pacific Franc (Cfp)
OFFICIAL LANGUAGE: Tahitian, French
MAJOR RELIGIONS: Protestants, Roman Catholics
Telephone: 689
Nat'l Holiday: Bastille Day, July 14
Official Time: 10 hrs. behind G.M.T.
Electricity: 110 volts
Exchange Rate: 1US$ = Cfp 88.35
Nat'l Airline: Polynesian Airlines

LAW REGARDING HOMOSEXUALITY: Homosexuality is accepted in French Polynesia. The islands are administered by French law. The minimum age of consent is 15, but it is advisable not to get sexually involved with under 18 years old. Homosexuality has been culturally accepted in Polynesia for centuries, and their sexuality developed outside the strict Judeo-Christian ethic.

HAAPITI MOOREA ✆ 689

✈ Tamae Airport (MOZ)

LOCATION: On the wildest coast of Moorea, Tahiti's sister island 20 km / 13 mi. off Tahiti. 7 min. by plane, and 45 minutes by boat.

POPULATION: Moorea (isl.) 6,000

CLIMATE: see Papeete.

DESCRIPTION: A French polynesian resort off Tahiti but close enough to enjoy the tranquility and lifestyle of an authentic Polynesian atmosphere with easy access to Papeete.

BAR Y RESTAURANT ¶¶

● A friendly bar and restaurant in Haapiti is **Le Bateau**, pub and restaurant, PK. 34 (56.15.35) located at the **Residence Linareva** (see description below). It is not a gay bar, just a friendly old Pub and Restaurant serving French cooking in a boat moored at the lagoon off the beach and connected to the resort.

⚜ ACCOMMODATIONS ⚜

RÉSIDENCE LINAREVA
BP 205 Temae, Haapiti - Moorea, French Polynesia. Tel: 561-535. USA/Canada reservations: Tel: (516) 944-5330 or (800) 257-5344, Fax: (516) 944-7540 or (800) 982-6571. TYPE: *Hotel*. CLIENTELE: Gay/Straight. LOCATION: 2 km. / 1 mi. from Haapiti on shore of a lagoon at the foot of green hills.

* Rooms: 7 w/priv. bath
  3 dbl / 3 triple/ 1 quad
* Balcony, garden, cooking facilities
* CTV, phone, A/C (Bahama fans)
* Restaurant/Bar: **Le Bateau**
* Sundeck, maid service, parking
* Clothing optional policy
* Beach: 10 m (30 ft.) mixed
* Gay Bars: 5 km / 3 mi.
* Airport: 25 km / 16 mi., taxi (30 min.)
* Reservations: 1 night deposit
* Credit Cards: MC/VISA
* Open: Year round
* Rates: on request
* *TAC:* 10%

DESCRIPTION: Small Polynesian bungalow resort with Tahitian style rooms, some with ocean view. Unique floating bar/restaurant. Prices include outrigger canoes, bikes, windsurfing, snorkel equipment, private sunbathing and pontoon.

PAPEETE TAHITI ✆ 689

✈ Tahiti-Faaa Int'l Airport (PPT)

LOCATION: On the northwestern coast of the island of Tahiti in French Polynesia.

POPULATION: 80,000

CLIMATE: Mild tropical climate with two seasons: warm and humid period between November and April, and dry season between May and October. Average annual temperature is 25°c

(77°F). The tropic sun is less filtered by the atmosphere. Sunscreen is necessary to prevent skin damage.

DESCRIPTION: Tahiti is an unspoiled paradise, exotic and mystic, where handsome young men and women walk around semi-dressed in colorful island outfits. The image of Tahiti was enhanced by Paul Gaugin's paintings, and countless stories and movies about the legendary Captain Cook and the 'Bounty'. Papetee, means in native language, 'water basket'.

Papeete has lovely sandy beaches and it is a wonderful place to explore by night. Horny young sailors and GIs cruise the beaches and the bars for women, Mahus (Tahitian transvestites) or anything that moves and they can lay their hands on. Clubs range from sleazy joints to posh discos. However, they are all expensive.

❖ Gay Beach: beach south of the **Maeva Beach Hotel**.

BARS ☿ RESTAURANTS 🍴

● Bars/Clubs (G/S): **Bounty Club**, disco with the 'loosest' ambience in town, mixed crowd of tourists, locals, GI's, and gays, rue des Écoles (upstairs) (429-300); **Club 106**, Front de Mer (427-292); **La Cave du Royal**, dance bar with mixed crowds, Blvd. Pomare (420-129); **Chez Jacky**,mixed cocktail bar at the **Royal Papeete**, 291 blvd. Pomare; **Lido**, gay bar, rue des Écoles (429-584); **Mayana Club Disco**, next to Pirate Bar, elegant and expensive (428-229); **Night Club** in Pirae, for after-hours crowds, 15 min. from the airport (281-05); **Vaima Bar**, Vaima Shopping Center (429-745).

● Restaurants (AW): **Le Gallieni**, French Polynesian, at the **Royal Papeete Hotel**, 291 blvd. Pomare; **Restaurant King**, L'Avenue Prince Hinoi (426-241); **Restaurant Acajou**, rue George Lagaroe, near Vaima Bar, Vaima Shopping Center (428-758).

🔑 ACCOMMODATIONS 🔑

MATAVAI
Box 32, Tipaerui, Papeete. Tel: 426-767. Fax: 423-690. TYPE: *Hotel*. CLIENTELE: Gay/ Straight. LOCATION: On the outskirts of town, some 1/2 mile / 800 m from downtown. 146 w/priv. bath, CTV, phone, bar, restaurant, pool. Rates: from cfp 10,000. *TAC:* 10%.

Royal Papeete

In downtown Papeete, across the street from the Moorea ferry boat dock

USA/Canada reservations
(800) 257-5344
Tel: (516) 944-5330
Fax: (516) 944-7540

DESCRIPTION: Unappealing architecture, popular with flight crews, and French GI's.

PRINCESSA HEIATA HOTEL
Pirae. Tel: 428-105. TYPE: *Hotel*. CLIENTELE: Mostly Straight. LOCATION: 2-1/2 mi. / 4 km from Papeete. 25 rooms, 13 bungalows, CTV, phone, pool. DESCRIPTION: Moderately priced, popular with French GI's and Foreign Legionnaires.

✪ ROYAL PAPEETE
291 Pomare Blvd., Papeete. Tel: 420129. USA/Canada Reservations: Tel: (516) 944-5330 or (800) 257-5344. Fax: (516) 944-7540 or (800) 982-6571. TYPE: *Hotel*. CLIENTELE: All Welcome. LOCATION: Town Center opp. Moorea Ferry Dock. 80 rooms w/priv. bath, phone, minibar, A/C, balcony, maid & room service, restaurant, American bar, parking, 10 min. to beach, gay bars nearby, Airport: 10 min., taxi. w/AB. Rates: (US) $140-$180. *TAC:* 10%. DESCRIPTION: Charming hotel built in Colonial motif. Refrigerators are available in deluxe rooms only.

GERMANY

AREA: 137,753 sq. mi. (356,780 sq. km)
POPULATION: 78,000,000
CAPITAL: Berlin
CURRENCY: Deutch Mark (DM)
OFFICIAL LANGUAGE: German
MAJOR RELIGIONS: Protestantism, Roman Catholicism.

LAW REGARDING HOMOSEXUALITY: Legal minimum age for consensual homosexuality is 18. Some acts of male homosexuality are punishable by 5-15 years in prison. In spite of Germany's liberal image homosexuality is discriminated against in various parts of the country, and right wing / skinheads violence against gays and foreigners is on the rise.

Telephone: 49
Nat'l Holiday: Unification Day, October 3
Official Time: G.M.T. + 1
Electricity: 220 volts
Exchange Rate: 1US$ = DM 1.50
National Airline: Lufthansa

BERLIN   ✆ 030

✈ Tegel Airport (TXL) West Berlin
  Schoenfeld Airport (SXF) East Berlin

LOCATION: Northeastern Germany 180 mi. / 285 km east of Hannover and 181 mi. / 290 km southeast of Hamburg.

POPULATION: 3,300,000

CLIMATE: Continental with cold, snowy winters and cool, pleasant summers. Average temperature for January is 28°F (-2°c), and for July is 64°F (18°c).

Gay Visitor Information
Mann-O-Meter: 216-8008

Lesbian Visitor Information
Lesbentelefon Tel: (030) 2152-000

DESCRIPTION: Berlin is the historic and cultural center of Germany and the capital of the nation since 1237 until its division after the Second World War. **East Berlin** is famous for **Alexanderplatz**; the **Unter den Linden Ave.**; the **Brandenburg Gate**, and the **TV Tower**. Berlin is a city of contrasts, a potpourri, where the conventional exists side by side with the extraordinary. It is a bohemian metropolis with old quarters and high rise buildings. The Berlin gay scene is spread out in various part of the city, however the highest concentration can be found in the Schöneburg area between Wittenbergplatz and Nollendorfplatz.

● Shopping: explore the two mile long stretch of **Kurfürstendamm** with its exclusive shops, department stores, boutiques and art galleries, or the ultra modern **Europa Center**.

❖ Beaches: for nude sunbathing and swimming check **Strandbad Wannsee**, lake beach with official nudist area (deck B), take the S-Bahn to Nikolassee station.

❖ **SPECIAL EVENT**: Every year in late winter Berlin hosts the **International Film Festival**.

BARS ♈ RESTAURANTS ♐

● Bars/clubs (GM): **Andreas Kneipe**, old-fashion Berlin bar, Ansbacher Straße 29 (218-3257); **Berlin Connection**, cafe bistro, Martin-Luther Str. 19 (213-1116); **Club 70**, rustic bar, gay films, video rentals, Ebersstraße 58 (784-1786); **Corner (Kne-Mo)**, elegant bar and café in the Kurfürstendamm area, Knesebeckstraße 35 (883-4547); **Dandy Club**, dance club, young clientele, drag shows, Urbanstraße 64 (691-9013); **Kleist-Casino**, disco, Kleiststraße 35 (213-4981); **Le Moustache**, leather bar, Gartenstraße 4 (281-7277); **Pinocchio**, rustic bar, young clientele, Fuggerstraße 3 (245-736); **Pool**, popular Fri.-Sat. night disco, young crowds, Motzstraße 19 (247-529); **Tom's Bar**, leather video bar, Motzstraße 19 (213-4570); **Twilight Zone**, leather bar, Welserstraße 24 (241-432).

● Bars/Clubs (GMW): **Hafen**, Motzstraße 19 (211-4118); **Schoppenstube**, Schönhauser Allee 44 (448-1689).

● Bars/clubs (GW): **Am Wasserturm**, dance bar, Spandauer Damm 168 (302-5260); **Artemisia** Hotel Bar, Branndenburgischerstr.

18 (878-905); **Begine**, café and cultural center, Potsdamer Straße 139 (215-4325); **Dinelo**, bar & cafe, Vorbergstraße 10 (782-2185); **Pour Elle**, bar & disco, Kalkreuthstraße 7 (247-533).

● Restaurants (GMW): **Le Bistrot**, bar restaurant, Rheinstraße 55, 1 Berlin 41 (852-4914) open 19:00-5:00; **Biberbau**, Old German decor, steaks and salads, Durlacherstraße 15 (853-2390); **Café Voltaire**, Stuttgarter Platz 14 (324-5028). Other (AW): **Fofi's Estiatorio**, where fashion designers, models, and film directors go for lunch or dinner, 70 Fasanenstraße (881-8785); **Paris Bar**, 152 Kantstrasse (313-8052) where Berlin's top painters, gallery owners, and art collectors go for lunch.

λ SERVICES λ

● Bookstore (GMW): **Prinz Eisenharz**, Berlin's premier Gay & Lesbian bookshop and café, Bleibtreustr. 52 (313-9936).

● Health Clubs: (GM) **Manuels Sportstudio**, gym, solarium, aerobics, sauna, membership required, Joachim-Friedrich-Straße 37/38 (892-2080); **Sport-Studio Apollo**, fitness gym, sauna, solarium, Hauptstraße 15 (784-8203); **Sports-Studio**, M. Bergmann St. 102.

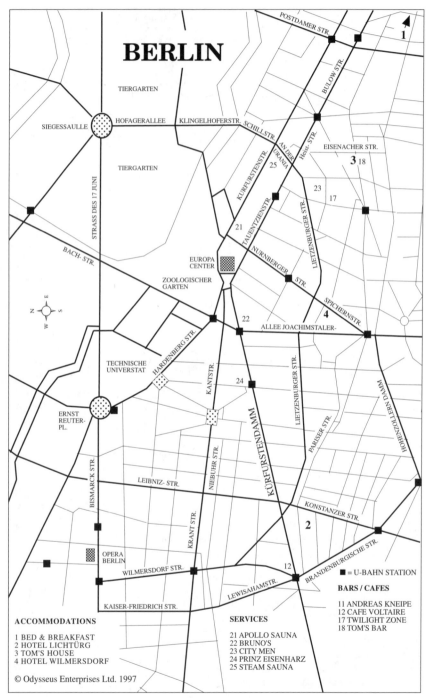

BERLIN

TIERGARTEN

SIEGESSAULLE

HOFAGERALLEE   KLINGELHOFERSTR.

TIERGARTEN

POSTDAMER STR.

BULOW STR.

SCHILL-STR.

AN DER URANIA

Heir. STR.

EISENACHER STR.

3 18

KURFURSTENSTR.

25

23

17

STRASS DES 17 JUNI

BACH- STR.

TAUENTZIENSTR.

21

NURNBERGER   STR.

LIETZENBURGER STR.

EUROPA CENTER

ZOOLOGISCHER GARTEN

SPICHERNSTR.

4

22   ALLEE JOACHIMSTALER-

N
W · E · S

TECHNISCHE UNIVERSTAT

HARDENBERG STR.

KANTSTR.

24

LIETZENBURGER STR.

PARISER- STR.

HOHENZOLLERN DAMM

ERNST REUTER-PL.

BISMARCK STR.

LEIBNIZ- STR.

NIEBUHR STR.

KURFURSTENDAMM

KONSTANZER STR.

2

KRANT STR.

OPERA BERLIN

WILMERSDORF STR.

LEWISAHAMSTR.

12   BRANDENBURGISCHE STR.

KAISER-FRIEDRICH STR.

■ = U-BAHN STATION

BARS / CAFES

11 ANDREAS KNEIPE
12 CAFE VOLTAIRE
17 TWILIGHT ZONE
18 TOM'S BAR

ACCOMMODATIONS

1 BED & BREAKFAST
2 HOTEL LICHTÜRG
3 TOM'S HOUSE
4 HOTEL WILMERSDORF

© Odysseus Enterprises Ltd. 1997

SERVICES

21 APOLLO SAUNA
22 BRUNO'S
23 CITY MEN
24 PRINZ EISENHARZ
25 STEAM SAUNA

● Publication (GMW): **✪ Gay Travel, the first** gay travel magazine in Europe, c/o Rosa Zone Verlag, Beurhausstraße 58, 44137 Dortmund. (231) 914-3072. **✪ Siegessäule**, Berlin's largest gay & lesbian magazine, Jackwerth Verlag GmbH, Lützowstraße 102-104, 10785 Berlin. (30) 230827-0. Fax: (30) 265-2805.

● Saunas (GM): **Apollo City Sauna**, large sauna, Kurfürstenstraße 101 (213-2424); **Steam Sauna Club**, Kurfürsten Str. 113 (244-060); **Treibhaus Sauna**, sauna, solarium, dark room, Schönhauser Allee 132 (448-4503).

● Sex-Shops: **Bruno's**, Kurfürstendamm 227 (882-4290); **City Men Shop & Video**, Fuggerstraße 26 (242-959).

 **ACCOMMODATIONS**

HOTEL ARCO
Geisbergstraße 30, Berlin 10777. Tel: (30) 218-2128. TYPE: *Hotel*. HOSTS: Jacques & Rolf. CLIENTELE: Gay/Straight. LOCATION: Central location, two blocks south of Littenberg-Platz.

* Rooms: 21; 11 w/priv. bath, 10 w/shared sgl 7/ dbl 7/triple 5/ quad 2
* Smoking allowed in rooms
* CTV, phone, safe box, C/H
* Maid service, off street parking
* Beach: 3 km / 2 mi (gay/nude)
* Gay Bars: 2-8 min. walk
* Health Club: 1.5 km / 1 mi. (Apollo)
* Airport(s): Tegel/Tempelhof, Schoenfeld 4km (2.5 mi.) / 6 km (4 mi.) / 12 km (8 mi.)
* Metro: Zoologischer Garten / Schoenfeld
* Languages: German, English, French
* Reservation: deposit required
* Open: Year round
* Rates: DM 85 - DM 175 w/Bb
* Check out time: 11 am
* *TAC:* 8%

DESCRIPTION: Budget hotel with renovated rooms, terrace and shady garden in the gay area.

✪ "BED & BREAKFAST"
11 Friesen Str., Kreutzberg, 10965 Berlin. Tel: (177) 693-8466. Fax: (30) 693-8466. TYPE: *Guest House / Rental Apts*. HOST: Uwe Hagemann, owner. CLIENTELE: Mostly gay men & women. LOCATION: Near Gneisenau St. (main cross street). M° Gneisenau.

* Rooms: 15, 4 w/priv., 11 w/shared bath 15 dbl / 3 triple / 2 quad
* Suites: 3 (1BR) w/lkitchen, terrace
* Smoking allowed in rooms

* CTV, VCR, phone, refrigerator, C/H, cooking facilities, hair dryer
* Bed types: single, double
* Parking (off street), pets w/prearrangement
* Gay Bars: 400 m / yards
* Health Club: 1 km / 0.8 mi. (mixed)
* Airport: Tempelhof 2 km / 1.4 mi.
* Languages: German, English
* Reservations: deposit required
* Cancellation: 2 weeks in advance
* No credit cards (bank transfer possible)
* Rates: DM 35 - 80 (per person) w/CB
* Check in / check out: any time, own key

DESCRIPTION: Affordable Gay & lesbian guesthouse and one bedroom apartment near gay bars and clubs. Shuttle service available from airport. Gay maps and information available.

✪ HOTEL LICHTBÜRG
Paderborner Straße 10. USA/Canada reservations - Tel: (516) 944-5330 or (800) 257-5344. Fax: (516) 944-7540. TYPE: *Hotel*. CLIENTELE: All Welcome. LOCATION: Heart of Berlin's gay scene near the Kurfürstendamm.

* Rooms: 64 w/priv. bath
* CTV, phone, radio, C/H
* Restaurant, indoor heated pool

* Parking and room service available
* Gay Bars: many nearby
* Airport: 7 km / 4 mi., taxi
* Train Station: 3 km / 2 mi. Zoo Station
* Season: Year round
* Rates: (US) $160-$230 w/bB
* *TAC:* 10% (from Odysseus)

DESCRIPTION: Nice 3-star hotel in a quiet residential area. Neatly furnished rooms, most are studio type with private bath. Friendly atmosphere.

TOM'S HOUSE

Eisenacherstraße 10, D-10777 Berlin. Tel: (030) 218-5544. TYPE: *Guest House*. HOST: Christoph Reinke. CLIENTELE: Gay men only. LOCATION: Centrally located near subway station Nollendorfplatz. 8 rooms w/shared shower. DESCRIPTION: House built in 1896. 3rd floor, no elevator, leather clientele.

❂ HOTEL WILMERSDORF

Schaperst. 36, 10719 Berlin. USA/Canada reservations - Tel: (516) 944-5330 or (800) 257-5344. Fax: (516) 944-7540. TYPE: *Hotel*. CLIENTELE: All Welcome. LOCATION: Heart of Berlin's gay scene near the Kurfürstendamm. 10 min. to Europe-Center.

* Rooms: 40 w/priv. bath
* CTV, phone, radio, minibar, C/H
* Breakfast room, parking
* Gay Bars: many nearby
* Metro: Zoo Station, 15 min. walk
* Airport: 7 km / 4 mi., taxi
* Train Station: 3 km / 2 mi. Zoo Station
* Season: Year round
* Rates: (US) $140-$190 w/bB
* *TAC:* 10% (from Odysseus)

DESCRIPTION: Friendly 3-star hotel in a central but quiet location. All rooms are spacious and tastefully furnished. Enjoy your breakfast with a view over the colorful roofs of Berlin.

DRESDEN   ℂ   0351

✈ Dresden Airport (DRS)
   7 mi. / 11 km northeast of Dresden

LOCATION: Saxony of Eastern Germany on the border with the Czech Republic.

POPULATION: 520,00

DESCRIPTION: Rebuilt practically from the

ashes after WWII, Dresden is still one of Europe's most beautiful baroque cities. The 'Old City' contains many interesting architectural gems.

BARS Ⓨ RESTAURANTS 🍴

● Bars/clubs (GM): **Apollo**, disco, Oskar-Mai-Straße 3 (432-1859); **Bunker**, leather cruise bar, c/o Lederclub Dresden, Florian-Geyer-Straße 3 (441-6143); **Mega-Drome**, dance club, Meißner Straße 507 (542-7731); **Stadt Riesa**, Wiener Straße 14 (432-8968).

● Restaurants (GMW): **Café Reinhardt**, Naumannstraße 8 (448-0847); **Kaffee Am Thor**, Platz der Einheit (513-27).

⬚ ACCOMMODATIONS ⬚

HOTEL MERCURE NEWA
St. Petersburger Straße 34, Dresden D-01069. Tel: (351) 481-40. TYPE: *Hotel*. CLIENTELE: All Welcome. LOCATION: Downtown near train station. 313 rooms w/priv. bath, sauna, solarium. Rates: on request.

DÜSSELDORF   ✆ 0211

✈ Düsseldorf Int'l Airport (DUS)

LOCATION: West of the country, 25 mi. /40 km east of the Dutch border 30 mi. / 48 km north of Cologne.

POPULATION: 1,103,770

CLIMATE: Continental with cold snowy winters and cool and pleasant summers.

Gay/Lesbian Visitor Information
LuSZD center: 330-292

DESCRIPTION: Düsseldorf is the capital of the State of Northern Rhineland-Westphalia. It is an important cultural and industrial center and a University town with a student population of over 13,000. Most of the gay scene is concentrated near the Hauptbanhof, at the intersection of Bismarktraße and Charlottenstraße.

BARS Ⓨ RESTAURANTS 🍴

● Bars/clubs (GM): **Comeback**, Charlottenstraße 60 (164-0978); **Goldenen Spiegel**, mature clientele, Ackenstraße 49 (164-0254); **Harlekin**, mature clientele, Corneliusstr. 1 (374-638); **Insider**, bistro, Gupellostraße 32 (364-218);

Musk, leather bar, Charlottenstraße 47 (352-154); **Wilma**, Charlotternstraße 60 (351-737).

● Bars/clubs (GMW): **Mau-Mau**, Kölner Straße 54 (358-268); **Papillons**, show bar, Friedrich-Ebert-Straße 13 (359-563); **Theater-Stube**, Luisenstraße 33 (372-244); **Valentino**, dance club, Bahnstraße 63 (362-959).

● Restaurants: **Bernath Café**, women's cafe, Telleringstr. 56 (35-4101); **Cancun**, Mexican, Ellerstraße 123 (74-2936); **La Strada**, cafe popular with gay men, Immermannstr. 32 (36-2428). Other (AW) **Müllers und Fest KD**, expensive, German cuisine, Königsalllee 12 (32-6001).

λ SERVICES λ

● Health Clubs (GM): **City Sauna**, Luisenstraße 129, Mintropplatz (373-973); **Phoenix Sauna**, Platanenstraße 11a (663-638).

⬚ ACCOMMODATIONS ⬚

ALT-GRAZ HOTEL
Klosterstraße 132, 4000 Düsseldorf 1. Tel: (211) 364-028. TYPE: *Hotel*. HOST: Gerhard Pichlhöfer. CLIENTELE: Gay/Straight. LOCATION: Center of town, near Central Train Station (Hauptbanhauf) and Old Town.

SAVOY HOTEL
Oststraße 128, Düsseldorf D-40210. Tel: (211) 360-336. USA/Canada (800) 257-5344 or (516) 944-5330. Fax: (516) 944-7540. TYPE: *Hotel*. CLIENTELE: All Welcome. LOCATION: Near gay clubs and bars. DESCRIPTION: First class modern hotel convenient to the local gay scene.

FRANKFURT   ✆ 069

✈ Frankfurt-Main Int'l Airport (FRA)

LOCATION: In the western part of West Germany, mid way between Cologne and Stuttgart.

POPULATION: 650,000

CLIMATE: Seldom too hot or too cold, cloudy, foggy and wet. Summer temperatures occasionally reach 80˚F (26˚c).

Gay/Lesbian Visitor Information
Gay Switchboard: 28-3535

DESCRIPTION: Frankfurt is Germany's

major international air hub. It is the country's seventh largest city, and an important industrial, commercial and financial center. **The Zeil** is the major shopping district, with large department stores. For a panoramic view visit the revolving glass-enclosed observation deck and restaurant of the 1,086 ft. (330 m) **Television Tower** near Rosa Luxemburgstraße in the Ginnheim section of northwest Frankfurt. Most gay bars are located on or near Alte Gasse north of the Zeil pedestrian mall, and northeast of the Stock Exchange.

BARS Y RESTAURANTS ¶¶

● Bars/clubs (GM): **Blue Angel**, disco, Brönnerstraße 17 (28 2772); **Come Back**, Alte Gasse 33-35 (29-3345); **Construction Five**, levy/leather oriented disco, Alte Gasse 5 (29 1356); **Harveys**, cafe/bar, Bornheimer Landstraße 64 (497-303); **Lucky's Manhattan**, bar/restaurant, Schäffergaße 27 (284-919); **Queer Bar**, Klinger Straße 26 (131-0589); **The Stall**, leather bar, Stiffstraße 22 (29-1880); **Zum Schwejk**, Schäfergaße 20 (29-3166).

● Bars/clubs (GW): **Club Madame**, Aller Heilingen St. 25 (28-3164); **La Gata**, Seehofstraße 3 (61-4581).

● Restaurants (GMW): **Bierbar Karussel**, dinner show, traditional cuisine, Porzellanhofstraße 10 (28-5293); **Liliput**, coffee shop, Sandhofpassage (28 5727); **Maurice**, Berger Straße 31-33 (493866); **Tonight**, restaurant/bar, nice crowd, good food, Altegaße 26, across from 'Construction 5'. Others (AW): **Restaurant Français**, at the Steigenberger Hotel Frankfurt Hof, Kaiserplatz (2 0251), elegant and expensive; **Wienhaus Brückenkeller**, leading restaurant with German cuisine in the heart of Old Town (expensive); **Rhinpfalz-Weinstuben**, wine tavern with local specialties, 1 Gutleutsraße (23-3870); **Café Schwille**, pastries and deserts 50 Grosse Bockenheimer Strasse (28-3054).

λ SERVICES λ

● Erotica (GM): **Dr. Müller's**, sex-cinema-center, Kaiserstraße 66 (25-2717); **Heaven**, all male cinema, videos, Holzgraben 9 (29-4655); **Pleasure**, books, videos, Kaiserstraße 51.

● Health Clubs (GM): **Club Sauna Amsterdam**, daily from 14:00-24:00, Waidmannstraße 31 (631-3371); **Palace**, Braubachstraße 1 / Ecke Fahrgaße (282-852).

 ACCOMMODATIONS

AMBASSADOR HOTEL
Moselstraße 12, Frankfurt 6000. Tel: (69) 251-077. US/Canada Reservations: Tel (516) 944-5330 or (800) 257-5344. Fax: (516) 944-7540 or (800) 982-6571. TYPE: *Hotel*. CLIENTELE: Gay/Straight. LOCATION: City center in the Adult entertainment area walk to gay village.

* Rooms: 94 w/priv. bath or shower
* CTV, phone, mini-bar
* Italian Restaurant, bar
* Limited room service
* Laundry/dry cleaning service
* Gay Bars: walking distance
* Train Station: 200 m/yards
* Airport: 20 km / 13 mi.
* Season: Year round
* Rates: (US) $120-$160
  ($190-$280 during International Fairs)
* *TAC:* 10%

DESCRIPTION: Small tourist class hotel, comprising of two connected buildings. Convenient location to explore the local gay scene.

BAUER HOTEL SCALA
Schafergaße 31, Frankfurt D-60329. Tel: (69) 271-110. US/Canada Reservations: Tel (516) 944-5330 or (800) 257-5344. Fax: (516) 944-7540 or (800) 982-6571. TYPE: *Hotel*. CLIENTELE: Gay/Straight. LOCATION: Downtown in the heart of the local gay village, near subway and tramway stations.

* Rooms: 44 w/priv. bath
* Rooms for non smokers
* CTV, phone, mini-bar
* Laundry/dry cleaning service
* Gay Bars: walking distance
* Train Station: 600 m/yards
* Airport: 20 km / 13 mi.
* Season: Year round
* Rates: (US) $160-$230. *TAC:* 10%

DESCRIPTION: Moderate first class downtown hotel, renovated in 1989. Excellent Gay Village location.

HAMBURG   ℂ   040

✈ Fuhisbuttel Airport (HAM)

LOCATION: Northern Germany, where the Elbe river flows into the North Sea.

POPULATION: 1,800,000

CLIMATE: Continental with cold snowy winters

and cool, pleasant summers. Average January temperature is 26°F (-4°c), and July is 64°F (18°c).

Gay/Lesbian Visitor Information
Magnus Hirschfeld Centrum: 279-0060

DESCRIPTION: Hamburg on the Elbe river is one of Europe's busiest ports. Founded by Charlemagne in 810, the city's prosperity depended on its trading activities. The first port was built in 1189, and by the mid 13th century the city entered into a mercantile partnership with neighboring cities to form the **Hanseatic League**. Hamburg is a fun city for gay visitors. At night gay life is at its best. The gay scene is in the St. Pauli area and in the trendy St. Georg district near the Hauptbanhof. Hamburg is famous for its leather scene with many leather oriented meetings and events during the year.

BARS ♈ RESTAURANTS 🍴

● Bars/clubs (GM): **Bel Ami**, Zimmerpforte 2 (280-1738); **Black**, leather bar, Danziger Str. 21 (24-0804); **Camelot**, dance club, Hamburger Berg 13; **Chaps**, levy/leather bar, Woltmannstraße 24 (23 0647); **Exquisit**, Spielbundenplatz 22 (31 4393); **Pit Club & Male**, disco nightclub with cruisy dark rooms upstairs, Pulverteich 17 (24-3380); **Paradiso**, Detlev-Bremer-Straße 52 (31-4988); **Piccadilly**, Silbersacktweite 1 (319-2474); **Ramrod**, Talstraße 10-12 (317-4580); **Rudi's**, Steindam 58 (247-274); **Spundloch**, dance bar/cabaret, Paulinenstraße 19 (31-0798); **Tom's Saloon**, leather cruise bar, dark room, Pulverteich 17 (280-3056); **Wunderbar**, dance bar, Talstraße 14 (317-4444).

● Bars/clubs (GMW): **Café/ Bar** at the Magnus Hirschfeld Center, Borgweg 8 (279-0060); **Tuc Tuc**, bar/disco, Oelkersallee 5 (430-0695).

● Bars/clubs (GW): **Cafe Schue**, relaxed ambience, Dammtorbahnhof; **Camelot**, Hamburger Berg 13 (314-164); **Frauenkneipe**, dance bar, Stresemannstraße 60 (436-377);**Ika-Stuben**, Budapestrerstr. 38 (310-998).

● Cabarets (G/S): **Crazy Boys**, male strippers, Pulverteich 12 (24-6285); **Pulverfass Cabaret**, drag show, Pulverteich 12 (24-9791).

● Restaurants (AW): **Alte Mühle**, old fashioned German restaurant, 34 Alte Mühle (604 9171); **Le Canard**, Classic French, one of the best restaurants in Germany, 11 Martinstrße (460 4830); **Old Commercial Room**, traditional German cuisine, popular stopover for sailors, 10 Englische Planke (36 6319).

λ SERVICES λ

● Erotica (GM): **Erotic-Kino**, Talstr. 2; **Henry's Show Center**, Steindamm 7 (24-3107); **Homo Kino**, Talstr. 8 (31-2495); **Homo Gay Kino**, Clemens-Schultz Str. 43 (31-5068); **New Man City**, Pulverteich 8 (240-149); **Sparta City**, cinema, shop, Lange Reihe 92 (280-2741).

● Health Clubs (GM): **Appollo Sauna**, Max-Brauer- Allee 277 (434-811); **Badehaus Hamburg**, steam room, sauna, fitness, Pulverteich 37 (240514); **Melidissa**, 24 hrs non stop, Max-Brauer-Allee 155 (380-9669); **Schwitzkasten**, Virchowstraße 12-14 (389-3133).

● Leather/Rubber (GMW): **Basta Boots**, rubber gloves/boots, Gurlittstr. 31-33 (245-979); **Mr. Chaps Leatherworks**, Schmilinskystr. 9 (243-109); **RIK Productions**, clothing, toys, Gurlittstr. 31-33 (245-979).

● Sex Shops (GM): **Homo Kino Hamburg**, Talstraße 8 (312495); **Revolt Shop**, Clemens-Schultz-Str. 77 (312-848); **Seventh Heaven**, Steindamm 24 and Talstr. 18.

 ACCOMMODATIONS

HOTEL ST. GEORG
Kirchenallee 23, 2000 Hamburg 1. Tel: (040) 241-141. USA/Canada reservations (800) 257-5344 or (516) 944-7540. Fax: (800) 982-6571. TYPE: *Hotel*. CLIENTELE: Gay/Straight. LOCATION: Midtown Hamburg, near the Central Railway Station. Shopping, nightlife and subway one minute walking.

* Rooms: 26; 15 w/shower
  sgl 9; dbl26; triple 12. Smoking allowed
* CTV (room), phone
* 24 hours room service; maid service
* Business phone/fax facilities
* Minibar, safety box, balcony,
  garden, room service, parking
* Gay Bars: 5 min. walk
* Airport: 14 km / 9 mi.,taxi, bus, metro
* Train Station/Metro: 2 minutes
* Languages: German, French, English,
  Greek, Italian, Dutch, Arabic
* Reservation: 1 night deposit
* Credit Cards: MC/VISA/AMEX/DC/EC
* Rates: (US) $95-210 w/full GB
* *TAC:* 10% (from Odysseus)

DESCRIPTION: Gay friendly hotel near the Central Train Station and main Shopping Center. Very clean, individually furnished rooms, attentive service.

✪ HOTEL VILLAGE
Steindamm 4, Hamburg 1. Tel: (40) 246137. USA/Canada reservations (800) 257-5344 or (516) 944-7540. Fax: (800) 982-6571. TYPE: *Hotel*. CLIENTELE: Mostly Gay. LOCATION: Near Central Train Station and the Gay Scene.

* Rooms: 17, 6 w/priv., 11 w/shared bath
  sgl 6 / dbl 9/ triple 2 (smoking allowed)
* CTV, phone, refrigerator
* Maid, room and laundry service
* Gay Bars: 2 minutes
* Health Club: 5 minutes
* Open: Year round
* Rates: (US) $120-$160
* *TAC:* 10% (from Odysseus)

DESCRIPTION: The largest gay hotel in Hamburg. All bars and clubs are walking distance.

✪ SARAH PETERSEN
Lange Reihe 88, D-20098 Hamburg 1. Tel/Fax: (40) 249-826. TYPE: *Guest House*. HOSTESS: Sarah Petersen, owner. LOCATION: City center, in the heart of the gay scene of St. Georg.

* Rooms: 4 (3 dbl / 1 triple)
* Smoking allowed in rooms
* CTV, refrigerator, hair dryer
* Laundry service
* Gay Bars: 2-5 min. walking
* Gay Sauna: 8 min. (gay)
* Airport: 20 min., w/direct bus
* Train Station/Subway: 8 min. walk
* Languages: German, English
* Reservations: 50% deposit
* Cancellation: 80% charges if not rerented
* Open: Year round
* Rates: DM 98-240 / (off) DM 89-210 w/eEb
* Check in by appointment / check out 11 am

DESCRIPTION: Artistic guest house on the first floor of an elegant art-nouveau house. The guest house is facing Lange Rihe - an old European street popular with trendy gays. Guest rooms are quiet and tastefully furnished.

KASSEL   ✆ 0561

✈ Kassel-Calden

LOCATION: Northeast of the central Hesse province. Near former E. Germany.

POPULATION: 203,000

CLIMATE: Continental climate with cold winters and mild summers.

Gay Visitor Information
Schwule Gruppe Kassel: 804-3819

DESCRIPTION: Kassel is the capital of the province and a major industrial center. The **Provincial Museum** and **Art Gallery** is one of the finest in the country. Nearby **Göttingen** is a University town with a medieval town hall and ambiance.

BARS 🍸 RESTAURANTS 🍴

● Bars/clubs (GMW): **Bubble Gum**, Wilhelmshöher Allee 110 (12-227); **Frisch & Fresch**, leather bar, Wilhelmsöher Allee 84 (775-252); **RUK-Zuck**, dance club, Frankfurter Straße 131 (22729); **Take Five**, Friedrich-Ebert-Straße 118 (18854); and the **Café Bar** at the Haus Lengen for hotel guests only (see information below).

λ SERVICES λ

● Health Clubs (GM): **Sauna im Pferdestall**, Erzbergerstraße 23 (16-801).

● Sex Shop (GM): **Sex Point**, gay cinema and sex shop, Kólnischestraße 18 (711-841).

 ACCOMMODATIONS

HAUS LENGEN
Erzbergerstraße 23-25, 3500 Kassel. Tel: (0561) 16801. TYPE: *Hotel*. HOST: Uwe C. Lengen. CLIENTELE: Mostly Gay. LOCATION: 5 minutes to Central Station. 7 rooms, CTV, cafe, bar, sauna. Rates: on request. Budget guest house.

KOLN   ℭ 221
(COLOGNE)

✈ Kolon-Bonn Airport (CGN)

LOCATION: North Rhein Province of West Germany, 20 mi. / 32 km north of Bonn.

POPULATION: 1,103,700

CLIMATE: Continental with average temperatures of 34°F (2°c) in January and 67°F (19°c) in July.

Gay/Lesbian Visitor Information
G& L Center (SCHULZ): 931-8800

HOTEL RHEINGOLD
★★★
Niveau in persönlichem Rahmen

USA / Canada Reservations
(800) 257-5344
Tel: (516) 944-5330 • (516) 944-7540

DESCRIPTION: Cologne is the largest city in the Rhineland and 4th largest in Germany. The city became famous for its *eau de cologne* over a century ago. Today it is an important trade center and a University town. Cologne has a lively gay scene with bars, discos, cafes and restaurants. Most of the gay scene is in or south of the **Old City** near **Neumarkt**.

❖ SPECIAL EVENT: ILGA World Conference, June 29-July 5, 1997 on the subject of "Challenge and Pride". Tel/Fax: (221) 9318-8016. Email: iglf@aol.com or Ilga@macman.org

BARS 🍸 RESTAURANTS 🍴

● Bars/clubs (GM): **Chains**, leather cruise bar, Stephanstr. 4 (238-730); **Come Back**, Alter Market 10 (257-7658); **Hands**, leather bar, Mathiasstraße 22 (24-3541); **Lu-Lu Tanzbar**, disco, dark room action, Hohenzollernring 16-18 (25-4433); **My Lord**, bar/restaurant, Mülenbach 57 (23 1702); **Steifelknecht**, leather/levi cruise bar, dark sex rooms with slings upstairs, Pipinstr. 9 (213-001); **Teddy Treff**, leather bar, Stephanstr. 1 (248-310); **Transfert**, cafe,bar on two levels, theme parties, outdoor terrace, Hahnenstraße 16 (258-1085).

● Bars/clubs (GMW): **Disco im SCHULZ**, Kartäuserwall 18 (931-8800); **Park**, Mauritiuswall 84 (21-3357).

● Bars/clubs (GW): **Candida**, Gladbacherstrasse 36 (524-633); **Georg Sand**, Marsilsteim 13 corner of Mauritiuswall (216-162); **Sappho II**, Pfeilstraße 17 (23-8837); **Sappho Klack**, Severinstraße 189 (317-233).

● Restaurants (GM): **Beim Pitter**, cafe popular with leather and jeans crowd, Alter Market 58; **Quo Vadis**, cafe, bistro, outdoor sitting area, Vor St. Martin 9-10 (258-1414). Other (AW): **Goldener Pflug**, expensive, 421 Olpener Straße (89 5509); **Spezialitäten-restaurant Balduinklause**, international atmosphere, 10 Balduuinstraße (23 8098).

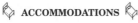

λ SERVICES λ

● Health Clubs (GM): **Badehaus am Römerturm**, elegant, outdoor pool, one of the best in Europe, Frienstraße 23-25 (230-253); **Club 30**, Mühlenbach 30 (21-7386); **Der Faun**, Händelstraße 31 (216-157); **Phoenix**, Kettengaße 22 (231-421); **Vulcano**, Marienplatz 3-5 (216-051).

● Sex Shops (GM): **Gay Sex Messe**, Mathiasstraße 13 (24-8217); **Sex & Gay Center**, Mathiasstraße 23 (23-5301) also Kettengaße 8; **Smoky**, Friesenplatz 5 (25-2652).

🔖 ACCOMMODATIONS 🔖

MERIAN HOTEL
Allerheiligenst. 1, Köln 50668. Tel: (0221) 16650. USA/Canada reservations - (800) 257-5344 or (516) 944-5330. Fax: (800) 982-6571 or (516) 944-7540. TYPE: *Hotel*. CLIENTELE: All Welcome. LOCATION: Near the Cathedral, shopping, and public transportation.

* Rooms: 31 w/priv. bath
* Apartments: 2 deluxe apts
* CTV, phone, minibar, hair-dryer
* Breakfast room
* Maid, laundry service, elevator, parking
* Gay Bars: walking distance
* Airport: 5 km / 3 mi.
* Season: Year round
* Rates: (US) $160-$220
  $250-$430 (during fairs and exhibitions)
* *TAC:* 10% (from Odysseus)

DESCRIPTION: Contemporary hotel with bright, newly furnished rooms and all modern amenities. Two exclusive apts on the 5th floor. One has an open fireplace with a cosy accom-

modations, the other one has a small kitchenette. Fantastic view of the Cathedral from the balconies of both apts.

○ **HOTEL RHEINGOLD**
Engelbertsraße 33-35 , 50674 Köln. Tel: (221) 924-090. USA/Canada reservations: Tel: 1 (800) 257-5344 or (516) 944-5330. Fax: 1 (800) 982-6571 or (516) 944-7540. TYPE: *Hotel*. CLIENTELE: All Welcome. LOCATION: Old City near Rudolfplatz and the gay scene.

* Rooms: 52 w/priv. bath; suites: 4
* Smoking allowed in rooms, soundproof
* CTV, phone, C/H, hair-dryer, safety box
* Bar, Sauna, Solarium, pool
* Parking: paid, off street
* Gay Bars: walking distance
* Health Club: 200 m / yards
* Airport: 20 km / 13 mi., taxi, bus
* Train Station: 10 minutes
* Languages: German, English, French
* Reservations: deposit required
* Credit Cards: VISA/AMEX
* Season: Year round (Trade Fair is high season, impossible to book)
* Rates: (US) $140 - $180 w/CBb
  $230-$410 during exhibitions
* *TAC:* 10% (from Odysseus)

DESCRIPTION: Traditional 3-star hotel with spacious and tastefully furnished rooms. Fine service and excellent location. Heavily booked during fairs.

LEIPZIG   ℂ   **041**

✈ Schkeuditz Airport (LEJ)

LOCATION: Central eastern Germany, 100 mi. / 160 km southwest of Berlin.

POPULATION: 565,000

CLIMATE: Cold winters, specially in January when the temperatures are below freezing. Summers are generally in the 70°'sF (21°c).

Gay/Lesbian Visitor Information
SVD: 590-0468

DESCRIPTION: Leipzig is the second largest city in former East Germany. It offers concerts, museums, and two international trade fairs of industrial and electronic goods each year (mid March and early September). During this period it is difficult to make hotel reservations, and the rates are normally higher. The gay scene is limited and is concentrated in the area between the **Central Train Station** and the **New Town Hall**. Most establishments cater to a mixed gay/lesbian clientele.

BARS ♈ RESTAURANTS ▯

● Bars/clubs (GMW): **Advokat**, Brühl 56; **Black Horse**, Roßstraße 12 (331-5267); **Café Vis-à-Vis**, Rudolf-Breitscheid-Straße 33 (29-2718); **Kutsche**, dance club, Wintergartenstraße 9 (211-4374).

● Restaurant (AW): **Auerbachs Keller**, Leipzig's best restaurant, at Grimmische Straße 2/4 in Madler passage (209-131); **Falstaff**, elegant restaurant near train station, Georgiring 9 (286-403); **Kaffeebaum**, authentic German beer-hall ambiance, 4 Kleine Fleischergaße (200-452); **Varadero**, Cuban cuisine, near the Markt at Barfussgässchen 8 (281-686).

λ SERVICES λ

● Sex Shop (G/S): **Erotik shop**, Universität straßer 18 (28-4144).

🗝 ACCOMMODATIONS 🗝

HOTEL CORUM LEIPZIG
Rudolf-Breitscheiderstr. 3. Tel: (341) 125-100. TYPE: *Hotel*. CLIENTELE: All Welcome. LOCATION: Downtown near gay bars. 122 rooms w/priv. bath. restaurant, bar, sauna.

LÜBECK   ℰ 0451

✈ Fuhlsbuttel Airport (HAM)

LOCATION: Schleswig-Holstein, the northern most province of Germany on the North Sea.

POPULATION: 235,000

CLIMATE: Cold winters, specially in January when the temperatures are below freezing. Summers are generally in the 70°'sF (21°c).

Gay/Lesbian Visitor Information
HIL: 746 -19

DESCRIPTION: Lübeck is an historic city which became the **Free Imperial City** in 1226. It is the hometown of Thomas Mann and Willy Brandt, both Nobel Prize winners. The

city is the capital of *marzipan*, a sweet almond paste, which is used in candies and pastries.

BARS ♈ RESTAURANTS ▯

● Bars/clubs (GM): **Chapeau Claque**, Hartengrube 25 (77 371); **Flamingo**, Marlesgrube 58 (704836); **Papa Gay**, Marlesgrube 61 (72 144); **Why Not**, Fischergrube 23 (754-56).

● Bar/club (GMW): **Dorian Gray**, Engelsgrube 72 (151-137).

● Restaurant (GMW): **Astoria Restaurant**, good food, Hotel Astoria (see description below). Other (AW): **J.G. Niederegger**, home of the famous Lübeck martzipans, coffee shop, pastries, 89 Breite Straße (71-036); **Schabbelhaus**, German baroque atmosphere, gourmet seafood, 48-52 Mengstraße (72 011); **Stadtrestaurant**, on the first floor of the central train station, considered the best in town, Swiss/German cuisine, 2-4 am Bahnhof (84-044).

🗝 ACCOMMODATIONS 🗝

HOTEL ASTORIA
Fackenburger Allee 68, 2400 Lübeck 1. Tel: (451) 46763 and 478100. Fax: (451) 476488. TYPE: *Hotel*. HOST: Manfred Dose. CLIENTELE: All Welcome. LOCATION: Old Town location near the gay scene and the Train station. 20 rooms w/priv. or shared shower. DESCRIPTION: Gay friendly hotel in Old Town near gay bars.

MUNICH   ℰ 089

✈ Riem Int'l Airport (MUC)

LOCATION: Southern Germany in the Province of Bavaria, 35 mi. / 56 km north of the Austrian border.

POPULATION: 1,314,860.

CLIMATE: Continental with cold snowy winters and cool and pleasant summers.

Gay/Lesbian Visitor Information
Gay Center: 260-3056

DESCRIPTION: Like many cosmopolitan cities, Munich has its own style in art and culture and a particular way of enjoying the little pleasures of life. Munich is the capital of Bavaria, the beer capital of the world and a cul-

HOTEL WALLIS
★ ★ ★
Hotelbar
Garage

USA/Canada reservations
(800) 257-5344
Tel: (516) 944-5330 • Fax: (516) 944-7540

tural center. The city enjoys an atmosphere of easy going tolerance which contrasts sharply with the puritanism of the north.

Munich has much to offer to visitors: museums, the **Royal Residence** and **Nymphenburg Palace**, the **National Theatre**, sidewalk cafes in *Schwabing*, Munich's Latin Quarter and if you venture into the countryside you will discover a magnificent land with forests, castles, lakes and snowy mountain peaks.

Munich's gay nightlife is legendary. You will certainly find your kind of entertainment. The gay scene is located in the historic downtown, south of Marien Platz and east of Sendlinger Straße.

❖ **SPECIAL EVENTS:** Munich loves to celebrate. The year starts with **Fasching** or the Carnival, then there are the famous **Starcbier** or the bock beer festivities, and during the year there are many more festivals and celebrations including the famous **Oktoberfest** the joyful beer drinking celebration that begins on the third Saturday in September and lasts until the first Sunday in October. 1996 dates: Sept. 21 - Oct. 6, 1996.

NOTE: During Oktoberfest it is impossible to book gay hotels in Munich, therefore if you

plan to visit Munich during Oktoberfest make your hotel reservations at least 6-4 months prior to your departure.

BARS Y RESTAURANTS ¶¶

● Bars/clubs (GM): **Bolt**, small leather bar, popular with Americans, Blumenstraße 15 (26-4323); **Cock**, leather bar, Augsburger Straße 21 (26-5995); **Fred's Pub**, dance bar with porno movies and shows, Reisinger Strasse 15 (266-138); **New York**, disco, Sonnenstraße 25 (59-1056); **Nil**, café bar, young crowd, Hans-Sachs-Straße 2 (26-5545); **Klimperkasten**, piano bar, Maistraße 28 (53-7639); **Morizz**, Klenzestraße 43 (201-6776); **Nil**, Hans-Sachs-Straße 2 (26-5545); **Ochsengarten**, leather bar, Müllerstraße 47 (266-446); **Pils-Stuben 2000**, bar, Dultstraße 1 (263-964); **Pop-As**, leather bar, Thalkirchner Straße 12 (260-9191); **Teddy Bar**, cruise leather bar, Hans-Sachs-Straße 1 (260-3359).

● Bars/clubs (GMW): **Mylord**, music bar, Ickstattstr. 2a (260-4448); **Prince**, Reichenbach-straße 55 (201-1655); **Soul-City**, dance club, Maximilianplatz 5 (553-301); **Together Again**, disco, show & cabaret, Müllerstraße 1 (263-469).

● Bars/clubs (GW): **Karotte**, dance bar, restaurant, Reichenbachstraße 37 (201-4294); **Na Und**, cocktail bar, Unterer Anger 16 (260-4304).

● Restaurants (GMW): **Deutsche Eiche**, (see hotel); **Girgl's Quelle**, Buttermelcherstrasse 9 (227-901); **Iwan**, bar & restaurant, Sonnenstr. 19 (554-933); **Sebastiansstubn**, Sebastianplatz 3 (260 4424). Others (AW): **Alois Dallmayr**, the most famous delicatessen, 14 Dienerstraße (21 35100); **Goldene Stadt**, famous Bavarian specialties, 44 Oberanger (26 4382); **Haxnbauer**, budget Bavarian restaurant, 5 Münz-straße (22 1922). To top your evening with local entertainment, check the sexy male strippers at **Die Spinne Cabaret**, Ringseisstraße 2 (53 5194).

λ SERVICES λ

● Cinema (GM): **Buddy**, gay cinema, Utzschneiderstraße 3 (26 8938).

● Health Club (GM): **City Sauna Club**, Lindwurmstraße 3 (265-554); **Dom Pedro**, sauna, solarium, massage, Fasaneriestr. 18 (129-3276); **TS 27**, Bavaria's largest sauna palace, Taunusstrße 27, 4th Fl. (359-7068).

● Leather: **Walter's Leder-Boutique**, Reichenbachstr. 40a (201-5062).

● Sex-Shop: **Cornelius Men**, leather and rubber sex boutique, Corneliusstraße 19 (201-4753); **Sex-World**, Sonnenstr. 12 (554-733).

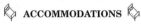 ACCOMMODATIONS

✪ HOTEL WALLIS

Schwanthalerstr. 8, Munich. USA/Canada reservations - Tel: (516) 944-5330 or (800) 257-5344. Fax: (516) 944-7540 or (800) 982-6571. TYPE: *Hotel*. CLIENTELE: All Welcome. LOCATION: Central near the Deutches Theater, Marienplatz, Main Station and Pedestrian Zone.

* Rooms: 54 w/priv. bath. Suites: 2
  4 sgl / 48 dbl / 2 triple
* Rooms for smokers and non smokers
* CTV, phone, radio, C/H
* Room & maid service, laundry, parking
* Bar: **Kerz'n Stübel** Bavarian style
* Airport: Franz-Joseph-Strauss
  35 km / 22 mi., direct connection to airport
* Train Station: 300 m /yards
* Metro: 50 m / 50 yards
* Gay bars: walking distance
* Season: Year round
* Rates: (US) $140- $260
  Suite: $190-$320 w/GbB
  higher rates during fairs and Oktoberfest
* Check in 12 noon / check out 12 noon
* *TAC:* 10% (from Odysseus)

DESCRIPTION: Nicely furnished Bavarian style hotel in a central location. Delicious breakfast buffet is served each morning. Very friendly atmosphere.

STUTTGART   ✆ 0711

✈ Echterdingen Airport (STR)

LOCATION: Southwestern Germany, near the Neckar Valley and a gateway to the Black Forest.

POPULATION: 650,000

CLIMATE: Very cold winters, specially in January when the temperatures are below freezing. Summers are generally in the 70"sF (21˚c).

DESCRIPTION: Stuttgart is the capital of the southwest German Federal State of Baden-Württemberg. It is a large, prosperous industrial center, the home of the famous Mercedes and Porsche automobiles. The city hosts many

hotel bergmeister

USA/Canada Reservations
(800) 257-5344

Tel: (516) 944-5330 • Fax: (516) 944-7540

important trade shows during the year. Stuttgart is an important art and culture center. The city is known for its excellent Opera, Philharmonic orchestra and ballet. This is also the third largest wine growing and producing region in Germany.

BARS ♀ RESTAURANTS 🍴

● Bars/clubs (GM): **Boots**, leather bar, Bopserstraße 9 (23-4764); **Eagle**, leather bar, Mozartsraße 51 (640-6183); **Eastend**, leather cruise bar, Haussmannstraße 235 (286-4702); **Kings Club**, disco, Calwer Straße 21 (22-4558); **Kings Pub**, Freidrichstraße / Boltzstraße (226-4127); **Monroe's**, Schulstraße 3 (226-2770).

● Bars/clubs (GMW): **Keller Küble**, Reuchlinstraße 12 (615-9744); **Laura Club**, dance club, Lautenschlagerstraße 20 (290-160); **Suspekt**, video bar, Ludwigstraße 55A (616-645).

● Bar (GW): **Lesbenkneipe**, bar and center, Kernerstaße 31 (296-432).

● Restaurants (GMW): **Café Janseitz**, coffee shop, Bebelstraße 25 (63-1303). Other (AW): **Alte Post**, old tavern, 43 Friedrichstraße (29 3079); **Ferensehturm**, good food, panoramic view, 120 Jahnstr., Degerloch suburb (24 6104).

λ SERVICES λ

● Health Club (GM): **Olympus Sauna,** Gerberstraße 11 (649-8919).

● Sex Shops (GM): **Binokel Sex Shop,** König-Karl-Straße 85 (569-347); **Insider Video,** MUohringer Srtaße 129 (649-4023).

ACCOMMODATIONS

AM WILHELMPLATZ
Wilhelmplatz 9, Stuttgart 70182. Tel: (711) 210241. USA/Canada reservations (800) 257-5344 or (516) 944-5330. Fax: (516) 944-7540. TYPE: *Hotel.* CLIENTELE: Gay Welcome. LOCATION: Central but quiet location. All rooms w/priv. bath, CTV, phone, minibar. Rates: $110-$160 w/CB.

✪ HOTEL BERGMEISTER

Rotenbergstraße 16, 70190 Stuttgart. Tel: (711) 283363. USA/Canada reservations (800) 257-5344 or (516) 944-5330. Fax: (516) 944-7540. TYPE: *Hotel.* CLIENTELE: Gay Welcome. LOCATION: Central but quiet location near Urachplatz.

* Rooms: 60 w/priv. bath
* CTV, phone, minibar, safe, balcony
* Room and maid service, laundry
* Fitness room, sauna, elevator, parking
* Hotel bar & restaurant
* Gay Bars: walking distance
* Airport: 30 min.

* Train Station: nearby
* Open: Year round
* Rates: $150-$220 w/CBb
* *TAC:* 10% (from Odysseus)

DESCRIPTION: Charming hotel with spacious guest rooms and modern and comfortable studio apartments. Tasteful decor and friendly staff.

WESTERLAND ✆ 4651

LOCATION: North Frisian Islands off the Schleswig Holstein coast and near the southern Danish border.

Ⴤ BARS Ⴤ

● Bars/clubs (GM): **Nanu,** Strandstrasse 23 (24-074); **Ringelspiel,** Andreas Dirkstrasse 2 (78-594); A mixed dance club for gay men and women is **Kleist-Casino,** Elisabethstrasse 1(24-228).

λ SERVICES λ

● Health Club (GM): **Gay Beach Club Sauna,** Bötticher Straße 3 (211-91).

ACCOMMODATIONS

MARIN HOTEL
Strand Straße 9, 25980 Westerland/Sylt. Tel: (4651) 92-800. TYPE: *Hotel.* CLIENTELE: Gay men. LOCATION: On the Strand. rooms w/priv. bath, CTV, bierbar. Season: summer only. Rates: on request.

GHANA

AREA: 92,099 sq. m. (238,536 sq. km)
POPULATION: 14,000,000
CAPITAL: Accra
CURRENCY: Ghana cedi (GC)
OFFICIAL LANGUAGE: Twi, Fante, English
MAJOR RELIGIONS: Tribal religions, Islam, Christianity
Telephone: 233
Nat'l Holiday: Independence Day, March 6
Official Time: G.M.T.
Electricity: 220 volts, 50 cycle AC
Exchange Rate: 1US$ = GC 1,407
National Airline: Ghana Airways

LAW REGARDING HOMOSEXUALITY: Homosexuality (male or female) is not mentioned in the Code of Law. Homosexual acts between men are punishable under the general sections concerning assault and rape. The society enjoys an uncomplicated open minded attitude towards sexual behavior.

ACCRA   ✆ 021

✈ Kotoka Airport (ACC) 11 km / 7 mi.

LOCATION: On the Gulf of Guinea and Gold Coast overlooking the Atlantic.

POPULATION: 1,200,000

CLIMATE: The rainy season is from April to June and in October.

Gay/Lesbian Visitor Information

Festus Owusu Sekyere
P.O.Box 282, Nkawkaw-E/R

DESCRIPTION: Large city spreading out in the English tradition. Getting around is a logistical hassle with few taxis around. Visit the **Harbour**, the colorful **Makola** market and the **National Museum**. The population is kind and friendly which compensate for the general atmosphere of chaos that prevails.

BARS Ⓨ RESTAURANTS ¶¶

There are no gay bars in the western sense, but some bars/clubs in international hotels can be of interest.

● Bars/clubs (G/S): **Ambassador Hotel Bars**, Independence Ave; **Apollo Theatre**, famous nightclub, **Blow Up**, restaurant & Nightclub (near Liberation Circle); **Keteke Club**, Osu R.E., 6th St.; **Lido Club**, Kokolemle; **Riviera Beach Club**, Black Star Square.

● Restaurants (AW): **Blow Up**, Lebanese/European (near Liberation Circle); **Maharaja**, Indian, Cantonments Rd. in front of Central Bus Station (772137); **Uncle Sam**, Kojo Thompson Rd.

❖ Gay Beaches: **Labadi Pleasure Beach** (near the Trade Fair); **Mark Cofie Tourist Beach**, Old Tema Rd; **Black Star Square Beach.**

🔷 ACCOMMODATIONS 🔷

AMBASSADOR HOTEL
Independence Ave., Accra. Tel: (21) 664646. Tlx: 2113. TYPE: *Hotel*. CLIENTELE: Mostly Straight. LOCATION: Central. 153 rooms w/priv. bath, bars. Rates: on request.

LABADI BEACH HOTEL
P.O. Box 1, Trade Fair, Accra. Tel: (21) 772-501. Fax: (21) 772-520. TYPE: *Hotel*. CLIENTELE: Mostly Straight. LOCATION: Great beach location with some gay action nearby. 104 rooms w/priv. bath, 4 suites, 15 min. from airport, A/C, phone, CTV, minibar, large balcony, pool, health center, restaurants and bars. Rates: (US) $165 - $380. *TAC:* 10%. DESCRIPTION: A 5-star hotel with world class comfort and amenities.

GREECE

AREA: 50,944 sq. mi. (131,945 sq. km)
POPULATION: 10,300,000
CAPITAL: Athens
CURRENCY: Drachme (DR)
OFFICIAL LANGUAGE: Greek
MAJOR RELIGIONS: 97% Greek Orthodox
Telephone: 30
Nat'l Holiday: Independence Day, Mar. 25
Official Time: G.M.T. + 2
Electricity: 220 volts
Exchange Rate: 1US$ = DR 233
National Airline: Olympic Airways

LAW REGARDING HOMOSEXUALITY:
Homosexuality is legal between adult men over
17. Homosexuality is discriminated against in
Greece in spite of the classic culture that considered homosexuality a well regarded lifestyle.
Many Greeks are bi-sexual, but will not admit
openly to be gay. There is a greater sense of freedom and tolerance on the island of Mykonos. The
main cities of Athens and Thessaloniki offer a
well established gay nightlife scene.

ALEXANDROUPOLIS ✆ 551

✈ Alexandroupolis Airport

DESCRIPTION: "Frontier" town and military
garrison close to the Turkish border. Good
beaches and popular Summer Festival. Many
lonely GI's. Locals are known for their erotic
prowess. Of interest to gay travelers: **Kokkina
vrachia (Red Rocks) beach**, some nudism;
The Park by the Waterfront at night; **Nea
Marki Beach** popular with conscripts. No
established gay nightlife in town. Bus service
to Istanbul (Turkey) about 5-6 hrs.

 **ACCOMMODATIONS**

ALEXANDER BEACH HOTEL
USA/Canada reservations call Odysseus (516)
944-5330 or (800) 257-5344. Fax: (516) 944-
7540 or (800) 982-6571. TYPE: *Resort Hotel*.
CLIENTELE: All Welcome. LOCATION: On a
beach, 1 km from downtown. 105 rooms w/priv.
bath, A/C, C/H, phone, CTV, minibar, balcony,
pool, free parking. Rates: on request.

ATHENS   ✆   1

✈ Helinikon Int'l Airport (ATH)

LOCATION: In Southeast Greece along the
Mediterranean Sea.

POPULATION: Metro: 4,350,000

CLIMATE: Mild Mediterranean climate year
round. Summers are hot with pleasant sea
breezes, average July temperature is 85°F
(29°c). Winters are windy, wet and cool with
average temperature for January of 50°F (10°c).

DESCRIPTION: Athens is a Mediterranean
city with rows of white cement houses, large
avenues, busy street cafes, interesting flea
markets, and countless souvenir gift shops
with modern replicas of ancient greek art.

Athens suffers from air pollution, which endan-
ger its historical monuments and disturbs the
life of locals and tourists. It is mainly a transit
destination for visitors who spend a few days in
Athens before proceeding to their favorite Greek
Islands eg. Mykonos, Santorini, Crete etc.

While in Athens discover the treasures of the
past: The **Acropolis**, built on a rock dominating the city, it is Athen's main tourist attraction. The **Acropolis Museum** tucked into the
northern end of the plateau has interesting
exhibits to help visitors visualize how the monument looked centuries ago; **The Agora**, at the
base of the Acropolis, was the center of Ancient
Athens business and commerce; **The Royal
Palace**, the home of the exiled King Constantine, a handsome French-style château, where
you can watch the colorful kilted soldiers per-
form their changing-of-the-guard ceremony;
The **Olympic Stadium**, a reconstruction in
white marble of an ancient stadium for the first
modern Olympic Games in 1896; **Lycabettus
Hill**, a limestone rock reaching 1000 ft. (300 m)
into the sky with an interesting white church at
the top. Take the funicular ride to enjoy a
panoramic view of the city and its environment.

If you like museums visit: **National Archeological Museum** - 1 Tositsa St., for the great treasures of Ancient Greek arts; **National Gallery** - 46 Vassilis Sofias Ave. for classic and contemporary paintings.

To absorb Greek colors visit the **Plaka** - a restored quarter on the northern slope of the Acropolis with tavernas, live entertainment and Bouzouki music and dance. Most of the Athens gay scene is now located at the fashionable **Kolonaki** area Around **Kolonaki** and **Syntagma Squares** are the main shopping centers and **Tsakalof St.** running off Kolonaki Square is Athens' most exciting shopper's street. For authentic Mediterranean ambience try the giant **Flea Market** centering on **Pendrossou St.**

The gay scene is centered at the Kolonaki area between the National Garden and the Likavitós. Kolonaki is residential with a chic, upscaled flavor. The famous cafés around Kolonaki Square have always attracted the young, the upper middle classes, and the fashionable gay crowds.

❖ Gay Beach: **"Limanakia" Beach**, just before Varkiza on the Saronic Coast, much action during the summer. Buses leave from the beginning of Marnis St., close to Vathis Square for Varkiza.

❖ SPECIAL EVENTS: **World Games** during August 1997. Accommodations will be scarce in Athens in August. Make your hotel reservations in Athens early 1997 at least 4-6 weeks in advance. Odysseus has great hotels in Athens so give us a call at (800) 257-5344 or (516) 944-5330. Fax: (516) 944-7540. Email: odyusa @odyusa.com.

BARS Ⓨ RESTAURANTS 🍴

● Bars/clubs (GM): **Alekos Island**, the oldest and friendliest gay bar in Athens, open daily: 10:30pm-2:00a, 42 Tsakalof, Kolonaki; **Alexander's**, late night cruise bar/disco, great atmosphere on week-ends, open: 11:00 pm - 4:00 am 44 Anagnostopoulou St., Kolonaki, (364-6660); **City Club**, popular western style gay club, 2 bars and large dance floor, 4 Koryzi St., off Vourvachi St., at the beginning of Syngrou Ave. (924-0740); **Dom**, Gothic style, mixed clientele, 112 Pireos & 31 Ikarieon St., Gazi; **Endechomeno**, Greek music, 5 Lembesi St. near the beginning of Syngrou St.; **Erection Club**, good shows and theme parties, 6 Trion Ierarchon St., Gefira Poulopoulou, Thession (342-0357); **Factory**, high energy dance club, go-go

boys, dark room, 116 Ermou St., entrance from Thessalonikis St. (345-6187); **Flying In**, best gay bar in Piraeus, Greek fun and drag shows after 1am, G. 34 Charilaou Trikoupi St. (453-3993); **Granazi**, greek music, 20 Lembesi St., off the beginning of Syngrou Ave. (325-3979); **Koukles**, behind Olympic Airways, Zan Moreas St. (921-3054); **Lambda**, Lembesti St., off Syngrou Ave. (922-4202); **Lizard**, neo-classical style club, 31 Apostolou Pavlou St., near Thesseion Square; **Oval**, Cafe by day and bar by night, frequented by the underground Athenian intellectual elite, 5 Tosita St. behind the National Archeological Museum on Patission St. (Exarcheia Square); **Porta**, pleasant bar, friendly atmosphere, 10 Phalirou, Makryianni; **Spyros**, popular, open late, Vourvachi St. begining of Syngrou Ave. (922-3982); **Ta Pedia**, popular, packed on weekends, 5 Lembesi St., below "Endechomeno"; **Test Me**, bar with regular mature clientele, 64 Pipinou St., Plateia Viktorias (822-6029); **Underwear**, opposite Hellenikon airport, local Summer tease.

● Bars/clubs (GW): **Alexander's**, fashionable dance club, mostly men but lesbians are welcome, 42 Anagnostopoulou St. (Kolonaki) (364-6660); **Mexico**, dance club popular with lesbians, 249 Thisseos St., at Malachia. Kallithea (951-0075); **Odyssia**, relaxed bar popular with lesbians, Greek music, 116 Ermou St., Thession.

● Restaurants (AW): **Grisgrago Cafe**, Odos Daidalou and Aggios (Plaka); **Dimokritos**, good tavern in a convenient location, 23 Dimokritou St. & Tsakalof (Kolonaki) (361-3588); **Dionyssos**, Greek specialties, good stop for a drink with a panoramic view, Mt. Lycabettus, accessible by the funicular, above Kolonaki Sq. (722 6374); **Ellinikon** (ΕΛΛΗΝΙΚΟΝ), excellent pastry shop, Kolonaki Square 19-20 (360-1858); **Fortouna**, excellent seafood, An. Polemou 22, Kolonaki (722-1282); **Kirki**, coffee shop just below "Lizard" popular in the evenings, 31 Apostolou Pavlou St.; **Montparnasse**, famous restaurant & bar, excellent cuisine, 32 Haritos St. (Kolonaki) (729-0746); **Neon**, self-service cafeteria, Omonia Sq. also in Tsakaloff St. (Kolonaki) and Gr. Labraki St., near the Square in Piraeus; **Oval**, Cafe by day and bar by night, frequented by the underground Athenian intellectual elite, 5 Tosita St. behind the National Archeological Museum on Patission St. (Exarcheia Square); **Stagecoach**, American Steakhouse, 6 Loukianou, Kolonaki (723-7902) moderately priced.

Note: **Kolonaki Square** is only a few blocks from the National Gardens and Syntagma, just off Vassilis Sofias. Here is the authentic meet-

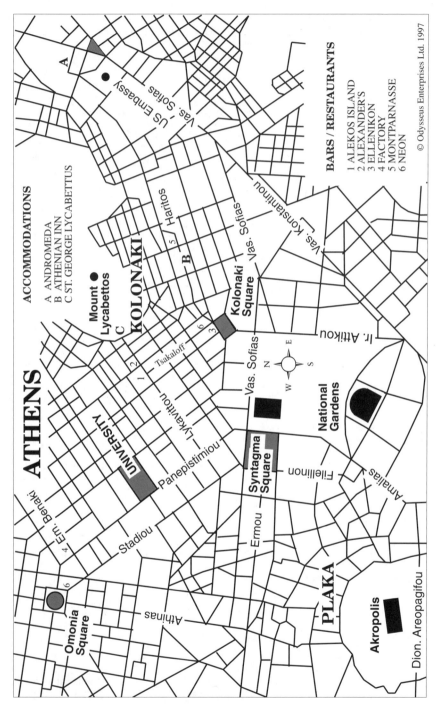

ATHENS

ACCOMMODATIONS

A ANDROMEDA
B ATHENIAN INN
C ST. GEORGE LYCABETTUS

BARS / RESTAURANTS

1 ALEKOS ISLAND
2 ALEXANDER'S
3 ELLENIKON
4 FACTORY
5 MONTPARNASSE
6 NEON

© Odysseus Enterprises Ltd. 1997

KOLONAKI

Mount
Lycabettos

Kolonaki
Square

National
Gardens

Syntagma
Square

UNIVERSITY

Omonia
Square

PLAKA

Akropolis

US Embassy

Vas. Sofias

Haritos

Vas. Sofias

Vas. Konstantinou

Ir. Attikou

Vas. Sofias

Tsakaloff

Lykavittou

Panepistimiou

Stadiou

Athinas

Em. Benaki

Ermou

Fillellinon

Amalias

Dion. Areopagifou

ing place where Athenians sip coffee, chat with their friends, and do their shopping.

λ SERVICES λ

● Adult Movies (G/S): **Athenaikon**, exclusive gay films, Plateia Dimarchiou (Kotzia) behind the Town Hall, Fri-Sat. 22:00 - 3:00 am; **Omonia**, gay cinema, Santovriandou St., (behind Omonia Square); **Star** (ΣTAP), the closest thing to a dark room in Greece, action on first and second floors, 10 Agiou Konstantinou St. (Omonia Square).

● Health Clubs (GM): **Athens Relax**, 3 floors of Greek action, 8 Xouthou St., (near Omonia Square, take a right at Sokratous St. and follow it down till you reach Xouthou) (522-2866); **Ira Baths**, 4 Zinonos St. (near Omonia Square) (523-4964).

● Videos (GM): **Videorama**, large selection of gay videos, 1 Emmanuil Benaki St., & Stadiou St. (2nd Fl.) open 10-22 (321-4738).

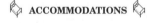 **ACCOMMODATIONS**

✪ ANDROMEDA ATHENS

Mavili Square, Athens. Information & Reservations: Odysseus Enterprises Tel: (516) 944-5330 or (800) 257-5344, Fax: (516) 944-7540 or (800) 982-6571. TYPE: *Deluxe Hotel*. CLIENTELE: Gay Welcome. LOCATION: Fashionable neighborhood of Athens near the US Embassy off Vassilis Sofia.

* Rooms: 17 w/priv. bath
* Suites: 9; 1 w/cooking facilities
* Studios: 4 (one-bedroom apartments)
* CTV, minibar, phone A/C, C/H, balcony
* Restaurant: **Michaelangelo** (Italian)
  open: lunch 13:00-15:00 / dinner 20:30-00:30
  breakfast buffet; 7:00am-10:00am
* Bar: mixed clientele
* Conference/banquet room, exercise room, laundry facilities
* Maid & room service, valet parking
* Beach: 10 km / 6 mi.
* Gay Bars: 5 min. by taxi
* Airport: 10 km / 6 mi., taxi, limo
* Open: Year round
* Rates: $190 - $390 w/AB
  Suites and Penthouse Rates on request
* **TAC:** 10% (from Odysseus)

DESCRIPTION: Exclusive, intimate boutique 5-star hotel offering the finest amenities and service. Rooms and suites are elegantly furnished and decorated. Highly recommended for

HOTEL FENIX

10 min. from the airport
Friendly hotel
comfortable rooms

USA/Canada reservations
(800) 257-5344

Tel: (516) 944-5330 • Fax: (516) 944-7540

GLYFADA - ATHENS

sophisticated travelers that need the very best. Quite, private and dignified. Special prices and warm welcome extended for Odysseus customers. *See color photos in the Travel Supplement*.

✪ ATHENIAN INN

22 Haritos St., Kolonaki. US/Canada Reservations: Odysseus (516) 944-5330 or (800) 257-5344. Fax: (516) 944-7540 or (800) 982-6571. TYPE: *Hotel*. CLIENTELE: Equal gay/straight. LOCATION: In the fashionable Kolonaki residential area, 2 blocks from Kolonaki Square, near the local gay scene.

* Rooms: 28 w/private bath or shower
  3 sgl / 22 dbl / 3 triple. Suites available
* Smoking allowed in rooms
* CTV, phone, C/H, A/C, safe box
  (CTV in room is available for extra charge)
* Cafeteria & bar
* Maid service, laundry service, elevator
* Gay Bars: walking distance
* Health Club: near Omonia
* Airport: 1/2 hour, taxi
* Open: Year round
* Rates: (US) $75 - $120
* Check in 12:30 / check out 12:30
* **TAC:** 10% (from Odysseus)

DESCRIPTION: 6-story Inn with rustic, stucco interiors. Breakfast lounge with CTV. Rooms have large double or twin beds, private showers, some with balcony and view of the Lycabettus Hill. Short walk to Kolonaki Square. *See color photos in the special Travel Supplement.*

✪ FENIX HOTEL

Glyfada, Athens. USA and Canada reservation/ information Tel: (516) 944-5330 or (800) 257-5344, Fax: (516) 944-7540 or (800) 982-6571. TYPE: *Hotel.* CLIENTELE: All Welcome. LOCATION: On Fleming Square, near Hellinikon AP, 10 mi. / 15 km from the center of Athens.

* Rooms: 138 w/priv. bath
* CTV, phone, hair dryer, balcony, A/C, C/H
* Restaurant, coffee shop, cocktail lounge swimming pool, free parking
* Beach: 200 m / yds
* Airport: 3 km / 2 mi., taxi
* Open: Year round
* Rates: (US) $75 - $140 w/CB
* *TAC:* 10% (from Odysseus)

DESCRIPTION: Moderate first class resort hotel near the Hellinikon International Airport. Large comfortable superior rooms and suites some with king size bed and balcony. Recommended for travelers who need to stay overnight close to the airport for early morning connection.

✪ ST. GEORGE LYCABETTUS

Lycabettus Hill, Athens. USA and Canada reservation/ information Tel: (516) 944-5330 or (800) 257-5344, Fax: (516) 944-7540 or (800) 982-6571. TYPE: *Hotel.* CLIENTELE: All Welcome. LOCATION: At foot of the Lycabettus Hill walk to Kolonaki bars, clubs and restaurants.

* Rooms: 162 w/priv. bath. Suites: 5
* CTV, phone, minibar, balcony (most)
* Room & maid service, laundry, parking
* Wheelchair access
* Rooftop pool, sun terrace, restaurants, bar
* Gay Bars: walking distance
* Health Club: near Omonia
* Airport: 1/2 hour, taxi
* Open: Year round
* Rates: (US) $210 - $660
* Check in 12:30 / check out 12:30
* *TAC:* 10% (from Odysseus)

DESCRIPTION: Deluxe hotel with Byzantine, Victorian and Greek art decorations throughout. Beautiful rooms and suites, some with panoramic views of the Acropolis. During the summer months enjoy rooftop swimming with refreshments served by the pool. Gourmet dining available at "Le Grand Balcon".

PATRAS   ⓒ   061

LOCATION: In northern Peloponese.

DESCRIPTION: The capital city and the largest town in the Peloponnese; the second major port of Greece (after Piraeus) connecting Greece with Italy, Yugoslavia and Turkey via boats and ferries, as well as some Ionian Islands. The ferry agents, railroad station and main KTEL bus station are all grouped on the harbor road Othonos Amalías. Patras is famous for its carnival before Lent, and it is a major destination for many incoming and outgoing tourists who are Italy bound. For gay travelers the cruising areas include: **Kolokotroni St.,** between Agiou Andreou and Othonos Amalias opposite the Railroad Station; The small square between Gounari, Kanari and Othonos Amalias St.. ❖ Gay Beach: **Kalgorias Beach**, behind the sand dunes (summer only); **Irminis Baths** summer only.

BARS 𝖸 RESTAURANTS 🍴

● Bar (GM): **Morgana**, 5 Paparrigopoulou St., off Riga Fereou St.

● Restaurants (AW): check out the tavernas and fast food places around Othonos Amalias and Ayiou Andhréou; **Psari**, good seafood taverna, Ayios Dhimitrios 75, open evenings.

ACCOMMODATIONS 🔑

GALAXY HOTEL
9 Agiou Nikolau, Patras. USA/Canada reservations call Odysseus Tel: (516) 944-5330 or (800) 257-5344. Fax: (516) 944-7540 or (800) 982-6571. TYPE: *Hotel.* CLIENTELE: All Welcome. LOCATION: Near harbor. 53 rooms and suites, priv. bath, A/C, C/H, room service, bar, free parking. Rates: on request.

PORTO RIO HOTEL
Rion, Patras. USA/Canada reservations call Odysseus Tel: (516) 944-5330 or (800) 257-5344. Fax: (516) 944-7540 or (800) 982-6571. TYPE: *Beach Hotel.* CLIENTELE: All Welcome. LOCATION: Convenient to Piers and ferry to Italy. 209 rooms w/priv. bath, 48 bungalows w/priv. garden, phone, A/C, minibar, pool, health center, free parking. Rates: on request.

λ SERVICES λ

● **Adult Movies (G/S): Armonia**29 Kitsou Tzavela & Agias Triados; **Ermis**, 58 Agias Sofias Str.

THESSALONIKI   ✆ 031

✈ Thessaloniki Airport (SKG)
10 mi. / 16 km southeast

LOCATION: In the northern province of Macedonia.

DESCRIPTION: Thessaloniki is a modern coastal city with a glorious history and beautiful natural setting. Also known as Salonika, it is the second largest city in Greece. The capital of Macedonia was the historic center of the Hellenic Empire under Alexander the Great. At the end of the 15th century it became home for Jews expelled from Portugal and Spain, and by the early 1900 Jews made up large part of the population and contributed to the cultural heritage of the city. Most of the Jewish community perished under the Nazi occupation of WWII. Visit the **Archeological Museum** for fascinating perspective on Macedonian history; the **Old Jewish Villas** now houses a Folk Museum and a municipal gallery. A short day tour is recommended to **Pella**, the ancient capital of Macedonia some 25 mi. / 40 km away.

The gay scene is located near **Vardari Square** and at the Park surrounding the **Zoological Garden**. At **Vardari Square** you can also find some cheap hotels that rent by the hour if interested. **"Kalachari"** bordered by Stratou Ave., and the new Byzantine Museum is an open car parking where some gay cruising is taking place (AYOR). Also check out the fashionable cafes on Nikis Avenue (on waterfront) "Thermaikos", "Achillion", "Issalos", "Iguana", "En Plo" and "Aroma".

BARS ☿ RESTAURANTS 🍴

● **Bars/clubs (GM): Ahududu**, drag shows, trendy, 3 Halkis St., Vas. Georgiou area (836-444); **Bachalo**, 6 Romanou Str., behind Dore (268.637); **Factory**, 51 Prox. Koromila St., trendy; **Taboo**, best gay bar in town, Kastritsiou St., off Agias Sophias St. (279-132).

● **Bar/club (GMW): Funky Mobile**, fashionable dance club, 29 Papandreou Str.

● **Restaurants (G/S): Bazaar**, coffee shop near Taboo bar, Kastritsiou St., off Agias Sophias St.; **Cyprus Corner**, atmospheric restaurant, classic Greek cuisine at the hilltop suburb of Panorama, Komninon 16, Panorama (941-220); **De Facto**, opposite cinema Ilisia, cafe-bar, jazz music, many artists and writers, 17 Pavlou Mela St.; **Ta Nissia**, seafood and *Mezedes*, Koromila 13 (285-991).

λ SERVICES λ

● **Adult Movies (G/S): Laikon**, Vardari Square area; **Vilma**, good action in the balcony, Diokitriou St., at plateia Vardari (Square).

● **Video Club (G/S): Rouge**, 67 Tsimiski St., Mon.-Fri. 11-23.

ACCOMMODATIONS

CAPSIS HOTEL
28 Onastirou St., Thessaloniki. Tel: (31) 521-321. TYPE: *Hotel.* CLIENTELE: All Welcome. LOCATION: Commercial district, near museums and ancient monuments.

* Rooms: 428 w/priv. bath
* CTV, mini bar, hair dryer, A/C, C/H
* Restaurants, bar, roof garden w/pool health studio, gym, sauna
* Airport: 16 km / 10 mi., taxi
* Open: Year round
* Rates: $120 - $190
* *TAC:* 10%

DESCRIPTION: Three star hotel with business class comfort and amenities.

EL GRECO
23 Egnatia, Thessaloniki. Tel: (31) 520-620. TYPE: *Hotel.* CLIENTELE: All Welcome. LOCATION: City center, 600 m / yards to train station. 90 rooms w/priv. bath, A/C, restaurant, bar. Rates: $75-$130.

THE GREEK ISLANDS

There are six groups of Greek Islands according to their geographical position and proximity to each other. Each group is connected with the mainland by ferry service or flight by **Olympic Airlines** via Athens Airport. There are scheduled ferry, catamaran and hydrofoil connections between the islands of each group. However, it is more complicated to switch from one group of islands to another. Very often the

FOR THE BEST GREEK ISLANDS VACATION
CALL: (800) 257-5344
Tel: (516) 944-5330 • Fax: (516) 944-7540
Email: odyusa@odyusa.com

only way is to do it via Athens or Piraeus.

★ Group #1: **The Ionian Islands**, located off the western coast of Greece in the Ionian Sea, include: **Zakynthos, Cephalonia, Ithaca, Lefkas, Paxos, Corfu.**

★ Group #2: **The Argo-Saronic Islands**, located off-shore from Piraeus and the Peloponnisos, include: **Aegina, Poros, Hydra, Spetses.**

★ Group #3: **The Cyclades**, the classic islands of the Aegean Sea: **Andros, Kea, Tinos, Syros, Mykonos, Kithnos, Naxos, Paros, Sifnos, Milos, Folegandros, Santorini, Ios.**

★ Group #4: **The Dodecanese Islands**, off the western coast of Turkey: **Karapathos, Rhodes, Halki, Tilos, Symi, Astipalaia, Nissyrnos, Kos, Kalymnos, Leros, Patmos, Lipsi.**

★ Group #5: **The North and East Aegean Islands**, off the northwestern Turkish coast and the Macedonian coast: **Ikaria, Samos, Chios, Lesbos, Lemnos, Samothraki, Thassos.**

★ Group #6: **The Sporades Islands**: off the eastern mainland coast: **Skyros, Skopelos, Alonissos, Skiathos.**

CLIMATE: Mild Mediterranean. Monthly temperatures are as follows: January 45°F-54°F (7°c-12°c); February 45°F-56°F (7°c-14°c); March 47°F-58°F (8°c-14°c); April 53°F-66°F (12°c-19°c); May 59°F-74°F (15°c-23°c); June 66°F-81°F (19°c-27°c); July 71°F-86°F (22°c-30°c); August 71°F-86°F (22°c-30°c); September 66°F-79°F (19°c-26°c); October 61°F-73°F (16°c-23°c); November 54°F-64°F (12°c-18°c); December 49°F-58°F (9°c-14°c).

❖ **TRAVEL SEASON INFORMATION:** The season on the Greek Islands is from April to mid-October with slight modifications depending on the island. **The high season is July - September** when the sea water temperature is just right and the evenings are warm and pleasant. As Europe goes on holiday from the third weekend of July through the end of August millions of Europeans (Italians, French & Germans) visit the islands and independent travel during high season is extremely difficult.

If you plan to vacation during the high season make your reservations as early as possible, at least 3 months before your departure. Also bear in mind that flights to and between the islands get very quickly booked up during high season, therefore make your airline reservations as soon as possible.

Although there are rapid boats, ferries and boat connections between the islands they are not as reliable as the flights and are subject to cancellation if the sea conditions are not favorable.

CHIOS © 0271

✈ Chios Airport

LOCATION: Eastern Aegean island, southwest of Lesvos near the Turkish Coast.

DESCRIPTION: Colonized by the Ionians in the 8th century, Chios had a long and tumultuous history as it was dominated by several regional powers. In 1822 the island was devastated by a massacre by the Turks and by an earthquake in 1881 which completed the destruction. Today, Chios offers a bustling capital on the east coast. Near Vrontado there is a monument to Homer, the author of the Odyssey, who according to sources was born on Chios. Unique to Chios are the fascinating *masticohora* fortified villages in the south of the island from the 14th and 15th centuries; they produced mastic for the courts and harems for the ruling Turks. Chios beaches are accessible by car or boat. The island has some gay life in winter and summer. Conscripts and locals are very friendly.

❖ Gay Beach: Check out the **Emborio** pebble beach in the south and **Daskalopetra** nudist beach; **Nagos Beach** at **Kardamyla**.

BARS ♈ RESTAURANTS 🍴

● Bars/Discos (G/S): **Graffiti**, bar; **Kahloua Cafe, No Name**, coffee shop; **Sail Inn**, bar.

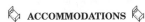
ACCOMMODATIONS

VILLA ARGENTIKON
Chios. USA/Canada reservations call Odysseus Tel: (516) 944-5330 or (800) 257-5344. Fax: (516) 944-7540 or (800) 982-6571. TYPE: Scenic Country Estate. CLIENTELE: All Welcome. LOCATION: Scenic location surrounded by walls. 6 suites, 3 villas in beautiful medieval Genovese architecture. Garden restaurant for dinners by candlelight. Rates: on request.

CORFU © 0661

✈ Kerkyra Airport (CFU)

LOCATION: Northern Ionian Islands off the northwestern coast of Greece.

POPULATION: 30,000

DESCRIPTION: Greek Island with a 14th century Venetian-style city capital, and distinguished British and French influences. The island's reputation started with Homer, who called it *'The beloved island of the gods'*, where the shipwrecked Odysseus was entertained by the lovely Nausica (a classic drag queen?). Today, modern Corfu is flooded with tourists, mostly the 'unsophisticated' kind from Great Britain. It is overcrowded, noisy and commercialized during high season. Visit: The **New** and the **Old Port**; **The Esplanade**, a large public square, garden and promenade; **Corfu Casino** is open year round at the **Achilleion Palace**; and the many charming island churches and monasteries.

❖ Beaches: **Agios Ioannis Peristeron** near **Benitses**; **Alekos Baths**, mixed beach close to the city; **Myrtiotissa** nudist beach near **Pelekas**.

❖ **HOW TO GET THERE**: by air charter flights from European cities (london, Geneva, Milan, Düsseldorf, Stuttgart & Frankfurt); by sea - daily ferry from Brindisi (Italy) 8 hrs., in the summer from Igoumenitsa every 1 1/2 hrs. (2 hrs.); twice daily from Paxos (3 hrs.), and daily from Ithaca (6 hrs.). There are two ferry boats a week Corfu -Piraeus and return. The voyage takes 18 hrs.

BARS ♈ RESTAURANTS ╟

● Bar/Disco (GM): **Blue Bar**, Emporiko Kentro, Ethnikis Anisteos, in the commercial centre of town; **Hippodrome**, in the centre, disco (43150); **Sweet Movie**, cosmopolitan bar, Agios Ioannis, close to Benitses (92335).

● Restaurants (AW): **Averof**, popular with locals and tourists, on the Esplanade; **Gisdakis**, Greek Island dishes, budget, near San Rocco Square.

⬙ ACCOMMODATIONS ⬙

GRECOTEL KOMENO BAY
Komeno Bay, Corfu 491 00. Tel: (0661) 9-1481. TYPE: *Resort Hotel*. CLIENTELE: Mostly Straight. LOCATION: Beachfront hotel 6 mi. (10 km) from Corfu Town. 308 rooms, 8 suites, bungalows, phone, CTV, A/C, restaurants, bars, disco. DESCRIPTION: Beachfront superior first class resort complex. An upscaled accommodations choice.

HILTON INT'L CORFU
P.O. Box 124, Kanoni, Corfu 491 00. Tel: (0661) 3-6540. Telex: 332148 HILT GR. Fax: (0661) 3-6540. TYPE: *Deluxe Hotel*. CLIENTELE: Mostly Straight. LOCATION: Hillside complex overlooking the sea and islands, 15 min. from town. 256 bungalows/suites w/priv. bath. DESCRIPTION: Deluxe hillside complex overlooking the sea and islands. Good choice for the upscaled.

KOMMENO VILLAS
Kommeno Bay, Corfu. USA/Canada reservations: Odysseus (516) 944-5330 or (800) 257-5344. Fax: (516) 944-7540 or (800) 982-6571. TYPE: *Villas*. CLIENTELE: All Welcome. LOCATION: In a large Olive Grove with magnificent seaview. 6 individual houses built in traditional island style, near Dassia in the vicinity of deluxe hotels. Every apartment is fully equipped with kitchen, private terrace or balcony. 7 twin-bed apartments with living room (sleeping 4-5) and 9 studios (sleeping 2-3). *TAC:* 10% (from Odysseus).

CRETE

✈ Heraklion Airport (HER)

HANIA   ℰ   0821

✈ Hania Airport (CHQ) 14 km / 9 mi.

LOCATION: 120 km / 75 mi. west of Heraklion, and 59 km / 37 mi. from Rethymnon the island's oldest inhabited city, on the beautiful western shore.

POPULATION: 45,000

DESCRIPTION: Hania is Crete's second largest city, a spiritual center, and a former capital. It is a charming town with a picture perfect Venetian harbor, artistic quarters and wonderful sandy beaches. Hania has the most bi-sexual population on the island. Visit the **Kastéli** the site of the town earliest Venetian and Turkish habitation; the inner (eastern) harbor; and the modern city. The Old City is a showcase of well-preserved traditional houses from many eras. For fine leather goods and genuine articles of Cretan folk art visit the **"Stivanadika"** (Schridolph St.).

❖ Gay cruising takes place at **Dimotikos**

Kipos, a public garden with small zoo and cafeteria near the Stadium, corner of Dimokratias & Valaoritou Sts.

❖ Beaches: all the beaches lie to the west of the city. The "Gay Beach" with its sand dunes and action is a short distance west of the town between the tavern and a holiday complex. The City Beach is only ten-minute walk, but for good sandy beach take the local bus to **Kalamáki Beach**.

BARS ♟ RESTAURANTS 🍴

● The nightlife is concentrated in the old town near the port area. Check **Adriani**, popular disco, Akti Tompazi 20, adjacent to the Port Police; **Canale**, dance club, young crowds, mostly tourists, Venetian Port (55527); **Dio Lux**, cafe bar beyond Neoria, mixed; **Faggoto**, the oldest and most authentic American style bar in town, jazz music, mixed clientele, 16 Angellou St., (57487); **Mythos**, meeting place of freaks from all over the world, rock music of the sixties, Venetian Harbour; **Nemesis**, youthful bar with good music and noisy atmosphere, Venetian Port (45828).

● Restaurants (AW): **Mathios**, grilledseafood, one of the oldest restaurants in town, right on the sea, Venetian Port (54291); **Elizabeth**, Seafood and great selection of cretan wines, Venetian Port (29150); **Tamam**, old Turkish hammam converted into restaurant, excellent home-like cuisine, 49 Zambeliou St. (58639).

 ACCOMMODATIONS

○ CASA DELFINO

Old Town, Hania. USA and Canada Information or Reservations: Odysseus (516) 944-5330, or (800) 257-5344. Fax: (516) 944-7540 or (800) 982-6571. TYPE: *All Suite Hotel*. CLIENTELE: All Welcome. LOCATION: Heart of the Old Town and the Venetian Harbor.

* Suites: 12 w/priv. bath
* VIP Suites: 4
* Phone, refrigerator, cooking facilities
* Maid & room service, fully A/C
* Beach: gay beach nearby
* Gay Bars: some mixed bars nearby
* Airport: 15 min. taxi
* Open: Year round
* Rates: $120-$180
* *TAC:* 10% (from Odysseus)

DESCRIPTION: Luxurious and independent apartments-suites, each with its own individ-

Luxurious lodge in the Old Town of Chania

CASA DELFINO
(800) 257-5344
Tel: (516) 944-5330 • Fax: (516) 944-7540

Halepa Hotel

Historic hotel in a quiet residential area near beaches and nightlife

USA/Canada Reservations
(800) 257-5344
Tel: (516) 944-5330 • Fax: (516) 944-7540
Email: odyusa@odyusa.com

ual touch in a renovated 17th century Venetian Palace, an historic monument in Old Town. Very beautiful, romantic and friendly. VIP Suites are spacious two bedroom units with full bath with jacuzzi, some with private terrace/ roof garden.

✪ HALEPA HOTEL

El. Venizelou Str., Hania. USA/Canada Information/Reservations: Odysseus (516) 944-5330, or (800) 257-5344. Fax: (516) 944-7540 or (800) 982-6571. TYPE: *Hotel.* CLIENTELE: All Welcome. LOCATION: Coastal road to Hania in the elegant Halepa district, 10 min. from Hania city center.

* Rooms: 46 rooms w/priv. bath
* 2 VIP suites
* Phone, radio, A/C, private parking
* Dining room, bar, garden, sun terrace
* Gay Bars: some nearby
* Beach: 50 m / yards
* Airport: 20 min.
* Open: Year round
* Rates: (US) $80-$160
* *TAC:* 10% (from Odysseus)

DESCRIPTION: Renovated 19th century historical hotel in a beautiful historical suburb of Hania. The New Classical building was used as the British Embassy to Crete during the period of Cretan democracy. Accommodations include standard rooms with twin beds, and traditional rooms which are larger and have large double beds. The hotel is close to the sea within walking distance to the beach.

HERAKLION   ✆ 081

✈ Heraklion Airport (HER)

LOCATION: Central north coast of Crete.

POPULATION: 90,000

DESCRIPTION: Heraklion is the capital of Crete, Greece's largest island, and the famous island of *Zorba the Greek*. Crete is ancient and modern. Here lie the ruins of Europe's first civilization, the Minoan, so wonderfully sophisticated and peaceful (the only weapons archeologist have found in the palace date from the later Mycenaean period). Heraklion is the central point for transport in Crete, with its busy international harbor and airport. **Heraklion's Archeological Museum** has the world's greatest collection of Minoan artifacts, and the **Grand Palace of Knossos** is only a short drive away. The Vene-

tians have left their mark on some of Crete's finest public buildings and churches.

❖ Gay Beach: **Chersonissos Nissaras**, Sissi Beach, nudism.

❖ **HOW TO GET THERE**: By Air - fly from Athens to Heraklion via Olympics domestic flight, also direct flights from London, and few flights a week from Rhodes, Santorini & Mykonos. By Boat - Crete is connected daily with Piraeus (12 hrs.), Karpathos (5 hrs.), Santorini (6 hrs.), and Kythera (4 hrs.); also ships from Alexandria (Egypt), Cyprus, Haifa (Israel) and Brindisi (Italy) call at Heraklion port once a week.

BARS ☿ RESTAURANTS ¶¶

● Bars/clubs (GM) are bars are mixed and located in Vanizelou Square: **Aman Café**; **Take Five** and the **Athina Disco**, Plateia Venizelou; **Atrium**, disco, behind the inter-city bus station (KTEL); **Flash**, packed in summer, at Korai Square; **Trapeza**, the gayest disco in town, at Bofor str; **Vavel**, beyond agios Titos

● Restaurants (AW): **Glasshouse**, fashionable Italian restaurant near the Xenia Hotel; **Victoria Pizza Café**, Plateia Eleftherias & Daedalou Street.

✑ ACCOMMODATIONS ✑

HOTEL ATLANTIS

Merambellou str., Heraklion, Crete. Tel: (081) 229-103. USA/Canada reservations: call Odysseus (516) 944-5330 or (800) 257-5344. Fax: (516) 944-7540. TYPE: *Hotel.* CLIENTELE: All Welcome. LOCATION: Downtown near the famous Minoan Museum.

* Rooms: 160 w/private bath. Suites: 4
  126 dbl / 34 single
* CTV, phone, balcony, A/C, C/H, minibar
  terrace (98 rooms), free safe box
* Rooftop garden with swimming pool
* 24 hour room service
* Restaurant, lounges, and bar
* Free off-street parking
* Airport: 8 km / 5 miles, taxi
* Season: open all year
* Rates: (US) $80-$140
* *TAC:* 10% (from Odysseus)

DESCRIPTION: Class A hotel with an air of restfulness while being in the town center. Gracious rooms with comfortable full bath with luxury amenities. A stone throw away from the Minoan Museum. Superb views of the harbour and the sea.

HYDRA   ✆   **0298**

No Airport or cars on the Island. The Island is only accessible by ferry or hydrofoil from Piraeus.

LOCATION: The Saronic Gulf Islands, about 1-1/2 hrs. by hydrofoil from Piraeus.

POPULATION: 2,000; 20,000 (summer)

DESCRIPTION: Small picturesque island and art colony within an easy reach from Piraeus. Hydra town is a charming steep-sided port known for its yacht marina, symmetry and clear, bright light. It is fashionable and expensive with chic boutiques, restaurants and cocktail bars. Since the 1960's Hydra has become a major destination for artists, jet-setters and movie stars.

 ACCOMMODATIONS

ORLOFF HOTEL
Hydra, Greece. Information/Reservations (USA/Canada) Tel: (516) 944-5330 or (800) 257-5344. Fax: (516) 944-7540. TYPE: *Guest House.* CLIENTELE: All Welcome. LOCATION: Central near the Port. 10 rooms w/priv. or shared bath, garden, bar, 200 m / yards to port. Season: year round. Rates: (US) \$110-\$190. *TAC:* 10%. DESCRIPTION: Restored old mansion. Hydra's finest and most elegant guest house. All rooms are unique and individually decorated.

IOS   ✆   **0286**

No Airport on the Island. The Island is accessible by boat from Athens, Santorini or Mykonos.

LOCATION: Cyclades north of Santorini. Ios can be easily reached from Santorini via boat or catamaran. The trip takes about 1-1/2 hrs. Take the Vantouris Sea Line and avoid the Ios Express.

POPULATION: 2,000

DESCRIPTION: Young people's paradise, the Island of Ios also known as the "Party Island" was adopted by the hippies in the 1960's, and today it is favorite with students and backpackers. The beaches are the main draw, many are clothing optional. At night the village

IOS PALACE
USA/Canada reservations
(800) 257-5344

swings with hi-energy disco music and beer drinking in the tavernas. Ios attracts mostly budget travelers, but can also offer a simple, laid-back, quite beach vacation for the 25+.

❖ Nude Beaches: **Milopota**, famous large sandy beach; **Manganari**, secluded superb beach at the southern end of Ios, accessible only by sea.

BARS ♟ **RESTAURANTS**

The nightlife concentrates in Hora (The Village), a short walk up the hill behind the port. It consists of loud discos and beer drinking tavernas. There is no established gay scene but check **Ios Club** for sunset cocktails and classical music; **Why Not**, drinking pub; and the **Far Out**, self-service cafeteria.

 ACCOMMODATIONS

✪ IOS PALACE HOTEL
USA/Canada Information or Reservations: Odysseus Enterprises Tel: (516) 944-5330 or (800) 257-5344, Fax: (516) 944-7540. TYPE: *Holiday Complex.* CLIENTELE: All Welcome. LOCATION: On the clothing optional sandy beach of Mylopota.

* Rooms: 70 w/priv. bath or shower
* Bungalows: 2 large rooms, A/C, CTV, phone kitchenette, minibar, large veranda, pool
* Phone, CTV, A/C, balcony
* Taverna, poolside bar, freshwater pool gym, health studio, nightly Jazz bar
* Maid service, parking area
* Beach: on the beach, nude beach
* Open: April - October; High season: July-August
* Rates: (US) $60 - $190 include all taxes, service and transfers
* *TAC:* 10% (from Odysseus)

DESCRIPTION: Attractive B-superior class hotel bungalow complex built in cycladic architecture, overlooking the Aegean sea. Standard rooms are not air-conditioned but have hi-fi music, phone, mini bar and large terraces overlooking the sea; deluxe rooms in the new section are fully air-conditioned with satellite CTV/video. Bungalows consist of two large rooms with a fully equipped kitchenette, satellite CTV, full air-condition, and extra large veranda, private swimming pool, umbrellas and sun beds. Best hotel in Ios for the friendliness of its staff and the amenities and services offered. Highly recommended.

ITHACA   ℰ   0674

LOCATION: One of the seven Ionian islands northeast of Cephalonia, the largest of the Ionian Islands. Off the western coast of the Peloponnisos.

POPULATION: 4,000

CLIMATE: Mild climate year round. In mid May the temperatures vary between 80˚F-90˚F (26˚c - 32˚c); winters are mild and pleasant.

DESCRIPTION: Ithaca is not a typical gay destination. As a matter of fact, it might very well be an unknown destination for many gays or travelers in general. We dedicate this chapter to the island which is known as **"Odysseus Island"** as a tribute to the wandering Greek King from which this guide derives its name. **Odysseus**, according to Homer's famous epic tale, returned to Ithaca, his beloved kingdom, after wandering 10 years in his journey home from the Trojan war. Today, a sign at the port welcome visitors saying "Every traveler is a citizen of Ithaca". Ithaca is a small mountainous island, narrow, rocky with no exceptional beaches, but its excellent harbor makes it a big favorite with sailors.

Ithaca is no longer a site of historical importance as it was in Odysseus times, but this tiny island, untouched by progress and technology, is waiting to be explored. Ithaca can be reached by bus from Athens to Patras, then by ferry to Ithaca in the afternoon.

❖ Beaches: **Myrtos**, magnificent white beach backed by cliffs; **Platis Yialos**, public beach with many hotels.

BARS ♈ RESTAURANTS

There are no gay bars and restaurants on the island. Meals are inexpensive. Many restaurants serve traditional Greek dishes in the Vathi harbor area.

ACCOMMODATIONS

HOTEL MENTOR
Georgiou Drakouli St., Vathi, Ithaca. Tel: (674) 32-433. TYPE: *Hotel*. CLIENTELE: Mostly Straight. LOCATION: Centrally located in the Vathi Harbor. 38 rooms. DESCRIPTION: Modern, clean and comfortable category 'B' hotel. Owner speaks English.

ODYSSEUS HOTEL
Vathi, Ithaca. Tel: (674) 32 381. TYPE: *Hotel*. CLIENTELE: Mostly Straight. LOCATION: Centrally located in front of the Vathi Harbor. 10 rooms. Rates: on request. DESCRIPTION: Category 'B' hotel. the island's second official hotel.

LESVOS   ℰ   0277

✈ Mytilini Airport

LOCATION: Lésvos belongs to the North-Eastern Aegean Islands, off the Turkish coast.

POPULATION: 24,000

CLIMATE: Mediterranean with hot summer tempered by cooling sea breezes with temperatures in the 80'˚sF (28˚c), mild winters with temperatures in the 60'˚sF (16˚c).

DESCRIPTION: This section on Lésvos is dedicated to all our sisters who are looking for a non conventional vacation spot in a spiritual search of their roots. Many lesbians go to Lesbos for camping on the **Skala Eressou**, a secluded sandy nude beach near the birth place of Sappho. Eressos is a small village on the northwestern part of Lésvos, some 100 km / 63 mi. west of Mytilini. There is no 'Lesbian colony' on Eressos, but the nearby Holiday Complex of **Aeolian Village** on Skala Eressos, one of the prettiest villages of Lesvos, is a perfect holiday destination for lesbians and gay men. The birth place of Sappho is only a short distance away. Some tours to Lésvos are occasionally organized by gay and lesbian oriented travel agents. **Odysseus** can help you with your accommodations in the Aeolian Village Skala Eressos.

Lésvos, or Mytilini as it is most commonly called after its principal city, is the third largest in Greece. It is famous for pastoral hills covered with olive trees, high mountains, and quaint villages. The island has a poetic aura attached to it. Sappho ran a marriage school for young ladies, to whom she dedicated many of her passionate love poems. The capital Mytilini is a large town with beautiful mansions, public buildings, and lovely public gardens. Visit the **Archeology Museum**, near the Tourist Police station.

Of special interest to visitors is the **Health Spa** at **Therma**; **Methymna** (known locally as **Molivos**), is the prettiest little village on the island with red-tiled roofs, and flower gardens located in north above the harbor. Molivos has a busy harbor with restaurants, bars, shops and fine beaches. Nearby **Eftalou** is a more upscaled and less crowded resort popular with gay men and lesbians. In the south-central area of Lésvos, west of Mytilini, there is the awesome **Mt. Olympos** (964m / 3162 ft.) the home of the mythological Greek gods; **Sigri** is a quiet fishing harbor with tavernas, lovely beach and an 18th century Turkish Castle; **Plomari** is an old town with ouzo distileries where you can buy authentic Lesbian Ouzo (great gift for your lesbian friends back home). Gay cruising is taking place at the **Municipal Theatre**, behind the building and in the park at the front; **The Waterfront Promenade** can be interesting at night.

❖ **HOW TO GET THERE**: Lésvos is connected by air twice a day from Athens; several times a week from Thessaloniki and Limnos. By sea - daily boats from Piraeus via Chios (14 hrs.), 2 weekly from Lemnos (6 hrs). In the summer, daily boats from Ayvalik (near ancient Assos) in Turkey.

BARS Y RESTAURANTS ¶¶

Lésvos does not have any lesbian or gay nightlife scene. We recommend the bars and restaurants at the Aeolian Village in Skala Eressos.

● Bars/Clubs (GMW): **Filoxenia**, popular breakfast and cocktail bar (Eressos); **Jimmy's**, popular bar; **An**, mixed disco at the seaside; **Sarai**, mixed clientele.

● Restaurant (AW): **Asteria** is a recommended restaurant in Mytilini; **Bennet's**, international & vegetarian (Eressos). Most of the beaches have fairly good tavernas serving local seafood.

🗝 ACCOMMODATIONS 🗝

GRECOTEL AEOLIAN VILLAGE
Skala Eressos, Lesvos. USA/Canada reservations or information Tel: (516) 944-5330 or (800) 257-5344. fax: (516) 944-7540. TYPE: *Holiday Village.* CLIENTELE: Gay men & lesbians welcome. LOCATION: 5 km / 3 mi. from Eressos the birthplace of Sappho.

* Rooms: 84 w/priv. bath. Suite: 1
* Bungalows & Maisonettes: 42
* CTV, phone, refrigerator, safe deposit C/H, A/C
* 24 hrs rooms service, maid service
* Restaurant: **Sappho** (breakfast / dinner)
* Pool, poolside bar & restaurant
* Watersports school, tennis, horseback riding
* Open: May - October
* Rates: on request
* *TAC:* 10% (from Odysseus)

DESCRIPTION: Peaceful and elegant village resort complex. The main building and bungalows are surrounded by extensive grounds with lawns and colorful gardens, adjoining a long sandy beach near the birthplace of Sappho.

MYKONOS   ⓒ   0289

✈ Mykonos Airport (JMK)
    7 mi. / 11 km Southeast

LOCATION: In the Aegean Sea within a circle of Greek Islands known as the Cyclades. It is one hour flight from Athens or a six-hour ferry ride, 3 hrs by catamaran from Piraeus.

POPULATION: 6,000 (plus 1 pelican). 25,000 during the summer

CLIMATE: Mediterranean. Summers are hot with pleasant sea breezes, average July temperature is 85°F (29°c). Winters are windy and cool with average January temperature of 62°F (16°c).

DESCRIPTION: Mykonos is a small island

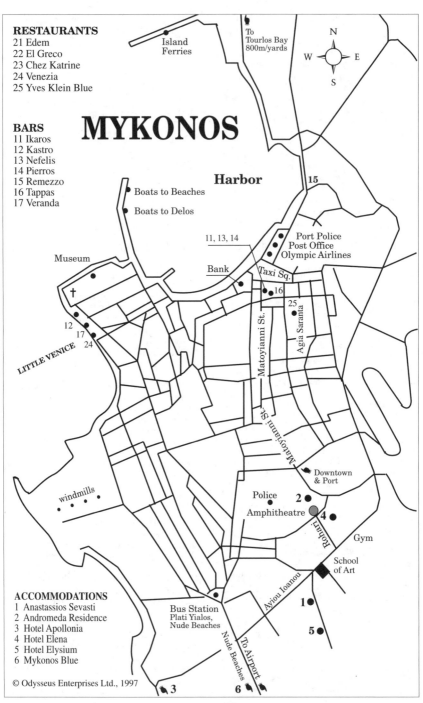

RESTAURANTS
21 Edem
22 El Greco
23 Chez Katrine
24 Venezia
25 Yves Klein Blue

BARS
11 Ikaros
12 Kastro
13 Nefelis
14 Pierros
15 Remezzo
16 Tappas
17 Veranda

MYKONOS

Island
Ferries

To
Tourlos Bay
800m/yards

N
W   E
S

Harbor

Boats to Beaches

Boats to Delos

Museum

11, 13, 14

Port Police
Post Office
Olympic Airlines

Bank

Taxi Sq.

16

25

Matoyianni St.

Agia Saranta

12
17
24

LITTLE VENICE

Matoyianni St.

Downtown
& Port

windmills

Police

Amphitheatre

2

4

Roberti

Gym

School
of Art

1

5

ACCOMMODATIONS
1 Anastassios Sevasti
2 Andromeda Residence
3 Hotel Apollonia
4 Hotel Elena
5 Hotel Elysium
6 Mykonos Blue

Bus Station
Plati Yialos,
Nude Beaches

Aviou Ioanou

Nude Beaches

To Airport

© Odysseus Enterprises Ltd., 1997

3

6

measuring only about 35 sq. mi. (90 sq. km) mostly made of grey rock. But it is a beautiful island, and one of the best world resorts for gay men and lesbians. The city of Mykonos is a wonderful place to spend an enjoyable carefree vacation in international ambience. The city is post-card beautiful with white mediterranean houses, lovely windmills, stucco Greek Orthodox churches, and a busy port around which most of the town's life revolves. Enjoy local seafood restaurants, art galleries and arts and crafts shops.

❖ Beaches: During the day you will spend most of the time on the island's nude gay beaches "Paradise", and "Super Paradise" which indicate the degree of intimacy, seclusion and nudism involved. 'Super Paradise' is the island's premier all gay nude beach with restaurant, bar and rocks above for heavy cruising day & night. A new gay nude beach is reported on Panorama Beach. Nude sunbathing is permitted on Elia Beach, which is popular with gays. Agrari Beach can be cruisy in early evening. In order to get to the nude beaches take a bus to Plati Yalos beach (10 minutes drive from Mykonos by local bus), then take a boat to the beach of your choice. All of these beaches have inexpensive and informal tavernas that offer lunch at the water's edge.

It is advisable to stay as close as possible to the town center to enjoy the convenience of gay nightlife and access to gay beaches. Take side trips to see other facets of the island including a trip to Ano Mera in the center of the island, or to Delos, a 45 minute ride by boat or caique. (Daily departures from the port except for Mondays). Delos is the sacred island with fascinating ruins of a 4000 year old town with shrines, statues and temples.

❖ HOW TO GET THERE: by air - many daily scheduled Olympic Air flights from Athens (45 minutes). By sea - twice daily ferry from Piraeus via Tinos and Syros (6 hrs.), twice daily from Rafina via Tinos and Andros (5hrs); from Paros/Naxos (2hrs.). A new rapid ferry service Catamaran I to Mykonos from Piraeus is now available which takes about 3 hours.

❖ SEASON TRAVEL INFORMATION: The season in Mykonos is lasting from April to October. The high season is July - September with August the peak of the high season. Most hotels close by mid-October. Winter travel to Mykonos is not recommended.

❖ SPECIAL EVENT: Greek Orthodox Easter, April 22-29, 1997. (dates change in '98)

BARS ♉ RESTAURANTS 🍴

Nightlife in Mykonos is a delightful experience which starts very late after midnight. Early crowds enjoy sunset and entertainment in the Cocktail bars along the sea in Little Venice behind the port.

● Bars/Clubs (GMW): **Factory** large disco above Ikaros; **Ikaros**, bar with balcony overlooking the square, Mantogianni St.,; **Manto**, mostly lesbians, Mantogianni near the Agia Kyriaki sector; **Nefelis**, above Pierro's with good view of the scene below, Plateia Agias Kyriakis (23183); **Pierro's Bar**, drag shows and dance floor, Mantogianni St., (Main Street) center of town, a few minutes from the harbor. **Pierros** opens onto a small square that is the central meeting place for the gay community and where cruising continues after the disco closes; **Porta**, near the Church of Panagia Paraportiani; **Tappas**, gay bar behind Ikaros; **Remezzo**, disco, mixed clientele, known as Mykonos favorite rendez vous for the int'l jet set.

● Cocktail Bars (G/S): **Kastro**, harbor views and relaxing classical music, near the Church of Panagia Paraportiani (23072); **Piano Bar** on Madon Martogenous Square is a place to be at sunset (225 28); **Veranda**, cocktails and sunset views, Little Venice; **Yves Klein Blue**, refined restaurant & piano bar, Aghia Saranta (27391).

● Restaurants (AW): Mykonos has many good restaurants and tavernas serving both Greek and International cuisine. Recommended restaurants (AW): **Antonini's**, in the taxi square, traditional Greek, inexpensive; **Edem**, superior Greek/ International, on main street going towards the port, turn left at Panos blanket shop; **Eva's Garden**, superb/expensive food; **Nikos**, inexpensive Greek, next to the windmill disco; **Katrins**, French, the most expensive on the island, Odos Nikiou; **Kounelas**, seafood restaurant and fish tavern next to Porta Bar near the Church of Panagia Paraportiani; **Philippi**, international cuisine in lovely garden setting, Odos Malamatenias; **Sesame**, wine bar/vegetarian, off main street next to the Nautical Museum; **Venezia**, fresh seafood, Little Venice; **Yves Klein Blue**, restaurant & piano bar, Aghia Saranta (27391).

λ SERVICES λ

● Rent a car (AW): ✪ **Mustang**, near bus station. USA/Canada make your car rental reservation through Odysseus Tel: (516) 944-5330 or (800) 257-5344. Fax: (516) 944-7540.

Photo: Julius Apuzzo

MYKONOS
LIVE THE LEGEND

ising out of the blue-green waters of the Aegean Sea, **Mykonos** is located in the heart of the Cyclades, a group of islands that surround the ancient holy island of Delos. **Mykonos** is like no other island in the world. Stony and hilly with very few trees, Mykonos is famous for its natural resources: Sun, Sand, Sea and the extraordinary people that live on the island. Mykonians are known for their hospitality, tolerance and adaptability. Gay and Lesbian travelers can be reassured of a genuine welcome. So whether you are interested in ancient history, or prefer the beaches, including the island's famous "nudist beaches" such as Paradise and Super Paradise, there is always something to do in **Mykonos**. And when the night falls, the town and harbor light up with thousands of points of light. This is the time to enjoy a romantic

sunset cocktail in the piano bars overlooking the harbor and live Myknos legendary nightlife to the fullest!

We at **ODYSSEUS** are very fortunate to have the best hotels and resorts in Mykonos: **The Andromeda Residence, Mykonos Blu, Anastassios Sevasti Hotel, Hotel Elysium, Hotel Elena** and **Hotel Apollonia**. We have sent more gay/lesbian clients to Mykonos since 1986 than any other travel agent / tour operator and are very proud to offer our clients the very best Mykonos has to offer. So, if you desire the very best give us a call now, we will be glad to help you with the best vacation of your life!

ODYSSEUS
P.O.Box 1548, Port Washington NY 11050 (USA)
Toll Free: (800) 257-5344
Email: odyusa@odyusa.com
Internet: www.odyusa.com

● Sex Shop (AW): **Sexy Shop**, F. Zouganeli & Matoyanni Sts. Open: 10:30am-2:30pm & 6pm-1am. (behind Pierros Bar).

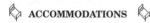

ACCOMMODATIONS

✪ ANASTASSIOS SEVASTI

Mykonos Town. USA/Canada Reservations: (800) 257-5344 or (516) 944-5330. Fax: (800) 982-6571 or (516) 944-7540. TYPE: *Hotel*. CLIENTELE: Gay Welcome. LOCATION: Scenic School of Art area, 300 yards/300m from the center of town, near buses to beaches. Short but steep uphill walk.

* Rooms: 60 w/priv. shower. Suite: 1
* Breakfast room, bar, TV Lounge
* Phone, radio, hair dryer, refrigerator, safe deposit box, ceiling fans, A/C
* Pool & poolside bar, gym
* Room & maid service
* Beach: buses nearby
* Gay Bars: 300 yards / 300 m
* Airport: 10 min.
* Reservations: thru Odysseus
* Open: April 1 - October 30
* Rates: (US) $110 - $190; (off) $60 - $110 w/CB, service, taxes and AP transfers
* *TAC:* 10% (from Odysseus)

DESCRIPTION: Two story hotel of Myconian architecture. Rooms have twins or double beds. most have balcony with seaview. Large fresh water pool with poolside bar. Traditional Greek hospitality in a clean, comfortable and conveniently located hotel. *See color photos in the Travel Supplement.*

✪ ANDROMEDA RESIDENCE

Mykonos Town. TYPE: *Luxury Villas.* Reservations: USA/Canada Odysseus (516) 944-5330 or (800) 257-5344. Fax: (516) 944-7540. CLIENTELE: Gay Welcome. LOCATION: Center of town, 5 min. walk to Port, near bus stop to beaches.

* Villas: 32 (studio, 1-3 bedroom apts)
* CTV (CNN), phone, A/C, patio
* Fully equipped kitchens
* Restaurant & poolside bar
* Pool & sunbathing area, garden
* Gay Bars: walking distance
* Beach: transportation required for gay beaches, buses nearby
* Airport: 15 min., taxi
* Reservations: thru Odysseus
* Open: April 10 - October 15
* Rates: (US) $95 - $270

Rates include service and all taxes.
* *TAC:* 10% (from Odysseus)

DESCRIPTION: The Andromeda Residence is a luxurious group of villas, maisonettes, and studios right in the heart of Mykonos Town. Amenities include: Large fresh water swimming pool, poolside bar and restaurant, full reception, 12 hours room service, direct dial phones in all units, fax service, travel assistance and more. Andromeda Residence offers the best accommodations in Mykonos Town. The ambiance is sophisticated and cosmopolitan. Recommended for upscaled travelers, couples and groups. *See color photos in the Travel Supplement.*

✪ HOTEL APOLLONIA

Agio Iannis, Mykonos. USA/Canada Reservations: (800) 257-5344 or (516) 944-5330. Fax: (800) 982-6571 or (516) 944-7540. TYPE: *Hotel.* CLIENTELE: All Welcome. LOCATION: Little harbor of Agio Yanis, 6 km / 4 mi.x from Mykonos town. 40 rooms w/CTV, phone, A/C, internal video-system, mini-bar, balcony with seaview, pool, parking. DESCRIPTION: Elegant beachfront hotel in a quiet location.

✪ HOTEL ELENA

Mykonos Town. USA/Canada Reservations: (800) 257-5344 or (516) 944-5330. Fax: (800) 982-6571 or (516) 944-7540. TYPE: *Hotel.* CLIENTELE: All Welcome. LOCATION: Mykonos Town center.

* Rooms: 28 w/ priv. shower
* Radio, phone
* Bar, balcony, garden, maid service
* Beach: buses to the beaches nearby
* Gay Bars: nearby
* Airport: 15 min., free pick up
* Reservations: thru Odysseus
* Open: year round
* Rates: (US) $60 - $170. w/CB, tax, service, and AP transfers
* *TAC:* 10% (from Odysseus)

DESCRIPTION: Two story Greek island style hotel with comfortable accommodations, and friendly hospitality. Conveniently located to Mykonos nightlife, and the bus station to the nude beaches. *See color photos in the Travel Supplement.*

✪ HOTEL ELYSIUM

Mykonos Town. School of Art area. USA/Canada Reservations: (800) 257-5344 or (516) 944-5330. Fax: (800) 982-6571 or (516) 944-7540. TYPE: *Hotel.* CLIENTELE: Mostly gay men & women. LOCATION: Mykonos Town School of

Art are with panoramic view of the Old City and the Sea.

* Rooms: 45 w/ priv. shower
  2 sgl / 36 dbl / 2 triple / 2 quad
* Suites: 3, 1 BR, 2 BR w/living room, full bath, kitchen, patio/terrace
* Smoking allowed in rooms
* Bed types: single, double, large (oversized) double, king size
* CTV (VCR), phone, refrigerator, safe box
* Maid and room service, laundry service
* Snack bar, balcony, garden
* Pool, sauna, jacuzzi, gym
* Free parking, pets w/prearrangement
* Beach: buses to the beaches nearby
* Gay Bars: nearby
* Airport: 15 min., free pick up
* Reservations: thru Odysseus
* Open: year round
* Rates: (US) $80 - $210
  w/ABb, tax, service, and AP transfers
* Check In - any time / check out 12pm
* *TAC:* 10% (from Odysseus)

DESCRIPTION: Built in 1989 with traditional Myconian architecture. The Elysium Hotel offers elegant rooms and suites with all modern amenities. Nice swimming pool, poolside bar, and fully equipped fitness center. *See color photos in the Travel Supplement.*

✪ MYKONOS BLUE

Psarou, Mykonos GR-846 00. Reservations (USA/Canada) (800) 257-5344 or (516) 944-5330. Fax: (516) 944-7540. Email: odyusa @odyusa.com. TYPE: *Deluxe Resort.* CLIENTELE: Gay Welcome. LOCATION: On Psarou beach, 5 km / 3 mi. from Mykonos Town.

* Bugalows: 146 w/priv. bath
* Bungalow Suites in garden: 4
* CTV (VCR), phone, refrigerator, safe deposit,balcony, hairdryer, A/C, C/H
* Restaurants: indoor and outdoor dining
* Cocktail bar, pool taverna, pool snack bar
* Seawater pool, lounges, terraces, TV room
* Gym, aerobics, evening shows
* Beach: on the beach
* Gay Bars: in town 10 min by car
* Airport: 15 min. (taxi, shuttle)
* Open: May-October
* Rates: $290 - $450
* *TAC:* 10% (from Odysseus)

DESCRIPTION: Mykonos most elegant 5-star resort complex on Psarou Beach. The main building and bungalows are surrounded by extensive gardens. The accommodations are pretty island style bungalows and bungalow suites with deluxe amenities. Friendly welcome to Odysseus clients.

PAROS   ✆   0284

LOCATION: Cycladic Islands between Naros and Antiparos and south of Mykonos.

POPULATION: 3,000

CLIMATE: Summers are hot with pleasant sea breezes, average July temperature is 85°F (29°c). Winters are windy and cool with average January temperature of 62°F (16°c).

DESCRIPTION: Paros is one of the largest and most fertile of the Cyclades. Underneath **Profitis Ilias Mountain** lies some of the finest, most translucent marble in the world. It is also the main building material of Paros' charming villages. Paros plays a close second to Mykonos in general public popularity.

Paros or **Parikia** is the island's chief town and main port. The main street is lined with shops, tourist and non-tourist. **Naoussa** in the north, is one of the most popular spots on the island with its picturesque port, narrow winding lanes, small medieval castle, and sex hungry Egyptian fishermen.

❖ Beaches: Paros is loaded with beaches. **Chryssi Akti** or Golden Shore on the east coast is the perennial favourite. Also popular with gays are the beaches at **Langeri** and **Monastiri**.

❖ **HOW TO GET THERE**: By ferry boat or hydrofoil from Piraeus, Mykonos, Tinos and Syros. Daily flights from Athens. **From Mykonos** daily hydrofoil at 8:45am, 45 min. trip. The Ferry leaves at 9:00am, 2 hrs trip. In case of windy weather the passengers are moved from the hydrofoil to the ferry.

BARS ⅄ RESTAURANTS 🍴

There is a hint of gay nightlife in the resort village of Naoussa in the north.

● Clubs/Bars (G/S): **Augosta** (Naoussa); **Chez Leonardo**, disco mixed clientele (Parikia); **Kavarnis Bar**.

● Restaurants (AW): **La Luna**, gay owned (51547); **Tavern Christos** near the Post Office (51225).

⅄ SERVICES ⅄

● Boutique (G/S): **Tango**, gay owned, stop for shopping and information.

🏠 ACCOMMODATIONS 🏠

⊙ ASTIR OF PAROS

Naoussa, Paros. USA/Canada reservations Tel: (516) 944-5330 or (800) 257-5344. Fax: (516) 944-7540 or (800) 982-6571. TYPE: *Class A deluxe Villas Resort.* CLIENTELE: All Welcome. LOCATION: between the village of Naoussa and the Kolymbithres beaches.

* Suites: 4 executive suites, 42 JR suites
* Rooms: 11 double rooms
* CTV, phone, A/C, minibar, full bath
* TV lounge, gourmet restaurant
* Pool, tennis court, jacuzzi, gym, sauna
* Beach: walking distance
* Airport: 15 min
* Open: April - October
* Rates: (US) $145 - $380 w/fAB
* *TAC:* 10% (from Odysseus)

DESCRIPTION: Beautiful Cycladic style holiday village with tradition of discreet and unadorned luxury in extensive gardens setting. Elegant and peaceful.

⊙ KALLISTI COMPLEX

Naousa, Paros. USA/Canada reservations Tel: (516) 944-5330 or (800) 257-5344. Fax: (516) 944-7540 or (800) 982-6571. TYPE: *Resort Complex.* CLIENTELE: All Welcome. LOCATION: 350 m / yards from the center of Naoussa.

* Rooms and studios: 30 w/priv. bath
* Phone, refrigerator, cooking facilities kitchenette in studios, balcony
* Pool (freshwater), bar, parking
* Beach: walking distance
* Airport: 15 min.
* Open: April - October
* Rates: (US) $145 - $380 w/fAB
* *TAC:* 10% (from Odysseus)

DESCRIPTION: Charming resort complex offering a unique balance between the relaxing environment of Kallisti and the nightlife of Naoussa. Accommodations vary from standard rooms to fully equipped studios and apts.

PAROS PHILOXENIA

Nea Chryssi Akti, Paros. USA/Canada reservations: (516) 944-5330 or (800) 257-5344. Fax: (516) 944-7540 or (800) 982-6571. TYPE: *Hotel & Villas.* CLIENTELE: All Welcome. LOCATION: On the eastern shore of Paros Island, overlooking the sea, 1.5 km from the fishing village of Piso Livadi.

* Rooms/Bungalows: 45, Singles, Doubles & Suites w/priv. bathrooms
* Phone, radio and veranda
* Restaurant, bar, pool, beach, windsurfing, sea sports
* Hotel bus from port & airport
* Season: April - October
* Rates: (US) $90-$140
* *TAC:* 10% (from Odysseus)

DESCRIPTION: Tastefully designed in Cycladic architectural style. The accommodations are spacious, beautifully designed and comfortably furnished.

PATMOS   ℂ   0247

LOCATION: In the northern Dodecanese, a group of Greek islands near the Turkish coast.

POPULATION: 3,000

CLIMATE: Mediterranean climate with two main seasons - hot dry summer from July to Sept. with average July temperature of 86°F

(30˚c) and wet/rainy winter from November to February with an average January temperature of 54˚F (12˚c).

DESCRIPTION: Patmos is a 14 sq.mi (36 sq. km) island of volcanic rock and deserted sweeps of sand. The island has long been a place of pilgrimage for those who believe that St. John the divine dictated on this island the text of Revelation to his pupil Prochoros. Today, Patmos is becoming a chic island, popular yet not overdeveloped. **Chora** is the main town, built high on a hill, with white mansions, surrounding the huge 17th century fortified **Monastry of St John**. Most resort and tourist activities are in **Skala** a relaxed harbor town that looks like Mykonos Town did some 40 years ago. Patmos offers unspoilt sand beaches where nude sunbathing is accepted on the less frequented beaches.

❖ Beaches: There are many secluded beaches on the island. **Lampi** is a secluded pebble beach in the north; **Kampos** offers a busy pebble beach with tavernas; and **Psilli Amos** is a superb remote sandy beach in the south.

❖ **HOW TO GET THERE**: By boat or hydrofoil from Piraeus. Ferries to Rhodes stop in Patmos. Any other combination is most unlikely to work.

BARS ♈ RESTAURANTS ♈

There is no established gay scene on Patmos. However the following tavernas can be suggested: **Olympia** and **Vagelis** on Plateia Ag. Levias Square (Chora); **Patmiam House**, elegant restaurant in an old mansion, excellent cuisine, run by a New York based couple (Chora).

🏠 ACCOMMODATIONS 🏠

ROMEOS HOTEL
Skala. Tel: (247) 31962. USA/Canada reservations Tel: (516) 944-5330 or (800) 257-5344. Fax: (516) 944-7540 or (800) 982-6571. TYPE: *Hotel*. CLIENTELE: Mostly Straight. LOCATION: In the port town of Skala.

* Rooms: 56, Suites: 2 w/priv. shower
* Phone (direct dial), bar, pool
* Open: April - October
* Rates: on request
* *TAC:* 10% (from Odysseus)

DESCRIPTION: Good quality accommodations and service. This hotel is the best choice on the island. Saltwater pool.

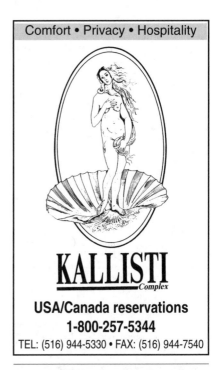
RHODES   ℭ   0241

✈ Maritsa Airport (RHO)

LOCATION: In the Dodecanese, a group of Greek islands near the Turkish coast.

POPULATION: 35,000

CLIMATE: Mediterranean climate with two main seasons - hot/dry summer from July to September with average July temperature of 86˚F (30˚c) and wet/rainy winter from November to February with an average temperature of 54˚F (12˚c).

DESCRIPTION: Rhodes is the capital of the Dodecanese, the fourth largest Greek Island and a port-of-call for cruise ships. Visit the **Old Town** with its medieval walled citadel and buildings from the 15th century; the **Commercial Harbour** with its smart yachting scene; the beautifully restored **Street of the Knights**; and the **Platiá ton Evréon Martirón** (The Square of the Jewish Martyrs) in memory of the large local Jewish community that was almost totally annihilated by the Nazis in 1943; the ornate synagogue is nearby. For gamblers there is a fast action at the tables of the international Casino at the deluxe Grand Hotel Astir Palace. For a gratifying trip visit the **Butterfly Valley** (Petaloudes) the island's #1nature attraction. The valley is filled with butterflies of all colors and shapes from June to September. Also worth visiting is the resort village of **Lindos** where sun, sea and sex have been the main agenda since the 60's (some 40 km / 25 mi. south along the coast). Lindos has a large harbor, sandy beaches, lively nightlife and bohemian type followers (see more information under Lindos).

The sleepy island of **Halkí** known as the "isle of peace and friendship" can be reached via the port of **Kamiros** scala on Rhode's less traveled northwestern coast. Lesbians may be interested to know that the island of **Tilos** is the home of the poetess **Erinna** which was a rival to **Sappho**. (we are not sure whether this means that Lesbians should visit this island or avoid it. Maybe a Lesbian reader could educate us on this matter).

❖ Beaches: There are many postcard-perfect beaches on the island. However for nude beach check **Faliraki Beach** (mostly straight or mixed) 10 km / 6 mi. south of Rhodes Town. Other beaches: **Kato Petres Beach** near hotel "33" on the road towards the villages.

❖ Public Cruising: **Park** opposite the Tourist Police and behind the Old Town Taxi Station; **Park** behind the church of St. Francis.

● **HOW TO GET THERE**: By air - fly from Athens, Heraklion, Santorini and Mykonos. By boat - daily ferry from Piraeus, 2 per week from Limassol (Cyprus) and Haifa (Israel). Frequent hydrofoils from Kos, Kalymnos, Patmos & Marmaris (Turkey).

BARS ⓨ RESTAURANTS ¶

● Bars/clubs (G/S): **Berlin**, close to Hotel Alexia, 47 Orfanidi St. (new town) near Pl. Arh Hrissanthou; **Blue Lagoon**, exotic pool bar, 25 Martiou St., (next to the Post Office) (32632); **Buzios disco**, 6 Kountourioti Sq., Paralia Elli (26800); **Tramp's Unlimited Club**, A. Diakou 30-32 (29048); **Valentino** (Old City); **Medoussa & Veggera**, both in the center of town, popular with mixed clientele.

● Restaurants (AW): **Argo**, seafood, Hippocratous 23-24 (34232); **Castello House**, fish tavern, terrace roof garden, 50, Orfeos Socratous St., Old Town (23616); **Symposium**, restaurant & bar, Archelou 3 (37509); **Karpathos**, coffee & pastry shop, Lahitos.

λ SERVICES λ

● Turkish Bath (G/S): **Hamam**, Old City.

⌖ ACCOMMODATIONS ⌖

○ CHEVALIERS PALACE

3 G. Grivas St., Rhodes Town. Tel: (241) 22781. USA/Canada booking: (516) 944-5330 or (800) 257-5344. Fax: (800) 982-6571 or (516) 944-7540. TYPE: *Hotel*. CLIENTELE: Mostly Straight. LOCATION: 5 min. from City Center.

* Rooms: 182 w/priv. bath. Suites: 26
* Phone, balcony, A/C, room & maid service
* Restaurant, bar, parking
* Sauna, solarium, seawater pools
* Beach: 30 m / yards
* Gay Bars: walking distance
* Airport: 10 min., taxi
* Open: Year round
* Rates: US$65 - $160. **TAC:** 10%

DESCRIPTION: Seven-story modern hotel in a central location with seaviews.

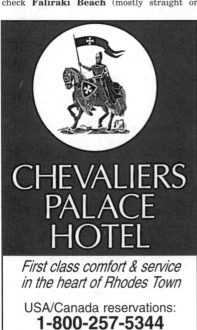

CHEVALIERS PALACE HOTEL

First class comfort & service in the heart of Rhodes Town

USA/Canada reservations:
1-800-257-5344

Tel: (516) 944-5330 • Fax: (516) 944-7540

LINDOS   © 0244

✈ Maritsa Airport (RHO)

LOCATION: About 40 km / 25 mi. south of Rhodes Town.

DESCRIPTION: Lindos boasts 4,500 years of history. The picturesque village is built on a hillside at the foot of the Acropolis. It will surprise you with its maze of white washed, cubed houses, ancient buildings, and golden sandy beaches. At night the village comes alive with music and dancing in the town's popular dance clubs and discos, and great dinning of local dishes in Lindo's famous garden restaurants.

BARS ☓ RESTAURANTS 🍴

Lindos does not have a gay/lesbian nightlife. The following are some general interest recommendations:

● Bars/Clubs (AW): **Acropolis**, the longest established disco in town; **Il Sogno**, cocktail music pub, 'where dreams come true', center of town; **The Lindian House**, center of Lindos, pool tables, garden courtyard, rock music, friendly; **Remejjos Pool Bar**, centre of Lindos, rock music, garden courtyard, friendly atmosphere.

● Restaurants (AW): **Calypso**, traditional & international, historic Sea Captain's house; **Cypriot Taverna**, Greek & Cypriot cuisine, lovely roof garden; **Grill on the Hill**, English & Continental, views of the Acropolis and Lindos Bay.

🗝 ACCOMMODATIONS 🗝

Note: we can offer a large selection of Self-catering villas, apartments and studios in Lindos and the nearby area. Prices and description of properties are available on demand. For information/reservation please call **Odysseus**. Tel: (516) 944-5330 or (800) 257-5344. Fax: (516) 944-7540 or (800) 982-6571.

✪ LINDOS MARE HOTEL

Lindos, Rhodes. USA/Canada Reservations: (516) 944-5330 or (800) 257-5344. Fax: (516) 944-7540 or (800) 982-6571. TYPE: *Luxury Hotel.* CLIENTELE: All Welcome. LOCATION: The most closely situated hotel to Lindos Village (2.5 km / 1.5 mi.).

* Rooms: 62 w/priv. bath. Suites: 4
* Phone, radio, refrigerator, A/C
* Balcony w/panoramic seaview
* Restaurant, bar, snack bar
* Pool, games room
* Mini-market
* Beach: 100 m / yards
* Gay Bars: mixed bars in Lindos
* Airport: 45 minutes
* Port: 45 minutes
* Open: Year round
* Rates: (US) $80-$260 w/CB
* *TAC:* 10% (from Odysseus)

DESCRIPTION: Deluxe hotel built recently into the hillside overlooking Vlicha Bay. It is of a modern architectural design ideal for a quiet and relaxing holiday. Car rental is necessary.

VILLA LINDOS
Lindos, Rhodes. Reservation/Information: Odysseus Tel: (516) 944-5330, or (800) 257-5344. Fax: (516) 944-7540 or (800) 982-6571. TYPE: *Villa.* CLIENTELE: All Welcome. Rates: on request. *TAC:* 10%. LOCATION: 5 minute walk to main beach. DESCRIPTION: Large secluded self-catering house with own courtyard, kitchen/diner, nice views, main room sleeps 3 with a traditional bed. Second room sleeps 2.

LINDOS MARE

USA/Canada reservations
(800) 257-5344

SAMOS   ✆   0273

✈ Samos Airport

LOCATION: The southernmost of the North-East Aegean Islands group. Just few miles off the Turkish coast with good daily ferry connection to Kusadasi (Turkey). If you take the hydrofoil to Kusadasi, you need to leave your passport with the travel agency overnight. Your passport will be delivered to you upon embarkation at the Custom's House. This is a standard procedure on both sides (Greece and Turkey).

POPULATION: 5,630

CLIMATE: Mediterranean.

DESCRIPTION: Densely forested large size island with a distinctive red-roofed turn-of-the century houses, near the exotic coast of Turkey. The island's famous Samian wine is popular with locals and visitors. According to Greek Mythology Samos was inhibited by Pelasgians who worshiped the goddess Hera, the wife of Zeus. Visit: **Vathi** (Samos Town); **Zoodochos Pigi**, monastery with panoramic view of the Strait of Mycale; The famous **Temple of Hera** the second largest Temple ever built in Greece is located near **Pithagorio**. The nicest place to stay on the island is **Kokkari Village**, just 10 km / 6 mi. from Samos Town. Kokkari is a beautiful traditional seaside village built on a hill. The town offers great beaches including a nude beach nearby, wonderful restaurants and lively nightlife.

❖ Gay Beach: **Tsamadou Beach**, gay nude beach near the popular resort village of Kokkari, about 10 km / 6 mi. northwest of Vathi along the coast.

HOW TO GET THERE: Daily flights from Athens. Daily ferry connection with Piraeus and Ikaria; once a week with Chios, Mythilini and Paros. Twice weekly, Tues. & Sat. night (23:30) by Dimitra boat from Mykonos, Frequent boats and hydrofoils to and from Kusadasi (Turkey).

BARS ♈ RESTAURANTS 🍴

● Bars/Clubs (GM): **Barino**, Kokkari Village (near Central Square) summer only; **Clary's Pub**, Samos Town, Central Square; **Dino's Pub**, Vathi (27-285); **Metropolis**, trendy and popular bar; **Totem Disco**, summer only, 5 min. by car from Samos Town (27-250); **Traffic**, mixed clientele, many young men, good rock music and inexpensive drinks, Them. Sofoulis St., Samos Town.

● Restaurants (AW): **The Cock's Egg**, Kokkari Village; **To Petrino** Vathi; **Vatzoulia's**, excellent Greek food, popular with locals, en route to temple of Aphaia.

🏠 ACCOMMODATIONS 🏠

ARION HOTEL
Kokkari, Samos Island.USA/Canada information/reservation Odysseus Tel: (516) 944-5330 or (800) 257-5344. Fax: (516) 944-7540 or (800) 982-6571. TYPE: *Deluxe Hotel & Bungalows.* CLIENTELE: All Welcome. LOCATION: In Kokkari near the beaches.

* Rooms: 86 w/priv. bath
* Bungalows: 12 w/priv. bath
* Phone, A/C, verandas w/seaview
* Wheelchair access, elevator
* Restaurant, bar, gym, sauna, pool
* Maid & room service, parking
* Beach: 400 m
* Gay Bars: mixed bars in town (5 min.)
* Airport: 25 min. / Port: 15 min.
* Open: Year round
* Rates: (US) $90-$160 HB
  American buffet breakfast + dinner
* *TAC:* 10% (from Odysseus)

DESCRIPTION: Traditional class 'A' fully air-conditioned hotel & bungalows complex set in a lush area with panoramic sea views near Kokkari village. Fine amenities and service.

OLYMPIA VILLAGE
Kokkari, Samos. USA and Canada information/reservation Odysseus Tel: (516) 944-5330 or (800) 257-5344. Fax: (516) 944-7540 or (800) 982-6571. TYPE: *Studios.* CLIENTELE: All Welcome. LOCATION: Near the beach in Kokkari village.

* Apartments: 25, 2-bedroom units
* CTV, Phone, radio, C/H
* Small bar on premises
* Beach: 50-100m/yards
* Gay Bars: walking distance in town
* Airport: 25 km / 16 mi. taxi
* Port: 16 km / 10 mi. taxi
* Open: Year round
* Rates: (US) $100-$140
* *TAC:* 10%

DESCRIPTION: Modern self-catering apartments and maisonettes in a garden setting with balcony, patio or terrace. Each apartment size is about 60 sq. m. (660 sq. ft.).

SANTORINI *✆* 0286

✈ Santorini Airport (JTR)

LOCATION: In the Aegean Sea, south of Mykonos. Between Mykonos and the island of Crete.

POPULATION: 4,000

DESCRIPTION: Santorini, known by its official Greek name Fira (spelled Thira), is an extraordinary island born of the eruption of an ancient Volcano. The island's eruption was recorded by ancient Egyptian and Hebrew scriptures. Some scientist believe that Santorini is actually the lost land of Atlantis. Today, it has become a chic island and a must stop on the path of many cruise ships in the Mediterranean.

Most visitors to Santorini start their tour at **Fira**, a post-card beautiful port, with traditional Greek island houses all in white. Fira is the main town of the island built on almost the center of the crater rim with a magnificent views of the sea and the volcanic islets. Thousands steps lead from the town to the port below with amazing views on each step of the way (just try to avoid those pesky donkey dongs while enjoying the enchanted scenery); take a motor launch to the tiny port of **Skala Fira**, and from there go on the famous donkey ride to the hill-top.

Ia or **Oia**, is the third port in Santorini. A quiet village with picturesque white houses, and resort hotels. It is less crowded than the capital Thira, and further away from the low budget tourism of Kamari in the south.

Important tourist sites include: **Ancient Thira**, the Dorian town on top of the Mesa Vouno mountain, one of the most interesting archeological sites on the island; **Monastery**, at the top of the mountain of Profitis Ilias, 668 m / 2,200 ft. high, great views of the island and a folk-museum run by monks; **Perissa**, on the southeast coast with its 8 km / 5 mi black beach with fine seafood tavernas and resorts; **Akrotiri**, the Minoan town destroyed by earthquake and coverd with volcano dust. Here were unearthed some of the most beautiful Minoan frescoes, but the originals are kept in a museum in Athens, in Akrotiri they show photos only.

❖ Gay Beach: **Avis Beach**, between Monolithos and Kamari, nudism; **Monolithos Beach**.

❖ **HOW TO GET THERE**: by air - daily flights from Athens, frequent air connections with Mykonos (40 minutes), Heraklion (Crete), and Rhodes. By sea - daily ferry from Piraeus (14 hrs). Summer connections with Milos, Serifos, Sifnos, Kimilos and Ag. Nikolaos (Crete). With Mykonos there is a connection by rapid boat (Catamaran or Nearchos) twice a week.

BARS ♀ RESTAURANTS ¶

Santorini is mostly a destination for straight tourists. It is a favorite stop for many cruise ships in the Aegean.

● Bars/clubs: **Casablanca**, mixed trendy disco; **Disco Hysteria Club**, the most high-tech disco this side of the caldera with European and American music (shopping center "Adonis"); **Franco's Bar**, mixed bar, Odós Marinatos (228-81); **Just Blue**, Central Square; **Minim's Bar**, mixed bar/café in Oia; **Tropical Bar** (near the cable car and Franco's).

● Restaurants (AW): **Archipelgo**, restaurant & bar, Fira (236-73); **Bonjour**, cafe/bar, (237-44); **Il Cantuccio**, elegant Italian, gay owned and operated, Firostefani (22082); **Kastro**, restaurant, cafeteria & bar (225-03); **Selene**, elegant restaurant, local and international specialties, Fira, behind the Atlantis Hotel (222-49); **Zotos**, pastry, coffeeshop, Fira (222-87).

ACCOMMODATIONS

☛ **Fira**

✪ DANA VILLAS

Fira, Santorini. Tel: (286) 22455. USA/Canada reservations: Odysseus - (516) 944-5330 or (800) 257-5344, Fax: (516) 944-7540. TYPE: *Hotel*. CLIENTELE: Gay/Straight. LOCATION: Panoramic location on the rim of a cliff in Firostefani, 15 min. walk from the center of Fira.

* Maisonettes: 10; Apts: 10; Studios: 10
* CTV, phone, A/C, terrace, kitchenette
* Safe deposit in each villa
* Pool, sundecks, bar, restaurant
* Daily cleaning service
* Airport: 25 min. taxi or shuttle (paid)
* Open: April 1- Oct. 31
  high season June 1 - Sept. 30
* Rates: (US) $140 - $280

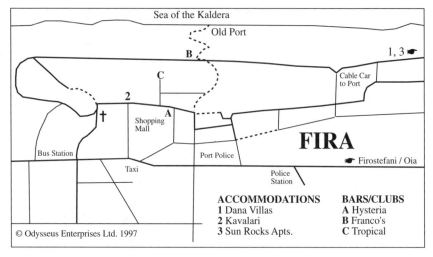

Sea of the Kaldera
Old Port
B
1, 3
C
Cable Car
to Port
2
A
Shopping
Mall
Bus Station
Port Police
FIRA
Taxi
Firostefani / Oia
Police
Station

ACCOMMODATIONS	BARS/CLUBS
1 Dana Villas	**A** Hysteria
2 Kavalari	**B** Franco's
3 Sun Rocks Apts.	**C** Tropical

© Odysseus Enterprises Ltd. 1997

* Breakfast, service & tax included
* **TAC:** 10% (from Odysseus)

DESCRIPTION: Charming villas and apartments complex in traditional architectural style. Quiet but panoramic location near Fira Town. Apartments consist of two bedrooms, and a suite is a large apartment with two bathrooms. *See color photos in the special Travel Supplement.*

GROTTO VILLAS
Firostefani. USA/Canada reservations: Odysseus - (516) 944-5330 or (800) 257-5344, Fax: (516) 944-7540 or (800) 982-6571. TYPE: *Hotel.* CLIENTELE: Gay/Straight. LOCATION: In Firostefani, 15 min. walk from Thira town center via the panoramic boardwalk.

* Villas: 10 (one & two bedroom)
* Kitchen, living room, terrace
* Pool and poolside bar
* Gay bars: 15 min. away
* Beach: 30 min. by car
* Open: May 1 - Oct. 31
* Rates: (US) $90 - $180
* **TAC:** 10% (from Odysseus)

DESCRIPTION: Traditional style holiday complex with panoramic view of the sea and the volcano. Quiet but scenic location.

✪ KAVALARI HOTEL
Fira, Santorini. Tel: (286) 22455. USA/Canada reservations: Odysseus - (516) 944-5330 or (800) 257-5344, Fax: (516) 944-7540 or (800) 982-6571. TYPE: *Hotel.* CLIENTELE: Gay/Straight. LOCATION: In the center of Fira, a short walk from restaurants, bars, and discos.

* Rooms: 13 w/priv. bath
* Deluxe Rooms: 5 w/cooking facilities
* Phone, terrace garden
* Maid service, no pets
* Beach: 15 km / 10 mi., 15 min. by bus. Mixed/nude beach
* Gay Bars: 5 minutes walk
* Airport: 12 km / 8 mi., taxi, bus
* Open: Apr. 1 - Oct. 31
* Rates: (US) $65 - $260 w/breakfast
* **TAC:** 10% (from Odysseus)

DESCRIPTION: The Kavalari occupies a traditional Sea Captain's house built on the Caldera (cliff) with an incomparable view of the volcano from the flower-decked terraces. Rooms are individually furnished in traditional style with private facilities. Deluxe rooms have living area, kitchenette and seaview. *See color photos in the special Travel Supplement.*

SUN ROCKS APTS
Firostefani, Santorini.USA/Canada reservations: Odysseus - (516) 944-5330 or (800) 257-5344, Fax: (516) 944-7540 or (800) 982-6571. TYPE: *Villas Complex.* CLIENTELE: All Welcome. LOCATION: In Firostefani, 700 m / yards from Thira town center via the panoramic boardwalk.

* Villas: 15, studio to one-bedroom
* Full kitchen, living room, phone, terrace
* Service: daily cleaning, laundry, groceries
* Pool, poolside bar, sundecks
* Gay bars: 15 min. away
* Beach: 30 min. by car
* Open: April 1 - Oct. 31
* Rates: (US) $130 - $290
* **TAC:** 10% (from Odysseus)

DESCRIPTION: Elegant apartments/villas complex in Firostefani. Elegant decor in traditional style and excellent service. Spacious terace with panoramic view of the Seagean and the Caldera.

THE TSITOURAS COLLECTION

Firostefani, Santorini.USA/Canada reservations: Odysseus - (516) 944-5330 or (800) 257-5344, Fax: (516) 944-7540 or (800) 982-6571. TYPE: *Deluxe Houses Complex*. CLIENTELE: All Welcome. LOCATION: In Firostefani, 700 m / yards from Thira town center via the panoramic boardwalk. DESCRIPTION: 5 traditional Cycladic style houses perched on the top of a 1000 ft / 300 m cliff with a spectacular view. Each house has spacious bedrooms, sittingroom, safe, full bath, minibar and full service. The houses are furnished and decorated with valuable antiques and *objets d'art*. This is the most elegant and luxurious complex of its kind in Santorini. Very popular with celebrities. Rates: from (US)$540/day. 3 days minimum stay requested. *TAC:* 10% (from Odysseus).

☛ Oia

OIA MARE VILLAS

Oia. USA/Canada reservations: Odysseus - (516) 944-5330 or (800) 257-5344, Fax: (516) 944-7540 or (800) 982-6571. TYPE: *Hotel*. CLIENTELE: Gay Welcome. LOCATION: In Oia, 20 min. by car from Fira town center.

* Villas: 7 (one & two bedroom)
* Studio: 1
* Kitchen, living room, terrace
* Phone, CTV, radio
* Gay bars: 20 min. by car (Fira)
* Beach: at footstep of the cliff
* Open: April 1 - Oct. 31
* Rates: (US) $130 - $210
* *TAC:* 10% (from Odysseus)

DESCRIPTION: Small complex at the edge of the tranquil village of Oia. Villas and apartments furnished and decorated in a typical Santorini style, built into the rock face overlooking the Aegean Sea. Narrow steps lead to a swimming beach nearby. Transfers and Continental breakfast are available at additional cost.

SKIATHOS   © 0427

✈ Skiathos Airport

LOCATION: In the Sporades off the eastern coast of Greece.

DESCRIPTION: Historic island which was ruled by the Maceonians, the Romans and the Turks. The island is noted for its greenery, its trees extending right to the golden beaches. Despite the crowds of tourists, Skiathos manages to preserve its quaint and laid back charm.

❖ Gay Beach: **Banana Beach** clothing optional next to Koukounaries Beach, to the right of the bus stop, go over a dune and an olive grove.

BARS ▼ RESTAURANTS ▮▮

● Bars/clubs (G/S): **Adagio**l, Evangelistrias & Papadiamanti; **Bonzai**, Papadiamanti; **La Piscine**, disco, city center; **Portofino** in the harbor.

ACCOMMODATIONS

AEGEAN EAGLE

Megali Ammos, Skiathos. USA/Canada reservations: Odysseus - (516) 944-5330 or (800) 257-5344, Fax: (516) 944-7540 or (800) 982-6571.TYPE: *Hotel*. CLIENTELE: Gay/Straight. LOCATION: 1 km outside Skiathos town in Megali Ammos. Very high standard complex of apartments / suites. Each apt/suite for 2-4 pax built in a unique combination of traditional architecture and contemporary luxury. A/C, sitting room w/fire place, kitchen, one bedroom, full bath, veranda. Amenities: gym, pool, snack bar, maid service once a week. Cost: $260 and up. *TAC:* 10% (from Odysseus).

Note: Odysseus has a variety of accommodations on the island of Skiathos from the economic to the luxurious. Please call Odysseus Tel: (516) 944-5330 or (800) 257-5344 for prices and details of various hotels and apartments.

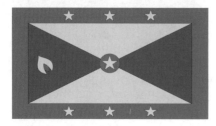

GRENADA

AREA: 133 sq. mi. (344 sq. km)
POPULATION: 110,000
CAPITAL: St. George
CURRENCY: EC$
OFFICIAL LANGUAGE: English, French
MAJOR RELIGIONS: Roman Catholicism, Protestantism
Telephone:
Nat'l Holiday: Independence Day, Feb. 7
Official Time: GMT - 4
Electricity: 220-240 volts A.C., 50 cycles
Exchange Rate: 1US$ = EC$2.70
National Airline: BWIA

LAW REGARDING HOMOSEXUALITY: Homosexuality is illegal in Grenada. However, the island is a popular international tourist destination with friendly people and lovely sandy beaches.

ST GEORGE

✈ Point Salines Int'l Airport (GND)
    9 mi. / 14 km southwest

LOCATION: Southwest near Point Salines and Grand Anse beach.

POPULATION: 30,000

CLIMATE: Two distinct seasons: dry and rainy. Dry season from January to May; Rainy season the rest of the year. Average temperature is 80°F (27°c).

DESCRIPTION: Sleepy island with popular white sandy beach at Grand Anse Beach near St. George. The "Spice Island" is an independent three-island nation. The air on Grenada is famous for its fragrance of exotic flowers and fruits. St. George the capital is one of the most spectacular ports in the West Indies with Georgian Colonial buildings and colorful Creole architecture. During your holiday enjoy scuba diving in an exotic underwater world with submarine gardens, colorful fish and coral reefs; and duty free shopping of imported goods and native gifts and spices.

❖ SPECIAL EVENT: **Carnival**, second weekend in August with colorful parades and festivities.

BARS ♈ RESTAURANTS 🍴

● Bars/Clubs (AW): **Fantazia 2001**. disco at the Gem Holiday Beach Resort, Morne Rouge Bay (444-2288).

● Restaurants (AW): **Coconut's Beach**, French/Creole, fresh seafood daily, Grand Anse Beach (444-4644); **La Belle Creole**, Creole/Seafood, West Indian specialties, at Blue Horizons, Grand Anse Beach (444-4316); **Sur La Mer**, dinner and cocktails, at the Gem (444-4224).

ACCOMMODATIONS

THE GEM HOLIDAY BEACH RESORT
Morne Rouge Bay, St. George. Tel: (809) 444-4224. USA/Canada reservations: Tel - (516) 944-5330 or (800) 257-5344. Fax: (516) 944-7540. TYPE: *Holiday Beach Resort*. CLIENTELE: All Welcome. LOCATION: On the beautiful white sandy beach at Morne Rouge Bay, just a few steps from the famous Grand Anse Beach, and minutes from St. George.

* Apartments: 17 (1BR / 2BR)
  Seaview or Ocean View w/balcony
* CTV, phone, full kitchenette, refrigerator, living room, dining room, ceiling fans, A/C
* Maid service, use of snorkeling equipment dry cleaning, free parking
* Cultural center, nightclub, restaurant
* Beach: on the beach
* Airport: 10 min.
* Open: Year round
* Rates: $90 - $200 (no meals)
  Meal Plan available on request
* *TAC:* 10% (from Odysseus)

DESCRIPTION: Apartment hotel complex on the beach. All units are fully air-conditioned one or two bedroom apartments. Tastefully furnished and private. Weekly entertainment includes BBQ with live music and West Indian buffet. Complimentary entrance to Grenada's #1 nightclub Fantazia 2001.

GUATEMALA

AREA: 42,042 sq. mi. (108,889 sq. km)
POPULATION: 8,042,000
CAPITAL: Guatemala City
CURRENCY: Quetzal (Q)
OFFICIAL LANGUAGE: Spanish, Mayan
MAJOR RELIGIONS: Roman Catholicism
Telephone: 502
Nat'l Holiday: Independence Day, Sept. 15
Official Time: G.M.T. - 6
Electricity: 120 volts
Exchange Rate: 1US$ = Q 5.96
National Airline: Aviateca

LAW REGARDING HOMOSEXUALITY: Homosexuality is not mentioned in the law, but is considered a taboo by the local population. The rich Mayan culture considered homosexuality a gift from gods to the society. Today, gays are frequently harassed by the police and discretion is recommended.

GUATEMALA CITY   *©*   2

✈ La Aurora Int'l Airport (GUA)

LOCATION: Southern Guatemala, situated on an elevated plateau of the Sierra Madre at an altitude of 5,000 ft. (1500 m).

POPULATION: 2,300,000

CLIMATE: Moderate, comfortable with average temperature of 75°F (24°c) year round. Cool nights 60°F (15°c), and hot days 80°F (27°c).

DESCRIPTION: Guatemala City has become one of the most active and progressive in Central America. It is internationally recognized by travelers and artists as the 'City of Sunshine', or the 'City of Eternal Spring' for its mild generous climate.

The best shopping area is the local market behind the Cathedral in the main square with best prices in the whole country for handicrafts, textiles, woodwork, pottery, jade, gold etc. Visit the **Ixchel Museum** for its fabulous collection of textiles and native dresses, the **Archeological Museum** near the airport has one of the best exhibitions of Mayan art. Gay life in Guatemala City is limited and subdued. Unemployment rate is high, therefore any contacts with locals must be cautious.

BARS ⅄ RESTAURANTS ¶¶

● Bars/Clubs: **Encuentro**, 6 Avenida 12; **Pandora Box**, Ruta 3 no. 3-08, Zona 4; **Kashe**, bar, 24 calle 2-37 (Zona 3)

● Restaurants: **Fu-Lu-Sho**, Chinese restaurant, 6a Avenida 12-09, Zona 1; **Las Vegas**, bar & restaurant, mixed clientele, 12 Calle 6-31, Zona 1.

 ACCOMMODATIONS

CAMINO REAL
Reforma Ave. & 14th St., Zone 10, Guatemala City. Tel: 680211-15. TYPE: *Hotel*. CLIENTELE: Mostly Straight. LOCATION: Exclusive Embassy District, 15 min. to downtown. 430 rooms, CTV, phone, A/C, balcony, garden, restaurant, bar, disco, pool, sundeck, tennis courts, Health club & sauna. DESCRIPTION: Modern hotel with attractive architecture. One of the best in Guatemala.

HOTEL DEL CENTRO
13 St., 4-55 Zone 1, Guatemala City. Tel: 81519, 80639. TYPE: *Hotel*. CLIENTELE: Mostly Straight. LOCATION: Downtown, in the old city. 60 rooms, CTV, phone, A/C, restaurant: International cuisine. DESCRIPTION: Modern building, all private facilities, convenient to the local gay scene.

PLAZA, MOTEL
Via 7, 6-16 Zone 4, Guatemala City. Tel: 63626, 62338. TYPE: *Motel*. CLIENTELE: Mostly Straight. LOCATION: Between the Airport and downtown.

* Rooms: 66 w/priv. bath
* TV, phone, balcony, garden
* Restaurant, pool & sundeck
* Room & maid service, parking
* Gay Bars: 5 min. walking
* Airport: 15 min., taxi
* Rates: (US) $65-$95. *TAC:* 10%

DESCRIPTION: Standard tourist motel near the gay scene.

HONDURAS

AREA: 43,277 sq. mi. (112,087 sq. km)
POPULATION: 3,700,000
CAPITAL: Tegucigalpa
CURRENCY: Lempira (L)
OFFICIAL LANGUAGE: Spanish
MAJOR RELIGIONS: Roman Catholicism
Telephone: 504
Nat'l Holiday: Independence Day, Sept. 15
Official Time: 6 hours behind G.M.T.
Electricity: 220 volts, 60 cycles
Exchange Rate: 1US$ = L 10.09
National Airline: Sahsa

LAW REGARDING HOMOSEXUALITY:
Honduras constitution 'guarantees' the civil
rights of 'all citizens'. There is no mention of
homosexuality in the Penal Code. However, the
emerging gay & lesbian community battles
homophobia and struggles for basic human
rights. Very few gay men or lesbians who are
out of the closet feel safe to be openly gay.

❖ Prior to 1985 existed a certain degree of tolerance for a 'semi-visible' gay community largely concentrated in major urban centers such as
Tegucigalpa and San Pedro Sula. Many gay
and lesbian bars were allowed to operate
because they were profitable for the military
that controlled the sale of liquor and extorted
protection fees from the bar owners. After 1985
the impact of AIDS sparked virulent homophobia in Honduras and the climate is today
unsafe for gay and lesbian travelers.

SAN PEDRO SULA   ℭ 53

✈ La Mesa Airport (SAP)

LOCATION: 58 km / 37 mi. south of Puerto
Cortés in northwestern Honduras.

POPULATION: 310,000

CLIMATE: Temperate and pleasant in the
cooler season October - March; hot and humid
in the summer.

DESCRIPTION: Second largest in Honduras
and one of the most rapidly growing urban centers in Central America. You can meet gay men
at the Central Park (AYOR) near the Gran
Hotel Sula.

● Side trip: visit the magnificent **Copán
Mayan** ruins, about 2 hrs. (186 km / 116 mi.)
from San Pedro Sula.

BARS ⛾ RESTAURANTS ⛾

● Bars/Clubs (GM): **Corcel Neuro** (525-075);
Terrazas Video Disco, 15 Avda 10 calle (Zona
Viva). ● Restaurant (AW): **French restaurant
and Steakhouse** at the Copanti Hotel & Club.

◈ ACCOMMODATIONS ◈

BOLIVAR HOTEL
Calle & 2a Ave., No. 8 El Centro. Tel: 53.32.24.
TYPE: *Hotel*. CLIENTELE: Mostly Straight.
LOCATION: Centrally near the train station.

* Rooms: 70 w/priv. bath
* Suites & Efficiency Apartments
* Bar, nightclub, pool, parking
* Airport: 5 mi. / 8 km
* Gay Bar: taxi required
* Open: Year round
* Credit Cards: MC/VISA/AMEX/DC
* Rates: (US) $59 - US$80 *TAC:* 10%

DESCRIPTION: Tourist class hotel.

COPANTI HOTEL & CLUB
Ctra Salida a Chamelecon, Apdo 1060. Tel: 53-
0900. Fax: (504) 57-3890. TYPE: *Hotel*. CLIEN-
TELE: Mostly Straight. LOCATION: In suburban area, 5 min. from town center.

* Rooms: 200 w/priv. bath. Suites: 7
* CTV, phone, A/C
* Restaurant, steakhouse, coffee shop
* Pool, bar, health club, sauna
* 4 lighted tennis courts
* Airport: 20 minutes
* Rates: (US) $80 - $180 *TAC:* 10%

DESCRIPTION: Resort hotel in a quiet suburban location. 2 hours from the famous Copan
Mayan ruins.

HONG KONG

AREA: 403 sq. mi. (1,044 sq. km)
POPULATION: 6,200,000
CURRENCY: Hong Kong Dollar (HK$)
OFFICIAL LANGUAGES: English, Cantonese
MAJOR RELIGIONS: Confucianism, Buddhism, Christianity, Islam, Taoism
Telephone: 852
Nat'l Holiday: Liberation Day, Aug. 26/28
Official Time: G.M.T. + 8
Electricity: 220 volts, 50 cycles
Exchange Rate: 1US$ = HK$ 7.73
National Airline: Cathay Pacific Airways

LAW REGARDING HOMOSEXUALITY: Criminal sanctions on homosexual relations between consenting adults over were lifted in Hong-Kong in 1991. It is now legal for two gay men over the age of 21 to have consensual sex. It was never illegal for two women to have sex in private. Hong Kong is in the process of considering Equal Rights Ordinance for gays.

There are no specific laws preventing anyone with AIDS or HIV from travelling to Hong Kong.

HONG KONG ISLAND KOWLOON

✈ Kai Tak Int'l Airport, Kowloon (HKG)

LOCATION: At the south-eastern tip of the People's Republic of China, just north of the Tropic of Cancer.

CLIMATE: Subtropical. Early spring (late March/April) and late autumn (Oct/Nov) are the most pleasant. Spring average temperature is 70°/77°F (21°/25°c) with low humidity. Summer's average temperature is 82°F (28°c) with very high humidity. Winter's average temperature is 59°F (15°c) with 75% humidity.

**Gay/Lesbian Visitor Information
Contacts Magazine**
GPO Box 13427, H.K.
Tel: 2817-9120. Fax: 2817-9447
E-mail: Band@HK.Super.Net.

Helpline: 2898-4422

DESCRIPTION: A soon to expire British Territory (colony); Hong Kong will be handed over to Mainland China in 1997. Hong Kong was founded as a place to conduct business and trade in the Far East. As a duty-free port, Hong Kong attracts million of tourists each year who come to savor the exotic charm of the island and indulge in low cost quality shopping. Hong Kong can be divided into four areas: **Hong Kong Island**, **Kowloon**, the **New Territories**, and the **Outlying Islands**, most of which are uninhabited. Hong Kong Island is the Colony's business hub, with high rise buildings, and shopping area. Kowloon is much smaller than the Hong Kong Island but with twice the population. It houses the islands main shopping area, restaurants, bars and hotels. The New Territories are the island's country side with small farming villages. Outlying Islands are mostly uninhabited.

❖ Public Cruising (AYOR): best after 8:30pm and before closing - **Oceaon Terminal Shopping Centre**, 3rd Fl., MTR Tsim Sha Tsui; **Pacific Place Shopping Mall**, MTR Admirality; **Times Square Shopping Mall**, MTR Causeway Bay.

❖ Gay Beaches (GM): **Kowloon Park Swimming Pool**, MTR Tsim Sha Tsui; **Middle Bay**, South Bay Road, Hong Kong, mainly frequented by gay men, especially on weekends; **The Rock Middle Bay**, area between Middle Bay and South Bay. Some nude sunbathing (illegal) and action in bushes (also illegal). Approach from South Bay Road. Steep path on the right hand (sea side); **South Bay**, South Bay Road, Hong Kong, clean, sandy beach, good for making contact. No action. Also used by straights; **Cheung Sha Beach**, Lantau Island. Note: **Middle Bay** is well-known for being dangerous (AYOR). For safety reason it is better to make the 1-hour trip to **Lantau Island** and walk to the remote **Cheung Sha Beach**. There are in fact two beaches - known as Upper and Lower Cheung Sha Beaches - the most exciting cruise beach is located right between these two beaches. Here the beach area is secluded and free of outsiders and police patrols.

BARS ϒ RESTAURANTS ¶¶

● Bars/clubs (AW): **Babylon**, large Karaoke lounge, 8:00pm - 2:00am, 5/F Kingspower Commercial Bldg., 409-413 Jaffe Rd., Wan Chai (2573-3978); **CE Top**,well appointed bar with disco and separate Karaoke room, 7:00pm-1:00am. 9/F 37-43 Cochrane St., Central, Hong Kong (2544-3581); **Club '97**, bar full of atmosphere and charm, only gay on Friday evenings 6-9pm and 1st Sunday of the month, 9, Lan Kwai Fong Central, Hong Kong (2810-9333); **Deviant Zone**, 1/F 21, D'Agular St., Central HK (2537-3345); **Members Connection**, small gay Karaoke bar, mainly Chinese, 7pm-3am (890-7731); **Petticoat Lane**, intimate Baroque-style bar with good choice of food and drinks, members only but overseas visitors welcome, 2, Tun Wo Lane, Central, 12 noon - 3pm / 7pm-2am (2973-0642); **Propaganda**, Hong-Kong's largest and best disco club, packed on weekends, disco hours 9:30pm-3:30am, Mon-Sat. (closed Sundays, except on Public holidays), 30-32 Wyndham St., Central (2868-1316); **Wally Matt Lounge**, 9 Cornwall Ave., Tsim Sha Tsui, 6pm-3am (2367-6874).

● Bars/clubs (GM): **AE**, uninspiring and cheaply decorated, mainly Chinese, 1/F Kwong Ah Bldg., 114, Thomson Rd., Wan Chai, Hong Kong, 2pm-1am (2591-0500); **H2O**, Karaoke bar, mainly Chinese, 5:00pm-3:00am, 2/F Hop Yee Bldg., Causeway Bay (2834-6451); **Members Connection**, small and sleazy Karaoke bar, mainly Chinese, 3/F 5 Lan Fong Rd., Causeway Bay, 7:00pm-3:00am (890-7731); **Why Not**, karaoke bar, open 8:00pm - 2:00am, 12/F Kyoto Plaza, 491-499 Lochart Rd., Causeway Bay HK (2572-7808).

● Restaurants (AW): **Stew & Steam**, 'in' place for good Cantonese food, popular with gays, G/F 21-23 Tai Wong St., East, Wan Chai; **White Stag, English** pub catering to mostly Chinese clientele, 72 Canton Rd. Tsimashatsui (2368-4612); **Ned Kelly's Last Stand**, Australian Pub with live Dixieland Jazz nightly from 9pm, 11A Ashley Rd. in Tsimshatsui (2366-0562).

λ SERVICES λ

● Health Clubs (GM): **AA**, open 1:00pm-2:00am, 1/F 19 Lan Fong Rd., Causeway Bay, HK (2577-3705); **AE**, 1/F Kwong Ah Bldg., 114 Thomson Rd., HK (2591-0500); **BA**, one of the original saunas, clean and well run, 1/F Flat D, Cheung Hong Mansion, 25-33 Johnston Rd., Wanchai, Hong Kong, 2pm-2am (527-7073); **Bobson Club**, 3/F Flat D, 35-37, Ma's Bldg.,

Hankow Rd., Kowloon, 3:30pm-1am (2376-2208); **Blue Blood**, fitness club, 3/F Perfect Commercial Bldg., 20 Austin Ave. TST (2302-0780); **Central Escalator**, small friendly and popular with locals and tourists, steam and sauna, drinks and food available, 1pm - 1am, 2/Fl., Cheung Hing Comm. Bldg., 37-43 Cochrane St., Central (2581-9951); **Game Boy's**, the biggest steam/sauna in HK, has been raided numerous times by police, mainly Chinese, 2/F 324 Lockhart Rd., Fook Yee Bldg., Wanchai 12 noon - 2am (574-3215); **JJ Park**, mainly Chinese but a few foreigners, 3/F Flat A, Fairview Mansion, 51 Paterson St., Causeway Bay, 3pm-1am (2882-2399); **KK**, drinks and food available, Larger than usual sauna with Karaoke room. Mainly Chinese. 16/F Block A, Fuk Kok Bldg., 19-21 Jordan Rd. Kowloon, 2pm-2am (2388-6138); **Robson Fitness Club**, 35-37 Hankow Rd., 3/F Flat D, Mag Bldg., Tsim Sha Tsui, Kowloon, open 3:30pm-1:00am (2376-2208); **Rome Club**, unfriendly not recommended, mainly Chinese, 2/F Chap Lee Commercial Bldg., 27 Ashley Rd., Tsim Sha Tsui, Kowloon, 3pm-12 midnight, (2376-0602).

● Organization (GMW): **10% Club**, voluntary group consisting of only Chinese speakers. Organizes some outdoor events for members. Does some political lobbying. G.P.O. Box 72207, Kowloon. (314-8726).

● Publication (GMW): **Contacts Magazine**, A4-size monthly publication, the only title being issued by the newly emergent gay community, 32 pages of local and international gay news. 12 issues annually subscription cost HK$300 for local residents and US$70 for overseas residents including airmail postage, Island Publishing Co., GPO Box 13427, Hong Kong. Tel: 2817-9447. Fax: 2817-9120. E-Mail BandT@HK.Super.Net.

● Shopping (G/S): **Fetish Fashion**, leather & rubber clothing, 1/F 52-60 Lynhurst Terrace, Central (2544-1155); **Gear**, beach and gym wear for men, 4 Anton St., Wan Chai (2527-1557); **Splash**, men's wear shop, 1/F Wah Fung Bldg., 245-251 Lockhart Rd., Wan Chai.

⬦ ACCOMMODATIONS ⬦

HARBOUR HOTEL

116-122 Gloucester Rd., Wanchai. Tel: 2574-8211. Fax: 2572-2185. TYPE: *Hotel*. CLIENTELE: Mostly Straight. LOCATION: In Wanchai across the harbour from Kowloon.

* Rooms: 200 w/priv. bath, telephone
* Coffeeshop, Chinese restaurant

* Sauna: popular with gays
* Gay Bars: 1 mi. (1.6 km)
* Airport: 6 mi. (10 km), taxi
* Credit Cards: MC/AMEX/DC
* Open: Year round
* Rates: (HK) $1,450 - $1,800
* *TAC:* 10%

DESCRIPTION: Business oriented hotel in the Central District. Rooms are of elegant simplicity. The Sauna attracts many local and visiting gays. Entrance to the Sauna is on Fleming Rd. Good massage.

HYATT REGENCY (HK)
67 Nathan Road, Kowloon. Tel: 2366-2321. TYPE: *Deluxe Hotel*. CLIENTELE: Mostly Straight. LOCATION: 5 min. walk from the Star Ferry, near the Tsimashtsui subway station and the gay scene.

* Rooms: 723 w/priv. bath. Suites: 17
* CTV, phone, A/C
* Restaurants, bar & coffee terrace
* Room & maid service, valet parking
* Gay Bars: nearby
* Airport: 4 1/2 mi. (7 km), taxi
* Credit Cards: MC/VISA/AMEX/CB/DC
* Open: Year round
* Rates: (HK) $1,730 - $1,930

* *TAC:* 10%

DESCRIPTION: Elegant hotel with hints of Chinese culture in the furnishings and architecture. Bathrooms with Italian marble.

REGAL MERIDIAN HOTEL
71 Mody Road, P.O. Box 98760, Kowloon. Tel: 2722-1818. TYPE: *Deluxe Hotel*. CLIENTELE: Mostly Straight. LOCATION: In the Tsimshatsui district of East Kowloon, convenient to the local gay scene.

* Rooms: 585 w/priv. bath. Suites: 34
* CTV, phone, A/C
* Restaurant: French, Cantonese
* Brasserie, coffee shop, disco
* Pool & Fitness Club
* Room & maid service, valet parking
* Gay Bars: in basement
* Airport: 3 mi. (5 km), taxi
* Credit Cards: MC/VISA/AMEX/DC/CB
* Open: Year round
* Rates: (HK) $1,650 - $6,000
* *TAC:* 10%

DESCRIPTION: French owned hotel. Tastefully decorated rooms and lobby with 18th century French antiques. Sound proof rooms, minibars, with three phones in each room.

HUNGARY

AREA: 35,919 sq. mi. (93,030 sq. km)
POPULATION: 10,700,000
CAPITAL: Budapest
CURRENCY: Forint (Ft)
OFFICIAL LANGUAGE: Hungarian
MAJOR RELIGIONS: Roman Catholicism, Protestantism
Telephone: 36
National Holiday: Liberation Day, April 4
Official Time: GMT +1
Electricity: 220 V
Exchange Rate: 1US$ = Ft 136
National Airline: Malev

LAW REGARDING HOMOSEXUALITY: The age of consent for homosexual relationship is 18. Prison terms of up to 3 years are enforced on violators. The Hungarian society is intolerant towards gays and lesbians. There is a movement towards the formation of a gay/lesbian activist group. Hopefully the current political liberalization will help. Hungary's Constitutional Court legalized common law gay marriages on March 8, 1995. (Civil and Church marriages remain off-limits). It is the first Eastern European nation to do so.

BUDAPEST   © 01

✈ Ferihegy Airport (BUD)

LOCATION: North central area over the two banks of the Danube river.

POPULATION: 2,000,000

CLIMATE: Continental. Summers are hot with July average of 82°F (28°c). Winters are cold with January average of 34°F (1°c). Spring and fall are the most pleasant seasons.

DESCRIPTION: The capital of Hungary is one of the most delightful historical cities in Europe. It is the center of government, industry and commerce. For the international travelers Budapest offers various attractions: **Matthias Church, Fisherman's Bastion, Hero's Square, St. Istram Basilica**and the **Parliament Buildings**. The **Thermal** is a world-class health spa on **Margaret Island**, and a fashionable casino gambling is available at the **Hilton Hotel casino**. Visit **Castle Hill**, the famous **Danube Bridges**, the **Inner City** in modern **Pest**; and **Old Buda**. Buda and Pest are separated by the Danube River. It is best to stay in Pest and take a cab to Buda if necessary.

Shopping is usually from 10am-6pm Mon-Fri, and 9am-1pm Sat. Shops are closed on Sundays. The water quality is very good and can be consumed by the immunologically compromised. Bottled water is available but not necessary.

Budapest has a small but lively gay/lesbian scene which is expanding and getting better every year. Public cruising is popular late night at **Népliget** (People's Park) on the blue line (M3) suburban stop. The Park is only a short walk from the metro. It is best to explore first with an Hungarian friend. The metro ceases service at midnight, but taxis are readily available (AYOR). Another cruisy area is along the Marriott Hotel/Danube walkway south to Elizabeth bridge (AYOR) some are hustlers.

❖ Gay Beach: **Palatinu Stranfürdo** (May 1 - Sept. 1) Margitsziget, swimming pools and sunbathing area. Some gays.

BARS ♈ RESTAURANTS 🍴

● Bars/clubs (GM): **Action**, small friendly bar with dark room, best place to meet locals and tourists, Mºm blue line at Perenciek tere, 7pm-4am; V. Magyar utca 42; **Angyal (Angel Club)**, bar/disco/restaurant, VII Szövetségutca 33, 10pm-6am, loud music, young crowd, Sat. night is best (113-1273); **Art 44**, open 7pm-4am, XI Halmi u. 44, shows Fri/Sat; **Club 93**, restaurant/bar, VIII, Vas u. 2, Mº red line at Blaha Lujza tér, 9pm-4am; **Darling**, gay pub in the Inner City, v. Szép utca 1, Mº blue line at Ferenciek Tere, 9pm-5am; **Lokál**, VII Kertész utca 31, Dob Utca; **Mystery**, open 9pm-4am (closed Sundays), Mº blue line at Arany János u., Nagásandor József utca 3 (112-1436).

● Restaurants (GMW): **Alföldi**, inexpensive, in the Inner City near Calvin Square, popular with University students, outdoor terrace in summer, Kecskeméti utca 4 (174-404); **Club**

93, restaurant and bar, Italian cuisine, VIII, Vas u. 2, M° red line at Blaha Lujza tér, 9pm-4am; **Cyrano's**, mixed restaurant with excellent food, very homoerotic outfits on all male gorgeous staff, appears to be gay owned, on Vaci Utca east of Deák Square in Pest; Other (AW): **Gerbeaud**, coffee house, capuccino and deserts,Deák Square; **Gündel**, in the City Park, XIV, Allatkerri Krt. 2 (121-3550); **Hanna**, Kosher restaurant near the Jewish Synagogue and Museum, Bob utca 35 (427-359); **Margitkert**, smart restaurant popular with locals and foreigners, Margit utca 15 (354-791); **Muzeum Kávéház**, next to the National Museum in downtown, VIII. Múzeum Krt. 12 (138-4221); **Robinson's**, good food, Városligeti 76 near Heros Square (345-0955); **Rózsadomb**, restaurant/beer hall between Castle Hill and Margaret Bridge, Bimbó ut 2 (353-847).

λ SERVICES λ

● Gay Liberation: **Homeros Lambda**, Jégverem utca 6 I. 6, 1111 Budapest (201-7333); **Kesergay**, Hungarian Jewish Gay & Lesbian group, P.O. Box 1489, 1464 Budapest. Tel/Fax: (135-2463); **Lambda Budapest**, Box 388, 1461 Budapest.

● Health Clubs (G/S): **Gellért Furdo** (baths), mixed sauna, massage, thermal bathing, nude sunbathing on roof at the Hotel Gellért, XI. Kelenhegyi úcta 4; **Lukács Iszapfürdö**, Mon-Fri 12-19, after darkness wild action in the open-air mud basin, II Frankel Leo utca 26-29, M° red line, Battyányi tér (115-4280); **Rácz**, best Sat. 14-19, I. Hadnagy u. 8-10, M° blue line to Ferenciek tere, take bus #7 to Buda, one stop (175-4449); **Rudas**, Mon-Fri. 6:30-19, Sat. 6:30-13, Sun. 6:30-12, I Döbrentei Tér 9, M° blue line to Ferenciek tere, take bus #7 to Buda, one stop. be discreet (156-1322); **Széchenyi**, Mon-Fri 6:30-19, Sat. 6:30-13, swimming pool, sunroof where gays meet, hot water basin, steam room, XIV Allatkerti u. 11, M° yellow line at Széchenyi fürdo, (121-0310).

● Health Service: **AIDS Segély**, anonymous HIV testing, Mon, Wed., Thu. 17-19, Tue., Fri. 10-12, XI Karlonia u. 35/b, (166-9283).

● Sex Shops (G/S): **Apollo Video Shop**, VI Teréz Kőrut 3 10am-6pm; **Eros Sex Shop**, VI Nyugati Pu, 10am-6pm.

 ACCOMMODATIONS

DUNA INTER-CONTINENTAL
Apaczai Csere Janos U., Budapest 1364. Tel: (01) 175-122. TYPE: *Deluxe Hotel*. CLIENTELE: Mostly Straight. LOCATION: On the Pest side of the Danube, between Chain Bridge and Elizabeth Bridge. 350 rooms w/priv. bath, CTV, phone, A/C, restaurants, club & terrace cafe, pool, fitness center, sauna. Gay Bars: nearby. Airport: 10 mi. (16 km). Credit Cards: MC/VISA/AMEX/ACC. Open: Year round. Rates: (US) $120 - $290. *TAC:* 10%. DESCRIPTION: Modern elegant hotel with fine amenities. Ibusz rated 5 stars.

GELLÉRT HOTEL
Szt. Gellért ter 1, Budapest 1111. Tel: (01) 1852-200. US/Canada reservations available from Odysseus Tel: (516) 944-5330, (800) 257-5344. Fax: (516) 944-7540 or (800) 982-6571. TYPE: *Moderate deluxe hotel*. CLIENTELE: Mostly straight. LOCATION: At the foot of the Gellért Hill, beside de Danube. 235 rooms w/priv. bath, CTV, phone, A/C, restaurant, coffeeshop, sauna, health spa. Rates: on request. *TAC:* 10%. DESCRIPTION: Grand style hotel with an internationally famous thermal health spa. The sauna is popular with certain gay clientele but it is not a gay sauna.

HOTEL KORONA
utca 12, Budapest H-1053. Tel: (1) 117-4111. TYPE: *Hotel*. CLIENTELE: Mostly straight. LOCATION: Downtown opp. the Nat'l Museum. 433 rooms w/priv. bath, CTV, phone, minibar, A/C, health center. Rates: on request. DESCRIPTION: Impressive downtown hotel. Rooms for non-smokers available.

RAMADA GRAND HOTEL
Margitsziget H-1138, Budapest. Tel: (1) 132-1100. USA/Canada reservations available from Odysseus Tel: (516) 944-5330 or (800) 257-5344. Fax: (516) 944-7540 or (800) 982-6571. TYPE: *Hotel*. CLIENTELE: Mostly Straight. LOCATION: On the northern end of Margaret Island near the Hotel Géllert. 163 rooms w/priv. bath, suites: 28, CTV, phone, mini-bar, A/C, restaurant, bar, nightclub, parking, pool, sauna, gym, health spa . Airport: 14 mi. / 22 km, taxi. Gay Bars: nearby. Open: Year round. Rates: (US) $120 - $250. *TAC:* 10%. DESCRIPTION: Old World-style hotel in a quiet setting.

ICELAND

AREA: 39,768 sq. mi. (103,000 sq. km)
POPULATION: 250,000
CAPITAL: Reykjavík
CURRENCY: Króna (IK)
OFFICIAL LANGUAGES: Icelandic
MAJOR RELIGIONS: Protestantism
Telephone: 354
Nat'l Holiday: Independence Day, Dec. 1
Official Time: G.M.T
Electricity: 220 volts
Exchange Rate: 1US$ = IK 64.44
National Airline: Icelandair

LAW REGARDING HOMOSEXUALITY: The legal age of consent for both homosexuals and heterosexuals is 14. In spite of the country's small population there are 2 gay and lesbian organizations and a thriving gay community.

REYKJAVIK   ✆   1

✈ Keflavik Airport (KEF)

LOCATION: Southwestern island location on the shores of the Atlantic Ocean.

POPULATION: 100,000

CLIMATE: Unpredictable, but temperate by the Gulf Stream. July is the warmest and the best time to visit Iceland. Iceland is the land of the midnight sun. In Reykjavík, the sun sets for few hours between 3:00am and 5:00am.

Gay/Lesbian Visitor Information
Félagid: 551-8330

DESCRIPTION: Reykjavík is the world's northernmost capital. It is the largest and most important city in Iceland with a population of almost half the total island population. Iceland is a mystical land of glaciers, fire spitting volcanoes, midnight sun, and ancient tales of epic stories.

BARS 𝖸 RESTAURANTS ❚❚

● Bars/Clubs (GMW): **Bar "22"**, popular dance club, Laugavegur 22; **Félagid**, Lindargata 46 (551-8330); **Reykjavik Gay Center**, coffee shop, Lindargata 49 (285-39); **Rosenberg**, dance club, Austurstræti 22b.

● Restaurants (AW): **Hersson**, Austurstræti 20; **Thrir Frakkar**, Baldursgata 14 (239-39).

λ SERVICES λ

● Health Club (G/S): **Vesturbæjar**, Hofsvallagata (150-04).

🗝 ACCOMMODATIONS 🗝

CITY HOTEL
Ranargata 4A, Reykjavik. Tel: (1) 8650. TYPE: *Hotel*. CLIENTELE: All Welcome. LOCATION: Quiet residential area few blocks from harbor or city center. 61 rooms w/priv. bath, phone, CTV, C/H, 24 hrs. room service, elevator, lounge, parking. Rates: (US) $100-$130. DESCRIPTION: Tourist class hotel with neatly furnished rooms.

LOFTLEIDER HOTEL
Reykjavik Airport, Reykjavik IS-101. Tel: (1) 22322. TYPE: *Hotel*. CLIENTELE: Mostly Straight. LOCATION: 15 min. from center of the city.

* Rooms: 218 w/private bath
* CTV, phone, C/H
* Restaurant, cafeteria, lounges
* Pool, sauna, parking
* Room & maid service
* Airport: 30 mi. (48 km)
* Gay Bars: nearby
* Credit Cards: AMEX/DC/EC
* Open: Year round
* Rates: (US) $130 - $180
* *TAC:* 10%

DESCRIPTION: First class hotel, the largest in Finland, with tastefully furnished rooms. Air terminal at the hotel. Long time favorite with international air stewards and flight attendants.

INDIA

AREA: 1,269,339 sq. mi. (3,287,588 sq. km)
POPULATION: 685,000,000
CAPITAL: New Delhi
CURRENCY: Indian rupee
OFFICIAL LANGUAGE: Hindi, English and many other ethnic languages
MAJOR RELIGIONS: Hinduism, Islam, Christianity, Buddhism, Sikhism
Telephone: 990
Nat'l Holiday: Independence Day, Aug. 15
Official Time: G.M.T. + 7
Electricity: 220 volts
Exchange Rate: 1US$ = rupees 34.85
National Airline: Air India

LAW REGARDING HOMOSEXUALITY: Homosexual acts between men are illegal under the Penal Code. Homosexuality is punishable with a maximum penalty of life imprisonment and a fine, but the trend is towards more liberal attitudes. Homosexual acts between women are not mentioned in the law.

BOMBAY   ✆ 022

✈ Bombay Int'l Airport (BOM)

LOCATION: On the northwestern coast of India and the Arabian Sea.

POPULATION: 6,000,000

CLIMATE: Hot and sticky, plenty of rainfall, cool nights.

DESCRIPTION: Bombay is a long and narrow island city founded by the British on the site of a Portuguese trading station. Today it has a mix of many cultures and races. Downtown has some splendid 19th century Indo-Gothic buildings which remind travelers of London. To absorb local scents and colors visit the **Chor**

Bazaar, the **Thieves Market** around **Mutton Street**.

❖ Beach: **Chowpathy Beach** at the end of Marina Drive.

BARS ▼ RESTAURANTS 🍴

● Bars/clubs (G/S): **Ambassador Hotel Bar**, some gays, Veer Nariman Rd., Churchgate extension; **Gaylord Café**, Churchgate near the Ambassador Hotel; **Ritz Hotel Bar**, some gays, 5 Jamshedji Rd., Churchgate; **Studio 29**, Dinoha Vaccha/Marine Drive (at Bombay Int'l Hotel); **President Hotel Disco**, mixed disco, 90 Cuffe Parade, Colaba (219-141).

● Restaurants: **Talk of the Town Patio**, Churchgate / Marine Drive, also check the **Gulzar Indian restaurant** at the Hotel President; and the restaurants at the Ambassador Hotel.

ACCOMMODATIONS

AMBASSADOR HOTEL
Veer Nariman Rd., Churchgate Extension. Bombay 400020. Tel: 204-1131. TYPE: *Hotel*. CLIENTELE: Mostly Straight. LOCATION: In Churchgate business district. 127 rooms w/priv. bath. Rates: (US) $65-$90. *TAC:* 10%. DESCRIPTION: Pleasant first class hotel in the business district.

HOTEL PRESIDENT
90 Cuffee Parade, Colaba, Bombay 400005. Tel: 495-0808. Fax: 495-1201. TYPE: *Hotel*. CLIENTELE: Mostly Straight. LOCATION: Near the heart of downtown Bombay, 40 min. from airport, 5 min. from ocean terminal. 319 rooms w/priv. bath, A/C, CTV, phone, 24 hrs. room service, 4 restaurants, bars, health club. Rates: (US) $80 - $100. *TAC:* 10%

CALCUTTA   ✆ 033

✈ Calcutta Int'l Airport (CCU)
   8 mi. / 13 km northeast

LOCATION: Northeastern India on the Bay of Bengal.

POPULATION: 10,860,000

CLIMATE: Weather is best between Nov. and Feb. From March on the temperatures rise sharply. Summer temperatures in July reach high of 90°F (32°c); winter temperatures in January reach a low of 55°F (12°c). The arrival of Summer rains lower the temperatures but raise the humidity.

DESCRIPTION: Founded by English merchants in 1690, Calcutta is India's second largest city and the capital of West Bengal. Calcutta epitomizes extreme poverty and deprivation, but it is also a cultural and intellectual center with great contribution to art, medicine and science.

BARS Y RESTAURANTS ¶¶

● Bars/clubs (G/S): **Ambar**, C.R. Avenue; **Metropol Hotel Bar**, Deccars Lane; **Park Hotel Pub**, 17 Park St., especially after midnight on weekends; **Trincas Bar**, Paile Street.

ACCOMMODATIONS

PARK HOTEL
17 Park St. Tel: (33) 249-7336. TYPE: *Hotel.* CLIENTELE: All Welcome. LOCATION: Fashionable Park Street, 1 km from downtown.

* Rooms: 170 w/priv. bath. Suites: 12
* CTV (CNN), phone, minibar, A/C
* Restaurant, Pub, cocktail lounge
* 24 hrs. room service
* Outdoor pool, shops, free parking
* Airport: 15 km / 10 mi.
* Open: Year round
* Rates: (US) $90 - $130

DESCRIPTION: Moderate first class hotel. Helpful room service staff. Male friends can stay overnight.

NEW DELHI © 011

✈ Indira Gandhi Int'l Airport (DEL)
14 mi. / 22 km south of Delhi

LOCATION: Northern India in the Uttar Pradesh province.

POPULATION: 4,500,000

CLIMATE: Three season year - hot (Feb-May), wet (June-Aug.) & cool (Oct. - Jan.).

DESCRIPTION: New Delhi is the capital of India and the busiest entrance point for over-

seas airlines. **Old Delhi** and **New Delhi**, the sections of interest to visitors are located on the west bank of the **Yamuna River**. The 'hub' of New Delhi is the great circle of **Connaught Place** and nearby sts. This is a business and tourist centre where most of the shops, restaurants, banks, travel agents and other businesses are located. Delhi's more expensive residential areas are located south of the New Delhi government areas.

New Delhi has a subdued gay scene for a large metropolis of its size. There are no established gay venues. The places where you may encounter other gay travelers are in bars of major hotels. Public cruising areas include the gardens in the centre of **Connaught Place** and the shopping mall known as **Connaught Circus**. **Nehru Park** in front of the Ashoka Hotel can be busy in the evening.

BARS Y RESTAURANTS ¶¶

● Bars (G/S): **Imperial Hotel Bar**, Janpath Rd. (31-151); **Janpath Hotel bar**, Janpath Rd. (350-070); **Nirulas Bar**, Nirulas Hotel, Connaught Circus (352-419).

● Restaurants (AW): **Lido**, near Connaught Place; **Nirula's**, light snacks, Janpath & Connaught Place.; **Wenger's**, pastry shop, Connaught Place.

λ SERVICES λ

● Health Club (G/S): **Claridges Hotel Health Club**, very cruisy sauna, popular with gays,12 Aurangzeb Rd., (545-2223).

ACCOMMODATIONS

CLARIDGE's HOTEL
12 Aurangzeb Rd., New Delhi 110011. Tel: (11) 545-2223. Fax: (11) 301-0625. TYPE: *Hotel.* CLIENTELE: Mostly Straight. LOCATION: 4km / 2 mi. from city center. 164 rooms w/priv. bath, CTV, phone, A/C, restaurant, coffee shop, health club, gym, sauna (popular with gay clientele), tennis, parking. Rates: (US) $85-$250. *TAC:* 10%.

IMPERIAL HOTEL
Janpath, New Delhi. Tel: (11) 332-5332. Fax: (11) 332-4542. TYPE: *Hotel.* CLIENTELE: Mostly Straight. LOCATION: In garden setting adjacent to Connaught Circus. 230 rooms w/priv. bath, CTV, phone, A/C, restaurant, bar, pool. Rates: (US) $65-$180. *TAC:* 10%.

AREA: 788,430 sq. mi. (2,042,034 sq. km)
POPULATION: 148,000,000
CAPITAL: Jakarta
CURRENCY: Rupiah
OFFICIAL LANGUAGE: Bahasa Indonesia,
Indonesian & Papuan languages, English
MAJOR RELIGIONS: Islam, tribal religions,
Christianity, Hinduism
Telephone: 62
Nat'l Holiday: Independence Day, Dec. 27
Official Time: G.M.T. + 7
Electricity: 220 volts
Exchange Rate: 1US$ = Rupiahs 2,283
National Airline: Garuda Indonesian Air.

LAW REGARDING HOMOSEXUALITY:
Homosexual acts are legal. The Indonesian culture is traditionally open and acceptable of male homosexuality. Many gay men marry, but continue to have homosexual relationships after marriage. The new middle-class and some religious movements express dislike of homosexuality. Although there are no laws which deal concretely with HIV or AIDS. Travelers with HIV or AIDS may risk denied entry or quarantine.

✔ Note: special thanks to Dédé Oetomo and Tom Boellstorff from **Gaya Nusantara** *(Indonesian National Gay Network)* for their important contribution to the preparation of this section on Indonesia.

BATAM ISLAND

BATAM   *℗*   778

✈ Batam Airport

LOCATION: In the Riau Archipelago, immediately south of Singapore.

DESCRIPTION: Heavily developed island which is almost an industrial suburb of Singapore. No need for a visa to enter or leave Indonesia through Batam Port or Airport. Cheap connection to Singapore by ferry several times daily. The Singapore dollar (S$) is a legal tender on the island and widely accepted.

❖ Public Cruising (AYOR): **Bukit Senyum** *(Smiling Hill)*, mostly at night, many transvestites; also at the **Batu Ampar** in the karaoke clubs.

BARS Ⴤ RESTAURANTS ❚❙

● Bars/clubs (G/S): **Club 5-0**, gay meetingplace at the New Holiday Hotel, many westerners; **Golden Gate**, disco / karaoke, gay men and westerners, Nagoya Plaza Hotel; **Regina Palace**, disco, discreet gay, best nights Sat-Sun nights; **Studio 21**, many gay men, very discreet club.

ACCOMMODATIONS

PANORAMA BATAM
Magoya, Batam. Tel: (778) 452-888. TYPE: *Hotel*. CLIENTELE: All Welcome. LOCATION: City center, 25 min. to the airport or ferry terminal to Singapore. 289 rooms, 12 suites w/priv. bath, CTV (movies), phone, minibar, restaurants, bars, pool, fitness center. Rates: on request.

BALI ISLAND

DENPASAR   *℗*   361

✈ Ngurah Rai Int'l Airport (DPS)

LOCATION: In the southern portion of the island of Bali.

POPULATION: 1,000,000

CLIMATE: Tropical, hot and sticky with rainfall heaviest from Nov. through April.

DESCRIPTION: Denpasar is the provincial capital. Not a tourist destination - a crowded urban necessity for those who live in Bali. Not worth the trip for most gay visitors with the exception of **Puputan Field** *(Lapangan Puputan)* between Surapati and Veteran

370   INDONESIA

Streets, the central civic park ringed by government buildings - a friendly social scene for local gay men who gather there from about 6-11pm nightly; The night scene for cross-dressers for hire is **Renon**, near Mathari department store.

λ SERVICES λ

● AIDS Organization (G/S): **Yayasan Usadha Indonesia**, Jalan Belimbing, Gang Y no. 4 (22620).

 ACCOMMODATIONS

See Kuta Beach.

KUTA BEACH   ℂ   361

✈ Ngurah Rai Int'l Airport (DPS)

LOCATION: On the island of Bali in eastern Indonesia.

POPULATION: 500,000

CLIMATE: Tropical, hot and sticky with plenty of rainfall; cool nights.

DESCRIPTION: Kuta Beach is a beach resort town along the Kuta Bay 5 mi. / 8 km northwest of Denpasar. It is popular with Australians on cheap holidays who enjoy drinking in local pubs. Gay life is thriving in Kuta Beach. The major gay scene focuses on a small strip of beach and night spots in nearby Seminyak. Many local 'rent-boys' offer their services for those who are interested.

❖ Public Cruising (AYOR): **Kuta-Legian Beach**.

❖ Gay Beaches: in **Seminyak**, beginning at the beach access road Jalan Dhyana Pura (by Bali Imperial Hotel), the gay scene flows north away from Kuta to Pura Petitenget (temple). There is a section that can be nudist, and along the way are several "massage stands" that offer cold drink and hot massage (most notable is one operated by "Mama Ketut" between the Bali Oberoi Hotel and Bali Pesona Hotel beachfronts). As sunset approaches, activity increases - not considered safe for those walking alone after dark. From 7pm-10pm the area of Kuta Beach across from the Sahid Jaya Hotel is active with rent-boys.

BARS ♈ RESTAURANTS 🍴

● Bars/clubs (G/S): **C-Line**, gay owned gallery, bar & art cafe, jl. kartika plaza 33, kuta near the Bali Bintang Hotel (1512-85); **Double Six Club**, late night gay scene on the beach in Seminyak near Jalan Dhyana Pura; **Gado-Gado**, nightclub, late night gay scene, Jalan Dhyana Pura at the beach; **Int'l Bali Beach Hotel**, beach, bar and pool; **Made's Warung**, lively cocktail bar after 7pm, Kuta; **Sari Club**, Legian St. Kuta; **Spotlight Disco**, same building as the Burger King, some gays, 95% Asians, Kuta.

● Restaurants (G/S): **Goa 2001**, seafood restaurant & bar, the bar area becomes more gay from 10pm-12midnight, Jalan Legian; **La Lucciolla Restaurant & Beach Club**, gay owned and operated on the gay beach with excellent Italian menu, jalan Oberoi & Pura Petitenget Beach.

λ SERVICES λ

● Island Tours (GMW): ✪ **Bali Spartacus**, gay friendly hotels and tours on the exotic island of Bali, Poppies Lane 1 #77, Kuta (756-454). USA/Canada call (800) 257-5344 or (516) 944-5330. Fax: (516) 944-7540.

 ACCOMMODATIONS

✪ BALI MANDIRA COTTAGES
Ji Padma, Kuta Beach. USA and Canada Reservations: Odysseus (516) 944-5330 or (800) 257-5344. Fax: (516) 944-7540. TYPE: *Beach Resort Complex*. CLIENTELE: All Welcome. LOCATION: On Kuta Beach near downtown.

* Cottages: 118 units w/priv. bath
* Phone, A/C, refrigerator, garden
* Wheelchair access, free parking
* Restaurant, bar, pool, tennis, Squash
* Beach: on the beach
* Gay Bars: some nearby
* Airport: 6 km / 4 mi., taxi
* Open: Year round
* High Season: July/August, 12/20/96-1/10/97
* Rates: (US) $80 - $200
   Tax & service included. No breakfast
* *TAC:* 10% (from Odysseus)

DESCRIPTION: Balinese-style cottage complex right on Kuta Beach where the action is. Accommodations offered vary from standard single cottages, beach front cottages and deluxe cottage suites.

✪ SANTIKA BEACH

Ji Kartika, Tuban Beach. USA and Canada Reservations: Odysseus (516) 944-5330 or (800) 257-5344. Fax: (516) 944-7540. TYPE: *Beach Resort Complex.* CLIENTELE: Gay Welcome. LOCATION: On Tuban Beach south of Kuta Beach.

* Rooms: 40 standard, 20 superior deluxe rooms 68 (twin or
* Bungalows: 14 (twin beds); 8 large with 1 dbl + 1 twin bed, 1 full bath
* Presidential Suite: with own pool
* Junior Suites: 10 (1BR)
* Phone, A/C, minibar, hairdryer, garden
* 24 hrs. room service, 24 hrs. security
* Wheelchair access, free parking
* Restaurant, bar, pool, tennis, Squash
* Beach: on the beach
* Gay Bars: some nearby
* Airport: 6 km / 4 mi., taxi
* Open: Year round
* High Season: July/August, 12/20/97-1/10/98
* Rates: (US) $100 - $180 w/AB
  Tax & service included
* **TAC:** 10% (from Odysseus)

DESCRIPTION: Elegant peaceful resort complex on the beach overlooking the ocean and surrounded by acres of lush tropical gardens. Art shops, boutiques, nightspots, art market and public transportation can be found just around the corner.

Bali Mandira Cottages
USA/Canada Reservations
(800) 257-5344

UBUD   ©   **361**

✈ Ngurah Rai Int'l Airport (DPS)

LOCATION: Inland about 45 min. north of Denpassar. One hour drive north from the Airport.

CLIMATE: Tropical, but tempered by elevation and breezes for cooler nights.

DESCRIPTION: Ubud is the small-town cultural heart of Bali - historically rich and artistically fertile. Visual and performing arts are exceptional, especially painting, dance and gamelan music. There is enough shopping variety to please most visitors, and the island's best selection of restaurant cuisines. Tourism is increasing, but Ubud remains a real community rather than a tourist development. There is no evident gay scene, but the night market, dance performances and restaurants provide some meeting opportunities.

Hotel Santika Beach
USA/Canada Reservations
(800) 257-5344

🗝 ACCOMMODATIONS 🗝

BALI SPIRIT HOTEL & SPA
Nyuh Kuning-Ubud, Bali. USA/Canada reservations or information. Tel: (516) 944-5330 or (800) 257-5344. Fax: (516) 944-7540. TYPE: *Hotel.* CLIENTELE: All Welcome. LOCATION: 1 km from Ubud.

* Suites: 5, Villas: 2
* Cooking facilities (in villas)
* Maid & room service, phone, balcony
* Restaurant, bar, shop, parking
* Pool, river beach, sundeck
* Clothing optional at river
* Beach: 1 hour
* Gay Bars: 1 hr., mixed bar on premises
* Airport: Denpasar, 1 hour, free pick up
* Languages: English, Indonesian
* Reservations: 1 night deposit
* Credit Cards: MC/VISA/AMEX
* Season: Year round
* Rates: (US) $110-$130; (off) $75-$110 w/AB. Tax: 15.5%
* *TAC:* 10% (from Odysseus)

DESCRIPTION: Moderate deluxe hotel overlooking small whitewater river and daily bathing scene of village life. Balinese traditional architecture on a grand scale with comfortable interiors showcasing fine textiles, teak and bamboo furniture. Offers performance stage and Holistic health spa with spiritual focus and traditional healing techniques. Experience "Local color" in a "Homo-Sensual" culture.

JAVA ISLAND

BANDUNG   🏳 21

✈ Husein Sastranegara Airport, 15 min.

LOCATION: West Java on high altitude, between Jakarta and Yogyakarata.

POPULATION: 1,500,000

DESCRIPTION: The capital of west Java and the third largest city in Indonesia. It is an important University town with well educated and affluent population. Visit the nearby volcano and the beautiful Puncak Pass.

❖ Public Cruising (AYOR): **Town Hall Park** *(Taman Balai Kota)* aka **BP** or **Badak Putih** "white rhinoceros", Merdeka St., at night; **Bandung Town Square** *(Alun-alun Bandung or A2B)* at night; **Sumatra St.**, many transvestites, alongside the office of Emergency Safety (Bala Keselamatan) and Ponderosa, mostly at night.

JAKARTA   🏳 21

✈ Soekarno-Hatta Int'l Airport (CGK)

LOCATION: On the northwestern coastal plain of the island of Java.

POPULATION: 7,000,000

CLIMATE: Hot and sticky; plenty of rainfall, cool nights.

VISITOR INFORMATION
Indonesian Tourist Office
3457 Wilshire Blvd.
Los Angeles CA 90010
Tel: (213) 387-2078

DESCRIPTION: Jakarta, the capital and the largest city in Indonesia, is a city of immigration with a substantial Chinese population. The various districts reflect the population's period of arrival and ethnic origin. The **Old City** is known as **Kota**. It is a part of **Glodok** a Chinese-dominated district. The Kota district retains some Dutch influence in its architecture, layout and the canals. It is the main commercial district with ethnic chinese shops, cafes, and restaurants. **Tanjung Priok**, the city's port, is the largest in Indonesia. Jakarta is a typical third world metropolitan, where the modern coexists along with the poor neighborhoods.

❖ Gay cruising (AYOR): **The Cinere Movie House**, *(Gedung Bioskop Cinere)* in the lobby, mostly young crowd, nighttime; **Cipuat - The Sahara Movie House** *(Gedung Bioskop Sahara)*, in the yard, mostly young crowd, nighttime; **Lapangan Bateng Park** near the Hotel Borobudur, Jalan Lapangan Benteng Selatan, mostly rent boys, 7pm-11pm (later is dangerous); **Sarina Market** at Jakarta Tower; **Shopping Centre** at Grand Hyatt, Jalan M.H. Thamrin.

λ SERVICES λ

● Cinema (G/S): **Cinema 21**, Gelael supermarket of Blok M Shopping Center.

BARS ♈ RESTAURANTS 🍴

The Gay Scene in Jakarta, like in many other Third World countries, is not well defined. Very often the meeting places are at the bars and coffee shops of the better tourist hotels. Some places that look straight, will turn 'gayer' at late hours.

● Bars/Clubs (G/S): **Klimax**, disco, organized by a gay group,every Sunday night, 10pm - 2am, Gajah Mada St.; **Matra**, disco, mostly lesbians, 24 hrs., daytime on Saturday has the most young men ("student night"), Grand Menteng Hotel, Matraman Raya St.; **The New Moonlight**, disco, popular with gay men and lesbians on Saturday night, intersection of Hayam Wuruk and Mangga Besar Streets; **Sofian Hotel Diskotik**, disco, mixed young crowd, heavy metal, some lesbians, 24 hrs., Saharjo St.; **Stardust**, 24 hrs., at the Jaykarta Tower Bldg., (*Gedung Jayakarta Tower*), Hayam Wuruk St.; **Tanamur**, disco, popular with gay men on Thursdays, lesbians on Sunday night, Tanah Abang Timur St., Central Jakarta; **Voilá**, mixed young men and transvestites, Sunday night, The Patra Jasa Bldg., (*Gedung Patra Jasa*), Rasuna Said St.

● Bars/Clubs (GW/S): **Matra**, disco, mostly lesbians, 24 hrs., Grand Menteng Hotel, Matraman Raya St.; **The New Moonlight**, disco, popular with lesbians on Saturday night, intersection of Hayam Wuruk and Mangga Besar Streets; **Sofian Hotel Diskotik**, disco, mixed crowd,lesbians, 24 hrs., Saharjo St.; **Tanamur**, disco, popular with lesbians on Sunday night, Tanah Abang Timur St., Central Jakarta;

 ACCOMMODATIONS

BOROBUDUR INTER-CONTINENTAL
Jalan Lapangan Banteng Salatan, Jakarta. Tel: (21) 370-333. Fax: (21) 380-9595. TYPE: *Deluxe Hotel*. CLIENTELE: Mostly Straight/ Few Gay. LOCATION: On the south side of Memorial Square, 5 minutes from City center.

* Rooms: 861 w/priv. bath. Suites: 57
* CTV, phone, A/C, minibar
* Restaurants, bar & disco - check bar on second floor, turns gay after 22 hour
* Health club, pool, parking
* Gay Bars: on premises
* Airport: 20 min. taxi
* Credit Cards: VISA/DC/CB/AMEX
* Season: Year round
* Rates: (US) $170-$400.
* *TAC:* 10%

DESCRIPTION: Moderate deluxe hotel with fine amenities. Suitable for business men or corporate travelers. Popular gay cruise park nearby.

HOTEL INDONESIA
JL. M.H. Thamrin, P.O. Box 54, Jakarta. Tel: (21) 320-008. Fax: (21) 321-508 TYPE: *Hotel*. CLIENTELE: Mostly Straight. LOCATION: City center near the night-club strip, near Embassies and the National Monument.

* Rooms: 610 w/pri. bath. Suites: 30
* CTV, phone, A/C, minibar
* Restaurants, bars, cabaret
* Room & maid service
* Gay Bars: nearby
* Airport: 45 km / 28 mi., taxi
* Credit Cards: MC/VISA/EC/DC/AMEX
* Season: Year round
* Rates: (US) $150 - $350
* *TAC:* 10%

DESCRIPTION: Deluxe hotel with fine amenities and service. The hotel is used as a central meeting place for gays in the evening: lobby, bar and coffee shop. No problem bringing a companion to you room if properly dressed.

JAKARTA HILTON
JL Gatot Subroto, Jakarta. Tel: (21) 570-3600 Fax: (21) 583-089. TYPE: *Hotel*. CLIENTELE: Mostly Straight. LOCATION: Next to the Jakarta Convention Hall & National Sports Center.

* Rooms: 1,080 w/priv. bath
* Suites: 77, Penthouse Suite + pool
* CTV, phone, A/C, minibar
* Restaurants, bars, disco, pool, sauna
* Room & maid service
* Gay Bars: check the disco
* Airport: 18 km / 11 mi., taxi
* Credit Cards: MC/VISA/EC/DC/ACC/AMEX
* Season: Year round
* Rates: (US) $135-$350
* *TAC:* 10%

DESCRIPTION: Deluxe hotel with fine amenities and service. Great restaurants, coffee shops, and a popular disco with many gay followers.

SURABAYA ⓒ 31

✈ Juanda Airport (SUB), 10 mi. / 16 km SE

LOCATION: Northeast Java on Selat Madura (Java Sea).

POPULATION: 2,100,000

DESCRIPTION: The capital of east Java, and a busy commercial port. Surabaya is the second largest city in Indonesia. It is a convenient stop between Java and Bali and one of the most 'Indonesian' of all the large cities.

❖ Public Cruising (AYOR): **Texas** (the Joyoboyo Bus Terminal) at night; **Irian Barat Street**, transgenders and gay men, every night; **Kalifor**, the street next to Surabaya Plaza near the World Trade Center, gay men, rent boys, after 10pm.

BARS ☿ RESTAURANTS ‖

● Bars/Clubs (G/S): **Atom**, disco, Wednesday night is gay night, Bunguran St.; **Calypso**, Saturday night is gay night, Wijaya Shopping Centre, Bubutan St.; **Qemi**, disco at the Elmi Hotel, Wednesday night is gay night, 42-44 Panglima Sudirman St.; **La Suraya**, disco, popular Thursday night after the drag show, gay men, transgenders, rent boys, behind Surabaya Mall; **Studio East**, Monday night is gay night, Simpang Dukuh St; **Taman Remaja**, popular drag show every Thursday night 9-10:30p., gay men and lesbian followers near the stage area.

● Restaurants (AW): Surabaya is dominated by Western-style fast food chains many are located at the **Surabaya Delta Plaza**; **Kiet Wan Kie**, excellent Chinese restaurant, Jalan Jembatan Kembang Jepun 51 (near the Jembatan Merah bus station).

λ SERVICES λ

● Organization (GMW): **Gaya Nusantara**, The Indonesian National Gay Network, Jalan Mulyosari Timur 46, Syrabaya 60112. Tel: 62-31-593-4924. Fax: 62-32-593-9070; 594-0300. E-Mail: doetomo@server.indo.net.id

 ACCOMMODATIONS

ELMI HOTEL
Jl Panglima Sudirman 42-44, Surabaya. Tel: (31) 522-571/9. TYPE: *Hotel*. CLIENTELE: All Welcome. LOCATION: downtown, 2 km from train station, 19 km / 12 mi. from Juanda airport. 142 rooms w/priv. bath, CTV, phone, refrigerator, room service, restaurant, coffee shop, bar, lounge, nightclub, pool, health club with sauna. Rates: on request. DESCRIPTION: Moderate first class hotel.

KALIMANTAN (BORNEO ISLAND)

BANJARMASIN   ✆   542

✈ Juanda Airport (SUB), 10 mi. / 16 km SE

LOCATION: Southern Kalimatan on Borneo Island.

POPULATION: 400,000

DESCRIPTION: One of the most beautiful cities in Indonesia. Banjarmasin is 'Venice like' criss-crossed by many canals lined with stilt houses and buildings on top of floating logs.

BARS ☿ RESTAURANTS ‖

● Bars/Clubs (G/S): **Bobo Disco**, popular with gay men and transgenders on Tuesday night; **Matt Disco**, gay men, transgenders, popular on Friday night; **Shinta Disco**, gay men, transgenders, Wednesday night.

 ACCOMMODATIONS

HOTEL SABRINA
Jalan Bank Rakyat 21, Banjarmasin. Tel: (342) 4442, 4721. TYPE: *Hotel*. CLIENTELE: All Welcome. LOCATION: Downtown. rooms with CTV and A/C. Rates: on request.

SULAWESI ISLAND

UJUNG PANDANG   ✆   423

✈ Ujung Pandang AP (UPG) 11 mi. / 18 km

LOCATION: Southwest Sulawesi on Selat Makassar Bay.

POPULATION: 710,000

DESCRIPTION: Capital of the Sulawesi province with an old Dutch style port. It is the largest and liveliest city on the island.

BARS ☿ RESTAURANTS ‖

● Bars/Clubs (G/S): **Belopa Disco**, dance club, popular on Saturday night and Sunday morning, Marannu City Hotel, Sultan Hasanuddin St. 3-5; **Jumbo Roller Disco**, Thursday & Saturday nights, many teenagers, Timor St; **Zig-Zag Disco**, Makassar Golden Hotel, Jalan Penghibur.

● Restaurants (G/S): along Pantai Losari; **Asia Bahru**, seafood, corner of Jalan Latimojong; **Losari**, beach pub & restaurant, Makassar Golden Hotel, Jalan Penghibur.

 **ACCOMMODATIONS**

MARANNU CITY HOTEL
Jl Sultan Hassanudin 3-5, Ujung Pandang. Tel: (411) 5087. TYPE: *Hotel*. CLIENTELE: All Welcome. LOCATION: Centrally near the Sports Field and the beach. 176 rooms w/priv. bath, CTV, phone, disco popular with gays. Rates: on request.

SUMATRA ISLAND

BANDAR LAMPUNG ℂ 721

✈ Branti Airport, 29 km / 18 mi

LOCATION: Southern Sumatra, 90 km / 56 mi. north of Bakauheni.

DESCRIPTION: Getaway town for the rest of Sumatra. Good daily ferry connection every hour with Java from nearby Bakauheni. The ferry crossing takes about 1-1/2 hrs.

❖ Public Cruising (AYOR): around the monument in front of the **Golden Movie House** *(Bioskop Golden)* Tanjunkarang district at night; between **Pemuda Street** and main crossroads, Tanjungkarang district, at night; near **King Supermarket**, at Tanjungkarang Plaza, daytime.

Y BAR Y

● Bar/Club (G/S): **Oya Disco**, Saturday night, Yos Sudarso St., Sukaraja, Telukbetung district, cloe to town center.

 **ACCOMMODATIONS**

SHERATON INN-LAMPUNG
Jl Wolter Monginsidi No. 175. Tel: (721) 486-666. TYPE: *Hotel*. CLIENTELE: All Welcome. LOCATION: Downtown close to Teluk Bay. 107

rooms, 6 suites, w/priv. bath, phone, CTV, restaurant, bar, pool, gym, sauna & massage. Rates: on request.

SUMATRA ISLAND

MEDAN ℂ 61

✈ Polonia Airport (MES) 1 mi. / 1.6 km

LOCATION: Northern Sumatra, 32 hrs.. by car from Jakarta via the Trans-Sumatran Hwy.

POPULATION: 1,400,000

DESCRIPTION: Capital of Sumatra. The city offers the ambiance of an old Dutch planter aristocracy, good antique shops, Mosques and museums.

❖ Gay Beach (G/S): check out the Swimming Pool area at the **Tiara Hotel**, Cut Mutia St. popular with Westerners and gay Indonesians.

BARS Y RESTAURANTS ¶

● Bars/Clubs (G/S): **Dynasty**, disco & pub, exclusive *rendezvous* at the Danau Toba Int'l Hotel, Imam Bonjol St., #17; **Fire Disco**, Thamrin Plaza; **Que Que Disco**, a gay "Chinatown" nightly, Olympia Plaza; **S'carpark**, disco, 50% gay, main floor of Istana Plaza; **Skyroom**, disco 90% gay on Saturday night, 8th floor of Olympia Plaza.

● Restaurants (AW): **TD Coffee shop**, Balia Kota St; **Olympia Plaza Cafe** at the Olympia Plaza; **Tip Top**, large veranda for people watching, good food, Jalan Ahmad Yani 92; **Lyn's Café**, Western menu, Jalan Ahmad Yani 98.

λ SERVICES λ

● Cinema (G/S): **Deli Plaza Theatre**, cruisy cinema.

● Massage Parlor (G/S): on Sei Wampu St. (**Yakestra**); many gay masseurs as well as meeting point; also on S Parman Street (**Sejatera**).

 **ACCOMMODATIONS**

DANAU TOBA INT'L HOTEL
Jl Imam Bonjol 17. Tel: (61) 327000. TYPE: *Hotel*. CLIENTELE: All Welcome. LOCATION:

Central location, 3 km / 2 mi. from airport. 260 rooms w/priv. bath, phone, CTV, refrigerator, restaurants, coffee shop, disco, pool, steam bath, massage. Rates: on request. DESCRIPTION: Attractive first class hotel. Disco popular with gays.

TIARA HOTEL
Jl Cut Mutia, Medang. Tel: (61) 516000. TYPE: *Hotel.* CLIENTELE: All Welcome. LOCATION: Downtown, 1 km / 1/2 mi. from Polonia Airport, 3 km / 2 mi. from train station. 185 rooms w/priv. bath, 11 suites, CTV, phone, rooms for non-smokers, 24 hrs. room service, restaurant, bar, outdoor pool (popular with gays), sauna, gym. Rates: on request. DESCRIPTION: First class international hotel.

PADANG   *①*   361

✈ Tabing Airport, 15 minutes

LOCATION: Central west coast of Sumatra, in the centre of the Matrilineal Minangkabau area.

POPULATION: 500,000

DESCRIPTION: Easy going town with a large Chinese population (15%). Traditionally the eldest female is the boss in this part of the world, and property is inherited through the female line.

❖ Public Cruising (AYOR): There is not much of a gay scene, but some cruising is taking place at the following places: **Taman Melati**, gay men and transgenders, at the Aditiawarman Museum Complex, near the Utama Theatre at the Taman Budaya; **Preside Music Room** and the **Duta Plaza** yard nighttime; **Padang Theatre**, night & day.

 ACCOMMODATIONS

HOTEL BUMI MINANG
Padang. Tel: (361) 88011. TYPE: *Hotel.* CLIENTELE: All Welcome. LOCATION: Downtown, 15 min. from the airport. 164 rooms w/priv. bath, CTV, phone, A/C, restaurants, pool, bar, health club. Rates: on request.

PALEMBANG   *①*   361

✈ Sultan Badarrudin Airport, 9 km / 5 mi.

LOCATION: Southern Sumatra, on the Musi River, 50 km / 31 mi upstream from the Sea.

POPULATION: 800,000

DESCRIPTION: Main export outlet for south Sumatra and a heavily industrialized city. Centre of the ancient highly developed Srivijaya civilization, but few relics of interest remain from this era. There is not much to see and do around Palembang for international travelers, and the gay scene is limited.

❖ Public Cruising (AYOR): **"Five days & Five Nights" monument** *(Tugu Lima Hari Lima Malam),* every night, especially gay men; **The "Nusa Indah" Park** *(Taman Nusa Indah),* every night, gay men and transgenders; **Talang Semut Park** *(Taman Talang Semut)* in the park and the vicinity, gay men, best on Saturday night.

ACCOMMODATIONS

SANDJAJA HOTEL
Jl Kapten Rivai 6193. Palembang. Tel: (711) 350-634. TYPE: *Hotel.* CLIENTELE: All Welcome. LOCATION: Residential area, 9 km / 6 mi from train station, 12 km / 8 mi. from airport. 182 rooms, 6 suites, w/priv. bath, A/C, CTV, phone, restaurant, bar, pool, sauna, massage. Rates: on request. DESCRIPTION: Attractive superior tourist class hotel.

IRELAND (EIRE)

AREA: 27,136 sq. mi. (70,282 sq. km)
POPULATION: 3,440,000
CAPITAL: Dublin
CURRENCY: Irish Pound (IR£)
OFFICIAL LANGUAGES: English, Gaelic
MAJOR RELIGION: Roman Catholicism
Telephone: 353
Nat'l Holiday: Independence Day, April 17
Official Time: G.M.T.
Electricity: 220 volts
Exchange Rate: 1US$ = IR£ 0.62
National Airline: Aer Lingus

LAW REGARDING HOMOSEXUALITY: Sexual acts between consenting males are legal. The age of consent is 17 same as it is for heterosexuals. On June 24, 1993 the infamous 132 year-old legislation banning homosexual acts was overturned. The move came 5 years after gay rights politicians took the case to the European Court of Human Rights.

CORK © 021

✈ Cork Airport (ORK) 3 mi. / 5 km south

LOCATION: 160 mi. / 256 km, or 4-1/2 leisurely hours, along the Irish Sea coast south of Dublin.

POPULATION: 175,000

Gay & Lesbian Visitor Information
Gay/Lesbian Information: (021) 271-087

DESCRIPTION: The second largest city in Ireland, Cork is an historic University town on the two branches of the River Lee. It offers an excellent shopping center, major department stores on **Patrick Street**, and quaint shops and boutiques along **Prince** and **Oliver Plunkett** Streets.

BARS ♼ RESTAURANTS ¶¶

● Bars/Clubs (GMW): **Loafers**, Douglas St; **Other Place**, mixed disco, wine bar, late cafe, 7/8 Augustine St. (317-660); **Other Side**, bookshop, cafe, relaxed atmosphere, 8 So. Main St. (317-660).

ACCOMMODATIONS

IMPERIAL HOTEL
14 Pembroke St., South Mall, Cork. Tel: (21) 274040. TYPE: *Hotel*. CLIENTELE: All Welcome. LOCATION: City center overlooking South Mall. 101 rooms, 1 suite. CTV, phone, trouser press, C/H, coffee/tea making facilities, 24 hrs. room service, maid service, free secured parking. Open: Year round (closed Christmas/New Year). Rates: I£75 - I£95. DESCRIPTION: Historic Old-World style moderate first class hotel. Good central location and excellent service.

DUBLIN © 01

✈ Dublin Airport (DUB)

LOCATION: Eastern shore of the Republic of Ireland on Dublin Bay with the River Liffey flowing through the city.

POPULATION: 600,000

CLIMATE: Maritime climate. Summers are pleasant, winters are mild. Average winter temperatures 40°F/4°c); average summer temperatures 67°F/19°c).

Gay/Lesbian Visitor Information
Hirschfield Center
10 Fownes St. D2. Tel: (01) 6710-939
Gay Switchboard: (01) 6721-055

Lesbian Visitor Information
Lesbian Line: (01) 6613-777

DESCRIPTION: Dublin is a romantic city with rich historical heritage dating back to the days of the Celts in 140 AD. Many cultures left their influence on Dublin since then, including the Vikings, the Normans, and the British in more recent history. In the 18th century, Dublin became an important seaport and raised to a rank of a prestigious European capital. The city is famous for its Georgian Streets, elegant squares, ancient churches and cathedrals. Today, with the decriminalization of male homosexuality in 1993 and the establishment of full legal equality with heterosexuality, Dublin is also a friendly destination for gay & lesbian travelers.

Visit: **Merrion Square**, a beautiful Georgian Square. Apartment #1 on the square is where the young Oscar Wilde lived with his parents; **National Museum** - has displays of gold objects dating from the Bronze Age to early Christianity; **Trinity College** - the oldest University in Ireland, founded by Elizabeth I of England on the site of a 12th century monastery; **Parliament House** - now the Bank of Ireland; **Guiness Brewery** - the famous stout brewery in the world on Crane St. (85-6701).

BARS ⅄ RESTAURANTS 🍴

● Bars/clubs (GM): **The Bailey**, popular on Saturdays afternoons only, 2 Duke St. D2 (477-3760); **Duke**, nightclub, Dame Lane (over George Bar); **Incognito**, 1/2 Bow Lane East, off Aungier St., (478-3504).

● Clubs (GMW): **George/Block**, popular dance club, bars, videos and lounge, 89th St. George St. (478-2893); **Horny Organ Tribe**, Rok Garden, Crown Alley, Temple Bar, mixed gay club, Sun. 11:30-2:30; **Marks Bros**, mixed coffee shop opposite the George, St. George St.; **Pod**, trendy nightclub, every Thurs., Harcourt St.; **Shaft**, bar, club, restaurant, 22 Ely Pl. D2 (711-638).

● Clubs (GW): **Salon**, at The Cellary, Fownes St., Sun. 9:30-3am women only.

● Restaurants (AW): **Max Bros**, trendy coffee shop, 7 South Great George's St.; **Well-Fed Restaurant**, vegetarian cuisine, 6 Crow St. D2.

λ SERVICES λ

● Health Clubs (GM): **The Gym**, video room, coffee bar, steam rooms, 14/15 Dame Lane (off South Great George's St.) D2 (679-5128); **Incognito Sauna**, video room, snack bar, 1-2 Bow Lane (678-3504).

 ACCOMMODATIONS

BLOOM'S HOTEL
Anglesea St., Dublin 2. Tel: (1) 471-5622. Fax: (1) 715-997. TYPE: Hotel. CLIENTELE: Mostly Straight. LOCATION: City Center, north of Dame Street. Near Trinity College and the gay scene.88 w/priv. bath. Suites: 2, restaurant & bar, CTV, phone, A/C, free parking. Rates: (IR) £90 - £110. *TAC:* 10%. DESCRIPTION: Named after the hero of James Joyce's 'Ulysses', this is a first class hotel with fine amenities and service.

DONNYBROOK VIEW
65 Morehampton Rd., Donnybrook, Dublin 4. Tel: (01) 468-0975. TYPE: *Bed & Breakfast.* HOST: John & Ray. CLIENTELE: Gay/Straight. LOCATION: 2 mi. / 3 km from Dublin City Center. 6 rooms w/shared bath, CTV, phone (reception), Rates: (IR) £15 -£30 w/IrB. DESCRIPTION: 19th century terraced house in a pleasant residential suburb.

FRANKIE'S
8 Camden Place (off Camden St.), Dublin 2. Tel: (01) 478-3087 or 475-2182. TYPE: *Guest House.* HOST: Joe & Frankie. CLIENTELE: Gay men and women. LOCATION: St. Stephen Green Park, Trinity College area. Walking distance to center and the gay nightlife scene.10 rooms (6 w/priv., 4 w/shared bath), CTV, phone, C/H, parking, pets accepted. Gay Bars: 5 minutes. Airport: 8 mi. / 13 km. Rates: £17-£49 w/IrB. DESCRIPTION: 150 years old mews style building in a convenient location.

MALLARD
76 Tyrconnell Rd., Dublin 8. Tel: (01) 535-040. TYPE: *Bed & Breakfast.* HOST: Donal Traynor. CLIENTELE: Gay Men & Women Only. LOCATION: City center, near the gay scene.

* Rooms: 6; 1 w/priv., 5 w/shared bath
* CTV, phone, A/C, Maid Service
* No Parking, No Pets
* Beach: 4 mi. / 6 km (nude)
* Gay Bars: 15 minutes
* Airport: 15 mi. / 24 km, taxi, bus
* Reservations: 10% deposit
* Open: Year round
* Rates: (IR) £15 - £25 w/IrB

DESCRIPTION: Mid-Victorian town house, fully central heated. Tea & coffee facilities, hot & cold water in room. Located on bus route.

SHELBOURNE HOTEL
27 St. Stephen Green, Dublin 2. Tel: (1) 476-6471. Telex: 93653. TYPE: *Deluxe Hotel.* CLIENTELE: Mostly Straight. LOCATION: Central location, overlooking St. Stephen's Green. Close to the local gay scene, and all points of interests. 172 rooms w/priv. bath. DESCRIPTION: Historic, prestigious, deluxe hotel. The constitution for the Irish Free State was drafted here in 1922.

GALWAY ✆ 091

✈ Galway Airport

LOCATION: 180 mi. / 290 km west of Dublin on the Galway Bay of central west Ireland.

POPULATION: 60,000

Gay & Lesbian Visitor Information
Gay/Lesbian Line: (09) 566-134

DESCRIPTION: A busy Seaport on Galway Bay, at the mouth of the River Corrib. Historic Galway is compact with narrow streets, quaint houses, lively shops, art galleries and restaurants. Galway is the gateway to Gaelic Country. The city hosts several festivals during the summer when hotel accommodations are hard to find.

BARS Y RESTAURANTS ¶¶

● Bars/clubs (GMW): **Blue Note**, mixed young crowd, gay friendly bar, off Domnicks St.; **Java**, coffee shop, mixed, gay friendly, lower Abbeygate St.; **Liberation**, Vagabonds, Salthill, 11-1:30a Sat.; **Neachtains**, mixed, low key pub, Quay St.

 ACCOMMODATIONS

GREAT SOUTHERN-EYRE SQUARE
Eyre Sq., Galway. Tel: (91) 753-181. TYPE: *Hotel*. CLIENTELE: All Welcome. LOCATION: Downtown adjacent to the train station. 116 rooms, 3 suites, CTV (movies), phone, C/H, 24 hrs. room service, parking (charge), restaurant, bars, rooftop pool, gym, sauna, steam room. Rates: (IR) £70-90. DESCRIPTION: Upscaled victorian hotel on a picturesque main square. The hotel's elegant central foyer is the center of the social life in the city.

LIMERICK ✆ 061

✈ Shannon AP (SNN) 16 mi. / 26 km west

LOCATION: 190 mi / 305 km southwest of Dublin on the mouth of the Shannon River.

POPULATION: 80,000

Gay & Lesbian Visitor Information
G& L Switchboard: (161) 310-101

DESCRIPTION: the fourth-largest city in Ireland, Limmerick offers wide streets, lovely Georgian houses and gracious historic buildings. The city was the center of the Irish revolt against the English in the 17th century. The famous Treaty of limerick of 1691 was to end hostilities between the English and the Irish and grant religious liberty to the Irish and Catholics. It is historically very interesting, but not much is going on in the city for gay and lesbian visitors.

 ACCOMMODATIONS

ROYAL GEORGE HOTEL
O'Connell St., Limerick. Tel: (161) 414-566. TYPE: *Hotel*. CLIENTELE: All Welcome. LOCATION: City center. 54 rooms w/priv. bath, CTV, hair dryer, C/H, trouser press, restaurant, bar. Rates: (IR) £45-65.

WATERFORD ✆ 051

✈ Waterford Airport

LOCATION: Southeast Ireland, about 160 mi. / 256 km south of Dublin on Waterford Harbor.

POPULATION: 45,000

Gay & Lesbian Visitor Information
Gay/Lesbian Line: (051) 79907

DESCRIPTION: Old Viking settlement with a fortification built by the Danes in 1003. The town is famous for its beautiful 18th century cathedral and crystal factory. Not much is known about the local gay scene which is small and low key. **Drogheda - Out Comers** Gays & lesbians meet every 2nd and 4th Fri. at 7:00pm at the Resource Center for the Unemployed, 8 North Quay.

 ACCOMMODATIONS

TOWER HOTEL
The Mall, Waterford. Tel: (51) 75801. TYPE: *Hotel*. CLIENTELE: All Welcome. LOCATION: Town center, along the Quay, opposite historic Reginald's Tower. 141 rooms w/priv. bath, 3 suites, CTV, phone, restaurant, lounge bar, wheelchair access, 24 hrs. room service, indoor pool, jacuzzi, health club. Rates: (IR) £55-75.

ISRAEL

AREA: 10,260 sq. mi. (26,265 sq. km)
POPULATION: 5,000,000
CAPITAL: Jerusalem
CURRENCY: Shekel (IS)
OFFICIAL LANGUAGES: Hebrew, Arabic
MAJOR RELIGIONS: Judaism, Islam, Christianity.
Telephone: 972
Nat'l Holiday: Independence Day, April 26
Official Time: G.M.T + 2
Electricity: 220 volts
Exchange Rate: 1US$ = NS 3.23
National Airline: El Al

LAW REGARDING HOMOSEXUALITY: Homosexuality is legal in Israel. Minimum legal age for consensual homosexuality is 18. The gay lifestyle is flourishing in Tel Aviv as more gays come out of the closet. In the rest of the country discretion is suggested. Homosexuality is now fully accepted in the Israeli Army and the Knesset (Israeli Parliament) passed a non-discriminative law concerning sexual-preference.

❐ Israel is now enjoying a new historic phase with the improvement of its relations with the Palestinians and the neighboring Arab countries. Both Egypt and Jordan have open borders with Israel. The Palestinians are working on their autonomy, and a break through with Syria to the north is possible. This new reality and the overall improvement of relations with the Arab countries signal a new era of peace and stability. Now, more than ever it is good time to visit Israel and enjoy the beaches, gay nightlife of Tel-Aviv (the best in the Middle East) and the country's countless religious and historic sites.

Odysseus has great connections in Israel. So if you plan to visit Israel, or as a travel agent you have clients going to Israel give **Odysseus** a call: (800) 257-5344 or (516) 944-5330, or fax: (800) 982-6571 or (516) 944-7540. We know Israel inside out and have the best hotels for the gay and lesbian clientele.

EILAT   ℂ   059

✈ Eilat Airport (ETH)

LOCATION: Southernmost tip of Israel, on the shores of the Red Sea and the Gulf of Eilat. Common border with Jordan & Egypt. Aquaba (Jordan) and Taba (Egypt) are easily accessible from Eilat. 5 minutes drive from the new **Arava** crossing with Jordan or to Egypt's **Taba** crossing into the Sinai.

POPULATION: 20,000

CLIMATE: Hot dry desert climate year round. Summers are extremely hot with temperatures reaching 110˚F (40˚c), evenings are slightly cooler. Winters are sunny and pleasant with temperatures in the 70˚F (21˚c), the lowest temperature in winter is 50˚F (10˚ c). Eilat has the same latitude as Southern Florida, with a water temperature of at least 70˚F (21˚c).

VISITOR INFORMATION
Government Tourist Information Center
Ha'Tmarim Blvd. Eilat. Tel: 722-68 or 767-37

DESCRIPTION: Eilat is a desert Oasis on the Red Sea, the "Sun and Fun Capital" of Israel. It is surrounded by mountains, man made lagoon and exotic palm trees. The hot sunny climate attracts tourism year round from Scandina and Europe. It is the only place where you can see from your hotel room four countries: Israel, Jordan, Saudi Arabia & Egypt, and two continents: Asia & Africa.

The ambience is of a total relaxation, sun worship and hedonism. Women can bath topless on public beaches. An Underwater Observatory, open to the public, offers a spectacular view of the exotic underwater wildlife and corals.

Eilat maintains a free trade zone status, and VAT has been abolished on goods and services. This helps bring Eilat prices of food and services to the level of the rest of the country. Although Eilat touches on the borders of Jordan and Egypt, both borders are now open for tourism into the Sinai, mainland Egypt and Aquaba and Jordan.

● Meeting Places: along the Beach near the Hotel 'Neptune'; **Um El Rash Rash** park near the 'Red Rock Hotel'.

BARS ⅄ RESTAURANTS 🍴

There are no gay bars, clubs or restaurants which cater exclusively to gay clientele.

● Discos: **Shiva disco**, mixed clientele, at the **King Solomon's Palace Hotel**, North Beach; **Spiral Disco**, hotels area, Saturday nights are for gays only.

● Restaurants (AW): check the Tourist Center, where you can find a variety of restaurants serving budget to more expensive meals; the **Hard Rock Café** on Elliot St., recommended for food and international ambience; **La Tour Eiffel**, French cuisine, opp. Post Office (714-04); **Pundak Habira**, 102/1 Ha'Almogim St. (374-562).

ACCOMMODATIONS

AMERICANA HOTEL

North Beach, Eilat. Tel: (7) 333-777. USA/ Canada Reservations Tel: (800) 257-5344 or (516) 944-7540. Fax: (800) 982-6571 or (516) 944-7540. TYPE: *Resort Hotel.* CLIENTELE: All Welcome. LOCATION: North Beach near the lagoon, across from the famous King's Wharf Center.

* Rooms: 106 w/priv. bath
  40 rooms w/priv. balcony,
  36 deluxe connecting rooms w/kitchenette
* CTV w/12 satellite channels,
  in house movies, phone, A/C, C/H
* Restaurant, coffee shop, steakhouse
  large dining room, dairy cafeteria
* Nightclub, TV room, gym w/sauna, pool
* Beach: walking distance
* Airport: 2 km / 1.5 mi., bus, taxi
* Open: Year round
* Rates: (US) $80 - $130
* *TAC:* 10% (from Odysseus)

DESCRIPTION: Lively 3-star hotel with a young, festive atmosphere and policy of doing everything possible to please the guests. The Americana Disco is popular with the 18-22 years old. Walk to the best sand beach in Eilat.

ORCHID RESORT

Almog Beach, Eilat. USA/Canada reservations Tel: (800) 257-5344 or (516) 944-5330. Fax: (800) 982-6571 or (516) 944-7541. CLIENTELE: All Welcome. LOCATION: Coral Beach, south of Eilat towards the Egyptian border.

* Chalets: 136 w/priv. bath
* Suites: 4 opulent suites w/kitchenette,
  jacuzzi, pool, garden
* CTV, phone, A/C, mini bar, personal safe
* Ceiling fan, air-dryer
* Restaurant, exotic cocktail bar
* Pool, sauna, fitness club, Thai massage

* Room & maid service.
* Airport: 2 km / 1.5 mi., taxi, bus
* Credit Cards: MC/VISA/BC/DC/EC/AMEX
* Open: Year round.
* Rates: (US) $90-$265.
* *TAC:* 10% (from Odysseus)

DESCRIPTION: Elegant Thai style resort with distinctive Thai design, exclusive location and relaxing ambiance. The resort village consists of colorful chalets made of wood and bamboo. The furnishings and decoration were all imported from the Far East. Exotic and delightful.

HAIFA   © 04

✈ Haifa Airport
   Ben Gurion Int'l Airport (TLV)

LOCATION: Northern Israel from the Port of Haifa to the top of Mt. Carmel, 90 km / 56 mi. north of Tel-Aviv.

POPULATION: 250,000

CLIMATE: Mediterranean. Sunny hot summers with temperatures in the high 80's (28°c); cool, windy and rainy winters with low temperatures in the 40's F (6°c).

Gay/Lesbian Visitor Information
Gay & Lesbian Community Center
1 Arlozorof St., (top floor). Tel: (04) 672-665

Gay & Lesbian Hotline (Kav Lavan)
Tel: (04) 525-352 Mon. 7-11pm

DESCRIPTION: Haifa is Israel's major port of entry for tourism and commerce. The city is beautifully situated on the slopes of Mt. Carmel overlooking a broad bay that stretches all the way to Acre in the north. Haifa is the only Israeli city that has a subway system called **'Carmelit'** which runs from the top of Mt. Carmel to the Port area via Hadar (mid-Town). A ride in the Carmelit is a fun way to explore the various facets of the city. Visit: **The Baha'i Temple** with its beautiful golden dome, vistas and Persian gardens; **Haifa University**; **Stella Maris** with its Italian church and the famous **Cave of Elijah**. Recommended side trips can include the nearby Druze villages, Nazareth, Tiberias, Acre and Sefad.

There is not much of an organized gay scene in Haifa. The tradition is to cruise mostly at night in the city's main parks: **Gan Ha'Zikaron**,

Hadar, across from Town Hall; **Gan Benyamin**, Hadar across from the Municipal Theatre.

❖ Beaches: Haifa has great sandy beaches which are easily accessible. There's great swimming and sunbathing at **Dado Beach**, **Carmel Beach**, and other beaches along the Bay of Haifa. The gay beaches for cruising and nude sunbathing are south of **Dado Beach** and **Atlit Beach** at the secluded Dunes area. **Hof Ha'Kishon** north of **Hof Kiryat Haim** can be interesting too.

BAR ♈ RESTAURANTS 🍴

● Bar (G/S): **Barock**, 2 Sarah St.

● Restaurants (AW): **Taiwan**, Chinese, 59 Ben Gurion Ave. (520-088); **Tequila's**, Mexican, 125 Hanassi Ave., Central Carmel (381-184); **UN Restaurant**, oriental cuisine, 20 Sderot Hatzionut (529-842); **Voila**, Swiss-French, 21a Nordau St. (664-529).

λ SERVICE λ

● Records/CD's (AW): **Tower Records**, Hozot Ha'Mifratz Super Mall, Zomet Vulcan (424-344).

● Sex Shop (G/S): **Eros**, gay videos, magazines, Ha'Neviyim 20, 1st. fl. 16 (621-242).

🔖 ACCOMMODATIONS 🔖

DAN CARMEL
85-87 Hanassi Ave., Haifa 31060. Tel: (4) 386211. Fax: (4) 387-504. TYPE: *Deluxe Hotel.* CLIENTELE: Mostly Straight. LOCATION: Top of Mt. Carmel overlooking Haifa Bay. 219 rooms w/priv. bath, CTV (CNN), phone, A/C, 24 hrs. room service, Pub, restaurant, pool, health club, parking. Season: Year round. Rates: (US) $95-$200. Elegant hotel in a panoramic location.

HAIFA TOWER
63 Herzel St., Haifa. Tel: (04) 677-111. USA/Canada Reservations: (800) 257-5344 or (516) 944-5330. Fax: (516) 944-7540. TYPE: *Hotel.* CLIENTELE: All Welcome. LOCATION: Central Hadar Hacarmel, in the shopping, tourism and entertainment center of town. 100 rooms w/priv. bath & CTV, bar, restaurant, parking, beach 20 min. by bus. Rates: on request. *TAC:* 10% from Odysseus). DESCRIPTION: Modern tower hotel in the heart of Haifa with views of the Carmel mountain range and Haifa Bay. Walk to shops, restaurants and the cruise areas of Independence Garden and Gan Benyamin (near the Municipal Theatre).

JERUSALEM   ✆ 02

✈ Atarot Airport (Jerusalem)
Ben Gurion Int'l Airport (TLV)

LOCATION: In the Judean Hills, surrounded by mountains and overlooking the Judean desert and the Dead Sea. 63 km (40 mi.) southwest of Tel Aviv.

POPULATION: 450,000

CLIMATE: Cool, dry and pleasant mountain climate. Summer temperature in the 80"'sF (27°c) dropping to 70"'s at night. Winter temperatures in the 50"'s (10°c) with occasional snow.

VISITOR INFORMATION
24 King George St. Jerusalem
Tel: (02) 241-281

DESCRIPTION: Jerusalem is the historic and contemporary capital of the State of Israel. It is a metaphysical, spiritual, and ageless symbol for millions of people of all faiths. David, king of Israel, established Yerushalayim (City of Peace in Hebrew) as the "stronghold of Zion". His son, Solomon, built the magnificent First Temple which for 400 years symbolized the spiritual attachment of the Jewish People to Zion and the Holy Temple. Although Christ lived and died in Roman times, it was not until the 4th century that churches began to appear in Jerusalem, and later Moslem mosques. Neither Judaism nor Christianity flourished in Jerusalem under the rule of the Moslem conquerors. The British Mandate ended with the War of Independence in 1948. Jerusalem was then divided into two sections. After the War of 1967 both parts of Jerusalem were again reunited and integrated.

Visitors can enjoy the freedom to visit all the holly sites including: **The Western Wall, The Mosque of Omar, El-Aqsa Mosque, Via Dolorosa**, the **Stations of the Cross**, and **Church of the Holy Sepulcher**. In modern Jerusalem, prominent features are: **The Knesset, New Great Synagogue, Israel Museum** - a great museum of art, biblical and archaeological exhibits; visit the **Shrine of the Book** for a look at the ancient **Dead Sea Scrolls**; **Yad Vashem** - the **Holocaust Museum**, **Jerusalem Miniature Model** (66 A.D.) adjacent the **Holyland Hotel** in Bayit Va'Gan. Other places of interest include the **Binyaney-Ha-ooma Congress Center**, the **Hebrew University**, and the **Hadassa Medical Center**. Jerusalem will fascinate you with its eternal beauty, colors, fragrances, and traditions.

The gay scene in Jerusalem has traditionally evolved around nightly, and sometime day cruising in the **Independence Garden** (Gan Ha'atzmauth), a recreation park bordered by the Plaza Hotel and Agron Street.

❖ Special Event: **Jerusalem 3000**, a 16 month celebration marking 3,000 years since the founding of Jerusalem as the capital of ancient Israel by the biblical king David. Enjoy festivals, sight and sound spectacles, concerts and exhibits of Jewish and arab art starting. Fall '95 - end of 1996.

BARS ▼ RESTAURANTS 🍴

There are no exclusive gay bars and restaurants in Jerusalem, most Jerusalemites travel to Tel-Aviv for nightlife and entertainment.

● Bar/Pub (G/S): **Cafe Akari**, gay friendly Cafe in the famous "Midrachov" pedestrian Street; **Shunra Pub**, Heleni Ha'Malka 9 (255-868); **Tmol Shilshom**, coffee shop/bookstore, Solomon 5; **Zman Amiti** (Real Time), pub/bar, Shlomo Ha'Melech St. (King Solomon St.).

● Meeting place: **Gan Ha'atzmauth** (Independence Garden) a beautiful public garden in the center of Jerusalem near the Sheraton Plaza Hotel.

● Restaurants (AW): **The Cow On The Roof**, expensive, French Nouvelle Cuisine, Sheraton Plaza Hotel (228 133); **Teppenyaki**, Japanese Cuisine, King Solomon Hotel (241 433); **Golda's**, Eastern European Jewish Cuisine, Moriah Hotel, 39 Keren Hayesod St. (232 232); **Marrakesh**, Moroccan specialties, 4 King Davis St. (221 208); **Philadelphia**, Middle Eastern restaurant in Arab East Jerusalem, Al-Zahara St. (289 770); **The Pie House**, budget cafe known for its fresh baked pies, 5 Hyrcanos st. (242 478).

λ SERVICES λ

● Bookstore (AW): **Tmol Shilshom**, also coffeeshop, 5 Solomon St. (232-758).

● Sex Shop (G/S): **Eros**, gay videos, magazines, King George 16 (231-688).

📷 ACCOMMODATIONS 📷

SHERATON JERUSALEM PLAZA
47 King George St., P.O.Box 7686, Jerusalem 91076. Tel: (02) 228-133, US (800)-325-3535.

TYPE: *Deluxe Hotel*. CLIENTELE: Mostly Straight. LOCATION: In the heart of Jerusalem, overlooking the Independence Park. 414 rooms & suites, CTV, phone, A/C, pool, sauna, room & maid service, free parking. Airport: 37 mi. / 60 km. Credit Cards: MC/VISA/EC/DC/BC/AMEX. Open: year round. Rates: (US) $95-$180. *TAC:* 10%. DESCRIPTION: 20-story luxury hotel situated in the heart of Jerusalem near the Independence Park (popular meeting place for Jerusalem gays). Close to all historic sites.

TEL AVIV ✆ 03

✈ Ben-Gurion Int'l Airport (TLV)
10 mi. / 16 km west

LOCATION: In the Coastal Plain, half way along the Israeli Mediterranean Sea coast.

POPULATION: 1,000,000 (metro)

CLIMATE: Mediterranean with two distinguished seasons: winter - a rainy season with frequent spells of sunshine, and summer - sunny, hot and clear with no rain. Average winter temperatures in January vary between 52˚F - 66˚F (11˚c-19˚c); average summer temperatures in August (the hottest month) vary between 72˚-86˚F (22˚-30˚c).

Gay Visitor Information
Haguda - (S.P.P.R.)
Soc. for Protection of Personal Rights
28 Nahmani St., P.O. Box 37604
Tel Aviv 61375
Tel: (03) 204-327. Fax: (03) 525-2341
Open: Mon. & Thurs. 7:00pm-10:00pm)

White Line Info: (03) 292-797
(7:30pm-11:30pm)

DESCRIPTION: Founded in 1909 on a barren strip of sand dunes, Tel Aviv ('Spring Hill' in Hebrew) is today the most modern and energetic city in the Middle East. Dominated by the **Shalom Tower**, the tallest building in Israel, with a roof-top observatory and the **Shalom Palace Wax Museum**, the city is compact and easy to explore. Most of the luxury hotels are along the Mediterranean on Hayarkon St. Here is also the **Independence Park**, (Gan Ha'Azmaut') next to the Hilton Hotel; where there is nightly gay action. During summer days, the beach strip just north of the Hilton Hotel is known unofficially as **Tel-Aviv's Gay Beach**, though not exclusively so. The liveliest part of Tel-Aviv is **Dizengoff St**, with restaurants, sidewalk cafes, milk bars and the famous *Dizengoff Center* where people relax near the famous 'Agam' fountain.

Tel-Aviv can finally boast the largest bus terminal in the Middle-East for the comfort of hundreds of thousands of locals and tourists alike. The new, seven story 600,000 sq. ft. terminal is fully air-conditioned, complete with shopping mall, and restaurants. It is conveniently located in the heart of the city near Levinsky Street.

Visit: **Beth Hatefutsoth Museum**, Tel-Aviv University Campus, Gate 2, Klausner Street, Ramat Aviv, with unusual exposition and reconstruction of jewish life in communities throughout the world; **Tel Aviv Museum**, 27 King Saul Blvd., with collection of Israeli and international art. A side tour to nearby **Old Port of Jaffa** - a reconstructed recreation area with Crusader walls, medieval stone passageways, art galleries, fine restaurants and cafes is recommended.

❖ Beaches: **Hilton Beach** and **Jerusalem Beach** (South Tel-Aviv near the Ambassador Hotel). Gay nude beach: **Gaash Beach**, 15 mi. / 24 km north of Tel-Aviv near Kibutz Gaash (north of Herzliya). The beach is secluded behind sand dunes and is mostly popular on Saturdays, private car required.

● Cruising (GM): The all time favorite for gay Tel-Avivians is the **'Independence Garden'** adjacent to the Tel-Aviv Hilton and opposite the Hotel Shalom, the garden is now brightly lit at night which makes it less intimate and cruisy; **Rakevet-Zafon** (Tel-Aviv North Train Station) **Park**, in the southeastern side of Namir Rd., and Arlozorov St. Junction.

BARS Y RESTAURANTS 🍴

● Bars/clubs (GMW): The gay club/nightlife scene in Tel-Aviv/Jaffa is unpredictable with bars and clubs closing and opening in a frenzy manner. **Abie's Bar**, video pub & cafe, open: 22:00 - 2:00 am Geula St. 40 near Allenby; **Habima Club**, Sun. from 21:00, Marmorek 10 (685-6917); **HeShe**, popular mixed bar, 8 Ha'Shomer, 1st floor, corner Ahuzat Benjamin, from 20 hrs; **Name's**, indoor/outdoor bar, large dance floor, great music, Ahad-Ha'am St., 22; **New Hangar**, dance club, Salme 54 Jaffa; **Playroom** , 58 Allenby St. Fri. nights only (near the Post-Office), dark room, cruisy; **Zman Amiti** (Real Time), Thur. nights, 22 Eilat Road, Jaffa (683-7788).

● Bar/club (GW): **Habima Club**, Fri. 13:00-20:00, Marmorek 10 (685-6917); **Sapho**, disco for lesbians only, 22 Ahad Ha'Am, Tuesdays only from 24:00.

● Coffee shop (GMW): **Nordau Cafe**, restaurant & bar on the second floor, 145 Ben Ye'Huda St., corner Arlozorov St. (524-0134).

● Restaurants (AW): **Babai at the Port**, excellent seafood, Hangar No. 1, Old Port of Jaffa by the main gate; **Cactus**, Tex-Mex, Hayarkon 66 (510-5969); **Casbah**, Moroccan cuisine, 32 Yirmiyhau Street (442-617); **Copenhagen**, cafe restaurant, Danish style, Kikar Ha'Medina, He Be'Yiar 10 (691-9289); **Danny's**, seafood, 54 Yirmiyhau Street (447-984); **Dolfin Yam**, seafood, Yordei Ha'Sira 1 (546-2235); **Hard Rock Café**, Dizengoff Center (525-1336); **Kapulsky**, best bakery, pastry shop, 168 Dizengoff Street (236-734); **Picaso**, Italian & International, Ha'Yarkon 88 (510-2784); **The Red Chinese**, Chinese & Thai, 326 Dizengoff St. (546-6347); **Stagecoach Pub/ Restaurant**, western movie-set decor, live music, hamburgers and salads, 216 Ha'Yarkon; also try the shops and restaurants at the popular Dizengoff Center; **Tony Roma's**, ribs and steaks, 98 Hayarkon St. (524-8219).

λ SERVICES λ

● Clothing/Gifts (AW): **American Bazaar**, Israel's largest selection of army surplus and souvenirs, 20 Salomon St., Old Central Bus Station (371-638); **Crazy Richard**, Israeli Army Surplus, T-Shirts, Kikar Atarim 358 (527-1058); & Dizengoff Center 769 (204-612).

● Escort Services (GM): **Boys** (699-7060); **Men to Men**, 24 hrs (683-2369).

● Gallery (AW): **Avi Soffer Galleries**, Kikar Kedumim, Old Jaffa (683-1054), 238 Dizengoff St. (546-0184).

● Laundry (AW): **Kabas-na**, coin-operated laundry, wash & dry in 1 hour, open 7am-8pm, 127 Ben-Yehuda (523-1605).

● Records/CD's (AW): **Tower Records**, Opera Tower, 1 Alenby St. (517-4044).

● Sauna (GM): **Thermos**, open from 13:00, Fridays close after midnight, 79 Shlomo Ha'Melekh St. (224-202).

● Pharmacy (AW): **Beny's Pharmacy**, Dizengoff 174 (222-386).

● Sex Shops (G/S): **Amsterdam Videos**, peep show, videos, Alenby 138 (560-1081), Neve Sheanan 25 (378-527), Ha'Migdalor branch, Alenby 21 (517-7005); **Eros**, gay videos, magazines, Ha'Hashmonaim 90 (561-0544); **Red Point**,

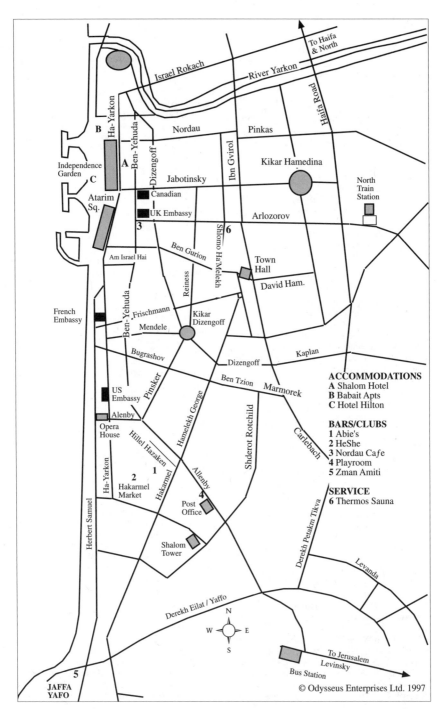

To Haifa & North

Israel Rokach

River Yarkon

Haifa Road

To Haifa & North

Ha-Yarkon

Ben-Yehuda

Dizengoff

Nordau

Pinkas

Ibn Gvirol

Kikar Hamedina

North Train Station

B

A

Independence Garden

C

Atarim Sq.

Jabotinsky

Canadian

UK Embassy

3

Arlozorov

Shlomo Ha'Melekh

6

Am Israel Hai

Ben Gurion

Reiness

Town Hall

David Ham.

French Embassy

Ben-Yehuda

Frischmann

Mendele

Kikar Dizengoff

Bugrashov

Dizengoff

Kaplan

Pinsker

Ben Tzion

Marmorek

Carlebach

US Embassy

Alenby

Opera House

Hillel Hazaken

Hamelekh George

1

Hakarmel

Allenby

Shderot Rotchild

Ha-Yarkon

2

Hakarmel Market

Post Office

4

Shalom Tower

Herbert Samuel

Derekh Petakh Tikva

Levanda

Derekh Eilat / Yaffo

N

W   E

S

5

JAFFA YAFO

To Jerusalem

Levinsky

Bus Station

© Odysseus Enterprises Ltd. 1997

ACCOMMODATIONS
A Shalom Hotel
B Babait Apts
C Hotel Hilton

BARS/CLUBS
1 Abie's
2 HeShe
3 Nordau Cafe
4 Playroom
5 Zman Amiti

SERVICE
6 Thermos Sauna

videos, sex toys, London Ministore (696-1216).

 ACCOMMODATIONS

SHALOM HOTEL

Ha'Yarkon St. Tel-Aviv 63405. USA/Canada reservations: Odysseus (516) 944-5330 or (800) 257-5344. Fax: (516) 944-7540 or (800) 982-6571. TYPE: *Hotel*. CLIENTELE: All Welcome. LOCA-TION: North Tel-Aviv across from Independence Park near Gay Beach, bars and restaurants.

* Rooms: 48 w/priv. bath or shower
  12 sgl / 36 dbl / some quads
* A/C, Central Heating
* Color cable TV (CNN), Telephone
* Restaurant/Pub: **Stagecoach**
* Beach: walking distance
* Gay Bars: walking distance
* Airport: 35 minutes; Airport bus
  shuttle stop nearby (#222)
* Reservations: through Odysseus
* Open: March 1-Nov. 15 / Dec. 20-Jan. 5
  (off) Nov. 16-Dec. 19 / Jan. 6-Feb. 28
* Rates: US$90-$160 w/IsB
* *TAC:* 10% (from Odysseus)

DESCRIPTION: A centrally located modern 3-star hotel. All front rooms have balconies with views of the Mediterranean and the Independence Park. All double rooms have private bath. Popular pub and restaurant in front of the hotel. Day tours/excursions can be arranged upon request to various destinations in Israel.

TEL-AVIV APARTMENTS - BABAIT

Tel-Aviv. USA/Canada reservations Tel: (800) 257-5344 or (516) 944-5330. Fax: (800) 982-6571. TYPE: *Rental Apartments*. CLIENTELE: Gay welcome. LOCATION: Central and north Tel-Aviv near the gay scene.

* Apartments: one & two bedrooms
  bedroom, living room, full bath, kitchen
* Villas: 3 bedrooms
* CTV, phone, A/C, C/H, balcony (some)
* Beach: walking distance (gay beach)
* Gay Bars: walking distance
* Airport: 20 min. (bus, taxi)
* Rates: from (US) $80/day; monthly rates
  from (US) $1,850
* Check in 3pm / check out 10am
* *TAC:* 10% (from Odysseus)

DESCRIPTION: Fully furnished apartments for short or long stay. Apartments across from the Sheraton Hotel in central Tel-Aviv are fully reno-vated with double bed in the bedroom. The small-er apartments have no balcony. Apartments north of the Hilton Hotel (near the Independence Park) are larger and more convenient for longer stay.

TEL-AVIV HILTON

Hayarkon St., Independence Park, Tel-Aviv 63405. Tel: (3) 520-2222. Fax: (3) 527-2711. TYPE: *Deluxe Hotel*. CLIENTELE: All Wel-come. LOCATION: Adjacent to the Indepen-dence Park and the 'gay beach'. 599 rooms w/priv. bath, CTV (CNN), phone, A/C, balcony, 24 hrs room service, 4 Kosher restaurants, bars, pool, tennis. Rates: (US) $235-$260. *TAC:* 10%.

TIBERIAS   ✆   03

✈ Ben-Gurion Int'l Airport (TLV)
   90 mi. / 140 km southwest

LOCATION: On the western shore of **Lake Kinnereth** - The Sea of Galilee in Northern Israel, 700 ft. / 210 m. below sea level.

POPULATION: 30,000

CLIMATE: Mild in the fall, winter and spring with temperatures in the 70°sF (21°c); but bru-tally hot in July and August with temperatures reaching 100°c (38°c).

DESCRIPTION: Year round resort town and tourism center for the Galilee and the Golan Heights. Built in A.D. 18 by Herod Antipas (son of Herod the Great), Tiberia is one of Israel's leading winter resorts. Tiberia's Hot Springs are known for their therapeutic values. Winter sports are available on Mount Hermon (1.5 hrs drive). **Kibutz Ein-Gev**, across the lake, offers its **Music & Folk Dance Festival** during Passover Week in the Spring.

❖ Public Cruising (AYOR): Tiberias does not have organized gay scene, however it has developed a good public cruising scene where you can meet locals and multinational UN peacekeepers. **Municipal Garden**, Ha'Galil St., corner Ha'yarden St. Old City; **Indepen-dence Garden**, near the Plaza Hotel and Pedestrian Street (evenings); **New Marina**, possible to meet at any time, check it out.

 ACCOMMODATIONS

HOTEL DAPHNE

Ha-Nassi St., Tiberias. Tel: (06) 792-261. TYPE: *Hotel*. LOCATION: Near the intersec-tion of Ha'Nassi & Ushishkin in the new town. 73 rooms w/priv. bath, A/C. DESCRIPTION: Moderately priced, some rooms with lake view.

ITALY

AREA: 116,303 sq. mi. (301,225 sq. km)
POPULATION: 57,140,000.
CAPITAL: Rome
CURRENCY: Lira (Lit.)
OFFICIAL LANGUAGE: Italian
MAJOR RELIGIONS: Roman Catholicism
Telephone: 39
Nat'l Holiday: Liberation Day, April 25
Official Time: G.M.T. + 1
Electricity: 220 volts
Exchange Rate: 1US$ = Lit 1,590
National Airline: Alitalia

LAW REGARDING HOMOSEXUALITY:
Homosexuality is legal in Italy. The legal minimum age for consensual homosexual activity is 16 years. Although the country has adopted liberal legislation since 1861, homosexuality is not well accepted everywhere in Italy. Generally the south is more hostile to homosexual lifestyle than the north; discretion is advisable.

BOLOGNA   🕐 081

✈ Guglielmo Marconi Airport (BLQ)
4 mi. / 6 km northwest

LOCATION: In the Northern Appenines 94 mi. / 150 km SW of Venice and 227 mi. / 363 km north of Rome.

Gay Visitor Information
ARCI Gay Nazionale
Tel: (051) 436-700

DESCRIPTION: Gastronomic capital of Italy, Bologna is a famous academic center. The University of Bologna is the oldest in Europe and it attracts many students from all over the world.

❖ Gay Beach: **Noce Di Reno**, 10 km / 6 mi.

from Bologna towards Noce, near the head of the line bus #16, nudism and action.

❖ Public Cruising (AYOR): **Piazza XX Settembre**, in the adjacent public gardens, evenings, many GI's and hustlers; **Stazione Centrale**, evenings, mostly elderly folks, GI's and hustlers.

BARS Y RESTAURANTS 🍴

● Bars/Clubs (GM): **Brief Encounter**, sex disco bar, dark room, open 19:00 till late, via Settima Strada 5, exit Padova Est, Zona Industriale Nord (776-073); **Cafe Chopin**, via Nazario Sauro 7b (236-766); **Cassero**, bar, videos, disco with young crowds on Sundays, piazza Porta Saragozza 2; **Caveau del Terzo Piano** c/o Circolo Culturale ARCI Gay, Via Giambologna 4 (533-074); **Il Pachito**, disco bar, Via Polese 47C; **Matilda**, disco, Via A. Righi 9 (226-566); **No Wall Bar**, artistic shows, Via Moline 2/F (228-971).

● Restaurants (AW): **Grassilli**, Bolognese Cuisine, via del Luzzo 3 (237-938); **Al Papagallo**, gastronomic cuisine, piazza della Mercanzia 3E (232-807); **Rostaria Antico Brunetti**, the oldest restaurant in town, just off piazza Maggiore in the heart of town, inexpensive but good, via Canduti di Cefalonia 5 (234-441).

λ SERVICES λ

● Health Club (GM): **Cosmos Club**, American bar, sauna, solarium, free massage, via Boldrini #22 interno 16, open: 12 noon - 1:30a (255-890); **New Vigor Club**, sauna, Turkish bath, bar, videos, via S. Felice 6b open: 11-2am (232507).

🏳️ ACCOMMODATIONS 🏳️

INTERNAZIONALE
via dell'Indipendenza 60, Bologna 40121. Tel: (51) 245-544. Fax: (51) 249-544. TYPE: *Hotel.* CLIENTELE: All Welcome. LOCATION: Central near the Convention Hall. 139 rooms w/priv. bath, A/C, CTV, minibar. Rates: $150-$210.

THE VECCHI
via dell'Indipendenza 47, Bologna 40121. Tel: (51) 231-991. Fax: (51) 224-143. TYPE: *Hotel.* CLIENTELE: All Welcome. LOCATION: Central, 5 min. walk from railway station. 96 room w/priv. bath, A/C, minibar, CTV. DESCRIPTION: Clean and bright moderate hotel. Rates: $120-$180.

CAGLIARI   ✆   **070**

✈ Elmas Airport (CAG) 5 mi. / 8 km SW

LOCATION: In the south of Sardinia, an island in the Mediterranean Sea south of Corsica.

❖ Gay Beaches: **Calafighera**, near Sella del Diavolo and Calamosca, the beach is also locally known as **"Calagay"**; **Calamosca**, from Cagliari take bus #11, many GI's; **Terra Mala**, popular with gays, nudism, young crowds.

❖ Public Cruising (AYOR): **Piazza Matteoti**, in the parks during evenings, can be dangerous; **Piazzale su Siccu**, by car or by feet, evenings only, some hustlers.

♈ BARS ♈

● Bars/Clubs (GM): **Black Samba**, via Mameli 122; **Pantheon**, gay bar, via Mameli 218 (21-03).

CAPRI   ✆   **081**

LOCATION: An island in the Tyrrhenian Sea south of Naples, off the tip of the Amalfi Coast.

POPULATION: 9,000

CLIMATE: Pleasant Mediterranean climate with warm summers and cool, windy and wet winters. Average January temperature is 48°F (9°c), and average July temperature is 78°F (26°c).

VISITOR INFORMATION
Azienda Soggiorno
Piazza Umberto, Capri 80073
Tel: (081) 8370-686

DESCRIPTION: Italy's most famous small rock-islet draws millions of visitors from around the world. The island is smart, intimate and fashionable. **Capri Town** on the mountain top is popular with the international jet-set. **Anacapri** the second town is located uphill and is quieter. The main attraction remains the **Blue Grotto**, but if you can not go down to the grotto, take a boat trip around the island for unforgettable views. Capri's Gay Scene centers around the famous **Piazzeta di Capri**, a 24 hrs. meeting and pick up location near the stairs at the bar by the cable-car.

❖ Gay Beach: **Via Krupp**, sunbathing and nudism at the foot of Via Krupp.

● **HOW TO GET THERE**: By boat - Catamaran - 2 daily from Fiumicino Seaport; Hydrofoils - 19 daily from Margellina terminal in Naples. Other boats from Sorrento or Positano.

BARS ♈ RESTAURANTS 🍴

● Bars/Clubs (G/S): **Piranha**, via Camerelle 61b (837-6011); **Number 2**, disco at the Hotel Quisisana, via Camerelle 2 (837-0788).

🏳 ACCOMMODATIONS 🏳

GRAND HOTEL QUISISANA
via Camerelle 2, Capri 80073. Tel: (81) 837-0788. Fax: (81) 837-6080. TYPE: *Deluxe Hotel*. CLIENTELE: Mostly Straight. LOCATION: Few steps from the Piazza with views of the sea.

* Rooms: 150 w/priv. bath. Suites: 18
* CTV, phone, mini-bar, balcony
* Wheelchair accessible, A/C
* Restaurant, bar, disco, nightclub
* Pools (2), roof garden, solarium
* Sauna, massage, gym, tennis
* Credit Cards: MC/VISA/AMEX/EC/DC
* Open: April - October
* Rates: (LIT) 270,000 - 340,000. *TAC:* 8%

DESCRIPTION: The grand hotel of Capri is a hub of activity from its front terrace bar, lavishly public spaces, the disco or the pools. All rooms are elegant and well appointed, but the best units (most expensive) are the poolside apartments.

FLORENCE   ✆   **055**

✈   Amerigo Vespuci Airport (FLR)
3 mi. / 5 km

LOCATION: In the province of Tuscany. The river Arno flows through the city.

POPULATION: 442,000

CLIMATE: Pleasant Mediterranean climate with warm summers and cool, windy and wet winters. Average January temperature is 48°F (9°c), and average July temperature is 78°F (26°c).

VISITOR INFORMATION
Tourist Information Center
Tel: (055) 217459

Gay Visitor Information
Arci Gay: (055) 239-8772

DESCRIPTION: Florence is a city of art with a distinguished Renaissance influence. The museums are loaded with priceless masterpieces of world famous painters, sculptors and artists from the 13th and 14th centuries. The palaces and cathedrals are fine examples of Medieval and Renaissance architecture.

Florence is a shopper's paradise for leather goods and jewelry. The quality is excellent and the prices are far lower than what you would pay in New York or Paris. For first time visitors the **Arno** is a good orientation point. Most of the city sits on the north, or right bank of the river. The main squares are the **Piazza del Duomo** - the religious heart of Florence, and the **Piazza della Republica** - the city's busiest commercial center.

Visit: **The Cathedral** (Duomo) Complex (downtown); **Uffizi Museum & Gallery** - a Renaissance Palace turned museum with 15 rooms dedicated to Florentine and Tuscan masterpieces; **Pitti Palace**, a palace turned museum and devoted to 17th century art; **Plazza Vecchio** - the Residence of the Medicis; on the third floor is a new permanent exhibition of 140 works of art removed from Italy by the Nazis; **The Academy** - where Michelangelo's original David is displayed; **Ponte Vecchio** - the only bridge in Florence that survived the 1944 destruction; the **Straw Market** - a 16th century covered market with good deal of shopping bargains.

❖ Public Cruising (AYOR): **Piazza Republica**, from Piazza della Republica to Piazza Santa Croce per Calimala, especiali in the evenings, young crowds; **Stadio Campo di Marte**, sports ground beside Viale P. Paoli, evenings only, also in cars mixed, can be interesting; **Parco le Cascine**, car park in the vicinity of the Ponte alla Vittoria, at night in car or on foot, possible encounters during the day too; **Motel Agip**, on the exit off the A1 Florence-Nord motorway, in the Agip motel car park, truck drivers and gay men in cars preferably at night.

BARS ⅄ RESTAURANTS 🍴

● Bars/clubs (GM): **Crisco Club**, video bar, backroom, leather/jeans,Via S. Egidio 43/R (248-0580); **Satanassa**, disco bar, games room, backroom, videos, open: 22:00 - 6:00 weekends, 10pm-3am during the week, closed Tues, Via

Pandolfini 26r (243-356); **Tabasco**, video cruise bar, Piazza Santa Cecillia 3r behind a Tobacco store in a small courtyard near the Uffizi, open: 21:00 closed: mon. (213-000).

● Bars/clubs (GMW): **Madi'Club**, music bar, art exhibition, Via delle Seggiole, 8r; **Piccolo Café**, snack bar, art exhibition, Borgo Santa Croce 27 (241-704); **Rose**, cafe, snack bar, Via del Parione 26r (287-090);

● Restaurants (AW): **Enoteca Pinchiorri**, expensive in a 15th century Ciofi-Iacometti Palace, Via Ghibellina 87 (242-7777); **Gauguin**, 24r Via degli Alfani (234-0616); **Harry's Bar**, popular with American tourists, traditional Italian fare plus hamburgers and fries, expensive, Lungarno Amerigo Vespucci 22r (296-700); **Trattoria Anita**, home cooking, Toscan specialties, via del Parlascio 2/R (218-698); **Vecchia Bettola**, Tuscan trattoria, inexpensive, viale Ariosto 32-34r (224-158); **La Vie En Rose**, Tuscan creative cuisine, 68r Borgo Allegri (245-860).

⅄ SERVICES ⅄

● Cinema (G/S): **Arlecchino**, Via dei Bardi 47r (284-332); **Italia**, Piazza Alinari, evenings only (211-069).

● Clothing (G/S):**Il Giardino d'Inverno**, sexy underwear for men and women, via del Melarancio 8 rosso (211-391).

● Erotica: **Cornice E'**, posters, magazines, via del Melarancio 15/R (215-831): **Frisco Int'l Imports**, show room, videos, condoms, Via Veracini 15 (357-351); **Magic America**, Via Guelfa 89-91/R (2128-40).

● Health Club (GM): **Florence Baths**, Sauna & Gym, Via Guelfa 93r (216-050).

● Leather Boutique: **Ring**, Via Galliano 29/R (357-351).

🔑 ACCOMMODATIONS 🔑

HOTEL CELLAI
via 27 Aprile 14, Florence. Tel: (55) 489-291. TYPE: *Hotel*. CLIENTELE: Gay/Straight. LOCATION: Historical and art district. 50 rooms w/priv. bath, CTV, phone, A/C. Rates: Lit. 100,000 - Lit. 250,000. DESCRIPTION: Central 3-star hotel. Rooms individually decorated and furnished.

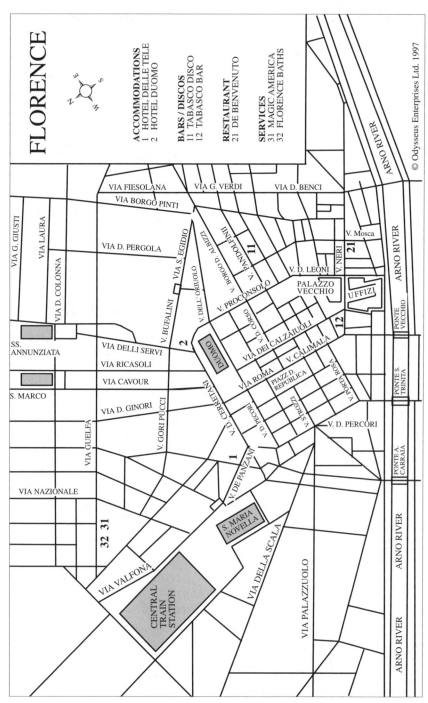

FLORENCE

ACCOMMODATIONS
1 HOTEL DELLE TELE
2 HOTEL DUOMO

BARS / DISCOS
11 TABASCO DISCO
12 TABASCO BAR

RESTAURANT
21 DE BENVENUTO

SERVICES
31 MAGIC AMERICA
32 FLORENCE BATHS

© Odysseus Enterprises Ltd. 1997

✪ HOTEL DELLE TELE

Via Panzani. Firenze. USA/Canada reservations: Odysseus: (516) 944-5330 or (800) 257-
5344. Fax: (516) 944-7540 or (800) 982-6571.
TYPE: *Hotel*. CLIENTELE: Gay/Straight.
LOCATION: Centrally located a short walk
from the train station, and the Cathedral.

* Rooms: 20 w/priv. bath or shower
* CTV, phone, A/C, frigo bar
* Breakfast room, bar, parking (nearby)
* Maid & room service, elevator
* Gay Bars: nearby
* Airport: 7 km / 4 mi., taxi
* Gay Bars: walking distance
* Reservations: through Odysseus
* Open: Year round
* Rates: (US) $100 - $190 w/CB
* *TAC:* 10%

DESCRIPTION: Elegant comfortable 3-star
hotel in a 17th century building. Many paintings on canvas ("tele") on display in the public
rooms, corridors and bedrooms. Clean airy
rooms, excellent and efficient service. Highly
recommended.

✪ HOTEL DUOMO

Piazza Duomo. Firenze. USA/Canada reservations: Odysseus: (516) 944-5330 or (800) 257-
5344. Fax: (516) 944-7540 or (800) 982-6571.
TYPE: *Hotel*. CLIENTELE: Gay/Straight.
LOCATION: Centrally located in famous Piazza Duomo. Entrance on 4th Fl., via elevator.

* Rooms: 30 w/priv. bath or shower
* CTV, phone, A/C, frigo bar
* Maid & room service, breakfast room
* Gay Bars: walking distance
* Airport: 7 km / 4 mi., taxi
* Reservations: through Odysseus
* Open: Year round
* Rates: (US) $100 - $190 w/CB
* *TAC:* 10%

DESCRIPTION: 3 star hotel in the Piazza
Duomo near all tourist attractions. Clean airy
rooms, excellent and efficient service. Highly
recommended.

HOTEL MONA LISA

Borgo Pinti 27, Florence. Tel: (55) 247-9751.
USA/Canada reservations: Odysseus: (516)
944-5330 or (800) 257-5344. Fax: (516) 944-
7540 or (800) 982-6571.TYPE: *Hotel*. CLIEN-
TELE: All Welcome. LOCATION: Historic center of town.

* Rooms: 30 w/priv. bath
  sgl 5 / dbl 20 / triple 4/ quad 1

Hotel delle Tele

USA/Canada reservations
(800) 257-5344
Tel: (516) 944-5330 • Fax: (516) 944-7540

Hotel Duomo

USA/Canada reservations
(800) 257-5344
Tel: (516) 944-5330 • Fax: (516) 944-7540

* Rooms for smokers and non-smokers
* CTV, phone, refrigerator, safe box, C/H, A/C, hairdryer
* American bar, garden
* Maid & room service, parking
* Airport: 3 mi. / 5 km, taxi
* Train Station: 1 mi. / 1.6 km
* Languages: Italian, Spanish, French, English, German
* Open: Year round
* Rates: Lit. 280,000 - Lit. 400,000 w/CBb
* Check in 2:00 pm / check out 12:00 noon
* *TAC:* 10% (from Odysseus)

DESCRIPTION: Elegant Renaissance Palace furnished with fine antique furniture, old oil paintings, and number of art treasures.

GENOVA   *✆* 010

✈ Christoforo Colombo Airport (GOA)

LOCATION: In the northern Province of Liguria along the shores of the Mediterranean Sea.

POPULATION: 787,000

CLIMATE: Pleasant Mediterranean climate with warm summers and cool, windy and wet winters. Average January temperature is 48°F (9°c); average July temperature is 78°F (26°c).

Gay Visitor Information
ARCI Gay: (010) 281-430

DESCRIPTION: Genova (Genoa) is a city of hills and sea, the largest commercial port in the Mediterranean and a busy international airport. It is a colorful mix of modern highrise buildings, picturesque seamen's quarters, aristocratic palaces and historic villas.

To explore the beauty of Genova, take an afternoon boat trip in the port, the city looks magnificent from the seaside. As a side trip visit **Savona** or **Nervi**, east of Genova a popular year round resort town.

❖ Public Cruising (AYOR): **Via XX Settembre**; **Mura delle Cappuccine**, at night and by car; **Stazione Principe** (Central Station) in front of Bar Principe.

❖ Gay nude beach: **Pieve Ligure**, 100 m (100 yards) by the Pieve Ligure Railway Station. Pieve Ligure is some considerable distance out

of Genova, car rental is necessary since bus and train service is unreliable.

BARS ⅄ RESTAURANTS

● Bars/clubs (GM): **Company**, American style bar/disco, via Smirne 2 (581-489); **Diva**, disco, P.zza Tommaseo 17/R. (362-8652); **La Cage**, American bar, disco, via Sampierdarena 167/R (454-555).

● Bar/Club (GMW): **L'Ibisco**, private club, bar & restaurant, via delle Casette 21 (384-388).

● Bar/club (GW): **Glamorama**, American bar, cabaret for women only, via Rivoli 12/R (581-685).

● Restaurants (AW): **Al Grillo**, home cooking, vico Domocculta 14 (546-511); **Bruno**, regional cuisine, vico Casana 9 (208-505).

λ SERVICES λ

● Health Club (GM): **Topkapi Sauna**, mixed clientele, via Casaregis 26/R (546-489).

● Cinema (GM): **Dionisio**, good action, via Colombo 11.

ACCOMMODATIONS

BRISTOL PALACE HOTEL
Via XX Settembre 35, Genova 16121. Tel: (010) 592-541. TYPE: *First Class Hotel*. CLIENTELE: Mostly Straight. LOCATION: In city center.105 rooms w/priv. bath, CTV, phone, A/C, mini-bar. Rates: (LIT) 280,000 - 510,000. *TAC:* 8%. DESCRIPTION: Old-World traditional hotel on main street in the center of town. Good amenities but formal atmosphere.

GROSSETO   *✆* 0564

LOCATION: Southern Tuscany near the spa town of Saturnia.

DESCRIPTION: A small village in the Tuscan Hills. Nearby Saturnia located on the hilltop is a famous spa town. In the valley below the village swirl the steaming sulfur springs of the **Terme di Saturnia**.

Public Cruising (AYOR): **Below the City Walls**, opposite the prison at night; **Follonica**, along the railway near Prato Ranieri; **Saturnia**

Baths, outdoor natural baths near the hotel **Terme di Saturnia.**

❖ Gay Beaches: **Grosseto-Alberese Marina,** beautiful natural beach, very popular; **Grosseto-Giannella-Orbetello,** 20 mi / 32 km south of Grosseto going towards Port S. Stefano; **Grosseto - Feniglia Beach - Orbetello,** between Orbetello and Port Ercole, pine forest, lagoon and dunes.

 ACCOMMODATIONS

MOTEL AGIP
SS Aurlia Sud, Grosseto 58100. Tel: (564) 24-100. TYPE: *Motel.* CLIENTELE: All Welcome. LOCATION: Central. 32 rooms w/priv. bath, phone, CTV. Rates: on request.

TERME DI SATURNIA
58050 Saturnia (Grosseto). Tel: (564) 601-061. TYPE: *Spa Hotel.* CLIENTELE: All Welcome. LOCATION: In the valley below the village. 104 rooms w/priv. bath, phone, CTV, A/C, restaurant, complete health spa. Rates: on request. DESCRIPTION: Elegant large spa hotel in a country setting.

LIGURIA

✈ Côte d'Azur Airport (NCE)
Nice/France 40 km / 25 mi.

DESCRIPTION: The Italian Riviera stretches across the northwestern part of the Mediterranean Coast from France/Monaco to an area just west of Genova. The Italian Riviera offers during the summer months many excellent beaches for nude sunbathing, some are popular with gay nudists.

❖ Gay nude beaches: **Pieve Ligure,** walk about 250 m / yards from the straight nude beach towards Recco; **Ventimiglia,** beautiful beach outside town at the S. Ludovico junction, nude sunbathing, gay action; **Monterosso,** walk beyond the cliffs, mostly young crowds; **Levanto,** near the old Railroad Station, nude sunbathing, some action; **Varigotti,** after Noli going towards Varigotti, part of the beach is exclusively gay, others are mixed. Good action.

ACCOMMODATIONS

For accommodations near the nude beaches of the Italian riviera check Genova or Nice (France). You can also stay in San Remo or Ventimiglia.

MESSINA   ✆ 090

LOCATION: Northeastern Sicily, across the Strait of Messina from the mainland.

Gay/Lesbian Visitor Information
ARCI GAY Messina. Tel: (090) 693-542

❖ Gay Beaches: **San Saba,** take bus #28 from Messina, nudism, good action; **Giampilieri,** near Messina.

BARS ⅄ RESTAURANTS 🍴

● Bars/clubs (GM): **Angolo del Buongustaio,** pub, open late, young crowds, via T. Canizzaro; **Safari,** tavern, mixed, Piazza Duomo.

MILANO   ✆   02

✈ Linate Int'l Airport (LIN)

LOCATION: Northern province of Lombardy, about 120 mi. / 192 km north of Genova, 40 mi. / 64 km southwest of Como.

POPULATION: 1,800,000

CLIMATE: Continental. Summers can be hot and airless with high temperatures reaching 85°F (29°c). Winters are cold and foggy with temperatures in the low 10°Fs (-12°c) with occasional snowfall.

Gay/Lesbian Visitor Information
Centro d'Iniziativa Gay (ARCI Gay)
Via Torricelli 19. Tel: 839-4604
Telefono Amico Arcigay
Numero verde 1678-27182

Lesbian Visitor Information
Telefona Amica: 839-4604

DESCRIPTION: Milan is the financial and commercial hub of Italy, and a world famous fashion and business center. Although the city is smaller in population than Rome, many Milanese consider their city to be the 'real' capital of Italy. The city is rich with 14th and 15th century history of Umbro-Etruscan origin.

Visit the **Piazza del Duomo,** and the **Castle of the Sforzas.** Art lovers can enjoy the city's fine art collections in the various museums. if you are a real 'Opera Queen', nothing will top your excitement at **La Scala** - the most famous opera house in the world. The best shopping street is **Via Montenapoleone**. The **Brera** area is a younger alternative and it is known as Milan's version of St.-Germain-de-Prés.

Milan is the undisputable 'gay capital' of Italy. It houses the national gay archives and the national headquarter of ARCI Gay, Italy's leading gay organization with branches all over the country. The gay publications **Hot Line** and **Babilonia** are published here.

❖ Gay Beaches: **Ticino**, beach on the left of Vigevano bridge, also nudism.

❖ Public Cruising (AYOR): **Bastioni di Porta Venezia**, opposite Palestro Park, M° Porta Venezia; **Fossa dei Leoni** (Lion's Pits), near Nord Stazione, dangerous at night, some rent boys and police control, M° Cadoma; **Ortomercato**, many gays, some truckers, viale Monte Cimone and streets nearby (evenings); **Via G.B. Sammartini**, Milano's famous 'Gay Street' on the west side of Central Station-Milano, many gay shops and meeting points; **Via Reggimenti Cavalleria di Savoia**, on the street, gardens and parkings (evening).

● Side trip from Milano: **Monza** - scene of the Italian Grand Prix in September and beautiful Lake Como.

BARS ☿ RESTAURANTS 🍴

● Bars/clubs (GM): **American Disaster**, gay disco, theme nights, Via Boscovich 48; **Argos**, disco, pub, dark room, glory holes, open daily 22:00-03:00, via Resegone #1 (607-2249); **Company Club**, cruise club, theme parties, V. Benadir #14 (282-9481); **HD**, gay disco, via Tajani 11 (718-990); **Hot Line Club**, bar & cultural center, open 24 hrs., Via G.B. Sammartini 23 (6698-3506); **Man 2 Man**, videos, strips, live shows, erotic massage, viale Umbria 120; **Menu**, restaurant, cabaret, piano bar, via Valassina 16 (668-8579); **Nuova Idea**, bar & disco entertainment complex, via de Castilla 30 (6900-7869); **One Way**, leather disco/bar, Via F. Cavallotti 204, Sesto San Giovanni (6900-7859); **Papè Satan**, gay disco on weekends only, Via Baracchini (M° Duomo); **Plastic**, gay disco only on Thu, viale Umbria 120; **Querelle**, bar, Via de Castillia 20 (683-900); **Rubicon Club**, Gay disco Wed, Thu & Fri, via S. Tecla 3 (8646-4255); **Segreto**, disco club, Pzza Castello 1 (860307); **Uiti Bar**, some rent-boys, via Monviso 14 (3315-996); **Zip Club**, private disco/club, darkroom, membership required, Corso Sempione 76 (331-4904).

● Bars/Clubs (GMW): **Cafeole**, disco bar, via Chiesa Rossa 69, open: 22 - 6; **Hot Line Club**, gay club affiliated with Arci Gay, mostly lesbians, via G.B. Sammartini 23 (669-88456); **Sottomarino Giallo** (Yellow Submarine), only women disco and bar, via Donatello 2 (294-01047).

● Bars/Clubs (GW): **Cicip e Ciciap**, restaurant & bar, Via Gorani (877-555); **Sottomarino Giallo**, disco, Via Donatello 2 (2940-1047).

● Restaurants (AW): **After Line Pub Restaurant**, video, shows, Via Sammartini 25 (669-2130); **Al Cucciolo**, Via Lecco 4 (225-387); **Bagutta**, homey hangout for Milan's literary, journalistic, and artistic crowd, 14 Via Bagutta (7600-2767); **Due Amici**, Via Borsieri 3 (668-4696); **La Risotteria**, gay friendly, via Dandolo 2 (551-81694); **Menù**, good cuisine, Via Vlassina 16 (668-8579); **Pizzeria al Quaranta**, via Panfilo Castaldi 40; **Torre di Pisa**, funky favorite in the Brera district, the crowd is a jumble of Milan's fashion, business, art and design worlds, 26 Via Mercato (874-877).

λ SERVICES λ

● Adult Cinemas (G/S): **Ambra**, via Clitumno corner via Padova; **La Fenice**, viale Bligny 52; **Roxy**, corso Lodi 128.

● Health Clubs (GM): **Alexander's Club**, private sauna, Via Pindaro 23 (255-0220); **Body Gym**, sauna, body building, bar, videos, via Lesmi 9 (894-02049); **Magic Sauna**, sauna, Turkish bath, videos, solarium, massage,Via Maiocchi 8 open: 12 - 24 (2940-6182); **La Nuova Sauna**, Via Gaudenzio Ferrari 6, open daily 12:00-23:00 (837-8207); **One Way Sauna**, Via Renzo e Lucia 3 (846-6148); **Teddy Sauna Club**, bar, sauna, massage, videos, via Renzo e Lucia 3 near Piazza Maggi (846-6148); **Thermas**, sauna, solarium, videos, body building, open 12 noon - 12 midnight, Via Rezzecca 9 (545-0355).

● Sex Shops (GMW): **Erotika**, gay video shop, sexy underwear, via Melzo 19 (2952-1849); **In Line Diffusion**, Via Scarlati 20 (225-976); **Magic America**, videos, magazines, Via Legnone 19 (688-1057); **Studio Know How**, gay videos, mail order, Piazza Duca d'Aosta 12 (669-87085).

🗝 ACCOMMODATIONS 🗝

HOTEL CENTRO
Via Broletto 46, Milan 20121. Tel: (02) 869-2821. TYPE: *Hotel*. CLIENTELE: All Welcome. LOCATION: Central historical area near the Duomo. 54 rooms w/priv. bath. DESCRIP-

TION: Pleasant and central 3-star hotel with rooms equipped to high standards.

HOTEL CITY
Corso Buenos Aires 42/5, Milan 20124. Tel: (2) 295-23382. TYPE: *Hotel.* CLIENTELE: All Welcome. LOCATION: Near the Bastioni di Porta Venezia park, Central Station and the Via Sammartini 'Gay Street'. 55 rooms w/priv. bath, CTV, phone. Rates: on request. DESCRIPTION: Moderate 3-star hotel convenient to Milan's gay scene.

HOTEL DURANTE
Pzza Durante 30, Milan 20131. Tel: (02) 282-7673. USA/Canada Reservations: 1-800-257-5344 or (516) 944-5330. Fax: 1-800-982-6571 or (516) 944-7540. TYPE: *Hotel.* CLIENTELE: Gay welcome. LOCATION: 100 m / yards from underground/M° Loreto-Pasteur and main shopping street (Corso Buenos Aires).

* Rooms: 12 w/priv. bath
  3 sgl / 9 dbl / 3 triple
* Smoking allowed in rooms
* CTV, phone, C/H
* Airport: 10 min. Linate / 1 hour Malpensa
* Train Station: 2 underground stops
* Season: Year round. Closed - August
  + 10 days over the Christmas Holidays
* Rates: (US) $60 - $110 w/CB
* Check in 14:00 / check out 11:00
* *TAC:* 10% (from Odysseus)

DESCRIPTION: Budget hotel in a convenient location welcoming gay clientele.

HOTEL SAN CARLO
Via Napo Torriani 28. (02) 669-2937. USA/ Canada reservations - Tel: (516) 944-5330 or (800) 257-5344. Fax: (516) 944-7540. TYPE: *Hotel.* CLIENTELE: All Welcome. LOCATION: Commercial center in front of railway Central Station. 75 rooms w/priv. bath, CTV, phone, A/C, minibar, restaurant, bar, 24 hrs safe box service. parking. DESCRIPTION: Good quality 3-star hotel.

NAPLES   ℭ   081

✈ Capodichino Airport (NAP)
4 mi. / 6km northeast

LOCATION: In the southern region of Campania, 136 mi / 218 km south of Rome.

CLIMATE: Warm and pleasant year round. Winter January temperatures average 50°F (10°c); and summer July average 83°F (28°c). Summer temperatures often exceed 90°F (35°c).

Gay Visitor Information
ARCI GAY Antinoo Napoli
Tel: (081) 552-8815

DESCRIPTION: Naples is a magnificent seaport set against the back drop of a crystal-blue sky and volcanic mountains. Many attraction inside the city and nearby: e.g. Pompeii, Capri, Ischia and Vesuvius, make Naples one of the top tourist destinations in Italy. Oscar Wilde once wrote about Naples: "The museum is full of lovely Greek bronzes. The only bother is that they all walk about the town at night."

❖ Public Crusing (AYOR): **Piazza Dei Martiri**, the gayest point in town, mostly in the evenings, anytime during the year; **Lungomare/Boardwalk** and environs, specially in the evening, quiet and secure; **Villa Comunale**, Zona Acquarium, public gardens, best by car, American sailors and GI's; **Piazza Municipo**, also near the Palazzo S. Giacomo, evenings only; **Molo di Mergellina**, only durning the summers in the evenings, good meeting place; **Piazza Vittoria**; **Stazione Centrale**, a bit of everything, gays, Arabs, hustlers, proceed with caution.

BARS Ⓨ RESTAURANTS

● Bars/clubs (GM): **Bagatto Club Privé**, disco, closed on Monday, via Dumas Padre 3/A; **Bibop**, meeting place, vico dei Sospiri, Chiaia.

● Bar/Club (GMW): **Blanche**, gay/lesbian disco, popular, via Crispi Gradini Amedeo 12, Tue/Thurs./Sat.

● Restaurants (AW): **La Fazenda**, authentic Napolitan cuisine, panoramic view of Capri, via Marechiaro 58A (769-7420); **La Sacrestia**, elegant Pasta/Seafood, one of the best in town, via Orazio 116 (761-1051); **Umberto**, atmospheric restaurant, right in the heart of Gay Naples, via Alabardieri 30 (418-555).

λ SERVICES λ

● Adult Cinema (G/S): **Arco**, popular among gays, via Poerio 4; **Casanova**, corso Garibaldi 330; **Eden**, via Sanfelice 15; **Roxy**, via Tarsia; **Trianon**, Piazza Calenda.

ACCOMMODATIONS

GRAND HOTEL VESUVIO
Via Partenope 45, Naples 80121. Tel: (81) 764-0044. TYPE: *Hotel.* CLIENTELE: All Welcome. LOCATION: Near Piazza dei Martiri, Chiaia and the Aquario, Naples main gay cruise areas.

* Rooms: 170 w/priv. bath. Suites: 15
* Phone, CTV, A/C, hairdryer, frigobar
* Restaurant: rooftop w/panoramic views
* American bar, Free parking
* Room & Maid Service
* Gay bars: walking distance
* Beach: walking distance
* Airport: 3 km / 2 mi.
* Open: Year round
* Rates: $150-$190
* *TAC:* 10%

DESCRIPTION: Traditional waterfront superior first class hotel. Great location to explore the flavors of Naples gay scene.

PALACE HOTEL
Piazza Garibaldi, Naples 80142. Tel: (81) 267-044. TYPE: *Hotel.* CLIENTELE: All Welcome. LOCATION: 100 m/yards from train station. Neatly furnished rooms w/bath, CTV, phone, restaurant. Rates: $100-$140.

PADOVA ✆ 049

✈ Marco Polo-Tessera Airport (VCE)
25 mi. / 40 km east

LOCATION: Padova is located 25 mi. / 40 km west of Venice and 50 mi. / 80 km east of Verona.

Gay Visitor Information
ARCI Gay "Circolo Nuovo"
Tel: (049) 875-6326

DESCRIPTION: Major art and University center on the main rail line between Venice and Milan. Padova's famous School of Medecine attracts students from all over the world.

BARS RESTAURANTS

● Bars/clubs (GM): **Alcazar**, disco, via Risorgimento 16, Fontaniva (Padova) (049-597-0475); **Etienne** (open), strada dei colli 18 (zona Brusegana) gay disco Sat. only (620-156); **La Dolce Vita**, bar and disco, via Monte Cero 40 open: 20:30 until late (897-6778); **Pick Up**, video dance and piano bar, via Longhin 41/a, Zona Stanga. Open: 6pm-2am; **Tartan's Pub**, mixed clientele, via C. Battisti 187 (875-6639).

● Restaurants (AW): **Ristorante Dotto**, elegant restaurant in the heart of the city, via Squarcione 23 (875-1490); **Trattoria da Placido**, good local food at moderate price, via Santa Lucia 59 (875-2252).

λ SERVICES λ

● Health Clubs (GM): **Concorde Club**, sauna, dark room, videos, open daily 2pm-2am, via Pelizzo #3 (4th Fl.) zona piazzale stanga, exit Hwy Padova East (776-464); **Paradise Club**, sauna, pool, videos, via Turazza 19 (Zona Stanga); **Olympus Club**, gay sauna, darkroom, Turkish bath, bar, via N. Tommaseo 96/A (807-5843).

ACCOMMODATIONS

HOTEL DONATELLO
piazza del Santo, 102-104. Tel: (49) 875-0829. Fax: (49) 875-0829. TYPE: *Hotel.* CLIENTELE: All Welcome. LOCATION: near the Basilica of St. Anthony. 42 rooms w/priv. bath. Well furnished rooms, centrally located. Fine restaurant. Rates: $80 - $130.

PALERMO ✆ 091

✈ Punta-Raisi Airport (PMO)
20 mi. / 32 km west

LOCATION: in northwestern Sicily, 145 mi. / 230 km west of Messina.

Gay Visitor Information
ARCI Gay Palermo
Tel: (091) 324-917

DESCRIPTION: The largest port and capital of Sicily. Palermo is a show case of Norman-Arabic culture. Many of its residents are surprisingly blond with blue eyes because they trace their ancestry to the Normans.

❖ Gay Beaches: **Mondello**, take bus #15 to Capo Gallo; **Barcarello**, peaceful nude beach, good action, near Capo Gallo.

❖ Public Cruising (AYOR): **Giardino Inglese**, popular with some military officers; **Viale della Libertà**, popular meeting place, good contacts; **Piazza Croci**, popular meeting place, evenings only; **Piazza Politeama**, active during the day, many hustlers; **Marina di Pulsano**, mixed, be descreet.

PISA ✆ 050

✈ G. Galilei Airport (PSA)
2 mi. / 3 km south

LOCATION: In Tuscany north of Livorno on the Arno river.

POPULATION: 100,000

DESCRIPTION: Medieval maritime port on the Arno famous for the leaning **Tower of Pisa.** Built circa 1174 it is one of the world's most recognizable attractions. Visit the city's old cathedrals, majestic piazzas and famous museums of art and paintings.

❖ Public Cruising (AYOR): **Lungarno Guadalongo,** in the parkside alongside the Arno River, at night (by car); **Opposite the Station** during the day; **Giardinni Scotto,** public gardens, Lungarno Ribonacci, daytime with caution; **Pontedera,** via della Repubblica, from the Piazza della Stazione to Piazza Garibaldi, alongside the railway line, evenings.

❖ Beaches: **Free Communal Beach,** between Tirrenia Square and Marina di Pisa, near the US Army beach; **Vecchiano Marina,** on the Aurelia Road to Migliarino Pisano.

BARS Y RESTAURANTS ¶¶

● Bar/club (GM): **Gao Bar,** closed Mon., Vicolo della Croce Rossa 5 (546-420).

● Restaurants (AW): **Bruno,** one of Pisa's finest restaurants, expensive, Via Luigi Bianchi 12 (560-818); **Emilio,** Tuscan cuisine, Via del Cammeo 42 (562-141); **Al Ristoro dei Vecchi Marcelli,** Tuscan cuisine, rustic decor, excellent seafood selections, Via Volturno 49 (20424).

λ SERVICES λ

● Health Clubs (GM): **Siesta Club 77,** three floors, Finnish sauna, videos, relax cabins, via di Porta a Mare 25-27 open: 15-1 (42075).

● Sex Shop (GM): **Tentazioni Sexy & Gay Shop,** 13E Via Rossellini (54054).

 **ACCOMMODATIONS**

LA PACE HOTEL
Via Gramasci Galleria 14, Pisa 56100. Tel: (50) 29353. TYPE: *Hotel.* CLIENTELE: All Welcome. LOCATION: Central location, 10 min. from the leaning tower of Pisa.

* Rooms: 67 w/priv. bath; 5 suites
* Phone, CTV, C/H, A/C
* Restaurant, American bar, free parking
* Maid service, elevator

* 24 hrs room service
* Airport: 2 km / 1 mi.
* Train Station: 500 m / yards
* Gay Bars: in town
* Open: Year round
* Rates: from $75 and up
* *TAC:* 10% (from Odysseus)

DESCRIPTION: Tourist class hotel in a central location. 6 tennis courts.

ROYAL VICTORIA
Lungarno Pacinotti 12. Pisa 56126. Tel: (50) 940-112. TYPE: *Hotel.* CLIENTELE: All Welcome. LOCATION: Centrally located overlooking the Arno River.

* Rooms: 67 most w/priv. bath
* Phone, CTV, C/H
* Restaurant, bar, parking garage
* Maid service, elevator
* Airport: 2 km / 1 mi.
* Train Station: 500 m / yards
* Gay Bars: in town
* Open: Year round
* Rates: from $75 and up
* *TAC:* 10% (from Odysseus)

DESCRIPTION: Traditional style tourist class hotel in a central location.

ROME   ℭ   06

✈ Leonardo de Vinci (Fiumicino) (FCO)
   16 mi. / 26 km southwest

LOCATION: In the Province of Latium, a midway west coast location, along the banks of the river Tiber.

POPULATION: 2,535,000

CLIMATE: Mediterranean. Summers are hot with July average high temperature of 82°F (28°c). Winters are cool, windy and rainy with January average low temperature 49°F (9°c).

**Gay/Lesbian Visitor Information
ARCI Gay Roma.** Tel: (06) 322-7791
Circolo Culturale Mario Mieli
Tel: (06) 541-3985

DESCRIPTION: Rome - 'The Eternal City', is one of the greatest centers of Christianity and Western civilization. Its origin lies in a confused mixture of legend, history and mythology. The name 'Roma' means City of the River. For

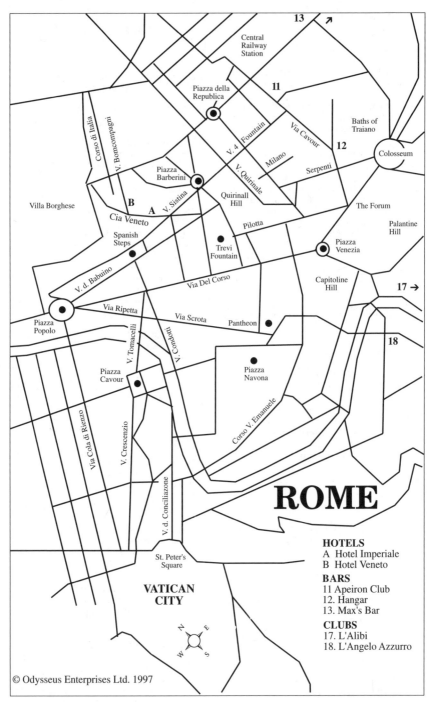

HOTELS
A Hotel Imperiale
B Hotel Veneto
BARS
11 Apeiron Club
12. Hangar
13. Max's Bar
CLUBS
17. L'Alibi
18. L'Angelo Azzurro

© Odysseus Enterprises Ltd. 1997

centuries Rome was the geographical, political and cultural center of the powerful Roman civilization.

Lovers of art and history will rejoice to visit some of the world's most magnificent architectural monuments and art treasures. For many Christians a visit to the Vatican City is a genuine spiritual uplift. For the rest of us the taste and smell of authentic Italian cooking can not be beat.

It is impossible to list all the wonderful places in Rome, yet do not miss the following: **Colosseum**, the best known symbol of Rome; **Vatican City** - a self administered city/country governed by the 'Holy See', where you can visit some exhibits of the largest art treasure collections of the world; **Saint Peter's Cathedral** one of the seven wonders of the world and the **Sistine Chapel** with its ceiling painted by Michelangelo; **Villa Borghese**, a park north of via Veneto with three exciting museums; **Museo Borghese**, **Museo Etrusco**, and the **Galleria Nazionale d'Arte Moderna**; the **Catacombs** - the underground city of the dead; The **Piazza di Spagna** (Spanish Steps) - 136 steps will take you up to a 16th century church **Trinità dei Monti**, for a breathtaking view of the town below.

Recommended side trips: **Tivoli**, one hour east of Rome, Italy's most magnificent water park with landscaped gardens and fountains; **Ostia Antica**, an ancient Roman Naval base and a classical prototype of a classical Roman city.

❖ Gay Beaches: **Il Buco**, via Anzio by Ostia, good action; **Spiaggia Libera**, Sulla via Aurelia at 46km, nudism, many gays; **Spiaggia dei 300 Scalini**, between Sperlonga and Formia towards Gaeta, nudism, good action.

❖ Public Cruising (AYOR): **Monte Caprino**, near the park of Villa Caffarelli, classic meeting place, can be dangerous; **Piazza Navona**, classic meeting point, good contacts; **Santa Maria in Trastevere**, good meeting place.

BARS Ⓨ RESTAURANTS 🍴

● Bars/clubs (GM): ✪ **Hangar**, Rome's premier cruise bar for 12 years, with excitement of nightclub without dancing, American-Italian owned near Coliseum, Roman Forum, sizzling videos mondays, packed every night, closed Tues. and 3 weeks in August, Via in Selci 69 (via Cavour) (488-1397); **l'Alibi**, via di Monte Testaccio 44 (574-3448); **Angelo Azzuro**, disco, young crowd, Via Cardinal Merry del Val 13 (580-0472); **Apeiron**, video bar/disco, Via dei

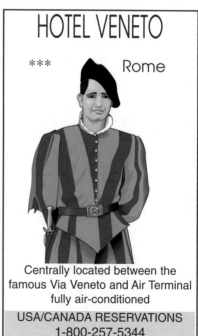

Quatro Cantoni 5 (487-1299); **Max's Bar**, bar, entertainment, Via Achille Grandi 7/a, Porta Maggiore (7030-1599); **Officina**, disco, bar, videos, via Ignazio Danti 20 (275-3508).

● Bars/clubs (GW): **Angelo Azzuro**, disco, young crowd, Fridays Ladies Night, Via Cardinal Merry del Val 13 (580-0472); **Joli Coeur**, lesbians only, v. Sirte 5.

● Restaurant (AW): **Arancio**, gourmet food and wine, via Dell'Arancio, closed Sun (687-6119); **Arancio d'Oro**, excellent food, via Monte d'Oro 17, closed Mon. (686-5026); **Babington's**, Old World English tea room, popular with foreigners, Piazza di Spagna 23 (678-6027); **Café Greco**, one of the oldest and most famous in the city, Via Condotti 86 (678-2554); **Cavour 313**, popular wine bar, Via Cavour 313 (678-5496); **Da Luigi**, large outdoor terrace in summer, closed Mon., Piazza Sforza Cesarini 24 (686-5946); **El Toulà**, Roman haute cuisine, expensive, near the Spanish Steps area, via della Lupa 29 (687-3498); **Nerone**, popular with gay clientele, closed Sun., via delle Terme di Tito 96 (474-5207); **Robin Hood**, everything pizza from appetizers to deserts, Via Cavour 158 (498-03511); **Sans Souci**, chic French, sophisticated dining, expensive, via Sicilia 20 (482-1814); **Piccolo Abruzzo**, popular pasta restaurant, via Sicilia 237 (482-0176).

λ SERVICES λ

● Cinemas (G/S): **Ambasciatori**, via Montebello 101; **Pussycat**, via Cairoli 98 (always open); **Volturno**, via V. Volturno; **Ulisse**, via Tiburtina.

● Health Club (GM): **Apollion Bath**ing pool, solarium, massages, via Mecenate 59/A (487-2316); **Mediterraneo**, saunurkish bath, massage, bar, via Pasquale Villari 3, open from 14:00 (7720-5934); **Terme di Roma**, always open, sauna, body center, body building, massage, solarium, via Persio 4 (718-4378).

● Sex Shop (G/S): **Cobra Porno Shop**, v. Barletta 23 (385-947); **Europa 92**, gay videos, via Boezio 96 (687-1210).

ᚥ ACCOMMODATIONS ᚥ

HOTEL IMPERIALE
Via V. Veneto, Rome. USA/Canada reservations: 1 (800) 257-5344 or (516) 944-5330. Fax: 1 (800) 982-6571 or (516) 944-7540. TYPE: *First Class Hotel.* CLIENTELE: All Welcome. LOCATION: Central tourist location on the fashionable Via Veneto. M° Barberini.

* Rooms: 85 w/priv. bath
* Apartments: 10
* CTV, phone, bath-rooms w/hydromassage, A/C, C/H, minibar, safe box, elevator
* High class restaurant, American bar
* Gay bars: some nearby
* Airport: 35 min. taxi, train
* Open: Year round
* Rates: (US) $155-$360
* *TAC:* 10% (from Odysseus)

DESCRIPTION: Elegant 4-star modernized 5-story hotel dated from 1700. All rooms and apartments are tastefully decorated in classic Roman style. Excellent central location and world class service.

✪ HOTEL VENETO

Via Piemonte, Rome. USA/Canada reservations Odysseus (516) 944-5330 or (800) 257-5344. Fax: (516) 944-7540. TYPE: *Hotel.* CLIENTELE: All Welcome. LOCATION: In the heart of historical Rome, between the fabulous Via Veneto and the Air Terminal.

* Rooms: 100 w/priv. bath
* CTV, phone, A/C
* Restaurant & American bar
* Roof garden, parking
* Gay bars: walking distance
* Air Terminal: nearby
* Airport: 45 min. taxi
* Open: Year round
* Rates: (US)$100 - $180 w/CB
* *TAC:* 10% (from Odysseus)

DESCRIPTION: 3-star renovated hotel in the heart of Rome. Spacious rooms tastefully decorated in traditional style. The hotel is fully air-conditioned. Quiet location and good service.

TAORMINA   ✆   0942

✈ Punta Raisi Airport (PMO) Palermo
  or Catania Fontanarossa

LOCATION: On the northeastern coast of Sicily, on the slopes of Monte Tauro looking out at Mount Etna and the Ionian Sea.

POPULATION: 10,000

CLIMATE: Mild mediterranean. Summers are hot, dry and sunny with a July average temperatures in the 80°sF (27°c). Winters are cold and rainy with average January temperatures of 52°F (11°c).

DESCRIPTION: Historic resort town known for centuries as a popular vacation destination for Europe's rich and famous. Taormina offers peace and relaxation combined with a beautiful natural scenery. The city has interesting medieval architecture, and many tourist attractions on or off the main street. For stunning views of the town and the sea stop at the Greek Theatre, or at the charming **Piazza IX Aprile**.

❖ Gay Beach: **Rocce Bianche**, near Spisone, good action; **Re del Sole**, near Spisone (mixed).

BARS Y RESTAURANTS

● Bars/Clubs (GM): **Casanova Pub**, bar, tavern, pizzas, via Paladine 4 (23-865); **Perroquet**, disco, cabaret, always open, Piazza S. Domenico 2 (24-808).

ACCOMMODATIONS

VILLA SCHULER
Via Roma 17, 98039 Taormina. Tel: (942) 23481. USA/Canada Reservations Odysseus: (516) 944-5330 or (800) 257-5344. Fax: (516) 944-7540 or (800) 982-6571. TYPE: *Hotel/Rental Apartments*. HOST: Gerardo Schuller Mgr. CLIENTELE: All Welcome. LOCATION: Panoramic position, 2 min. from "Corso Umberto", 5 min. to the famous Greek Theatre and Bus Terminal.

* Rooms: 26; 22 w/priv., 4 w/shared bath
   sgl 5/ dbl 13/ triple 4/ quad 4
* CTV, phone (in room), C/H
* Balcony, garden, roof solarium, sundeck
* Bar: (24 hrs. service inside/outdoors)
* Room & maid service, free parking,
* Beach: 1.5 mi. / 2 km (gay/mixed)
* Gay Bars: 1/2 mi. / 800 m
* Airport: 30 mi. / 48 km, taxi, limo, bus
* Train St'n: Taormina Giardini
   2 mi. / 3 km, taxi, bus
* Reservations: through Odysseus
* Open: Year round
* Rates: US$90-$160 w/expanded CB
* *TAC:* 10% (from Odysseus)

DESCRIPTION: Traditional villa surrounded by its own extensive gardens. Spacious rooms with priv. bath, balcony, seaview.

TRIESTE   © 040

✈ Ronchi Legionari Airport
   35 km / 22 mi.

LOCATION: In northeastern Italy on the border with Slovenia and the Adriatic Coast.

DESCRIPTION: Trieste is an important Adriatic Seaport and a Getaway to the Nude beach colonies of the Adriatic Coast. Slovenia and Croatia's Adriatic Coast is known for its nudist colonies and a major center for organized nudism or "naturism" in Southern Europe.

❖ Gay Beach: **Grado**, along the sea at the Grado Public Beach, near the solarium area.

❖ Public Cruising (AYOR): **Giardini Campo Marzio**, many GI's; **Giardini Di Bracola**, mostly GI's.

 ACCOMMODATIONS

HOTEL AL TEATRO
Corso Cavour 7, 34132 Trieste. Tel: (40) 366220. Fax: (40) 366560. TYPE: *Hotel*. CLIENTELE: All Welcome. LOCATION: Few steps from the piaza dell'Unita, 10 min. walk from the station. 46 rooms, 34 w/priv. bath or shower. Budget hotel with simply furnished rooms. The hotel was favorite of many of Trieste's visiting Opera stars. Rates: $70-$130.

DUCHI D'AOSTA HOTEL
Piazza Unita d'Italia, Trieste. Tel: (40) 7351. Fax: (40) 77733. TYPE: *First Class Hotel*. CLIENTELE: All Welcome. LOCATION: Set on Main Square overlooking the sea near air terminal. 50 rooms w/priv. bath. Rates: $160-$350.

BARS Y RESTAURANTS

● Bar/Club (G/S): **Bananas**, bar/disco, via Madonna del Mare.

● Restaurants (AW): **Antica Trattoria Suban**, country tavern, local cuisine, via Comici 2 (54368); **Al Bragozzo**, best seafood restaurant at the port, riva Nazario Sauro 22 (303001); **Harry's Grill**, expensive but excellent restaurant at the Hotel Duchi d'Aosta, piazza dell'Unita d'Italia 2 (7351).

TURIN   © 011

✈ Caselle Airport (TRN)

LOCATION: In northwestern province of Piemonte, near the French border.

POPULATION: 1,300,000

Gay Visitor Information
Informagay: (011) 436-5000

DESCRIPTION: Turin is the richest city in Italy and the hard working capital of Piemonte. Via Roma is dotted with luxury shops, fashion boutiques and antique treasures. The heart of the city is dominated by the Mole Antonelliana 300 ft. tower (100 m) that offers spectacular views of the town. **Piazza San Carlo** is an impressive architectural gem in the heart of the city; of interest is the **Old Turin Synagogue**, art museums and 18th century palaces.

❖ Gay Beach: **Fiume Orco**, past the bridge on the MI-TO highway entry at Chivasso. Nudism in the summer.

❖ Public Cruising (AYOR): **Parco Valentino** near Corso Polonia and Molinette Hospital (evenings); **Piazza d'Armi** (Army Square), many military officers, in the evening; **Giardini Reali**, corner Corso Regina and Corso S. Maurizio (evening); **Via Roma** near Piazza Castello and Bar Blu.

BARS ▼ RESTAURANTS ¶¶

● Bars/clubs (GM): **Area**, disco, Wed./Sun. gay nights, via S. Massimo (832-668); **Charming Club**, video bar, disco, V.P. Clotilde 82 (484-116); **Il Centralino**, Sunday evenings gay only, via Rosine 16/A (837500); **Matisse**, bar, via Garibaldi 13 (547-338); **Queen**, Wed. evening gay disco, via Madonna di Campagna 1 (corner via Stradella) (259450); **Velver Pub**, alternative bar and restaurant, popular with gays, via Ormea 78/D (650-3590); **Virgin Disco**, gay disco, via Ventimiglia 152 (663-7462)

λ SERVICES λ

● Adult Cinema (G/S): **Hollywood**, 24 hrs, Corso Regina Margherita 106; **Major**, Corso Giulio Cesare 105; **Roma Blue**, via San Donato 40 bis; **Zeta Sexy Movie**, via Cibrario 88.

● Erotica: **Carpe Diem**, sex shop, leather, videos, Via Marco Polo 32 bis (590-735).

● Health Club (GM): **Antares**, gay fun complex, bar, sauna, restaurant, Mon. closed, Via Pigafetta 73 (501-645).

🔯 ACCOMMODATIONS 🔯

STARHOTEL MAJESTIC
Corso Vittorio Emmanuele 54, Turin I-10123. Tel: (011) 539-153. TYPE: *Hotel*. CLIENTELE:

Mostly Straight. LOCATION: Downtown hotel, across from the central train station and bus terminal. 137 rooms w/priv. bath, CTV, phone, A/C, restaurant, bar. Rates: on request. DESCRIPTION: Traditional first class tourist hotel in a convenient location.

VENICE   ℰ   041

✈ Marco Polo-Tessera Airport (VCE)
8 mi. / 13 km north

LOCATION: In northern Italy on the Adriatic Coast, 267 km / 167 mi. east of Milan, and 528 km / 330 mi. north of Rome.

POPULATION: 390,000

CLIMATE: Mild year round. Winters are rainy with an average January temperature of 41°F (5°c). Summers are warm and humid with an average July temperature of 70°F (21°c).

Gay/Lesbian Visitor Information
ARCI Gay: (041) 721-842

DESCRIPTION: Venice is mysterious, moody, fascinating and decaying. The city can be confusing in the complexity of its narrow streets and waterways. A good map of the town is always necessary. The city looks like a Theme Park with medieval architecture, palazzo façades, and romantic gondolas. Visit the famous **Piazza San Marco** and the **Doge's Palace**. For a bird view of Venice take the elevator to the top of the **Campanile di San Marco** in the **Piazza San Marco**.

❖ Gay Beaches: **Lido degli Alberoni**, free beach with pine forest, some nudism, almost exclusively gay; **Lido di Sottomarina Chioggia**, check the dunes area; have some green bucks ready; **Lido San Nicoló**, good luck! Outside Venice: **Jesolo** behind the piazza Mazzini; **L'Isola Del Morto** at Jesolo, excellent possibilities; **Ponte di Vidor**, Cavolo di Pederobba (TV) from Vidor drive pass the bridge, then the first street to the left, walk until you reach the river (Piave), good action, nudism; **Baia Delle Sirene**, near S. Vigilio, nudism and some action.

❖ Public Cruising (AYOR): **Muro del Pianto**, along the seaside of the Reali gardens, mostly young crowds; **Ponte di Rialto**, at Campo Rialto Nuovo.

❖ **SPECIAL EVENT**: Venice draws many gay

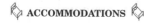

and lesbian visitors from all over Europe for the **Carnevale di Venezia**. The Carnival of Venice known for its outrageous costumes and masks takes place in February. It officially starts 18 days before the beginning of Lent but the dates change from one year to another.

BARS RESTAURANTS

● Bar/club (GMW): **Al Miracoli**, private club, Campiello Miracoli 6075 (523-0616).

● Restaurants (AW): **Ai Canottieri**, dining and show, Cannaregio 690 (715-408); **Al Cherubino** (see above); **Al Carletto**, calle delle Bande, Castello 5272 (522-7944); **Al Covo**, true Venetian fare, 3698 Campiello della Pescaria Castello (522-3812); **Da Arturo**, restaurant/tavern, S. Marco 3656; **Da Carletto**, Castello 5272; **Montin**, Venetian cuisine, 17th century inn and garden setting, 1147 Fondamenta Eremita, Giudecca (522-7151).

ACCOMMODATIONS

AL SOLE PALACE
S. Croce Fondamenta Minotto, Venice. USA/ Canada reservations Tel: (514) 254-5330 or (800) 257-5344. Fax: (516) 944-7540 or (800) 982-6571. TYPE: *Hotel.* CLIENTELE: All Welcome. LOCATION: Facing the Tolentini's canal in the heart of Old Venice. 100 rooms w/priv. bath, phone, C/H, safe box, elevator, restaurant, bar, TV lounges, 24 hrs. room service, maid service. Rates: (US) $130-$210. *TAC:* 10% (from Odysseus). DESCRIPTION: Gothic Venetian Palace Hotel with authentic atmosphere and a charming garden restaurant. Rooms with simple modern furnishings.

✪ HOTEL BASILEA
S. Croce, Venice. USA/CANADA Reservations Odysseus (516) 944-5330 or (800) 257-5344. Fax: (516) 944-7540 or (800) 982-6571. TYPE: *Hotel.* CLIENTELE: All Welcome. LOCATION: On a typical Venetian canal in the historical heart of Venice near the Railway Station and Air Terminal.

* Rooms: 30 w/priv. bath or shower
* CTV, phone, radio, mini-bar, A/C
* Breakfast room, lounge
* Gay Bar: walking distance (mixed bars)
* Airport: 15 km / 9 mi.
* Train Station: 10 minutes
* Open: Year round
* Rates: (US) $90-$260 w/CB
* *TAC:* 10% (from Odysseus)

**USA/Canada reservations
(800) 257-5344**

Hotel Basilea
★★★

DESCRIPTION: Comfortable 3-star hotel. All rooms and public areas are tastefully furnished and decorated in classic Venetian style. Guest rooms are spacious with large double beds, full bath, carpets and draperies.

VICENZA   ✆   0444

LOCATION: In northern Italy, 51 km / 32 mi. northeast of Verona.

POPULATION: 110,000

Gay Visitor Information
ARCI Gay: (0444) 323-391

DESCRIPTION: At the foot of the Berici Mountains, Vicenza is known for the beauty of its 16th century buildings by the master architect Andrea Palladio a native to this city. Nearby Verona is a noble city known for its magnificent Roman, Medieval and Renaissance buildings and monuments.

BARS RESTAURANTS

● Bars/clubs (GM): Vicenza - **Athos Top Bar**,

Contra Corpus Domini 31 (327187). Verona - **Lucio's**, mixed club, many soldiers, via Unità d'Italia 100; **Alter Ego**, disco, young crowd, via Torricelle 9 (915-130).

● Health Clubs (GM): Vicenza - **Rainbow Club**, sauna, via Valscura 21A (522-647); Verona - **Selenia Club**, sauna, solarium, video bar, via Apollo 15, corner via Selenia (543-396).

● Leather Club (Vicenza): **Moto Leather Club**, c/o Tiziano Bedin, C.P. 259 (321-290).

 **ACCOMMODATIONS**

AGIP MOTEL
Via degli Scaglieri 68. Vicenza I-36100. Tel: (444) 564-711. Fax: (444) 566-852.   TYPE: *Motel*. CLIENTELE: All Welcome. LOCATION: 5 km from train station. 132 rooms w/priv. bath, color TV, minibar, rooms for non smokers, restaurant, bar. Rates: Lit. 120,000 - Lit. 150,000.

VIEST MOTEL
241 Strada Pelosa, Vicenza I-36100. Tel: (444) 582-677. Fax: (444) 582-434. TYPE: *Motel*. CLIENTELE: All Welcome. LOCATION: At Exit Vicenza East Tollgate Venice-Milan Motorway. 61 rooms w/priv. bath, hair dryer, CTV, phone, minibar, parking. Rates: Lit. 120,000 - Lit. 180,000.

JAMAICA

AREA: 4,411 sq. mi. (11,424 sq. km)
POPULATION: 2,300,000
CAPITAL: Kingston
CURRENCY: Jamaican Dollar (JM$)
OFFICIAL LANGUAGE: English
MAJOR RELIGIONS: Protestantism,
Roman Catholicism
Telephone: 809
Nat'l Holiday: Independence Day, Aug. 6
Official Time: GMT - 5
Electricity: 110/220 volts 50c AC
Exchange Rate: US$ 1 = JM$ 36
National Airline: Air Jamaica

LAW REGARDING HOMOSEXUALITY:
Homosexual acts are prohibited by law. The
punishment can be severe and includes imprisonment with hard labor for up to ten years.
However the law is rarely enforced. The attitude of the population is rather homophobic,
and the existence of the harsh laws has a
demoralizing effect on the local gay population.

KINGSTON

✈ Norman Manley Int'l AP (KIN)

CLIMATE: Tropical year round with day time
temperatures in the mid 80°sF (30°c).

Gay/Lesbian Visitor Information
Gayfriends: (809) 926-6562
Box 1152, Kingston 8

DESCRIPTION: Jamaica's capital is the
island's center of commerce and government.
The town is undergoing a cultural and architectural renaissance. ❖ Gay Beaches: **Mosquito Beach** (off Hillshire Rd.); **Fort Clarence
Beach** (about 30 minutes away).

BARS ♀ RESTAURANTS 🍴

● Bars/Clubs (GMW): **2001**, 3 Dumfries Rd.,
Kingston 10; **Speakeasy**, Constant Spring
Rd., Mary Brown's Corner.

● Restaurants (AW): **Cleo's**, Kingsway Ave corner of Hope Rd.; **Norma**, fancy restaurant in
New Kingston (929-4966); **Talk of the Town**,
Caribbean/Continental, views of the town from
atop the Jamaica Pegasus Hotel (926-3690).

 ACCOMMODATIONS

JAMAICAN PEGASUS HOTEL
81 Knutsford Blvd. Kingston. Tel: 926-3691.
Fax: 929-5855. TYPE: *Hotel*. CLIENTELE:
Mostly Straight. LOCATION: Fashionable suburb of Kingston. 350 rooms, CTV (CNN),
phone, A/C, restaurant, cocktail lounge, cafe.
DESCRIPTION: First class 17 story hotel with
beautiful rooms and suites. Excellent service.

MONTEGO BAY

✈ Donald Sangster Int'l Airport (MBJ)
2 mi. / 3 km east

DESCRIPTION: Montego Bay is a quaint
town with fascinating monuments, tropical
gardens and handsome Georgian homes. The
Montego Bay Craft Market is one of the
cleanest and best organized in the Caribbean.
The beaches are long and wide with many
expensive beach hotels. ❖ Gay Beach: **Doctor's Cove Beach**

BARS ♀ RESTAURANTS 🍴

● Dance bar (G/S): **Cascade Bar**, at Doctor's
Cove Beach Hotel; **Cave Disco**, at Seawind
Beach Resort (953-2250).

 ACCOMMODATIONS

DOCTOR's CAVE BEACH HOTEL
Doctor's Cave Beach, Montego Bay. Tel: 952-
4355. Fax: 952-5204. TYPE: *Hotel*. CLIEN-
TELE: Mostly Straight. LOCATION: Heart of
resort area across from Doctor's Cave Beach.
90 rooms w/priv. bath, CTV, phone, A/C, pool,
jacuzzi, gym. Rates: on request. DESCRIP-
TION: Moderate first class beach resort hotel
set in lush tropical gardens with colorfully decorated rooms across from the action beach.

JAPAN

AREA: 145,730 sq. mi. (377,441 sq. km)
POPULATION: 120,000,000
CAPITAL: Tokyo
CURRENCY: Yen (¥)
OFFICIAL LANGUAGE: Japanese
MAJOR RELIGIONS: Buddhism, Shintoism
Telephone: - 81
Nat'l Holiday: Foundation Day, Feb. 11
Official Time: G.M.T. + 9
Electricity: 100 volts A.C. (50 - 60 cycles)
Exchange Rate: 1US$ = ¥101.15
National Airline: Japan Air Lines (JAL)

LAW REGARDING HOMOSEXUALITY:
The minimum legal sexual age of consent is 13, but raised to 17 by some municipalities. Legally, homosexuality does not exist. There is no law governing homosexuality, and it is not considered a criminal offense when conducted in private between consenting adults. The Japanese Society of Psychiatry and Neurology has removed homosexuality from its list of disorders. The society now accepts WHO disease-classification, which considers gayness OK. Foreigners may not be welcomed in some gay saunas or baths because of AIDS concern.

BEPPU   ©   **0977**

✈ Oita Airport

LOCATION: In the Oita Prefecture of the northeastern coast of the island of Kyushu, Japan's southernmost island.

POPULATION: 134,000

CLIMATE: Four distinct seasons. Summer starts with a rainy season from mid-June to mid-July. Winters are mild and pleasant. Spring is Cherry Blossom season, and Fall is known for the beauty of the foliage.

DESCRIPTION: Beppu is Japan's leading hot springs resort town. Millions of tourists come to Beppu to relax, experience a Japanese Spa vacation and 'take the water' for cure or rejuvenation. The city is located on Beppu Bay with steep mountains at the backdrop. Major attractions: the **Hell or Jigoku**, steaming, bubbling springs, and the **Exotic Bathing**, at the local bathhouses.

BARS ♈ RESTAURANTS 🍴

● Bars/clubs (GM): **Don Quixote**, (25-0710); **New Bon Bar**, 3-10 Ekimae-cho (next to car park at the Train Station) (23-0604).

● Restaurants (AW): **Chikuden**, Japanese menu, Sushi & Sashimi, 1-6-1 Kithama (25-2277), moderately priced, 15 minutes walk from the Beppu Station; **Bistro Soen**, Japanese & Western menu, 1-1 Higashi-soen-cho (26-0583).

 ACCOMMODATIONS

IKOI HOTEL
6-21 Kyomachi, Beppu. Tel: (0977) 22-6460. TYPE: *Hotel / Sauna*. CLIENTELE: Gay men only. LOCATION: In Beppu. Rates: ¥2000-¥5000. Note: foreigners are welcome.

SUGINOI HOTEL
Kankaiji, Beppu 874. Tel: (0977) 24-1141. Telex: 7734-67 SUNGNOI J. TYPE: *Hotel*. CLIENTELE: Mostly Straight. LOCATION: On a wooded hill with breathtaking view of the harbor.

* Rooms: 600 w/priv. bath, 80 Western style,
  Suites: 51CTV, phone, A/C
* Japanese restaurant & bars
* Exotic Public Baths
* Gay Bars: car needed
* Airport: 1 hour
* Credit Cards: MC/VISA/AMEX/DC
* Rates: ¥19,000-¥34,000
* *TAC:* 10%

DESCRIPTION: Deluxe Spa Hotel. Popular with Japanese and International tourists who come to experience their exotic large public mineral baths.

HIROSHIMA   ©   **082**

✈ Hiroshima Airport

LOCATION: In southern Honshu.

POPULATION: 980,000.

CLIMATE: Winter is cold with almost no snow. Summer can be hot and humid.

DESCRIPTION: Hiroshima is a bustling modern city full of vitality that was rebuilt over the ashes of a terrible horror. It was the first city ever to be destroyed by atomic bomb on August 6, 1945. Although there are no historic buildings and tourist sites, Hiroshima draws millions of visitors every year to the **Peace Memorial Park** and the adjacent museum. Side trips from Hiroshima are recommended to Miyajima, one of the most scenic spots in Japan about 45 minutes by boat.

BARS Y RESTAURANTS 🍽

● Bars/clubs (GM): **Akademie**, Honshu Kaikan Bldg., 4F, 6-10 Shinten-Ji, Naka-ku (244-3041); **Hiroshima 26 Snack**, Shoei Bldg., 3F, Tanaka-machi 1-13, Naka-ku (249-0013); **Hoge**, 5-3 Nagaregawa-machi, Naka-ku (246-7937).

ACCOMMODATIONS

ANA HOTEL HIROSHIMA
7-20 Naka-machi, Naka-ku, Hiroshima 730. Tel: (82) 241-1111. Fax: (82) 241-9123. TYPE: *Hotel.* CLIENTELE: Mostly Straight. LOCATION: Near Peace Memorial Park.

* Rooms: 431 w/priv. bath. Suites: 8
* CTV, phone, minibar, A/C
* Wheelchair access
* Bar, restaurant, lounges
* Health Club, gym, sauna
* Room & maid service, parking
* Gay Bars: nearby
* Airport: 15 minutes
* Credit Cards: MC/VISA/AMEX
* Open: Year round
* Rates: ¥ 20,000 - ¥ 25,000. *TAC:* 10%

DESCRIPTION: First class twenty-story downtown hotel.

KOBE   ℂ   078

✈ Airport (OSA)

BARS Y RESTAURANTS 🍽

● Bars/clubs (GW): **Badteeth**, entrance fee ¥1,600 + 1 drink), 3F, Hiroshikawa Bldg., 2-4-6, Kita-Nagasa-Dori, Chuuoh-ku, Kobe (333-8658).

KYOTO   ℂ   075

✈ Osaka Int'l Airport (OSA)

LOCATION: In western Honshu 38 mi. / 60 km north of Osaka.

POPULATION: 1,500,000

CLIMATE: Four seasons are well distinguished. Winter is cool with average mean temperature in January of 41°F (5°c). Spring and fall are pleasant with average temperatures in the 60°'sF (16°c). Summer is warm with average temperature in July of 75°F (24°c).

DESCRIPTION: Ancient capital of Japan, Kyoto is Japan's most romantic city. It is the only Japanese city which was spared from bombing during the second world war, and therefore all of its historic buildings and quarters remain intact. Explore the narrow streets, charming canals, and serene gardens and temples. Visit: **Nijo Castle**; the famous **Ryoanji Rock Garden** and the **Imperial Palace**.

BARS Y RESTAURANTS 🍽

● Bars/clubs (GM): **Apple**, young crowd, Daiichi Kobashi Kaikan, 3F, Torishijo Torishijo Nishikiamachi, Shimogyo-ku (256-0258); **C'est Bon**, Shijo Kawaramachi dori-Agaru, Futasujime, Higashi-iru, Nakagyo-ku (211-0385); **Friend**, ARK Bldg., B1, Shijokudaru, Kiyamachi, Shimogyo-ku, (351-1228); **Ken**, Dai-ichi Kobashi Kaikan, 2F, Hitosuji-me Agaru, Shimogyo-ku (255-2954)

ACCOMMODATIONS

KYOTO GRAND HOTEL
Shiokoji-Horikawa, Shimogyu-ku, Kyoto 600. Tel: (75) 341-2311. Fax: (75) 341-3073. TYPE: *Hotel.* CLIENTELE: Mostly Straight. LOCATION: Downtown.

* Rooms: 500 w/priv. bath. Suites: 6
* CTV, phone, A/C, wheelchair access
* Restaurants, bars, shopping center
* Heated pool, sauna
* Gay Bars: nearby
* Airport: 42 km / 26 mi.
* Train Station: 300 m / yards
* Credit Cards: MC/VISA/AMEX/JCB
* Open: Year round
* Rates: ¥ 12,000 - ¥17,000
* *TAC:* 10%

DESCRIPTION: First class large commercial hotel.

PALACE-SIDE HOTEL
Shimodachiuri-agaru,Karasuma-dori, Kami-gyo-ku, Kyoto 602. Tel: (75) 431-8171. Fax: (75) 414-2018. TYPE: *Hotel.* CLIENTELE: Mostly Straight. LOCATION: west of the Old Palace.

* Rooms: 120 w/priv. bath
* Restaurant, Bar, Parking
* Gay Bars: car needed
* Airport: 1 hour by taxi
* Train Station: 8 minutes
* Credit Cards: MC/VISA/AMEX
* Open: Year round
* Rates: ¥ 7,000 - ¥ 15,000. *TAC:* 10%

DESCRIPTION: Tourist class hotel with western style rooms. English spoken.

NAGOYA   ℂ   052

✈ Komaki Airport (NGO)
11 mi. / 18 km northeast

LOCATION: Between Tokyo and Kyoto on the Ise Bay. About 180 miles / 300km west of Tokyo.

POPULATION: 2,000,000.

CLIMATE: Winter is cold and exceedingly dry with almost no snow. Summer is hot and humid.

DESCRIPTION: Nagoya, the fourth largest city in Japan, is the only stop on the fast Tokaido Shinkansen train's itinerary. Though not a popular tourist destination, it is a gateway to two of Japan's most exciting sightseeing regions: Ise and Tobe to the south, and Hida to the north.

The history of Nagoya starts in the 17th century when the great shogun Tokugawa built his castle. This was followed by settlements that grew into a major urban center. Nagoya became an important center for military and aircraft industries in the 1930's, and was badly destroyed during WW II. Today, it is a modern city, well planned with clean streets and remarkably efficient subway system.

Visit: **Nagoya Castle**, a faithful copy of the original castle; **Atsuta Shrine**, one of the oldest in the country, popular with pilgrims. **Nagoya City Center - Sakae**, dominated by the 180m (590 ft.) TV tower, is the section of town where it all happens. Here you will find the city's major departments stores, bars,

restaurants and cinemas. A 60 min. bus ride from the town center is **Meiji Mura**, a masterpiece of Meiji period (1868-1912) Japanese architectural history.

BARS ♆ RESTAURANTS

● Bars/clubs (GM): **Hakuba**, Grand Nishiki Bldg., B1, 5-19-1 Meieki, Nakamura-ku (231-8805); **Nan Nan**, Near Hirokoji Station, young clientele, hours 6pm-2am (201-4740); **Megamix**, 4-18-3 Ei, Naka-ku (252-7827); **Noboru**, hours 6pm-2am, Tokyo Bldg 4F, 4-11-10 Sakae, Naka-ku (241-2852); **Ratori**, Moriman Bldg, B1, 16-8-3 Nishiki-cho, Naka-ku (971-2449).

● Restaurants (AW): **Shoufukuro**, Kaiseki restaurant with beautiful view of the city, 2-14-19 Meieki Minami (586-0005); **Miyako**, moderately priced restaurant at the Miyako Hotel, 4-9-10 Meieki (571-3211); **Beer Garden**, cheap but good food on the roof top of the Miyako Hotel in the summer.

λ SERVICES λ

● Health Club(GM): **Futogawa-Ryo Hotel**, 2-2 Sanae-cho, Nishi-ku, 3 pm - 10 am (451-7667) open to Japanese only.

⬙ ACCOMMODATIONS

CORONA CLUB
3-3 Meieki-minami, Nakamura-ku, Nagoya 460. Tel: (052) 571-2444. TYPE: *Hotel/Sauna/ Bar.* CLIENTELE: Gay men only (only Japanese welcome). 64 private rooms, some gorgeous with pool.

NAGOYA TOKYU HOTEL
624-1, Sakae 4-chome, Naka-ku. Nagoya 460. Tel: (052) 251-2411. TYPE: *Hotel.* CLIENTELE: Mostly Straight. LOCATION: In the Nightlife district of Sakae in the heart of Nagoya, near the local gay scene.

* Rooms: 568, w/priv. bath. Suites: 15
* CTV, phone, A/C
* Restaurants, bar & cocktail lounge
* Room & maid service
* Pool, gym & sauna
* Gay Bars: some nearby
* Airport: 25 min., taxi, limo
* Credit Cards: MC/VISA/EC/DC/BC/AMEX
* Open: Year round
* Rates: ¥ 15,500 - ¥ 17,000.
* *TAC:* 10%

DESCRIPTION: Modern first class hotel in a convenient location close to the local gay scene.

OSAKA   ℂ   06

✈ Osaka Airport (OSA) 10 mi. / 16km
northwest of city

LOCATION: Western Honshu, 38 mi. /60 km
south of Kyoto, 55 min. flight from Tokyo.

POPULATION: 2,779,000

CLIMATE: Four seasons are well distinguished. Winter is cool with average mean temperature in January of 41°F (5°c). Spring and fall are pleasant with average temperatures in the 60°'s F (16°c). Summer is warm with average temperature in July of 75°F (24°c).

DESCRIPTION: Osaka, the third largest city in Japan, is a major industrial center with a huge concentration of factories. Unlike Tokyo and Kyoto, there are very few tourist attractions. English-language signs are rare. There is no foreigner-oriented information service in Osaka, which makes life difficult to the non Japanese speaking tourists. Of interest to visitors are: **The Minami**, downtown section with fine restaurants, new kabuki theatre, and a world famous bunraku puppet theatre. **Osaka Castle**, first built in 1615 and restored in 1931 after being twice destroyed.

Downtown Osaka is divided into two sections: north (**Kita**) and south (**Minami**). Kita is elegant with posh tourist hotels and expensive department stores, Minami is where the nightlife action is - near Namba subway Station. A few blocks north of Namba is the famous **Dotonbori**, a pedestrian street which runs east-west parallel with the river of the same name. Dotonbori has many excellent restaurants, many specialize in local cuisine.

● The gay scene in Osaka is active and interesting, most of the bars are located in the Kita-ku district running south from the Osaka Station.

❖ **SPECIAL EVENTS:** Osaka has many colorful and folklore festivals year round, one of the most interesting is the **Doya-Doya Naked Festival** on the 14th of January at the Shitennoji Temple near Tennoji Station. In this festival two teams of young men wearing only loin clothes, compete against each other in cold water austerities, and fight their way to a sacred stick in the center of the temple, a sort of a Japanese version of all male 'wet pants' contest in the middle of the winter.

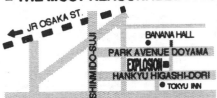

A different festival and a very beautiful one is the traditional **Cherry Blossoms** at the Mint Bureau in mid-April. The precinct of the Mint Bureau is open to the public for viewing the new double petaled cherry blossoms. The **Mint Garden** is open to the public every year during the cherry blossom festivities.

BARS ⵨ RESTAURANTS 🍴

● Bars/clubs (GM): **Adonis**, Kirishima-Leisure Bld. 2F, 23-8 Doyama-cho, Kita-ku (312-2429); **Christopher**, dance bar with leather clientele, lesbians welcome, disco/bar, best place for foreign visitors to Osaka, closed Tuesday, 16-4 Doyama-cho, Kita-ku (The Pearl Leisure Building B1) (315-1380); **Crazy 8**, box-like rooms for groping (632-8010); **Garçon**, host bar, hours 6pm-1am, Taiko Center, B1, 4-8-12 Nanba, Minami-ku (643-6539); **In and Out**, video room and glory holes (633-1525); **Jungle Box**, cruise bar, dark room (366-4450); **Limelight**, OK Bldg., 2F, 16-6, Doyama-cho, Kita-ku, (361-4336); **Pipeline Nanba**, in the basement of Takeda Bldg. B1 (632-0441); **Popeye**, Dai-ichi Matsue Kaikan, 3F, 6-15 Doyama-cho, Kita-ku (315-1502); **Stork Club**, piano bar and entertainment club, Stork Bldg. 2F, 17-3 Doyama-cho, Kita-ku (361-4484); **Stork South**, Coq d'Or Bldg., B2, 5-72 Namba Shin-cho, Minami-ku (643-4001); **Yacht**, Nanshin Kaikan Bldg., 2F, 4-7-9 Namba, Minami-ku (643-6734).

● Bar/club (GMW): ✪ **Explosion**, the largest and best permanent gay disco in Japan, English speaking staff. The most reasonable prices in Japan, no cover charge, B1 Sanyo-Kaikan 8-23, Kita-ku (312-5003).

● Bar (GW): **Happy Valley**, 1-34-5 Shinmachi, Nishi-ku, (533-0446); **Yurikago**, entrance ¥1,800 with food and 1 drink, 3F, Nippou Friend Bldg., 8-12, Kamiyama-cho, Kita-ku, Osaka-shi (363-4934).

● Restaurants (AW): Kita-ku area - **Kagaman**, Kaiseki Restaurant near ANA Sheraton Hotel, Japanese, 1-1-11 Sonezaki-shinchi (341-2381); **Suehiro Ashai**, steaks, 1-5-2 Sonezaki-shinchi (341-1760); Western style cuisine at the **ANA Sheraton Hotel Rose Room**, Elegant French, 1-3-1 Dojimahama (347-1112).

λ SERVICES λ

● Bookstore: **E.T.C. Box**, Cosmo Plaza, Doyama Bldg., B1, 11-2 Doyama-cho, Kita-ku (316-0095).

● Health Clubs (GM): **Hokuo-kan**, only Japan-

ese welcome, see description under accommodations; **Royal**, bathhouse, sauna, older clientele, only Japanese welcome, 1-2-4 Ebisu Higashi, Naniwa-ku, (643-0001).

● Massage: **Suehiro**, 2-4-18 Ebisu Higashi, Naniwa-ku (643-6458) Japanese only welcome.

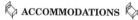 ACCOMMODATIONS

ANA SHERATON HOTEL
1-3-1 Dojimahama, Kita-ku, Osaka 530. Tel: (06) 347-1112. TYPE: *Hotel*. CLIENTELE: Mostly Straight. LOCATION: Downtown in the Kita-ku district.

* Rooms: 500 w/private bath
* CTV, phone, A/C, wheelchair access
* Restaurant: The Rose Room - French
* English style Pub
* coffee shop & bar
* Indoor pool & sauna
* Room & maid service, valet parking
* Gay Bars: some nearby
* Airport: 8 mi. / 13km, limo
* Credit Cards: MC/VISA/DC/AMEX
* Open: Year round
* Rates: ¥16,000 - ¥20,000.
* *TAC:* 10%

DESCRIPTION: Deluxe modern hotel with fine amenities, and comfortable rooms. Conveniently located to explore the local gay scene.

HOKUOKAN
Manzaicho 3-13, Kita-ku, Umeda district, Osaka City 530, Osaka Pref. Tel: (06) 361-2288. TYPE: *Hotel /Sauna*. CLIENTELE: Gay men only. LOCATION: In Umeda district, the center of downtown Osaka, just 2 blocks from the subway and the Hankyu Department store.

* Rooms: public or private w/bath
* Balconies, A/C
* Restaurant, cafe, sauna
* Maid service, parking
* Gay Bars: near Pipeline
* Airport: 40 min. taxi
* Open: Year round
* Rates: on request

DESCRIPTION: 5-story building in a remarkable architectural design. Lounges and the central hall are beautifully decorated with original art. The ambience is homey and friendly. All private rooms are clean and comfortable. No problem to bring pick-ups to your room. Note: this place is OK for foreigners who speak Japanese or who are accompanied by Japanese friends.

OSAKA TERMINAL HOTEL
3-1-1 Umeda, Kita-ku, Osaka 530. Tel: (06) 344-1235. Telex: 523-3738 OSATER J. TYPE: *Hotel*. CLIENTELE: Mostly Straight. LOCA-TION: Adjacent to the Osaka Station in Kita-ku.

* Rooms: 665 w/private bath. Suites: 2
* CTV, phone, A/C
* Restaurants, bar, coffee shop, pub
* Wheelchair access, maid service
* Ground floor access to Train Station
* Gay Bars: some nearby
* Airport: 20 min., limo, taxi
* Credit Cards: MC/VISA/JCB/DC/AMEX
* Open: Year round
* Rates: ¥ 13,000 - ¥ 17,000
* *TAC:* 10%

DESCRIPTION: Moderately priced hotel featuring quality, western style accommodations. The cheapest units face the courtyard. The are quieter, but do not have a view of the city. First floor is connected with the Train Station. Good location to enjoy the local gay nightlife.

SAPPORO   ©   011

✈ Chitose Airport (CTS);
Okadama Airport (OKD)

LOCATION: In western Hokaido, the northernmost island of Japan.

POPULATION: 1,250,000

CLIMATE: 4 distinct seasons. Summers are cool without rain. Winters are cold and snowy with temperatures below freezing.

DESCRIPTION: Sapporo is a modern city with little historic heritage. It is located on the fascinating island of Hokkaido which is the winter snow play land of Japan. The city is famous for its beer production, the famous Sapporo Snow Festival in February, and its vicinity to some nearby popular hot springs. Hokkaido is the home island of the ancient Ainu people which have Caucasian features and immigrated to Hokkaido some 8 centuries ago.

❖ Visit: **Eki-Mae Dori**, the main venue going through the heart of the city; **Clock-Tower**, with local history museum inside; **Odori** - wide popular boulevard; **Odori Park** - where the Summer Festival is celebrated, often with beer gardens and live shows; **Aurora & Pole Towns** with their boutiques and restaurants;

and the **Batchelor Museum** - dedicated to the study of the ancient Ainu people and their unique culture.

● Sapporo has a well established gay scene. There is a good selection of gay bars to choose from. Most are located in the Susukino Nightlife District.

BARS ⟁ RESTAURANTS 🍴

● Bars/clubs (GM): **Chaplin**, S.A. Bldg., 5F, Minami 6, Nishi 6, Chuo-ku (531-1334); **Ciao**, young clientele, hours: 7:30pm - 2:30am, 5-jyo, Shinmachi, 2F, Chuo-ku (531-9331); **James**, cozy bar, S.A. Bldg. 1F, Minami 6-jyo, Nishi 6-chome, Chuo-ku (512-2997); **La Cave**, bar with friendly staff, S.A. Bldg. 2F, Minami 6, Nishi 6, Chuo-ku (531-6734).

● Restaurants (AW): **Sapporo Bier Garten**, open air restaurant June-August, inside dining during winter at the Sapporo Beer Hall a 19th century brick building where the Sapporo Brewery was originally built, Nishi 6, E9 (742-1531); **Hyosetsu-no-Mon**, specializing in giant king crab, seafood, S5 W2 (521-3046), a Western style restaurant is located next to the main restaurant; **Zenniku**, authentic Sapporo cuisine at the ANA Hotel close to the Sapporo Station, N1 W3 (221-4411).

🏠 ACCOMMODATIONS 🏠

ANA HOTEL
1-2-9 Kita-Sanjo-Nishi, Chuo-ku, Sapporo 060. Tel: (11) 221-4411, Fax: (11) 221-0819. TYPE: *Hotel*. CLIENTELE: Mostly Straight. LOCA-TION: Center of business and shopping district.

* Rooms: 460 w/priv. bath. Suites: 2
* CTV, phone, A/C
* Restaurants, lounges, sauna, parking
* Maid & room service
* Gay Bars: some nearby
* Airport: 50 min., taxi, bus
* Train Station: 3 min. away
* Credit Cards: VISA/AMEX/JCB
* Open: Year round
* Rates: ¥ 14,500 - ¥ 21,000
* *TAC:* 10%

DESCRIPTION: Centrally located high rise first class hotel. Restaurants serve western cuisine.

MOMOHA RYOKAN
Minami 5, Nishi 5, Chuo-ku, Sapporo 060. Tel: (011) 531-7075. TYPE: *Japanese Inn/Ryokan*. CLIENTELE: Gay men. LOCATION: Susukino

Nightlife District.

* Rooms: Japanese style
* Phone, A/C, room & maid service
* Gay Bars: many nearby
* Train Station: 15 minutes
* Rates: on request

DESCRIPTION: Gay family type Ryokan (Japanese Inn) and the only one of its kind in Japan. Open to Japanese only.

TOKYO   © 03

✈ Haneda Int'l Airport (HND); Narita Int'l Airport (NRT)

LOCATION: On the eastern shore of central Honshu along the Tokyo Bay.

POPULATION: 11,000,000

CLIMATE: The four seasons are well defined. Spring, beginning in March is mild and pleasant but sometimes rainy with average temperature of 56°F (13°c). Summer is hot and humid with average temperature of 90°F (32°c). The winter is sunny and dry with occasional light snowfall. Average Jan. temperature is 39°F (4°c).

Gay/Lesbian Visitor Information
International Friends/Passport Japan
C.P.O. Box 180, Tokyo 100-91
Tel: (03) 5693-4569
e-mail: *odyjapan@passport.org*

❖ **Note: International Friends / Passport Japan** does not provide: escorts, meet planes, or send someone to your hotel. If you have *Odysseus*, you have enough information to have a good time in Japan.

DESCRIPTION: Tokyo, the capital of Japan, is a gigantic urban agglomeration and an exhilarating blend of the old and new. Edo became the administrative capital of Japan in the 17th century and was renamed Tokyo - 'eastern capital' in 1868.

Modern Tokyo is confusing and intriguing for western visitors. Signs are unreadable, streets are not named, and houses are not numbered the way we are used to in the west. They are numbered in the order which they were built, which adds to the general feeling of confusion and frustration. The best way to get around in Tokyo is by taxi or the subway. Always keep a small map

of the area of your destination in English and Japanese, with at least one major landmark. Do not forget to keep the address where you wish to return to written down in Japanese.

❖ Visit: the **Imperial Palace**, in the center of Tokyo across from the Marunouchi business district. **The Ginza** ('Silver Mint'), area south east of the palace (Ginza subway), is an elegant part of town with prestigious entertainment clubs and department stores e.g. **Mitsukoshi** and **Wako**.

➤ **Shinjuku** is the gayest district of Tokyo with many gay bars, porno shops, bathhouses (not for non-Japanese), and accommodations. Shinjuku is divided into two parts by the Yamanote line. The western section has modern high-rise buildings and elegant restaurants, the northeastern section of Shinjuku Station is called **Kabuki-cho** which is a playground for straights, but also has famous gay bathhouses. These gay bathhouses are not open for non Japanese or Asian clients. **Shinjuku Gyoen**, to the southeast, is one of Tokyo's most beautiful public gardens. The largest concentration of gay bars is just to the north of this park, in Shinjuku Ni-chome (pronounced *Knee-cho-may*). **Roppongi**, southwest of Tokyo's central area is famous for its nightlife which is more elegant than that of Shinjuku. Roppongi is a popular residential area for foreigners living in Tokyo and also where many of the foreign embassies are located.

❖ Nearby attraction: Of special interest is the town of **Kamakura**, about 1 hour by train from Tokyo. Here you explore many temples, shrines and the impressive 42 ft. / 13 m. tall statue of the **Great Buddha**. *Reader recommendation.*

BARS 🍸 RESTAURANTS 🍴

There are hundreds of gay bars in Tokyo, mostly for gay men. Many of the gay bars popular with foreigners are located in Shinjuku 2 - chome area. To get there take the Marunouchi subway line to Shinjuku 3-chome Station, or the Yamanote train line to Shinjuku Station (in direction of Isetan Department store). The following bars can be recommended to non Japanese speaking tourists on the merit of their popularity with foreigners and also because English is often spoken.

If you are not sure wether you'll be welcome in a bar, call first. Your language ability in Japanese, English, French or other major language may be enough to make you welcome. Otherwise, pick another place where you can be understood and where you can understand what is going on. Not all bars listed have Eng-

Manufacturers and Publishers: Let us bring your products to Japan's gay marketplace!

弊社取扱い商品カタログご希望の方は、
80円切手同封の上お申し込みください。

Photo: courtesy OG Magazine

We are the exclusive distributors of many fine products and publications. Why not yours?

PASSPORT JAPAN, C.P.O. BOX 180, TOKYO 100-91 JAPAN
TEL: 81•3•5693•4569 ✻ FAX: 81•3•5694•3775

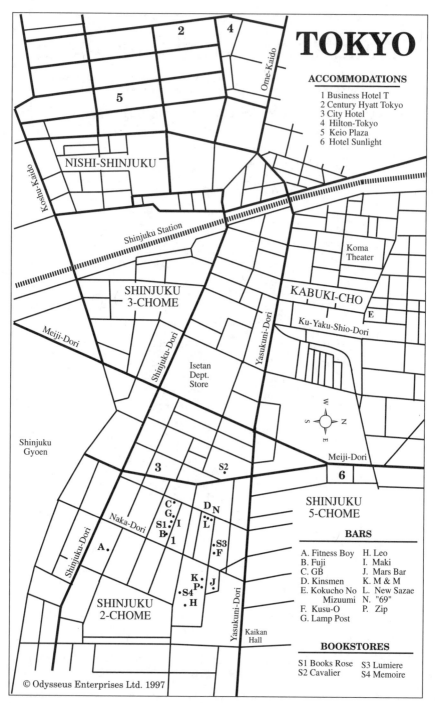

TOKYO

ACCOMMODATIONS

1 Business Hotel T
2 Century Hyatt Tokyo
3 City Hotel
4 Hilton-Tokyo
5 Keio Plaza
6 Hotel Sunlight

BARS

A. Fitness Boy
B. Fuji
C. GB
D. Kinsmen
E. Kokucho No Mizuumi
F. Kusu-O
G. Lamp Post
H. Leo
I. Maki
J. Mars Bar
K. M & M
L. New Sazae
N. "69"
P. Zip

BOOKSTORES

S1 Books Rose
S2 Cavalier
S3 Lumiere
S4 Memoire

© Odysseus Enterprises Ltd. 1997

ODYSSEUS '97/98

lish speaking staff. A little knowledge of Japanese may be helpful.

➤ **Shinjuku** ● Bars/Clubs (GM): **Arty Farty**, spacious gay bar, Old American West decor, ¥500 cover charge, 2-17-4 Shinjuku, Shinjuku-ku (3356-5388); **Club Dragon**, hot new bar with a genuine dance floor, a rarity in Tokyo; just across the alley from GB, in the same building as the Pit Inn jazz club, Accord Bldg., 2-12-4-B1 Shinjuku (3341-0606); **Couple**, open 18:00-3:00, Fujita Bldg., 2F, 2-15-13 Shinjuku (3350-6180); **Delight**, dance bar, some nights are gay only, Daini Hayakawa Bldg., B1F, 2-14-6 Shinjuku (3352-6297) from 8pm; **Fitness Boy**, Vella Heights Bldg., #310, 2-7-3 Shinjuku, Shinjuku-ku, body builders bar (3341-8994); **Fuji Bar**, New York style, karaoke, mixed age, Sentofo Bldg., B1, 2-12-16-B104, Shinjuku, Shinjuku-ku, (3354-2707); **Colt**, across the street from GB, small dance floor, good music; **GB**, American style bar, **recommended for tourists**, Shinjuku Plaza Bldg., B1, 2-12-3 Shinjuku, Shinjuku-ku (3352-8972); **Goshu**, a traditional Japanese "snack", open 19:00-2:00, Yuni Bldg., 2F, 2-14-13 Shinjuku (3350-0566); **J Club**, English & Thai language OK, Futami #9 Bldg., 2F, Shinjuku (3352-4969); **Kinsmen**, mixed clientele, mainly gay men but some lesbians and straight women, popular after midnight, Oda Bldg. 2F, 2-18-5 Shinjuku 2F, Shinjuku-ku (3354-4949); **Kokucho No Mizuumi**, Club/disco, nightly live entertainment, where boys will be girls, good entertainment, clientele is not necessarily gay, Kabuki-cho area (see map); **Kusuo**, (meaning Kyushu Men), short-hair Kansai types, Sunflower Bldg., 3F, 2-17-1 Shinjuku, Shinjuku-ku (3354-5050); **Lamp Post**, piano bar, 7pm-3am, Yamahara Heights #201, 2-12-15 Shinjuku, 2F, Shinjuku-ku (3354-0436); **Leo**, some foreigners, Tsutsui Bldg., 2F, 2-14-36 Shinjuku, Shinjuku-ku (3354-7699); **Lynch**, Dairoku Tenko Bldg., 6F, Shuinjuku (3359-4799); **M&M**, video movies, concerts, caters to Westerners and Japanese who like them, Wakao Bldg., 2F, 2-14-10 Shinjuku, Shinjuku-ku (3354-0474); **Maki**, Yamahara Heights Bldg., #404, 2-12-15 Shinjuku, Shinjuku-ku (3341-8991); **Matt Bianco**, Nakae Bldg., 2F, Shinjuku (3356-7295); **Moto**, open 16:00-3:00, Sentofo Bldg., 2F, 2-12-16 Shinjuku (3350-5140); **New Sazae**, late night spot, especially young men who go for body piercing, Ishikawa Bldg, 2F, 2-18-5 Shinjuku, Shinjuku-ku, (3354-1745); **Page One**, open 20:00-4:00, Dai 1 Tenkka Bldg., 3F, 2-15-10 Shinjuku (3354-4640); **Poplar**, across the hall from Fuji, caters to older men, open 18:00-2:00, Sentofo Bldg., #B103, 2-12-16 Shinjuku (3350-6929); **Position**, open 19:30-3:00, Yamahara Heights #503, 2-12-15 Shinjuku (3341-5980); **Ryuu (Dragon)**, open 19:30-3:00,

Sakagami Bldg., 2F, 2-14-5 Shinjuku (3354-1680); **'69'**, mixed clientele, Reggae music, Daini-Seiko Bldg B1, 1st Fl., 2-18-5 Shinjuku-Ku (3341-6358); **Sugichan**, open 19:00-3:00, Dai 6 Tennla Bldg., 4F, 2-10-10 Shinjuku (3341-4554); **Tokyo**, Yuri Bldg., 2F, 2-14-3 Shinjuku (3354-0457); **Torch Bar**, open 20:00, Sunny Coop, 1F, 2-7-2 Shinjuku (3354-9156); **Transistor Glamour**, Futami Bldg., 2F (3356-1166); **Club Zip**, young Japanese clientele, 1F, 2-14-11 Shinjuku (3356-5029); **Zukkero**, for men with ample figures and those who like them, open 18:00-2:00, Sentofo Bldg., 3F, 2-12-16 Shinjuku (3354-9174).

● Bars/clubs (GW): **E. Cup**, new bar, entrance fee about ¥2,800, 2-15-8, Shinjuku (5379-5085); **Madonna Bar**, Fujita Blvd., 1F, 2-15-13 Shinjuku, Shinjuku-ku (3354-1330); **Mars Bar**, the oldest women's bar, entrance fee ¥3,500 with food and 1 drink), Hosono Bldg., 3F, 2-15-13 Shinjuku, Shinjuku-ku, (3354-7923); **Monalisa Pink**, lesbian night every third Thursday from 22:00hrs at Bar Delight, a club with young fashionable women crows, very popular, entrance fee ¥2,500 with a drink, Hayakawaya Bldg., B1, 2-14-6, Shinjuku (3352-6297); **Kinswomyn**, most popular women's bar, reasonable prices, about ¥800 per drink, Daiichi Tenka Bldg., 2-15-10 Shinjuku, open 7pm-3am, English spoken, Non Japanese welcome (3354-8720). Lesbians are also welcomed in the following gay bars: **Fuji**, **69**, **Himiko** at **New Sazae**, every fourth Saturday, friendly atmosphere, Ishikawa Bldg., 2F, 2-18-5 Shinjuku, ¥1,800 (1 drink), and **Kinsmen**. For more information about the Tokyo Lesbian scene write to: **International Feminists of Japan**, c/o **AGORA**, 1-9-6 Shinjuku, Shinjuku-ku, Tokyo 160 (3792-4110/3793-6241).

➤ **Outside Shinjuku**
● Bars/clubs (GM): **Dokkoisho**, soft porn video bar, 4-32-25 Kitazawa, 1F, Setagaya-ku (3460-8637); **Goshoguruma (Palace Carriage)**, open 18:00-1:00, Sun. 15:00-1:00, closed Wed., 2-25-4 Asakusa, Taito-ku (3845-1474); **Hige (Beard)**, hairy type clientele, To-ou Bldg., 3F, 7-7-4 Ueno,Taito-ku (3844-1261); **Lax**, Fuyo Bldg, 3F, 2-8 Sakuragaoka, Shibuya-ku (3469-4190); **Peppermint**, caters to younger (20's-30's) crows, open 19:00-4:00, Mimasu Bldg., B1F, 4-20-1 Higashi-ueno, Taito-ku (3844-1261); **7 (Sebun)**, open 15:00-23:30, Makino Bldg., 2F, 2-10-7 Nishi-asakusa, Taito-ku (5828-4440); **24 Snack Asakusa**, open 18:00-2:00, Sat. 16:00-3:00, Sun. 15:00-2:00, 2-28-28 Asakua, Taitou-ku (3843-4424); **24 Snack Ueno**, open 18:00-2:00, affiliated with 24 (pronounced "Ni-Yon") Kaikan (Sauna) and has a shuttle van to take customers there,

Shinei Bldg., 1F, 7-7-11 Ueno, Taito-ku (3845-1942); **Utaya (Song)**, open 19:00-3:00, 4-10-9 Higashi-ueno, Taito-ku (3844-2538); **X Bar**, SM type clientele, Dai-go, Maejima Bldg., B1, 2-2-7 Nishi Ikebukuro, Toshima-ku (3982-8747) hours: 6pm-1am.

λ SERVICES λ

● Adult Bookstores (GMW): ✪ **Cavalier**, Muraki Bldg., B1, 3-11-2 Shinjuku, Shinjuku-ku (3354-7976); **C'est Bien**, erotic adult shop, Yoshida Bldg., B1, 2-29-12, Dohgenzaka, Shibuya-ku; **Apple Inn**, 1-13-5 Shimbashi, 2F, Minato-ku (3574-1477); **Books Rose**, Yamahara Heights, B1, 2-12-15 Shinjuku, Shinjuku-ku (3341-0600) (lesbians are welcome); **Lumiere**, Sunflower Bldg., 1F, 2-17-1 Shinjuku, Shinjuku-ku (3352-3378); **Memoire**, 2-14-8 Shinjuku, Shinjuku-ku (3341-1776); **Paradise** (Hokuo Shoji), 2-13-3 Yoyogi, Shibuya-ku (3370-5641).

● Computer Bulletin Board (GM): **GayNet Japan (GNJ)**, Japan's first computer bulletin board service (BBS) for gay people encouraging a friendly, supportive "at home" atmosphere. Cooperate with International Friends (if) in social events and membership fees. Tel: (03) 5330-2581. Fax: (03) 5330-2451. Email: gnjsupport@gnj.or.jp. WEB: www.gnj.or.jp/gaynet/ Modem: (03) 5330-0721.

● Health Clubs (GM): Bathhouses welcoming foreign visitors (none in Shinjuku): **Hotel Jinya**, situated on four floors near the Ikebukuru Station (JR Yamanote line), Sento (Japanese style public bath), dry sauna, hot pools, video rooms and hot action, the staff welcome foreigners, but it helps to speak some Japanese, 2-30-19 Ikebukuro, Toshima-ku (5951-0995); **Ichijo**, near Ueno station, 1-1-15 Negishi, Taito-ku (3844-4567); **24 Kaikan Asakusa**, 2-19-16 Asakusa, Taito-ku (near Asakusa Kannon) (3841-7806); **Seibuen**, 24 hrs. sauna, only Japanese welcome, 1-11-2 Minami Ikebukuro, Toshima-ku (3985-8678)

● Massage (GM): **Century Massage**, Daisan Tenka Bldg., 6F, 2-14-8 Shinjuku, Shinjuku-ku (3356-1628) ¥9,500; **Happiness**, Daisan Fujiwara Bldg., 3F, 2-14-14 Shinjuku, Shinjuku-ku, ¥8,500 (3356-3003), English is not spoken.

 **ACCOMMODATIONS**

Note: there are no gay hotels in the western sense. Most gay accommodations are a bath/sauna/accommodation complex, or love hotels where you pay and play by the hour. In the list-

ing for Tokyo we include hotels that are conveniently located and English is spoken.

BUSINESS HOTEL T
2-12-3 Shinjuku, Tokyo 160. Tel: (03) 3352-5524. TYPE: *Love Hotel*. CLIENTELE: All Welcome. LOCATION: Next door to bar GB, around the corner from bar Fuji. DESCRIPTION: Typical love hotel, seems to allow male couples and mixed Japanese and non-Japanese. No English spoken.

CENTURY HYATT TOKYO
2-7-2 Nishi-Shinjuku, Shinjuku-ku, Tokyo 160. Tel: (03) 3349-0111. US (800) 228-9000. TYPE: *Luxury Hotel*. CLIENTELE: Mainly Straight. LOCATION: Shinjuku shopping and entertainment district, 25 min. walk to the local gay scene. 800 Rooms w/priv. bath. Suites: 20, CTV, phone, A/C, Restaurants, bars, disco. Rates: ¥22,000 - ¥39,000. *TAC:* 10%. DESCRIPTION: Luxury western style hotel with a 7-story Atrium Lobby. 5 min. to Shinjuku Station. No problem taking people to your room.

CITY HOTEL
3-8-10 Shinjuku, Shinjuku-ku, Tokyo 160. Tel: (03) 3341-7861. TYPE: *Hotel*. CLIENTELE: Mostly Straight. LOCATION: Across from Shinjuku-Ni-chome. DESCRIPTION: 10 story building. All rooms with air-conditioning, priv. bath and color TV. Excellent Korean BBQ restaurant on premises. Do not allow two men to stay together, but can be recommended for cheap single accommodations Rates: ¥6,000-¥9,000.

HILTON-TOKYO
6-6-2 Nishi-Shinjuku, Shinjuku-ku, Tokyo. Tel: (03) 3344-5111. TYPE: *Luxury Hotel*. CLIENTELE: Mostly Straight. LOCATION: West side of Shinjuku, 25 minutes from the local gay scene. 808 Rooms w/priv. bath. CTV, phone, A/C, Restaurants, bars, lounges, pub, pool, gym, sauna, tennis courts, 24 hrs. room service, parking, Credit Cards: MC/VISA/AMEX/JCB. Rates: ¥29,000 - ¥37,000. *TAC:* 10%. DESCRIPTION: Western style luxury hotel in the Hilton tradition. Conveniently located to the Shinjuku bars and baths.

KEIO PLAZA
2-2-1 Nishi-Shinjuku, Shinjuku-ku, Tokyo 160. Tel: (03) 3344-0111. TYPE: *Luxury Hotel*. CLIENTELE: Mainly Straight. LOCATION: In the heart of Shinjuku's entertainment area, 25 min. to gay scene. 1,500 Rooms w/priv. bath, Suites: 23, CTV, phone, A/C, Restaurants, bars, lounges, Tea Room, room & maid service, pool, sauna, massage, Credit Cards: MC/VISA/AMEX/JCB.Rates: ¥22,000 - ¥25,000. *TAC:*

10%. DESCRIPTION: Giant western style luxury hotel in the heart of Shinjuku's entertainment center, near the gay scene.

LISTEL SHINJUKU
5-3-20 Shinjuku, Shinjuku-ku, Tokyo 160. Tel: (03) 3350-0123. Fax: (03) 3350-0123. TYPE: *Hotel.* CLIENTELE: Mostly Straight. LOCATION: Five minutes from Shinjuku Ni-chome the gay area.Rooms & suites w/priv. bath, CTV, phone, A/C, Restaurant, room & maid service, Gay Bars: nearby. Rates: ¥8,500 - ¥9,500. DESCRIPTION: Hotel in the Shinjuku Go-chome district. Reservations are accepted from foreign travelers. Weekly, monthly rates are available too.

SHINJUKU INN (Business Hotel)
5-1-4 Shinjuku, Shinjuku-ku, Tokyo 160. Tel: (03) 3341-0131. Rates: ¥7,200 - ¥15,900. Seems to have no policy against men staying together. Business hotels only accept on-the-spot reservations. Do not try to make reservation by phone or through your travel agent. No credit cards accepted. LOCATION: few blocks from the gay scene.

SHINJUKU PRINCE HOTEL
1-20-1 Kabuki-cho, 1-chome, Shinjuku-ku, Tokyo 160. Tel: (03) 3205-1111. Fax: (03) 3205-1952. TYPE: *Hotel.* CLIENTELE: Mostly Straight. LOCATION: On the 10th-24th floors of the Seibu Shinjuku Station. Rooms: 571 w/priv. bath, A/C, Restaurant, sky lounge, Gay Bars: some nearby, Airport: 1/2 hr. Haneda, Credit Cards: MC/VISA/AMEX/JCB, Rates: ¥ 15,000 - ¥17,000. *TAC:* 10%. DESCRIPTION: First class tourist hotel near the gay scene.

✪ HOTEL SUNLITE

5-15-8 Shinjuku, Shinjuku-ku, Tokyo 160. Tel: (03) 3356-0391. USA/Canada: Tel: (516) 944-5330 or (800) 257-5344. Fax: (516) 944-7540 or (800) 982-6571. TYPE: *Hotel.* CLIENTELE: Gay/Straight. LOCATION: East side of Shinjuku station. 10 min. from Shinjuku station on foot or 5 min. by taxi.

* Rooms: 72 w/priv. bath
* CTV, phone, refrigerator
* Restaurant: **Floret** 7:30am - 9:30pm
* Bar: **Plato** bar lounge 10am-10pm
* Maid service, laundry service
* Gay Bars: some nearby
* Airport: Narita, limousine bus 85 min, express train 59 min, rapid train
* Train Station: 10 minutes
* Season: Year round
* Rates: from (US) $120 and up
* *TAC:* 10% (from Odysseus)

**USA/Canada reservations
(800) 257-5344**

hotel **Sun Lite**
shinjuku

DESCRIPTION: Sleek Business hotel in a convenient location. Rooms are cheerful and immaculately clean. Rooms type 'A' are smaller with tiny bathrooms and no refrigerator. Rooms type 'C' are about 2 sq.m. / 22 sq.ft. larger with refrigerator. If you plan to stay out late doors close at 1:30am.

YOKOHAMA   ℂ   045

✈ Haneda Int'l Airport (HND);
   Narita Int'l Airport (NRT)

LOCATION: 30 min. by train SW of Tokyo.

POPULATION: 2,900,000

DESCRIPTION: Serving as the capital city's port Yokohama is a modern city with large foreign and Chinese population. Yokohama was a tiny fishing village when Commodore Perry arrived in the mid 19th century and it became the first port to open for international trade. Yokohama's main gay area is in Naka-ku, near Sakuragicho station. There are several gay bars in this area and a good sauna to start you out right.Yokohama can be easily reached by train for a day trip from Tokyo.

Y BARS Y

● Bars/clubs (GM): **Daruma**, Naka-ku, Takagawa-cho (242-8385); **Friend Bar**, Nogecho, Naka-ku (242-9747); **Three Box**, Sky Bldg., 2F, Naka-ku, Nage-cho 2-90 (242-4570).

λ SERVICES λ

● Health Club (GM): **Doanji**, mixed room, sauna, snack bar, ¥1,700 admission, 3-93 Miyagawa-cho (242-6255).

 **ACCOMMODATIONS**

HOTEL YOKOHAMA
6-1 Yamahita-cho, Naka-ku, Yokohama 231. Tel: (045) 662-1321. TYPE: *Hotel*. CLIENTELE: All Welcome. LOCATION: Facing Yokohama harbor.

* Rooms: 166 w/priv. bath. Suites: 2
* CTV, phone, refrigerator, A/C, C/H
* Maid & room service, laundry
* Restaurants: French & Japanese
* Coffee shop, bar, cocktail lounge
* Beauty Salon, free parking
* Gay Bars: some nearby
* Airport: 30 min.
* Train Station: 10 min.
* Open: Year round
* Rates: from ¥25,000

DESCRIPTION: Tasteful 4-star 13 story hotel. Beautiful decor, elegant details, quality service.

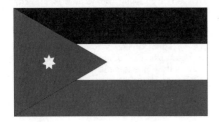

JORDAN

AREA: 35,000 sq. mi. (90,650 sq. km)
POPULATION: 2,800,000
CAPITAL: Amman
CURRENCY: Jordanian dinar (JOD)
OFFICIAL LANGUAGE: Arabic
MAJOR RELIGIONS: Islam
Telephone: 962
Nat'l Holiday: Independence Day, 25 May
Official Time: GMT + 2
Electricity: 220 volts 50c AC
Exchange Rate: US$1 = JOD 0.70
National Airline: Royal Jordanian

LAW REGARDING HOMOSEXUALITY: Homosexuality is illegal. The attitude towards homosexuality can be hostile, although bisexuality is relatively widespread. Most men are open at one time or another to a gay experience, but will never admit to being homosexual. There are no gay groups or organizations.

❖ **Note:** visit **Petra**, the mysterious ancient (3000 BC) Nabatean city with a magnificent temple curved in the red rock. Petra is 262 km / 160 mi. south of Amman and north of Aqaka.

AMMAN   ℭ   06

✈ Queen Alia Int'l AP (AMM)

LOCATION: Northwestern Jordan.

POPULATION: 1,110,000

CLIMATE: Hot and dry desert climate, with cool evenings. Rainfall from November to March.

DESCRIPTION: The biblical town of Rabat-Amon, and Philadephia during Roman times, is now the capital city of Jordan. A new town that expanded rapidly since Jordan's independence. The most impressive sight is a second century Roman amphitheatre in the center of town.

❖ Public Cruising (AYOR): **Park Hashamite**, center of town, the promenade near the park and the **Roman Amphitheatre**.

♟ BARS ♟

● Bars/Clubs (AW): **After Eight Bar**, next to Hotel Granada; **Venus Night Club**, Rainbow St.

 ACCOMMODATIONS

CAMEO HOTEL
Jabal Amman. Tel: (6) 644515. TYPE: *Hotel*. CLIENTELE: Mostly Straight. LOCATION: City center. 44 rooms w/priv. bath, CTV, phone, 24 hrs room service, restaurant, bar, terrace. DESCRIPTION: Tourist class hotel.

AQABA   ℭ   03

✈ Aqaba AP (AQJ) 8 mi. / 13 km west
Eilat Airport (ETH / Israel)

LOCATION: On the Red Sea. Jordan's southernmost tip facing the Israeli resort town of Eilat.

DESCRIPTION: A fun resort town and Jordan's only seaport. Now it is easy to cross to Eilat and enjoy the cosmopolitan nightlife and facilities west of the border.

♟ BARS ♟

● Bars/Clubs (AW): **Holiday International Bar**, Kings Blvd., beachfront; **Omar Bar**, Hotel Alcazar (241-31). Also check information for Eilat (Israel).

ACCOMMODATIONS

ALCAZAR HOTEL
Al-Corniche St. Aqaba. Tel: (3) 31431. TYPE: *Hotel*. CLIENTELE: Mostly Straight. LOCATION: 250 m / yards from the beach. 132 rooms, phone, A/C, restaurants, pub, bar, pool, health club, sauna. DESCRIPTION: Modern hotel.

HOLIDAY INT'L
Kings Blvd. Aqaba. Tel: (3) 312-426. TYPE: *Hotel*. CLIENTELE: Mostly Straight. LOCATION: Seashore location. 156 rooms, phone, CTV (movies), A/C, restaurant, bar, pool, beach bar. DESCRIPTION: First class beach hotel.

KOREA (SOUTH)

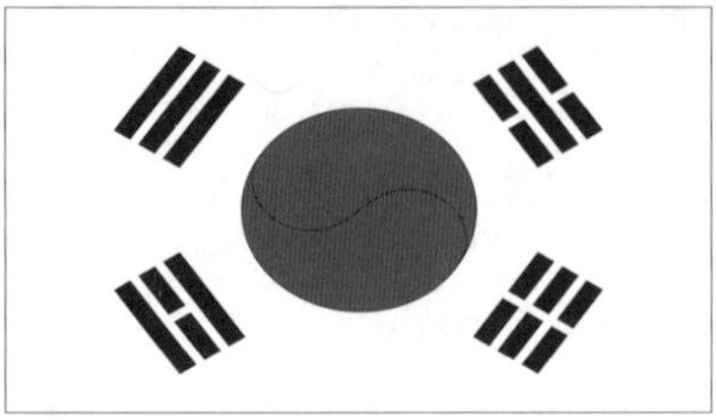

AREA: 38,175 sq. mi. (98,873 sq. km)
POPULATION: 37,500,000
CAPITAL: Seoul
CURRENCY: Won
OFFICIAL LANGUAGE: Korean
MAJOR RELIGIONS: Confucianism, Buddhism, Ch'ondogyo, Christianity
Telephone: 82
Nat'l Holiday: Foundation Day, Oct. 3
Official Time: G.M.T. + 9
Electricity: 100 volts
Exchange Rate: 1US$ = Wons 769
National Airline: Korean Airlines (KAL)

LAW REGARDING HOMOSEXUALITY: Homosexual acts between consenting adults in private are not considered to be an offense according to the South Korean law. Bisexuality is common between Korean men, and it is easy to establish contacts with Koreans in bars or other meeting places.

SEOUL ✆ 02

✈ Kimpo Int'l Airport (SEL)
16 mi. / 25 km northwest

LOCATION: Northwestern South Korea.

POPULATION: 9,500,000

CLIMATE: Cold, dry winter & hot, wet summer. The most desirable seasons are spring or fall. The average low winter temperature is 33°F (1°c), and average high summer temperature is 81°F (26°c).

VISITOR INFORMATION

Korea Nat'l Tourism Corp.
460 Park Avenue, New York, NY 10022
Tel: (212) 688-7543

DESCRIPTION: Seoul is the capital and the cultural heart of the Republic of Korea. Founded by Yi Song-gye in 1392 as the capital of the Yi dynasty, it proudly traces its history to the 14th century. Today, the contemporary city coexists with its traditional past.

Of interest to visitors: **Yongdong** (New Seoul and Olympic Village) across the Hang-gang River; **Youido**, the 'Manhattan' of Seoul in the middle of the Han-gang River with the famous MBC building and more.

BARS RESTAURANTS

There are a few gay establishments in Seoul located near the Pagoda Park. The bars are coffee shops or Japanese style singing bars with a master who greets and introduces customers to each other.

● Bars/clubs (GM): **Alexander**, cozy little bar near OB bar for directions call the owner Roh-Seung-Hwdn (743-8264); **Berkeley**, nice bar, good music, friendly staff, call (742-1151) they will pick you up; **Kalib**, 62-2 Nakwon-Dong, Chong Ro Gu (743-3880); **Namjung**, Between Pagoda Park & Victory Town Garage 2nd Fl.); **OB Beer** (742-4836). Call bars for directions; **Tunnel**, popular with foreigners, in the Itaewon Area, near the main street where the Hamilton Hotel and Burger King are located. Call Joo Chun for directions (797-2283); **Utopia**, large bar between Bimon St., & Nagwon Arcade.

λ SERVICES λ

● Cinema (GM): **Pagoda Cinema**, 1st fl.

● Health Clubs (G/S): **Pagoda Hotel Sauna** (2nd fl); **Shin Shin Sauna**, traditional bathhouse near the Bank of Korea, 9343 Buckchang-Dong, Chung-ku, 2nd Fl. (777-9331).

ACCOMMODATIONS

SEOUL ROYAL HOTEL
6, 1-Ka, Myong-dong, Chung-ku, Seoul 100. Tel: (2) 771-45. TYPE: *Hotel.* CLIENTELE: Mostly Straight. LOCATION: in downtown Myong-dong area. 310 rooms. 21 suites. CTV, phone. Japanese & Western restaurants, nightclub & bar. 20 km / 12 mi. to Airport. Credit Cards: MC/VISA/ DC/AMEX. Rates: (US) $95-$140. ***TAC:*** 10%. DESCRIPTION: First class, 28-story hotel in downtown area. No problems bringing visitors to your room.

LATVIA

AREA: 25,174 sq. mi (65,000 sq. km)
POPULATION: 2, 700,000
CAPITAL: Riga
CURRENCY: Lats (Lvl)
OFFICIAL LANGUAGE: Latvian
MAJOR RELIGIONS: Protestantism
Telephone: 371
Nat'l Holiday: Nat'l Day, 18 November
Official Time: G.M.T. +2/4
Electricity: 220 volts
Exchange Rate: 1US$ = Lvl 0.53
National Airline: Latvian Airlines

LAW REGARDING HOMOSEXUALITY: Homosexuality between two consenting adult men has been decriminalized, and the age of consent is now 18 for homosexual activity and 16 for heterosexual activity.

RIGA ℭ 0132

✈ Spilve Airport (RIX)
4.5 mi. / 7 km northwest of the city

LOCATION: Western Latvia on the Gulf of Riga in the Baltic Sea.

POPULATION: 2,700,000

CLIMATE: Damp climate with over 600mm / 24" of precipitation a year. July is the warmest and wettest month with temperatures reaching 22°c (72°F). Winters are cold and snowy with temperatures below freezing (30°F).

Gay/Lesbian Visitor Information
LASV (Latvian Assoc. for Sexual Equality) P.O. Box 460 Riga LV-1001

DESCRIPTION: Riga is the biggest and the most vibrant city in the Baltic states. For cen-

turies Latvia was ruled by many different countries and regional powers. There is a distinguished German connection which is manifested itself in the architecture style and the number of tourists from Germany. Visit: Old Riga, with square rows of 17th century German buildings; Riga Castle dated from the 13th Century; and New Riga, with is manicured parks and 19th century blvds.

❖ Cruising (AYOR): Square behind the **Hotel Latvia**, and Square opposite the Opera; and at the **Arkadijas Parken**.

BARS Ŷ RESTAURANTS ⑪

● Bars/clubs (GMW): **Baren**, 40 Tallinas iela; **Cafe Nara**, across from the Dailes Theatre; **Cleo Bar**, A Caka Iela 120; **Loks**, bar/disco, Lördagar / Brivibas iela 197 (22-06); **Oaze**, dance club, Karla Ulmana Gatve 2 (629-200); **Osiris Cafe**, corner of Kr. Barona and Lacplesis; **Salus**, Leona Paegles iela 1 (22-06).

● Restaurants (AW): **Sena Riga**, Aspazias bulvaris 22, Old Riga, behind the Hotel de Rome; **Cafe Forums**, shiny cafe restaurant, young clientele, Kalku iela 24.

λ SERVICES λ

● Erotica (GM): **Berlin-Riga**, sexshop, Lacplesa iela 47; **Labi**, videos and shows, Lacpleasa iela 61; **Luteks**, sexshop, Avotu iela 38/40; **Sexland**, Terbatas iela 47.

● Health Club (GM): **Varaviksne**, Kugu iela 17.

ACCOMMODATIONS

HOTEL de ROME
Kalku iela 28, Riga, Latvia LV-9985. Tel: (0132) 223171. TYPE: *Hotel*. CLIENTELE: Mostly straight. LOCATION: Old Riga. 90 rooms w/priv. bath, phone, fax, minibars. Rates: (US) $70-$120. DESCRIPTION: Finnish run hotel, tastefully decorated rooms, good service.

LATVIA HOTEL
55 Elizabetes St., Riga, Latvia LV-9985. Tel: (0132) 229-020. TYPE: *Hotel*. CLIENTELE: Mostly Straight. LOCATION: Opposite Park, near Museum of Fine Art. 356 rooms w/priv. bath, 2 suites, CTV, phone, restaurants, bar, sauna, elevator. Rates: (US) $80-$180. *TAC:* 10%. DESCRIPTION: Striking 26-storey downtown hotel. Clean rooms and good views.

LITHUANIA

AREA: 25,174 sq. mi. (65,200 sq. km)
POPULATION: 4,200,000
CAPITAL: Vilnius
CURRENCY: Litas
OFFICIAL LANGUAGE: Lithuanian
MAJOR RELIGIONS: Roman Catholicism
Telephone: 370
Nat'l Holiday: Independence Day, Feb. 16
Official Time: G.M.T. +2/4
Electricity: 220 volts
Exchange Rate: 1US$ = L 4
National Airline: LAL - Lithuanian Airlines

LAW REGARDING HOMOSEXUALITY: Lithuania was the first Baltic State to liberate itself from the former URSS, but it was also the last Baltic State to abolish the penal code for homosexuality. The Lithuanian Parliament abolished the criminal code that outlawed gay male sexual activity in July 1993. However, the attitude of the general population remains mostly intolerant and homophobic.

BALTIC RESORTS ℭ 02

Klaipeda and Palanga are popular beach resorts. Klaipeda's male nude beach is in **Smiltyne** (a 5 min. boat trip). Palanga's male nude beach is in the northern part of town.

BARS ⅄ RESTAURANTS ⑪

● Bars/clubs (G/S): **Klaipeda**, first floor cafe and bar at the Klaipeda Hotel; **Goda** Cafe, near male beach in Palanga.

VILNIUS ℭ 02

✈ Vilnius Airport (VNO)

LOCATION: Southeastern Lithuania on the Neris River near the Russian border.

POPULATION: 600,000

CLIMATE: June to August are the hottest and warmest months with temperatures reaching 22°c (72°F). Winters are cold and snowy with temperatures below freezing (30°F).

Gay/Lesbian Visitor Information
Vilnius Gaytel: 266894 or 766583

DESCRIPTION: The lively capital of Lithuania has an ancient history that can be traced back to as early as the 5th century. Historic links to Catholic Poland is manifested by many Catholic churches and Central European architecture. Between WWI and WWII the jewish population was about one-third of the total population, and Vilnius became known as the 'Jerusalem of Lithuania'. Visit: **Old Vilnius** with its quaint houses and streets from the 15th and 16th century. The streets west of Pilies gatvé were once the heart of Vilnius **Jewish Quarter**; **Castle Hill**; **New Town**.

● Two of the most popular cruising spots in Vilnius include: **Lukiskiu Square** in the Summer; and the bars at the **Opera Theatre** during night performances, Vienuolio 1.

BARS ⅄ RESTAURANTS ⑪

● Bars/clubs (GM): **Amsterdam Club**, P.D. 429, Vilnius 2038 (266894 or 766583); **Akimirka**, Gedemino Prospekt 31 (617-417); or the bar at the **Lietuva Hotel** (see description below); **Stikliai**, beer bar, Stiklin 7.

● Bars/clubs (GMW): **Stijkiai Cafe**, 18 Stiklin; **Satyras Disco**, Kalvariju gatre.

● Restaurants (AW): **Opera**, cafe, Tylioji 4; **Kavine Alumnatas**, cafe popular with students, Uni-versiteto gatvé 4; **Restoranas Stikliai**, English menu, old city location, Stikliu gatvé 7 (627-971); **Satyras**, Kalvariju 125l; **Stikliai**, cafe, Stikliu 18

◈ ACCOMMODATIONS ◈

LIETUVA HOTEL
20 Ukmerges/Paleckio St., Vilnius 232600. Tel: (0122) 356074. Fax: (0122) 356-270. TYPE: *Hotel*. CLIENTELE Mostly Straight. LOCATION: On the right bank of the River Neris. 337 rooms, 17 suites, CTV, phone, restaurants, bars, pool, sauna. Rates: (US) $80-$120.TAC: 10%. DESCRIPTION: Moderate first class hotel.

LUXEMBOURG

AREA: 999 sq. mi. (2,587 sq. km)
POPULATION: 364,000
CAPITAL: Luxembourg
CURRENCY: Luxembourg Franc (LF)
OFFICIAL LANGUAGE: Luxembourgeois, French, German
MAJOR RELIGIONS: Roman Catholicism
Telephone: 352
Nat'l Holiday: Liberation Day, Sept. 9
Official Time: G.M.T. + 1
Electricity: 220 volts
Exchange Rate: 1US$ = LF 29.04
National Airline: LuxAir

LAW REGARDING HOMOSEXUALITY: Homosexuality between consenting adults over 18 years is legal. Violation of the law may carry imprisonment for up to six months and fines up to LF 10,000. Luxembourg is a tiny Grand Duchy with a conservative population. It is becoming more open and cosmopolitan due to its position within the EEC.

LUXEMBOURG CITY ✆ 352

✈ Findel Int'l Airport (LUX)
3 mi. / 5 km northeast

LOCATION: In the south of Luxembourg Alzette River Valley, 219km / 137mi. southeast of Brussels (Belgium), and 190 km / 118 mi. southwest of Bonn (W. Germany).

POPULATION: 78,300

CLIMATE: Continental climate. Average temperatures vary from 54˚F to 72˚F in the summer (12˚c - 22˚c), and 32˚F to 43˚F in the winter (0˚c - 6˚c).

Gay/Lesbian Visitor Information
(IGHL-Info): 48-576

DESCRIPTION: Luxembourg City is the nation's 1000 year old capital. Its location on a high plateau overlooking the Alzette River, leaves a dramatic impression on visitors. Visit the medieval buildings, cathedrals and churches. **Place d'Armes**, popular square with coffee shops, restaurants and boutiques. Some gay cruising is possible at the **Parc Municipale** (near RTL) or the main railway station (AYOR).

BARS 𝕐 RESTAURANTS 🍴

● Bars/Discos (GMW): **Big Moon**, 14 rue Vauban (431-746); **Bistro d'Art Scène**, 6, rue Sigefroi (228-363); **Boulevard Café**, 49, Blvd. Royal (465-074); **Café Chez Mike**, international meeting place, 30 Ave. Emile Reuter (453-284); **Chez Gusty et Francis**, drag shows, 101 rue d'Eich (431-223); **Pulp Club**, dance club, 36 Blvd. d'Avranches (496-940); **Rosegarden**, dance club, 3 rue du Pleebiscite (492-486).

● Restaurants (AW): **Auberge des Cygnes**, restaurant, brasserie, Pizzerie, in Remisch on the Moselle River (698-852); **De La Source**, cafe/restaurant, 5 rue Chimay (461-763); **Mesaverde**, vegetarian cuisine, 11 rue du Saint-Esprit (464-126); **Roma**, Italian cuisine, 5 rue Louvigny (223-692); **Times**, 8 rue Louvigny (222-722).

λ SERVICES λ

● Health Club (G/S): **Piscine Olympique**, pool and sauna, 2 rue Léon Hengen (436-060).

● Radio Program (GMW): **XL on Radio ARA**, information about local and international gay scene and events, 2 rue de la Boucherie (222-288).

● Sex Shops (G/S): **Boutique Amour**, 8 Blvd. d'Avranches; **Erotic Video Center**, 7 rue de Bonnevoie (481-455); **Sex-Shop-Kino-Video**, 35 Ave. de la Liberté (491-410).

 ACCOMMODATIONS

ALFA HOTEL
16 Place de la Gare, Luxembourg City, L-1616. Tel: 49-0011. USA/Canada reservations - (516) 944-5330 or (800) 257-5344. Fax: (516) 944-7540. TYPE: *Hotel.* CLIENTELE: All Welcome. LOCATION: Opposite train station and air-terminal. 100 rooms most w/priv. bath, CTV, phone, soundproof, brasserie, restaurant, lounge, parking. Airport: 3 mi. / 5 km. Gay Bars: nearby. Credit Cards: MC/VISA/ACC/BC/DC. Open: Year round. Rates: (US) $85 - $160 w/CB. *TAC:* 10% (from Odysseus). DESCRIPTION: Eight story tourist class hotel in a convenient location.

MACAU

AREA: 6 sq. mi. (16 sq. km)
POPULATION: 448,000
CAPITAL: Macau
CURRENCY: Pataca (MOP) / HK$ (widely used)
OFFICIAL LANGUAGE: Chinese,
Portuguese
MAJOR RELIGIONS: Confucianism,
Buddhism, Taoism, Christianity
Telephone: 853
Nat'l Holiday: Portuguese Independence Day
Dec. 1; Dragon Boat Festival (June)
Official Time: G.M.T. + 8
Electricity: 110/220 volts
Exchange Rate: 1US$ = MOP 8

LAW REGARDING HOMOSEXUALITY:
Macau is a Portuguese territory. As in Portugal
homosexuality is not mentioned in the Code of
Law, but "Acts against nature" maybe used
against gay men. Macau reverts back to the
People's Republic of China in 1999 at which
time it will be administered under the People's
Republic of China law.

MACAU CITY

✈ Macau Int'l Airport

LOCATION: 65 km / 40 mi. west of Hong Kong
with frequent ferry/hydrofoil connection.

CLIMATE: Same as Hong Kong with cool sea
breeze during summer nights.

DESCRIPTION: Macau is divided into three
main sections, the Macau Peninsula attached
to Mainland China at the northern tip, and the
two islands of Taipa and Coloane. Macau main

attraction for international travelers is gambling at the islands casinos. But there are also
luxury holiday resorts on the mainland and the
islands. There is not much of a gay scene in
Macau, some cruising (AYOR) takes place in
front of the **Lisboa Hotel**. It is possible to
make contacts with gay travelers at the bars
and coffee shops of the deluxe international
hotels, especially late at night. The coffee shop
at the **Sintra Hotel** on the 1st floor can be
cruisy, but it is not a official gay establishment
and discretion is recommended.

 ACCOMMODATIONS

HOTEL LISBOA & CASINO
Ave. de Amizade. Tel: 577666. TYPE: *Hotel &
Casino*. CLIENTELE: All Welcome. LOCA-
TION: Pearl River Estuary near the harbor.
1049 rooms w/priv. bath, CTV, phone, A/C, 12
restaurants, 24 hrs. coffee shop, nightclub/
disco, 24 hrs casino, pool, sauna, gym. 10 mi. /
16 km to Coloane beach. Rates: (US) $110 -
230. DESCRIPTION: First class elaborately
designed international hotel and casino complex.

SINTRA HOTEL
Avda De D. Joao IV. Tel: 710111. TYPE: *Hotel*.
CLIENTELE: All Welcome. LOCATION: Near
casinos and business area. 240 rooms w/priv.
bath, CTV, phone, A/C, restaurant, coffee shop,
sauna. Rates: (US) $90-$130. DESCRIPTION:
Moderate first class hotel with spectacular
view of Praia Grande Bay.

COLOANE

DESCRIPTION: Coloane is the larger of the
two islands and it is famous for its beautiful
beaches. It is less developed and largely
unspoiled.

 ACCOMMODATIONS

WESTIN RESORT MACAU
Estrade De Hac Sa, Coloane Island. Tel: 871-
111. TYPE: *Resort Complex*. CLIENTELE: All
Welcome. LOCATION: Northern tip of the
island, overlooking private beach. 208 rooms
w/priv. bath, CTV, phone, A/C, hairdryer, 24 hrs
room service, restaurant, pool bar, gym, sauna,
indoor and outdoor pools. Rates: (US)$160-
$230. DESCRIPTION: Dramatic terraced
deluxe resort.

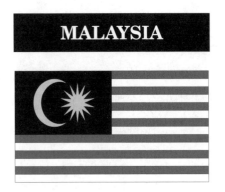

MALAYSIA

AREA: 128,308 sq. mi. (332,318 sq. km)
POPULATION: 13,500,000
CAPITAL: Kuala Lumpur
CURRENCY: Ringgit (R)
OFFICIAL LANGUAGE: Malay, Chinese, English, Tamil
MAJOR RELIGIONS: Islam, Confucianism, Buddhism, tribal religions, Christianity
Telephone: 60
Nat'l Holiday: National Day, August 31
Official Time: G.M.T. + 8
Electricity: 220 volts
Exchange Rate: 1US$ = R 2.54
National Airline: Malaysia Airlines

LAW REGARDING HOMOSEXUALITY: Homosexuality is illegal according to section 377 of the Penal Code. It is subject to harsh penalty with prison terms from 2 - 20 years. Sex between consenting adults is not reported or persecuted. Female homosexuality falls under same section of the law, however, there are no known prosecutions of lesbians.

KUALA LUMPUR ℰ 03

✈ Subang Int'l Airport (KUL)

LOCATION: Central west coast.

POPULATION: 960,000

CLIMATE: Temperatures are about 70˚F - 90˚F (21˚c-32˚c) year round with heaviest rainfall between May and September. March and April best months for travel.

Gay/Lesbian Visitor Information
Pink Triangle Group
P.O. Box 118 59, Kuala Lumpur 50760
Tel: (03) 981-2863 Fax: (03) 981-2864

DESCRIPTION: Kuala Lumpur (K.L) is located at the confluence of the Klang and the Gombak rivers. The city is a mix of races and cultures with impressive Islamic, Gothic, Tudor and Colonial styles. It is one of Asia's most gracious cities. Visit the Masjid Negara (National Mosque) one of the largest in Southeast Asia.

⅄ BARS ⅄

● Bar/club: (GM): **Blue Boy**, 54 Jalan Sultan Ismail (48-4179); **Shangri La Hotel Bar**, mixed bar at the hotel, 11 Jalan Sultan Ismail (232-2388).

ACCOMMODATIONS

SHANGRI-LA HOTEL
11, Jalan Sultan Ismail, Kuala Lumpur 50250. Tel: (03) 232-2388. TYPE: *Hotel*. LOCATION: Downtown business & entertainment center. 721 rooms w/priv. bath. 36 suites, CTV, phone, minibar, restaurants, bars, disco, pool, gym, sauna, massage. DESCRIPTION: Deluxe hotel. The hotel's bar is popular with gay clientele.

PENANG ℰ 04

✈ Penang Int'l Airport (PEN) 11 mi. / 18 km W

LOCATION: Island off the northeastern coast of Malaysia in the straits of Melaka.

DESCRIPTION: Penang is the oldest British settlement in Malaysia. It is also one of the country's major tourist attractions with lovely beach resorts and historical sites.

❖ Gay Beach: **Batu Feringgi** Beach.

⅄ BAR ⅄

● Bar/Club (G/S): **Casa Blanca**, near the Jockey Club on the beach.

ACCOMMODATIONS

GOLDEN SANDS
Batu Feringgi Beach. Penang. Tel: (4) 811-911. TYPE: *Resort Hotel*. CLIENTELE: All Welcome. LOCATION: Beachfront. 395 rooms w/priv. bath, CTV, phone, A/C, minibar, restaurants, pub, disco, pool. DESCRIPTION: Superior first class resort hotel set in tropical gardens. Convenient "gay beach" location.

MALTA

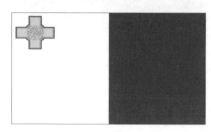

AREA: 122 sq. mi. (316 sq. km)
POPULATION: 350,000
CAPITAL: Valletta
CURRENCY: Maltese Pound
OFFICIAL LANGUAGE: Maltese, English
MAJOR RELIGIONS: Roman Catholicism
Telephone: 356
Nat'l Holiday: Republic Day Dec. 13
Official Time: GMT +1
Electricity: 240 volts
Exchange Rate: US$1 = M£ 0.35
National Airline: Air Malta

LAW REGARDING HOMOSEXUALITY:
Homosexuality is legal between men 18 years
and older. Homosexual acts between women
are not mentioned in the law. Due to the small
size of the island,Catholic influence, and
Mediterranean culture, homosexuality is a
subject of discretion.

ST. JULIAN's

 BARS Y

● Bars/Clubs (GM): **Axis**, dance club, Paceville;
Why Not, dance club, Saturday night only, Burl-
ing Centre, Dragonara Rd. (1st Fl).

⬨ ACCOMMODATIONS ⬨

MALTA HILTON
St. Julian's. Tel: 336201. TYPE: *Deluxe Hotel*.
CLIENTELE: All Welcome. LOCATION: On
the beach, 15 min. from Valletta. 201 rooms
w/priv. bath, CTV, phone, A/C, minibar, balcony, restaurants, bars, pools. Rates: (US)
$140-$210. DESCRIPTION: Graceful hotel in a
garden setting. Cruisy swimming pool area.

VALLETTA

✈ Luqa Airport (MLA) 4 mi. / 6 km southwest

CLIMATE: Mediterranean. Long warm sum-
mers with temperatures in the 80°sF (26°c).
Winter from November to March is mild with a
January average 50°F (10°c).

DESCRIPTION: Malta is a small island in the
Mediterranean, an independent republic with
a British Commonwealth membership. The
island was mentioned in ancient Greek mythology as the place where Odysseus was held cap-
tive by Calypso. The island offers interesting
sites of old civilizations including medieval
buildings, fortifications, cathedrals and
citadels. The capital Valletta is reminiscent of
the Knights of St. John; the city was built by the
French Grand Master of the Knights. Nearby
Sliema is a coastal resort with a long sea front
promenade and an attractive hotel section with
shops and cafes. Malta's main seaport is at
Grand Harbor, Valletta.

● **HOW TO GET THERE**: By ferry service to
Naples, Barcelona, Piraeus & Izmir. The
island's airport has frequent flights to and from
major European cities.

● Entertainment: **Dragonara Palace Casino**, a moderate deluxe hotel resort and casino
in Sliema offering European style casino
games, and resort activities, on a peninsula
along St. Julian's Bay.

BARS Y RESTAURANTS 🍴

● Bars (GM): Vallerta - **Lantern**, bar &
restaurant, 20 Sapper St.;**The Site**, 186
Dimech St., Balluta Bay (311-390); Bugibba -
Didies Bar, mixed bar, many women, Turists
St., (47-6266).

● Restaurant (AW): **Scalini**, International cuisine, 32, south St., (60 62 21) in Valletta.

⬨ ACCOMMODATIONS ⬨

OSBORNE HOTEL
50 South St., Valletta. Tel: 243656. TYPE:
Hotel. CLIENTELE: Mostly Straight. LOCA-
TION: City's highest point. Rooms and suites
w/priv. bath, CTV, phone, radio, pool, sun terrace. Rates: (US) $50 - $90. *TAC:* 10%.

MARTINIQUE

AREA: 425 sq. mi. (1,093 sq. km)
POPULATION: 360,000
CAPITAL: Fort de France
CURRENCY: French Franc (FF)
OFFICIAL LANGUAGE: French, Creole
MAJOR RELIGIONS: Roman Catholicism
Telephone: 596
Nat'l Holiday: Bastille Day, July 14
Official Time: GMT - 4
Electricity: 240 volts
Exchange Rate: US$1 = FF 4.86
National Airline: Air France

LAW REGARDING HOMOSEXUALITY: Martinique is a French department and it is governed by French law. Homosexuality is accepted in France. The legal minimum age of consent is 15, but it is not advisable to get sexually involved with under 18 because of possible legal complications. Gay men and lesbians are protected against discrimination on the job. The law also protects HIV+ and PWA against discrimination by employers.

FORT DE FRANCE

✈ Lamentin AP (FDF) 3.5 mi. / 6 km southeast

LOCATION: Martinique is the northernmost of the Windward (eastern) islands in the Lesser Antilles. It is located near Dominica, Guadeloupe and St. Lucia. Fort-de-France is midway the western coast on the Caribbean side.

POPULATION: 96,000

CLIMATE: Tropical Caribbean. The average year round temperature is 79°F (26°c). The weather is humid during the day, but cools off at night. Summer days are tempered by trade winds.

DESCRIPTION: Tropical Martinique offers a taste of France in the tropics. The capital Fort-de-France looks like a small scale of Nice combined with the ambiance of New Orleans. Visitors can enjoy duty free shopping with many French imports such as crystals, porcelains, fashion wear and fragrance. Sports lovers can enjoy boating, hiking, horseback riding and scuba diving.

❖ Gay Beaches: Martinique is not famous for its beaches, but there is a good beach at **Le Diamant**. Topless sunbathing is OK for ladies on beaches and poolside; **Plage de Salines** at the south end of the island near Savane des Petrifications, is popular with gays mostly on weekends; **Plage Madiana**, in Schoelcher, can be cruisy.

❖ **SPECIAL EVENT: Carnaval**, parades, masquarades and lot's of fun starting just before *Lent*.

BARS  RESTAURANTS

● Bars/Clubs (AW): nightspots in Martinique close around midnight. Most large hotels offer bars, clubs and restaurants for cruise ship tourists. Check out **Le Bakoua**, dinner dancing, fun limbo shows and live bands; **le Top 50**, popular disco club at Quartier Bac (584-336).

ACCOMMODATIONS

L'ANSE BLEUE
Dizac, Le Diamant. Tel: (596) 762191. TYPE: *Beachfront Hotel*. CLIENTELE: All Welcome. bungalows with priv. bath, kitchenette. Rates: from (US) 100/day.

LE VILLAGE DU DIAMANT
La Dizac, Diamant. Tel: (596) 762189. TYPE: *Beachfront Hotel*. CLIENTELE: All Welcome. LOCATION: On Diamant Beach in front of Diamond Rock. 59 rooms w/priv. bath, phone, A/C, kitchenette, restaurant, bar, outdoor pool, free parking. Rates: (US) $95 - $130.

HAMEAU de BEAUREGARD
Rte de Salines, Ste-Anne. USA/Canada reservations Tel: (800) 257-5344 or (516) 944-7540. Fax: (800) 982-6571 or (516) 944-7540. TYPE: *Apartmernt Hotel Complex*. LOCATION: Near the small market of Ste Anne. 85 apartments with A/C, CTV, phone, fully equipped kitchenette, private entrance and balcony. Amenities - restaurant, bar, pool and beaches nearby. Rates: (US) $90-$140. *TAC:* 10%. DESCRIPTION: Tastefully furnished apartments in a convenient location. Gay beach nearby.

MEXICO

AREA: 761,601 sq. mi. (1,972,545 sq. km)
POPULATION: 67,396,000
CAPITAL: Mexico City
CURRENCY: Mexican Peso
OFFICIAL LANGUAGE: Spanish
MAJOR RELIGIONS: Roman Catholicism
Telephone: 52
Nat'l Holiday: Independence Day, Sept. 16
Official Time: 6 - 8 hrs. behind G.M.T.
Electricity: 110 volts
Exchange Rate: 1US$ = Peso 7.63
National Airline: Aeroméxico

LAW REGARDING HOMOSEXUALITY:
Homosexuality is not mentioned in the Federal
code of law but nevertheless it is considered a
taboo by most Mexicans. Gay establishments
are sometimes harassed by the police. Gay
lifestyle is better accepted in large cities and
international tourist resorts.

ACAPULCO   ℭ   748

✈ Juan N. Alvarez Airport (ACA)

LOCATION: In the southwest Mexican
province of Guerrero, on the Pacific Ocean 252
miles / 405 km south of Mexico City.

POPULATION: 600,000

CLIMATE: Warm year round with average
temperature of 80˚F (27˚c). Humidity varies,
and during the rainy season (August - October)
the showers are short and the days are sunny.

DESCRIPTION: Acapulco, one of Mexico's
most popular seaside resorts and an old
favorite with gay travelers is a beautiful city,
surrounded by mountains and more than 20
fine sand beaches around the Acapulco Bay.

● The gay area is located at the expensive and
crowded Condesa Beach in front of Beto's with
many seaside restaurants and cafes. The portion of the Costera between the Exelaris Hyatt
Regency and the Ritz Hotel, is known as the
'strip' and one of Acapulco's sassiest and most
exciting areas.

❖ Shopping: **Plaza Bahia**, boutiques, cinemas,
next to Acapulco Plaza; **La Gran Plaza**, elegant boutiques, in front of the Ritz Hotel.

❖ Gay Beach: **Condesa Beach** is where the
boys are. The "Gay Beach" stretches from the
rock on the south side to Beto's Restaurant at
Avenida Costera Miguel Alemán 99, Acapulco
Dorado.

BARS ♈ RESTAURANTS 🍴

Acapulco is famous for its busy and titillating
nightlife. Discos usually open at 10:00 pm and
stay open until the last customer leaves. Many
bars and discos have international reputation,
and cater to the fun loving jet-setters from
around the world such as **Baby'O**, at the end of
the Costera, Horacio Nelson.

● Bars/clubs (GM): **Del Puerto**, neighborhood
bar, younger crowd, Calle Benito Juárez 4,
Centro; **La Malinche**, male strippers, small
disco, Calle La Picuda, Plaza Condesa; **Open
House**, disco/bar, videos, pool table, Calle La
Picuda, Plaza Condesa; **Las Puertas**, behind
Cathedral in downtown, bar, male strip shows,
lots of hustlers, Calle Medero 7 in Zocalo, Main
Square, (820-142); **Relax**, video dance bar,
male strippers, Lomas del Mar 7 (across from
Denny's) (40-421).

● Bars/clubs (GW): **Queens Club**, mostly lesbians but men are welcome, Calle Adolfo López
Mateos 8, Fraccionamiento Las Playas.

● Restaurants (AW): **Beto's Beach**, the five-
star darling of the beach-side restaurants,
Mexican and seafood specialties, Condesa
Beach (40-473); **Casanova**, glamorous and
expensive, about $125 pp, Las Brisas; **Le
Bistroquet**, Int'l cuisine, mixed clientele,
Andrea Doria #5, Costa Azul (846-860); **El
Campanario**, popular with spectacular views;
Kookaburra, Mexican/French, great view
from Las Brisas; **Madeiras**, beautiful views,
chic clientele, reservations a must; **Spicey**,
Thai cuisine w/Mexican spices, Las Brisas;
Villa Hotel & Racquet Club Restaurant,
great for people watching (40 333).

🕮 ACCOMMODATIONS 🕮

✪ ACAPULCO LAS PALMAS

155 Ave. Las Conchas, Fracto. Farallon, Acapulco C.P. 39690. Tel: (74) 870843. Fax: (74) 871282. USA/Canada reservations available from Odysseus (516) 944-5330 or (800) 257-5344, Fax: (516) 944-7540 or (800) 982-6571. TYPE: *Guest House / Villas*. HOSTS: Bobby Munson & David Ramer. CLIENTELE: Gay men only. LOCATION: Heart of the 'Golden Zone' a short distance from the Costera's beaches, restaurants and nightclubs. 10 min. to the Craft Market and the 'Zocalo' (town square).

* Rooms: 15 w/priv. bath
* CTV (VCR), phone, A/C, safe box
* Suites: 2 (1BR) w/full bath, jacuzzi, patio
* Bed Types: twin, doubles
* Services: maid, room, laundry
* Recreation: fishing, boat-trips, para-sailing
* Bar: **El Bar**; Restaurant: **'Las Palmas'** continental (on request)
* Garden, pool, sun terrace, jacuzzi
* Clothing optional policy
* Beach: 2 minutes by taxi, 10 min. walk to the famous gay 'Condesa' beach
* Gay Bars: 2 min. by taxi, 10 min. walk
* Airport: 20 min.
* Languages: English, Spanish
* Open: Year round

* Reservations: deposit required
* Rates: (US) from $100-$260/day w/CB minimum 3 nights stay required
  Full menu available (HB) breakfast + lunch
* Check In 2:00pm / check out 12:00 noon
* **TAC:** 10% (from Odysseus)

DESCRIPTION: Acapulco's newest guest house. Elegant villa resort complex in local Colonial style. Relax in the mosaic tiled jacuzzi on the sundeck terrace. Enjoy a long drink at the bar overlooking the magnificent Acapulco Bay.

CASA LE MAR

Lomas Del Mar, Acapulco. USA/Canada Reservations: Odysseus (516) 944-5330 or (800) 257-5344, Fax: (516) 944-7540 or (800) 982-6571. TYPE: *Guest House*. HOST: Richard Dean. CLIENTELE: Gay men & women only. LOCATION: In the "Condesa Beach" area.

* Rooms: 4 dbl w/priv. bath.
* Penthouse: 1 w/balcony, patio, dbl bath
* CTV, phone, A/C
* Garden, pool, sundeck, maid service
* Beach: 3 minute walk
* Gay Bars: nearby
* Airport: 15 min.,
* Open: Year round

* Reservations: deposit required
* Rates: (US) $70-$260/day; whole house and weekend rates on request
* **TAC:** 10% (from Odysseus)

DESCRIPTION: Mexican style open-air house accommodating up to 8 people near beach, shopping & nightlife. The whole house can be rented with maid and cook.

VILLA CASA BLANCA
La Condessa, Acapulco. Odysseus (516) 944-5330 or (800) 257-5344, Fax: (516) 944-7540 or (800) 982-6571. TYPE: *Villa*. CLIENTELE: All Welcome. LOCATION: High on a hill near Fiesta Mexicana with view of Acapulco Bay. 4 air-conditioned bedrooms, 5 bathrooms, dining and living rooms, fresh water filtered pool overlooking Acapulco Bay. Modern kitchen, fountain, 3 CTV's and VCR. 2 car garage, 5 telephones and servants' quarter. 3 full time servants (cook, gardner and handyman) take care of the villa and hotel guests. Rates: from (US) $500/day.

CABO SAN LUCAS   ℭ   0114

✈ Los Cabos Airport (SJD)

LOCATION: At the southernmost tip of the Baja California peninsula.

POPULATION: 9,000

CLIMATE: Mild and pleasant year round with temperatures in the 80°Fs (25°c).

DESCRIPTION: Rapidly growing international fun resort town popular with north American tourists. Although there is no established gay scene cruising is possible on **Medano Beach** between the Las Palmas Restaurant and the Hacienda Beach Resort; also check the **Boulevard Marina** at night (AYOR) between the Papagallos Restaurant and Señor Suchi Restaurant.

 ACCOMMODATIONS

HACIENDA BEACH RESORT
Land's End, Cabo San Lucas Bay. Tel: (114) 30122. TYPE: *Hotel*. CLIENTELE: All Welcome. LOCATION: On the 'Gay Beach' walking distance of the village.

* Rooms: 114 w/priv. bath. Suites: 12
* Cabanas: 30 / Townhouses: 10
* CTV, phone, balcony, patio

* Restaurants, bars, pool, marina
* Room and maid service
* Gay Beach: walking distance
* Airport: 20 km / 13 mi.
* Open: Year round
* Rates: (US) $120 - $280
* **TAC:** 10%

DESCRIPTION: Club-like beachfront hotel with a wide variety of accommodations. Beautiful Mexican architecture, gardens and fountains.

MARINA CABO
Blvd. de la Marina 39, Cabo Sabn Lucas. Tel: (114) 30898. TYPE: *Condominium Hotel Complex*. CLIENTELE: All Welcome. LOCATION: Center of resort area, part of the Marina. DESCRIPTION: Studios with kitchenette, balcony, view of the bay, daily maid service. Rates: on request.

CANCÚN   ℭ   098

✈ Cancún Int'l Airport (CUN)

LOCATION: An island in the Caribbean Sea off the east coast of the Yucatan Peninsula.

POPULATION: 600

CLIMATE: Tropical climate. Hot and humid year round with temperatures in the mid 90°sF (34°c) between May - November and in the mid 80°sF (30°c) October-March. It rains heavily between May - September.

DESCRIPTION: An international resort and the doorway to *Mundo Maya* (Maya World), with beautiful beaches, water sports including

scuba diving, luxury resort complexes and superb nightlife. Take a day cruise to the nearby undeveloped **Isla Mujeres** and explore a quieter, laid back and informal island popular with younger tourists.

❖ Gay Beaches: **Shangri La**, nude beach with active gay section among the dunes and bushes, 40 minutes south of Cancun near the town of **Playa del Carmen**. Around Cancun none of the beaches are exclusively gay, but worth mentioning are: **The Mirador**, beautiful stretch of beach at the end of the hotel zone across from the Ruinas del Rey; right next to **Club Med** there is a large rock formation jutting out into the sea with a small beach on either side with some action; the beach at the **Sheraton** is quite cruisy.

Casa de las Palmas
USA/Canada reservations: (800) 257-5344

❖ Public Cruising (AYOR): **El Mirador**, small white lighthouse type building behind the El Camino Hotel good for late afternoon cruising; **Palapa Park**, late afternoon / early evenings, located one block north of Avda Tulum, between Tulipanes Sts in downtown.

BARS 🍸 RESTAURANTS 🍴

● Bars (GM): **Cocodrilos Bar**, video dance club, drag shows, Margaritas 28 (46-024); **Picante**, mixed disco, Av. Tulum 20 S.M. (inside the Centro Commercial Cancun, Plaza Galerias).

● Restaurants (AW): Check out the following restaurants at the Krystal Cancun Resort, Paseo Kalkulcan Lote 9: **Aquamarina**, local & international; **Barotonga** seafood; **Bogart's**, Int'l cuisine; **El Mortero**, Mexican.

λ SERVICES λ

● Cinema: **Cine Perlita**, porno movies, mixed clientele, calle 10, in front of Blanco Dept. Store.

🖐 ACCOMMODATIONS 🖐

CAMINO REAL
PO Box 14, Punta Cancun 77500. Tel: (98) 830-100. TYPE: *Deluxe Hotel*. CLIENTELE: Mostly Straight. LOCATION: Beachfront hotel on Cancun's northern tip. 381 rooms w/priv. bath, CTV, phone, VCR, pool w/swim up bar. DESCRIPTION: Deluxe beachfront resort hotel near the gay beach.

❍ CASA DE LAS PALMAS

Tenkah Beach, Yucatan Mexican Riviera. Reservations: USA/Canada Tel - (800) 257-5344 or (516) 944-5330. Fax: (516) 944-7540. TYPE: *Villas*. HOST: Scott, owner. CLIENTELE: Mostly gay men & women. LOCATION: 68 mi. / 109 km south of Cancun on a private beach called Tankah.

* Rooms: 12; 4 w/priv., 8 w/shared bath
* Suite: 1, Villas: 3 (4 x 1BR)
  w/full bath, patio, ceiling fans
* Bed Types: twin, king size
* Services: maid, laundry
* Sundeck, clothing optional policy
* Recreation: coral reefs, scuba dive,
  Maya temples, ecological parks
* Parking: free, no pets
* Beach: 50 yards / m
* Gay Bars: 75 mi. / 120 km (Cancun)
* Airport: 65 mi. / 109 km (Cancun Int'l)
* Airport Transportation: pick up, bus, limo
* Languages: Spanish, English

* Open: Sept. 1 - May 31
* Rates: $110 - $1,200 w/AB
* Check in / Check out: any time
* *TAC:* 10% (from Odysseus)

DESCRIPTION: One-story Stucco Mexican houses located on private beach in Tanakah a natural habitat community. Casa de Las Palmas does not have air conditioning, but relies on trade winds from the Caribbean. TV is limited but videos are available for your pleasure. Hot and cold gravity fed water is available for bathing and bottled water is available for drinking. Mayan ruins are located in Tulum and Coba, both within one hour drive.

SHERATON CANCUN RESORT
Blvd. Kukulcan, Cancun. Tel: (98) 831-988. Fax: (98) 850-083. US Reservations: 1-800-325-3535. TYPE: *Resort Complex.* CLIENTELE: Mostly Straight. LOCATION: On the beach. 748 rooms w/priv. bath, satellite TV, phone, A/C, restaurants, disco, entertainment, pools, gym, tennis courts. DESCRIPTION: Superior first class resort complex comprising of 3 six-story pyramid shaped buildings and 7-story V-shaped building.

ENSENADA ✆ 066

✈ General Abelardo Rodriguez AP (TIJ)

LOCATION: In Baja California, one hour south of Tijuana.

POPULATION: 250,000

DESCRIPTION: Baja's third city and leading seaport. A delightful city on the northern shore of the Bahia de Todos Santos. Tourist activity concentrate along Av. López Mateos where most of the hotels, bars and restaurants are located.

Ⴎ BAR Ⴎ

● Club (GM): **La Ola Verde**, calle 2da, corner of Gastelum in downtown.

λ SERVICES λ

● Health Clubs (G/S): **Baños Floresta**, mostly Straight bathhouse, Calle 2 No. 1357; **Baños Los Arcos**, Calle 2 between Calles Gastelum and Miramar behind the Hotel San Carlos.

 ACCOMMODATIONS

CORTEZ HOTEL
Ave. López Mateos 1089, Ensenada. Tel: (667) 82307. Fax: (667) 83905. TYPE: *Hotel.* CLIENTELE: Mostly Straight. LOCATION: Downtown on the famous Av. López Mateos. 79 rooms w/priv. bath. Rates: (US) $40-$75. *TAC:* 10%. DESCRIPTION: Best Western hotel in a convenient location.

HOTEL PLAZA
Av. López Mateos 540, Ensenada. TYPE: Hotel. CLIENTELE: *Mostly Straight.* LOCATION: Central. DESCRIPTION: Plain clean hotel with rooms facing the street.

GUADALAJARA ✆ 036

✈ Miguel Hidalgo Int'l Airport (GDL)

LOCATION: On a mile-high plain surrounded by rugged countryside, 150 mi. / 240 km east of Puerto Vallarta and 300 mi. / 480 km northwest of Mexico City.

POPULATION: 2,500,000

CLIMATE: Delightful moderate climate with an average daily maximum of 73°F (23°c) in January and 79°F (26°c) in July.

DESCRIPTION: A picturesque colonial town with Spanish influence, beautiful parks and fountains. The city was one of the first to fall to Father Miguel Hidalgo in 1810 during the war with Spain and slavery was outlawed here 50 years before Lincoln issued his emancipation proclamation. Guadalajara is attracting many visitors due to its balmy climate, elegant hotels, and talented craftsmen. Although it is a conservative town, there is an interesting nightlife scene for gay travelers.

BARS Ⴎ RESTAURANTS ‖

● Bars/Clubs (GM): **El Botanero**, Javier Mina & 54th St., sect. Libertad; **Chivas**, Calles Degollado and López Cortilla, Centro; **La Malinche**, dance bar, Alvaro Obregón 1230, sect. Libertad; **Monica's**, dance bar, 1713 Alvaro Obregón, sect. Libertad, (643-9544); **El Teller**, disco, calle 66 #30 (between Gigantes & 12 de Octubre) sect. Reforma.

● Bars/Clubs (GMW): **Gerardos**, 2529 Lapaz Ave. Sector Juarez; **Romano's**, disco, 54th St. (before Lacomanche Nightclub) Sector Libertad; **S.O.S.**, popular disco, 1413 La Paz Ave.,

Sector Juarez (626-4179).

● Restaurants (GMW): **Brasserie**, 1171 Prisciliano Sanchez St. Sector Juarez; **Copa de Leche**, 414 Juarez Ave., sector Juarez (614-5347); **Las Sombrillas**, service outdoor in the Plaza, very cruisy, Plaza Las Sombrillas.

λ SERVICES λ

● Health Clubs (Mixed): **Baños Galena**, mixed, 167 Galena St. Sector Juarez; **Baños Guadalajara**, 634 Federalismo sur Ave., Sector Juarez; **Baños Jordan**, 72 Los Angeles St., Sector Reforma; **Baños Nueva Galicia**, steam room, gym, at the basement of the Hotel Abasto, Avda Leazaro Cárdenas 2412, sector Juárez.

ACCOMMODATIONS

CARLTON HOTEL
Av. Ninos Heros & 16 de Septiembre, Guadalajara 44100. Tel: (36) 147272. Fax: (36) 135539. TYPE: *Hotel.* CLIENTELE: Mostly Straight. LOCATION: In a commercial area, 2 blocks from Train Station.

* Rooms: 222 w/priv. bath. Suites: 5
* Floor for non-smokers
* CTV, phone, balcony
* Room & maid service
* Restaurants, Coffee Shop, Nightclubs
* Heated pool, free parking
* Gay Bars: some nearby
* Airport: 9 mi. / 14 km
* Open: Year round
* Rates: (US) $90 and up. *TAC:* 10%

DESCRIPTION: First class 20-story hotel with Mexican-Colonial decor.

ISLA MUJERES   🕻 987

✈ Cancún Int'l Airport (CUN)

LOCATION: Off the coast of Cancun in the Caribbean Sea. 6 mi. / 10 km north of Cancun. Direct boat connection from Puerto Juarez.

HOW TO GET THERE: From Cancun by taxi to Puerto Juarez (10 min.). From Puerto Juarez by boat/ferry, daily/hourly departure from 6:00am - 8:30pm. The crossing takes about 15 min. and cost about US$3. Return service to Cancun operates daily and hourly between 6am-8:30pm.

CLIMATE: Tropical climate. Hot and humid

year round with temperatures in the mid 90°sF (34°c) between May - November and in the mid 80°sF (30°c) October-March. It rains heavily between May - September.

DESCRIPTION: Long and narrow island resort with sandy beaches, palm trees and clean blue water. Extremely informal, it is popular with younger people. The main activity in the evening takes place in the square near the church. The island offers fine beaches, water sports, deep sea fishing and scuba diving.

ACCOMMODATIONS

VILLAS HI-NA-HA
Isla Mujeres. USA/Canada reservations - (516) 944-5330 or (800) 257-5344. Fax: (516) 944-7540. TYPE: *Resort Complex.* CLIENTELE: Gay men & women welcome. LOCATION: On the most tranquil part of the island, right on sandy ocean beach.

* Suites: 6 one-bedroom w/priv. bath
* Villas: 3 two-bedroom
* A/C, phone, CTV, balcony, ocean view
* Snack bar: breakfast & lunch
* Pool, private pier, beach, dive shop
* Gay bars: see Cancun
* Beach: on the beach
* Airport: Cancun (45 min.) taxi, boat
* Open: Year round
* Rates: (US) $90-$240 w/AB
* *TAC:* 10% (from Odysseus)

DESCRIPTION: Beach resort complex. Each villa consists of 2 bedrooms and 3 bathrooms with kitchenette. It can be rented as 6 independent rooms w/priv. facilities. Great for small groups for a quiet and relaxing getaway in the Caribbean Sun.

IXTAPA/ZIHUATANEJO 🕻 753

✈ Ixtapa/Zihuatanejo Airport (ZIH)
5 mi. / 8 km northeast of Ixtapa

LOCATION: About 150 mi. / 237 km up the coast north of Acapulco by paved Route 200. 3 hrs by bus from Acapulco, 30 min. flying from Mexico City.

DESCRIPTION: Zihuatanejo is a lovely fishing port and a quiet beach resort. It offers beautiful beaches such as **La Madera Beach** and **La Ropa Beach**. **Las Gatas Beach** is secluded and can be reached by boat from the town center. **Ixtapa** is a booming seaside resort with sandy beaches and luxury resort hotels.

BARS ♈ RESTAURANTS ♉

● Bar (G/S): **Splash**, mixed bar and restaurant, c/. Ejido Esquina and c/. Vicente Guerrero (408-80).

● Restaurants (AW): check out the restaurants at the Krystal Ixtapa, Blvd. Ixtapa, Zona Hoteliera: **Aquamarina**, Mexican & International; **Barotonga** seafood; **Bogart's**, International; **La Pasta Nostra** Italian.

ACCOMMODATIONS

KRYSTAL IXTAPA
Blvd. Ixtapa s/n, Zona Hoteliera, 40800 Ixtapa. Tel: (753) 303-33 or Toll Free (800) 232-9860. Fax: (753) 302-16. TYPE: *Deluxe Hotel.* CLIENTELE: All Welcome. LOCATION: Center of town near La Puerta Shopping Center and Playa El Palmar. 235 rooms w/priv. bath, suites, rooms for smokers and non smokers, CTV, phone, safe box, A/C, C/H; room, maid, laundry service; wheelchair access, elevator, free parking, 4 restaurants, bars, disco, pool, beach. Gay Bar: 4 mi / 6 km. Health Club: walking distance (mixed). Airport: Zihuatanejo Int'l 8.7 mi / 14 km. Languages: English, Spanish. Reservation: 1 night deposit, payment in full three weeks prior to arrival. Cancellation: 4 day prior notice full refund, less than 4 days 1 night penalty. Credit Cards: MC/VISA/ AMEX/DC. Open: Year round. Rates: season 12/24-4/15 $142-$824; (off) 4/16-12/23 $99-$435. Tax: 15%. Check in time 3pm / check out 12 noon. DESCRIPTION: Moderate deluxe resort hotel. All rooms have ocean view with private balcony. The private village of Ixtapa/Zihuatanejo is one of the preferred holiday destination for Mexican tourists. It offers relaxation, recreation and culture.

JUAREZ ℭ 016

✈ Abraham Gonzalez Int'l Airport (CJS) 12 mi. / 19 km southeast of Juarez

LOCATION: Just opposite El Paso (TX) with a quick bus connection between the two cities.

POPULATION: 1,200,000

CLIMATE: Dry and sunny. Summer temperatures are high but not extreme with a July average of 82°F (28°c). Winters are mild with low humidity and a January average of 55°F (13°c).

DESCRIPTION: Ciudad Juarez is a bustling metropolis specializing in cross boarder industry. It is the largest *maquiladora* city in the world. The center of the gay action is in the center of Juarez near the northbound Paseo del Norte Bridge to El Paso.

BARS ♈ RESTAURANTS ♉

● Bars/Clubs (GM): **Club Nebraska**, Calle Mariscal 251; **Club Olimpico**, popular, some lesbians, Avenida Lerdo 210 sur; **El Angel Azul**, Avda Pronaf 369; **El Herrardo Country Club**, western style, Avda Juárez near Calle Colón; **Omare**, popular fun place specially on weekends,, corner of Calle Corona and Calle Ignacio de la Peña; **Ritz**, attractive neighborhood bar, Calle Ignacio de la Peña.

● Restaurants (AW): **Taco Cabaña**, Calle de las Peña; **El Gordo #2**, Francisco Madero. Both have great tacos and burritos.

λ SERVICES λ

● Health Clubs (GM): **Baños Jordan**, all gay but rather dirty, Calle Santos Degollado; **Polo's Baños**, expensive and fashionable, not exclusively gay but recommended, Avda 16 de Septiembre 558.

ACCOMMODATIONS

You may stay in nearby El Paso (TX) or if you prefer to stay in Juarez you may select the following hotel.

SYLVIA's HOTEL
Av 16 de Septiembre 1977 Ote. Juarez. Tel: (16) 50442. TYPE: *Hotel.* CLIENTELE: All Welcome. LOCATION: 5 mi. / 8 km from Train Station. 100 rooms, priv. bath, pool.

MAZATLÁN ℭ 069

✈ Rafael Buelna Intl AP (MZT) 15 mi. / 24 km southeast

LOCATION: Pacific coast resort in the province of Sinaloa, just south of the Tropic of Cancer at the foot of the Sierra Madre overlooking Olas Altas Bay.

POPULATION: 800,000

CLIMATE: Hot summers and pleasantly moderate winters. The water temperature in the winter is 68°F (20°c), and 75°F (24°c) in the summer.

DESCRIPTION: Pacific paradise resort town with tourism mostly in the Zona Dorada area. This is one of the most popular resorts and active ports in all of Mexico. Mazatalán, is striking with its long white beaches, beachfront hotels and resorts, seafood restaurants, good nightclub, and bright lights. Mazatlán is close to the USA/Mexico border with excellent international flights connection from Denver, Los Angeles and San Francisco. However, many American tourists arrive by car. Beaches of interest include: **Olas Altas Beach** near Centro; **Zona Costera** and the fashionable **Zona Dorada**. For public gay cruising check the famous **Avenida Del Mar** along the boardwalk, or the shady park at the **Plaza de la Revolucion, Centro**.

❖ **SPECIAL EVENT:** Celebrate **Carnival** (Mardi Gras), one of the best fiestas in Mexico, from Wed. to Tue. before Ash Wednesday. A Queen is crowned and prices are awarded. Let the best Queen win!

BARS ♈ RESTAURANTS 🍴

● Bars/Clubs (GMW): ✪ **Pépé Toro**, the most popular bar/disco in town. Meet the local people and welcome to Paradise. Open on weekend 9:00 pm, Av. de las Garzas #18, Zona Dorada (14-41-76). Other (G/S): **Dragon Rojo**, drag shows, Calle José Mariá Pino Suarez, Colonia Francisco Madero; **El Caporal**, Calle Paseo Claussen; **El Jaripeo**, mixed bar at the Hotel Posada de Don Pelayo, Avda del Mar 111, Zona Costera; **Señor Frog**, popular and crowded disco, Avda del Mar, Zona Costera. Also check out the discos on Avda Camarón Sábalo, Zona Dorada.

● Restaurants (AW): **Boca Mar**, seafront restaurant and bar, Avda del Mar, Zona

Costera (81-6008); **Shrimp Bucket** and **Señor Frog**, Olas Altas 11 and Ave. del Mar.

🏠 ACCOMMODATIONS 🏠

EL RANCHO
Playa los Cerritos. USA/Canada reservations Tel: 1 (800) 257-5344 or (516) 944-5330. Fax: 1 (800) 982-6571 or (516) 944-7540. TYPE: *Tropical Ranch*. CLIENTELE: All Welcome. LOCATION: On the beach 1 mi / 1.6 km to the Zona Dorada.

Bar PePe Toro

Av. de las garzas #18
Zona Dorada
MAZATLAN MEX.
http://www.mazcity.com.mx/pepetoro

* Villas: 28 (2-bedroom / 2 bathrooms)
* CTV, full kitchens, A/C
* Restaurant, bar
* Tropical garden, pool, jacuzzi, parking
* Extensive sunbathing beach
* 24 hrs. security
* Open: Year round
* Rates: (US) $100 - $280
* *TAC:* 10% (from Odysseus)

DESCRIPTION: Tourist complex of 28 comfortable villas with a harmoniuos decoration in Mexican motif. Each villa can accommodate up to 4 adults.

LAS FLORES SUITES
Avda Rodolfo T. Loaiza 212. Mazatlan. Tel: (69) 135-022. USA/Canada reservations (800) 257-5344 or (516) 944-5330. Fax: (800) 982-6571. TYPE: *All Suite* Resort *Hotel*. CLIENTELE: All Welcome. LOCATION: Opposite beach in the famous Zona Dorada, 10 min. from downtown.

* 119 Suites, studios & standard rooms
* CTV, phone, A/C
* Room service, elevator, parking
* Restaurant, bar, pool, sundeck
* Beach: walking distance
* Gay Bars: walking distance
* Airport: 5 mi. / 8 km

* Open: Year round
* Rates: (US) $65-$130

DESCRIPTION: Modern beach resort hotel. All rooms and suites w/AC some with terrace and seaview.

MEXICO CITY   © 05

✈ Benito Juarez Int'l Airport (MEX)

LOCATION: In Mexico's Federal District (D.F.), in central Mexico 1,820 km (1,140 mi.) south east of the US border at an high altitude of 2,240 m (7,350 ft).

POPULATION: 14,000,000

CLIMATE: An 'eternal spring' type weather, with daytime temperatures usually between 66°F - 84°F (19°c - 29°c). However, winters can be cold at night.

VISITOR INFORMATION
Ministry of Tourism: (05) 250 0123

DESCRIPTION: Mexico-City, the capital of Mexico, is a fascinating city and a show place of Spanish and pre-Columbian art and culture. Visitors to Mexico City will also encounter a growing problem of poverty, unemployment, and overpopulation. Problems which are normally associated with third world countries. The colonial heart of the city is the Zocalo, the main square with the Palacio Nacional and the Cathedral Metropolitana. The city's main avenue is the Paseo de la Reforma, a 19th century Mexican version of the Parisian Champs Elysées.

● The gay area of Mexico City is in the **Zona Rosa**; it is also an elegant commercial and shopping area with gourmet restaurants and hotels.

❖ Note: Life in Mexico City is hard combined with traffic problems, air pollution and high crime rate outside the Zona Rosa. Visitors should always be careful on the streets and subways.

BARS ▼ RESTAURANTS ¶¶

● Bars/Clubs (GM): **L'Baron**, disco, male strippers, Av. Insurgente Sur 1231; **El Vaquero**, levi/leather cruise bar, Insurgentes sur 1231; **Dandy's Le Club**, dance bar, Martin del Campo 118, Col. Moctezuma; **Dark Room**, male strippers, videos, Bajio 339, Tue-Sun. 9:30pm; **Enigma**, bar & restaurant, Morelia

esq. Alvaro Obregón, Col. Roma; **Bar Fancy**, dance bar, Artículo 123 #66-D, Centro; **El Famoso 42**, dance bar, drag shows, male strippers, Republica de Cuba 42, Zona Centro; **Men**, bar/restaurant, Pensador Mexicano 11, Centro; **Spartacus**, disco, 8 Cuauhtémoc Ave., Nezahualcoyotl City (taxi necessary to get there); **El Taller**, disco, male strippers, Florencia 37-A (basement) Zona Rosa; **El Vaquero**, leather/levy video bar, Insurgentes Sur 1231; **Zipper**, male strippers, many GI's, Av. Reforma y Colon.

● Bars/Clubs (GMW): **Alquimia**, disco, drag shows, male strippers, Ponciano Arriaga 31; **Anyway**, disco, Monterrey 47 (2nd fl.), Col. Roma, 9:00pm - 3:00am daily; **Botas**, disco, drag shows, male strippers, Niza 45, Zona Rosa; **Butterfly**, super disco, Av. Izazaga 9 y Eje Central Lazaro Cardenas 8, Jose Maria Izazaga centro, daily from 9:30pm; **Chocho's Le Club**, pub/tavern, Plaza Garibaldi, Zona Centro, open 24 hrs, **5 Avenida**, disco, drag shows, various events, Bucareli 48; **Dandys Le Club**, disco, drag shows, Martin del Campo 118, Col. Moctezuma; **El Paseo**, mixed bar, mature clientele, Av. Paseo de la Reforma 148, Col. Juárez; **Exacto**, nightclub, popular with lesbians, cocktails and drag shows, Monterey 47, 1st Fl. Col. Roma; **Gina's Place**, 85 Oxaca Col. Condesa; **Bar Mata**, Filomeno Mata 11, Esq. 5 de Mayo, Zona Centro; **Mayday**, popular, clean cut bar, 200 San Agustin St. (Colonia Echegaray); **La Opera**, 5 de Mayo #10, Esq. Filomeno Mata, Zona Centro.

● Restaurants (GMW): **Enigma**, bar & restaurant, Morelia esq. Alvaro Obregón, Col. Roma; **Fonda San Francisco**, typical mexican cuisine, Velasquez de León 126, Col. San Rafael; **El Secreto**, Cafeteria, Espacio Cultural, Xola 1454 Col. Narvarte; **El Viena**, Cafeteria, Cuba 3, centro. Other restaurants (AW) in the Zona Rosa area: **Bugambilia**, Fine food, live music, Cuauhtémoc Ave. & Luz Saviñon St.; **El Olivo**, natural food, 13 Varsovia St, Zona Rosa; **Regine's**, gourmet restaurant on the 21st floor of the Hotel Century Zona Rosa (see information under accommodations); **El Paseo**, piano bar, fine food, 148 Reforma Ave. Other (AW): check out the following restaurants at the Krystal Rosa Hotel, Liverpool No. 155, Zona Rosa **Kamakura**, Japanese; **Cafe Martinique**, local and international.

λ SERVICES λ

● Health Clubs (G/S): Note: the saunas listed are not exclusively gay. Gay men prefer the public steam bath facilities, or use the "special" massage services when offered. **Baños Finis-**

terre, Calle Manuel María Contreras 11, priv. steam cabins, "special" massage service, (M° San Cosme); **Baños San Cristobal**, priv. and general steam cabins, Via Morelos y Av. Revolución, Ciudad Ecatepec; **Baños San Juan**, "special" massage service, Lopez 120 (510-4602); **Baños Torre Nueva**, sauna, steam bath, "special" massage service, 42 Alvaro Obregon (Colonia Roma); **Baños Señorial**, Isabel Católica, Zona Centro, steam room, "special" massage service.

 **ACCOMMODATIONS**

ARISTOS HOTEL
Paseo de la Reforma 276, Mexico City 06600. Tel: (525) 211-0112. TYPE: *Hotel*. CLIENTELE: All Welcome. LOCATION: Zona Rosa across from the US Embassy.

* Rooms: 360 w/priv. bath, Suites: 20
* CTV, phone, radio, A/C, Wheelchair access
* Restaurant, cafeteria, bar, nightclubs
* Sundeck, saunas, parking (charge)
* Gay Bars: walking distance
* Airport: 15 min., taxi
* Open: Year round

DESCRIPTION: First class lively hotel.

HOTEL CENTURY ZONA ROSA
Liverpool 152 & Amberes, Mexico City D.F. 06600. Tel: (05) 584-7111. TYPE: *First Class Hotel*. CLIENTELE: Mostly Straight. LOCATION: Heart of the Zona Rosa.

* Rooms: 143 w/priv. bath. Suites: available
* CTV, phone, A/C
* Restaurants, Bar w/live entertainment
* Pool (heated), sauna, massage
* Room & maid service, parking
* Car rental, currency exchange
* Laundry & valet service, house doctor
* Gay Bars: walking distance
* Airport: 30 min., taxi, limo
* Credit Cards: MC/VISA/AMEX/DC
* Open: Year round

DESCRIPTION: Striking 22-story modern hotel in the center of the Zona Rosa. Superb amenities, accommodations and service.

KRYSTAL ROSA
Liverpool no. 155, Zona Rosa, Mexico City D.F. Tel: (5) 211-0092 or Toll Free (800) 232-9860. Fax: (5) 511-3490. TYPE: *Hotel*. CLIENTELE: All Welcome. LOCATION: Heart of the Pink Zone (Zona Rosa) walk to clubs and restaurants. 302 rooms w/priv. bath, suites, rooms for smokers and non smokers, CTV, phone, safe box,

A/C, C/H; room, maid, laundry service; wheelchair access, elevator, free parking. 2 restaurants, bar, shops, pool. Gay Bars: walking distance. Health Club: on premises. Airport: Benito Juarez 7.5 mi. / 12 km. Train Station: 3.5 mi. / 6 km. Languages: Spanish, English. Reservation: 1 night deposit, payment in full three weeks prior to arrival. Cancellation: 4 days full refund, less than 4 days 1 night penalty. Credit Cards: MC/VISA/AMEX/DC. Open: Year round. Rates: season $120 - $1,000; call for specials for weekend rates. Tax: 15%. Check in time 3pm / check out 1pm. DESCRIPTION: Superior first class hotel in the heart of the famous Pink Zone, the financial and upscale commercial district of Mexico City. It has the perfect location to discover the historical delights of the city for business and pleasure.

HOTEL ROYAL ZONA ROSA
Amberes 78, Col. Juarez, Mexico-City DF 06600. Tel: (905) 525-4850. Fax: (905) 514-3330. TYPE: *Hotel*. CLIENTELE: Mostly Straight. LOCATION: In the heart of the Zona Rosa. 163 rooms. rates: from (US) $80. Moderate first class hotel.

MONTERREY   *©*   08

✈ Mariano Escobedo Intl AP (MTY)
   15 mi. / 24 km northeast

LOCATION: Northeastern Mexico, 253 km / 160 mi. south of the USA border, 915 km / 570 mi from Mexico City.

POPULATION: 3,000,000

CLIMATE: Very hot summers and very cold winters.

DESCRIPTION: Capital of the Nuevo León State, Monterrey is basically a large, industrial and polluted town. Inspite of its touristic shortfalls, the town some interesting opportunities for gay nightlife. Areas of interest to gay visitors are: **Zona Rosa**; **Plaza Hidalgo** and **Plaza Morelos**.

Y BARS Y

● Bars/Clubs (GM): **Arcano**, dance club, Calle Ruperto Martinez Oriente; **Botana**, Calle Matamoros, Poniente 164; **La Napoleon**, video bar, Calle Garibaldi Sur 727 y 731.

● Bars/Clubs (GMW): **Fridays**, neighborhood

bar, Calle Padre Mier, Poniente; **Scorpio**, disco club, drag shows, male strippers, Calle Padre Mier, Oriente 860.

λ SERVICES λ

● Health Clubs (GM): **Baños Capri**, mixed clientele, large and clean, Calle Domínguez Poniente 957; **Baños Orientales**, exclusively gay sauna, good action, Calle Hidaldgo Oriente 310, Ciudad Guadalupe (672-843).

ACCOMMODATIONS

AMBASSADOR HOTEL
Hidalgo 310 Oriente. Monterrey. Tel: (8) 340-6390. TYPE: *Hotel.* CLIENTELE: Mostly Straight. LOCATION: Downtown at Civic Center. 240 rooms w/priv. bath.

HOTEL RIO
Padre Mier 194, Poniente. Monterrey. Tel: (8) 344-9040. TYPE: *Hotel.* CLIENTELE: Mostly Straight. LOCATION: Center of town.

PUERTO VALLARTA © 322

✈ Gustavo Diaz Ordaz Airport (PVR)
4 mi. / 6 km north

LOCATION: In northwestern Jalisco on the Pacific Ocean.

POPULATION: 70,000

CLIMATE: Hot summers (80°F / 30°c) and warm winters (68°F / 20°c).

DESCRIPTION: Puerto Vallarta was the site of classic film "Night of the Iguana". The town is divided by the River Cuale. The expensive hotels, resorts, the airport and the port are located north of the river, and the cheap hotels, and the bus terminal are located south of the river. The resort offers beaches, sports and camping. Puerto Vallarta is rapidly becoming one of the hottest up & coming gay destination.

❖ **TRAVEL SEASON:** The high season for travel is **October 15 - April 30** where prices for accommodations generally double and are in short supply. A six to four month notice is necessary to secure reservations during this period. The most popular time of the year to be in Puerto Vallarta are: Haloween, Thanksgiving, Christmas and New Year. During holidays a minimum stay of 7 nights is requested.

❖ Gay Beaches: **Blue Chairs Beach** in front of Tito's Bar, it is the town's official "gay beach" towards the southern end of Playa de Los Muertos, South of Rio Cuale; Beach opposite Océano Palace Hotel, **Playa del Sol Beach**, and **Dorado Beach**.

BARS ♈ RESTAURANTS 🍴

● Bars/Clubs (GMW): **Los Balcones**, circular bar with balcony tables, restaurant disco, Juárez 182 & Liberdad (246-71); **Café Sierra**, bar, café and restaurant, Insurgentes 109 (227-48); **Espejos**, dance bar, Juárez 182 at Libertad; **Club Paco Paco**, entertainment complex, bars, cantina, large disco, Ignacio L. Vallarta 278, Col. Emiliano Zapata (21899); **Paco's Ranch**, video dance bar with strip shows daily, Venustiano Carranza 239 (around the bloc from Club Paco); **El Rancho**, C&W dance bar, lots of locals, happy hour, Ignacio Vallarta 264; **Xanadu**, dance club, look for the huge palapa on the east side of the hill off Hwy 200 on the left just after the Pemex gas station; **Zotano**, basement disco and upstairs bar, Morelos 101 Plaza Rio.

● Restaurants (GM): **Club Paco Paco**, Mexican cantina, Ignacio L. Vallarta 278, Col. Emiliano Zapata (21899); Others (AW): **Adobe Cafe**, stuff chili, Hidalgo 224 near Libertad (31374); **Le Bistro**, Art Deco dining on an island in the middle of the River **Café Olé**, upscale French, Basilio Badillo 300 (22-877); **Chez Elena**, garden restaurant, local cuisine, Matamoros 520; **Choco Banana**, 147 C/ Amapas (behind El Dorado); **Los Balcones**, restaurant & bar, Juárez 182 & Liberdad (246-71); **Bombos**, Corona 327, Col. El Centro; **Mama Mias**, do your own taco restaurant, Diaz Ordiaz 840; **La Palapa**, seafood, beach location, Amapas & Pulpito; **Red Cabbage**, regional cuisine in a funkie decor, c/ rio Ribera 206-A; **Santos**, restaurant & bar, Francisca Rodriguez 136, Col. Olas Altas. Also check out the following restaurants at the Krystal Vallarta Resort, Ave. de las Garzas s/n.

λ SERVICES λ

● Cooking Classes (GMW): **Memo's Pancake House**, learn art of Mexican cooking, Basilio Badillo 289.

● Health Clubs (GM): **Spa 564**, Olas Altas 564 at Manuel Dieguez).

● Massage (GM): **Karl Winkler**, wonderful relaxing, and rejuvenating legitimate massage (90-329-21921).

● Reservation Service (GMW):**Doin' It Right Travel**, villas, condos, gay hotels & tours in Puerto Vallarta, 150 Franklin #208, San Francisco, CA 94102. Tel: (415) 621-3576, or (800) 936-3646. Fax: (415) 708-4356. Email: skinner@aol.com

ACCOMMODATIONS

○ CASA PANORAMICA

Apt. Postal 114, Puerto Vallarta, Jal 48300. Tel: (011-52-322) 2-3656. USA - Tel: (800) 745-7805. Fax: (808) 324-1401. TYPE: *Bed & Breakfast.* HOST: Jim H. O'Daniel. CLIENTELE: Mostly Gay. LOCATION: South Puerto Vallarta in the Conchas Chinas area. 3/4 mi. / 1 km to Main Square. Taxis and buses in front of the house.

* Rooms: 6 dbl w/priv. bath. Suite: 1
* Smoking allowed in rooms
* CTV (lounge), phone (public), terraces
* Cooking facilities, maid service
* No wheelchair access
* Pool, sundeck, free parking
* Beach: 3 blocks (mixed)
* Gay Bars: 5 - 14 blocks
* Health Club: 5 blocks
* Airport: 8 km / 5 mi., taxi
* Languages: English, Spanish
* Reservations: 1 night deposit
* Cancellation: 30 days in advance
* Credit Cards: MC/VISA/AMEX/DISC
* Open: Year round (closed in August)
* Rates: (US) $70-$95 (Nov.-May 31); $50-$75 (June - Oct. 31) w/AB. Tax: 15%
* *TAC:* 10%
* Email: casapano@ pvnet.com

DESCRIPTION: Dramatic 11,000 sq.ft. villa on 5 levels, perched on the side of the majestic Sierra Madre mountains with views of the bahia Banderas and the coastline. All rooms have spectacular views. *IGTA*

FONTANA DE MAR

Puerto Vallarta. USA/Canada reservations - Tel: (516) 944-5330 or (800) 257-5344. Fax: (516) 944-7540. TYPE: *Resort Hotel.* CLIENTELE: All Welcome. LOCATION: One block from Playa de los Muertos beach, 5 min. walk to downtown.

* Rooms: 42 w/priv. bath
* 9 Jr suites w/kitchenettes
* CTV, phone, A/C, balcony (some)
* Restaurant, bar, rooftop pool & sundeck
* Beach: nearby (1 block)
* Open: Year round
* Rates: (US) $40-$70 w/CbB
* *TAC:* 10%

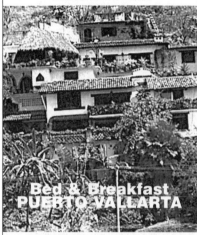

casa panoramica

A ROOM WITH A VIEW...

Bed & Breakfast
PUERTO VALLARTA

**FOR INFORMATION AND RESERVATIONS
CALL 1-(800)-745-7805 (USA)
OR 011-52-322-23656 (MEXICO)**

DESCRIPTION: Tourist class Spanish colonial style hotel. Rooms are simply furnished but clean and comfortable.

KRYSTAL VALLARTA

Ave. de Las Garzas, Puerto Vallarta 48300. Tel: (322) 408-02 or Toll Free (800) 232-9860. Fax: (322) 402-22. TYPE: *Deluxe Hotel.* CLIENTELE: All Welcome. LOCATION: On 25 acres of private beach between Playa del Posada and Playa de Oro. 420 rooms w/priv. bath, 57 suites, 33 villas (99 villas rooms), rooms for smokers and non smokers, CTV, safe box, C/H, A/C; room, maid, laundry service; wheelchair access, elevator, free parking, 5 restaurants, bar, club, shops, 3 pools (3). Beach: on the beach (mixed). Gay Bars: 3 mi / 5 km (several bars). Health Club: 2.5 mi / 4 km. Airport: Gustavo Diaz Ordaz 1.9 mi / 3 km. Languages: Spanish, English. Reservation: 1 night deposit, payment in full three weeks prior to arrival. Credit Cards: MC/VISA/AMEX/ DC. Open: Year round. Rates: season 12/24-4/15 $130-$455; (off) 4/16-12/23 $110-$385 Tax: 15%. call for specials. Check in time 3pm/ check out 12 noon. DESCRIPTION: Hacienda-style self-contained tropical paradise resort. Guest can relax in the plush tropical gardens and enjoy moonlit strolls along cobblestone paths and bubbling fountains. Electric golf carts provide on site transportation on request.

○ MOLINO DE AGUA

Puerto Vallarta. USA/Canada reservations -
Tel: (516) 944-5330 or (800) 257-5344. Fax:
(516) 944-7540. TYPE: *Resort Hotel.* CLIEN-
TELE: All Welcome. LOCATION: Right on
Playa de los Muertos beach in town.

* Rooms & Suites: 64 w/priv. bath & A/C
* Private terrace, garden or ocean view
* Maid service, parking
* Pools (2), jacuzzi, restaurant, cafeteria
* Gay bars: walking distance
* Beach: on the beach
* Season: Year round
* Rates: (US) $80-$140
* *TAC:* 10% (from Odysseus)

DESCRIPTION: Charming seaside resort.
Units vary from small pool or garden side cabins, to large ocean-side suites and junior suites.
All units are fully air-conditioned. A short walk
to everything. No need for taxi.

○ PLAYA LOS ARCOS

Puerto Vallarta. USA/Canada reservations -
Tel: (516) 944-5330 or (800) 257-5344. Fax:
(516) 944-7540. TYPE: *Resort Hotel.* CLIEN-
TELE: All Welcome. LOCATION: Beachfront
on the main beach "Playa del Sol" on the south
shore of Puerto Vallarta, a 5 min. walk from
downtown.

* Rooms: 146 w/priv. bath
* Suites: 11 kitchenette suites
* CTV, phone, A/C most w/oceanview balcony
* Room service, maid service, laundry
* Restaurant: **La Mision** w/dinning terrace
  Mexican and seafood
* Bar: **Palapa Bar** live music
* Pool, solarium, tennis court
* Maid and laundry service, glass elevator
* Open: Year round
* Rates: (US) $70 - $130 w/Bb
* *TAC:* 10% (from Odysseus)

DESCRIPTION: First class beach resort complex. All rooms are fully air-conditioned with 2
double beds or kingbed. Large master suites
w/kitchenette. Excellent location and service.

TIJUANA   ✆   066

✈ General Abelardo Rodriguez AP (TIJ)

LOCATION: Border town, 17 mi. / 27 km south
of downtown San Diego (CA).

POPULATION: 1,500,000

CLIMATE: see San Diego (USA)

Gay/Lesbian Visitor Information
Tijuana Gay Community Info Hotline
Tel: (066) 880267

DESCRIPTION: Tijuana is probably the most visited city in the world with over 55 million people legally crossing the border each year. A city exploding with poor population, sharing a dream to be on the other side of the border. Due to recent government efforts, the town received new life with planned renovation and reconstruction. For those who wish to venture into the Tijuana experience there is a trolley reaching the border from San Diego, and US and Mexican customs are open 24 hours a day.

❖ Gay Beaches: **Rosarita Beach**, 30 minutes south of Tijuana, and along the coast from Playa Tijuana to Punta Bandera off of Hwy 1, or the Tijuana-Ensenada Toll Road.

❖ Note: It is best not to drive to Tijuana from San Diego, unless you are going to Ensenada. Traffic at the border crossing is chaotic and the Customs return wait is about one hour until late at night.

BARS 🍴 RESTAURANTS 🍴

Most of the gay bars and clubs are located in downtown Tijuana.

● Bars/Clubs (GM): **El Ranchero**, 1949 Plaza Santa Cecilia (85-2800); **El Taurino**, the oldest gay bar in town, some hustlers, 189 Niños Héros (85-2478); **Emilio's**, popular café, live music, America Parking Complex on 3rd, 1810 Calle Tercera #11 (3 St.) (88-0267); **Los Equipales**, dance bar, young crowd, 2024 7th St. (88-3006) across from the "Jai Alai Palace"; **Mi Kasa**, bar & disco, 1923 4th St. (81-7091); **Mike's Disco**, on Revolucion near the corner of 6th.

● Bars/Clubs (GMW): **Jardin de Ala**, popular café, live music, Constitución 808, 2nd fl.; **Noa-Noa**, disco & bar, some hustlers, fun atmosphere, 150 "D" Ave. corner Calle Primera, centro (86-2207); **Paradigm**, dance club, connected to Emilio's Cafe, America Parking Complex

on 3rd St., 1810 Calle Tercera #11; **Tare**, dance bar, Calle Tercera y Av. Jalisco, Pueblo Nuevo.

 ACCOMMODATIONS

If possible stay overnight in San Diego which is only 30 minutes across the border. San Diego offers a variety of gay oriented accommodations which are clean, comfortable and range from the budget to the more luxury oriented. If you must stay in town overnight the El Conquistador Hotel is a good choice.

EL CONQUISTADOR HOTEL
Blvd. Agua Caliente 700, Sur. Tijuana B.C. 22420. Tel: (706) 681-4801/2. Telex: 566-741 HCOMME. TYPE: *Hotel.* CLIENTELE: Mostly Straight. LOCATION: Opposite Tijuana Country Club. 110 rooms w/priv. bath, 5 suites, wheelchair access, CTV, phone, maid & room service, restaurant, bar & poolside bar pool, sauna & jacuzzi. Gay Bars: some nearby. Airport: 15 mi. / 24 km, taxi. Credit Cards: MC/VISA/BC/AMEX. Open: Year round. Rates: (US) $60 - $150. *TAC:* 10%. DESCRIPTION: Moderate first class hotel with fine amenities including 3 tennis courts.

LUCERNA HOTEL
10902 Paseo de los Heroes, Tijuana 22320. Tel: (66) 342000. Fax: (66) 342400. TYPE: First Class Hotel. CLIENTELE: Mostly Straight. LOCATION: In a quiet section of Tourist Zone. 170 rooms w/priv. bath, 9 suites, CTV, phone, A/C, restaurants, pool w/patio. Gay Bars: some nearby. Airport: 5 mi. / 8 km. Rates: (US) $60 and up. *TAC:* 10%. DESCRIPTION: First class commercial hotel in a central location. Convenient to the local gay scene.

PLAZA de ORO
calle 2da, Benito Juárez y Av. D. Miguel F. Marínez, Tijuana. Tel: (66) 851437, 853776, 853891. TYPE: *Hotel.* CLIENTELE: Mostly Straight. LOCATION: Central downtown, close to gay bars, 10 min. to the USA border. 36 rooms w/priv. bath, CTV, phone, A/C, restaurant, bar, pool, parking. Gay Bars: One block from the Noa Noa club, and a short cab ride from the other gay clubs. Airport: 25 min., taxi. Season: Year round. Rates: (US) $40-$65. *TAC:* 10%. DESCRIPTION: Contemporary style Best Western hotel offering good accommodations in a central location.

MONACO

AREA: 368 acres
POPULATION: 30,000
CAPITAL: Monaco Ville
CURRENCY: Monégasque Franc or FF
OFFICIAL LANGUAGES: French
MAJOR RELIGIONS: Roman Catholicism
Telephone: 377
Nat'l Holiday: Nov. 19, Fête Nationale
Official Time: G.M.T. + 1 or 2
Electricity: 11o/240v 50c AC
Exchange Rate: 1US$ = FF 4.86
National Airline: none

LAW REGARDING HOMOSEXUALITY:
The age of consent that can be tolerated according to the law for sexual relationship between two men is 16. However, the Principality is very small and conservative. There is no established gay scene in Monaco. The nearest city with established gay nightlife is Nice (France), which is only 30 min. away by car, bus or train.

MONTÉ CARLO

✈ Côte d'Azur Airport (NCE)
(Nice / France 15 mi. / 24 km SW)

LOCATION: On the Mediterranean at the foot of the southern Alps.

POPULATION: 25,000

CLIMATE: Pleasant Mediterranean climate. Warm and sunny summers, temperate winters.

DESCRIPTION: The tiny one-square mile principality is comprised of four districts. Monte Carlo is located in a scenic setting overlooking the blue Mediterranean bay. Monaco is synonymous with all that is luxurious and glittering in the world of travel.

❖ Recreation: The principality offers world class casinos: **Casino de Monte Carlo**, Place du Casino; Loews Monte Carlo, American style casino, 12 ave. des Spelugues; **Monte Carlo Sporting Club & Casino**, Ave. Princesse Grace; and the **Cafe de Paris**, a large walk in casino at the Place du Casino. An international health spa is located at the **Loews**.

The gay scene in Monte Carlo is very limited. There is some gay cruising in the following public places: Avenue Princesse Grace, Promenade de St.-Bache; Place du Casino and Ave. St. Martin (avenue and gardens).

⊻ BARS ⊻

● Bars (G/S): **Sea Club**, Ave. Princesse Grace; **Tip-Top**, Ave. de Spélugues. For more gay fun check the information for Nice (France).

 ACCOMMODATIONS

HOTEL BALMORAL
Monte Carlo. USA/Canada reservations/information - Odysseus Tel: (516) 944-5330 or (800) 257-5344. Fax: (516) 944-7540 or (800) 982-6571. TYPE: *Hotel*. CLIENTELE: All Welcome. LOCATION: On main avenue overlooking the harbor, walking distance to the casinos.

* Rooms: 77 w/priv. bath
* CTV, phone, A/C
* Restaurant, bar, terrace, parking
* Gay bars: mixed bars nearby
* Airport: 25 km / 16 mi. (Nice)
* Open: Year round
* Rates: (US) $100-$190
* *TAC:* 10%

DESCRIPTION: Traditional hotel, renovated in 1988, with comfortable but simply furnished rooms and suites. Restaurant is closed on Sunday/Monday and holidays.

HOTEL DE PARIS
Place de Casino. Tel: 163-000. TYPE: *Deluxe Hotel*. CLIENTELE: All Welcome. LOCATION: On Casino Square in Monte Carlo. 210 rooms w/priv. bath, luxury suites, elegant restaurant, rooftop restaurant with panoramic views, bars, wine cellar, indoor pool, sauna, health spa. Casino nearby. Rates: $300 and up. DESCRIPTION: Exquisite renowned Palace Hotel dating from 1863. Luxuriously appointed accommodations and first class service.

MOROCCO

AREA: 172,414 sq. mi. (446,550 sq. km)
POPULATION: 20,300,000
CAPITAL: Rabat
CURRENCY: Dirham (D)
OFFICIAL LANGUAGES: Arabic, Berber, French
MAJOR RELIGIONS: Islam, Judaism, Christianity
Telephone: 212
Nat'l Holiday: National Day, May 23
Official Time: G.M.T.
Electricity: 110 volts
Exchange Rate: 1US$ = D 8.35
National Airline: Royal Air Maroc

LAW REGARDING HOMOSEXUALITY: Male or female homosexuality is illegal with a penalty of 6 months to three years in prison or a fine. However, the facts of life are that many Moroccan men do not shun homosexuality and practice it in one time or another.

Note: Morocco is not an easy travel destination. There are some safety problems, and foreign travelers may be hassled for money or drugs. However, it is exotic and fascinating.

AGADIR   ✆ 08

✈ Inezgane Airport (AGA)

LOCATION: Southern resort city on the Atlantic Ocean.

POPULATION: 65,000

CLIMATE: Sub-tropical with plenty of sunshine year round. Winters average temperature in January is 69°F (20°c); Summers average temperature in July is 81°F (27°c).

DESCRIPTION: Popular beach resort between the Atlas Mountains and the Atlantic Sea where sun seekers from France, Britain and other European countries flock in by the plane load in search of sun, sea and wide sandy beaches. Agadir is probably one of the most relaxed Moroccan cities where gay travelers can have fun without too much trouble.

❖ Beach: The best beaches are north of Agadir. The further you go you'll discover beautiful sandy coves. **Inezgane Beach** at the mouth of the River Sousse, 8 km / 5 mi. from Agadir can be interesting.

BARS ⅄ RESTAURANTS ¶¶

● Bars/Clubs (G/S): **Bahaia Club**, fashionable, mixed dance club at the Sud Bahia Hotel, rue des Administrateurs -Publiques (237 41); **Dome**, Ave. Hassan II; **Steak Bar** next to Tislit Apts.

🖾 ACCOMMODATIONS 🖾

PYRAMID HOTEL
Route d'Inezgane, Bensergaou. Tel: (8) 307-05.
TYPE: *Hotel.* CLIENTELE: Gay/Straight.
LOCATION: In a wooded area near the beach.
25 rooms, swimming pool.

TAGADIRT HOTEL
Blvd. du 20 Août, Agadier. Tel: (8) 840630.
TYPE: *Hotel.* CLIENTELE: Mostly Straight.
LOCATION: On a main blvd. facing the beach.

* Rooms: 150 w/priv. bath
* Apartments: 95 (1-4 persons)
* Restaurant, grill, nightclub
* Pool, parking
* Beach: on the beach
* Bars: some mixed bars nearby
* Airport: 6 mi. / 8 km
* Open: Year round
* Rates: on request

DESCRIPTION: Tourist class hotel & apartment complex. Apartments have kitchen, priv. bath, patio, terrace. Weekly house cleaning and linen change. Very private.

CASABLANCA   ✆ 02

✈ Mohamed V Int'l Airport (CMN)
   16 mi. / 25 km south

LOCATION: On the Atlantic Coast between Rabat and El Jadida.

POPULATION: 3,600,000

DESCRIPTION: The largest and most cosmopolitan city in Morocco. Casablanca is a modern city with a European flair; a principal port and the country's commercial and industrial center. In spite of the size of its population, it does not have much of a gay scene, and the attraction to gay visitors is minimal.

BARS ♈ RESTAURANTS 🍴

● Bars/Clubs (G/S): **Café de France**, rue P. Sorbier (223-679); **Int'l Seamen's Center**, Zanqat Azilal (by the docks); **Tour D'Ivoire**, rue de Quiberon (258-120).

● Restaurants (AW): for inexpensive food try the restaurants in the Medina; for quality cuisine try the restaurants at the larger hotels. For excellent seafood check the restaurants along the coast. For Moroccan specialties try **Al Mounia**, 95 rue Prince Moulay Abdallah (222-669).

🏠 ACCOMMODATIONS 🏠

RIAD SALAM
Blvd. de la Corniche, Ain Diab. Tel: (2) 392-244. Fax: (2) 391-345. TYPE: *Beach Complex.* CLIENTELE: All Welcome. LOCATION: On the Corniche, 30 min. from the airport. 150 rooms, 50 bungalows, CTV, phone, minibar, thalassotherapy, nightclub, restaurant, pools, sauna, gym. Rates: US$110-$260. *TAC:* 8%. DESCRIPTION: Fashionable beach resort complex.

MARAKECH ☎ 04

✈ Menara Airport (RAK)
3-1/2 mi. / 6 km southeast

LOCATION: Heart of the country at the foot of the snow-capped Atlas Mountains.

CLIMATE: Hot and dry desert climate. Winter average temperature in January is 52°F (11°c), but winter nights can be cold; summers are hot with highs in the 100°F's (38°c). Spring is the best season to visit Marakesh.

DESCRIPTION: Once the capital of Morocco, Marakesh is a great Imperial city and a meeting place of Arab & African cultures. The exotic Oasis attracts international travelers to its fashionable resort hotels, casino, mosques, palaces and oriental souks. For gay travelers, the coffee shops around the **Djemaa El F'naa**,

the huge square in the old part of town, are great places to sip coffee, enjoy the scene and make some good contacts.

BARS ♈ RESTAURANTS 🍴

● Bar/Club (G/S): **Renaissance Bar**, Ave. Mohamed V (near Hotel les Ambassadeurs).

● Restaurants (NG): **La Maison Arabe**, rue Derb El Ferrane (442-604); **Les Ambassadeurs**, 6 av. Mohammed V (431-451); **Le Petit Poucet**, 56 Av. Mohammed V (431-188).

λ SERVICES λ

● Health Club (G/S): **Bains de la Ville**, hammam, sauna, some possibilities late at night, Djema'a el Fna.

🏠 ACCOMMODATIONS 🏠

CLUB MED VILLAGE
Djemaa El Fna Square, Marakesh. Tel: (4) 444-018. Fax: (4) 444-647. TYPE: *Resort Complex.* CLIENTELE: All Welcome. LOCATION: Famous El'Fna Square in the heart of the Old City. 190 rooms w/priv. bath, pool, Turkish bath, bars, restaurants, 10 min. to airport, Club Med membership required. DESCRIPTION: Moroccan style village with shaded patios and fountains.

EL SAADI HOTEL
Av. Quadissia, Marakesh. Tel: (4) 448-811. TYPE: *Hotel.* CLIENTELE: All Welcome. LOCATION: In Palm Grove adjacent to Casino & nightclub.

* Rooms: 150 w/priv. bath
* Bungalows w/priv. entrance & solarium
* CTV, Telephone, minibar, balcony
* Restaurants, Bars, Pool, Gym, Sauna
* Open: Year round
* Rates: US$120 - $350.
* *TAC:* 8%

DESCRIPTION: Superior first class hotel and private bungalows complex.

TANGIER ☎ 09

✈ Boukhalf Airport (TNG)

LOCATION: Northern Morocco on the Strait of Gibraltar.

POPULATION: 200,000

CLIMATE: Healthy warm climate year round. Sunny and pleasant summer with temperatures soaring to around 38 c (100 F); autumn/ spring are temperate.

DESCRIPTION: Tangier's is Africa's closest port to Europe. The city has an international flavor with a picturesque old town overlooking the port, colorful souks, 17th century kasbah and popular beaches east of the city. The flourishing gay scene of yesteryear no longer exists. The local authorities eradicated most signs of homosexual existence in this city.

❖ Beaches: **Atlas Beach**, **Coco Beach**, **Neptuno**, **Mustapha Beach Club**.

BARS ☙ RESTAURANTS 🍴

● Bars/clubs (GM): **Balima Hotel Bar**, 12 rue

Magellan (39-346); **Café Central**, Petit Socco at Hotel Mauritania (34-677); **Café de Paris**, Place de France; Chez Miami, Tangier's beach; **Scott's Disco**, 8 re el-Mouhtanabi (31-141), off Blvd. Pasteur.

● Restaurants (AW): **Nautilus**, 9 rue Khalid Ibn Oualid (off blvd. Pasteur); **San Remo**, Italian cuisine, 15 rue Ahmed Chaouki (38-451).

ACCOMMODATIONS

RIF HOTEL
Av. d'Espagne, Tangier. Tel: (9) 935-908. TYPE: *Hotel*. CLIENTELE: Mostly Straight / Few Gay. LOCATION: On the beach, overlooking Straits of Gibraltar. 129 rooms w/priv. bath, restaurant, piano bar. DESCRIPTION: The place to stay in Tangier. First class hotel in a prime beach location and tropical garden setting. Exotic Moorish interior, spacious rooms.

NEPAL

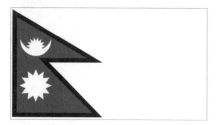

AREA: 54,663 sq. mi. (141,577 sq. km)
POPULATION: 14,180,000
CAPITAL: Kathmandu
CURRENCY: Nepali Rupee (N.Rs)
OFFICIAL LANGUAGE: Nepali, Maithili
MAJOR RELIGIONS: Hinduism, Budhism
Telephone: 977
Nat'l Holiday: King's Birthday, 28 Dec.
Official Time: G.M.T. + 5 3/4
Electricity: 220 volts
Exchange Rate: 1US$ = 54.25 NRs
National Airline: Royal Nepal Airlines

LAW REGARDING HOMOSEXUALITY:
Homosexual behavior is illegal. Foreigners
involved in homosexual contacts can be
expelled. Homosexuality is a taboo. The only
gay and lesbian group NQS is only 2 years old.
The group fights for gay freedom and human
rights. Nepalis are very prudish. Women travelers are not bothered by local men, but are
safer traveling in groups.

KATHMANDU   © 020

✈ Tribhuvan Int'l AP (KTM)
    4 mi. / 6 mi east of Kathmandu

LOCATION: In the Kathmandu Valley surrounded by the Central Hills of eastern Nepal.

POPULATION: 700,000

CLIMATE: 5 seasons prevail in Nepal.
Autumn (Oct/Nov) is clear, dry and not too cold;
Winter (Dec/Jan) is snowy and cold; Spring
(Feb-mid April) is warmer with longer days
and many local festivals; Pre-Monsoon (mid-
April/early June) is hot and dusty; Monsoon
(June-Sept) is the rainy season.

Gay/Lesbian Visitor Information
Nepal Queer Society
G.P.O. 8975, Attn: K.P. Sharma
Katmandu, Nepal

DESCRIPTION: Kathmandu is Nepal's
biggest and most cosmopolitan city. **Thamel** in
the Old City area with ageless temples, shrines
and parks with the appeal of Disneyland to foreign travelers. Thamel offers the best lodgings,
restaurants, cafés, American diners and English pubs. Visit: **Durbar Square** the site of the
Old Royal Palace with dozens of temples and
monuments; **Freak Street** (Jhochhen Tol) was
popular with hippies in the 1960's, but little
remain of this hippy heyday venue due to strict
immigration and drug laws since 1974.

❖ Public Cruising (AYOR): **Basantapur**
(Freek Street); **Ratna Park**.

BARS ⊤ RESTAURANTS ⊪

● Bars/clubs/Restaurants (G/S): **Asta Mangal**
at the Pilgrims House, popular with international tourists; **Bangalore Coffee House**,
Indian vegetarian, corner of Jamal and Durbar
Marg near the American Express; **Cosmopolitan**, pasta, steaks; **La Dolce Vita**, Upscaled
Italian, Thamel; **Manglo Pub**, Durbar Marg,
one of the rare places to meet young Nepalese;
Oasis, patio dining on Freak Street.

⬙ ACCOMMODATIONS ⬙

PILGRIMS HOTEL
Thamel, P.O. Box 3872, Kathmandu. Tel: (1)
416-910. USA/Canada reservations (800) 257-
5344 or (516) 944-5330. Fax: (800) 982-6571 or
(516) 944-7540. HOST: Pradeep. CLIENTELE:
All Welcome. LOCATION: Central location
near the Royal Palace with mountain views,
only two minutes walk to the heart of Thamel.

* Rooms: standard, deluxe and suites
* 24 hrs. running hot/cold water
* 24 hrs. electricity
* Same day laundry service
* Restaurant, bar, cafe, garden restaurant
* Season: Year round
* Rates: (US) $45 - $70
* *TAC:* 10% (from Odysseus)

DESCRIPTION: 5 story economy hotel with
tastefully furnished rooms and suites in traditional style. Rooftop sunbathing. Indoor garden
with restaurant, cafe and bar.

NETHERLANDS

AREA: 15, 892 sq. mi. (41,160 sq. km)
POPULATION: 14,227,000
CAPITAL: The Hague
CURRENCY: Dutch Guilder/florin, (Dfl)
OFFICIAL LANGUAGE: Dutch
MAJOR RELIGIONS: Protestantism, Roman Catholicism.
Telephone: 31
Nat'l Holiday: Liberation Day, May 5
Official Time: G.M.T. + 1
Electricity: 220 volts
Exchange Rate: 1US$ = Dfl 1.58
National Airline: KLM

LAW REGARDING HOMOSEXUALITY: Homosexuality is legal in the Netherlands. The minimum legal age for consenting homosexuality is 16. Dutch law is tolerant when it comes to protection of minorities and this includes the gay community. Homosexuality is openly accepted in Amsterdam, but discretion is appropriate in other parts of the country. The Netherlands will legalize gay marriages in 1995.

AMSTERDAM   ✆   020

✈ Schipol Airport (AMS)

LOCATION: In the Province of North Holland, on the intersection between the North Sea Canal and the sea.

POPULATION: 987,000

CLIMATE: Cool, wet, windy winter, with infrequent snow. Temperatures fall below 32°F (0°c). Summer is nice and cool thanks to the tempering effect of the North Sea.

Gay/Lesbian Visitor Information
Switchboard Amsterdam
Tel: (020) 623-6565 (10am-10pm)

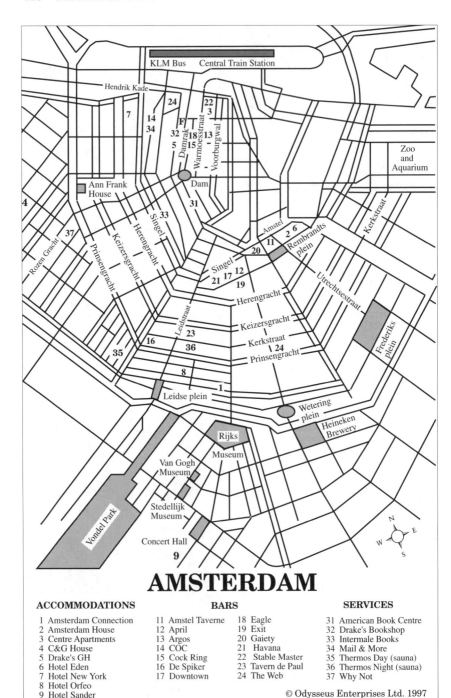

AMSTERDAM

ACCOMMODATIONS	BARS	SERVICES

ACCOMMODATIONS

1 Amsterdam Connection
2 Amsterdam House
3 Centre Apartments
4 C&G House
5 Drake's GH
6 Hotel Eden
7 Hotel New York
8 Hotel Orfeo
9 Hotel Sander

BARS

11 Amstel Taverne
12 April
13 Argos
14 COC
15 Cock Ring
16 De Spiker
17 Downtown
18 Eagle
19 Exit
20 Gaiety
21 Havana
22 Stable Master
23 Tavern de Paul
24 The Web

SERVICES

31 American Book Centre
32 Drake's Bookshop
33 Intermale Books
34 Mail & More
35 Thermos Day (sauna)
36 Thermos Night (sauna)
37 Why Not

© Odysseus Enterprises Ltd. 1997

LIST OF OFFICIAL EVENTS

GAY GAMES AMSTERDAM 1998

AUGUST 1-8

CULTURE	SPORT		FESTIVITIES
Community art	Badminton	Judo	Sport climbing	Rainbow Tour for
Exhibitions	Ballroom dancing	Karate	Swimming	the End of AIDS
Choir festival	Basketball	Marathon	Table Tennis	Opening Ceremony
Storytelling festival	Billiards	Martial arts	Tennis	Amstel Nights
Film festival	Bowling	Physique	Track and Field	Parties
Performing arts	Bridge	Power lifting	Triathlon	Closing Ceremony
	Chess	Rowing	Volleyball	
	Cycling	Squash	Waterpolo	
	Ice Dancing	Softball	Windsurfing	
	Ice Hockey	Soccer	Wrestling	

Gay Games Amsterdam 1998   1000 CV Amsterdam   fax: +31 20 626 1998
PO Box 2837   The Netherlands   E-mail: info@gaygames.nl

DESCRIPTION: Amsterdam is a great city with a gentle humane size. Old brick houses are built along city canals with no high rise buildings. Amsterdam is a major industrial and banking center, with the largest freshwater harbor in Europe. Enjoy a stroll in **Volden Park**, Amsterdam's largest park known to attract modern time hippies during the day, and gay cruising at night. Another tourist attraction is the **Red-Light-District** east of the Dam where heterosexual men line up to satisfy their sexuality as if it was a doctor's prescription.

Amsterdam is known for its museums: **The Rijksmuseum**, (42 Stadhouderskade), is filled with Dutch art and history; the **Vincent Van Gogh Museum** (7 Paulus Potterstraat) with hundreds of the artist's paintings and drawings; The Stedelijk (13 Paulus Potterstraat) devoted to modern art; the **National Shipping Museum** (1-7 Kattenburgplein), the famous **Anne Frank House** (263 Prinsengracht); and **Rembrandt's House** (4-6 Jodenbreestraat). If you are tired of visiting museums and tourist attractions do not worry, Amsterdam is thriving with gay life and activity 24 hrs. a day.

Most Gay bars and clubs are within one to five minutes walking distance of either the Leidsplein or Rembrandtsplein in Amsterdam. The main homosexual organization **C.O.C.**, Rozenstraat 14 (623-4079), operates a club which is geared towards mature, professional clientele.

❖ Gay/Nude Beach: **Zandvoort**, 18 mi. / 29 km west of Amsterdam.

❖ **SPECIAL EVENTS**: **Queen's Birthday** April 30, very difficult to find hotel accommodations for the last week of April and first week of May; **Gay Games V**, August 1-8, 1998, get your hotel reservations early to secure accommodations in Amsterdam for the Gay Games event of this century, accommodations will be hard to get. Book your accommodations with **Odysseus** NOW. Tel: (800) 257-5344 or Fax: (800) 982-6571 (USA/Canada). Tel: (516) 944-5330 or Fax: (516) 944-7540. *TAC:* 10%

BARS ¥ RESTAURANTS ¶¶

● Bars/clubs (GM): **Amstel Tavern**, Amstel 54 (623-4254); **April's**, popular men's disco with dark room, Regulierdswarsstraat 42 (625-8788); **Cockring**, disco, leather clientele, Warmoesstraat 96 (623-9604); **Exit**, disco, backroom, Reguliersdwarsstraat 42 (625-8788); **Fellows**, elegant bar, Amstel 50 (626-3343); **Gaiety**, Amstel 14 (624-4271); **Havana**,

WHY NOT

AMSTERDAM'S
TOTALLY UNIQUE HOUSE OF BOYS

GO-GO BOYS

SEMI-NUDE BOYS LIVE ON STAGE EVERY DAY
18:00 TO 19:00
22:00 TO 23:00
FREE ENTRY

LIVE SEX SHOWS

2 BOYS IN EROTIC SEX SHOWS
THU • FRI • SAT - 20:00
ENTRY - FL 40.00

STRIPTEASE SHOWS

4 BOYS NUDE ON STAGE
THU • FRI • SAT - 23:00
FREE ENTRY

PLUS

BOYS ★ BOYS ★ BOYS

GOODLOOKING GUYS ALWAYS AVAILABLE
2 BARS - CINEMA
S&M PLAYROOM - UNIQUE MASSAGE SERVICE
ESCORT & CALL BOY SERVICE

ESCORTS • INFO. CALL (020) 6274 374
OPEN 7 DAYS 12:00 - 02:00

N.Z. VOORBURGWAL 28
1012 RZ AMSTERDAM

WRITE FOR OUR FREE ILLUSTRATED BROCHURES
BOYS ARE OVER 18 YEARS OF AGE

BLUE BOY

Cuban style disco/bar, no dress or entry restriction, one of the best in Amsterdam, Reguliersdwarsstraat 17 (620-6788); **It**, large popular disco, Amstelstraat 24 (625-0111); **Krokodil**, Amstelstraat 34 (626-2243); **Mankind**, relaxed canalside bar, Weteringstraat 60 (638-4755); **Le Montmartre**, Dutch sing-a-long music bar, campy atmosphere, drag shows, Halvemaansteeg 17 (620-7622); **Roxy**, Weds gay disco in old movie theatre, Singel 465-467 (620-0354); **Shako**, artists' bar, 's Gravelanddseveer 2 (624-0209); **Tavern De Pul**, Dutch bar, Kerkstraat 45 (622-1506);

● Bars in hotels (GM): ✪ **Orfeo Bar** (Orfeo Hotel); ✪ **New York bar** (New York Hotel).

● Leather bars (GM): **Argos**, Europe's oldest leather bar, heavily macho and cruisy, Warmoesstr. 95 (622-6595); **Club Jaques**, relaxed bar, Warmoesstraat 93 (622-0323); **Cockring**, huge, cruisy, men only disco on the edge of the Red Light district, Warmoesstraat 96 (623-9604); **Company**, American style, Amstel 106 (625-3028); **Cuckoo's Nest**, Nieuwezijds Kolk 6 (627-1752); **The Eagle**, Warmoersstraat 86 (627-8634); **De Spyker**, American style leather/jeans bar, dark room, Kerkstraat 4 (620-5919); **Stablemaster Bar**, JO / Safe Sex parties, Warmoersstraat 23 (625-0148); **The Web**, busy after-noons, 2 backrooms, porn videos, roof garden, Jacobs Straat 6 near Central Station (623-6758).

● Bars/clubs (GMW): **Casa Maria**, Warmoersstraat 60 (627-6848); **COC**, Rozenstraat 14 (623-4079); **Sinners**, mixed gay cultural club, Wagenstraat 3 (620-1375); **Trut**, disco, 165 Bilderdijkstraat.

● Bars/clubs (GW): **Cafe Saarein**, best-known lesbians only bar, Elandstraat 119 (623-4901); **Clit Club**, Prinsengracht 472 (Thur. 9pm-2:30am); **Ellen Schippers**, leather & latex for women, 3rd fl., 1st Jan Steenstraat 112 (618-5879); **Homolulu**, 'Cheers' style lesbian disco, Kerkstraat 23 (624-6387); **Roxy**, popular monthly **Pussy Lounge** dance party on Sunday, Singel 465-467 (620-0354); **Saarein**, Women-only bar, Elandstraat 119 (623-4901); **Van Den Berg**, restaurant, dance club, Lindergracht 95 (622-2716); **Vive-la-Vie**, lively women's bar on the edge of the Rembrandtsplein, Amstelstraat 7 (624-0114); **Vrouwenkafée**, Nieuwpootkade 7 (681-8153).

● Restaurants (GMW): **Backstage**, Knitwear boutique/café, Utrechtsedwarsstraat 67 (622-3638); **Baldur**, vegetarian cuisine, popular with lesbians, Wteringssschans 76 (624-4672); **Galerie Françoise**, lesbian owned mixed café, regular exhibitions by women artists, Kerkstraat 176 (624-0145); **Huyschkaemer**, friendly designer bar/restaurant, mixed artistic crowd, Utrechtstraat 137 (627-0575); **It Café**, popular, good ambiance, Amstelstraat 27 (420-0935); **Le Monde**, Coffee Shop, Rembrandsplein 6 (626-9922); **Le Palais**, French, 65 Leidsstraat (622-8154); **Tempo Doeloe**, Indonesian, 75 Utrechtsestraat (625-6718).

λ SERVICES λ

● Book Stores (GMW): ✪ **The American Book Center**, center of Amsterdam near many gay bars, for books in English only, special gay & lesbian books & magazines section in the basement. Also mail order, gifts and videos. Open: Mon-Sat 10am-8pm, Thurs 10am-10pm, Sun 11am-6pm, Kalverstraat 185 Tel: (20) 625-5537. Fax: (20) 624-8042. E-mail: base@abc.nl. Internet: http://www.abc.nl/gaypage.html; ✪ **Intermale**, Europe's largest gay bookstore, large selection of (English language) books on a diversity of subjects relating to homosexuality. Write for a free brochure, Spuistraat 251, 1012 VR Amsterdam. Tel: (20) 625-0009. Fax: 620-3163.

● Business Services (G/S): ✪ **Mail & More**, postal, communication and business services,

Nieuwezijds Voorburgwal 86, 1012 SE Amsterdam. Tel: (20) 638-2836. Fax: (20) 638-3171.

● Cinemas (GM): **Adonis**, American videos on large screen, coffee, back room, Warmoesstr. 92 (627-2959); **Why Not**, Nieuwezijds Voorburgwal 27 (627-4374).

● Erotica (GM): **Drake's**, magazine, videos, cruisy video cabins, Damrak 61, NL-1012 LM Amsterdam (627-9544); **The Bronx**, sex & video shop, Kerkstraat 53-55 (623-1548); **Man to Man**, gay cinema, video rooms, Warmoesstraat 92 (627-2959); **Le Salon**, Nieuwendijk 20-22 (622-6565).

● Escort (GM): ✪ **People**, the leading gay-escort service in Benelux, first class young men for discreet home/hotel visits, or sightseeing. For exquisite collection of young men call 24 hours a day (662-9990). (From USA 011-31-20-662-9990). Internet: http://www.axxel.nl/Business/People. e-mail: people@axxel.nl

● Health Club (GM): **Manadate**, Gay Fitness Center, Prinsengracht 715, 1017 JW Amsterdam (625-4100); **Modern**, mature Dutch clientele, Jacob van Iennepstraat 311, noon-6pm daily; **Thermos Day Sauna**, Raamstraat 33,

noon-11pm, best 4-7pm (623-9158); **Thermos Night Sauna**, Kerkstraat 58-60, 12 noon - 8 am, packed weekends (623-4936).

● Leather (GM): **Mister B**, leather/rubber, SM toys, mail order, Warmoessstraat 89 (422-0003); **Wrapped**, leather & latex clothes made to measure, Singel 434 (420-4022).

● Mail Order/Videos (GMW): ✪ **The American Book Center**, center of Amsterdam near many gay bars. Open: Mon-Sat 10am-8pm, Thurs 10am-10pm, Sun 11am-6pm, Kalverstraat 185 (625-5537).

● Rentals (G/S): ✪ **Amsterdam House**, short or long term rentals, apartments and houseboats, Amstel 176a, 1017 AE Amsterdam (6262-577) Fax: (6262-987).

● Sex Clubs (GM): ✪ **Why Not**, gay porno cinema, two bars, luxury relax rooms, daily free go-go boy shows, live sex shows and striptease, body to body Thai massage, call boy escort service, totally unique and fully licensed gay bordello, N.Z. Voorburgwal 28 (6274-374).

● Sex Shop (GM): **Drake's**, gay store and porno cinema, Damrak 61 (638-2367).

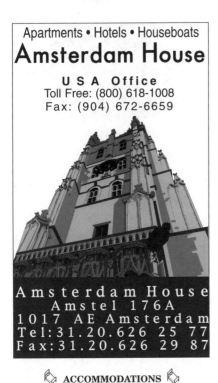

Apartments • Hotels • Houseboats
Amsterdam House
U S A Office
Toll Free: (800) 618-1008
Fax: (904) 672-6659

Amsterdam House
Amstel 176A
1017 AE Amsterdam
Tel:31.20.626 25 77
Fax:31.20.626 29 87

🔖 ACCOMMODATIONS 🔖

NOTE: The demand for accommodations in gay hotels in Amsterdam often exceeds the supply. We recommend that you make your hotel reservation at least 2-3 months before your departure. April 30 is the **Queen's Birthday** and rooms are hard to find, April & May are difficult months for reservations because of the **Spring Break** and the invasion of young UK college students. During the summer months all the hotels request a minimum stay of 3 nights during weekends (Fri/Sat/Sun). **New Year** is very much in demand. Any booking for the New Year period must be at least 7 days and prepaid in advance. A last minute reservation during these periods is almost impossible.

AMSTERDAM CONNECTION
Amsterdam. USA/Canada reservations available from Odysseus Tel: (516) 944-5330 or (800) 257-5344, Fax: (516) 944-7540 or (800) 982-6571.TYPE: *Rental Apartments.* Apartments: studio, one or two rooms w/private or shared bath, use of kitchen & dining room, CTV, radio, tape cassette player, Tea/Coffee making facilities, C/H, phone. Rates: from (US) $110/day. *TAC:* 10% (from Odysseus). DESCRIPTION: Furnished apartments near gay bars. Own key.

✪ APART'HOTEL CENTRE APARTMENTS AMSTERDAM
P.O. Box 15.889, 1001 NJ Amsterdam . Tel: (20) 627-2503. Fax: (20) 625-1108. TYPE: *Rental Apartments.* CLIENTELE: Gay men only. LOCATION: Near the Central Station, Damrak and the gay scene.

* Studios & Apartments: 14
  (one or three room apartments)
* CTV, radio, video/CD record player, A/C
* Cooking facilities, refrigerator, C/H
* Parking: In front of Central Station
* Gay Bars: 5 min. walking distance
* Beach: 20 min. (gay/nude)
* Health Club: 10 min. (Splash)
* Airport: 10 mi. / 16 km, taxi, bus
* Train Station: 5 min. walk
* Languages: Italian, French, German,
  Spanish, English, Portuguese
* Reservations: deposit required + $200
* Open: Year round
* Rates: studio Dfl 145-165 / Apt Dfl 175-195
* Tax: 6%

DESCRIPTION: Self-catering quality apartments furnished in contemporary design. Each with double bedroom, lounge, modern kitchen with microwave and dishwasher. The larger apartments have a separate single bedroom for a third guest. *Note: we must know your arrival time in advance. IGTA.*

✪ C&G Bed & Breakfast HOUSE
Tel: (20) 422-7996. TYPE: *Private Housing.* CLIENTELE: Gay men only. LOCATION: Center of Old Amsterdam, in the heart of the beautiful 'Jordaan' residential area. Walk to bars, clubs, shops and restaurants.

* Houses: 2 w/living-dining room
* Rooms: deluxe rooms w/shared bath/toilet
* CTV, radio, safe-box, phone (in living room)
* Coffee & tea facilities
* TV lounge, roof garden, sundeck
* No pets, smoking permitted
* Gay Bars: walking distance
* Health Club: nearby
* Airport: 20 mi. / 16 km, taxi
* Languages: Dutch, English, Spanish,
  Italian, German, Portuguese, French
* Open: Year round.
* Rates: Dfl 100 w/CB
* Tax: 6%

DESCRIPTION: Two modern houses to share with gay owners. Deluxe rooms some furnished with antiques, each individually decorated.

The shared bath/toilets are modern and clean. *Note: we must know your arrival time in advance.*

✪ DRAKE's GUEST HOUSE

Damrak 61, 1012 LM Amsterdam. Tel: (20) 638-2367. TYPE: *Guest House.* CLIENTELE: Gay men only. LOCATION: 500 m south of Central Station near Dam Square.

* Rooms: 8 w/priv. shower
* CTV (in house gay video channel), mini-bar, safe box, C/H, hair dryer
* Bed Types: double, queen size
* Maid service, no pets
* Shop: Drake's Gay Sex Store / cinema
* Gay Bars: many within walking distance
* Train Station: 500 m / yards
* Languages: English speaking staff
* Reservations: 1 night deposit
* Cancellation Policy: 72 hrs in advance
* Credit Cards: MC/VISA/AMEX/DC/EC
* Rates: Dfl 125 - 225 / (off) Dfl 100-225 (breakfast not included)
* Check in 1:00pm / check out 12:00 noon
* **TAC:** 10%

DESCRIPTION: Guest house with casual Dutch atmosphere. Each room has double bed, private shower, most with en-suite toilet. Free ticket to Drake's Sex Cinema.

✪ HOTEL EDEN

Amstel 144, 1017 AE Amsterdam.USA/Canada from Odysseus (516) 944-5330 or (800) 257-5344. Fax: (516) 944-7540. TYPE: *Hotel.* CLIENTELE: All Welcome. LOCATION: Heart of the city overlooking the Amstel River near Rembrandtsplein. Public transportation - tram 4 or 9 to Rembrantsplein.

* Rooms: 198 w/priv. bath Single/double/triple/quad rooms
* Rooms for non-smokers
* CTV, phone, hairdryer, A/C, C/H
* Bed Types: twin, queen, king
* Wheelchair Accessibility, elevators
* Bar/Restaurant: **Captain's Table**
* Brasserie: **The Garden of Eden** view of the Amstel River (drink, lunch, dinner)
* Public Parking: 'Stopera' opposite hotel
* Safety deposit boxes, elevators, lounge
* Gay Bars: 5 min. walking distance
* Train Station: 5 km / 3 mi.
* Airport: 12 km / 8 mi., bus or taxi
* Reservations: through Odysseus
* Open: Year round
* Rates: $90 - $180 w/CB

In the heart of the city overlooking the Amstel River

€den*hotel*

For reservation/information
1-800-257-5344
Tel: (516) 944-5330
Fax: (516) 944-7540

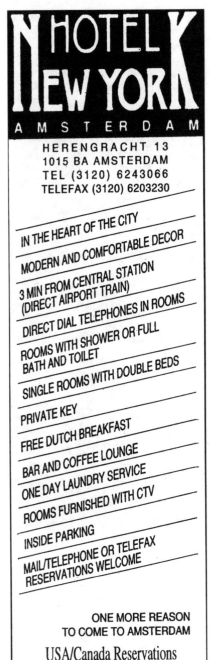

**HERENGRACHT 13
1015 BA AMSTERDAM
TEL (3120) 6243066
TELEFAX (3120) 6203230**

IN THE HEART OF THE CITY

MODERN AND COMFORTABLE DECOR

3 MIN FROM CENTRAL STATION
(DIRECT AIRPORT TRAIN)

DIRECT DIAL TELEPHONES IN ROOMS

ROOMS WITH SHOWER OR FULL
BATH AND TOILET

SINGLE ROOMS WITH DOUBLE BEDS

PRIVATE KEY

FREE DUTCH BREAKFAST

BAR AND COFFEE LOUNGE

ONE DAY LAUNDRY SERVICE

ROOMS FURNISHED WITH CTV

INSIDE PARKING

MAIL/TELEPHONE OR TELEFAX
RESERVATIONS WELCOME

ONE MORE REASON
TO COME TO AMSTERDAM

USA/Canada Reservations
1-800-257-5344

* *TAC:* 10% (from Odysseus)

DESCRIPTION: Fully renovated (1990) comfort-able 3-star hotel in a 17th century building. Individual smoke detectors. All guest rooms are modern with private facilities. Most with twin beds, but some rooms have queen or king size beds. Excellent location for the local gay scene. Specially furnished apartments on request.

✪ HOTEL NEW YORK

Herengracht 13, 1015 BA Amsterdam-C. Tel: (020) 624-3066. Booking available in the USA/Canada from Odysseus: 1-800-257-5344. Tel: (516) 944-5330. Fax: (516) 944-7540. TYPE: *Hotel*. HOST: Arno. CLIENTELE: Mostly Gay men. LOCATION: Central location along one of the most famous canals in Amsterdam. Convenient to gay bars, shopping, and the Royal Palace.

* Rooms: 20 w/priv. bath
  6 sgl / 11 dbl / 2 triple / 1 quad
* Smoking allowed in rooms
* CTV, TV Lounge, phone, refrigerator, safe deposit, C/H, soundproof
* Business fax/phone facilities
* Room & maid Service, paid parking
* Fire Safety Permit
* Beach: 30 min. (mixed)
* Gay Bars: 15 minutes
* Health Club: 2 min. (mixed)
* Airport: 30 min., taxi, bus
* Train Station: 5 min. Central Station
* Languages: Dutch, German, English, Portuguese, Spanish
* Credit Cards: MC/VISA/AMEX/DC/EC
* Open: Year round
* Rates: $150 - $250 w/DB
* Check In: 08:00 / Check Out: 12:00 noon
* *TAC:* 10% (from Odysseus)

DESCRIPTION: Amsterdam's elegant gay hotel consisting of newly renovated 17th century houses joined together into a charming hotel. All rooms have private facilities. Single rooms have double beds. Deluxe rooms are spacious with CTV, full bath and refrigerator. Own Key.

✪ ORFEO HOTEL

Leidsekruisstraat 14, 1017 RH Amsterdam. Tel: (020) 623-1347. Booking also available in the USA and Canada from Odysseus (516) 944-5330 or (800) 257-5344. Fax: (516) 944-7540 or (800) 982-6571. TYPE: *Guest House*. HOST: Avi & Peter. CLIENTELE: Gay men only. LOCATION: In the center of Amsterdam convenient to all the gay action, a few steps from the Leidseplein and Kerkstraat. 5 min. walk to museums and concert hall.

* Rooms: 24; 16 w/shared bath/shower 8 w/priv. shower & CTV, safe box, C/H direct dial phone
* Apartments: fully equipped 1 and 2 bedroom apts w/weekly maid service
* Services: room, maid and laundry
* Smoking allowed in rooms
* Bar (fully licensed)
* Sauna (no extra charge)
* Parking facilities nearby
* Beach: 30 km / 19 mi.
* Gay Bars: many nearby
* Airport: 20 minutes
* Train Station: 10 min.; transfers: taxi, St. car # 1,2, or 5 stop at Prinsengracht
* Reservations: 1 night deposit
* Credit Cards: MC/VISA
* Open: Year round
* Rates: (US) $80-$160 w/DB
* *TAC:* 10% (from Odysseus)

DESCRIPTION: Warm and friendly all male guest house in the center of Amsterdam. Rooms with private facilities have color TV and refrigerator. Off season (winter) special weekly rates. The Orfeo has been serving the gay community since 1969. Own key.

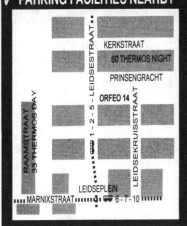

HOTEL SANDER

★★★★

hotel
sander

10 min. from Kerkstraat

Jacob Obrachstraat 90, 1071 KJ Amsterdam
Tel: 020-662-7574 • Fax: 020-679-6067

✪ HOTEL SANDER

Jacob Obrechstraat 69, 1071 KJ Amsterdam.
Tel: (20) 662-7574. Fax: (20) 679-6067. HOST:
F. Lamèns. CLIENTELE: All Welcome. LOCA-
TION: Downtown near World Trade Center
and major entertainment and shopping areas.

* Rooms: 20 w/priv. bath
  3 sgl / 10 dbl / 4 triple / 3 quad
* Smoking allowed in rooms
* CTV, phone, safe box
* Maid, room and laundry service
* Bar: **The Portal** intimate hotel bar
* Garden, terrace, elevator, parking
* Gay bars: 10 min.
* Health Club: 1 block (mixed)
* Airport: 6 km / 4 mi, taxi, bus, train
* Train Station: Zuid Station 2 km / 1.5 mi
* Languages: Dutch, English, French,
  German, Italian, Spanish, Portuguese
* Reservations: 1 night deposit or CC#
* Cancellation: 48 hrs
* Credit Cards: MC/VISA/AMEX/DISC/EC/JCB
* Open: March - November
* Rates: DFL 125-340; (off) DFL 125-250
  w/CB. Check in 8 am / check out 11 am
* *TAC:* 10%

DESCRIPTION: Elegant 4 story hotel. All

rooms are tastefully furnished some with balcony. The hotel overlooks tennis courts which
can be reserved for guests. *IGTA*

❖ Many gay travelers experience the difficulty
of booking a gay hotel in Amsterdam. As a general rule always make your reservations a few
months in advance and longer for the hot periods mentioned earlier. Most gay hotels will not
accept booking for one day during the weekend
(e.g. Friday, Saturday or Sunday). Therefore
never plan to book only part of the weekend. If
you still find it difficult to find a room you can
always consult the **Odysseus** office in the
USA. Tel: (516) 944-7540. Fax: (516) 944-7540.
As a last resort alternative you may consider
the following hotels:

THE HAGUE   ✆ 070
SCHEVNINGEN

✈ Rotterdam Airport (RTM) 13 mi. /20 km
    southeast; Schipol Airport (AMS)
    28 mi. / 45 km northeast

LOCATION: Near the North Sea Coast in the
south of Netherlands (Zuid Holland). 60 km /
38 mi. to Amsterdam and 26 km / 16 mi. to Rotterdam. Nearby Schevningen is a famous seaside resort.

POPULATION: 450,000

CLIMATE: see Amsterdam or Rotterdam

Gay Visitor Information
HIG-COC: 365-9090

DESCRIPTION: The capital of the Netherlands and the third largest city. The Hague is
mostly a residential city favored by retired people who appreciate its neat appearance and
cultural and administrative status. Visit the
Old Town and the **Binnenhof** where the Parliament and ministries are located. Nearby
Schevningen is a fashionable seaside resort
with white sandy beaches, recreation area and
a casino.

BARS ℉ RESTAURANTS ¶

● Bars/clubs (GM): **De Landman**, Dennweg
48 (346-7727); **Stairs**, bar/disco some leather,
Nieuwe Schoolstraat 11 (364-8191); **De Vink**,
Schoolstraat 30 (365-0357).

● Bar/club (GMW): **Boko Bar**, Nieuwe Schoolstraat 1 (364-2374); **Strass**, disco, Balistraat 1 (363-6522).

● Restaurants (GMW): **De Haagse Graaf**, Gortstraat 12 (364-3240); **Wilhelm Tell**, Laan Van Meerdervoort 324 (360-5609). Other (AW): **Café Schlemmer**, cappuccino or light meal, 17 Houtstraat (360-9000); **Tampat Senang**, elegant Indonesian, summer garden, 6 Laan van Meerdervoort (363-6787); **Westbroek-park**, open glass pavilion restaurant in a middle of a beautiful park, French specialties, 35 Kapelweg (354-6072).

λ SERVICES λ

● Bookstore (GMW): ○ **The American Book Center**, books in English only, special gay & lesbian books & magazines section. Also mail order, gifts and videos, Lange Poten 23 (364-2742).Open: regular store hours. Fax: (70) 365-6557. E-mail: base@abc.nl. Internet: http://www.abc.nl/gaypage.html

● Health Clubs (GM): **Eldorado**, Hoge Zand 90 (346-0037); **Fides**, sauna, non-stop video bar, Veenkade 20 (346-3903).

🗝 ACCOMMODATIONS 🗝

CORONA HOTEL
Buitenhof 39-42, The Hague NL-2513. Tel: (70) 363-7930. Fax: (70) 361-5785. TYPE: *Hotel*. CLIENTELE: Mostly Straight. LOCATION: Central location near Houses of Parliament.

* Rooms: 26 w/priv. bath. Suites: 3
* CTV, phone, C/H
* 24 hrs. Room Service
* French restaurant & terrace, sidewalk cafe, brasserie, parking
* Gay Bars: walking distance
* Airport: 40 minutes
* Season: Year round
* Credit Cards: MC/VISA/AMEX
* Rates: (Dfl) 230 - 330.
* *TAC:* 8%

DESCRIPTION: Small appealing 4-story hotel in a central location.

PULLMAN HOTEL CENTRAL
Spui 180, The Hague NL-2511. Tel: (70) 363-6700. Fax: (70) 363-9398. TYPE: *Hotel*. CLIENTELE: Mostly Straight. LOCATION: In the heart of the city, next to the music and dance Theatre.

* Rooms: 159 w/priv. bath. Suites: 8
* 1 Wheelchair Unit

* Rooms for non smokers
* CTV, phone, minibar
* Restaurant, coffee shop, bar, lounge
* Fitness center w/sauna, parking
* Gay Bars: walking distance
* Distance to Airport: 40 min.
* Season: Year round
* Rates: (Dfl) 235 - 450.
* *TAC:* 8%

DESCRIPTION: Sleek elegant first class hotel in a central location.

➤ **Schevningen**
BADHOTEL
Gevers Deynootweg 15, Schevningen NL-2586. Tel: (70) 325-6265. Fax: (70) 355-5870. TYPE: *Hotel*. CLIENTELE: Mostly Straight. LOCATION: Near the beach and the casino. 92 rooms w/priv. bath, rooms for non smokers, French restaurant, bar, lounge, free parking. Rates: (Dfl) 129 - 205. *TAC:* 8%. DESCRIPTION: Tourist class hotel near the beach.

EUROPA HOTEL
Zwolsestraat 2, Schevningen, NL-2587. Tel: (70) 351-2651. Fax: (70) 350-6473. TYPE: *Hotel*. CLIENTELE: Mostly Straight. LOCATION: Near the beach, 15 min. from Hague.

* Rooms: 174 w/priv. bath. Suite: 1
* Rooms for non smokers
* CTV,phone, balcony, C/H
* French restaurant, brasserie, bar
* Pool, Fitness room, sauna, solarium
* Beach: 200 m / yards
* Gay Bars: car needed
* Airport: 40 min.
* Season: Year round
* Credit Cards: MC/VISA/AMEX/DC/EC
* Rates: (Dfl) 200-285. *TAC:* 8%

DESCRIPTION: First class international hotel near the beach and the casino.

ROTTERDAM ✆ 010

✈ Rotterdam Airport (RTM)
6 mi. / 10 km northwest

LOCATION: On the delta of the Rijn (Rhein) and the Maas (Meuse), 40 mi. / 63 km southwest of Amsterdam and 16 miles / 25 km southeast of Den Hague.

POPULATION: 560,000

CLIMATE: see Amsterdam

DESCRIPTION: The largest seaport in the world, Rotterdam was badly damaged during WWII but was reconstructed in a modern and progressive fashion. To visit the city, take a tram tour, and a boat tour around the harbor.

Rotterdam has excellent museums: **The Museum Boymans-Van Beuningen** with great classic and modern art collections, **De Buffel** with maritime objects portraying naval history of the Dutch. **The Groothandelgebouw**, the Wholesale Center, is one of the largest complexes of its kind in Europe.

BARS ⅄ RESTAURANTS 🍴

● Bars/clubs (GM): **Bonaparte**, Nieuwe Binnenweg 117 (436-4100); **Café Keerwéér**, Keerweer 14 (433-615); **Cosmo**, Schiedamse Singel 133-137 (412-3668); **Eye**, disco, leather clientele, Zomerhofstraat 15 (465-6533); **Shaft**, leather bar, Schiedamsesingel 137.

● Bars/clubs (GMW): **Gay Palace**, disco with videos and dark room, Schiedamse Singel 139 (414-1486); **Hommeles**, Schiekade 8 (467-8974); **Roze Musketier**, Schiedamsevest 12 (411-9471); **Sweet Sixties**, Schiedamsevest 146 (213-2032).

● Bar (GW): **De Kanjer**, Maashaven O.Z. 32A.

λ SERVICES λ

● Health Clubs (GM): **Cosmo**, Schiedamsesingel 133 (412-3668); **Finland**, Grondherndijk 7 (429-7029); **Spartacus**, 's Gravendijkwal 130 (436-6285).

🏠 ACCOMMODATIONS 🏠

CENTRAL HOTEL
Kruiskade 12, 3012 EH Rotterdam. Tel: (010) 414-0744. Fax: (010) 412-5325. TYPE: *Moderate First Class Hotel*. CLIENTELE: Mostly Straight. LOCATION: City center near Lijnbaan shopping center.

* Rooms: 64 w/priv. bath or shower
* CTV, phone, C/H, wheelchair access
* Restaurant, cafe, TV Room
* Maid & room service
* Gay Bars: walking distance
* 100 m from air terminal
* Credit Cards: MC/VISA/AMEX/ACC/BC/DC
* Season: Year round

* Rates: (Dfl) 95 - 180
* *TAC:* 8%

DESCRIPTION: 5 story hotel in city center, neatly furnished rooms. Rooms at front are soundproof.

UTRECHT   🕾 030

✈ Amsterdam Schipol Int'l AP (AMS)

LOCATION: In the province of Utrecht, about 30 min. southeast of Amsterdam.

POPULATION: 250,000

CLIMATE: same as Amsterdam

DESCRIPTION: Utrecht is a major city and the capital of the Utrecht province. Founded in the 7th century it is one of the oldest towns in the Netherlands. Utrecht is ideally located to explore the historic castles in the surrounding countryside. The Gay Scene in Utrecht is concentrated in the central part of the town on Oude Gracht along the canal.

BARS ⅄ RESTAURANTS 🍴

● Bars/clubs (GMW): **Body Talk**, cafe terrace, Oudegracht 64, (315-747); **De Roze Wolk**, bar and disco, Oude Gracht 221 (322-066); **Wolkenkrabber**, bar with outdoor terrace in summer, many lesbians, Oudegracht 47 (319-768).
● Restaurant (GMW): **Around the World**, Vredenburgpassage 98.

λ SERVICES λ

● Health Club (GM): **Silver Lion**, Th. à Kempisplantsoen 7-8 (942-332).

🏠 ACCOMMODATIONS 🏠

SCANDIC CROWN HOTEL
Westplein 50, 3531 BL Utrecht. Tel: (030) 925-5200. Fax: (030) 925-199. TYPE: *First Class Hotel*. CLIENTELE: Mostly Straight. LOCATION: Centrally located near Central Station. 120 rooms w/priv. bath, Wheelchair access, CTV, phone, minibar, restaurants, bar, jacuzzi & sauna. Credit Cards: MC/VISA/AMEX/EC/DC. Rates: (Dfl) 250-325. *TAC:* 8%.

NEW CALEDONIA

AREA: 7,358 sq. mi. (19,058 sq. km)
POPULATION: 164,000
CAPITAL: Nouméa
CURRENCY: CFP Franc (Cfp)
OFFICIAL LANGUAGE: French
MAJOR RELIGIONS: Roman Catholicism,
Telephone: 687
Nat'l Holiday: 14th of July, Bastille Day
Official Time: GMT +11
Electricity: 220 volts, 50c AC
Exchange Rate: 1US$ = Cfp 88.35
National Airline: Air France

LAW REGARDING HOMOSEXUALITY: As
a French territory, homosexuality is accepted
here as in France. The legal minimum age of
consent is 15, but it is not advisable to get sexually involved with under 18 because of possible legal complications. Gay men and lesbians
are protected against discrimination on the job.
The law also protects HIV+ and PWA against
discrimination by employers.

NOUMÉA   © NO AREA CODES

✈ Tontouta Airport (NOU) / Magenta (GEA)
30 mi. / 48 km northwest

LOCATION: Southern New Caledonia.

POPULATION: 56,000

DESCRIPTION: The capital of New Caledonia. New Caledonia is a sunny island in the
South Pacific Ocean under French jurisdiction
with a limited autonomous administration.
The island has a pleasant climate year round
and it is popular with Japanese and Australian
tourists.

❖ Beach: **Plage des Nouville**, gay nude beach

near the Kuendu Beach Resort.

BARS RESTAURANTS

● Bars/Clubs (GM): **"421"** , New Center, Rte. 1
(285-700); **Le Babylos**, 44 rue Anatole France
(281-436); **Boite à Bijoux**, 55 rue de
Sébastopol (at Hotel Mon Logis); **Café de
Paris**, Rue de Sébastopol; **Eden**, disco, 55 Ave.
de Sébastopol (at Hotel Mon Logis); **Joker
Club**, rue Surleau (271-777); **Paris Club**, 45-
47 Ave. de Sebastopol.

ACCOMMODATIONS

KUENDO BEACH RESORT
Nouméa. Tel: 278989. TYPE: *Melanesian style
resort*. CLIENTELE: All Welcome. LOCATION:
On the Ile Nou peninsula, 6 km / 4 mi. from
downtown Nouméa.

* Bungalows: 20 w/priv. bath
* CTV, phone, A/C, washing machine
* Bars (2), restaurants (2), pool
* Gay Bars: in town
* Gay Beach: walking distance (nude beach)
* Airport: 50 km / 31 mi.
* Open: year round
* Rates: (US) $130 and up

DESCRIPTION: Beach resort complex.

PARADISE PARK MOTEL
45 rue du Roman. Tel: 272-541. TYPE: *Motel*.
CLIENTELE: All Welcome. LOCATION: In a
park, 5 min. from city. 62 studio rooms w/priv.
bath, A/C, phone, CTV (on request), 2 swimming pool, supermarket nearby. Rates: (US)
$90-$120. DESCRIPTION: Tourist class informal motel. You may bring a friend to your room
but be discreet.

LE PARIS HOTEL
45 rue Sébastopol, Nouméa. Tel: 281-700.
TYPE: *Hotel*. CLIENTELE: All Welcome.
LOCATION: Downtown.

* Rooms: 48 w/priv. bath. Suites: 4
* CTV (VCR), phone, A/C, refrigerator
* Restaurant, bar, coffeeshop, nightclub
* Gay bars: walking distance
* Beach: nearby
* Open: Year round
* Rates: (US) $75 and up

DESCRIPTION: Downtown hotel near ocean
and terminal.

NEW ZEALAND

AREA: 103,736 sq. mi. (268,676 sq. km)
POPULATION: 3,176,000
CAPITAL: Wellington
CURRENCY: New Zealand Dollar (NZ$)
OFFICIAL LANGUAGE: English, Maori
MAJOR RELIGIONS: Protestantism, Roman Catholicism.
Telephone: 64
Nat'l Holiday: New Zealand Day, Feb. 6
Official Time: G.M.T. + 12
Electricity: 230 volts
Exchange Rate: 1US$ = NZ$1.40
National Airline: Air New Zealand

LAW REGARDING HOMOSEXUALITY:
Homosexual acts between consenting males aged 16 and over are legal. Gays and lesbians are still subject to discrimination in areas of housing, jobs and military service but the Reform Bill is a victory for the gay community in New Zealand.

AUCKLAND   ℭ   09

✈ Auckland Int'l Airport (AKL)
14 mi. / 22 km south

LOCATION: On the shores of the Waitemata Harbor, surrounded by water and volcanic hills, 660 km / 412 mi. north of the Capital Wellington.

POPULATION: 770,000 (metro area)

CLIMATE: Subtropical, with lack of extreme cold or hot temperatures. Seasons are reversed. Summer January average is 23°c (73°F). Winters are cool and pleasant, with July average of 14°c (57°F). Average annual rainfall is 1268 mm (50").

Gay/Lesbian Visitor Information
Gayline : 303-3584

DESCRIPTION: Auckland the 'Queen City ' is

New Zealand's largest port and main entry point for most travelers. The city's main drag is Queen Street which runs all the way from the busy waterfront uphill to Karangahape Rd. near Myers Park, which is also the center of the local Maori population. Visit **Parnell Village**, a restored area with art galleries, shops, restaurants and one of the most appealing streets in Auckland.

BARS ⅄ RESTAURANTS 🍴

● Bars/clubs (GM): **Brad's Bar**, at Club Westside Sauna, 1F, 45 Anzac Ave.; **The Bar**, Cnr. Albert/Wolfe Sts. (373-5407); **Depot**, cruise club, 354A Karangahape Rd. (356-731); **Legend**, dance bar, 335 Karangahpe Rd. (377-6062); **Staircase**, dance club/ cabaret, 17 Albert St. (3770-303).

● Restaurants (G/S): **Bayou Cafe**, 422 Richmond Rd. (3767-055); **Le Brie**, Chancery Lane & O'Connel (3744-393); **Hebourside**, seafood, Ferry Bldg., Quay St. (3774-113); **Olé**, Latin cuisine restaurant & bar, 161 Ponsonby Rd., Ponsonby (376-1130); **Pasta Mania**, 25 Ponsonby Rd., Ponsonby (376-5166); **Olé**, restaurant & bar, 161 Ponsonby Rd., Ponsonby (376-1130); **Thailand**, 55 Albert St., St Patrick's Square (303-3890).

⅄ SERVICES ⅄

● Cinema (GM): **Cardinot Gay Cinema**, gay movies, 10 Gore St., 10am-2am (373-3771).

● Drag Shop (GM): **Desiree Costumes**, drag fashion galore, everything for the sophisticated queen, 41 Anzac Ave. (373-2491)

● Health Clubs (GM): **NZCI**, sauna, gym, 151 Beach Rd., (366-1781); **Westside**, sauna, cruise & health club, 45 Anzac Ave., (3777-771); **Wingate Club**, architect-designed sauna and spa complex, end of Wingate St., Avondale (828-0910).

● Leather (GM): **Chameleon**, leather, PVC, latex fashion, 374 Karangahpe Rd. (307-3331).

● Massage (GM): **Golden Eagle**, massage, creative relaxation, 3226 Great North Rd., New Lynn (827-1901).

◈ ACCOMMODATIONS ◈

DRYDEN LODGE
27 Dryden St., Auckland. Tel: (09) 3781-892. Fax: (09) 3781-282. TYPE: *Hotel*. HOST: Peter & Lance. CLIENTELE: All Welcome. LOCATION: 10 mins. from downtown. 45 rooms w/shared bath, restaurant, gym, parking.

DESCRIPTION: Budget hotel.

HEATHMAUR LODGE
75 Argyle St., Herne Bay, Auckland. Tel: (9) 376-3527. USA/Canada reservations (800) 257-5344. TYPE: *Bed & Breakfast.* CLIENTELE: Gay/Straight. LOCATION: Close to city center and cafes of Herne Bay. Rooms w/priv. or shared bath, TV lounge, sun room, sunny verandah. Walk to beach. Rates: (US) $80-$120. *TAC:* 10% (from Odysseus). DESCRIPTION: Restored Edwardian style lodge.

REMUREA HOUSE
500 Remurea Road, Auckland. Tel: (09) 524-7794. TYPE: *Guest House.* HOST: Ray King. CLIENTELE: All Welcome. LOCATION: 10 mins. from downtown. 10 rooms, sundeck, 6 km / 4 mi. to beach, 15km / 10 mi. to airport. Rates: NZ$39-58 w/EB. DESCRIPTION: 2-story Colonial House providing old fashioned comfort.

CHRISTCHURCH   ✆ 03

✈ Christchurch Int'l Airport (CHC)
  7 mi. / 11 km northwest

LOCATION: Pacific Coast of the South Island overlooking Pegasus Bay.

POPULATION: 290,000

CLIMATE: Temperate and pleasant. Summer's January average is 22°c (72°F). Winters are cooler with a July average of 12°c (54°F).

Gay/Lesbian Visitor Information
Gay Information Line: 379-3990 24 hrs.

DESCRIPTION: Christchurch is the most English city outside of England, with the picturesque Avon river flowing through its center. The city was named after after the famous Christ Church college. The city can be leisurely explored with a bicycle. The closest beaches are **North Beach**, **South Brighton**, and **Taylors Mistake** - a great sheltered surfers beach.

❖ Gay Beach: **North Beach** is also known as "Waimairi Beach". Walk north along the beach until you reach a deserted area, head into sand dunes for the gay action.

BARS ▼ RESTAURANTS ¶¶

● Bars/clubs (GM): **Colombo**, at Colombo Sauna, 661 Colombo St.; **Menfriends**, cruise

club/sauna, Upstairs 83 Lichfield St. (377-1701); **Nonames**, bar/club, 674 Colombo St. (3662-558); **UBQ**, 112 Hereford St. (379-1821).

λ SERVICES λ

● Health Clubs (GM): **Colombo Sauna**, 661 Colombo St., top of stairs (667-352); **Menfriends**, cruise club/sauna, Upstairs 83 Lichfield St. (377-1701).

🗝 ACCOMMODATIONS 🗝

QUALITY INN CHRISTCHURCH
Cnr. Durham & Kilmore Sts. Tel: (03) 54-699. TYPE: *Hotel.* CLIENTELE: Mostly Straight. LOCATION: In the heart of the city adjacent to Town Hall. 161 rooms w/priv. bath.

TOAD HALL
162 Lichfield St., Christchurch 8002. Tel: (03) 365-9666. TYPE: *Bed & Breakfast.* HOSTS: Don & Chris. CLIENTELE: Gay men. LOCATION: Town center location, walk to cafes, and bars.

NELSON   ✆ 03

✈ Nelson Airport

🏠 ACCOMMODATIONS 🏠

AUTUMN FARM
RDI Takata, 7172 Golden Bay. Tel: (03) 525-9013. TYPE: *Farm Guest House*. HOSTS: Peter or Richard. CLIENTELE: Gay men. LOCATION: Off the beaten track.

PALM GROVE
Cambria & Tasman Sts., Nelson. Tel: (03) 548-4645. TYPE: *Guest House*. CLIENTELE: Gay men. clean, comfortable, free parking.

ROTORUA   ℭ   07

✈ Rotorua Airport (ROT)

LOCATION: About 158 mi. / 254 km southeast of Auckland on the North Island on the shores of Lake Rotorua.

POPULATION: 50,000

CLIMATE: Temperate year round. Summer January average 60°F (15°c), and winter July average 50°F (10°c).

Gay/Lesbian Visitor Information
Gayline: 348-3598

DESCRIPTION: Rotorua is a popular hot-springs resort town on the shores of Lake Rotorua. The town is famous for it thermal water, and active geysers.

🍴 RESTAURANTS 🍴

.● Restaurants (AW): **Aorangi Peak**, elegant with panoramic views, Mountain Rd (470-046); **Passage to India**, Indian cuisine, 44 Hinemoa St. (485-258); **Rendezvous Restaurant**, lamb specialties, 116 Hinemosa St. (489-273); **Zanelli's**, Italian, Amohia St.

🏠 ACCOMMODATIONS 🏠

ROTORUA INT'L
Froude St., P.O. Box 1048, Rotorua. Tel: (07) 381-189. Fax: (07) 371-620. TYPE: *First class hotel*. CLIENTELE: Mostly Straight. LOCATION: In thermal area. 2 mi. (3 km) from town center. 163 rooms w/priv. bath. DESCRIPTION: Elegant hotel in the thermal area.

WELLINGTON   ℭ   04

✈ Wellington Int'l Airport (WLG)

LOCATION: On the southwestern tip of the North Island, 660 km / 412 mi. south of Auckland.

POPULATION: 350,000

CLIMATE: Temperate Oceanic climate, cooler than Auckland. Average daily temperature in mid Summer (January) is 20°c (68°F), and in mid-winter (July) 11°c (52°F).

Gay/Lesbian Visitor Information
Gay Switchboard: 385-0674

DESCRIPTION: Wellington is the Capital of New Zealand and the seat of the Government. The city sprawls around a natural harbor and is surrounded by green undulating hills.

BARS ♈ RESTAURANTS 🍴

● Bar/club (GMW): **Casper's**, dance bar & cafe, 120-126 Victoria St. (384-1333).

● Restaurants (AW): **Nicholson's Brasserie & Bar**, Band Rotunda, Oriental Bay (843-835); **As You Like It Cafe**, 32 Riddiford St., (893-983); **Preview Brasserie**, 134 Cuba St., (828-780); **Pierre's**, 342 Tinakori Rd., (726-238); **Victoria Cafe**, 59 Brougham St., Mt. Victoria (842-420).

λ SERVICES λ

● Health Club (GM): **Wakefield**, sauna, bar, videos, bunk room, gym, 62 Dixon St., 1st Fl. (385-4400).

🏠 ACCOMMODATIONS 🏠

AMBASSADOR TRAVELODGE
287 The Terrace, Wellington. Tel: (04) 4845-697. Fax: (04) 485-7215. TYPE: *Motel*. HOST: Phil Smees. CLIENTELE: Gays Welcome. LOCATION: City center, near gay scene and the University. 39 rooms, 4 cottages, CTV, phone, A/C.

HAMPSHIRE HOUSE
305 The Terrace, P.O. Box 101, Wellington. Tel: (04) 4843-051. TYPE: *Hotel*. HOST: Cees (Case) M. Kooge. CLIENTELE: Mostly Straight. LOCATION: 5 min. walk from town center. 9 rooms. Rates: on request. DESCRIPTION: budget accommodations.

NORWAY

AREA: 125,053 sq. mi. (323,887 sq. km)
POPULATION: 4,100,000
CAPITAL: Oslo
CURRENCY: Krone (NK)
OFFICIAL LANGUAGE: Norwegian
MAJOR RELIGION: Protestantism
Telephone: 47
Nat'l Holiday: Independence Day, May 17
Official Time: G.M.T. +1
Electricity: 220 Volts
Exchange Rate: 1US$ = NK 6.22
National Airlines: SAS

LAW REGARDING HOMOSEXUALITY:
Discrimination against gay men and lesbians is
prohibited by the law. Homosexuals have the
same legal status and rights as heterosexuals.
The law also protects gay men and lesbians in
the work place and in the society in large. The
legal age of consent is 16. Norway is the second
country in the world after Denmark to allow
same sex partners to register as official partners. Some problems are caused by religious
fundamentalist groups which vehemently
oppose to homosexual lifestyle.

BERGEN   ℂ   055

✈ Flesland Airport (BGO)
   12 mi. / 19 km southwest

LOCATION: Southwestern coast, in a harbor
under Mt. Fløyen, about 300 mi. / 480 km
northwest of Oslo.

POPULATION: 215,000

CLIMATE: See Oslo

DESCRIPTION: Picturesque gingerbread village with a distinctive 18th century grace. It is

one of Norway's most cosmopolitan, cultural
and beautiful cities. Bergen is the home town
of the legendary Vikings. Don't forget to place
this magnificent town on your Scandinavian
itinerary.

Gay/Lesbian Visitor Information
HBB-Bergen
P.O. Box 312, N-5001 Bergen
Tel: 5531-2139 Fax: 5596-1210

BARS ㅜ RESTAURANTS

● Bars/clubs (GM): **Café Opera**, Engen 24 (5523-
0315); **Fincken**, Nygårdsgate 2a (23-1316).

λ SERVICES λ

● Health Club (GM): **Tropic Sauna**, Nye
Sandviksvei 28, open 16:00-23:00 (32-6533).

ACCOMMODATIONS

HORDAHEIMEN HOTEL
C. Sundtsgt 18, Bergen. N-5004. Tel: (55) 23-
2320. USA/Canada reservations: Tel (516) 944-
5330 or (800) 257-5344. Fax: (516) 944-7540 or
(800) 982-6571. TYPE: *Hotel*. CLIENTELE: All
Welcome. LOCATION: Facing the harbor. 69
rooms w/priv. shower/bath, CTV, phone, hot &
cold water, cafeteria, cafe, CTV. DESCRIP-
TION: Tourist class hotel.

OSLO   ℂ   022

✈ Fornebu Int'l Airport (FBU)
   5 mi. / 8 km southwest

LOCATION: In Norway's southeastern coast,
at the end of the long Oslofjord.

POPULATION: 470,000

CLIMATE: From April to September, nights
are very short in Oslo, as the sun shines 24
hours a day above the Arctic Circle. Summers
art short, but pleasant with occasional showers. Winter temperatures are about 20°F (-6°c)
in January, and Summer temperatures are
about 70°F (21°c) in July.

Gay/Lesbian Visitor Information
HOLT: (02) 113660 or 382331

DESCRIPTION: Oslo, the capital of Norway,
is the oldest of all the Scandinavian capitals.

The size of the city is very large, but only a small portion is urban, the rest is a great outdoor playground for the residents of Oslo and tourists from around the world. The principal boulevard in town, and its major orientation point is **Karl Johansgate** which runs from the Central Station to the Royal Palace. Visit: **Rådhust** (City Hall), built in 1950 and houses series of mural paintings celebrating the town's 900th anniversary; the **Resistence Museum** at the **Akershut Castle & Fortress**; the **Viking Museum**, where you can see well preserved Viking ships from the year 800; **Oslo Harbor**; and the **Royal Palace** at the west end of Karl Johansgate.

❖ Beaches: **Bygday**, close to the museums, popular on sunny summer days; **Homolulu**, little sandy/rocky beach some 10 min. walk from Bygday through the forest; **Huk**, a beach on the island of Bygdøy. Take bus Nr. 30 to Bygdøy from the central station (Jernbanetorvet), Weselsplass just behind the parliament building, or from the National theatre; **Sognsvann**, inland lake 7 mi. / 11 km from Oslo, check out the lakelet (Svartkulp) for the nude gay area; **Svartskog**, beautiful beach along the Oslo Fjord where you can find more than just sardines. Take bus Nr. 75 from Strandgata by the Stock Exchange (Børsplassen) to Svatskog.

❖ Cruising: gay cruising takes place at the following public parks AYOR: **Frogenparken** mainly during early evening, nights; **Sofienbergparken**, between Church and school in the evenings; **Stensparken**, evenings and nights.

BARS ♈ RESTAURANTS 🍴

● Bars/clubs (GM): **Andy Capp**, Fritdjof Nanses Plass 4 (414-165); **Den Sorte Enke**, Oslo's largest disco, 3 bars, yard open in the summer, Møllergatan 23 (110-560); **London Pub**, C.J. Hambross Plass 5 (414-126); **Potpourrie**, dance club, øvreVollgate (2241-1440).

● Café/Clubs (GW): **Coco Chalet**, Ostre Slotsgate 8; **Centrum Scene**, Arbeidersamfunnens Plass 1; **London Pub**, Hambros Plass 5 (22:00-04:00).

● Restaurants (GMW): **Molina**, coffee shop, St. Olavs Plass 2 (2236-1594); Other (AW):

Annen Etage, French and Norwegian Cuisine, Hotel Continental, Stortings Gate 24/26 (41 90 60); **Étoile**, French and Norwegian cuisine, on the top floor of the Grand Hotel, Karl Johans Gate 31 (42 93 90); **La Mer**, best fish and seafood restaurant in Oslo, Pilestredet 31 (203445); **Theatrecaféen**, Oslo favorite restaurant, much frequented by artists, at the Hotel Continental, Stortings Gate 24/26 (41 90 60); **Cafe Sjakk Matt**, popular Oslo Cafe, Haakon VII's gate 5, near Vika (42 32 27), moderately priced.

λ SERVICES λ

● Erotica (GM): **Gay International**, Rodstedsgate 2 (203-736).

● Health Clubs (GM): **Club Hercules**, sauna, solarium, videos, gym, Stenersgate 22a (171-735); **My Friend Club**, sauna, solarium, videos, Calmeyersgt. 15 (36-2221).

🔑 ACCOMMODATIONS 🔑

ANSGAR HOTEL
Moellergrt 26, Oslo N-0179. Tel: (2) 204-735. Fax: (2) 205-453. TYPE: *Hotel*. CLIENTELE: All Welcome. LOCATION: Central, over shops near Youngstroget Market Place. 58 rooms w/shared or priv. bath, phone, bath on each floor, dining room, lounge, parking Gay Bars within walking distance, health club sauna nearby; 13 km / 8 mi., to airport; 1 km / 800 yards to train station; Open year round. Rates: (US) $80 - $130. *TAC:* 8%. DESCRIPTION: Tourist class hotel in the heart of the gay scene.

HOTEL CONTINENTAL
Stortingsgaten 24/26, Oslo 1. Tel: (2) 41 90 60. TYPE: Hotel. CLIENTELE: Gay/Straight. LOCATION: Between the National Theatre and Town Hall, overlooking the Palace Park. 169 rooms w/priv. bath. 12 Suites, CTV, phone, A/C, French restaurant, Vienna style cafe, room & maid service; Gay Bars on premises, other nearby; 5 mi. (8 km) to airport. Credit Cards: MC/VISA/AMEX/DC/ACC; open year round. Rates: (US) $220-$280. *TAC:* 10%. DESCRIPTION: Graceful Victorian deluxe hotel with spacious and charmingly appointed rooms and suites. The bars and restaurants at the hotel are known for their quality and attract many artists and gay customers.

PANAMA

AREA: 29,761 sq. mi. (77,082 sq. km)
POPULATION: 2,500,000
CAPITAL: Panama City
CURRENCY: balboa (b)
Panama is one of the few countries in the world which issue no paper money. US bank notes are used exclusively called balboas. Silver coins are called pesos.
OFFICIAL LANGUAGE: Spanish
MAJOR RELIGION: Roman Catholicism
Telephone: 507
Nat'l Holiday: G.M.T. -5
Official Time: Nov. 4, Independence. Day
Electricity: 220 volts
Exchange Rate: 1US$ = b 1.00
National Airlines: Copa, Ansa

LAW REGARDING HOMOSEXUALITY:
Homosexuality is not mentioned in the Code of Law.

PANAMA CITY

✈ Tocumen Int'l Airport (PTY)
17 mi. / 28 km north of city

LOCATION: On the Pacific Ocean end of the Panama Canal.

POPULATION: 430,000

CLIMATE: Tropical climate with heavy rainfall between April and December. Temperatures range from 21°c (70° F) at night to 32°c (90° F) by day.

DESCRIPTION: The capital is a curious blend of old Spain, American modernism, and the bazaar atmosphere of the East. Most of the interesting sites are in the old part of the city. Visit the **Plaza de Francia** and the **Paseo de las Bóvedas** with a panoramic view of the **Bahia de Panama**. Panama City offers good quality hotels, restaurants, and several international casinos in the commercial center.

❖ Safety is a major concern for international visitors. Thieves abound and mugging are frequent. Do not walk on any street alone after dark.

BARS Ⓨ RESTAURANTS 🍴

● Bars/clubs (GMW): **Bar Disco**, Avda 1 & calle 9; **Boys Bar**, Avda Industrial, Esperanza, Tumba Muerto; **Ecos Bar**, Avda de las Martires; **Michelle's**, via Brasil near via España.

λ SERVICES λ

● Cinema (G/S): **Cine Eldorado**, erotic movies, mixed, Avda Central; **Cine Tropical**, c/ Monteserrin.

 ACCOMMODATIONS

CARIBE HOTEL
Av Peru & Calle 28 Este. Tel: 27-2525. TYPE: *Hotel.* CLIENTELE: All Welcome. LOCATION: Near business district. 175 rooms w/priv. bath, CTV, phone, A/C, restaurant, rooftop pool, casino, free parking. Rates: (US) $50-$90. DESCRIPTION: Moderate first class hotel popular with locals.

EL PANAMA HOTEL
via España, Panama City. Tel: 69-5000. Fax: 23-6080. TYPE: *Hotel.* CLIENTELE: Mostly Straight. LOCATION: On via España where the boys are. 345 rooms w/priv. bath, phone, CTV, A/C, 24 hrs. room service, restaurant, bar, disco, casino. Rates: $115-$525. *TAC:* 10%. DESCRIPTION: Modern highrise hotel.

SUITES COSTA DEL SOL
via España, Panama City. Tel: 20-3333. Fax: 69-4559. TYPE: *All Suite Hotel.* CLIENTELE: Mostly Straight. LOCATION: On via España. 242 suites, CTV, kitchenette, restaurant, bar, swimming pool, sauna, jogging in roof garden. Rates: $70-$120. *TAC:* 10%. DESCRIPTION: Four story hotel in a convenient location.

TOWER HOUSE SUITES
Calle 51 #36, Bella Vista. Tel: 69-2526. TYPE: *All Suite Hotel.* CLIENTELE: All Welcome. LOCATION: In banking and commercial area. 42 suites, CTV (CNN), phone, A/C, coffee shop, free parking, kitchenette, pool, laundromat. Rates: (US) $60 and up. DESCRIPTION: Hotel complex with studios and 1BR suites.

PARAGUAY

AREA: 157,047 sq. mi. (406,752 sq. km)
POPULATION: 4,600,000
CAPITAL: Asunción
CURRENCY: guarani
OFFICIAL LANGUAGE: Spanish
MAJOR RELIGION: Roman Catholicism
Telephone: 595
Nat'l Holiday: Independence Day, May 14-15
Official Time: GMT - 3
Electricity: 100 volts 60c AC
Exchange Rate: 1US$ =
National Airlines: Aéreas Paraguayas (LAP)

LAW REGARDING HOMOSEXUALITY: Homosexuality is not mentioned in the code of law as being a criminal offense. But it can be punishable under certain circumstances when specific charges of "corruption of minors" and "offenses against public morals" are introduced. There are no support groups in the country advocating gay and lesbian rights. The society is too conservative to openly accept homosexual lifestyle.

ASUNCIÓN ✆ 021

✈ Silvio Pettirossi AP (ASU) 10 mi. / 16 km

LOCATION: South west Paraguay, on small rolling hills on the east bank of the Rio Paraguay, close to the border with Argentina.

POPULATION: 800,000

CLIMATE: Humid and warm during most of the year. Summer day temperatures in the 70's or 80's (25°c) from September to April and in the 60's (18°c) from May to August. Rainfall is significant during the rainy season.

DESCRIPTION: The first permanent settlement in southern South America, Asunción was founded in 1537 by Spanish explorers. Today, the capital of Paraguay is a small, clean city with an atmosphere of a colonial South American town. **Plaza de los Héros** and the streets near the **Hotel Guarani** are right at the heart of the city. The area is also known to attract gay cruising after dark (AYOR).

BARS RESTAURANTS

● Bars/clubs (GMW): **Aloha Pub**, small bar with restaurant, c/ Ayolas 1038; **Barca**, dance club, Presidente Franco near Hotel Ambajador; **Stop**, small bar, good music, 14 de Mayo 477.

● Restaurants (AW): **La Pérgola Jardin**, expensive restaurant, international menu, 240 Av. Perú (200-777); **Le Grand Café**, international menu, 476 c/ Oliva (446-180); **Le Pérgola del Bolsi**, inexpensive and popular, 399 Estrella corner Alberdi (491-841).

ACCOMMODATIONS

HOTEL GUARANI
Calle Oliva y Independencia Nacional, Asunción. Tel: (21) 491-131. Fax: (21) 443-647. TYPE: *Hotel.* CLIENTELE: All Welcome. LOCATION: Main Square in the heart of town.

* Rooms: 168 w/priv. bath
* Suites: 28 w/balcony
* CTV, phone, minibar, A/C, hairdryer
* 24 hrs. room service, parking
* Casino, restaurants, coffee shop
* Pool, sauna, gym, jogging track
* Gay Bars: walking distance
* Airport: 18 km / 10 mi., taxi
* Train Station: 6 blocks
* Open: Year round
* Rates: $120 - $195
* ***TAC:*** 10%

DESCRIPTION: Popular first class hotel.

ZAPHIR HOTEL
C/. Estrella 955, Asunción. Tel: (21) 490-025. TYPE: *Hotel.* CLIENTELE: All Welcome. LOCATION: Downtown city center.

* Rooms: 69 w/priv. bath
* CTV, phone, A/C
* Restaurant, bar, laundry service
* Airport: 12 km / 8 mi., taxi
* Train Station: 1 km / 3/4 mi.
* Open: Year round
* Rates: $60-$90

DESCRIPTION: Small downtown tourist hotel. All rooms with private facilities.

PERU

AREA: 496,222 sq. mi. (1,285,215 sq. km)
POPULATION: 17,100,000
CAPITAL: Lima
CURRENCY: Peru New Sol (PEI)
OFFICIAL LANGUAGE: Spanish, Quechua
MAJOR RELIGION: Roman Catholicism
Telephone: 51
Official Time: G.M.T. - 5
National Holiday: July 28, Independ. Day
Electricity: 220 volts
Exchange Rate: US$1=PEI 2.25
National Airline: Aero Peru

LAW REGARDING HOMOSEXUALITY: Homosexuality in private or between consenting adults is not illegal. However, homosexuality is considered reason for discharge from the military and police forces or a ground for separation or divorce. Laws referring to 'public morality' can be used against gays or lesbians.

Note: Reports were received that the travel conditions to Peru may still be dangerous. The poverty level has already made the streets unsafe.

LIMA   © 14

✈ Jorge Chavez Int'l Airport (LIM)

LOCATION: Mid-way the western coast of Peru on both sides of the Río Rímac, at the foot of the Cerro San Crisóbal.

POPULATION: 4,000,000

CLIMATE: Though Lima is close to the equator, its climate is temperate due to the high altitude. The Humboldt Current cools the air, but the humidity is high exceeding 90% in winter (May - October). It is warmer between Nov. - April but with lower humidity level.

Gay/Lesbian Visitor Information
MHOL - Perú
Tel: (14) 336-375. Fax: (14) 335-519

DESCRIPTION: Lima the capital of Peru was the chief city of Spanish South America since the 16th century. It is an important political, economic and cultural center. The city represents a mixture of contradictions: extreme wealth and poverty, beauty and ugliness. Visit the heart of the city to appreciate its unique colonial style. **La Jirón** de la **Unión** is the main shopping street. In spite of the oppressive influence of the Catholic church, there is a relatively developed gay culture and nightlife in Lima.

❖ *Note:* Peru is one of the cheapest destinations in South America, however there is a serious problem of security, and theft from tourists. Avoid drinking tap water for risk of contamination. Drink bottled mineral water only.

BARS Y RESTAURANTS ¶¶

● Bars/Clubs (GMW): **Abracadabra**, disco, Camino Real 149, San Isidro, Miraflores; **Contacto's**, Ignacio Merino 2399; **Paulina's**, video bar, Centro Commercial San Felipe 60 (619-009); **Perseo Club**, disco, Cuadra 25, Avda Aviacion, San Borja.

● Restaurants (G/S): **Haiti**, some gay clientele, Avenida Diagonal / Primera Cuadra (in Miraflores opposite Parque Kennedy); Other (AW): **The Sky Room** and Grill La Balsa at the Hotel Crillón in central Lima (description below).

λ SERVICES λ

● Health clubs (GM): **Baños Turcos J. Padro**, some gay clientele, Avenida José Pardo 192, Miraflores (near Plaza Kennedy); **Las Vegas**, Avenida Colonial 2527 (270051).

🏠 ACCOMMODATIONS 🏠

CRILLÓN HOTEL
Ave. Nicolas de Pierola 589. Tel: 283-290. Fax (14) 280-682. TYPE: *Hotel*. CLIENTELE: Mostly Straight. LOCATION: Central location near commercial district. 547 rooms w/bath, 91 Suites, CTV, phone, A/C, restaurants, bars, nightclub, sauna, All major Credit Cards. Open: year round.Rates: (US) $80 - $130.**TAC:** 10%. DESCRIPTION: High rise first class hotel in a central location.

PHILIPPINES

AREA: 115,707 sq. mi. (299,681 sq. km)
POPULATION: 48,000,000
CAPITAL: Manila
CURRENCY: Peso
OFFICIAL LANGUAGES: Pilipino, English, Spanish
MAJOR RELIGIONS: Roman Catholicism, Islam, Protestantism
Telephone: 63
Nat'l Holiday: Independence Day, June 12
Official Time: G.M.T. + 8
Electricity: 220 volts
Exchange Rate: 1US$ = peso 26.19
National Airline: Philippines Airlines

LAW REGARDING HOMOSEXUALITY:
Homosexuality is not illegal. The age of consent is 18. Homosexual relationship between adult males are socially acceptable. However, sexual offenses against minors are severely punishable under the laws referring to 'Public Morality' and may lead to 'deportation for sexual perversion'

CEBU   ℂ   032

✈ Mactan Int'l Airport (CEB) 5 mi. / 8 km

LOCATION: On the eastern coast of the island of Cebu in the Central Visayas.

POPULATION: 500,000

CLIMATE: Climate is subject to monsoons. December to May is the dry season. Temperatures hoover around 80˚F (21˚c) with slight variation between the winter and summer.

DESCRIPTION: Cebu, known as the "Queen City of the South", is the oldest city in the Philippines. Supported by a large and prosperous Chinese population, it has achieved an impressive level of urbanization, second only to Manila. The city's most famous landmark is a large wooden cross from the 16th century which symbolizes the archipelago's first encounter with the West. Cebu is famous for its hand crafted guitars and string instruments. Off the southern tip of Cebu Island is **Smilon Island**, a marine park with exotic corals and sea life.

♣ Entertainment: Casino complex with slots, table games, music lounge and a bar featuring live entertainment, **Casino Filipino Cebu**, Casino Filipino Building, Nivel Hills, Lahug, Cebu City (536-21).

λ SERVICES λ

● Cinemas (G/S): **Majestic**, Colon St. (771-24); **Ultravistarama**, Legaspi Street (964-26).

 ACCOMMODATIONS

MAGELLAN INT'L HOTEL
Gorordo Ave., P.O. Box 409, Cebu City 6401. Tel: (032) 74613 or 95154. TYPE: *Hotel*. CLIENTELE: Mostly Straight. LOCATION: 7 min. from downtown. 180 rooms w/priv. bath. DESCRIPTION: First class hotel with a variety of entertainment and sports facilities. Swimming pool with poolside restaurant and Dinner Theatre, tour offices, car rental, golf course nearby.

MANILA   ℂ   02

✈ Manila Int'l Airport (MNL)

LOCATION: Southwest of the main island Luzon, overlooking the Manila Bay.

POPULATION: City - 2,000,000;
                    Metro - 8,000,000

CLIMATE: see Cebu

DESCRIPTION: Metro Manila with a population of over 8 million people, is a difficult city to manage from a social and political stand point. The city is heavily depended on foreign tourism. It is known for its easy going, hedonistic lifestyle.

● Gay tourism traditionally popular with some gays, is a touchy subject, because it is often associated with the sexual exploitation of the poor, underage and uneducated Philippinos.

Visit: **Rizal Park** with its monument to the

hero; **Japanese & Chinese Gardens, Museum of Philippines Costumes & Museum of Contemporary Art** in Ermita; **Malate Church & Plaza**; **Ayala Avenue** in Makati - the 'Wall Street' of the Philippines; Manila's **Chinatown** in Binondo; **Divisoria** - Manila's popular bargain hunting basement towards the western end of Recto Avenue.

BARS ♈ RESTAURANTS 🍴

● Bars/clubs (GM): **Chico's**, disco, fashion shows, 1668 Rodriguez Str. Blvd. Quezon City (79 96 34); **Cine-Café**, Roces Ave., Quezon City; **Club 690**, popular bar, sex shows, 690 N.S. Amoranto St., Quezon City (712-3662); **Library**, 1779 Adriatico St., Malate (50 92 95); **Music Box**, popular bar, 1 Timog Ave., Quezon City (921-1743); **Question Mark**, bar & escort service, 1193 Maria Orosa St., Ermita (521-2346); **Solution**, 569 Libertad St., Pasay City (833-1641);**Vocals**, Pedro Gil & Aguinaldo Sts.

● Restaurants (AW): **Aristocrat**, good food, reasonably priced, can be cruisy, Roxas Blvd/San Andreas, Metro Manila (50 26 21); **Barrio Fiesta**, Buendia Ave. Makati (87 47 28); **Josephine**, seafood, near Holiday Inn, 1800 Conception St./ Roxas Blvd. (50 31 25); **Zamboanga Restaurant**, 8739 Makati Ave., grilled lobster, and seafood, entertainment nightly with Filippino folk dances (89 49 32).

● Entertainment: **Casino Filipino Silahis** at the Silhais Int'l Hotel, Roxas Blvd. Manila. 24hrs. casino action, try the **"Stargazer"** & Sushi bar a popular gathering place for Manila's youngsters at the top of the hotel; and Casino Filipino Hilton, at the Manila Hilton, U.N. Ave, Ermita, Manila. 24 hrs. gambling, fine dining at the "Rotisserie".

 ACCOMMODATIONS

ADMIRAL HOTEL
2138 Roxas Blvd., Malate 1004. Tel: (02) 521-0711. Fax: (02) 522-2018. TYPE: *Hotel.* CLIENTELE: Mostly Straight. LOCATION: City center facing the bay. 110 rooms w/priv. bath. 13 Suites, CTV, phone, marble bath, A/C, 24 hrs.

room service, Sushi bar, restaurant, bar, disco, pool, massage, gift shop, free parking, gay bars within walking distance, 8 km / 5 mi. to airport. open year round. Credit Cards: MC/VISA/ AMEX. Rates: (US) $110-$220. *TAC:* 10%. DESCRIPTION: Moderate first class multi-story hotel in a convenient location near Convention Center, shopping, zoo, museums and gay bars. No problem taking friends to your room.

AMBASSADOR HOTEL
2021 A. Mabini St., Malate 2821. Tel: (02) 50 60 11/19. TYPE: *Hotel.* CLIENTELE: Mostly Straight. LOCATION: In tourist belt, 10 minutes from Seaport. 268 rooms w/private bath, 12 Suites, CTV, phone, A/C, Chinese & Japanese restaurants, revolving disco, rooftop pool, room & maid service. 6 km / 4 mi. to airport. Credit Cards: MC/VISA/EC/DC/AMEX. open year round. Rates: (US) $60-$90. *TAC:* 10%. DESCRIPTION: Moderate first class hotel, renovated in 1986. Popular with groups. Cruising Manila disco on the 6th floor is gay oriented.

HOLIDAY INN MANILA
3001 Roxas Blvd., Pasay City, Manila 1300. Tel: (2) 597961. Fax: (2) 522-3985. TYPE: *Hotel.* CLIENTELE: Mostly Straight. LOCATION: City center overlooking Manila Bay. 265 rooms w/priv. bath, 28 Suites, CTV, phone, A/C, wheelchair access, maid & 24 hrs. room service, restaurant, coffee shop, bars, pool, health club, gym, sauna. many gay bars nearby, 6 km /4 mi. to airport. Credit Cards: MC/VISA/ AMEX/DC . open year round. Rates: (US) $110-$160. *TAC:* 10%. DESCRIPTION: Sleek high rise first class hotel in the heart of the gay scene.

MANILA MIDTOWN HOTEL
Pedro Gil, Ermita. Tel: (2) 57 39 11. Fax: (2) 522-2629. TYPE: Hotel. CLIENTELE: Mostly Straight. LOCATION: In the heart of Manila's tourist belt, near the gay scene. 600 rooms w/priv. bath, 162 suites, CTV, phone, A/C, maid & room service, restaurants, lounges, disco, pool, health club, sauna, jacuzzi , nearby gay bars, 9 km / 6 mi. to airport. Credit Cards: MC/VISA/ AMEX/DC. open year round. Rates: (US) $90 - $110. *TAC:* 10%. DESCRIPTION: First class high rise hotel In a commercial complex in the heart of Manila with theatres and shopping.

POLAND

AREA: 120,725 sq. mi. (312,678 sq. km.)
POPULATION: 38,000,000
CAPITAL: Warsaw
CURRENCY: Zloty (Zl)
OFFICIAL LANGUAGE: Polish
MAJOR RELIGIONS: Roman Catholicism
Telephone: 48
Nat'l Holiday: National Day, July 22
Official Time: GMT +1
Electricity: 220 V
Exchange Rate: 1US$ = Zl 2.47
National Airlines: LOT

LAW REGARDING HOMOSEXUALITY:
Homosexuality is not mentioned in the Code of
Law since 1932. The age of consent is 15 for
both straight and gay people. In recent years
few gay groups were established in large cities.
In February 1990 they were officially recognized by the Polish Government. The general
attitude of the Polish society towards homosexuality is that of intolerance and ignorance.

CRACOW   ✆ 012

✈ Balice Int'l Airport (KRK)

LOCATION: In southern Poland.

POPULATION: 660,000

CLIMATE: Cool Northern European climate
with summer temperatures averaging 68°F
(20°c), and winter 26°F (-3°c).

Gay/Lesbian Visitor Information
Lambda Cracow: 562-456

DESCRIPTION: Old University town and the
capital of Poland until 1611. It is the only major
Polish city to escape war devastation. Modern
Cracow is a lively cultural center with fine his-

toric buildings, towers, dungeons and churches.

❖ **SPECIAL EVENTS**: June is the time when
most events take place in Cracow - **International Biennale of Graphic Arts** (even numbered years); **Polish International Short
Film Festival**; **Folk Art Fair**; and the colorful **Lajkonik Pageant**, celebrating the historic day when a young Cracovian craftsman
drove back a Tartar invasion.

BARS 🍸 RESTAURANTS 🍴

● Bars/clubs (GM): **Hades**, Ul. Stavowwislna
60 (219-369); **Disco Club**, Fri-Sat dance club,
Ul. Rejtana 4 (562-456).

λ SERVICES λ

● Health Clubs (G/S): **Laznia Finska**, Ulica
Rejtana4 (562-456); **Spartakus Sauna**, Ulica
Krupnicza 29 (340-243).

🏠 ACCOMMODATIONS 🏠

HOTEL CRACOVIA
1 Puzskina St., Cracow 30-111. Tel: (12) 228-666.
Fax: (12) 219-586. TYPE: *Hotel*. CLIENTELE:
Mostly Straight. LOCATION: On city's inner
ring road.425 rooms w/priv. bath. Suites: 10,
phone, Radio, C/H, restaurant, bar, cafe, parking. Rates: (US) $50- $100. DESCRIPTION:
Moderate first class hotel in a central location.
Bar popular with gay followers on premises.

HOLIDAY INN
7 Koniewa St., Cracow 30-150. Tel: (12) 375-044.
Fax: (12) 375-938. TYPE: *Hotel*. CLIENTELE:
Mostly Straight. LOCATION: 4 km / 2.5 mi. from
downtown. 306 rooms w/priv. bath. Suites: 2,
CTV, phone, A/C, C/H, restaurant, coffee shop,
bar, pool, sauna, solarium, parking. Rates: (US)
$40 - $110. DESCRIPTION: Modern first class
hotel decorated to reflect Polish culture. Popular
bar with gay followers on premises.

GDANSK   ✆ 058

✈ Rebiechowo Airport (GDN)

LOCATION: On Poland's Baltic Coast.

POPULATION: 380,000

CLIMATE: Cool Northern European climate
with temperatures averaging 68°F (20°c) in the

summer, and 26°F (-3°c) in the winter.

Gay/Lesbian Visitor Information
Lambda Gdansk: 316-125

DESCRIPTION: Gdansk is a picturesque sea-faring town on the Baltic Coast. The city gained international fame with Solidarity's struggle during the communist era to form a Trade Union at the Gdansk Shipyard. Visit the 18th century **Main Town**, or the nearby beach resorts of **Sopot** and **Gdynia**.

λ SERVICES λ

● Health Clubs (G/S): **Hotel Posejdon**, Ul. Kapliczna 30, Jelitkowo; **Hotel Marina**, Ul. Jelitkowska 20.

 ACCOMMODATIONS

MARINA ORBIS HOTEL
ul. Jelitkowska 20, Jelitkowo 80-342. Tel: 53-20-79. TYPE: *Hotel*. CLIENTELE: Mostly Straight. LOCATION: In Jelitkowo near Gdansk, close to the Baltic Sea. 193 rooms, restaurant, cafe, bar & nightclub, sauna: some gay clientele, indoor pool, bowling. Rates: (US) $50 - $80. DESCRIPTION: Government rated 4 star well equipped hotel.

POSEJDON-JELITKOWO
30 Kapliczna, Jelitkowo 80-341. Tel: 53-18-03. Telex: 512783 P. TYPE: *Hotel*. CLIENTELE: Mostly Straight. LOCATION: In Jelitkowo near Gdansk and the Baltic Sea. 147 rooms w/priv. bath. Suites: 2, A/C (available), restaurant & cafe, pool & sauna: popular with gays. Rates: (US) $50 - $140 (suite). DESCRIPTION: Modern motel-like hotel rated 4 stars.

WARSAW   © 022

✈ Okecie Int'l Airport (WAW)

LOCATION: In the heart of Eastern Poland on both sides of the Vistula river.

POPULATION: 1,700,000

CLIMATE: Temperate continental climate with 6 distinguished seasons. Winters are snowy with a mean average temperature of -2°c (28°F); Summers are pleasant with average mean temperature in July of 18°c (65°F); Fall is dry, sunny known as the "Polish golden autumn".

Gay/Lesbian Visitor Information
Pink Service. Tel: 253-911

DESCRIPTION: Poland's historic capital since the 17th century, lies on the Vistula, it is the industrial, administrative and cultural centre of Poland. The historic city was 2/3 destroyed by the Nazis during WWII. Most of the city's once thriving Jewish population was totally annihilated. Today, Warsaw is a new city raised from the ashes of a devastating war. The Old Town district was completely reconstructed to preserve the spirit of the the authentic old town.

BARS Y RESTAURANTS ¶¶

● Bars/clubs (GMW): **Kozia Pub**, Ul. Kozla 10/12, near Nowy Rynek Sq. (313-288); **Red Club**, dance bar, Marszalkowska; **Rudawka**, Fri gay disco, Ulica Elblaska 53.

λ SERVICES λ

● Health Clubs (GM): **Fantom Sauna**, sauna, sex shop, dark room, Ul. Bracka 20A.

 ACCOMMODATIONS

EUROPEJSKI
13 Krakowskie Przedmiescie St., Warsaw 00-071. Tel: (22) 265051. Telex: 813615, 812521. TYPE: *First Class Hotel*. CLIENTELE: Mostly Straight. LOCATION: Near the Old Town. 250 rooms w/priv. bath, suites: 11, C/H, phone, restaurant, parking. Rates: (US) $95 - $138. DESCRIPTION: Famous traditional hotel, rated 3 stars. Some rooms with antique furnishings.

FORUM
Nowogrodzka St., 24/26, Warsaw 00-511. Tel/Fax: (22) 210-271. Telex: 814704, 812521. TYPE: *First Class Hotel*. CLIENTELE: Mostly Straight. LOCATION: City center near the Palace of Culture and Sciences. 751 rooms w/priv. bath. Suites: 13, CTV, phone, room service, restaurants & bar. Rates: (US) $115 - $135. DESCRIPTION: 4 star hotel with good amenities. Restaurant/bar popular with gay followers.

VICTORIA INTER-CONTINENTAL
Krolewska 11, Warsaw 00-065. Tel: (22) 278011. TYPE: *Deluxe Hotel*. CLIENTELE: Mostly Straight. LOCATION: Victory Sq. opposite Opera House. 370 rooms w/priv. bath; Suites: 36, CTV, phone, A/C, room service, restaurant, bar/lounge, nightclub, sauna, massage, solarium, pool, gym. Rates: (US) $180 - $210. DESCRIPTION: Elegant hotel with international amenities. Good entertainment.

PORTUGAL

AREA: 35,549 sq. mi. (92,072 sq. km)
POPULATION: 9,933,000
CAPITAL: Lisbon
CURRENCY: escudo (P$)
OFFICIAL LANGUAGE: Portuguese
MAJOR RELIGIONS: Roman Catholicism
Telephone: 351
Nat'l Holiday: Independence Day, Dec. 1
Official Time: G.M.T.
Electricity: 220 volts
Exchange Rate: 1US$ = P$147.84
National Airline: TAP Air Portugal

LAW REGARDING HOMOSEXUALITY: Homosexuality is not mentioned in the Code of Law, but 'acts against nature' are used against gay men. Police can be hostile and the society in general is intolerant as a result of religious pressures. Gay men and lesbians are excluded from military service and suffer from certain civil discrimination.

ALGARVE ⟨ℭ⟩ 89

✈ Faro Int'l Airport (FAO)

LOCATION: Southern coast of Portugal.

CLIMATE: The weather is never cold. The best time for holidays is from the end of January through the end of October. The temperatures are in the mid 70°sF to mid 80°sF (24°c). Winter temperatures are in the high 50°sF (14°c).

DESCRIPTION: Popular resort area for Europeans with fine sandy beaches, historic villages, hidden coves, luxury resort hotels and casinos. There are many picturesque small town and villages close to each other all the way from the border with Spain on the east to the Atlantic ocean on the west.

❖ Beaches: **Armaçao de Pêra**, nude sunbathing on the sand dunes; **Pêra**, nude sunbathing at the dunes and bamboo grove near Carlos Bar; **Lagos**, nude beach at the end of Meia Praia by the dunes.

HOW TO GET THERE: by flight to the Faro Airport, or to Lisbon and by car to the Algarve (about 4 hrs. drive). Alternatively, fly to Seville (Spain) and from there about 256 km / 160 mi (2-1/2 hrs.) by car. There are no customs or annoying boarder crossing check points, you drive right in from Spain crossing a large bridge. The roads are good and easy to drive.

BARS ♈ RESTAURANTS 🍴

● Bars/Clubs (GM): Almansil - **Options**, EN 125; **Outside-In**, Santa Barbara de Nexe; **Memories**, EN 125. Armaçao de Pêra - **Mai um Bar**, Rua Dr. Martinho Simões 23. Lagos - **Britaica**, Rua Marqês de Pombal 7; **Club Fechadura**, Rua Vasco de Gama 37; **Kilt**, Cais Herculano 1; **Lui Sol**, rua de S. José 21, Lagos (082-761-794); **Roterdão Bar**, Av. 25 de Abril; **Snoopy**, S. Gonçalo.

ACCOMMODATIONS

✪ CASA MARHABA

Alfanzina, Algarve. USA/Canada reservations - Tel: (516) 944-5330 or (800) 257-5344. Fax: (516) 944-7540. TYPE: *Guest House*. HOST: Tony. CLIENTELE: Gay men. LOCATION: Small village in the sunny Algarve, close to beaches and tourist attractions.

* Rooms: 5 dbl w/priv. bath
* CTV lounge w/video facilities
* Early evening bar
* Pool, sundecks, garden
* Gay bars: car rental necessary
* Beaches: many nearby
* Airport: Faro 50 km / 30 mi.
* Open: Year round
* Rates: (US) from $480/week; daily rates available on request
* *TAC:* 10%

DESCRIPTION: Intimate guest house in the peaceful Algarve. Recommended for those in search of sun, beach and relaxation. Bountiful breakfast with a seasonal selection of fresh fruit, pastries, fresh coffee and juice is served daily on the sunny terrace. Car rental is necessary to explore the beauty of the area, to access nearby beaches, gay bars and restaurants.

CASA MARHABA
Algarve · Portugal

USA/Canada reservations: (800) 257-5344. Email: odyusa@odyusa.com

LISBON   ©   1

✈ Portela Int'l Airport (LIS)
  5 mi. / 8 km north

LOCATION: Halfway down the Atlantic coastline of Portugal.

POPULATION: 1,100,000

CLIMATE: Warm and pleasant year round.
Winters are cool with average low Jan. temperature of 46°F (7°c). Summers are hot, dry with
average high July temperature of 81°F (27°c).

DESCRIPTION: Lisbon is a romantic city
sprawling across seven hills on the right bank
of the Tagus river. Founded by seafaring
Phoenicians, it later became the center of dis-
coveries and colonial explorations. Today, with
more than a million inhabitants, it still con-
serves a colorful small village atmosphere full
of spirit and excitement.

The gay scene in Lisbon is concentrated on the
northern periphery of the **Bairro Alto** (Upper
Town) near the **Botanical Garden**, where
most of the city's fado houses, bars and restaurants are located.

Visit: **The Alfama**, the **Moorish Quarter**;
Castle St. George - a castle of Visigoth origin;
The Cathedral; and the **Belém**.

❖ Beaches: **Costa de Caprica**, is a charming
stretch of sandy beaches 30-60 min. outside
Lisbon where nudity is possible and tolerated.
A mini-railway runs along 8 km / 5 mi of dunes
(in season only). Take the fun narrow gauge
railroad to post #17 where the gay nude beach
is located; **Estoril**, a major coastal resort town
with a cosmopolitan casino and a golf course;
Praia do Meço, 30 km/19 mi. south of Lisbon
offers nude sunbathing.

BARS ⅄ RESTAURANTS 🍴

● Bars/Clubs (GM): **Alcazar**, drag shows, Rua
da Imprenta Nacional 104; **Bricabar**, intimate
dance club, Rua Cecilio de Sousa, 82-84 (342-
8971); **Finalmente**, fashionable disco, daily
drag shows, (22-04), rua Cecílio de Soussa; **O
Duche**, Largo da Liberdade 33B; **Trumps**,
large disco, Rua da Imprensa Nacional 104-B
(671-0 59); **Xecque-Mate**, cruise bar/ disco,
Rua de Sâo Marçal 170 (372-830).

● Bars/Clubs (GMW): **Alcântra-Mar**, disco, Rua da Cozinha Economica 11 (363-7176); **Harry's Bar**, snack bar, eclectic clientele, rua de São Pedro de Alcântara 57 (360-760); **Memorial**, disco/bar, restaurant, rua de Gustavo de Matos Squeira 42a (668-891).

● Restaurants (GMW): **Bota Alta**, Travessa da Queimada (327-959); **Puente Na Bicha**, Portuguese specialties, Travessa da Agua da Flor 38 (325-924); Others (AW): **Bizarro**, Rua da Atalaia (371-899); **Fidalgo**, gourmet seafood, fashionable hangout for arts and media professionals, rua da Barroca 27 (342-2900); **Memorial**, rua de Gustavo de Matos Squeira 42a (668-891); **Xele Banana**, Praça das Flores 29 (660-515).

λ **SERVICES** λ

● Health Clubs (GM): **Descan**, Avda Republica 83; **Estrella**, Avda Infante Santo 361; **Grecus**, rua do Telhal 77-4 (4th floor) (370-578); **Iys**, Rua Borges Carneiro 42; **Spartacus**, Rua de Emenada.

 **ACCOMMODATIONS**

HOTEL BRITANIA
Rua Rodrigues Sampaio 17, Lisbon. Tel: (1) 315-5016. USA/Canada reservations (800) 257-5344 or (516) 944-5330. Fax: (800) 982-6571 or (516) 944-7540. TYPE: *Hotel*. CLIENTELE: All Welcome. LOCATION: Center of town near the Botanical Gardens.

* Rooms: 30 w/priv. bath
* CTV (CNN), phone, A/C, minibar, bidet
* Maid, laundry and limited room service
* Bar, TV Lounge, free parking
* Gay Bars: some nearby
* Airport: 8 km / 5 mi, taxi, bus
* Open: Year round
* Rates: (US) $90 - $160
* *TAC:* 10% (from Odysseus)

DESCRIPTION: Charming renovated 3-star downtown hotel near the gay scene. Rooms are tastefully furnished, bathrooms with marble fixtures, bidet. Pleasant and central.

CAPITOL HOTEL
Rua Eca de Queiroz 24. Tel: (1) 536-811. USA/Canada reservations (800) 257-5344 or (516) 944-7540. Fax: (800) 982-6571 or (516) 944-7540. TYPE: *Hotel*. CLIENTELE: All Welcome. LOCATION: City center next to Marques de Pombal Square.

* Rooms: 57 w/priv. bath
* CTV, A/C, C/H, phone, minibar

* Maid service, room service, laundry service
* Restaurant, bar, cafeteria
* Gay Bars: some nearby
* Airport: 20 min. taxi, bus
* Open: Year round
* Rates: (US) $65 - $160
* *TAC:* 10% (from Odysseus)

DESCRIPTION: Centrally located tourist hotel.

HOTEL REX
Rua Castilho 169. Tel: (1) 388-2161. USA/ Canada reservations (800) 257-5344 or (516) 944-7540. Fax: (800) 982-6571 or (516) 944-7540. TYPE: *Hotel*. CLIENTELE: All Welcome. LOCATION: City center opposite Edward VII Park.

* Rooms: 68 w/priv. bath
* Suites: 9 w/living room and terrace
* CTV, A/C, C/H, phone, minibar
* Maid service, room service, laundry service
* Restaurants:2
* Gay Bars: some nearby
* Airport: 20 min. taxi, bus
* Open: Year round
* Rates: (US) $65 - $160
* *TAC:* 10% (from Odysseus)

DESCRIPTION: Moderate first class hotel in a central location.

YORK HOUSE
32 rua das Janelas Verdes 1, Lisbon 1200. Tel: 396-2435. TYPE: *Pension*. CLIENTELE: Mostly Straight. LOCATION: West of the heart of the city, next to the National Art Gallery. 32 rooms w/priv. bath, restaurant. Airport: 20 min. Gay Bars: car needed. Rates: from (US) $120/ and up. DESCRIPTION: A restored 17th century convent surrounded by patio and gardens. All rooms are tastefully decorated with antiques. Popular with writers.

MADEIRA ISL.   ℐ   91

✈ Funchal Airport (FNC)
15 mi. / 24 km NE of Funchal

LOCATION: 400 mi. / 640 km off Morocco's Atlantic Coast, and 600 mi. / 960 km southwest of the Portugese mainland.

POPULATION: 100,000

CLIMATE: Spring-like year round. Winter temperatures are in the mid 50°Fs (15°c); and mid 60°sF (18°c) in the summer, with warm periods pushing up sometimes to the 80°Fs

(28°c). July/August is the high season.

DESCRIPTION: Island rising precipitously from sea level to mountaintop offering dramatic beauty but no sandy beaches. The only existing beaches are small and rocky along the shoreline. Funchal is the main town and port of call. Visit: **Old Town** and the **Casino de Madeira** at the ultramodern **Casino Park** for gaming, entertainment and fine dining.

BARS ♈ RESTAURANTS 🍴

● Bars/Clubs (G/S): **Café Apolo** & **Café Funchal**, Largo da Sé Sq.; **Greenwood Pub**, Old City; **Why Not**, Largo Corpo Santo 29 (307-77).

● Restaurants (AW): **Quinta Magnólia**, hotel-school restaurant in elegant old mansion amidst botanical gardens, moderate, 10 rua do Dr. Pita (64614); **São José**, local specialties, 11 Largo do Corpo Santo (23214); **Viking**, rua de Alegria 1 (457-90).

🔑 ACCOMMODATIONS 🔑

CASINO PARK
Quinta da Vigia, Funchal 9000. Tel: (91) 33111. Fax: (91) 32076. TYPE: *Deluxe Hotel*. CLIENTELE: Mostly Straight. LOCATION: 10 min. walk from town center. 400 rooms w/priv. bath, 42 Jr Suites, swimming pool, Health Center w/Sauna, Jacuzzi, Nightclub, Casino, Restaurants, Bars. Season: Year round. Rates: US$125-$225. *TAC:* 10%. DESCRIPTION: Elegant hotel with sweeping views of the harbor and town.

HOTEL ESTRELICIA
Caminho Velho da Ajuda, Funchal 9000. Tel: (91) 30131/3. USA/Canada reservations: Tel: (516) 944-5330. Fax: (516) 944-7540. TYPE: *Hotel*. CLIENTELE: All Welcome. LOCATION: In the heart of Funchal's tourist center. 148 rooms w/priv. bath, restaurant, bar, pool, parking. Gay Bars: walking distance. Season: Year round. Rates: US$60-$120. *TAC:* 10% (from Odysseus). DESCRIPTION: Tourist class modern high-rise hotel in a convenient location.

SANTA MARIA
Rua Joao de Deus 24-26. Tel: (91) 252-71/3. USA/Canada reservations: Tel: (516) 944-5330. Fax: (516) 944-7540. TYPE: *Hotel*. CLIENTELE: All Welcome. LOCATION: Center of town. 83 rooms w/priv., bath, balcony, 8 suites, restaurant, bar & lounge, panoramic rooftop terrace w/swimming pool & bar. Gay Bars:

walking distance. Airport: 20 km / 13 mi. (bus shuttle). Season: Year round. Rates: US$ 65-95. *TAC:* 10% (from Odysseus). DESCRIPTION: Tourist class hotel with clean but simply furnished rooms.

PORTO   Ⓒ   02

✈ Petros Rubras Int'l Airport (OPO) 10 mi. / 16 km NW

LOCATION: Northern Portugal.

POPULATION: 500,000

DESCRIPTION: Portugal's second largest city is famous for its celebrated wine, and rich history and culture. Visit the **Old City** and the picturesque **Barredo quarter** and tour the wine "lodges" for a unique wine tasting experience. The gay scene is located near the **Brasilia Shopping Center**.

BARS ♈ RESTAURANTS 🍴

● Bars/Clubs (GM): **Bustos**, Rua Guades de Azevedo 203-1 (314-876); **Swing**, pub & disco with gay/lesbian followers, 766 Praçeta Engenheiro Amaro de Costa (609-0019).

● Restaurants (AW): **Boavista**, glass enclosed with views of the Foz fortress and the Douro estuary, 58 Esplanada do Castelo, Foz do Douro (680-083); **Tripeiro**, fine regional cooking, 195 rua Passos Manuel (200-5886).

λ SERVICES λ

● Health Clubs (GM): **Gimno**, fitness center, Avda da Boavista 949 (615-67); **Oasis**, Rua Guedes Azeuedo 205 (31-7533); **Polisauna**, Rua Formosa 400-3 (247-04).

🔑 ACCOMMODATIONS 🔑

DOM HENRIQUE
Rua Guesdes de Azevedo 179, Porto 4000. Tel: (2) 200-5755. TYPE: *Hotel*. CLIENTELE: Mostly Straight. LOCATION: Central location. 112 rooms w/priv. bath, CTV (CNN), phone, A/C, mini-bar, rooftop restaurant & lounge, bar, coffeeshop. Gay Bar: walking distance. Airport: 30 min. (taxi). Season: Year round. Rates: US$125-$230. *TAC:* 10%. DESCRIPTION: First class hotel in a convenient location.

ROMANIA

AREA: 91,699 sq. mi. (237,500 sq. km)
POPULATION: 23,250,000
CAPITAL: Bucharest
CURRENCY: Leu (ROL)
OFFICIAL LANGUAGE: Romanian
MAJOR RELIGIONS: Eastern Orthodoxy
Telephone: 40
Nat'l Holiday: Liberation Day, Aug. 23
Official Time: G.M.T.
Electricity: 220 volts
Exchange Rate: 1US$ = ROL 2,539
National Airline: Tarom

LAW REGARDING HOMOSEXUALITY:
The Romanian government has honored its international obligations by decriminalizing homosexual activity in private between consenting adults. Reforms to the penal code repeal the total ban on lesbian and gay sex; but the reformed penal code continues to ban involvement in any "propaganda" for the purposes of "enticing and seducing a person to practice same sex acts". The penalty will be of up to 5 years in prison. Gay organizations in Romania may be illegal.

BUCHAREST   ℂ   01

✈ Otopeni Int'l AP (OTP) 11 mi. / 18 km No.

LOCATION: Southern Romania on both banks of the Dimbovita River.

POPULATION: 2,000,000

CLIMATE: Temperate and free of extremes, but snow is possible as late as April. January low is 19°F (-7°c); Summer high is 86°F (30°c).

DESCRIPTION: Bucharest became the capital of Romania in the 17th century. Like Paris it has gracious buildings, large boulevards and

neo-Classical 19th century character and it is at best in the Spring. For gay travelers there is not much of a gay scene in Bucharest. Cruising (AYOR) is possible at: **Plata Universitei** (around International Hotel) and the **Park of Opera Roumania** (near U-Eroilor).

♈ BARS ♈

● Bars/clubs (G/S): **Club R**, Calea Setbau Voda 70, Sector 4 (233-450); **Remitz Bar**, Calea Doro-banti; **Martin Disco**, Ses. Stefan cel Mare (321-4945).

λ SERVICES λ

● Health Clubs (G/S): **Baia Grivita**, Sf. Voievozi 137 (near Gara de Nord on Calea Grivita).

ACCOMMODATIONS

NORD HOTEL
Calea Grivitei 143, Bucharest 78102. Tel: (1) 506-081. TYPE: *Hotel*. CLIENTELE: Mostly Straight. LOCATION: Near Gara de Nord and the sauna. 245 w/priv. bath, 7 suites, phone, C/H, videos, restaurant, bar, brasserie, parking. Rates: (US) $70-$140. *TAC:* 10%.

CONSTANTA   ℂ   016

LOCATION: On the Black Sea.

POPULATION: 300,000

DESCRIPTION: Romania's second largest city, Constanta is an historic seaport. Nearby are some of Romania's better known seaside resorts. Cruising (AYOR): **Park** in front of the **Old Casino**; **Park of the Musical Theatre**; and the beach near Hotel Belona and Hotel Europa (Eforie Nord).

BARS ♈ RESTAURANTS 🍴

● Bars/clubs (G/S): **Café de Vin**, mixed bar attracting gay clientele late at night, Bulvardul Republici 20 (at Hotel Continental)

ACCOMMODATIONS

PALAS HOTEL
Str. Opreanu 5-7, Constanta 8700. Tel: (16) 14696. TYPE: *Hotel*. CLIENTELE: Mostly Straight. LOCATION: Historic Center. Rates: upon requests.

RUSSIA

AREA: 6,592,812 sq. mi. (137,551,000 sq. km)
POPULATION: 147,400,000
CAPITAL: Moscow
CURRENCY: Ruble (R)
OFFICIAL LANGUAGE: Russian
MAJOR RELIGIONS: Russian Orthodoxy, Islam, Judaism, Protestantism
Telephone: 7
Nat'l Holiday: Independence Day, June 12
Official Time: GMT +2
Electricity: 220v
Exchange Rate: 1US$ = R 5,450*
* unstable currency
National Airlines: Aeroflot, Transaero

LAW REGARDING HOMOSEXUALITY: The notorious article 121 of the Russian Penal Code that criminalized homosexuality was abolished in 1993 and since than there are no specific laws against gays in Russia. The age of consent is set to 16 for both gays and straight (since January 1, 1997). The situation is steadily improving, no major discrimination is noted in everyday life, gays even prevail on TV, radio and the press. A liberal attitude exists mostly in Moscow and St. Petersburg. With their fast growing gay scene they offer some of the best destinations for gay travelers in Eastern Europe. Other cities and communities in Russia are still very conservative.

❖ **HIV/AIDS Travel:** On February 24, 1995 the State Duma of Russia adopted a special AIDS law. According to this law there are no restrictions for incoming or outgoing from Russia for people with AIDS who stay less than 3 months. Foreigners that intend to stay in Russia for more than 3 months are required to produce a certificate that they are HIV negative, submit for testing, or leave the country. There are no other restrictions for foreigners visiting Russia. (information supplied by *The Kremlin Tours*, Moscow).

● National Organizations (GMW): **Gay Busi-**

ness **Association of Russia**, promoting gay business projects and legal assistance to gay managed or operated businesses. E-mail: Kremln@dol.ru; **Treugolnik** (Triangle), gay rights group, PO Box 7, 105037 Moscow. (163-8002). Email: triangle@glas.apc.org

Gay/Lesbian Visitor Information
Gay Russia National Website
http://www.gayrussia.msk.ru

MOSCOW   ℰ   95

✈ Domodedovo Airport (DME)
Sheremetievo Airport (SVO)
Int'l Airport 34 km / 21 mi.
Vnukovo Airport (VKU)

LOCATION: Central zone of the great Russian Plain, between the Rivers Volga and Oka, on the banks of the Moskva.

POPULATION: 10,800,000

CLIMATE: Changeable climate. Cold winters with plenty of snowfall and temperatures below freezing (average about -10°c / -23°F).The best time to see Moscow in snow is February, the sunniest winter month. Summers are mild with temperatures in the 60"sF (15°c). May, June and September are the best months to visit Russia. July and August are the hottest months.

Gay/Lesbian Visitor Information
✪ **The Kremlin Tours**
Tel/Fax: 274-7421/464-1814
Email: kremln@dol.ru

DESCRIPTION: Founded in 1147 by Kievan Prince Yuri Dolgoruky, Moscow has been the Russian capital more than 500 years. The town was built by Peter the Great as Russia's "window onto Europe", and today it's most recognized international symbols are the **Red Square** and the magnificent **Kremlin**, whose mighty medieval walls had been already built when Columbus discovered America in 1492. Moscow is known for its magnificent ballet productions at the National **Bolshoi Theatre** and the great Circus shows.

❖ Public Cruising (AYOR): to meet local gays, take a stroll in the small park right in front of the **Bolshoi Theatre** (a few minutes walk from Red Square), relax on one of the comfortable benches around the fountain (the "hottest" area), or just stand next to the entrance to the

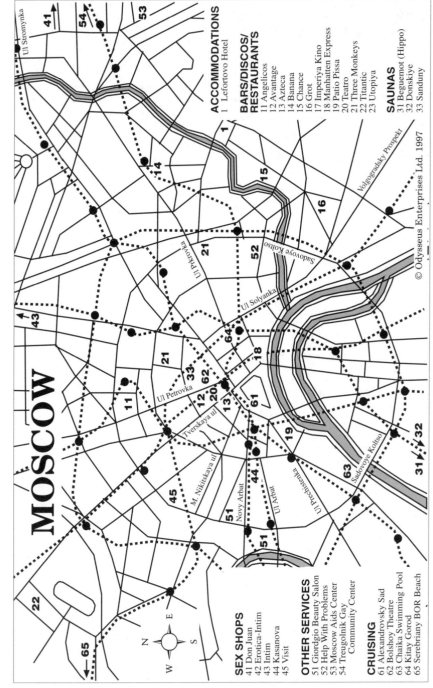

MOSCOW

ACCOMMODATIONS
1 Lefortovo Hotel

BARS/DISCOS/RESTAURANTS
11 Angelicos
12 Avantage
13 Azteca
14 Banana
15 Chance
16 Grot
17 Imperiya Kino
18 Manhatten Express
19 Patio Pissa
20 Teatro
21 Three Monkeys
22 Titantic
23 Utopiya

SAUNAS
31 Beguemot (Hippo)
32 Donskiye
33 Sanduny

SEX SHOPS
41 Don Juan
42 Erotica-Intim
43 Intim
44 Kasanova
45 Visit

OTHER SERVICES
51 Giorgio Beauty Salon
52 Help With Problems
53 Moscow Aids Center
54 Treugolnik Gay
   Community Center

CRUISING
61 Alexandrovsky Sad
62 Bolshoy Theatre
63 Chaika Swimming Pool
64 Kitay Gorod
65 Serebriany BOR Beach

© Odysseus Enterprises Ltd. 1997

nearest **Okhotny Riad** metro (from 21 hrs). Visit the **Staraya Ploshchad** (Old Square) and the cruisy **Iliyinsky Park** near the **Gueroyam Plevny** (Heroes of Plevna) monument (M° Kitai Gorod). Try also the **Alexandrovsky Garden** just next to the Kremlin Wall, very cruisy even during day time. If you are into the military, try your luck in a park next to **Prospekt Vernadskogo** metro station (red line), popular in the afternoon.

❖ Gay Beach (GM): **Serebriany Bor**, M° Shchukinskaya (violet line). Find the bridge across the river, reach a peninsula and go to the left from the bridge, keep walking about 10-15 min.

BARS 🍴 RESTAURANTS 🍴

● Bars/Clubs (GM): **Banana**, bar and disco daily, 23-06 hrs, 50/12 Baumanskaya Ul. (M° Baumankaya - yellow line) (267-4504); **Chance**, disco, in the old Hammer & Sickle House of Culture, two dance floors, occasional strip show, 11/15 Volochaeskaya Uliza, M° Ploschad Ilicha (yellow line) (298-6247); **Imperya Kino** (Cinema Empire), popular with younger gays and hustlers, entrance fee US$10, at Teatr Kinoaktiora, 33 Povarskaya Ul., next to the US Embassy, M° Barrikadnaya - violet line), Fri-Fri 23-06 hrs (290-3725); **Techno Bar**, dance club Mon-Wed, big disco Thu-Sun. 23-06 hrs., the club is surrounded by aquariums with a show at 2:00 am featuring naked boys swimming with the fish (lucky fish aren't they). Thecno Bar is a part of the **Chance** complex, popular on weekends; ✪ **Tri Obeziany** (**Three Monkeys**), private gay club for members only access system, a must for any foreign visitor, bar/disco daily 18-09 hrs., very popular on weekends when special shows are arranged, live entertainment, male strippers. Entrance fee on Fri. and Sat. US$10 including one drink. For guest card(s) call the Kremlin Tours in Russia. In the USA call Odysseus (800) 257-5344 or (516) 944-5330. Foreign visitors are admitted with Passport.

● Bars/Clubs (GW): **Dyke**, live entertainment, 4 Trubnaya Ploschad, at the Three Monkeys Club, Sat. 18-23 hrs. (163-8002).

● Bars/Clubs (AW): **Advantage**, cruise bar, hustlers, 11-24 hrs., 2 Pushkinskaya Ul. M° Okhotny Riad - red line; **Manhattan-Express**, American style bar and disco, not gay but popular with many gays, entrance fee about US$30, 23-06 hrs. in the North-West wing of the Rossiya Hotel, 6 Varvarka Ul., M° Kitai-Gorod, orange or violet line (298-5354); **Titanik**, most prestigious and expensive disco in Moscow, not gay but popular with young and wealthy gays, entrance fee

about US$30, 23-06 hrs, in the Stadion Yunykh Pionerov (Pioneer's Stadium), 31 Leningradsky Prospekt (M° Dinamo - Green line) (213-4581); **Utopiya**, not gay but popular with younger gays in the Rossiya Cinema, 2 Bolshaya Dmitrovka Ul. M° Pushkinskaya - violet line, or M° Tverskaya - green line, 23-06 hrs. (229-0003).

● Restaurant (GM): ✪ **Angelicos**, Mediterranean cuisine, friendly service, 12-02 hrs., 6/1 Bolshoy Karetny Per (M° Tsvetnoy Bulvar - grey line) (299-3696); **Banana**, international cuisine, open 24 hrs., 50/12 Baumanskaya Ul. in the Banana Club (267-4504); ✪ **Three Monkeys**, international & Russian cuisine, open: 24 hrs., at the Tri Obeziany Club, 4 Trubanaya Sq. (208-4637). Other (AW): **Azteca**, Mexican cuisine, popular with gays, cruising in the area, open: 24 hrs., 3/5 Tverskaya Ul. next to the Intourist Hotel, M° Okhothny Riad - red line; **Grot**, international cuisine, 10 Dobrovolcheskaya Ul., M° Toganskaya - Circular or violet line, 12-02 hrs. (911-2141); **Teatro** at Hotel Metropol, 1/4 Teatralny Proezd (927-6000).

λ SERVICES λ

● Advertising (GMW): ✪ **Kremlin Advertising**, first gay advertising agency in Russia.

ЛЕФОРТОВО
H   O   T   E   L

USA/Canada reservations (800) 257-5344

Advertising and promotional campaigns in Russia and abroad. Ads design and layout, legal consulting, distribution of international publications in Russia, PO Box 44, 105318 Moscow E-318. Tel: 251-1438. Fax: 250-5700. Email: kremln@dol.ru

● Beauty Salon (GM): ✪ **Giordgio**, massage, solarium, body correction, tatoo, bar, 17 Protochny Per., M° Smolenskaya - dark blue line, (241-4083) phone may change in Spring '97.

● Escort Service (GM): ✪ **Alexander**, the only reliable escort service in Moscow, 24 hrs., catalogues available, moderate prices. Also models agency and trans-show "Urals Gems" (219-5031). Pager: 974-0111 or 25-612 or 33-638. Email: alexandr@investur.perm.su. Internet: http://nevod.perm.su/partners/investur or http://gayrussia.msk-ru

● Health Care: **AIDS Center**, 14/2 Vosmaya (8th) Ul. Sokolinoy Gory, M° Semionovskaya - dark-blue line, 9-18 hrs. (365-5665).

● Health Clubs (GM): **Beguemot** (Hippo), private sauna club, entrance fee about US$10, M° Profsoyuznaya, orange-line, 12-02 hrs. For guest cards and other information call Kremlin

Tours; **Nemo**, sauna, 25 Novoalekseevskaya Ul., M° Alexeevskaya - Orange line.

● Health Club (AW): **Health & Swim Club**, gym, sauna, pool, solarium, popular with wealthy gays especially foreigners, at the Radisson Slavianskaya Hotel, 7-22 hrs., 2 Berezhkovskaya Naberezhnaya, M° Kievskaya - circular Blue or dark blue line (941-8020); **Sanduny**, popular with gays, magnificent interior, dom la Pervy (First) Neglinny Pereulok, M° Kuznetsky Most - violet line, 9-22 hrs. closed Tues. (925-4631).

● Video/Mail Order (GM): ✪ **Moscow Gay Service**, All gay Russian videos, magazines, leather etc., PO Box 11, 115563 (394-2689).

● Sex Shops (G/S): there are no specific sex shops for gays in Russia, but at any shop listed below you can find sex toys and erotica for gays. **Intim**, 6 Zemlianov Val, closed: sunday, M° Kurskaya - circular or dark blue line (916-0659); **Intim**, dom 29, stroenie 3 Pervaya (1st) Tverskaya-Yamskaya Ul.; **Kazanova**, dom 4, stroyenie 3 Stary Arbat, open: 10-19 hrs., M° Arbatskaya - dark blue line (203-5434).

● Tourism (GMW): **Kremlin Tours**, travel arrangements, visas, accommodations, special VIP services for businessmen, PO Box 44, Moscow E-318. Tel/Fax 274-7421 or 464-1814. Email: kremln@dol.ru.

◈ ACCOMMODATIONS ◈

ACCOMMODATIONS NETWORK
Private apartments in downtown Moscow. Prices from US$50. Available from Kremlin Tours Tel/Fax: (95) 916-0659. In the USA/Canada from Odysseus (800) 257-5344 or (516) 944-5330. Fax: (516) 944-7540.

BELGRADE HOTEL
Smolenskaya Square, Moscow 119121. Tel: (95) 248-7848. TYPE: *Hotel*. LOCATION: Sadovoye ring in city center. CLIENTELE: Mostly tourists. 920 Rooms w/bath. 145 Suites. phone, radio, A/C. restaurant, bars, cafe. medical room, currency exchange. 20 mi. (32 km) to Airport. Rates: (US) $120-$160. DESCRIPTION: 3 star hotel in the center of Moscow.

✪ LEFORTOVO HOTEL
1/4 Pervy Krasnokursantsky Proezd, M° Aviamotornaya - yellow line. Reservations: Kremlin Tours Tel/Fax: (95) 916-0659. In the USA/Canada from Odysseus (800) 257-5344 or (516) 944-5330. Fax: (516) 944-7540. TYPE: *Hotel*. CLIENTELE: Gay Welcome (mostly businessmen).

LOCATION: Lefortovo District, next to River Yauza embankment, 10 min. driving distance from the Kremlin.

* 56 rooms w/bath, 6 suites,
* Satelite CTV, phone, C/H, writing desk
* 24 hrs room service, restaurant, 2 bars, beauty salon, fitness center, sauna, massage, solarium
* Gay Bars: many nearby
* Airport: 30 min. (taxi)
* Open: year round
* Rates: US$120-$200 W/RB
* *TAC:* 10%

DESCRIPTION: Gay friendly elegant boutique hotel with unique Russian atmosphere in the heart of Moscow. Tastefully furnished guest rooms with excellent service and welcoming staff. Moscow style breakfast served in room.

HOTEL METROPOL
1/4 Tatralny Proezd, Moscow 10312. Tel: (501) 927-6000. TYPE: *Hotel.* CLIENTELE: All Welcome. LOCATION: Downtown Moscow, few minutes walk to Red Square. 403 rooms w/priv. bath, CTV (CNN), minibar, satelite phone/fax, 70 plush old world suites, fitness center, gym, sauna, massage, Metropol restaurant & cafe. Rates: $440 - $1,800. DESCRIPTION: Elegant deluxe landmark hotel.

SAVOY MOSCOW HOTEL
3 Roshdestvenka St., Moscow 103012. Tel: (59) 929-8500, Fax: (59) 230-2186. TYPE: *Hotel.* LOCATION: Near the Bolshoi Theatre, Kremlin, and the Red Square. CLIENTELE: Foreign Tourists. 86 Rooms w/private bath. 4 Suites. CTV, phone, minibar, room service, restaurant, bars, art gallery, limo & travel service. 3 km (2 mi.) to Train Station. Credit Cards: MC/VISA/AMEX/CB/DC. Rates: (US) $240 - $380. DESCRIPTION: Victorian style Russian/Finnish run hotel in a great location with international amenities.

UKRAINA HOTEL
2/1 Kutuzovsky Pr., Moscow. Tel: (95) 243-3021. TYPE: *Hotel.* CLIENTELE: Foreign Tourists. LOCATION: on a curve of the Moskva River, 20 min. drive from town center. 1500 rooms w/priv. bath. 24 suites, phone, radio, A/C, restaurant & rooftop café, currency exchange, parking. 1 km (2/3 mi.) to train station. Rates: (US) $120 - $240. DESCRIPTION: Giant 30-story 3 star hotel. Gays sometimes meet at the rooftop cafe.

ST. PETERSBURG   © 812

✈ Pulkovo Airport (LED)
11 mi. / 18 km south

LOCATION: On the shores of the Baltic close to Finland.

POPULATION: 4,600,000

CLIMATE: Changeable weather, humid and foggy. Fairly mild for the northern location. In January the average temperature is about -8°c (17°F), and in July it is 18°c (64°F).

Gay/Lesbian Visitor Information
Kremlin Tours: 246-9292
Email: kremln@dol.ru

DESCRIPTION: St. Petersburg is the most European of all the Soviet cities. Founded in 1703 it was the Russian capital under the Czars. St. Petersburg became Leningrad after the Russian Revolution and became a symbol of bravery when the German invading armies where stopped at the city's gate during WWII at a very high cost in human life and property. Today, it is a thriving city known for its architecture, history and culture.

● To meet local gays: the crusiest place in town is **Dumskaya Ulitsa**, next to the **Gostiny Dvor**, M° Gostiny Dvor - yellow line, with its small open-air cafes always popular with local guys and arcades of Gostiny Dvor; also take a late evening walk (10 or 11 pm) on **Nevski Prospekt**, try the small park next to the Katherine the Great monument on Nevsky Prospekt. On a sunny day try sunbathing on the Neva embankment along the walls of **Peter's Fortress**. St. Petersburg is full of sailors from all over the Baltic countries.

BARS ♈ RESTAURANTS 🍴

● Bars/clubs (GMW): **Amadey**, club & cafe, disco on Fri & Sat. 23-07 hrs, 12 Sverdlovskaya Naberezhnaya (embankment) at DK "Krasny Vyborzhets" M° Finliandsky Vokzal - red line (174-5120 or 112-8335); **Mayak**, very popular club with late night shows, 23 Galernaya Ul., at the DK "Mayak" M° Nevsky Prospekt - blue line, Fri. & Sat. nights only 24-06 hrs., (311-4311).

● Bars/clubs (AW): **Candy Man**, Kosygina Prospekt 23-06 hrs, M° yellow line; **Domenicos**, 70 Nevsky Prospekt, M° Mayakovskaya - green line (272-5717); **Piramida**, 23-06 hrs., 3 Lomonosova Ul. M° Nevsky Prospekt - blue line; **Tribunal**, 12-03 hrs., Senatskaya Ploschad (Square) at the corner of the Angliyskaya Noberezhnaya (English Embankment).

● Restaurants (AW): **Cat**, moderate prices, friendly gay waiters, 12-24 hrs., 24 Kravannaya Ul., M° Nevsky Prospekt - blue line (315-3900); **Literaturnoye Cafe**, Russian & International cuisine, 12-24 hrs., elegant restaurant popular with wealthy gays, 18 Nevsky Prospekt, M° Nevsky Prospekt - blue line (312-8543); **Metropol**, the oldest restaurant in St. Petersburg with the best Russian food, 22 Sadovaya St., (no English spoken); **Sadko**, tourist restaurant, corner of Nevsky Prospekt & Brodsky St.

λ SERVICES λ

● Advertising (GMW): ✪ **Poleff Group**, advertising & legal consulting, PO Box 70, 191025. Tel: 272-6538. Fax: 272-6562. Email: poleff@mail.nevalink.ru

● Health Club (G/S): **Yamskie Bani**, Very cruisy sauna, especially in the afternoon, try the third floor and dark staircase leading to the attic, Wed.-Sun., 9-21 hrs., 9 Dostoevskogo Ul. M° Vladimirskaya - red line (312-5836).

● Sex Shops (G/S): **Intim**, 10-19 hrs., 2 Vosstaniya Ul. M° Ploschad Vosstaniya - red line (279-5761); **Kolos**, 10-19 hrs., 58 Liteiny Prospekt, M° Mayakovskaya - green line (279-9855); **Soneks**, 10-19 hrs., 1 Shepetovskaya Ul., M° Novocherkasskaya - yellow line (224-2937).

● Tourism (GMW): ✪ **Kremlin Tours**, gay travel, visas, multi entry 1 year visas, guides, accommodations. Tel/Fax: 246-9292. Email: kremln@dol.ru.

🏠 ACCOMMODATIONS 🏠

ACCOMMODATIONS NETWORK
Private apartments in downtown Moscow. Prices from US$50. Available from Kremlin Tours Tel/Fax: (812) 246-9292. In the USA/Canada from Odysseus (800) 257-5344 or (516) 944-5330. Fax: (516) 944-7540.

EUROPEYSKAYA HOTEL
1/7 Brodsky St., St. Petersburg 191031. Tel: (812) 210-3295.TYPE: *Hotel.* CLIENTELE: Tourists. LOCATION: Center of town overlooking Arts Square near Nevsky Prospect. 225 Rooms some w/bath. 78 Suites. restaurants, bars, cafeteria, sauna. Rates: on request. DESCRIPTION: A 5-story old-fashioned hotel. Rooms are decorated with antiques. Some gays at the Hotel bar.

MOSKVA HOTEL
2 Aleksandra Nevskogo Pl., M° Ploshchad Aleksandra Nevskogo, green or yellow line. Tel: (812) 274-2100. TYPE: *Hotel.* CLIENTELE: Mostly Tourists. LOCATION: Very convenient downtown location next to metro station. 770 rooms w/bath, restaurants, bars, sauna, beauty salon, 22 km / 14 mi. from airport. Rates: US$120-$160. Special lower rates available through Kremlin Tours or Odysseus. DESCRIPTION: A 7-story modern hotel rated 3-stars.

SOCHI   ℭ   812

✈ Adler Airport

LOCATION: Southwestern Russia on the Black Sea, at the foot of the Caucasus Mts.

CLIMATE: Excellent subtropical climate year round. The average winter temperature in January is 43˚F (6˚c); and the average summer temperature in July is 85˚F (29˚c).

DESCRIPTION: Sochi is the largest and best known of Russia's Seaside resorts. It offers beautiful beaches, health spas and casino gaming at the Radisson Hotel Lazurnaya.

❖ Beach: **Teatraluju**, nude beach across the street from the Hotel Magnolie.

BARS Y RESTAURANTS 🍴

● Bars/clubs (G/S): **Bar** at Hotel Leningrad; **Café** at Hotel Primorskaya.

🏠 ACCOMMODATIONS 🏠

ZHEMCHUZHINA HOTEL
3 Chernomorskaya St., Sochi 354076. Tel: (8622) 922-060. TYPE: *Hotel.* CLIENTELE: All Welcome. LOCATION: 2 km / 1 mi from city center overlooking the Black Sea.

* Rooms: 993 w/priv. bath. Suites: 41
* Rooms for non smokers, wheelchair access
* CTV, phone, balcony
* Restaurants (6), bars (15), sauna, pool
* Rates: $90-$140

DESCRIPTION: Nineteen story tourist class hotel in a convenient beach location.

SAINT MARTIN
(FRENCH WEST INDIES)

AREA: 20 sq. mi. (52 sq. km)
POPULATION: 28,000
CAPITAL: Marigot
CURRENCY: French Francs (FF), US$ is accepted everywhere.
OFFICIAL LANGUAGE: French
ONLY RELIGION: Roman Catholicism
Telephone: 590
Nat'l Holiday: Bastille Day, July 14
Official Time: G.M.T. - 4
Electricity: 110v 60c AC
Exchange Rate: 1US$ = FF 4.86
National Airline: N/A

LAW REGARDING HOMOSEXUALITY: Saint Martin is a French overseas territory and it is subject to French jurisdiction. Homosexuality is accepted and the law is the same as it is in france. People are generally friendly and homosexuality does not seem to be a problem.

❖ Due to the devastating effect of Hurricane Marilyn on St. Martin during late summer of 1995, some of the information given in this section may not be accurate.

MARIGOT

✈ Esperance Airport (SFG)
 Juliana Airport (SXM)

LOCATION: On the island of St. Martin, 100 mi. / 160 km off the east coast of the US Virgin Islands, on the French northern part of the island. Marigot sits on an open bay.

POPULATION: 14,000

CLIMATE: Always pleasantly warm, though it can be humid. Temperatures vary between 60°F - 80°F (16°c-26°c) with little seasonal change. Evenings are cooled by ocean trade winds.

VISITOR INFORMATION
French West Indies Tourist Board
610 5th Ave., NY, NY 10020
Tel: (212) 757-1125

DESCRIPTION: The tiny island is divided between the French and the Dutch. **Marigot** the capital of the French section is characterized by small gingerbread homes. Although French is the official language, English is widely spoken. The island offers nude beaches in the French part, duty free shopping and casinos in the Dutch part.

❖ Beaches: **Cupecoy Beach**, north of the Dutch-French border, check the the 'clothing optional' beach at the far end of Cupecoy.

BARS ♈ RESTAURANTS 🍴

● Bar/Club (GM): **L'Atmosphere**, dance club with gay following, on the Marina in Marigot (875-024); **La Bodega'y**, bar, disco, Marina Royale (872-993).

● Restaurants (AW): **David's**, steak and seafood, rue de la Liberté (875-158); **La Brasserie**, French/Seafood, rue du Général de Gaulle (879-443).

🏠 ACCOMMODATIONS 🏠

LA SAMANA HOTEL
Cupecoy Bay. Tel: 875-122. TYPE: *Hotel.*
CLIENTELE: All Welcome. LOCATION: On Cupecoy Beach, nude beach nearby.

* Rooms: 85 w/priv. bath
* CTV, phone, A/C
* Cooking facilities
* Restaurant, bar, disco
* Pool, gym, sauna, tennis, parking
* Beach: mixed nude beach nearby
* Airport: 10 minutes
* Open: Year round
* Rates: (US) $275-$530
* *TAC:* 10%

DESCRIPTION: Exotic resort resembling a luxurious Moorish Mediterranean village, situated on 55 remote acres on a secluded beach. Beachfront rooms and apartments with dining area, and spacious patio.

SAUDI ARABIA

AREA: 829,995 sq. mi. (2,149,687 sq. km)
POPULATION: 8,500,000
CAPITAL: Riyadh
CURRENCY: Saudi Riyal (SR)
OFFICIAL LANGUAGE: Arabic
ONLY RELIGION: Islam
Telephone: 966
Nat'l Holiday: National Day, 23 September
Official Time: G.M.T. + 3
Electricity: 110 volts
Exchange Rate: 1US$ = S$3.75
National Airline: Saudia

LAW REGARDING HOMOSEXUALITY: In this fanatic Islamic country, all homosexual acts between men as well as women can be punished with the death penalty. However, the law only applies in extreme cases. It is necessary for gay visitors or business persons to be extremely cautious.

AL-KHOBAR / DAMMAN / DHAHRAN   © 03

✈ Dhahran Int'l Airport (DHA)
8 mi. / 13 km southeast

 ACCOMMODATIONS

HOTEL AL-KHOBAR
Corniche Blvd., P.O. Box 1266, Al-Kobar 31952. Tel: (03) 864-6000. TYPE: *Superior First Class Hotel*. CLIENTELE: Mostly Straight. LOCATION: On the edge of a residential area over looking the Gulf and private beach. Rooms: 339 w/ priv. bath, 22 suites, Villas: 13, CTV, phone, minibar, restaurants, gym. Rates: (US) $80-$160. *TAC:* 10%. DESCRIPTION: An international hotel with possible cruising in the sauna.

JEDDAH   © 02

✈ King Abdul Aziz Int'l Airport (JED)
11 mi. / 18 km north

DESCRIPTION: Important port on the Red Sea and the country's commercial and diplomatic capital. ❖ Beaches at "**The Creek**" and "**29 Palms**" provide cruising opportunities for Europeans and other foreigners.

 ACCOMMODATIONS

ALBILAD HOTEL MOEVENPICK
Al Cornish Hwy. Tel: (02) 691-0111. Fax: (02) 681-2208. TYPE: *Hotel*. CLIENTELE: Mostly Straight. LOCATION: On the Red Sea. 363 rooms, 40 suites, CTV, phone, A/C, coffee shop, jacuzzi, gym, private beach. Rates: (US) $70-$160. *TAC:* 10%. DESCRIPTION: First class hotel with some possible cruising in the sauna and the jacuzzi.

RIYADH   © 01

✈ King Khaled Int'l Airport (RUH)
22 mi. / 35 km north

DESCRIPTION: The capital of Saudi Arabia is a modern city. Apart from the Royal Palace and some museums it boasts the largest commercial airport in the world.

BARS Y RESTAURANTS ¶¶

● There are no gay bars or restaurants in Riyadh. In general rule the bars and restaurants at the better international hotels are the best place to meet other gay people at late hours. Also check **Hardi's Burger Coffee Shop**, popular among young saudis.

 ACCOMMODATIONS

MARRIOTT RIYADH HOTEL
P.O. Box 16294. Riyadh 11464. Tel: (01) 477-9300. Fax: (01) 477-9089. TYPE: *Hotel*. CLIENTELE: Mostly Straight. LOCATION: Downtown Riyadh location. 369 rooms, 23 suites, CTV, phone, A/C, restaurant, coffee shop, pool, health club, sauna. Rates: (US) $110 - $140. *TAC:* 10%. DESCRIPTION: Deluxe downtown hotel with fine amenities. Some cruising in the sauna and swimming pool area.

SEYCHELLES

AREA: 108 sq. mi. (280 sq. km)
POPULATION: 69,000
CAPITAL: Victoria
CURRENCY: Seychelles Rupee (SCR)
OFFICIAL LANGUAGES: English, French
MAJOR RELIGIONS: Roman Catholicism
Telephone: 248
Nat'l Holiday: Independence Day, June 29
Official Time: G.M.T. + 4
Electricity: 240 volts 50c AC
Exchange Rate: 1US$ = SCR 503
National Airline: Air Seychelles

LAW REGARDING HOMOSEXUALITY:
Homosexual acts are illegal. Probably as a result of an outdated Colonial British law. There is no support for gay and lesbian rights as there may not be that many on the island. Seychelles rely heavily on tourism and therefore it is very unlikely that gay tourists will encounter problems as long as they are discreet.

MAHÉ ISLAND

✈ Seychelles Int'l Airport (SEZ)

LOCATION: The Seychelles islands (about 115 islands) are located off the coast of Eastern Africa in the Indian Ocean, between the equator and the 10th parallel south.

CLIMATE: The temperature is a constant and comfortable 24°c-29°c (75°F-85°F) year round. Seasons are defined by the beginning and end of the south-east trade winds usually from May to October. The rest of the year is a rainy northwest monsoon climate. Seychelles are outside of the cyclone zone and are therefore safer for November to April travel.

DESCRIPTION: Mahé is the largest of the Seychelles islands and the home of Victoria the capital and business center of the islands. About 85% of the country's tourism infrastructure is on this island. The islands are official haven for tropical birds, fish with parts of the islands designated as marine national parks. For gay visitors the main meeting points are between the Beau Vallon Bay Hotel and Fisherman'sCove Hotel.

❖ Beaches: **Beau Vallon Beach** one of the largest and the most popular beach in the Seychelles; **South Mahé Beaches**, quieter prettier and more secluded beaches.

BARS ♈ RESTAURANTS ♍

Check out the bars and clubs at the major tourist hotels as there is no established scene for gay or lesbian travelers. The resort hotels offer live entertainment, good restaurants, dances and films.

ACCOMMODATIONS

BERJAYA BEAU VALLON BAY HOTEL
Beau Vallon, Mahe. Tel: 247-382. TYPE: *Hotel.* CLIENTELE: All Welcome. LOCATION: Beau Vallon Bay.

* Rooms: 182 w/priv. bath. Suite: 1
* CTV, phone, minibar, A/C, hairdryer
* Restaurants (3), bar, casino
* Maid Service, room service, laundry
* Pool, poolside bar, games room, boutiques
* Diving center, water sports, tennis
* Beach: on the beach
* Airport: 20 km / 13 mi.
* Open: Year round
* Rates: $250 - $360

DESCRIPTION: First class beach front resort complex and casino.

CASUARINA BEACH
Anse aux Pins, Mahe. Tel: 376-211. TYPE: *Guest House.* CLIENTELE: All Welcome. LOCATION: Barrier Reef of Anse aux Pins, south of the International Airport.

* Rooms: 14 w/priv. bath
* A/C, terrace, Ocean views
* Restaurant, dinning terrace, bar
* Airport: 3 mi. / 5 km
* Rates: $110 - $160

DESCRIPTION: Beachfront hotel & restaurant. Excellent diving and snorkeling nearby.

SINGAPORE

AREA: 226 sq. mi. (618 sq. km)
POPULATION: 2,480,000
CAPITAL: Singapore
CURRENCY: Singapore Dollar (S$)
OFFICIAL LANGUAGES: English (Most commonly spoken), Mandarin, Malai & Tamil.
MAJOR RELIGIONS: Christianity, Islam, Hinduism and various Chinese religions.
Telephone: 65
Nat'l Holiday: National Day, Aug. 9
Official Time: G.M.T. + 8
Electricity: 220 volts
Exchange Rate: 1US$ = S$1.41
National Airline: Singapore Airlines

LAW REGARDING HOMOSEXUALITY:
Homosexuality is punishable by 10 years to life imprisonment. Gay men are barred from night-clubs, bars and discos with frequent crackdown and harassment by the police. Undercover officers pose as homosexuals and pray on gay men near the park or the central district areas. Homosexual acts between women is not mentioned in the Code of Law.

SINGAPORE   © 65

✈ Changi Int'l Airport (SIN)
11 mi. / 18 km northeast

LOCATION: Island city-state at the southern tip of the Malay Peninsula in South East Asia.

POPULATION: 3,000,000. 76% Chinese, 15% Malay, 7% Indian, 2% Others.

CLIMATE: Hot and humid year round with an average daily temperature of 80°F (27°c) and 80% humidity. Average annual rainfall 95" (2327mm).

Gay & Lesbian Visitor Information
Gay Liberation Singapore
PO Box 299, Raffles City Post Office 9117

DESCRIPTION: Singapore is a compact Police-City-State in the heart of South-East Asia; on the tip of the Malaysian peninsula. Most travelers or business persons to the Orient usually consider Singapore as one of their many destinations. Here they can enjoy the comforts of a modern, cosmopolitan city with international banking facilities, cleanliness and easy access to places within and outside the country. Formerly known as a "shoppers' paradise", Singapore has lost much of its competitive edge to Hong Kong and Taiwan. But the city is not as congested or densely populated as other major Asian cities.

The main attraction is the diversity of the population: there are different ethnic festivals and celebrations, ethnic quarters, places of worship, shrines, monuments and cultural performances. This ethnic diversity adds to the country's exotic cuisine which most visitors cannot forget. Since Singapore is a tropical country with summer year round, many visitors simply relax on the beaches or take tours to several outlying islands.

❖ The gay community in Singapore is under constant human rights violations and surveillance by the local authorities. Nightclubs that cater to gay clientele are often harassed and their patrons abused by the police. If you have enough gay pride skip Singapore, and spend your gay money somewhere else. In Singapore they do not only forbid to play with a butt, they will destroy yours for doing it.

In absence of established gay scene such as clubs, bars and discos, gay men known locally as PLU's (people like us) either meet in private homes or take to public cruising. Popular cruising exists mostly in the **Orchard Road - Scotts Road** hub. During the day time guys cruise along the shopping malls and food centers. The popular malls are: **The Far East Plaza, Lucky Plaza, Scotts Center, Plaza Singapura, Raffles City Shopping Center**, especially 3rd floor around atrium escalator, Raffles City is fast becoming the new cruisy spot in Singapore ; and **Liang Court**. All within the Orchard Road - Scotts Road nexus.

❖ Beaches: **Sentosa Island** is the most frequented island resort for families and gay men alike. It is accessible by a ferry or a cable car. Gays prefer the portion near the golf course which is cruisy on Sundays. Skinny dipping is common since the area is away from where the families are. **Marine Parade Beach** (East Coast Parkway) is another popular beach with gay crowds. Go to the area of the beach near the **Big Splash Seafood** restaurant popular with young gays. Another gay beach known to locals as **"Obayashigumi"** is located about a mile from the Big Splash Restaurant and close to the **People's Association** campsite. This beach is more secluded, therefore more sexually active. Another place to cool off in a cruisy gay atmosphere is the **River Valley** (RV) Swimming Pool, just opposite Liang Court/ Daimaru, directly opposite the Hotel New Otani. This is the only gay place in Singapore that is timeless; gays cruise here day and night, weekdays or weekend.

BARS Y RESTAURANTS ᛁᛁ

❖ Note: due to constant police harassment of gays in Singapore, gay bars and clubs regularly move premises.

● Bars/Clubs (GM): **Babylon**, 52 Tanjong Pagar Rd. (227-7466); **Exchange**, 304 Orchard Rd.#06-01 Lucky Plaza (733-1943); **Gate**, dance club, Orchard Hotel, 442 Orchard Rd. (734-7766); **Velvet Underground**, dance club, 21 Jiak Kim St. (738-2988); **Vincent**, 304 Orchard Rd. #06-05 Lucky Plaza (736-1360).

ACCOMMODATIONS

Note: There are no gay hotels in Singapore. Most hotels require guests to register the people they bring back to their rooms.

HOTEL BENCOOLEN
47 Bencoolen St., Singapore 0718. Tel: 336-0822. TYPE: *Hotel*. CLIENTELE: Mostly Straight. LOCATION: On the edge of Tourist Belt (Orchard Road), in the heart of the city, 5 minutes to commercial area (Wall Street of Singapore) & 5 minutes to shopping centres. 68 rooms w/priv. bath, CTV (lounge), phone, A/C,

coffee house for snacks. Rates: S$80-$135. DESCRIPTION: Economic, 16-Story high hotel in the middle of town, provides sufficient security and basic comfort. Quiet, ideal for bringing people back to your room with no problems.

ORCHARD HOTEL
442 Orchard Rd., Singapore 0923. Tel: 734-7766. TYPE: *Hotel*. CLIENTELE: All Welcome. LOCATION: Shopping & entertainment district.679 w/priv. bath. Suites: 15, rooms for non-smokers, CTV (CNN, movies), phone, minibar, A/C, hair dryer, coffee/tea making facilities, restaurants, pool, poolside bar, lounges, disco on premises. Rates: $140 - $260 *TAC:* 10%. DESCRIPTION: Superior first class hotel with fine amenities and service in a central location.

RIVER VIEW HOTEL
382 Havelock Rd., Singapore 0316. Tel: (65) 732-9922. Fax: (65) 732-1034. TYPE: *Hotel*. CLIENTELE: All Welcome. LOCATION: Riverside, 5 min. from business district.

* Rooms: 472 w/priv. bath. Suites: 8
* CTV, phone, minibar, marble bath
* Non-smokers rooms, wheelchair access
* Bar, disco, coffee shop
* Pool, poolside bar, health club, sauna
* Gay friendly disco on premises
* Airport: 20 mi. / 32 km, taxi
* Rates: S$180-$260.
* *TAC:* 10%

DESCRIPTION: First class hotel near Orchard Rd. and Chinatown.

TANGLIN COURT HOTEL
2-4 Kim Yam Road, Singapore 0923. Tel: 737-3581, 737-8802. TYPE: *Hotel*. CLIENTELE: Mostly Straight. LOCATION: Good location, 5 minutes walk from Orchard Road. Easy transport nearby (buses and taxis). Rooms: w/shared/priv. bath. Rates: S$68/day. DESCRIPTION: Quiet hotel, with private rooms located near shopping and the gay scene.

SINT MAARTEN
(DUTCH WEST INDIES)

AREA: 37 sq. mi. (96 sq. km)
POPULATION: 21,000
CAPITAL: Philipsburg
CURRENCY: NA Florins (Naf), US$ is accepted everywhere.
OFFICIAL LANGUAGE: Dutch
ONLY RELIGION: Protestantism, Roman Catholicism
Telephone: 590
Nat'l Holiday: St. Maarten's Day, Nov. 11
Official Time: G.M.T. - 4
Electricity: 110/220v 60c AC
Exchange Rate: 1US$ = Naf 1.79
National Airline: ALM

LAW REGARDING HOMOSEXUALITY: St Maarten is a Dutch overseas territory and it is subject to Dutch jurisdiction. Homosexuality is legal and the law is the same as it is in the Netherlands. People are generally friendly and homosexuality does not seem to be a problem.

▲ Due to the devastating effect of Hurricane Marilyn on St. Maarten during late summer of 1995, some of the information given in this section may not be accurate.

PHILIPSBURG

✈ Juliana Airport (SXM)
  Esperance Airport (SFG)

LOCATION: On the island of St. Maarten, 100 mi. / 160 km off the east coast of the US Virgin Islands, on the Dutch southern part of the island. Philipsburg sits on Great Salt Pond & Great Bay.

POPULATION: 16,000

CLIMATE: Always pleasantly warm, though it can be humid. Temperatures vary between 60°F - 80°F (16°c-26°c) with little seasonal change. Evenings are cooled by ocean trade winds.

VISITOR INFORMATION
St. Maarten Tourist Information
275 7th Ave., NY, NY 10020
Tel: (212) 989-000

DESCRIPTION: The tiny island is divided between the Dutch and the French. **Philipsburg** the capital of the Dutch section curves like a toy village along Great Bay. The historic town still retains some of its unique shingles architecture. Although Dutch is the official language, English is widely spoken. The island offers nude beaches in the French part, duty free shopping and casinos in the Dutch part.

❖ Beaches: **Cupecoy Beach**, north of the Dutch-French border, check the the 'clothing optional' beach at the far end of Cupecoy; **Oyster Pond Beach**, popular with bodysurfers; **Dawn Beach** famous for its underwater exotic beauty and reefs. Clothing optional not allowed on all the Dutch beaches.

BARS ⛾ RESTAURANTS 🍴

● Bars/Clubs (G/S); **Cheri's Cafe**, next to Maho Beach Resort, live reggae and latin music (5995-53361); **Music News Café**, Simpson Bay.

● Restaurant (AW): **The Greenhouse**, bar & restaurant with dance floor, Bobby's Marina, Philipsburg (5995-22941).

ACCOMMODATIONS

RAMA APARTMENTS
Point Blanche Bay. Tel: 5-22582. TYPE: *Rental Apts.* CLIENTELE: All Welcome. LOCATION: Overlooking the ocean, walking distance to Philipsburg. 22 Apts, 6 Suites, CTV, phone, A/C, balcony (some), pool, grocery store, free parking, restaurant & beaches nearby. Rates: (US) $70 - $90. DESCRIPTION: Simply furnished apts overlooking the ocean.

MAHO BEACH RESORT & CASINO
Maho Bay. Tel: 5-52115. TYPE: *Resort Hotel & Casino.* CLIENTELE: All Welcome. LOCATION: Beachfront on rocky cliff at Maho Beach. 600 rooms w/priv. bath, 40 suites, CTV, phone, A/C, jacuzzi, kitchenette, nightclub, pool, health club. Rates: (US) $120 - $320. DESCRIPTION: Elegant first class resort.

SLOVAKIA

AREA: 18,928 sq. mi. (49,035 sq. km)
POPULATION: 5,300,000
CAPITAL: Bratislava
CURRENCY: Slovak Crown (Sk)
OFFICIAL LANGUAGE: Slovak
MAJOR RELIGIONS: Roman Catholicism, Protestantism
Telephone: 42
Nat'l Holiday: Independence Day
Official Time: GMT +1
Electricity: 220 volts
Exchange Rate: 1US$ = Sk 29.39
National Airline:

LAW REGARDING HOMOSEXUALITY: Homosexuality between consenting adults is not illegal. The legal age of consent is 15 years.

BRATISLAVA ✆ 07

✈ Ivanka Airport (BTS) 7.5 mi. / 12 km N.

LOCATION: Western Slovakia, 35 mi. / 56 km east of Vienna (Austria).

POPULATION: 380,000

Gay/Lesbian Visitor Information
Ganymedes: (07) 253-888
Box 4, Bratislava 830 00

DESCRIPTION: The capital of Slovakia. Bratislava is rich in history and has a fairly active cultural life. Visit: the **Old Town**, the Gothic-Renaissance square of Primaciálne námestie; the **Old Town Hall** and the elegant **Primate's Palace**. The gay scene is very limited. There is some action at the Park near the Slovak National Theatre, and the Park at state Hospital (Americké neamestie).

BARS ▼ RESTAURANTS ¶¶

● Bars/Clubs (GM): **Apollon**, dance club, Panenska 24 (5311-536); **Kamel Klub**, Molecova ul. - Karlova ves. Brat. (362-390).

λ SERVICES λ

● Health Club (G/S): **Kúpele Grössling**, mainly gay, Kúpelná ulica.

ACCOMMODATIONS

HOTEL CARLTON
Hviezdoslavovo nám. 7, Bratislava 811 00. Tel: (7) 331851. TYPE: *Hotel*. CLIENTELE: Mostly Straight. LOCATION: Center of town. 276. Class A (w/priv. facilities) and B rooms, Attractive view of Bratislava's most picturesque Square. Rates: $60 and up.

KOSICE ✆ 095

✈ Kosice Airport

LOCATION: Southeastern Slovakia near the Hungarian border.

POPULATION: 200,000

DESCRIPTION: The second largest city in Slovakia. Kosice is a large tourist center with a major gypsy population. It is historically and ethnically close to Hungary.

BARS ▼ RESTAURANTS ¶¶

● Bars/Clubs (AW): **Klub Folklorneho suboru & Carnica**, Löfflerova 1; **Micro Bar**, Biela Ulica; **Wine Cellar** at the Interhotel Slovan (see info below).

● Restaurants (AW): **Miskolc**, Hungarian cuisine, Hlavná ulica 65; **Yalta**, Hlvaná ulica 69.

ACCOMMODATIONS

INTERHOTEL SLOVAN
Hlavná 1, Kosice. Tel: (89) 95227. TYPE: *Hotel*. CLIENTELE: Mostly Straight. LOCATION: Center of town in busy shopping area. 212 rooms w/priv. bath, phone, radio, restaurants, wine cellar, day bar, summer terrace. Rates: on request. DESCRIPTION: Popular hotel.

SLOVENIA

AREA: 7,814 sq. mi. (20,251 sq. km)
POPULATION: 2,100,000
CAPITAL: Ljubljana
CURRENCY: Slovenian Tolar (Slt)
OFFICIAL LANGUAGE: Slovene
MAJOR RELIGIONS: Roman Catholicism
Telephone: 38
Nat'l Holiday: Dec. 26 Independence Day
Official Time: GMT + 1 or 2
Electricity: 220 volts, 50c AC
Exchange Rate: 1US$ = Slt 122.41
National Airline: Adria Airways

LAW REGARDING HOMOSEXUALITY:
The age of consent for homosexual and heterosexual sex is 16.

LJUBLJANA   © 61

✈ Barnik Airport (LJU)
   8 mi. / 13 km Northwest

LOCATION: Heart of Slovenia.

POPULATION: 200,000

Gay/Lesbian Visitor Information
ROZA Club
Kersnikova 4, 61000 Ljubljana
Tel: (61) 124-089 (Tue/Thu 12-14h)

DESCRIPTION: The capital of the Republic of
Slovenia, Ljubljana is the cosmopolitan and
economic center of the nation. The city is
known for its baroque palaces and churches
and has interesting mix of architectural styles
from the 15th - 20th century. Visit the **National Museum**, 20 Presernova, is one of the oldest
in Europe. For gay travelers, the cruisy areas
are: **Old Lubljana**; a Park behind a gas station (area between Dunajska St., Celovska St.
and the Railway Line AYOR can be dangerous
at night)

❖ Beach: **The Left bank of River Sava**.
Straight from the city by Dunajska Street, at the
Crnuce bridge turn to the left and at the Zagar's
Inn turn to the river. Only in the summer.

♈ BARS ♈

● Bars/Clubs (GMW): **Galerija**, cafe, Mestni
trg 5; **Kavarna Union (Café Union)**, Miklosiceva St.; **Klub K4** (The Pink Disco), Kersnikova 4, every Sunday from 22h-4h. (closed
August); **Magnus Cafe**, Metelkova; **Opéra
Bar**, Cankarjeva Cesta, across from the US
Cultural Center.

λ SERVICE λ

● Sauna (GM/S): **Sauna Zlati Klub**, Straight
sauna with mostly gay men clientele, (at Tivoli).

ACCOMMODATIONS

HOLIDAY INN
Miklosiceva 3, Ljubljana 61000. Tel: (61) 150-
023. Fax: (61) 150-323. TYPE: *Hotel*. CLIEN-
TELE: Mostly Straight. LOCATION: Historic
Old Town. 133 rooms w/priv. bath, CTV, telephone, A/C, restaurant, swimming pool, fitness
center. Open: year round. Rates: US$130 and
up. *TAC:* 10%.

SLON HOTEL
Titova 10, Lubljana 61001. Tel: (61) 151-232.
TYPE: *Hotel*. CLIENTELE: Mostly Straight.
LOCATION: Heart of the city. 185 rooms
w/priv. bath or shower, CTV, telephone, C/H,
cafe, nightclub, popular restaurant, free parking. Season: Year round. Rates: US$60 and up.
TAC: 10%. DESCRIPTION: Pleasant business
and group oriented hotel.

SOUTH AFRICA

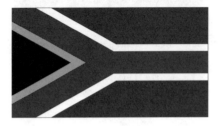

AREA: 455,318 sq. mi. (1,127,200 sq. km)
POPULATION: 43,000,000.
CAPITAL: Cape Town, Pretoria
CURRENCY: Rand (R)
OFFICIAL LANGUAGE: English, Afrikaans, and 10 indigenous languages
MAJOR RELIGIONS: Protestantism, Tribal religions, most major religions well represented
Telephone: 27
Nat'l Holiday: Republic Day, May 31
Official Time: G.M.T. + 2
Electricity: 250 volts / 50 cAc
Exchange Rate: 1US$ = R 4.65

National Airline: SAA

LAW REGARDING HOMOSEXUALITY: The South African Parliament is currently debating a proposal to outlaw discrimination on the basis of sexual orientation. If the law passes as it is expected to be, South Africa will have one of the most enlightened official attitudes towards homosexuality in the world.

❖ The dramatic changes in South Africa since the abolishment of apartheid and the establishment of a democratic society are having a tremendous impact on international tourism to this country. The liberalization of the laws regarding gays and lesbians and the existence of first class nightlife and entertainment businesses are making South Africa a excellent vacation destination for the international gay travellers.

CAPE TOWN   ✆   021

✈ D.F. Malan AP (CPT) 14 mi. / 22 km SE

LOCATION: Southwestern tip of South Africa on the Atlantic Ocean.

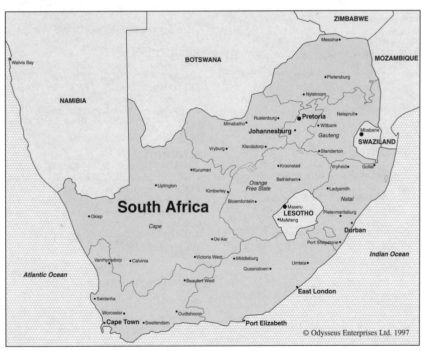

© Odysseus Enterprises Ltd. 1997

POPULATION: 860,000

CLIMATE: Sunny and temperate. South of the Equator, South Africa's seasons are the reversed of the northern hemisphere. June/ July is mid-winter, Christmas/Hanuka falls in midsummer. Summer average temperature is 22°c (72°F), and winter average temperature is 13°c (55°F).

Gay/Lesbian Visitor Information
Abigale: (021) 24-1532
(Association for bi-sexual, gay & lesbians)

DESCRIPTION: The oldest city in South Africa and the country's legislative capital. Founded by Dutch settlers in the 17th century, Cape Town has grown to become a true modern cosmopolitan city. The backdrop of the Table Mountain, and the blue Ocean add natural beauty to the city. The Cape Peninsula that stretches south of Cape Town is a miniature world with quaint fishing villages, secluded beaches and beautiful marine drive. Nearby **Sea Point**, close to the city centre is a traditional seaside holiday destination. A popular attraction is the entertainment offered by the **Victoria & Alfred Waterfront** adjacent to the Cape Town harbor.

❖ Beaches: **Clifton Beach**; **Graaf's Pool**, men-only nudist beach, across from the Winchester Mansions Hotel (Sea Point); **Sandy Bay Beach**, secluded nude beach used by all and accessed by walking from Llandudno, about 20 min. drive towards **Hout Bay**; also check the many beaches and the waterfront between **Sea Point** and **Camps Bay**.

BARS 🍸 RESTAURANTS 🍴

● Bars/clubs (GM): **Angels**, bar/disco, excellent music, 27, Somerset Rd. Greenpoint, wed/fri/sat 11pm till late (21-2958); **Brusnwick**, bar, mature clientele, Bree St. (25-2739); **Cafe Erte**, club, Astria Bldg., 265a Main St., Sea Point (434-6624); **Carte Blanche**, Trill Rd., Observatory (448-2266); **Don Pedro's**, 113 Roodebloem Rd., Woodstock (47-4493).

● Restaurants (GMW): **Al Gambero**, Bree St. (217-147); **Chaplin's Theatre Restaurant**, cafe, cabaret, live entertainment, excellent service and food, 253a Main Rd., Sea Point (434-8409); **Clementine's**, restaurant, live entertainment, Wolfe St., Chelsea Village, Wynberg (797-6168); **Eauver the Top**, restaurant, live entertainment, 77 Main Rd., Kalk Bay (788-3746); **Elaine's**, curry bistro, 105 Lower Main Rd., Observatory; **Mario's**, Italian, Main Rd., Greenpoint; **The Vox**, bar & cafe, video night (mon), 95 Lower Main Road, observatory (448-6894).

λ SERVICE λ

● Community Center (GMW): **Triangle**, 41 Salt River Rd., (448-3812).

● Health Club (GM): **Steamers**, steamroom, sauna, heated pool, bar. Open: 12 noon - 2am, weekends 24 hrs, Wembley & Solan St., Gardens (461-6210).

 ACCOMMODATIONS

CAPETONIAN HOTEL
Pier Place, Heerengracht Cape Town, P.O. Box 6856 Roggebaai 8012. Tel: (021) 21-1150. TYPE: *Hotel*. CLIENTELE: Mostly Straight. LOCATION: Centrally located, overlooking the harbor and Table Mountain. 170 rooms w/priv. bath. Suites: 50, CTV, phone, A/C, restaurant, coffee shop, bars, sauna, gym, wheelchair access. Rates: (R) 185 - 240. DESCRIPTION: Standard first class tourist hotel, government rated 4 stars, in a good central location. *Protea Hotels & Inns*.

CAPE TOWN INN
54 Bree St., Cape Town 8001. Tel: (021) 23-5116. Fax: (021) 24-2720. TYPE: *Hotel*. CLIENTELE: All Welcome. LOCATION: City centre, south-west corner of Bree and Strand Streets.

* Rooms: 84; 80 w/priv., 4 w/shared bath 3 sgl / 59 dbl / 15 triple / 7 quad
* Smoking allowed in rooms
* CTV, phone, A/C
* Suite: 1, 2-bedroom, full bath, kitchen
* Maid service, laundry service, elevator
* Restaurant: **La Copa** (Italian) & bar
* Gay Bars: 200 m / yards
* Health Club: 500 m / yards (mixed)
* Airport: Cape Town Int'l, 20 km / 13 mi.
* Train Station: Cape Town Central, 500 m / yards taxi, bus, walk
* Languages: English, French, Dutch, German, Afrikaans
* Reservations: 20% deposit
* Cancellation: details on request
* Credit Cards: MC/VISA/AMEX/DC
* Open: Year round
* Rates: (R) 195 per room (all taxes included)
* Check in 18:00 / Check out 10:30a

DESCRIPTION: 10-story newly appointed building with conference facilities and restaurant. City centre location. 3 star quality.

NEW REGENCY HOTEL
90 Regent Rd., Sea Point, Cape Town. Tel: (21) 439-6101. USA/Canada reservations: 1 (800) 257-5344. Tel: (516) 944-5330. Fax: (516) 944-

7540. TYPE: *Hotel.* CLIENTELE: All Welcome. LOCATION: Corner of Queens & Regent Rd.close to all beaches and famous waterfront.

* Rooms: 42 w/priv. bath
  8 sgl / 19 dbl / 8 triple / 7 quad
* Rooms for non smokers
* CTV, phone, safe box
* Room service, laundry service, elevator
* Bar: Guys and Dolls, Manhattan theme pool room. Jokers: Casino club
* Free parking
* Beach: 2 km / 1.5 mi. gay/nude
* Gay Bars: 2 km / 1.5 mi.
* Airport: DF Maion 30 km / 20 mi.
* Train Station: Cape Town 10 km / 6 mi.
* Languages: English, Afrikaans, German
* Credit Cards: MC/VISA/AMEX/DC
* Rates: R 165 - R 335; (off) R 117 - R 285 w/Eb. Check in 11:00a / Check out 11:00a
* *TAC:* 10%

DESCRIPTION: Totally refurbished hotel. All rooms are tastefully furnished, most with private balconies.

THE QUARTERS
De Waterkant, Cape Town. Tel: (82) 557-0824. Fax: (82) 419-1479. TYPE: *Guest House.* CLIENTELE: Gay men only. LOCATION: Walking distance to gay bars and clubs, 5 minutes to waterfront.

STONEHURST
3 Frere Rd., Sea Point 8001 (Cape Town). Tel: (021) 434-9670. USA/Canada reservation/information: Odysseus Tel: (516) 944-5330 or (800) 257-5344. Fax: (516) 944-7540 or (800) 982-6571. TYPE: *Guest House.* HOST: Jan Ludik. CLIENTELE: All Welcome. LOCATION: Off main road Sea Point, close to Adelphi Shopping Centre. 3 km / 2 mi. from Cape Town.

* Rooms: 18; 7 w/priv. bath, 11 w/shared sgl 6/ dbl 8/ triple 1/ quad 3
* Rooms for smokers and non smokers
* CTV (lounge), phone (public), cooking facilities, balcony, garden
* Wheelchair access, free parking
* Beach: 500 m/yards (gay/mixed/nude)
* Gay Bars: 1 km / 1/2 mi.
* Health Club: 1 km / 1/2 mi.
* Airport: 10 km / 6 mi, bus, taxi
* Train Station: Cape Town 1.5 km / 1 mi.
* Reservations: deposit required
* Cancellation: no refund
* Open: Year round
* Rates: (R) 60 - 150
* *TAC:* 10% (from Odysseus)

DESCRIPTION: 100 years old Victorian build-ing furnished with antiques. Fully equipped. Central kitchen open at all times. Self-catering rooms and flats.

WINCHESTER MANSIONS HOTEL
221 Beach Rd., Sea Point 8001. Tel: (21) 434-2351. USA/Canada: Tel: (516) 944-5330 or (800) 257-5344. Fax: (516) 944-7540 or (800) 982-6571. TYPE: *Hotel.* CLIENTELE: All Welcome. LOCATION: Cape-Town's Atlantic Promenade, overlooking the sea and a nude gay beach.

* Rooms: 47 w/priv. bath. Suites: 22
* CTV, phone, A/C (some rooms)
* Wheelchair accessibility
* Restaurant & courtyard, Café, pool
* Beach: across from nude gay beach
* Gay bars: in Capetown (2 km / 1.5 mi.)
* Airport: 12 km / 8 mi., bus, taxi
* Open: year round
* Rates: (R) 220 - 485. *TAC:* 10%

DESCRIPTION: Elegant Mansion-like hotel. Classic English style rooms and large executive suites with fresh flowers and polished furniture. 7 nights minimum stay mid-December to mid-January. No children under 12.

DURBAN   Ⓒ   031

✈ Louis Botha Airport (DUR)
10.5 mi. / 17 km SW

LOCATION: Eastern South Africa on the Indian Ocean.

POPULATION: 750,000

CLIMATE: Average July temperatures in the winter 48°F (9°c); average January temperature in the summer 66°F (19°c).

DESCRIPTION: An intriguing blend of East, West and native African, Durban offers a subtropical carnival atmosphere year round. Here you can enjoy endless summer, beautiful ocean coast lined with golden beaches, world class resorts and cosmopolitan nightlife scene. Explore a world of mosques, temples, oriental festivals, Zulu culture and exotic bazaars. Visit: **Durban's Flower Market, Seaworld,** and the **Victoria Street Market.**

BARS ♈ RESTAURANTS ♨

● Bar/club (GM): **Grumpy's**, 124 Point Rd. (368-1625).

● Restaurants (GMW):**Two Moon Junction**, 45 Windermere Rd., Morningside (303-3078); **Late Night Galleon**, coffee bar, Nedbank Centre, Cnr Point & West St. (32-4689).

🏠 ACCOMMODATIONS 🏠

THE BEACH HOTEL
Marine Parade. Tel: (31) 37-4222. TYPE: *Hotel*. CLIENTELE: All Welcome. LOCATION: Beachfront near shopping, 10 min. from city centre. 106 rooms w/priv. bath, CTV, phone, A/C, restaurant, bars. Rates: (US) $80 - $120.

EAST LONDON   ✆   0431

✈ Ben Schoeman Airport (ELS)

LOCATION: Southeastern South Africa, about 310 km / 195 mi. northeast of Port Elizabeth on the Atlantic Coast.

POPULATION: 120,000.

CLIMATE: see Cape Town.

DESCRIPTION: East London gained its place in South African history as a 'border' town on the frontier separating the white settlers from the native black tribes. It is the country's only river port on the mouth of the Buffalo River which is busy handling export of goods and agricultural produce. The town is a famous holiday resort with fine sandy beaches, and delightful mountain retreats.

❖ The 'Gay Beach' is at the end of the promenade after the 'Holiday Inn' in the sandy area. Best hours are late afternoons. Gay nightlife in this resort town is rather subdued. We do not know of any gay oriented bars or restaurants.

BARS 🍸 RESTAURANTS 🍴

● Bar/club (GMW):**Pandora's Box**, 35 Dyer St., Arcadia (call Dean at 432996 or 433570).

🏠 ACCOMMODATIONS 🏠

HOLIDAY INN
John Bailie Rd & Moore St., P.O. Box 1255, East London 5200. Tel: (0431) 27-260. Telex: 250021 SA. TYPE: *Hotel*. CLIENTELE: Mostly Straight. LOCATION: Walking distance of the 'Gay Beach'.

* Rooms: 173 w/priv. bath. Suites: 2
* Restaurant, coffee shop, bars
* CTV, phone, A/C, wheelchair accessible
* Pool, room & maid service
* Beach: near gay beach
* Gay Bars: none in area
* Airport: 6 mi. / 10 km
* Airport Transportation: taxi
* Credit Cards: MC/VISA/DC/BC/AMEX
* Open: Year round
* Rates: (R) 135 - 190. *TAC:* 10%

DESCRIPTION: Moderate first class 3-story hotel, government rated 3 stars. not gay oriented, but conveniently located to East London's 'Gay Beach'.

JOHANNESBURG   ✆   011

✈ Jan Smuts Int'l Airport (JNB)

LOCATION: In Gauteng, in the centre of the northern half of South Africa, 36 mi. (58 km) south of Pretoria.

POPULATION: City 645,230;
Metro 2,000,000

CLIMATE: Southern Hemisphere. Mild weather year round with average July temperatures of 48°F (9°c) in the winter, and average January temperature in the summer of 66°F (19°c), but can reach the mid 80°'s (26°c). Summer is a rainy season with late afternoon showers, winters are usually dry.

Gay/Lesbian Visitor Information
GLOW: (011) 336-5081

DESCRIPTION: Johannesburg, the largest city in South Africa, is also known known as the 'Golden City'. It stands 1,753 m (5,785 ft.) above sea level on an elevated ridge in the Gauteng's highland. Gauteng means "place of gold" in Sotho. Born as a gold mining camp in 1886, Johannesburg developed quickly into the largest city in South Africa. The city is modern with many highrise buildings; it offers multitudes of entertainment and recreation. **Yeoville**, is the counter-cultural or avantguard capital of South Africa with a large gay and lesbian population. It offers many informal and unpretentious restaurants, bars, and cafes along Rockey Street.

A short trip north of Johannesburg will take you to **Pretoria**, South Africa's administrative capital, founded in 1855. The city history is linked to Paul Kruger's pioneer days, and it is an elegant city with colorful gardens, tree-lined streets, and fine buildings. 250 miles (400 km) northeast is the famous **Kruger National Park**, one of the greatest game sanctuaries in the world. Here, on a huge area of 19,500 sq. km (7,529 sq. mi.) is the natural habitat of hundred of species of animals and birds.

BARS 🍸 RESTAURANTS 🍴

● Bars/clubs (GM): **Bob's Bar**, 76 Op De Bergen St., Fairview (624-1894); **Champions**, upscaled bar, corner Wolmarans and Loveday Sts., Braamfontein (720-6605 or 725-2697); **Club Zoo**, strictly leather bar, open: 10pm - 5am Wed-Sat., Hopkins St. behind CNA next to Checkers parking, Yeoville (447-1608); **Connections**, 1 Pretoria St., Pretoria Gate Bldg., Hillbrow (642-8511); **Gotham City**,dance club, leather bar, peep show cubicles. G-holes, coffee shop, erotic shows, safe and secure parking, open 12 noon daily, 58 Pretoria St., Hillbrow (447-1620); **Krypton**, bar, restaurant, Constantia Center, Tyrwhitt Ave., Rosebank, opposite house of sports cars (788-4708); **Pandora's**, piano lounge, 77 Cargo Cnr, Tyrwhitt Ave., Rosebank (447-3066); **Skyline**, Harrison Reef Hotel, Pretoria St., Hillbrow.

● Bars/clubs (GMW): **Champs-Elysées**, pub, club & coffee house, 70A Rockey St., Yeoville (082-410-1517 or 487-2465).

● Restaurants (AW): **Blue Crane**, Vierdelaan 15, Florida (472-3300); **Hamiltons**, The Colony Shopping Ctr, Jan Smutslaan, Craighall Park (442-6446); **Elaine's**, curry bistro, 9a Rockey St., Bellevue (648-0801); **Jose's**, late night Bar & Grill, 21 4th Ave., Parkhurst (788-4308); **Quasimodo**, bistro & bar, international menu, 430 Commissioner St., E. Fairview (614-5585); **Tea Room**, fully licensed coffee shop, breakfast & lunch, 17, Constantia Centre, below Krypton, Tyrwhitt Ave. Rosebank (442-4706); **Iyavaya**, African cuisine, 42 Hunter St., Yeoville (648-3500).

λ SERVICES λ

● Erotica (GM): **Priapus**, gay adult bookshop, videos, magazines, cnr. Victory & Quinn, Parkhurst (880-8316).

● Publication (GMW): **Exit**, South Africa's Gay & Lesbian newspaper keeps the world informed about social, political and constitutional developments. Also travel and other features, P.O. Box 32472, Braamfontein 2017. Tel: 011-614-9866. Fax: 011-618-3165.

🔑 ACCOMMODATIONS 🔑

BRAAMFONTEIN PROTEA
120 DeKorte St., Braamfontein 2017. Tel: (11) 403-5740. Fax: (11) 403-2401. TYPE: *All Suite Hotel*. CLIENTELE: All Welcome. LOCATION: Near Civic Center.

* Suites: 294 w/priv. bath
* Suites for non-smokers
* CTV, phone, A/C, minibar, balcony
* Restaurant, lounge, gym, sauna
* Gay Bars: some nearby
* Airport: 30 km / 19 mi., taxi
* Train Station: 1 km / 800 yards
* Open: Year round
* Credit Cards: MC/VISA/AMEX/DC
* Rates: R 275 - 330. *TAC:* 10%

DESCRIPTION: Multistory all-suite hotel. Renovations in 1992.

ROSEBANK HOTEL
Tyrwhitt & Sturdee Ave., Rosebank 2132. Tel: (11) 788-1820. Fax: (11) 788-4123. TYPE: *Hotel*. CLIENTELE: All Welcome. LOCATION: Quiet garden suburb, near Rosebank Shopping Center.

* Rooms: 212 w/priv. bath. Suites: 24
* CTV, phone, A/C
* Wheelchair accessible
* 24 hrs. room service
* Bar, restaurants
* Gay Bars: some nearby
* Airport: 26 km / 16 mi., taxi
* Open: Year round
* Credit Cards: MC/VISA/AMEX/DC
* Rates: from R 370
* *TAC:* 10%

DESCRIPTION: Smart business oriented hotel in a safe area.

PIKETBERG MTS   ✆ 0261

LOCATION: One and a half hour's drive from Cape Town.

🔑 ACCOMMODATIONS 🔑

NOUPOORT GUEST FARM
P.O. Box 101, Piketberg 7320. Tel: (261) 5754. TYPE: *Guest House*. HOST: Dr. J.K. Lipinski. CLIENTELE: Equal Gay/Straight. LOCATION: High on the western slopes of the Piketberg Mts. 10 cottages, pool, gym, sauna, jacuzzi, Rates: from R130. *TAC:* 10%

PORT ELIZABETH ✆ 041

LOCATION: Southern tip of the Eastern Cape.

POPULATION: 395,000

CLIMATE: Mediterranean climate. Pleasant and warm year round with plenty of sunshine. Midwinter occurs in June/July, midsummer Dec/Jan. Average maximum temperatures vary from 26.5°c (80°F) in January to 19.5°c (67°F) In July.

DESCRIPTION: Located in the scenic Eastern Cape, Port Elizabeth is a popular year round resort. Here you can find unlimited opportunities throughout the year for swimming, surfing, deep sea fishing, diving, yachting and sports. For culture there is museums, historical buildings, botanical gardens, and nature reserves. Visit: **Historic Market Square**, The **Oceanarium**; the **Snake Park House** and the **Tropical House** with its colorful display of exotic birds.

BARS ▼ RESTAURANTS ¶¶

● Bars/clubs (GMW): **Oscar's**, above Karieba Batteries, Hancock St., North End; **Priscilla's**, coffee shop, cnr Clyde & Lawrence Sts, central; **Rich's**, open 6 days (Tues.-Sun.) cnr Strand & Kemp Sts, Port Elizabeth Central (992-1664).

● Restaurant (GMW): **Galleri**, 95 Parliament St., Central.

🗝 ACCOMMODATIONS 🗝

BEACH HOTEL
Beach Rd., Humewood. Tel: (41) 53-2161. TYPE: *Hotel.* CLIENTELE: All Welcome. LOCATION: Overlooking Hobie Beach. 63 rooms w/priv. bath, CTV, phone, A/C, bars, restaurants. Friendly hotel with country club atmosphere. Rates: $60-$110.

PRETORIA ✆ 12

✈ Jan Smuts Int'l Airport (JNB)

LOCATION: In a fertile valley, less than an hour drive north from Johannesburg.

POPULATION: 560,000

CLIMATE: Slightly hotter than it is in Johannesburg.

Gay/Lesbian Visitor Information
GLOP: (012) 469-888
Gay & Lsbian Organization
of Pretoria

DESCRIPTION: Pretoria is the administrative capital of South Africa. It is a University and Science center specially noted for its fine buildings, colorful gardens and tree lined streets. City attractions include: **The aquarium**, exotic fishes and reptiles; **The Union Buildings**, housing government offices, great view over Pretoria, **Arcadia location**; **The South African Mint**, coin collection from all over the world; **Pretoria Art Museum** etc.

BARS ▼ RESTAURANTS ¶¶

The Pretoria Gay scene seems to be located near or around the Railway Station.

● Bars/clubs (GM): **Club 113**, bar, dance floor, dark rooms, weekend nudist party, splash pool, Rosslyn, Pretoria (542-4928); **Cock's Eye**, bar & restaurant, Gerard Moerdyk St., Oeverzicht Art Village, Sunnyside (341-06941); **Pancake Palazzo**, cocktail bar, Gerard Moerdyk St., Oeverzicht Art Village, Sunnyside; **Steamers**, most popular clubs in town, restaurant, disco, drag and strip shows, Paul Kruger & Railway Sts., Opp. Station (322-6278).

● Restaurants (GMW): **Die Opstal**, excellent food, great prices, Derdepoort Recreation Resort, 15 min. drive from Pretoria (808-2036); **Pavarotti's**, Sammy Marks Centre, 330 Church St. (323-4221). Other (AW): restaurants at the **Belgrave Hotel**, at the **Manhattan Hotel**, and at the **Continental Hotel**.

λ SERVICE λ

● Erotica (GM): **Adam**, videos, imported magazines, books, sex toys, 226 Duncan St. (342-4395/6).

🗝 ACCOMMODATIONS 🗝

CONTINENTAL HOTEL
152 Visagie St., Pretoria. Tel: (012) 3-2241. TYPE: *Hotel.* CLIENTELE: Gay/Straight. LOCATION: Opposite City Hall (corner of Bosman St.) near the Railway Station.

* Rooms: 60 w/private bath
* CTV Lounge, phone

Exit, P.O. Box 28827, Kensington 2101
Tel: (011) 614-9866. Fax: (011) 618-3165

* Bar: **Scrupules**
* Near Pretoria Railway Station
* Rates: R 50 and up

DESCRIPTION: Budget accommodations in the center of the Gay Scene.

EARL'S COURT B&B
PO Box 1739, Groenkloof, Pretoria 0027. Tel: (012) 463-141. TYPE: *Bed & Breakfast.* HOST: G. Manning, owner. CLIENTELE: Gay men. LOCATION: On Sir Herbert Baker St., in Groenkloof near Pretoria. 9 rooms w/shared bath. DESCRIPTION: Sixties style Bed & Breakfast mansion. Stunning views of Pretoria for the discerning clients.

MANHATTAN HOTEL
247 Schieding St., Pretoria 0007. Tel: (012) 28-6061. TYPE: *Hotel.* CLIENTELE: Mostly Straight. LOCATION: near town center and Burgers Park, north of the Railway Station, in the center of the Gay Scene.

* Rooms: 297 w/priv. bath. Suites: 10

* CTV, phone, roof garden, restaurant, bar, lounge, pool & sauna
* Room & maid service
* Gay Bars: behind Belgrave Hotel
* Airport: 22 mi. / 35 km, courtesy bus
* Credit Cards: MC/VISA/EC/DC/CB/AMEX
* Rates: (R) 105 - 140. *TAC:* 10%

DESCRIPTION: Modern 8-story hotel decorated in New York's Manhattan style. Government rated 3 stars. Fine amenities and conveniently located to the gay scene.

SIMON's TOWN   ✆   021

✈ D.F. Malan AP (CPT) 28 mi. / 45 km SE

LOCATION: Cape Peninsula, 45 min. by car or 2 hrs by train along the coast to Cape Town.

DESCRIPTION: Small historic town with victorian houses, scenic walks and home base to the South african marines. Nice beaches nearby including **Boulders Beach** with its famous penguin colony.

ACCOMMODATIONS

BAYVIEW B&B
12 Harington Rd., Seaforth / Simon's Town 7995. Tel/fax: (21) 786-3387. TYPE: *Bed & Breakfast.* HOSTS: Stephan & Keith. CLIENTELE: Gay men. LOCATION: 300 m / yards from Seaforth Beach. 1 room w/dbl bed shared bath, 2-bedroom apt with separate entrance. Rates: on request.

VAAL RIVER   ✆   082

LOCATION: Near Vanderbijlpark

ACCOMMODATIONS

THE BIRDCAGE
PO Box 3368, Vanderbijlpark 1900. Tel: (82) 87-2348. TYPE: *Guest House.* HOSTS: Rudy & Gawie. CLIENTELE: Gay men only. LOCATION: Vaal River opposite Cloudy Creek bird sanctuary. 5 rooms, pool, roman bath, jacuzzi, watersports. Rates: from R 445.

SPAIN

AREA: 194,881 sq. mi. (504,742 sq. km)
POPULATION: 37,430,000
CAPITAL: Madrid
CURRENCY: Peseta (PTS)
OFFICIAL LANGUAGE: Spanish
MAJOR RELIGIONS: Roman Catholicism
Telephone: 34
Nat'l Holiday: Nat'l Day. Oct. 12
Official Time: G.M.T. + 1
Electricity: 220 volts
Exchange Rate: 1US$ = PTS 126
National Airline: Iberia

LAW REGARDING HOMOSEXUALITY:
Homosexuality has been legalized since 1978,
but the Military Code still punishes homosexuality in the army with up to 6 years in prison.
In spite of the general trend towards liberalism
of the Spanish society that began after the
death of Franco, homosexuality remains a difficult issue for the local gay community. Spain's
parliament in April 1995 banned discrimination based on sexual orientation.

ALICANTE   ✆ 96

✈ Alicante Airport (ALC) 8 mi. / 13 km SW

LOCATION: Southeast Spain on the Mediterranean Sea, 168 km / 105 mi. south of Valencia.

POPULATION: 270,000

DESCRIPTION: Capital of the busy Costa
Blanca with good beaches and lively nightlife
in season.

❖ Beaches: try **San Juan de Alicante**, about
6 km / 4 mi. outside town reached by bus from
the Plaza del Mar or via train; **Playa Libre**,
just outside town where nudism is permitted,
between Playa Agua Amarga and Playa del Sal-

adar/Urbanova. For fabulous beaches take a day
trip to **Isla de Tabarca** to the south. Boats leave
from Explanada de España daily in summer.

BARS ♟ RESTAURANTS ♟♟

● Bars/Clubs (GM): **Boys**, video cruise bar, c/
Cesar Elguezabal 11; **Enigma**, c/ Arquitecto
Moret 23; **Jardineto**, c/ Baron de Finestrat 5;
Missing, dance club, dark room, porno videos,
c/ Gravina 4 (521-6728); **Montecristo**, cocktail
bar, c/ Ab-el-Hamet 1 (512-3189); **Rosses**, gay
disco, c/ San Juan Bosco 6.

● Restaurants (AW): **Auberge de France**,
French cuisine, La Albufereta Beach, Finca Las
Palmeras (526-0602); **Dársena**, regional cooking, on the quayside (520-7589); **El Delfin**, good
fresh food, c/ Esplanada de España 12 (521-4911).

λ SERVICES λ

● Erotica (GMW): **Quintana**, c/ Poeta Quintana 41; **Cosmopolitan**, sex shop, c/ Rafael
Altamira 5 (514-4822); **Sexyland**, c/ Segura 18
also c/ Mariano Luiña 9 (Elche).

● Health Clubs (GM): **Sauna 26**, Quintana 26,
1st Fl.; **Sauna Yogasaun**, c/ Marques de
Molins 34.

 ACCOMMODATIONS

PALAS HOTEL
Cervantes 5, Alicante E-03002. Tel: (6) 520-
9211. TYPE: *Hotel*. CLIENTELE: All Welcome.
LOCATION: Town center, 50 yards/m from
beach. 1 km from train station, 8 km / 6 mi.
from airport. Walk to gay clubs. 40 rooms
w/priv. bath, phone, CTV, room service, restaurant, lounge, parking. Rates: from $80/day.

BALEARIC ISLANDS

IBIZA   ✆ 971

✈ Ibiza Airport (IBZ) 2 mi. / 3 km South

LOCATION: An island in the Mediterranean
Sea off the east coast of Spain, the third largest
of the Balearic Archipelago. The island can be
reached by plan or boat. Distance from

Barcelona is 162 mi. / 260 km, and from Valencia 100 mi. / 160 km, boat crossing takes 8 hours.

POPULATION: 50,000

CLIMATE: Mediterranean with hot summers tempered by cool breezes, and cooler but sunny winters. Summer temperatures are in the 80°'sF (28°c), and winter temperatures are in the mid 60°'sF (18°c).

DESCRIPTION: Ibiza is one of the Balearic islands in the Mediterranean Sea. The island was "discovered" by hippies in the 1960s. Today the idyllic island with its gentle rolling green hills and mild sunny climate offers dream vacations. The beaches are magnificent, and the Mediterranean light is constant. Ibiza Town, the island's capital, also known locally as Eivissa, is a fairytale city with its Old Town (D'Alt Vila) at the top of a hill overlooking the harbor, surrounded by ancient walls. D'Alt Vila is Europe's most ancient fortress city with a history going back to the Phoenicians and Romans. The Old City at night is a sexual fantasyland for gays, with many bars, discos and clubs that cater to their whims. Ibiza attracts jet setters, celebrities and people from the fashion industry, and of course a large number of gays and lesbians.

Visit the **Archeological Museum** on Via Romana, with interesting collection of Punic relics, all of which were discovered on the island, and leisurely explore the **Vara De Rey** and the Harbor. Other tourist areas are **San Antonio**, with a beautiful Ibiza style church and lovely bay, and **Santa Eulalia del Rio**, a favorite beach resort with bohemians, painters and writers.

❖ Gay Beaches: There are two busy nude beaches in Ibiza: **Es Cavallet** (exclusively gay) and **Las Salinas**. Both are located south of Ibiza town. Bus to Las Salinas leaves from the bus terminal in Ibiza Town every 30 min. If you drive, go towards the Airport (Sant Jordi) and take the road called Canal. When you reach the bar called **Chiringay** you are in **Es Cavallet**. The beaches of Ibiza allow the practice of all water sports year round. In Formentera, the official nude beach is **Las Illetas**, but most of the other island beaches are available for nude bathing. To access the nude beaches in Formentera take the regular ferry service from Ibiza Port. **Figueretes**, is the nearest public beach, "Miami Beach" style.

❖ **TRAVEL SEASON**: April - October. High Season: July-September.

BARS ☨ RESTAURANTS 🍴

SPAIN 503

The gay scene in Ibiza is mostly geared to gay males, but some of the bars are mixed. Most of the gay bars are located in the Old Town (D'Alt Vila) or near the Port in or around the famous Calle de la Virgen 'Gay Street'.

● Bars/clubs (GM): **Angelo**, mixed disco, Paseo Maritime, opposite the harbor, walking distance from Ibiza Town; **Benidorm**, Sa Carossa 11; **Bronx**, Sa Carossa 4; **Capricho**, c/ La Virgen 42 (192-471); **Catacumbas**, cellar bar at the Hotel Marigna, Carrer de Al Sabini 18, Figueretas; **Catwalk**, c/ de la Virgen 42 (31-4279); **Crisco**, leather bar, dark room downstairs with porno videos, c/ Ignacio Riquier (301719); **Galeria**, c/ de la Virgen 64; **Garabato**, c/ Ignacio Riquer 17; **Geminis**, bar/cafeteria, Paseo de la Pitiusas s/n (392-565); **Incognito**, Calle Santa Lucia 23, Ibiza Town; **JJ Bar**, calle de la Virgen 79 (31-0247); **Leon**, cruise bar, c/. La Virgen 62; **Kinky**, C/. De Passdais 18; **Monroe's**, bar/cafeteria, c/ Ramon Muntaner 33, Figueretas (392-541); **Movie**, calle Mayor 34 (31-1526); **La Muralla**, Sa Carossa 2, (30-1883); **Paris Folie's**, show bar, c/ La Virgen 27 (313-555); **Samsara**, show bar, c/ La Virgen 44 (191-692); **Teatro**, cabaret/ entertainment complex, Virgen 83 (30-1719).

● Bars/clubs (GMW): **Anfora**, Ibiza's only exclusive gay disco, sleek, elegant and high energy, young crowd, San Carlos 5 (Old Town).

● Restaurants (AW): **Ca'n den Parra**, calle San Rafael 3 (39-1114); **Chiringay**, beach bar & restaurant at **Es Cavallet** gay nude beach; **El Olivo**, Plaça de la Vila (30-0680); **Dalt Vila**, cafe/restaurant, Plaza de Vila 3 (805-524); **Foc I Fum**, calle de la Virgen 55 (313-380); **The Casino Restaurant**, excellent restaurant inside the Ibiza casino, paseo Maritime, near the marina. (313-312); ✪ **El Portalon**, excellent food, great service, Pza Desamparados 1-2 (30-3901); **Escalon**, calle Santa Cruz 6 (302-3 79); **El Gordo**, French, catering to both gay men and lesbians, on the road to Santa Eulalia (331-717); **Jackpot Pizzeria**, for light meals 24 hrs. a day at the Ibiza Casino, paseo Maritime; **Montesol**, society cafe at the popular Vara dei Rey; **Pomelo**, C/. La Virgen 53 (313-122); **Sam Restaurant**, excellent seafood, affordable, near the harbor; **Sa Torre**, calle de la Virgen 78, Ibiza town; **S'Oficina**, elegant restaurant, Basque cuisine, Avda España 6 (301-116); **Teatro Pereyra**, C/. Abel Matutes s/n 1 (300964); **West Side**, Calle de la Virgen 4 (315-514).

❖ **SPECIAL BUY: Herbas Ibicencas**, Ibiza's own specialty herb liquor. This delightful liquor is not available anywhere else. Makes a great gift or souvenir.

λ **SERVICES** λ

● Erotica: **Sex Shop Non Stop**, Via Romana 48 (39-1473).

● Health Service: **Asociacion Antisida de Ibiza**, Aragón 85, 2º5a. (39-0414).

 **ACCOMMODATIONS**

✪ APARTHOTEL NAVILA

c./ San Luis 1, Ibiza. USA/Canada information/reservation: Odysseus - Tel: (516) 944-5330 or (800) 257-5344. Fax: (516) 944-7540 or (800) 982-6571. TYPE: *Apartments*. LOCATION: Central Old Town near many gay bars, shops and restaurants.

* Apartments: 13, 1 bedroom apts sleeping 2-4 people w/maid service
* Kitchenette, A/C, balcony, seaview (some)
* Rooftop pool, sundecks w/spectacular view
* Beach: 15 min. to gay beach
* Gay Bars: walking distance
* Airport: 15 min., taxi
* Season: Year round
* Rates: (US) $140 - $230
* *TAC:* 10% (from Odysseus)

DESCRIPTION: Renovated 500 years old mansion. Each apartment is individually decorated and different in style. All apartments are spacious with high ceilings, living room, kitchen and dining area, large bedroom, and large full bath, some with sky light. The best choice in the Old Town of Ibiza.

CLUB PARADISE

Playa Talamanca, Ibiza.USA/Canada reservations - Odysseus (800) 257-5344. Tel: (516) 944-5330. Fax: (516) 944-7540. TYPE: *Resort Complex*.CLIENTELE: Gay Welcome. LOCATION: On the beautiful Talamanca Beach overlooking the Old Town.

* Rooms: 210 w/priv. bath
* Phone, CTV, balcony
* Restaurant, bar, fitness center
* Pool, poolside bar
* Airport: 20 min. (taxi)
* Beach: on the beach, 20 min. to nude beach
* Gay Bars: 10 min. by car
* Open: May - October
* Rates: $160 - $240 w/CB
* *TAC:* 10% (from Odysseus)

DESCRIPTION: Beachfront holiday complex with excellent restaurant, large pool and fitness center. Popular with Italian tourists.

BARS
A Angels
B Anfora
C Crisco
D Gayleria
E Incognito
F La Muralla
G Teatro

RESTAURANTS
H Foc I Fum
J El Olivo
K Portalon

ACCOMMODATIONS
1 Aparthotel Navila
2 Delfino Verde
3 Hotel Marigna

Mediterranean Sea

Paseo Maritimo

Casino

Calle Virgen

OLD CITY

DALT VILA

S. Rafael
S. Carlos
C. Mayor

Puerto de Ibiza
Port size not to scale

Av. Andenes

Av. Ramon Y Tur Conde

Santa Eulalia del Rio

Vara del Rey

N E S W

IBIZA

Bull Ring

Pedro Frances

Av. Ignacio Wallis

Av. de España

Calle Leon

To Airport & Nude Beaches

To San Rafael

© Odysseus Enterprises Ltd. 1997

ODYSSEUS '97/98

DELFIN VERDE

c/. Garigo 2. USA/Canada reservations - Odysseus (800) 257-5344. Tel: (516) 944-5330. Fax: (516) 944-7540. TYPE: *Apartments Hotel*. CLIENTELE: Gay men. LOCATION: Port area near the gay clubs of c/. de la Virgen.

* Apartments: 20 w/priv. bath
* CTV, phone, A/C, small kitchenette
* Restaurant & bar
* Beach: 15 min. to nude beach (by car)
* Gay Bars: walking distance
* Airport: 15 min. (taxi)
* Open: May - October
* Rates: on request
* *TAC:* 10% (from Odysseus)

DESCRIPTION: Apartment-hotel in the port area near many gay bars and clubs. The location right in the middle of the nightclubs area is noisy day and night. Suitable mostly for younger guys who like to party.

✪ HOTEL MARIGNA

Carrer de Al Sabini 18, Playa Figueretes, Ibiza.USA/Canada information/ reservation: Odysseus - Tel: (516) 944-5330 or (800) 257-5344. Fax: (516) 944-7540 or (800) 982-6571. TYPE: *Hotel*. CLIENTELE: Gay men only.

LOCATION: In Playa Figueretes, 15 min. from the Old Town and gay bars. Bus stop to gay beach only 2 min. from the hotel.

* Rooms: 44 w/priv. bath. Studios: available 2 sgl / 39 dbl / 3 triple
* Smoking allowed in rooms
* Phone, safe box, balcony (some)
* Bar: **Catacomb** cellar bar
* Pool, sundeck, parking (off street)
* Beach: 10 min (gay beach)
* Gay Bars: 1 mi. / 1.6 km (Old Town)
* Health Club: 50 yards / meter
* Airport: 4 mi. / 6 km, taxi
* Languages: Spanish, German, Dutch, English
* Reservations: through Odysseus
* Open: April 1 - October 31
* Rates: from US$75 - $120 w/bB
* Check in time 2pm / check out 12 noon

DESCRIPTION: Ibiza's largest all gay hotel and the largest in Europe. Completely refurbished the hotel includes 2 bars, 2 lounges, huge breakfast hall, roof terrace, gay shop and coffee terrace.

PIKES

San Antonio, Ibiza. USA/Canada information/ reservation: Odysseus - Tel: (516) 944-5330 or

(800) 257-5344. Fax: (516) 944-7540 or (800) 982-6571. TYPE: *Resort Complex*. LOCATION: Countryside, away from tourist areas, 14 km / 9 mi. to Ibiza town (10 min. by car).

* Suites & Rooms: 24 w/priv. bath
* CTV (CNN/Satellite), phone, music unit, minibar, A/C, C/H, patio, terrace
* Restaurant: gourmet int'l cuisine
* Bar, pool, tennis court, sauna, swim spa, jacuzzi, gym
* Beach: 15 min (gay nude beach)
* Gay Bars: 15-20 min. by car
* Open: Year round
* Rates: (US) $230 and up
* *TAC:* 10% (from Odysseus)

DESCRIPTION: Low key secluded hideaway resort in a renovated 15th century Spanish pueblo style. All the rooms and suites are lavishly furnished and include all the modern comforts. The most elegant VIP suite is very spacious with private jacuzzi, open fire-place, kitchenette, personal gazebo and splendid views.

PALMA DE MALLORCA ✆ 971

✈ Palma de Mallorca Int'l AP (PMI)
5.5 mi. / 9 km east

LOCATION: On the island of Mallorca, the largest of the Balearic Islands.

POPULATION: 330,000

CLIMATE: Mediterranean with plenty of sunshine. Summers are warm with temperatures in the 80's F (27°c) cooled by sea breeze. Winters can be cold and windy with temperatures in the low 50's F (10°c). Spring and fall are mild and pleasant.

DESCRIPTION: A bustling cosmopolitan resort on the beautiful Bay of Palma and Spain's busiest port in the Mediterranean. Founded by the Romans, the city manifests distinguished architecture and influence of various periods that include: Arab, Medieval, Christian and Jewish. Visit the Old Quarter - **La Portella**, the busy port area **Paseo Maritime**; the spectacular **Casino de Mallorca** at the end of the Andraitx motorway in the Urbanizacion Sol de Mallorca (681-500).

The gay scene is concentrated around the Plaza Gomila on Avda Joan Miró in the center of town near the Centro Commercial.

BARS ♈ RESTAURANTS ▯▯

● Bars/clubs (GM): **Abaco**, cocktail bar, c/ San Juan s/n; **Aries**, C/. Parras 3 (at Av. Joamn Mirro) (737899); **Black Cat**, disco, Avda Joan Miró 75; **Ca'n Jordi**, video dance club, Pl. Mediterrráneo 2-4; **Channa-A**, dance club, Av. Joan Miró 75; **Finalmente**, private club, c/ Bartolome Quetglas 4 (Chalet) Cala Mayor (40-3548); **Obsession**, dance club, dark room, c/ Cabo Martorell Roca 15 (Cala Mayor); **Status**, popular pub, international ambiance, Avda Joan Miró 38 (454-030); **La Yedra**, Joan Miró 47 (737-493); **Yuppi**, Av. Joan Miró 106.

● Restaurants (GMW): **Don Sit**, Avda Joan Miró 49 (286-348); **El Jardin**, Avda Joan Miró 57 (454973); **La Pergola**, Plaza Atarazanas 13 (714-808).

λ SERVICES λ

● Erotica (GM): **Amsterdam**, gay videos, magazines, Av. Argentina 34 (73-9734); **Libreria Sexologica**, sex shop, c/ Vallori 2 (727-865); **Non Stop**, Joan Miro 30 (45-6340).

● Health Club (GM): **Aries**, C. Porras 3 (73-7899); **Spartacus**, gym, sauna, solarium, c/ Santo Espiritu, 8 bajos (72-5007).

ACCOMMODATIONS

HOTEL ROSAMAR
Joan Miro 74, 07015 Palma de Mallorca. Tel: (71) 732-723. TYPE: *Hotel*. CLIENTELE: Gay Welcome. LOCATION: On the famous Av. Joan Miro near the bay. DESCRIPTION: Economy two-star hotel with clean rooms.

PALMA BAY APTS
Palma de Mallorca. USA/Canada reservations - (800) 257-5344. Tel: (516) 944-5330. Fax: (516) 944-7540. TYPE: Apartments. CLIENTELE: Gay Welcome. LOCATION: City Center near the beaches. 5 fully equipped apartments, private and discreet, own key.

ROYAL CRISTINA APTS
Arenas de Bilbao, Playa de Palma. Tel: (71) 492550. TYPE: *Aparthotel*. CLIENTELE: All Welcome. LOCATION: Near the beach.

* Studios & Apts: 326
* CTV (CNN/Satellite), phone, minibar, terrace, A/C, cooking facilities
* Maid service, 24 hrs reception, free parking
* Restaurants, snack bar, cafeteria/pizzeria bars (3), water sports, billards

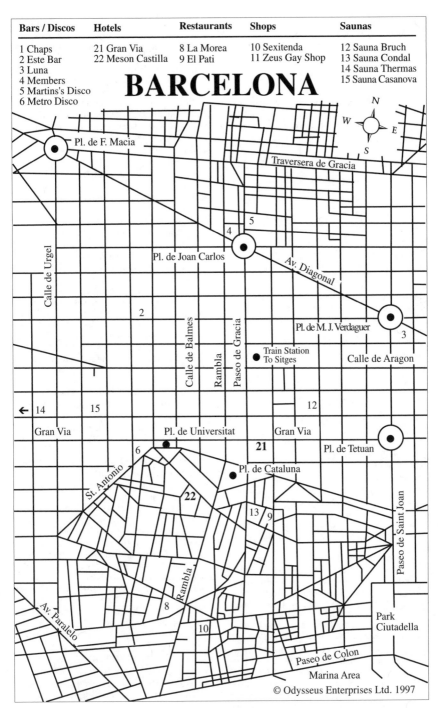

Bars / Discos	Hotels	Restaurants	Shops	Saunas
1 Chaps	21 Gran Via	8 La Morea	10 Sexitenda	12 Sauna Bruch
2 Este Bar	22 Meson Castilla	9 El Pati	11 Zeus Gay Shop	13 Sauna Condal
3 Luna				14 Sauna Thermas
4 Members				15 Sauna Casanova
5 Martins's Disco				
6 Metro Disco				

BARCELONA

Pl. de F. Macia

Traversera de Gracia

N
W E
S

Calle de Urgel

Pl. de Joan Carlos

Av. Diagonal

2

Calle de Balmes

Rambla

Paseo de Gracia

Pl. de M. J. Verdaguer

3

Train Station
To Sitges

Calle de Aragon

14   15

12

Gran Via

Pl. de Universitat

Gran Via

Pl. de Tetuan

6

21

Pl. de Cataluna

St. Antonio

22

Paseo de Saint Joan

13 9

Rambla

8

Av. Paralelo

10

Park
Ciutadella

Paseo de Colon

Marina Area

© Odysseus Enterprises Ltd. 1997

* Indoor & outdoor pools, sports center
* Beach: 100 m / yards
* Gay Bars: walking distance
* Open: Year round
* Rates: (US)$90 and up
* *TAC:* 10% (from Odysseus)

DESCRIPTION: Holiday apartments complex. Studios and one-bedroom apts with kitchenette, living room, and terrace.

BARCELONA   *©* 03

✈ Barcelona AP (BCN) 6.2 mi. / 14 km SW

LOCATION: On the Costa Dorada. A northeastern coast location on the Mediterranean Sea, northeast of Sitges.

POPULATION: 1,800,000

CLIMATE: Mild, moderate Mediterranean climate. Summer's high temperature averages 20°c (68°F). Average winter temperature is 10°c (50°F); Its climate is kept tempered by the vicinity to the sea and the semi circling mountains protect the city from cold north and west winds.

Gay/Lesbian Visitor Information
F.A.G.C.: 545-6398
Telefono Rosa: 237-7070 (18h-22h)

DESCRIPTION: Barcelona, Catalan in spirit and European in appearance, stretches out across the Catalonian plain between the Llobregat and Besós rivers, at the foot of the Tibidado Mountain. The city is rich with history which dates back to the Romans of 200BC who developed the port. Early in this century, Barcelona became an important art center where world famous artists and painters learned their fare and created great masterpieces. Some of the famous names include Joan Miró, Pablo Picasso and Juan Gris.

The people of Barcelona are known for their warmth, love of food, and cheerful spirit. Visit: **Barrio Gótico**, the Old Quarter with buildings representing 15 centuries of architectural history; **The Ramblas**, an open air market in the heart of the **Gothic Quarter**; the **Seaport**; and the **Columbus Monument**, completed in 1868 it is a fifty-meter (150ft) high column with the bronze statue of the Discoverer of America on top.

The gay spirit of Barcelona is reflected in its lively gay scene. Bars, shops and restaurants are located in or near the **Granvia**, **Avenida Diagonal** and the **Ramblas**. The gay scene is spread out, and nightlife starts late after midnight. Clubs open late and stay open until the early morning hours. Public cruising take place at the **Jardines Montjuic (Gardens)** (AYOR).

❖ Beaches: most town beaches are crowded with polluted water. **Playa San Sebastián** is the nearest gay beach. **Playa de Chernobil** is a nudist beach. For better/gayer beach travel to Sitges (40 km /25 mi.) down coast.

BARS ᵧ RESTAURANTS 🍴

● Bars/Clubs (GM): **Bananas**, dance club, c/ Moia 1; **Café de la Calle**, Calle Vic 11 (218-3863); **Colours**, Riera de San Miguel 59; **Este Bar**, Consell de Cent 257; **Fluxus**, bar, cafe, Diagonal 365 (215-5365); **James & Punto Club**, vda. Meridiana 244; **La Luna**, disco, Diagonal 323; **Martin's**, popular disco, porno videos, P² de Gracia 130 (228-1973); **Metro**, popular disco, Sepulveda 185 (323-5227); **Monroe's**, c/ Lincoln 3; **New Chaps**, leather bar, Avda Diagonal, M° Diagonal, 365 (215-5365); **Oh Patmos**, c/ Pádua 68; **Paris-Dakar**, Sant Marc 18-20; **Punto BCN**, Muntaner 63-65; **Que Te Dije**, c/ Riera de San Miguel 55; **Roma**, Alfonso XII, 41; **Taller**, disco, Méjico 7; **Tatu**, dance club, c/ Cayo Celio 7; **Topxi**, show bar/disco c/ Valencia 358.

● Bars/Clubs (GMW): **Bahia**, Séneca 12; **Café de la Calle**, Vic. 11; **Divertido**, c/. Moiá 1; **Este Bar**, consejo de Ciento, 257; **Gris**, Riera S. Miguel 59; **Punto BCN**, c/ Muntaner 63-65; **Roma**, c/ Alfons XII 41 (201-3513)..

● Bars/Clubs (GW): **Daniels**, calle Sta Petronila, Plaza Cardona (209-9978); **La Nostra Illa**, R. Benet 3; **La Rosa**, Brusi 39; **Members**, disco, calle Seneca 3.

● Restaurants (AW): Barcelona has great restaurants, the Ramblas is a popular place to experience local authentic cuisine, try **Amaya**, excellent Basque food, Ramblas Santa Mónica 24 (302-1037); **El Egypto**, inexpensive, popular and Bohemian, located behind the Boquería Market, Calle Jerusalen 12 (317-7480). Gay oriented restaurants: **Café de la Opera**, mixed coffee shop, cruisy during the day, Rambla 74; **El Patio**, pizzeria, calle Amargos 13 (302-0036); and **La Morera**, Plaza San Augustin 1 (318-7555).

λ SERVICES λ

● Health Clubs (GM): **Bruch**, bar, videos, jacuzzi, c/ Bruch 65 (487-4814); **Casanova**,

Barcelona's most modern gay men's health club, gym, fitness, solarium, snack bar, c/ Casanova, 57, 7th fl. open: 11pm-6am (323-7860) do not confuse with the next door Casanova Sauna on #59 which is for straights only; **Condal**, Barcelona's first all male health club & sauna, downtown near Pça. Catalunya, bar, video room, Finnish sauna, Espolsasacs 1, (301-9680): **Padua**, c/ La Gleva 34 (212-1654); **Thermas**, Disputació 46.

● Sex-Shops (GMW): **Libreria Sexologica**, c/ Diputació 222 (317-8939); **Sextienda**, c./ Raurich 11 (318-8676); **Zeus**, gay shop, videos, and information center, Riera Alta 20 (442-9795).

 **ACCOMMODATIONS**

HOTEL ALFA
Calle K, s/n Zona Franca, Barcelona. Tel: (93) 336-2564. USA/Canada: Tel: (516) 944-5330 or (800) 257-5344. Fax: (516) 944-7540 or (800) 982-6571. TYPE: *Hotel*. CLIENTELE: All Welcome. LOCATION: 2 mi. / 3 km from Airport and 20 min. from city center (courtesy van shuttle).

* Rooms: 99 w/priv. bath. Suite: 1
* CTV, phone, A/C, minibar, safe box
* Restaurant, bar, sauna, gym, pool
* Free parking, pets allowed
* Gay Bars: 30 min.
* Airport: 5 min., courtesy shuttle
* Open: Year round
* Rates: (US) $120 - $250
* *TAC:* 10% (from Odysseus)

DESCRIPTION: Superior tourist class hotel near the airport for travelers with early morning departures.

○ **HOTEL GRANVIA**
Gran Via 642, 08007 Barcelona. USA/Canada - Tel: (516) 944-5330 or (800) 257-5344. Fax: (516) 944-7540 or (800) 982-6571. TYPE: *Hotel*. CLIENTELE: Gay/Straight. LOCATION: Center of Barcelona near Pça. Cataluña.

* Rooms: 54 w/priv. bath
* CTV, phone, C/H, A/C
* Terrace cafe, restaurant
* Formal Antique filled Salon
* Parking nearby
* Beach: 30 min. (Sitges) gay/nude
* Airport: 10 km / 6 mi., taxi
* Gay Bars: many nearby
* Beach: 20 min. gay nude beach
* Health Club: walking distance
* Open: Year round
* Rates: US$ 110 - $180 w/CB
* *TAC:* 10% (from Odysseus)

DESCRIPTION: Late 1800 palatial style atmospheric three star hotel. Sweeping neoclassical staircase, complete with columns and arches, and a mirrored breakfast salon. Spacious rooms with twin or Queen size beds. Large full bath. Public spaces are tastefully decorated with antiques and objets d'art. The hotel is equipped with modern security and safety systems. **See advertisement in special Travel Supplement.**

MESON CASTILLA
Valldoncella 5, 08001 Barcelona. USA/Canada - Tel: (516) 944-5330 or (800) 257-5344. Fax: (516) 944-7540 or (800) 982-6571. TYPE: *Hotel*. CLIENTELE: Gay Welcome. LOCATION: Center of Barcelona near Plazas Castilla, Univesidad & Cataluña, walk to the Ramblas.

* Rooms: 60 w/priv. bath
* Phone, full bath, C/H
* Restaurant, bar
* Parking nearby
* Beach: 30 min. (Sitges) gay/nude
* Airport: 10 km / 6 mi., taxi
* Gay Bars: many nearby
* Beach: 20 min. gay nude beach
* Health Club: walking distance
* Open: Year round
* Rates: US$95 - $160 w/CB
* *TAC:* 10% (from Odysseus)

DESCRIPTION: Traditional style two-star hotel in a central location. Guest rooms and public areas are tastefully furnished with antique and period furnishings. Colorful ambiance and warm welcome to Odysseus customers.

BENIDORM   ℭ   96

✈ Alicante Airport (ALC)
55 km / 35 mi. south of Benidorm

LOCATION: On the famous Costa Blanca near Alicante. About 2 hrs. south of Valencia.

POPULATION: 30,000, swelling to 250,000 tourists during the high season.

CLIMATE: Hot summers with temperatures in the 90's°F (32°c) in July. Winter temperatures in January are mild around 61°F (16°F). Sunshine alternates with clouds and rain. Rainfall rarely last more than a day or two.

DESCRIPTION: The Old Fishing village of Benidorm is long gone. Today it is a mega resort, playground for the not-so-rich and famous.

'Hong-Kong by the sea', it is catering to package tours from England, France and Belgium. The Beaches are wide and sandy. The famous Playa Levante and Playa Poniente resemble Copacabana beach with high rise hotels and tourist developments. Benidorm offers some good gay nightlife in the Old City. It attracts mature gay and lesbian clientele to the bars on Alicante, Vicente and Santa Faz that run parallel to each other. It is a great holiday destination even with a grey hair or two. Here it does not really matter.

BARS ♈ RESTAURANTS 🍴

● Bars/Clubs (GM): **42nd Street**, video dance bar, Avda Uruguay (near Hipercondor); **Adonis**, c/ Santa Faz 39 (585-2045); **Chaplin**, c/ San Vicente 9; **David**, c/Mayor 9; **Eros**, c/ Santa Fez 24; **The Gardens**, friendly pub, c/ Alicante 18 / San Vincente 15; **Horpheos**, dance club, Plaza de la Constitucion 4; **People**, the most popular video/cruise bar in Benidorm, c/ Santa Fez 31; **Via Veneto**, dance bar, live shows, c/ Martinez Oriola 18;

● Bars/Clubs (GMW): **Exit**, popular disco, c/ Gerona (Hotel La Peña); **Mister Me**, c/ San Vicente 17; **Opción**, disco, c/ Mayor 8; **Peppermint**, C. San Vicente 11; **Zanzibar**, late night show bar, C. Santa Fez 5 (586-7807).

● Restaurants (AW): **Duomo**, gourmet pizzeria and and crêperia, excellent cuisine and service, c/ San Vicente 7 (586-5118); **El Puerto**, excellent seafood selection, Paseo Colón 1; **Posada Del Mar**, fresh seafood, Paseo Colón.

λ SERVICES λ

● Erotica (GM): **Sex Shop Benidorm**, cabins, videos, magazines, c/ San Roque 10.

● Health Clubs (GM): **Adonis Sauna**, c/ Venezuela 4 (585-7958); **Sauna Scorpio**, Finnish & steam sauna, massage, videos, c/ Ruzafa, Edif. Carrasco.

 ACCOMMODATIONS

LES DUNES SUITES
Playa Levante. USA/Canada reservations - Tel: (516) 944-5330 or (800) 257-5344. Fax: (516) 944-7540. TYPE: *Apartment Resort Complex.* CLIENTELE: All Welcome. LOCATION: Heart of the famous Levante Beach facing the sea, 10 min. walk to the Old Town.

* Apartments: 88 suite type
* CTV (Satellite), phone, safety box,

private terrace with seaview
* Light maid service (every 4 days)
* Laundry service, medical service
* Restaurant: full menu
* Pool, coffee lounge, garden solarium
* Free parking
* Gay Bars: 10 min. walk
* Beach: across the street, nude beach nearby
* Airport: Alicante 40 min (taxi/bus)
* Open: Year round
* Rates: (US)$80-$180
 High Season: July/Aug/Sept.
 Christmas and Holly Week
* TAC: 10% (from Odysseus)

DESCRIPTION: High rise holiday apartment complex in the heart of the Levante Beach. Each suite consists of: full kitchen, living room, dining area, double bedroom and a full bath. The apartments are suitable for 1 or 2 persons. Communicating apartments can be arranged for larger party.

LOS PELICANOS / LAS OCAS
C. Gerona, Playa Levante. USA/Canada reservations - Tel: (516) 944-5330 or (800) 257-5344. Fax: (516) 944-7540. TYPE: *Resort Complex.* CLIENTELE: All Welcome. LOCATION: 300 m / yards from the Levante Beach, 15 min. walk to the Old Town. 400 rooms w/priv. bath, phone, C/H, balcony. Facilities include: swimming pools, indoor and poolside bar, games rooms, all you can eat fixed price lunch/dinner. Rates: on request.

BILBAO　　　　　🍷　94

✈ Sondica Airport (BIO) 7 mi. / 11 km No.

LOCATION: Basque Country of Northern Spain 100 km / 63 mi. west of San Sebastian, 395 km / 250 mi. north of Madrid.

POPULATION: 370,000

DESCRIPTION: Founded in 1300, Bilbao is the industrial hub of Northern Spain. The city stretches along the narrow valley of the Nervion. Visit the **Casco Viejo**, the old city on the east bank of the river for bars, restaurants, antique shops and vibrant nightlife.

BARS ♈ RESTAURANTS 🍴

● Bars/Clubs (GM): **Este Bar**, cruise bar, c/ Hernani 3; **Bohemios**, c/ El Cristo 16; **Otxoa**, c/ Heros 9; **Sperma**, c/ Dos de Mayo 6; **Tevere**, popular video bar, c/ Lamana 1.

● Restaurants (AW): **Goizeko Kabi**, c/ Particular de Estraunza 4; **Gredos**, traditional cuisine, c/ Alameda de Urquijo 50 (443-5001);**Rogelio**, Basque cuisine, Basurto-Castrejana 7 (431-3021).

λ SERVICES λ

● Erotica (GM): **American's**, c/ Nicolas Arcorta 5; **Sex Shop**, c/ Ledesma 2.

● Health Clubs (GM): **Rodas**, c/ Garcia Salazar 14; **Oasis**, c/ Atxuri 43.

 ACCOMMODATIONS

HOTEL LOPEZ DE HARO
Obispo Orueta 2-4, Bilbao E-48009. Tel: (4) 423-5500. TYPE: *Hotel*. CLIENTELE: All WElcome. LOCATION: Heart oif commercial district, near museum and theatre. 53 rooms w/priv. bath, CTV, phone, A/C. minibar, safe, 24 hrs room service, restaurants, Tea Room. Rates: from $120/day.

CADIZ   ℂ   956

✈ San Pablo Airport (SVQ)

LOCATION: Costa de la Luz of Southern Spain. About 1-1/2 hrs drive from Seville.

DESCRIPTION: The oldest settlement in Spain. Cadiz reached its greatest period in the 18th century when it had the monopoly on the Spanish-American gold and silver sea trade. Visit the Old City **Inner Cadiz** with its historic quarters, open squares and sailors' alleyways.

Y BARS Y

● Bars/Clubs (GM): **El 20**, club, disco, entertainment, C. Cánovas del Castillo 27 (227-951); **El Desvan**, coffee shop, c/ Santo Cristo 8.

λ SERVICES λ

● Sex Shop (GMW): **Internacional**, c/ Pintor Murillo 2.

 ACCOMMODATIONS

LOS HELECHOS
Plaza Madre de Dios 9, 11540 Sanlúcar de Barameda. Tel: (56) 361349 or 367655. USA/

Canada reservations: (516) 944-5330 or (800) 257-5344. Fax: (516) 944-7540. TYPE: *Hotel*. CLIENTELE: All Welcome. LOCATION: Parque nacional de Doñana. 50 rooms w/priv. bath, CTV, phone, A/C, bar. Gay bars: nearby. Rates: $90-$125. *TAC:* 10% (from Odysseus).

CANARY ISLANDS

LAS PALMAS   ℂ   928

✈ De Grand Canaria Int'l Airport, Las Palmas (LPA) 30 km / 18 mi. south

LOCATION: Northern tip of Gran Canaria.

POPULATION: 370,000

DESCRIPTION: The seat of the autonomous government of the Canary Islands. Las Palmas is a major port city and a chief stop over for many commercial and holiday cruise ships.

BARS Y RESTAURANTS ||

● Bars/clubs (GM): **Bridge**, c/ Mariana Pineda 17; **Complice**, dance club, c/ Joaquin Cazlá 48; **Flash**, dance club, c/ Bernardo de la Torre 86; **Lady Pepa**, c/ Sargenta Llagas 32; **Las Marismas del Racio**, c/ Bernardo de la Torre 57 (278-476); **Metal**, dance club, dark room, c/ Dr. Miguel de la Rosa 37; **Punto de Encuentro**, dance club, c/ Ripoche 22; **Rio Bar**, Parque Santa Catalina; **Vertigo**,

λ SERVICES λ

● Health Clubs (GM): **Bronx**, c/ Bernardo de la Torre 37-39; **Trebol**, c/ Tomás Miller 55.

 ACCOMMODATIONS

CONCORDE HOTEL
Tomas Miller 85, Las Palmas. Tel: (28) 262750 TYPE: *Hotel*. CLIENTELE: All Welcome. LOCATION: 1 block from the beach, close to shopping and nightclubs. 128 rooms w/priv. bath, CTV, phone, A/C, minibar, rooftop restaurant, bars, rooftop pool and solarium. Rates: (US) $80-$130. DESCRIPTION: Impressive ultra-modern resort hotel overlooking the bay.

MASPALOMAS   © 928
PLAYA del INGLES

✈ De Grand Canaria Int'l Airport,
Las Palmas (LPA) 30 km / 18 mi. N.

LOCATION: Gran Canaria island is located in the Atlantic Ocean about 70 miles / 112 km off the Moroccan Coast. Maspalomas/Playa del Ingles is located on the southern tip of the Gran Canaria island, 43 km / 27 mi. south of Las Palmas, and about 30 km / 18 mi. south of the De Gran Canaria Int'l Airport.

POPULATION: 25,000

CLIMATE: Sub-tropical, with plenty of sunshine year round accompanied with little variation in temperatures. Winters average temperature in January is 69°F (20°c), and Summers average temperature in July is 81°F (27°c).

DESCRIPTION: Playa del Ingles, located at the extreme south of Gran Canaria has a pleasant sunny climate year round and some of the finest sand beaches on the island. **Las Palmas**, the largest city on the northern part of the island, is a popular resort for straight tourists, but has its own gay scene and certainly worth a visit. **Playa del Ingles** is the gay holiday playground of the Canary Islands attracting many northern European gays year round. All of the gay resorts in Playa del Ingles are exclusively all male, and so are most of the gay bars.

❖ Gay Nude Beach: **Playa de Maspalomas**, take the Avenida de las Dunas (by the lagoon) to the dunes or stroll along the gay part of the nudist beach. Or take a taxi/bus to El Faro (the Lighthouse) then proceed walking past the busy commercial center to the public beach. The gay beach is at the end of the official FKK nude beach.

❖ **TRAVEL SEASON**: Year round. High season is December to April.

BARS 🍴 RESTAURANTS 🍴

Most of the gay bars are located in the town's commercial centers: **Yumbo Center,** and **El Nilo**.

● Bars/clubs (GM): **Café Berlin**, intimate bar with a distinctive "Berliner" ambiance, Yumbo Center (3rd floor); **Centre Stage**, leather bar, Yumbo Center; **Cockpit**, Nilo Center; **Comeback**, Yumbo Center, 2nd floor; **Cruise,**

leather bar, Yumbo Center 2nd Fl.; **Hummel-Hummel**, café/bar, Yumbo Center (769-973); **Johny's**, Nilo Center; **Kings Club**, disco, Nilo Center & **Kings Club II** at the Yumbo Center; **La Belle Café**, where the fun never stops, mixed crowds, Yumbo Center (2nd floor); **Metropole**, late night disco, videos, back room, Yumbo Center (4th fl.); **Mykonos**, popular late night disco, Yumbo center, (4th floor); **Nestor**, pub, Yumbo Center, ground floor.

● Restaurants (AW): **Aubergine**, Yumbo Center (771-172); **Casa Richard**, Dutch cuisine, Yumbo Center; **Casa Vieja**, San Augustin; **Copper Kettle**, on the roundabout just before the Yumbo Center; **Bistro**, steak house, Sandia Center; **Movie**, cafe restaurant, Yumbo center, local 211-01, 2nd floor; **Valentine's**, Singapore style, Yumbo Center.

λ SERVICES λ

● Health Club (GM): **Nilo Sauna**, Nilo Center (765-464).

● Sex-Shops: **Men's Plaza**, Yumbo Center (1st fl.) 161 #4. Hrs. 17:00-3:00.

🔖 ACCOMMODATIONS 🔖

CATARINA HOTEL
Avda de Tirajana 1, Playa del Ingles. ReservationsUSA/Canada. Tel: (516) 944-5330 or (800) 257-5344. Fax: (516) 944-7540 or (800) 982-6571. TYPE: *Resort Complex.* CLIENTELE: All Welcome. LOCATION: Quiet area. Walk to gay nude beach and Yumbo Center.

* Rooms: 400 w/full bath
* Phone, radio, A/C, balcony, seaview (some)
* Restaurants, grill room, bars
* Fresh water pools (3), tennis courts, parking
* Airport: 40 min. Las Palmas
* Rates: (US) $120-$250 w/CB
* **TAC:** 10% (from Odysseus)

DESCRIPTION: First class 4-star resort hotel with a view of the dunes of Maspalomas. 400 spacious rooms divided in living room, bedroom, each 40 m² / 440 sq.ft. with balcony. Excellent quality and location to enjoy the nude beaches and nightlife.

✪ LOS ROBLES

Campo Int'l, Maspalomas. Reservations: USA/Canada. Tel: (516) 944-5330 or (800) 257-5344. Fax: (516) 944-7540 or (800) 982-6571. TYPE: *Resort Complex.* CLIENTELE: Gay men only.

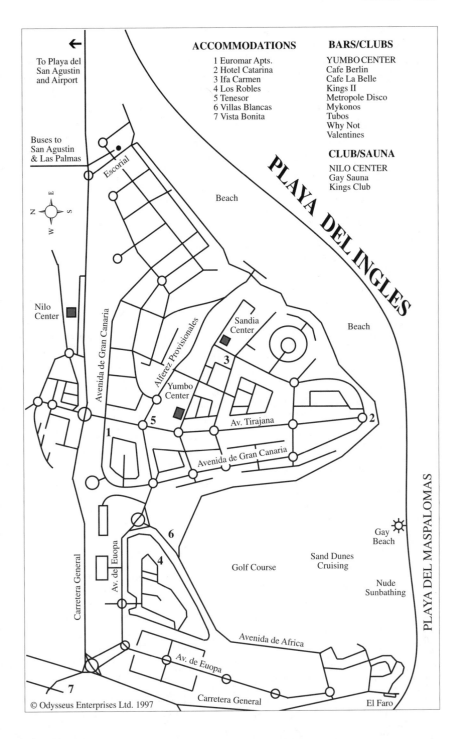

To Playa del
San Agustin
and Airport

ACCOMMODATIONS

1 Euromar Apts.
2 Hotel Catarina
3 Ifa Carmen
4 Los Robles
5 Tenesor
6 Villas Blancas
7 Vista Bonita

BARS/CLUBS

YUMBO CENTER
Cafe Berlin
Cafe La Belle
Kings II
Metropole Disco
Mykonos
Tubos
Why Not
Valentines

CLUB/SAUNA

NILO CENTER
Gay Sauna
Kings Club

Buses to
San Agustin
& Las Palmas

Escorial

PLAYA DEL INGLES

N E S W

Beach

Nilo
Center

Avenida de Gran Canaria

Alferez Provisionales

Sandia
Center

Beach

3

Yumbo
Center

5

Av. Tirajana

2

1

Avenida de Gran Canaria

Carretera General

Av. de Euopa

6

4

Golf Course

Sand Dunes
Cruising

Gay
Beach

Nude
Sunbathing

PLAYA DEL MASPALOMAS

Avenida de Africa

Av. de Euopa

7

Carretera General

El Faro

© Odysseus Enterprises Ltd. 1997

LOCATION: Quiet area near beaches, nightlife and shopping.

* Bungalows: 22 (sgl/dbl/triple)
* CTV, in house VCR, phone (reception) security safe, refrigerator
* Kitchenette, patios, garden
* Pool, sundecks, poolside bar
* Clothing optional policy
* Beach: 35 min. walk (gay/nude)
* Gay Bars: 15 min. walk
* Airport: 45 min., taxi, transfers
* Open: Year round
* Rates: US$720 and up complete packages from Amsterdam including roundtrip flights; US$590 and up weekly (Sun-Sun or Wed.-Wed.) US$85 and up daily
* *TAC:* 10% (from Odysseus)

DESCRIPTION: Secluded and well protected all male gay bungalow holiday complex in a tropical garden setting. All bungalows are spacious and offer bedroom with two single beds, kitchenette, dining area, living room with sofa bed, full bath and two patios. The bungalows sleep comfortably 2-3 persons. Formerly known as "Beach Boy Bungalows". **See advertisement in Special Travel Supplement.**

TENESOR APARTMENTS
Playa del Ingles. USA/Canada reservations (800) 257-5344 or (516) 944-7540. Fax: (800) 982-5344 or (516) 944-7540. TYPE: *Apartments Complex.* CLIENTELE: All Welcome. LOCATION: Centrally situated near the Yumbo Center, walk to gay bars and clubs. Frequent bus service nearby.

* Apartments: 60 (1BR / 2BR) living room, kitchen, full bath, balcony
* Restaurant, pool bar, pool, sundecks
* Wheelchair access, 2 elevators
* Parking, cleaning (5 days)
* Gay Bars: 200 m / yards
* Beach: 20 min. walk
* Airport: 35 km / 22 mi.
* Open: Year round
* Rates: from US$70/day. *TAC:* 10%

DESCRIPTION: Simply furnished apartments complex in a central convenient location accommodating from 2-4 people. Each bedroom has two twin beds. Garden view.

❂ VILLAS BLANCAS

Campo de Golf, Maspalomas. USA/Canada reservations Tel: (800) 257-5344 or (516) 944-5330. Fax: (516) 944-7540. Email: odyusa @odyusa.com. TYPE: *Resort Complex.* CLIENTELE: Gay men only. LOCATION: Campo de Golf area, 5 min. taxi ride from Playa del Ingles

and the famous Yumbo Center.

* Bungalows: 24 w/priv. bath one-bedroom each, living room, full bath, kitchen, patio/terrace, refrigerator, safe box,
* Smoking allowed
* Bed Type: twins (two single beds)
* Maid service, wheelchair access
* Bar: poolside serving drinks, snacks, light meals, and breakfast
* Pool, sundeck, clothing optional policy
* Free Parking, pets w/prearrangement
* Beach: 3 km / 2 mi (gay/nude)
* Gay Bars: 2 km / 1.5 mi.
* Health Club: next door (mixed)
* Airport: Las Palmas (LPA) 52 km / 32 mi.
* Airport Transfers: $100 R/T (1-3 pax)
* Languages: English, Spanish, German, French
* Reservations: prepaid
* Open: Year round
* Rates: $80 - $120 w/CB
* Check in - arrival / check out 10:30 am
* *TAC:* 10% (from Odysseus)

DESCRIPTION: Gran Canary's newest all male international resort complex. Near Maspalomas beaches and dunes. Bungalows with swimming pool and bar are surrounded by well tended tropical gardens. Poolside and garden sunbeds. Villas Blancas welcome you with a drink, weekly BBQ and bar tour of the Yumbo Center.

❂ VISTA BONITA

Sonnenland, Maspalomas. USA/Canada reservations Tel: (800) 257-5344 or (516) 944-5330. Fax: (516) 944-7540. TYPE: *Resort Complex.* CLIENTELE: Gay men only. LOCATION: On a hill overlooking Maspalomas and Playa del Ingles. Public transportation nearby.

* Villas: 22 w/priv. bath
* Kitchenettes: fully equipped w/microwave
* CTV, phone, balcony, garden
* Pool, poolside bar, sundecks
* Clothing optional policy
* Beach: 3 km / 2mi. (gay/nude)
* Gay Bars: 2 km / 1.5 mi.
* Airport: 30 km / 19 mi.
* Rates: (US) $80-$130/day w/EB
* *TAC:* 10% (from Odysseus)

DESCRIPTION: Elegant duplex villas and Penthouses with large living room, patio and kitchenette. Double bedroom with full marble bath on the second floor.

FURNISHED APTS/STUDIOS
Odysseus can offer several furnished apartments and studios in a central location near the Yumbo Center. Call: (800) 257-5344.

CORDOBA   ✆ 971

✈ Airport de Cordòba

LOCATION: In the heart of sunny Andalusia in southern Spain. 143 km / 90 mi. northeast of Seviile, 173 km / 108 mi. north of Malaga.

POPULATION: 304,000
CLIMATE: Mild and pleasant year round

Gay/Lesbian Visitor Information
LGC - Tel: 484-459

DESCRIPTION: Founded by the Carthaginian, Cordoba became the capital of the Moorish emirate in 711. It prospered and become the epicenter of western civilization during the 10th century. Its mosque became the world's largest after Mecca. Visit the **Mosque-Cathedral** lavishly decorated with forest of columns and arches of the Mihrab and the richly decorated Catholic church inside; the **Alcazar de los Reyes Cristianos** and the **Jewish District** with its XIV century synagogue, the only one preserved in Andalusia. Cordoba was the home of the famous *Maimonides*, a Jewish doctor and philosopher. A statue for Maimonides is located in the heart of the **Juderia** (Jewish Quarter).

BARS ⅄ RESTAURANTS ¶¶

● Bars/Clubs (GM): **El Cinco de Oros**, Angel de Saavedra 4-6; **El Peruano**, cantina, c/El Reloj s/n; **Juda Levi**, cafe & bar, Plaza de Juda Levi 1.

● Restaurants (AW): **Ciro's**, international cuisine, Paseo de la Victoria 19 (290-464); **El Blasón**, regional cuisine, select atmosphere, c/ José Zorilla s/n (480-625); **El Triunfo**, regional cuisine, c/ Corregidor Luis de la Cerda 79.

🗝 ACCOMMODATIONS 🗝

EL TRIUNFO
c/ Corregidor Luis de la Cerda, 79. 14003 Cordoba. USA / Canada reservations: Odysseus (516) 944-5330. Fax: (516) 944-7540. TYPE: *Hotel*. CLIENTELE: All Welcome. LOCATION: Adjacent to the famous Mosque-Cathedral. 70 rooms, bar, restaurant, parking.

GRANADA   ✆ 958

✈ Granada Airport (GRX)
11 mi. / 18 km west of Granada

LOCATION: Southern Spain in Andalusia in the fertile vale of the Genil river near the Sierra Nevada Mountains.

POPULATION: 300,000

Gay/Lesbian Visitor Information
NOS - Tel: 200-602

DESCRIPTION: Granada is the very finest of Spain's historic cities. This well preserved city is a landmark of romantic Moorish art and culture. The **Alhambra** palace and gardens is the main attraction and it is one of the greatest historic buildings in the world.

BARS ⅄ RESTAURANTS ¶¶

● Bars/Clubs (GMW): **Angel Azul**, dance bar, c/ Lavadero de las Tables 15; **Rayma**, dance bar, porno videos, dark room, good music and ambiance, c/ Arriola 15 (161-384).

● Restaurants (AW): **Baroca**, International cooking, c/ Pedro Antonio de Alarcón 34 (265-061); **Cunini**, seafood, c/ Capuchina 14 (263-701); **Sevilla**, opened by a famous bullfighter in 1930, c/Oficios 12 (221-223).

λ SERVICES λ

● Health Clubs (GM): **Boabdil**, Crta. de la Sierra 34/C, Trevenque s/n (221-073); **Ziries**, c/ Ziries 1, bajo (956-493).

🗝 ACCOMMODATIONS 🗝

VICTORIA HOTEL
Puerto Real 3, Granada E-18005. Tel: (58) 257-700. TYPE: *Hotel*. CLIENTELE: All Welcome. LOCATION: Busy central location near Cathedral, Royal Chapel and shopping. 1.5 km / 1 mi. to train station, 15 km / 10 mi. to airport. 69 rooms w/priv. bath, phone, CTV, room service, restaurant, small bar. Rates: from $90/day.

MADRID   ✆ 1

✈ Barajas Int'l Airport (MAD)
8 mi. / 13 km northeast

LOCATION: In the heart of Spain.

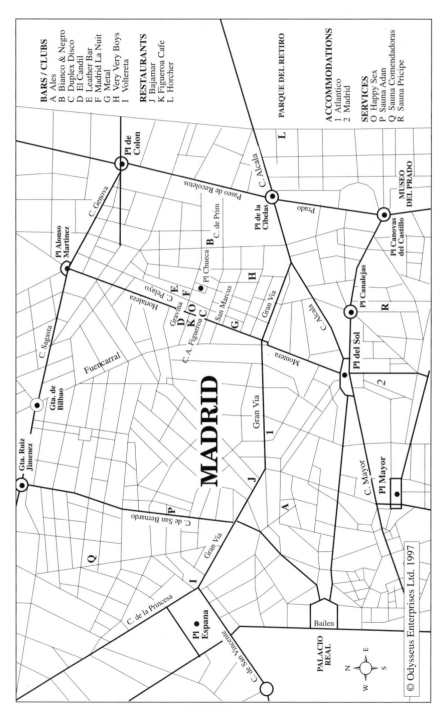

BARS / CLUBS
A   Ales
B   Bianco & Negro
C   Duplex Disco
D   El Candil
E   Leather Bar
F   Madrid La Nuit
G   Metal
H   Very Very Boys
I   Voltereta

RESTAURANTS
J   Bajamar
K   Figueroa Cafe
L   Horcher

ACCOMMODATIONS
1   Atlantico
2   Madrid

SERVICES
O   Happy Sex
P   Sauna Adan
Q   Sauna Comendadoras
R   Sauna Pricipe

© Odysseus Enterprises Ltd. 1997

POPULATION: 3,000,000

CLIMATE: Continental. Mid-winter can be cold with temperatures below freezing. In January, the average daily temperature dips to 40˚F (4˚c). May and October are the most comfortable months. Summers are hot and dry. The average temperature in August is 75˚F (24˚c).

Gay/Lesbian Visitor Information
Gay Inform - Tel:523-0070

DESCRIPTION: Madrid, the capital of Spain, is a cosmopolitan city that offers a fine selection of entertainment, historic sightseeing, fine food etc. The cradle of the Spanish Empire is a city of contrasts, where the old coexists with the ultra-modern. History buffs will enjoy exploring the distinguished periods in Spanish history from Medieval times, through the 19th century till today.

Visit: The world-famous **Prado Museum**; the magnificent **Royal Palace**; the historic **Plaza Mayor**; the large boulevards; and the hectic **Rastro** ("Thieves Market") **Flea Market**, great for lovers of bargains and antiques. Recommended side trips: **El Pardo**, **Pardo Palace**, the now infamous royal-style residence of General Franco; **El Greco's House**; **El Escorial - Felipe II's** famous castle-monastery with a fine exhibition of paintings, and royal antiquities; and of course the **Museo Picasso** in **Buitrago**, 47 miles / 75 km northeast of Madrid.

Madrid is a great city for gay entertainment. Many of the gay bars are located near metro Chueca and Hortaleza. The gay scene in Madrid is almost totally gay male oriented.

BARS Y RESTAURANTS ▮▮

● Bars/Clubs (GM): **Ales**, large popular disco, Veneras 5, M˚ Domingo y Sol (548-2022); **Azul**, gay pub, c/ Pelayo 30; **Bachelor**, popular disco with shows, Reina 2, M˚ Gran Via; **Bar de Copas**, cruise bar, Pelayo 11; **Blanco & Negro** (Black & White), popular bar, Libertad 34, M˚ Chueca (531-1141); **Bubu**, calle del Cid 1 (431-2282); **Candil**, video cruise bar, Hernán Cortes 21; **Cathedral**, large bar/restaurant complex, c/ Fuencarral 28; **Cruising**, leather dance bar, dark room, Pérez Galdós 5, M˚ Chueca (521-5143); **Cueros**, video bar, Pelayo 2 M˚ Chueca; **Daniel's**, cocktail bar, c/ Hortaleza 43; **Dulce Ó Salao**, dance club, dark rooms, porno videos, c/ Libertad 34 (531-1141); **Griffins**, dance bar, drag shows, mature clientele, Villalar 8, M˚ Banco; **Heaven**, dance club, c/ Veneras 2 (548-2022); **Larra**, Calle Lara 21 (221-5705); **LL**,

video bar, C. Pelayo 11; **Leather Bar**, American bar, porno videos and American music, Pelayo 42 or 48, M˚ Chueca (308-1462); **Lord Byron**, day-time coffee shop, mature clientele, Recoletos 18; **Madrid La Nuit**, disco bar, Pelayo 31 (522-9978); **Metal**, disco, Hortaleza 43 (531-8614); **Mirador**, c/ Pelayo 30; **New Kueros**, c/ Pelayo 2; **Refugio**, disco, Dr. Cortezo 1, basement of Teatro Calderón, open at midnight; **Strong Center**, large popular disco with the biggest dark room in Madrid, Trujillo 7, M˚ Domingo y Sol; **Sueño Eterno**, cocktail bar, c/ Pelayo 37; **Topxi**, c/ Augusto Figueroa 16; **Troyans**, leather video bar, C. Pelayo 4 (521-7358); **Very Very Boys**, Libertad 4; **Video Show Bar**, dance bar, dark rooms, porno videos, c/ Barco 32.

● Bars/Clubs (GW): **Ambient**, drinks and pizzas, San Mateo 21; **Bolero**, gravina 10, M˚ Chueca (532-8921); **Derroche Cafe - Croissant Shop**, Caladrava 6, M˚ Latina; **Metal**, disco, Hortaleza 43 (531-8614); **La Rosa**, disco, C. Tetuán 27 (531-0185).

● Restaurants (GMW): **Figueroa Café**, coffee shop popular with local gays, Figueroa 17; **Bajamar**, fine seafood, Gran Via 78; **Las Cuatro Estaciones** ('Four Seasons'), attractive in elegant setting, General Ibanez Ibero 5, corner of San Francisco se Sales 41; **Horcher**, superb, intimate restaurant, near the gay area, traditional cuisine, Alfonso XII 6; **Momo**, c/ Augusto Figueroa 41 (532-7162).

λ SERVICES λ

● Escort (GM): **Adan's**, discreet escort service, hotel or home, Toll Free 908-508-887; **Boys**, 24 hrs escort service (361-5595); **Macho's**, young men, bodybuilders, home or hotel, 24 hrs (355-2939).

● Health Clubs (GM): **Adan**, bar/sauna, Hydro-therapy, Calle San Bernardo 38, M⁰ Noviciado (532-9138); **Alameda**, open: 12 noon - 24 hrs., c/ Alameda 20; **Comendadoras**, Plaza Comendadoras 9, M⁰ Noviciado (532-8892); **Cristal**, c/ Augusto Figueroa (531-4489); **Internacional 2**, Finnish sauna, massage, dark cabins, c/ Altamirano 37 (541-8198); **Internacional 3**, largest and most popular sauna in Madrid, Olivar 1 (429-6219), Calle Maestro Arbós 23 M⁰ Legazpi (228-6050) and Altamirano 37 (541-8198); **Sauna Paraiso**, c/ Norte 15, M⁰ Noviciado (522-4232); **Sauna Principe**, modern sauna, cafeteria, massage, C/. Principe 15 (429-3949) M⁰ Sol.

● Sex-Shops (GM): **California**, c/ Valverde 20;

Manhattan II, sex-shop, videos, magazines, Avda. Guadalajara 18; **Manhattan Sex Center**, Camino Viejo de Leganees 96 (525-4442); **Sex Shop Gay**, Barco 43, M⁰ Tribunal (532-2896).

● Social Club (GMW): **Cogam**, social and political organization, Aptdo 18165. (523-0070).

 ACCOMMODATIONS

✪ HOTEL ATLANTICO

Gran Via 38, Madrid. USA/Canada Reservations/Information. Odysseus Tel: (516) 944-5330 or (800) 257-5344. Fax: (516) 944-7540 or (800) 982-6571. TYPE: *Hotel.* CLIENTELE: All Welcome. LOCATION: Heart of Madrid main shopping center and nightlife.

* Rooms: 60 w/priv. bath
* Phone, CTV, minibar, safety box, A/C hair dryer, maid & room service
* 24 hrs. laundry service
* Cafeteria, pub, parking nearby
* Gay Bars: many nearby
* Health Club: walking distance
* Airport: 14 km / 9 mi., taxi
* Train Station: 3 km / 2 mi.
* Open: Year round
* Rates: (US) $100-$140 w/CB
* *TAC:* 10% (from Odysseus)

DESCRIPTION: Charming 3-star hotel with amenities far superior to its category. Spacious and tastefully decorated rooms, sparkling clean bathrooms. Excellent location for the Madrid gay scene and nightlife.

HOTEL MADRID
Carretas 10, Madrid. USA/Canada reservations Tel: (516) 944-5330 or (800) 257-5344. Fax: (516) 944-7540 or (800) 982-6571. TYPE: *Hotel.* CLIENTELE: All Welcome. LOCATION: Downtown near Pueta del Sol.

* Rooms: 71 w/priv. bath or shower
* Phone, A/C
* Bar lounge, maid & laundry service
* Gay Bars: walking distance
* Health Club: walking distance
* Airport: 14 km/ 9 mi.
* Train Station: 3 km / 2 mi.
* Open: Year round
* Rates: (US) $85 - $130 w/CB
* *TAC:* 10% (from Odysseus)

DESCRIPTION: Moderately priced 3-star downtown hotel with basic but clean rooms, simply furnished with private facilities. Short walk to gay clubs, bars and saunas.

Hotel Atlántico S.A.

USA/Canada
Reservations
800-257-5344

MALAGA ✆ 95

✈ Malaga Airport (AGP) 6 mi. / 10 km SW

LOCATION: Costa del Sol

DESCRIPTION: The second largest city in Andalusia (after Seville) Malaga is an agglomeration of small fishing villages and new resort development. Malaga offers the best seafood cafes in the province.

BARS ☕ RESTAURANTS 🍴

● Bars/Clubs (GM): **Akelarre**, c/ Mariblanca 4; **El Convento**, Madre de Dios 21; **La Gata Loca**, disco, Pasaje de Campos 13; **Sabor Pub**, snack bar, American billard, private cabins, c/ Martinez Campos 11 (260-1519); **WC**, Plaza del Teatro s/n.

● Restaurants (AW): **Antonio Martin**, Malaga cuisine served on a fine seafront terrace, Paseo Maritimo 4 (222-113); **Café de Paris**, Int'l cuisine, Malagueta District (225-043); **La Alegria**, classic cuisine, c/ Marin Garcia 10 (224-143).

λ SERVICES λ

● Erotica (GM): **Amsterdam Sex Shop**, Tomas Heredia 20 (222-7097); **Cosmopolitan**, c/ Muelle de Heredia 12 (222-1583); **Hamburgo**, c/ Casas de Campo 11.

● Escort (GM): **Mamma Louiss**, escort service (255-9430).

 ACCOMMODATIONS

DON CURRO HOTEL
Sancha de Lara 7, Malaga E-29015. Tel: (5) 222-7200. TYPE: *Hotel.* CLIENTELE: All Welcome. LOCATION: Near Iberia Airlines terminal and 400 yards / m to the harbor. 105 rooms w/priv. bath, restaurant, lounge.

MARBELLA   ✆   95

✈ Malaga Airport (AGP)
   35 mi. / 56 km northeast

LOCATION: On the famous Costa del Sol, (Sunshine Cost) south of Malaga.

POPULATION: 90,000

CLIMATE: Mediterranean climate with mild winters and sunny dry summers. Winter temperature remain at an average 12˚c (60˚F) in January; Summer temperatures are in the mid 20's˚c (80's˚F) in July.

DESCRIPTION: Marbella is an upmarket seaside resort, playground for the beautiful people, with 28 km / 18 mi. of beaches, luxury hotels and marinas. It is popular with celebrities, jet setters and wealthy Arab sheiks and has the highest concentration of Rolls Royce cars per capita in the world. Visit the town's famous **Puerto Baños Marina**, the new 'Hollywood' of Europe, where the talented and gorgeous mix with the uppercrust.

❖ Beaches (G/S): **Cabopino**, popular nudist beach, accessible via the Coastal Hwy N-340 towards Torremolinos near Hotel Artola. Check out the dunes area near "Las Dunas" beach bar; **Costa Natura**, a famous nudist beach (not gay) near Estepona.

BARS Ⴘ RESTAURANTS 🍴

● Bars/Clubs (GM): **Boccacio**, video bar, Puer-

ta del Mar; **Eros**, dance club, drag shows, center of town, c/ Juan Ruiz Muñoz 12; **Ojo**,video bar, c/ Perta del Mar 9; **Oscar's**, bar/restaurant, c/ Aduar 1; **Platano**, gay bar, open air terrace, c/ Antonio Belon 4.

● Restaurants (AW): **Antonio**, good local cuisine, nice terrace,Muelle Ribera, Puerto Banús (281-1091); **La Fonda**, regional cuisine in an attractive 18C Andalusian house, Pl. Santo Cristo 9 (277-2512); **La Meridiana**, fashionable elegant restaurant, Andalusian cuisine, Camino de la Cruz s/n behind the Mosque in Las Lomas (277-6190).

λ SERVICES λ

● Erotica (GM): **International**, c/ Rivera, Casa Y/Z (Puerto Banus).

 ACCOMMODATIONS

VILLA COLON
29660 Nueva Andalucia. USA/Canada reservations / information Tel: (516) 944-5330 or (800) 257-5344. Fax: (516) 944-7540 or (800) 982-6571. TYPE: *Resort Complex.* CLIENTELE: Gay men only. HOSTS: Peter and Fred. LOCATION: San Pedro de Marbella, 300 m / yards to city center.

* Rooms: 6 w/priv. bath (sgl/dbl/triple)
* Suite: 1 (3-bedroom w/patio)
* CTV, VCR, phone, refrigerator, C/H, A/C
* Maid service, room service & laundry
* Pool, sundeck, free parking
* Beach: 15 min. (nude beach)
* Gay Bars: 5 min.
* Airport: Malaga 40 min., taxi, bus, car
* Languages: German, French, Spanish, Eng.
* Reservations: through Odysseus
* Rates: (US) $75 - $140 w/GerB. *TAC:* 10%
* Check In until 18 hrs / check out 12 noon

DESCRIPTION: Large villa in a tropical garden setting 'Key West' style. Nice pool area, covered terrace with drinks, TV video lounge, breakfast room, patio.

SEVILLE   ✆   954

✈ San Pablo Airport (SVQ)
   8 mi. / 13 km northeast

LOCATION: Strategic inland port in the south of Spain with ready access to the Mediterranean and the Atlantic. 215 km / 135 mi. north west of Málaga, and 547 km / 340 mi. south of Madrid.

POPULATION: 700,000

CLIMATE: Best weather from May to mid-June and from September through October. Summers are hot with highs in the 100's°F (38°c). Winters can be chilly and wet with unpredictable warm spells.

DESCRIPTION: Seville is Spain's 4th largest city, lying on the banks of the Guadalquivir River. In its glorious days it became the capital of the New World during the days of great explorations. It is the spiritual heart of Moorish Andalusia; the city of famous Opera characters such as Carmen, Don Juan and that famous barber; a world of fascinating Gypsies and moody flamenco.

Visit the **Sierpes** - a popular pedestrian street with restaurants, shops and galleries; the famous 15th century **Cathedral**, the bell tower **Giralda** a splendid example of Moorish art and the fortified walls and gardens of the **Alcázar**; the **Barrio de Santa Cruz** - the former Jewish Quarter before the expulsion by the Catholic kings Ferdinand & Isabella. The quarter is almost a stereotype of Spain with its people, sounds and fragrances. A side trip is recommended to the nearby historic city of Cordova. Take a train for a 30 minute scenic ride

from the Central Train Station. In Cordova visit the famous **Mosque-Cathedral** (Mezquita-Cathedral) and the ancient Jewish Quarter.

BARS ¥ RESTAURANTS ¶¶

● Bars/Clubs (GM): **Itaca**, disco with dark room, porno videos, and hot crowd, calle Amor de Dios 25a; **Isbiliya**, bar/restaurant, P° Colón 2; **La Mirada**, dark room TV, c/ Luis de Vargas s/n; **Memory**, c/ Fernán Caballero 6 (421-4789); **Pub 27**, cruise bar, porno videos, young crowd, c/. Trastamara 19; **Valentino**, dark rooms, porno videos, Marqués de Paradas 25 (near the Estacion de Cordoba)

● Restaurants (AW): **Egaña Oriza**, one of Seville's most fashionable restaurants serving Basque specialties, San Fernando 41 (227-211); **El Bacalao**, Andalusian Seafood, Plaza Ponce de Léon 15 (216-670); **San Francisco,** French cuisine, old convent decor, Plaza San Francisco 10 (222-056).

λ SERVICES λ

● Health Club (GM): **Hispalis**, c./ Céfiro 3 (458-0220); **Nordik**, Finnish sauna, calle Resolana 38 (437-1321).

● Sex Shops (G/S): **Internacional**, calle Sierpes 48 (Galeria) (456-0729); **Sex Shop**, Gravina 86 (421-1194).

ACCOMMODATIONS

✪ BECQUER HOTEL
Reyes Catolicos 4, Seville 41001. Tel: (95) 422-8900. USA/Canada Reservations: (516) 944-5330 or (800) 257-5344. Fax: (516) 944-7540 or (800) 982-6571. TYPE: *Hotel.* CLIENTELE: Mostly Straight. LOCATION: Centrally located near commercial center of town.

* Rooms: 120 w/priv. bath
* CTV, Phone, A/C
* Breakfast room, bar, parking
* Room & maid service
* Gay Bars: 10 min. walk
* Airport: 14 km / 9 mi., bus, taxi
* Credit Cards: MC/VISA/AMEX/BC/CB
* Open: Year round
* Rates: (US) $110 - $190
* *TAC:* 10% (from Odysseus)

DESCRIPTION: Moderately priced dignified hotel with spacious and artistically decorated public areas. Guest rooms are pleasantly decorated in local style. Large marble baths.

Hotel Bécquer — Sevilla

USA/Canada reservations (800) 257-5344

SITGES   © 73

✈ Barcelona Airport (BCN)
30 km / 20 mi. northeast

LOCATION: Along the Mediterranean shores of Catalonia's Costa Dorada (Golden Coast), 20 miles (30 km) southwest of Barcelona. 25 min. by car to downtown Barcelona, 30 min. to Barcelona Airport (BCN), 60 min. to Tarragona.

POPULATION: 13,000

CLIMATE: Mild with an average annual high of 60°F (15°c). Winters are mild. Most of the year there is a pleasant sea breeze.

DESCRIPTION: Sitges is a popular seaside resort with great appeal to gay travelers. It is an old seafaring city which abounds in conservative charm and colors. The great Catalonian painter Santiago Rusiñol discovered Sitges at the end of the last century. Now it is a famous vacation spot for tourists from all over the world who enjoy the city's big esplanade and its fine sandy beaches.

Visit the **Cau Ferrat Museum**, founded by Rusiñol and installed in a Gothic building, contains famous paintings by El Greco, Picasso and Catalonian artists; **Romantic Museum**, an unusual and beautiful 18th century structure with a display on the evolution of 19th century fashion; the **parish church** in Baroque style.

❖ Beaches: the main 'Gay Beach' in town is in the centre of the seafront across from the **Calipolis Hotel**; **Playas del Muerto**, two small beaches between Sitges and Vilanova i la Geltru are *nudist beaches* about 1 mi. / 1.5 km out of town to the south-west, on the far side of the golf course. The first is mixed, but the second is exclusive for gay nudism. If you do not have a car ask the taxi driver to take you to the **Atlantida Disco** and walk from there following the track that runs parallel to the railway line. The Pine Forest across the railway track tends to be quite cruisy too.

❖ **SPECIAL EVENTS**: Sitges offers a variety of interesting cultural, religious and artistic events and festivals year round. Here is a partial list of events. The dates are subject to change: February 13 & 15: **Carnival**; March 6: **Antique Car Rallye**; March 9: **"Menjar de Tast"** (Food Festival); May 29 - June 5: **Theatre Festival**; June 12-20: **Carnation Exhibition**; June 13

(aprox.): **Corpus Christi** (Carpet of Flowers); June 23: **Sant Joan**; July & August: **Open Air Concerts**; August 23-25: **Festa Mejor** (biggest display of fireworks in Spain) festival in honor of Saint Bartholomew the patron saint of Sitges; September 17-19: **Grape Harvest Festival**; September 27: **World Tourism Day**; October 1-9: **Int'l Fantastic Film Festival**; October 23: **Invitation to the Artists**; October 30: **Winter Rallye - "Villa de Sitges"**

❖ *Note:* Sitges is a popular European holiday destination. July and August is the high season and it is impossible to book on a short notice. If you plan to travel to Sitges during these months make your reservations many months ahead of time.

BARS ⅄ RESTAURANTS 🍴

● Bars/clubs (GM): **Azul**, Carrer San Buenaventura 10; **Bari**, c/ Nueva 7; **Blau**, c/ Sant Pere 29; **Bourbon's**, Calle San Buenavantura 9 (894-3347); **El Candil**, video dance bar, Calle de la Carreta 9; **Christopher's**, c/ Santa Tecla 6; **Company**, cafe/bar, San Francisco 36; **El Horno**, Amsterdam style leather bar, carrer Juan Tarrida Ferratyes 6 (894-0909); **El 7**, musical bar, c/ Nueva 7; **Lord's**, dance club, porno videos, c/ Marquees de Montroig 16 (894-1522); **Mediterraneo**, San Buenaventura 6; **Mitja Luna**, C. Santa Tecla 8 (894-5157); **New Comodin**, Calle Tacó 14 (894-5074); **Parrot's**, Plaza Industria, c/ 2 de Mayo; **Perfil**, leather/music bar, Espalter 7; **Puchero**, c/ San Jose 22; **Reflejos**, music bar, San Buenaventura 19; **Spray**, San Buenaventura 37; **Trailer**, exclusively gay disco, c/ Angel Vidal 14.

● Bars/clubs (GMW): **Azul**, Calle San Buenaventura 10; ✪ **La Renaixença**, friendly men's bar at the Hotel La Renaixença, c/ Isla de la Cuba 7 (894-8375); ✪ **Romantic Corner**, mixed 'Old Fashioned' bar at the Hotel Romantic, c/ Sant Isidre 33 (894-0643); **San Francisco**, c/ Sant Francesc 36.

● Restaurants (AW): **Casa Willy**, c/ Parellades 80; **Chez Jeanette**, c/ Sant Pau 23 (894-0048); **Chez Nous**, P° de Villafranca; **Flamboyant**, c/. Pau Barrabeig; **El Jardin**, c/ Pau Barrabeig 4; **Ma Maison**, c/. Bonaire 28; **Miami**, c/ Sant Pau 11; **El Trull**, Pge. M. F. Clará 3; **El Xalet**, elegant garden restaurant, Carrer Isla de Cuba 35 (894-5579).

⅄ SERVICES ⅄

● Antiques/Collectibles (AW): **El Desuan**, Pas-

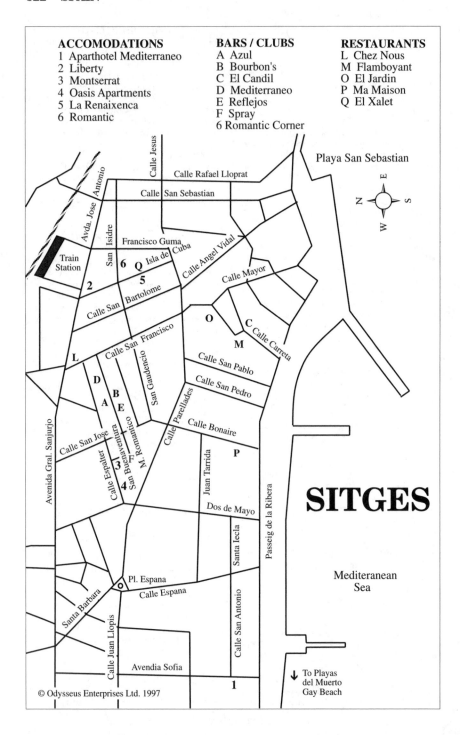

ACCOMODATIONS
1 Aparthotel Mediterraneo
2 Liberty
3 Montserrat
4 Oasis Apartments
5 La Renaixenca
6 Romantic

BARS / CLUBS
A Azul
B Bourbon's
C El Candil
D Mediterraneo
E Reflejos
F Spray
6 Romantic Corner

RESTAURANTS
L Chez Nous
M Flamboyant
O El Jardin
P Ma Maison
Q El Xalet

Calle Jesus

Calle Rafael Lloprat

Playa San Sebastian

Calle San Sebastian

Avda. Jose Antonio

Francisco Guma

Train Station

San Isidre

Isla de Cuba

Calle Angel Vidal

Calle Mayor

Calle San Bartolome

Calle San Francisco

Calle Carreta

Calle San Pablo

Calle San Pedro

San Gaudencio

Calle Parellades

Calle Bonaire

Calle San Jose

Avenida Gral. Sanjurjo

Calle Espalter

San Buenaventura

M. Romanico

Juan Tarrida

Dos de Mayo

Passeig de la Ribera

SITGES

Santa Iecla

Santa Barbara

Pl. Espana

Calle Espana

Calle Juan Llopis

Calle San Antonio

Mediteranean
Sea

Avendia Sofia

↓ To Playas
del Muerto
Gay Beach

© Odysseus Enterprises Ltd. 1997

seig Vilanueva #25 near the Supermarket.

● Gyms (AW): **The Gym**, mixed clientele, St. Bartolomeo 9; **Mediterraneo**, elegant gym and health club, mixed clientele, Avda Sofia 3

● Health Club (GM): **Sauna Sitges**, open daily year round, Calle Espalter 11 (894-2863).

● Laundry/Dry Cleaning (AW): **Bugaderia Blanca Subur**, Sant Bonaventura 7.

● Spanish Studies (G/S): ✪ **Hola! Idiomas**, Language School in Sitges teaching "Spanish for Foreigners". 2 to 4 weeks intensive programs and tailor made courses (either one to one or groups). Spain: Tel: (34-3) 894-9621. Email: hola.idiomas@interplanet.es. Internet http://www.interplanet.es/hola. **USA/Canada reservations:** Odysseus Tel: (800) 257-5344 or (516) 944-5330. Fax: (516) 944-7540.

 ACCOMMODATIONS

HOTEL LIBERTY
Isla de Cuba 45, Sitges 08870. Tel: (3) 811-0872. USA/Canada reservations: (800) 257-5344 or (516) 944-5330. Fax: (800) 982-6571 or (516) 944-7540. TYPE: *Hotel*. HOST: Thomas.

CLIENTELE: Mostly gay men. LOCATION: Central near the Train Station. 14 rooms, CTV, phone, refrigerator, A/C. DESCRIPTION: Turn-of-the century small hotel with bright rooms and modern facilities. Two rooms have access to a large, sunny terrace. Breakfast buffet served until 12 noon.

MEDITERRÀNEO APART-HOTEL
Av. Sofia 3. Sitges 08870. USA/Canada reserva tions: Odysseus (516) 944-5330. Fax: (516) 944-7540. TYPE: *Luxury Apartments*. CLIENTELE: Gay/Straight. LOCATION: Right on the beach, walking distance to gay nude beach and gay bars.

* 60 Fully equipped apartments
* Full bathroom and kitchen
* CTV (CNN), VCR, phone, A/C
* 24 hrs. room service, maid service
* Restaurant, snack bar, parking
* Solarium, gym, sauna, spa, massage
* Beach: on the beach
* Gay Bars: walking distance
* Health Club: on premises
* Airport: 30 km / 19 mi., train, taxi
* Season: Year round
* Rates: $170 - $265
* *TAC:* 10% (from Odysseus)

DESCRIPTION: 4-star modern apartments-hotel complex. Fully furnished and equipped elegant apartments with double bedroom, living room, European kitchen. Panoramic seaview from the balcony. Highest quality and standard for the upscale travelers.

HOTEL MONTSERRAT
San Bonaventura 33, Sitges 08870. TYPE: *Hotel.* CLIENTELE: Gay men & women welcome. Reservations: USA/Canada - Odysseus (516) 944-5330, Fax: (516) 944-7540. LOCATION: In the heart of historic Sitges, walk to gay bars, discos and restaurants.

* Rooms: 28 w/priv. bath
* CTV, phone, C/H, safety box
* Balcony: 50% of rooms
* Handicapped facilities: 20% of rooms
* Reception hall, lounge bar w/CTV
* Conference room, breakfast lounge
* Sun terrace, elevator
* Gay bars: walking distance
* Parking: public parking nearby
* Beach: 300m/yards (mixed)
  1-1/4 mi. (2 km) to gay nude beach
* Gay Bars: many nearby
* Health Club: 50m / yards
* Airport: 15 mi. / 25 km. taxi, train
* Train Station: 5 min. walk
  direct line to Barcelona (35 minutes)
* Reservations: through Odysseus
* Season: April 1 - October 30
* Rates: $80 - $110/day
  including breakfast, service & taxes
* *TAC:* 10% (from Odysseus)

DESCRIPTION: Modest but clean, comfortable and friendly 2-star hotel on Sitges most famous gay street 'calle San Bonaventura' with many gay bars, clubs and discos at the door step. Many rooms with double beds and refrigerator, large bathrooms. Court view rooms with priv. bath and refrigerator. Street view rooms with priv. bath and CTV. Rooms with balcony available at extra charge. Breakfast buffet served from 8:30am - 11:00am.

'OASIS APARTMENTS'
Sitges, Spain.USA/Canada - Odysseus (516) 944-5330 or (800) 257-5344. Fax: (516) 944-7540. TYPE: *Apartment Complex.* CLIENTELE: Gay men & women. LOCATION: Heart of Sitges walk to all gay bars, clubs, shops and restaurants.

* Apartments/Studios: 17 (1-4 rooms)
* Living room, kitchen, full bath, balcony
* CTV, phone, fan, intercom
* Parking: public parking nearby
* Beach: 300m/yards (mixed)
  1-1/4 mi. (2 km) to gay nude beach

* Gay Bars: many nearby
* Health Club: 50 m / yards
* Airport: 15 mi. / 25 km. taxi, train
* Train Station: 5 min., walk
  direct line to Barcelona (35 minutes)
* Reservations: through Odysseus
* Open: Year round
* Rates: $80 - $160/day
  including breakfast, service & taxes
* *TAC:* 10% (from Odysseus)

DESCRIPTION: One and two bedroom apartments, each with a living room, full bath, kitchen and balcony. Some bedrooms with large double beds. Fans available in the summer. Excellent choice for the independent travelers. 7 day min. in low season, 10 day min. in high season or 10% surcharge for shorter stay. Refundable deposit of PTS 8,000 required upon check in. Own key.

○ LA RENAIXENÇA
Isla de la Cuba, Sitges 08870 . TYPE: *Hotel.* CLIENTELE: Gay men & women only. Reservations: USA/Canada - Odysseus (516) 944-5330 or (800) 257-5344. Fax: (516) 944-7540. LOCATION: Heart of Sitges near the Hotel Romantic. Short walk to train station. Excellent connection to Barcelona-Center (30 min.).

* Rooms: 16 w/private bath, balcony
* Breakfast room: Hotel Romantic
* Rooftop solarium, maid service
* Beach: walking distance
* Gay Bars: nearby
* Airport: 30 km (19 mi.), taxi
* Train Station: 25 m / 80 ft.
  direct train line to Barcelona (35 min.)
* Open: Year round
* High Season: July 11 - August 11
* Rates: $80-$110/day
  including breakfast, service & taxes
* *TAC:* 10% (from Odysseus)

DESCRIPTION: Catalan style economy Hotel, annex to the Hotel Romantic, furnished with antiques and period furniture to reflect its artistic character. The hotel provides complete freedom and privacy. Guests can use the reception service day and night at the Hotel Romantic. Welcome drink to Odysseus guests.

○ HOTEL ROMANTIC
Carrer de Sant Isidre 33, Sitges 08870. Tel: (93) 894-0643. USA/Canada reservations: Odysseus (516) 944-5330 or (800) 257-5344. Fax: (516) 944-7540 or (800) 982-6571. TYPE: *Hotel.* HOST: Gonçal Sobré. CLIENTELE: Mostly Gay. LOCATION: In the heart of Sitges, near beach,

art museums, theatres, night clubs and all places of interest to gay visitors. Short walk to Sitges train station with excellent connection to Barcelona-Center (30 min. by express train)

* Rooms: 74; 68 w/priv., 6 w/shared bath
  20 sgl / 54 dbl
* Smoking allowed in rooms
* Public TV Lounge, phone, safety deposit
* Balconies (some): overlooking garden
* Bar: **Romantic Corner**
* Room & maid service
* Ocean beach nearby, solarium
* Parking: public parking nearby
* Beach: 300m/yards (mixed)
  1 1/4 mile (2 km) to gay nude beach
* Gay Bars: many nearby
* Health Club: 50 m / yards
* Airport: 15 mi. / 25 km., taxi, train
* Train Station: 5 min. walk
  direct line to Barcelona (35 minutes)
* Reservations: through Odysseus
* Season: April 1 - October 30
* Rates: $80 - $110/day
  including breakfast, service & taxes
* **TAC:** 10% (from Odysseus)

DESCRIPTION: Old fashioned two-star historic artistic hotel, conserved and restored in

the style of the period (1882). Collections of painting, ceramics and sculptures make the Hotel Romantic a living work of art. Enjoy its elegant interiors and the international bar. Breakfast is served in the indoor dining room or in the delightful Mediterranean garden. Welcome drink to Odysseus guests. *See color photos in the Travel Supplement.*

TORREMOLINOS   Ⓒ   **95**

✈ Malaga Airport (AGP) 4 mi. / 6 km north

LOCATION: Fashionable seaside resort on the Costa Del Sol near Malaga.

POPULATION: 50,000

CLIMATE: The most important characteristic of the Costa del Sol is the gentleness of its winters, with a January mean temperature of 56°F (13°c). Summers are warm but agreeable with mean temperature in July of 76°F (24°c). The water temperature in the winter (January) is 60°F (15°c), and 76°F (24°c) in the summer (August). There are few rainy days, but rainfalls are usually intense.

DESCRIPTION: Sitting on a rocky headland, Torremolinos is so close to Malaga that it is difficult to separate the two. It is an international resort at the foot of the **Mijas Range**. While **Montemar** is the residential district with private homes and posh hotels, **La Carihuela** is a typical fishing village with splendid beaches and large resort hotels. The fabulous beaches of Malaga and Torremolinos are blossoming with nude bathers. Many of the hotels down to Torremolinos are topless. Over the years, an international artists' colony has developed with painters from all over the world. The **Tolox Spa**, famous for its medicinal waters, is only 27 mi. / 43 km away. While staying at Torremolinos a visit to nearby Malaga is a must.

BARS ℧ RESTAURANTS ¶¶

● Bars/Clubs (GM): **Bavaria**, dance club, Edificio Centro Jardin (near Rey Sol); **Bronx**, dance club, Edificio Centro Jardin (38 73 60); **Budy's**, cruise bar, porno videos, Edificio Centro Jardin (237-0824); **Chessa**, gay bar, terrace, La Nogalera, local 408; **Contacto**, shows and entertainment, dark rooms, porno videos, open air terrace, La Nogalera, local 204; **Esquina**, disco pub, live shows, La Nogalera, local #203; **La Gorila**, C/. Casablanca, Pueblo

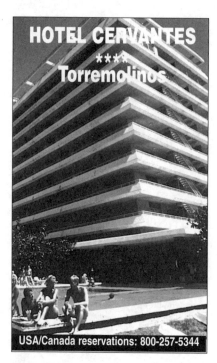

Blanco; **Malu**, good ambiance, open air terrace, La Nogalera, local 1103, Calle Guateria; **Men's Bar**, cruise video bar, La Nogalera local 714; **Moon**, superdisco, Avda. Carlota Alexandra; **Movies**, pub, La Nogalera, local 405; **Parthenon**, disco, La Nogalera, local No. 716; **Pourquoi Pas?**, La Nogalera local 703, bloc 7; **Rosa Negra**, gay bar, Pasaje Rio Mundo (Pasaje Pizarro); **Tension**, video cruise bar, La Nogalera local 524; **Zatanazza**, good music, open air terrace, La Nogalera, local 306.

● Restaurants (AW): **La Bóveda**, Spanish cuisine, Cuesta del Tajo 22 (38 11 85); **La Brocherie**, next to Pourquoi Pas Bar, La Nogalera 704; **El Comedor**, Calle Casablanca Pueblo Blanco (38-3881); **Sala de Tokyo**, Japanese cuisine, Carretera Cadiz corner Avenida Imperial (38-2193); **Las Rosas**, International/Spanish cuisine, Calle Maestre Miret (37 19 49).

λ SERVICES λ

● Health Club (GM): **Sauna Miguel**, c/ Carlota Alessandri 166 (238-8740).

● Sex-Shop (GM): **Internacional**, Avda. Los Monantiales, Edif. Tres Torres, (37-1196).

ACCOMMODATIONS

○ CERVANTES HOTEL

Las Mercedes, Torremolinos 29620. USA/Canada Reservations: Tel: (516) 944-5330 or (800) 257-5344. Fax: (516) 944-7540 or (800) 982-6571. TYPE: *Resort Hotel*. CLIENTELE: All Welcome. LOCATION: Center of city on hillside plateau above beach adjacent to a colorful shopping center - La Nogalera, where the gay scene is located.

* Rooms: 400 w/priv. bath or shower
* TV (on request), phone, A/C
* Restaurant, rooftop grill, bars, cafeteria
* Indoor and rooftop pool, sauna
* Room & maid service, parking
* Beach: walking distance
* Gay Bars: walking distance
* Airport: 5 km (3 mi.), taxi
* Train Station: nearby
* Credit Cards: MC/VISA/AMEX/EC/DC
* Open: Year round
* Rates: (US) $70-$130 w/CB. *TAC:* 10%

DESCRIPTION: Lively 4-star 10 story resort hotel. All rooms are spacious and comfortable. some have king size beds, all have balcony, full bath, wall-to-wall carpeting and piped music. Excellent reports from Odysseus customers.

PATIO DE CABALLOS

Cerro Del Toril, Torremolinos. USA/Canada reservation/information Tel: 1 (800) 257-5344 or (516) 944-5330. Fax: 1 (800) 982-6571 or (516) 944-7540. TYPE: *Resort complex*. HOST: Gaudin. CLIENTELE: Gay men only. LOCATION: 5 min. from the center of Torremolinos by car.

* Villas: 4 (one-bedroom)
* Living room, kitchen, patio, full bath
* Refrigerator, safe box, cooking facilities
* Pool, sundeck, clothing optional, seaview
* Gay bars: 2 km / 1.5 mi.
* Health Club: 2 km / 1.5 mi. (mixed)
* Airport: Malaga, 10 min.
  (airport transfers are included)
* Train Station: Torremolinos or El Pinillo 800 m / yards, walk or taxi
* Languages: English, French, Spanish, Dutch, German
* Reservations: through Odysseus
* Open: April 1 - October 15
* Rates: from $840/week
* *TAC:* 10% (from Odysseus)

DESCRIPTION: Exclusive gay holiday complex. 4 luxury villas decorated in Moorish style to a very high standard with individual sun terrace and sun beds around a private pool.

Private and secluded with spectacular views of the Costa del Sol, the Sierra Nevada mountains and the Mediterranean. One week minimum stay requested. Price include: welcome drink and a diner party once a week. Car rental reservations available.

VALENCIA   ℂ   96

✈ Manises Airport (VLC)
8 mi. / 13 km northwest

LOCATION: About halfway the Eastern Coast of Spain on the Gulf of Valencia, 361 km (225 mi.) southwest of Barcelona.

POPULATION: 800,000

CLIMATE: Hot sunny summers with July average temperature of 84°F (29°c); winters are mild and pleasant with a January average temperature of 61°F (16c).

Gay/Lesbian Visitor Information
Collectivo Lambda: 380-2211
Info Rosa: 380-3222

DESCRIPTION: Valencia is the third largest city in Spain with a reputation for clothing and furniture design. The architecture is distinctively Valencian with a wealth of elaborate baroque façades. Although Valencia does not offer an exciting gay scene such as in Barcelona or Madrid, it is a popular destination for many Spanish gays who come for a weekend or the winter months.

Visit: **Palacio del Marques de dos Aguas**; **Museo Nacional de Céramica**; **Colegio de Patriarca** with its excellent Art Museum displaying rare works by El Greco, Morales, and Ribalta; **Plaza Zaragoza**; and **Valencia's Cathedral**.

❖ For those who wish to visit the Balearic Islands and Ibiza, ferries leave daily for Mallorca, and twice weekly for Ibiza. Information and tickets are available through Trasmediterranea, or any local travel agent.

BARS Ⓨ RESTAURANTS 🍴

The gay scene in Valencia is not concentrated in any one particular area. Car rental while in Valencia is recommended.

● Bars/Clubs (GM): **Ales**, dance club, dark rooms, porno videos, c/ La Sangre 9; **Balkiss**,

disco, c/ Dr. Monserrat 23 (331-7081); **Central**, leather cruise bar, C. Quart 47 (391-0981); **La Guerra**, cruise bar, C/. Quart 47; **Metal**, c/ Plaz. Picadero 3; **North Dakota**, western style, Pza. Margarita Valldaura 1 (357-5250); **Oh Valencia**, c/ Murillo 26; **Pol's**, live shows, private cabins, c/ Del Mar 45; **Studio 17**, dance bar, young clientele, Calle Cerrajeros 17, Plaza Redondo, (331-8203); **Venial**, fashionable bar, c/ Quart 26; **Xandro's**, large complex, videos, C. Derechos 30.

● Bars/clubs (GMW): **Contramano**, c/ Murillo 12; **Venial**, fashionable dance club, open 24:00, C. Quart 26.

● Restaurants (AW): **Cafe Atlas**, popular with gay clientele, c/ Dr. Montserrat 30-32; **Canela y Clavos**, mixed gay & lesbian clientele, c/ Roteros 21 (331-7421); **La Hacienda**, the best and most expensive in town, c/ Navarro Reverter 12 (373-1859); **Bar Pilar**, cheap seafood, corner c/ Moza Zeit, off Pl. del Esparto.

λ SERVICES λ

● Health Clubs (GM): **Olimpic**, Calle Vivóns 17 (373-0418); **Quart**, Calle San Miguel (391-9694).

● Sex Shops (GMW): **Afro**, sex shop, Gran Via Germania 53; **Blue Sex Factory**, **European Sex Center**, Avda. Constitución 26 (347-4427); **Moncho Inter-nacional**, c/ Dr. Zamenhoff 15 (382-3349); **Spartacus**, exclusively gay, Flassaders 8 (352-5662).

🗝 ACCOMMODATIONS 🗝

HOTEL INGLÉS
Marqués de Doa Aguas 6, Valencia 46002. Tel: (96) 3214-555. TYPE: *Hotel*. CLIENTELE: Mostly Straight. LOCATION: Central location near Pl. de Zaragosa (Plaza de la Reina).

* Rooms: 63 w/priv. bath
* CTV, phone, A/C
* Room & maid service
* Gay Bars: some nearby
* Airport: 15 min., taxi
* Credit Cards: MC/VISA/ACC
* Season: Year round
* Rates: on request

DESCRIPTION: Good convenient hotel.

REINA VICTORIA
Barcas 4-6, Valencia 46002. Tel: (96) 352-0487. TYPE: *First Class Hotel*. CLIENTELE: Mostly Straight. LOCATION: In the heart of the city (Plaza del Ayuntamiento).

* Rooms: 100 w/priv. bath
* CTV, phone, A/C
* Restaurant, piano bar
* Room & maid service, parking
* Gay Bars: some nearby
* Airport: 15 min. taxi
* Season: Year round

DESCRIPTION: First class hotel in a convenient location.

ZARAGOZA   Ⓥ 976

✈ Zaragoza Airport

LOCATION: Provincial capital of Aragon in the northeast of Spain.

POPULATION: 600,000

Gay/Lesbian Visitor Information
LYGA - Tel: 395-577

DESCRIPTION: Zaragoza is the lively city with excellent bars and restaurants. The city preserves many impressive Gothic and Romanesque Cathedrals and buildings. Visit the **Aljaferiá Palace**, the most spectacular Moorish monument outside of Anadlusia.

BARS ♈ RESTAURANTS

● Bars/Clubs (GM): **El Eden**, c/ Veronica s/n; **La Carcel**, video cruise bar, dark room, dance floor, c/ Jusepe Martinez 7; **Atuaire**, c/ Contamina 13; **Cruising**, c/ San Feliz 4; **Pub Bear**, cocktail bar, c/ Coso 148 (infront of Hotel Ramiro); **Sphinx**, dance club, c/ Madre Rafols 2.

λ SERVICES λ

● Erotica (GM): **El Tubo**, c/ Cuatro de Agosto 15; **Pignatelli**, c/ Ramon de Pignatelli 44.

● Health Club (GM): **Nordik**, Finnish and Turkish bath, c/ Andres Grupide 4.

🗝 ACCOMMODATIONS 🗝

PALAFOX HOTEL
Casa Jimenez, Zaragoza E-50004. Tel: (76) 237700. TYPE: *Hotel*. CLIENTELE: All Welcome. LOCATION: Near Train Station. 20 min. to airport. 200 rooms w/priv. bath, CTV, minibar, suites, restaurant, bar, pool, sauna, solarium. garden, parking. Rates: from $130.

SRI-LANKA

AREA: 25,332 sq. mi. (65,610 sq. km)
POPULATION: 17,000,000
CAPITAL: Colombo
CURRENCY: Sri Lanka rupee (LKR)
OFFICIAL LANGUAGE: Sihala, Tamil English
MAJOR RELIGION: Buddhism, Hinduism, Christianity, Islam
Telephone: 94
Nat'l Holiday: Independence day, Feb. 4
Official Time: G.M.T. + 51/2
Electricity: 220 volts, 50 cycles
Exchange Rate: 1US$ = Lkr 53
National Airline: Air Lanka

LAW REGARDING HOMOSEXUALITY: Homosexual acts between men regardless of age is prohibited by the penal code. Punishment can be up to 10 years in prison. The law is applied frequently and the number of convictions is on the rise.

COLOMBO   🕭   31

✈ Katunayake Int'l AP (CMB) 20 mi. / 26 km

LOCATION: Central western coast.

POPULATION: 1,900,000

DESCRIPTION: Capital of Sri Lanka, Colombo is a major harbor. The **Fort** south of the harbor is the city's main commercial center. For gay travelers there is not much of a gay scene.

❖ Gay beach: coast area between Galle Face Hotel and the lighthouse; beach at Wellawatta railway station.

 ACCOMMODATIONS

GALLE FACE HOTEL
2 Kollupitiya Rd. Tel: (1) 541-010. TYPE: *Hotel.* CLIENTELE: Mostly Straight. LOCATION: On the seafront at the southern end of Galle Face Green. 60 rooms w/priv. bath, 21 suites, phone, TV lounge, 24 hrs. room service, ocean-view dining, pool, private beach. Rates: (US) $70-$120. DESCRIPTION: First class resort hotel on a strip of coast where the boys are.

NEGOMBO   🕭   31

✈ Katunayake Int'l AP (CMB) 9 km / 6 mi. S.

LOCATION: 24 mi. / 38 km north of Colombo on Sri-Lanka's western coast.

POPULATION: 60,000

CLIMATE: Tropical climate tempered in the south by the altitude and affected by the monsoons.

DESCRIPTION: Coastal town north of Colombo and a popular gay resort. A task force was created in the town to prevent the spread of AIDS, not through safer-sex education, but rather by the arrest and reform of local male prostitutes.

 ACCOMMODATIONS

BLUE OCEANIC BEACH HOTEL
Ethukala. Tel: (31) 2642. Fax: (31) 4277. TYPE: *Informal Resort Hotel.* CLIENTELE: Mostly Straight. LOCATION: On the beach. 129 rooms w/priv. bath. Suites: 3, phone, minibar, ceiling fan, A/C, restaurants, bars, pool, tennis, scuba. Rates: (US) $40-$80. *TAC:* 10%. DESCRIPTION: Friendly hotel with attractive chalet-type rooms. 25 units are air-conditioned.

BROWN'S BEACH HOTEL
175 Lewis Place, Negombo 40. Tel: (31) 2076. Fax: (31) 2639. TYPE: *Hotel.* CLIENTELE: Mostly Straight. LOCATION: On the beach. 145 rooms w/priv. bath, 10 beach bungalows, 4 suites, phone, balcony, A/C, room & maid service, restaurants, bar, nightclub, pool, gym, sauna, parking, on the beach. Rates: (US) $60-$90. *TAC:* 10%. DESCRIPTION: First class hotel on private beach in tropical garden setting.

ST. BARTHÉLEMY

AREA: 8 sq. mi. (21 sq. km)
POPULATION: 5,000
CAPITAL: Gustavia
CURRENCY: French Franc (FF) or US$
OFFICIAL LANGUAGE: French
MAJOR RELIGION: Roman Catholicism
Telephone: 590
Nat'l Holiday: Bastille Day, July 14
Official Time: G.M.T. - 5 (6 in winter)
Electricity: 220 volts, 50 cycles
Exchange Rate: 1US$ = FF 4.86
National Airline: Air St. Barthélemy

LAW REGARDING HOMOSEXUALITY:
Homosexuality is accepted. The legal minimum
age of consent is 15, but it is not advisable to
get involved in homosexual relationship with
under 18 years old. St. Barthélemy is a French
territory and it is subject to the French legal
system.

GUSTAVIA   ℭ   NO AREA CODE

✈ St. Jean Airport (SBH) 2 mi. / 3 km NW.

LOCATION: Western coast of the island on the
three protective sides of Port de Plaisance harbor.

POPULATION: 1,500

CLIMATE: Hot and sunny year round beach
climate with average day time temperatures
75˚F-84˚F (24˚c-30˚c).

DESCRIPTION: St. Barthélemy is a tiny paradise island offering eight hours of warm sunshine every day and twelve superb beaches
with golden sand. Known as the St. Tropez of
the Caribbean it offers topless sunbathing, elegant shopping, gourmet restaurants and colorful beach cafés. Topless sunbathing is permit-

ted on all the beaches. While nude bathing is
practiced on secluded beaches such as **Saline**
and **Gouverneur** it is not exactly legal.

St. Barts holds an unusual high ratio of ten
men for every one women. (Can you imagine
this place to be anything but Paradise?). Handsomely tanned young men, like those in sleek
fashion-stud magazines can be seen parading
past the island's famous *haute couture* shops,
or sunbathing on the beaches.

❖ **SPECIAL EVENTS: The Festival of St.
Barthélemy**, three fun days French Fair style
in late August, and **Carnival** and **Mardi Gras**
with black & white parades and parties in Late
January.

BARS ▼ RESTAURANTS ▮▮

● Bars/Clubs (G/S): **Autour Du Rocher**,
nightclub, increasingly gay after 11pm; **Chez
Ginette S.O.S.**, late-night lost boys hangout,
near Anse de Cayes (27-6611); **Club La
Banane**, evening *à La Cage aux Folles* (276-
825) l'Oubli Café, yuppie style; piano bar at
the **Hibiscus Hotel**; **Le Pélican**, pub, St.
Jean (276464); **Le Sélect**, major local
bar/hangout, rue Général de Gaulle, Gustavia.

● Restaurants (AW): **3 Forces**, French Creole
vegetarian at the Hostellerie de 3 Forces (see
description below); **Au Trois Gourmands**,
award winning French cuisine, expensive (27-
71-83); **Au Port**, French restaurant overlooking the harbor (27-62-36).

⬧ ACCOMMODATIONS ⬧

BAIE DES ANGES HOTEL
Baie de Flamandes, Gustavia. USA/Canada
reservations: Odysseus (516) 944-5330 or (800)
257-5344. Fax: (516) 944-7540 or (800) 982-
6571. TYPE: *Hotel*. LOCATION: Beachfront. 9
air-conditioned rooms w/priv. bath and terrace,
bungalows w/kitchenette. Water sports.

HOSTELLERIE DES 3 FORCES
Vitet. USA/Canada reservations: Odysseus
(516) 944-5330 or (800) 257-5344. Fax: (516)
944-7540 or (800) 982-6571. TYPE: *Hotel*.
HOST: Hubert. CLIENTELE: Gay/Straight.
LOCATION: High on a mountain, 3 mi. / 5 km
east of the Capital. 8 one-bedroom cottages,
bar, restaurant. Rates on request. DESCRIP-
TION: Mountaintop Cottage complex. Each
cottage complements the sign of the zodiac.
Superior cottage has bahama fans, deluxe cottage is fully air conditioned.

ST. KITTS/NEVIS

AREA: 104 sq. mi. (269 sq. km)
POPULATION: 45,000
CAPITAL: Bassetere
CURRENCY: East Caribbean Dollar (XCD)
OFFICIAL LANGUAGE: English
MAJOR RELIGION: Protestantism
Telephone: 809
Nat'l Holiday: Independence Day, Sept. 19
Official Time: G.M.T. - 4
Electricity: 220 volts, 60 cycles
Exchange Rate: 1US$ = XCD 2.70
National Airline: Winair

LAW REGARDING HOMOSEXUALITY: No information is available concerning the status of homosexuality on this island.

ST. KITTS/NEVIS

✈ Golden Rock Airport (SKB)

2 mi. / 3 km west of Basseterre

LOCATION: Volcanic island in the British Leeward Islands.

CLIMATE: Hot and sunny year round beach climate with average day time temperatures 75°F-84°F (24°c-30°c).

DESCRIPTION: Sleepy Caribbean island that is becoming popular for a quiet laid back vacation. The Capital Basseterre, is a 18th century port with quaint waterfront and colonial houses.

❖ Beaches: the best beaches on the island are **Banana Bay** and **Friar's Bay**.

BARS ⅄ RESTAURANTS 🍴

● Bars/Clubs (G/S): **Kititian Monkey Bar**,

Timothy Beach (465-8050); **Why Not Bar**, small video cruise bar, Fort St., Basseterre (465-2858).

● Restaurants (AW): **Ballahoo**, Caribbean cuisine, overlooking the town center from Fort Street (465-4197); **Golden Lemon**, Creole and Continental, Dieppe Bay (465-7260); **The Patio**, Caribbean & International, Frigate Bay Beach (465-8666); **Turtle Beach Bar & Grill**, popular seafood buffet with live entertainment;

🏠 ACCOMMODATIONS 🏠

FORT THOMAS HOTEL
Basseterre, St. Kitts. Tel: 465-2695. TYPE: *Hotel*. CLIENTELE: All Welcome. LOCATION: Amid tropical gardens on the site of the old fort. 64 rooms w/priv. bath, CTV, phone, balcony, mountain or ocean view, restaurant, terrace bar, outdoor pool, parking. Rates: (US) $80-$120. DESCRIPTION: Moderate first class hotel in a central location, 4 mi. / 7 km from beach.

FOUR SEASONS RESORT
Pinneys Beach, Nevis. Tel: 469-1111. TYPE: *Resort Hotel*. CLIENTELE: All Welcome. LOCATION: On Pinney's Beach on the island's leeward side. 196 rooms w/priv. bath, 17 suites, CTV, VCR, phone, hairdryer, minibar, room service, restaurants, bars, outdoor pool, tennis, gym, parking. Rates: (US) $190 - $650. DESCRIPTION: Deluxe resort complex.

ISLAND PARADISE BEACH VILLAGE
Frigate Bay, St. Kitts. Tel: 465-8035. TYPE: *Apartments Complex*. CLIENTELE: All Welcome. LOCATION: On Frigate Bay. 62 apartments (1,2,3BR), ceiling fan, A/C, CTV, phone, balcony or verandah, full kitchen, living/dining area,pool. Restaurants, casino, beach and tennis nearby. Rates: (US) $120 - $210. DESCRIPTION: Limited service quality oceanfront apartment.

TIMOTHY BEACH RESORT
Frigate Bay, St. Kitts. Tel: 465-8597. TYPE: *Condominium Resort*. CLIENTELE: All Welcome. LOCATION: Waterfront on Frigate Bay.

* Rooms: 30 w/priv. bath
* Suites: 31 w/1 or 2BR (w/kitchen)
* A/C, phone, minibar, balcony, patio
* Cafe, bar, pool, tennis, free parking
* Open: Year round
* Rates: (US) $120 - $260

DESCRIPTION: Charming and informal waterfront condominium resort.

AREA: 55,144 sq. mi. (142,823 sq. km)
POPULATION: 400,000
CAPITAL: Paramaribo
CURRENCY: Suriname guilder (Sfl)
OFFICIAL LANGUAGE: Dutch, Hindi, Indonesian
MAJOR RELIGION: Christianity, Islam, Hinduism
Telephone: 597
Nat'l Holiday: Independence Day, Nov. 25
Official Time: G.M.T. -3
Electricity: 127/220 volts, 60 cycles
Exchange Rate: 1US$ = Sfl 438
National Airline: Suriname Airways (SLM)

LAW REGARDING HOMOSEXUALITY: Homosexual acts between consenting adults are not mentioned in the Code of Law as being a criminal offense. However, homosexual acts with minors under the age of 18 can be punished with imprisonment up to four years according to article 302 of the Surinamese penal code. The age of consent for heterosexual sex is 16.

PARAMARIBO

✈ Zaderij Int'l AP (PBM) 30 mi. / 48 km So.

LOCATION: Northern Suriname on the Atlantic Ocean.

POPULATION: 198,000

CLIMATE: Tropical with high humidity but not very hot. In the coastal area temperatures vary between 23°c-30°c (73°F-86°F). April - August is the main dry season.

DESCRIPTION: The capital and the chief port, lies on the Suriname river. It has many attractive colonial buildings and the population is mainly Creole. One of Suriname's main problem is the ethnic tension between Creoles and East Indians. There are no great beaches, and the sea and rivers in the coastal area are muddy. Mosquitoes can be a real problem.

BARS Υ RESTAURANTS ¶¶

● Bars/Clubs (G/S): **Midnight Store**; **Touché** dance club, Cartousji; **Saramaca Bar** at the Torarica Hotel & Casino, L.J. Rietbergplein.

● Restaurants (AW): **Sarinah**, Indonesian, Verlengde Gemenelandsweg 187; **La Bastille**, Kleine Waterstraat opp. Torarica Hotel; **Fa Tai**, Chinese, Maagdenstraat 64.

 ACCOMMODATIONS

TORARICA HOTEL-CASINO
L.J. Rietbergplein 1. Tel: 471500. TYPE: *Hotel & Casino*. CLIENTELE: All Welcome. LOCATION: Beautiful garden setting on the banks of the Suriname River.

* Rooms: 132 rooms w/priv. bath
* Suites: 9 (1 BR) w/kitchen
* Rooms for non smokers
* CTV (CNN), VCR, phone, A/C, minibar
* Room & maid service, wheelchair access
* Restaurant, bar, casino, pool, sauna
* Airport: 45 km / 28 mi.
* Open: Year round
* Rates: (US) $110 - $130

DESCRIPTION: First class hotel & casino.

STARDUST HOTEL
Cordon St., Leonsberg. Tel: 50689. TYPE: *Motel*. CLIENTELE: All Welcome. LOCATION: Near the Suriname River & Seashore, 4 mi / 6km from downtown (shuttle).

* Rooms: 137 w/priv. bath
* Suites: 17 penthouse suites
* Condominiums: 55
* CTV, phone, A/C, balcony (most)
* Restaurant, bars, roof garden, pool
* Sauna, gym, tennis, golf, free parking
* Airport: 28 mi. / 45 km (free shuttle)
* Open: Year round
* Rates: (US) $45-$85

DESCRIPTION: Resort complex with fine amenities.

SWEDEN

AREA: 173,665 sq. mi. (449,792 sq. km)
POPULATION: 8,300,000
CAPITAL: Stockholm
CURRENCY: Swedish Kronen (SK)
OFFICIAL LANGUAGE: Swedish
MAJOR RELIGION: Protestantism
Telephone: 46
Nat'l Holiday: Flag Day, June 6
Official Time: G.M.T. + 1
Electricity: 220 volts
Exchange Rate: 1US$ = SK 6.60
National Airline: SAS

LAW REGARDING HOMOSEXUALITY: Homosexuality is not mentioned in the Swedish Law, but the minimum legal age for consensual homosexuality is 15. Homosexuality in Sweden is generally accepted as an alternative lifestyle with no problems.

GOTHENBURG   *©*   031

✈ Landvetter Int'l Airport (GOT)
15.5 mi. / 25 km east

LOCATION: On the Göta river on the west coast of Sweden.

POPULATION: 700,000

CLIMATE: See Stockholm

Gay/Lesbian Visitor Information
RFSL: 711-6151

DESCRIPTION: The second largest city in Sweden and the most continental of all Swedish cities. Founded by king Gustav II Aldof in the 17th century, it is one of the youngest cities in Sweden. The west coast of Sweden with Gothenburg in its center, is a popular summer resort with a scenic coastal strip with sandy beaches.

The busy harbor serves as home port for many shipping companies. The city is connected with Fredeikshavn in Denmark by ferry, and it is only one hour flight from Stockholm. Visit: the **Old Town**, a delightful Dutch-built section alongside canals; **Kungsportavenyn**, the city's main boulevard dotted with shops, cafes and restaurants; **Liseberg**, an amusement park popular in the summer; The **University of Göterborg** founded in 1891. Gay cruising takes place at the **Slottskogen Park** in the summer only.

BARS  RESTAURANTS

● Bars/clubs (GM): **Bacchus**, restaurant/disco, Bellmansgatan 9 (132-043); **Café Hellmans**, café at RFSL center, Esperantoplatsen 7 (711-1420); **Touch**, pub nights, disco, Esperantoplatsen 7 (near tram/bus stop Järntorget) run by volunteers of RFSL (711-1420).

● Bars/clubs (GW): **RFSL center** (711-1420); **Kvinnohuset**, activities for women, call for directions (211-465); **Touch**, lesbian nights, disco, Esperantoplatsen 7 (near tram/bus stop Järntorget) run by volunteers of RFSL .

λ SERVICES λ

● Erotica (GM): **Videolook**, Andra Långgatan 16; **Blue Video**, Andra Langgatan 32.

● Leather (GM): **Barbarella**, Fjärde Långgat. 6, Box 31172. Tel/Fax (147-968).

🗝 ACCOMMODATIONS 🗝

CARL JOHAN HOTEL
Karl Johansg. 66-70, Göteborg S-41455. Tel: (031) 420-020. TYPE: *Hotel*. CLIENTELE: Mostly Straight. LOCATION: Near the international ferry harbor.

* Rooms: 149 w/priv. bath
* CTV, phone, C/H, wheelchair Access
* Restaurant, bar, sauna
* Room & maid service, parking
* Gay Bars: walking distance
* Airport: 16 km (10 mi.), taxi
* Credit Cards: MC/VISA/AMEX/EC/DC
* Open: Year round
* Rates: (SK) 400 - 950
* *TAC:* 10%

DESCRIPTION: Contemporary hotel in a convenient location.

KIRUNA ✆ 0980

✈ Kiruna Airport

LOCATION: About 720 mi. / 1200 km north of Stockholm in Lapland.

POPULATION: 25,000

DESCRIPTION: 'Old Klondike' style mining town. The city sprawls across wild region unconquered by men of Arctic Scandinavia. It has the same sort of fascination usually reserved to exotic places. There is no gay scene in this land of the 'Midnight Sun' but it is unique and worth exploring.

 ACCOMMODATIONS

ICE HOTEL
63 Marknadsvegen, 98191 Jukkasjarvi. Tel: (980) 21190. USA/Canada reservations available from Odysseus Tel: (516) 944-5330 or (800) 257-5344. Fax: (516) 944-7540 or (800) 982-6571. TYPE: *Ice Hotel.* CLIENTELE: All Welcome. LOCATION: 7 mi. / 11 km from Kiruna. 60 beds, some in common rooms, others in rooms sleeping 2 people. DESCRIPTION: Large Ice Igloo hotel built on the grounds of an existing all cabin hotel. The beds are made of hard snow covered with reindeer hide. Down sleeping bags are provided. Most of the furniture is made of ice. Shared toilet facilities in a separate building. Price includes breakfast and morning sauna. 3 hrs. dog sled excursions for up to 4 pax can be arranged. Rates: on request. *TAC:* 10% (from Odysseus).

MALMÖ ✆ 040

✈ Sturup Int'l Airport (MMX)
19 mi. / 30 km southeast

LOCATION: Southern Sweden across the Öresund from Copenhagen.

POPULATION: 240,000

CLIMATE: Mild due to the tempering effect of the Gulf Stream. Summers average 61°F-77°F (16°c-25°c). Winter temperatures seldom drop below 30°F (-1°c).

Gay/Lesbian Visitor Information
G & L Switchboard: 611-9944

DESCRIPTION: Located across a narrow gulf from Copenhagen, Malmö is a lively city where you can catch frequent hydrofoil boats to Copenhagen (45 min. crossing) and the European continent.

BARS ♈ RESTAURANTS ♨

● Bars/clubs (GM): **4:AN**, disco, Snapperupsgatan 4 (230-311); **RFSL Indigo**, pub, cafe & disco, Monbijougatan 15 (611-9962).

● Restaurants (AW): **Don Quijote**, Bergsgatan 10 (971-226); **Gustav Adolf**, restaurant & cafe on main square, Gustav Adolf Torg 43 (611-2272); **Pars**, Iranian cuisine, Ängelholmsgatan at Kristianstadgatan; **Victors**, cafe and bar, Lilla Torget.

 ACCOMMODATIONS

✪ HOTEL PALLAS
Norra Vallgatan 74, S-21122 Malmö. Tel: (40) 611-5077. USA/Canada: (800) 257-5344. TYPE: *Hotel.* HOST: Michael Henderson. CLIENTELE: Equal Gay/ Straight. LOCATION: Central location near Main Railway Station. Few minutes walk to main restaurants and shopping area, and the hydrofoils to Copenhagen.

* Rooms: 19 w/shared bath
  12 sgl / 7 dbl / 6 triple / 6 quad
* Smoking allowed in rooms
* CTV, phone (reception), C/H, cooking facilities, sundeck, parking
* Beach: 500 m / yards
* Gay Bars: 100 m / yards
* Health Club: 250 m / yards
* Airport: 20 min., taxi
* Train Station: 100 m / yards walking
* Languages: Swedish, English, German
* Open: Year round
* Rates: (US) $70-$110 w/CB
* *TAC:* 10% (from Odysseus)

DESCRIPTION: Budget hotel. The double room are large with a small living area (20 sq.m. / 220 sq.ft.). All rooms have wash basin and CTV. Showers and toilets are located in a hallway just outside the rooms. Friendly atmosphere.

SAVOY HOTEL
Nora Vallgatan 62. Tel: (40) 70230. TYPE: *Hotel.* CLIENTELE: All Welcome. LOCATION: Near Air Terminal, Train Station, overlooking busy square.

* Rooms: 100 w/priv. bath. Suites: 7

* CTV (CNN), phone, minibar, balcony
* Bar, restaurant, parking nearby
* Beach: 15 min. mixed
* Gay Bars: walking distance
* Open: Year round
* Rates: Skr 500 - 1,500
* *TAC:* 8%

DESCRIPTION: First class traditional hotel in a central location. All rooms are tastefully furnished. Good service.

STOCKHOLM   ©   08

✈ Arlanda Int'l Airport (ARN)
6 mi. / 10 km east

LOCATION: Waterfront city in the Southeastern Sweden spreading over 14 islands on the coast of the Baltic Sea.

POPULATION: Metro 1,500,000;
City 665,500

CLIMATE: Winter days are short and cold with abundance of snow and temperatures in the 30°'sF (-2°c). Summer has long days, and by the end of June the sun shines 19 hours. The summer temperature is mild and pleasant, ranging from mid to high 70°F (20°c) and the air is dry.

Gay/Lesbian Visitor Information
Gay Community Center: 736-0212

DESCRIPTION: Stockholm is a dynamic city with a delicate balance between urbanism and respect for nature. A city of islands, it is dominated by the sea and shipping activities. The original **Old Town** (Gamla Stan) is popularly known as the 'City between the Bridges'.

Taking the Old City as an orientation point Stockholm can be divided into the following parts: to the north, Norrmaln, is the business quarter, to the west, Kungshomen, is the administrative quarter, and to the south, Slussen, and Södermaln, the popular quarters. The best way to see and feel the impulse of this great city is to take a boat ride. You may take a tour from the front of the Grand Hotel and get off any place to rejoin the boat later.

Visit museums, **Skansen**, **Tivoli** - amusement park with a beautifully illuminated Arabian Nights Palace; **Deer Park** (Djurgården), where you can see the amazing Wasa - a restored 350 year old Viking war ship that sank in 1628.

Hotell Pallas
Malmö - SWEDEN

USA/Canada reservations
1-800-257-5344
TEL: (516) 944-5330 • FAX: (516) 944-7540

❖ Beaches: "The beautiful people" go to **Rålambshovsparken**; The island of **Långholmen** lies directly opposite Riddarfjärden. The gay beach is located on the west side; **Frescati** near the University, take the underground to Universitetet then walk under the motorway towards the water.

BARS ¥ RESTAURANTS ¶

● Bars/clubs (GM): **Boy Bar**, dance club, c/o le Garage, Herculesgaten 11; **Hjärter Dam**, mixed leather bar & **Kinky Bar**, private leather bar, Polhemsgatan 23; **Hus1**, restaurant, bar, disco, Sveavägen 57 (315-533); **OZ**, disco, St. Eriksterassen 63 (653-8750); **Patricia**, Stadsgårdskajen 152; **SLM**, (Scandinavian Leather Men), disco, bar & leather club, Wollmar Yxkullsgatan 18 (643-3100).

● Bars/clubs (GW): **Kvinnohuset**, cafe/library, Snickarbacken 10; **Lesbisk Nu Disco**, at Lesbisk Center, Kocksgatan 28 (644-0802); **RFSL-Huset**, Tuesday is women's night at the disco, 57 Sveavägen (736-0212).

● Restaurants (GMW): **Alice B**, the only gay restaurant in Stockholm, Sveavägen 57 (315-533) at the RFSL Huset; **Bon Apetit**, restau

"The Queen of Lake Mälardrottningen
In the Heart of Stockholm
USA/Canada reservations (800) 257-5344

rant and pub, Ringvägen 153 (640-2013); **Café Diva**, Sveavägen 57 (344-222); **Hermans Lilla Gröna**, Katarina Bang. 17; **OZ**, also bar & disco, St. Eriksterassen 63 (653-8750); **Vau de Ville**, between Kungsträdgårdsg. and Hamngatan; Other (AW): **Blå Gåsen**, gourmet restaurant, Karlvägen 28; **Monte Carlo**, bar/restaurant corner of Sveavägen and Kungsgatan; The Old Town is famous for its authentic cellar restaurants: try **Diana**, unconventional with mixed clientele, Brunnsgränd 2 (10 73 10); and **Fem Små Hus**, fine Old Town restaurant for intimate dining, Nygränd 10 (10 04 82).

λ SERVICES λ

● Sex shops (G/S): **Foxy**, gay films, Tomtebogatan 13 (10-22 daily); **Haga Video**, Hagagatan 56 (335-544); **Manhattan**, Hantverkargatan 49 (653-9210); **Revolt**, Nytorgsgatan 21A (643-7950); **Roxy**, Döbelnsgatan 4; **US Video**, Regeringsgatan 85.

 ACCOMMODATIONS

MALARDROTTNINGEN HOTEL
Riddarholmen, Stockholm S-11128. Tel: (8) 243600. USA/Canada reservations - (800) 257-5344. Tel: (516) 944-5330. Fax: (516) 944-7540. TYPE: *Botel*. CLIENTELE: All Welcome. LOCA

TION: Berthed on the waterfront, few blocks from the Old Town and major attractions.

* Rooms: 59 w/shower
* CTV, phone, radio, A/C
* Restaurant, Grill, Captain's Bar
* Sauna, tennis court
* Gay Bars: walking distance
* Train Station: 800 m/ yards
* Airport: 40 km / 25 mi.
* Open: Year round
* Rates: $120-$280
* *TAC:* 10% (from Odysseus)

DESCRIPTION: Unique floating hotel converted from a luxury yacht. Great location and ambiance.

SCANDIC CROWN HOTEL
Guldgrand 8, S-10465 Stockholm. Tel: (8) 702-2500. TYPE: *Hotel*. CLIENTELE: All Welcome. LOCATION: City Center near the Old Town.

* Rooms: 264 w/priv. bath. Suites: 16
* Relax Center w/Sauna, pool, solarium
* Rates: SKR 1253 - 1,661

DESCRIPTION: Striking superior first class hotel. Comfortable rooms with excellent amenities.

SWITZERLAND

AREA: 15,943 sq. mi. (41,292 sq. km)
POPULATION: 6,366,000
CAPITAL: Bern
CURRENCY: Swiss Franc (SF)
OFFICIAL LANGUAGES: Swiss German Dialect, French, Italian
MAJOR RELIGIONS: Protestantism, Roman Catholicism
Telephone: 41
Nat'l Holiday: Confederation Day, Aug. 1
Official Time: G.M.T + 1
Electricity: 220 volts
Exchange Rate: 1US$ = SF 1.14
National Airline: Swissair

LAW REGARDING HOMOSEXUALITY: Legal minimum age for consensual homosexual activity is 20. The attitude of the Swiss society towards homosexuality is that of intolerance because of the religious and conservative nature of the Swiss society.

BASEL   ✆   061

✈ Mulhouse Int'l Airport (BSL)
7 mi. / 11 km northwest

LOCATION: On the Rhine, in the meeting point of France, West Germany, and Switzerland.

POPULATION: 200,000

CLIMATE: Continental with cold winters with plenty of snow, and temperatures in the 20˚F's (-6˚c); summers with sunny and dry weather in the upper 70˚F's (25˚c).

Gay/Lesbian Visitor Information
Arcados, Rhingaße 69
Tel: (061) 681-3132

DESCRIPTION: Basel is the second largest town in Switzerland. Historic city on the Rhine and a meeting point of three great European countries: France, Germany, and Switzerland. Basel, is known as the city of Humanists and capital of the Swiss chemical industries. Enjoy the city's distinguished architecture: medieval cathedrals, streets, and squares, colorful fruit and vegetable market near the 16th century **Town Hall** - Rathaus; the **Old City**; and many excellent art museums.

❖ **SPECIAL EVENT**: February Carnival, which is a 3-day medieval, and gothic carnival following Ash Wednesday.

BARS ♟ RESTAURANTS ♟♟

Most of the gay scene is located in the Old Town around the Clara Platz tram station.

● Bars/clubs (GMW): **Dupf**, bar/club, Rebgasse 43 (692-0011); **Elle et Lui**, Rebgasse 39 (325-479); **Isola Club**, dance bar, Gempensrasse 60, near the SBB train station; **Zisch-Bar**, Klybeckstraße 1B.

● Bar/club (GW): **Frauzentrum**, women's center with lesbian bar night and events, 2 Klingentalgraben.

● Restaurants (GMW): **Basler Stübli**, Hegenheimerstrasse 14 (44 91 66); **Dupf**, Rebgasse 43 (692-0011); **Ku-Fong** Restaurant, Petersgraben 21 (25 31 13). There are many reasonably priced restaurants in Basel, for good, simple food, try **Restaurant Zum Stadtkeller**, Marktgasse 11. This is not a gay oriented restaurant but it recommended; **Schelz & Kegelkino**, bar/restaurant, 55 Gartnerstraße.

λ SERVICES λ

● Health Club (GM): **Mawi**, St. Alban-Vorstadt 76 (23-2354) 2nd fl.; **Sauna Brunnhof**, steam bath, massage, sun terrace, Brunngasse 8.

● Shops (GMW): **Arcados**, Rheingaße 69 (681-3132); **Kiosk 18**, Schneidergaße 18 (261-1986).

🏠 ACCOMMODATIONS 🏠

DREI KÖNIGE AM RHEIN
8, Blumenrain, CH-4001 Basel. Tel: (61) 252 153. TYPE: *Deluxe Hotel*. CLIENTELE: Mostly Straight. LOCATION: On the bank of the Rhein, near the Tourist Office. 90 rooms w/priv. bath. Rates on request.

BERN   © 031

✈ Belp Airport (BRN) 6 mi. / 10 km SE

LOCATION: On a peninsula of the winding Aare river in the Canton of Berne in northwestern Switzerland.

POPULATION: 142,000

CLIMATE: Continental with cold winters with plenty of snow, and temperatures in the 20°F's (-6°c); summers with sunny and dry weather in the upper 70°F's (25°c).

Gay/Lesbian Visitors Information Bern's Gay Center, Muhleplatz 11 Tel: (031) 311-1197

DESCRIPTION: Bern is the capital of both Switzerland and the country's second largest canton. It is an administrative center and a lively University town. Visit: the arcaded streets of the **Old Town** dominated by the Minster (Basilica). The charming older part of Bern still preserves its original layout.

BARS ♈ RESTAURANTS 🍴

● Bar/club (GM): **Ursus Club**, bar & disco, Junkergaße 1 (311-7406).

● Bars/clubs (GMW): **ISC Club**, Neubrückenstr. 10; **Samurai**, Aarbergergaße 35 (311-7406).

● Bar/club (GW): **The Women's Center**, bar/disco,lesbian evenings, 1 Langmauerweg.

● Restaurants (AW): **La Terasse**, expensive restaurant at the Bellevue Palace, great view and atmosphere, 3-5 Kochergaße (224-581); **Schulteiss-Stube**, gourmet, expensive, at the Scweizerhof hotel, 11 Bahnhofpl. (224-501); **Klötzlikeller**, old wine tavern, local specialties, inexpensive, 62 Gerechtigkeitsgaße (227-456).

λ SERVICES λ

● Health Clubs (GM): **Al Peter's Sun Deck**, sauna, fitness club, Länggass-Straße 65 (302-4686); **Studio 43**, Monbijoustraße 123 (462-827).

● Gay Shop (GM): **Loveland**, sex shop, cinema, videos, Gerechtigkeitsgaße 39 (224-533).

🪶 ACCOMMODATIONS 🪶

METROPOLE HOTEL
Zeughusgaße 26-28, Bern CH-3011. Tel: (31) 225021. TYPE: *Hotel*. CLIENTELE: All Welcome. LOCATION: City center near Town Hall.

* Rooms: 60 w/priv. bath
* CTV, phone, A/C
* Restaurant, bar, diet meals available
* Elevator, parking
* Gay Bars: walking distance
* Airport: 20 min.
* Rates: (US) $120-$160
* *TAC:* 8%

DESCRIPTION: Superior tourist class historic hotel in a convenient location.

GENEVA   © 022

✈ Cointrin Int'l Airport (GVA) 3 mi. / 5 km northwest

LOCATION: At the western tip of Lake Geneva , between the Alps and the Jura, sharing a common border with France.

POPULATION: 160,000

CLIMATE: Continental, with temperatures never very hot or too cold. The average summer temperature is 65°F (18°c), and 34°F(1°c) in the winter. Rain does not last very long, but fog can be persisting.

Gay/Lesbian Information/Dialogai Tel: (022) 340-0000

DESCRIPTION: Geneva, is a trim and proper postcard city on Lake Geneva, with the snow covered Alps in the backdrop. It is a cosmopolitan city, in the heart of Europe, with a distinguished French culture and Swiss efficiency. Many of the worlds international organizations maintain in Geneva their headquarters and offices, including the U.N., the International Red Cross, etc. The gay scene of Geneva is in the Old City near the Place Neuve.

BARS ♈ RESTAURANTS 🍴

● Bars/clubs (GM): **La Bretelle**, mixed bar, rue des Etuves (732-7596); **Le Concorde**, bar and restaurant, 3 rue de Berne (731-9680); **Le Declic**, dance club, 28 Blvd. du Pont d'Arve (320-5914); **Dialogai**, 5 rue Rossi (731-8446); **La Garçonniere**, drag shows, 22 Pl. Bémont (28-2161); **Le Grillon**, dance club, 40 rue du

Rhone, 1st Fl. (310-1111); **Hippocampe**, 47 rue des Paquis (732-0800); **Le Musicol**, club/disco, 5 rue Richemont (32-6710); **Le Tube**, 3 rue de l'Université, 21:00 - 02:00 hrs. (329-8298).

● Bars/clubs (GW): **Le 1900**, Place Pradier (731-2124); **La Bretelle**, mixed bar, rue des Etuves (732-7596).

● Restaurants: **Concorde**, 3 rue de Berne (731-9680); **l'Evidence**, rue des Grottes 13 (731-8446). Other restaurants (not gay): **Le Duc**, best seafood restaurant in Switzerland,7 Quai du Mont-Blanc (731-7330) expensive; **Edelweiss**, Swiss chalet with regional specialties, 2 Pl. de la Navigation (31 49 40); **Les Armures**, inexpensive restaurant for local specialties in the heart of Old Town, 1 rue du Puits-St.-Pierre (728-3442).

λ SERVICES λ

● Health Clubs (GM): **Sauna Gemeaux**, gay men only, 4 bis rue Prévost-Martin (720-0463); **Pradier Sauna**, 8 rue Pradier, Cornavin (732-2857); **Sauna Club**, sauna, solarium, fitness, mixed clientele Tue/Wed., Ave. de Baptista, Avanchet-Parc (near the airport) (796-9066).

ACCOMMODATIONS

CENTURY HOTEL
Ave. de Frontenex 24, Geneva CH-1207. Tel: (022) 736-8095. Fax: (022) 786-5274. TYPE: *Hotel*. LOCATION: Near center, within walking distance of the lake. 138 rooms w/priv. bath, CTV, phone, bar, terrace. Rates on request.

CHANTILLY HOTEL
27 rue de la Navigation, Geneva CH-1201. Tel: (22) 731-1107. TYPE: *Hotel*. CLIENTELE: Mostly Straight. LOCATION: Downtown, near the lake and the gay scene. 62 rooms w/priv. bath. CTV, phone, minibar. Rates on request. DESCRIPTION: Tourist class hotel in the heart of Geneva's gay scene.

LAUSANNE   © 021

✈ Cointrin Int'l Airport (GVA)

LOCATION: On the north shore of Lake Geneva, 70 km / 44 mi. northeast of Geneva.

DESCRIPTION: University town and convention hub, ranking with Geneva as a major cultural center of French speaking Switzerland.

BARS Y RESTAURANTS

● Bars/clubs (GM): **New Scotch**, dance club, 1 rue Ennig (234041); **Pink Side**, Avenue Tivoli 1 (311-3300); **Le Saxo**, rue de la Grotte 3 (323-4683).

● Bars/clubs (GMW): **Café de Négotiants**, 10 place du Tunnel (312-9766); **New Scotch**, Enning 1 (234-041); **Vagabond**, 4 ave. Béthusy (205-214).

λ SERVICES λ

● Health Clubs (GM): **New Relax Club**, sauna, massage, solarium, Galeries St. François A (4th fl.) (312-6678); **Pink Beach**, 9 ave. de Tivoli (311-0605); **Top Club**, sauna, massage, snack bar, Bellefontaine 6 (312-2366).

ACCOMMODATIONS

CONTINENTAL HOTEL
2 Place de la Gare, Lausanne CH-1001. Tel: (21) 201-551. Fax: (21) 237-679. TYPE: *Hotel*. CLIENTELE: Mostly Straight. LOCATION: Opposite Train Station, convenient to gay clubs. 120 rooms w/shower or bath, bar, club, disco, 3 restaurants, room service. Season: Year round. Rates: (SF) 170 - 210. *TAC:* 10%.

LUCERNE   © 041

✈ Kloten Intl Airport, Zurich (ZRH)
45 mi. / 72 km NE of Lucerne

LOCATION: In the Canton of Lucerne at the north end of Lake Lucerne.

POPULATION: 68,000

Gay & Lesbian Visitor Information
Halu Gay & Lesbian Group: 513532

DESCRIPTION: Capital of the Canton of Lucerne. This well preserved medieval town on **Vierwaldestätter See** is one of the greatest tourist attractions in Switzerland. Visit the **Old Town** - a wonder of Italian Renaissance style architecture, and the famous **Kapelbrücke** (Chapel Bridge) one of the best preserved wooden bridges in the country (partially damaged by fire recently).

BARS Y RESTAURANTS

● Bars/clubs (GMW): **Halu Disco**, 2nd and last Sat., Geissensteinring 14.

λ SERVICES λ

● Health Clubs (GM): **Discus**, sauna, bar, solarium, gym, Geissensteinring 26. Open: 13:00-23:00 daily (44-8877); **Tropica**, Fri. night sauna, Neuweg 4 (231150).

🏠 ACCOMMODATIONS 🏠

HOTEL DREI KOENIGE
Buchstrasse 35, Lucerne CH-6003. Tel: (41) 228-833. TYPE: *Hotel*. CLIENTELE: Mostly Straight. LOCATION: Heart of the city, walking distance of the Old Town.

* Rooms: 68 w/priv. shower/bath WC
* CTV, phone, radio
* Restaurants: 2
* Gay Bars: some nearby
* Train Station: 3 km / 2 mi.
* Open: Year round
* Rates: SF 130 - SF 230
* *TAC:* 8%

DESCRIPTION: Traditional tourist class hotel in a central location.

GRAND HOTEL NATIONAL
Haldenstrasse 4, Lucerne CH-6002. Tel: (41) 501111. TYPE: *Hotel*. CLIENTELE: Mostly Straight. LOCATION: Banks of Lake Lucerne with views of the Alps.

* Rooms: 80 rooms w/priv. bath
* Suites: 7 some w/fireplace & balcony
* CTV, phone, A/C, minibar
* 24 hrs. room service
* Piano bar, gym, sauna, pool
* Restaurants: French, Italian Chinese
* Gay Bars: walking distance
* Train Station: 1 km / 800 yards
* Airport: 45 mi. / 72 km
* Open: Year round
* Rates: SF 355 - SF 555
* *TAC:* 8%

DESCRIPTION: Deluxe Classic style hotel with fine amenities. Special service include complimentary fruit basket with flowers and chocolate.

NYON   ℂ   022

✈ Cointrin Int'l Airport (GVA)

LOCATION: NW shore of Lake Geneva, half way between Geneva and Lausanne.

POPULATION: 11,000

DESCRIPTION: Old world little town on Lake Geneva with interesting Roman relics. Visit the **Old Town**; its medieval church; and the **Historical Museum** in the five-towered castle on top of the hill. The **Musée Léman** offers interesting collection of antiquities.

BARS ▼ RESTAURANTS ¶¶

There are no exclusive gay bars and restaurants in town. The nearest gay oriented scene is in nearby Lausanne or Geneva. However, try the gay friendly bar and restaurants at the **Hôtel Rotisserie du Nord** (description below).

🏠 ACCOMMODATIONS 🏠

HOTEL ROTISSERIE du NORD
Rue Saint Jean 26, 1260 Nyon. Tel: (022) 361-3035. USA/Canada reservations Tel: (516) 944-5330 or (800) 257-5344. Fax: (516) 944-7540 or (800) 982-6571. TYPE: *Hotel*. HOST: Hansjorg J. Fluckiger. CLIENTELE: All Welcome. LOCATION: Centrally located. 20 rooms w/priv. bath, CTV, phone, minibar, restaurant, cocktail bar, terrace, parking: near the hotel, 5 min. lake beach. DESCRIPTION: Good quality 3-star hotel with a popular Grill restaurant and Cocktail Bar. Some rooms with lake view.

ZURICH   ℂ   01

✈ Kloten Int'l Airport (ZRH)
   7 mi. / 11 km northeast

LOCATION: On the northern tip of Lake Zurich in northern Switzerland, on both sides of the river Limmat.

POPULATION: 360,000

CLIMATE: Atlantic influenced weather, with the moderating effect of the Alps. Winter is mild around 32°F (0°c), and summers are pleasant with temperatures seldom getting higher than 80°F (26°c).

Gay/Lesbian Visitor Information
Gay & Lesbian Center - HAZ
Sihlquai 67, Zürich 8005
Tel: (01) 271-2250

DESCRIPTION: Zurich, is Switzerland's largest city and the main port of entry for many tourists. It is a captivating city with medieval architecture; a bustling financial center: and a shoppers paradise with quality goods, watches, jewelry, entertainment and leisure activities.

Visit: **Uetliberg**, for a view of the city from the mountain top; **Kunsthaus**, art collection from the Middle Ages to contemporary, one of the finest in Europe, Heimplatz 1; **Lindenhoff Hill**, Old Roman Fort, now splendid gardens in the center of town; **Ritberg Museum**, fine collection of non-European art, Gablerstraße 15; **Boat Tours**, of the lake or the Limat River.

BARS RESTAURANTS

● Bars/clubs (GM): ✪ **T & M Club**, gay disco with cyber bar and drag show at 10pm, Marktgaße14 (252-5944); **Bagpiper**, Zähringerstraße 11 (251-4756); **Barfüsser**, two bars, one leather oriented and restaurant, Spitalgasse 14 (251-4064); **Blue Box**, 13 Konradstraße; **Carrousel**, Zähringerstrs. 33 (251-4600); **Fanny Hill**, 113 Ankerstraße; **Tip Top**, Seilergaben 13 (251-7822) .

● Bars/clubs (GMW): **Club Hey**, disco, Rämistraße 6 / Bellevue Entrance (252-3210); **Mascotte**, disco, Theatrestraße 10 (252-4481).

● Bar/club (GW): **Frauzentrum**, women's center with bar and disco, 27 Mattengaße.

● Restaurants (GMW): ✪ **Montmartre**, mixed cuisine, spare ribs, at the Goldenes Schwert Hotel, Marketgaße 14 9266-1818); **Buurstube**, French, and **Edelweiss**, Swiss specialties at the Rothus Hotel (252 1530); **Trattoria La Gondola**, Italian menu, Heinrichstraße 83 (272 5703); **Café Marion**, Mühlegaße 22 (42 27 26); **Odéon Café**, Limmatquai 2 (251 16 50). Other restaurants (AW): **Oepfelchammer**, "Old Zurich" specialties in a cozy ambience, Rindermarkt 12 (251 2336); and for homesick Americans there is **California**, featuring California wines and American food with English menu, Asylstraße 125 (53 56 80) inexpensive.

λ SERVICES λ

● Health Clubs (GM): **Adonis**, Mutschellenstr. 17 (201-6416); **Apollo**, Seilergarben 41 club, sauna and Turkish bath (474 952); **Club David**, Kanzleistraße 84 (241-7800); **Moustache**, bar, solarium, sauna and massage, Badenerstraße 156b, entrance Engelstr. 4 (241-1080); **Paragon Relax Club**, fitness, solarium, steam bath, videos, bar, Mühlgaße 11 (252-

6666); **Reno's Relax**, club sauna, Kernstraße 57 near Hevetiaplatz (291-6362).

● Gay Shops (G/S): **Condomia**, Zentralstraße 62 (463-4819); **Gero Schweiz**, gay videos, Uetlibergstraße 12 (451-2616); **Macho Men's Shop**, leather, videos, Engelstr. 62 (241-3215); **Wild House**, rubber, leather, video, toys, magazines, escort service, Spitalgaße 12, 8001 Zurich (251-9140).

🏠 ACCOMMODATIONS 🏠

✪ GOLDENES SCHWERT

Marketgaße 14, 8001 Zurich. Tel: (1) 266-1818. Fax: (1) 251-3924. USA/Canada reservations available from Odysseus Tel: (800) 257-5344 or (516) 944-5330. Fax: (800) 982-6571 or (516) 944-7540. TYPE: *Hotel*. CLIENTELE: Mostly gay men & women. LOCATION: Heart of Old Town near the financial district and 2 min. away from the famous "Banhofstraße" shops.

* Rooms: 31 w/priv. bath
  sgl 5 / dbl 24 / triple 3
* Smoking allowed in rooms
* CTV, VCR, phone, safe box, C/H, hairdryer
* Suites: 3 w/living room, full bath, kitchen
* Bed Types: single, twin, double
* Services: maid, laundry, elevator, gym
* Restaurant: Montmartre
* Bar & Disco: **T&M** gaybar / shows
* Gay Bar: on premises
* Health Club: 2 min. Paragon
* Airport: 15 km / 10 mi., taxi, bus
* Metro: Rathusplatz 1 min. walk
* Languages: German, English, French
* Reservations: 1 night deposit
* Credit Cards: MC/VISA/AMEX/DC
* Open: Year round
* Rates: SF 99 - SF 350
* Check in 24 hrs / Check out 12 noon
* *TAC*: 10% (from Odysseus)
* Email: hotel@rainbow.ch
* URL: http://www.gaybar.ch

DESCRIPTION: 3-star hotel in Zurich's Old Town. Large guest rooms, 8 theme rooms, and 3 suites. All rooms with private bath, cosmetic box, some with private balcony.

ROTHUS HOTEL
Maktgaße 17, Zurich 8001. Tel: (01) 252-1530 Fax: (1) 251-3924. TYPE: *Hotel*. CLIENTELE: Gay Men. LOCATION: Centrally located in Old Town near Rathausbrücke.

* Rooms: 80; 37 w/priv. bath, 8 w/shower
* TV lounge, phone, C/H
* Restaurants, bars, club, no parking

* Gay Bars: on premises
* Airport: 6 km / 4 mi., bus, taxi
* Train Station: 1 km (0.6 mi.)
* Credit Cards: MC/VISA/AMEX/DC/EC
* Season: Year round
* Rates on request.
* *TAC:* 10%

DESCRIPTION: Hotel & entertainment complex for gay men. T & M Club offers the best drag show this side of the Rhine.

❍ HOTEL WELLENBERG

Niederdorfst. 10, CH-8001 Zurich. USA/Canada Reservations or Information: (800) 257-5344 or (516) 944-5330. Fax: (516) 944-7540. TYPE: *Hotel.* CLIENTELE: All Welcome. LOCATION: Heart of Zurich's Old Town.

* Rooms: 45 w/priv. bath
* Rooms for smokers and non smokers
* Rooms for disabled persons
* CTV (VCR), phone, A/C, C/H, minibar, hairdryer, patio, wheelchair access
* Individual safe deposit box in room
* Restaurant, breakfast room, Bars (2)
* Service: room, maid, turndown
* Parking (charge), health club, tennis
* Airport: 8 mi. / 13 km, taxi
* Train Station: 1/2 mi. / 800 m.
* Gay Bars: walking distance
* Health Club: on premises (mixed)
* Open: Year round
* Rates: $190 - $270 w/CBb
* *TAC:* 10% (from Odysseus)

DESCRIPTION: Modern and comfortable mod-

Hotel Wellenberg
Four-Star comfort in the heart of Old Town

USA/Canada reservations
(800) 257-5344

erate first class hotel in the heart of Old Zurich. All rooms are soundproofed with elegant furniture and decor. The rooms offer a unique view over the roofs and gardens of the Old Town. A friendly hotel with great charm and hospitality.

AREA: 71,498 sq. mi. (185,180 sq. km)
POPULATION: 12,000,000
CAPITAL: Damascus
CURRENCY: Syrian Pound (S£)
OFFICIAL LANGUAGES: Arabic, Armenian
MAJOR RELIGIONS: Islam, Christianity
Telephone: 963
Nat'l Holiday: Revolution Day, March 8
Official Time: G.M.T. + 2/3
Electricity: 110/220 volts, 60 cycles AC
Exchange Rate: 1US$ = S£42
National Airline: Syrian Airlines

LAW REGARDING HOMOSEXUALITY: Homosexual behavior is illegal. Section 520 of the Penal Code criminalizes any "carnal knowledge against the order of nature" with a maximum penalty of 3 years in prison. Homosexuality is a taboo and there are no gay and lesbian support groups.

ALEPPO   ✆   021

✈ Nejrab AP (ALP) 6.5 mi. / 10 km

DESCRIPTION: One of the oldest and best preserved cities in the Middle East. Possible gay cruising (AYOR) at the **Municipal Garden** and the Square on Ibrahim Hararo St.

ACCOMMODATIONS

CHAHBA CHAM PALACE
Aleppo. Tel: (21) 248-572. TYPE: *Hotel*. CLIENTELE: Mostly straight. LOCATION: Downtown. 249 rooms w/priv. bath, A/C, CTV, minibar. Rates: (US) $160-$230.

DAMASCUS   ✆   011

✈ Damascus Int'l AP (DAM) 18 mi. / 29 km

LOCATION: Southwestern Syria to the east of the Anti Lybanon mountains.

POPULATION: 923,000

CLIMATE: Hot dry summers and cold winters.

DESCRIPTION: 4,000 years old Damascus is the political, commercial and cultural center of Syria. The central feature of Damascus is the **Ummayyad Mosque** which is the site of St. John the Baptist tomb.The city has exotic *souq* (bazaar), mosques and age old quarters. For gay visitors some possible cruising (AYOR) takes place at the **Souq-el-Hallabeiah**; near the international Omayad Hotel; at the **Sabki-Ziki Alarsouzi gardens** and the famous **Hassan Al Kharrat Square.**

BARS ♀ RESTAURANTS 🍴

● Bars/clubs (G/S): **As-Shark el Awsat**, coffee shop, Basha St; **Sham Palace**, bar, Ave. Maysaloun (232-300).

λ SERVICES λ

● Hamams (AYOR) (G/S): **Al Mokadam**, Afif St.; **Al Jadid**, Bab Srijeh; **Hamam Al Wared**, Ain el Kuresh St.; **Nour-El Dine Al Shahid**, Bzourieh souq.

ACCOMMODATIONS

CHAM PALACE
Maysaloun St. Tel: (11) 232-300. TYPE: *Hotel*. CLIENTELE: Mostly Straight. LOCATION: Downtown in business district. 313 rooms w/priv. bath, 72 suites, marble full bath, CTV, phone, minibar, 24 hrs. room service, sauna, massage, steam bath, solarium, outdoor pool, restaurants, cafes, disco. Rates: (US) $280 - $350. DESCRIPTION: Moderate deluxe hotel.

OMAYAD HOTEL
4 Brazil St. Tel:(11) 221-7700. TYPE: *Hotel*. CLIENTELE: Mostly Straight. LOCATION: Residential area near government offices, embassies and business district. 75 rooms w/priv. bath, CTV, phone, hairdryer, minibar, balcony (some), suites (6), restaurant, American bar, nightclub, roof garden, free parking. Rates: (US) $130-$190. DESCRIPTION: First class older hotel.

TAIWAN

AREA: 13,971 sq. mi. (36,185 sq. km)
POPULATION: 16,800,000
CAPITAL: Taipei
CURRENCY: Taiwan dollar (T$)
OFFICIAL LANGUAGES: Chinese, Formosan
MAJOR RELIGIONS: Confucianism, Buddhism, Taoism, Christianity
Telephone: 886
Nat'l Holiday: Retrocession Day, Oct. 25
Official Time: G.M.T. + 8
Electricity: 110 volts, 60 cycles AC
Exchange Rate: 1US$ = T$27.24
National Airline: CAL (China Airlines)

LAW REGARDING HOMOSEXUALITY: No Sodomy Law. Homosexual acts between consenting adults in private are not considered an offense. The general attitude towards alternative lifestyles seems to be more relaxed since the death of Chiang Ching-kuo.

❖ **SPECIAL EVENT: Chinese New Year**, the longest and most important festival in Taiwan, Feb. 19, 1997.

KAOHSIUNG   ✆ 07

✈ Kaohsiung Int'l Airport 7 mi. / 11km

LOCATION: Southwestern Coast of Taiwan

POPULATION: 1,300,000

DESCRIPTION: Taiwan's second largest city is a major economic and industrial center and home to the island's largest international seaport. The city offers tourist attractions, temples, beaches and bargain shopping. Cruising (AYOR): **Love River** near shopping area and **Kaohsiung Main Railway Station**.

BARS ♈ RESTAURANTS

● Bars/clubs (GM): **Ba Chen Too**, 9F, 289-3 Chung Hwa 3rd Rd (282-0516); **Color Plate**, Tayou St. 5, 2nd Fl. (551-3757); **Men's Talk**, B1 32 Ming Shing St. (211-7049); **Private Life**, dance club, 278 Chi Hsien 3rd Rd. (561-1100).

λ SERVICES λ

● Health Clubs (GM): **Han Chin**, steam room, sauna, relax room, massage, 101 Hou Nan 2nd Rd. (216-7073); **Michaelangelo**, popular during weekends or late evenings, good looking guys, 12F 21 Gee Kuan St. (216-9052).

ACCOMMODATIONS

GRAND HOTEL
Cheng Ching Lake, Kaohsiung. Tel: (7) 383-5911. TYPE: *Hotel.* CLIENTELE: All Welcome. LOCATION: Lakefront, 4 mi. / 6 km from the city. 108 rooms w/priv. bath, CTV, phone, A/C, refrigerator, restaurants, coffee shop, bar, outdoor pool, gym, sauna, tennis. RATES: (US) $110-$140. DESCRIPTION: World famous hotel resembling Imperial Palace.

KINGDOM HOTEL
42 Wu-Fu 4th Rd., Kaohsiung. Tel: (7) 241-0121. TYPE: *Hotel.* CLIENTELE: All Welcome. LOCATION: Downtown hotel in shopping and business area near Love River. 290 rooms w/priv. bath, 9 suites, CTV, restaurants, coffee shop, piano bar, nightclub, outdoor pool, free parking. Rates: (US)$150-$180. DESCRIPTION: First class hotel in city center. Some gay cruising nearby at Love River shopping Mall.

TAICHUNG   ✆ 04

✈ Shuey-Nan Airport 4 km / 3 mi.

LOCATION: Central Taiwan.

POPULATION: 650,000

DESCRIPTION: The island's third largest city, Taichung was founded in the 17th century and it is now Central Taiwan's economic, cultural and communications center. Taichung's attractions include international harbor, classical Chinese-style parks, temples and museums. Visit the **Taiwan Museum of Art** with 24 galleries, the **Encore Garden**, for a daily riot of colors and blossoms, 10 km / 6 mi. northeast. For special souvenirs and artcrafts visit **Sanyi** a small village with the best wood carvers in Asia, 40 km / 25 mi. north of Taichung. Public cruising (AYOR) **Main Railway Station** and **Taichung Park**.

BARS Y RESTAURANTS ¶¶

● Bars/clubs (GM): **Ai Chiao**, 216 Chen Kung Rd. (221-1975); **Eternal Love**, 8F-3 12, Tzi Yu Rd., Sec. 2 (223-2348); **Hollywood**, 141, Chung San Rd. (220-2126).

λ SERVICES λ

● Health Clubs (GM): **Hawaii**, 364 San Ming Rd. (237-2447); **King Siaw**, 2F, 71 Ming Chuan Rd. (227-6707).

ACCOMMODATIONS

PARK HOTEL
17 Kung Yuan Rd., Taichung. Tel: (4) 220-5181. TYPE: *Hotel*. CLIENTELE: All Welcome. LOCATION: Commercial center overlooking Taichung Park. 127 rooms w/priv. bath, 11 suites, CTV, phone, refrigerator, restaurant, coffee shop, bar, nightclub. Rates: (US) $80-$110. DESCRIPTION: Moderate first class hotel.

TAICHUNG HOTEL
87 Min Chuan Rd., Taichung. Tel: (4) 224-2121. TYPE: *Hotel*. CLIENTELE: All Welcome. LOCATION: Downtown near train station. 180 rooms w/priv. bath, 15 suites, CTV, phone, airdryer, refrigerator, restaurants, free parking. Rates: (US) $80-$120. DESCRIPTION: Tourist class hotel in a convenient location.

TAIPEI ℭ 02

✈ Chiang Kai Shek Int'l Airport (TPE) 25 mi. / 40 km west

LOCATION: In northern Taiwan.

POPULATION: 2,500,000

CLIMATE: Subtropical hot and humid. January average temperature is 60°F (16°c): July average is 80°F (27°c).

DESCRIPTION: Taipei, a rapidly growing city has all the problems of Third World urban development. New buildings and construction are everywhere. Air pollution is one of the city's biggest, more urgent problems. Taipei is still very Chinese at heart. Throughout the city there are timeless scenes from the world's oldest civilization. Visit the **Lungshan Temple**, the city's oldest and most famous, 211 Kuangchou St. near the famous Huahsi St. Night Market; **Chiang Kai-Shek Memorial Hall**, the island's most impressive monument to the country's great hero; the **National Theatre** at the Chiang Kai-Shek memorial offers one of the best and most spectacular Chinese Operas in the world. The gay scene is friendlier and more easy going than in Hong Kong. The central gay meeting point is the **Taipei New Garden**; casual gay encounters are always readily available.

BARS Y RESTAURANTS ¶¶

● Bars/clubs (GM): **Art**, 2F 147 Lin Sen North Rd. (571-3540); **Buffalo Town**, 289 Linsen North Rd., 12th fl. (564-1172); **Funky**, karaoke bar, B1, No. 10, Sec. 1, Han Chou Rd., S (394-2162); **Jupiter**, 154 Po Ai Rd. (311-8585); **Kiss**, dance club, c/o Mandarin Hotel, 3rd fl.; **President**, karaoke bar, 9 Teh Hwei St. (595-1251); **Tchaikovsky**, 35 Lane 30, Chin Chou St., across from Hotel 666, (542-0270); **Traffic Fish**, mature clientele, 5 Chun Shan N. Rd., Sec. 2, Lane 6 (562-7123).

● Restaurants (AW): **Cupid**, restaurant & pub, New Garden Park (Xin Gong Yuan) (311-8585); or check the coffee shop, **Hilton Taipei Hotel**, 38 Chung Hsiao West Road, 2nd fl. (311-5141).

λ SERVICES λ

● Health Clubs (GM): **Hans Men's Sauna**, busy on weekends and late evenings, relax cabins, massage, 2F, 195 Chung-Shioo West Rd. Section 1 (381-1859); **Hilton Hotel Sauna**, mixed gay/straight, good massage; **Nong Lai**, steam room, sauna, massage, good loking men, 5F, 155 Shin-Ning South Rd. (381-0891); **Royal Palace**, 20 Hsi Ning South Rd. (381-5900).

ACCOMMODATIONS

HILTON TAIPEI
38 Chung Hsiao W. Rd., Section 1. Taipei. Tel: (2) 311-5151. Fax: (2) 331-9944. TYPE: *Hotel*. CLIENTELE: Mostly Straight. LOCATION: Opposite train station, 1 mi. / 2 km from downtown, 20 mi. /32 km from airport. 415 rooms. A/C, color TV, Telephone. 24 hour room service. restaurants, lounge, health club, roof garden w/jacuzzis. Rates: T$4,000 - T$5,900. DESCRIPTION: Deluxe hotel with excellent amenities. The hotel's lobby and coffee shop can be cruisy. The sauna is popular with local and foreign gays.

TANZANIA

AREA: 363,708 sq. mi. (942,003 sq. km)
POPULATION: 24,800,000
CAPITAL: Dar es Salaam
CURRENCY: Tanzanian Shilling (TZS)
OFFICIAL LANGUAGE: Swahili, English
MAJOR RELIGION: Tribal religions, Christianity, Islam
Telephone: 255
Nat'l Holiday: Independence Day, Dec. 9
Official Time: G.M.T. + 3
Electricity: 220/230 volts, 50 cycles
Exchange Rate: 1US$ = TZS 602
National Airline: Air Tanzania

LAW REGARDING HOMOSEXUALITY: Homosexual acts between men are illegal under article 154-157 of the Penal Code. Such acts between two men can be penalized by up to 14 years in jail. The number of known persecutions under this article is minimum, however the attitude of the general population can be described as hostile.

DAR ES SALAAM   © 051

LOCATION: Central eastern Tanzanian coast on the Indian Ocean.

POPULATION: 2,200,000

CLIMATE: The coastal strip along the Indian Ocean have a hot, humid, tropical climate alleviated by sea breezes. The long rainy season is from March to May.

DESCRIPTION: Dar es Salaam "Haven of Peace" is the capital of Tanzania and its largest city. It is mostly low rise city with colonial character and a busy harbor. For exotic flavors explore the **Kariakoo Market** between Mkuguni and Tandamuti streets.

BARS ♈ RESTAURANTS 🍴

● Bars (G/S): **Bahari Beach Hotel bar**, on the beach, 15 mi / 24 km north from city; **Hotel Embassy Bar**, near the main Post Office, mixed bar, friendly crowd; **Mbowe Bar**, at the Hotel Mbowe; **Seaview Bar**, Ocean Road.

● Restaurants (AW): **Sheesh Mahal**, Indian food, India St.; **Imran Restaurant**, Chagga St., Indian cuisine; **Supreme Restaurant**, vegetarian Indian, Nkrumah St.

◊ ACCOMMODATIONS ◊

BAHARI BEACH HOTEL
Daar es Salaam. Tel: (51) 47101. TYPE: *First Class Hotel*. CLIENTELE: Mostly Straight. LOCATION: On the beach north of Daar es Salaam. 100 rooms w/priv. bath, A/C, phone, balcony, restaurants, lounges, bars, outdoor pool, free parking. Rates: (US) $120-$150. DESCRIPTION: Unique hotel in exotic African Village theme.

EMBASSY HOTEL
24 Garden Ave., Daar es Salaam. Tel: (51) 30074. TYPE: *Hotel*. CLIENTELE: Mostly Straight. LOCATION: City Center across from the Main Post Office. 150 rooms w/priv. bath, A/C, suites with living room area, refrigerator, room service, restaurant, bar, pool. Rates: $110 - $160. DESCRIPTION: Five story business hotel in a central location.

ZANZIBAR   © 054

LOCATION: Island off the coast of Tanzania.

DESCRIPTION: Exotic island known as the Spice Island popular holiday destination with the famous " beach boys" that hassle travelers trying to sell anything from dope to who knows what. Popular hang out bar for gays are the **Tarumbeta Club** disco next to the Stone Town Inn, and the bar at the Zanzibar Hotel.

◊ ACCOMMODATIONS ◊

STONE TOWN INN
Shangani St., Tel: (54) 33658. TYPE: *Hotel*. CLIENTELE: All Welcome. LOCATION: Near the beach. single/doubles with communal bath, and self contained rooms. DESCRIPTION: Mid range hotel with Zanzibari character.

THAILAND

AREA: 198,455 sq. mi. (513,998 sq. km)
POPULATION: 46,455,000
CAPITAL: Bangkok
CURRENCY: Baht
OFFICIAL LANGUAGES: Thai, Lao, Chinese
MAJOR RELIGIONS: Buddhism
Telephone: 66
Nat'l Holiday: Nat'l Day, Aug. 12
Official Time: G.M.T. + 7
Electricity: 220 volts
Exchange Rate: 1US$ = Baht 25.55
National Airline: Thai Airways Int'l

LAW REGARDING HOMOSEXUALITY: There are no laws that make reference to homosexuality in the Code of Law. Homosexual acts between men seem to be accepted. Thais are open about sexual matters, they are subtle and pleasure seeking people. There is little physical violence against lesbians in Thailand. However, most lesbians are pressured to get married. There are references in Thai history to Lesbians in particular in the royal court.

❖ SPECIAL EVENT: The year 1996 is a Golden Jubilee Year with special events and festivities to celebrate the 50th anniversary of the current king's coronation.

BANGKOK   ℭ   2

✈ Bangkok Int'l Airport (BKK)
18 mi. / 29 km northeast

LOCATION: A port city on the Gulf of Thailand.

POPULATION: Metro 2,500,000;
            City 1,870,000

CLIMATE: There are three well defined seasons: the Hot Season (March-April), the Rainy Season (May-October), and the Cool Season (November-February). Average temperatures are about 83°F (28°c), ranging in Bangkok from 96°F (34°c) in April to 62°F (14°c) in December.

VISITOR INFORMATION
Tourism Authority of Thailand
Five World Trade Center, Suite 2449
New York NY 10048
Tel: (212) 432-0433.

Lesbian Visitor Information
Anjaree
P.O. Box 322, Rajdamnoen BKK 10200
Lesbian feminist group in Bangkok

DESCRIPTION: Bangkok, Krung Thep in Tahi, is the orient in its mystical sense. It can be sweaty, noisy and confusing, but if you give it a chance, it will reveal its hidden beauty. The city sits on an endless web of klongs (water canals) that serve communications, transportation and commerce. Bangkok is a blend of rich pagodas, modern hotels and poor dwellings of the less privileged, but it is always wrapped in exotic veils of colors and smells.

This is a heaven for bargain hunters and compulsive shoppers. You will find a profusion of stunning merchandise: silks, leather, sparkling sapphires, exotic art and craft. Many goods can be imported to the U.S. duty free.

Bangkok offers exciting places to visit: the fabulous Emerald Buddha Temple, and the Grand Palace Complex; the Pasteur Institute's Snake Farm - where poisonous snakes are fed and 'milked' daily, the world's largest Crocodile Farm, and the 200-acre open-air museum called the Ancient City. Take a pleasant excursion on the klongs to the the famous 'Edleweiss' Restaurant for a superb lunch or early dinner and get ready to enjoy the legendary nightlife. After dark the city becomes more relaxed, then you will discover the sensuous, tolerant if a little seedy nature of the commercial sex industry.

❖ We recommend for safer sex reason to carry a supply of good quality condoms (American made or others), because they may not be available in the clubs.

BARS ♉ RESTAURANTS 🍴

There are many gay oriented bars and cabarets in Bangkok. Most of the gay bars at the Silom-Suriwongse Area, Patpong District, are within walking distance from the hotels mentioned in this guide. Other areas require a taxi ride.

● Bars/clubs (GM): **Barbeiry**, cruise dance bar, live nude male shows, 35 / 3-4-5 Suriwongse Road (235-1078); **Divine**, dance club, 98-104 Silom Road, Soi 4, above Sphinx (234-7249); **Harrie's**, late night disco with cabaret shows, 8-10 Silom Rd. (235-8079); **Lionceau**, cocktail lounge, live shows, 128/14-16 Soi Silom 6 (234-8997); **My Way**, small, intimate bar with male dancers, 944/4 Rama IV Road, opposite Chulalongkorn Hospital (233-9567); **Sphinx**, popular disco, cabaret, and karaoke bar, 98-104 Silom Road Soi (234-7249); **Super Lex**, one of the best and friendliest bars in Bangkok, live sex shows on weekends, 39/19 Soi Anumarnrachathon & Tantawan, off Suriwongse Road (211-6946); **Tawan**, go-go boys, 135/25 Suriwongse Road (234-5506); **Telephone Bar**, popular cruise bar, across from the Rome Club, 114/11 Soi 4 (Jaruwan) Silom Rd. (234-5506); **Twilight**, 38-40 Suriwongse Rd., Opposite Suriwongse Hotel (237-0837).

● Restaurants (AW): **Bobby's Arms**, Patpong II Rd., Carpark Bldg. 2F (233-6828); **Sea-Food Restaurant**, 388 Sukhumvit Rd. (258-0218); **Sky High Restaurant**, 16 Rajdamnoen Ave. (224-1947); **Thai Room**, 30/37 Patpong 2 Rd. (233-7920).

λ SERVICES λ

● Health Clubs (GM): **Colony**, elegant sauna, 117 soi Charonsuk, Sukhumvit soi 55 (391-4393); **The Obelisks**, large sauna/entertainment complex, 39/3 Sukhumvit 53 Rd. (662-4377); **Volt**, 235/18 soi CS Apartment (258-3832).

 ACCOMMODATIONS

AMBASSADOR HOTEL
171 Sukhumvit Road, BKK 10110. Tel: (2) 254-0444.TYPE: *Hotel*. CLIENTELE: Mostly Straight. LOCATION: Near business, entertainment districts, and the gay scene. 976 rooms w/priv. bath, CTV, phone, A/C, restaurant, disco. Rates: Bt 2,800 - Bt 3,000.

BEL-AIR PRINCESS
16 Sukumwit Rd., Sukhumwit Soi 5, BKK 10110. Tel: (2) 253-4300. USA/Canada reservation/information Odysseus Tel: (516) 944-5330 or (800) 257-5344. Fax: (516) 944-7540 or (800) 982-6571. TYPE: *Hotel*. CLIENTELE: All Welcome. LOCATION: On a quiet street off main shopping center, near the gay scene. 160 rooms w/priv. bath. Suites: 15, CTV, A/C, phone, hair dryer, minibar, refrigerator, coffee shop, restaurant, pool & bar, fitness center, free parking. DESCRIPTION: Attractive superior first class Californian-style hotel. All rooms are comfortable and tastefully decorated.

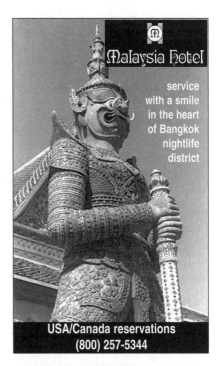

✪ MALAYSIA HOTEL
54 Soi Ngamduplee, Rama IV Rd.. USA/Canada reservations Tel: (516) 944-5330 or (800) 257-5344. Fax: (516) 944-7540. TYPE: *Hotel*. CLIENTELE: All Welcome. LOCATION: Downtown near Lumpini Park, Silom Rd. and Patpong Rd., in the heart of the gay scene.

* Rooms: 120 rooms w/priv. bath, 5 suites
* CTV, phone, A/C, refrigerator
* Restaurants (2), pool, giant screen TV
* 24 hrs room service
* Gay Bars: walking distance
* Health Club: walking distance
* Airport: 30 km / 19 mi., taxi, bus
* Open: Year round
* Rates: (US) $60 - $80, suites rates higher
* *TAC:* 10%

DESCRIPTION: Charming economic class hotel. Accommodations vary from small standard rooms to spacious and tastefully furnished deluxe rooms. No problem to bring friends to your room.

TAWANA RAMADA
80 Surawongse Rd., Bangkok 10500. Tel: (2) 236-0361. TYPE: *Hotel*. CLIENTELE: Mostly Straight. LOCATION: Downtown location in

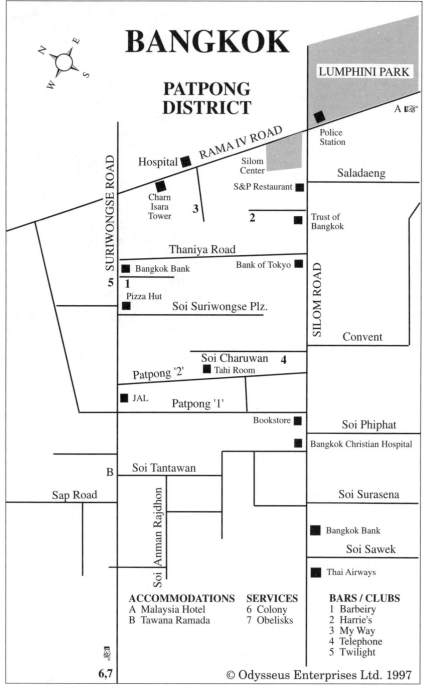

BANGKOK

PATPONG DISTRICT

LUMPHINI PARK

RAMA IV ROAD

SURIWONGSE ROAD

Hospital

Silom Center

Police Station

A ☞

Saladaeng

Charn Isara Tower

3

S&P Restaurant

2

Trust of Bangkok

Thaniya Road

Bangkok Bank

Bank of Tokyo

5   **1**

Pizza Hut

SILOM ROAD

Soi Suriwongse Plz.

Convent

Soi Charuwan   **4**

Tahi Room

Patpong '2'

JAL

Patpong '1'

Bookstore

Soi Phiphat

Bangkok Christian Hospital

B   Soi Tantawan

Sap Road

Soi Anman Rajdhon

Soi Surasena

Bangkok Bank

Soi Sawek

Thai Airways

ACCOMMODATIONS	SERVICES	BARS / CLUBS
A Malaysia Hotel	6 Colony	1 Barbeiry
B Tawana Ramada	7 Obelisks	2 Harrie's
		3 My Way
		4 Telephone
6,7		5 Twilight

© Odysseus Enterprises Ltd. 1997

ODYSSEUS '97/98

the heart of the business, shopping and nightlife district. 265 rooms w/priv. bath, 11 suites, CTV, phone, restaurant, disco. Rates: Bt 3,500 - Bt 4,800. *TAC:* 10%. DESCRIPTION: Modern first class hotel right on the foot steps of the Patpong District's gay scene.

CHIANG MAI   ✆   053

✈ Chiang Int'l Airport (CNX)

LOCATION: 700 km / 438 mi. north of Bangkok, the valley of Chiang Mai introduces you to the charm and culture of the North.

POPULATION: 150,000

CLIMATE: see Bangkok

DESCRIPTION: Chiang Mai is one of the oldest cities, and the second largest in Thailand, dating back to the 13th century when it was the capital of the Lannathai Kingdom. The temples of that era and the charm of the local population remain its greatest tourist assets. Day trips from Chiang Mai takes you to temple caves, waterfalls, elephant work camps and historic villages of great beauty.

BARS ᵞ RESTAURANTS 🍴

● Bars/clubs (GM): **Butterfly Room**, go-go male dancers, 126 Loi Khroh Rd., (279-315); **Coffee Boy**, nightly "Go-Go" boy show and a spectacular cabaret, 8pm-2am, 248 Toong Hotel Rd. (2444-5850); **Danny's Bar**, 161/90 Chotana Rd., Soi 4, Sri-bhum Changpuek (225174); (**New Lanterns**, 25/1 Rajchiangsaen Road, Soi 2 (271-022).

● Restaurant: **Lotus**, Thai & International cuisine, Café/pub with live music and shows on week-ends, the Lotus Hotel.

 ACCOMMODATIONS

○ COFFEE BOY COTTAGE

248 Toong Hotel Rd., Chiangmai 50000. Tel: (53) 247-021. USA/Canada Reservation/information: Tel (516) 944-5330 or (800) 257-5344. Fax: (516) 944-7540. HOST: Narong. TYPE: *Guest House*. CLIENTELE: Gay men only. LOCATION: 1 km / 800 yards from center of Old Town near bus and RR stations.

THE COFFEE BOY COTTAGES

CHIANG MAI THAILAND

* Rooms: 13 w/priv. bath / 4 sgl / 9 double
* Wheelchair accessibility, parking
* Smoking allowed in rooms
* CTV, phone, A/C
* Safety deposit, garden
* Bar: **Coffee Boy Bar**
* Recreation: local and regional tours
* Gay Bars: many nearby
* Airport: 4 km / 2.5 mi. (free pick up)
* Train Station: 1/2 km / 800 yards
* Languages: English, Thai
* Reservations: deposit required
* Credit Cards: MC/VISA
* Season: Year round
* Rates: (US)$80-$120 w/AB
* *TAC:* 10%

DESCRIPTION: Thailand's leading gay bar and guest house. Resort hotel in Northern Thailand architectural flavor and design offering luxury accommodations in 9 cottages and a 3-bedroom house. Each cottage has air-condition, king-sized beds, fully equipped bath with hot water, 8 cottages have their own living room. Nightly "Go-Go" boy show at the Coffee Boy Bar & Cabaret 8pm-2am daily.

LOTUS HOTEL
2/25 Viangbua Rd., Tambol Chang-phuak,

Amphur Muang, Chiang Mai, Thailand 50.500. Tel: (53) 215-376 or 215-462. Fax: (53) 221-340. TYPE: *Hotel*. HOST: Mr. Chaiwat Denprapat. CLIENTELE: Mostly Gay. LOCATION: Downtown 10 min. from Night Bazaar. 11 rooms w/priv. or shared bath, phone, CTV, minibar, A/C, restaurant, bar. DESCRIPTION: Units vary from the economic to the luxurious.

NONG KHAI   ℭ   042

✈ Udon Thani Airport

LOCATION: Northeastern Nong Khai province, directly on the Mekong River. Thabo is a bustling town about 25 km / 16 mi. from the provincial capital Nong Khai.

POPULATION: Nong Khai - 25,000; Thabo - 16,000

CLIMATE: Three distinctive seasons - hot (March - June), rainy (July - October), and cool and dry (November - February). The north of Thailand is not as humid as the rest of the country, and the temperatures can drop to 13°c (55°F) and even lower at night during the cool season.

DESCRIPTION: Nong Khai Town is located 620 km / 388 mi. from Bangkok and 55 km / 35 mi. from Udon Thani Town. It is located at the end of Route 2 the Friendship Highway at the Makong River. Across the river is Laos. The region is rich in historical and archeological sites with distinguished Laos and Khmer influence. Nearby Thabo is an agricultural center and the "Gateway" to Loei.

🍴 RESTAURANT 🍴

● Restaurant: **Black & White**, modern fashion corner restaurant at the Isan Orchid guest lodge (042) 431-665. (see description below).

🗝 ACCOMMODATIONS 🗝

ISAN ORCHID
87/9 Growarawud Road, Thabo, Nong Khai 43110. Tel: (042) 431-665. TYPE: *Bed & Breakfast*. HOST: Saiyon or Don. CLIENTELE: Gay/Straight. LOCATION: In Thabo near Nong Khai. 6 rooms w/shared or priv. bath, CTV lounge, phone, cooking facilities. Rates: Bt 500 - Bt 850 w/breakfast. DESCRIPTION: Large Thai style private home.

PATTAYA   ℭ   038

✈ Don Muang Int'l Airport

LOCATION: 130 km / 82 mi. southeast of Bangkok on the Gulf of Thailand.

POPULATION: Small resort

CLIMATE: See Bangkok

DESCRIPTION: Thailand's most popular seaside resort is about 2 1/2 hrs. drive from Bangkok. It is world famous as Thailand's premier sex, sand & sin destination. You can get there by flight or aboard air conditioned coach. The resort offers complete facilities from golf courses to cruises aboard charter boats. But it is mostly famous for its exceptional scuba diving centers.

BARS 🍸 RESTAURANTS 🍴

● Bars/clubs (GM): **Adam & Eve**, Cocktail Lounge & Massage, nude shows, Pattaya Inn, 380 Beach Road, Pattaya Soi 2, North Pattaya, Chonburi (418-400, or 418-718/9; **The Body Guard**, show bar, 325/77 Pattayaland soi 2; **Gentleman Club**, 325/27 Pattayaland soi1, Pattaya City (429867); **Boys, Boys, Boys**, disco, nightclub, 325/91 Pattaya Land Soi 3 (424-099); **Le Cafe Royale**, piano bar with outside terrace, 103-5 Pattaya Land Soi 3, (428-303); **Cockpit**, Pattaya's largest dance bar/restaurant, 325/106 Pattaya Land Soi 3, South Pattaya Beach; **15 Club**, go-go dancing, sex shows, 109/33 M. Soi 15, South Pattaya (710-281); **Memory Club**, bar, cabaret, escort, go-go boys, 157/104 Soi 18 M5, North Pattaya (420-147); **Why Not?** 325/24 Pattaya Land Soi 1, South Pattaya.

● Restaurants (GM): **Le Café Royale**, International & Thai cuisine, 102-5 Pattayaland Soi 3 (428-303); **Dolf Riks**, Dutch, Indonesian and Thai Cuisine, Sri Nakorn Centre (418-269); **Nang Nual**, cruisy, 214-10 South Pattaya Beach (418-478); **Papa's**, Swiss/Int'l, 219/66-67 Soi Samanmit (426-374).

❖ Gay Beach: **Jomtieh Beach**, transportation required, near 'Cobra' wind surfing.

🗝 ACCOMMODATIONS 🗝

Note: The gay scene is concentrated in South Pattaya. We recommend choosing a hotel in South Pattaya.

AMBIANCE INN
325/89 Pattayaland Soi 3, Pattaya Chonburi, 20260. Tel: (38) 424-099. Fax: (38) 424-824. TYPE: *Hotel*. HOST: Jim Lumsden. CLIENTELE: Gay men only. LOCATION: South Pattaya off Pattaya Beach Rd. and Pattayaland 2. 18 rooms, 3 suites, CTV, phone, bar, disco, sundeck. DESCRIPTION: Thai style inn.

LE CAFÉ ROYALE
102-5, Pattayaland Soi 3, South Pattaya, Cholburi 20260. Tel: (38) 428-303, 423-515. Fax: (38) 424-579. TYPE: *Hotel*. HOST: Robert & Ian. CLIENTELE: Mostly Gay. LOCATION: In South Pattaya near gay beach. 20 rooms w/priv. bath, 2 suites, CTV, phone, A/C, restaurant, bar. DESCRIPTION: Hotel/entertainment complex.

ROYAL CLIFF BEACH HOTEL
Pattaya Beach Resort. Tel: (38) 418-511. TYPE: *Luxury Hotel*. CLIENTELE: Mostly Straight. LOCATION: On the beach. 724 rooms w/priv. bath, balcony, ocean view, CTV, phone, A/C, bar, coffee shop. Rates: Bt 2,400 - Bt 22,000. *TAC:* 10%. DESCRIPTION: Luxury resort for business travelers.

PHUKET   © 076

USA/Canada reservation
(800) 257-5344

✈ Phuket Int'l Airport (HKT)

LOCATION: Provincial island in the Andaman Sea, 890 km / 556 mi. south of Bangkok.

POPULATION: 35,000

CLIMATE: Tropical. Hot summers from March to June with temperatures in the mid 80°sF (30°c); rainy season lasts from July through October. November through February is the cool season with temperatures in the high 70"s (25°c).

DESCRIPTION: Phuket is an exotic beach resort destination with appeal to mainstream straight tourism. Coconut trees, sugar palms and long sandy beaches are the draws.

BARS ⅄ RESTAURANTS ⊺⊺

● Bars/clubs (GM): **Black & White**, dance bar, 70/123 Paradise Complex, Rat-Uthit Rd. (430-758); **My Way II**, go-go dancers, 70/157 Paradise Complex, Tat-Uthit Rd. (342-163); **Pow-Wow Pub**, Arizona style decor, see Home Sweet Home; **Pup Pup Pub**, dance bar, strip boys, 70/12 Paradise Complex; **Tangmo**, popular cabaret, dance club, male dancers, 70/50-55 Paradise Complex near the Royal Paradise Hotel (3409-42/3); **Uncle Charly's**, 77/64 Aaronson Plaza, Rat-Uthit Rd. (opp. Patong Bay Shore Hotel).

● Restaurants (GM): **Hot Gossip**, 70/16 Royal Paradise Complex; **Ka Jok Sea**, 26 Takuapa Rd., Muang; **Kamyan**, 1 Thoong-Kha Road, Phuket City (214-201); **Pow-Wow**, Thai and Western cuisine, see Home Sweet Home; **Rendez-Vous**, 70/179-80 Paradise Complex, Raj-Uthit Rd., Patong (214-201).

🖼 ACCOMMODATIONS 🖼

HOME SWEET HOME
70/179-180 Paradise Complex, Rat-Uthid Rd., Patong Beach, Phuket. Tel: (76) 340756. USA/Canada reservations: (516) 944-5330 or (800) 257-5344. Fax: (516) 944-7540. TYPE: *Guest House*. CLIENTELE: Gay men. LOCATION: In the heart of Patong Beach.

* Rooms: 8 dbl w/priv. bath
* Smoking allowed in rooms
* CTV, phone, minibar, safety deposit
  A/C, soundproof rooms
* Bar & restaurant: **Pow-Wow Pub**
* Maid & room service, Parking, sundecks

THE ROYAL PARADISE HOTEL
Paradise Complex - Pattaya

**USA/Canada reservations
(800) 257-5344**

* Beach: 300 m / 900 ft.
* Gay Bars: 200 m / 600 ft.
* Airport: 40 km / 25 mi
* Season: Year round
* Rates: US$70 - $90
* *TAC:* 10% (from Odysseus)

DESCRIPTION: Low rise 3 story beachfront Oasis. Each room is individually furnished and decorated in eclectic Thai and Western style. The accommodation suite style consists of a separate bedroom, large sitting area, and spacious bathroom. Airport transfers and English speaking guides are available at extra charge.

PATONG BEACH HOTEL
P.O. Box 25. Phuket 83121. Tel: (076) 321-301/2). TYPE: *Hotel*. CLIENTELE: Gay/Straight. LOCATION: Opposite beautiful Phuket Beach on the west coast of the island. 122 rooms w/priv. bath, bungalows, restaurant, pool, bars, disco. Rates: Bt 1,210 - Bt 1,700. *TAC:* 10%. DESCRIPTION: Lodge-like hotel.

PHUKET MARLIN HOTEL
158/1 Yawari Rd., Phuket 83000. Tel: (76) 12866/70. Fax: (76) 216-429. TYPE: *Hotel*. CLIENTELE: Mostly Straight. LOCATION: 1 km from downtown with easy access to Phuket beaches. 180 rooms w/priv. bath, 5 suites, CTV, phone, A/C, restaurant, disco. Rates: Bt 850 - Bt 1,250. *TAC:* 10%. DESCRIPTION: Modern hotel near downtown.

○ ROYAL PARADISE HOTEL
Paradise Complex, Patong Beach Phuket. USA/Canada reservations: (800) 257-5344 or (516) 944-5330. Fax: (516) 944-7540. Email: odyusa@odyusa.com. TYPE: *Hotel*. CLIENTELE: All Welcome. LOCATION: On Patong Beach near exciting gay nightlife.

* Rooms: 250 deluxe w/priv. bath
* CTV, phone, balcony
* Restaurants, coffee shop, poolside bar
* Games room, disco, Sky lounge
* Pool, health club, massage center
* Beach: on the beach
* Gay Bars: walking distance
* Airport: 40 km / 25 mi
* Season: Year round
* Rates: US$220 - $360
* *TAC:* 10% (from Odysseus)

DESCRIPTION: Elegant tower style hotel with first class amenities. Each deluxe room offers 2 queen sized beds. Most with private balcony and a stunning view of the tranquil Andaman Sea.

TRINIDAD & TOBAGO

AREA: 1,980 sq. mi. (5,128 sq. km)
POPULATION: 1,212,000
CAPITAL: Port of Spain
CURRENCY: Trinidad Dollar (TTD)
OFFICIAL LANGUAGE: English, Hindi
MAJOR RELIGION: Christianity, Hinduism, Islam
Telephone: 809
Nat'l Holiday: Independence Day, Aug. 31
Official Time: G.M.T. -4
Electricity: 110/220 volts, 50 cycles
Exchange Rate: 1US$ = TTD 6.14
National Airline: BWIA

LAW REGARDING HOMOSEXUALITY: Homosexual acts between men or women are illegal under section 13 of the Penal Code. "Buggery" defined as anal intercourse can be punished with life in prison, if committed on a minor, and 10 years if committed on adult, 18 years or older. According to article 8 par. 18/1 of the Immigration Act, homosexual men and women are not allowed to enter the country. Homosexuals risk police harassment and violence.

TRINIDAD / TOBAGO

LOCATION: Southernmost of the Caribbean islands just off the northeastern coast of Venezuela.

POPULATION: 70,000 (Port of Spain)

CLIMATE: Tropical climate year round, with constant trade winds and temperatures ranging from 75°F-85°F (24°c-30°c). The rainy season runs from May to November.

DESCRIPTION: Trinidad is very different from any other island in the Caribbean. Visi-

tors are attracted to the swinging rythem and sounds of the islands calypso, limbo, and steel-drum bands. Port of Spain is the islands capital, a busy port and major commercial center. The island has a cosmopolitan population made of Syrians, Chinese, Americans, Europeans and West Indians. Tobago is sleepier, less crowded, but offers stunningly beautiful landscape, with a generous dose of lovely beaches for sun and fun.

❖ Beaches: Trinidad beaches are undeveloped. The closest better beach **Maracas** is 18 mi. / 29 km from Port of Spain. Tobago has better beaches such as **Back Bay**, 8 min. walk from Mount Irvine Bay Hotel; **Man-O-War Bay**, natural harbor with long sandy beach; **Pigeon Point**, the island's most popular bathing area.

BARS ♟ RESTAURANTS ⑪

● Bars/Clubs (GM): **The Attic**, Maraval Shopping Center, Maraval; **Cocoa House**, popular with gays, 46 Ariapita Ave., Port of Spain (628-3176); **Gayelle**, Cipriani Blvd., Trinidad; **The Pelican Club**, the oldest gay hangout in town, 204 Colbentz Ave, Port of Spain (next to the Hilton); **Pier One**, mixed seaside bar, Chaguanas; **Smoky & Bunty**, popular mixed bar, open late, Western Main Rd., St. James;

● Restaurants (AW): **Michael's**, excellent Italian cuisine, 143 Long Circular Road, Port of Spain Trinidad (628-0445); **Rouselles**, West Indian/International, Bacolet St., Scarborough, Tobago (639-4738).

 ACCOMMODATIONS

TRINIDAD HILTON
Port of Spain. Tel: 624-3211. TYPE: *Hotel Complex.* CLIENTELE: All Welcome. LOCATION: 1 mi / 1.6 km from downtown. 394 rooms w/priv. bath, CTV, phone, A/C, balcony, minibar, restaurants, bars, pools, tennis. Rates: (US) $150-$230. DESCRIPTION: Elegant resort complex and conference center. Walk to gay bar.

REX TURTLE BEACH
Great Cortland Bay. Tel: 639-2851. TYPE: *Resort Hotel.* CLIENTELE: All Welcome. LOCATION: Beachfront tropical garden setting, 5 mi / 8 km from Scarborough. 125 rooms w/priv. bath, phone, radio, A/C, balcony, restaurants, bars, private beach, parking, scuba diving. Rates: (US) $90-$210. DESCRIPTION: First class informal resort hotel with fine amenities and service.

TUNISIA

AREA: 63,170 sq. mi. (163,610 sq. km)
POPULATION: 8,300,000
CAPITAL: Tunis
CURRENCY: Tunisian Dinar (TND)
OFFICIAL LANGUAGE: Arabic, French
MAJOR RELIGION: Islam
Telephone: 216
Nat'l Holiday: Independence Day, March 20
Official Time: G.M.T. + 1 or 2
Electricity: 110/220 volts, 50 cycles
Exchange Rate: 1US$ = TND 0.99
National Airline: Tunis Air

LAW REGARDING HOMOSEXUALITY: Homosexual acts between men or women are illegal under section 230 of the Penal Code.

SOUSSE ℭ 3

LOCATION: Central coast of Tunisia.

POPULATION: 70,000

CLIMATE: Mediterranean. Hot summers with highs in the 80's (28°c); rainy and windy winters with high in the 40's (10°c).

DESCRIPTION: A large port with interesting medina and kasbah. The city is a popular summer beach resort. Check the beach beyond the Hotel Salaam at the extreme end of the bay.

BARS ♈ RESTAURANTS ╢

● Bar (G/S): **Topkapi**, Ave. Habib Bourgiba.

● Restaurants (AW): **Restaurant de Sportifs**, 25 Ave. du Président Habib Bourgiba (251-18); **Restaurant Sheriff**, 4 rue Ali Belhouane (259-48).

ACCOMMODATIONS

NEJMA APARTMENT HOTEL
Rte. de la Corniche. Tel: (3) 226-811, TYPE: *Apartment Hotel Complex*. CLIENTELE: All Welcome. LOCATION: On the promenade near the beach in the heart of Sousse. 127 apartments w/priv. bath, kitchenette, balcony, restaurant, bars, pool, free parking. Rates on request.

TUNIS ℭ 1

✈ Cartage Airport (TUN) 5 mi. / 8 km NE.

LOCATION: Northern Tunisia, at the western end of the Lake of Tunis.

POPULATION: 550,000

CLIMATE: Mediterranean. Hot, sunny and humid in the summer with temperatures in the mid 80's F (28°c). Winters are cold and rainy with some snowfall, average temperature is about 50°F (11°c).

DESCRIPTION: The capital city is plain, but with easy-going and unhurried atmosphere. The medina with its mosques, bazaars, cafés and hammams are interesting. For gay visitors the Avenue Habib Bourgiba near Café de Paris is where 'things' sometimes happen.

BARS ♈ RESTAURANTS ╢

● Bars/clubs (GM): **Café de Paris**, Avenue Habib Bourgiba corner Avenue de Carthage; **Le Drugstore** at Hotel Africa Meridien, 50 Ave. Habib Bourgiba; **Tunis Club**, Avenue Habib Bourgiba, opposite Café de Paris.

● Restaurant (AW): **Carcassone**, cheap but good food, 8 Ave. de Carthage; **Le Cosmos**, French, 7 Ave. Ibn Khaldoun (241-610); **L'Etoile**, best value in town, 3 rue Ibn Khaldoun.

ACCOMMODATIONS

L'AFRICA MERIDIEN
50 Ave. Habib Bourgiba. Tel: (1) 347-477. TYPE: *Hotel*. CLIENTELE: Mostly Straight. LOCATION: City Center near Medina & Souks. 168 rooms w/priv. bath, CTV, refrigerator, 24 hrs. room service, restaurants, bars, solarium, pool, rooftop club. Rates on request.

TURKEY

AREA: 300,946 sq. mi. (779,450 sq. km)
POPULATION: 46,000,000
CAPITAL: Ankara
CURRENCY: Turkish Lira (T£)
OFFICIAL LANGUAGE: Turkish
MAJOR RELIGION: Islam
Telephone: 90
Nat'l Holiday: Republic Day, October 29
Official Time: G.M.T. + 2
Electricity: 220 volts, 50 cycles
Exchange Rate: 1US$ = T£ 103,952
National Airline: Turkish Airlines

LAW REGARDING HOMOSEXUALITY:
Homosexuality is not mentioned in the code of
law. Homosexuality and bi-sexuality is not
uncommon among Turkish men. However,
most Turks will not wish to be openly known as
gays. Society and police can be hostile towards
flaunting homosexuals.

❖ Turkey is undergoing tremendous changes. It
is a modern democratic country, a moslem country with increasing westernized influence.
Turkey offers the warm hospitality of its people
with an opportunity to explore the country's treasures of natural and historical sites. Since the
1970's most of the tourism to Turkey comes from
Europe and the USA. Regarding homosexuality,
Turkish people are not against homosexuality,
but they do not support it either. It is considered
an offense for two men to kiss in public, or for a
gay man to flaunt his homosexuality. Turkish
men may react in a hostile manner if they are
approached and proposed to practice homosexuality. The Turkish society has a limited place
where homosexuals can play a prominent public
role. Most gay men who are nationally famous
are either classical singers, pop stars or other
entertainers. Because of the high unemployment
(20%) and disregard for homosexuals, many gay
men are forced into prostitution to earn a living.
This reinforces the biased attitude of the Turkish
population regarding homosexuality. Gay visitors

should bear in mind that Turkish people in general don't have prejudice and show same hospitality and kindness to anyone regardless of their
sexual preference. The Turkish attitude may be
ambiguous, but as a gay traveler it is safer to be
discreet and avoid a flaunting behavior.

BODRUM   ✆   **252**

LOCATION: In the southern Aegean on the Gulf
of Gökova across from the Greek island of Kos.

POPULATION: 33,000

CLIMATE: Mediterranean. Hot summers with
highs in the 80°s (28°c); rainy and windy winters with high in the 40°s (10°c). Spring and fall
are most pleasant.

DESCRIPTION: Attractive resort (the ancient
Greek city of Halicarnassos) with white washed
square houses, subtropical gardens, busy port
and marina. Visit: **Castle of St. Peter** built by
the knights of St. John; the famous **bazaar**,
and the **ancient amphitheater**. For possible
cruising join the crowd on the **promenade**
from the bazaar out to the east cove where
everybody checks everybody else.

❖ Beach: **Gümbet**, beach resort 3 km / 2 mi.
west of Bodrum packed with lounges, sun-
bathers and windsurfers.

BARS ⅄ RESTAURANTS ᭟

● Bars/clubs (G/S): **Adamik**, cafe & bar, Eski
Banka Sok. 23; **Halikarnas**, the ultimate disco
for the beautiful people in town, mixed clientele, great music and laser show, Cumhuriyet
Caddesi; **Sensi Bar**, latest sound, seaside
tables, Cumhuriet Cad. 143; **Sunny's Bar**, the
most entertaining bar in Bodrum, Cumhuriyet
Cad. 107.

● Restaurants (AW): The classy restaurants
are in the harbor area close to the water. The
less expensive are in the bazaar area. **Ali
Baba**, seafood, port area; **Amphora**, seafood &
grilled meat, facing the yacht marina, Neyzen
Tevfik Caddesi 164 (2368); **Dolphin**, Turkish
& Int'l, seaside dining, Uslu Pasaji; **Pekin**, traditional Chinese cuisine, Cumhuriyet St., 12
(62851); **Karadeniz**, outdoor terrace, watch
people go by, Kilise Meydani; **Kortan**, seafood,
Comhuriyet Caddesi (1300).

λ SERVICES λ

● Health Club (NG): **Hammam** (Turkish Sauna), Dere Umurca Sokagi, daily 8am-5pm. Wed-Sat afternoon Women only.

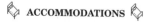 **ACCOMMODATIONS**

HOTEL GÖZEGIR
Cumhuriyet Cad. 157, Bodrum. USA/Canada reservation/information- Odysseus Tel: (516) 944-5330 or (800) 257-5344. Fax: (516) 944-7540 or (800) 982-6571. TYPE: *Hotel.* CLIENTELE: All Welcome. LOCATION: Central location along the promenade.

* Rooms: 50 w/priv. bath
* Phone, central music, hot water
* Terrace pool, restaurant, poolside bar
* Bus Station: 10 min. by car
* Open: Year round
* Rates: on request
* *TAC:* 10% (from Odysseus)

DESCRIPTION: Holiday resort in the heart of Bodrum offering Turkish hospitality, comfortable rooms and professional service.

HOTEL GÖZEN
Cumhuriyet Caddesi, Bodrum. Tel: (252) 316-1227. USA/Canada reservation Tel: (516) 944-5330 or (800) 257-5344. Fax: (516) 944-7540 or (800) 982-6571. TYPE: *Hotel.* CLIENTELE: All Welcome. LOCATION: Centre of town.

* Rooms: 22 w/priv. bath or shower
* CTV, phone, balcony, rooftop terrace
* Beach: 10 min. to Gümbet Beach
* Bus Station: 10 min. by car
* Open: Year round
* Rates: on request. *TAC:* 10% (from Odysseus)

DESCRIPTION: Traditional hotel in a central location. Simply furnished rooms with seaview.

HOTEL MAGNIFIC
Gümbet, Bodrum.USA/Canada reservation Tel: (516) 944-5330 or (800) 257-5344. Fax: (516) 944-7540 or (800) 982-6571. TYPE: *Hotel.* CLIENTELE: All Welcome. LOCATION: Gümbet Beach, 7 min. from Bodrum by mini-van or taxi.

* Rooms & Suites: 67 w/priv. bath
* Restaurant, cafe, atrium garden
* Pool, private beach, TV lounge
* Bus Station: 25 min. by taxi
* Open: April-October
* Rates: on request. *TAC:* 10%

DESCRIPTION: Charming holiday village complex with fine service and amenities on the popular Gümbet beach.

ISTANBUL   ℭ 212

✈ Ataturk Int'l Airport, Yeslikoy (IST)
15 mi. / 24 km southwest

LOCATION: On the Bosphorus at the crossroads between Asia and Europe.

POPULATION: 2,860,000

CLIMATE: Hot, sunny and humid in the summer with temperatures in the mid 80°sF (28°c). Winters are cold and rainy with some snowfall, average temperature is about 40°F (5°c).

VISITOR INFORMATION
Turizm Danisma Bürolari
Mesrutiyet Cad. 57,
57/B Galatasaray, Istanbul
Tel: 154-6393

DESCRIPTION: On the crossroads between Asia and Europe, Istanbul is a fascinating city with a magic mixture of East and West. Constantine the great founded Byzantine in the 4th century as the new capital of the Roman Empire in the East. The city flourished under different cultures until it became the moslem capital of the Ottoman Empire. The best view of the city is from the sea as you approach the harbor when the famous Istanbul skyline spreads before your eyes: the **Blue Mosque** and the **Church of the Holy Wisdom** or **Santa Sophia**, the **Sultan Palace, Dolmabace Sarayi**, **Selamlik Harem** and **Topkapi**. There are many sites to visit in Istanbul, the most famous are the places mentioned above, but do not forget to check the **Grand Bazaar** the largest covered shopping center in the world; after a busy day relax in a Turkish Bath - **The Hamam**. The most famous Hamam is **Cagaloglu Hamami**, a refurbished 16th century building in the Old City with separate facilities for men and women, near Sultanahmet Sq. on Hilaliahmer Caddesi (522-2424) for $30 you can have a sauna experience fit for a pasha.

❖ Beaches: **Florya Plajlari Beach**, at Florya a suburb of Istanbul on the European coast of the Sea of Marmara. Take a bus "F" to the beach from Taksim Square. **Günes Plaji** is the more interesting one.

BARS ♀ RESTAURANTS �|♦

The gay scene is concentrated near or around the famous Taksim Square the main business and shopping area.

● Bars/clubs (GM): **Privé**, cave-like club just off Taksim Square in the new town, Tarlabasi Caddesi 28, Taksim (235-7999); **Pub 14**, pleasant gay club on a tiny side street off Cumhuriyet Caddesi near Privé, Abdülhak Hamit Caddesi 63 (near Taskim), Belediye Dükkanlari 14 (256-2121); **Pub 1001**, gay club off Taksim Square, Siraselviler Cad. 53; (adjacent to the Keban hotel); **Valentino**, Siraselviler Cad.; **Yesil Bizans**, café/bar, Siraselviler cad. 176/5, Taksim (151-8925).

● Disco (GMW): **20-19 The Last Door**, gay friendly dance club, Abdülhak Hamit Cad. No. 75, Talimhane (near Pub 14) (156-2121).

● Restaurants (AW): near Taksim Square **Haci Baba**, popular spot for Turks and tourists, Taksim Istiklal Caddesi 49 (244-1886); **Kazan**, Turkish restaurant, central location, nice atmosphere, self-service buffet, Cumuhuriyet Cad. No. 151/1 (232-7216); **Konyali**, elegant cafeteria overlooking the water, Topkapi Palace grounds, Topkapi Sarayi (513-9697); **McDonald's**, American fast food, Taksim Gezi Dükkanlari 5; **Pandorosa**, Taksim Square, some gays at the back bar; **Sarnic**, Turkish & French cuisine, located in an old Roman cistern, Soguk Cesme Sokagi (512-4291); Orther locations: **Urcan**, seafood restaurant, Orta Cesme Cad. 2/1, Sariyer (242-0367); **Ulus 29**, trendy restaurant with panoramic view of the Bosporus, Akatlar Parki, Ulus (265-6198).

🏛 ACCOMMODATIONS 🏛

AYASOFIA PENSIYONLARI
Soguk Cesme Sokagi, Istanbul. Tel: (212) 513-3669. USA/Canada Tel: (516) 944-5330 or (800) 257-5344. Fax: (516) 944-7540 or (800) 982-6571.TYPE: *Hotel /Apartments complex.* CLIENTELE: All Welcome. LOCATION: Taksim Square area. Converted townhouses behind Agia Sofia. Each house has 5-10 rooms, 19 century furnishings, warming atmosphere of armchairs with tassels, velvet curtains, views of St. Sophia from the windows. Very private, own key. Rates: (US) $110 - $220. *TAC:* 10% (from Odysseus).

HOTEL ARCADIA
Dr. Imran Öktem Cad., No. 1, Sultanahmet, Istanbul. Tel: (212) 516-9696. USA/Canada reservations: Odysseus Tel: (516) 944-5330 or (800) 257-5344. Fax: (516) 944-7540 or (800) 982-6571. TYPE: *First Class Hotel.* CLIENTELE: All Welcome. LOCATION: Main shopping and leisure centre of Istanbul, 500 m. from the Grand Bazaar, near St. Sophia, the Blue Mosque and Topkapi Palace.

* Rooms: 48 w/priv. bath, Suites: 7
* CTV, phone, A/C, C/H, safe deposit, bath phone, hairdryer
* Restaurant: Turkish & International
* Lobby Coffee Bar
* 24 hrs room service
* Gay Bars: walking distance
* Airport: 15 km / 9 mi. (taxi)
* Open: Year round
* Rates: (US) $110 -$140 w/CB
* *TAC:* 10% (from Odysseus)

DESCRIPTION: Elegant 4-star hotel with a traditional local hospitality in a central location. All rooms are elegantly furnished to the highest standards.

HOTEL RICHMOND
Istiklal Cad. 445, Tünel 80670, Istanbul. Tel: (212) 252-5460. USA/Canada reservations: Odysseus Tel: (516) 944-5330 or (800) 257-5344. Fax: (516) 944-7540 or (800) 982-6571. TYPE: *First Class Hotel.* CLIENTELE: Mostly Straight. LOCATION: Main shopping and leisure centre of Istanbul, 2 km / 1 mi. from Taksim Square, 10 min. walk to Old Town.

* Rooms: 101w/priv. bath
* Suites: 2 regular
* Business suite: 6 w/jacuzzi
* CTV, phone, hair dryer, A/C, minibar safe deposit
* Room & maid service, laundry, parking
* Gay Bars: walking distance
* Airport: 19 km / 12 mi (taxi)
* Open: Year round
* Rates: (US) $90-$140
* *TAC:* 10% (from Odysseus)

DESCRIPTION: Elegant 4-star hotel. All rooms and suites are tastefully decorated to the highest standards. Excellent location and service.

RIVA HOTEL
Aydede Caddesi 8, Taksim, Istanbul TR-80090. Tel: (212) 156-4420. USA/Canada reservations: Odysseus Tel: (516) 944-5330 or (800) 257-5344. Fax: (516) 944-7540 or (800) 982-6571. TYPE: *First Class Hotel.* CLIENTELE: Mostly Straight. LOCATION: Taksim Square.

* Rooms: 70 w/priv. bath. Suites: 7
* CTV (CNN), phone, minibar, A/C, C/H
* Restaurant & bar
* Maid & 24 hrs. room service
* Gay Bars: some nearby
* Airport: 25 km / 16 mi., taxi
* Train Station: 5 km / 3 mi.
* Credit Cards: MC/VISA/AMEX
* Season: Year round
* Rates: (US) $90 - $140. *TAC:* 10%

DESCRIPTION: Elegant business oriented hotel in a convenient location.

YESIL EV
Kabasakal Caddesi 5, Sultanahmet - Istanbul. Tel: (212) 517-6786. USA/Canada reservations: Odysseus Tel: (516) 944-5330 or (800) 257-5344. Fax: (516) 944-7540 or (800) 982-6571. TYPE: *Hotel.* CLIENTELE: All Welcome. LOCATION: Taksim Square area.

* Rooms: 19 rooms w/priv. bath
* Pasha Room (#31) w/Turkish Hammam
* Gay Bars: walking distance
* Airport: 19 km / 12 mi. (taxi)
* Open: Year round
* Rates: (US) $120-$160 w/CB
  Pasha Room - $260 w/CB
* *TAC:* 10% (from Odysseus)

DESCRIPTION: World-class renovated 19th century mansion in the historic Beyazit-Sultanahmet district. All rooms are elegantly furnished with brass bedsteads, velvet curtains and period furnishings. The Pasha Room includes authentic Turkish Hammam. Friendly staff.

KUSADASI   ℭ   256

✈ Adnan Menderes AP, Izmir (ADB)

LOCATION: On the Aegean coast, 1.5 hrs. by car south of Izmir.

POPULATION: 36,000

CLIMATE: Hot, sunny and humid in the summer with temperatures in the mid 80°sF (28°c). Winters are cold and rainy, average temperature is about 40°F (5°c).

DESCRIPTION: A seaside vacation resort and port where many Aegean cruise ships touring the Greek Islands stop to visit the ancient city of **Ephesus**. Ephesus, about 17 km / 10 mi. away offers a magnificent selection of ancient architectural gems such as **The Library of Celsus**, the **Magnesian Gate**, the **Gymnasium of Vedius**, the **Thermal Baths of Scholastika** and the **Great Amphitheater**. From Kusadasi one can also visit the ancient cities of Priene, Miletus and Didyma, and even inland to Aphrodisias. If you have time include **Pamukkale**, one of Turkey's most enchanting sites, mineral hot pools in a cotton-white plateau some 400 ft. high. Pamukkale is about 50 km / 32 mi. east of Kusadasi.

❖ **HOW TO GET THERE**: Kusadasi is a port of call for many cruise ships in the Mediterranean. You may take a short 3 day cruise from Athens to Kusadasi and back, or fly to the Greek Island of Samos from Athens and catch a boat from there to Kusadasi (about 2-1/2 hours). If you take a boat or hydrofoil (flying dolphin) from Samos, you need to leave your passport with the travel agency that arranges your boat ticket. You will receive your passport upon embarkation near the Customs House at the port.

🍴 RESTAURANT 🍴

● Restaurants (AW): **Club Caravanserail**, elegant Ottoman style restaurant for lunch or dinner at the Club Méditeranée, Atatürk Bulvari at Barbaros Caddesi (14-115); **Özurfa**, Turkish, Cephane Sok. 7 (614-6070); **Sultan Han**, old house built around a courtyard and gigantic tree, excellent seafood specialties, Bahar Sokak 8 (13-849); Also check the seafood restaurants on the waterfront **Toros Canli Balik** (11-144), **Kazim Usta'nin Yeri** (11-226) or **Diba** (11-063).

λ SERVICES λ

● Turkish Bath (G/S): **Hammam**, corner of Tuna Sok. & Yedieylul Sok behind the Mosque, 8am-10pm daily.

 ACCOMMODATIONS

BAHAR PANSIYON
Cephane Sokak 12, Kusadasi. USA/Canada Tel: (516) 944-5330 or (800) 257-5344. Fax: (516) 944-7540 or (800) 982-6571. TYPE: *Hotel.* CLIENTELE: All Welcome. LOCATION: Centre of town near the Bazaar and the promenade.

* Rooms: 30 w/priv. bath or shower
* Phone, roof terrace & restaurant
* Beach: walking distance
* Port: 10 min. walk
* Open: year round
* Rates: (US) $45 - $70 w/TB
* *TAC:* 10% (from Odysseus)

DESCRIPTION: Colorful & traditional Turkish hotel. Friendly atmosphere and pleasant rooms.

CLUB CARAVANSÉRAIL
Okuz Mehmet Pasa Kervansarayi, Tel: (636) 14115. USA/Canada Tel: (516) 944-5330 or (800) 257-5344. Fax: (516) 944-7540 or (800) 982-6571. TYPE: *Hotel.* CLIENTELE: Mostly Straight. LOCATION: In the center of town near the Bazaar and the port at the seaside end of Barbaros Hayrettin Caddesi.

* Rooms: 40 w/priv. bath
* Phone, courtyard
* Restaurant, nightclub, bar
* Airport: 70 km / 43 mi. / Izmir
* Port: 5 min. walk
* Open: Year round
* Rates: on request

DESCRIPTION: 300 year old atmospheric castle-like Ottoman style hotel, refurbished and elegant. Best accommodations choice in Kusadasi.

HOTEL EFE
Güvercinada Caddesi, Kusadasi. USA/Canada reservations/information Odysseus Tel: (516) 944-5330 or (800) 257-5344. Fax: (516) 944-7540 or (800) 982-6571. TYPE: *Hotel.* CLIENTELE: All Welcome. LOCATION: Centre of town near the Bazaar and the promenade.

* Rooms: 44 w/priv. bath or shower
* Phone, hot water, C/H, elevator
* Restaurant, Pub, American Bar, Cafe
* Room & maid service, parking
* Beach: walking distance
* Port: 10 min. walk
* Open: Year round
* Rates: on request. *TAC:* 10%

DESCRIPTION: Good quality hotel in a central location. Rooms are pleasant, attractively furnished. All have balcony with seaview.

MARMARIS   ⓒ 252

LOCATION: About 60 mi. / 96 km southeast of Bodrum along the Mediterranean coast.

POPULATION: 16,000

CLIMATE: See Bodrum

DESCRIPTION: Sleepy little fisherman's village that is expanding into a resort town. Yet it retains a simple unexploited charm. Marmaris has a large Marina, and is a major ferryboat hub between the Turkish Coast and the Island of Rhodes (Greece). Any travel agent in town can book you on a boat for a 2-1/2 hrs daily voyage (except on Sunday) to Rhodes.

BARS Ⓨ RESTAURANTS 🍴

● Bars (NG): There is no established gay scene in Marmaris. Drinking takes place along the east marina. **Bar Ivy**, attracts young backpacking crowd after dark; **Palm Tree**, pleasant garden bistro.

● Restaurants (AW): **Birtat**, seafood, at the marina behind the Tourism Info Office (11-076); **Tat**, self-service cafeteria, Mustafa Kemal Pasa Sokak 16 (15-903).

λ SERVICES λ

● Turkish Bath (AW): **Yesil Marmaris**, Turkish Bath & Massage Saloon, right in the Shopping District (Bazaar) behind the Old Mosque #3. Very touristic oriented (24406).

🏠 ACCOMMODATIONS 🏠

OTEL 47
Atatürk Cad. 10, 48700 Marmaris. USA/Canada Tel: (516) 944-5330 or (800) 257-5344. Fax: (516) 944-7540 or (800) 982-6571. TYPE: *Hotel.* CLIENTELE: All Welcome. LOCATION: Centre of town near the beach, Bazaar and the promenade. 60 rooms w/priv. bath or shower, phone, balcony w/seaview, hot water, cafeteria, restaurant, TV lounge, maid service, parking, elevator, beach, 5 min. to port by taxi, season year round. DESCRIPTION: 3-star seaside hotel in an excellent location with large, comfortable Turkish style rooms and fine European standards. Rates: on request. *TAC:* 10% (from Odysseus).

UKRAINE

AREA: 233,089 sq. mi. (603,700 sq. km)
POPULATION: 51,000,000
CAPITAL: Kiev
CURRENCY: Uryvna (U)
OFFICIAL LANGUAGE: Ukrainian
MAJOR RELIGIONS: Russian Orthodoxy, Catholicism
Telephone: 380
Nat'l Holiday: Independence Day
Official Time: G.M.T.
Electricity: 220v 50c AC
Exchange Rate: US$ = Uak 1.88
Nat'l Airline: Air Ukraine

LAW REGARDING HOMOSEXUALITY: As of December 1991, article 122 of the Penal Code that criminalized homosexuality was abolished and homosexuality is no longer a crime in the Ukraine. The general age of consent is 16. The attitude of the majority of the population remains hostile to homosexuality.

KIEV   ⦅ 4

✈ Zhulhani Airport (IEV) 7mi. / 11 km South
  Borispol Airport (KBP) 24 mi. / 38 km SE.

LOCATION: Eastern Ukraine on the Dniepper River.

POPULATION: 2,500,000

CLIMATE: Winters are windless, but snowy and very cold with average temperatures of -15˚F-0˚F (-26˚c - -17˚c); summers are warm with temperatures reaching 80˚F-85˚F (26˚c-29˚c).

Gay/Lesbian Visitor Information
Two Colours: 211-0327

DESCRIPTION: The capital of the Ukraine and the cradle of East Slavic culture, Kiev is one of Eastern Europe's oldest cities. Modern Kiev is pleasant with splendid rococo, baroque and Art Deco architecture, medieval monastries and acres of green parklands and wide, attractive boulevards. Visit the **Verkhny Horod** (Upper Town); the famous **Khreshcatik** - the city's bustling main blvd., ; the **Golden Gate** corner of Volodymyrska Vullytsia and Yaroslaviv Val; and the **Babi Yar** memorial to Kievans and others killed during WWII. There is not much of a gay scene in Kiev. Places where you can meet other gays in town include: **Kreshatik St.,** (at the University) and the Main Railway Station.

Y BAR Y

● Club (GMW): **Dwa Kolori** (Two Colors), Parchomenko Str. 38-41 (211-0327).

λ SERVICES λ

● Sex Shop (G/S): **Salon Intym**, vul. Gorkago 24a (220-5409).

ACCOMMODATIONS

LYBID HOTEL
Victory Sq., Kiev. Tel: 74-0063. TYPE: *Hotel*. CLIENTELE: Mostly Straight. LOCATION: Central opposite Kiev Circus near Train Station. 280 rooms w/priv. bath, 14 suites, room service, restaurants, bar. Rates: US$80 - $250.

ODESSA   ⦅ 48

✈ Central Airport (ODS) 8mi. / 13 km S.

LOCATION: Southwestern Ukraine on the Black Sea.

POPULATION: 1,100,000

CLIMATE: Winters can be cold and snowy with average temperatures of -15˚F-0˚F (-26˚c - -17˚c); summers are warm with temperatures reaching 80˚F-85˚F (26˚c-29˚c).

DESCRIPTION: The "Pearl of the Black Sea" Odessa is a charming port town with ancient and diverse history and culture. It has an important Jewish heritage, impressing 18th and 19th century architecture, panoramic sea view and vibrant street scenes. A colorful city with legacy of writers, performers, musicians. The end of summer **Odessa Film Festival**

recreates an ambience of Cannes of Eastern Europe. The gay scene is limited. Meeting places include: Main railway station, Park Lenina and Kulikov Pole. Beach of interest to gay visitors is **Arcadia Beach**.

BARS ⊤ RESTAURANT 🍴

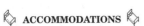

● Bars/clubs (G/S): **Turcomplex bar**, Genuezskaya St.; **Kafe Russkiy Chai**, Kulikovo Pole.

● Restaurant (NG): **Gambrinus**, atmospheric beer cellar, 31 Deribasovskaya Ulitsa (212911).

λ SERVICES λ

● Health Club (G/S): **Banja No. 2**, steam room, sauna, massage, Torgovaya St. opp. Ljesi Ukraniki Theathre.

🏠 ACCOMMODATIONS 🏠

ARCADIA HOTEL
24 Shechenko Naberezhnaya, Odessa. Tel: (48) 637527. TYPE: *Hotel*. CLIENTELE: Mostly Straight. LOCATION: On the famous Arcadia Beach. 150 rooms, some w/priv. bath.

CHERNOYE MORE HOTEL
159 Lenin St., Odessa. Tel: (48) 240123. Fax: (48) 240031. TYPE: *Hotel*. CLIENTELE: Mostly Straight. LOCATION: 2 km / 1.5 mi. to train station, 3 km / 2 mi. from sea terminal. 195 rooms, some w/priv. bath. CTV, telephone, 24 hrs. 195 rooms service, cafe, restaurants, bars. Rates: US$70-$120.

LONDONSKAYA
11 Primorsky Bulvar, Odessa. Tel: (48) 228-787. TYPE: *Hotel*. CLIENTELE: Mostly Straight. LOCATION: On the seawall promenade, overlooking the harbor. 60 rooms, most w/priv. bath, grill/bar, breakfast courtyard, English speaking concierge, business services. One of the best hotels in Odessa.

UNITED ARAB EMIRATES

AREA: 32,278 sq. mi. (83,600 sq. km)
POPULATION: 1,700,000
CAPITAL: Abu Dahbi
CURRENCY: Dirham (Dh)
OFFICIAL LANGUAGE: Arabic
MAJOR RELIGIONS: Islam
Telephone: 971
Nat'l Holiday: National Day, December 2
Official Time: G.M.T. + 4
Electricity: 220v 50c AC
Exchange Rate: US$ = Dh 3.67
Nat'l Airline: Gulf Air

LAW REGARDING HOMOSEXUALITY:
Homosexual behavior is illegal. Homosexual
acts are considered as "unnatural offenses"
that can be punishable with a maximum of
fourteen years in prison. Open homosexuality
is a "conduct at odds with public morality".
These "obscene acts" can be punishable for a
maximum of two years. Homosexuality is a
social taboo. There is no visible social support
organizations for gay and lesbian rights.

❖ **Note**: the population of the UAE consists
mainly of Bedouins, a proud and hospitable
race that changed over the years from nomad
lifestyle to modern city living. Bedouin guests
are often offered as a welcome gesture a special
brew of coffee flavored with a bit of cardamon,
or sugary mint tea.

ABU DHABI   © 2

✈ Abu Dhabi Int'l Airport (AUH)
   27 mi. / 43 km southeast

LOCATION: On the Persian Gulf.

CLIMATE: Hot and humid desert climate.
Pleasant climate from December to March;
extremely hot and damp from May to October.

Rainfall is negligible.

DESCRIPTION: Flat and sandy with huge
modern buildings, Abu Dhabi is the largest of
the Emirates. Public Cruising (AYOR): check
out the Sheraton Hotel on Corniche Road near
the volcano fountain.

♈ BARS ♈

● Bars/Clubs (AW): **Hemingway**, at the
Hilton International (661-900); **Tequiliana**,
disco, at the Hilton International.

 ACCOMMODATIONS

HILTON INTERNATIONAL
Corniche Ave., Abu Dhabi. Tel: (661-900).
TYPE: *Hotel*. CLIENTELE: All Welcome.
LOCATION: Facing the Arabian Gulf, 25 mi /
40 km from airport. 200 rooms w/priv. bath,
CTV, phone, A/C, 24 hrs. room service, outdoor
pool, tennis, beach club, restaurants (8), coffee
shop, lounge. Rates: $150-$240.

SHERATON HOTEL & RESORT
Corniche Rd., Abu Dhabi. Tel: (773-333). TYPE:
Resort Hotel. CLIENTELE: All Welcome.
LOCATION: On the Corniche within walking
distance of banks, shops and restaurants. 260
rooms w/priv. bath, CTV, phone, minibar, A/C,
24 hrs room service, restaurants (7), 2 pubs,
tennis, jacuzzi, outdoor pool, gym, private
beach. Rates: $144 - $220.

DUBAI   © 6

✈ Dubai Int'l Airport (DXB) 2.5 mi. / 4 km E.

LOCATION: On the Persian Gulf.

CLIMATE: See Abu Dhabi

DESCRIPTION: Called the "Venice of the
Gulf" Dubai has a remarkable deep-water
creek, and a busy commercial center. At Dubai
Creek in the early 20th century, the local
Bedouin population lived on fishing and pearl
diving. But since the economic prosperity of the
1950's the massive growth of Dubai is associated with gold trade and oil. Visit the newly renovated **Dubai Museum** set within a fort for
interesting insight into traditional aspects of
early life in Dubai.Public cruising (AYOR)
along the road and beside the Creek in Deira;
and around the busy **Al Nasr Square** (City
Center).

BARS 🍸 RESTAURANT 🍴

● Bars/clubs (AW): **Carlton Tower Bar**, at the Carlton Tower Hotel, Beniyas Rd. (22-71-11); **English Pub**, at the Hotel Intercontinental, Bin Yass St. (22-71-71); **Jules Bar**, at the Forte Grand Hotel, Airport Rd., (48-40-40); **Premier Disco**, dance club at the Hyatt Regency, Deira Sea Corniche (21-18-68).

● Restaurant (AW): check out the restaurants at the **Carlton Tower Hotel, Hotel Intercontinental, Forte Grand Hotel**, and the **Hyatt Regenc.**

 ACCOMMODATIONS

CARLTON TOWER HOTEL
Beniyas Rd., Dubai. Tel: (4) 227-111. TYPE: *Hotel.* CLIENTELE: All Welcome. LOCATION: 5 km / 3 mi. from the airport. 154 rooms w/priv. bath, CTV, phone, A/C, restaurants, pub, nightclub. Rates: $90 - $120.

FORTE GRAND DUBAI
Airport Rd., Dubai. Tel: (4) 824-040. TYPE: *Hotel.* CLIENTELE: All Welcome. LOCATION: 1/2 km / 800 yards from the airport. 384 rooms w/priv. bath, CTV, phone, A/C, restaurants, cocktail lounge, disco, sauna, gym. Rates: $190 - $320. DESCRIPTION: Deluxe dramatic business oriented hotel.

HOTEL INTERCONTINENTAL
Bin Yass St., Dubai. Tel: (4) 227-171. TYPE: *Hotel.* CLIENTELE: All Welcome. LOCATION: Waterfront overlooking Dubai creek, on main route to airport. 281 rooms w/priv. bath, CTV, phone, A/C, health club, sauna, jacuzzi, restaurants, bars, coffee shop (some gays meet here), outside pool. Rates: $225 - $430.

UNITED KINGDOM

AREA: 94,399 sq. mi. (244,493 sq. km)
POPULATION: 55,670,000
CAPITAL: London
CURRENCY: British Pound Sterling (£)
OFFICIAL LANGUAGE: English
MAJOR RELIGIONS: Protestantism,
Roman Catholicism.
Telephone: 44
Nat'l Holiday: Queen's Birthday, June 15
Official Time: G.M.T.
Electricity: 240 volts, AC.
Exchange Rate: 1$ = £0.61
Nat'l Airline: British Airways

LAW REGARDING HOMOSEXUALITY:
Homosexual acts between consenting adults is
not mentioned in the law of being a criminal
offense. Minimum legal age for consensual
homosexual activity for men is 18 as of Nov. 3,
1994. The age of consent for heterosexual and
lesbian act is 16. There is a new upsurge of
homophobia with the institution of a law
against the promotion of homosexuality by
local authorities or schools (Clause 28 of the
1988 Local Government Act).

BATH   *C*   1225

✈ Bristol Airport, Lulsgate (BRS)
  8 mi. / 13 km west of Bath

DESCRIPTION: Britain's oldest and most
famous Spa town. The city is known for the
magnificent 18th century architectural style,
elegant squares and exquisite crescent streets.

BARS ℐ RESTAURANTS 🍴

● Bar/club (GMW): **Green Room**, The Garrick's
Head, St. John's Place (448-819); **Dark Horse**,
gay friendly bar, 4 Northampton St. (425-944).

● Restaurants (NG): check the restaurants,
pubs and wine-bars at the popular **Northumberland Passage.**

🔖 ACCOMMODATIONS 🔖

HODGKINSON'S
South Parade, Matlock, Bath, Derbyshire DE4
3NR. Tel: (1629) 582-170. TYPE: *Hotel &
Restaurant.* HOSTS: Malcolm and Nigel.
CLIENTELE: Gay Welcome. Restored Georgian hotel. All rooms with private bath.

KENNARD HOTEL
11 Henrietta St., Bath. Tel: (1225) 310-472.
TYPE: *Hotel.* HOST: Malcolm & Richard.
CLIENTELE: Equal Gay/Straight. LOCATION: Over Pulteney bridge, a short walk to
the Abbey and Roman Baths. 13 rooms.
DESCRIPTION: Converted Georgian townhouse. Rates: £52-£62. *TAC:* 10%.

BIRMINGHAM   *C*   121

✈ Birmingham Int'l Airport (BHX)

LOCATION: Heart of England, about 100 mi.
(160 km) northwest of London.

POPULATION: 1,058,000.

Gay/Lesbian Visitor Information
Gay Switchboard:622-6589 (nightly)

DESCRIPTION: Birmingham is the "capital"
of one of Britain's most important regions. The
nearby region is known as the Shakespeare
Country with historical towns such as Stratford-Upon-Avon, Shakespeare's birthplace, Warwick, Kenilworth, and Royal Leamington Spa.

BARS ℐ RESTAURANTS 🍴

● Bars/clubs (GM): **Fountain Inn**, 102 Wrentham St., (622-1452); **Jester**, Horsefair, Holloway Circus, Queensway (643-0155); **Nightingale**, large entertainment complex, 40
Thorp St. (622-1718); **Peacocks**, disco bar, 311
Westcourt, Bull Ring Center; **Route 66**,
cabaret, bar, 139/147 Hurst St. (622-3366).

● Bar (GMW): **Partners**, gay pub/disco, Hurst
St. (622-4710).

λ SERVICES λ

● Health Clubs (GM): **Spartan Sauna**, sauna, solarium, massage, book shop, 127 George Rd., Erdington (382-3345); **Warehouse Health Club**, 16 Fleet St. (233-3090).

 ACCOMMODATIONS

THE FOUNTAIN INN
102 Wrentham St., Birmingham B5 6QL. Tel: (121) 622-1452. TYPE: *Bed & Breakfast*. HOST: Chris Hands. CLIENTELE: Gay men & women. LOCATION: City center, near gay bars. 5 rooms, gay pub. Rates: £25-£35. *TAC:* 10%. DESCRIPTION: 100 years old Victorian public house.

OAKLEAVES
22 Gibson Dr., Handsworth Wood, Birmingham. Tel: (021) 551-6510. HOST: Robert. TYPE: *Hotel*. CLIENTELE: Gay men only. LOCATION: Central near gay bars. 7 rooms. Rates: on request.

THE VILLAGE
152 Hurst St., Birmingham B5 6RY. Tel: (121) 622-4742. TYPE: *Hotel*. CLIENTELE: Gay men. LOCATION: Gay Village. All rooms w/priv. bath, breakfast served in room. busy gay bar. Rates: on request.

BLACKPOOL   ℭ 1253

✈ Blackpool Airport (BLK)

LOCATION: A seaside resort town in Northern England on the Irish Sea.

POPULATION: 149,000

CLIMATE: Cold Northern climate. Summers are cool and pleasant, winters are cold and snowy, with temperatures below freezing.

Gay Visitor Information
Gay Helpline: 770-378

DESCRIPTION: Blackpool is a down-to-earth resort town for the Northwestern region of England. It is rarely visited by foreign tourists who consider it to be too blue collar and too far removed. Visit nearby **Liverpool**, the hometown of the Beatles only 26 mi. / 42 km south, and the Lake District to the north.

BARS Y RESTAURANTS ⑪

● Bars/clubs (GM): **Basil's on the Strand**, 9 the Strand (294-109); **Flamingos**, entertainment complex, 176 Talbot Rd. (24-901); **Funny**

Girls, drag shows, Queen St. 291 (291-114); **Lucy's Bar**, drag shows, live DJ, below TFG Talbot Square (293-204); **Pepes Bar**, 94 Talbot Rd., (26691).

λ SERVICES λ

● Health Club (GM): **Galaxy**, sauna, jacuzzi, TV lounge, 25 Springfield Rd., open 1pm-11pm (Near Metropole Hotel) (294-610).

ACCOMMODATIONS

GYNN HOUSE
20 Gynn Ave., Blackpool, Lancs. Tel: (1253) 352-285. TYPE: *Hotel*. HOST: Mike Bristow. CLIENTELE: All Welcome. LOCATION: 10 min. walk from main rail and bus station. 10 rooms w/shared shower. Rates: £15-£20 pp w/EB. Victorian terraced hotel.

SUNNYSIDE HOUSE
27 Vance St., Blackpool FY1 4QD. Tel: (1253) 23752. TYPE: *Guest House*. HOST: Eric or Dave. CLIENTELE: Gay men. LOCATION: Near Flamingo disco. DESCRIPTION: Most rooms with private facilities. Rates: £8.50 - £10.

TRADES HOTEL
51/53 Lord Street, Blackpool FY1 2BJ. Tel: (1253) 26401. TYPE: *Hotel*. CLIENTELE: Gay men. LOCATION: Town center, 2 min. from Flamingo Club and North Railway Stn. DESCRIPTION: Small hotel with sauna and solarium. Rates: £10-£33.

BOURNEMOUTH   ℭ 1202

✈ Bournemouth Int'l Airport, Hurn AP

LOCATION: In the south of England along the shores of the English Channel. 96 minutes by train from London Waterloo Station.

POPULATION: 144,100

CLIMATE: Continental, tempered by the Gulf Stream.

Gay/Lesbian Visitor Information
Dorset G&L Helpline: 318-822

DESCRIPTION: Beach resort on the English Channel with 7 mi. / 11km of soft sands backed by sandstone cliffs. During the winter, many internationally known "stars" visit the town on their UK tours.

❖ Gay Beach: "**Shell Bay**", five minutes ferry ride across from Sandbanks to Studland, where you'll find a straight/gay nude beach with very open and active gay cruising in the sand dunes off of the beach.

BARS  RESTAURANTS

● Bars/clubs (GMW): **Exchange Bar**, mixed disco, 4 The Triangle (294-321); **Legends**, cafe, bar, 53 Bourne Ave. (310-100); **Queens Hall**, 14 Queens Rd., Westbourne (764-416); **Triangle**, leather disco club, weekend cabaret, 30 The Triangle (297-607).

● Restaurants (GMW): **Falcon**, 10 Drummond Rd. (309-808); **Orchard**, 15 Alumdale Rd, Alum Chine (767-767); **Zorba's**, 218 Old Christchurch Rd. (28-125).

λ SERVICES λ

● Health Club (GM): **121 Gentlemen's Health Spa**, 121 Poole Rd., Westbourne. Open: 12 noon - 10pm daily (757-591)

🔖 ACCOMMODATIONS 🔖

THE CREFFIELD
7 Cambridge Rd., Bournemouth, BH2 6AE. Tel: (1202) 317-900. TYPE: *Hotel*. CLIENTELE: Gay men. LOCATION: Central. All rooms w/priv. bath, CTV, hair dryers. Single rooms have double beds. Rates: on request.

THE ORCHARD
15 Alumdale Rd., Bournemouth, BH4 8HX. Tel: (1202) 767-767. HOST: Andrew & Alan CLIENTELE: Gay men & women only. LOCATION: 1 mi. / 2 km from the center of town near the beach. 10 rooms. Rates: £14-£18 w/B. *TAC:* 10%

ST. GERMAINE
24 Derby Rd., Bournemouth, Derby BH1 3QA. Tel: (1202) 557-923. TYPE: *Hotel*. CLIENTELE: Gay men & women. LOCATION: 6 min. from town and sea. 15 rooms most w/priv. bath, CTV, phone, free transport to clubs and pubs.

BRIGHTON   ✆   1273

✈ Gatwick Airport (LGW),
   Heathrow Airport (LHR)

LOCATION: In East Sussex of southeast Eng-

land along the shores of the English Channel. About 50 mi. / 80 km south of London, on A23 and M23 motorway.

POPULATION: 156,500

CLIMATE: Continental with tempering effect of the Gulf Stream.

Gay Visitor Information
Gay Switchboard: 690-825
Lesbian Visitor Information
Lesbian Line: 603-298

DESCRIPTION: Brighton is known as "London by the Sea" and together with neighboring **Hove** are considered the grand dames of the English seaside. For shopping, explore the antique shops around the 'Lanes' and Gloucester Road area. The Brighton Antique Fair takes place in July. For elegant shops, try the East St. and the Regent Arcade.

❖ Beach: the official nude beach is 50 m (150 ft.) east of the main town promenade, near the Peter Pan's Playground, Drive Madeira and Dukes Mound area.

BARS  RESTAURANTS

● Bars/clubs (GM): **Aquarium**, cruise bar, all ages, 6 Steine St. (605-525); **Bulldog**, 36 St. James' St., popular pub, mostly mature men (684-097); **Legends**, karaoke/cabaret, 31-32 Marine Parade (624-462); **Marlborough**, popular gay pub, Princes St. (570-028); **Oriental**, cabaret, drag shows, 5 Montpelier Rd. (728-808); **Revenge**, leather club and disco, 32 Old Steine, opp. Palace Pier (606-064); **Schwartz Bar**, leather uniforms cruise bar, basement 31/32 Marine Parade (New Europe Hotel); **Secrets**, 25 Steine St. (609-672); **Zanzibar**, bar/brasserie, 129 St. James' St. (622-100); **Wild Fruit**, Paradox, 78 West St., (321-628).

● Bars/Clubs (GMW): **Black Horse**, 112 Church St. (606-864); **Brighton Belle**, piano bar, 2 St. George Place (609-713); **Mix Bar**, 8 Queens Rd.; **Queen's Head**, 10 Steine St. (602-939); **Village**, bar,disco, lounge, 74 St. James St. (622-260).

● Bar/club (GW): **Blue Moon**, women's dance club, 37 New England Rd. (709-040); **Club Cheeky**, dance club, at Zenon's, 15 King's Rd (326-848); **Pink Promotions**, women's disco twice monthly, call Lisa (01903-723-625).

● Restaurants (AW): **Albatross Cafe**, popular with gay men and lesbians, 27 Middle St. (329-

462); **Chez Carcajou**, Swiss/French cuisine, intimate candlelit ambiance, 15 New Road (256-48); **Choys**, Cantonese/Peking cuisine, 2-3 Little East Street (253-05, 253-28); **Fudges**, King's Road, Seafront (205-852); **Latin in the Lane**, Italian, 10 Kings Road (328-672); **Market Wine House**, Brighton's oldest bar with superb seafood and Continental dishes, 20 Market Street (238-29).

λ SERVICES λ

● Health Clubs (GM): **Bright'n Beautiful**, sauna club, 9 St. Margaret's Pl. (328-330); **Denmark Sauna**, 84-86 Denmark Villas, Hove (723-733); **Fitness Camp**, sauna, 90 St. James St. (674-455).

● Shops (GMW): **Cardome**, 47a St. James St. (692-916); **Sin-A-Matique**, gay shop, leather, rubber, magazines, 22 Preston St. (329-154); **Wildcat Collection**, body piercing, jewelry, 16 Preston St. (323-758).

 ACCOMMODATIONS

ALPHA LODGE
19 New Steine, Brighton, BN2 1PD. Tel: (1273) 609-632. TYPE: *Guest House.* CLIENTELE: Mostly gay men. HOST: Derrick & Charles. LOCATION: Regency Sq. overlooking the sea and the Victorian Pier. 10 rooms, bar, sauna. Rates: £20-£33 pp. *TAC:* 10%.

BENSONS
16 Egremont Place, Brighton, BN2 2GA. Tel: (1273) 698-852. TYPE: *Guest House.* HOST: Gill or Barbara. CLIENTELE: Gay women. LOCATION: Close to the sea and clubs. 5 rooms. Season: Year round.

COWARD's
12 Upper Rock Gardens, Brighton BN2 1QE. TYPE: *Guest House.* HOST: Gerry & Cyril. CLIENTELE: Gay men & women. LOCATION: Off James Street, 5 min. to city center. 6 rooms. DESCRIPTION: Refurbished Regency guest house (built 1807). All rooms have private facilities are tastefully furnished and painted in classical style.

HUDSONS
22 Devonshire Place, Brighton BN2 1QA. Tel: (1273) 683-642. TYPE: *Guest House.* HOST: Frank & Graham. CLIENTELE: Gay men & women only. LOCATION: Near town center. 9 rooms w/showers. CTV, phone, C/H. Rates: £28 - £47. DESCRIPTION: 19th century Regency residence. *TAC:* 10%.

NEW EUROPE HOTEL
31-32 Marine Parade, Brighton BN2 1TR. Tel: (1273) 624-462. TYPE: *Hotel.* CLIENTELE: Gay men. LOCATION: Central. All rooms w/priv. bath. Most with seaview. Rates: from £20 pp.

SHALIMAR HOTEL
23 Broad St., Brighton BN2 1TJ. Tel: (1273) 605-316. TYPE: *Hotel* HOST: Kevin & Lawrence. CLIENTELE: Gay men only. LOCATION: Centrally located near the Palace, Pier and the Gay Scene. 11 rooms, 6 w/priv.; 4 w/shared bath, CTV, phone, refrigerator, C/H, hairdryer, tea/coffee, ironing board, maid and room service, bar, Rates: £15-£25; (off) £15-£20. DESCRIPTION: Brighton's most central gay hotel, decorated to high standard.

VICTORIA HOUSE
23 Wilbury Rd., Hove BN3 3PB. Tel: (1273) 26838. TYPE: *Bed & Breakfast.* HOST: Brian or Arthur. CLIENTELE: Gay men. LOCATION: Near seafront. Rooms w/priv. bath. Luxury holiday apartment sleep up to 5. Rates: on request.

CANTERBURY   ✆ 01831

⅄ BAR ⅄

● Bar/club (GMW): **Carpenters Arms**, Wed & Sat. from 7pm, Black Griffin Lane.

 ACCOMMODATIONS

THE LINCOLN
Nr. Canterbury. Tel: (1831) 749302. TYPE: *Hotel.* CLIENTELE: Gay men only. LOCATION: 15 min. drive to Canterbury. Restaurant, close to ferries and Channel Tunnel.

CARDIFF   ✆ 01222

✈ Cardiff-Wales Airport (CWL)

LOCATION: On the Taff River, on the Bristol Channel, about 130 mi. / 210 km west of London. 2-1/2 hrs. from London by car or train.

POPULATION: 276,880

CLIMATE: Same as London

Gay Visitor Information
Friend - Tel: (01222) 340-101

DESCRIPTION: An important seaport, administrative and industrial center of Great Britain. The city's ancient origin is indicated by the foundation of a Roman fort, dating from 75 A.D., on the site of the **Cardiff Castle** built by the Normans. In 1955 it was officially declared the capital of Wales. While the city is of ancient origin, it is modern, and noted for its civic center, fine University and spacious parks. The gay scene is limited.

BARS Y RESTAURANTS ⫬

● Bar/clubs (GM): **Bel Air/Scene**, bar/cabaret, Riverside Hotel, 53-59 Despenser St. (378-866); **Club X**, 39 Charles St. Wed.-Sat (645-721); **Exit Bar**, 48 Charles St. (640-102); **King's Cross**, gay pub,The Hayes/Caroline St.

● Restaurant (GMW): **Charlies**, gay diner, WEsley Lane, off Charles St.; **Courtfield**, à la carte, fully licensed, Mixed crowd (G/S) 101 Cathedral Rd. (227-701).

λ SERVICES λ

● Health Club (GM): **Locker Room**, sauna, gym, TV lounge, cafe, 50 Charles St. (220-388).

ACCOMMODATIONS

COURTFIELD HOTEL
101 Cathedral Road, Cardiff CF1 9PH. Tel: (01222) 227701. TYPE: *Hotel*. HOST: Norman. CLIENTELE: Mostly Straight. LOCATION: Central location near National Sports Center. 16 rooms. Rates: on request. DESCRIPTION: Tourist hotel in an authentic Victorian street, adjacent to the Cardiff Castle. *BHRCA*

LIVERPOOL   *©* 051

✈ Liverpool Airport, Speke (LPL)

LOCATION: England's northwest, on the banks of the River Mersey, overlooking the Liverpool Bay, 35 mi. / 56 km west of Manchester.

POPULATION: 650,000

CLIMATE: See Manchester

Gay Visitor Information: 708-9552

DESCRIPTION: Liverpool started as a small fishing village in the 12th century, and reached its heyday in the 18th century as a major trade post with the New World. Today, the city is mostly associated with 'Beatles' memorabilia, and soccer (European football) games.

BARS Y RESTAURANTS ⫬

● Bars/clubs (GM): **Garlands**, disco & club, 8-10 Eberle St. (236-3946); **Lisbon Bar**, mixed pub popular with gays, 35 Victoria St.; **Paco's**, 25 Stanley St. (236-9737); **Time Out**, young cruise bar, 30 Highfield St., junction Cockspur St. & Pownal Sq. (236-6768).

● Bars/clubs (GMW): **The Curzon Club**, member club, Temple Lane (236-5160); **Reflections**, large dance club, opposite Curzon Club, Temple Lane (236-3946).

ACCOMMODATIONS

ATLANTIC TOWER HOTEL
Chapel St., Liverpool L3 9RE. Tel: (051) 227-4444. TYPE: *Hotel*. CLIENTELE: Mostly straight. LOCATION: Adjacent to St Nicholas Church at Center Pier near the train station. 226 rooms w/priv. bath, restaurant, gym. gay bars nearby. DESCRIPTION: Dramatic first class hotel.

LONDON   *©* 071/081

✈ Heathrow Airport (LHR);
Gatwick Airport (LGW)

LOCATION: In the southeast of England in the Greater London County along the banks of the River Thames.

POPULATION: 12,332,900

CLIMATE: Continental. Winters are cold with occasional snowfalls from December through February. January average mean temperature is 39°F (4°c). Fall and Spring are cool and pleasant. Summers are cool with average temperature for July of 63°F (17°c).

Gay/Lesbian Visitor Information
Gay Switchboard: 837-7324 (24 hrs.)

DESCRIPTION: London is a city where hundreds of years of tradition live side-by-side with the ultra modern, eccentric and the avant-garde. The city extends over 600 sq. mi. with historical monuments, parks, shops, tourist attractions and recreational areas.

London is famous for its theatre productions and shopping. The main shopping streets are **Oxford St.**, **Regent St.**, **Bond St.**, for male fashion and luxury goods, **Kensington High St.**, and **King's Road** in Chelsea, for young 'in' fashion, and with a variety of shops including the spectacular **Harrods.**

❖ **SPECIAL EVENTS**: **Fine Arts and and Antiques Fair**, June 6-16 at the Grand Hall, Hammersmith Rd., W14 (370-8211); **Gay Pride**, last Saturday in June. The march assembles at Hyde Park from 11am and moves off at 12 noon; The **City of London Festival**, July 7-24 (for info call 377-0540); **Lord Mayor's Procession & Show**, Nov. 9 (for info call 606-3030); **Lighting Up the Christmas Tree**, Trafalgar Square, December 5.

BARS Ⲩ RESTAURANTS ⅠⅠ

● Bars/clubs (GM): **Anvil**, leather S/M bar, dress code, 88 Tooley St. SE1 (407-0371); **Attitude**, cruise bar, at Trafalgar, 46 Sumner Rd. Peckham (701-2175); **Backstreet**, leather rubber cruise bar, Wentworth Mews, Burdett Rd. E3 (980-8557); **Brief Encounter**, 41 St. Martins Lane WC2 (240-2221); **Bar Code**, 3-4 Archer St., W1 (734-3342); **Bromptons**, cruise bar, disco, 294 Old Brompton Rd. (370-1344); **City of Quebec**, older gays, 12 Old Quebec St., Marble Arch (629-6159); **Dante's Inferno**, male's strip pub, 425 New Kings Rd., SW6 (736-2324); **Earls & Club 180**, 180 Earls Court Road, SW5 (835-1826); **Halfway to Heaven**, bar on 2 levels, 7 Duncannon St., off Trafalgar Square, Charing Cross (930-8312); **Heaven**, Europe's largest gay disco, The Arches, Craven St., WC2 (839-2520) Charing Cross or Embankment tube; **Hoist**, leather rubber fetish cruise bar, South Lambeth Rd., Vauxhall Cross, SW8 (735-9972); **Limelight**, gay tea dance sunday 6-11, 136 Shaftsebury Ave. W1 (434-0572); **Phoenix**, 37 Cavendish Sq. W1.; **79CXR**, 79 Charing Cross Rd.; **Substation South**, leather, rubber, uniforms, young crowd, 9 Brighton Terrace, SW9 (737-2095); **Zeebrabar**, classy Soho bar, 62 Frith St., Soho (437-4018).

● Pubs (GM): **The Black Cap**, London's best known drag pub, bar/cabaret, 171 Camden High St., NW1 (484-1742); **The Colherne**, Britain's oldest and most famous gay pub, 261 Old Brompton Rd. (373-8356); **Kings Arms**, Soho's oldest pub, 23 Poland St. (734-5907); **Queen's Head**, Chelsea Pub, 27 Tyron St. SW3 (589-0262); **Vauxhall Tavern**, popular drag pub, 372

Kennington Lane SE11 (582-0833).

● Bars/clubs (GMW): **Balans**, busy brasserie, 60 Old Compton St.W1 (437-5212); **Balans West**, stylish brasserie with bar, 239 Old Brompton Rd. SW5; **Duke of Wellington**, mixed pub, 119 BallsPond Rd. N1 (249-3729); **Freedom**, cafee/bar, mixed Soho crowd, 60 Wardour St. W1 (734-0071);

● Bars/clubs (GW): **Ace of Clubs**, older women, 52 Piccadilly W1, Sat. 9:30p - 4am (408-4457); **Diva Dive**, well established dyke's bar for the 30+ crowd, 64 Wilton Rd. SW1 (0956-477724); **Drill Hall**, busy Monday night women's only bar, 16 Chenies St. WC1 (631-1353); **Girl Bar** (at The Box) Sun. 7-11, 32-34 Monmouth St., WC2 (240-5828); **Glass Bar**, private women only club for gay and straight professional women, 190 Euston Rd. NW1; **Rossana's**, Weds single night, Thurs & Fri 7-11, 17 Strutton Ground, off Victoria St., SW1 (233-1701).

● Restaurants (GMW): **Club 29**, lounge and restaurant, professional, 29 Clarges St. Mayfair (629-5221); **Detour**, leather crowd, above the Colherne Pub, 261 Old Brompton Rd.; **Mildreds**, restaurant/cabaret, 4 Inverness St. Camden Town NW1; **La Liberté**, French cuisine, 32 Philbeach Gardens SW5 (244-6884); **The Saloon**, 206 Fulham Rd., (352-6828); **Steph's**, 39 Dean St., W1 (734-5976); **Tapas**, 34 D'Arblay St. W1 (439-7099).

λ SERVICES λ

● Erotica (GMW): **Studio**, gay store, 40 Berwick St. W1 (437-0811).

● Escort/Massage (GM): **A.A. Adams**, Suite 302, Radnor House, 93 Regent St., (437-0703).

● Health Club (GM): **Burlington Health Club**, 23 Old Bond St. (493-2265); **Covent Garden Health Spa**, 29 Endell St. Covent Garden WC2 (836-2236); **Holland Park Sauna**, 156 Shepherds Bush Shopping Centre W12 (743-3264); **Society Sauna**, 180 Royal College St., Camden Town (267-5021); **Star Steam & Sauna**, open 11:00 am until late, 38 Lavender Hill, Battersea SW11 (924-2269).

● Leather (GM): **Expectations**, leather & rubber store, 75 Great Eastern St. (EC); **Rob of London**, clothing and toys, 24 Wells St. W1 (735-7893).

 **ACCOMMODATIONS**

ACCOMMODATIONS

1 New York
2 Redcliffe

BARS / CLUBS

11 Bromptons
12 The Coleherne
13 Copa
14 Duke of Cornwall
15 Heaven
16 Kings Arm
2 Manhattan's
18 The Phoenix
19 Vauxhall

■ = UNDERGROUND STATION

© Odysseus Enterprises Ltd. 1997

ODYSSEUS '97/98

✪ HOTEL NEW YORK

32 Philbeach Gardens, London SW5 9EB. Tel:
(171) 244-6884. USA/Canada Tel: (516) 944-
5330 or (800) 257-5344. Fax: (516) 944-7540 or
(800) 982-6571. TYPE: *Hotel*. CLIENTELE:
Gay men & women. LOCATION: Earls Court,
near underground.

* Rooms: 15 most w/priv. bath
* CTV (cable), phone, hair dryer, iron and
  ironing board, tea/coffee making facilities
* 24 hrs room service, maid service
* Restaurant: **La Liberté** - French
* Jacuzzi, sauna, licensed bar
* Gay Bars: on premises, other nearby
* Health Club: walking distance (gay)
* Underground: Earls Court 2 min. walk
* Airport: 15 mi. / 24 km (Heathrow) taxi
* Open: Year round
* Rates: (US) $120 - $190 w/EB
* **TAC:** 10% (from Odysseus)

DESCRIPTION: London's premier all gay hotel
in a convenient Earls Court location. Spacious
well decorated rooms, relaxed luxury lounge,
and private rear garden.

✪ REDCLIFFE HOTEL

268 Fulham Rd., London SW10. Tel: (171) 351-
2467. USA/Canada Tel: (516) 944-5330 or (800)
257-5344. Fax: (516) 944-7540 or (800) 982-
6571. TYPE: *Hotel*. CLIENTELE: Gay men.
LOCATION: Central Chelsea location, walking
distance to Earl's Court.

* Rooms: 16 w/priv., bath
  2 sg / 14 dbl / 4 triple or quad
* CTV, phone, safety box, C/H
* Gay Bars: walking distance
* Health Club: 5 min.
* Airports: Heathrow 7 mi. / 11 km
  Gatwick 15 mi. / 24 km, taxi, subway
* Subway: Earls Court 15 min.
* Open: Year round
* Rates: $110-$180 w/EB
* **TAC:** 10% (from Odysseus)

DESCRIPTION: Victorian 4-story building. All
rooms with en-suite bathroom. Luxury doubles
are spacious with ironing table, iron trouser
press and tea/coffee making facilities. Quality
all male gay hotel.

MANCHESTER   ℂ   0161

✈ Manchester Int'l Airport (MAN)
10 mi. /16 km southwest

USA/Canada reservations
(800) 257-5344

USA/Canada reservations
(800) 257-5344

LOCATION: Northwest England, some 30 mi. / 45 km west of Liverpool.

POPULATION: 500,000

CLIMATE: Unpredictable but on the cool side, Summers are pleasant with temperatures in the 70°F's (21°c), and winters can be cold with snowfall.

Gay/Lesbian Visitor Information
Manchester L& G Center: 274-3814

DESCRIPTION: Manchester, the 2nd largest city in the UK and the capital of Northern England, is located near some of England's loveliest countryside, and the famous Lake District of the North West.

BARS Y RESTAURANTS ¶¶

● Bars/clubs (GM): **Central Park**, dance club, cabaret, Sackville St. (236-5196); **Green Room**, theatre, licensed bar, 54-56 Whitworth St. W (236-1677); **M.E.N.**, uniform, denim, fetish cruise bar, 48 Princess St.; **Monroe's**, bar/hotel, 38 London Rd., (236-0564); **Napoleon's**, disco, leather club at the Cellar, Sackville St. (236-8800); **New York**, entertainment complex, 98 Bloom St. (236-6556); **Paradise Factory**, dance club, 112 Paradise St. (273-5422); **Rembrandt Hotel**, bar, restaurant and accommodations, 33 Sackville Street (236-2435/1311).

● Bars/clubs (GMW): **Central Park**, cabaret, Sackville St. (236-5196); **Dickens**, 74a Oldham St. (236-5196); **New Union**, mixed pub, Princess and Bloom Sts. (228-1492); **Rembrandt Hotel**, bar & restaurant, **Universal** - women's night on Sat. 10:00-2:00, Village Edge, below Blooms Hotel.

● Restaurants (GMW): **Bloom St. Cafe**, mixed gay diner, 39 Bloom St. (236-3433); **Blue Cafe**, Briish/European cuisine, 29 Sackville St. (236-0074); **Boodles**, weekends dinner till 10pm, 34 Canal St. (237-9117).

λ SERVICES λ

● Health Clubs (GM): **Bath House Sauna**, 749 Moston Lane M10 (682-2405); **Euro Sauna**, 202 Hill Lane, Blackley (740-5152).

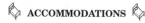 **ACCOMMODATIONS**

MONROE's
38 London Rd., Manchester. Tel: (161) 236-0564. TYPE: *Hotel & Bar*. HOSTS: Alan &

Chris. CLIENTELE: Gay men only. LOCATION: Next to Rockies.

REMBRANDT HOTEL
33 Sackville St., Manchester M1 3LZ. Tel: (161) 236-1311/2435. TYPE: *Hotel*. CLIENTELE: Gay men & women. LOCATION: Heart of Manchester's Gay Village. 6 rooms w/shared shower, bar. Rates: on request. DESCRIPTION: The oldest gay establishment in Manchester.

NEWCASTLE-upon-TYNE ✆ 0191

Gay/Lesbian Visitor Information
Friend: 261-8555
Lesbian Line: 261-2277

BARS Y RESTAURANTS ¶¶

● Bars/Clubs (GMW): **Courtyard**, 2 Scotswood Rd. (232-2037); **Heavens Above**, mixed gay bar, Churchill St. (232-2037); **Henry's Bar**, The Barking Dog, Marlborough Cres. W only upstairs **Powerhouse**, mixed with men only bar at rear, Blenheim St / Waterloo St. (261-4507); **Rockies**, pub/disco, 78 Scotswood Rd., (232-9648); **Strings**, mixed pub popular with lesbians, 29 Blenheim St. (232-3530).

● Restaurants (GMW):**Village**, Sunderland St. next to the Powerhouse, open nightly; **Heaven Cafe**, cafe and art gallery, good food, open late.

 **ACCOMMODATIONS**

CHEVIOT VIEW
194 Station Rd., Wallsend, Newcastle-upon-Tyne NE28 8RD. Tel: (191) 262-0125. TYPE: *Guest House*. HOST: C. Brownlee. CLIENTELE: Gay men & women. LOCATION: 10 min. from Newcstle city centre. 5 rooms w/priv. or shared bath, CTV, phone, C/H, cocktail bar. Rates: £17-£25. Victorian style.

OXFORD ✆ 1865

✈ Heathrow Airport (LHR); 45 mi. / 72 km Gatwick Airport (LGW)

Gay/Lesbian Visitor Information

L&G Center, North Gate Hall, St. Michael's St., Oxford OX1 2DU (01865) 793-759

Gay Switchboard: (01865) 793-999
Lesbian Line: (01865) 242-333

☿ BARS ☿

● Bars/clubs (GMW): **Jolly Farmers**, Paradise St. (off Westgate Ctr) (793-759); **Boy Zone, L&G Center**, North Gate Hall, St. Michael's St., (200-249).

ACCOMMODATIONS

EASTGATE HOTEL
The High St., Oxford OX1 4BE. Tel: (1865) 248-244. Fax: (1865) 791-681. TYPE: *Hotel*. CLIENTELE: All Welcome. LOCATION: Town center overlooking the ancient examination halls. 43 rooms w/priv. bath, CTV, phone, restaurant, bar, rooms for non smokers, free parking. Rates: from £110.

KINGS ARMS HOTEL
Horton-cum-Studley Nr. Oxford. Tel: (1865) 351-235. TYPE: *Hotel*. HOSTS: Keith and Mark. CLIENTELE: Gay/Straight. LOCATION: 7 mi. / 11 km from city center close to M40. All rooms w/priv. bath, restaurant, bar.

SCARBOROUGH   ✆   1723

LOCATION: East coast of Yorkshire near York.

ACCOMMODATIONS

INTERLUDES
32 Princess St., Scarborough Y011 1QR. Tel: (1723) 360513. Fax: (1723) 368597. TYPE: *Hotel*. HOSTS: Ian & Bob. CLIENTELE: Equaly Gay/Straight. LOCATION: Near the 12th Century Castle, overlooking the harbor. 5 rooms, 4 w/priv. bath, CTV, C/H. Rates: £22-£26.

TORQUAY   ✆   1803

✈ Exeter Airport (EXT)

LOCATION: South Devon coast.

POPULATION: 109,900

Gay Visitor Information
Gay Community: 292-055

DESCRIPTION: Torquay is located on the

fashionable 'English Riviera'. It offers a delightful blend of seaside resort, fine sandy beaches, and scenic coastal roads.

BARS ☿ RESTAURANTS ¶¶

● Bars/clubs (GM): **Cliff House Hotel**, bar, sauna, entertainment, St. Marks Rd. Meadfoot Beach (294-656); **Double 2 Club**, Rock Road (222-79); **Judy G's**, disco, Belgrave Rd. (213-232); **Meadfoot Inn**, pub overlooking the habor, 7 Meadfoot Lane (297-112); **Monroe's**, large club, Victoria Rd. (291-149).

ACCOMMODATIONS

CLIFF HOUSE HOTEL
St. Marks Road, Meadfoot Beach, Torquay, Devon. Tel: (01803) 294-656. TYPE: *Hotel*. HOST: Alan Wilson. CLIENTELE: Gay men & women only. LOCATION: At the edge of the sea along the Riviera. 16 rooms w/priv. bath, restaurant, bar, sauna, gym. Rates: £20-£26 pp.

LINDON HOUSE HOTEL
97 Braddons Hill Rd., East, Torquay TQ1 1HF. Tel: (01803) 292-074. TYPE: *Hotel*.   HOST: David & Robert. CLIENTELE: Gay men. LOCATION: Central location, 500 m / yards from the harbor. 7 rooms w/shared bath, restaurant. Rates: on request. *TAC:* 10%.

NORTHERN IRELAND

BELFAST   ✆   0232

✈ Belfast Int'l Airport (BFS) 13 mi. / 20 km west; or Belfast City Airport (BHD) 2 mi. / 3 km east of Belfast

LOCATION: Western Northern Island on the River Lagan.

POPULATION: city 295,000; metro 500,00

DESCRIPTION: Belfast, known as "Athens of the North" is a major port city that grew rapidly during the late 18th and early 19th centuries. The town center is dominated by the large Renaissance style **City Hall**. Visit the **Castle Court**, Ireland's largest covered shopping mall. After many decades of violent religious struggle, Northern Ireland has finally chosen the road for peaceful reconciliation.

Gay Visitor Information
N. Ireland Gay Right Assoc: 664-1111
Lesbian Line: (0232) 238-668
Thur. 7:30pm-10pm

BARS ꓬ RESTAURANTS ꣺

● Bars/clubs (GMW):**Crow's Nest**, mixed clientele, Skipper St. (off High St.); **Parliament Bar**, Dunbar St.; **Limelight**, Ormeau Ave.,; **Pink Beach Club**, Fridays only at the Orpheus, York St. 9; **Cara-Friend**, Cathedral Bldg., Lower Donegall St., drop in Sat. 1:30-5:00pm, ring bell marked CF (322-023).

● Restaurant (AW): **Renshaws**, high quality cuisine, popular neighborhood restaurant, mostly straight clientele, 15 Brunswick St. (333-5555).

✦ ACCOMMODATIONS ✦

RENSHAWS HOTEL
15 Brunswick St., Belfast. USA/Canada reservations/information Tel: (516) 944-5330 or (800) 257-5344. Fax: (516) 944-7540. TYPE: *Hotel*. LOCATION: Suburb of Queen's University, near the Belfast Museum, Botanic Gardens and Railway Station.

* Rooms: 45 w/priv. bath
* CTV, phone, laundry, dry cleaning service
* Parking (on street or private parking)
* Restaurant, bar, conference room
* Gay Bars: some nearby
* Airport: 20 min., bus or taxi
* Open: Year round
* Rates: $110 - $160
* *TAC:* 10% (from Odysseus)

DESCRIPTION: Renovated turn of the century hotel completely restored to its original splendor. Renshaws offer a quiet relaxation at the lovely Victorian terrace and the availability of a city and its amenities.

SCOTLAND

AYR ℂ 01292

LOCATION: 35 mi. / 56 km south of Glasgow.

Gay/Lesbian Visitor Information
G&L Switchboard: 619-000

✦ ACCOMMODATIONS ✦

ROSELAND
15 Charlotte St., Ayr, So. Ayrshire KA7 1DZ. Tel/Fax: (1292) 283435. TYPE: *Bed & Breakfast*. HOST: Ron. CLIENTELE: All Welcome. LOCATION: Near Wellington Square; 2 min. from Seafront. Glasgow 35 mi. / 4 rooms w/shared bath. Rates: £10-£25. DESCRIPTION: Edwardian Town House.

EDINBURGH ℂ 131

✈ Turnhouse Airport (EDI)
6 mi. / 10 km west

LOCATION: Southeast Scotland on the Firth of Forth.

POPULATION: 510,000

CLIMATE: Temperate continental. July average is 70°F (21°c), and January average is 35°F (2°c). Spring and fall have a delightful weather, winters can be foggy with frequent rain or snowfall.

Gay/Lesbian Visitor Information
Gay Switchboard: 556-4049

DESCRIPTION: Edinburgh is the Scottish capital. The beautiful city is dominated by the **Edinburgh Castle** which sits on a rock 270 ft. high (90 m), and has been a fortress since the 11th century. The **'Old Town'** or **Royal Mile** extends from the Castle to **Holyrood Palace**, the Royal residence used by Her Majesty on her visits to Scotland.

The **New Town** development started over two centuries ago - the result is a remarkable grid of spacious crescents and wide streets. Visit the **National Gallery of Scotland**, the **Gallery of Modern Art**, or the **Scottish National Portrait Gallery**. Edinburgh is an ideal place to start and end your vacation in Scotland, from here you can easily explore the rest of this enchanting land; medieval mansions, handsome kilt wearing Scots, 70 mile long Whisky Trail, or the eternal mystery of Loch Ness in the north.

BARS ꓬ RESTAURANTS ꣺

● Bars/clubs (GM): **Cafe Kudos**, stylish bar, young crowd, 22 Greenside Place (556-4349); **CC Blooms**, cafe, bar, disco, karaoke, 23 Greenside Place (556-9331); **Lord Nelson**,the Linden Hotel, 9-13 Nelson St. (557-4344);

Newtown, men only cruise bar, 26 Dublin St. (538- 7775); **Over The Rainbow**, cafe bar, 32C Broughton St. (557-8969); **Route 66**, dance bar, 6 Baxter's Place; **Star Tavern**, 1 Northumberland Place (556-2760).

● Bars/clubs (GW): **Tolerance**, women only monthly disco, call for info (226-4224); **Wee Red Bar**, women's disco once a month, c/o Edinburgh College of Art (557-0751).

● Restaurants (GMW): **Black Bo's**, vegetarian gay friendly restaurant and bar, 57/61 Blackfriars St. (557-6136); **Blue Moon Cafe**, light meals, adjacent to the Gay Community Center, 60-A Broughton St. (556-2788); **Buntoms**, Thai cuisine, at the Hotel Linden, 9/13 Nelson St. (557-4344).

λ SERVICES λ

● Community Center: **Edinburgh Gay Community Center**, 58a Broughton St. Edinburgh EH1 3SA (556-2788).

● Health Club (GM): **Bodytech**, 29a Haddington Place, Leith Walk (557-2294).

ACCOMMODATIONS

AMARYLLIS
5, Upper Gilmore Place, Edinburgh. Tel: (131) 229-4669. TYPE: *Guest House*. HOST: L. Melrose. CLIENTELE: All Welcome. LOCATION: 15 min. from city center. 5 rooms w/shared bath, CTV, phone, C/H. Rates: £14-£20.

LINDEN HOTEL
9/13 Nelson St., Edinburgh EH3 6LF. Tel: (131) 557-4344. TYPE: *Hotel*. CLIENTELE: Gay/ Straight. LOCATION: Close to Centre of Edinburgh, beside Queens Gardens. 20 rooms w/priv. shower, CTV, phone, safe box, C/H, Thai restaurant, lounge bar. Rates: £20-£65. *TAC:* 10%. DESCRIPTION: Townhouse hotel.

MANSFIELD HOUSE
57, Dublin St., Edinburgh EH3 6NL. Tel: (31) 556-7980. USA/Canada: (516) 944-5330 or (800) 257-5344. Fax: (516) 944-7540 or (800) 982-6571. TYPE: *Guest House*. CLIENTELE: Gay men. LOCATION: Centrally located within minutes of bars and clubs.

* Rooms: 5 dbl/sgl w/shared or priv. bath
* Color TV, tea/coffee making facilities
* Open: Year round
* Rates: $90-$120
* *TAC:* 10% (from Odysseus)

DESCRIPTION: Small elegant guest house in a convenient location. Large rooms with one or two double beds. One room with private facilities.

RIMSWELL HOUSE
33 Mayfield Gardens, Edinburgh EH9 2BX. Tel: (131) 667-5851. TYPE: *Hotel*. HOST: Peter T. Fraser. CLIENTELE: Gay/Straight. 20 rooms, 4 w/priv. bath, 16 w/shared bath, CTV, refrigerator, maid service. Rates: £13.50 - £18.50. DESCRIPTION: Low budget hotel.

GLASGOW ✆ 0141

✈ Glasgow Airport (GLA)
Prestwick Airport (PIK)

LOCATION: Southwestern Scotland on the banks of the River Clyde.

POPULATION: 1,700,000

CLIMATE: see Edinburgh

Gay/Lesbian Visitor Information
Switchboard: 221-8372
Lesbian Line: 552-3355

DESCRIPTION: Glasgow is the industrial, commercial and artistic center of Scotland. Built on fourteen hills, it strikes the visitor with a spectacular, almost contemporary skyline. But a second glance reveals a rich historic heritage dating back to the sixth century. Glasgow offers many museums, historic buildings, cultural centers, and great parks. Don't miss the **Scottish Design Center** with its unique shops selling Scottish made goods and craft, with an exhibition area and coffee shop, 72 St. Vincent Street (221-6121).

BARS ▼ RESTAURANTS ▮▮

● Bars/clubs (GMW): **Austin's**, happy hour every evening, 183A Hope St. (332-2707); **Bennets**, dance bar, 80-90 Glassford St. (552-5761); **Club X**, popular with the smarter set, 25 Royal Exchange Sq. (204-4599); **GHQ**, disco/cabaret nightly, 8/10 Queen St. (332-8005); **GLC Cafe**, popular with younger crowd, 11 Dixon St.; **Madame Gillespies**, cabaret, 26 Cheapside St. (226-5468); **Squires**, elegant pub, 106 West Campbell Street (221-9184); **Waterloo**, video bar, 308 Argyle St. (221-7359).

● Bar/club (GW): **Sappho's**, women's bar nightly, Sadie Frost's, 8-10 W. George St. (332-8005).

● Restaurant (GMW): **Delmonicas**, 68 Virginia St. (552-4803); **Eat Out**, licensed cafe, at GHQ, George Sq. (332-7060); **Mother India**, 28 Westminster Terrace, Sauchiehall St. (221-1663).

 ACCOMMODATIONS

CREST HOTEL
377 Argyle St., Glasgow G2 8LL. Tel: (41) 248-2355. TYPE: *Hotel*. CLIENTELE: Mostly Straight. LOCATION: In the center of town, close to bus/air terminal and the central station. Conveniently located to the local gay scene. 121 rooms w/priv. bath, restaurant, bar, lounge. Rates: £50-£78. *TAC:* 8%. DESCRIPTION: Modern hotel in the center of town. Not gay, but convenient to the Glasgow gay scene.

INVERNESS ✆ 047

✈ Dalcross Airport (INV) 9 mi. / 15 km NE.

LOCATION: Northern Scotland, 156 mi. / 250 km north of Edinburgh.

POPULATION: 50,000

CLIMATE: see Edinburgh

DESCRIPTION: Major tourist area of the Scottish Highlands. Enjoy true Scottish folklore such as highland dancing, pipe bands and sexy Scotts in mini-skirts.

ACCOMMODATIONS

AUCHENDEAN LODGE HOTEL
Dulnain Bridge, Grantown-on-Spey, Morayshire PH26 3LU. Tel: (047) 985-347. TYPE: *Hotel*. HOST: Eric Hart & Ian Kirk. CLIENTELE: Gay Welcome. LOCATION: 10 mi. / 16 km from Aviemore. 8 rooms. Rates on request.

URUGUAY

AREA: 157,047 sq. mi. (406,752 sq. km)
POPULATION: 4,500,000
CAPITAL: Asunción
CURRENCY: Uruguay peso (UYU)
OFFICIAL LANGUAGE: Spanish, guarani
MAJOR RELIGIONS: Roman Catholicism
Telephone: 598
Nat'l Holiday: Independence Day, August 25
Official Time: G.M.T-3
Electricity: 220 volts, 50 cycles.
Exchange Rate: 1US$ = peso 8.63
Nat'l Airline: Uruguaya

LAW REGARDING HOMOSEXUALITY:
Homosexuality is not mentioned in the Code of
Law. Since the democratization of the country
in 1985 the status of the local gay population
has improved.

MONTEVIDEO   ✆ 02

✈ Carrasco Airport (MVD)
10 mi. / 16 km northeast

LOCATION: Southern Uruguay on the
Atlantic Ocean.

POPULATION: 1,500,000

CLIMATE: Warm, temperate and slightly
humid. Summer (Dec-Feb) temperatures are in
the 80's°F (26°c). Winter (June-Sept.) temperatures are in the 40°sF (8°F).

DESCRIPTION: Capital city of Uruguay,
Montevideo is the largest city in the country. It
has colonial atmosphere and one of the best
educated population in South America.

❖ Gay Beaches: nine sandy beaches extend
along the metropolitan waterfront from Playa

Ramirez to Playa Carrasco. The gay beaches
are at **Playa Miramar**; and **Playa Turisferia**

❖ **SPECIAL EVENT: Carnaval Week**, 4-8
day celebration ending on February 28.

BARS ▼ RESTAURANTS 🍴

● Bars/clubs (GMW): **Avanti**, Avda Fernandez
Crespo y Lima; **Ecology**, General Paz 1431;
874, dance club, San José 874 (915-040);
Lobizón, Zelmar Michelini 1264 (911-334);
Metropolis, pub, Cerro Lago 1281; **Spok**,
disco/pub, San jose y Santiago de Chile, open
Mon-Fri from 10:00 pm.

● Restaurant (AW): **Doña Flor**, French cuisine, Blvd. Artigas 1034 (785-751); **El
Entrevero**, local cuisine, 2774 21 de Septiembre, Pocitos (700-481); **Le Gavroche**, one of
the city's top French restaurants, 1989 Rivera
(497-371); **Morini**, seafood, on top of the Mercado Central, 1229 Ciudadela (959-733).

λ SERVICES λ

● Sex Shops (G/S): **Atlas II**, Uruguay 1167 (906-
477); **Cinema Yi**, Carlos Quijano 1275, Sariano
(913-368); **Sesh**, Soriano 786 #104 (915-868).

ACCOMMODATIONS 🏠

BALMORAL PLAZA
Plaza Libertad 1126, Montevideo. Tel: (2) 922-
393. TYPE: *Hotel*. CLIENTELE: All Welcome.
LOCATION: Facing Plaza Libertad the main
square in Montevideo.

* Rooms: 75 w/priv. bath, Suites: 3
* CTV (movies), phone, minibar, hairdryer
* 24 hrs. room, laundry & valet service
* Rates: (US) $80-$120

DESCRIPTION: Modern highrise hotel.

INTERNACIONAL HOTEL
Colonia 823, Montevideo. Tel: (2) 920-001.
TYPE: *Hotel*. LOCATION: Centrally 5 min.
from beach and casino.

* Rooms: 95 w/priv. bath, Suites: 5
* CTV, phone, refrigerator, A/C
* 24 hrs. room service
* Restaurant, lounge, free parking
* Airport: 24 mi / 38 km
* Rates: (US) $60-$90

DESCRIPTION: Moderate first class hotel
near theatres and shopping.

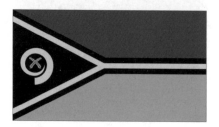

VANUATU

AREA: 5,700 sq. mi. (14,763 sq. km)
POPULATION: 155,000
CAPITAL: Port Vila
CURRENCY: Vatu (VUV)
OFFICIAL LANGUAGE: Bislama, English
MAJOR RELIGIONS: Christianity, animist
Telephone: 678
Nat'l Holiday: Independence Day, July 30
Official Time: G.M.T + 11
Electricity: 220/240 volts, 50 cycles.
Exchange Rate: 1US$ = VT 109.50
Nat'l Airline: Air Vanuatu

LAW REGARDING HOMOSEXUALITY:
Homosexuality between consenting adults is
not mentioned in the Code of Law as a criminal
offense. The local 93% Malenesian population
have no problem dealing with homosexuality.

PORT VILA

✈ Baurefield Airport (VLI)
4 mi. / 6 km north of Port Vila

LOCATION: On the central Efate island
between the picturesque harbor and Erakor
Lagoon. Vanuatu is a Y-shaped chain of 82
islands between New Caledonia and the
Solomon Islands in the South Pacific.

POPULATION: 15,000

CLIMATE: Tropical climate with high temperatures average about 84°F (23°c). Evenings are
usually in a comfortable 70°F (21°c) year round.

DESCRIPTION: Port Villa is the cosmopolitan little capital of Vanuatu. The chic stores
along the port stock elegant Parisian fashion,
but outside town or in further away islands
women wear grass skirts and men only *nambas*
(penis sheaths).

BARS Y RESTAURANTS ¶¶

● Bars/clubs (G/S): **Henri Crocq Bar** at the
La Lagon Hotel, 3 km / 2 mi. from Port Villa
(22313); **Hotel Rossi Bar**, at the Radisson
Royal Palms , Tassiriki Park (22040).

● Restaurant (AW): **Cheng's**, Chinese, Kumul
Hwy, opposite market (24374); **Chez Gilles et
Brigitte**, French cuisine, Pango Rd.; **Water-
front Bar & Grill**, steaks and seafood, Kumul
Hwy (23490).

❖ Entertainment: Casino games are available
at the **Windsor Int'l Hotel** on Kumul Hwy
opposite le Rendez Vous restaurant; and at the
Vanuatu Club behind the post office.

 ACCOMMODATIONS

IRRIKI CENTRE VILLE HOTEL
rue Higginson, Port Villa. Tel: 22464. TYPE:
Hotel. CLIENTELE: All Welcome. LOCATION:
Shopping complex in town center. 21 rooms
w/priv. bath, 4 suites, phone, A/C, coffee maker,
refrigerator, some w/kitchen, restaurant, bar,
free parking. Rates: (US) $90 - $130.
DESCRIPTION: Small stylish hotel in a central location.

KAVITI VILLAGE MOTEL
Port Villa. Tel: 24684. TYPE: *Holiday Village*.
CLIENTELE: All Welcome. LOCATION: 5 minutes from town center. 37 self catering studios
and 2BR apartments, all with kitchen, ceiling
fan and private shower, some with A/C or balcony. Pool and poolside bar, free parking.
Rates: (US) $80-$130.

LE LAGON HOTEL
Erakor Laggon, Port Villa. Tel: 22313. TYPE:
Resort Hotel. CLIENTELE: All Welcome.
LOCATION: 2 mi / 3 km from Port Villa, 4 mi.
/ 6 km from airport. 108 rooms with priv. bath,
6 suites, 28 bungalows, phone, refrigerator,
A/C, room service, restaurants, bar, pool and
poolside bar. Rates: (US)$160-$210. DESCRIP-
TION: Popular resort hotel combining native
designs with contemporary comfort.

WHITE SANDS
Port Villa. Tel: 22090. TYPE: *Bugalow Com-
plex*. CLIENTELE: All Welcome. LOCATION:
On white sandy beach 3/4 mi. / 1 km from Port
Vila. 1-2BR bungalows, refrigerator, bar, ter-
race w/ocean view, restaurant, bar, scuba.
Rates: (US) $60-$110.

VENEZUELA

AREA: 352,143 sq. mi. (912,050 sq. km)
POPULATION: 18,000,000
CAPITAL: Caracas
CURRENCY: Bolívar
OFFICIAL LANGUAGE: Spanish
MAJOR RELIGIONS: Roman Catholicism
Telephone: 58
Nat'l Holiday: Independence Day, 19 April
Official Time: 4 hrs. behind G.M.T
Electricity: 110 volts, 60 cycles.
Exchange Rate: 1US$ = Bolívars 473.25
Nat'l Airline: Viasa

LAW REGARDING HOMOSEXUALITY:
Homosexuality is not mentioned in the
Venezuela Code of Law. Local attitude towards
gays vary from the progressive and liberal in
Caracas, to openly hostile outside the capital.
Although there is an important gay and lesbian
community in Caracas, they are not politically
organized. Venezuelan gay and lesbian bars
have been raided and there are reports that
some of those arrested being physically
assaulted.

CARACAS   © 02

✈ Simon Bolivar Airport (CCS)
   12 mi. / 19 km northeast

LOCATION: Caracas, lies in a small forest
surrounded basin in the Central Highlands
region of Northern Venezuela. The mountains
rise spectacularly from the green Ocean shores
to heights of 2,000 - 3,000 m. (6,600 - 9,900 ft.).

POPULATION: 5,000,000.

CLIMATE: Temperatures are moderate, average 25°c (77°F). July / August maximum temperatures reach 32°c (89°F). Occasional low

temperature of 9°c (66°F) can be registered in
January and February.

DESCRIPTION: Caracas, the capital, was
founded in 1567. It remained a sleepy Spanish
colonial town until Oil was discovered and
brought with it wealth and development. Today
Caracas is the cosmopolitan capital of the richest country in Latin America. Quaint colonial
buildings have given way to high-rise buildings. Sprawling on a narrow 9 mile / 15 km valley, the city is located about 12 miles / 19 km
south of the Caribbean Coast. The city is
known for its mellow weather, and as a gateway to the nearby mountains.

Caracas has three opulent shopping centers:
the **Centro Comercial Tamanaco**; the **Centro Comercial Chacaíto**; or the **Centro
Comercial Sabana Grande**. Interesting open
air markets where you can find fine work by
native artisans include: **Quinta Crespo**; **La
Pastora**; **Chacao** and **El Junquito**. Visit:
Plaza Bolivar, a traditional center with the
statue of Simon Bolivar; **The Capitol**; **The
Cathedral**, just east of the Plaza Bolivar, is
famous for its stained glass windows; **The
National Pantheon**, where the national hero
Bolivar was buried; The **Museo de Arte Con-
temporaneo**, Caracas well known showplace
of modern art collection. **The Plaza
Venezuela** and the section adjoining, **Sabana-
Grande**, are the major areas for nightlife in
Caracas.

BARS ￦ RESTAURANTS ￦

Gay nightlife flourishes in Caracas. Bars open
late 11:00pm and stay open till 6:00am. There
are reports by local gay group of police raiding
gay bars/clubs in Caracas and verbally and
physically mistreating some patrons.

● Bars/clubs (GM): **A Mi Manera**, private
dance club, need passport to enter, c/. Madrid,
Quinta Avileña, Las Mercedes (929-672); **La
Cotorra**, Centro Commercial, Paseo de Las
Mercedes (920-608); **Dos Barras**, bar &
restaurant, callejón Asuncion, Sabana Grande
(729-406); **El Gaban**, Calle San Antonio 38,
Sabana Grande (762-7807); **Ibis Club**, Centro
Commercial Bello Campo, popular with North
Americans 8pm-4am; **Palacio Imperial**, show
bar, Av. Venezuela, El Rosal District; **Le
Punch**, disco, Avda. Casanova, Centro Com-
mercial C-diaz, Sabane Grande; **Hotel
Tomanco Bar**, sunday nights only, Avda Las
Mercedes; **Zig Zag**, most popular club/disco in
Caracas, drag show every sunday, Av. Liberta-
dor, edificio La Linea, near the Crillon Hotel.

● Bars/clubs (GMW): **El Gusto**, bar, in front of Plaza Bolivar Esq. Principal; **Ice Palace**, high tech dance club, Edificio Teatro Altamira (downstairs) 9pm-5:30a (Closed Sunday); **La Tortilla**, bar, Calle San Antonio, Sabana Grande, bet. Av. Abraham Lincoln/Casanova, M° Pl. Venezuela.

● Bar/Club (GW): **Torremolinos**, bar, Callejón Asuncion, Sabana Grande.

● Restaurant (AW): **El Buffet Vegetariano**, vegetarian cuisine, Calle Los Jardines, La Florida; **Le Coq d'Or**, the oldest French restaurant in Caracas, fine food, no reservations accepted, Ave. Los Mangos. Urb. Las Delicias; **Gazebo**, the best restaurant in Caracas featuring Creole cuisine, Ave. Rio de Janeiro. Urb. Las Mercedes (925-568); **Iguana Café & Grill**, Avda Las Mercedes, near El Tolon Park; **El Parque**, informal restaurant where the literati, businessmen and politicians gather, good musical shows and fine food, Parque Central (573-2976).

❖ Gay Beaches: **Camuri Chico** in the suburb seaside resort of La Guaira; **Playa Bahia de Cata** (Maracay, 3 hrs. from Caracas); **Playa Macuto Sheraton** (next to the hotel).

λ SERVICES λ

● Health Club (GM): **Baños Turcos Del Este**, Av. Principal Sabana Grande (corner Torre Miracielo) 9pm-4am; **Baños Turcos Suecos**, c/ el Mango, Urb. San Antonio.

🏨 ACCOMMODATIONS 🏨

PASEO LAS MARCEDES
Av. Principal de las Mercedes, Aptdo 61182, Caracas 1060-A. Tel: (2) 910-444. TYPE: *Hotel*. CLIENTELE: Mostly Straight. LOCATION: In Las Mercedes Shopping Center. 200 rooms w/priv. bath, CTV, phone, A/C, restaurants, lounge, pool w/terrace. Rates: from US$85. *TAC*: 10%. DESCRIPTION: 9-story hotel in fashionable Las Mercedes Shopping Mall, near a popular gay bar. Fine service and helpful staff. The hotel is not gay oriented, it is suggested for your convenience.

TAMANACO INTER-CONTINENTAL
Aptdo 467, Las Mercedes, Caracas. Tel: (2) 924522. TYPE: *Deluxe Hotel*. CLIENTELE: Mostly Straight. LOCATION: Residential section on a hillside 10 min. from downtown and Las Mercedes Mall.

* Rooms: 584 w/private bath, minibar

* Suites: all w/private terrace
* CTV (movies), phone, A/C
* Restaurants, lounges, pool, tennis
* Health Club w/ sauna and massage
* Room & maid service: 24 hrs.
* Gay Beach: 45 min.
* Gay Bars: 10 min.
* Airport: 15 mi. / 25 km, taxi
* Credit Cards: MC/CB/DC/AMEX
* Open: Year round
* Rates: from US$190 and up
* *TAC:* 10%

DESCRIPTION: Deluxe hotel surrounded by tropical gardens. Sunday evenings the mixed cocktail lounges are popular with affluent gays.

ISLA MAGARITA   091

LOCATION: A small island in the Caribbean Ocean off the northern coast of Venezuela.

POPULATION: 200,000

CLIMATE: Exceptionally good, but dry climate year round.

DESCRIPTION: Venezuela's main Caribbean holiday destination with undeveloped beaches, small villages, national parks and fascinating lagoon. Most of the International resort hotels are at **Porlamar**, about 11 km / 7 mi. from the airport.

❖ Gay Beaches: **El Agua Beach**, **Playa Bella Vista**, behind Mosquito Coast (AYOR); **Playa el Morro** in front of Sol Y Mar (AYOR).

BARS 🍸 RESTAURANTS 🍴

There is no established gay scene on the island, although it is popular with American and Canadian gay tourists. The following bars in Parlamar can be of some interest:

● Bars/Clubs (GMW): **Club d'Elite**, dance club, Avda Santiago Marino, Porlamar (at the Margarita Suites Hotel); **Margarita Concorde Hotel bar**, El Morro, Porlamar; **Mosquito Coast**, disco, Avde behind the Bella Vista Hotel; **Village**, Avda Santiago Mariño.

🏨 ACCOMMODATIONS 🏨

MARGARITA CONCORDE HOTEL
El Morro, Parlamar. Tel: (95) 613-333. TYPE: *Resort Hotel*. CLIENTELE: All Welcome.

LOCATION: Overlooking the Caribbean. 475 rooms w/priv. bath, CTV, phon, A/C, restaurants, pool, marina, nightclub. Rates on request.

MARGARITA INT'L RESORT
Av. Bolivar, Urb. Dumar Country Club, Bella Vista. Tel: (95) 614332, TYPE: *All Suite Resort.* CLIENTELE: All Welcome. LOCATION: 1 mi / 2km from downtown, 13 mi / 20 km from the airport. 212 suites 1 or 2BR with full bath, kitchenette, CTV, A/C, phone, balcony, restaurants, bar, 2 pools, gym, sauna. Rates: US$60-$120. DESCRIPTION: First class all suite resort. Nice beach location.

LA GUAIRA / MACUTO
Caracas Beaches   ℭ   02

✈ Simon Bolivar Airport (CCS)

LOCATION: On the Caribbean Sea, only 45 minutes from Caracas if traffic is light.

POPULATION: About 70,000

CLIMATE: Mean temperature 25˚c (84˚F).

DESCRIPTION: **La Guaira** is Venezuela's main port. **Macuto** to the east is the largest, most pleasant seaside resort serving the Caracas population. It has a fine tree lined promenade (Paseo del Mar) and a splendid yacht marina.

❖ Gay Beaches: **Camuri Chico** in the suburb seaside resort of La Guaira; **Playa Bahia de Cata** (Maracay, 3 hrs. from Caracas); **Playa Macuto Sheraton** (next to the hotel).

 ACCOMMODATIONS

MACUTO SHERATON
Aptdo 65, La Guaira, Caraballeda. Tel: (31) 91801/19. Fax: (31) 944-318. TYPE: *First Class Hotel.* CLIENTELE: Mostly Straight. LOCATION: On the beach between the Caribbean Sea and Andes Mtns.

* Rooms: 500 w/private bath. Suites: 9
* Phone, TV, Air-conditioning
* Restaurants, Dining Room
* Pool Side Bar: **El Merinero**, popular with gays and airline crews.
* Disco: **El Cordero**, weekend hot spot for straight couples and closet gays.
* Tennis courts, sauna, steam baths
* Room & maid service

* Beach: near 'gay' beach
* Gay Bars: on premises
* Airport: 15 mi. (24 km)
* Credit Cards: MC/VISA/AMEX/DC/CB
* Open: Year round
* Rates: from US$110
* *TAC:* 10%

DESCRIPTION: The Macuto Sheraton is the gay tourist's best choice. It features a bar and disco where gays can meet, socialize and cruise. Although it lacks a private beach, the nearby municipal beach is a great place to suntan and soak local colors.

MELIA CARIBE HOTEL
Caraballeda Beach, P.O. Box 285, La Guaira. Tel: (31) 945-555. Fax: (31) 941-509. TYPE: First Class Hotel. CLIENTELE: Mostly Straight. LOCATION: On the exclusive Caraballeda Beach, overlooking the Yacht Club.287 rooms w/private bath, CTV, phone, A/C, pool, gym & sauna, Rates: US$120 and up. *TAC:* 10%. DESCRIPTION: Fine hotel on an exclusive beach. Great appeal to international jetsetters, airline crews, and gay travelers. Gay cruising possible with discretion.

PUERTO LA CRUZ   ℭ   081

✈ Barcelona Airport

LOCATION: Caribbean Coast east of Caracas.

DESCRIPTION: A bustling commercial port and resort city with lovely beaches and excellent weather year round. Easy connection to nearby islands including Isla Margarita (4 hrs by ferry).

 BARS Y RESTAURANTS ¶

● Bars/Clubs (GMW): **Con Sabor Latino**, dance club, c/ Bollivar (Edificio Alsyru, 2F); **El Hato**, c/ Democracia 6.

 ACCOMMODATIONS

DORAL BEACH HOTEL
Av. Americo Vespucio, Puerto La Cruz. Tel: (81) 812222. TYPE: *Hotel & Villas.* CLIENTELE: All Welcome. LOCATION: Beachfront on the El Morro peninsula. 1312 rooms and villas w/priv. bath, CTV, phone, phone, terrace, restaurants, coffee shop, pool, island cruises nearby. DESCRIPTION: Moderate first class holiday complex.

AREA: 188,321 sq. mi. (487,792 sq. km)
POPULATION: 13,500,000
CAPITAL: San'a
CURRENCY: Yemeni Rial (Yr)
OFFICIAL LANGUAGE: Arabic
MAJOR RELIGIONS: Islam
Telephone: 967
Nat'l Holiday: Revolution Day, Sept. 26
Official Time: GMT+ 3
Electricity: 220 / 240v 50c AC
Exchange Rate: 1US$ = Yr 120
Nat'l Airline: Yemenia Airways

LAW REGARDING HOMOSEXUALITY:
Yemen is an Islamic state. The law regarding
homosexuality in this country is similar to the
law in Egypt or Jordan. Homosexuality (for gay
men) isn't 'morally' approved among the people
of the country. It is advisable not to display
homosexual behavior in public and be very cautious when dealing with the local population.
In privacy however this is not much of a problem.

❖ **Note:** international telephone is available in
all cities in Yemen. But international calls are
very expensive. A call to the USA costs about
US$3 per minute and to fax US$4 per page.

SANA'A   © 01

✈ Sana'a Int'l AP (SAH) 15 mi. / 20 km north

LOCATION: Centrally located in the Republic
of Yemen

POPULATION: 160,000

CLIMATE: Climate varies considerably with
altitude and geological nature of the location.
The coastal plain is hot, humid and dusty. The

highlands are more pleasant in the summer
and moderately cold in winter. The rainy season is between July and September.

DESCRIPTION: Sana'a a city of 64 minerats
is one of the world's first human settlements. A
world heritage city and one of Arabia's oldest
living cities, supposedly founded by Shem, one
of the three sons of Noah. In the second century it was the main highland garison town of the
Sabean Kingdom. The city name Sana'a meant
"fortified place". The old city of Sana'a with its
amazing architecture contains houses that are
more than 400 years old. Visit: **Suq al-Milh**
Sana's main market where a wide variety of
goods are on sale; **Bab-el-Yemen**, the main
gate to the city; **The National Museum** formerly a royal palace from the 1930's with articrafts
of the ancient Kingdoms of Saba, Marib, Main,
and Hymyar; and the exotic **Turkish baths**.

❖ Public cruising (AYOR): **Abdul Nasar St.**;
Abdul Mohni St.; and **Bab el Yemen
Square**.

 ACCOMMODATIONS

SULTAN PALACE HOTEL
Sana'a city. USA/Canada reservation/informa-
tion - Odysseus (800) 257-5344 or (516) 944-
5330. Fax: (516) 944-7540. TYPE: *Hotel*.
CLIENTELE: All Welcome. LOCATION: Heart
of the Old City near downtown.

* Rooms: 15 w/shared bath
* Restaurant: Yemeni food & western cuisine
* Yemeni musical soiree on demand
* Open: Year round
* Rates: on request
* *TAC:* 10% (from Odysseus)

DESCRIPTION: Yemeni style tourist hotel
with enviable good reputation. The house of an
ancient Sultan coserving the culture and history of Yemen's ancient ancestors. Famous
evenings for tourists with Yemeni traditional
music and dance.

ZIMBABWE

AREA: 150,803 sq. mi. (390,580 sq. km)
POPULATION: 11,000,000
CAPITAL: Harare
CURRENCY: Zimbabwe Dollar (Z$)
OFFICIAL LANGUAGE: English, Shona
MAJOR RELIGIONS: Tribal, Protestantism
Telephone: 263
Nat'l Holiday: Independence Day, April 18
Official Time: GMT +2
Electricity: 220 / 240v 50c AC
Exchange Rate: 1US$ = Z$10.76
Nat'l Airline: Air Zimbabwe

LAW REGARDING HOMOSEXUALITY:
Homosexuality between adult males over 18 is
not a crime, but sodomy is. The climate for
homosexuals in Harare has worsened recently.
According to the president of Zimbabwe Mr.
Robert Mugabe Homosexuals have no legal
rights in Zimbabwe and are "worse than pigs or
dogs". Homosexuality, according to the president, is a white vice imported with the British
Colonialism. Black lesbians have the hardest
time in this male-dominated society. Many are
forced to get married and raise children.

HARARE   *C*   04

✈ Harare Airport (HRE) 7.5 mi / 12km south

LOCATION: North Zimbabwe.

POPULATION: 1,000,000

CLIMATE: Temperate conditions year round,
moderated by the country's altitude and its
inland position. October is the hottest month
with high daily temperatures in the 30°sC (mid
80°sF); Mid-winter temperatures in July are
around 15°sC (60°sF).

DESCRIPTION: Harare is the capital and the
largest city in Zimbabwe. It is divided like
many other towns into a commercial center
with its sprawling white suburbs and the high
density black townships. Much of the city's
activity concentrates in **Mbare musika** the
country's largest market and bus terminal. On
Sundays visit the popular **arts and crafts
market** in the Harare Public Gardens. The
small gay community finds it very difficult to
organize and fights for the rights of gay men
and lesbians in the prevailing "gay bashing"
atmosphere.

❖ Public cruising (AYOR): **Central Park
Ramble**; **The Botanical Gardens**; **Cecil
Square**.

BARS ☩ RESTAURANTS ⑪

● Bars/clubs (G/S): **Archipelgo**, popular with
white Zimbabwens, in Liquenda House, 58
Baker Street; **Sandro's**, Union Ave. / Julius
Niere Way; **Sahara's Club**, near the Sheraton
Hotel, Stanley Ave. (704-637); **Sportsman's
Bar**, at Jameson Hotel building, Union Ave.

● Restaurants (AW): **Holiday Inn Restaurant**, all you can eat buffet breakfast, Samora
Machel Ave.; **Homegrown**, all-you-can-eat
salad bar, Speke Ave. near Leopold Takawira
St; **Sheratons Hotel Restaurant**, great
lunch and dinner buffets, Pennefather Ave.;
Terrace Restaurant, sunny café on the 3rd
level of Barbour's Dept. Store.

❖ Gay Beach: **City Swimming Pool**

 ACCOMMODATIONS

HOLIDAY INN
Samora Machel Ave. & Fifth St., Harare. Tel:
(4) 795-611. Fax: (4) 735-695. TYPE: *Hotel*.
CLIENTELE: Mostly Straight. LOCATION:
City center, 3 km / 2 mi. from the Botanical
Gardens. 178 rooms w/priv. bath, CTV, phone,
minibar, balcony, 24 hrs. room service, restaurant, lounge, nightclub, outdoor pool. Rates:
$110 - $220.

SHERATON HARARE HOTEL
Pennefather Ave., Harare. Tel: (4) 729-771.
Fax: (4) 728-450. TYPE: *Hotel*. CLIENTELE:
Mostly Straight. LOCATION: downtown hotel
near city center. 309 rooms w/priv. bath, CTV,
phone, minibar, 24 hrs. room service, restau-
rant, coffee shop, outdoor pool, sauna, gym.
Rates: $140-$315.

AIRLINES

Aer Lingus	1-800-223-6537
Aeroflot	1-800-995-5555
Aerolineas Argentinas	1-800-333-0276
Aeromexico	1-800-237-6639
Aero Peru	1-800-255-7378
Air Aruba	1-800-677-7888
Air Canada	1-800-776-3000
Air France	1-800-237-2747
Air India	1-800-223-7776
Air Jamaica	1-800-523-5585
Air Malta	1-800-756-2582
Air Nevada	1-800-634-6377
Air New Zealand	1-800-262-1234
Air Sunshine	1-800-327-8900
Alaska Airlines	1-800-426-0333
Alitalia	1-800-223-5730
All Nipon Airways (ANA)	1-800-235-9262
ALM-Antillean Airlines	1-800-327-7230
Aloha Airlines	1-800-227-4900
American Airlines	1-800-433-7300
America West	1-800-235-9292
Ansett (Australia)	1-800-366-1300
Asiana	1-800-227-4262
Austrian Airlines	1-800-843-0002
Avensa (Venezuela)	1-800-428-3672
Avianca	1-800-284-2622
Bahamas Air	1-800-222-4262
British Airways	1-800-247-9297
BWIA	1-800-327-7401
Canadian Int'l	1-800-426-7000
Cape Air	1-800-352-0714
Carnival Airlines	1-800-824-7386
Cathay Pacific	1-800-233-2742
Cayman	1-800-422-9626
China	1-800-227-5118
Continental	1-800-525-0280
Delta	1-800-221-1212
El Al Israel	1-800-223-6700
Empire Airways	1-800-392-9233
Ecuatoriana	1-800-328-2367
Finnair	1-800-950-5000
Garuda (Indonesia)	1-800-342-7832
Gulf Air	1-800-553-2824
Hawaiian	1-800-367-5320
Iberia	1-800-772-4642
Icelandair	1-800-223-5500
Japan	1-800-525-3663
KLM	1-800-374-7747
Korean Air	1-800-438-5000
Lan Chile	1-800-244-5366
Lot Polish	1-800-223-0593
Lufthansa	1-800-645-3880
Malaysia Airlines	1-800-421-8641
Malev Hungarian	1-800-262-5380
Martinair	1-800-627-8462
Mexicana	1-800-531-7921
MGM Grand Air	1-800-275-4646
Midwest Express	1-800-452-2022
Mount Cook (NZ)	1-800-468-2665
Northwest Airlines	1-800-225-2525
Olympic	1-800-223-1226
Philippine	1-800-435-9725
Quantas	1-800-227-4500
Royal Air Maroc	1-800-292-0081
Sabena	1-800-955-2000
Saudi Arabian	1-800-472-8342
Scandinavian (SAS)	1-800-221-2350

Singapore	1-800-742-3333
SAA	1-800-722-9675
Southwest	1-800-531-5601
Swissair	1-800-221-4750
TAP	1-800-221-7370
Thai Airways	1-800-426-5204
Tower Air	1-800-452-5531
TWA, TWA Express	1-800-221-2000
United	1-800-241-6522
US Air	1-800-428-4322
UTA-French Airlines	1-800-282-4484
Varig Brazilian Airlines	1-800-468-2744
VIASA	1-800-327-5454
Virgin Atlantic	1-800-862-8621

BOOKSTORES

AUSTRALIA
Adelaide (08)
Imprints Booksellers, 80 Hindley, Adelaide. 8531-4454.
Melbourne (03)
The Beat, 157 Commercial Rd., Prahran. 9241-8748.
FOE Bookshop, 222 Smith St., Collingwood. 9419-8700.
Gemini Adult Bookshop, 164 Acland St., St. Kilda. 9534-6074.
Hares & Hyeneas, 135-137 Commercial Rd., So. Yarra. 9824-0110 also 360 Brunswick St., Fitzroy 9419-4445.
Hartwig's Books, 245 Brunswick St. Fitzroy. 9417-7147.
International Bookshop, 2nd fl., 17 Elizabeth St. 9614-2859.
Readings Bookshop, Toorak Rd., So. Yarra. 9866-8586.
Perth (08)
Arcane Bookshop, 212 William St., Northbridge. 9328-5073.
Sydney (02)
The Bookshop, 207 Oxford St., Darlinghurst. 9331-1103.
The Bookshop Newtown, 186 King St., Newtown. 9514-244.
Gleebooks, 191 Glebe Point Rd., Glebe. 9660-2578.

AUSTRIA
Salzburg (0662)
American Discount, Alter Market 1. 845-640
Vienna (01)
American Discount, Rechte Wienzeile 5, Wien 4. 587-5772; Neubaugasse39. 523-3707; Donaustadt-stasse1, 203-9518.
Shakespeare & Co., Sterngaße 2. 535-5053

BELGIUM
Antwerpen (03)
Groene Waterman, Wolstratt 7. 232-9394
Brussels (02)
Artemys, Galerie Boritiergalerij 8 (near Central Station) 512-0347.
Chez Ingride, Rue Théodore Verhaegenstraat 136. 534-1898.
Librairie Darakan, Rue du Midi / Zuidstraat 9. 512-2076.
Librairie FM-Presse, Rue d'Arenbergstraat 40. 512-9684.

CANADA
Calgary (403)
Calgary Books 'n Books, 738A 17th Ave SW. 228-3337.
A Woman's Place, 1412 Center St., South. 263-5256.
Montréal (514)
L'Androgyne, 3636 St-Laurent, H2X 2V4. 842-4765.

○ **Priape**, Montréal's #1 gay shop, books, videos, clothing, gifts and much more. 1311 Ste-Catherine E., H2L 2J5. 521-8451.
Ottawa (613)
After Stonewall, 105- 4th Ave., 2nd fl., ON K0A 1V0. 567-2221.
Ottawa Women's Bookstore, 272 Elgin St., ON K2P 1M2 (613) 230-1156.
Toronto (416)
Glad Day Bookshop, 598A Yonge St., M4Y 1Z3. 961-4161.
○ **Priape**, books, videos, clothing, gifts and much more. 465 Church St., ON M4Y 2C5. 586-9914.
This Ain't The Rosedale Library, 483 Church St., M4Y 2C6. 929-9912.
Toronto Women's Bookstore, 73 Harbord. 922-8744.
Vancouver (604)
Blacksheep Books, 2742 W. 4th Ave. 732-5087.
Little Sisters Books & Art, 1221 Thurlow St., V6E 1X4. 669-1753.
Victoria
Everywoman's Books, 641 Johnson St. (604) 388-9411.

DENMARK
Copenhagen
Pan, Knabrostræde 3. 3311-1961.

FINLAND
Helsinki (090)
Baffin Books, Eerikinkatu 33694-7078.

FRANCE
Paris (01)
Funambule, 48 rue Jean-Pierre Timbaud (10th) 4806-7494).
Kiosque de Forum, 10 rue Pierre Lescot (1st) 4026-3704.
Kiosque des Amis, 29 Blvd. des Italiens (2nd) 4265-0094.
Les Mots à la Bouche, 6, rue Ste Croix de la Bretonnerie. 4278-8830.
Librarie des Artistes, 23 Blvd. Clichy (9th) 4282-1190.
Librarie des Femmes, 74 rue de Seine (6th) 4329-5075.
Librarie Erotique Kama Sutra, 19 rue Pierre Lescot (1st). 4026-2183

GERMANY
Berlin (030)
Adam, Jungstraße 31. 292-3089
Bruno's, Kurfürstendamm 227 Ku'damm-Eck, 1st fl. 882-4290.
Prinz Eisenherz Buchalden, Bleibtreustraße 52, D-10623 Berlin. 313- 9936.
Cologne (0221)
Der Andere Buchladen, Wahlenstraße 1. 520-579
Ganymed, Kettengaße 3. 251-110
Düsseldorf (0211)
Gegen des Strich, Bilker Straße 23A. 323-7938
Schrobsdorff'sche Buchandlung, Königsalee 22. 84-211.
Frankfurt (069)
Land in Sicht, Rotteckstraße 11-13. 443095
Oscar Wilde, Alte Gaße 51. 281260
Wohlthat Cultur-Centrale, Neue Kräme 14-16. 280-064.
Hamburg (040)
Blendwerk, Lange Reihe 113. 240-003
Männerschwarm, Neuer Pferdemarkt 32. 436-093.
Revolt Shop, Clemens-Schultz-St. 77. 312-848.
Munich (089)
Max & Milian, Ickstattstraße 2. 260-3320

IRELAND
Dublin (01)
Books Upstairs, 36 College St., 796-687.
Waterstones, 7 Dawson St. 679-1415
Winding Stair, 40 Lower Ormond Quay. 873-3292

ITALY
Florence (055)
Magic America, via Guelfa 89-91/R. 212-840
Milano (02)
Libreria Babele, Via Sammartini 21, 20125 Milano. 669 2986.
Magic America, via Legnone 19, 20158 Milano 688-1057.
Padova (049)
Il Mercatino, via Accademia 2. 875-4898

JAPAN
Osaka (06)
E.T.C. Box, Shin Doyama Bldg. 1F, 11-2 Doy-ma-cho, Kita-ku, Osaka 530. 316-0095.
Tokyo (03)
Apple Inn, 1-13-5 Shimbashi, 2F, Minato-ku, Tokyo 105. 3574-1477.
Books Rose, Yamahara Heights, B1, 2-12-15 Shinjuku, Shinjuku-ku, Tokyo 160. 3341-0600.
Cavalier, Muraki Bldg., B1, 3-11-2 Shinjuku, Shinjuku-ku, Tokyo 160. 3354-7976; 3354-7976.
Lumiere, Sunflower Bldg., 1F, 2-17-1 Shinjuku, Shinjuku-ku, Tokyo 160. 3352-3378.
Memoire, 2-14-8 Shinjuku, Shinjuku-ku, Tokyo 160. 341-1775.
Paradise, (Hokuo Shoji) 2-13-3 Yoyogi, Shibuya-ku, Tokyo 151. 3370-5641.

NETHERLANDS
Amsterdam (20)

○ **The American Book Center**, center of Amsterdam near many gay bars, for books in English only, special gay & lesbian books & magazines section in the basement. Also mail order, gifts and videos. Open: Mon-Sat 10am-8pm, Thurs 10am-10pm, Sun 11am-6pm, Kalverstraat 185. Tel: 625-5537. Fax: 624-8042. E-mail: base@abc.nl. Internet: http://www.abc.nl/gaypage.html
The Bronx, Kerkstraat 53-55, 1017 GC. 623-1548.
Bruna, Leiderstraat 89. (020) 622-0578.
○ **Drake's**, Damrak 61, 1012 LM. 627-9544, Fax: 627-6702.

○ **Intermale**, Europe's largest gay bookstore, large selection of (English language) books on a diversity of subjects relating to homo sexuality. Write for a free brochure, Spuistraat 251, 1012 VR Amsterdam. Tel: 625-0009. Fax: 620-3163.
Salon International, Nieuwendijk 20-22, 622-6565.
Vrolijk, Paleisstraat 135. 623-5142.

Den Haag (70)
○ **The American Book Center**, books in English only, special gay & lesbian books & magazines section. Also mail order, gifts and videos. Open: regular store hours, Lange Poten 23, 2511 CM, The Hague. 364-2742. Fax: 365-6557. E-mail: base@abc.nl. Internet: http://www.abc.nl/gaypage.html
Roode Hond, Prins Hendrikstraat 138. 364-88861.
Ruward, Spuistraat 231. 363-0879.
Rotterdam (010)
Boekenbeurs, 1e Middellandstraat 23. 412-5640.

NEW ZEALAND
Auckland (09)
OUT! Bookshop, 45 Anzac Ave. Auckland. (09) 377-7770.
Onehunga Book Exchange, 163 The Mall, Onehunga. 622-1766
Christchurch (03)
David's Book Exchange, 181 High St. 366-2057
OUT! Bookshop, c/o Colombo Health Club, 661 Colombo St. 667-352.
Menfriends, Upstairs 83 Lichfield st. 377-1701
Wellington (04)
OUT! Bookshop, Dixon St., & Cuba Mall, 1st fl. (next to Alfie's) 584-400.

NORWAY
Oslo (02)
Gay International, Rodstegate 2, Oslo 1. 203-736.
Tronsmo Bokhandel, Kristian August Gate 19, 0130 Oslo. 202-509.

SOUTH AFRICA
Johannesburg (011)
Exclusive Books, 48 Pretoria St., Hillbrow, Johannesburg. 642-5068.
Phambili Books, 55 Kruis St., Johannesburg. 29-4944.
Tadpole Books, PO Box 1893, Houghton 2041. 883-9740
Pretoria (012)
Adam, 226 Duncan St. 342-4395

SPAIN
Barcelona (93)
Sextienda, Calle Raurich 11, 08002, Barcelona. 318-8676.
Zeus, Riera Alta 20, 08001 Barcelona. (93) 442-9795.
Madrid (91)
Libreria Berkana, Gay & Lesbian bookstore, C/. La Palma 39, 28004 Madrid (532-1393).
Seville (95)
Internacional Sex Shop, Calle Sierpes 34 (Galeria).

SWEDEN
Gothunberg
Rosa Rummet, Esperantoplatsen 7.
Stockholm (08)
Rosa Rummet, Sveavägen 57. 736-0215.

SWITZERLAND
Basel (061)
Arcados, Rheingaße 69. 681-3132.
Kiosk 18, Schneidergaße 18, Basel 4051. 251-986.
Bern (031)
Loveland, Gerechtigkeitsgaße 39. 22-4533.
Zurich (01)
BS-Laden, Anwandstraße 67. 241-0441.
Wild House, Spitalgaße 12. 251-9140.

UNITED KINGDOM
Brighton (1273)
Out! Brighton, 4 & 7 Dorset St.., off Edward St. 623-356.
Public House Bookshop, 21 Little Preston St., 28-357.
Edinburgh (131)
Better Books, 11 Forrest Rd. 225-1515.
West and Wilde Bookshop, 25a Dundas St., Edinburgh EH3 6QQ. 556-0079.
Glasgow (141)
Changes Bookshop, 340 W. Princess St. 357-3631.
Third Eye Centre, 350 Sauchihall St.
Liverpool (151)
News from Nowhere, 100 Whitechapel Rd., Liverpool L1 6EN. 708-7270.
London (171)
Clone Zone, 1 Hogarth Rd., Earls Court, SW5. 373-0598.
Colletts Int'l Bookshop, 129-131 Charing Cross Rd, WC2. 734-0782.
Gay's The Word, 66 Marchmont St., W.C. 1. 278-7654.
Studio 40, 40 Berwick St., London W1V 3RE. 437-0811.
Manchester (161)
Clone Zone, 37/39 Bloom St., The Basement. 236-1398.
Cornerhouse Books, 6-8 Oxford Rd. 228-7621.

USA

ALABAMA
Birmingham (205)
Lodestar Books, 2020 11th Ave. S., 939-3356.

ALASKA
Anchorage (907)
Alaska's Women's Bookstore, 2440 E. Tudor Rd., Frontier Mall. 562-4716.
Bona Dea, 2440 E. Tudor Rd., 562-4716.
Cyrano's, 413 'D'St. 274-2599.

ARIZONA
Mesa (602)
Borders Books & Music, 1361 S. Alma School Rd., Mesa, AZ 85210. 833-2244.
Phoenix (602)
The Adult Shoppe,111 S. 24th St. Phoenix, AZ 85034. 306-1130.

Castle Boutique, 24 hrs., 5501 E. Washington. 231-9837.
Obelisk, 24 W. Camelback, Suite A. Phoenix, AZ 85013. 266-2665.
The Short Skirt, 33 W. Camelback Rd. 235-9610.
Unique on Central, 4700 N. Central Ave., Phoenix, AZ 85012. 279-9691.

Tempe

The Book Connection, 6434 S. McClintock Dr., Tempe AZ 85283 (602) 820-2953.

Tucson

Antigone Books, 403 E. 5th St. (520) 792-3715.

ARKANSAS
Little Rock (501)

Twisted Entertainment, 7201 Asher Ave. 568-4262
Wild Card, 400 N. Bowman. 223-9071.
Women's Project, 2224 Main St. 372-5113.

CALIFORNIA
Laguna Beach (714)

A Different Drummer, 1294C S. Coast Hwy, Laguna Beach, CA 92651. 497-6699. Fax: (714) 497-0471. email: ddrummer@ix.netcom.com

Los Angeles (213/310)

A Different Light, 4014 Santa Monica Blvd., Los Angeles, CA 90029. (213) 668-0629.
A Different Light, 8853 Santa Monica Blvd. (310) 854-6601.
Books on the Edge, 2433 Main St., Santa Monica (310) 399-3399.
Circus of Books , 8230 Santa Monica Blvd., (310) 656-6533; 4001 Sunset Blvd., Silverlake. (213) 666-1304.
Drake's, 7566 Melrose Ave., Los Angeles, CA 90028. (213) 651-5600.
Either Or Bookstore, 124 Pier Ave., Hermosa Beach (310) 374-2060.
Lavender Books,1213 N. Highland Ave., (213) 464-0029.
Pleasure Chest, 7733 Santa Monica Blvd. (213) 650-1022.
Unicorn Bookstore, 8940 Santa Monica Blvd., West Hollywood, CA 90069. (310) 652-6253.

Long Beach (310)

Chelsea Books, 2501 E. Broadway. 434-2220
Dodd's Bookshop,4818 E. 2nd St.438-9948
Hot Stuff, 2121 E. Broadway. 433-0692
Pearls Booksellers, 224 Redondo Ave. 438-8875.

Oakland/Berkeley (510)

Mama Bears Culture Center, 6536 Telegraph Ave. 848-8443.

Palm Springs (619)

Bloomsbury Books, 555 S. Sunrise Way #105, Palm Springs, CA 92264. 325-3862
Between The Pages Bookstore, 214 E. Arenas Rd., Palm Springs, CA 92262. (619) 320-7158
Perez, 68-366 Perez Rd. 321-5597
Worldwide Books, 68-300 Ramon Rd., Cathedral City, CA 92234 (619) 321-1313

Sacramento (916)

Lioness Books, 2224 J St.,442-4657.

San Diego (619)

Blue Door Bookstore, 3823 5th Ave., San Diego, CA 92103. 298-8610.
Obelisk The Bookstore, 1029 University Ave. San Diego, CA 92103. 297-4171.

San Francisco (415)

A Different Light, 489 Castro St., San Fran-cisco, CA 94114. 431-0891
Bernal Books, 401 Cortland Ave. 550-0293
Good Vibrations, 1210 Valencia St. 550-7399
Le Salon, 1118 Polk St. 673-4492.

Modern Times Bookstore, 888 Valencia St., San Francisco, CA 94110. 282-9246.
Small Press Traffic, 3599 24th St. 281-9338.

COLORADO
Denver (303)

Category Six, 1029 E. 11th Ave. Denver, CO 80218. 832-6263.
Tattered Cover, 2955 E. 1st Ave. 322-7727.

CONNECTICUT
Hartford (203)

MetroStore, 493 Farmington Ave. 231-8845.
Reader's Feast, 529 Farmington Ave., Hart-ford, CT 06105. 232-3710.

DELAWARE
Rehoboth Beach (302)

Lambda Rising, 39 Baltimore Ave., Rehoboth Beach, DE 19971. 227-6969.

DISTRICT OF COLUMBIA
Washington D.C. (202)

Lambda Rising, gay & lesbian books and magazines, 1625 Connecticut Ave., NW, Washington, D.C. 20009. 462-6969. Toll Free (800) 621-6969. Fax: 462-7257.
The Map Store, 1636 'I' St., NW 628-2608.
Kramerbooks & Afterwards, 1517-21 Connecticut Ave. NW. 387-1400.
Lammas Women's Shop, 1426 21st St NW (near Dupont Circle), Washington, D.C. 20036. 775-8218.

FLORIDA
Fort Lauderdale (305)

Outbooks, 1239 E. Las Olas Blvd., 764-4333

Key West (305)

Bargain Books & News, 1028 Truman Ave. 294-7446.
Bookstore Named Desire, 420 Applerouth Lane. 296-1000.
Blue Heron Books, 538 Truman Ave. 296-3508.
Caroline St., Books & Cafe, 800 Caroline St. 294-3931.
Key West Island Books, 513 Fleming St., 294-2904.
Leather Master, 418-A Applerouth Lane. 292-5051.

Miami / Miami Beach (305)

GW Miami Beach, 718 Lincoln Rd., Mall, Miami Beach. 534-4763.
Lambda Passages, 7545 Biscayne Blvd. Miami, FL 33138. 754-6900.

Orlando (407)

Alobar, 709 W. Smith St. 841-3050.
Out & About Books, 930 N. Mills Ave., 896-0204.

St. Petersburg (813)

Brigit Books, 3434 4th St. N. 522-5775.
Lifestyle Books, 3150 5th Ave. N. 323-5857.

Tampa (813)

Tomes & Treasures, 202 1/2 South Howard Ave., Tampa, FL 33606. 251-9368.

GEORGIA
Atlanta (404)

Borders Bookshop, 3655 Roswell Rd., Tuxedo Festival, Atlanta, GA 30342. 237-0707.
Brushstrokes, Ansley Square, Atlanta, GA 30324. 876-6567.
Charis Books & Moore, 1189 Euclid Ave. 524-0304.
Outwrite, 931 Monroe Drive, Suite #108, Atlanta, GA 30308. 607-0082. Fax: 607-0092. Philip Rafshoon, pres.
Phoenix & Dragon, 5531 Roswell Rd., Sandy Springs. 255-5207
Poster Hut, 2175 Cheshire Bridge Rd., Atlanta, GA 30324. 633-7491.

HAWAII
Honolulu (808)
Eighty Percent Straight, 2131 Kuhio Ave. Honolulu HI 96815. 923-9996.

ILLINOIS
Chicago (312)
People Like Us, 3321 North Clark Street, Chicago, IL 60657. 248-6363.
Unabridged Bookstore, 3251 North Broad-way, Chicago, IL 60657. 883-9119.

INDIANA
Indianapolis (317)
Bookland, 137 W. Market St. 639-9864.
Dreams & Swards, 828 E. 64th St., 253-9966.

LOUISIANA
Baton Rouge (504)
Hibiscus Bookstore, 635 Main St., Baton Rouge, LA 70802. 387-4264.
New Orleans (504)
Faubourg Marigny Books, 600 Frenchmen St., New Orleans, LA 70116. 943-9875.
Sidney's Newstand, 917 Decatur. 524-6872.

MAINE
Portland (207)
Ananael, 521 Congress St. 780-0830.

MARYLAND
Baltimore (410)
Lambda Rising, 241 West Chase St., Baltimore, MD 21201. 234-0069 or (800) 621-6969. Fax: (202) 462-7257.
Louie's Bookstore Café, 518 N. Charles St., Baltimore, MD 21201. 962-1224.

MASSACHUSETTS
Boston (617)
Glad Day Bookshop, 673 Boylston St. Boston, MA 02116. 267-3010. Fax: (617) 267-5474.
Globe Corner, 1 School St. 523-6658.
New Words, 186 Hampshire St., Cambridge, MA 02139. 876-5310.
Unicorn Books, 1210 Massachusetts Ave., Arlington. 646-3680.
Waterstone's, 26 Exeter. 859-7300
We Think the World of You, 540 Tremont St. 423-1965.
Wordsworth, 30 Brattle St. 354-5201
Northampton (413)
Pride & Joy, 20 Crafts Ave., Northampton, MA 01060. 585-0683.
Provincetown (508)
Now Voyager, 357 Commercial St., Provincetown, MA 02657.487-0848.
Provincetown Bookshop, 246 Commercial St., 487-2313.
Recovering Hearts, Books & Gifts, 4 Stan-dish St., 487-4875.

MICHIGAN
Ann Arbor (313)
Borders Books, 303 S State St. 668-7652.
Common Language, 214 S 4th Ave. 663-0036.
Detroit (810)
Chosen Books, 120 W. 4th St., Royal Oak MI 48067. 543-5758.

Grand Rapids
Sons & Daughters, 962 Cherry St., NE, Grand Rapids, MI 49503. 458-2123.

MINNESOTA
Minneapolis (612)
A BrothersTouch, 2327 Hennepin Ave., Minneapolis, MN 55405. 377-6279.
Amazon Bookstore, 1612 Harmon Pl., Minneapolis, MN 55403. 338-6560.

MISSOURI
St. Louis (314)
Left Bank Books, 399 N Euclid Ave. 367-6731.
Our World Too, 11 So. Vandeventer, St. Louis, MO 63108. 533-5322.

MONTANA
Missoula (406)
Fantasy for Adults only,2611 Brooks St., Missoula, MT 59801. 543-7760.

NEBRASKA
Omaha (402)
New Realities,1026 Howard St. NB 68102. 342-1863.

NEVADA
Las Vegas (702)
Get Booked, 4640 Paradise. 737-7780.
Reno (702)
Grapevine Books, 1450 S. Wells Ave. Reno, NV 89502. 786-4869.

NEW JERSEY
Denville (201)
Perrin& Treggett Bookseller , 3130 Route. 10 West Denville, NJ 07834. 328-8811.
Englewood (201)
Pandora Book Peddlers, 9 Waverly Place. Madison, NJ 07940. 822-8388.

NEW MEXICO
Albuquerque (505)
Full Circle Books, 2205 Silver SE, Albuquerque, NM 87106. 266-0022
Madrid (505)
○ **Diva Divine**, exotic, esoteric gift boutique celebrating the sensual with body products, gifts, erotic and spiritual jewelry, books, B&D toys, leather & PVC clothing and accessories, adult sex toys. A luscious empo-rium of smells, sounds and colors. Open daily - 10am - 5pm, 2850 State Hwy 14 (438-4360). Email: diva@nets.com
Santa Fe (505)
Galisteo News, 201 Galisteo Street Santa Fe. NM 87501. 984-1316.

NEW YORK
Albany (518)
Romeo's, 299 Lark St. 434-4014
Video Central, 37 Central Ave. 463-4153
Ithaca (607)
Borealis Bookstore, 111 No. Aurora St. 272-7752
Long Island (516)
Heaven Sent Me, 108 Cain Dr., Hauppauge, Industrial Park. 434-4777

New York City (212)

A Different Light, large selection of gay & lesbian books, magazines & videos, 151 W. 19th St. 989-4850. Order (800) 343-4002.

Ann Street, Adult Entertainment Center, large selection of videos, magazines and toys, 21 Ann Street (Btwn. B'way & Nassau) 267-9760.

Christopher Street, large selection of videos, magazines and toys,500 Hudson St. (at Christopher St.) 463-0657.

○ **Les Hommes Book Shop**, large selection of videos, magazines and toys,217 West, 80th St., (Btwn. B'way & Amsterdam).

Oscar Wilde Memorial Bookshop, 15 Christopher St., NY 10014. 255-8097.

NORTH CAROLINA
Charlotte (704)

○ **White Rabbit Books & Things**, large selection of gay & lesbian books and magazines, 314 Rensselaer Ave #1 377-4067.

Greensboro (910)

○ **White Rabbit Books & Things**, large selection of gay & lesbian books and magazines, 1833 Spring Garden St. 272-7604.

Raleigh (919)

○ **White Rabbit Books & Things**, large selection of gay & lesbian books and magazines, 309 W. Martin St. 856-1429.

OREGON
Portland (503)

Laughing Horse, 3652 SE Division. 236-2893.
Looking Glass, 318 SW Taylor. 227-4760.
Powell's Books, 1005 W. Burnside St. 228-4651.
Twenty Third Ave, 1015 NW 23rd Ave. 224-5097.
Widdershins, women's books & café, 1996 SE Ladd Ave. 232-2129.

PENNSYLVANIA
New Hope (215)

Book Gallery, 19 W. Mechanic St. 862-5110.

Philadelphia (215)

Afterwords, 218 S. 12th St. 735-2393.
Book Trader, 501 So. St., 925-0219.
Borders, 1727 Walnut St. 568-7463.
Giovanni's Room, 345 S. 12th St., Philadelphia, PA 19107. 923-2960. Fax: (215) 923-0813. Ed Hermance owner
Travelers Emporium, 210 S. 17th St. 546-2021.

RHODE ISLAND
Providence (401)

Visions & Voices, 255 Harris Ave., Providence, RI 02909. 273-9757.

TENNESSEE
Memphis (901)

Brentano's, 3773 Hickory Ridge #521. 360-8423

TEXAS
Austin (512)

Liberty Books, 1014-B N. Lamar Blvd., Austin, TX 78773. 495-9737.

Dallas (214)

Crossroads Books, 3930 Cedar Springs, Dallas, TX 75219. 521-8919.
Curious Times, 4008-D Cedar Springs, Dallas, TX 75219. 528-4087.

Lobo, 4008C Cedar Springs, Dallas, TX. 75219. 522-1132.

Houston (713)

Inklings, 1846 Richmond Ave., Houston, TX. 77098. 521-3369.

VIRGINIA
Virginia Beach (804)

Outright Books, 485 So. Independence, Blvd., Suite 110, Virginia Beach, VA 23452. 480-8428.

WASHINGTON
Seattle (206)

Balley/Coy Books, 414 Broadway Ave. E. 323-8842.
Beyond the Closet Books, 1501, Belmont Ave., Seattle, WA 98122. 322-4609.
Freemont Place, 621 N. 35th St. 547-5970.
Pistill Books, 1013 E. Pike St. 325-5401.
Red & Black Books, 432 15th Ave. E. 322-7323.

WISCONSIN
Madison (608)

Going Places, 2860 University Ave. 233-1920.
Pic-a-Book, 506 State St. 256-1125.

Milwaukee (414)

AfterWords, 2710 N. Murray. 963-9089.
People Books, 3512 N. Oakland Ave. 962-0575.
Schwartz, 209 E. Wisconsin Ave. 274-6400.

LODGING

AUSTRALIA

VICTORIA
Richmond

○ **PALM COURT BED & BREAKFAST**, 22 Grattan Place, Richmond 3121 Victoria. Tel: 0419-777-850 Tel/Fax: +61-3-9427-7365. Postal Address: PO Box 184, East Melbourne 3002 Victoria. *TYPE:* B&B. OWNER: Trevor Davis. CLIENTELE Gay men & women. LOCATION: Overlooking Melbourne Parkland & Cricket Ground. 4 R ooms 2 dbl, 2 tpl, shared bath, CTV, phone, refrigerator, room and laundry service, free parking. 1.5 mi. to gay bars & health club. 3 mi to beach. Rates: A$ 40-60. DESCRIPTION: 2 story restored Victorian home.

PALM COURT

Bed & Breakfast

22 Grattan Place
Richmond, 3121
Victoria, Australia

Tel: (0419)
777-850

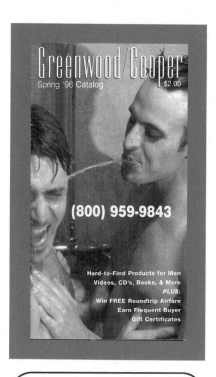

USA

FLORIDA
Orlando

○ **GARDEN COTTAGE,** 1309 E. Washington St., Orlando, FL 32801-2153. Tel: (407) 894-5395. Fax: (407) 894-3809. TYPE: *Cottage.* OWNERS: Lisa & Sherry. CLIENTELE: Gay men and women only. LOCATION: Downtown Orlando, 4 blocks east of Lake Eola. 1BR cottage in historic gay neighborhood. Rates: $70-$80. *TAC:* 10%. Email: talmadge@aol.com

MASSACHUSETS
Boston

○ **Just Right Reservations,** hotels, inns, and guest houses in Boston, Provincetown, and New York City. Office hours: Mon-Fri 9am-4pm EST. James Koumpouras, managing partner, 18 Piedmont St., 2nd Fl. (617) 423-3550.

MAIL ORDER

CANADA

Montréal (QC)
● Business (GMW):
○ **In-fo,** the listing & guide company all about gay Canada, PO Box 42, Stn "M", Montréal, QC H1V 3L6.

● Clothing / Mail Order (G/S/M):
Fireboy, erotic clothing and accessories for men only. **Free Catalog** CP/Box 116 Succ. P.A.T., Montréal, QC H1B 5K1.

● Erotica (GM):
○ **Priape,** sexy clothing, leather, videos, books, gifts etc., 1311 Ste-Catherine E., Montréal, QC H2L 2H4 (514) 521-8451 or (800) 461-6969.

MAIL ORDER - MAPS - PUBLICATIONS 593

Fax: (514) 521-1309.

Toronto (ON)
● Erotica (GM):
○ **Priape**, sexy clothing, leather, videos, books, gifts etc, 465 Church St., Toronto ON M4Y 2C5 (586-9914) or Toll Free (800) 461-6969. Fax: (416) 586-0212 or (416) 586-0150.

USA
California

Laguna Beach
● Jewelry (GMW):
○ **Jewelry by Poncé**, specializing in Commitment and Pride rings (traditional, rainbow, triangles); body jewelry, watches, unique gifts. Visit our store or call 800-969-RING for brochures. Wholesale inquiries welcome. See our ad in the *Odysseus Travel Supplement*. URL: www.jewelrybyponce.com. Email: jewelry@jewelrybyponce

North Hollywood
● Erotica (GM):
In Touch Products, gay videos, magazines, 13122 Satico St., No. Hollywood, CA 91605 (800) 637-0101.

West Hollywood
Greenwood/Cooper, hard to find catalog of products for men, videos, CD's, books and more, P.O. Box 691979, W. Hollywood, CA 90069-1979. (800) 959-9843. Email: order@alluvial.com

---

MAPS

USA/INTERNATIONAL

○ **Columbia FunMaps Inc.**, free Gay & Lesbian guide maps for 63 destination locales across the USA, Canada and the US Virgin Islands. 118 E. 28th St., Ste 308, New York NY 10016. (212) 447-7877. Fax: (212) 447-7876. Alan H. Beck, publisher.

PUBLICATIONS

AUSTRALIA
Brother Sister, Gay & Lesbian News, Queensland edition, 210 Constance St., Fortitude Valley QLD 4006. (07) 3852-2155. Fax: (07) 3852-2822.
Campaign Australia, P.O. Box A228, Sydney South, NSW 2000. (02) 9332-3620 Fax: (02) 9361-5962.
Melbourne Star Observer, (03) 9419-9877. Fax: (03) 9419-0827.
Queensland Pride, P.O. Box 591, Mt. Gravatt, QLD

4122. Tel: (07) 3349-1613. Fax: (07) 3849-7184.
Sydney Star Observer, Australia's largest Gay & Lesbian publication, PO Box 179, Dar-linghurst, NSW 2010. Tel: (02) 9380-5577. Fax: (02) 9331-2118.

BELGIUM
Gay Mag, rue des Teinturiers 18/7. (02) 512-3108. Fax: (08) 511-9396.
La Gazette, Ave. des Saisons 59. (02) 646-2583
Regard, BP 215, 1040 Brussels 4. (02) 733-1024
Tels Quels Magazine, rue de Marché au Charbon 81. (02) 512-4587.
Tenue de Ville, Rue des Riches Claires 17. (02) 502-4318.

BULGARIA
Flamingo, P.O. Box 63, Sofia 1680.

CANADA
Angles, 1170 Bute St., Vancouver, BC, V6E 1Z6. (604) 688-0265. Fax: (604) 688-5405.
Fugues, Québec's leading gay entertainment publication, C.P. 335 Succ. "C" Montréal, Qc H2L 4K3. (514) 848-1854.
Gazelle, Québec's leading lesbian entertainment publication, 1212 rue st-Hubert, Montréal, Qc H2L 3Y7. Tel: (514) 499-9994.
Icon, 467 Church St., 3rd Fl., Toronto, ON M4Y 2C5. (416) 960-9607. Fax: (416) 960-0655
○ **QC Magazine**, Alberta's premier gay & lesbian lifestyle, entetainment and news magazine, PO Box 64292, 5512-4th St., NW, Calgary AB T2K 6J1. (403) 630-2061. Fax: (403) 275-6443. Email: qcmag@nucleus.com. WEB: mindlink.net/moworks/club_z.html
○ **RG Magazine**, Québec's gay news magazine, CP 5245 Succ. C, Montréal, Qc H2X 3M4. (514) 523-9463.

CZECH REPUBLIC
○ **Amigo**, P.O. Box 60, 180 00 Praha 8, gay & lesbian information service and entertainment monthly magazine,Tel/Fax: (02) 684-6548. Email: amigoint@mbox.vol.cz
○ **Czech Mate**, complete guide to all gay & lesbian businesses in the Czech Republic and Slovakia in English, Amigo, P.O. Box 60, 180 00 Praha 8,Tel/Fax: (02) 684-6548. Email: amigoint@mbox.vol.cz
Soho Revue, National Gay & Lesbian magazine with news, event calendar, stories, poetry, photos, personals, 40 pages. Orbis, Vinohradska 46, 120 41 Praha 2. Tel/Fax: (02) 25-7891.

DENMARK
PAN, Knabrostaede 3, Box 1023, Copenhagen K. (09) 11.19.61.

FRANCE
Idol, monthly lifestyle magazine, artistic male nude photos, Groupe Illico, 64 rue Rambuteau, 75003 Paris. (1) 4804-5800. Fax: (1) 4804-0592.
Illico, monthly gay information magazine, guide the the Paris gay scene, Group Illico, 64, rue Rambureau, Paris 75003. (1) 4804-5800. Fax: (1) 4804-0592.
Men, erotic magazine, glossy nude photos, French version of the Advocate Men, Groupe Illico, 64 rue Rambuteau, 75003 Paris. (1) 4804-5800.

594   PUBLICATIONS

Trixx, 99 rue de la Verrerie. (01) 4804-5800

GERMANY

Magnus, news and entertainment magazine, Jackwerth Verlag GmbH, Lützowstraße 102-104, 10785 Berlin. (30) 230827-0 Fax: (30) 265-2805.

✪ Rosa Zone, monthly news and entertainment magazine with "gay travel" section, Beurhausstraße 58, 44137 Dortmund. (231) 914-3072. Fax: (231) 914-3071. Email: rosazone@t-online-de

✪ Siegessäule, Berlin's largest gay & lesbian magazine, Jackwerth Verlag GmbH, Lützowstraße 102-104, 10785 Berlin. (30) 230827-0. Fax: (30) 265-2805.

GREECE

To Kraximo (ΚΡΑΞΙΜΟ), periodical with radical view on homosexuality, P.O. Box 4228, Athens 102 10.

HONG-KONG

Contacts Magazine, monthly publication, the only gay magazine in Hong-Kong. Island Publishing Co., G.P.O. Box 13427, Hong Kong. 2817-9447. Fax: 2817-9120.

HUNGARY

Mások,monthly newspaper, news, advertising, photos, P.O. Box 388, 1461 Budapest 1.

ITALY

Babilonia, Via Ebro 11, 20141 Milano. (02) 5696-468.

Hot Line, via G.B. Sammartini No. 21, 20125 Milano. Tel: (02) 669-83506 or 667-10015. Fax: (02) 669-86533.

Marco, The magazine of Gay Contacts, nude classified photos/ads, Edizioni Moderne, Casella Postale 17160, 20170 Milano.

Rome Gay News, v. Einaudi 33, 00040 Frattocchie (Roma). Tel: (06) 9354-7567. Fax: (06) 9354-7483. Luciano Consoli, editor.

JAPAN

Adon, 201 Hohyu Bldg., 2-11-9 Yotsuya, Shinjuku-ku, Tokyo 160. (03) 359-5856.

Barazuku, Daini-Shobo Limited, 5-2-11.

Daizawa, Setagaya-ku, Tokyo 155. (03) 421-5462.

Sabu, San Bldg., 26-3 Sanei-cho, Shinjuku-ku, Tokyo 160. (03) 359-2341.

Samson, P.O. Box 66, Shitaya Post Office, Taito-Ku, Tokyo 110-91. (03) 841-2091.

The Gay, T.I.Y. Shuppan, P.O. Box 209, Shinjuku-ku, Tokyo 160-91. (03) 363-5197.

LITHUANIA

Amsterdamas, P.O. Box 2862, Vilnius 2000. Tel: (370-2) 266994 or 766583. Fax: (370-2) 223451.

MEXICO

Apolo, Editorial NVH, Concha #126, Col. el Caracol, México, D.F.

Del Otro Lado, the Gay magazine of Mexico and Latin America, write for subscription and advertising information, c/o CIDHOM, Aptdo Postal 13-424, México, D.F. - C.P. 03500.

Frontera Gay, c/o FIGHT, A.C., Aptdo Postal 3302, Tijuana, Baja California, C.P. 22000.

Hermes, Mexico's premier entertainment and cultural magazine, Febo Editores SA de CV, A.P. 73-025, C.P. 03311, México, D.F. (211-5291) Fax: (286-4009).

THE NETHERLANDS

De Gay Krant, Postbus 161, 5680 AD Best. (4998) 91-000 Fax: (4998) 72638.

Expreszo, c/o Stichting Hoezo, PO Box 618, 3000 AC. (20) 612-3791. Fax: (20) 623-9761

HOMologie, PO Box 165 84, 1001 RB Amsterdam. (20) 618-8045

MaGAYzine, c/o Best Publishing, PO Box 10, 5680 AA Best. (0499) 390-000. Fax: (0499) 390-603.

Rainbow Magazine, Gerard Doustraat 160F, 1073 VZ Amsterdam. (20) 679-9188.

XL, Nieuwezijds Voorburgwal 68-70, 1012 SE Amsterdam. (20) 623-4596. Fax: (20) 626-7795

NEW ZEALAND

✪ Out!, Private Bag, Auckland 1. (09) 779-031. Fax: (09) 777-767.

RUSSIA

Risc, P.O. Box 157, 129224 Moscow.

Tema, P.O. Box 11, 109180 Moscow.

1/10, c/o Dima Lychov, Poste Restante, 111123 Moscow E-123. (305-5737), Fax: (141-8315).

You Magazine, P.O. Box 9, 107120 Moscow.

SLOVENIA

Revolver, Roza Klub, Kersnikova 4, 61000 Ljubljana.

SOUTH AFRICA

Exit, South Africa's leading national gay news magazine, P.O. Box 32472, Braamfontein 2017. Tel: (011) 614-9866. Fax: (011) 618-3165.

Outright, Alternative lifestyle magazine, PO Box 2464, Houghton 2041. (011) 648-5032/8909. Fax: (011) 648-3800.

The Quarterly, gay women's news magazine, Box 84527, Greenside 2034. (011) 442-8662. Fax: (011) 880-3593.

South African Gay Pages, free guide to holiday places, annual phone book, P.O. Box 1050, Melville JHB 2109. (011) 726-1560. Fax: (011) 726-6948. e-mail: family@iafrica.com

SPAIN

MENsuel, monthly, articles, photos, ads, classifieds, Ediciones Pedro Sanchez, Templaris 2, 08002 Barcelona. Tel: (93) 412-5380. Fax: (93) 412-3357.

SWEDEN

Reporter,Box 17 218, 104 62 Stockholm (08) 669-0012. Fax: (08) 669-0424.

SWITZERLAND

Dialogai INFO, P.O. Box 1430, 1211 Genève 1. (022) 219-157.

Kontakt, Belami-Verlag AG, Box 319, 8051 Zürich. (01) 321-4180.

Kontiki, Box 7679, CH-8023 Zurich. (01) 271-7011.

THAILAND

My Way, c/o Mr. Wallop. Box 1947, Bangkok 10501. (02) 233-9567.

UK / SCOTLAND

Gay Times, 283 Camden High St., London NW1 7BX. (171) 482-2576.

Gay Scotland, 58A Broughton St., Edinburgh. (131) 557-2625.

UKRAINE

Two Colours, P.O. Box 501, 252150 Kiev 150. publishers of **K.G.T.** and **Bogdan** magazines. (044) 419-5773. Fax: (044) 244-3811.

USA

The Advocate, 6922 Hollywood Blvd., Los Angeles, CA 90028. (213) 871-1225.

Ambush, 828-A Bourbon St., New Orleans, LA 70116-3137. (504) 522-8049. Fax: (504) 522-0907. Email: info@ambushmag.com

✪ **Art & Understanding**, The International Magazine of Literature and Art about AIDS, 25 Monroe St., Ste #205, Albany NY 12210. (518) 426-9010. Fax: (518) 436-5354. Emily Hoffman.

Au Courant, 2124 South St., Philadelphia, PA 19146. (215) 790-1179.

Baltimore Alternative, gay & lesbian publication serving the Baltimore/Washington community. P.O. Box 2351, Baltimore, MD 21203. (410) 235-3401. Fax: (410) 889-5665.

✪ **Baltimore Gay Paper**, #1 Gay & Lesbian paper in Maryland, P.O. Box 22575, Baltimore, MD 21203. (410) 837-7748. Fax: (410) 837-8512.

✪ **Bay Area Reporter**, 1528 15th St., San Francisco, CA 94103. (415) 861-5019.

✪ **Bear Magazine**, a magazine devoted to all American hairy men, exclusively for gay men, Brush Creek Media, 2215-R Market St., #148, San Francisco, CA 94114. (415) 552-1506. (800) 234-3877. Fax: (415) 552-3244. Contact: Richard Meyerson.

Beau, gay erotic magazine, P.O. Box 470, Port Chester, NY 10573.

BLK, The National Black Lesbian & Gay Newsmagazine, P.O. Box 83912, Los Angeles, CA 90083-0912. (310) 410-0808. Fax: (310) 410-9250.

Bunkhouse, magazine for ranchers & rough-ridin' men, published by Brush Creek Media, 2215-R Market St., #148, San Francisco, CA 94114. (415) 552-1506. Fax: (415) 552-3244

✪ **Columbia Fun Maps**, publishers of City Maps to 63 Gay & Lesbian friendly destinations in the USA, Canada and the US Virgin Islands, 118 E. 28th St., #308, New York NY 10016. (212) 447-7877. Fax: (212) 447-7876.

Detour, entertainment with style art magazine, Edward T. Stein & Assoc., 201 N. Service Rd., Melville, NY 11747. (212) 675-3680. Fax: (212) 675-3284.

Drummer, leather, sex & bondage magazine for gay men, color photos, Desmodus Inc., P.O. Box 410390, San Francisco, CA 94141-0390. (415) 252-1195. Fax: (415) 252-9574.

Etcetera, newsmagazine for Atlanta and the South, P.O. Box 8916, Atlanta, GA 31106. (404) 525-3821. Fax: (404) 525-1908.

Echo, P.O. Box 1808, Phoenix, AZ 85001-1808. Magazine of the southwest. (602) 266-0550. Fax: (602) 266-0773.

Edge, 6434 Santa Monica Blvd., Los Angeles, CA 90038. (213) 962-6994. Fax: (213) 962-8744.

50/50 Magazine, glossy magazine for creative Gay & Lesbian journalism, 2336 Market St., Ste #20, San Francisco, CA 94114. (415) 861-8210. Fax: (415) 621-1703.

First Hand, PO Box 1314, Teaneck, NJ 07666. (201) 836-9177. Fax: (201) 836-5055.

✪ **The Front Page**, The Carolina's oldest and most read Gay & Lesbian biweekly newspaper, P.O. Box 27928, Raleigh, NC 27611. Tel: (919) 829-0181. Fax: (919) 829-0830. front page@ aol.com. Jim Duely, editor

✪ **Frontiers**, 7985 Santa Monica Blvd., Ste. 109, West Hollywood, CA 90046. Tel: (213) 654-7782. Fax: (213) 656-8784.

Gay Chicago, 3121 No. Broadway, 2nd level, Chicago IL 60657. (312) 327-7271.

✪ **Gayellow Pages**, complete listing of US & Canada gay-friendly resources & businesses available in bookstores, Renaissance House, PO Box 533-OD, Village Stn. NY, NY 10014. (212) 674-0120. Fax: (212) 420-1126.

The Gay & Lesbian Times, Southern California's most widely read weekly newsmagazine, tabloid format, cut and stapled, Uptown Publications, P.O. Box 34624, San Diego, CA 92163-4624. (619) 299-NEWS (6397), Fax: (619) 299-3430. Michael Portantino, publisher.

The Gayly Oklahoman, P.O. Box 60930, Oklahoma City, OK 73146. (405) 528-0800; Tulsa (918) 599-9380.

Genre, 1509 N. Crescent Heights, Suite #7, Los Angeles CA 90046. (213) 896-9778.

✪ **Hot Spots**, Florida's largest gay entertainment publication, 5100 NE 12th Ave., Ft. Lauderdale, FL 33334. (305) 928-1862. Toll Free (800) 522-8775. Fax: (305) 772-0142. Internet: http://www.hotspotsmagazine.com.

Houston Voice, a weekly community news publication, 811 Westheimer, Suite #105, Houston, TX 77006. (713) 529-8490 or (800) 729-8490. Fax: (713) 529-9531.

✪ **HX / Homo Xtra**, The totally biased politically incorrect party paper, Two Queens Inc., 19 West 21st St., #703, New York NY 10010. (212) 627-0747. Fax: (212) 627-5280.

Identity Northview, Box 200070, Anchorage AK 99520-0070.

Island Lifestyle, P.O. Box 240515, Honolulu, HI 96824-0515. (808) 737-6400. Fax: (808) 735-8825.

Lambda Rising News, 1625 Connecticut Ave. NW, Washington DC 20009. (202) 462-6969.

Las Vegas/Reno Bugle, Newspaper Service Associates, P.O. Box 19360, Las Vegas, NV 89132-0360. (702) 369-6260. Fax: (702) 369-9325.

✪ **Long Island Pride Press**, resource for the Long Island (NY) gay & lesbian community. Publishers of **LIPP** & the **Long Island Pride Guide** distributed free every Pride Month (June), PO Box 2303, N. Babylon, NY 11703. Tel: (516) 225-7900. Fax: (516) 225-7918.

Manifest Reader, S&M, bondage magazine, Alternate Publishing, PO Box 14695, San Francisco, CA 94114-4695. Fax: (415) 863-7625

✪ **Metro Arts & Entertainment Weekly (MW)**, Washington's only gay & lesbian entertainment guide, look for us at family-friendly establishments throughout the Metropolitan Area. 1649 Hobart St. NW DC 20010. (202) 588-5220. Fax: (202) 588-5219.

Naked, magazine for men who like to get naked, published by Serengeti Publishing Corp., 7985 Santa Monica Blvd., #109-232, West Hollywood, CA 90046. (800) 962-5330

New Mexico Rainbow, the newspaper for New Mexico's Lesbian & Gay communit. Write to: P.O. Box 4769, Albuquerque NM 87196-4769. (505) 244-1824. Fax: (505) 244-1679. email: summers@rt66.com

Next, NYC's entertainment & lifestyle magazine, 121 Varick St. 3rd Fl., NYC, NY 10013. (212) 627-0165. Fax: (212) 627-0633

North View, Identity Inc., PO Box 200070, Anchorage, AK 99520-0070. (902) 258-4777.

Nosotros Magazine, News and entertainment magazine for the Latin community, P.O. Box 451454, Miami, FL 33245-1454. (305) 820-5006. Fax: (305) 558-2985. Ernesto Delgado.

Oblivion, San Francisco's Gay, Lesbian & Bizexual arts, entertainment and information guide, 519 Castro St. #24, San Francisco, CA 94114. (415) 487-5498.

Odyssey Magazine, 584 Castro St., #302, San Francisco, CA 94114-2500; **Odysseys Magazine Hawaii**, 1750 Kala-kua Ave., Ste 3247 Honolulu, HI 96826-3709. (808) 944-3307. Fax: (808) 955-8889.

On The Wilde Side, Long Island's largest entertainment and lifestyle magazine, 106 Cain Drive, Brentwood, NY 11717. (516) 434-1000. (800) 988-6583. Fax: (516) 435-0808

○ **Our World**, Our World Publishing, monthly gay & lesbian travel magazine, excellent travel articles and tips for the international globe trotters, call for subscription rates, 1104 Nova Rd., Ste 251-D, Daytona Beach, FL 32117. (904) 441-5367. Fax: (904) 441-5604. Wayne Whiston publisher

Out, 110 Greene St., Ste #800, New York NY 10019. (212) 334-9119.

Out & About, PO Box 120112, Norfolk, VA 23502. (804) 583-7468 or 471-5373.

Out Publishing, 747 South Ave., Pittsburgh, PA 15221. (412) 243-3350. Fax: (412) 243-4067.

○ **Outlines**, Indiana's leading Gay & Lesbian magazine, information, news, articles, bar scene, all you need to know about what's hot in Indiana, 133 W. Market St., #105, Indianapolis, IN 46204. (317) 574-0615.

OutSmart, Houston's Gay & Lesbian monthly magazine, 3406 Audubon Place, Houston, TX 77006-4412. Tel: (713) 520-7237. Fax: (713) 522-3275. Greg Jeu, Publisher.

Parlée Plus, Box 430, Babylon, NY 11702. (516) 587-8669.

Passport, Int'l Wavelength, 2215-R Market St., No. 829, San Francisco, CA 94114. Tel: (415) 749-1100. Fax: (415) 928-1165

Patlar, Box 22402, Sacramento, CA 95822. (916) 452-0769. 800-833-0769.

Philadelphia Gay News (PGN), 254 S. 11th St., Philadelphia, PA 19107. (215) 625-8501.

Pillar, Utah's premier monthly "Alternative Lifestyle" newspaper, P.O. Box 520898, SLC UT 84152-0898. Tel: (801) 265-0066. Fax: (801) 261-2923.

Positive Planet, PP Media, 323 Broadway Ave. E #1205. Seattle, WA 98102. (206) 828-1775. Fax: (206) 329-6091.

○ **Powerplay Magazine**, Homosexual acts of the male species, exclusively for gay men, Brush Creek Media, 2215R Market St.,

#148, San Francisco, CA 94114. (415) 552-1506 or (800) 234-3877. Fax: (415) 552-3244. Contact: Richard Meyerson.

POZ, A magazine for those HIV positive, Box 1279 Old Chelsea Station, New York, NY 10113-1279 (212) 242-2163 or (800) 883-2163. Fax (212) 675-8505. Sean O'Brien Strub, Executive Editor.

○ **Provocateur**, art, fashion and entertainment magazine, beautiful male/nude photography from the world's most famous photographers, published by **Alluvial Entertainment**, 8599 Santa Monica Blvd., West Hollywood, CA 90069. (800) 959-9843.

○ **San Francisco Bay Guardian**, the best weekly main stream newspaper in California. Free every Wednesday in stores all over town. Internet: www.fyisf.com. (394-0999).

San Francisco Bay Times, the Bay Area's outstanding gay and lesbian newspaper, 525 Bryant, San Francisco, Ca 94107. (415) 227-0800.

○ **SF Frontiers**, Bay Area's premier bi-weekly newsmagazine offering cutting edge information to the Gay & Lesbian community, 2370 Market St., 2nd Fl., San Francisco, CA 94114. (415) 487-6000. Fax: (415) 487-6060. David Gardner, Dir. of Sales.

SF Sentinel, 500 Hayes St., SF CA 94102. (415) 861-8100.

SGN (Seattle Gay News), 704 E. Pike St., Seattle WA 98122. (206) 324-4297.

SEG (Southern Exposure Guide), 819 Peacock Plaza, Ste. 575, Key West, FL 33041. Tel/Fax: (305) 294-6303.

Southern Exposure, 819 Peacock Plaza, Suite 575, Key West, FL 33040. (305) 294-6303. Fax: (305) 295-9597. Email: editor@kwest.com

Southern Voice, P.O. Box 18215, Atlanta, GA 30316. (404) 876-0789.

TWISL Magazine, P.O. Box 8068, Alton, IL 62002-8068. (618) 465-9370.

This Week In Texas Magazine (TWIT), Texas' Leading Gay & Lesbian Publication since 1975, published weekly. News, entertainment and classifieds, the best source for what's on in Texas, 3300 Reagan St., Dallas, TX 75219. (214) 521-0622. Fax: (214) 520-8948.

Victory, the National Gay & Lesbian entrepreneur magazine, 2261 Market, Suite 296, San Francisco, CA 94114.

Washington Blade, 1408 'U' St., NW, 2nd fl., Washington, DC 20009-3916. (202) 797-7000. Fax: (202) 797-7040.

The Weekly News (TWN), 901 NE 79th St., Miami, FL 33138. (305) 757-6333.

Windy City Times, 970 West Montana, Chicago, IL 60614. (312) 935-1790.

The Wisconsin Light, 1843 N. Palmer, Milwaukee, WI 53212. (414) 372-2773. Fax: (414) 289-0789.

RAILROADS

Rail Europe, U.S. ticketing agent for Eurailpass. (800) 438-7245 or (914) 682-5172).

RENT-A-CAR

GREECE / Mykonos
☺ **Mustang Rent-a-Car**, Mykonos Town. Best selection of cars and best prices in Mykonos, Friendly service. USA/Canada reservations: Tel: (516) 944-5330 or (800) 257-5344. Fax: (516) 944-7540 or (800) 982-6571. *TAC:* 10%

USA

Advantage	1-800-777-5500
Alamo	1-800-327-9633
American International	1-800-527-0202
Avis	1-800-331-1212
British Car Rental	1-800-448-3936
Budget	1-800-527-0700
Budget (Canada)	1-800-268-8900
Dollar	1-800-421-6868
Enterprize	1-800-325-8007
General	1-800-327-7607
Hertz	1-800-654-3131
National	1-800-227-7368
Rent-a-Wreck	1-800-421-7253
Snappy	1-800-669-4802
Thrifty	1-800-367-2277
Ugly Duckling	1-800-843-3825
Value Rent-a-Car (FL)	1-800-327-2501

RESERVATION SERVICES

CANADA
QUÉBEC / Montréal
☺ **Cachet Accommodations Network (C.A.N.)**, reservation service, Box 42-A, Stn "M", Montréal, QC H1V 3L6. Tel: (514) 254-1250. Fax: (514) 252-9954.

MEXICO
Puerto Vallarta
Doin' It Right Travel, villas, condos, gay hotels & tours in Puerto Vallarta, 150 Franklin #208, San Francisco, CA 94102. Tel: (415) 621-3576, or (800) 936-3646. Fax: (415) 708-4356.
Email: skinner@aol.com

USA
ARIZONA / Scottsdale
☺ **B&B Inn Arizona**, 13802 N. Scottsdale Rd., Scottsdale, AZ 85254. Tel: (602) 368-9250. Toll Free (800) 266-7829. TYPE: *Accommodations Service.* CLIENTELE: All Welcome. LOCATION: Arizona and throughout the country. DESCRIPTION: Free reservation service for thousands of bed & breakfasts, inns and ranches throughout the country. This free service can be accesses on the WEB at http:// bnbreservations.com Email: president@bnbreservations.com

INTERNATIONAL
New York / USA
☺ **Odysseus Worldwide Reservation System®** **(OWRS)**, efficient reservation service for quality gay & lesbian resorts, packages, cruises in: Greece & Greek Islands, Turkey, Israel, Spain, Europe, Eastern Europe, Thailand, Indonesia, Mexico and the Caribbeans. Tel: (516) 944-5330 or (800) 257-5344. Fax: (516) 944-7540 or (800) 982-6571. Call or fax for our FREE color brochure. *TAC:* 10%.

TOUR OPERATORS

AUSTRALIA
Sydney
☺ **Jornada**, Australia's largest and most innovative outbound tour operator. Specialists in tailoring individual and group packages to Australia, South Pacific and Asia. Commission payable to agents, level 1, 6 Manning Rd., Double Bay NSW 2028. Tel: (02) 9862-0909, Toll Free (800) 672-120. Fax: (02) 9362-0788. Email: justask@jornada.com.au

USA
Advance Damron Vacations, One Greenway Plaza, suite 890, Houston, TX 77046. (800) 695-0880
Atlantis, 8335 Sunset Blvd., West Hollywood, CA 90069. (800) 6-Atlantis
Olivia Records & Travel, 4400 Market St., Oakland, CA 94608. (800) 631-6277
RSVP, 2800 University Ave. SE, Minneapolis, MN 55414-3293. (612) 379-4697. Fax: (612) 379-0484

TRAVEL AGENTS

AUSTRALIA
Adelaide
Harvey World Travel, 70 Glen Osmond Rd. Parkside, SA 5063. Brian Bebbington. (08) 274-1222. Fax: (08) 272-7371.
Oatley
Off Road Australia Pty, Ltd., 107 Myall St., Oatley NSW 2223. Geoff Mason. Fax: (02) 570-9200.
Petersham
Queen Street Travel, GPO Box 413, Peter-sham NSW 2040. (02) 955-7550. Fax: (02) 955-7550. Hugh Clark, Dir. *IGTA, AGLTA.*
Surfers Paradise
Gold Coast Fun Leisure Holidays, P.O. Box 7260, Surfers Paradise, QLD 4217. (75) 922-223. Fax: (75) 922-223. Peter J. Turner.
Sydney
Alumni Travel, P.O. Box C235,100 Clarence St., Sydney. (02) 9290-3856. Fax: (02) 290-3857. Rob
Beyond the Blue, Ste 205, 275 Alfred St., N. Sydney, NSW 2060. (02) 9955-6755. Fax: (02) 922-6036.
HHK Travel, 50 Oxford St., Paddington, 2021 NSW. (02) 332-4299. Fax: (02) 9360-2164.

○ **Jornada**, Level 1, 6 Manning Road, Double Bay, 2028 NSW. (02) 9362-0900. (800) 672-120 (Australia only). Fax: (02) 9362-0788. Email: justask@jornada.com.au

Now Voyager, "804 Cliveden", 4 Bridge St., Sydney. (02) 9252-1799. Fax: (02) 9252-2065. Gary Ilich.

Oxford St. Flight Center, 26 Oxford St., Woollahara, NSW 2025. (02) 9360-2277. Fax: (02) 9360-5665.

CANADA
Edmonton
Algonquin Travel, Real Canadian Superstore, 17303 Stony Plain Rd., Edmonton, AB T5S 1B5. (403) 483-8778. Fax: (403) 481-5206.

Hamilton
Dennis Heming Travel, 150 James St., So. Hamilton ON L8 (905) 523-6500. Fax: (905) 523-7358.

Montréal
Alternative Travel, your connection to gay Montréal, 42 Pine Ave. West #2, H2W 1R1 (514) 845-7769 or (800) 267-7769. Fax: (514) 845-8421. Peter Gaty.

Terre des Hommes Voyages, 1122 Blvd. de Maisonneuve E., Montréal, QC H2L 1Z5. (514) 522-2225. Fax: (514) 522-7987. Anne Marie.

Voyage Express, 1481 rue Amherst, Montréal, QC H2L 3L2. (514) 526-2877. Fax: (514) 526-7355. Pascal.

Toronto
La Fabula Travel, 551 Church St., Toronto, ON. M4Y 2E2. (416) 920-3229 or (800) 667-2475. Fax: (416) 920-9484. Robert Bell.

Travel Cuts, 49 Front Street East, Toronto, ON M5E 1B3. (416) 365-0545. Fax: (416) 601-0855. Tim O'Brien.

Richmond
OCD Tours, 7680 River Road, Richmond, BC V6X 1X6. (604) 270-0033. Fax: (604) 273-6380.

Vancouver
APEX Travel, 982 Denman St., Vancouver, BC V6G 2M1. (604) 687-8200. Fax: (604) 687-8207.

Partners Travel, 1120 Davie St., Vancouver BC V6E 1N2. (604) 687-3837. Fax: (604) 687-7937.

Progressive Travel, 1120 Davie St., Vancouver, BC V6E 1N2. (604) 687-3837. (800) 910-1120. Fax: (604) 687-7937.

COSTA RICA
San José
Dos Libras,calle 3 bis, Av. 9 y 11 #936, San José. Tel: (506) 223-7961. Fax: (506) 257-7668.

GREECE
Mykonos
○ **Odysseus Worldwide Reservation System® (OWRS)**, the best hotels and villas in Mykonos and the Greek Islands. P.O. Box 1548, Port Washington, NY 11050. (516) 944-5330 or (800) 257-5344. Fax: (516) 944-7540 or (800) 982-6571. *TAC:* 10%.

NEW ZEALAND
Auckland
Travel Desk (NZ), Box 3175, Auckland, New Zealand. (09) 779-031.

RUSSIA
Moscow
○ **The Kremlin Tours**, P.O. Box 44, 105318 Moscow, E-318. Tel: (7-095) 962-9178, Fax: (7-095) 178-9847. Tlx 411700 MOTIVE box 18863. Email: kremln@dol.ru

SPAIN
Madrid
Lifestyle Travel, c/. Molino de la Navata 65, 28420 La Navata Madrid. (91) 858-5826.

SOUTH AFRICA
Highland North
Niche Travel Marketing, P.O. Box 64217, Highland North 2037. (27-11) 648-0730. Fax: ((27-11) 648-7140. Gerrie de Beer.

Johannesburg
Fu-An Travel, Safari and Tour Operator company for individuals and groups in South Africa and Southern Africa, P.O. Box 696, Bedfordview 2008. Tel: (27-11) 450-1923/4. Fax: (27-11) 455-2173. Jonathan

Queenstown
Liberty Tours, PO Box 580, Queenstown 5320. (27451) 88760. David Barron.

USA
ARIZONA
Phoenix/Scottsdale
Compass Travel, 4201 N. 16th St. #150, Phoenix, AZ 85016. (602) 266-5390. Fax: (602) 266-0013. David.

Dillards Travel, 7014 E. Camelback Rd., Scottsdale, AZ 85251. (602) 581-7977. Fax: (602) 945-6559.

FirsTravel, Ltd., 5150 N. 7th St., Phoenix, AZ 85014. (602) 265-0666. Fax: (602) 265-0135. Sam Worthington.

Pichard Travel, 4144 No. 44th St., Phoenix, AZ 85018. (602) 956-2152. Fax: (602) 956-1010.

Select Travel Services, 77 E. Weldon Ave., Ste #280, Phoenix, AZ 85012-2076. (602) 279-7500. (800) 743-3550. Fax: (602) 279-7600.

Tucson
Cortez Travel, 3101 No. Swan, Tucson AZ 85712. (602) 327-6038. Fax: (602) 327-6085.

CALIFORNIA
Anaheim
Travel Advisors, 2223 W. Ball Rd., Anaheim, CA 92804. (714) 535-1174. Michael Davis.

Beverly Hills
Uniquest Travel, 8306 Wilshire Blvd., Ste #893, Beverly Hills, CA 90211. (213) 656-3500. Fax: (213) 656-0205. Douglas Upchurch.

Wilson's Travel Agency, 9359 Wilshire Blvd., Beverly Hills, CA 90210. (213) 272-5124. Fax: (310) 550-3991. Lee Walkup.

Cathedral City
Canyon Travel, 67-555 Hwy 111, Suite C-110, Cathedral City, CA 92234. (619) 324-3484. Fax: (619) 324-0298.

Huntington Beach
Golden Eagle Travel, 7238 Heil Ave., Huntington Beach, CA 92647. (714) 848-9090. Fax: (714) 842-6494.

Irvine
Sundance Travel, 19800 MacArthur Blvd., Ste #100, Irvina, CA 92612.

Laguna Beach
California Riviera 800, 1400 So. Coast Hwy. Laguna Beach, CA 92652. (714) 376-0305. Fax: (714) 497-9077. Steven Crawford.

Long Beach
Savoy Travel Mgmt., 311 Cedar Ave., Long Beach, CA 90802-2818. Dana B. Morae, Pres. (310) 495-0123.

Touch of Travel, 3918 Atlantic Ave., Long Beach, CA 90807 A. V. Barney, C. Murphy. (310) 427-2144. Fax: (310) 427-3424.

Los Angeles

Adore Travel, 1494 So. Robertson Blvd., Los Angeles, CA 90035. (310) 859-8740.

Atlas Travel, 8923 So. Sepulveda Blvd., Los Angeles, CA 90045. (310) 670-3574. Fax: (310) 670-0725.

American Express Travel, 8493 W. 3rd St., Los Angeles, CA 90048. (310) 659-1682. Fax: (310) 659-1151. Monica or Janis.

Carlson Travel Network, 2616 Hyperion Ave., Los Angeles, CA 90027. (213) 660-2946. Fax: (213) 661-4518.

Travel Lab, 1943 Hillhurst Ave., Los Angeles, CA 90027. (213) 660-9811. Fax: (213) 660-9814. Tom Ziegert.

Travel Management, 832 N. La Brea Ave., Hollywood, CA 90046. (213) 993-0444. Fax: (213) 993-0456. Jan Olsson.

Travel Store, 11601 Willshire Ave., Los Angeles, CA 90025. (310) 575-5540. Fax: (310) 575-5541.

Los Gatos

Yankee Clipper Travel, 260 Saratoga Ave., Los Gatos CA 95030. (408) 354-6400. Fax (408) 395-4453. Jim Boin.

Redondo Beach

Calpro Travel, 328 S. Catalina Ave., Redondo Beach, CA 90277. (310) 318-2511. Fax: (310) 372-6221.

Sacramento

Aladdin Travel, 818 'K' Street Mall, Sacramento, CA 95814. (916) 446-0633. Fax: (916) 924-5910. Rob Thorbin.

San Diego

Byrd House Travel, 5338 Balboa Ave., San Diego, CA 92117. (619) 576-9447. Fax: (619) 576-6403.

Hillcrest Travel, 431 Robinson, San Diego, CA 92103. (619) 291-0758. Fax: (619) 291-3151. Tom Leonard.

Jerry & David's Travel, 1025 West Laurel St., San Diego, CA 92101. (619) 233-5199. Fax: (619) 231-0641.

Man on Vacation, 4715 30th St., Ste #6, San Diego, CA 92116. (619) 641-7085. Fax: (619) 641-7088.

Midas Travel, 525 University Ave., San Diego, CA 92103. (619) 298-1160.

Mission Center Travel, 3108 Fifth Ave., Suite A, San Diego, CA 92103-5829. (619) 299-2720. Dave Allen.

Sun Travel, 3545 Midway Drive, San Diego, CA 92110. (619) 222-2786. Fax: (619) 222-9591.

Sundance Travel, 1040 University Ave., #B-207, San Diego, CA 92103. (619) 497-2100. Fax: (619) 293-4615.

San Francisco

Above & Beyond Travel, 3568 Sacramento St., San Francisco, CA 94118. (415) 922-2683.

Bottom Line Travel, 1236 Castro St.,San Francisco CA 94224. (415) 826-8600. Fax: (415) 826-8698.

Carlson Wagon Lit, 1245 Market St. ,San Francisco, CA 94103. (415) 558-9796. Fax: (415) 558-8960.

Castro Travel, 435 Brannan St., Ste #104, San Francisco, CA 94107. (800) 861-0957. Fax: (415) 357-0221.

Now Voyager Travel, 4406 18th St., San Francisco, CA 94114. Jonathan Klein. (415) 626-1169. Fax: (415) 626-8626.

Orchid Travel, 4122 20th St., San Francisco, CA 94114. (415) 552-2468. Fax: (415) 552-9264.

Passport To Leisure Travel, 2265 Market St., San Francisco, CA 94114. (415) 621-8300. Fax: (415) 621-8304.

Starlite Travel, 758 Sacramento St., San Francisco, CA 94108. (415) 981-2350. Fax: (415) 956-1587.

Sundance Travel, 660 Market St., 5th Fl., San Francisco, CA 94104.

Travel Time, 4005 24th St., San Francisco, CA 94114. (415) 647-4303. Fax: (415) 826-4838.

○ **Travel Trends**, full service travel agency 431 Castro St., San Francisco, CA 94114. (415) 558-6922. Fax: (415) 558-9338.

Travel Zone, 1630 Union St., San Francisco, CA 94123. (415) 474-6400. Fax: (415) 771-9399.

Winship Travel, 2321 Market St., San Francisco, CA 94114-1688. (415) 863-2555. Fax: (415) 863-2473. Douglas.

San José

All Points Travel, 615 Stockton Ave., San José, CA 95126. (408) 288-3820. Fax: (408) 993-8134. Joe Butler.

Santa Clara

Rainbow Travel, 1055 Monroe St., Santa Clara, CA 95050. (408) 246-1414. Fax: (408) 983-0677.

West Hollywood

Classic Travel, 7985 Santa Monica Blvd., Ste #103, West Hollywood CA 90046. (213) 650-8444. Fax: (213) 656-7898.

Club Travel, 8739 Santa Monica Blvd., West Hollywood CA 90069. (310) 358-2200. Fax: (310) 358-2222.

Embassy Travel Service, 906 N. Harper Ave., Ste B, West Hollywood, CA 90046. (213) 656-0743. Fax: (213) 650-6968.

Gunderson Travel, 8543 Santa Monica, #8, W. Hollywood, CA 90069. (310) 657- 3944. Fax: (310) 652-4301. Ron Gunderson.

Select Travel, 8380 Santa Monica Blvd., W. Hollywood, CA 90069. (213) 848-2211. Fax: (213) 848-9064. Rand.

COLORADO

Boulder

Pathways Travel, 1700 28th St., Ste #108, Boulder, CO 80301. (303) 449-0099. Fax: (303) 449-4585. Cathy.

Denver

Carlson Travel (CTN), 1485 So. Colorado Blvd., Ste #260, Denver, CO 80222. (303) 759-1318. Fax: (303) 758-5390.

Compass Travel, 1001 16th St., Ste A150, Denver, CO 80265. (303) 534-1292. Fax: (303) 534-8061.

Travel Boy, 201 Steele St., Ste 2B, Denver, CO 80206. (303) 333-4855. Fax: (303) 333-8559.

Travel 16th St., Masonic Bldg., 16th St., Denver, CO 80202. (303) 820-0311. Fax: (303) 595-0313. Ron Douglas or John Coxhead.

CONNECTICUT

Hamden

Adler Travel, 2323 Whitney Ave., Hamden, CT 06518. (203) 288-8100. Fax: (203) 230-8416.

Southbury

Rainbow Destinations, P.O. Box 776, Southbury, CT 06488. (203) 791-1535. Fax: (203) 791-1535. Joe.

DISTRICT of COLUMBIA

Washington, DC

Executive Travel, 1100 17th St., NW Ste #400, Washington, DC 20036. (202) 828-3501. Fax: (202) 785-2566.

Great Escape Travel, 1227 25th St., NW, Ste #590, Washington DC 20037. (202) 331-3322. Fax: (202) 331-1109. Mitch.

Passport Executive Travel, 1025 Thomas Jefferson St., N.W., Washington DC 20007. (202) 337-7718. Fax: (202) 342-7475. Allen Peterson.

Personalized Travel, 1325 'G' St., NW #915, Washington DC 20005. (202) 508-8656. (800) 237-6971. Fax: (202) 637-8454.

Travel Escape, 1725 K. St. NW, Washington, DC 20006. (202) 223-9354. Fax: (202) 296-0724. Garbo Afarian, pres.

Uptown Travel, 3504 Connecticut Ave., NW, Washington DC 20008. (202) 244-8652. (800) 999-4698. Fax: (202) 244-8676. Bill Murphy or Ginger.

FLORIDA
Ft. Lauderdale

Atlantic Travel, 2746 Commercial Blvd., Ft. Lauderdale, FL 33308. (800) 929-1234. Fax: (954) 772-2831.

Sun & Fun Tours, 2700 West Oakland Park Blvd., Ste #25, Ft. Lauderdale, FL 33311. (954) 731-2579. Fax: (954) 731-1210.

Miami / Miami Beach

Connection Tours, 169 Lincoln Rd., Ste #302, Miami Beach, FL 33139. (305) 673-3153. Fax: (305) 673-6501.

St. Petersburg

Fantasy Adventures, 138 Beach Drive NE, St. Petersburg, FL 33701. (813) 821-0880. Fax: (813) 822-0892.

Tampa

Tampa Bay Travel, 4830 W. Kennedy Blvd., Tampa, FL 33609. (813) 286-4202. Fax: (813) 286-4204. Jim Locke.

GEORGIA
Atlanta

All Points Travel, 1544 Piedmont Ave, Suite 135, Atlanta, GA 30324. (404) 873-3631. Fax: (404) 873-3633.

Conventional Travel, 1658 La Vista Rd., NE 6A, Atlanta, GA 30329. (404) 315-0107. Fax: (404) 315-0206.

Midtown Travel, 1830 Piedmont Rd., Ste F, Atlanta, GA 30324. (404) 872-8308. Fax: (404) 881-6322.

Northcreek Travel, 3715 Northside Pkwy, Atlanta, GA 30327. (404) 231-0332. Fax: (404) 231-2249.

Uniglobe Advisors, 945 E. Paces Ferry Rd., Atlanta, GA 30326. (404) 231-5257. Fax: (404) 231-5682. Loyal.

Marietta

Piedmont Travel, 2550 Sandy Plains Rd., Marietta, GA 30066. (404) 578-1946. Fax: (404) 565-5614.

Travel Affair, 1205 Johnson Ferry Rd., #116, Marietta, GA 30068. (404) 977-6824. Fax:(404) 977-0770. Gary Potts.

HAWAII
Honolulu

Bird of Paradise Travel, P.O. Box 4157, Honolulu, HI 96812. (808) 735-9103. Fax (808) 735-1436.

Outrigger Int'l Travel, 150 Kaiulani Ave., Honolulu, HI 96815. (808) 923-2377. Fax: (808) 923-9649. Mark Glasser.

Lahaina

❍ **Gay Hawaii Excursions**, activities and tours for all the Hawaiian islands designed exclusively for gays and/or lesbians: dinner cruises, helicopter tours, horseback riding, snorkeling at Molokini crater, sunset sails, bike down Halekale crateor, 256 Front St., Lahaina, HI 96761. (808) 667-7466. (800) 311-4460. Fax: (808) 667-5401. Albert Molina, *IGTA*.

ILLINOIS
Chicago

All Points Travel, 3712 North Broadway, Chicago, IL 60657. (312) 525-4700. Fax: (312) 525-7600.

ASAP Travel, 3745 North Halsted St., Chicago IL 60613. (312) 975-3900. Fax: (312) 975-3995.

CRC Travel, 2121 North Clybourn, Chicago, IL 60614. (312) 525-3800. (800) 874-7701. Fax: (312) 525-8762.

CTN/Travel Brokers, 18420 So. Halsted St., Glenwood, IL 60425. (708) 755-3350. Fax: (708) 755-7968.

Envoy Travel, 740 N. Rush St., Chicago, IL 60611. (312) 787-2400. Fax: (312) 787-7109

Gone With The Wind Travel, 212 S. Marion Suite 5, Oak Park, IL 60302-3159. (708) 383-6960. Fax: (708) 383-6984.

Hemingway Travel, 1640 No. Wells, Chicago, IL 60614. (312) 440-9870. Fax: (312) 440-9851.

Vacation Hotline, 1501 Fullerton Ave., Chicago, IL 60614. (312) 880-0030. Fax: (312) 880-5373.

World Travel Partners, 1341 W. Fullerton Ave., Ste #109, Chicago, IL 60614. (312) 244-2682.

KENTUCKY
Louisville

Travel 2000, 981 So. 3rd St., Suite #410, Louisville, KY 40203. (502) 584-1799. Fax: (502) 581-9063.

LOUISIANA
New Orleans

Alternative Tours & Travel, 1001 Marigny St., New Orleans, LA 70117. (504) 949-5815. Fax: (504) 949-5917.

MARYLAND
Silver Spring

Central Travel, 8767 Georgia Ave., Silver Spring, MD 20910. (301) 589-9440. Fax: (301) 587-3870.Buz Lowman.

MASSACHUSETTS
Boston

5 Star Travel, Caribbean experts, customized agents for individuals or groups, 164 Newbury St., Boston MA 02116. (617) 536-1999. Fax: (617) 236-1999. Paul or Stephen.

Travel Plus, 1401 Centre St., Boston, MA 02131, Boston, MA 02131. (617) 469-5500. Fax: (617) 469-5505. Park

Provincetown

In Town Reservations, P.O. Box 614, Provincetown, MA 02657. (508) 487-1883. Steve Kacouros

Wakefield

Always Travel, 413 Lowell St., Wakefield, MA 01880. (617) 246-3646. Maureen.

MICHIGAN
East Lansing

Anderson Travel, 2740 East Lansing Dr., East Lansing, MI 48823. (517) 337-1300.

MINNEASOTA
Minneapolis/St. Paul

All Airlines Travel, 111 E. Kellogg Blvd., Ste #225, St. Paul, MN 55101-1235. (800) 832-0304. Fax: (612) 222-2168. Larry.

The Travel Company, 2800 University Ave. SE, Minneapolis, MN 55414-3293. (612) 379-9000, Fax: (612) 379-8258.

NEVADA
Las Vegas

Cruise One, 5030 Paradise Rd., Suite B101, Las Vegas, NV 89119. (702) 256-8082. (800) 200-3012. Fax: (702) 256-8052. Jeff

Seawind Travel, 216 S. 4th St., Las Vegas, NV 89101.
(702) 387-5566. Fax: (702) 387-1312. Terry
Reno
Deluxe Travel, 102 California Ave., Reno NV 89509.
(702) 686-7000. Fax: (702) 686-6717.

NEW JERSEY
Edison
Galla Travel, 63 Chatsworth Court, Edison, NJ
08820. (908) 603-7239. (908) 603-7238
Pennington
Hobbit Travel Services, One Michael Way, Penning-
ton, NJ 08534. (609) 737-2257. Fax: (609) 737-2344.
Vernon
All About Travel, 280 Rte 94, Vernon NJ 07462.
(201) 827-3320. Fax: (201) 827-8097.

NEW MEXICO
Albequerque
Travel Scene, 2424 Juan Tabo Blvd. NE, Albuquer-que,
NM 87112. (505) 292-4343. Fax: (505) 294-2252.

NEW YORK
Albany
Atlas Travel Center, 1545 Central Ave., Albany NY
12205-5044. (518) 464-0271. Fax: (518) 464-0273.
Greg Belleville.
Great Neck
Courtyard Travel, 770 Middle Neck Rd., Great Neck
NY 11024. (516) 773-3700. Fax: (516) 829-5427.
Hartsdale
Choice Travel, 267 So. Central Park Ave., Harsdale,
NY 10530. (914) 993-3300. Fax: (914) 993-0361
New York City
All Continent Tours, 227 E. 56th St., New York NY
10022. (212) 371-7171. Fax: (212) 888-6828.
Sue Martino.
DC Worldwide Travel, 251 W. 19th St., 4th Fl., New
York, NY 10011. (212) 243-7529. Fax: (212) 647-
1629. Peter
Islanders Kennedy Travel, 183 West 10th St., New
York NY 10014. (212) 242-3222. Fax: (212) 929-
8530. Joe.
Jamar Travel, 60 E. 42nd St., New York NY 10165.
(212) 599-0577. Fax: (212) 599-3288.
Liberty Travel, 170 7th Ave. South, New York, NY
10014. (212) 675-2704. Fax: (212) 675-7049. Jackie.
Union Tours, 245 5th Ave., New York, NY 10016. (212)
683-9500. Fax: (212) 683-9511.
Worldwide Travel, 200 Court St., Suite 4L, Brooklyn,
NY 11201. (718) 797-0837. Fax: (718) 797-0431. David
Port Washington (L.I.)
⚪ Odysseus Travel, P.O. Box 1548, Port
Washington, NY 11050. Eli Angelo, Joseph
Bain. (516) 944-5330 or (800) 257-5344.
Fax: (516) 944-7540 or (800) 982-6571.
Email:odyusa@odyusa.com
Reservation service for quality hotels &
resorts in Athens, Mykonos, Santorini, and
all the Greek Islands. Also Canary Islands,
Ibiza, Barcelona, Madrid, Sitges, Rome,
Florence, Venice, Taormina (Sicily),
Amsterdam, London, Zurich, Paris,
Cannes, Nice. Cruises of the Greek Islands,
private yacht chartering in Caribbean or
Eastern Mediterranean. Special air prices
and complete packages to Athens, Istanbul,
Buenos Aires, Costa Rica, Rio de Janeiro

and Canary Islands. Special Gay Games
1998 hotels and air packages.
Proudly serving the travel needs of the gay
community since 1984. *TAC:* 10%. *IGTA,
ASTA, CLIA, AGLTA.*

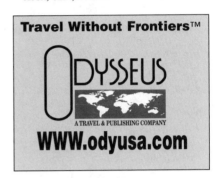

Travel Without Frontiers™

ODYSSEUS

A TRAVEL & PUBLISHING COMPANY

WWW.odyusa.com

Rochester
De Prez Travel, 145 Rue de Ville, Ste 1, Rochester,
NY 14618. (716) 234-3615. Ray Breslin.

NORTH CAROLINA
Durham
The Travel Store, 4711 Hope Valley Rd., Durham, NC
27707. (919) 489-9498. Fax: (919) 489-0830. Mary Beth.
Gasconia
All Travel,1708 E. Garrison Blvd., Ste A, Gasconia, NC
28054. (704) 853-1111. Fax: (704) 853-1115. Ann.

OHIO
Dayton
Horizon Travel, 6129 Far Hills Ave., Dayton, OH
45459. (513) 433-2206. (513) 433-2852

OREGON
Portland
Advantage Travel, 812 SW Washington St., #200,
Portland OR 97205. (503) 225-0186. Fax: (503) 225-
0313. Helmut Kogler.
Gulliver's Travel, 514 NW 9th Ave., Portland OR
97209. (503) 221-0013. Fax: (503) 223-6945.
Norman Nevers TC.
Prestige Travel, 4551 N. Channel Ave., Portland, OR
97217. (503) 285-2552. Fax: (503) 285-2459. Kathy.
Travel Agents Int'l, 917 SW Washington St., Portland,
OR 97205. (503) 223-1100. Fax: (503) 497-1015.

PENNSYLVANIA
Ephrata
Zeller Travel, 4213 Oregon Pike, Ephrata, PA 17522.
(717) 859-4710. (717) 859-3638. Terry Bigler.
Philadelphia
Liberty Travel, 220 South 16th St., Philadelphia, PA
19102. (215) 981-1000. Fax: (215) 981-1112.
Sigmund Travel Bureau, 262 So. 12th St., Ste. 206,
Philadelphia, PA. 19107. (215) 735-0090. Fax: (215)
735-9387. Henry Siegel.
Travel Now, 1 Franklin Plaza, Philadelphia, PA
19102. (215) 988-0848. Fax: (215) 988-0355. Dona.
Whole World Travel, 2 Logan Square #625, Philadelphia,
PA 19103. (215) 561-4545. Fax: (215) 561-5626. Janet
Will Travel, 118 So. Bellevue Ave., Langhorn, PA 19047.
(215) 741-4492. Fax: (215) 741-5156. Pat Wilson.

604   TRAVEL AGENTS

Pittsburgh
Pittsburgh Travel, The Shops at Station Square, Pittsburgh PA 15219. (412) 321-8511. Fax: (412) 261-9915.

Reading
Berkshire Travel, Box 14686, Reading, PA 19612. (610) 374-2204. Fax: (610) 372-6074.

TEXAS
Austin
Creative Travel, 8670 Spicewood Springs #10, Austin, TX 78759. (512) 331-9560. Fax: (512) 331-6230. Larry Harley

Dallas
Earth Movement Travel, 4140 Lemmon Ave., Ste #172, Dallas, TX 75219. (214) 526-6200. Fax: (214) 526-6272.
Oak Cliff Travel, 120 Wynnewood. Dallas, TX 75224. (214) 946-6496. Fax: (214) 946-8785
Precision Travel, 7557 Rambler Rd., Suite #150, Dallas, TX 75231. (214) 739-1991. Fax: (214) 739-2968
Travel Friends, 8080 N. Central, #320, Dallas TX 75206. (214) 528-6344.

Houston
Advance Damron Travel, 1 Greenway Plaza #890, Houston TX 77046-0100. (713) 888-1023. (800) 695-0880. Fax: (713) 888-1010.
Sojourns Travel, 3400 Montrose Blvd., Ste #909, Houston, TX 77006. (713) 528-2299. Fax: (713) 528-6767.
Woodlake Travel, 2513 S. Gesner, Houston, TX 77063. (713) 789-7500. Fax: (713) 789-2951. Randy Herriage.

Humble
After 5 Travel, 2602 Killdeer Lane, Humble, TX 77396-1826. (800) 335-1369. Fax: (713) 441-1275

San Antonio
Carlson Travel Network, 2313 NW Military, Suite 101, San Antonio, TX 78231. (210) 341-6363. Fax: (210) 341-6392.

VIRGINIA
Alexandria
Passport Executive Travel, 105 N. Washington St., #201, Alexandria, VA 22314. Tel: (703) 549-5559. Fax: (703) 549-3048. Bob McNeal.

WASHINGTON
Seattle
Royalty Travel, 1200 5th Ave., IBM Plaza Level West, Seattle, WA 98101. (206) 623-7474. Fax: (206) 623-8283. Greg Smith.
Sunshine Travel, 519 N. 85th St., Seattle, WA 98103. (206) 784-8141. Fax: (206) 784-8143.

WISCONSIN
Milwaukee
Milwaukee Travel, 7665 N. Port Washing-ton, Milwaukee, WI 53217. (414) 351-3010. Fax: (414) 351-7059. James.

TRAVEL INSURANCE

✪ **CSA Travel Protection**, W.C. International, travel insurance and assistance services, P.O. Box 3150, San Diego, CA 92163. Tel/Fax: (619) 280-0363.

ADVERTISERS INDEX

333 West 88th Assoc.	148
Acapulco Las Palmas	429
Admiral's Landing	107
Agence Fleche	203
Alexander's GH	59
Ambiance Inn	553
American Book Center	447
Ampersand Guesthouse	109
Amsterdam House	454
Anastassios Sevasti	348 TS
Andrea & Janet's Maui Vacations	83
Andromeda (Athens)	333 TS
Andromeda Residence (Mykonos)	348 TS
Anfora's Dreams	84
Astir of Paros	350
Athenian Inn	333 TS
Atherton Hotel	31
Au 727 Guest House	209
Auberge du Centre - Ville	204
Aurora Winds	3
Axial Beauborg Hotel	308
B&B Inn Arizona	5
Bali Mandira Cottages	371
Bar L'Ascenseur	303
Basic Plumbing	15
Beck's Motor Lodge	33
Bed & Breakfast Berlin	317
Belvedere Hotel	133
Benchmark Inn & Annex	107
Best Western Laguna Brisas Spa Hotel	11
Blancan aux Lodge	251
Bob Howard Real Estate	131
Brickfield Hill B&B	227
Brush Creek Media	595
C & G B&B House	453
Cachet Accommodations	200
Cajun	199
Camp Palm Springs	19
Carl's Guest House	110
Carousel Guest House	134
Carnaval in Rio	255
Casa De Las Palmas	431
Casa Delfino	339 TS
Casa Marhaba	475
Casa Panoramica	439
Cass Hotel	90
Centre Apartments Amsterdam	452
Charleston Beach B&B	165
Chelsea Pines Inn	146
Chevaliers Palace Hotel	352
Chicago Int'l Indoor Tennis Classic	89
City Suites	91
Club Comanche	177
Coconut Plaza Hotel	87
Colonial House Inn	146
Columbia Fun Maps	II, 15, 50, 63, 137

Community Bar & Grill	140	hotel Rheingold	323
Contacts Magazine	263	Hotel Romantic	525 TS
Czech Mate	283	Hotel Saintonge	309 TS
Dana Villas	355 TS	Hotel Sander	458
Diva Divine, Madrid NM	127	Hotel Santika Beach	371 TS
Dorothy's Surrender	37	Hotel Sunlite	417 TS
Drake's	445	Hotel Ulysse	302
Dreamdates	195	Hotel Urania	239
Eden Hotel	445	Hotel Vendome	247
El Mirasol Villas	19	Hotel Veneto	399
El Portalon	502	Hotel Village	321
Elephant Walk Inn	107	Hotel Wallis	326
Embassy GH	161	Hotel Wellenberg	543
Essex Hotel	34	Hotel Wilmersdorf	318
Exit	500	In•fo Canada	592
Explosion	409	Inn Exile	20
Fire Island Land Co.	133	Inn of The Turquoise Bear	129
Fire Island Pines	131	Intensity / José Arroyo Photography	XII
Frontiers	13	Intermale	447
Garden Cottage	592	International Mr. Leather	89
Gay Hawaii Excursion	83	Ios Palace	341
Gay Travel	315	Island Properties	133
Gayellow Pages / Renaissance House	597	Jefferson House	67
Greenwood & Cooper Inside Front Cover	I	Jewelry by Poncé	9
Hale Kipa O' Pele	76	Joluva Guest House	275
Halepa Hotel	339 TS	Jornada	225
Hangar	399	Just Right Reservations	105, 592
Hawaiian Hotels & Resorts	77	Kailua Maui Gardens	82
Hillcrest Inn	25	Kalani Eco-Resort	78
Hola! Idiomas	523	Kalorama Guest Houses	51
Homo Xtra Magazine	145	Kallisti Complex	351
Hot Spots Magazine	55	Kasa Korbett	26
Hotel 17	147	Kavalari Hotel	356 TS
Hotel Apollonia	348	Key West Business Guild	57
Hotel Arcadia	TS	King Henry Arms	56
Hotel Atlantico	518 TS	Kremlin Tours	481, 483
Hotel Basilea	403	Land's End Inn	111
Hotel Bécquer	520	La Renaixenca	524
Hotel Bergmeister	327	La Track	199
Hotel Blancaneaux	251	Le Chasseur Guest House	206
Hotel Bourbon	205	Le Dome	199
Hotel de la Couronne	207	Le Hommes Book Shop	141
Hotel Cervantes	526	Le Montrose	39
Hotel de Paris	299	Le Stade B&B	208
Hotel Delle Tele	391 TS	Leland Hotel	35
Hotel Duomo	391 TS	Liberty Open	137
Hotel Elena	348 TS	Lindos Mare	353
Hotel Elysium	348 TS	Los Robles	TS
Hotel Fenix	333	Macarty Park Guest House	99
Hotel Goldenes Schwert	541	Madrid (NM)	127
Hotel Gounod	304	Mahina Kai	79
Hotel Koruna	285	Mail & More	452
Hotel le Saint Andre	208	Mälardrottningen	536
Hotel Lichtburg	318	Malaysia Hotel	549
Hotel Luxeford Suites	115	Maui Kai	84 TS
Hotel Madeleine	247	Maui Vacation Rentals	83
Hotel Marigna	TS	Metro Art & Entertainment Weekly	49
Hotel New York - Amsterdam	456	Movo Media	Inside Backcover
Hotel New York - London	573	Molino de Agua	440
Hotel Orfeo	457	Mykonos Blu	349 TS
Hotel Pallas	535	Mykonos Live the Legend	346, 347

Navila Aparthotel	502 TS	Siegessaule	315
Neighborhood Inns of Chicago	91	Simonton Court	63
New World Marketing Group	203	Splash Bar	139
Oasis Guest House	105	Studio Six / Surfside Guesthouse	123
Ocean Walk GH	161	Sunset Inn	107
Olde Yard Inn	260	Surf Inn	91
Our World Magazine	597	St. George Lycabettus Hotel	334 TS
Out Magazine	463	Taverne du Village	199
Outlines	93	Ten Cawthra Square B&B	195
Palm Court Bed & Breakfast	591	The 1998 Amsterdam Gay Games	449
Park Brompton Inn	91	The Bad Boy Club Montréal	200
Park Lodge Hotel	227	The Beach Place	25
Park Manor Suites	26	The Chateau Tivoli	33
Passport Japan	413	The Coffee Boy Cottages	551
Pension David	285	The Front Page	149
People Escort Service	450	The Peach Atlanta	71
Pepe Toro	435	The Pines Guest House	61
Personal Chat line	5	The Plantation Inn	85 TS
Playa los Arcos	440	The Rainbow Club	283
Priape	587	The Ranch	111
Prieure des Granges	311	The Royal Paradise Hotel	554
Provincetown Precious Properties	107	The Shore Inn	47
qc magazine	187	The Volcano Ranch	79
RBR Farms	75	The WEB / Club 58	141
RG Magazine	201	Tradewinds Inn	112
Rathbone Inn	99	Travel Trends	601
Redcliffe Hotel	573	Triton Hotel	288
Renegade Resort	47	Unicorn	143
Richmond Hotel	67	Victoria Oaks Inn	43
Royal Hawaiian / Maui Surfing	82	Villas Blancas	TS
Royal Papeete	313	Vista Bonita	TS
Rue Royal Inn	100	WC International	TS
Sago Palms	21	Why Not / Blue Boy	451
San Francisco Bay Guardian	29	William Anthony House	63
San Vicente Inn Resort	40	William Lewis House	51
Santiago Resort	21	Wilton Palace Hotel	217
Sarah Petersen Guest House	321		

1997

JANUARY 1997
S	M	T	W	T	F	S
			1	2	3	4
5	6	7	8	9	10	11
12	13	14	15	16	17	18
19	20	21	22	23	24	25
26	27	28	29	30	31	

FEBRUARY 1997
S	M	T	W	T	F	S
						1
2	3	4	5	6	7	8
9	10	11	12	13	14	15
16	17	18	19	20	21	22
23	24	25	26	27	28	

MARCH 1997
S	M	T	W	T	F	S
						1
2	3	4	5	6	7	8
9	10	11	12	13	14	15
16	17	18	19	20	21	22
23/30	24/31	25	26	27	28	29

APRIL 1997
S	M	T	W	T	F	S
		1	2	3	4	5
6	7	8	9	10	11	12
13	14	15	16	17	18	19
20	21	22	23	24	25	26
27	28	29	30			

MAY 1997
S	M	T	W	T	F	S
				1	2	3
4	5	6	7	8	9	10
11	12	13	14	15	16	17
18	19	20	21	22	23	24
25	26	27	28	29	30	31

JUNE 1997
S	M	T	W	T	F	S
1	2	3	4	5	6	7
8	9	10	11	12	13	14
15	16	17	18	19	20	21
22	23	24	25	26	27	28
29	30					

JULY 1997
S	M	T	W	T	F	S
		1	2	3	4	5
6	7	8	9	10	11	12
13	14	15	16	17	18	19
20	21	22	23	24	25	26
27	28	29	30	31		

AUGUST 1997
S	M	T	W	T	F	S
					1	2
3	4	5	6	7	8	9
10	11	12	13	14	15	16
17	18	19	20	21	22	23
24/31	25	26	27	28	29	30

SEPTEMBER 1997
S	M	T	W	T	F	S
	1	2	3	4	5	6
7	8	9	10	11	12	13
14	15	16	17	18	19	20
21	22	23	24	25	26	27
28	29	30				

OCTOBER 1997
S	M	T	W	T	F	S
			1	2	3	4
5	6	7	8	9	10	11
12	13	14	15	16	17	18
19	20	21	22	23	24	25
26	27	28	29	30	31	

NOVEMBER 1997
S	M	T	W	T	F	S
						1
2	3	4	5	6	7	8
9	10	11	12	13	14	15
16	17	18	19	20	21	22
23/30	24	25	26	27	28	29

DECEMBER 1997
S	M	T	W	T	F	S
	1	2	3	4	5	6
7	8	9	10	11	12	13
14	15	16	17	18	19	20
21	22	23	24	25	26	27
28	29	30	31			

1998

JANUARY 1998
S	M	T	W	T	F	S
				1	2	3
4	5	6	7	8	9	10
11	12	13	14	15	16	17
18	19	20	21	22	23	24
25	26	27	28	29	30	31

FEBRUARY 1998
S	M	T	W	T	F	S
1	2	3	4	5	6	7
8	9	10	11	12	13	14
15	16	17	18	19	20	21
22	23	24	25	26	27	28

MARCH 1998
S	M	T	W	T	F	S
1	2	3	4	5	6	7
8	9	10	11	12	13	14
15	16	17	18	19	20	21
22	23	24	25	26	27	28
29	30	31				

APRIL 1998
S	M	T	W	T	F	S
			1	2	3	4
5	6	7	8	9	10	11
12	13	14	15	16	17	18
19	20	21	22	23	24	25
26	27	28	29	30		

MAY 1998
S	M	T	W	T	F	S
					1	2
3	4	5	6	7	8	9
10	11	12	13	14	15	16
17	18	19	20	21	22	23
24/31	25	26	27	28	29	30

JUNE 1998
S	M	T	W	T	F	S
	1	2	3	4	5	6
7	8	9	10	11	12	13
14	15	16	17	18	19	20
21	22	23	24	25	26	27
28	29	30				

JULY 1998
S	M	T	W	T	F	S
			1	2	3	4
5	6	7	8	9	10	11
12	13	14	15	16	17	18
19	20	21	22	23	24	25
26	27	28	29	30	31	

AUGUST 1998
S	M	T	W	T	F	S
						1
2	3	4	5	6	7	8
9	10	11	12	13	14	15
16	17	18	19	20	21	22
23/30	24/31	25	26	27	28	29

SEPTEMBER 1998
S	M	T	W	T	F	S
		1	2	3	4	5
6	7	8	9	10	11	12
13	14	15	16	17	18	19
20	21	22	23	24	25	26
27	28	29	30			

OCTOBER 1998
S	M	T	W	T	F	S
				1	2	3
4	5	6	7	8	9	10
11	12	13	14	15	16	17
18	19	20	21	22	23	24
25	26	27	28	29	30	31

NOVEMBER 1998
S	M	T	W	T	F	S
1	2	3	4	5	6	7
8	9	10	11	12	13	14
15	16	17	18	19	20	21
22	23	24	25	26	27	28
29	30					

DECEMBER 1998
S	M	T	W	T	F	S
		1	2	3	4	5
6	7	8	9	10	11	12
13	14	15	16	17	18	19
20	21	22	23	24	25	26
27	28	29	30	31		